# VISUAL STUDIO® 2010 AND SIX-IN-ONE

MW01378712

INTRODUCTION . . . . . . . . . . . . . . . . . . . . . . . . . . . . . . . . . . . . . . . . . . . . . . . . . . . . . . . . . . . . . . . . . . . . xxxiii

▶ PART I   VISUAL STUDIO

CHAPTER 1    History of Visual Studio . . . . . . . . . . . . . . . . . . . . . . . . . . . . . . . . . . . . . . . . . . 3
CHAPTER 2    Visual Studio UI Enhancements . . . . . . . . . . . . . . . . . . . . . . . . . . . . . . . . . 15
CHAPTER 3    Visual Studio Code Snippets . . . . . . . . . . . . . . . . . . . . . . . . . . . . . . . . . . . .31
CHAPTER 4    Visual Studio Templates . . . . . . . . . . . . . . . . . . . . . . . . . . . . . . . . . . . . . . . 65
CHAPTER 5    Getting the Most Out of the IDE . . . . . . . . . . . . . . . . . . . . . . . . . . . . . . 127
CHAPTER 6    Visual Studio Extensibility . . . . . . . . . . . . . . . . . . . . . . . . . . . . . . . . . . . . 201

▶ PART II   .NET 4

CHAPTER 7    .NET Framework Version History . . . . . . . . . . . . . . . . . . . . . . . . . . . . . . 279
CHAPTER 8    Modern UI Frameworks (WPF and Silverlight) . . . . . . . . . . . . . . . . . . . 297
CHAPTER 9    Windows Communication Foundation (WCF) . . . . . . . . . . . . . . . . . . . . 375
CHAPTER 10   Enhancements to the .NET Core Framework . . . . . . . . . . . . . . . . . . . . .399
CHAPTER 11   Enhancements to the .NET Workflow Framework . . . . . . . . . . . . . . . . .489
CHAPTER 12   Enhancements to the .NET Data Framework . . . . . . . . . . . . . . . . . . . . .563
CHAPTER 13   Enhancements to the .NET Communication Framework . . . . . . . . . . . 581
CHAPTER 14   .NET Charting Components . . . . . . . . . . . . . . . . . . . . . . . . . . . . . . . . . . .593

▶ PART III   ASP.NET 4.0

CHAPTER 15   ASP.NET Version History . . . . . . . . . . . . . . . . . . . . . . . . . . . . . . . . . . . . .653
CHAPTER 16   ASP.NET Charting Controls . . . . . . . . . . . . . . . . . . . . . . . . . . . . . . . . . . .669
CHAPTER 17   ASP.NET Dynamic Data . . . . . . . . . . . . . . . . . . . . . . . . . . . . . . . . . . . . . . 711
CHAPTER 18   ASP.NET Model View Controller (MVC) . . . . . . . . . . . . . . . . . . . . . . . . .751
CHAPTER 19   ASP.NET Ajax Improvements . . . . . . . . . . . . . . . . . . . . . . . . . . . . . . . . . . 837
CHAPTER 20   ASP.NET Ajax Control Toolkit and jQuery . . . . . . . . . . . . . . . . . . . . . . .893

▶ **PART IV**   **VB.NET**

**CHAPTER 21**   History of Visual Basic . . . . . . . . . . . . . . . . . . . . . . . . . . . . . . . . . . . . 981

**CHAPTER 22**   Visual Basic 10.0 Language Improvements. . . . . . . . . . . . . . . . . . . . 1007

▶ **PART V**   **C#**

**CHAPTER 23**   History of C#. . . . . . . . . . . . . . . . . . . . . . . . . . . . . . . . . . . . . . . . . . . . .1041

**CHAPTER 24**   C# 4.0 Language Improvements. . . . . . . . . . . . . . . . . . . . . . . . . . . . . 1065

▶ **PART VI**   **F#**

**CHAPTER 25**   Visual F# and the Other .NET Languages. . . . . . . . . . . . . . . . . . . . .1103

**INDEX**. . . . . . . . . . . . . . . . . . . . . . . . . . . . . . . . . . . . . . . . . . . . . . . . . . . . . . . . . . . 1173

# Visual Studio® 2010 and .NET 4

## SIX-IN-ONE

# Visual Studio® 2010 and .NET 4

## SIX-IN-ONE

István Novák
András Velvárt
Adam Granicz
György Balássy
Attila Hajdrik
Mitchel Sellers
Gastón C. Hillar
Ágnes Molnár
Joydip Kanjilal

WILEY

Wiley Publishing, Inc.

Visual Studio® 2010 and .NET 4 Six-in-One

Published by
Wiley Publishing, Inc.
10475 Crosspoint Boulevard
Indianapolis, IN 46256
www.wiley.com

Copyright © 2010 by Wiley Publishing, Inc., Indianapolis, Indiana

Published simultaneously in Canada

ISBN: 978-0-470-49948-1

ISBN: 978-1-118-00113-4 (ebk)

ISBN: 978-1-118-00295-7 (ebk)

ISBN: 978-1-118-00298-8 (ebk)

Manufactured in the United States of America

10 9 8 7 6 5 4 3 2 1

# ABOUT THE AUTHORS

 **ISTVÁN NOVÁK** is an associate of Grepton, a Hungarian IT services company. He works as a software architect and community evangelist. In the last 20 years, he participated in more than 50 enterprise software development projects. In 2002, he co-authored the first Hungarian book about .NET development. In 2007, he was awarded with the Microsoft Most Valuable Professional (MVP) title. He holds a master's degree from the Technical University of Budapest, Hungary, and also has a doctoral degree in software technology. He lives in Dunakeszi, Hungary, with his wife and two daughters. He is a passionate scuba diver. You may have a good chance of meeting him underwater at the Red Sea in any season of the year.

 **ANDRÁS VELVÁRT** is a Silverlight MVP, with a passion for user experience. As an accomplished speaker, he gives talks at numerous conferences where Windows Presentation Foundation (WPF) or Silverlight is the topic. Chapter 8 of this book feeds from his experience at teaching many Silverlight and WPF classes and work-shops. He is also the owner of Response Ltd. (www.response.hu), a small consulting and WPF/Silverlight development company in Hungary.

**ADAM GRANICZ** is the CEO of IntelliFactory, a leading provider of F# training, development, and consulting services, as well as technologies that enable rapid functional, reactive web development. As one of the first F# users, he is a key community member and an active F# evangelist. He has been the co-author of two F# books with Don Syme, the designer of the language. He is a regular speaker at developer conferences and various industry partner events.

 **GYÖRGY BALÁSSY** teaches web portal development as a lecturer at Budapest University of Technology and Economics. He is a founding member of the local MSDN Competence Centre (MSDNCC), having an important role in evangelizing the .NET platform as a speaker, book author, and consultant. He provided leadership in the foundation of the Hungarian .NET community as a key evangelist on Microsoft events, technical forums, and as the head of the Portal Technology Group in the MSDNCC. He is a regular speaker on academic and industrial events, presenting in-depth technical sessions on .NET, ASP.NET, Office development, and ethical hacking, for which he won the Best Speaker and the Most Valuable Professional (MVP) Awards in SharePoint and ASP.NET multiple times. He was selected to be the member of the ASPInsiders group. Since 2005, he has been the Microsoft Regional Director in Hungary.

**ATTILA HAJDRIK** has worked in the IT industry for more than 14 years. He is the founder and lead architect of Eyedea Ltd., a small independent software vendor (ISV) specializing in Rich Internet Application (RIA) development. Before founding his own company, he worked for 6 years at Microsoft as an Application Development Consultant, and later as a Senior Consultant in Microsoft Services. He specialized in .NET-based custom development projects. In 2004, He was awarded an

ASP.NET Most Valuable Professional (MVP) title. He has experience with all .NET-related technologies from the back end to the front end. He is addicted to Doman Specific Languages, model-based development, and a big believer in design patterns. His favorite technologies are Silverlight, Windows Presentation Foundation (WPF), and ASP.NET Model View Controller (MVC).

**MITCHEL SELLERS** specializes in software development using Microsoft technologies. He is the CEO of IowaComputerGurus Inc., a Microsoft C# MVP, a Microsoft Certified Professional, and experienced technical writer. He enjoys spending time sharing information with the development community through books, blog postings, and public speaking events. He is also an active participant in the DotNetNuke development community. For more information on him, visit his website at http://www.mitchelsellers.com.

**GASTÓN C. HILLAR** has been working with computers since he was 8 years old. He began programming with the legendary Texas Instruments TI-99/4A and Commodore 64 home computers in the early 1980s. He has worked as developer, architect, and project manager for many companies in Buenos Aires, Argentina. He is now an independent IT consultant working for several American, German, Spanish, and Latin American companies, and a freelance author. He has written four books in English, contributed chapters to two other books, and has written more than 40 books in Spanish. He contributes to *Dr. Dobb's* Go Parallel programming portal (http://www.ddj .com/go-parallel/), *Dr. Dobb's* (http://drdobbs.com), and is a guest blogger at Intel Software Network (http://software.intel.com). He lives with his wife, Vanesa, and his son, Kevin. When not tinkering with computers, he enjoys developing and playing with wireless virtual reality devices and electronic toys with his father, his son, and his nephew, Nico. You can reach him at gastonhillar@hotmail.com. You can follow him on Twitter at http://twitter.com/ gastonhillar. His blog is at http://csharpmulticore.blogspot.com.

**ÁGNES MOLNÁR** has been working with Microsoft technologies and SharePoint since 2001. After a few years of working as a developer and SharePoint expert, she founded a SharePoint consulting company in Hungary, Central Europe. She's been working as a senior consultant, and has led SharePoint implementations at numerous Central European companies. Her main focus is on architecture, governance, information and knowledge management, and enterprise search. She's a frequent speaker at conferences around the globe, and is also the co-author of various SharePoint books.

**JOYDIP KANJILAL** was awarded a Microsoft Most Valuable Professional (MVP) title in ASP.NET in 2007, 2008, and 2009. He has more than 12 years of industry experience in IT, with more than 6 years experience in Microsoft .NET and its related technologies. He was selected as MSDN Featured Developer of the Fortnight (MSDN), and was also selected as Community Credit Winner at www.community-credit.com several times. He has authored numerous books on ASP-related topics.

# ABOUT THE TECHNICAL EDITOR

**DOUG PARSONS** is a software architect and the director of Ohio Operations for NJI New Media. His expertise is in web development with a specialization in political websites. Most notably, he has worked on the 2008 John McCain presidential campaign website and, more recently, Mitt Romney's official book tour website. In his downtime, he enjoys spending time with his lovely fiancée, Marisa, and their four puppies.

# CREDITS

**ACQUISITIONS EDITOR**
Paul Reese

**PROJECT EDITOR**
Kevin Shafer

**TECHNICAL EDITOR**
Doug Parsons

**PRODUCTION EDITOR**
Rebecca Anderson

**COPY EDITOR**
Christopher Jones

**EDITORIAL DIRECTOR**
Robyn B. Siesky

**EDITORIAL MANAGER**
Mary Beth Wakefield

**FREELANCER EDITORIAL MANAGER**
Rosemarie Graham

**ASSOCIATE DIRECTOR OF MARKETING**
David Mayhew

**PRODUCTION MANAGER**
Tim Tate

**VICE PRESIDENT AND EXECUTIVE GROUP PUBLISHER**
Richard Swadley

**VICE PRESIDENT AND EXECUTIVE PUBLISHER**
Barry Pruett

**ASSOCIATE PUBLISHER**
Jim Minatel

**PROJECT COORDINATOR, COVER**
Lynsey Stanford

**PROOFREADERS**
Josh Chase, Word One New York
James Saturnio, Word One New York

**INDEXER**
J & J Indexing

**COVER DESIGNER**
Michael E. Trent

**COVER IMAGE**
© Andreas Bauer/istockphoto.com

# ACKNOWLEDGMENTS

**THIS BOOK WOULD NOT BE SO CLEAR** in its voice without the contribution of Kevin Shafer, who not only fixed our typos and grammar, but added a lot of value by improving our thoughts put down to paper and ironed out our tangled sentences. Doug Parsons examined the technical content very carefully, tried all the sample code we prepared, and gave us a lot of suggestions to improve the understandability of examples. Without his thorough work, samples would contain many more bugs and ambiguous code details.

—ISTVÁN NOVÁK

**I WOULD LIKE TO THANK** my wife and family for their support, and coping with the long hours and nights of writing. A special thank you goes to my friend, István Novák, who got me to write the Modern UI Frameworks chapter, and kept the project alive even if it meant that he had to write more than half of the book — a lot more than what his share was.

—ANDRÁS VELVÁRT

**I WOULD LIKE TO THANK** István Novák for his help and useful tips he gave me to write this book. Last but not least, I would like to thank Tamás Varga for inspiring me to get this book done."

—ATTILA HAJDRIK

**THIS BOOK STARTED OUT AS MY IDEA** and I was the original sole author. However, because of software release delays and schedule conflicts, that ended up not being feasible, and I wasn't sure what would happen with the book. Other authors were brought on to help with the writing. I am very grateful for the hard work and dedication that each of them gave toward this book. Without their efforts, the book would have never made it past the overall concept.

This is the second book that I have been an author on with Wiley/Wrox, and I have to say that their entire team deserves a pat on the back. I would like to call special attention to two individuals. Paul Reese (Acquisitions Editor) put up with my schedule and availability changes, while still allowing me the opportunity to be an author on the book. Kevin Shafer (Project Editor) was yet again a great person to work with, and helped keep everything moving through the process smoothly. The technical editors and all other individuals on the project were critical to getting the book finalized and ready to release.

—MITCHEL SELLERS

**I WISH TO ACKNOWLEDGE** Paul Reese and Kevin Shafer. Paul gave me the opportunity to be part of another project of this size and scope. Kevin improved my paragraphs and found the right place for each code snippet. The reader will notice his great work. Special thanks go to my wife, Vanesa S. Olsen, because she understood that I needed to work with many computers and mobile devices at the same time to test each code snippet.

—GASTÓN C. HILLAR

# CONTENTS

*INTRODUCTION*                                                        *xxxiii*

## PART I: VISUAL STUDIO

**CHAPTER 1: HISTORY OF VISUAL STUDIO**                                      3

Roots                                                                        4
The First Breakthrough: Visual Basic                                         4
Other Languages and Tools                                                    4
Visual Studio 97 and 6.0                                                     5
Visual Studio.NET 2002 and 2003                                              5
Visual Studio 2005                                                           7
Visual Studio 2008                                                           8
Visual Studio 2010                                                          10
Changes in Editions                                                         10
What's New in Visual Studio 2010                                            12
Shift to WPF                                                                12
Summary                                                                     13

**CHAPTER 2: VISUAL STUDIO UI ENHANCEMENTS**                                15

Basic IDE Overview                                                          15
Exploring the Start Page                                                    15
Understanding Window Management                                             16
New Project Dialog Window                                                   17
Creating New Projects in a New Way                                          19
Using the Add Reference Dialog Window                                       19
Using the Extension Manager                                                 20
Exploring New Daily Development Features                                    20
Exploring the Code Editor Window                                            20
Code Navigation                                                             22
Generate From Usage                                                         24
Exploring the Visual Designers                                              25
WPF Designer                                                                26
XML Schema Designer                                                         27
New Tools for Architects                                                    27
Summary                                                                     29

## CHAPTER 3: VISUAL STUDIO CODE SNIPPETS — 31

**Understanding Code Snippets** — **32**
Using Code Snippets — 34
HTML, SQL, and JScript Code Snippets — 37
**Creating Code Snippets** — **38**
Creating a Simple Code Snippet — 38
The Code Snippet File Structure — 41
**Managing Code Snippets** — **51**
The Code Snippet Manager — 52
Code Snippet Storage — 53
Adding and Removing Snippets — 54
Importing Snippets — 54
**Advanced Code Snippet Features** — **56**
Multiple Snippets in a File — 56
Code Snippets in Other Languages — 58
Building Online Code Snippet Providers — 59
**Snippet Editors** — **59**
Export as Code Snippet Add-In — 60
Snippet Designer — 61
Snippet Editor — 62
**Summary** — **63**

## CHAPTER 4: VISUAL STUDIO TEMPLATES — 65

**The Role of Templates** — **66**
Project Templates — 67
Item Templates — 69
**Creating Templates** — **70**
Creating a Simple Project Template — 71
Creating a Simple Item Template — 76
**Template Storage Structure** — **81**
Template Folders — 82
The Template Manifest File — 84
**Customizing Templates** — **98**
Template Parameters — 98
Custom Template Parameters — 99
Wizards — 101
**Deploying Templates** — **110**
Exporting and Importing Templates — 111
Creating a Template Installation Kit — 114
**Summary** — **125**

## CHAPTER 5: GETTING THE MOST OUT OF THE IDE     127

### Window Management                                    128
Visual Studio Window Architecture                        128
Tool Windows                                             131
Document Windows                                         132
Arranging Windows                                        134

### Customizing Menus and Toolbars                       138
The Customize Dialog                                     139
Adding Menus and Commands                                140
Creating and Rearranging Toolbars                        144
Context Sensitivity                                      145

### IDE Configuration                                    145
The Options Dialog                                       145
Changes in Option Pages                                  147
Visual Studio Settings                                   150

### Reducing Efforts with Keyboard Shortcuts            155
Command Routing and Command Contexts                     155
Working with Keyboard Shortcuts                          157
Working with Keyboard Mapping Schemes                    160

### Custom Start Pages                                   162
Creating Your First Custom Start Page                    163
Changing the StartPage.xaml File                         173
Accessing the Visual Studio Context                      176
Accessing the Visual Studio Object Model                 182
A Few More Points About Start Pages                      186

### Customizing the Toolbox                              186
A Lap Around the Toolbox                                 186
Customizing Toolbox Tabs                                 189
Adding Items to the Toolbox                              190
A Few More Points About Toolbox Customization            193

### Visual Studio Gallery                                193
Browsing the Visual Studio Gallery                       194
Downloading and Installing Components                    196
Adding Your Own Contributions to the Gallery             197
Working Together with the Community                      198

### Summary                                              198

**CHAPTER 6: VISUAL STUDIO EXTENSIBILITY**     **201**

**The Visual Studio Shell and Packages**     **202**
Package Integration     203
**Extensibility Out of the Box**     **204**
Extending Visual Studio by Customization     204
Using Macros to Automate Common Tasks     208
Visual Studio Add-Ins     209
**Extensions with Visual Studio SDK**     **210**
The Full Power of Extensibility     210
Visual Studio Package Development     211
Editor Extensibility     212
**Creating Visual Studio Macros**     **213**
Understanding the Structure of Macros     213
Using the Macros IDE     218
Recording and Developing Macros     221
Macro Samples     225
**Creating Visual Studio Add-Ins**     **229**
Add-In Architecture     229
Creating a Simple Add-In     230
Using the Automation Model     239
Going on with Add-In Development     241
**Visual Studio Packages in a Nutshell**     **242**
Creating a Package with a Simple Menu Command     242
Debugging the Package     254
**Extending the New Editor**     **255**
Extending the Editor with the Managed Extensibility Framework     256
Editor Extensibility Points     258
Creating a Simple Classifier     260
**Summary**     **275**

**PART II: .NET 4**

**CHAPTER 7: .NET FRAMEWORK VERSION HISTORY**     **279**

**Before the .NET Framework**     **279**
Win/Win32 Programming in C     279
C++ Programming     280
Programming in Visual Basic     280
Programming in Delphi     281
COM Programming     281

The Origin and Goals of the .NET Framework                          282
Evolution of the .NET Framework                                     283
  .NET Framework 1.0                                                286
  .NET Framework 1.1                                                286
  .NET Framework 2.0                                                286
  .NET Framework 3.0                                                287
  .NET Framework 3.5                                                287
  .NET Framework 4.0                                                288
  .NET Compact Framework                                            289
  .NET Micro Framework                                              289
.NET Framework Architecture                                         289
  Common Language Run-time (CLR)                                    290
  Base Class Library                                                291
  Services of the .NET Architecture                                 292
Main Benefits of the .NET Framework                                 293
Summary                                                             294

CHAPTER 8: MODERN UI FRAMEWORKS (WPF AND SILVERLIGHT)               297

The Importance of User Experience                                   297
Developers Are from Vulcan, Designers Are from Venus                299
A New Generation of Presentation Frameworks                         301
The Ten Pillars of Silverlight                                      303
  XAML                                                              304
  Tools for Working with Silverlight (and WPF)                      313
  Layout                                                            315
  Data Binding                                                      322
  Styles                                                            330
  Templates                                                         332
  Animations                                                        341
  Media                                                             345
  Networking                                                        352
  Other Features                                                    355
Windows Presentation Foundation                                     359
  WPF Features not Available in Silverlight                         361
Choosing Between WPF and Silverlight                                366
Designer - Developer Cooperation in Silverlight and WPF             367
  A Common Solution Format                                          367
  Blendability                                                      368
  Design Time Sample Data in Blend                                  369

SketchFlow 370

Triggers, Actions, and Behaviors 371

Model-View-ViewModel Pattern 372

**Summary** **373**

**CHAPTER 9: WINDOWS COMMUNICATION FOUNDATION (WCF)** **375**

**WCF Versus ASMX Web Services** **375**
**A Quick Look at SOA** **376**

Service 377

Service Provider 377

Service Consumer(s) 377

Service Registry 377

Service Contract 377

Service Proxy 378

Service Lease 378

Message 378

Service Description 378

Advertising and Discovery 378

**Building Blocks of the WCF Architecture** **378**
**Getting Started With WCF** **381**

Creating the WCF Service 382

Defining Data Contracts 386

Specifying the Binding Information 387

Hosting the WCF Service 388

Creating the Service Proxy 389

Creating the Service Client — The Service Consumer 391

**Working with an Ajax-Enabled WCF Service** **392**
**REST and WCF** **394**
**Implementing a WCF Service Declaratively** **394**

Defining the Service Contract 395

Hosting the Service 396

Implementing the Service Logic Declaratively 396

**Summary** **398**

**CHAPTER 10: ENHANCEMENTS TO THE .NET CORE FRAMEWORK** **399**

**Changes in Common Language Run-time** **400**

In-Process Side-By-Side Execution 400

DLR Integration 402

Type Equivalence 411

| | |
|---|---|
| **Parallel Computing** | **415** |
| The Challenge of Many-core Shift | 416 |
| The Microsoft Approach | 418 |
| Parallel LINQ | 421 |
| Task Parallel Library | 428 |
| **Code Contracts** | **455** |
| **Managed Extensibility Framework** | **463** |
| The Challenge | 463 |
| A Simple MEF Example | 465 |
| Basic MEF Concepts | 471 |
| Composition | 477 |
| A Few More Points on MEF | 486 |
| **Summary** | **487** |

| | |
|---|---|
| **CHAPTER 11: ENHANCEMENTS TO THE .NET WORKFLOW FRAMEWORK** | **489** |

| | |
|---|---|
| **An Introduction to WF 4.0** | **490** |
| The Workflow Design Surface | 491 |
| The Hello Workflow Application | 492 |
| **Creating Flowcharts and Coded Workflows** | **499** |
| Flowcharts in WF 4.0 | 500 |
| Code-Only Workflows | 505 |
| **Workflow Architecture** | **509** |
| WorkflowApplication and Hosts | 510 |
| Activities | 511 |
| Extensions | 512 |
| Workflow Activity Model Changes | 513 |
| **Workflow Activity Library** | **517** |
| Primitive Activities | 518 |
| Flow Control Activities | 518 |
| Workflow Run-Time Activities | 520 |
| Flowchart Specific Activities | 521 |
| Error-Handling Activities | 522 |
| Transaction Handling Activities | 523 |
| Collection-Handling Activities | 524 |
| Messaging Activities | 525 |
| **Using the Compensating Transaction Model** | **527** |
| The ConferenceWorkflow Example | 527 |
| Implementing Cancellation, Confirmation, and Compensation | 528 |
| Cancellation | 530 |
| Compensation | 530 |

**Persistence and Human Interactions** **532**

The DomainNameWorkflow Project 533

Workflow Tracking 544

**Workflow Services** **551**

Creating a Workflow Service 551

Using WorkflowServiceHost 553

**Summary** **562**

**CHAPTER 12: ENHANCEMENTS TO THE .NET DATA FRAMEWORK** **563**

**Language Integrated Query (LINQ)** **563**

LINQ Operators 564

LINQ Implementations 566

**Parallel LINQ (PLINQ)** **572**

**Entity Framework** **573**

Entity Framework Architecture 573

**The Entity Data Source Control** **579**

**Choosing Between LINQ to Entities and LINQ to SQL** **579**

**Summary** **579**

**CHAPTER 13: ENHANCEMENTS TO THE .NET COMMUNICATION FRAMEWORK** **581**

**Enhancements in WCF Framework 3.5** **581**

**Enhancements in WCF Framework 4.0** **583**

Simplified Configuration 583

Standard Endpoints 585

Discovery 586

REST Improvements 588

Routing Service 589

**Summary** **592**

**CHAPTER 14: .NET CHARTING COMPONENTS** **593**

**Creating Charts** **594**

Creating a Simple Chart 594

Adding Data to the Chart Programmatically 598

Adding Charts to WPF Applications 603

**Using Chart Controls** **605**

Elements of a Chart 606

The Chart Class 607

Chart Types 609

Chart Coordinate System 617

Three-Dimensional Charts 619
Appearance of Chart Elements 621
Axes and Related Chart Elements 623
Data Points 630
**Advanced Chart Manipulation** **633**
Annotations 633
Binding Data to Series 638
The DataManipulator class 641
More Chart Manipulations 648
**Summary** **649**

**PART III: ASP.NET 4.0**

**CHAPTER 15: ASP.NET VERSION HISTORY** **653**

**Development of the Web and Web Development** **653**
**Enter ASP** **654**
**Enter ASP.NET** **655**
**ASP.NET Version History** **657**
ASP.NET 1.0 659
ASP.NET 1.1 659
ASP.NET 2.0 659
ASP.NET 3.0 664
ASP.NET 3.5 665
ASP.NET 3.5 SP1 667
ASP.NET 4.0 667
**Summary** **668**

**CHAPTER 16: ASP.NET CHARTING CONTROLS** **669**

**Creating Charts** **670**
Adding a Chart Control to a Page 670
Setting up Charts in an Event Handler Method 671
Binding Data to the Chart 676
**Rendering ASP.NET Charts** **679**
Image URL Rendering 680
Using Charts with Legacy Web Sites 683
Binary Stream Rendering 684
**Chart State Management** **688**
Saving Chart State 688
Advanced Chart State Management 690

| | |
|---|---|
| **User Interactivity** | **694** |
| Using Tooltips | 694 |
| Handling Clicks on Data Points | 696 |
| Interactivity With Ajax | 697 |
| A Few More Points on User Interactivity | 709 |
| **Summary** | **709** |

| | |
|---|---|
| **CHAPTER 17: ASP.NET DYNAMIC DATA** | **711** |
| **Creating a New Dynamic Data Web Site** | **711** |
| Working Against a Data Model | 711 |
| Displaying Data from Existing Tables | 716 |
| Creating Simple CRUD Applications | 718 |
| Creating a Dynamic Data Application for Master-Detail Relationships | 725 |
| **Working to Modify Implementation to Fit Business Needs** | **730** |
| Understanding Dynamic Data's Structure | 730 |
| Customizing the Look and Feel | 732 |
| Working with Page Templates | 735 |
| Working with Field Templates | 738 |
| Working with Entity Templates | 741 |
| Working with Filter Templates | 744 |
| Creating Custom Pages | 746 |
| Customizing Validations | 747 |
| **Summary** | **750** |

| | |
|---|---|
| **CHAPTER 18: ASP.NET MODEL VIEW CONTROLLER (MVC)** | **751** |
| **Introduction to MVC** | **752** |
| Similar Design Patterns | 753 |
| Microsoft and the Web Platform | 753 |
| What Is Microsoft ASP.NET MVC 2? | 754 |
| Extensibility in MVC | 760 |
| **Creating an MVC 2 Application** | **761** |
| The Project Structure | 763 |
| How Does it Work? | 764 |
| **Adding New MVC 2 Pages** | **771** |
| Create a Database | 771 |
| Create a Model | 772 |
| Listing Books | 773 |
| Adding Book Actions | 779 |

| | |
|---|---|
| **Customization in MVC 2** | **790** |
| Model Binding | 790 |
| Validation | 795 |
| UI Customization | 804 |
| **Routing Details** | **816** |
| Controller Factory | 816 |
| Influencing the Execution Flow | 817 |
| Authorization | 819 |
| Action and Result Filtering | 821 |
| Exception Filtering | 822 |
| ActionResult | 822 |
| **Testing with MVC 2** | **824** |
| Refactoring AcmeLibrary | 824 |
| Creating and Running Unit Tests | 831 |
| **A Few More Points on MVC 2** | **834** |
| Areas | 834 |
| Metadata Providers | 834 |
| Value Providers | 834 |
| Model Binders | 835 |
| Child Actions | 835 |
| Asynchronous Controllers | 835 |
| **Summary** | **835** |
| | |
| **CHAPTER 19: ASP.NET AJAX IMPROVEMENTS** | **837** |
| | |
| **Understanding Ajax** | **838** |
| The XMLHttpRequest Object | 839 |
| ASP.NET and Ajax | 840 |
| **Using the ASP.NET Ajax Server Controls** | **841** |
| Refactoring the Framework Libraries | 844 |
| Using the Microsoft CDN | 846 |
| **Using the Microsoft Ajax Library** | **848** |
| Working with DOM Elements | 852 |
| The Script Loader | 855 |
| Client Side Data Binding with Templates | 859 |
| Advanced Data-Binding Scenarios | 872 |
| Working with Server-Side Data | 878 |
| **Summary** | **892** |

**CHAPTER 20: ASP.NET AJAX CONTROL TOOLKIT AND JQUERY** | **893**

**First Look at the Ajax Control Toolkit** | **894**
Installing the Ajax Control Toolkit | 894
Creating a Simple Web Application with the Toolkit | 896
**Using the Controls of the Toolkit** | **908**
New Server Controls | 915
Control Extenders | 938
Animations | 957
**The jQuery Library** | **962**
"Hello, World" with jQuery | 963
Selectors and Filters | 965
Chaining and Utility Functions | 970
Eventing Model and Event Handlers | 971
Visual Effects and Animations | 975
jQuery Ajax Features | 976
**Summary** | **977**

**PART IV: VB.NET**

**CHAPTER 21: HISTORY OF VISUAL BASIC** | **981**

**The Roots of Visual Basic** | **982**
Structured and Unstructured BASIC | 982
Moving to "Visual" | 984
Visual Basic in the 1990s | 985
**Visual Basic in the .NET Framework** | **986**
Design Goals and Debates | 986
Visual Basic .NET (7.0) and .NET 2003 (7.1) | 987
Visual Basic 2005 (8.0) | 989
Visual Basic 2008 (9.0) | 997
**Summary** | **1005**

**CHAPTER 22: VISUAL BASIC 10.0 LANGUAGE IMPROVEMENTS** | **1007**

**New Productivity-Improving Syntax** | **1008**
Implicit Line Continuation | 1008
Auto-Implemented Properties | 1010
Collection Initializers | 1012
Multiline Lambda Expressions | 1018
**Working with Dynamic Objects** | **1020**
Late Binding in Visual Basic 2010 | 1021
Accessing an IronPython Library | 1023

| | |
|---|---|
| **Variance** | **1026** |
| Type Substitution | 1026 |
| Variance in Visual Basic 2010 | 1029 |
| A Few More Points on Variance | 1033 |
| **Summary** | **1038** |

## PART V: C#

### CHAPTER 23: HISTORY OF C# — 1041

| | |
|---|---|
| **The Evolution of C#** | **1041** |
| Design Goals | 1042 |
| Short History | 1042 |
| Implementations | 1043 |
| **C# 1.0** | **1044** |
| Type System | 1044 |
| Memory Management | 1045 |
| Syntactic Sugar | 1046 |
| C# 1.1 | 1047 |
| **C# 2.0** | **1047** |
| Generic Types | 1048 |
| Partial Types | 1050 |
| Static Classes | 1051 |
| Iterators | 1052 |
| Anonymous Methods | 1052 |
| Delegate Inference | 1053 |
| Delegate Covariance and Contravariance | 1053 |
| Nullable Types | 1054 |
| Property Accessors | 1055 |
| Null-Coalesce Operator | 1056 |
| Namespace Aliases | 1056 |
| **C# 3.0** | **1056** |
| Local Variable Type Inference | 1057 |
| Extension Methods | 1057 |
| Anonymous Types | 1058 |
| Lambda Expressions | 1059 |
| Query Expressions | 1060 |
| Expression Trees | 1061 |
| Automatic Properties | 1062 |
| Object Initializers | 1062 |
| Collection Intializers | 1063 |
| Partial Methods | 1063 |
| **Summary** | **1064** |

## CHAPTER 24: C# 4.0 LANGUAGE IMPROVEMENTS — 1065

### Pains with Interoperability — 1066
Creating the PainWithOffice Application — 1066
Frustrating Issues — 1069
Remove the Pain — 1070

### Dynamic Lookup — 1072
Dynamic Binding — 1072
The dynamic Type — 1073
Dynamic Operations — 1074
The Dynamic Language Run-time — 1077

### Named and Optional Parameters — 1078
Using Optional Parameters — 1079
Using Named Parameters — 1081
Overload Resolution — 1082

### COM-Specific Interoperability Features — 1084
Dynamic Import — 1084
Omitting ref from Parameters — 1084
Indexed Properties — 1085
Compiling Without PIAs — 1086

### Variance — 1087
Type Substitution — 1087
Bird's-Eye View of Variance — 1089
Variance in C# 4.0 — 1090
A Few More Points on Variance — 1094

### Summary — 1099

## PART VI: F#

## CHAPTER 25: VISUAL F# AND THE OTHER .NET LANGUAGES — 1103

### A Brief History of F# — 1104
### F# at First Glance — 1105
Trying Things Out with F# — 1106
Understanding Syntax — 1107

### Your First F# Project — 1112
### Programming with F# — 1113
Namespaces and Modules — 1113
Attributes — 1115
Literals and Bindings — 1115
Expressions — 1120
Values and F# Types — 1124

Type Augmentations     1137
Computation Expressions     1138
Sequences     1141
Range Expressions     1143
Sequence Expressions     1143
Asynchronous Workflows     1144
Pattern Matching     1146
Active Patterns     1149
Exceptions     1154
Units of Measure     1157
Lazy Computations     1159
Quotations     1160
Working with Database Queries     1161
**A Larger Application in F#**     **1163**
The Ast Module     1164
The Language Module     1164
The Evaluator Module     1166
The FunctionPlotter Module     1167
Running the Function Plotter     1170
**Other .NET Languages**     **1170**
IronRuby     1170
IronPython     1170
**Summary**     **1171**

*INDEX*     *1173*

# INTRODUCTION

**IN THE .NET DEVELOPMENT WORLD,** we have seen massive improvements and enhancements to the framework over the last several years. Since 2006, we have seen releases of .NET 3.0, .NET 3.5, and .NET 4. We have also seen the introduction of many new technologies such as Windows Communication Foundation (WCF), Windows Presentation Foundation (WPF), Windows Workflow, and Silverlight that came as parts of the various releases.

Keeping up with all of this change can be difficult for all developers, both those new to the industry and those who have been using .NET since its inception almost ten years ago. To help keep up with this rapid change, this book serves as an "all-in-one reference" for the major changes and enhancements and provides a glimpse into the specifics of the new technologies.

## WHO THIS BOOK IS FOR

This book was written with the experienced .NET developer in mind. Many of the chapters talk specifically about the enhancements or changes that have been introduced with the new versions of the .NET Framework. However, even those readers who are not fluent in .NET development should be able take a lot out of the detailed examples provided in this book.

For the experienced reader, a few "history" chapters have been added to help identify when various functionality has been added so that you can quickly identify the needed toolset to be able to adopt a specific feature.

## WHAT THIS BOOK COVERS

This book focuses on enhancements that have been added to .NET and Visual Studio 2010 over previous versions. In certain chapters and sections, a more historical view is presented to help provide context. For example, in the chapters discussing WCF, an examination of WCF basics and features added in .NET 3.5 are needed to help provide a full understanding of the functionality provided in the 4.0 release.

This book is intended to be an overview of Visual Studio and .NET as a whole. It is *not* a book on any single topic, but rather a more macro-level overview. As such, many concepts will be introduced in one or two chapters to provide an overview of the functionality and how it can be leveraged. For many of the topics such as WCF, Silverlight, and WPF, there are several entire books dedicated to the topic. The goal of this book is to provide an introduction to the technology, allowing you the capability to make a selection of the next area to study in more detail.

# HOW THIS BOOK IS STRUCTURED

Given the broad scope of this book, it has been divided into six distinct sections that will help you quickly locate the content most relevant to you. It is not necessarily structured in a manner to be read cover-to-cover, although chapters are tied together to make that reading style as cohesive as possible.

The following sections provide you with a section-by-section and chapter-by-chapter breakdown of the content included.

## Part I: Visual Studio

This section is dedicated to the discussion of the Visual Studio 2010 Integrated Development Environment (IDE), and the enhancements and features available to developers.

➤ *Chapter 1: "History of Visual Studio"* — This chapter provides an important introduction to the history of how the Visual Studio product has evolved from the foundation to the current product it is today. Major milestones and supported languages are discussed, along with major enhancements included in each release.

➤ *Chapter 2: "Visual Studio UI Enhancements"* — This chapter focuses on the major User Interface (UI) changes between the Visual Studio 2008 and Visual Studio 2010 products. The conversion of Visual Studio to use Windows Presentation Foundation (WPF) provided an incredible amount of new UI features and functionality, which are all discussed in this chapter.

➤ *Chapter 3: "Visual Studio Code Snippets"* — From a developer productivity standpoint, Visual Studio's Code Snippets functionality is one of the biggest timesavers when it comes down to reducing total keystrokes. This chapter is dedicated to discussing how to use and create code snippets to improve productivity.

➤ *Chapter 4: "Visual Studio Templates"* — In addition to code snippets, Visual Studio provides a robust template system that allows for templates to be created for projects or specific items. This chapter focuses on introducing the various template types, and how they can be used to improve the development process.

➤ *Chapter 5: "Getting the Most Out of the IDE"* — The feature set included in Visual Studio 2010 is massive, and the number of configuration items can be mind-boggling, even to those who have been using Visual Studio for a long time. This chapter focuses on ways to get the most out of the IDE, including customization, window management, shortcuts, and the gallery.

➤ *Chapter 6: "Visual Studio Extensibility"* — In addition to the robust configuration and other features included with Visual Studio, there is additional support for extensibility in the form of plug-ins, macros, and the like. This chapter illustrates how Visual Studio is set up to allow for extension by developers.

# Part II: .NET 4

The second portion of the book is dedicated to functionality provided by the 4.0 version of the .NET Framework. Each of these chapters dives into new functionality that has been added across the various technology sections of the .NET Framework.

➤ *Chapter 7: ".NET Framework Version History"* — Before individual enhancements can be discussed, it is important to understand the history of the .NET Framework. With such rapid change in .NET over the past few years, this chapter helps to level-set the times, versions, and release cycles that introduced new or improved functionality to the framework.

➤ *Chapter 8: "Modern UI Frameworks (WPF and Silverlight)"* — Recent releases of Visual Studio have added two new UI frameworks. This chapter provides a quick overview to answer the three most important questions when looking at new frameworks: when it should be used, why it should be used, and how it should be used.

➤ *Chapter 9: "Windows Communication Framework (WCF)"* — This chapter is dedicated to WCF as it functions within the .NET 4 and Visual Studio 2010 environment.

➤ *Chapter 10: "Enhancements to the .NET Core Framework"* — This chapter examines the new functionality added to the framework that can support development using various other framework portions. You will learn about changes to the Common Language Runtime (CLR), the addition of parallel computing, code contracts, and the Managed Extensibility Framework (MEF).

➤ *Chapter 11: "Enhancements to the .NET Workflow Framework"* — Windows Workflow is another of the .NET framework pieces that has seen a large number of changes with past releases of Visual Studio. This chapter is dedicated to discussing the major changes that have been introduced in the .NET 4 release.

➤ *Chapter 12: "Enhancements to the .NET Data Framework"* — Microsoft has been dedicated to providing object relational mapping (ORM) style tools for developers and, as such, items such as the entity framework and the like have seen a number of massive changes in recent releases. This chapter is dedicated to the enhancements included within the Data portions of the framework.

➤ *Chapter 13: "Enhancements to the .NET Communications Framework"* — This chapter about communications discusses the enhancements and changes that have been introduced with .NET 4. This chapter is most helpful for readers who are moving forward from older versions of WCF.

➤ *Chapter 14: ".NET Charting Components"* — Although available as part of .NET 3.5 Service Pack 1 (SP1), the .NET charting components are a very powerful and recent addition to the .NET Framework. This chapter examines the usage and benefits provided by the built-in charting components that are available with .NET 4.

# Part III: ASP.NET 4.0

The third portion of this book focuses on ASP.NET 4.0 and related items. For web application developers, this section pulls together all of the new features and enhancements into one location, making it easy to find the items specific to web functionality.

➤ *Chapter 15: "ASP.NET Version History"* — Similar in nature to the .NET Framework as a whole, it is important to remember major milestones with regard to the previous releases of ASP.NET to ensure that you are aware of new or changed functionality that has been introduced. This chapter provides that needed foundation.

➤ *Chapter 16: "ASP.NET Charting Controls"* — This chapter examines .NET Charting components in a general manner. Here you will learn about the controls within the context of an ASP.NET application, and the steps necessary to properly leverage the controls.

➤ *Chapter 17: "ASP.NET Dynamic Data"* — Microsoft recently added support for dynamic data, and this chapter is dedicated to discussing the features, benefits, and options available when using dynamic data.

➤ *Chapter 18: "ASP.NET Model View Controller (MVC)"* — Microsoft has added a new project template type that supports web application development using the well-known MVC design pattern. The introduction of MVC to the ASP.NET feature set has added a number of items that can be used by developers of both MVC and Web Forms applications, and this chapter is dedicated to those discussions.

➤ *Chapter 19: "ASP.NET Ajax Improvements"* — ASP.NET Ajax is the foundational component for creating a rich user experience with an ASP.NET application. A number of enhancements were added to ASP.NET Ajax implementation, and this chapter is dedicated to outlining all new features.

➤ *Chapter 20: "Ajax Control Toolkit, jQuery, and More"* — In addition to the base ASP.NET Ajax offering, Microsoft maintains a secondary download of the Ajax Control Toolkit, which provides a robust set of additional controls. Microsoft has also embraced and added support for the jQuery Open Source JavaScript library. This chapter discusses these items and how they can relate within your applications.

# Part IV: VB.NET

This section of the book is dedicated to discussing new features and enhancements that have been added to the Visual Basic language. This is a short section because of the limited changes that impact the Visual Basic language only.

➤ *Chapter 21: "History of Visual Basic"* — To help get an understanding of the changes to the Visual Basic language, it is important to understand the history of the language, and when certain features were added. This chapter provides the needed introduction.

➤ *Chapter 22: "Visual Basic 10 Language Enhancements"* — This chapter focuses on additions and enhancements to the Visual Basic language as provided by Visual Studio 2010.

## Part V: C#

This section of the book is dedicated to discussing new features and enhancements that have been added to the C# Language. This is a short section because of the limited changes that impact the C# language only.

➤ *Chapter 23: "History of C#"* — To help get an understanding of the changes to C# included with Visual Studio 2010, this chapter has been provided to set up the history of the language with a short summary of major enhancements provided in past releases.

➤ *Chapter 24: "C# 4.0 Language Enhancements"* — This chapter examines the new language features that have been added to C# for version 4.0. Items such as covariance and other language enhancements are discussed with examples.

## Part VI: F# and Other .NET Languages

The final section of this book discusses the F# language and other .NET languages such as IronRuby and IronPython. This section contains Chapter 25, which is the final chapter of the book. This extensive chapter introduces the F# language with detailed examples and explanations that will allow you to quickly get up and running with F#. The chapter finishes with information on IronRuby and IronPython.

## WHAT YOU NEED TO USE THIS BOOK

Readers will need access to an edition of Visual Studio 2010; this book uses the Premium edition of Visual Studio 2010 for most of the examples. However, other editions (including the Express editions) will work.

## CONVENTIONS

To help you get the most from the text and keep track of what's happening, we've used a number of conventions throughout the book.

*Boxes with a warning icon like this one hold important, not-to-be-forgotten information that is directly relevant to the surrounding text.*

*The pencil icon indicates notes, tips, hints, tricks, or asides to the current discussion.*

As for styles in the text:

➤ We *highlight* new terms and important words when we introduce them.

➤ We show keyboard strokes like this: Ctrl+A.

➤ We show filenames, URLs, and code within the text like so: `persistence.properties`.

➤ We present code in two different ways:

```
We use a monofont type for most code examples.
We use bold to emphasize code that is particularly important in the present
    context, or to show changes from a previous code snippet.
```

## SOURCE CODE

As you work through the examples in this book, you may choose either to type in all the code manually, or to use the source code files that accompany the book. Some of the source code used in this book is available for download at `www.wrox.com`. When at the site, simply locate the book's title (use the Search box or one of the title lists) and click the Download Code link on the book's detail page to obtain the source code for the book. Code included on the website is highlighted by the following icon:

**Available for download on Wrox.com**

Listings include the filename in the title. If it is just a code snippet, you'll find the filename in a code note such as this:

*Code snippet filename*

 *Because many books have similar titles, you may find it easiest to search by ISBN; this book's ISBN is 978-0-470-49948-1.*

Once you download the code, just decompress it with your favorite compression tool. Alternately, you can go to the main Wrox code download page at www.wrox.com/dynamic/books/ download.aspx to see the code available for this book and all other Wrox books.

## ERRATA

We make every effort to ensure that there are no errors in the text or in the code. However, no one is perfect, and mistakes do occur. If you find an error in one of our books, like a spelling mistake or faulty piece of code, we would be very grateful for your feedback. By sending in errata, you may save another reader hours of frustration, and at the same time, you will be helping us provide even higher quality information.

To find the errata page for this book, go to www.wrox.com and locate the title using the Search box or one of the title lists. Then, on the book details page, click the Book Errata link. On this page, you can view all errata that has been submitted for this book and posted by Wrox editors. A complete book list, including links to each book's errata, is also available at www.wrox.com/misc-pages/booklist.shtml.

If you don't spot "your" error on the Book Errata page, go to www.wrox.com/contact/techsupport.shtml and complete the form there to send us the error you have found. We'll check the information and, if appropriate, post a message to the book's errata page and fix the problem in subsequent editions of the book.

## P2P.WROX.COM

For author and peer discussion, join the P2P forums at p2p.wrox.com. The forums are a web-based system for you to post messages relating to Wrox books and related technologies, and interact with other readers and technology users. The forums offer a subscription feature to email you topics of interest of your choosing when new posts are made to the forums. Wrox authors, editors, other industry experts, and your fellow readers are present on these forums.

At p2p.wrox.com, you will find a number of different forums that will help you, not only as you read this book, but also as you develop your own applications. To join the forums, just follow these steps:

1. Go to p2p.wrox.com and click the Register link.

2. Read the terms of use and click Agree.

3. Complete the required information to join, as well as any optional information you wish to provide, and click Submit.

4. You will receive an email with information describing how to verify your account and complete the joining process.

 *You can read messages in the forums without joining P2P, but in order to post your own messages, you must join.*

Once you join, you can post new messages and respond to messages other users post. You can read messages at any time on the web. If you would like to have new messages from a particular forum emailed to you, click the "Subscribe to this Forum" icon by the forum name in the forum listing.

For more information about how to use the Wrox P2P, be sure to read the P2P FAQs for answers to questions about how the forum software works, as well as many common questions specific to P2P and Wrox books. To read the FAQs, click the FAQ link on any P2P page.

# PART I
# Visual Studio

▶ **CHAPTER 1:** History of Visual Studio

▶ **CHAPTER 2:** Visual Studio UI Enhancements

▶ **CHAPTER 3:** Visual Studio Code Snippets

▶ **CHAPTER 4:** Visual Studio Templates

▶ **CHAPTER 5:** Getting the Most Out of the IDE

▶ **CHAPTER 6:** Visual Studio Extensibility

# 1

# History of Visual Studio

Although this book is dedicated to Visual Studio 2010 and .NET Framework 4.0, having a good historical background in Visual Studio can help you better understand the features treated in the subsequent chapters. Regardless of whether you are old friends with Visual Studio or it is new for you, it is always worth knowing where it started and how it's been evolving.

The roots of Visual Studio go back for almost 19 years, back to the point somewhere between the release of Windows 3.0 and 3.1. It is incredible how the development tool has evolved enormously during almost two decades! The road behind Visual Studio was never smooth or flat; it was full of bumps and curves. However, one thing stayed constant during the years: Microsoft created this tool with developers in mind, and made amazing efforts to build a strong developer community surrounding the product.

In this chapter, you'll read a short story of Visual Studio's past and present, with emphasis on the roots of this great tool, as well as the situations and motivations that led to the integrated development environment (IDE) you use today.

---

**VISUAL STUDIO DOCUMENTARY**

At PDC 2009 (held between November 17 and 19, 2009, in Los Angeles), Microsoft published a screencast with the title, "Visual Studio Documentary." This one-hour video is a great source for "company secrets" surrounding Visual Studio from the ancient ages to the present-day stage. A number of Microsoft (and ex-Microsoft) celebrities such as Anders Hejlsberg, Alan Cooper, Bill Gates, Tim Huckaby, Sivaramakichenane Somasegar, Dan Fernandez, Tony Goodhew, Jason Zander, Scott Guthrie, and Steve Balmer are featured in this video. They add interesting personal commentaries on history, motivations, technology context, competitors, and nitty-gritties that paved the road for Visual Studio.

You can download this two-part documentary from http://channel9.msdn.com/ shows/VisualStudioDocumentary/The-Visual-Studio-Documentary- Part-One, where you can also find the link for the second part of the video.

## ROOTS

For a long time, Windows development was a field where only C and C++ programmers could play. They had to carry out a lot of tasks for creating the simplest user interface — such as defining and registering Windows classes, implementing the Windows message loop, dispatching Windows messages, painting the client in Windows, and so on. The smallest "Hello, World" program for Windows was about a hundred lines of code, where you could not meet any explicit statement to print out the "Hello, World" text. Instead, you had to draw this text to an absolute window position as a response to the WM_PAINT message. At that time, the user interface (UI) was defined by static text files that were compiled into binary resources and linked to the application. The UI missed the concept of controls — there were windows and child windows, all of them represented by HWNDs (or window handles).

At that time, developers accepted this way of Windows software creation as a price for interacting with a graphical user interface (GUI).

## The First Breakthrough: Visual Basic

The first tool that dramatically changed Windows application development was Visual Basic 1.0, released in May 1991. Visual Basic introduced (or, perhaps, invented) such concepts as forms, controls, code-behind files — all of which are still in use in contemporary development tools. Instead of writing resource files and addressing UI elements through 16-bit constants, you could drag-and-drop predefined UI controls to your forms and program their events. The hundred-line "Hello, World" program was so simple with Visual Basic:

```
Private Sub Form_Load()
    MsgBox("Hello, World!")
End Sub
```

You did not have to care about programming the message loop or event dispatching code! Visual Basic allowed you to create an application represented by an icon on the Windows desktop. When you double-clicked on that icon, the application started and ran just as Word or Excel — which, at that time, was a delightful experience. Visual Basic revolutionized the application development platform, because it made Windows programming available for the masses.

## Other Languages and Tools

The whole visual composition aspect of Visual Basic was something that could be applied for the C++ and other languages as well. In the few years following the release of Visual Basic, a plethora of tools was created by Microsoft:

➤ Visual C++ 1.0 was released in February 1993 with Microsoft Foundation Classes (MFC) 2.0 and proved that C++ programming for Windows could be more productive than ever before — while still keeping the full and granular control over the operating system.

➤ In 1992, Fox Technologies (the creator of FoxBASE and FoxPro) merged with Microsoft, and, at the end of 1995, Visual FoxPro 3.0 was released.

➤ The emergence of the Java programming language in 1995 motivated Microsoft to create its own Java language implementation. It was Visual J++1.0 that conformed to the Sun specification and used Microsoft's Java Virtual Machine (JVM).

Having so many separate languages and tools, the architect teams recognized that the whole visual aspect could be separated from the languages. Why create separate IDEs for all the languages and tools if they could fit into the same environment? That was when the idea of Visual Studio was born.

## Visual Studio 97 and 6.0

In 1997, Microsoft built a single environment to integrate multiple languages into one application surface. This was released as Visual Studio 97, bundling Microsoft development tools for the first time. This package contained Visual Basic 5.0, Visual C++ 5.0, Visual FoxPro 5.0, and Visual J++ 1.1 from the set of existing tools. The bundle was also extended with Visual InterDev, a new tool for developing dynamically generated Web sites using the Active Server Pages (ASP) technology. A snapshot of the Microsoft Developer Network Library was also a part of the package.

At this time, the IDE named Developer Studio integrated only Visual C++, J++, Visual InterDev, and MSDN. The name "Visual Studio" was rather the name of the bundle (because Visual Basic and Visual FoxPro had their own IDEs).

The famous and long-lived logo of Visual Studio that resembles the sign of infinity (or to the Moebius strip) was introduced with the first version. You can clearly recognize it from the package cover shown in Figure 1-1.

Shortly after the 1997 version, in June 1998, Visual Studio 6.0 was released. It did not contain too many new things, but fixed early integration issues to make the product more robust. The version numbers of all of its constituent parts also moved to 6.0 to suggest a higher level of integrity among the individual tools. However, instead of three IDEs in Visual Studio 97, version 6.0 had four, because Visual C++ got its own IDE.

Microsoft understood the challenge of the Java phenomenon. Not only the language, but also the managed nature of the Java platform inspired the company to make a huge leap in regard to a development platform shift. The huge amount of research and development work done between 1998 and 2002 led to the introduction of the .NET Framework. This new platform entirely changed the future of Visual Studio.

**FIGURE 1-1:** The Visual Studio 97 package

## VISUAL STUDIO.NET 2002 AND 2003

In July 2000, the .NET Framework was first announced publicly at Professional Developers Conference (PDC) in Orlando, Florida. At PDC, Microsoft also demonstrated C#, and announced ASP+ (which was later renamed to ASP.NET) and Visual Studio.NET. It took more than a year and a half, but, in February 2002, .NET Framework 1.0 was released as part of a pair with Visual Studio.NET (the latter of which is often referred as Visual Studio .NET 2002).

Visual Studio.NET had an IDE that finally integrated the tools and languages into the same environment. Because (except for Visual C++) all the languages were new (even Visual Basic .NET could be considered as new, because it had been fundamentally changed), the toolset had to be re-designed and re-implemented. Microsoft had a better chance to ultimately integrate the pieces into a single IDE, and it did so remarkably. Figure 1-2 shows the splash screen of Visual Studio.NET Enterprise Architect Edition, which indicates that constituent languages and tools share a common IDE.

**FIGURE 1-2:** Visual Studio.NET splash screen

The set of languages Microsoft integrated into the product were established with long-term support for the .NET Framework in mind. At that time, developers could use four languages out-of-the-box:

➤   *Visual C#* — This completely new language was developed (by a team led by Anders Hejlsberg) and enormously used by Microsoft itself to develop the Base Class Library of the framework. This new language attracted a lot of developers both from the former Visual Basic and C++ camps, and became very popular. It uses C-like syntax ("curly-braced-language"), but its constructs are more readable than those of C or C++.

➤   *Visual Basic .NET* — The former Visual Basic versions just scratched the surface of object-oriented programming (OOP), but the real innovations were missing from the language for a long time. The clear object-oriented nature of .NET required a new Visual Basic. Microsoft recognized the popularity of the language and created Visual Basic .NET with full .NET and OOP support.

➤ *Visual C++* — With the ascension of .NET, there were still many software development areas with native (Win32 API) Windows development rules (for example, device driver implementation). Visual C++ provided this capability. Besides, Visual C++ was able to interoperate with managed code, and additional grammatical and syntactic extensions (Managed Extensions for C++) allowed compiling code targeting the .NET Common Language Run-time (CLR).

➤ *Visual J#* — This language was considered as a replacement for Visual J++. However, this language had a Java syntax. It could build applications targeting only the .NET Framework's CLR. Now having a competing platform against Java, after replacing J++, Microsoft no longer created any language running on the JVM.

The .NET Framework's Base Class Library was established as a common infrastructure for developers, thus making it easy and natural to solve common tasks such as using data access and Web services. Visual Studio .NET provided a rich set of built-in tools to leverage the infrastructure provided by the framework. The IDE was designed with extensibility in mind, and allowed developers to integrate their own custom tools into the IDE.

A bit more than a year after Visual Studio.NET was released, a new version, Visual Studio .NET 2003, was shipped together with .NET Framework 1.1. Microsoft had a lot of work to do to stabilize the framework, and, of course, dozens of critical bugs were fixed. A few things (such as the security model) were also changed, and new features were added to the framework (such as built-in support for building mobile applications, IPv6 support, and built-in data access for ODBC and Oracle databases). Also, the CLR became more stable from version 1.0 to 1.1.

Visual Studio.NET (the one released with .NET 1.0) was not able to compile applications for the new CLR version, so the 2003 version had to undertake this task. Thanks to the robustness and stability of Visual Studio .NET 2003, it became very popular, and is still in use because of the large number of business applications developed for .NET 1.1.

## VISUAL STUDIO 2005

Released in November 2005, Visual Studio 2005, together with .NET Framework 2.0, brought fundamental changes to the tool, as well as to the languages. The Common Type System (CTS) of the framework introduced generic types. This concept affected all languages, because they must have been prepared to handle the feature of generics, and development tools also needed to encapsulate support for this. The shift of CTS also touched ASP.NET and ADO.NET.

Web application development had some pain in the former Visual Studio versions. Developers had to install and use Internet Information Server (IIS) locally on their machines, and it meant confrontation with system administrators who did not want to have IIS on desktops for security reasons. Visual Studio 2005 installed a local development Web server on desktops and resolved this particular situation.

With this release, Microsoft widened the camp of programmers using Visual Studio with two new editions:

➤ *Express Editions* — These editions (they are free) targeted students, hobbyists, and other developers coding for fun. Instead of giving a "geese" version of Visual Studio for free, Microsoft created language-related kits with the names of Visual C# 2005 Express, Visual Basic 2005 Express, Visual Web Developer, and Visual C++ 2005 Express, equipped with the full language feature set, but with limited tool support.

➤ *Team System Editions* — Microsoft wanted to move Visual Studio out of the box of development tools and position it among the high-end enterprise development tools. Team System Editions provided out-of-the-box integration with Microsoft's Team Foundation Server 2005, and added powerful productivity tools for specific development project roles. There are four editions for Developers, Testers, Architects, Database Designers, and a fifth one, Visual Studio Team Suite, which includes all of the features of these four editions in a single package.

Compare the list of installed products in the splash screen of Visual Studio 2005 Team Edition for Software Developers (shown in Figure 1-3) with the list shown in Figure 1-2. The eye-catching difference tells you how many tools were added to the new editions.

Following the initial release, a few special-purpose products were also shipped and integrated into the IDE (such as Visual Studio Tools for Office and Visual Studio Tools for Applications).

An unusual thing happened in November 2006: .NET Framework 3.0 was released without any accompanying Visual Studio version. This major .NET version kept the CLR untouched

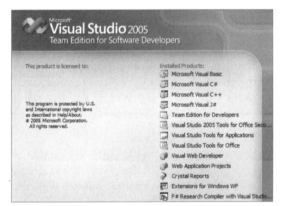

**FIGURE 1-3:** Products installed with Visual Studio 2005 Team Edition for Software Developers

and added infrastructure components to the framework — Windows Workflow Foundations (WF), Windows Communication Foundations (WCF), Windows Presentation Foundation (WPF), and CardSpace. Developers could download Visual Studio extensions to use these new .NET 3.0 technologies.

## VISUAL STUDIO 2008

In November 2007, one year after .NET 3.0, Visual Studio 2008 was shipped together with .NET Framework 3.5. Although the .NET CLR was still version 2.0, the new query expression syntax (LINQ) feature in .NET 3.5 demanded changes to the existing tools.

The most popular feature of version 2008 was multi-targeting. With this, Visual Studio developers could specify the target framework (.NET 2.0, .NET 3.0, and .NET 3.5) of their projects, or even mix projects with different targets in their solutions. Because one native Win32 process could host only one CLR at the same time, .NET 1.1 (because it uses CLR 1.1) was not in the list of available targets.

Both Visual Basic and C# went through fundamental changes to support the new LINQ syntax. As an addition, Visual Basic 9.0 was given support for XML literals (including plain XML text in the source code); C# 3.0 was extended with new initializer syntax. Both languages were equipped with new constructs (including type inference, anonymous types, extension methods, and lambda expressions) to support LINQ and reduce syntax noise.

The J# language was retired in Visual Studio 2008; the last version supporting it was Visual Studio 2005. Microsoft made this decision because the use of J# started to decline. However, the last version of J# will be supported until 2015.

The LINQ technology was about moving data access and data processing toward the functional programming paradigm. This new paradigm (new for Microsoft development tools) gained momentum as Microsoft Research started to work on a new functional programming language called F#. The first community technology preview (CTP) of the language appeared in Visual Studio 2005 (take a look again at the last product item in Figure 1-3), and Visual Studio 2008 hosted a few more new CTPs.

In addition to the main themes of .NET Framework 3.5, Visual Studio has other great features and changes:

➤ Built-in support for the three foundations released in .NET 3.0 and refreshed in 3.5:

  ➤ WPF has a visual designer for XAML layouts.

  ➤ WCF has a few project types out-of-the-box.

  ➤ WF has visual a designer to create workflows graphically.

➤ JavaScript programming is now supported with IntelliSense and a debugger.

➤ Web developers can use a new and powerful XHTML/CSS editor.

After the initial release, Microsoft's new technologies were also integrated with Visual Studio:

➤ One of the new emerging technologies was Silverlight. With the initial Visual Studio release in November 2007, only Silverlight 1.0 was available, and that was based on JavaScript. In August 2008, Silverlight 2.0 was shipped, implementing the same full CLR version as .NET Framework 3.0, and so it could execute programs written in any .NET language. In July 2009, Silverlight 3.0 was released. All versions had their own toolset that can be down loaded and integrated with Visual Studio 2008.

➤ In August 2008, a service release was issued with .NET Framework 3.5 SP1 and Visual Studio 2008 SP1. This version added new ADO.NET data features to the framework and also designers to the IDE:

  ➤ *ADO.NET Entity Framework* — This raises the level of abstraction at which programmers work with data to the conceptual level.

> ➤ *ADO.NET Data Services* — This is first-class infrastructure for developing dynamic Internet components by enabling data to be exposed as REST-based data services.

> ➤ *ASP.NET Dynamic Data* — This provides a rich scaffolding framework that allows rapid data driven development without writing any code.

Visual Studio 2008 did not change the structure of editions in version 2005. All editions (including Visual Studio Team System 2008 and Visual Studio 2008 Express Editions) were released together.

## VISUAL STUDIO 2010

The latest version of Visual Studio has 10.0 as the internal version, and its name is officially Visual Studio 2010.

No doubt, Microsoft takes Visual Studio into account as the ultimate tool for developers creating applications and business solutions on the Windows platform. This intention can be caught on the messages called "the pillars of Visual Studio 2010":

> ➤ *Creativity Unleashed* — You can use prototyping, modeling, and visual design tools to create solid, modern, and visionary solutions through software development. You can leverage the creative strengths of your team to build your imaginations together.

> ➤ *Simplicity through Integration* — Visual Studio helps simplifying common tasks, and helps you explore the depth of the platform you and your team work with. It has an integrated environment, where all team members can use their existing skills to model, code, debug, test, and deploy a growing number of application types, including the solutions for the cloud platform.

> ➤ *Quality Code Ensured* — The toolset of Visual Studio includes everything that helps you with maintaining source code, finding and fixing bugs, and managing your projects. Testers and developers on your team can use manual and automated testing, as well as advanced debugging tools, from the very beginning. Utilizing these tools, you can be confident that the right application is built, the right way.

These messages are a very brief and straightforward summary of what Visual Studio 2010 offers for experts — software developers, testers, architects, business analysts, project managers — working on software development tasks and projects.

## Changes in Editions

While Visual Studio 2008 had many editions — such as Standard, Professional, and Team System Editions (including Development, Database, Architecture, and Test Editions) — you will be able to choose from three main version (of course, free Express editions are still available):

➤ *Microsoft Visual Studio 2010 Professional with MSDN* — This version is intended to be the essential tool for basic development tasks to assist developers in easily implementing their ideas.

➤ *Microsoft Visual Studio 2010 Premium with MSDN* — This provides a complete toolset to help developers deliver scalable, high-quality applications.

➤ *Microsoft Visual Studio 2010 Ultimate with MSDN* — This version (as its name suggests) is a comprehensive suite of application life-cycle management tools for software teams to help ensure quality results from design to deployment.

The feature sets of these editions are formed so that editions contain every feature the lower editions have, plus add their own functionality on top of them.

Microsoft's intention with Visual Studio 2010 is clear from the features all editions have in common:

➤ *Development platform support* — All important platforms (Windows, Web, Office, SharePoint, and cloud development) are available with a common tool set.

➤ *Team Foundation Server integration* — There is no difference among the Visual Studio editions in the Team Foundation Server support they have! All of them are shipped with the Visual Studio Team Explorer 2010 to instantly access Team Foundation Server with the entire feature set, including source control and work item management, build automation and test case management, Team Portal, Business Intelligence (BI), and reporting.

➤ *Debugging and Diagnostics* — The efficient debugging and diagnostics tools (with a number of new Visual Studio 2010 innovations) help developers to become more productive than ever before. Now, post-mortem debugging, multi-threaded application debugging through the Parallel Stack and Tasks window, and 64-bit support for mixed mode debugging are available for every developer independently of the edition he or she uses.

These editions are bundled with MSDN subscriptions. This is a great benefit — especially for Premium and Ultimate users who receive additional software for production use (such as Expression Studio 3, Office Plus 2010, Visio Premium 2010, and Project Professional 2010). All users get the standard MSDN subscription benefits, such as priority support on MSDN Forums, technical support incidents, *MSDN* magazine, and so on.

As a result of setting up the editions as treated, small developer teams with the Professional edition now can work together in a way that was possible only with one of the Team System editions with the previous versions. The Premium edition adds new tools for database development, testing, and advanced functions for debugging and diagnostics. Users of the Ultimate edition have architecture, modeling, and test lab management tools shipped with the product, a benefit they never got before with Visual Studio.

## What's New in Visual Studio 2010

Addressing what is new in Visual Studio is not tackled here in its entirety. Each chapter of this book contains sections dedicated to this topic. Moreover, many chapters are especially about treating Visual Studio new features with all nitty-gritty details.

Without the need of completeness, here is a short list to whet your appetite:

➤ Cloud development (Windows Azure) and SharePoint development is now supported.

➤ Test Driven Development (TDD) is available in Visual Studio. You can follow the Consume-First-Declare-Later approach during code writing.

➤ The code editing experience has been significantly enhanced:

    ➤ Visual Studio now understands your code, provides you with Call Hierarchy, and highlights references.

    ➤ With the Quick Search function, you can easily navigate within your code — not just in the current code file but in the entire solution.

    ➤ IntelliSense has been improved. It now has substring matching, helping you when you do not remember exact member names.

    ➤ The new code editor is extensible, and creating extensions has been significantly simplified.

➤ Online Visual Studio Gallery is integrated directly into Visual Studio. With the Extension Manager, you can browse online content (tools, controls, and templates) and immediately install third-party extensions.

➤ You are not obliged to create new projects from the templates already installed on your machine. You can create your project right from online project templates with the New Project dialog.

➤ Multi-core and multi-threaded applications are now first-class citizens in Visual Studio. You can debug your applications with their nature of using multiple parallel tasks and threads. The new tools and views allow you to look for and focus on those details (race conditions, blockings, interoperation, and so on) that were invisible in previous versions.

➤ Modeling, designing, and validating architecture now are organic parts of Visual Studio. Not only can architects benefit from these features, but those can be used for communication among team members or with customers.

## Shift to WPF

Maybe it sounds weird, but the majority of Visual Studio's code base is unmanaged code — large pieces of this code come from the COM era, and did not really change over time. With Visual Studio 2010, the development team undertook the challenge of a technology shift: the UI technology of the shell and a major part of the IDE was changed from GDI/GDI+ to WPF — that is, a managed technology. The new design of the product (the new splash screen is shown in Figure 1-4) communicates this new approach.

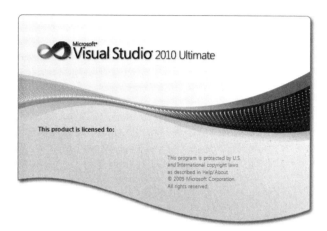

**FIGURE 1-4:** The splash screen reflects the brand new design of Visual Studio 2010

The formerly angular and multi-colored "infinity sign" logo became a round-cornered and gradually-colored one, emphasizing the smooth integration among the tools within the IDE.

The new code editor of Visual Studio has been totally rewritten to use WPF as its display technology, new functions such as the modeling tools, the new parallel task debugger, and many, many more features also were implemented with WPF.

## SUMMARY

The name of Visual Studio is about 13 years old, but the roots of the product go back almost two decades. The first milestone on the road was definitely Visual Basic 1.0. Up until 1997, other programming languages and tools also picked up the visual composition aspect that had distinguished Visual Basic from the formerly used development tools. Visual Studio was born by packaging these tools (Visual Basic, Visual C++, Visual FoxPro, Visual J++, Visual InterDev, and MSDN) into a bundle.

With the introduction of the .NET Framework in 2002, Visual Studio started to gain big momentum. The languages and tools encapsulated into the product changed, together with the state-of-the-art paradigms and trends. The surrounding developer community has experienced a spectacular growth in the last eight years.

After seven major versions (five of which leveraged the .NET Framework), Visual Studio transformed from a single development tool into a rock-solid software development environment. It supports a wide audience, from students and hobbyists, to large-enterprise IT groups with full application life-cycle management functionality needs.

As of this writing, you can use Visual Studio 2010 released together with .NET Framework 4.0. Its functionality has been significantly extended since Visual Studio 2008.

In Chapter 2, you'll learn about the new enhancements of the IDE's user interface.

# Visual Studio UI Enhancements

In Chapter 1, you read about the major product changes for Visual Studio 2010, and gained an historical overview of previous versions. If you have used any of the previous versions of Visual Studio, you will see with Visual Studio 2010 that Microsoft is adding more and more features, as well as enabling features for the free Express editions of Visual Studio.

This chapter highlights the major differences between the 2008 and the 2010 version of the product, but focuses only on the User Interface (UI) without going into greater detail about the features.

## BASIC IDE OVERVIEW

Visual Studio 2010 does not have a piece that has remained untouched from the 2008 version. As you read in Chapter 1, this is because Visual Studio 2010 is based on Windows Presentation Foundation (WPF), and now all features and modules seamlessly integrate with the Visual Studio Shell without serious Component Object Model (COM) interoperability operations. The interoperability and communication between different parts is accomplished through a new component in the .NET Framework 4.0 called *Managed Extensibility Framework (MEF)*.

 *Chapter 8 provides more on the basic principles of WPF, or, if you'd like, you can read more about MEF, and how the modularity and extensibility work, in Chapter 6.*

## Exploring the Start Page

When you start Visual Studio, the integrated development environment (IDE) presents a familiar screen to the user — the Start Page shown in Figure 2-1. The Start Page is familiar to those who have used Visual Studio 2008, but this one is a brand new part. If you navigate between the pages and subpages of the Start Page, you will discover that this is the first place where you'll see some glimpse of WPF — icons look more detailed, and selected items smoothly animate.

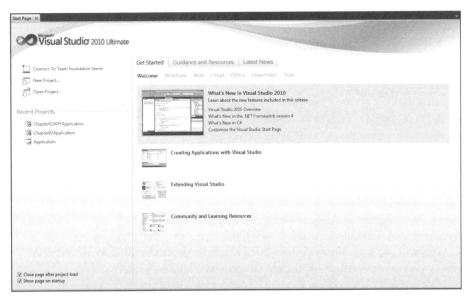

**FIGURE 2-1:** Visual Studio 2010 Start Page

One of the new features in Visual Studio 2010 is the capability to connect to a Team Foundation Server straight from the Start Page. Another new feature is that the Recent Projects list can be pinned, which makes the opening of a solution more accessible.

When Visual Studio 2010 is used under Microsoft Windows 7, the IDE leverages a new feature in the operating system, and the same pinning functionality for recently opened projects is available when you right-click the Visual Studio icon on the taskbar. Projects are pinned and can be opened with a single click as well. The difference is that a new instance of Visual Studio will be started for this operation.

The first extensibility point is right in front of you. The Start Page itself is a pure WPF window, and its content is freely customizable. This is loaded by the IDE from the directory <Visual Studio Install Directory>\Common7\IDE\StartPages\en\StartPage.xaml. This is valid for the English version of the Visual Studio.

> *You can read more about Start Page customization at* http://msdn.microsoft.com/en-us/library/aa991992(VS.100).aspx.

## Understanding Window Management

In previous versions of Visual Studio, two kinds of windows were defined within the IDE: *tool windows* and *document windows.* You were not able to dock a tool window with a document window. Rather, a tool window was dockable only with other tool windows, or to the edge of the

IDE. However, with tool windows, the user had the capability of dragging them out onto a second monitor, and this solution proved to be perfect for the docking problem.

For Visual Studio 2010, Microsoft has enhanced window management. This new version unifies the concept of windows, and the differentiation between the two kinds of windows has disappeared from the UI perspective. Now you can dock these windows as you like. Figure 2-2 shows how an output window can be docked into the tabbed document area of the IDE.

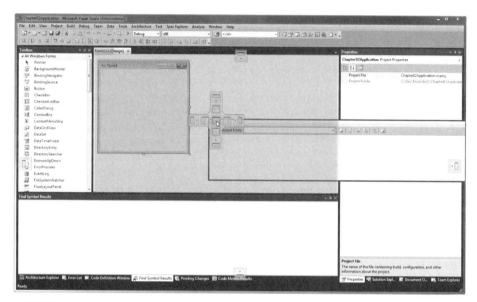

**FIGURE 2-2:** Output window dragged into the tabbed document area

The visual feedback about the result of a window-docking operation also is much improved, so the user will know where the currently dragged window will be exactly positioned after releasing the left mouse button.

As development tasks become more complex, every developer needs more than just a code editor window. One display surface, regardless of its size and resolution, cannot fulfill all of the developer's requirements. That's why the Visual Studio team added the multi-monitor support to Visual Studio 2010. Now, any window from the IDE can be dragged out and aligned onto a second, third, and so on, monitor, and the IDE will remember your settings correctly. It will even reuse them for future Visual Studio starts. This feature is extended in such a way that you can have your own multi-monitor setup for, say, development and debug modes.

Another useful feature is that when you hold down the Ctrl key and double-click the header of a dragged-out window, the window is docked in its original position.

## New Project Dialog Window

The next new thing to note occurs when starting a new project or solution. By choosing the New Project command from the Start Page, you now see the New Project dialog shown in Figure 2-3.

**FIGURE 2-3:** New Project dialog

In the New Project dialog, you now have three options to begin a new project:

➤ Select a project type from the recently used templates.

➤ Select a project type from the Installed Templates (which is the old way).

➤ Select a project type from the Online Templates (which are the ones submitted by other developers).

You can filter on project type names by entering search criteria into the textbox in the upper-right corner of the dialog.

For every new project, you can specify which framework you would like to use for that project. However, if you have Silverlight 3 and Silverlight 4 developer tools installed, this framework version selection doesn't have any effect. For a Silverlight project, you must specify the Silverlight version for the project after you have clicked the OK button to create the project. Figure 2-4 shows the ensuing Silverlight version selection dialog.

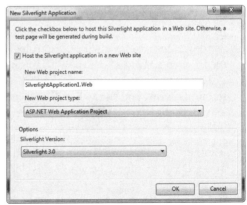

**FIGURE 2-4:** Silverlight version selection

# Creating New Projects in a New Way

Often, a developer will have some old code files somewhere on his or her computer, or a complete project in a directory, but not organized into a project. In Visual Studio 2008, you had to manually create a new project and add those files by hand. In Visual Studio 2010, you invoke the Project From Existing Code wizard from the File ➪ New Project ➪ Project From Existing Code menu selection.

The first step of the wizard is to provide some brief information, including specifying the language of the project you would like to create.

In the next wizard step, you name the project and specify the directory where your files are stored. You also tell the IDE what type of project you would like to create.

Let's say that you have the following files in a directory:

➤  Program.cs

➤  Data\City.cs

➤  Data\Country.cs

➤  Data\Person.cs

After you have clicked the Finish button, Visual Studio 2010 is unfolding the default project template for the selected language and, after it has collected all the files from the given directory, it is adding them to the project. When the wizard has finished its job, you get a ready-to-compile console application.

# Using the Add Reference Dialog Window

The Add Reference dialog window is one of the most used windows within Visual Studio. As you might expect, since multi-targeting became a core functionality of the whole project system within the IDE, every part of the IDE offers some functionality that is somehow dependent on a version of the .NET Framework. Because of this, the given project targets must be smarter and more developer-friendly.

That's why this dialog box has been enhanced for Visual Studio 2010. Take a look at the Runtime column in Figure 2-5. In the upper part of the figure, you can see how the window is opened for a project that has the .NET 2.0 Framework as its target. In the lower part of the figure, you can see that same information for a .NET 4-targeted project. This dialog not only filters based on the .NET Framework version, but also based on the type of the project.

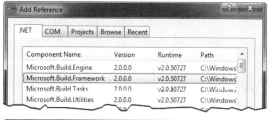

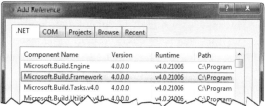

**FIGURE 2-5:** Add Reference dialog for .NET Framework 2.0 and 4.0 base project

## Using the Extension Manager

In Visual Studio 2008, extensions were often troublesome. Neither their installation nor the development was easy.

In Visual Studio 2010, the installation experience has been radically changed. Extension developers can still use a product install experience based on the Windows Installer, and a distribution based on a website, but leveraging the online extension manager gallery is just providing developers with a better opportunity to have their extensions installed on more developer machines. The Extension Manager now shows available online extensions that are regularly updated, and these can be installed with a single click of a button.

 *Chapter 5 provides more information about the functionality of the Extension Manager.*

# EXPLORING NEW DAILY DEVELOPMENT FEATURES

The following discussion examines the new features that Visual Studio 2010 provides to simplify your daily development tasks.

## Exploring the Code Editor Window

This is one area within Visual Studio where most developers spend significant time authoring code. The code editor of Visual Studio 2010 is built from scratch, and with extensibility in mind.

A lot of features available in Visual Studio 2008 only through third-party extensions are now available in the IDE. The code editor now displays important information to the developer in a clear, visual form. Figure 2-6 shows the code editor. Let's take a closer look at some of the features in the code editor.

Take a look at the vertical line on the left margin, under the row of the class definition. The editor is using different colors to mark the lines that were changed before the last save operation and the lines which was modified after the last save operation.

**FIGURE 2-6:** Code editor

In the upper-right corner of the editor, above the scrollbar, you will find a splitter button. By dragging that, you can split your window and navigate within the same file in the two different windows. Although this functionality is not that new, another new feature capitalizes on the power of WPF — you can zoom your code to any level you need. You no longer must change the font size when doing code-only presentations. Now you can change the zoom level by holding down the Ctrl key and moving the mouse wheel, and everyone will see the code (even from the last row of the audience).

WPF and a brand new editor provide the opportunity to greatly enhance text selection within the code editor. Box selection can be activated by holding down the Alt key, in addition to the normal selection keys (for example, Shift and the arrow keys, as well as other navigation keys). As shown in Figure 2-7, when you're doing an empty block selection, you can start to type, and the typed-in characters will appear in all rows.

```
static class Program
{
    privat string Name { get; set; }
    privat int Age { get; set; }
    privat bool IsHappy { get; set; }
```

**FIGURE 2-7:** Empty box selection for typing in multiple rows simultaneously

Notice the thin vertical line following the "privat" text in Figure 2-7, which is an empty block selection. Delete and overwrite operations also work for box selection.

The code editor now incorporates the concept of a visualizer. Different extensibility points now are available for you to develop your own extension, which provides a richer, more customized presentation of code. For example, the default comment presentation now displays in italics.

Another powerful feature of the IDE is the IntelliSense functionality. If you activate an IntelliSense visualizer extension, you are presented with a much richer IntelliSense presentation, as shown in Figure 2-8. Visual Studio provides a full WPF feature set to use when developing extensions for the editor.

IntelliSense also now includes a new function for filtering on code. This feature is called *Pascal cased IntelliSense lookup,* and it is very powerful because you must type less during your daily work, which enables a faster delivery time for projects.

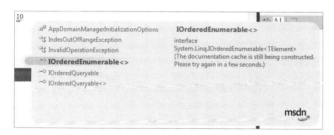

**FIGURE 2-8:** Rich IntelliSense presentation via an extension

IntelliSense can operate in two modes: *Consume First* mode and *regular IntelliSense* mode. You can switch between the two modes by using the Ctrl+Alt+Space keyboard combination.

As an example, say you entered **IOE** and pressed the space key in Consume First mode. The editor inserts the first match — `InvalidOutOfRangeException`, in this case — at the caret position, as shown in Figure 2-9. In regular mode (Figure 2-10), "IOE" remains as typed text, since you did not make an explicit selection from the available items with the up arrow and down arrow keys, followed by a Tab or Enter key.

**FIGURE 2-9:** IntelliSense pop-up selection in Consume First mode

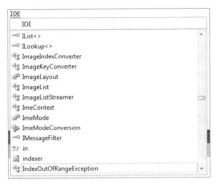

**FIGURE 2-10:** IntelliSense pop-up selection in Regular mode

## Code Navigation

This section examines other new code-navigation features included in Visual Studio 2010.

### Reference Highlighting

*Reference highlighting* is a function that helps with the reading of code. If you set the cursor on a variable name, for example, all the other occurrences of that identifier are highlighted in the editor, as shown in Figure 2-11.

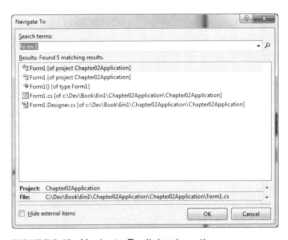

**FIGURE 2-11:** Reference highlighting on Name property

### Search and Replace

Visual Studio 2008 included Find and "Find in Files" with their Replace complements for code navigation and searching, as well as incremental search. A new feature in Visual Studio 2010 called Navigate To can be activated with the Ctrl+comma key sequence. This provides a powerful way to quickly search for something when you don't know what kind of text you're looking for. The executed search is very relaxed (for example, whitespace characters are not taken into account).

As shown in Figure 2-12, the Navigate To dialog is very simple and does not clutter the code editor window.

**FIGURE 2-12:** Navigate To dialog in action

## Call Hierarchy

A new function called Call Hierarchy can also be used to navigate code. This function can be invoked by positioning the caret in a method's name and pressing Ctrl+K, followed by the T key. The function is also available from the context menu.

Call Hierarchy shows what methods the selected function is calling, or who is calling the selected method. This function helps you to understand code execution and code flow in more complex solutions. Call Hierarchy display can go to any depth in function calls. One caveat of this function is that when someone is using interfaces heavily, this function cannot resolve a "default implementation" class for a given interface.

Figure 2-13 shows the Call Hierarchy function in action on a simple class.

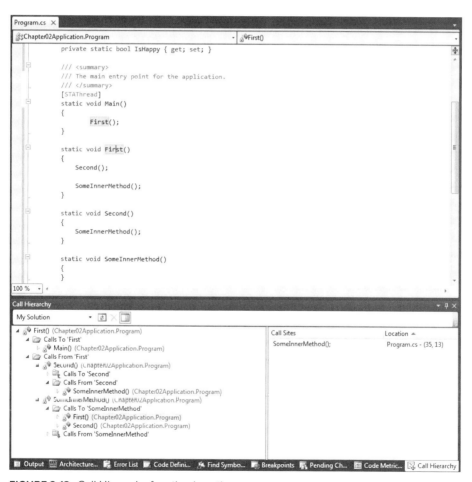

**FIGURE 2-13:** Call Hierarchy function in action

## Code Definition

In previous versions of Visual Studio, it was very tedious to look up a class definition or its implementation. To navigate this task, you had to use Go To Definition, but this function took your eye from the current code position to a new code file. In Visual Studio 2010, a new Code Definition Window automatically navigates to the given type as you move the caret around in your code.

Figure 2-14 shows that, as soon as you move to the `form1` text, the Code Definition window opens the `Form1.cs` file and navigates to the class definition of the `form1` class.

**FIGURE 2-14:** Code Definition window in action

## Debugging

The last feature to note regarding the code editor window is related to debugging. In Visual Studio 2010, you can utilize much better management options for breakpoints. One of the most powerful functions is the capability to label breakpoints.

For example, let's say that you have a `NameLabels` label assigned to all parts of the code that have something to do with the `Name` property. In the Breakpoints tool window, you can filter on labels, which is very helpful if you have organized labels within the solution, and, say, you must debug based on a dedicated, assigned label.

# Generate From Usage

The Generate From Usage feature was designed to help Test Driven Development (TDD). When following the principles of TDD, developers write the unit and other tests for the project based on the specification, before the actual code that will be tested is written. When the developers are finished with the tests, the classes and functions are implemented, and, as the process advances, more and more tests will succeed. TDD makes for a very tedious process to implement all the classes, constructors, and methods used by a given test.

However, now, the Generate From Usage feature is making all this really simple. With this feature, you can create classes, constructors, and methods without actually leaving the current editing position. Consider the following `CalculatorTest` class:

```
[TestClass]
public class CalculatorTest
{
    [TestMethod]
    public void AddTestSuccess()
    {
        var calculator = new Calculator();

        var result = calculator.Add(5, 6);

        Assert.AreEqual(result, 11);
    }
}
```

Visual Studio underlines `Calculator` type name, since that's not defined anywhere in the solution.

If you open the smart tag and select the Generate New Type command, the ensuing dialog asks you to tell the IDE the following things:

➤   What kind of item you would like to create (for example, Class, Struct, Enum, or Interface)

➤   The accessibility of the item you are about to create

➤   A target project for the item from the solution

➤   An existing file (or an existing file within the project) where the generated item will be appended

As soon as the class is generated, the previously underlined line becomes valid, and then all you must do is add the definition of the `Add` method by invoking the same dialog again, and, following that, add the implementation of the method.

Now, if you run the unit test, it will succeed.

## EXPLORING THE VISUAL DESIGNERS

Visual Studio has included a lot of new designers from release to release, and included enhancements to existing ones. In Visual Studio 2010, the following designers have been added or greatly enhanced:

➤   WPF/Silverlight Designer

➤   XML Schema Designer

This section discusses some new features without going into detail about a specific feature (since you can get more information about them in the following chapters).

# WPF Designer

The WPF Designer was added in Visual Studio 2008, with a basic design-time experience, and targeted to WPF projects. For Silverlight, the design surface was in read-only mode. In Visual Studio 2010, the editor has been enhanced to provide a unified design-time experience for WPF and Silverlight developers alike.

Figure 2-15 shows time-related windows within the IDE using the WPF Designer. A few things in this figure should be noted.

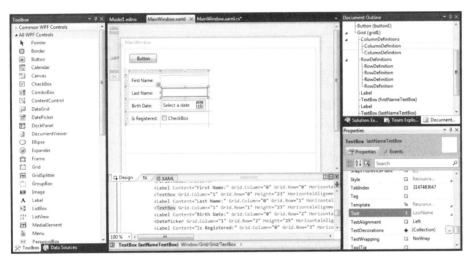

**FIGURE 2-15:** WPF development related windows

In the Toolbox window, you'll notice the full range of controls for both platforms, with drag-and-drop support to the editor surface.

On the right side of Figure 2-15, you can see a Document Outline window. This is really handy when you'd like to look at the visual tree and structure of the currently opened XAML file. Under that, you can see the Properties grid. This grid is not the one you may have used during Windows Forms development. It's a brand new, extensible, WPF-based property grid.

The Properties grid features two tabs: Properties and Events. You can sort the properties alphabetically, or you can sort them by categories. However, in Visual Studio 2010, you can type in partial property names to filter on them. This way, when you are looking for a property, it's sometimes faster to type in a few letters, rather than trying to find it by scrolling.

In the middle of Figure 2-15, you'll notice there is the split view of the design surface. You can switch between the split and normal view, or you can even vertically split (instead of horizontally) the Design and XAML views. On the left side of the design surface is a zoom control that enables you to zoom in and out in a fairly high range to get the ideal zoom factor for the given operation.

As you see in Figure 2-15 the Last Name text box is selected in the editor surface, and the selection is automatically synchronizing the XAML view (TextBox). When a new element is selected either in the XAML view or in the design view, the default property of the given element is also selected in the property grid.

A powerful feature of the property grid is that it has a full-blown binding editor embedded. The binding editor can be activated by clicking the property type dependent symbol on the right side of the property name cell. The binding editor itself is represented with an Accordion control, and every aspect of the data binding can be edited here. All edit operations are reflected instantly in the XAML view as well.

For debugging purposes, Visual Studio 2010 includes a WPF tree visualization that enables the run-time inspection of the visual tree of an element. It can be activated from a data tip, Watch window, Autos window, or from the Locals window by clicking the magnifying glass icon next to the name of a WPF object.

## XML Schema Designer

XML Schema Designer is a new addition to the IDE. In previous versions of Visual Studio, developers could only author XML schema through an XML Schema Explorer.

XML Schema Designer is a WPF-based graphical designer that aids with the visualization of the of XML schema sets at different levels of abstraction, including the following:

➤ *XML Schema Explorer* — This helps the navigation within the XML Schema definition.

➤ *Start View* — This is the entry point into this designer. Other functions are accessible from here.

➤ *Graph View* — This visualizes the relationships between the schema elements.

➤ *Content Model View* — This visualizes the details of the schema elements, and supports expansion of included types.

## NEW TOOLS FOR ARCHITECTS

The architect role was first addressed in Visual Studio 2008 Team System, but missing from the product were a lot of tasks and tools that can help the architects to do their daily work (such as designing systems, validating existing code against an architecture, or architecting) within the IDE.

Visual Studio 2010 incorporates unified modeling language (UML) support with forward- and reverse-engineering. Architecture Explorer helps you navigate a solution from the architecture point of view, and layer diagrams enable the mapping and validation of a logical architecture to the physical solution.

The new IDE offers a new project type named Modeling. All architectural items are contained within this project. Figure 2-16 shows a sample business n-tier application structure that includes a Modeling project.

**FIGURE 2-16:** Solution structure with Modeling project

The example solution contains a client application, a service, and some business logic classes. The architect can define the architecture of such system in a layer diagram by creating the boxes for each part of the system and adding dependencies. A *layer diagram* is a logical representation of the system. The architect can assign projects, namespaces, and types with each element in the diagram. During regular development or at every build, the architecture in the layer diagram can be validated against the physical solution structure.

Figure 2-17 shows the layer diagram for the sample solution. Notice the numbers in each box. The UI layer has one `ClientApplication` project associated, the Service layer has one WCF Services project assigned, and the Business layer has four business logic classes assigned. The first two assignments were done by dragging and dropping the projects themselves onto the boxes representing each layer. The business logic assignment was done from the Architecture Explorer view.

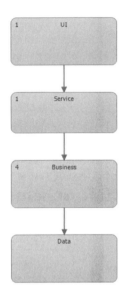

**FIGURE 2-17:** Layer diagram

As shown in Figure 2-18, the Architecture Explorer supports easy navigation within the solution:

➤ *Class view* — The first level is the namespace level, second level is the class level, and, going beneath that, the member level (the last level) is the level of method calls.

➤ *Solution view* — The first level is the project level, the next is the file level, and, from there, the same levels are available as when you navigate through the Class view.

➤ *File System navigation* — This has been added to make the files outside a solution navigable, too.

➤ *Saved DGQL Query mode* — This makes the navigation possible based on a saved Directed Graph Query Language (DGQL) file.

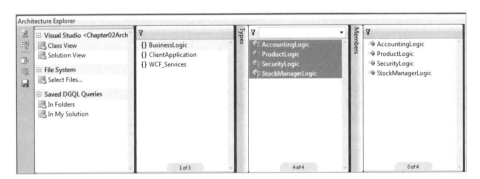

**FIGURE 2-18:** Architecture Explorer Window

As mentioned, full UML editing support is available within the modeling project. One of the powerful features is the capability to reverse a method into a sequence diagram by executing a command from the context menu.

## SUMMARY

This chapter discussed the new UI-related features and functions of Visual Studio 2010. You learned about changes to the Shell itself, including the new window management and multi-monitor support. You learned about the new code editor features and the extensibility possibilities. The new visual designers and their features were also introduced. Finally, you got a glimpse of the functions available for architects in the new IDE.

Chapter 3 provides an in-depth exploration of Visual Studio code snippets and some features that can help you become more productive in your daily work.

# 3

# Visual Studio Code Snippets

When you develop applications, you spend a huge amount of time typing source code. Even if there are many designers and wizards in Visual Studio generating code skeletons, resource information, and many code related files, at the end of the day, each developer writes code. Sometimes, typing is very tedious. For example, let's assume you have the Name property defined with the following pattern in C#:

```csharp
private string _Name;

public string Name
{
  get { return _Name; }
  set
  {
    _Name = value;
    PropertyChanged("Name", value);
  }
}
```

It almost could be written with the automatic property syntax of C# (this syntax was introduced in C# 3.0), but, unfortunately, you have a PropertyChanged call in the property setter requiring a backing field and manually created getter-setter definitions. If you have other properties such as Title, Description, Active, and so on, following the same pattern as Name, you must type the previous pattern in addition to a lot of replacing for the occurrences of Name and _Name with the appropriate identifiers.

The work of Visual Basic programmers becomes even dustier, because they must type a bit more, as shown here:

```vb
Private _Name As String
Public Property Name() As String
  Get
    Return _Name
  End Get
```

```
      Set(ByVal value As String)
        _Name = value
        PropertyChanged("Name", value)
      End Set
    End Property
```

What if you could create a lot of properties with these semantics by only typing their names? Well, you can if you use code snippets!

Early versions of Visual Studio did not include any features that could prevent developers from having to do this kind of repetitive work. One of the most requested features was adding some tool into Visual Studio that was capable of creating code based on some template mechanism in order to simplify typing. Code completion helped a lot, because it could save about every second keystroke, but it was not efficient enough.

Visual Studio 2005 introduced the concept of *code snippets*. The idea behind this concept was (in satisfying the wishes of the community) to enable developers to declare a template of code, and then use it as many times as they wanted in their source code files. A template had zero, one, or more placeholders that could be changed by users — a change in one place altered all the placeholder's occurrences in the template. This concept was successful in compensating the feature developers, compensation that was missed in the two early .NET-related versions of Visual Studio.

Code snippets are easy-fitting tools for developers who are fastidious about spending their time on useful things. This chapter provides details that that will help you learn about code snippets. After reading this chapter, you will be familiar with the following:

- ➤ *Understanding the concept of code snippets.* — This chapter provides a brief explanation about what code snippets are, and how to use them. You will also learn about a few language-dependent snippet features that highlight differences between the C# code editor and the Visual Basic Editor.

- ➤ *Creating code snippets.* — You will create a very simple snippet and integrate it with the Visual Studio integrated development environment (IDE), and learn about the details of a file format to define a code snippet.

- ➤ *Managing code snippets.* — During your everyday work, you may use not only one, but more programming languages, and a few dozen code snippets. In this chapter, you will look at how snippets are stored on your computer, and learn how to use the Code Snippets Manager to manage them.

Toward the end of this chapter, you will learn about a few advanced features and extension opportunities, as well as a few great community tools to help you with code snippet development.

## UNDERSTANDING CODE SNIPPETS

The concept behind code snippets is simple and powerful. Snippets are source code pieces that may range from one character to pages of text, and can be easily inserted into the code. The code to be inserted is defined with a template mechanism that allows defining *placeholder*s and changing them when the template is about to be applied. Of course, the same placeholder can be put into many places within the template, and altering the text of one placeholder triggers changes to all of its occurrences accordingly.

Let's revisit that earlier code to define a property:

```
private string _Name;

public string Name
{
  get { return _Name; }
  set
  {
    _Name = value;
    PropertyChanged("Name", value);
  }
}
```

Here you see five occurrences of Name used as identifier or string literal. A code template for this property could look like this:

```
private string _%Name%;

public string %Name%
{
  get { return _%Name%; }
  set
  {
    _%Name% = value;
    PropertyChanged("%Name%", value);
  }
}
```

When it is time to insert the code template, the %Name% value can be changed to a current value to be applied together with the template.

Although code snippets are simple, there are a few implementation details that you should know about:

➤ From a functional point of view, there are two kinds of snippets. With *expansion snippets*, the code template is simply inserted into the current editor position. With *surrounding snippets*, you let the snippet embrace the code that you select. A good example is a snippet that creates a try...catch statement block around selected code. Snippets can be defined so that they are simultaneously expansion and surrounding types.

➤ C# and Visual Basic code snippet implementations are different with respect to a few features. There are features available in one language context but not in the other, and vice versa.

➤ There are no language-independent code snippets that insert the appropriate snippet depending on the context in which they are used.

➤ In C#, code snippets are also used for refactoring. Behind a large number of refactoring actions, code snippets bear the brunt of the work.

➤ Visual Studio 2008 and 2010 allow multi-targeting. You might have snippets that are target framework-dependent. They can be inserted but may not compile with the wrong target.

Of course, the most important thing is that you can use not only the code snippets shipped with Visual Studio, but you can also create your own snippets and integrate them with the IDE. Your snippets are totally coequal with the ones included with Visual Studio. To understand how you can build your own snippets, first let's see how to use them.

## Using Code Snippets

There are several ways to invoke code snippets. To use them, you must have at least one code editor window open. The expansion and surrounding type of code snippets can be activated with separate shortcuts. The reason behind this is that a certain snippet can be an expansion and surrounding snippet at the same time. If you have selected text in the code editor, the expansion type snippet should replace the selection with the inserted code template, while the surrounding type snippet should embrace the selection into the template.

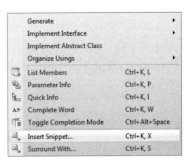

**FIGURE 3-1:** Invoking code snippets from the Edit ➪ IntelliSense menu

With a C# code file open, you can invoke the code snippets from the Edit ➪ IntelliSense menu, as shown in Figure 3-1.

As you can see, pressing the Ctrl+K keys, and then the X key, is a shortcut to the Insert Snippet function, while Ctrl+K, and S represent the shortcut key combination to the Surround With function. The same functions presented on the Edit menu are also available on code editor's context menu (accessed by using a right mouse-click), as shown in Figure 3-2.

Let's have a look at how to insert a code snippet.

## Inserting a Snippet

Select a position in the code editor where you want to insert a snippet, and select the Insert Snippet menu command, or use the Ctrl+K, X shortcut combination. Visual Studio displays a navigation line and a list of virtual folders that groups the available code snippets by their category. Figure 3-3 shows the list of top-level snippet categories for C#.

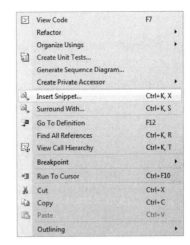

**FIGURE 3-2:** Code snippet functions in the context menu

You can use the up arrow, down arrow, and Enter keys, or the mouse, to select a category. Categories may have subcategories. As you traverse through them, the navigation line displays the path. Using the Backspace key, you can go back to an upper-category level. When you reach the level of code snippets, the list displays the names of available snippets. When you select any of the available snippets, the related tooltip displays their descriptions and their shortcuts, as shown in Figure 3-4.

```
using System;
using System.Collections.Generic;
using System.Linq;
using System.Text;

namespace ConsoleApplication1
{
  class Program
  {
    static void Main(string[] args)
    {
    }

    Insert Snippet: |
                   📁 My Code Snippets
  }              📁 NetFX30
}              📁 Office Development
               📁 Other
               📁 Test
               📁 Visual C#
```

**FIGURE 3-3:** Snippet categories that are displayed

```
using System;
using System.Collections.Generic;
using System.Linq;
using System.Text;

namespace ConsoleApplication1
{
  class Program
  {
    static void Main(string[] args)
    {
    }

    Insert Snippet: Other > workflow > |
  }              📄 Add DependencyProperty - EventHandler
}              📄 Add DependencyProperty - Property
```

**FIGURE 3-4:** Traversing through snippet categories

At the snippet level, you invoke the selected snippet by using the Tab or the Enter keys, or by using a mouse-click.

Using these ways of inserting a snippet is practical when you are just getting acquainted with the variety of available snippets, but not really useful when you know exactly which snippet you want to invoke. A much more efficient way of accessing snippets is through their shortcuts. Of course, that means you must remember the shortcut — or at least the first few characters. Let's have a look at how this method works.

Open a project with a C# file, or create a new C# project just for testing purposes. There is a snippet with shortcut `propfull` that inserts a property with a backing field.

```
{
  pro|
}  ⚬ IFormatProvider
   ⚬ InvalidProgramException
   ⚬ IQueryProvider
   ⚬ IServiceProvider
   🔧 Program
   📄 prop
   📄 propa
   📄 propdp
   📄 propfull
   📄 propg
```

**FIGURE 3-5:** Code-completion list with snippets

Because you know its shortcut, you can use it to invoke the snippet. Start typing `propfull`. As you type, the IntelliSense code-completion list appears. This list contains the code snippets matching the keys you've already typed. Figure 3-5 shows that all code snippets starting with "pro" on this list.

When you select the code snippet to invoke (either by using a mouse-click, or by pressing Enter and then Tab, or pressing Tab twice), the snippet template is inserted into the code, indicating the placeholders you can change, as shown in Figure 3-6.

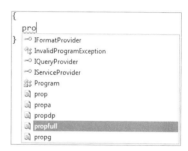

```
class Program
{
  private int myVar;

  public int MyProperty
  {
    get { return myVar; }
    set { myVar = value; }
  }
}
```

**FIGURE 3-6:** Code template with placeholders

When the code snippet is inserted, the focus is set on the first placeholder (int in Figure 3-6). Also, the other occurrence of the int placeholder is marked to indicate that editing first one will automatically change the other. By pressing Tab, you can move to the next placeholder; by pressing Shift+Tab, you can go back to the previous one. While you are in a placeholder, you can replace its content at any time. As you move to another placeholder, the content change will be propagated to other occurrences of the placeholder. When you press the Enter key, you will be finished with code template editing, and placeholder highlights are removed.

While you are in the code template editing mode, you can page up and page down in the code. You can even select and copy code details, and then replace the placeholder with them. However, when you try to edit any other part of the text outside of the code template, editing is terminated.

## Surrounding the Selected Code with a Snippet

You should now be familiar with how to use the expansion snippets. Surrounding snippets are very similar, and you can use them exactly the same way as expansion snippets. The only difference is how you invoke them.

Invoking a surrounding snippet with its shortcut (just as you did previously with expansion snippets) will work, but will embrace empty text. If you want it to encapsulate the selected text, you cannot use the shortcut-based approach — typing in the first key of the shortcut will replace the selected text.

So, the only way is to select the surrounding text and then invoking the Surround With command from the menu, or using the Ctrl+K, S key combination. Visual Studio will display the same navigation line as you saw with expansion snippets, and enable you to traverse through the snippet categories, similar to what you did previously. When you invoke the snippet, you can edit the placeholders exactly as described earlier.

The bad news for Visual Basic developers is that surrounding type snippets are not supported by the Visual Basic Editor. To compensate for this lack of support, the Visual Basic Editor provides some nice features not implemented in other editors.

## Visual Basic Specific Features

The Visual Basic Editor enables you to define code snippets by means of what they contain — type or method definitions, method body statements, and so on. The IntelliSense code completion and the Insert Snippet command are smart enough to offer only the list of snippets available at the current Editor position.

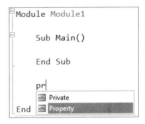

Let's say that you are using the shortcut Property to insert a property declaration. If you type it within a module or class, but outside of a method body, the snippet is offered on the code-completion list, as shown in Figure 3-7.

**FIGURE 3-7:** Property can be inserted here

Now, let's say you move the caret into the body of a method and try to invoke the Property snippet with its shortcut. This time, the snippet is not displayed in the completion list. As shown in Figure 3-8, only the `PropertyCollection` class (which starts with the "`Property`" prefix) is displayed.

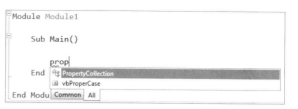

**FIGURE 3-8:** Property cannot be inserted here

This is not the only feature unique for Visual Basic. In other languages, you can edit the template of the code snippet while you edit placeholders. As you try to edit something else outside of the placeholders, template editing is terminated.

Visual Basic is different, however, in at least a couple of ways. First, when you press Enter while editing a placeholder, you are allowed to put a new line into the placeholder. Second, you can edit the placeholders in the code templates, not just directly after you invoke the snippet. If you use the Edit ⇨ IntelliSense ⇨ Show Snippet Highlighting command to highlight all placeholders in the active code document, you are allowed to edit them. If you insert several code snippets into the document, all of their placeholders will be highlighted, as shown in Figure 3-9.

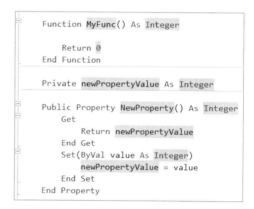

**FIGURE 3-9:** Show Snippet Highlighting

Similarly, with the Edit ⇨ IntelliSense ⇨ Hide Snippet Highlights command, you can disable placeholder editing. When you close the code file, and open it again, you lose the opportunity to edit template placeholders.

## HTML, SQL, and JScript Code Snippets

Visual Studio 2005 was the first version that implemented the code snippet feature, and it shipped with a few dozen snippets out-of-the-box. At that time, Visual C#, Visual Basic, and Visual J# were supported.

Visual Studio 2008 was the first version to support .NET 3.0 and .NET 3.5. This version added new snippets to the existing ones, many of them related to Workflow Foundation (WF) and to Windows Presentation Foundation (WPF). Visual Studio 2008 abandoned supporting Visual J#, so the corresponding snippets were also removed. However, it added great snippet support for extensible markup language (XML) and XML Schema Definition (XSD) files.

Visual Studio 2010 adds code snippet support for the HTML, SQL, and JScript languages. There are a few dozen code snippets supporting ASP.NET out-of-the-box, and Visual Studio does not skimp with JScript snippets. This should definitely be good news for web developers. SQL developers also benefit because Visual Studio 2010 ships with about two dozen SQL snippets.

## CREATING CODE SNIPPETS

Without a doubt, code snippets would not provide enough value if you were constrained to using only snippets shipped with Visual Studio. Of course, you can always add your own snippets to the library of existing ones. You don't have to stop at creating general-purpose code snippets, since you can also tailor them to your special needs.

In the following discussions, you will learn how easy it is to create a code snippet using XML format, as well as the nitty-gritty details of this particular format.

## Creating a Simple Code Snippet

Create a new XML file by selecting File ➪ New ➪ File, and then select the XML file format from the listed options. Change the name of the file to `ConsoleSnippet.snippet` and create it.

 *The* `.snippet` *extension is reserved by Visual Studio for code snippet definitions.*

Select the document window of the newly created file and view its properties. To enable the IntelliSense support for editing, assign the appropriate XSD file to this `.snippet` file with help of Schemas in the property window. By clicking the ellipsis button belonging to this property, you can set this schema with the ensuing dialog.

Toward the middle of the list, you will find the target namespace ending with `CodeSnippet` with a filename `snippetformat.xsd`. Right-click on this row, and click on the "Use selected schemas" item in the context menu, as shown in Figure 3-10. Close the dialog with OK.

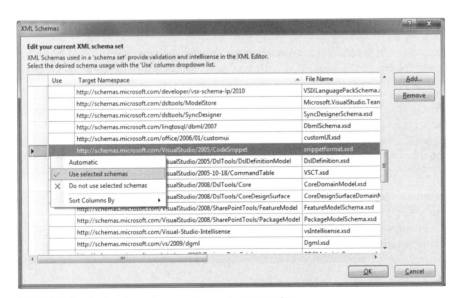

**FIGURE 3-10:** Assign the schema to the code snippet file

## Writing the Code Snippet Definition

You now can type in the definition of the snippet. Listing 3-1 shows the text you should type in. IntelliSense and code completion will help you accelerate the typing.

**LISTING 3-1:** ConsoleSnippet.snippet

```xml
<?xml version="1.0" encoding="utf-8"?>
<CodeSnippets xmlns="http://schemas.microsoft.com/VisualStudio/2005/CodeSnippet">
  <CodeSnippet Format="1.0">
    <Header>
      <Title>Write a message to the console</Title>
      <Shortcut>wmc</Shortcut>
      <Author>Istvan (DiveDeeper) Novak</Author>
      <Description>
        This snippet inserts a "Console.WriteLine" invocation into the code.
      </Description>
      <SnippetTypes>
        <SnippetType>Expansion</SnippetType>
      </SnippetTypes>
    </Header>
    <Snippet>
      <Code Language="CSharp">
        <![CDATA[
        Console.WriteLine("This is a message");
        ]]>
      </Code>
    </Snippet>
  </CodeSnippet>
</CodeSnippets>
```

Save the file in one of your working folders.

## Importing the Code Snippet

To make the snippet available in Visual Studio, go to the Tools ➪ Code Snippets Manager dialog. In the Language drop-down, select Visual C#. Below the Language drop-down, you will see a few folders listed. Select the `My Code Snippets` folder and click on the Import button.

A Code Snippets Directory file-selection dialog pops up on the screen to enable you to select a `.snippet` file. Select the `ConsoleSnippet.snippet` file from the folder where you previously saved it. Click Open. The Import Code Snippet dialog then opens to enable you to select the location of the specified snippet file. Click Finish to signal that you accept the location.

The new code snippet file is imported. You can see it in the Code Snippets Manager when you expand the `My Code Snippets` folder, as shown in Figure 3-11.

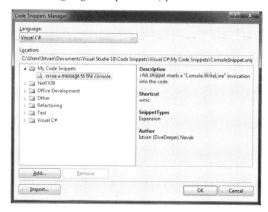

**FIGURE 3-11:** The imported code snippet

In the folder list, you see the title of the snippet, and, to the right, you will recognize the details you specified in the <Header> section of Listing 3-1.

Let's try using the snippet.

## Accessing and Using the New Snippet

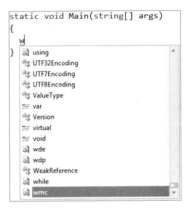

To begin, create a C# console application and open the Program. cs file. Look for a position where a statement can be inserted, and press the "w" key. IntelliSense automatically opens a list of possible completions for "w," as shown in Figure 3-12.

The "wmc" item in the list is highlighted as the best suggestion, and its icon unambiguously indicates that "wmc" is a code snippet shortcut. Pressing the Tab key twice invokes the code snippet, and the code for the snippet appears in the editor, as shown in Figure 3-13.

**FIGURE 3-12:** Code-completion list with code snippet suggestions

Although the snippet is working, you still have a few things to polish. First, you have unnecessary line breaks above and below the inserted statement. Second, you definitely would not like to use the default message but rather should type the one fitting with the source code context. Before typing this custom message, select the default one. Now you must struggle a bit with whether to use either the mouse or the keyboard.

```
static void Main(string[] args)
{
    |
    Console.WriteLine("This is a message");

}
```

**FIGURE 3-13:** The result of applying the snippet

Let's remove these small pains and modify the <Snippet> section shown previously in Listing 3-1. Listing 3-2 shows the modified code.

---

**LISTING 3-2:** The Modified <Snippet> Section

```xml
<?xml version="1.0" encoding="utf-8"?>
<CodeSnippets xmlns="http://schemas.microsoft.com/VisualStudio/2005/CodeSnippet">
  <CodeSnippet Format="1.0">
    <Header>
      <Title>Write a message to the console</Title>
      <Shortcut>wmc</Shortcut>
      <Author>Istvan (DiveDeeper) Novak</Author>
      <Description>
        This snippet inserts a "Console.WriteLine" invocation into the code.
      </Description>
      <SnippetTypes>
        <SnippetType>Expansion</SnippetType>
      </SnippetTypes>
    </Header>
    <Snippet>
```

```
      <Declarations>
        <Literal>
          <ID>message</ID>
          <ToolTip>The message to write to the console</ToolTip>
          <Default>Message</Default>
        </Literal>
      </Declarations>
      <Code Language="CSharp">
        <![CDATA[Console.WriteLine("$message$");]]>
      </Code>
    </Snippet>
  </CodeSnippet>
</CodeSnippets>
```

Note the addition of a `<Declarations>` section to the `<Snippet>` section defining a literal parameter named `message`. Also note that the `Code` element has been modified by removing the unnecessary line breaks and adding a reference to the `message` literal enclosed in dollar signs.

Save and import the modified snippet declaration again. The Code Snippets Manager recognizes that you are importing a snippet file that has already been added to the folder. It pops up a dialog to enable you to decide whether you want to rename or overwrite, or maybe skip it. Choose to overwrite, and the modified snippet will replace the original one.

Let's try that out. After typing "wmc" and pressing the Tab key twice, the snippet's code is inserted and the "Message" text is automatically selected, allowing you to replace it with the text you type in, as shown in Figure 3-14.

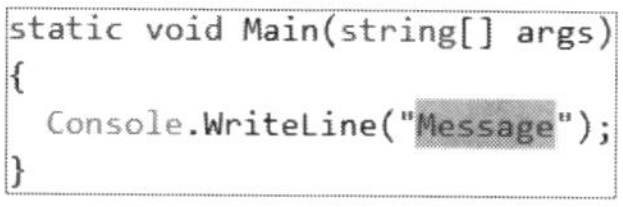

```
static void Main(string[] args)
{
  Console.WriteLine("Message");
}
```

**FIGURE 3-14:** The snippet selected the text to override

You can see how easy it is to declare a new code snippet. Now let's look behind the structure of the code snippet definition file.

## The Code Snippet File Structure

The structure of a code snippet file is simple. It doesn't have too many XML nodes, and its structure can be reflected with the following skeleton:

```
<?xml version="1.0" encoding="utf-8"?>
<CodeSnippets xmlns="http://schemas.microsoft.com/VisualStudio/2005/CodeSnippet">
  <CodeSnippet Format="1.0">
    <Header>
      <!-- General information goes here -->
    </Header>
    <Snippet>
      <!-- Here goes the code template -->
    </Snippet>
  </CodeSnippet>
</CodeSnippets>
```

All elements in the file should be in the `http://schemas.microsoft.com/VisualStudio/2005/CodeSnippet` namespace, as indicated in the `<CodeSnippets>` section. A single `.snippet` file may contain one or more snippets, with each of them represented by one `<CodeSnippet>` element. This element is valid only with its mandatory `Format` attribute set to the version number of the format used. For Visual Studio format numbers, the major number is 1. Although you can use just about any minor version number, you cannot leave the minor version tag empty.

Each `<CodeSnippet>` must have two mandatory sections:

➤ `<Header>` — This section defines general information about the snippet. The Code Snippets Manager leverages information from this section to display snippet properties.

➤ `<Snippet>` — This section defines the body, or the code template.

The schema definition requires that the `<Header>` be specified before `<Snippet>`. However, you can import the snippet even if this condition is not satisfied.

## The <Header> Element

Child nodes of the `<Header>` element contain general information about the code snippet — such as its title, a detailed description, the shortcut to activate it, and so on. Table 3-1 summarizes the available children of `<Header>`.

**TABLE 3-1:** Child Elements of <Header>

| ELEMENT | DESCRIPTION |
|---------|-------------|
| `<Author>` | This element is a placeholder to specify the author of the snippet and any other related information (such as trademarks, copyright symbols, and so on). |
| `<Title>` | This is a short title or name of the snippet. This name is indicated in the folder list of Code Snippets Manager. You should keep it short but expressive. |
| `<Description>` | The name often does not tell enough about the snippet. This element allows you to add a more verbose description to the snippet, and this description is displayed in the Code Snippets Manager when the snippet is selected in the folder list. |
| `<Shortcut>` | This element defines the shortcut text used with the snippet. Typing this shortcut and pressing the Tab key will activate the snippet, and the related code template is processed. When code completion is enabled, this shortcut also appears on the completion list with an icon indicating that this shortcut is going to invoke a code snippet. |
| `<Keywords>` | This element acts as a container for the `<Keyword>` child elements. Each `<Keyword>` child contains a custom keyword for the snippet. Although this is currently not used by Visual Studio, it represents a standard way of keywording code snippets for online content providers. |

| ELEMENT | DESCRIPTION |
| --- | --- |
| `<SnippetTypes>` | This element is a container for zero, one, or more `<SnippetType>` elements that can have one of the following values:<br><br>`Expansion` — This snippet is inserted at the cursor.<br><br>`SurroundsWith` — The snippet can be placed around the text that is selected in the editor.<br><br>`Refactoring` — This snippet is used for Visual C# refactoring operations, and cannot be invoked with a shortcut. When you put this value into your custom snippets, those can be imported into the snippet directory, but they will not work. Moreover, they will not be displayed in the code-completion list.<br><br>If you do not specify any `<SnippetType>` value, your snippet can be placed anywhere in code. |
| `<HelpUrl>` | This element contains a link for any additional online support and help information you write for the snippet. Currently, this tag is only supported by Visual Basic. |

All the elements shown in Table 3-1 are optional, so, in theory, you could create a snippet with empty header information. You can do that, and your snippet will be imported, but with no header information, it will not work. For example, if you do not specify a `<Shortcut>`, you cannot invoke the snippet directly from the editor, only through menu commands. You should define at least the `<Shortcut>`, `<Title>`, and `<Description>` elements.

## The <Snippet> Element

This element holds the information determining the snippet behavior. Child nodes under the `<Snippet>` element define the code template, and the context of the snippet. This is only a container for child elements. The following discussions describe these children in detail.

### Defining the Code

The `<code>` element is a placeholder for the code template. As you saw in the source of the earlier `ConsoleSnippet` sample, this template has a few parameters that can be substituted after the default text of the snippet has been inserted. Generally, this template contains multiple lines, so the content of `<code>` is enclosed in an XML CDATA section to keep all whitespaces during the XML parsing process, as shown here:

```
<Code Language="csharp"><![CDATA[enum $name$
{
    $selected$ $end$
}]]>
```

You can use special placeholders in the code, such as $end$ and $selected$ in the previous example. $end$ marks the location to place the cursor after the code snippet is inserted. $selected$ represents text selected in the document that is to be inserted into the surrounding-type snippet when it is invoked.

For example, let's say that you have selected the following text in the editor:

```
Value1,
Value2,
Value3,
```

Applying the `enum` snippet here with the Surround With function will result in the following code:

```
enum MyEnum
{
  Value1,
  Value2,
  Value3
}
```

The caret will be placed after `Value3`.

The code element has a few attributes with the following semantics:

➤ `Language` — This is a required attribute specifying the language to which the snippet is related. The editor uses this value to enumerate the code snippets that can be applied in a specific language context. The supported values are `CSharp`, `HTML`, `JScript`, `SQL`, `VB`, and `XML`.

➤ `Delimiter` — This defines the character to be used in the literals and placeholders. By default, it is the dollar sign ("$"). You can change it, and, of course, you must then modify the code template accordingly, as shown in the following sample:

```
<Code Language="CSharp" Delimiter="%">
  <![CDATA[Console.WriteLine("%message%");]]>
</Code>
```

➤ `Kind` — This specifies the kind of code that the snippet contains and, therefore, the location at which a code snippet must be inserted. This can have the values `method body`, `method decl`, `type decl`, `file`, and `any`. This attribute is used by the Visual Basic Editor, but is ignored by the C# editor. The Visual Basic Editor allows invoking a code snippet only at the right location. For example, you cannot activate a `type` declaration code snippet when you are within a `method` body. The C# editor does not make any kind of checks, and it allows activating the snippet at any editor source code position.

## Declaring Literals and Objects

In the code template, you can use placeholders for literal parameters and objects in order to let the user change default values. For example, in a class declaration snippet, the name of the type can be a literal parameter.

These placeholders are nested in the `<Declarations>` element that is placed directly in the `<Snippet>` element. Literal parameters are described with the `<Literal>` object, while object references are defined with the `<Object>` element.

Literal parameters and object references are very similar from the user's point of view. The Visual Studio team designed the code snippet feature with the following separation in their semantics:

➤ `<Literal>` — This element is used to identify a replacement for a piece of code that is entirely contained within the snippet, but will likely be customized after it is inserted into the code. For example, literal strings, numeric values, and some variable names should be declared as literals.

➤ `<Object>` — This element is used to identify an item that is required by the code snippet, but is likely to be defined outside of the snippet itself. For example, Windows Forms controls, ASP.NET controls, object instances, and type instances should be declared as objects.

Both elements have an optional Boolean attribute named `Editable` that is `true` by default. You can set its value to `false` (or `0`) to disable user edits after the snippet code is inserted. You might wonder, if the `Editable` attribute is useful, why you should make a literal read-only at all. Later in this chapter, you will learn about code snippet functions, and you will then see why to use read-only literals.

Table 3-2 defines the elements that can be nested in `<Literal>` or `<Object>`.

**TABLE 3-2:** Child Elements of <Literal> and <Object>

| ELEMENT | DESCRIPTION |
| --- | --- |
| `<ID>` | This required element specifies the identifier of the literal parameter or object. This identifier is put into the code template enclosed between the delimiters (dollar sign, by default). You must use exactly one `<ID>` element. The identifier cannot be `end` or `selected` because these are reserved. |
| `<Default>` | This required element specifies the default value of the object or literal parameter when the code snippet is inserted. However, you can omit this element and, in this case, a literal is replaced with a space character. |
| `<Type>` | Specifies the type of the literal or the object. This parameter is processed only for `<Object>`. However you can set it even for `<Literal>`. There must be exactly one `<Type>` element in the `<Object>` definition. |
| `<Tooltip>` | This optional element specifies the hint to be displayed for the literal parameter or object. You should describe the expected value and the intended usage of the literal or object. |
| `<Function>` | This optional element specifies a function to execute when the literal receives focus in Visual Studio. Currently, this element is used only with snippets written in C#. For other language contexts, this element is ignored. |

## Language-Dependent Features

As mentioned previously, a few code snippet features are implemented in different ways, depending on the language context. For example, Visual Basic does not support surrounding-type snippets, while the other languages do. In contrast, Visual Basic allows showing and hiding code template placeholders after the code template has been inserted and placeholder editing is terminated.

The following sections examine a few language-specific features that are related to the structure of the snippet file.

### <Imports> and <References>

There are two child elements of the `<Snippet>` section that are supported only in Visual Basic. When you insert a piece of code into the existing code text, even if that is syntactically correct, it may prevent the full source file from compiling for several reasons. One of the most important is that type and member references used in the inserted code cannot be resolved in the context they are used.

You can use the `<Imports>` element to define namespaces that should be added to the code as soon as the code snippet is being inserted. For example, if your code snippet is about creating and using streams or files, it probably uses types from the `System.IO` namespace. Instead of putting the full type names with the `System.IO` namespace prefix in the code template, you can add the following element to the `<Snippet>` section:

```
<Imports>
  <Import>
    <Namespace>System.IO</Namespace>
  </Import>
</Imports>
```

`<Imports>` is a container holding one or more `<Import>` element, each of them having exactly one `<Namespace>` element.

Sometimes the inserted code applies types that are in assemblies not referenced by the project where the snippet is used. The `<References>` element is a container holding one or more `<Reference>` elements to provide a way to add references to assemblies when the code snippet is being inserted into the code. The following extract shows how to use `<References>`:

```
<References>
  <Reference>
    <Assembly>System.Data.dll</Assembly>
    <Url>http://msdn.microsoft.com/en-us/library/system.data(VS.100).aspx</Url>
  </Reference>
  <Reference>
    <Assembly>
      MyCompany.Widgets.dll, Version=1.0, Culture=neutral,
        PublicKeyToken=0123456789abcdef
    </Assembly>
    <Url>http://mycompany.com/Widgets/overview.html</Url>
  <Reference>
</References>
```

The `<Reference>` element has two nested elements:

➤   `<Assembly>` — This is mandatory, and it contains the name of the assembly to be referenced. The name can be either the short name of the assembly (such as `System.Data.dll` shown in the previous example) or its strong name (such as `MyCompany.Widgets.dll`).

➤   `<Url>` — This is an optional element that can be set to a link providing more information about the assembly and types encapsulated.

## Code Snippet Functions

The `<Literal>` and `<Object>` elements may contain a child element named `<Function>`, which is processed only by the C# code editor. `<Function>` contains a name with arguments, and it is executed when a literal or object placeholder receives the focus in the editor.

Table 3-3 summarizes the function names that can be processed by the C# code editor:

**TABLE 3-3:** Code Snippet Functions

| FUNCTION | DESCRIPTION |
| --- | --- |
| `ClassName()` | Retrieves the name of the class that contains the snippet being inserted. This function is very useful when creating constructor or destructor declaration code or instantiation statements. |
| `GenerateSwitchCases(EnumLiteral)` | Generates a `switch` statement with the related `case` statements according to the type defined by `EnumLiteral`. The `EnumLiteral` parameter can be either an enumeration type or a reference to a `<Literal>` with an enumeration type. |
| `SimpleTypeName(TypeName)` | Reduces the name in the `TypeName` parameter to the simplest form in the context in which the snippet is being inserted. This function helps you make your code readable by removing unnecessary namespace tags in type references. |

Let's create a sample to show how these code snippet functions can be used. The sample shown in Listing 3-3 is a bit enforced and probably does not have too much practical use, but it does help to illustrate the functions. It will create an enumeration member field and a public constructor writing out debug information and providing a `switch` statement.

**LISTING 3-3: Code Snippet Functions by Example**

```
<?xml version="1.0" encoding="utf-8"?>
<CodeSnippets xmlns="http://schemas.microsoft.com/VisualStudio/2005/CodeSnippet">
  <CodeSnippet Format="1.0">
    <Header>
```

*continues*

**LISTING 3-3** *(continued)*

```xml
      <Title>Enumeration logger</Title>
      <Shortcut>loge</Shortcut>
      <Author>Istvan (DiveDeeper) Novak</Author>
      <Description>Creates a logger method for an enumeration.</Description>
    </Header>
    <Snippet>
      <Declarations>
        <Literal>
          <ID>type</ID>
          <ToolTip>Enum member type</ToolTip>
          <Default>EnumType</Default>
        </Literal>
        <Literal Editable="false">
          <ID>Debug</ID>
          <Function>SimpleTypeName(System.Diagnostics.Debug)</Function>
        </Literal>
        <Literal Editable="false">
          <ID>className</ID>
          <ToolTip>Class name</ToolTip>
          <Function>ClassName()</Function>
          <Default>ClassNameDefault</Default>
        </Literal>
        <Literal>
          <ID>enumExpr</ID>
          <ToolTip>Enumeration to switch on</ToolTip>
          <Default>switchExpr</Default>
        </Literal>
        <Literal Editable="false">
          <ID>cases</ID>
          <Function>GenerateSwitchCases($enumExpr$)</Function>
          <Default>default:</Default>
        </Literal>
      </Declarations>
      <Code Language="CSharp">
        <![CDATA[

      private $type$ _EnumValue;

      public $className$($type$ enumValue)
      {
        _EnumValue = enumValue;
        $Debug$.WriteLine("Value : {0}", _EnumValue);
        switch ($enumExpr$)
        {
          $cases$
        }
      }
      ]]>
      </Code>
    </Snippet>
  </CodeSnippet>
</CodeSnippets>
```

As you can see, Listing 3-3 contains five literals, and three of them are read-only having an `Editable` attribute with `false` value. This is intentional, because these literals are to define function values, and not to be edited by the user.

The `Debug` literal uses `SimpleTypeName` function to reduce the full type name according to the context where it is used. Should you have a `using` clause for the `System.Diagnostics` namespace, the `Debug` name is used. Not having this `using` clause, the full `System.Diganostics.Debug` type name would be inserted before the `WriteLine` member invocation.

The `className` literal uses the `ClassName` function to be substituted by the name of the class where the snippet is being inserted.

The most compound part of the Listing 3-1 is the use of the `cases` literal that depends on the `GenerateSwitchCases` function. As you can see, this function's argument is another literal, `enumExpr`, which can be edited by the user.

After importing this snippet, you can use the `loge` shortcut to invoke it. Figure 3-15 shows how it was used within the `Program` class of a C# console application.

```csharp
class Program
{
    static void Main(string[] args)
    {
        Console.WriteLine(" ");
        Console.WriteLine("Haho");
    }


    private EnumType _EnumValue;

    public Program(EnumType enumValue)
    {
        _EnumValue = enumValue;
        Debug.WriteLine("Value : {0}", _EnumValue);
        switch (switchExpr)
        {
            default.
        }
    }

}
}
```

**FIGURE 3-15:** Invoking the snippet

You can replace the `EnumType` placeholder with an enumeration type such as, for example, with `System.IO.FileShare`. When you press Tab, all occurrences of `EnumType` are changed accordingly, and the focus is set to the `switchExpr` placeholder, as shown in Figure 3-16.

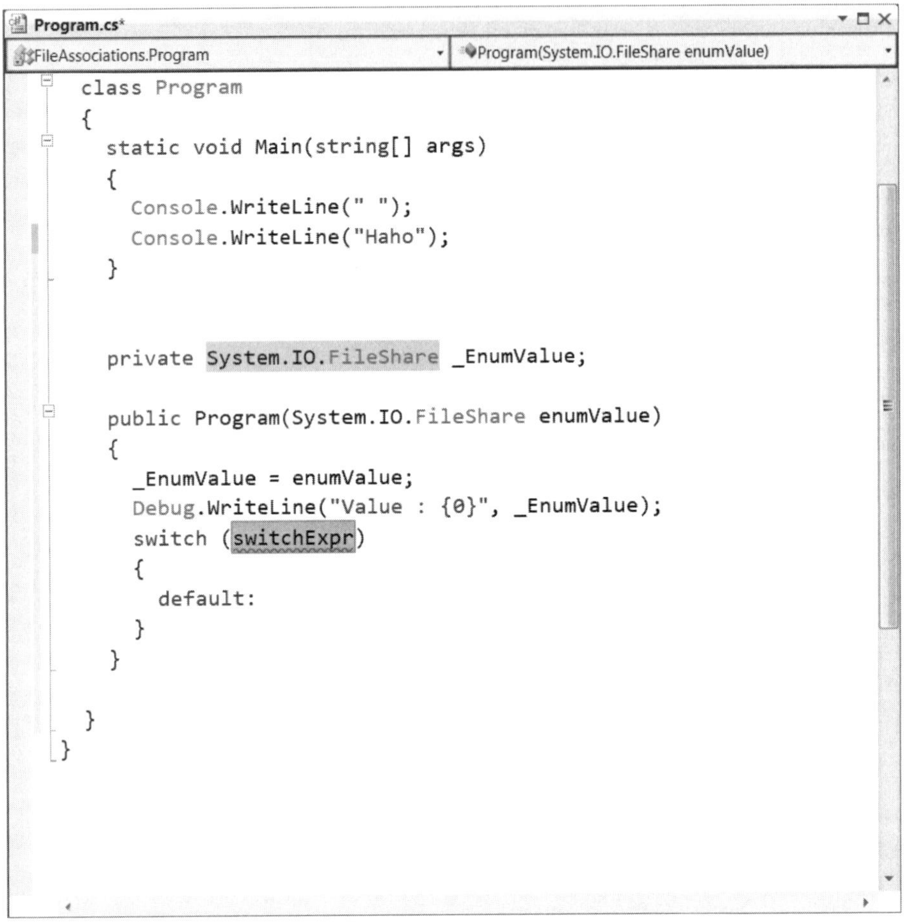
Program.cs*
FileAssociations.Program
Program(System.IO.FileShare enumValue)
class Program
{
static void Main(string[] args)
{
Console.WriteLine(" ");
Console.WriteLine("Haho");
}
private System.IO.FileShare _EnumValue;
public Program(System.IO.FileShare enumValue)
{
_EnumValue = enumValue;
Debug.WriteLine("Value : {0}", _EnumValue);
switch (switchExpr)
{
default:
}
}
}
}

**FIGURE 3-16:** Inserting an enumeration type

Now, let's say that you substitute `switchExpr` with `_EnumValue` and press Tab twice. The editor recognizes that `_EnumValue` is an enumeration type field, and automatically generates case statements according to the value set of `System.IO.FileShare`, as shown in Figure 3-17.

```
Program.cs*                                                    ▼ □ ×
FileAssociations.Program              ▼    _EnumValue                  ▼

      private System.IO.FileShare _EnumValue;

      public Program(System.IO.FileShare enumValue)
      {
        _EnumValue = enumValue;
        Debug.WriteLine("Value : {0}", _EnumValue);
        switch (_EnumValue)
        {
          case System.IO.FileShare.Delete:
            break;
          case System.IO.FileShare.Inheritable:
            break;
          case System.IO.FileShare.None:
            break;
          case System.IO.FileShare.Read:
            break;
          case System.IO.FileShare.ReadWrite:
            break;
          case System.IO.FileShare.Write:
            break;
          default:
            break;
        }
      }

    }
```

**FIGURE 3-17:** Case statement generation

You can play with the snippet to see how it behaves in several contexts. For example, you could try the following actions:

➤ Use a non enumerated type for EnumType

➤ Replace switchExpr with an expression resulting a non-enumerated type

➤ Insert the snippet outside of a class declaration

## MANAGING CODE SNIPPETS

Visual Studio ships with a few hundred code snippets out-of-the-box, and you can also create dozens of your own custom snippets. When you must handle so many of them, you definitely need some tool to categorize them. As you have already seen, Visual Studio 2010 has a tool called Code Snippets Manager that helps you with this activity. Let's take a look at some details.

# The Code Snippet Manager

Use the Tools ➪ Code Snippets Manager command, or press the Ctrl+K and then Ctrl+B key combination, to display the dialog to help you in managing code snippets integrated with Visual Studio. Figure 3-18 shows this dialog in action, where a concrete snippet is selected.

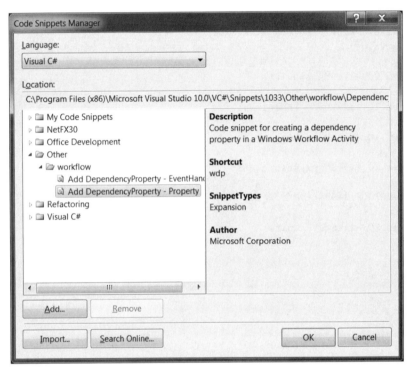

**FIGURE 3-18:**  Code Snippets Manager

At the top of the dialog, you see the Language drop-down box that you can use to filter all code snippets based on a language. The largest part of the dialog screen is occupied by the tree view on the left displaying the hierarchy of code snippets belonging to the specified language. The details pane on the right displays the most relevant properties of the snippet selected in the tree view.

Above the panes, you see the Location field that defines the full path of a folder or snippet selected in the tree view. You can copy the content of the Location field when you need it for further use — for example, to open the specified folder in Windows Explorer.

Below the panes, you find the Add and Remove buttons that let you add a new snippet folder to the list of existing ones and remove a folder from the list. You can also import a snippet file or search for more information online.

## Code Snippet Storage

By now, you should realize that, at the lowest level, code snippets are stored in XML files with the `.snippet` extension. The Code Snippets Manager works with a set of folders containing `.snippet` files. Actually, it stores only paths to those folders, and discovers subfolders and code snippet files dynamically. There are two kinds of folders:

➤ *System folders* — These are added to the Code Snippets Manager's list of folders at Visual Studio setup time.

➤ *User folders* — These can be added by users at any time. One user folder stored in your user profile is added for each language at Visual Studio setup time.

Table 3-4 summarizes the root of the system folders and default custom folders for each language supported by Visual Studio 2010 out-of-the-box.

**TABLE 3-4:** Code Snippet Folders

| LANGUAGE | SYSTEM FOLDER | USER FOLDER |
| --- | --- | --- |
| HTML | `%InstallRoot%\Web\Snippets\HTML` | `Visual Web Developer\My HTML Snippets` |
| JScript | `%InstallRoot%\Web\Snippets\ JScript` | `Visual Web Developer\My JScript Snippets` |
| Visual Basic | `%InstallRoot%\VB\Snippets` | `Visual Basic\My Code Snippets` |
| Visual C# | `%InstallRoot%\VC#\Snippets` | `Visual C#\My Code Snippets` |
| XML | `%InstallRoot%\xml\Snippets` | `XML\My Xml Snippets` |
| SQL | `%InstallRoot%\VSTSDB\Snippets` | `SQL\My Code Snippets` |

Visual Studio puts the custom code snippet folders in your `My Documents` virtual folder under the `Visual Studio 10\Code Snippets` subfolder. Depending on your user name, profile type, and operating system, `My Document` can be located in different places. For example, in a notebook computer using Windows 7, the Visual C# custom snippets would be in the `C:\Users\<username>\Documents\Visual Studio 10\Code Snippets\Visual C#\My Code Snippets` folder.

System folders are under the Visual Studio installation folder (`%InstallRoot%`) in the subfolders shown in the Table 3-4. Each folder contains a subfolder depending on the language of Visual Studio, and snippets are under the language folder. For example, if you have installed Visual Studio 2010 with English language, Visual C# snippets can be found in `%InstallRoot%\VC#\Snippets\1033` folder.

Code snippets can be grouped into a hierarchical folder structure. For example, Visual C# snippets have the following folders:

➤ `NetFX3` — These are snippets for .NET 3.0 new features.

➤ `OfficeDevelopment` — These are code snippets helping in Microsoft Office development tasks.

➤ `other` — This is the folder for other code snippets. Currently, a few WF snippets can be found here.

➤ `Refactoring` — These are code snippets used by the C# language service for refactoring functions.

➤ `Visual C#` — These are general-purpose snippets related to the C# language (properties, events, classes, and so on).

System folders can have so-called index files to enumerate snippets. The existence and the name of these files are language service-dependent. This file is called `SnippetIndex.xml` for Visual Basic, and `SnippetsIndex.xml` for the other languages. The format of these index files is beyond the scope of this book, but their structure is really simple. Feel free to open and examine them.

## Adding and Removing Snippets

The Code Snippets Manager allows you to add your own custom folders with snippets. As mentioned previously, Code Snippets Manager stores only paths to folders. So, by using the Add button, you can add only top-level folders to the selected language. When you click the Add button, a folder-selection dialog with Code Snippets Directory caption is popped up to let you specify the folder to add. After you add the selected folder to the directory, it is displayed in the folder list. You can immediately browse its content.

When you select a folder in the list and click the Remove button, you can draw it off from the library. Of course, this operation does not delete the content of the folder; it just omits it from the list handled by the Code Snippets Manager. You can remove only top-level folders. The Remove button is disabled when you select a subfolder or a snippet.

Be careful about removing system folders. The Code Snippets Manager allows you to remove them, and does not even ask for confirmation. Should you accidentally remove a system folder, you can add it later by selecting the physical folder you drew off. After adding it again, Visual Studio recognizes it is a system folder and handles it accordingly.

## Importing Snippets

If you have a lot of snippets organized in a folder, you can add the folder to the appropriate language with Code Snippets Manager. However, if you have `.snippet` files that have not been organized in any folder, you can import them, and make the snippets within them a part of your library.

After you select one or more `.snippet` files, click the Import button to start importing snippets. The Import Code Snippet dialog shown in Figure 3-19 is displayed to let you select the import folder for each file.

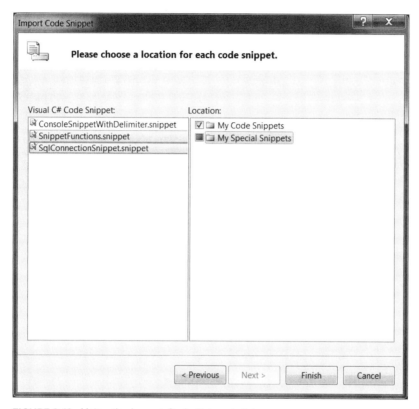

FIGURE 3-19: Using the Import Code Snippet dialog

The left pane of the window displays the code snippet files, while the right pane lists the user folders into which to import the snippets. When a snippet file is imported, the file is physically copied into the selected folder. As you can see from Figure 3-19, you can set the import folder for each individual file. One file can be copied into one or more than one folder. Figure 3-19 illustrates a situation when both the selected snippets are to be imported into the My Code Snippets folder, and only one of them is about to be put into the My Special Snippets folder.

The Code Snippet Manager allows you to import snippets only into the top-level user folders.

You can select code snippet files supporting different languages. The Import Code Snippet dialog groups them according to their host languages. You can click the Previous and Next buttons to page among the languages and set the appropriate folder. The label above the snippet pane on the left side of the dialog tells you the host language of the files listed in the pane.

When you click the Finish button, the snippet files will be instantly imported into the selected folders and are ready to use.

## ADVANCED CODE SNIPPET FEATURES

Thus far in this chapter, you have learned about the concept of code snippets, about the `.snippet` file format, and about the role of Code Snippets Manager. Let's take a look at some advanced features for code snippets.

## Multiple Snippets in a File

The `.snippet` file's structure was intentionally designed to be able to describe one or more snippets. The `<CodeSnippets>` element is a container that may hold one or more `<CodeSnippet>` elements, as shown in Listing 3-4.

**LISTING 3-4:** Multiple Code Snippets in One File

```xml
<?xml version="1.0" encoding="utf-8"?>
<CodeSnippets xmlns="http://schemas.microsoft.com/VisualStudio/2005/CodeSnippet">

  <!-- First snippet -->
  <CodeSnippet Format="1.0">
    <Header>
      <Title>Write an empty line</Title>
      <Shortcut>wel</Shortcut>
      <Author>Istvan (DiveDeeper) Novak</Author>
      <Description>
        This snippet inserts a "Console.WriteLine()" invocation into the code.
      </Description>
    </Header>
    <Snippet>
      <Code Language="CSharp">
        <![CDATA[Console.WriteLine();]]>
      </Code>
    </Snippet>
  </CodeSnippet>

  <!-- Second snippet -->
  <CodeSnippet Format="1.0">
    <Header>
      <Title>Write a message</Title>
      <Shortcut>wm</Shortcut>
      <Author>Istvan (DiveDeeper) Novak</Author>
      <Description>
        This snippet inserts a "Console.Write()" invocation into the code.
      </Description>
    </Header>
    <Snippet>
      <Declarations>
        <Literal>
          <ID>message</ID>
          <ToolTip>The message to write to the console</ToolTip>
```

```
        <Default>Message</Default>
      </Literal>
    </Declarations>
    <Code Language="CSharp">
      <![CDATA[Console.Write("$message$");]]>
    </Code>
  </Snippet>
</CodeSnippet>

<!-- Third snippet -->
<CodeSnippet Format="1.0">
  <Header>
    <Title>Write a message with a new line</Title>
    <Shortcut>wml</Shortcut>
    <Author>Istvan (DiveDeeper) Novak</Author>
    <Description>
      This snippet inserts a "Console.WriteLine()" invocation into the code.
    </Description>
  </Header>
  <Snippet>
    <Declarations>
      <Literal>
        <ID>message</ID>
        <ToolTip>The message to write to the console</ToolTip>
        <Default>Message</Default>
      </Literal>
    </Declarations>
    <Code Language="CSharp">
      <![CDATA[Console.WriteLine("$message$");]]>
    </Code>
  </Snippet>
</CodeSnippet>
</CodeSnippets>
```

When you import the snippet file, you will see all the snippets displayed in the Code Snippets Manager, as shown in Figure 3-20.

Having multiple snippets in a file makes it easy for you to manage and deploy the snippets — if you put a reasonable number of <CodeSnippet> elements into a file. A good rule of thumb is if you put two to five snippets sharing some common behavior into a file, this should be pretty easy to handle. However, if you put more into one file, or have snippets with very separate behavior in one file, manageability becomes difficult, and, moreover, can lead to complications.

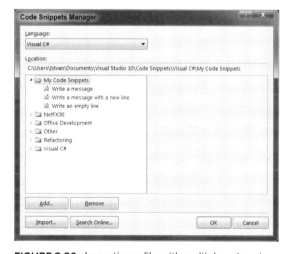

**FIGURE 3-20:** Importing a file with multiple snippets

# Code Snippets in Other Languages

As mentioned previously, Visual Studio 2010 supports code snippets for HTML, JScript, Visual Basic, Visual C#, XML, and SQL out-of-the-box. However, the infrastructure for code snippets is available for any other language. Visual Studio allows creating *language services* to implement other languages, and these languages can use the code snippet infrastructure to create their own snippet support.

Language services can be customized to determine how they use code snippets, and what kind of support they provide in the code editor related to the specific language. As you can imagine, there is a big difference between the Visual Basic implementation and other languages when handling snippet kinds (for example, type declaration, method declaration, method body, and so on), as well as providing surrounding-type snippets.

Language providers can decide if they implement code snippets at all, or, if they do, they can decide what features they support. For example, you can install IronPython Studio for Visual Studio 2008 that provides a language service for the IronPython language, and does, indeed, implement the code snippets. Figure 3-21 shows Code Snippets Manager with a language filter for Python and the Python snippets installed.

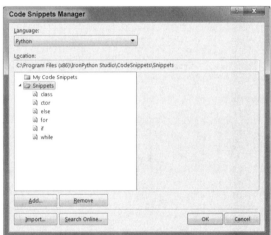

**FIGURE 3-21:** Code Snippets Manager with a language filter for Python

When you look into the Python snippet files, you see that they use the standard code snippet infrastructure, with the well-known snippet schema. You can definitely recognize from the `<Code>` element that these snippets belong to the Python language:

```
<Snippet>
  <Declarations>
    <Literal>
      <ID>expression</ID>
      <ToolTip>Expression to evaluate</ToolTip>
      <Default>true</Default>
    </Literal>
  </Declarations>
  <Code Language="python">
<![CDATA[while $expression$:
  $selected$$end$
]]>
  </Code>
</Snippet>
```

 *The Nemerle programming language has also been integrated with Visual Studio 2008 and supports code snippets.*

## Building Online Code Snippet Providers

With code snippets, you can create an online repository where you can select snippets categorized by your interest, and then download them to your machine. While snippets can be converted into the .snippet file format, you can either import them with Code Snippets Manager or create your own custom setup tool.

When you have a code snippet, you can also upload it to a site with its native .snippet file format. The structure of a snippet file contains a few elements (such as the <Keywords> and <HelpUrl> child elements of <Header>) intended to be used by online snippet providers to help with the categorization and organization of snippets.

You can even add new information to your code snippets, although the current code snippet scheme does not allow creating your own elements or attributes. Despite this schema constraint, you can add your own elements and attributes, as shown in the following extract:

```
<Snippet>
  <Code Language="CSharp" myAttr="myValue">
    <![CDATA[Console.WriteLine();]]>
  </Code>
  <MyElement>$$##</MyElement>
</Snippet>
```

Here, MyElement and myAttr are invalid elements by schema definition, but, in reality, the Code Snippets Manager does not validate the .snippet file against the schema. While the Code Snippets Manager finds the elements it looks for, it remains happy, and simply does not take care of other elements and attributes.

 *Although you can do this trick, it is not recommended. You cannot be sure that a future release of Visual Studio will not change this undocumented behavior. If you want to provide some kind of extension, you can use the* kind *attribute of the* <code> *element or the* <Function> *element nested into* <Object>.

## SNIPPET EDITORS

Editing .snippet files in Visual Studio is easy when you attach the appropriate XSD schema file to it, because IntelliSense helps a lot by listing elements, attributes, and values available in the current context. However, the user experience through editing the XML file (even with IntelliSense) is not always pleasant. Generally, the less complex part of your XML file is the <code> element encapsulating the body of the code template. The more complex code template you create, the longer the <Declaration> part is. As your code with the declarations gets longer than one or two pages on the screen, you can easily lose the focus. You must page up and down to understand what the code template is about.

The community recognized that the built-in Visual Studio snippet editing support can be improved with other tools that provide code template editing similar to editing the original code. Table 3-5 shows a few code snippet editors created and supported by the community.

**TABLE 3-5:** Code Snippet Editors and Tools

| NAME | URL |
| --- | --- |
| Snippy | http://www.codeplex.com/snippy |
| Export as Code Snippet Add-In | http://exportascodesnippet.codeplex.com |
| Snipp Dogg | http://snippdogg.codeplex.com/ |
| Snippet Builder | http://snippetbuilder.codeplex.com/ |
| Snippet Designer | http://snippetdesigner.codeplex.com/ |
| Snippet Editor | http://www.codeplex.com/SnippetEditor |

Let's take a quick look at three of these, each using a separate approach to help with code snippet development.

## Export as Code Snippet Add-In

This add-in was created by Alessandro Del Sole, and it works only with Visual Studio 2008. However, the full source code of the add-in can be downloaded, so you can update it to work with Visual Studio 2010 as well.

This is a good add-in because it is simple to use and helps you create snippets directly from your code. Often, you get the idea of making a snippet from a part of code right when you are typing the text and recognize that is reusable. With this add-in, you simply right-click on the selected code (this would be the base of the code template), and your snippet is about to be created. Figure 3-22 shows this step.

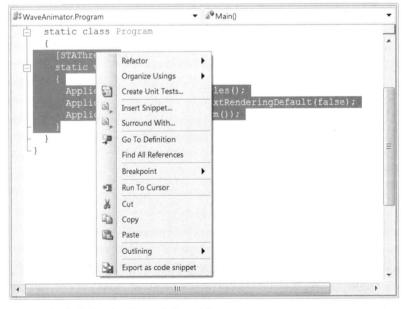

**FIGURE 3-22:** Selecting the code template

Next, you can add metadata attributes to the code template by filling in the form shown in Figure 3-23.

When you click the Export button, you can save the snippet into a file and use it just like other snippet files.

## Snippet Designer

This utility provides an even better user experience than Export as Code Snippet. Although, as of this writing, the utility was available only for Visual Studio 2008, the full source code is available, and it requires only small changes and recompilation to work with Visual Studio 2010.

You can start developing your snippets in two ways. The first is to use the File ⇨ New ⇨ File command and select Code Snippet File from the General category. The second is to select a piece of code while you are in the text editor, and use the "Export as Snippet" command from the context menu.

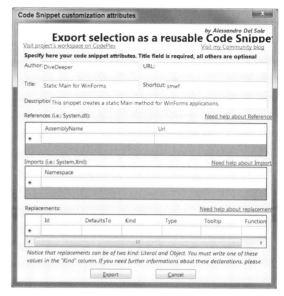

**FIGURE 3-23:** Add metadata to the code template

Independently of how you start, you can edit your `.snippet` file in a custom editor, as shown in Figure 3-24.

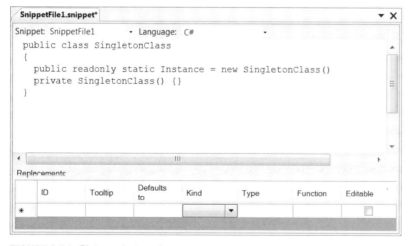

**FIGURE 3-24:** Plain code template

The code template you can edit here does not provide any placeholders, but you can add them easily with the context menu. Also, snippet metadata can be edited in the Properties window, as shown in Figure 3-25.

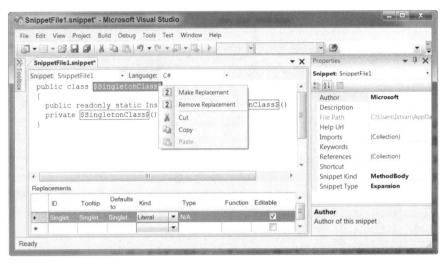

**FIGURE 3-25:** Code editing with Snippet Designer

Snippet Designer supports Visual Basic, Visual C#, and XML snippets.

## Snippet Editor

The previous two utilities are integrated with Visual Studio to help in code snippet editing. Snippet Editor is an external tool running out of Visual Studio. The great benefit of this tool is that is simultaneously supports Visual Studio 2005, 2008, and 2010. While it allows you to focus on editing a simple snippet, it also allows you browsing the snippet library. Figure 3-26 shows this application in action.

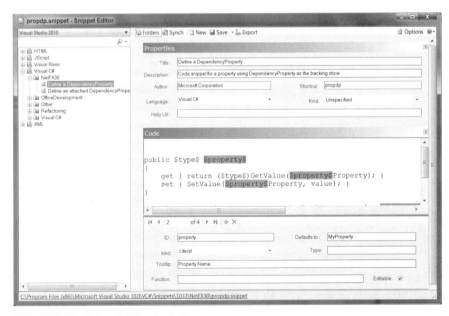

**FIGURE 3-26:** Snippet Editor in Action

The drop-down box at the top of the pane allows you to select one of the Visual Studio versions installed on your machine. In the left pane of the screen, you can manage the library of your snippets. The tree view displays the languages as top-level folders, and, under them, you can see the directory of snippets similar to what you can do with Code Snippets Manager. When you double-click on a snippet, you see its properties — including the code template — and you can immediately edit them.

The editor highlights the placeholders and allows the setting of their properties. In addition to being able to save the snippets, you can also export `.vsi` files and use them with the Visual Studio Community Content Installer tool to deploy the snippet.

If you intend to use this tool often, use the Tools ⇨ External Tools command to set up Snippet Editor so that it can be launched from the IDE.

## SUMMARY

Visual Studio code snippets play important role in personal productivity. The concept behind them is simple and powerful. Snippets are source code pieces that may range from one character to pages of text, and can easily be inserted into the code. The code to be inserted is defined with a template mechanism that allows defining placeholders and changing them when the template is about to be applied.

Visual Studio 2010 supports code snippets for the HTML, JScript, Visual Basic, Visual C#, SQL, and XML languages. There are minor differences in features available, depending on the host language.

The IDE ships with a few hundred code snippets altogether, and you can easily add your own snippets to the directory. By creating an XML file with the `.snippet` extension following the predefined schema, and then importing this file with Code Snippets Manager, you can put your snippets in practice in a few minutes.

In addition to Visual Studio, you can use community tools to create and manage snippets. Some of these tools are integrated with the IDE; some of them are external applications. Generally, they provide a better user experience than pure XML `.snippet` file editing.

In Chapter 4, you will learn about the concept of Visual Studio templates. In addition to familiarizing you with using the built-in project and item templates, the chapter will teach you how to create your own templates and integrate them with Visual Studio.

# Visual Studio Templates

Any time you start developing a new application with Visual Studio, you start by creating a new project or adding a new project to an existing solution. Because you can start with a new console application, Windows service, ASP.NET site, or whatever application type you use, you may underestimate the work that the IDE does behind the scenes when generating a project skeleton.

Let's enumerate a few activities done by the IDE that help you start with a project:

➤ A project file is created that controls the build process.

➤ The project's properties related to build, debug, and so on, are set up according to the project type.

➤ Source code items and resources are added to the project.

➤ In several cases, helpful documentation is generated.

In the heart of Visual Studio, project creation is based on the concept of *project templates*. When you start a new project, a template determines how your project's build process is established, what properties are set up (and to which values), and what kind of items are generated for you.

Visual Studio 2010 ships with almost a hundred project templates supporting the Visual Basic, C#, F#, and Visual C++ languages. The built-in templates are very useful, and, in many cases, they are a perfect place for you to start with a new application.

However, there are cases in which a customized project type would be a great benefit for your current work. Here are a few examples:

➤ When you create user interface (UI) intensive applications, you may use third-party UI controls and frameworks, and you would like to have the related assemblies added to the list of referenced assemblies.

➤ You have special notes and guidelines for developers using your company's domain-specific framework. Having those notes embedded into the project helps the team focus on core activities.

➤ You are using special build methods to compile, test, or deploy a specific application type. Keeping these methods together with the project provides a great value for your test and deployment specialist.

You'll surely not be surprised to learn that Visual Studio project templates support all of these scenarios. The template system is designed with extensibility in mind. You can even use third-party project templates and add them to Visual Studio.

The template system also allows you to work with *item templates*. When you work with your project, you can add items such as code files, Windows forms, Windows Presentation Foundation (WPF) forms, user controls, and so on to the existing project code. Just like project templates, item templates also can be defined by you. In cases where you use special frameworks, classes, and patterns, customizing project items for your need is especially useful.

This chapter explores the template system of Visual Studio, and delves into the following topics:

➤ *The categories and role of templates* — You'll learn why templates are an honorable friend, and what you can do with project and item templates.

➤ *Creating templates* — Without going too deep into the structure and anatomy of templates, you will build a very simple project and an item template, and learn how to integrate them with Visual Studio.

➤ *Template storage structure* — You will discover the details surrounding the anatomy of templates, and how the New Project and Add New Item dialogs provide a list of available templates.

➤ *Customizing templates* — There are great ways you can start from a simple template and create a few "flavors" from it by utilizing customization. In this chapter, you learn how to use custom template parameters, and how to build template wizards.

➤ *Deploying templates* — You will learn about the many ways to deploy your project and item templates. Visual Studio 2010 has a brand new feature called Extension Manager that makes it easy to share and deploy your templates through the Visual Studio Gallery, all of which you will learn about here.

Visual Studio project and item templates represent ideal candidates to use to tailor Visual Studio to your everyday needs. Patterns represented with project and item templates can prevent a lot of common mistakes from turning into miscommunication.

## THE ROLE OF TEMPLATES

The role of Visual Studio templates can be best characterized with the word "reusability." Templates are useful concepts because they save you from the burden of writing code from the scratch for each project, source code, form, and other types of items every time you start creating any instance of them. Templates not only save you time, but also help you avoid common mistakes by providing you skeletons for your frequently used artifacts. Templates provide consistency among your projects independently of who uses them and how.

You can leverage the reusability offered by templates in a variety of ways, including the following:

> ➤ At the most basic level, you can use the templates shipped with Visual Studio for the tasks you want to solve. For example, when you create an application with graphical user interface (GUI), you could start with the Windows Forms Application or the WPF Application template, but usually not a Console Application or a Class Library. Maybe it sounds strange, but you can start a GUI application even with the Console Application project template or with a Class Library and turn it to a graphical application by changing project properties, application entry point method, referenced assemblies, and so on. Of course, this is not the best practice, but, in theory, it could be done.

> ➤ You can create your first project and item templates by customizing existing ones. For example, you could create a new WPF Application template that contains a main form tailored to your company's design, or even add an About dialog to the project.

> ➤ You could create totally new project templates by changing the whole structure of existing ones, and even adding wizards that guide the user through the startup process.

> ➤ At a very high level, you could create templates extended with samples and documentation to adjust them to the methodology you use within your company.

The template system has been a part of Visual Studio from the first release. As new versions of Visual Studio have been released, new templates have been added to the IDE to support young languages and fresh technologies. With Visual Studio 2008, many templates arrived because of the new foundations (WF, WCF, and WPF) in .NET 3.0 and .NET 3.5. Visual Studio 2010 also ships new templates that are primarily related to the F# programming language and the Silverlight technology.

Visual Studio supports two categories of templates:

> ➤ Project templates
> ➤ Item templates

The template system also provides a way to compose *multi-project templates* that contain two or more related project templates.

The following discussions examine project and item templates to show you their common characteristics and behavior, as well as differences between them.

## Project Templates

Any time you start creating a new solution with Visual Studio, one of the first steps in the IDE is the File ➪ New ➪ Project command used to start a project. You expect this project to compile, to run, and to be ready for adding source code to give birth to your application. The command pops up the New Project dialog, where you can select one of the installed project templates, as shown in Figure 4-1.

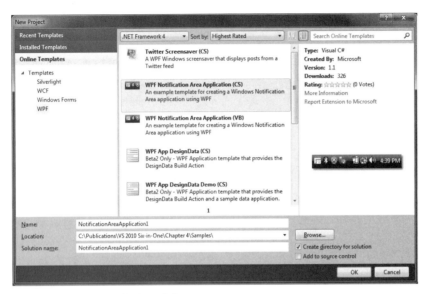

**FIGURE 4-1:** The New Project dialog

You probably use this dialog so often and so intuitively that you don't even think about the mechanisms moving small cogs behind the scenes resulting in this UI. The left pane of the dialog shows the categories from which you can select templates. This dialog changed a lot with Visual Studio 2010. For example, as you can see, you can quickly access the templates you've recently used. Another new feature is the capability to browse online templates and create your project based on one of them. Figure 4-2 shows the online WPF templates that were available as of this writing.

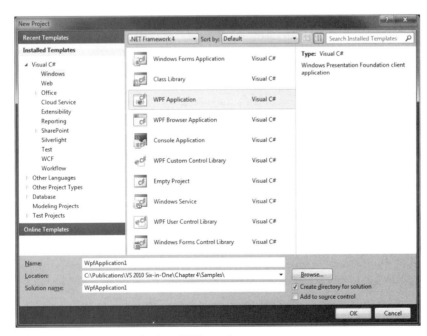

**FIGURE 4-2:** Illustration of online WPF templates

All the items you see in the middle pane of the New Project dialog are templates that cover an entire project, including the project file (with the properties set up), all source files (including resources, content files, associated document files, and so on), and the references used by the project.

The project files templates also contain some other metadata that is used by the IDE to display information about the template. For example, a short description of the project is shown on the right pane of the dialog. Data also includes information to categorize templates on the UI. Templates also can influence the behavior of the New Project dialog — for example, they can disable the Browse button.

When you create a project instance from the selected project template, the template system copies all files from the template to a specified location. Two important mechanisms are provided in addition to the copy operation:

➤ The template system can replace strings in the filenames and in the content of the files. For example, the project name can replace the project filename, and also the default namespace specifications in the source code files.

➤ A wizard can be started that collects some more information about the project and uses this information when generating project artifacts.

Let's say that you create a new WPF application with the name of `MyWpfApp`. Figure 4-3 shows the template system that enables you to start with the project.

The project template contains all the files shown in Figure 4-3. As you see, the project filename has been changed to `MyWpfApp`. If you open the `App.xaml.cs` file, you would see that the root namespace has also been renamed to `MyWpfApp`.

**FIGURE 4-3:** The new project in Solution Explorer

## Item Templates

When you create your project based on a specific template, you often add new items to this project, and you would like to start with a well-defined item skeleton instead of an empty code file. This is where the item templates come into the picture.

During your everyday activities, you generally work with a few stereotypes of project items such as forms, entity classes, service and controller types, database scripts, and so on. Visual Studio provides a great number of item templates you can add to your project with the Add New Item dialog. Figure 4-4 shows the items you can choose when working with a WPF application.

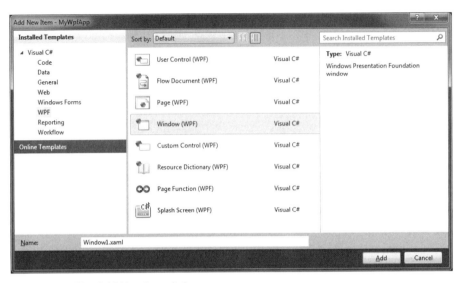

**FIGURE 4-4:** The Add New Item dialog

This dialog is very similar to the New Project dialog, and so are the mechanisms behind the UI. The template system works approximately the same way for item templates as for project templates — all item template files are copied to the appropriate project folder. Replacements and wizards are also supported for item templates.

Item templates provide a feature to enable you to add assembly references to the project hosting the item. In the template definition, an item can enlist referenced assemblies that the item is about to use for successful compilation. When the item is added to the project, all referenced assemblies that are not yet assigned to the project are also added.

Items and files are separate concepts. Although most items hold a single file, a few of them are composed of several files — such as forms and resources that may contain two (or even three) dependent files represented as a hierarchy within the Solution Explorer. An item template is definitely not a file template, so each file composing an item can be (and should be) added to the item template.

An item template may include files that will add more items to your project. For example, you may create an item template for an entity class that adds two files using partial class declaration with the intention that the user should customize only one of them. These files are separate items (that is, you can handle them separately), and, in the project, there is no information to indicate that they were added in a single step.

## CREATING TEMPLATES

By now, you are familiar with the idea of project and item templates. Let's have a look at how these concepts work in practice. In this section, you create a simple project template and a related item template. The activities here can be repeated for your own project and item templates.

The creation process starts with actually implementing the application, library, page, form, class, or whatever artifacts on which you intend to base your template. When these artifacts are ready, you can use the Export Template Wizard in Visual Studio to physically create the template definition, and integrate it with the IDE. Later, you can add customization points to the template.

# Creating a Simple Project Template

To demonstrate the steps of template creation, let's build a console application that receives commands from the user and executes them. Of course, the application will be very simple and not really robust, because this sample focuses on template development.

## Creating the Startup Project

Create a new C# project with the File ➪ New ➪ Project command and select the Console Application from the Windows project category. Name this new application `ConsoleBase` and click OK. Visual Studio creates a new console application with `Program.cs` and `AssemblyInfo.cs` files. (You can display this latter file when extending the Properties folder.) This application does not run any useful code by default. So, let's change the `Program` class to implement a very simple console application's logic, as shown in Listing 4-1.

**LISTING 4-1: Program.cs**

```csharp
using System;

namespace ConsoleBase
{
  class Program
  {
    const string PromptText = "#> ";
    const string QuitCommand = "quit";

    static void Main(string[] args)
    {
      DisplayWelcomeMessage();
      Console.Write(PromptText);
      string command;
      string pars;
      while (String.Compare((command = ReadCommand(out pars)),
        QuitCommand, true) != 0)
      {
        ProcessCommand(command, pars);
        Console.Write(PromptText);
      }
    }

    static void DisplayWelcomeMessage()
    {
      Console.WriteLine("Welcome to the BaseConsole application!");
      Console.WriteLine();
    }
```

*continues*

**LISTING 4-1** (*continued*)

```
    static string ReadCommand(out string pars)
    {
      var commandLine = Console.ReadLine().Trim();
      var command = commandLine;
      pars = string.Empty;
      var pos = commandLine.IndexOf(' ');
      if (pos > 0)
      {
        command = commandLine.Substring(0, pos);
        pars = commandLine.Substring(pos).Trim();
      }
      return command;
    }

    static void ProcessCommand(string command, string pars)
    {
      Console.WriteLine("{0}({1}) processed", command, pars);
    }
  }
}
```

*Code file [Program.cs] available for download at Wrox.com*

The class is very simple. It displays welcome text and loops with processing commands typed in by the user unless a `"quit"` command arrives, at which time it terminates. When you build and start it without debugging, you can see how it works. Figure 4-5 shows some sample output.

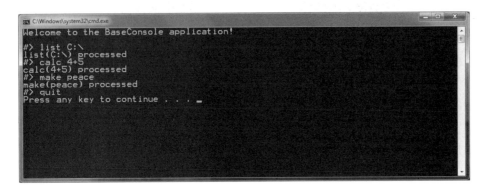

**FIGURE 4-5:** Sample output from BaseConsole

You are now ready to create a project template from this application. Go to the File menu and select the Export Template command. A new dialog, the Export Template Wizard, pops up on the screen. This wizard has a few pages, the first of which enables you to select the template type you intend to export, as shown in Figure 4-6.

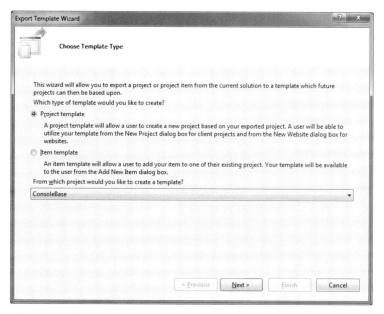

**FIGURE 4-6:** The Choose Template Type page

You want to export `BaseConsole` as a project template, so select that option. At the bottom of the page, you can select the project the template is based on. This list shows projects in the current solution.

Click the Next button, and the wizard moves you to the Select Template Options page, where you can specify a few attributes. Fill these options as shown in Figure 4-7.

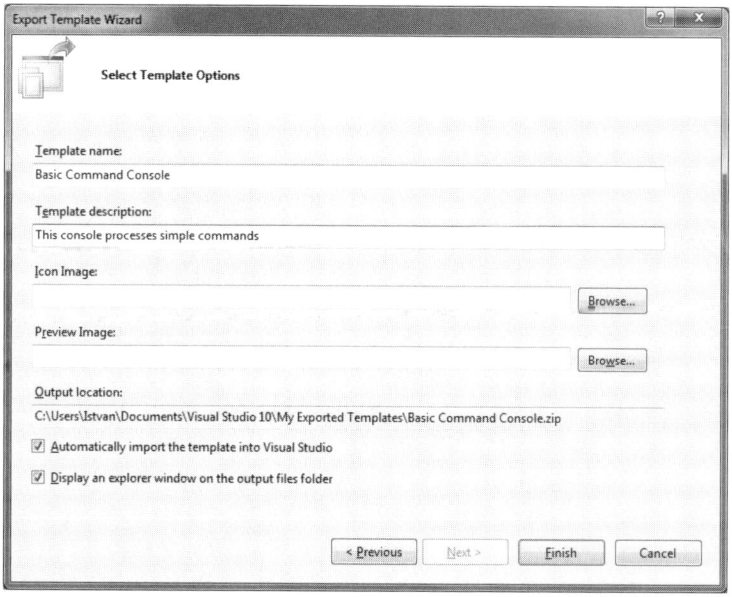

**FIGURE 4-7:** The Select Template Options page

Notice that the "Output location" field contains a path within your user profile. The template itself is a ZIPped archive that is about to be exported into the `Visual Studio 10\My Exported Template` folder under your profile's documents folder.

When you click Finish, the wizard collects all the files to include in the project template and puts them into a `.zip` archive. At the end of the process, the output folder is opened in a new Windows Explorer instance, and you can see the `Basic Command Console.zip` file there. Open this archive to have a look at its content. You will see a folder and four files, as illustrated in Figure 4-8.

| Name | Type |
| --- | --- |
| Properties | File folder |
| _TemplateIcon.ico | Icon |
| ConsoleBase.csproj | Visual C# Project file |
| MyTemplate.vstemplate | Visual Studio Project/Item Template File |
| Program.cs | Visual C# Source file |

**FIGURE 4-8:** Project template content

In addition to the original files of the project, you should note two new files created by the wizard: `__TemplateIcon.ico` and `MyTemplate.vstemplate`. Later in this chapter, you'll learn what these files are and what their roles are in Visual Studio's template infrastructure.

Close the Windows Explorer instance and go back to Visual Studio. The exported template is ready to be consumed. Create a new Visual Studio project with the File ➪ New ➪ Project command, and scroll down to the bottom of the template list within the Visual C# category. You should see the `Basic Command Console` template there, as shown in Figure 4-9.

**FIGURE 4-9:** The template is ready to be consumed.

Accept the default project name and click OK. Visual Studio creates the project from the `Basic Command Console`, and, when you run it, you can see that it behaves exactly the same as the original `BaseConsole` application from which you created the template.

## Adding a Small Customization

As you see, in just a few steps, you have created a new Visual Studio project template. Now, let's take this a step further. Let's add a small customization to the template. The first project you created from the template wrote the same welcome message ("Welcome to the BaseConsole application") to the console as the template itself. Let's modify the template so that the current project name given by the user in the New Project dialog is now used.

Open the `BaseConsole` project again, and change the `DisplayWelcomeMessage` method in the `Project.cs` file to the following:

```
static void DisplayWelcomeMessage()
{
  Console.WriteLine("Welcome to the $safeprojectname$!");
  Console.WriteLine();
}
```

The `$safeprojectname$` placeholder is a template parameter. When a new template is created, this parameter is replaced with the name of the current project transformed to a name conforming to the identifier syntax, so "unsafe" characters and spaces are removed.

Export the `BaseConsole` project to a project template exactly the same way you did before. The Export Template Wizard will warn you that the output file already exists. Confirm that you want to delete the existing file, and the original `Basic Command Console.zip` template will be replaced.

Now, create a new project using the refreshed template, and give the `My Customized Console` name to the application. Build and start the application. The welcome message now shows what the effect of the `$safeprojectname$` template parameter is, as illustrated in Figure 4-10.

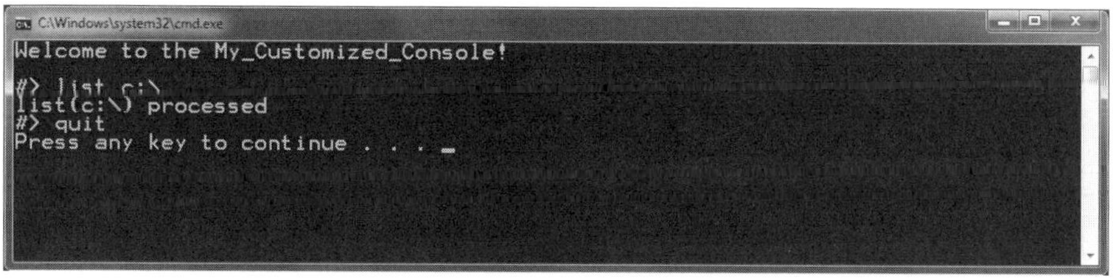

**FIGURE 4-10:** The effect of $safeprojectname$ parameter

As you can see, the `My Customized Console` project name was transformed to an identifier-safe version — spaces were changed to underscores.

# Creating a Simple Item Template

You can make the `BaseConsole` application more sophisticated by creating classes responsible for processing commands and creating an item template for the command processor classes. First, let's make a small change in the application architecture, and add the `CommandProcessor.cs` file shown in Listing 4-2 to the `BaseConsole` project.

Available for download on Wrox.com

**LISTING 4-2:** CommandProcessor.cs

```
namespace ConsoleBase
{
    internal abstract class CommandProcessor
    {
        public abstract void ProcessCommand(string pars);
    }
}
```

*Code file [CommandProcessor.cs] available for download at Wrox.com*

This will be the base class of types responsible for processing a simple command. You associate a class with the related command by using the `DisplayName` attribute. Create a new `CommandProcessorItem.cs` file to the project with the source code shown in Listing 4-3.

Available for download on Wrox.com

**LISTING 4-3:** CommandProcessorItem.cs

```
using System;
using System.ComponentModel;

namespace ConsoleBase
{
    [DisplayName("list")]
    class CommandProcessorItem: CommandProcessor
    {
        public override void ProcessCommand(string pars)
        {
            Console.WriteLine("list of  {0}", pars);
        }
    }
}
```

*Code file [CommandProcessorItem.cs] available for download at Wrox.com*

`CommandProcessorItem.cs` will be the base of the project item template you will export. In its current form, it acts as a real working class responsible for processing the command `"list"`. To prepare the application for the command processor semantics, let's modify the `Program.cs` file. Add the following `using` directives to the top of the file:

```csharp
using System.Reflection;
using System.ComponentModel;
```

Change the `ProcessCommand` method to seek the appropriate command processor class, as shown here:

```csharp
static void ProcessCommand(string command, string pars)
{
  foreach (var type in
    from type in Assembly.GetExecutingAssembly().GetTypes()
    where type.IsSubclassOf(typeof(CommandProcessor))
    select type)
  {
    var attrs = type.GetCustomAttributes(typeof(DisplayNameAttribute), false);
    if (attrs.Length == 0) continue;
    var displayName = (attrs[0] as DisplayNameAttribute).DisplayName;
    if (String.Compare(displayName, command, true) == 0)
    {
      var processor = Activator.CreateInstance(type) as CommandProcessor;
      if (processor != null) processor.ProcessCommand(pars);
    }
  }
}
```

At this point, your console application is refactored so that it supports command processor classes. When you start the application, you can check that it understands the `"list"` and `"quit"` commands but nothing else. Figure 4-11 shows the modified console.

**FIGURE 4-11:** The refactored console knows the list command

Now, let's extract an item template from this project. Because the modification you will apply to `CommandProcessorItem.cs` will result a syntactically invalid file, change the Build Action property of this file to `None` in the Properties window. Replace a few parts of the file with the `$safeitemname$` template parameter, as shown here:

```csharp
using System;
using System.ComponentModel;

namespace ConsoleBase
```

```
    {
      [DisplayName("$safeitemname$")]
      class $safeitemname$: CommandProcessor
      {
        public override void ProcessCommand(string pars)
        {
          Console.WriteLine("list of  {0}", pars);
        }
      }
    }
```

The `$safeitemname$` parameter will replace the item name specified in the Add New Item dialog with an identifier-safe name by transforming "unsafe" characters and spaces.

Because you have modified the project template, first export it again using the same settings as before, and be sure that the `Basic Command Console` name is used. Then, use the Export Template wizard to publish a project item template.

In the first step, you select the Item Template option, as shown in Figure 4-12.

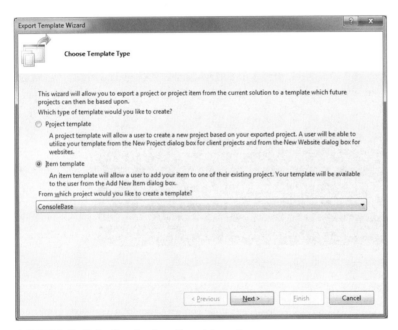

**FIGURE 4-12:** Selecting the Item Template option

The next step is to select the items of the project that are to be published as item templates. Select the `CommandProcessorItem.cs` file as shown in Figure 4-13. This is the only file you want to use as item template.

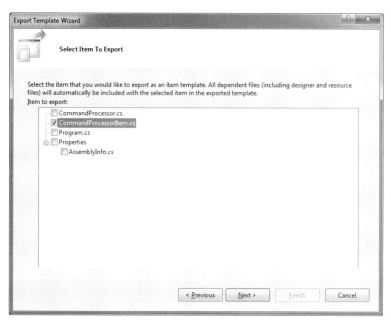

**FIGURE 4-13:** Selecting the items to export

The item template may have types and namespaces referencing to specific assemblies. In the next wizard page, you select these assemblies from the ones that are added as references to the host project. Figure 4-14 shows this page where only the System assembly is selected, because your item template references only this one:

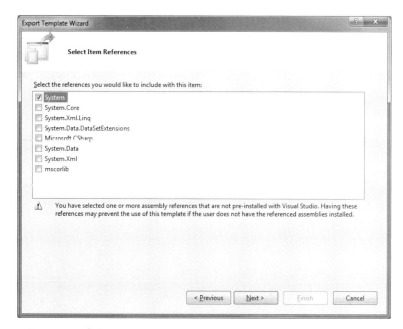

**FIGURE 4-14:** Selecting referenced assemblies

The last page of the wizard enables you to specify template options. The page here is the same as for project templates. Fill in the fields of the page as shown in Figure 4-15, and then click the Finish button to export the item template.

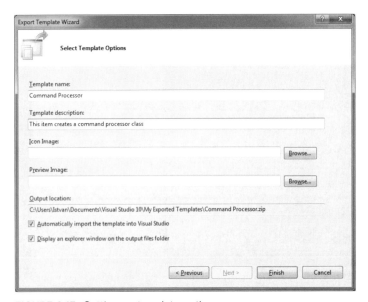

**FIGURE 4-15:** Setting up template options

The `.zip` archive representing the item template is put into the same directory as the `Basic Command Console` archive. When you open the archive, beside the `CommandProcessorItem.cs` file, you see the `__TemplateIcon.ico` and `MyTemplate.vstemplate` files as well, just as you did with the exported project template.

Let's see how this new item template works. Create a new project with the `Basic Command Console` project type, and name it `MySimpleCommandConsole`. When the project is created, add a new Command Processor item as shown in Figure 4-16 and give it the name `EchoProcessor.cs`.

**FIGURE 4-16:** Adding a new Command Processor item

Change the `DisplayName` attribute and the body of the `ProcessCommand` method as shown in Listing 4-4.

**LISTING 4-4:** EchoProcessor.cs

```csharp
using System;
using System.ComponentModel;

namespace MySimpleCommandConsole
{
  [DisplayName("Echo")]
  class EchoProcessor : CommandProcessor
  {
    public override void ProcessCommand(string pars)
    {
      Console.WriteLine(pars);
    }
  }
}
```

*Code file [EchoProcessor.cs] available for download at Wrox.com*

When you run the project, you can try the `echo` command, as shown in Figure 4-17.

**FIGURE 4-17:** Echo command in use

You have now built and exported a simple project template and an item template. Let's dive in a bit deeper and examine how Visual Studio stores and processes templates.

## TEMPLATE STORAGE STRUCTURE

As you just learned, project and item templates are stored as `.zip` archives. This archive stores files that will be artifacts when the template is transformed to a concrete project or item, and some other files with "accessory" information. When you created the project and item templates earlier, the Export Template wizard added two files to the archives:

➤   `__TemplateIcon.ico` — This file is used by Visual Studio as the icon representing the project or item template.

➤ `MyTemplate.vstemplate` — This is the most important file in the archive — the *template manifest.* The IDE recognizes the `.zip` file as a template from this manifest. This file is also used to describe information the IDE leverages to put the project or item template into the appropriate category within the New Project and New File dialogs, and also defines some behavior-related attributes.

Later in this chapter, you'll see a detailed description of the structure and the usage of the manifest file. But first, let's take a look at the template directory storage structure.

# Template Folders

All `.zip` archives representing project and item templates are stored in folders with a specific location. There are two kinds of folders:

➤ *System folders* — These are installed with Visual Studio setup, and all users of the machine can access them. The root of the system folders can be found under the Visual Studio installation folder in the `Common7\IDE\ProjectTemplates` and in the `Common7\IDE\ItemTemplates` folders, respectively.

➤ *User folders* — These are located within the current user's profile, and templates stored here can be accessed only by the user owning the profile. User folders can be found under the `My Documents` folder in the `Visual Studio 10\Templates\ProjectTemplates` and `Visual Studio 10\Templates\ItemTemplates` folders.

In addition to the system folders, you can find two other folders under `Common7\IDE` — `ProjectTemplatesCache` and `ItemTemplatesCache`. The internal structure of these folders is the same as the structure of `ProjectTemplates` and `ItemTemplates` folders, but, instead of `.zip` files, you can find folders with the `.zip` extension representing the extracted content of the corresponding template files. Visual Studio uses these cache folders because of performance reasons.

Visual Studio scans the template information in the `ProjectTemplates` and `ItemTemplates` folders when you open the New Project or Add New Item dialogs. When you examine the content of the system folders, it's difficult to understand how the folder structure and the `.zip` files are mapped to the structure you see in the dialogs. In addition to the folder structure, Visual Studio uses some other information to build up the category hierarchy.

## Understanding the Project Template Hierarchy

To map the folders and template archives into the categories that can be seen in the New Project dialog, the IDE counts on other information, including the following:

➤ Visual Studio looks up the system registry to build up the category structure in the dialog. This information can be found under the `HKEY_CURRENT_USER` hive in the Visual Studio 2010 configuration key root (`Software\Microsoft\Visual Studio\10.0_Config`) in the `NewProjectTemplates` key.

➤ A few template folders contain an XML file with `.vstdir` extension. These files are used to declare localized names and sort orders for the templates in the folder in which the `.vstdir` file is located.

As shown in Figure 4-18, the New Project dialog displays three types of project template hierarchy nodes:

➤   *Project type root nodes* — These are related to languages, or, more precisely, language service packages such as Visual C# or Visual Basic. Figure 4-18 shows examples for Visual C#.

➤   *Pseudo folder nodes* — These are parent folders for a few project type root nodes. Other Languages and Other Project Types provide good examples in Figure 4-18.

➤   *Template folder nodes* — These are the children of project root nodes, and they are mapped to physical folders having template files under them. In Figure 4-18, the Windows, Web, and Silverlight nodes under Visual C# are examples of them.

**FIGURE 4-18:** Project template node types

The whole procedure of creating the template node hierarchy is a bit complex, so this discussion does not include all the details. Instead, here are a few points to help you understand the basics:

➤   To produce the project template hierarchy, Visual Studio uses the .vstemplate files within the .zip archives, registry keys, and values stored in the NewProjectTemplates key mentioned earlier, resources in the language packages (determined with the help of registry values), physical template folder structure, and .vstdir files.

➤ Project type root nodes and pseudo folder nodes are described in the registry with localized names, sort order information, and folder nesting information.

➤ The template folder node hierarchy follows the structure of the folders in the `ProjectTemplates` folders. For machine templates (templates installed with Visual Studio 2010), the location is `Common7\IDE\ProjectTemplates\` under the Visual Studio installation folder. For user templates, the location is `\My Documents\Visual Studio 10\Templates\ProjectTemplates\`. The folder hierarchies from these two locations are merged to create the project types hierarchy. If there is a `.vstdir` file in any of these subfolders, it can describe the sort order of the template folder within its parent.

When the user clicks on a template folder, all templates in that folder are displayed. The IDE scans the folder for files with the `.zip` extension and the embedded template manifest to recognize project templates. When an appropriate file has been found, the IDE uses the template manifest to display information (icon, name, description, and so on) about the project template.

Looking at the New Project dialog, you can see that several project templates appear not only in the template folder, but also in other folders. The template manifest may contain a `<NumberOfParentCategoriesToRollUp>` entry that can declare a parent category level above the physical folder where the template should also be displayed.

### Understanding the Item Template Hierarchy

The Add New Item dialog also uses a hierarchical approach to list available item templates, just like the New Project dialog.

When you add a new item to a project, the hosting project's root type determines the physical folder under `ItemTemplates`. For machine templates (templates installed in Visual Studio 2010), the location is `Common7\IDE\ItemTemplates` under the Visual Studio installation folder. For user templates, the location is `\My Documents\Visual Studio 10\Templates\ItemTemplates`. The folder hierarchies from these two locations are merged to create the project item category hierarchy. If there is a `.vstdir` file in any of these subfolders, it can describe the sort order of the template folder within its parent.

Visual Studio scans this folder structure for `.zip` files with a template manifest stating the template is an item template. It uses the information in the manifest file to display item templates in a specific folder.

The root project type may filter the item templates. In the registry, there is an `AddNewItemFilters` key for the Visual Studio packages that represents the project type, and this key may list template directories or concrete template names that should be excluded from the list. The template manifest file has two entries named `<TemplateID>` and `<TemplateGroupID>` that can be used for further filtering and categorization of item templates based on the project's root type.

## The Template Manifest File

By now, you know the manifest file is the key component of templates. The template manifest is an XML file with the `.vstemplate` extension, and Visual Studio's template system uses it primarily with the following purposes:

➤ It recognizes that a `.zip` file in a template folder is not a simple `.zip` archive, but rather a template definition file.

➤ It uses the manifest to display information about templates in the New Project or Add New Item dialogs.

➤ It retrieves the list of items to be created for the new project or project item.

The following discussions describe the structure of the manifest file in detail and show a few samples to help you perform common tasks related to templates.

## The General Structure of the Manifest File

The `.vstemplate` file contains three fundamental, and two optional, elements representing its general structure:

```
<VSTemplate Type="_type" Version="2.0.0"
  xmlns="http://schemas.microsoft.com/developer/vstemplate/2005">
  <TemplateData>
    ...
  </TemplateData>
  <TemplateContent>
    ...
  </TemplateContent>
  <WizardExtension>
    ...
  </WizardExtension>
  <WizardData>
    ...
  </WizardData>
</VSTemplate>
```

The `<VSTemplate>` element has a `Type` attribute used to identify the template as a project or item template. It can have the values `Project` or `Item`, respectively. As a special template type, it also can have the value of `ProjectGroup` that will be explained a bit later.

The `Version` attribute specifies the version number for the template. Since Visual Studio 2005, this value has been `2.0.0`.

Following are the two other fundamental elements:

➤ `<TemplateData>` — This provides template categorization information and display characteristics for the New Project and Add New Item dialogs.

➤ `<TemplateContent>` — This specifies the files included in the template.

Visual Studio allows using wizards that can add custom functionality to templates. The `<WizardExtension>` and `<WizardData>` elements are responsible for specifying the assembly implementing the wizard and for passing information used by the wizard. These two elements are optional.

Let's look into the manifest file of the `Command Processor` item template you created earlier. Listing 4-5 shows the file.

**LISTING 4-5:** Manifest of the Command Processor Item Template

```
<VSTemplate Version="2.0.0"
  xmlns="http://schemas.microsoft.com/developer/vstemplate/2005" Type="Item">
  <TemplateData>
    <DefaultName>Command Processor.cs</DefaultName>
    <Name>Command Processor</Name>
    <Description>This item creates a command processor class</Description>
    <ProjectType>CSharp</ProjectType>
    <SortOrder>10</SortOrder>
    <Icon>__TemplateIcon.ico</Icon>
  </TemplateData>
  <TemplateContent>
    <References>
      <Reference>
        <Assembly>System</Assembly>
      </Reference>
    </References>
    <ProjectItem SubType="" TargetFileName="$fileinputname$.cs"
      ReplaceParameters="true">CommandProcessorItem.cs</ProjectItem>
  </TemplateContent>
</VSTemplate>
```

Instead of explaining all the details here (which will be done shortly), let's decrypt what this template definition is about.

## The <TemplateData> Element

This element plays a key role in providing categorization and display information about the template, and also defines a few points influencing the behavior of the New Project and Add New File dialogs. <TemplateData> has no attributes, but it may contain many child elements. Table 4-1 summarizes elements responsible for the display characteristics of the template.

**TABLE 4-1:** <TemplateData> Child Elements — Display Characteristics

| CHILD ELEMENT | DESCRIPTION |
|---|---|
| <Name> | This required element specifies the name of the template as it appears in the New Project or Add New Item dialogs. |
| <Description> | This specifies the description of the template as it appears in either the New Project or Add New Item dialog box. This element is required. |
| <Icon> | This specifies the path and the filename of the image file that serves as the icon for the template, which appears in either the New Project or the Add New Item dialog box. |

| CHILD ELEMENT | DESCRIPTION |
|---|---|
| `<PreviewImage>` | This specifies the path and the filename of the image file that serves as the preview image for an online template. This preview image is displayed in the New Project and Add New Item dialogs, as well as in the Visual Studio Gallery. |
| `<DefaultName>` | This element is required. For projects, this element specifies the name of the directory that stores the project on disk. For items, it specifies the file name of the source file. |
| `<ProvideDefaultName>` | This optional element specifies whether the Visual Studio project system will generate a default name for the template in the Add New Item or New Project dialog box. The text of this element must be either `true` or `false`, and the default is `false`. |
| `<Hidden>` | This element specifies whether the template appears either in the New Project or in the Add New Item dialog box. The text of this element must be either `true` or `false`, and the default is `false`. |
| `<SortOrder>` | This optional element defines the order of a project or item template in the dialogs. This is ignored for user templates, because those are always sorted alphabetically. The default value is `100`, and all values must be multiples of ten. Templates that have low sort order values appear in either the New Project or New Add Item dialog box before templates that have high sort order values. |
| `<NumberOfParentCategoriesToRollUp>` | This optional value specifies the number of parent categories up to the template folder that also will display the template in the New Project or Add New Item dialog box. For example, if a template with this metadata is placed two folder levels below the top-level Visual C# node, and this value is set to 2, the template will appear also under the Visual C# category node in the New Project dialog box. If this node is not set, the template only appears in the node in which it is physically located. |
| `<LocationFieldMRUPrefix>` | This specifies the most recently used paths in the New Project and Add New Item dialogs. |

The `<Name>`, `<Description>` and `<Icon>` elements can get their content from resources embedded into Visual Studio packages. In that case, the `Package` and `ID` attributes of these nodes should be used for the package GUID and the resource identifier, respectively.

Templates are assigned with project types and can be language-specific or language-independent. The child elements shown in Table 4-2 describe these characteristics.

**TABLE 4-2:** `<TemplateData>` Child Elements — Project and Language

| CHILD ELEMENT | DESCRIPTION |
|---|---|
| `<ProjectType>` | This value specifies the type of project the template will create and must contain one of the following values:<br><br>`CSharp, FSharp, Visual Basic` — The template creates a Visual C#, F# or Visual Basic project or item, respectively.<br><br>`Web` — Specifies that the template creates a web project or item. In this case, the language of the project or item is defined in the `<ProjectSubType>` element. |
| `<ProjectSubType>` | This is an optional element and provides a subcategory to the `<ProjectType>` element. This value is used in two scenarios.<br><br>If the project is a smart device project, the `SmartDevice-NETCFv1` and `SmartDevice-NETCFv2` values indicate that the template targets the .NET Compact Framework version 1.0 or 2.0, respectively.<br><br>If `<ProjectType>` is `Web`, this element specifies the programming language of the template. In this case, the available values of `CSharp` and `VisualBasic` are related to the Visual C# and Visual Basic languages, respectively. |

The other child elements of `<TemplateData>` are processed only by project templates or by item templates. You can put these elements into any manifest file, and unparsed elements are simply ignored by the template type. Table 4-3 summarizes those child elements that are processed by item templates.

**TABLE 4-3:** `<TemplateData>` Children — Item Template Specific Elements

| CHILD ELEMENT | DESCRIPTION |
|---|---|
| `<TemplateID>` | This optional element represents an identifier for an item template that is categorized into a group of item templates by the `<TemplateGroupID>` element. If this element is omitted, the `<Name>` is used as the identifier of the item template. This element is to be used in advanced scenarios where a Visual Studio package defines an item template. |
| `<TemplateGroupID>` | This value is optional and specifies an identifier for a category of item templates. This element is to be used in advanced scenarios where a Visual Studio defines an item template. |

| CHILD ELEMENT | DESCRIPTION |
|---|---|
| `<SupportsMasterPage>` | This optional element is used only for web item templates, and specifies whether or not the Select Master Page checkbox is enabled on the Add New Item dialog box. The text of this element must be either `true` or `false`, and the default is `false`. |
| `<SupportsCodeSeparation>` | This optional element is used only for web item templates, and specifies whether or not the "Place code in separate file" check box is enabled in the Add New Item dialog box. The text of this element must be either `true` or `false`, and the default is `false`. |
| `<SupportsLanguageDropDown>` | This optional element is used only for web item templates and specifies whether or not the Language option is enabled in the Add New Item dialog box. This option enables you to choose the programming language of the new item that you want to create from the template. The text of this element must be either `true` or `false`, and the default is `false`. |

Table 4-4 summarizes `<TemplateData>` child elements that are specific to project templates.

**TABLE 4-4:** `<TemplateData>` Children — Project Template Specific Elements

| CHILD ELEMENT | DESCRIPTION |
|---|---|
| `<BuildOnLoad>` | This element specifies whether to build the solution when a project is created from the template. The text of this element must be `true` or `false`, and the default is `false`. |
| `<CreateInPlace>` | This specifies whether to create the project and perform parameter replacement in the specified location, or perform parameter replacement in a temporary location and then save the project to the specified location. If the value of this element is `true` (this is the default), the project is created, and parameter replacement is performed in the location specified in the New Project dialog box. If `false`, parameter replacement is performed in a temporary location, and the project is then copied to the specified location. |
| `<CreateNewFolder>` | This specifies whether a containing folder is created on instantiation of the project. The text of this element must be either `true` or `false`, and the default is `true`. The project system hosting the specified template must support this option. |

*continues*

**TABLE 4-4** *(continued)*

| CHILD ELEMENT | DESCRIPTION |
|---|---|
| `<PromptForSaveOnCreation>` | This specifies whether the user is prompted for a project save location via the New Project dialog box when creating a project. If this element is set to `true`, then the user is prompted for a save location. If `false`, then the user is not prompted, and, in this case, a temporary project is created. |
| `<EnableLocationBrowseButton>` | In the New Project dialog box, the Location text box specifies the directory where a new project is saved. The Browse button helps you modify this directory by displaying the Project Location dialog box, which enables you to easily navigate to a different directory available from your computer, and then choose it as the directory where the new project is saved. The text must be either `true` or `false`, indicating whether or not to display the Browse button on the New Project dialog box. The default value is `true`. |
| `<LocationField>` | The Location text box in the New Project dialog box enables users to change the default directory in which new projects are saved. This element specifies if this text box should be enabled, disabled, or hidden. Thus, the element values are `Enabled`, `Disabled`, and `Hidden`. |

Now that you are familiar with the `<TemplateData>` element, you can understand what the following definition in the `Basic Command Console` project template stands for:

```
<TemplateData>
  <Name>Basic Command Console</Name>
  <Description>This console processes simple commands</Description>
  <ProjectType>CSharp</ProjectType>
  <ProjectSubType>
  </ProjectSubType>
  <SortOrder>1000</SortOrder>
  <CreateNewFolder>true</CreateNewFolder>
  <DefaultName>Basic Command Console</DefaultName>
  <ProvideDefaultName>true</ProvideDefaultName>
  <LocationField>Enabled</LocationField>
  <EnableLocationBrowseButton>true</EnableLocationBrowseButton>
  <Icon>__TemplateIcon.ico</Icon>
</TemplateData>
```

Not all child elements are described here, but, rather, let's focus on what the result is. So, the project template is for the Visual C# language and the project template will be placed somewhere at the end of the project template list. The New Project dialog will provide a default name for the project that is to be created in a new folder, and the user is allowed to select this folder's location.

You should now understand the meaning of the `<TemplateData>` section of the `Command Processor` item template:

```
<TemplateData>
  <DefaultName>Command Processor.cs</DefaultName>
  <Name>Command Processor</Name>
  <Description>This item creates a command processor class</Description>
  <ProjectType>CSharp</ProjectType>
  <SortOrder>10</SortOrder>
  <Icon>__TemplateIcon.ico</Icon>
</TemplateData>
```

## The <TemplateContent> Element

While the `<TemplateData>` element is responsible for providing information about template categorization, appearance, and defining simple behavior attributes, the `<TemplateContent>` element defines the structure of template files and related elements (such as referenced assemblies in project templates). Depending on the template type (that is, the `Type` attribute of the `<VSTemplate>` element), the following child elements can be used:

➤  Project templates should use the `<Project>` child element that defines the project file and keeps a list of files and folders to be added to the project. In this case, the referenced assemblies are defined in the project file.

➤  Item templates should use the `<ProjectItem>` and `<References>` child elements to define the files included in the item template and assembly references that should be added to the project when the item is inserted into the project, respectively.

➤  The `<ProjectCollection>` child element should be used with a third kind of template, the `ProjectGroup` type. This element describes the links to projects in multi-project templates.

Independently of the template type, the optional `<CustomParameters>` child element can be used in addition to the ones just described. This element groups custom parameters that are passed to the template wizard when the wizard makes parameter replacement.

### Defining Files and Folders in Project Templates

When the `Type` attribute of `<VSTemplate>` is set to `Project`, the `<Project>` child element should be used under `<TemplateContent>` to define all files and folders to be added to the project. You can use only one instance of `<Project>` that has the following attributes:

➤  `File` — This attribute is required, and names the project file in the `.zip` archive defining the template.

➤  `TargetFileName` — This optional attribute specifies the name of the project file when a project is created from the template. If this attribute is omitted, the name in `File` attribute or the user-specified project name is used.

➤  `ReplaceParameters` — This attribute specifies whether the project file has parameter values that must be replaced when a project is created from the template. The default value is `false`.

`<Project>` has two child elements, `<ProjectItem>` and `<Folder>`, that define the files and folders to be added to the project, respectively. While `<ProjectItem>` cannot contain any child element, `<Folder>` can nest both `<ProjectItem>` and `<Folder>` element recursively to represent the hierarchical structure of files and folders.

`<Folder>` has the following two attributes:

➤ `Name` — This attribute is required and indicates the name of the project folder in the `.zip` archive.

➤ `TargetFolderName` — This attribute is optional and can define the name of the folder when it is being created. If this attribute is omitted, the folder name in the `.zip` archive (as the `Name` attribute tells) is used. This attribute is also useful for using parameter replacement to create a folder name, or for naming a folder with an international string that cannot be used directly in the `.zip` file.

The `<ProjectItem>` element's value contains the filename in the `.zip` archive that should be added to the project. However, you should use only a simple filename without any path information. The element has about a half dozen attributes summarized in Table 4-5.

**TABLE 4-5:** `<ProjectItem>` Attributes For Project Templates

| CHILD ELEMENT | DESCRIPTION |
|---|---|
| `TargetFileName` | This attribute specifies the name and path of the project item when a project is created from the template. This attribute is useful for creating a directory structure different from the directory structure in the template `.zip` file, or for using parameter replacement to create an item name. The `TargetFileName` attribute can also be used to rename files with parameters. |
| `ReplaceParameters` | This optional value specifies whether the item has parameter values that must be replaced when a project is created from the template. The default value is `false`. |
| `OpenInEditor` | This attribute specifies whether the item should be opened in its respective editor in Visual Studio when a project is created from the template. If this value is `true`, the `OpenInWebBrowser` and `OpenInHelpBrowser` attributes are ignored. This attribute is optional, and its default value is `false`. |
| `OpenInWebBrowser` | This optional attribute specifies whether the item should be opened the web browser when a project is created from the template. Only HTML files and text files that are local to the project can be opened in the web browser. External URLs cannot be opened with this attribute. The default value is `false`. |

| CHILD ELEMENT | DESCRIPTION |
|---|---|
| OpenInHelpBrowser | This optional attribute specifies whether the item should be opened in the Help viewer when a project is created from the template. Only HTML files and text files that are local to the project can be opened in the Help browser. External URLs cannot be opened with this attribute. The default value is `false`. |
| OpenOrder | This optional attribute specifies a numeric value that represents the order in which items will be opened in their respective views (editors, web browser, or Help browser). All values must be multiples of ten. Items with lower `OpenOrder` values are opened first. |

The `<TemplateContent>` section of the `Basic Command Console` manifest is as follows:

```
<TemplateContent>
  <Project TargetFileName="ConsoleBase.csproj" File="ConsoleBase.csproj"
    ReplaceParameters="true">
    <ProjectItem ReplaceParameters="true" TargetFileName="CommandProcessor.cs">
      CommandProcessor.cs
    </ProjectItem>
    <ProjectItem ReplaceParameters="true"
      TargetFileName="CommandProcessorItem.cs">
      CommandProcessorItem.cs
    </ProjectItem>
    <ProjectItem ReplaceParameters="true" TargetFileName="Program.cs">
      Program.cs
    </ProjectItem>
    <Folder Name="Properties" TargetFolderName="Properties">
      <ProjectItem ReplaceParameters="true" TargetFileName="AssemblyInfo.cs">
        AssemblyInfo.cs
      </ProjectItem>
    </Folder>
  </Project>
</TemplateContent>
```

You can see here that all files — including the project file — preserve their original names in the `.zip` archive, and are ready for parameter replacement. As you saw in Table 4-5, the `TargetFileName` attribute can also be used to rename files with parameters. For example, in this template, you could replace the `Program.cs` filename with the project name by changing the related `<ProjectItem>` element to the following:

```
<ProjectItem ReplaceParameters="true" TargetFileName="$safeprojectname$.cs">
  Program.cs
</ProjectItem>
```

Attributes with the `OpenIn` prefix also can be very useful. With them, you can automatically open the files you intend (or recommend to your template's users) to edit, and you can also display help files. Because you cannot redirect the web browser or the Help browser to external URLs, you should follow these steps:

1. Create one or more HTML pages as a part of your template's documentation. You should put it in a separate documentation folder, especially if you have more than three of them.

2. Add the OpenInWebBrowser attribute with a true value to the index page of your documentation, and set its OpenOrder value so that it will be the page opened last.

3. If you need to redirect the user to external pages, create appropriate links in the documentation pages.

## Defining Files and Referenced Assemblies in Item Templates

When the Type attribute of <VSTemplate> is set to Item, you can use the <ProjectItem> and <References> child elements under <TemplateContent> to define all files and referenced assemblies to be added to the project. Even if you are using item templates, you can add more files to the project. Items such as Windows (or WPF) forms and web pages are composed from more than one file. If there are more files in your item template, you can add one <ProjectItem> element for each of them directly under <TemplateContent>.

 *Be careful not to confuse the <ProjectItem> element used for project templates with the ones used for item templates. The names may be the same, and both may describe files to be added to the project, but their attributes are different according to the context in which they are used.*

The <ProjectItem> elements for item templates do not have any child elements. Their values contain the filename in the .zip archive that should be added to the project. <ProjectItem> elements in this context can have three optional attributes:

➤ TargetFileName — This attribute's semantics are the same as in case of project templates. This attribute specifies the name and path of the project item when a project is created from the template, and accepts parameter-replacement expressions.

➤ SubType — This attribute specifies the subtype of an item in a multi-file item template. This value is used to determine the editor that Visual Studio will use to open the item. The possible values depend on the project system. For more information about SubType, open the project file with the XML editor and look at what kinds of subtypes are used for specific project items.

➤ ReplaceParameters — This attribute specifies whether the item has parameter values that must be replaced when a project is created from the template. The default value is false.

While referenced assemblies are the part of the project file in project templates, item templates do not know in advance the project context they will be added to. The <References> element provides a way that item templates can declare the code within them is about to use types defined in particular assemblies. When the item is added to the project, the information here is used to add the referenced assembly to the project (if not already added).

If you know that certain assemblies are already added to the project, you can omit those references from the item template definition. For example, if you create custom forms and dialogs as item templates, and you generally add them to Windows Forms projects, you may not need to specify System.Windows.Forms as a reference, because that assembly is already added to the project. As a good practice, you should always add those references to the item template definitions.

<References> is only a container for a <Reference> element that itself is a container for exactly one <Assembly> element. The value of an <Assembly> element must be the short name or the strong name of the assembly.

Following is a sample extract from an item template to demonstrate the usage of <ProjectItems> and <References>. The item is a simple Windows form intended to be the base of main application forms.

```
<TemplateContent>
    <References>
      <Reference>
        <Assembly>System.Windows.Forms</Assembly>
      </Reference>
      <Reference>
        <Assembly>VSXtra</Assembly>
      </Reference>
    </References>
    <ProjectItem SubType="Form" TargetFileName="$fileinputname$.cs"
      ReplaceParameters="true">
      MainForm.cs
    </ProjectItem>
    <ProjectItem SubType="" TargetFileName="$fileinputname$.Designer.cs"
      ReplaceParameters="true">
      MainForm.Designer.cs
    </ProjectItem>
  </TemplateContent>
```

Here you see two references added to the item template. One is the "mandatory" System.Windows .Forms assembly, and the other is a third-party one. The assemblies here use simple names. Before deploying the template, you should change them to strong names to work everywhere.

You can also see that the item is composed from two files. In both file definitions, the TargetFileName attributes use the $fileinputname$ replacement parameter that is changed to the filename specified by the user in the Add New item dialog. The ReplaceParameters attributes are also set to true.

## Advanced Features

So far, you have learned about project and item templates. Actually, there is a third type of template called *multi-project template* that is like a project template and contains not only one, but two or more projects. The `Type` attribute of the `<VSTemplate>` element should be set to `ProjectGroup` to sign the manifest describes a multi-project template:

```
<VSTemplate Version="2.0.0" Type="ProjectGroup"
    xmlns="http://schemas.microsoft.com/developer/vstemplate/2005">
```

Using a multi-project template creates more projects in the same solution. When a project based on a multi-project template is created from the New Project dialog box, every project in the template is added to the solution.

A multi-project template must include the following items, compressed into a `.zip` file:

> ➤ *A root* `.vstemplate` *file for the entire multi-project template* — This root manifest file contains the metadata that the New Project dialog box displays, and specifies where to find the `.vstemplate` files for the projects in this template. This file must be located at the root of the `.zip` file.

> ➤ *One or more folders that contain the files required for a complete project template* — This includes all code files for the project, and also a `.vstemplate` file for the template.

The root of the `.zip` archive can contain only the root `.vstemplate` file, and all the other `.vstemplate` files should be put in subfolders within the archive.

For example, a multi-project template `.zip` file that has two projects (`WinFormsApp` and `FormLibrary`) could have the following files and directories:

> ➤ `Application.vstemplate`: root `.vstemplate` file

> ➤ `WinFormsApp\WinFormsApp.vstemplate`: `.vstemplate` file for the `WinFormsApp` project

> ➤ `WinFormsApp\WinFromsApp.csproj`

> ➤ `WinFormsApp\Properties\AssemblyInfo.cs`

> ➤ `WinFormsApp\MainForm.cs`

> ➤ `WinFormsApp\MainForm.Designer.cs`

> ➤ `FormLibrary\FormLibrary.vstemplate`: `.vstemplate` file for the `FormLibrary` project

> ➤ `FormLibrary\FormLibrary.csproj`

> ➤ `FormLibrary\Properties\AssemblyInfo.cs`

> ➤ `FormLibrary\UserEntities.cs`

> ➤ `FormLibrary\SystemEntities.cs`

To describe this multi-project template, you can use the `<ProjectCollection>` element nested into `<TemplateContent>`. You can nest the following elements in `<ProjectCollection>`:

> ➤ `<ProjectTemplateLink>` — This element represents a project in a multi-project template. It contains a required `ProjectName` attribute that specifies the name of the project. The value of this element is the path to the `.vstemplate` file describing the specific project template within the `.zip` archive.

➤ `<SolutionFolder>` — This element represents a virtual solution folder in a multi-project template used to group projects. It has a required `Name` attribute specifying the solution folder name. The element can nest further `<SolutionFolder>` and `<ProjectTemplateLink>` elements recursively to represent the hierarchy of solution folders and projects.

Listing 4-6 shows the root `.vstemplate` file describing this multi-project template.

**LISTING 4-6: Application.vstemplate**

```
<VSTemplate Version="2.0.0" Type="ProjectGroup"
  xmlns="http://schemas.microsoft.com/developer/vstemplate/2005">
  <TemplateData>
    <CreateNewFolder>true</CreateNewFolder>
    <Name>Multi-project Application</Name>
    <DefaulName>MultiProjectApp</DefaultName>
    <Description>Demonstrates how a multi-project template looks like<Description>
    <Icon>MultiProjAppIcon.ico</Icon>
  </TemplateData>
  <TemplateContent>
    <ProjectCollection>
      <ProjectTemplateLink ProjectName="Application project">
        WinFormsApp\WinFormsApp.vstemplate
      </ProjectTemplateLink>
      <ProjectTemplateLink ProjectName="Library project">
        FormLibrary\FormLibrary.vstemplate
      </ProjectTemplateLink>
    </ProjectCollection>
  </TemplateContent>
</VSTemplate>
```

As you see from Listing 4-6, the values of the two `<ProjectTemplateLink>` elements simply refer to the included `.vstemplate` files for the projects.

You can use solution folders to group the projects within the multi-project template. Assuming that you created separate solution folders for `WinFormsApp` and `FormLibrary`, you could use the `<SolutionFolder>` nodes to specify the virtual location of the projects:

```
<TemplateContent>
  <ProjectCollection>
    <SolutionFolder Name="Application">
      <ProjectTemplateLink ProjectName="Application project">
        WinFormsApp\WinFormsApp.vstemplate
      </ProjectTemplateLink>
    </Solution>
    <SolutionFolder Name="Libraries">
      <ProjectTemplateLink ProjectName="Library project">
        FormLibrary\FormLibrary.vstemplate
      </ProjectTemplateLink>
    </Solution>
  </ProjectCollection>
</TemplateContent>
```

Multi-project templates cannot be created with the Export Template Wizard. You must manually establish the multi-project structure and the required manifest files. Actually, you are able to export templates for the individual projects into .zip archives, but you must write the root .vstemplate file by hand, and also repackage the .zip archives manually.

## CUSTOMIZING TEMPLATES

The New Project and Add New Item dialogs provide very limited customization for project templates. You could use placeholders in the content of template files to replace them with the project or item names specified in the dialogs. In many scenarios, however, these simple replacements do not provide an appropriate solution.

In this section, you will learn about the following two customization techniques:

➤ *Using custom parameters* — You can add custom parameters to the template manifest by specifying placeholders and their current replacement values.

➤ *Custom template wizards* — You can develop a wizard that can be run when the template is used. This wizard can collect information from the user and initiate actions according to this information.

Both techniques are very useful, especially template wizards that provide sophisticated customization opportunities.

## Template Parameters

In the samples presented thus far, you have already used the $safeprojectname$ and $safeitemname$ template parameters. There are a few more predefined ones, as shown in Table 4-6.

**TABLE 4-6:** Template Parameters

| PARAMETER | DESCRIPTION |
| --- | --- |
| clrversion | Current version of the common language run-time (CLR). |
| guid[1-10] | A GUID value to be used in the project file, or in any other source files. You can specify up to ten unique GUIDs (for example, guid1). Visual Studio generates the GUID values and replaces them consistently (for example, the same value replaces guid1 at every occurrence). |
| itemname | The name provided by the user in the Add New Item dialog box. The default extension is automatically cut from the name. |
| machinename | The current computer name. |
| projectname | The name provided by the user in the New Project dialog box. |

| PARAMETER | DESCRIPTION |
| --- | --- |
| registeredorganization | The registry key value from `HKLM\Software\Microsoft\Windows NT\CurrentVersion\RegisteredOrganization`. |
| rootnamespace | The root namespace of the current project. This parameter is used to replace the namespace in an item being added to a project. |
| safeitemname | The name provided by the user in the Add New Item dialog box, with all unsafe characters removed and spaces replaced by underscores. |
| safeprojectname | The name provided by the user in the New Project dialog box, with all unsafe characters removed and spaces replaced by underscores. |
| time | The current time in the format `DD/MM/YYYY 00:00:00`. |
| userdomain | The current user domain name. |
| username | The current user name. |
| webnamespace | The name of the current web site. This parameter is used in the web form template to guarantee unique class names. If the web site is at the root directory of the web server, this template parameter resolves to the root directory of the web Server. |
| year | The current year in the format `YYYY`. |

## Custom Template Parameters

The `<TemplateContent>` element has an optional child element named `<CustomParameters>` that can be used independently if the template is a project or item template. `<CustomParameters>` is a container that can hold one or more `<CustomParameter>` elements, each of which holds two mandatory attributes: `Name` and `Value`. A `<CustomParameter>` describes a placeholder substitution, where `Name` is the placeholder to be replaced with `Value`.

Let's assume you have the following `<TemplateContent>` section in the manifest file:

```
<TemplateContent>
  <!-- ... -->
  <CustomParameters>
    <CustomParameter Name="$className$" Value="EventClass" />
    <CustomParameter Name="$idPropertyType$" Value="long" />
    <CustomParameter Name="$idProperty$" Value="SeqNo" />
    <CustomParameter Name="$displayNameProperty$" Value="ShortName" />
  </CustomParameters>
</TemplateContent>
```

The placeholders between dollar signs will be replaced with the associated `Value` attribute in all files having a `true` value in their `ReplaceParameters` attribute. Let's assume one of your files in the template looks like this:

```
using System;

namespace MyRootNamespace
{
  public class $className$
  {
    public $className$($idPropertyType$ _$idProperty$,
      string _$displayPropertyName$)
    {
      $idPropertyName$ = _$idPropertyName$;
      $displayNameProperty$ = _$displayNameProperty$;
    }

    public $idPropetyType$ $idPropertyName$ { get; private set; }

    public string $displayNameProperty$ { get; private set; }
  }
}
```

The template system will replace the placeholders with their proposed values in the `<CustomParameters>` section of the manifest file. For the previous file, the following source code will be added to the project:

```
using System;

namespace MyRootNamespace
{
  public class EventClass
  {
    public EventClass (long _SeqNo,
      string _ShortName)
    {
      SeqNo = _SeqNo;
      ShortName = _ShortName;
    }

    public long SeqNo { get; private set; }

    public string ShortName { get; private set; }
  }
}
```

Similar to the predefined template parameters, custom parameters also work for filenames. For example, you could use the `$className$` custom parameter in the `<ProjectItems>` section like this:

```
<ProjectItems>
  <!-- ... -->
    <ProjectItem ReplaceParameters="true" TargetFileName="$className$.cs">
```

```
        Class.cs
      </ProjectItem>
    <!-- ... -->
  </ProjectItems>
```

# Wizards

Wizards are great tools to customize templates. If you have ever created a Visual Studio Add-In, Shared Add-In, C++ ATL project, or many other types of projects where a wizard helps to create an application, you definitely know the efficiency of this approach.

This is not solely a privilege of the Visual Studio development team at Microsoft to create wizards! This extensibility point is open for every Visual Studio developer. In following discussions, you will learn how easy it is to add your own wizard to a custom project template.

Wizards are simple .NET classes implementing the `IWizard` interface that can be found in the `Microsoft.VisualStudio.TemplateWizard` namespace in the `Microsoft.VisualStudio` `.TemplateWizard` assembly. If you implement `IWizard`, you can count on the following features:

- ➤ Collect information through your own UI and use that information to create a code skeleton.

- ➤ Extend the replacement dictionary (placeholder/replacement associations) dynamically.

- ➤ Declare each file that is part of the original template as to whether it should be added to the target project.

- ➤ Access (and even change) the project or the item from the template after Visual Studio has finished generating them.

- ➤ Run custom actions before items are opened in their corresponding editors.

## Comment Selector Sample

To demonstrate the features available through the `IWizard` interface, let's take a look at a simple example implementing a one-page wizard that allows the user to select a heading comment from a list. This example uses this wizard to put the selected comment into the header of the `Program.cs` file in a console application.

Start the wizard by creating a C# class library project, and name it `SimpleCommentWizard`. Delete the `Class1.cs` file, because you do not need it.

The wizard uses a WPF dialog as its user interface, so add the following assembly references to the project: `PresentationCore`, `PresentatioFramework`, and `WindowsBase`. To access the `IWizard` interface, you must also add references for the `EnvDTE` and `Microsoft.VisualStudio` `.TemplateWizardInterface` assemblies.

Because the wizard should be put into the Global Assembly Cache (GAC) so that Visual Studio can find and load it, you must sign it with a key to ensure it has a strong name. Go to the project properties and, on the Signing tab, click the "Sign the assembly" checkbox and select the <New...> item from the "Choose a strong name key file" combo box. Specify a key filename in the dialog appearing (for example, `Key.snk`) and clear the "Protect my key file with a password" checkbox. Click OK, and the key file is immediately added to the project.

The user interface of the wizard is actually a simple list box, as shown in Figure 4-19.

The user interface of the wizard is a WPF form using embedded WPF resources and data binding to keep the UI logic very simple. Add a WPF User Control item to the project with the `CommentSelector.xaml` name. Listing 4-7 shows the XAML file defining the UI.

**FIGURE 4-19:** The UI of the Simple Comment Wizard

**LISTING 4-7:** CommentSelector.xaml

```xml
<Window x:Class="SimpleCommentWizard.CommentSelector"
  xmlns="http://schemas.microsoft.com/winfx/2006/xaml/presentation"
  xmlns:x="http://schemas.microsoft.com/winfx/2006/xaml"
  xmlns:mc="http://schemas.openxmlformats.org/markup-compatibility/2006"
  xmlns:d="http://schemas.microsoft.com/expression/blend/2008"
  xmlns:src="clr-namespace:SimpleCommentWizard"
  mc:Ignorable="d"
  d:DesignHeight="300" d:DesignWidth="300" ResizeMode="NoResize"
  Title="Simple Comment Wizard"
  Width="300" Height="220" WindowStartupLocation="CenterScreen">
  <Window.Resources>
    <src:CommentDescriptorCollection x:Key="CommentTypes">
      <src:CommentDescriptor
        ShortName="No restriction"
        Description="You can use this application with no restriction."/>
      <src:CommentDescriptor
        ShortName="AS IS"
        Description="The application is provided as it is."/>
      <src:CommentDescriptor
        ShortName="No commercial use"
        Description="The application cannot be used in commercial products."/>
    </src:CommentDescriptorCollection>
  </Window.Resources>
  <DockPanel>
    <DockPanel DockPanel.Dock="Bottom" Height="36" Margin="4">
      <Button Name="OkButton" IsDefault="true" DockPanel.Dock="Right"
        Width="80" Margin="4" Click="OkButton_Click">OK</Button>
      <Button Name="CancelButton" HorizontalAlignment="Right"
        DockPanel.Dock="Right" Width="80" Margin="4"
        Click="CancelButton_Click">Cancel</Button>
    </DockPanel>
    <StackPanel Margin="4">
      <TextBlock Margin="4">Select a comment:</TextBlock>
      <ListBox x:Name="CommentListBox" Margin="4" SelectedIndex="0"
        ItemsSource="{StaticResource CommentTypes}"
```

```
          DisplayMemberPath="ShortName" />
        <Border BorderBrush="DarkGray" Margin="4" BorderThickness="2">
          <TextBlock HorizontalAlignment="Stretch" TextWrapping="Wrap"
            VerticalAlignment="Stretch" Padding="8,8,8,8"
            Text="{Binding ElementName=CommentListBox, Path=SelectedItem.Description}"
              Background="LightGoldenrodYellow" />
        </Border>
      </StackPanel>
    </DockPanel>
  </Window>
```

*Code file [CommentSelector.xaml] available for download at Wrox.com*

Although you have added a WPF user control, you changed it to a WPF window, as you can see from Listing 4-7. The code-behind file of the XAML definition is very simple. It responds the OK and Cancel buttons, as shown in Listing 4-8.

**LISTING 4-8:** CommentSelector.xaml.cs

```csharp
using System.Windows;

namespace SimpleCommentWizard
{
  public partial class CommentSelector : Window
  {
    public string SelectedComment { get; set; }
    public CommentSelector()
    {
      InitializeComponent();
    }

    private void OkButton_Click(object sender, RoutedEventArgs e)
    {
      var comment = CommentListBox.SelectedItem as CommentDescriptor;
      SelectedComment = comment == null ? null : comment.Description;
      Close();
    }

    private void CancelButton_Click(object sender, RoutedEventArgs e)
    {
      SelectedComment = null;
      Close();
    }
  }
}
```

*Code file [CommentSelector.xaml.cs] available for download at Wrox.com*

The SelectedComment property holds the value of the comment to be inserted into the source code. CancelButton sets it to null, while the OkButton assigns it with the value of the description belonging to the comment type selected in the list.

The CommentListBox control is responsible for listing the comments from which the user can select. It binds a collection of CommentDescriptor items defined in Listing 4-9.

**LISTING 4-9:** CommentDescriptor.cs

```csharp
using System.Collections.Generic;

namespace SimpleCommentWizard
{
  class CommentDescriptor
  {
    public string ShortName { get; set; }
    public string Description { get; set; }
  }

  class CommentDescriptorCollection : List<CommentDescriptor>
  {
  }
}
```

*Code file [CommentDescriptor.cs] available for download at Wrox.com*

Add a new class file with name CommentDescriptor.cs to the project and copy the content of the listing into the file. The CommentSelector.xaml file defines a resource with the key CommentTypes bound to CommentListBox.

## Implementing IWizard

Table 4-7 shows a few methods to implement with the IWizard interface.

**TABLE 4-7:** The IWizard Interface Methods

| METHOD | DESCRIPTION |
| --- | --- |
| BeforeOpeningFile | Runs the wizard logic after the code generation, when an item is about to open in the IDE with its corresponding editor. The method accepts an input parameter with the type of EnvDTE.ProjectItem that describes the item to be opened. When you implement this method, you can obtain information about the item to be opened, or even change the item's properties. |

| METHOD | DESCRIPTION |
|---|---|
| ProjectFinishedGenerating | Runs the wizard logic when a project has finished generating. This method is called by the IDE only when the wizard belongs to a project template. The method has an input parameter with the type of EnvDTE.Project that describes the project. You can use this method to obtain information about the project or even to change the project structure or properties. This method is a good placeholder for activities to add new files to the projects — or change existing ones — according to the information collected from the user. |
| ProjectItemFinishedGenerating | Runs the wizard logic when a project item has finished generating. This method is called by the IDE only when the wizard belongs to an item template. The method has an input parameter with the type of EnvDTE.ProjectItem that describes the item generated. You can use this method to obtain information about the item or even to change its properties. |
| RunFinished | Runs wizard logic when the wizard has completed all the tasks. You can use this method to clean up resources used by the wizard. |
| RunStarted | Runs custom wizard logic at the beginning of a template wizard run. This is the method where the user interface of the wizard should be displayed. The user interface can collect information from the user and build the template accordingly. This method has four parameters: automationObject — This is a reference to an automation object, allowing access to the EnvDTE instance representing IDE objects and services. replacementsDictionary — This is a dictionary associating placeholders and their replacement values. This method can extend this dictionary with new key and value pairs. runKind — This is an instance of WizardRunKind that tells the template type (project, item, or multi-project) the wizard is working on. customParams — This is an array of objects representing the key and value pairs defined in the <WizardData> section of the template manifest file. |
| ShouldAddProjectItem | Indicates whether the specified project item should be added to the project. The parameter of the method is the full path to the file to be added. |

The order of the methods shown in Table 4-7 does not reflect the order and mode they are fired in during the template-generation process. Following is the real order these methods are called:

1. Before any other activities happen, for any kind of wizard, the `RunStarted` method is called to let you initialize your wizard logic and collect information from users through the displayed UI.

2. The template system uses the replacement dictionary (the `RunStarted` method can override the default one), and creates the list of files to be added to the project. `ShouldAddProjectItem` is called for each file with the full physical path of the file. These filenames combine name replacements and file redirections (through the `TargetFileName` attribute). With this method, you can decide whether to include the file in the project. Returning `true` from this method tells the template system to add the file and carry out replacements in the original template file.

3. When all files have been added, one of the `ProjectFinishedGenerating` or the `ProjectItemFinishedGenerating` methods is called, depending on whether it is a project or an item template. In both cases, the automation object representing the project or the item is passed to the appropriate method.

4. For each file where the `OpenInEditor` attribute was set to `true` in the template manifest file, the `BeforeOpeningFile` method is called, passing the automation object representing the file.

5. At the very end, the `RunFinished` method is called.

The `IWizard` interface implementation is really not as complex as it may seem according to Table 4-7 and the steps just described. Listing 4-10 shows how the Simple Comment Wizard does this job.

**LISTING 4-10: CommentWizard.cs**

```csharp
using System.Collections.Generic;
using Microsoft.VisualStudio.TemplateWizard;
using EnvDTE;

namespace SimpleCommentWizard
{
  class CommentWizard: IWizard
  {
    public void BeforeOpeningFile(ProjectItem projectItem)
    {
    }

    public void ProjectFinishedGenerating(Project project)
    {
    }
```

```csharp
public void ProjectItemFinishedGenerating(ProjectItem projectItem)
{
}

public void RunFinished()
{
}

public void RunStarted(object automationObject,
  Dictionary<string, string> replacementsDictionary,
  WizardRunKind runKind, object[] customParams)
{
  var form = new CommentSelector();
  form.ShowDialog();
  if (form.SelectedComment != null)
  {
    replacementsDictionary.Add("$headercomment$", form.SelectedComment);
  }
}

public bool ShouldAddProjectItem(string filePath)
{
  return true;
}
    }
  }
```

*Code file [CommentWizard.cs] available for download at Wrox.com*

As you see, the logic is implemented by adding functionality to two methods. `ShouldAddProjectItem` returns `true` for all files, and `RunStarted` implements the logic that allows the user to select the appropriate comment.

`RunStarted` displays the user interface and adds the selected comment to the replacement dictionary with the `$headercomments$` key.

## Integrating the Wizard with the Template

Now that all pieces of the puzzle are ready, you just have to put them together:

➤ Earlier in this chapter, you created the `Basic Command Console` project template. Let's change it to use the wizard.

➤ You have the `SimpleCommentWizard` assembly containing the `CommentWizard` class that implements the wizard functionality.

To make the wizard work in the `Basic Command Console` project template, you must follow these steps:

**1.** Build and insert the `SimpleCommentWizard.dll` into the GAC. If you do not remember how to do it, here are the steps to help you:

    **a.** Start the Visual Studio 2010 command prompt. If you use Vista, Windows Server 2008, or Windows 7, you must start it in administrative mode. (You will find it in the All Programs Menu under Visual Studio 2010 ➪ Visual Studio Tools.)

    **b.**   Set the current folder with the `cd` command to the one into which the `SimpleCommentWizard.dll` was compiled.

    **c.**   Add the assembly to the GAC with `gacutil -i SimpleCommentWizard.dll` command.

**2.**   Put down the full name of the `SimpleCommentWizard.dll` assembly, because you need it to integrate the wizard with the project template. The easiest way is to use the `gacutil -1 SimpleCommentWizard` command line that writes out the full name of the assembly.

**3.**   Modify the `Program.cs` file and the template manifest within the `Basic Command Console.zip` to integrate the wizard and the new enhanced project template.

The last step requires some workaround, because it is not easy to modify files within a `.zip` archive.

The easiest way to do this is to extract the content of `Basic Command Console.zip` into a temporary folder. When you are ready with the modifications, zip the temporary folder again and override the original `Basic Command Console.zip` file with it. Keep in mind the following things:

➤   When zipping the temporary folder, select all the files in the folder, and zip those (not the folder itself). If you zip the folder, the template system will not find the manifest file and will ignore your template.

➤   The `Basic Command Console.zip` file you should override is in your `My Documents` folder under `Visual Studio 10\Templates\ProjectTemplates`.

So, modify the `Program.cs` file by adding the following lines to the top:

```
// =========================================================================
// $headercomment$
// =========================================================================
```

The `$headercomment$` is the placeholder for the file header comment. The `RunStarted` method of the wizard will provide the value for `$headercomment$`.

Let's take the last step. Modify the original template manifest to be the one shown in Listing 4-11.

**LISTING 4-11:** The Modified Template Manifest (MyTemplate.vstemplate)

```
<VSTemplate Version="2.0.0"
  xmlns="http://schemas.microsoft.com/developer/vstemplate/2005" Type="Project">
  <TemplateData>
    <Name>Basic Command Console Wizard</Name>
    <Description>This console processes simple commands</Description>
    <ProjectType>CSharp</ProjectType>
    <ProjectSubType>
```

```
    </ProjectSubType>
    <SortOrder>1000</SortOrder>
    <CreateNewFolder>true</CreateNewFolder>
    <DefaultName>Basic Command Console</DefaultName>
    <ProvideDefaultName>true</ProvideDefaultName>
    <LocationField>Enabled</LocationField>
    <EnableLocationBrowseButton>true</EnableLocationBrowseButton>
    <Icon>__TemplateIcon.ico</Icon>
  </TemplateData>
  <TemplateContent>
    <Project TargetFileName="ConsoleBase.csproj"
      File="ConsoleBase.csproj" ReplaceParameters="true">
      <ProjectItem ReplaceParameters="true"
        TargetFileName="CommandProcessor.cs">CommandProcessor.cs
      </ProjectItem>
      <ProjectItem ReplaceParameters="true"
        TargetFileName="CommandProcessorItem.cs">CommandProcessorItem.cs
      </ProjectItem>
      <ProjectItem ReplaceParameters="true" TargetFileName="Program.cs"
        OpenInEditor="true">Program.cs
      </ProjectItem>
      <Folder Name="Properties" TargetFolderName="Properties">
        <ProjectItem ReplaceParameters="true" TargetFileName="AssemblyInfo.cs">
          AssemblyInfo.cs
        </ProjectItem>
      </Folder>
    </Project>
  </TemplateContent>
  <WizardExtension>
    <Assembly>
      SimpleCommentWizard, Version=1.0.0.0, Culture=Neutral,
      PublicKeyToken=641eb7314f7120d3
    </Assembly>
    <FullClassName>SimpleCommentWizard.CommentWizard</FullClassName>
  </WizardExtension>
</VSTemplate>
```

As you can see, there are just minor modifications in the <TemplateData> section — now the name ends with Wizard. The real change is the insertion of the <WizardExtension> section that contains two child elements:

➤ <Assembly> — This names the assembly where the class implementing the wizard logic is implemented. Here, an assembly name should be specified that can be resolved in the GAC. Use the name here you put down when inserting your assembly into the GAC. With simply copying, the name out from the listing prevents your wizard from working, because it probably has a different public key token.

➤ <FullClassName> — This specifies the full name of the class implementing the wizard logic to be used in the template. This class must be the part of the assembly and implement the IWizard interface. As you might guess, one assembly can hold not only one but more wizard classes.

If you followed the steps in this section and copied the modified `Basic Command Console.zip` to the user project template folder, all pieces of the puzzle are now in the right place. Start Visual Studio 2010 and select File ⇨ New ⇨ Project. In the Visual C# root category, you will find the Basic Command Console Wizard. When you create the project, the wizard is displayed, as shown in Figure 4-19. Select the "AS IS" option and click OK.

After the project is generated, the `Program.cs` file opens and you can recognize the selected header comment:

```
// =========================================================================
// The application is provided as it is.
// =========================================================================
using System;
using System.Linq;
using System.Reflection;
using System.ComponentModel;

namespace Basic_Command_Console1
{
  class Program
  {
    // ...
  }
}
```

Now you are ready to learn about template deployment.

## DEPLOYING TEMPLATES

While it is useful to create templates only for your own consumption, the value of templates can grow significantly when reused by a team or by a large community.

A few months after the release of Visual Studio 2008, Microsoft introduced *Visual Studio Gallery* (`http://www.visualstudiogallery.com`). This is a new portal for Visual Studio-related products and extensions, including free and paid accessories such as custom controls, tools and utilities, templates, starter kits, and so on. In a very short time, Visual Studio Gallery become a central place for the Visual Studio community members. As of this writing, about 1,400 components were available on the gallery, including more than 300 of them for free!

With the release of Visual Studio 2010, the value of this gallery has grown significantly. The new IDE has a new feature called Extension Manager that can be used to download and install tools, controls, and templates directly from Visual Studio Gallery. Also, the New Project and Add New Item dialogs were extended to browse templates uploaded to the gallery. When you find an online template you want to work with — or just want to try — you can immediately start using it.

In the following discussions, you will learn about the options from which you can choose when deciding to export your templates and make them available for your team, or even for the ecosystem formed by the developer community.

# Exporting and Importing Templates

Thus far in this chapter, you have created a few project and item templates, including a simple wizard. During these exercises, you have exported and imported templates several times. Mostly, you have used the Export Template Wizard, but you have also integrated your templates with Visual Studio manually.

## Manual Export

The .zip file representing a project template or an item template can be created and exported manually. You can either start from an existing template by extracting the .zip archive into a working folder, or by creating it from scratch. Here are a few hints to help you creating your templates manually:

➤ Copy all the files to be included in the template into the working folder, keeping the hierarchy of folders. If you have not prepared placeholders for replacements yet, you can do it now.

➤ Create the template manifest file. Be sure to use the correct information in the `<TemplaData>` section, and be sure to use the correct filenames and paths in the `<TemplateContent>` section. Do not forget that all paths should be relative to the working folder representing the .zip archive.

➤ Create icon and preview image files for the template. You can omit them, but, in this case, the default icon and no preview image will be used by the IDE for your template.

➤ When zipping the files, do not send the parent folder into the .zip archive! When Visual Studio scans the folders for templates, it would find your .zip file, but would not recognize it as a template definition because there would be no manifest file directly in the root of the archive.

## Using the Export Template Wizard

Earlier in this chapter, you used the Export Template Wizard, so you should have a have a solid understanding of it. As you saw, the wizard has four pages:

➤ Choose Template Type (Figure 4-12)

➤ Select Item To Export (Figure 4-13)

➤ Select Item References (Figure 4-14)

➤ Select Template Options (Figure 4-15)

When you create a project template, only the first page (Choose Template Type) and the last page (Select Template Options) are displayed by the wizard, while for item templates, all pages enable you to specify template data. You can use the wizard intuitively, because it provides enough help to tell what fields and options should be filled in. However, the last page (Select Template Options) requires some explanation.

Figure 4-20 shows the Select Template Options page filled in with tips to help you see where specific template information will be displayed.

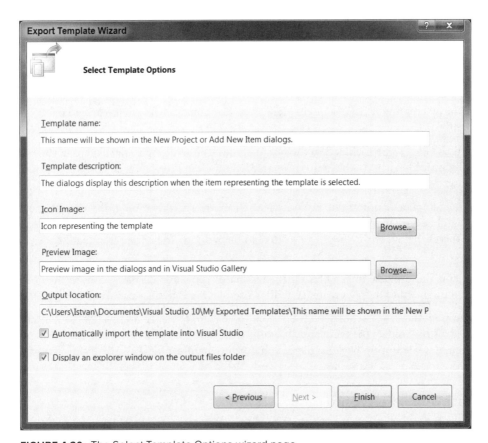

**FIGURE 4-20:** The Select Template Options wizard page

The Preview Image field is totally new in Visual Studio 2010. It allows you to assign an image (even bigger than the template icon) to your template, and this item is displayed in right pane of the New Project and Add New Item dialogs when the template is selected. This icon also can be used in the Visual Studio Gallery as a preview image of your shared extension. Figure 4-21 shows a sample of how the preview image is displayed for a template:

**FIGURE 4-21:** Preview image of a template

Figure 4-20 (the Select Template Options page) also shows you the output location with the full filename where your template will be exported. You can use this field to copy the filename for later use.

There are two useful checkboxes on this page that provide a couple of key options:

➤ You can tell the wizard that, in addition to exporting the template, you intend to immediately import it into Visual Studio.

➤ You can ask the wizard to display the output folder.

The exported template is copied to the `Visual Studio 10\My Exported Templates` directory under your `My Documents` folder. However, when you select the automatic import option, your template file will also be copied to the `Visual Studio 10\Templates\ProjectTemplates` or `Visual Studio 10\Templates\ItemTemplates` folder, depending on its type.

## Deploying the Template Files

In the meantime, your template contains a simple `.zip` file. If you want to deploy more templates, you can handle their `.zip` archives together. When you implement one or more custom template wizards, you must move assemblies representing them into the GAC, or to a location Visual Studio uses for assembly resolution.

While you have only a simple .zip file, you can use any type of file copy mechanism when you put the templates into the right user folder. You can use simple batch files, automatic tools, login scripts, or whatever you find useful.

This approach may work seamlessly for a small number of .zip files. However, when you have wizards included within your set of template definition files, you should create an automatic installation tool (for example, with Visual Studio) to deploy your template files and make them instantly work without any manual workaround.

## Creating a Template Installation Kit

You have many options for creating installation kits, even if you decide to use Visual Studio instead of any other sophisticated setup kit-composition tools. Rather than going through these options, let's take a look at a new technology, *Visual Studio Installer for Extensions (VSIX)*, introduced with Visual Studio 2010 and especially easy to use from both the developer side and from the user side.

The great thing about this new installer technology is that it connects Visual Studio Gallery with the Extension Manager in Visual Studio 2010 to provide you with a user experience similar to using Windows Update for keeping your operating system up-to-date.

This connection entails following these simple steps:

1.  Create a VSIX installation kit for your template.

2.  Upload the installation kit to Visual Studio Gallery.

3.  Use the Extension Manager (or the New Project or Add New Item dialogs) to install and use the template in any computer using Visual Studio 2010.

Let's extend the `Basic Command Console` sample with `SimpleCommentWizard` to demonstrate how VSIX, Visual Studio Gallery, and Extension Manager work together.

### Creating the VSIX Installation Kit

The VSIX installation kit is actually a .zip archive created with the Open Packaging Convention (see http://msdn.microsoft.com/en-us/magazine/cc163372.aspx for more details). You could create it manually just like zip archives representing templates. However, there is a better way.

The Visual Studio 2010 SDK contains a project type for generating a VSIX installation kit. To use it, you must install the Visual Studio Software Development Kit (VS SDK). This kit is free, and you can download it from the Microsoft Visual Studio Extensibility Development Center (http://msdn.com/vsx). When you visit this center, the download link is available right from the home page.

 *Note that there are separate versions of SDKs for the 2005, 2008, and 2010 versions of Visual Studio, and you must be sure to download the right one. Should you have more Visual Studio versions installed on your machine, you can download and install the right SDK for each of them, and they will work side-by-side.*

Installing VS SDK is very simple, so when you download the setup kit, you can immediately run the setup file. Follow the instructions on the screen, and, in a few minutes, VS SDK is ready to work with.

Start a new VSIX Project by selecting the appropriate template from the Extensibility subcategory under Visual C#, as shown in Figure 4-22. Name it `BasicCommandConsoleInstaller`.

FIGURE 4-22: Creating a new VSIX project

The project template contains a few files, as shown in Figure 4-23, viewed in Solution Explorer.

You will not need the `VSIXProject.cs` file, so you can remove it. There are two image files in the project. You can think of them as the icon and preview images in the case of template definitions. These images are used similarly for the installation kit when browsing in the Visual Studio Gallery. The most important file of the project is `extension.vsixmanifest`. As its name suggests, this is the file that tells everything about the installation kit.

You have two artifacts to put into an installation kit: the `Basic Command Console.zip` file representing

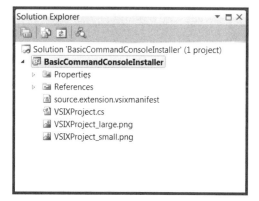

FIGURE 4-23: Files in the VSIX project

the template definition, and `SimpleCommandWizard.dll` holding the custom wizard logic. The installation kit can be created by following these steps:

**1.** Add the `SimpleCommandWizard.dll` to the project with the Add Existing Item command. Search for this file in the output directory of the `SimpleCommandWizard` project.

**2.** Create a folder named `Template`. By design, template archives must be put into a folder within the `.vsix` file, and you can name this folder as you want. Create a subfolder within `Template`, and name it `Console`. Now, use the Add Existing Item command to add the `Basic Command Console.zip` file in the `Console` folder. Be sure to select the version you've used, together with the `SimpleCommentWizard`. Rename the file to `BasicCommandConsole.zip` by removing spaces from the original filename.

**3.** Go to the Properties windows and set Build Action to Content, and "Include in VSIX" to True. Repeat this action for `SimpleCommandWizard.dll`, `VSIXProject_large.png`, and `VSIXProject_small.png` files. Omitting this step will prevent these files from being included in installation kit.

At this point, all artifacts are added to the VSIX project. Figure 4-24 shows how the structure of your project should look when viewed in Solution Explorer.

You are not able to build the installation kit yet, because you must modify the manifest to sign what kind of content is included in this kit. Listing 4-12 shows the original state of the manifest file.

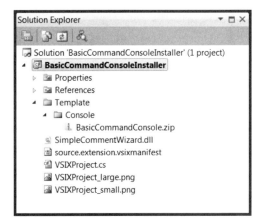

**FIGURE 4-24:** Files in the VSIX project after adding our artifacts

Available for download on Wrox.com

**LISTING 4-12: source.extension.vsmanifest**

```xml
<?xml version="1.0" encoding="utf-8"?>
<VSIX xmlns="http://schemas.microsoft.com/developer/vsx-schema/2010">

  <Identifier ID="BasicCommandConsoleInstaller.Microsoft.
           a866dfe1-d5bd-4402-85ab-a44f2a45e31e">
    <Name>BasicCommandConsoleInstaller</Name>
    <Author>Microsoft</Author>
    <Version>1.0</Version>
    <Description>Empty VSIX Project.</Description>
    <Locale>1033</Locale>
    <Icon>VSIXProject_small.png</Icon>
    <PreviewImage>VSIXProject_large.png</PreviewImage>
    <SupportedVSEdition version="10.0">
      <Edition>VST_All</Edition>
      <Edition>Pro</Edition>
```

```
      </SupportedVSEdition>
      <SupportedFrameworkRuntimeEdition minversion="4.0" maxversion="4.0" />
    </Identifier>

    <References>
      <!--Add References here-->
    </References>

    <Content>
      <!--Add Content here-->
    </Content>

  </VSIX>
```

*Code file [source.extension.vsmanifest] available for download at Wrox.com*

As you can see, the manifest is an XML file just like a template manifest, but it has a different schema. Use the View Code command (accessible from the context menu of `extension .vsixmanifest`) and use the XML editor to take a look at the content of the file. Without going too deep into the details of this file's schema, let's note a few things about it.

The `ID` attribute of the `<Identifier>` and `<Version>` elements identifies your installation kit. These values are also used to recognize new updates for an extension already installed. The `<SupportedVSEdition>` element enumerates all Visual Studio versions supporting the extension, which, in this case, is the Professional edition and all Team System editions.

The `<Content>` element is the one where you can put the payload information for the installer. Its child elements determine what actions to carry out during the installation. To add your artifacts to the payload, modify the manifest as shown in Listing 4-13.

**Available for download on Wrox.com**

**LISTING 4-13: The modified source.extension.vsixmanifest file**

```
<?xml version="1.0" encoding="utf-8"?>
<VSIX xmlns="http://schemas.microsoft.com/developer/vsx-schema/2010">
  <Identifier ID="DiveDeeper.BasicCommandConsoleInstaller">
    <Name>Basic Command Console Installer</Name>
    <Author>DiveDeeper</Author>
    <Version>2.0</Version>
    <Description>
      This kit installs the Basic Command Console template.
    </Description>
    <Locale>1033</Locale>
    <Icon>VSIXProject_small.png</Icon>
    <PreviewImage>VSIXProject_large.png</PreviewImage>
    <SupportedVSEdition version="10.0">
      <Edition>VST_All</Edition>
      <Edition>Pro</Edition>
    </SupportedVSEdition>
```

*continues*

**LISTING 4-13** *(continued)*

```
    <SupportedFrameworkRuntimeEdition minversion="4.0" maxversion="4.0" />
  </Identifier>
  <References />
  <Content>
    <ProjectTemplate>Template</ProjectTemplate>
    <Assembly assemblyName="SimpleCommentWizard, Version=1.0.0.0, Culture=Neutral,
      PublicKeyToken=641eb7314f7120d3">SimpleCommentWizard.dll</Assembly>
  </Content>
</VSIX>
```

*Code file [source.extension.vsmanifest] available for download at Wrox.com*

As you can see, a few options have been changed within `<Identifier>`, but the most important change is in `<Content>`:

➤ The `<ProjectTemplate>` element indicates that the installer will look in the `Template` folder and copy it into the `Extensions` folder within the local application data of Visual Studio.

➤ The `<Assembly>` element specifies that `SimpleCommentWizard.dll` is an assembly, and it should also be copied to the `Extensions` folder.

After you have followed these steps, the installation kit is ready to build. Use the Build ⇨ Rebuild Solution command to create the `.vsix` file representing the kit. Close Visual Studio 2010 and open the output folder (`bin\Debug` under your VSIX project folder, by default) and you can see the `BasicCommandConsoleInstaller` `.vsix` file there. Opening this file will start the Visual Studio Extension Installer tool, as shown in Figure 4-25.

Click the Install button and, in a few seconds, the utility does what you expect, as shown in Figure 4-26.

**FIGURE 4-25:** Visual Studio Extension Installer

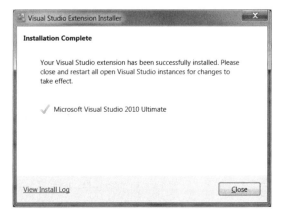

**FIGURE 4-26:** The template is installed

Start Visual Studio 2010 and check the success of the installation by creating a new project. You can see a new subcategory named Console under Visual C# in the New Project dialog, and, within this new category, you can find your template, as shown in Figure 4-27.

**FIGURE 4-27:** Verifying template installation

When you create a new project with this template, the Simple Comment Wizard is displayed, so you can check that not only the template definition, but also the wizard assembly, have successfully installed.

## Uploading Templates to the Visual Studio Gallery

You now have an installation kit for your template that can be deployed quite easily. Copy the `BasicCommandConsoleInstalles.vsix` file to a machine where Visual Studio 2010 is installed, and then open it. The Visual Studio Extension Installer runs and does the rest of the work.

Now, let's do something exciting. You can upload your template to the Visual Studio Gallery so that community members can find, download, install, and, of course, use it. In the following discussions, you will see how easy the upload process is. These discussions include screenshots of Visual Studio Gallery. By the time you read this book, the gallery may have another design, or even work a bit differently, but this examination at least provides a point of reference.

To upload your own extensions to Visual Studio Gallery, you must log in with your Live ID. If you have used Live Messenger, Hotmail, Live Mesh, Microsoft Connect, or some other community services from Microsoft, you have a Live ID. If you do not have one, it is very easy to create one.

You can visit the Visual Studio Gallery by navigating to `http://www.visualstudiogallery.com`. You can browse the gallery without signing in. Figure 4-28 shows a typical screen presented when you visit the gallery.

**FIGURE 4-28:** Visual Studio Gallery

Locate the Upload button in the upper-right part of the screen, just below the search box. Click it to start the upload process. You can upload an extension by following a few simple steps.

The first step is to select the kind of extension you want to upload, as shown in Figure 4-29.

☐ **Step 1: Extension Type***

What type of extension are you uploading?

○ Tool
○ Control
◉ Project or Item Template (Only supported in Visual Studio 2010)

[Next]

Select this if you want to add a template to the Visual Studio Gallery so that other developers can download it. Package the template as a .vsix file so that New Project dialog, and the Extension Manager in Visual Studio 2010 can recognize it, download it, and install it correctly, and the New Project dialog box can display it. (How to create a VSIX file?)

**FIGURE 4-29:** Select the type of extension to upload

Click Next. In the second step, you must select the `.vsix` file containing your template. Select it directly from the output folder of the `BasicCommandConsoleInstaller` project, as shown in Figure 4-30.

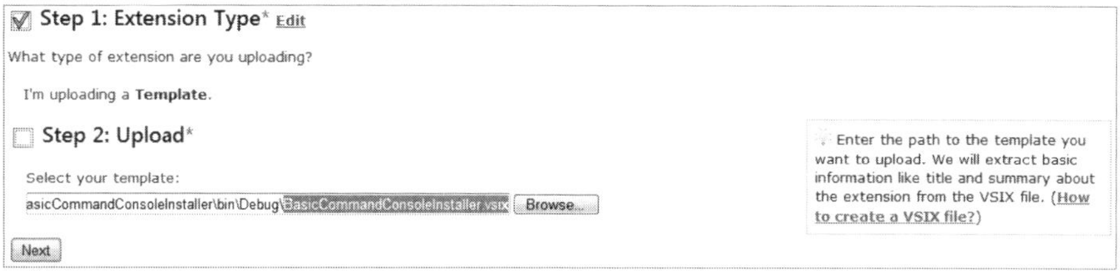

**FIGURE 4-30:** Select the .vsix file to upload

Click Next to move to the third step, where you can edit some more information about the template. Visual Studio Gallery extracts basic information from the `.vsix` manifest and lets you edit some other information to help to categorize your template. Figure 4-31 illustrates this step.

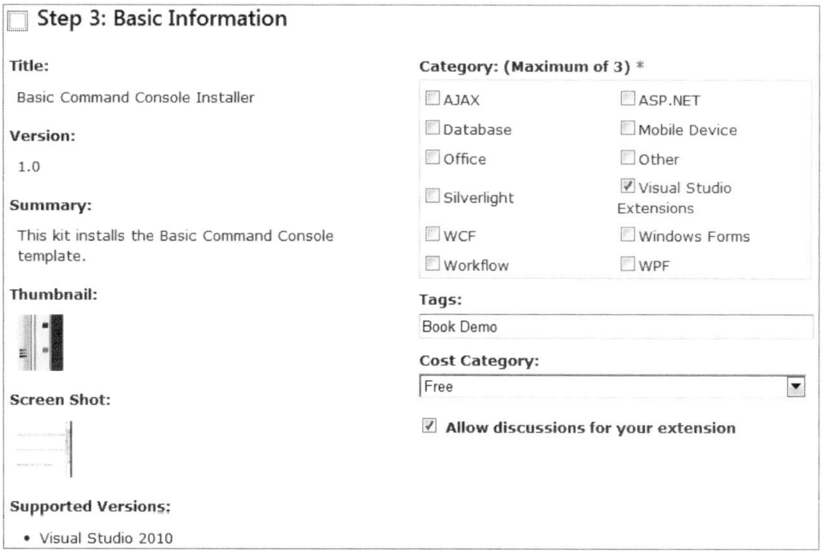

**FIGURE 4-31:** Editing basic template information

The information page (although it is not shown in Figure 4-31) also contains an editable description of the template. By using a rich text editor, you can specify information to be displayed with your uploaded template. You must also check the "I agree to the Contribution Agreement" checkbox, and then click Create Contribution to finish the template upload.

Once you complete these steps, the template is uploaded to Visual Studio Gallery, as shown in Figure 4-32. However, it is not yet published. You can edit it, if you feel you have missed something, or you can even delete it.

**FIGURE 4-32:** The template is uploaded

When you click on the "publish" link in the header, the template is immediately published. You and any other users of Visual Studio Gallery will be able to find it and download it. Later, you can edit, un-publish, or delete your template when signing in to the Gallery and going to the My Contributions page — it can be accessed directly from the home page. Figure 4-33 shows that the published template can be accessed from the Visual Studio Extensions category.

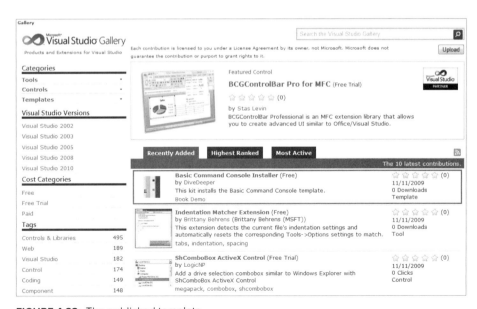

**FIGURE 4-33:** The published template

You have now shared your template with the community. Let's look at how community members can find and install it from within the Visual Studio IDE.

## Installing Templates with the Extension Manager

Visual Studio 2010 has a great new feature called *Extension Manager* to help with discovering, downloading, and managing Visual Studio Extensions from Visual Studio Gallery. By using this feature, community members can find the template you uploaded to the gallery.

You can go to the Tools menu and click on the Extension Manager command. The dialog has three panes:

➤ The left pane shows categories of extensions. This is where you can focus on installed extensions, browse the online gallery, or check updates for the installed components.

➤ The middle pane lists the extensions in the selected category.

➤ The right pane shows detailed information about the extension selected in the middle pane.

The template you have uploaded to the gallery can be found in the Visual Studio Extensions category under the Online Gallery, as shown in Figure 4-34.

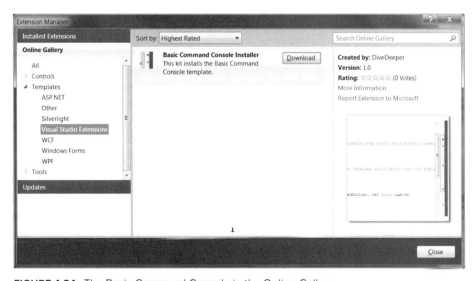

**FIGURE 4-34:** The Basic Command Console in the Online Gallery

Any community member who decides to try the template can click on the Download button. Extension Manager downloads the `.vsix` file representing the installation kit of the template and asks for a confirmation, as shown in Figure 4-35.

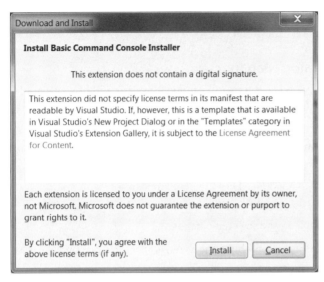

**FIGURE 4-35:** The template is about to be installed.

Clicking on Install immediately integrates the template with Visual Studio. Generally, after installing components, Extension Manager asks you to restart Visual Studio and provides a button to do this. However, template installation does not require a restart, and so you can instantly work with the new template.

Online templates do not require an explicit installation through Extension Manager. You can also access published templates in the Gallery through the New Project and Add New Item dialogs (you will notice that their user interface is very similar to Extension Manager). Figure 4-36 shows the `Basic Command Console` template found among other online templates.

**FIGURE 4-36:** Online templates in the New Project dialog

When you start a project from an online template, Visual Studio first installs the template just as though you installed it explicitly with Extension Manager, and then creates the project. When you try it with the `Basic Command Console` template, after installation, the Simple Comment Wizard starts instantly.

## SUMMARY

Templates are useful concepts because they save you from the burden of writing code from the scratch for each project and source code item. They help you avoid common mistakes by providing you with skeletons for your frequently used artifacts, and by providing consistency among your projects independently of who uses it and how.

Visual Studio supports two kinds of templates: project templates and item templates. They can be used from the New Project and Add New Item dialogs, respectively. The template system has been designed with extensibility in mind. You can easily integrate your own templates with Visual Studio. The easiest way of creating templates is by building the template just like a concrete project or item, and then using the Export Template Wizard to create the template definition file.

Template definitions are `.zip` archives containing all files that build up the project or the item. The heart of the definition is the template manifest with the extension of `.vstemplate`. This manifest contains the metadata required to place the definition into the right category within the IDE.

Templates can be customized with parameters. When a new project or item is created from a template definition, placeholders can be replaced with concrete values. You can also create wizards and attach them to templates. Before creating the concrete instance from the template, the wizard collects information from the user, and the project or item skeleton can be generated according this data.

Because template definitions are simple `.zip` archives, it is very easy to deploy them. Visual Studio 2010 offers great improvements in this area. It has a new feature called Extension Manager that allows you to browse and install templates from an online gallery called Visual Studio Gallery, which is a central repository for tools, controls, and extensions related to Visual Studio. In addition to the capability to browse this gallery, you can easily upload and publish your own templates, and share them with the community.

Chapter 5 provides an overview about great IDE features focusing on customization. Among others, you will learn about window management, configuration options, menu and toolbar customizations, and defining your own keyboard shortcuts. The chapter will teach you to create custom Start Pages, and introduces you to the Visual Studio Gallery.

# 5

# Getting the Most Out of the IDE

Visual Studio is a popular development tool offering more and more functions with every new release. The IDE targets not only programmers — coders — but actually every role that adds essential value to a software development project, including project managers, business analysts, architects, developers, database experts, testers and deployment experts. Can you imagine that all people in these roles will use the IDE in the same way?

The answer is obvious — each role uses a well-defined set of Visual Studio's functionality, and, of course, it is different for an architect than for a tester, or for a member with another role. But even two developers may use the IDE in different ways. Just think about the first dialog you face when you start Visual Studio the first time after installation! The IDE asks you to select the profile you would like to use. If you select C#, you will work with a different set of tool windows and other configuration settings than a developer selecting the C++ profile.

The IDE was designed with many customization options in mind. One of the most important goals of its design was to enable developers to create a modern, ergonomic, and productive environment they can utilize to create the best software. In this chapter, you will learn about many aspects of Visual Studio 2010's customization so that you can get the most out of the IDE.

Following is how this chapter is organized:

> *Window management* — Visual Studio provides great window management to help developers establish and manage their workspace. You will learn the architecture behind tool windows and document windows, as well as the available operations to arrange windows on your workbench.

> *Customizing menus and toolbars* — Menus and toolbars in Visual Studio can be tailored to fit your needs. In this section of the chapter, you'll learn about creating new menus and toolbars, as well as changing and rearranging commands associated with them.

➤ *IDE configuration* — There are hundreds of options you can set to configure the behavior of the IDE. In this section, you learn how to manage them with the Options dialog. The IDE provides a mechanism to export and import these configuration settings. This section of the chapter also teaches you to use it with the Export and Import Settings Wizard.

➤ *Keyboard shortcuts* — Visual Studio delivers more than a thousand commands available in the IDE. You do not need to use the mouse to invoke them through menu or toolbar items. You can associate keyboard shortcuts with them. In this section, you learn about this customization process.

➤ *Custom Start Pages* — You can change the Start Page of Visual Studio. Although this extensibility option was already available in the first Visual Studio.NET version, Visual Studio 2010 delivers essential changes and lowers the barrier for entering Start Page customization. This section examines several samples to help you to learn how to use the Custom Start Page Template.

➤ *Customizing the Toolbox* — The Toolbox is one of the most frequently used tool windows in the IDE. In this section, you'll learn the options to tailor the Toolbox to your needs.

➤ *Visual Studio Gallery* — This is a website that provides a catalog showcasing free and commercial products complementing or extending Visual Studio. In this section, you learn about browsing the Gallery, downloading components, and adding your contributions to its repository.

Visual Studio 2010 is extensible. When you miss a function or some features from the IDE, you can develop and integrate your own components into the IDE. Chapter 6 is dedicated entirely to this topic. However, before developing any new extensibility component for Visual Studio, stop for a moment! Maybe, what you would like to solve through development can be sorted out with simple customization. This chapter will help you with this decision.

## WINDOW MANAGEMENT

The Visual Studio IDE was designed to provide an ergonomic workbench for its users. During application development, many types of information are displayed on the surface of this workbench. Today, more and more developers use two or sometimes even more monitors to place all editors, tools, information, and message windows in order to be more productive.

Visual Studio provides great window management to help developers establish and manage their workspace. The IDE contains two basic window types: *tool window*s and *document window*s. These two window types behave in slightly different ways.

## Visual Studio Window Architecture

Visual Studio uses well-organized windows to establish a developer workspace. There is an exact boundary of responsibilities between a window and the IDE. The IDE provides a mechanism to maintain the list of windows, takes care of positioning and moving them, saves the layout, and so on — all without knowing what the window contains and how it is used. In contrast, a window takes care of painting its client area, responding to repositioning and resizing events — all without knowing how the IDE implements windowing logic.

The clear separation of these responsibilities is provided by the following roles:

➤ The IDE uses the concept of a *window frame* that is responsible for hosting the client area of the window, called a *window pane*. This frame integrates the pane with the IDE and controls the visual properties and behavior of the pane.

➤ The window provides a window pane object that can be hosted in a window frame instantiated by the IDE. This pane works as a controller for implementing the interaction logic behind the UI.

➤ The window frame also can provide a toolbar for commands understood by the pane. At initialization time, the pane tells the frame that a toolbar should be displayed in the window. When a command is invoked, the frame notifies the pane, giving it a chance to respond to that command.

Figure 5-1 helps to illustrate these concepts. There are a few windows highlighted with a border representing how the frame and the pane form a functional window.

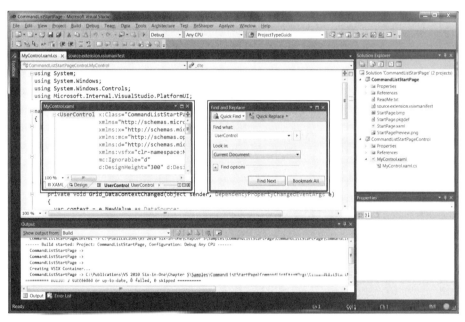

**FIGURE 5-1:** Windows in Visual Studio

The frame hosting the pane also adds some extra decoration and behavior to the hosted pane. For example, the "Find and Replace" window uses a floating frame that adds a title bar with a close button, a resizable tool-window border around the pane, and a toolbar. Every control in the window below the "Find what" label (including the label itself and pushbuttons at the bottom) are managed — painted and controlled — by the pane. The Quick Find button is drawn by the frame that is part of the toolbar.

The Solution Explorer on the right contains a pane with the tree view of the solution structure. The frame hosting this pane is docked at the right side of the main IDE window, and so it provides a different border than the floating window. The frame also contains a pin button to turn on or off the auto-hide property of the window.

The Output window at the bottom is docked exactly at the same location as the Error List window, but the latter is sent to the back. The window frame uses small tabs at the bottom for each pane in order to allow clicking it to bring the pane to the front. Just as with the other windows, the toolbar here is also the part of the window frame.

The Toolbox window at the left is an example of a window that is hidden at the moment. The small rectangle is the frame, indicating the pane is automatically hidden. As you hover the mouse over the frame, the window pane flies in.

The largest part of the screen behind the "Find and Replace" window is covered by two windows representing the `MyControl.xaml.cs` and `source.extension.vsixmanifest` files. These are so-called tabbed document windows. The frame provides the tabs with the names of the files and all other parts of the editor window belong to the pane. The `MyControl.xaml` window to the left of the "Find and Replace" window is a floating document window.

In the previous versions of Visual Studio, you had to choose between tabbed documents or multiple documents. The behavior of multiple documents was very different from floating document windows, as Figure 5-2 shows.

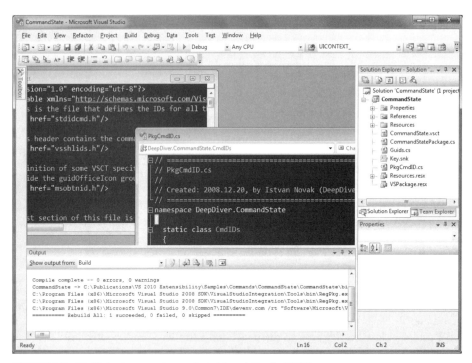

**FIGURE 5-2:** Multiple documents mode in Visual Studio 2008

Visual Studio 2010 now allows using both tabbed and floating document windows at the same time. Developers using multiple monitors can now drag any document window to the secondary display, which is especially helpful during debug sessions.

## Tool Windows

Most of the windows displayed in the Visual Studio IDE are *tool window*s. They generally surround document windows used to edit source code, or to design forms and web pages. The Server Explorer, Output window, Error List, Properties window, and Solution Explorer are only a few examples of them. Tool windows are typically single-instanced. However, they can be multi-instanced, like the web browser window shown in Figure 5-3.

**FIGURE 5-3:** Multiple instances of Web Browser tool window

When Visual Studio runs, there are generally a number of tool windows displayed on the screen, with a majority of them containing valuable information or resources continuously used by developers. Tool windows can float, or they can be docked to the edges of the main window to provide a practical workbench. They also can be tabbed with other tool windows, or they can even be put to the area of document windows. Docked tool windows can be set to hide automatically when the mouse leaves them. Figure 5-4 shows a good illustration of the following concepts:

➤ The "Find and Replace" window floats. Floating windows can be moved outside of the boundaries of the Visual Studio IDE as Figure 5-4 illustrates.

➤ The Solution Explorer and Properties window are docked at the right edge of the IDE's main window. The Toolbox is docked at the left edge of the IDE and is also auto-hidden.

➤ The Output window is docked at the bottom edge of the main window, and Error List is tabbed with it — they share the same visual frame with a single title bar. When they are moved by dragging the title bar, both tool windows move together. When they are dragged by their tabs at the bottom, only the captured tool window moves.

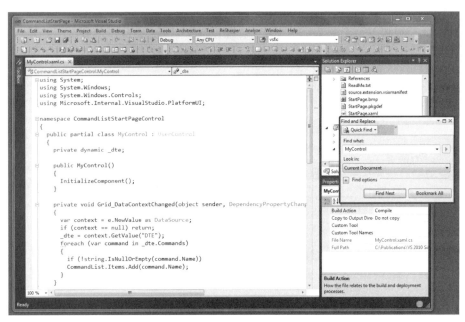

**FIGURE 5-4:** Floating tool windows can be dragged out of main window boundaries

Figure 5-3 shows two instances of the Web Browser tool window that are tabbed as document windows. They share the workspace in the center of the main window that is generally surrounded by tool windows. In this figure, the Solution Explorer and Properties windows are docked to the right. Because a Web Browser tool window generally requires a large space, it is tabbed with document windows by default.

## Document Windows

The other type of windows supported by the IDE is called a *document window*. In contrast to tool windows, document windows are always multi-instanced. They can occupy only the middle area of the main window, optionally surrounded by docked tool windows. Although, document windows cannot be docked, they can float, and they can also be split into horizontal and vertical groups, as shown in Figure 5-5.

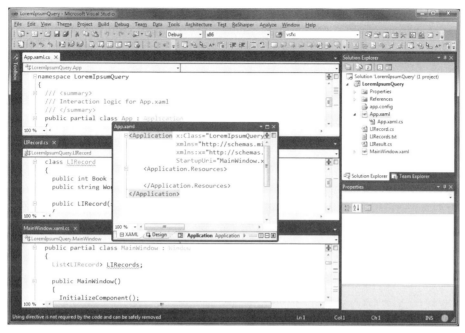

**FIGURE 5-5:** Document windows in horizontal tabs

The term "document window" reflects that any instance of them is associated with a logical entity called a *document* and is owned by a so-called *hierarchy*. The document and the hierarchy are abstractions that can have many different physical manifestations.

For example, the documents behind document windows in Figure 5-5 are the in-memory representations of the source files named in the title bars. The source files are not the documents; they are only the persisted forms of the abstraction called "document." Should you edit a SQL Server table within the IDE, the editor (that is, a document window) would have an in-memory representation of the document that is persisted as a table in a SQL Server database instance.

The hierarchy represents a collection of documents and other resources that are used to build the artifacts of a solution composed from one or more projects. A *project* is the smallest unit of related documents that can be used to build an artifact (for example, C# source files and referenced assemblies that can be compiled into a class library). In Solution Explorer, each project is a hierarchy.

The document windows in Figure 5-5 are owned by the LoremIpsumQuery project (hierarchy) in the Solution Explorer. Hierarchies in the Server Explorer can also own document windows. For example, through data connections created in Server Explorer, you can edit the content of SQL Server tables or modify stored procedures. Document windows used in this case are owned by the hierarchy representing the data connection.

The fact that document windows are owned by hierarchies and they are associated with documents adds a lot of functionality to them out-of-the-box. For example, you can have multiple document windows (or, with another term, *views*) for the same document. When you want to close the last open document window associated with the same document, Visual Studio prompts you with a dialog asking if you want to save that document or ignore all the changes. Another example is that document windows know if they have been modified since you last opened them, and this is how the Save All function knows which documents are to be saved.

# Arranging Windows

Depending on the phase of the software development lifecycle you are in, or on the tasks you are assumed to do, you may need to arrange your windows in the workspace differently. For example, while you are writing code, you may not need to see the toolbar or Server Explorer, and you may want to provide as much space for the code windows as you can. When you are debugging an application, you probably move the application to the second monitor and dock many tool windows around the code you are debugging to see local variables, the call stack, threads, and debug history.

Visual Studio provides several ways to arrange windows in the IDE:

➤ You can tab-dock document or tool windows to the editing frame.

➤ You can dock tool windows to the edge of a frame in the IDE, or tab-dock them to the editing frame.

➤ You can float windows over or outside of the IDE.

➤ You can display windows on multiple monitors.

➤ You can minimize (auto-hide) tool windows along the edge of the IDE.

➤ At any time, you can reset window placement to the original layout with the Window ➪ Reset Window Layout command.

## Floating Windows

If you have document or tool windows docked to the editing frame or to any other frames, you can make them float easily. Drag the title bar of the docked window and move it to another position within or outside of the IDE. You can even move a window to another monitor. When you double-click the title-bar, the window gets maximized on the current display. Double-clicking on a maximized window will return it to its position, and size it as it was before it was maximized.

When you press the Ctrl key while double-clicking the window, it is docked back to the frame it was docked to before you undocked it — and it works independently of how many times you moved, maximized, or resized the floating window.

For example, assume that you drag the `LIRecord.cs` file in Figure 5-5 to a floating position, move it around, and then maximize it by double-clicking on its title bar. As soon as you press Ctrl and double-click it, `LIRecords.cs` will return to its original docked position exactly as you see in Figure 5-5.

When several windows are docked side-by-side (for example, Solution Explorer and Team Explorer in Figure 5-5), dragging them by the title bar will move all the windows docked in the same frame. If you move the Solution Explorer in Figure 5-5 by the title bar, the Team Explorer will move together with it. If you want to move only one of the windows sharing the same frame, instead of dragging the title bar, drag the tab of the window.

## Docking Tool Windows

Tool windows can be fastened to one side of a frame in the IDE. When you start to move a tool window, a guiding diamond appears in the middle of the frame where the mouse is pointing to. The four arrows of the diamond point toward the four sides of the editing pane. An additional four arrows point to the four edges of the IDE, showing other positions where the tool window can be docked. As you move the window over another frame, the guide diamond changes to represent dock positions within that frame.

When you move the window and the mouse pointer overlays any of the guiding icons, a "ghost frame" shows you the new dock position. If you want to accept this dock position, simply finish dragging and release the left mouse button. Figure 5-6 shows what you see when the "Find and Replace" tool window is dragged over the guiding icon that fastens the window to the right edge of the editing area.

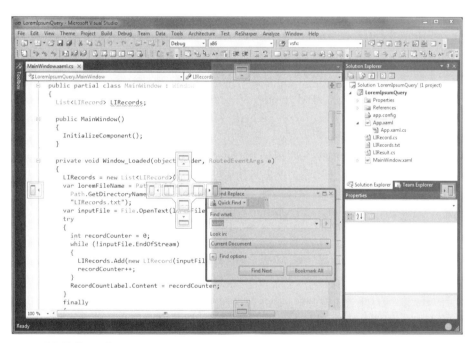

**FIGURE 5-6:** Dragging a tool window to a new dock position

When you start dragging a window while you keep the Ctrl key pressed, no guiding icons are displayed. In this mode, you cannot dock the window, only move it to another floating position. When you release the Ctrl key, the guiding icons are displayed again.

## Docking Document Windows

By default, document windows (designer windows and editor windows that display documents) are arranged on tabbed panes in the editing frame of the IDE. You can dock them only to one of the tab groups, but not to the edges of any frames.

When you drag document windows to a dock position, the guiding icons help you exactly the same way as in the case of tool windows. However, because of the docking restrictions of document windows, fewer icons are displayed.

## Auto-hiding Tool Windows

Tool windows docked to the edge of the main window frame can be set so that they are automatically hidden as they lose the focus. This is a very useful function to save space in the document area. When all tool windows at a certain edge of the main window are auto-hidden, the document window area is automatically extended to that direction as soon as tool windows docked to that edge get hidden.

As you move the mouse pointer over the title bar of an auto-hidden tool window, the window is displayed, unless the pointer leaves that tool window. If you activate the tool window (for example, click on it with the mouse) it will be displayed, unless you change the focus to any other document or tool window.

You can turn on the auto-hide mode for a tool window with the Window ⇨ Auto Hide command, and turn off this mode with the Window ⇨ Dock command. In the title bar of tool windows docked to any edge of the main window, you can see a pin icon. Click on it to turn on or off the auto-hide mode. When the pin points to the bottom, it indicates that the tool window is docked. When the pin points to the left, the window is in auto-hide mode.

## Organizing Document Tab Groups

Although document windows cannot be docked to the edges of frames, you can organize document windows into tab groups. Figure 5-5 shows you how three document windows are separated into three horizontal tab groups.

You can move the active document into a new group with the Window ⇨ New Horizontal Tab Group or Window ⇨ New Vertical Tab Group commands, which can be also accessed from the context menus of the document windows when you right-click on their tabs. In addition to these menu commands, you can drag document windows. The guiding icons escorting you during the drag-and-move operation allow you to place the window to a new vertical or horizontal group.

You can move documents among tab groups either by dragging them to another vertical or horizontal tab group, or using the Window ⇨ Move to Next Tab Group or Window ⇨ Move to Previous Tab Group commands that are also available in document tab context menus.

You can create either vertical or horizontal tab groups. When you divide the document area horizontally or vertically the first time, the next time only the New Horizontal Tab Group or New Vertical Tab Group commands are offered, respectively.

## Splitting and Duplicating Document Windows

When your source code files are very long, you often have to jump from one area of the file to another one, and back. If these areas are quite far away from each other, you must spend a lot of time with paging. You can make your work easier if you split the document window or duplicate it. Figure 5-7 shows you three document windows demonstrating these concepts.

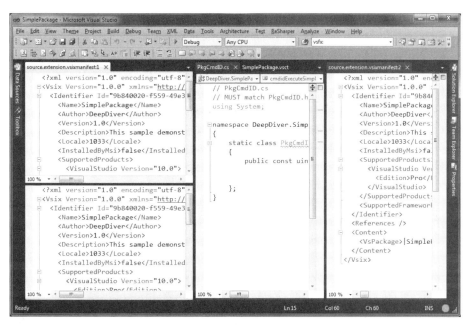

**FIGURE 5-7:** You can split and duplicate document windows

In this figure, the `source.extension.vsixmanifest` document window is split and duplicated.

Use the Window ⇨ Split command to divide the document window area into two vertical panes. You can scroll within the upper and lower panes independently, or even resize them by dragging the split bar between them into a new position. The two panes cannot be moved to separate tab groups; they always move together with the document window. You can unite the two panes with the Window ⇨ Remove Split command, or by resizing one of the panes to a zero height.

Sometimes it is very useful to have separate document windows for the same document. That is when the Window ⇨ New Window command comes into the picture. It creates an additional document window by cloning the active one, and indicates that by appending "index 1" to the original document window and "index 2" to the new window title. You can use the New Window command for the same window several times, so you can create more document window instances as well. The great thing about this approach is that you can move the cloned windows separately from the original one, even though you cannot do this operation with the panes of a split window.

When you split a document window or duplicate it, changes in one window (or window pane) will instantly appear in the other windows (other window pane).

## Setting the Position of New Document Windows

By default, when you open a new document, the related document window will be put to the leftmost location in the current tab group. You can change this behavior on the Documents tab of the Options dialog shown in Figure 5-8.

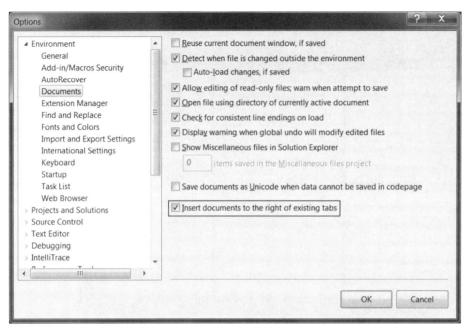

**FIGURE 5-8:** Changing the default position of document windows

Check the "Insert documents to the right of existing tabs" option and close the Options dialog with OK. The next time you open a document, the related window will be put to the rightmost position in the current tab group.

## CUSTOMIZING MENUS AND TOOLBARS

The Visual Studio IDE is a complex product that offers hundreds of functions to the user. These commands are organized into menus and toolbars so that you'll be able to find and launch them in the current context. For example, you need a separate command set for writing code and debugging your application. Even when you edit code, you may need a separate command set, depending on the file type. For example, while you are working with C# files, several refactoring functions help you; when you deal with XML files, formatting commands could provide a comfort zone for you.

The Visual Studio IDE team spent a lot of energy on research in the last few years to establish the menu and toolbar layout you can use with great productivity. However, one structure does not fit for all. Even within your team, you can find developers with different opinions about a certain layout.

The whole menu and toolbar structure was designed with extensibility and customization in mind. If you feel you can enhance the IDE by changing this structure and create a more productive development environment, you are free to do so. Visual Studio provides you with easy-to-use customization functions to tailor the IDE menus and toolbars to your needs:

➤  You can add commands to menus and toolbars — and, of course, you can remove them.

➤  You can add separators between commands to provide a better grouping of them.

➤ If you need, you can create your own menus, or change the order of the existing ones.

➤ You do not have to live only with the existing toolbars. You can create your own toolbars and fill them with existing commands.

➤ You can also reorganize the toolbars in the main docking area, and change their docking position.

If, at any time, you feel lost in the customization, you can reset menus and toolbars to their original state.

---

**RIBBONS IN VISUAL STUDIO**

Microsoft spent a lot of research time on establishing an intuitive user interface (UI) for applications with hundreds of commands. The Microsoft Office ribbon-based user interface is a good example of the results achieved. In the beginning, this new UI was very unusual for Office users, but — according to community feedback — after learning the ribbon basics, most of them loved it.

The first CTPs of Visual Studio were met with a frequently returning question: Why does Visual Studio not have ribbons? Well, the development team was also thinking about introducing ribbons to Visual Studio, but, after a while, they threw out this idea.

Ribbons are great because they are context-sensitive and offer functionality according to the context the user works in. For example, when you are editing a table in Word, new ribbon tabs appear that are customized to help you changing the layout and design of your tables. With applications that have only a few and easily identifiable contexts, this approach works well.

However, in Visual Studio, you have too many contexts. Editing the code itself is at least as complex from this aspect as the entire Word application itself. Of course, you do not have tables or pages, but instead you have namespaces, types, methods, and so on. Depending on where you are in the code, you would like to access different commands — for example, different code refactoring functions or code snippets.

So, the development team concluded that, because of this complexity, changing the Visual Studio menus and toolbars to ribbons would not be productive or intuitive.

---

## The Customize Dialog

Visual Studio provides the Customize dialog as the central place to tailor any menus or toolbars to your needs. You can easily access this dialog with the Tools ➪ Customize command. You do not have to go into the Tools menu. You can right-click on the main menu bar or any toolbars, and invoke the Customize command from the context menu popping up. (You'll find it at the bottom.) The Customize dialog contains two tabs. Figure 5-9 shows the Toolbars tab, while Figure 5-10 shows the Commands tab.

**FIGURE 5-9:** The Toolbars tab of the Customize dialog

**FIGURE 5-10:** The Commands tab of the Customize dialog

 *At the bottom of the dialog, you can see the Keyboard button that can be used to change or assign keyboard shortcuts to Visual Studio Commands. Later in this chapter, you will learn how to reduce efforts with keyboard shortcuts.*

At the right edge of toolbars you can see a small drop-down arrow. When you click it, the Add or Remove Buttons menu appears. When you move the mouse over this menu, it drops down a context menu with the Customize command on it. Launching the Customize dialog from this point will navigate directly to commands of the toolbar you invoked the customization from.

## Adding Menus and Commands

In the Commands tab of the Customize dialog, you can easily create your own menus or extend the existing ones with commands. The best way to learn these options is to walk you through the creation of a custom menu.

Let's assume that you want to create a new menu named Build Tasks in order to collect all the tasks of a simple build process in one place. You intend to place this new menu in the main menu bar of Visual Studio, just before the original Build menu. When you finish the customization, the new menu will look like the one shown in Figure 5-11.

**FIGURE 5-11:** The new Build Tasks menu

## Adding a Menu to the Main Menu Bar

To create this menu, follow these steps:

**1.** Open the Customize dialog and select the Commands tab. Because you want to add the new menu to the main bar, you are in the right place within the dialog. Under the "Choose menu or Toolbar to rearrange" label, the Menu bar option is selected with the Main Menu. In the Controls list, you can see all menus that can be displayed in the main menu bar. This list contains many more menu bars than are displayed in the main menu. Certain menu bars appear only in a specific context— for example, when you edit the code or debug a project.

**2.** Select the Refactor menu in the control list and click the Add New Menu button. This action will insert a New Menu placeholder into the list just before the Refactor menu. Using the Move Down button, move this placeholder before the Build menu. Of course, if you originally selected the Build menu, the Add New Menu button would place it right at its final location.

**3.** With New Menu selected, in the list click the Modify Selection drop-down button, and then change the name to Build Tasks.

At this point, you have a new menu that does not yet contain any commands. You can close the Customize dialog and look at the main menu bar. As you see (and is shown in Figure 5-12), the new menu is dimmed. There is no command you can invoke from here.

**FIGURE 5-12:** Build Tasks is dimmed

## Adding Commands to a Menu

Now, let's add commands to the Build Tasks menu. Follow these steps:

**1.** Open the Customize dialog, and move to the Commands tab. This time, you want to add a command to the Build Tasks menu, so you must first select it from the combo box to the right to the Menu bar option. When you drop down the combo box, it displays all menus and nested submenus. Scroll down to the items starting with Project, and you will find Build Tasks nearby, just before the Build menu. As soon as you select Build Tasks, the controls list becomes empty, indicating that there are no commands associated with this menu yet.

**2.** Click the Add New Commands button to choose a command from the dialog that appears on the screen shown in Figure 5-13. There are more than a thousand commands you can choose from. The Add Command dialog helps you to find the one you are looking for by categorizing the commands.

**3.** Select Build from the Categories list, then Build Solution from the Commands list, and click OK. This new item immediately appears on the controls list.

**4.** You can change the text displayed with the command. Click the Modify Selection button and change the name to "1) Build".

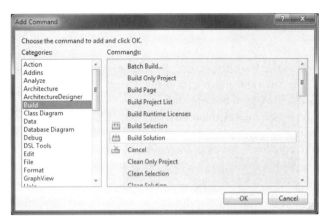

**FIGURE 5-13:** The Add Command dialog

When you close the Customize dialog, your first command is ready to run. Of course, while you do not have any solution or project loaded, the Build command will be disabled. However, when you load a solution, you can immediately try the new command to see that it works as expected.

Repeat the steps described earlier to add four more commands to the Build Tasks menu. Table 5-1 shows the category and command you should select in the Add Command dialog, as well as the name of the command to display in the menu.

**TABLE 5-1:** New Commands to Add to the Build Tasks Menu

| CATEGORY | COMMAND | NAME |
| --- | --- | --- |
| Test | Run All Tests in Solution | 2) Test |
| Analyze | Run Code Analysis on Selection | 3) Analyze |
| Analyze | Calculate Code Metrics for Solution | 4) Code Metrics |
| Debug | Start Without Debugging | 5) Start |

When you add a command, use the Move up and Move Down buttons to rearrange the buttons so that each of them will be in the right place.

Now, you are almost done. To establish the final form of the new menu, select the "2) Test" command, drop down the Modify Selection button, and check the Begin Group option to add a separator line before the command. Repeat the same for the "5) Start" button. Close the Configuration dialog. Your menu should now look similar to Figure 5-11.

## Removing Menus and Commands

If you added a command or a menu to the wrong place — for example, to another menu than the one you originally intended — you can simply remove it. Select the menu item or command in the controls list (of course, first you must select the appropriate menu that lists the command) and use the Delete button to remove it.

*Be careful. The IDE does not ask you for confirmation; it immediately removes the selected item. If you delete an item by accident, you must re-create the affected command or menu from the beginning. If you remove a predefined menu or command — for example, if you delete the File menu from the main menu bar — you can use the Reset All button to restore the original state of the menu or toolbar.*

## Adding Menus and Commands to Toolbars

You can add new commands and menus not only to the main menu bar or to one of its submenus, but also to toolbars and context menus. When you open the Customize dialog, on the Commands tab, you have three options under the "Choose a menu or toolbar to rearrange" label:

➤ *Menu bar* —You used this option in the walkthrough to add the Build Tasks menu to the main menu bar and commands to this menu.

➤ *Toolbar* — You can select any toolbars to customize or rearrange items. If you selected a toolbar from here in the previous examples, the Build Task menu with all of its newly added commands would have been added to that toolbar.

➤ *Context menu* — This option allows you to select any of the context menus to customize.

Instead of adding the Build Tasks menu to the main menu bar, you can select the "Project and Solution Context Menus | Project" item from the Context menu combo box, and place the Build Tasks commands in the controls list — exactly the same way as you did it before. Figure 5-14 shows the Build Tasks menu added to the project nodes' context menu in the Solution Explorer.

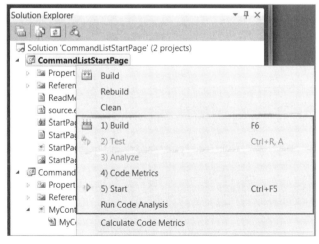

**FIGURE 5-14:** Adding custom commands to the Solution Explorer context menu

## Creating and Rearranging Toolbars

In Visual Studio, you can find two types of toolbars:

➤ *Global toolbars* — These are the toolbars that belong to the entirety of the IDE, such as the standard toolbar right below the main menu bar, the Build, Formatting, and Debug toolbars, and many more.

➤ *Tool window toolbars* — Tool windows can have their own toolbars. For example, the Output window has a toolbar where you can choose which output pane to display. You can find messages, navigate among them, and so on.

The customization is available only for the global toolbars. You cannot change or rearrange the commands in tool window toolbars. You have several options to rearrange or change the commands assigned to toolbars:

➤ Go to the Customize dialog and, on the Commands page from the combo box beside the Toolbar option, select the toolbar to change. The Controls list shows the commands assigned to the selected toolbar. You can use the Move Up and Move Down buttons to change the order of the commands. With the Modify Selection drop-down button, you can change the name of the toolbar command, set whether the text or the icon of the command should be displayed, and, with the Begin group option, you can place a separator item before the command.

➤ When you drop down the Add or Remove Buttons context menu of a specific toolbar (that is, click the small drop-down arrow belonging to the toolbar), the menu contains one item for each command. By clicking on the menu items, you can show or hide the related command on the toolbar. The tick mark to the left of the command indicates whether it is shown or hidden. Figure 5-15 shows the context menu belonging to the Debug toolbar.

**FIGURE 5-15:** The context menu of the Debug toolbar

The Toolbars tab of the Customize dialog (shown in Figure 5-9) displays all toolbars you can display in Visual Studio. Each item in the list on this tab contains a checkbox that you can check or uncheck to show or hide the related toolbar, respectively. This tab allows you more customization:

➤ Click the New button to add your own toolbar to the list. As soon as you type a non-blank name for the new toolbar in the New Toolbar dialog and click OK, the toolbar will be added to the list. You can use the Commands page to set up the command items assigned to this toolbar. You can do this customization the same way you did earlier with menu commands.

➤ Click the Delete button if you want to remove a toolbar from the list. This button is disabled for built-in toolbars, so, fortunately, you cannot delete any of them by accident. Before the toolbar is removed, you must confirm your intention.

➤ The Modify Selection drop-down button allows you to change the name of your custom toolbars. However, this function is not available for the pre-defined toolbars. This button also provides you with options to select the edge of the main window you want to dock the toolbar to. Choose one of the options (Top, Left, Bottom, Right), and the toolbar is set to the new position immediately. Of course, this option is available both for predefined and custom toolbars.

You do not have to go to the Customize dialog to show or hide a toolbar. You can control visibility through the View ➪ Toolbars menu, or with the toolbars' context menus.

## Context Sensitivity

Earlier, when you added the new menu item to the main menu, you could see that the Controls list in the Commands tab of the Customize dialog contained many items that cannot be seen when you load Visual Studio (take a look at Figure 5-10). Also, when you use Visual Studio, several toolbars are automatically displayed or hidden, depending on your activity. For example, when you start debugging an application, the Debug toolbar is automatically shown, and when you leave the debug mode, the toolbar is hidden.

The visibility of predefined toolbars may be bound (and most of them are) to so-called *UI contexts*. When the IDE enters a certain context, toolbars bound to that context are automatically displayed. As the IDE leaves that context, the toolbars get hidden again. This is the mechanism that controls, for example, the visibility of the Debug toolbar.

To add some spice to this behavior, you can "override" it during run-time by showing or hiding toolbars manually:

➤ If a toolbar is displayed when the IDE enters into a specific context, even if you leave the context, the toolbar does not get hidden. Try this scenario by showing the Debug toolbar before you start debugging. When you leave the debug mode, the Debug toolbar stays visible.

➤ If the toolbar is hidden when you leave the context it is bound to, even if the IDE enters to that context the next time, the toolbar stays hidden. Try this by hiding the Debug toolbar while debugging an application. When you start debugging again, you must manually enable the toolbar if you intend to use it.

## IDE CONFIGURATION

By now, you should have a good perspective of arranging windows in the IDE, and customizing menus, toolbars, and commands associated with them. You can configure many other things influencing the appearance and behavior of Visual Studio and the installed extensions. All of the customization techniques share several common mechanisms. In this section, you will learn more about them.

## The Options Dialog

The Options dialog box is a central place in Visual Studio 2010 to access and modify settings that influence the behavior of the IDE. It can be accessed from the Tools ➪ Options menu.

The Options dialog box is divided into two parts: a navigation pane on the left and a display area on the right. The tree control in the navigation pane includes categories (folder nodes), such as Environment, Projects and Solutions, Source Control, Text Editor, Debugging, and many more. Several categories (for example, the Text Editor) include subcategories. Expand any category node to list the pages of options it contains.

When you select the node for a particular page, its options appear in the display area. When you select a category node, the first available page node (named General, in most cases) is displayed. Figure 5-16 shows the Options dialog where the General page of the Environment category is selected.

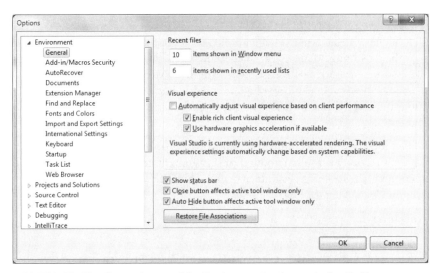

**FIGURE 5-16:** The General page of the Environment category in the Options dialog box

The content of categories and pages may vary depending on the Visual Studio 2010 edition you are using. Installed add-ins and extensibility components can also add their own categories and pages to the Options dialog. Table 5-2 summarizes the most frequently used option categories. (Note that this table is by no means complete.)

**TABLE 5-2:** Option Categories

| CATEGORY | DESCRIPTION |
| --- | --- |
| Environment | This category lists about a dozen pages that provide options to influence the general behavior of the IDE. For example, here you can set the fonts and colors used all around in the IDE, change how often auto-recover information should be saved, the way the environment should reflect to file changes outside of the IDE, and options for the "Find and Replace" dialog. Of course, this category contains many more options than enumerated here. |

| CATEGORY | DESCRIPTION |
|----------|-------------|
| Projects and Solutions | This category allows you to set up project and user template folders, as well as providing options for the Build and Run commands. You can also specify Visual Basic defaults and general Visual C++ project settings. |
| Source Control | Visual Studio can integrate with source control providers. In this category, you can select the provider you want to work with, and you can set up the selected provider's options. Also, you can influence how the environment interacts with the provider. For example, you can define whether a file should be automatically checked out when you start modifying it. |
| Text Editor | This category provides general and language-specific pages to define the behavior of the text editor in a specific context. The All Languages page defines options (such as handling tabs and indentations) that should be used globally for all languages. Language-specific pages allow you to override the global options and define language-specific options. For example, the Basic page lets you define whether End constructs should be automatically inserted into your code. |
| Debugging | This category provides six pages with almost a hundred options for configuring the debugging experience. |
| Test Tools | This category allows you configuring tools related to testing. Among the other options, you can set up the language of the default test project, define the test execution environment, and set the default actions for the dialog boxes displayed while tests are running. |

You can navigate to any page and change any settings there. When you are ready with the changes, click OK, and the Options dialog saves all settings on all pages. Clicking Cancel on any page cancels all change requests, including changes made on other pages. Some changes to option settings (such as Language settings) will only take effect after you close and restart Visual Studio. In this case, closing the Options dialog will display a message to let you know that you need to restart the IDE.

## Changes in Option Pages

Visual Studio 2010 added lots of functions to the IDE compared to the Visual Studio 2008 version. In addition to these functional enhancements, Visual Studio 2010 was built with new technologies. For example, the IDE now uses Windows Presentation Foundation (WPF) as the UI technology for most of the visual elements in the shell.

This section lists a number of the most important changes in the Options dialog as a result of either the functional enhancements or the technology improvements in Visual Studio 2010.

## Visual Experience Options

As you have learned, Visual Studio 2010 changed how document windows are handled in the IDE. While Visual Studio 2008 allowed you to select between tabbed documents and multiple documents mode (have a look at Figure 5-2), Visual Studio 2010 handles tabbed documents, and allows floating document windows with multiple monitors. These options have been removed from the General page of the Environment category.

Because of the WPF shift, the General page contains new visual experience options, as shown in Figure 5-16. These options include the following:

➤   *Automatically adjust visual experience based on client performance* — WPF is a technology that allows a rich user experience that includes such visual effects as gradients, animations, and media. This option specifies whether Visual Studio sets the adjustment to the visual experience automatically, or you set the adjustment explicitly. This adjustment may change the display of colors from gradients to flat colors, or it may restrict the use of animations in menus or pop-up windows.

➤   *Enable rich client experience* — This enables the full visual experience of Visual Studio, including gradients and animations. Clear this option when using Remote Desktop connections or older graphics adapters, because these features may result in poor performance in those cases.

➤   *Use hardware graphics acceleration if available* — WPF can leverage the hardware acceleration built into graphics adapter cards. With this option, you can declare that you want to use hardware graphics acceleration if it is available, rather than software acceleration. As shown in Figure 5-16, the page always displays a message below this option that tells you whether Visual Studio is using software or hardware acceleration.

## Extension Manager Page

As discussed in Chapter 2, the extension installation experience in Visual Studio 2010 has been radically changed. The new Extension Manager dialog now shows available online extensions that are regularly updated, and these can be installed with a single click of a button.

The Environment category contains a new page, Extension Manager, where you can set up the behavior of this dialog.

As shown in Figure 5-17, you can use the following options:

➤   *Enable access to extensions on the Visual Studio Gallery* — This option is checked by default. It allows you to browse, download, and install extensions within the Extension Manager dialog. If the checkbox is unchecked, you cannot browse the Gallery. Instead, a message warns you that you must first enable this option.

➤   *Automatically check for updates to installed extensions* — The VSIX deployment mechanism used in Visual Studio 2010 recognizes that a new extension is an update of an old one. If you check this option, the Extension Manager will automatically search the Visual Studio Gallery to discover available updates for your installed extensions.

➤   *Load per-user extensions when running as administrator* — Extensions are installed on a per-user basis. This option controls whether the per-user extensions should be loaded when you start Visual Studio in elevated mode (with the "Run as Administrator" command). If this option is unchecked, all extensions are disabled in elevated mode. The Extension Manager will list those extensions, but does not integrate them with the IDE. This option can be changed only in elevated mode.

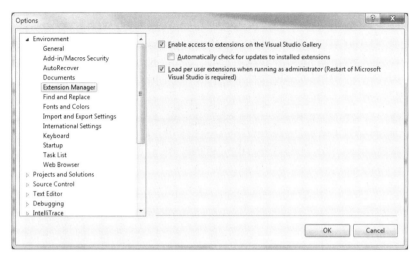

**FIGURE 5-17:** The Extension Manager options page

## Projects and Solutions

In Visual Studio 2010, the Visual C++ project system (that is, the behavior of Visual C++ projects in the Solution Explorer, the related functionality, such as build, configuration, and deployment) has been fundamentally changed. The VC++ Directories page under the "Projects and Solutions" category has been deprecated. Of course, developers can still set the C++ directories, but now these options can be accessed on a user property sheet that is added by default to all C++ projects. To access this page, you must click on the Properties item in the context menu of a C++ project.

## Text Editor

Because of the new Visual Studio editor, and changes in languages, there have been slight changes in the Text Editor category. These include the following:

➤ Two options ("Go to selection anchor after escape" and "Include insertion point movements in Undo list") have been dropped from the General page. They are no longer supported in Visual Studio 2010.

➤ Because F# has become a standard part of Visual Studio 2010 (assuming, of course, that you did not uncheck the F# language option when installing Visual Studio), the Text Editor category now contains a page for F#.

➤ The Basic category contains a new option in the VB Specific page — the "Enable highlighting of references and keywords" checkbox. When you check it, the text editor can highlight all instances of a symbol, or all of the keywords in a clause, such as `If..Then`, `While...End While,` or `Try...Catch...Finally`. You can navigate between highlighted references or keywords by pressing Ctrl+Shift+down arrow or Ctrl+Shift+up arrow.

➤  Visual Studio 2008 included several pages related to Transact-SQL scripts (SQL Script, T-SQL, TSQL7, T-SQL80, and T-SQL90). In Visual Studio 2010, the language services behind Transact-SQL changed, and you can configure them on the SQLCE, Transact-SQL, and T-SQL90 pages.

## Visual Studio Settings

When you tailor the IDE to fit your needs, the current set of configuration values is persisted. So, the next time you launch Visual Studio, your settings are retrieved. There are many things you can configure in Visual Studio, including tool windows, menus and toolbars, IDE options, keyboard shortcuts, the Toolbox, and many more.

Visual Studio provides several persistence mechanisms. For example, it stores the window layout in XML files, as well as the toolbar and menu settings in a binary file. The term "Visual Studio Settings" is cumbersome and has the following two interpretations:

➤  All settings in Visual Studio that you can configure anywhere in the IDE.

➤  The set of configuration values that can be saved to Visual Studio Settings files and load from them — that is, the configuration you can change in the Options dialog, as shown in Figure 5-18.

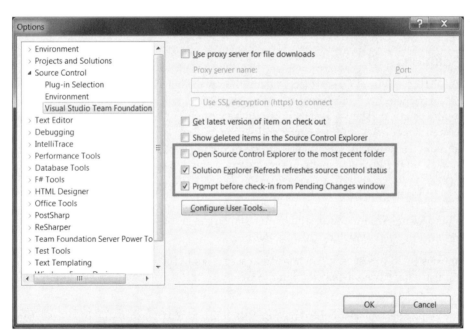

**FIGURE 5-18:** Options dialog

In articles, whitepapers, and Visual Studio documentation, these interpretations are not explained very well, and sometimes it is not clear what is meant by "settings." This section uses the second interpretation — and this is the one mostly used in MSDN documentation.

*For the easiest interpretation, you can put an equals sign between "Visual Studio Settings" and "configuration values set in the Options dialog." However, the IDE allows persisting settings that you cannot find in the Options dialog, such as the Code Analysis settings. Extensions integrated with Visual Studio also can provide persisted settings that cannot be modified in the Options dialog.*

## The Export and Import Settings Wizard

Visual Studio settings can be saved to files, and those files can be loaded into Visual Studio 2010 — even into an instance running on another machine, or into another user profile. This functionality allows you to manage settings, and use them for a number of purposes:

➤ You can back up the settings you currently use. Later, after changing the settings intentionally or accidentally, you can import the saved settings and restore the former state.

➤ You can save and load a part of the current settings. For example, if you want to store (and later restore) only the "Fonts and Colors" settings, you can do it.

➤ You can move settings from one computer to another. For example, you can manually synchronize the Visual Studio settings between your company notebook and home computer.

➤ Settings can be shared among a team of Visual Studio users — for example, among team members involved into the same software development project.

The key to settings management is the Import and Export Setting Wizard that you can access from the Tools menu. When the wizard starts, it offers you three options on its Welcome page, as shown in Figure 5-19.

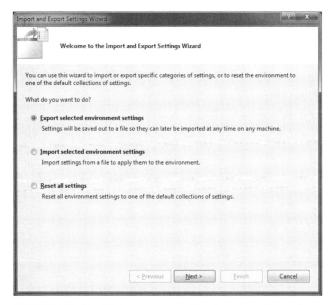

**FIGURE 5-19:** The Welcome page of the Export and Import Settings Wizard

You can use the following options:

➤ Export all environment settings or a selected subset of them into a `.vssettings` file.

➤ Import all settings from a saved `.vssettings` file, or a subset of settings saved into that file.

➤ Reset all settings by selecting one from the default collections of settings shipped with Visual Studio.

## Exporting Settings

To save the current settings, choose the "Export selected environment settings" option in the Welcome page and click Next. The wizard moves you to the "Choose Settings to Export" page, where you can define the subset of settings to export. By default, all settings except the "Import and Export Settings" are selected, but you can change this definition by checking and unchecking items in the tree view.

You can expand the nodes in the tree and select or unselect settings under any folder node. Figure 5-20 shows a configuration where only the "Fonts and Colors" settings are chosen to export.

Once you have defined the settings to export, click Next to move to the "Name Your Settings file" page. Specify the name of your settings file and the folder where you want to save that file. Click Finish. The Wizard exports the file immediately. It creates a

**FIGURE 5-20:** The "Choose Settings to Export" page

default filename for you that contains the date, but you can overwrite it. The default extension of the file is `.vssettings`. If you omit the extension, the Wizard appends it to the filename.

## Importing Settings

You can import the saved settings by choosing the "Import selected environment settings" option on the Welcome page. Click Next, and you get to the Save Current Settings page, where you can specify a folder and a file to save a backup of the current settings.

Although this page allows you to skip creating a backup file (as Figure 5-21 shows), it is always recommended to create a backup. Once you have imported a `.vssettings` file, the only real rollback option is to re-import the backup file. Otherwise, you must manually configure each setting that does not meet your expectations — and this reconfiguration can be laborious and painful.

**FIGURE 5-21:** The Save Current Settings page

Click Next to move to the "Choose a Collection of Settings to Import" page shown in Figure 5-22. The tree view on this page displays the collection of default settings files shipped with Visual Studio. Under the My Settings folder node, you see your recently used .vssettings files. By clicking the Browse button, you can select any other files to import. You can select any files with a valid settings file schema, even if those do not have the .vssettings extensions in their names.

When you have selected the settings file, click Next to move to the "Choose Settings to Import" page. This page follows the same logic as the "Choose Settings to Export" page (Figure 5-20), but here you can select a subset of the settings persisted in the chosen file. Click Finish to create the optional backup file and import the selected setting.

**FIGURE 5-22:** The "Choose a Collection of Settings to Import" page

## Reset All Settings

The third option you can choose in the Export and Import Settings Wizard lets you reset all settings to one of the predefined profiles. The use of this option is very similar to the import option. In the first step ("Save Current Settings page"), you can specify an optional backup file. In the second step, you can choose a default collection of settings (profile). When you click Finish, the backup file is created (assuming you have specified one), and settings are reset to the selected profile.

## Export and Import Options

In the Options dialog box, you can specify a few options that influence how Visual Studio handles setting files:

➤ *Automatically save my settings to this file* — This textbox displays the location and name of the .vssettings file you are currently using. When you close the IDE, any changes you have made (such as environment options or debugger and text editor settings) are saved to the current file. The next time you start the IDE, your settings are loaded. Change this textbox if you want to save these settings to a different file or location

➤ *Use team settings file* — When this checkbox is selected, you can share common settings (which are saved to a shared network location) among team members. You can navigate to this shared .vssettings file using the Browse button. This settings file is automatically re-applied each time Visual Studio detects whether a newer version of the file is available.

## Looking into the .vssettings Files

By now, you can imagine what kinds of settings are stored in a `.vssettings` file. This file has an XML format (unfortunately its schema is not published), and looking into it gives you hints about how Visual Studio stores the settings you've saved. The following code snippet shows an extract from a `.vssettings` file:

```
<UserSettings>
  <ApplicationIdentity version="10.0"/>
  <ToolsOptions>
    <ToolsOptionsCategory name="Environment" RegisteredName="Environment">
      <ToolsOptionsSubCategory name="Documents" RegisteredName="Documents"
          PackageName="Visual Studio Environment Package">
        <PropertyValue name="ShowMiscFilesProject">true</PropertyValue>
        <PropertyValue name="AutoloadExternalChanges">false</PropertyValue>
        <PropertyValue name="CheckForConsistentLineEndings">true</PropertyValue>
        <PropertyValue name="SaveDocsAsUnicodeWhenDataLoss">false</PropertyValue>
        <PropertyValue name="InitializeOpenFileFromCurrentDocument">true
            </PropertyValue>
        <PropertyValue name="ReuseSavedActiveDocWindow">false</PropertyValue>
        <PropertyValue name="DetectFileChangesOutsideIDE">true</PropertyValue>
        <PropertyValue name="DontShowGlobalUndoChangeLossDialog">true
            </PropertyValue>
        <PropertyValue name="AllowEditingReadOnlyFiles">true</PropertyValue>
        <PropertyValue name="DocumentDockPreference">0</PropertyValue>
        <PropertyValue name="MiscFilesProjectSavesLastNItems">0</PropertyValue>
      </ToolsOptionsSubCategory>
      <ToolsOptionsSubCategory name="FindAndReplace" RegisteredName=
          "FindAndReplace" PackageName="Visual Studio Environment
          Package">
        <PropertyValue name="ShowWarningMessages">true</PropertyValue>
        <PropertyValue name="InitializeFromEditor">true</PropertyValue>
        <PropertyValue name="ShowMessageBoxes">true</PropertyValue>
        <PropertyValue name="HideWindowAfterMatchFromQuickFindReplace">
            false</PropertyValue>
      </ToolsOptionsSubCategory>
      <!-- ... -->
    </ToolsOptionsCategory>
  </ToolsOptions>
  <!-- ... -->
</UserSettings>
```

If you look closely, you can recognize several categories, pages, and settings in the Options dialog. The `<ToolsOptions>`, `<ToolsOptionsCategory>`, and `<ToolsOptionsSubCategory>` elements form the page hierarchy within the Options dialog. `<PropertyValue>` elements define settings you can manage in a page.

You can find the `.vssettings` files for predefined profiles under the Visual Studio 2010 installation directory in the `Common7\IDE\Profiles` folder. You should take the time to examine these files to get more information about settings.

# REDUCING EFFORTS WITH KEYBOARD SHORTCUTS

Visual Studio has many commands that you can start from the menus or toolbars of the IDE. Although, you can launch all commands by moving the mouse pointer and clicking the appropriate menu or toolbar item, in many cases, this may be disturbing because you must interrupt your work. For example, when you edit code and want to comment out a block of instructions, you must follow these steps:

1. Even if the caret is at the beginning of the block to uncomment, you must move the mouse to the caret position, click the left mouse button, and hold it down while selecting the whole text.

2. Move your mouse over the Edit main menu item, and click on it.

3. Locate the Advanced item in the Edit menu, and move the mouse over it (or click it). The Advanced menu items are displayed on the screen.

4. Click the Comment Selection item.

The real issue with these steps is that you must raise your hand from the keyboard, find the mouse, look at the screen, and press mouse buttons several times; so you are interrupted in your typing of code.

You are not obliged to use the mouse! Press the Shift+down arrow keys and keep them pressed while all the lines to comment out are selected. Then, simply press Ctrl+K and then Ctrl+C, and you are ready. There is no need to remove your hands from the keyboard, and no need to use the mouse. The Ctrl+K, Ctrl+C key sequence is a shortcut to the Edit ➪ Advanced ➪ Comment Selection command.

This was just a very simple example of how useful keyboard shortcuts are. Many commands have shortcuts associated with them. You may find some of them are easy to remember, while some of them are difficult to use — depending on how often and in which context you use them.

The IDE allows you full control over the keyboard shortcuts assigned to commands. You can tailor them to your fit needs and to reduce the efforts required to carry out the most frequently used tasks.

## Command Routing and Command Contexts

There are more than a thousand commands available in Visual Studio 2010. You can imagine how difficult it is to find a keyboard shortcut for each of them (and even much more challenging to learn them by heart). There is no reason to make this full mapping, because many commands are very rarely used. If you counted the commands you frequently use while working in the IDE, you'd end up with a few dozen commands, but no more. By Pareto's principle, you should assign shortcuts to the most frequently used 20 percent of these commands to improve your productivity by 80 percent.

 *During installation, Visual Studio 2010 applies a default shortcut key combination scheme, depending on the settings you have selected. Visual Studio 2010 also includes six other keyboard mapping schemes, each of which differs from the others in the shortcut key combinations assigned by default to various UI elements. For a list of these combinations, organized by mapping scheme, see "Pre-defined Keyboard Shortcuts" at* `http://msdn.microsoft.com/en-us/library/da5kh0wa.aspx`.

Commands in Visual Studio are tightly coupled with command targets (entities that know how to interpret and execute a command in a certain context). For example, the Cut, Copy, and Paste commands work differently in certain contexts. If you are in the text editor, the Copy command copies the current selection. If you use the WPF designer, the currently selected object is copied. The text editor and the WPF designer are both *command targets*, and they know what to do when the Copy command is sent to them.

Visual Studio uses a routing algorithm to forward commands to the command targets. Instead of getting into all the nitty-gritty details of this algorithm, this discussion simply provides a high-level overview.

In the route to find its command target, the command bubbles up from level to level. The current level is called the *active command scope*. This scope has the chance to handle the command or to refuse it, and then the bubble goes on its way. The routing algorithm defines the following scopes from the leaves to the root:

➤ *Present Add-ins and special extensions (Visual Studio Packages) scope* — Commands first are offered to the registered and loaded add-ins, or specially registered Visual Studio Packages.

➤ *Context (shortcut) menus scope* — If the user initiates a command from a context menu, the command target object belonging to this menu has the first chance to handle the command. If it does not, then the normal route (starting from Present Add-Ins) is applied.

➤ *Focus window scope* — The window having the focus is the next entity that could undertake command handling. This can be either a tool window or a document window (for example, a window related to an editor). The management of the command is different depending on what kind of window is focused.

    ➤ *Document window scope* — Document windows are composed logically from two separate parts: a document view that is responsible for displaying the UI representing the document, and a document data object that is responsible for handling the information set behind the document. Both the document view and the document data can be command targets. The command first goes to the document view, and goes on to the document data if the view does not support the command.

    ➤ *Tool window scope* — A tool window can handle the command with its own logic. There are tool windows that route the commands within themselves to nested command targets. The Solution Explorer window is an example of these. Within Solution Explorer, a command is routed according to the hierarchy composed from the elements of the Solution Explorer where each node type (file, folder, project, solution, and so on) has the capability to handle the command. This internal route also goes from the lower hierarchy levels to the upper ones.

➤ *Current project scope* — The current project gets the opportunity to process the command. If it does not handle it, the command goes up in the hierarchy of projects to the level of solution. All nodes on this route can manage the command just like other command target objects.

➤ *Global scope* — If a command is not handled during the previous levels, the environment attempts to route it to the appropriate package (Visual Studio extension). If necessary, Visual Studio loads the appropriate package into memory.

Commands with shortcut key combinations that are part of the Global scope can be superseded by commands in other scopes, depending on the current context of the IDE. For example, if you are editing a file, commands that are part of the Text Editor scope have precedence over commands in the Global scope that start with the same key combination. For example, if several Global commands have key combinations that start with Ctrl + K and the Text Editor also has several commands with key combinations that start with Ctrl + K, when you are editing code the Text Editor key combinations will work, and the Global key combinations will be ignored.

## Working with Keyboard Shortcuts

The Keyboard page under the Environment category in the Tools ➪ Options dialog is your starting point for managing keyboard shortcuts. This page contains every piece of information you need to do the following:

➤   Determine the shortcut key assigned to a command

➤   Change shortcut keys of commands

➤   Create new custom shortcut keys

Figure 5-23 shows the Keyboard page displaying information about the `Edit.CommentSelection` command.

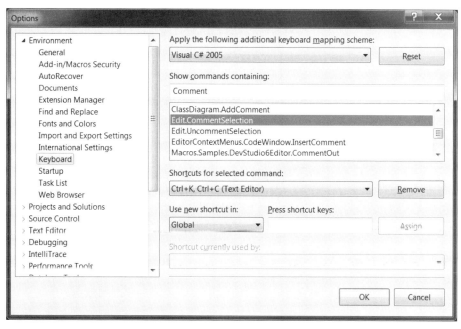

**FIGURE 5-23:** The Keyboard option page

The combo box at the top of the page lets you choose the keyboard mapping scheme to use while working in the IDE. If you click the Reset button, you can reset the mapping schemes to their initial state.

The list in the middle of the page enumerates all Visual Studio commands available for keyboard shortcut assignment. This list is very long, so finding commands by scrolling would be laborious. You can use the textbox above the list to type a part of the command name, and the list will be filled only with the command names matching your search definition.

Under the list box, you will see several controls that help you determine if there is any shortcut key associated with the command, and these controls also help you to define shortcuts for the selected command.

## Determine the Shortcut Key Assigned to a Command

The main menu of the Visual Studio IDE displays the keyboard shortcuts to the right of the menu item names, so you can easily find which shortcut to use for a specific command. However, there are commands that are either not visible in the main menu, or it is difficult to locate them. With the Keyboard page you can find the associated shortcut for any commands.

Type a part of the command name into the text box over the command list to help you locate a command in the list. Figure 5-23 shows how the "Comment" word helps to locate the `Edit. CommentSelection` command.

Directly below the list box, you can see the combo box showing the keyboard shortcuts associated with the command. You can associate zero, one, or more keyboard shortcuts with each command. If there is no shortcut assigned to the command, the combo box is disabled. You can drop down the combo box to display all shortcuts belonging to the command. For example, when you select the `Edit.Paste` command, the list contains two items, Ctrl+V and Shift+Ins, both defined in the Global scope.

The list shows the keys you must press to invoke the command, and shows the name of the scope the shortcut is associated with. Figure 5-23 shows that the `Edit.CommentSelection` command has a keyboard shortcut in the Text Editor scope (Ctrl+K, Ctrl+C). You can use up to two keystrokes for a shortcut.

## Removing a Shortcut

You can remove a shortcut easily. Select the one you want to delete from the combo box of shortcuts, and click the Remove button. The selected item will be removed from the list without any confirmation question. When you remove every item, the combo box and the Remove button are disabled, indicating that no more shortcuts are associated with the command.

## Creating a New Keyboard Shortcut

In most cases, you would like to assign a new keyboard shortcut to a command because of the following reasons:

➤ The command does not have any shortcuts yet.

➤ You would like to change an existing shortcut, or add another shortcut for the same command.

➤ You would like to override the shortcut defined in the Global scope.

Each of these can be handled with the "Use new shortcut in" combo box and the "Press shortcut keys" text box.

First, select the scope from the "Use New shortcut in" combo. In most cases, you want to use the Global or Text Editor scopes, but you can see that there are many other scopes to define a shortcut for. Next, click on the "Press shortcut keys" text box, and press one or two keys (key combinations) to associate with the command. The keys with the modifiers will be displayed in the text box.

> *Shortcuts can contain the Shift, Alt, and/or Ctrl keys in combination with letters, digits, function keys, or several symbols. Although you can use the Shift+Alt+Ctrl combination with a functional key, it is not recommended, because you must press and hold down four keys at the same time.*
>
> *The following keys cannot be assigned to a command in Global scope: Print Scrn/Sys Rq, Scroll Lock, Pause/Break, Tab, Caps Lock, Insert, Home, End, Page Up, Page Down, Windows logo keys, Application key, any of the arrow keys, or Enter; Num Lock, Del, or Clear on the numeric keypad; or Ctrl+Alt+Delete.*

You may select a key combination that is already assigned to another command (or even to more commands in different scopes). The "Shortcut currently used by" combo box displays every collision. You can find all of them by dropping down the list.

Click the Assign button to associate the new keyboard shortcut with the selected command. When the shortcut is already assigned to another command in the same scope where you define it, the previous association is removed, and the shortcut will belong to the new command.

> *Generally, the Options dialog does not save any changes when you close it with the Cancel button. However, the Keyboard page immediately saves the changes in a keyboard scheme as soon as you click the Assign button. So, changes made using the Assign button are not cancelled if you click the Cancel button.*

## Using the Keyboard Exclusively

Earlier in this chapter, you learned about the window management features of the IDE. Many features (such as moving, docking, auto-hiding, and showing windows) selecting the active document were treated there, so you may be thinking that you need the mouse for those actions. However, you can access all features treated there by using the keyboard exclusively.

You can move the focus to any of the tool windows or the document windows. You have two key combinations that allow you change the active window:

➤ *Alt+F7* — This key combination cycles the focus among tool windows.

➤ *Ctrl+Tab* — This key combination cyclically changes the active document window.

Press any of the keys, and the focus goes to the next tool or document window, depending on the key combination you use.

You can use the following combinations in enhanced mode:

➤ Press one of the combinations (Alt+F7 or Ctrl+Tab), and release the functional key (F7 or Tab), but keep the modifier key (Alt or Ctrl) pressed.

➤ A pop-up window appears in the center of the main window (shown in Figure 5-24) that helps you navigate among the tool windows and documents.

➤ Press F7 or Tab to move to the next window in the list, and release the Alt or Ctrl keys when the selection is on the window you want the focus to move to.

In addition to changing the focus, you can move and dock windows. First, set the focus to the window you want to move and/or dock, using the Alt+F7 or Ctrl+Tab key combinations as described earlier. Then, press Alt+Space and use the arrow keys to navigate to the Move command in the window menu. Press Enter.

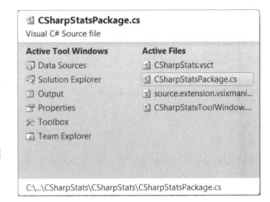

**FIGURE 5-24:** Pop-up window helping navigation among tool and document windows

Now you can use the arrow keys to move the floating window. As you move the window, the mouse pointer follows the window. After the first keystroke, the guiding icons appear on the screen. When you move the mouse pointer over any guiding icon (of course, with the arrow keys, and not with the mouse), you can see where the floating window gets docked. Press Enter to dock the window to the indicated position (or release it in the current position).

You can press Esc any time to abort the operation.

## Working with Keyboard Mapping Schemes

When Visual Studio is installed, it sets up five keyboard mapping scheme files that can be found under the Visual Studio installation root in the `Common7\IDE folder` with the `.vsk` extension. These are binary files that represent how shortcuts are associated with commands in that particular scheme:

➤ `Visual Basic 6.vsk`

➤ `Visual C# 2005.vsk`

➤ `Visual C++ 2.vsk`

➤ `Visual C++ 6.vsk`

➤ `Visual Studio 6.vsk`

You can find these filenames in the combo box at the top of the Keyboard options page. When you select a keyboard mapping scheme, the IDE uses the combinations found in the selected mapping scheme.

When you create shortcut keys for commands, they are stored as changes related to the shortcuts defined in the selected scheme. Later, when you reset the scheme, the changes you have already applied are simply removed.

## Exporting and Importing Keyboard Mapping Schemes

Earlier in this chapter, you learned about exporting and importing settings. The shortcuts you define in the Keyboard page of the Options dialog are the part of the exported set by default. If you want to export only the keyboard mappings, you must select only the Keyboard item on the "Choose Settings to Export" page of the Import and Export Settings Wizard.

## Keyboard Shortcuts in the Settings File

When you export the keyboard mappings, the `.vssettings` file contains only the differences (removed and newly created shortcuts) you have applied to the selected mapping scheme.

Let's take a look at an example to see what that means. Follow these steps:

**1.** On the Keyboard options page, select the Visual C# 2005 mapping scheme and click on Reset.

**2.** Add a new Text Editor shortcut for the `Edit.CommentSelection` command (let's say, Ctrl+Q, Ctrl+C).

**3.** Remove the Ctrl+C shortcut defined in the Global scope from the `Edit.Copy` command.

**4.** Export the mapping scheme with the Export and Import Settings Wizard to a location you can remember.

**5.** Open the saved `.vssettings` file in Visual Studio 2010 to examine it.

Listing 5-1 shows an extract of the `.vssettings` file.

**LISTING 5-1:** Keyboard Settings Persisted

```
<UserSettings>
  <ApplicationIdentity version="10.0"/>
  <ToolsOptions>
    <ToolsOptionsCategory name="Environment" RegisteredName="Environment"/>
  </ToolsOptions>
  <Category name="Database Tools" RegisteredName="Database Tools"/>
  <Category name="Environment_Group" RegisteredName="Environment_Group">
    <Category name="Environment_KeyBindings"
       Category="{F09035F1-80D2-4312-8EC4-4D354A4BCB4C}"
       Package="{DA9FB551-C724-11d0-AE1F-00A0C90FFFC3}"
       RegisteredName="Environment_KeyBindings"
       PackageName="Visual Studio Environment Package">
       <Version>10.0.0.0</Version>
       <KeyboardShortcuts>
         <ScopeDefinitions>
           <!-- ... -->
           <Scope Name="Text Editor" ID="{8B382828-6202-11D1-8870-0000F87579D2}"/>
```

*continues*

**LISTING 5-1** (*continued*)

```
        <!-- ... -->
        <Scope Name="Global" ID="{5EFC7975-14BC-11CF-9B2B-00AA00573819}"/>
        <Scope Name="Class Diagram" ID="{59B0B277-7DDF-4E36-A3ED-02DAC5B9E2FA}"/>
        <Scope Name="UML Activity Diagram" ID=
            "{950C3878-B510-4BC5-9051-42798A870364}"/>
        <Scope Name="UML Use Case Diagram" ID=
            "{FCFECC7C-3151-4B48-A85A-909F50500A70}"/>
        <!-- ... -->
      </ScopeDefinitions>
      <DefaultShortcuts/>
      <ShortcutsScheme>Visual C# 2005</ShortcutsScheme>
      <UserShortcuts>
        <Shortcut Command="Edit.CommentSelection"
          Scope="Text Editor">Ctrl+Q, Ctrl+C</Shortcut>
        <RemoveShortcut Command="Edit.Copy"
          Scope="Global">Ctrl+C</RemoveShortcut>
      </UserShortcuts>
    </KeyboardShortcuts>
  </Category>
 </Category>
</UserSettings>
```

Without understanding all the details in this listing, you can immediately recognize a few elements in this file. The `<ShortcutsScheme>` element names the keyboard mapping scheme used on the Keyboard options page. The `<UserShortcuts>` element encapsulates the changes you have applied to the scheme. In this file, it has two child nodes:

➤ `<Shortcut>` describes the new mapping you have added to the `Edit.CommentSelection` command.

➤ `<RemoveShortcut>` names the Ctrl+C key you have removed from the `Edit.Copy` command.

The file contains a `<ScopeDefinitions>` section that enumerates all scopes you can associate a keyboard shortcut with. Most of the definitions are omitted from this listing, but the remaining ones tell you their structure. Each scope definition has a name displayed on the Keyboard options page, and each has an identifier used in the Visual Studio IDE to track the scope.

## CUSTOM START PAGES

The first Visual Studio version released in February 2002 introduced the concept of the Start Page. When you launch Visual Studio, the Start Page appears and offers you a few options, such as creating a new project, opening one of your recent projects, reading the latest news, getting some guidance, and so on.

The format and content of the Start Page changed with each new Visual Studio version. Debates about the content of the Start Page have been ongoing in the community, with some finding it useful, while others suggesting changes. The Visual Studio Start Page was customizable already in its first version. At that time, so-called Tab Definition files with a well-defined XML schema were used to describe custom-defined portions of the page.

Visual Studio 2010 puts more emphasis on the Start Page and its customization. For example, it provides you two checkboxes at the bottom-left corner of the page to let you decide whether you want to display the Start Page at all. You can declare that you always want to close the page right after you load a project.

Instead of simply customizing the Start Page installed with Visual Studio 2010, you can define additional Start Pages and select which one you would like to use. Start the Tools ➪ Options dialog and go to the Startup option page under the Environment category, as shown in Figure 5-25.

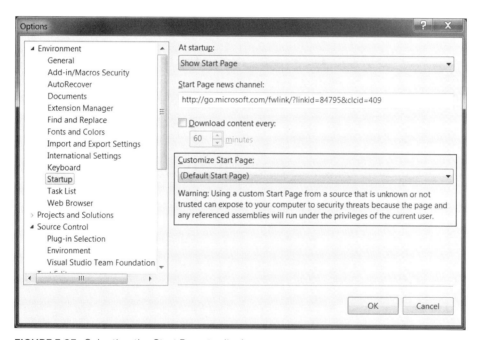

**FIGURE 5-25:** Selecting the Start Page to display

Locate the Customize Start Page combo box that provides a list of installed Start Pages, and you can see that it contains only the default one unless you add some more.

The designers of the new Visual Studio Shell changed the internal implementation of the Start Page. Now, the Start Page is a WPF Grid control; it is defined by a XAML file. If you want to define your own Start Page, you simply create your own XAML file and deploy it for Visual Studio 2010.

## Creating Your First Custom Start Page

Creating your own Start Page requires writing a Visual Studio extension and integrating it with the IDE — similar to the way you installed Visual Studio templates in Chapter 4. However, although you could create templates immediately after installing Visual Studio, Start Page development requires the Visual Studio 2010 SDK.

*Chapter 6 discusses in detail the Visual Studio SDK, and shows several examples of its application, including Visual Studio Packages and Editor extensions. You can download Visual Studio 2010 SDK through the Visual Studio Development Center (*http://msdn.com/vsx*). It is about 12 MB. Its installation is straightforward and takes about two minutes.*

Microsoft created a Visual Studio project template to develop Start Pages. This template can be found among the online templates. The first time you want to create a project with this template, select the File ➪ New ➪ Project command to display the New Project dialog. Click the Online Templates tab and select the Visual Studio Extensions category. In this category, you can locate the Custom Start Page Project Template, as shown in Figure 5-26.

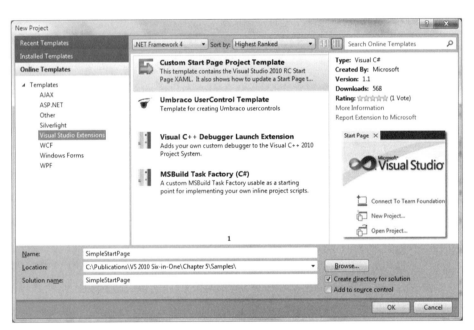

**FIGURE 5-26:** Locating the Custom Start Page Project Template

Name the project SimpleStartPage. When you click OK, Visual Studio downloads the project template and starts installing it, asking you for a confirmation. After you confirm the installation, the project is created. The next time you want to create a Start Page, you'll find the template under the Installed Template tab, so you do not have to download it again.

Build and run the project without debugging by pressing Ctrl+F5. When you start it, a new instance of Visual Studio (the Experimental Instance) is launched, and it uses the default Start Page. Go to Tools ➪ Options and select the Startup option page under the Environment category, as shown in Figure 5-25. Now, drop down the Customize Start Page combo box and select the "[Installed Extension] SimpleStartPage" item. When you click OK, the page is changed to the new one that is implemented by the SimpleStartPage project, as shown in Figure 5-27.

**FIGURE 5-27:** The new Start Page

The new Start Page is a clone of the default one and adds a new information tab (MyControl) to the existing ones. Close the Experimental Instance and go back to the project source code to look at its structure.

## The Structure of the Start Page Solution

When you develop a new Start Page, you can create it from the scratch and use something totally different from the default one, or (and this is the recommended way) add your own tabs to the existing ones. The Custom Start Page Project Template uses the second approach.

The solution it creates contains two projects. The first one (SimpleStartPage) contains the Start Page with its XAML definition and all accessories that allow it to deploy as a Visual Studio Extension. The second project (SimpleStartPageControl) defines a WPF user control that is used on the MyControl tab of the Start Page. Figure 5-28 shows the entire solution structure.

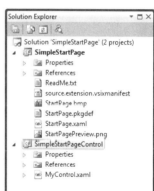

**FIGURE 5-28:** Start Page Solution Structure

Table 5-3 summarizes the roles of the most important files in the solution.

**TABLE 5-3:** The Start Page Solution Structure Files

| FILE | DESCRIPTION |
| --- | --- |
| Readme.txt | This file contains a brief explanation and description of running and deploying the solution. |
| source.extension.vsixmanifest | This file defines the deployment manifest information that is used during the installation of the extension. |
| StartPage.bmp | This file contains the icon representing the extension in the Extension Manager, and on the Visual Studio Gallery. |
| StartPage.pkgdef | This file describes the information to be merged into the registry during deployment. |
| StartPage.xaml | This XAML file defines the visual appearance of the start page. It is a clone of the default Start Page that adds a new MyControl information tab to be customized. |
| StartPagePreview.png | This file contains the preview image representing the extension in the Extension Manager, and on the Visual Studio Gallery. |
| MyControl.xaml<br>MyControl.xaml.cs | These files can be found in the SimpleStartPageControl project. They define the WPF user control representing the MyControl tab. |

In addition to these source files, the two projects of the solution reference a few assemblies. Table 5-4 summarizes their roles and descriptions.

**TABLE 5-4:** The Start Page Solution Structure Assemblies

| ASSEMBLY | DESCRIPTION |
| --- | --- |
| Microsoft.VisualStudio.Shell.10.0 | This assembly is shipped with Visual Studio 2010 SDK. It contains types and resources related to the new Visual Studio 2010 shell. Both projects reference this assembly, and use it to access shell-related resources (such as predefined pens and brushes to draw the UI of the IDE). |
| Microsoft.VisualStudio.Shell.StartPage | This assembly is shipped with Visual Studio 2010 SDK. Types and resources defined here are to be used in the Start Page. For example, this assembly contains a definition for MruListBox to display the recently used projects, or image resources used in the Start Page. |

| ASSEMBLY | DESCRIPTION |
|---|---|
| UIAutomationProvider, UIAutomationTypes | These two assemblies are used to create UI automation providers so that UI controls can be accessed not only through human interaction, but also through automation objects. In the default source code generated by the Custom Start Page Template, these assemblies are not used. |

## The Definition of the Start Page

The StartPage.xaml file in the SimpleStartPage project defines the essence of the Start Page. You can see that StartPage.xaml does not have a code-behind file, and its Build Action property is set to Content. The reason is that Visual Studio will load and parse the XAML file on-the-fly at startup time, and not its binary representation from the SimpleStartPage assembly.

Of course, that does not mean you cannot assign code to the StartPage.xaml, but you must do it so that the page uses some user-defined controls implemented in external assemblies. The code you intend to use should be placed into these external assemblies. The template follows this pattern; you can add code to the MyControl WPF user control class located in the SimpleStartPageControl assembly.

Open the StartPage.xaml file by double-clicking it in the Solution Explorer. If you have not compiled the solution yet, the XAML editor may warn you that it cannot display the preview of the page in the WPF Designer. After building the solution, you can reload the page.

The first thing you can observe is that the style of the page is different from the one you can see in the live Start Page. The cause of this phenomenon is that styles in the XAML file reference resources defined by Visual Studio. The Start Page must be loaded in the context of a running Visual Studio instance so that those styles can be accessed.

The structure of the XAML definition is simple, as the extract in Listing 5-2 shows.

**LISTING 5-2:** StartPage.xaml (Extract)

Available for download on Wrox.com

```
<Grid
    xmlns="http://schemas.microsoft.com/winfx/2006/xaml/presentation"
    xmlns:x="http://schemas.microsoft.com/winfx/2006/xaml"
    xmlns:sp="clr-namespace:Microsoft.VisualStudio.PlatformUI;
      assembly=Microsoft.VisualStudio.Shell.StartPage"
    xmlns:vs="clr-namespace:Microsoft.VisualStudio.PlatformUI;
      assembly=Microsoft.VisualStudio.Shell.10.0"
    xmlns:vsfx="clr-namespace:Microsoft.VisualStudio.Shell;
      assembly=Microsoft.VisualStudio.Shell.10.0"
    xmlns:my="clr-namespace:SimpleStartPageControl;
      assembly=SimpleStartPageControl"
    mc:Ignorable="d"
```

*continues*

**LISTING 5-2** *(continued)*

```
xmlns:d="http://schemas.microsoft.com/expression/blend/2008"
xmlns:mc="http://schemas.openxmlformats.org/markup-compatibility/2006"
d:DesignHeight="600"
d:DesignWidth="800">

<Grid.Resources>
  <ResourceDictionary>
    <ResourceDictionary.MergedDictionaries>
      <ResourceDictionary Source="/Microsoft.VisualStudio.Shell.StartPage;
        component/Styles/startpageresources.xaml" />
    </ResourceDictionary.MergedDictionaries>
  </ResourceDictionary>
</Grid.Resources>

<Grid x:Name="LayoutRoot"
  Background="{DynamicResource {x:Static vsfx:VsBrushes.StartPageBackgroundKey}}"
  Style="{DynamicResource StartPage.OuterGridStyle}">
  <!-- Grid definition omitted -->
</Grid>
</Grid>
```

*Code file [StartPage.xaml] available for download at Wrox.com*

The most eye-catching thing in the listing is that its root element is a `Grid` and not a `Window`, a `Page`, or a `UserControl` element. This `Grid` is a container holding the resources and defining the layout of the Start Page. As you can see from the attributes of the opening `Grid` tag, it defines `xmlns` tags for a few namespaces used by the referenced assemblies summarized in Table 5-4, and also a tag for the `SimpleStartPageControl` assembly.

The Start Page uses resources defined in a resource assembly of Visual Studio. The `<Grid.Resources>` element makes them available for the page.

The nested `Grid` with the `LayoutRoot` name defines the content of the Start Page. Visual Studio nests this `UIElement` into the Start Page. You can see how the `StartPageBackgroundKey` property of the `VsBrushes` class (defined in the `Microsoft.VisualStudio.Shell.10.0` assembly) is used to set up the background color of the grid.

 *Visual Studio places a lot of* `System.Windows.Media.Brush` *instances into the* `Application.Current.Resources` *collection. The* `VsBrushes` *class contains the keys (more than 100) to reference these resources.*

The `LayoutRoot` grid contains more than 200 lines defining the UI of the page. It is worth taking a look at a few details of this XAML code, because this will help you to understand how the Start Page is composed.

## Command Button Definitions

The Visual Studio 2010 Ultimate Edition's Start Page contains three command buttons in its top-left part under the logo, as shown in Figure 5-29.

These buttons are defined with the XAML code extract shown in Listing 5-3.

**FIGURE 5-29:** Command buttons on the Start Page

**LISTING 5-3:** StartPage.xaml (Command Button Definitions)

```
<Grid x:Name="commandButtonsGrid" MinWidth="270" Grid.Row="0"
    Margin="0,15,0,30" HorizontalAlignment="Left">
  <Grid.RowDefinitions>
    <RowDefinition Height="Auto"/>
    <RowDefinition Height="3"/>
    <RowDefinition Height="Auto"/>
    <RowDefinition Height="3"/>
    <RowDefinition Height="Auto"/>
  </Grid.RowDefinitions>

  <vs:ImageButton
    x:Uid="ConnectToTSButton"
    Margin="15,2,15,2"
    Width="Auto"
    Content="Connect To Team Foundation Server"
    Visibility="{Binding Path=TeamFoundationClientSupported,
      Converter={StaticResource boolToVisibilityConverter}}"
    Style="{DynamicResource StartPage.ProjectCommand.ButtonStyle}"
    Command="{x:Static sp:VSCommands.ExecuteCommand}"
    CommandParameter="Team.ConnecttoTeamFoundationServer"
    ImageNormal="../ConnectToTFS.png"
    ImageHover="../ConnectToTFSMouseOver.png"
    ImagePressed="../ConnectToTFSMouseDown.png">
  </vs:ImageButton>

  <vs:ImageButton
    Grid.Row="2"
    x:Uid="NewProjectButton"
    Margin="15,2,0,2"
    Width="Auto"
    Content="New Project..."
    Style="{DynamicResource StartPage.ProjectCommand.ButtonStyle}"
    Command="{x:Static sp:VSCommands.ExecuteCommand}"
    CommandParameter="File.NewProject"
    ImageNormal="../NewProject.png"
    ImageHover="../NewProjectMouseOver.png"
    ImagePressed="../NewProjectMouseDown.png">
  </vs:ImageButton>

  <vs:ImageButton
    Grid.Row="4"
```

*continues*

**LISTING 5-3** *(continued)*

```
    x:Uid="OpenProjectButton"
    Margin="15,2,0,2"
    Width="Auto"
    Content="Open Project..."
    Style="{DynamicResource StartPage.ProjectCommand.ButtonStyle}"
    Command="{x:Static sp:VSCommands.ExecuteCommand}"
    CommandParameter="File.OpenProject"
    ImageNormal=".../OpenProject.png"
    ImageHover=".../OpenProjectMouseOver.png"
    ImagePressed=".../OpenProjectMouseDown.png">
  </vs:ImageButton>
</Grid>
```

*Code file [StartPage.xaml] available for download at Wrox.com*

Each command button is defined by a `vs:ImageButton` type (which is implemented in the `Microsoft.VisualStudio.Shell.10.0` assembly) and contains a few properties influencing its appearance and behavior. The `ImageNormal`, `ImageHover`, and `ImagePressed` properties name the image resources to be displayed for the specific states of command buttons. In Listing 5-3, only partial paths are indicated. Look in the original `StartPage.xaml` file for the full resource URIs.

The `x:Uid` properties define the unique identifiers of buttons that can be used to access them programmatically. Their associated `Command` is defined so that they execute the Visual Studio IDE Shell command identified with the name in the `CommandParameter` property. The names used here are exactly the same you can use in the Command Window (View ➪ Other Windows Command Window).

As you see, the context of the Start Page contains properties to check the availability of certain Visual Studio features. For example, the Connect To Team Foundation Server button contains the following binding for its `Visibility` property:

```
Visibility="{Binding Path=TeamFoundationClientSupported,
  Converter={StaticResource boolToVisibilityConverter}}"
```

Here, the `TeamFoundationClientSupported` binding flag allows showing or hiding this command button, depending on whether the loaded Visual Studio edition supports Team Foundation integration or not.

## The Recent Projects Definition

The Start Page displays the list of recent projects below the command button definitions, as shown in Figure 5-30.

This list defines a context menu shown in Figure 5-30. This part of the Start Page is defined by the XAML definition shown in Listing 5-4.

**FIGURE 5-30:** List of Recent Projects

**LISTING 5-4:** StartPage.xaml (Recent Project List Definitions)

```xaml
<StackPanel Grid.Row="0" Margin="0,0,0,10" Orientation="Horizontal">
  <TextBlock Text="Recent Projects" VerticalAlignment="Top"
    Style="{DynamicResource StartPage.HeadingTextStyle}"
    x:Uid="RecentProjects"/>
  <Path VerticalAlignment="Center" Margin="6,0,0,-4" Width="Auto"
  Height="1" Stretch="Fill" StrokeThickness="1" StrokeLineJoin="Round"
  Stroke="{DynamicResource {x:Static vsfx:VsBrushes.StartPageSeparatorKey}}"
  Data="F1 M 0.5,0.5L 199.5,0.5"/>
</StackPanel>
<!-- MRU List Container -->
<ScrollViewer Grid.Row="1" HorizontalAlignment="Stretch"
  Style="{DynamicResource StartPage.ScrollViewerStyle}"
  VerticalAlignment="Stretch"  VerticalScrollBarVisibility="Auto">
  <sp:MruListBox
    DataContext="{Binding RecentProjects}"
    ItemsSource="{Binding Path=Items}"
    Background="Transparent"
    BorderThickness="0"
    AutomationProperties.AutomationId="MruList"/>
</ScrollViewer>
```

*Code file [StartPage.xaml] available for download at Wrox.com*

The `sp:MruListBox` WPF control implements the behavior shown in Figure 5-30. It simply binds the list to the `RecentProjects.Items` property of the Start Page's context.

## The MyControl User Control

The Custom Start Page Template added a simple customization point to the Start Page — the MyControl tab you can see in Figure 5-27. The `StartPage.xaml` file adds this tab to the definition as a simple tab of the `TabControl` displaying the "Get Started," "Guidance…," and other tabs:

```xaml
<Grid Grid.Column="2" Grid.Row="1" Margin="0,-35,15,15">
  <TabControl Style="{DynamicResource StartPage.TabControlStyle}"
    SelectedIndex="{Binding SelectedTabItemIndex, Mode=TwoWay}">
    <TabItem Header="Get Started" Height="Auto" ...>
      <!-- ... -->
    </TabItem>
    <TabItem Header="Guidance and Resources" Height="Auto" ...>
      <!-- ... -->
    </TabItem>
    <TabItem Header="Latest News" ...>
      <!-- ... -->
    </TabItem>
    <TabItem Header="MyControl" Style="{DynamicResource StartPage.TabItemStyle}">
      <my:MyControl/>
    </TabItem>
  </TabControl>
</Grid>
```

The `MyControl` tab item uses the `StartPage.TabItemStyle` dynamic resource just like the other tab items to provide the predefined appearance. The content of this tab is set to an instance of the `MyControl` WPF user control defined in the `SimpleStartPageControl` project.

The `MyControl.xaml` file defines the user control's appearance, as shown in Listing 5-5.

**LISTING 5-5: MyControl.xaml**

```xaml
<UserControl x:Class="SimpleStartPageControl.MyControl"
    xmlns="http://schemas.microsoft.com/winfx/2006/xaml/presentation"
    xmlns:x="http://schemas.microsoft.com/winfx/2006/xaml"

    xmlns:mc="http://schemas.openxmlformats.org/markup-compatibility/2006"
    xmlns:d="http://schemas.microsoft.com/expression/blend/2008"
    xmlns:vsfx="clr-namespace:Microsoft.VisualStudio.Shell;
      assembly=Microsoft.VisualStudio.Shell.10.0"
    mc:Ignorable="d"
    d:DesignHeight="300" d:DesignWidth="300">

    <Grid Background="{DynamicResource {x:Static
      vsfx:VsBrushes.StartPageBackgroundKey}}">
        <Border Margin="20" CornerRadius="10" BorderThickness="3"
          BorderBrush="{DynamicResource {x:Static
            vsfx:VsBrushes.StartPageSeparatorKey}}">
            <StackPanel HorizontalAlignment="Center"
              VerticalAlignment="Center"
              TextBlock.Foreground="{DynamicResource {x:Static
                vsfx:VsBrushes.StartPageTextBodyKey}}">
                <TextBlock Text="My Start Page Control" FontSize="18"
                  HorizontalAlignment="Center" />
                <TextBlock Text="{Binding Path=DTE.Name}" FontSize="12"
                  HorizontalAlignment="Center"/>
            </StackPanel>
        </Border>
    </Grid>

</UserControl>
```

*Code file [MyControl.xaml] available for download at Wrox.com*

As you see from the listing, the user control definition intensively uses the resource keys defined by the `VsBrushes` class to define the appearance attributes. The user control encapsulates two `TextBlock` elements; the second displays the name of the application (Microsoft Visual Studio). This name is obtained through data binding. The tool window displaying the Start Page creates a data context where a `DTE` object (the root object of the Visual Studio run-time object model that can be used from extensions such as macros, add-ins, or VSPackages) is passed through the `DTE` property. So, the `DTE.Name` binding path retrieves the application name.

# Changing the StartPage.xaml File

Although the Custom Start Page Template creates a clone of the Visual Studio Start Page so that you can customize it through the MyControl tab, you are not obliged to do so. If you want to create a simple Start Page and even omit the information tabs you can see there by default, you can simplify the StartPage.xaml file.

Create a new Start Page project with the Custom Start Page Template, just as you have already done with the SimpleStartPage project. Now, name this new project ModifiedStartPage. When the solution has been generated, remove the ModifiedStartPageControl project — you won't need it at all.

Instead of using the user control, you will change the StartPage.xaml file in the SimpleStartPage project so that all information tabs will be omitted. Instead of the original command buttons, you will add two new ones that display the Task List and display the Add New File dialog, respectively. The list of recent projects will be extended with a TextBlock displaying the number of items in the list.

Listing 5-6 shows the modified StartPage.xaml file. If you do not want to type it manually, just open the ModifiedStartPage project that can be found in the downloaded source code of the book at www.wrox.com.

**LISTING 5-6:** StartPage.xaml (ModifiedStartPage Project)

```xml
<Grid xmlns="http://schemas.microsoft.com/winfx/2006/xaml/presentation"
    xmlns:x="http://schemas.microsoft.com/winfx/2006/xaml"
    xmlns:sp="clr-namespace:Microsoft.VisualStudio.PlatformUI;
      assembly=Microsoft.VisualStudio.Shell.StartPage"
    xmlns:vs="clr-namespace:Microsoft.VisualStudio.PlatformUI;
      assembly=Microsoft.VisualStudio.Shell.10.0"
    xmlns:vsfx="clr-namespace:Microsoft.VisualStudio.Shell;
      assembly=Microsoft.VisualStudio.Shell.10.0"
    mc:Ignorable="d"
    xmlns:d="http://schemas.microsoft.com/expression/blend/2008"
    xmlns:mc="http://schemas.openxmlformats.org/markup-compatibility/2006"
    d:DesignHeight="600" d:DesignWidth="800">

  <Grid.Resources>
    <ResourceDictionary>
      <ResourceDictionary.MergedDictionaries>
        <ResourceDictionary
          Source="/Microsoft.VisualStudio.Shell.StartPage;
            component/Styles/startpageresources.xaml" />
      </ResourceDictionary.MergedDictionaries>
    </ResourceDictionary>
  </Grid.Resources>

  <Grid x:Name="LayoutRoot"
    Background="{DynamicResource {x:Static vsfx:VsBrushes.StartPageBackgroundKey}}"
    Style="{DynamicResource StartPage.OuterGridStyle}">
    <Grid Width="Auto" Grid.Column="0" Grid.Row="1" Margin="15,0,0,15"
      VerticalAlignment="Stretch">
```

*continues*

**LISTING 5-6** (*continued*)

```xml
<Grid.RowDefinitions>
  <RowDefinition Height="Auto"/>
  <RowDefinition Height="*"/>
</Grid.RowDefinitions>

<!-- Command buttons -->
<Grid x:Name="commandButtonsGrid" MinWidth="270" Grid.Row="0"
  Margin="0,15,0,30" HorizontalAlignment="Left">
  <Grid.RowDefinitions>
    <RowDefinition Height="Auto"/>
    <RowDefinition Height="Auto"/>
    <RowDefinition Height="3"/>
    <RowDefinition Height="Auto"/>
  </Grid.RowDefinitions>
  <TextBlock Text="My custom commands" VerticalAlignment="Top"
    Style="{DynamicResource StartPage.HeadingTextStyle}"
    x:Uid="MyCustomCommands"/>
  <vs:ImageButton
    Grid.Row="1"
    x:Uid="ViewTaskListButton"
    Margin="15,2,0,2"
    Width="Auto"
    Content="View Task List"
    Style="{DynamicResource StartPage.ProjectCommand.ButtonStyle}"
    Command="{x:Static sp:VSCommands.ExecuteCommand}"
    CommandParameter="View.TaskList"
    ImageNormal="pack://application:,,,/Microsoft.
      VisualStudio.Shell.StartPage;component/Images/StartPage/
      OpenProject.png"
    ImageHover="pack://application:,,,/Microsoft.
      VisualStudio.Shell.StartPage;component/Images/StartPage/
      OpenProjectMouseOver.png"
    ImagePressed="pack://application:,,,/Microsoft.
      VisualStudio.Shell.StartPage;component/Images/StartPage/
      OpenProjectMouseDown.png">
  </vs:ImageButton>
  <vs:ImageButton
    Grid.Row="3"
    x:Uid="NewFileButton"
    Margin="15,2,0,2"
    Width="Auto"
    Content="New File..."
    Style="{DynamicResource StartPage.ProjectCommand.ButtonStyle}"
    Command="{x:Static sp:VSCommands.ExecuteCommand}"
    CommandParameter="File.NewFile"
    ImageNormal="pack://application:,,,/Microsoft.
      VisualStudio.Shell.StartPage;component/Images/StartPage/
      OpenProject.png"
    ImageHover="pack://application:,,,/Microsoft.
      VisualStudio.Shell.StartPage;component/Images/StartPage/
      OpenProjectMouseOver.png"
    ImagePressed="pack://application:,,,/Microsoft.
```

```
                    VisualStudio.Shell.StartPage;component/Images/StartPage/
                    OpenProjectMouseDown.png">
                </vs:ImageButton>
            </Grid>
            <!-- Recent Projects -->
            <Grid Grid.Row="1" HorizontalAlignment="Left" Width="779">
                <Grid.RowDefinitions>
                    <RowDefinition Height="Auto" />
                    <RowDefinition Height="Auto" />
                    <RowDefinition Height="Auto" />
                </Grid.RowDefinitions>
                <TextBlock Text="Recent Projects" VerticalAlignment="Top"
                    Style="{DynamicResource StartPage.HeadingTextStyle}"
                    x:Uid="RecentProjects"/>
                <ScrollViewer Grid.Row="1" HorizontalAlignment="Stretch"
                    Style="{DynamicResource StartPage.ScrollViewerStyle}"
                    VerticalAlignment="Stretch"
                    VerticalScrollBarVisibility="Auto">
                    <sp:MruListBox
                        DataContext="{Binding RecentProjects}"
                        ItemsSource="{Binding Path=Items}"
                        Background="Transparent"
                        BorderThickness="0"
                        AutomationProperties.AutomationId="MruList"/>
                </ScrollViewer>
                <!-- Recent project count label -->
                <WrapPanel Grid.Row="5"
                    TextBlock.Foreground="{DynamicResource
                        {x:Static vsfx:VsBrushes.StartPageTextBodyKey}}">
                    <TextBlock Grid.Row="2" Text="Number of recent projects: " />
                    <TextBlock Text="{Binding Path=RecentProjects.Items.Count}" />
                </WrapPanel>
            </Grid>
        </Grid>
    </Grid>
</Grid>
```

*Code file [StartPage.xaml] available for download at Wrox.com*

Although this listing looks long, it is much shorter than the original StartPage.xaml in the template. Most of the code in the original file was related to the information tabs, and those are removed. This listing uses the same pattern as Listing 5-3 to define command buttons, and the same code as written is Listing 5-4 to implement the recent project list. The command buttons have been changed to invoke the View.TaskList and File.NewFile commands — have a look at the CommandParameter properties of the vs:ImageButton elements.

The recent project count label is composed from two TextBlock elements embedded into a WrapPanel. The Text property of the second element is simply bound the RecentProjects.Items .Count path to display the counter.

Build and run the project. Then go to the Tools ⇨ Options dialog to select the "[Installed Extension] ModifiedStartPage" item in the Customize Start Page combo box to display the new Start Page. Figure 5-31 shows how this new page looks.

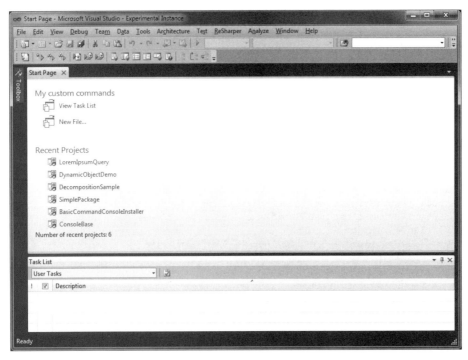

**FIGURE 5-31:** The Start Page implemented in the ModifiedStartPage project

## Accessing the Visual Studio Context

The previous example showed that the Start Page accesses the current Visual Studio context. For example, the list of recent projects was bound to its list box with the following declaration (in Listing 5-4 and Listing 5-5):

```
<sp:MruListBox
   DataContext="{Binding RecentProjects}"
   ItemsSource="{Binding Path=Items}"
   Background="Transparent"
   BorderThickness="0"
   AutomationProperties.AutomationId="MruList"/>
```

Here the DataContext property of the MruListBox control is bound to the RecentProjects data source property of the control's parent.

You might also have noticed how the MyControl property displays the name of the application with the following binding:

```
<TextBlock
   Text="{Binding Path=DTE.Name}"
   FontSize="12"
   HorizontalAlignment="Center"/>
```

Here the DTE.Name property of the parent control's data context provides that name.

The Start Page is a XAML file that is loaded and parsed by Visual Studio at start-up time, or when you change the current Start Page in the Options dialog. After the XAML file is loaded, the LayoutRoot grid is instantiated, and its DataContext property is set to an instance of the Microsoft.Internal.VisualStudio.PlatformUI.DataSource class that can be found in the Microsoft.VisualStudio.Shell.10.0.dll assembly.

Table 5-5 summarizes the properties of the data context set for the LayoutRoot grid.

**TABLE 5-5:** Visual Studio Context Properties

| PROPERTY | DESCRIPTION |
| --- | --- |
| CustomizationEnabled | This flag indicates whether the customization of the Shell (menus, toolbars) is enabled. |
| ClosePageOnOpenProject | This flag indicates whether the Start Page should be closed when a project is opened. |
| ShowPageAtStartup | This flag indicates if the Start Page should be displayed at Visual Studio Startup. |
| Source | This property shows the full file name of the Start Page currently used. |
| ExtensionId | This string shows the identifier of the extension defining the Start Page currently used. |
| WebProjectsSupported | This flag indicates whether the Visual Studio instance running supports web projects. |
| TeamFoundationClientSupported | This flag indicates whether the Visual Studio instance running supports accessing Team Foundation Server access. |
| Links | This data source property allows access to the links that can be found on the Start Page tabs. |
| Background | This data source property allows accessing data related to information to be painted in the background, such as the logo bitmap and the application name. |
| Rss | This data source property can be used to access RSS information displayed on the Latest News Start Page tab. |
| RecentProjects | This data source property can be used to access the list of recent projects. |

*continues*

**TABLE 5-5** *(continued)*

| PROPERTY | DESCRIPTION |
|---|---|
| SelectedTabItemIndex | This integer index stores the index of the tab currently selected on the Start Page. |
| SelectedSubitem1Index, SelectedSubitem2Index, SelectedSubitem3Index, SelectedSubitem4Index | These integer properties allow providing up to four hierarchical levels under the Start Page tabs. Each property stores the index of the current selection at the related level. |
| DTE | This property allows you to access the root DTE object of Visual Studio (the root object of the Visual Studio run-time object model that can be used from extensions). |

While you are using these properties from XAML, you can use the {Binding} markups. However, to access them from code, you need a workaround.

Let's create a new Start Page extension so that you can see how these properties can be used programmatically. When this extension runs, it displays information about the context properties summarized in Table 5-5, as shown in Figure 5-32.

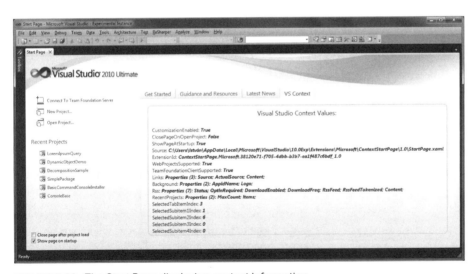

**FIGURE 5-32:** The Start Page displaying context information

Create a new project with the Custom Start Page Template and name it ContextStartPage. Change the name of the MyControl tab in the StartPage.xaml file to "VS Context" (you'll find this TabItem almost at the very end of the source file):

```
<TabItem Header="VS Context" Style="{DynamicResource StartPage.TabItemStyle}">
  <my:VSContextControl/>
</TabItem>
```

You are going to use a few interoperability types that can be found in the `Microsoft.VisualStudio` `.Shell.Interop.10.0` assembly (it's deployed with Visual Studio 2010 SDK), so add a reference to it from the `ContextStartPageControl` project. Instead of displaying a simple text, the Start Page control will display information about the data context properties.

Rename the `MyControl.xaml` file to `VSContextControl.xaml` and the `MyControl` user control to `VSContextControl`. Change the body of the user control to encapsulate a `ListBox` control, as shown in Listing 5-7.

**LISTING 5-7:** VSContextControl.xaml

```xaml
<UserControl x:Class="ContextStartPageControl.VSContextControl"
    xmlns="http://schemas.microsoft.com/winfx/2006/xaml/presentation"
    xmlns:x="http://schemas.microsoft.com/winfx/2006/xaml"
    xmlns:mc="http://schemas.openxmlformats.org/markup-compatibility/2006"
    xmlns:d="http://schemas.microsoft.com/expression/blend/2008"
    xmlns:vsfx="clr-namespace:Microsoft.VisualStudio.Shell;
       assembly=Microsoft.VisualStudio.Shell.10.0"
    xmlns:my="clr-namespace:ContextStartPageControl"
    mc:Ignorable="d"
    d:DesignHeight="300" d:DesignWidth="300">

    <Grid Background="{DynamicResource
        {x:Static vsfx:VsBrushes.StartPageBackgroundKey}}"
        DataContextChanged="Grid_DataContextChanged">
      <Border Margin="20" CornerRadius="10" BorderThickness="3"
        BorderBrush="{DynamicResource
          {x:Static vsfx:VsBrushes.StartPageSeparatorKey}}">
        <DockPanel HorizontalAlignment="Stretch"
          VerticalAlignment="Top"
          TextBlock.Foreground="{DynamicResource
            {x:Static vsfx:VsBrushes.StartPageTextBodyKey}}">
          <TextBlock DockPanel.Dock="Top" FontSize="18"
            HorizontalAlignment="Center" Margin="0,8,0,16">
            Visual Studio Context Values:</TextBlock>
          <ListBox x:Name="ContextValues" HorizontalAlignment="Stretch"
            Margin="8" BorderThickness="0" Background="Transparent">
            <ListBox.ItemTemplate>
              <DataTemplate>
                <StackPanel Orientation="Horizontal"
                  TextBlock.FontSize="14"
                  TextBlock.Foreground="{DynamicResource
                   {x:Static vsfx:VsBrushes.StartPageTextBodyKey}}">
                  <TextBlock Text="{Binding Name}" />
                  <TextBlock Text=": " />
                  <TextBlock FontWeight="SemiBold"  FontStyle="Italic"
                    Text="{Binding Value}" />
                </StackPanel>
              </DataTemplate>
            </ListBox.ItemTemplate>
          </ListBox>
```

*continues*

**LISTING 5-7** (*continued*)

```
        </DockPanel>
      </Border>
    </Grid>

  </UserControl>
```

*Code file [VSContextControl.xaml] available for download at Wrox.com*

This code does not contain anything special. Instead of using the default `ListBox` appearance, this source defines a simple `ItemTemplate` for the list box shown in Figure 5-32. Add the `ContextItem.cs` file to the `ContextStartPageControl` project to encapsulate information about context properties. This contains a very simple data object, as shown in Listing 5-8.

**LISTING 5-8:** ContextItem.cs

**Available for download on Wrox.com**

```
namespace ContextStartPageControl
{
    public class ContextItem
    {
      public ContextItem(string name, string value)
      {
        Name = name;
        Value = value;
      }

      public string Name { get; private set; }
      public string Value { get; private set; }
    }
}
```

*Code file [ContextItem.cs] available for download at Wrox.com*

The lion's share of the work is done in the code-behind file of the `VSContextControl`. It responds to the events when the control's `DataContext` property is set, or any of the properties behind the current data context change. When any of these changes occurs, the content of the `ListBox` is refreshed, as shown in Listing 5-9.

**LISTING 5-9:** VSContextControl.xaml.cs

**Available for download on Wrox.com**

```
using System.Windows;
using System.Windows.Controls;
using Microsoft.Internal.VisualStudio.PlatformUI;
using System.Linq;

namespace ContextStartPageControl
```

```
{
  public partial class VSContextControl : UserControl
  {
    public VSContextControl()
    {
      InitializeComponent();
    }

    private void Grid_DataContextChanged(object sender,
      DependencyPropertyChangedEventArgs e)
    {
      var context = e.NewValue as DataSource;
      if (context == null) return;
      context.PropertyChanged += ContextPropertyChanged;
      RefreshContext(context);
    }

    void ContextPropertyChanged(object sender,
      System.ComponentModel.PropertyChangedEventArgs e)
    {
      var context = sender as DataSource;
      if (context != null) RefreshContext(context);
    }

    private void RefreshContext(DataSource context)
    {
      ContextValues.Items.Clear();
      AddIntrinsicPropertyValue(context, "CustomizationEnabled");
      AddIntrinsicPropertyValue(context, "ClosePageOnOpenProject");
      AddIntrinsicPropertyValue(context, "ShowPageAtStartup");
      AddIntrinsicPropertyValue(context, "Source");
      AddIntrinsicPropertyValue(context, "ExtensionId");
      AddIntrinsicPropertyValue(context, "WebProjectsSupported");
      AddIntrinsicPropertyValue(context, "TeamFoundationClientSupported");
      AddDataSourcePropertyValue(context, "Links");
      AddDataSourcePropertyValue(context, "Background");
      AddDataSourcePropertyValue(context, "Rss");
      AddDataSourcePropertyValue(context, "RecentProjects");
      AddIntrinsicPropertyValue(context, "SelectedTabItemIndex");
      AddIntrinsicPropertyValue(context, "SelectedSubitem1Index");
      AddIntrinsicPropertyValue(context, "SelectedSubitem2Index");
      AddIntrinsicPropertyValue(context, "SelectedSubitem3Index");
      AddIntrinsicPropertyValue(context, "SelectedSubitem4Index");
    }

    private void AddIntrinsicPropertyValue(DataSource source, string propName)
    {
      var prop = source.GetValue(propName);
      ContextValues.Items.Add(new ContextItem(propName, prop.ToString()));
    }

    private void AddDataSourcePropertyValue(DataSource source, string propName)
    {
      var props = source.GetValue(propName) as DataSource;
```

*continues*

---

**LISTING 5-9** *(continued)*

```
        if (props == null) return;
        var propNames = string.Concat(
          props.Properties.Select(prop => prop.Name +"; "));
        ContextValues.Items.Add(
          new ContextItem(propName, string.Format("Properties ({0}): {1}",
            props.Properties.Count(), propNames)));
      }
    }
  }
```

*Code file [VSContextControl.xaml.cs] available for download at Wrox.com*

---

The `Grid_DataContextChanged` method catches the event when the control's data context is set. This event is raised when Visual Studio parses the `StartPage.xaml` file and instantiates the `LayoutRoot` grid. The context can be accessed through the `e.NewValue` property, and its type should be an instance of the `DataSource` class (declared in the `Microsoft.Internal.VisualStudio.PlatformUI` namespace). The method body subscribes to the `PropertyChanged` event with the `ContextPropertyChanged` handler method. You can experiment with how the page responds to property changes. You can check or uncheck the "Close page after project load" and "Show page on startup" checkboxes. On the VS Context tab, the "CustomizationEnabled" and "ClosePageOnOpenProject" property values will change accordingly.

If either the data context or one of its properties is changed, the `RefreshContext` method will set up the list according to the current property values. The intrinsic properties (with Boolean or string values) are handled by the `AddIntrinsicPropertyValue` method, while other properties with `DataSource` values are displayed with the `AddDataSourcePropertyValue` method.

The `DataSource` class provides a `GetValue` method to query the value of the property named in its argument. The value returned by this method is a `System.Object` that can be cast to the native type behind the property. For all the intrinsic properties, the `ToString()` method retrieves the string representation of the property value, and so it can be directly displayed.

There are properties (for example "Links") that retrieve a `DataSource` when querying their values with `GetValue`. With the `Properties` enumeration — be aware, it is not a collection — you can obtain metadata-like type and name about the properties of the `DataSource` instance. As shown in Listing 5-9, the `AddDataSourcePropertyValue` simply concatenates these property names.

## Accessing the Visual Studio Object Model

Table 5-5 listed the DTE property as a part of the Start Page data context. Using this property, you can access the object model of Visual Studio. The root of this model is the DTE object (with the same name as its accessor property), and you can utilize it to programmatically carry out miscellaneous tasks with Visual Studio.

*The DTE object model covers more than hundred object types with more than a thousand methods and properties. DTE is used by macros, add-ins and VSPackages heavily. Chapter 6 provides more information about using DTE in several scenarios.*

To have a simple example of using DTE, let's create a new Start Page that lists all available Visual Studio commands and allows the user to execute them. Figure 5-33 show this Start Page in action.

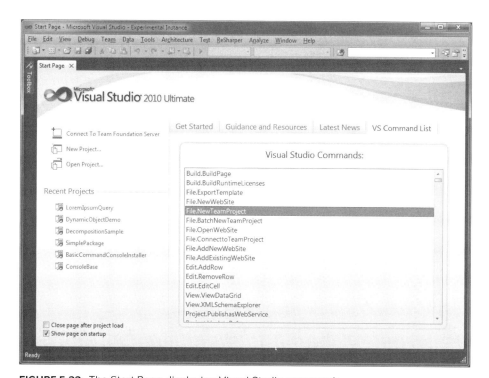

**FIGURE 5-33:** The Start Page displaying Visual Studio commands

Create a new Start Page project and name it `CommandListStartPage`. Add the `Microsoft.VisualStudio.Shell.Interop.10.0` assembly to the `CommandListStartPageControl` project. Modify the `StartPage.xaml` file to rename the `MyControl` tab's header:

```
<TabItem Header="VS Command List" Style="{DynamicResource StartPage.TabItemStyle}">
    <my:MyControl/>
</TabItem>
```

Change the `Grid` within the `MyControl.xaml` file to define a `ListBox` control holding the collection of the Visual Studio commands:

```
<Grid Background="{DynamicResource {x:Static
  vsfx:VsBrushes.StartPageBackgroundKey}}"
  DataContextChanged="Grid_DataContextChanged">
  <Border Margin="20" CornerRadius="10" BorderThickness="3"
    BorderBrush="{DynamicResource {x:Static
    vsfx:VsBrushes.StartPageSeparatorKey}}">
    <DockPanel HorizontalAlignment="Stretch"
      VerticalAlignment="Stretch"
      TextBlock.Foreground="{DynamicResource
        {x:Static vsfx:VsBrushes.StartPageTextBodyKey}}">
      <TextBlock DockPanel.Dock="Top" FontSize="18" HorizontalAlignment="Center"
        Margin="0,8,0,8">Visual Studio Commands:</TextBlock>
      <ListBox x:Name="CommandList" HorizontalAlignment="Stretch"
        VerticalAlignment="Stretch"
        ScrollViewer.VerticalScrollBarVisibility="Auto"
        Margin="8" Background="Transparent"
        FontSize="14"
        Foreground="{DynamicResource
          {x:Static vsfx:VsBrushes.StartPageTextBodyKey}}"
        MouseDoubleClick="CommandList_MouseDoubleClick">
      </ListBox>
    </DockPanel>
  </Border>
</Grid>
```

The application logic is defined in the `MyControl.xaml.cs` file, and it is very straightforward. The `Grid_DataContextChanged` method catches the moment when the data context is set, and uses it to obtain the list of Visual Studio commands. The `CommandList_MouseDoubleClick` method executes the selected command. Listing 5-10 shows this simple code-behind file.

**LISTING 5-10:** MyControl.xaml.cs (CommandListStartPage)

```
using System;
using System.Windows;
using System.Windows.Controls;
using Microsoft.Internal.VisualStudio.PlatformUI;

namespace CommandListStartPageControl
{
  public partial class MyControl : UserControl
  {
    private dynamic _dte;

    public MyControl()
    {
      InitializeComponent();
    }

    private void Grid_DataContextChanged(object sender,
```

```
        DependencyPropertyChangedEventArgs e)
    {
      var context = e.NewValue as DataSource;
      if (context == null) return;
      _dte = context.GetValue("DTE");
      foreach (var command in _dte.Commands)
      {
        if (!string.IsNullOrEmpty(command.Name))
        CommandList.Items.Add(command.Name);
      }
    }

    private void CommandList_MouseDoubleClick(object sender,
      System.Windows.Input.MouseButtonEventArgs e)
    {
      var command = CommandList.SelectedValue;
      if (command == null) return;
      try
      {
        _dte.ExecuteCommand(command);
      }
      catch (SystemException ex)
      {
        MessageBox.Show(ex.Message);
      }
    }
  }
}
```

*Code file [MyControl.xaml.cs] available for download at Wrox.com*

 *This code uses a new feature of the C# 4.0 language called dynamic binding. This feature allows the compiled program to resolve operations such as method calls, property and index accessors at run-time, and provide late binding to the COM object model. Chapter 10 provides more information about the .NET feature (Dynamic Language Runtime) that makes this behavior possible. Chapter 24 discusses how to use dynamic binding in C#.*

The `Grid_DataContextChanged` method obtains the DTE object through the `GetValue` method of the `DataSource` object representing the data context, and immediately stores it into the `_dte` member that was declared as `dynamic`. The subsequent `foreach` cycle uses the `Commands` collection of DTE to populate the list with the command names.

`CommandList_MouseDoubleClick` uses the `ExecuteCommand` method to carry out the command selected in the list. Several commands can be executed only within a specific context (for example, they require a solution to be loaded) or with parameters. The method catches the exceptions coming from the command execution, and shows the related error messages.

## A Few More Points About Start Pages

As you have seen, creating Start Page extensions is really simple with the Custom Start Page Template. You can tailor this page to your fit your needs in just a few minutes. Although the samples presented here show only a few aspects of customizing the Start Page, you can add more complex functionality to your extensions.

Here are a few hints about what else you can do with Start Pages:

➤ Examine the `StartPage.xaml` file created by the template. Look at how the "Get Started" and "Guidance and Resources" tabs implement their functionality. You can use them as a pattern if you want to create more tabs, thus providing information for your Visual Studio users.

➤ The "Latest News" tab is a good source to see how Visual Studio displays information coming from RSS feeds.

➤ Several properties of the `DataContext` can be modified with the `SetValue` method.

➤ If you want to change the layout and appearance of the Start Page, you can do it more radically than you have seen with the `ModifiedStartPage` sample. Although, you can use your own colors, brushes, and styles, you should use the ones defined by Visual Studio. You can iterate through the content of `MergeDictionaries` collection in the `Application.Current.Resources` object to find out which resources can be used.

## CUSTOMIZING THE TOOLBOX

The ancestor of Visual Studio Toolbox was introduced in Visual Basic 1.0, almost 20 years ago. Developers could use it to drag a visual control to the design surface instead of manually typing code to create an instance of that control. Over the years, this original function of the Toolbox did not change. However, it has been improved from release to release. Today, the Toolbox is such a common part of the IDE (like menus, toolbars, and the text editor) that developers use it almost unconsciously.

## A Lap Around the Toolbox

The Toolbox is a dynamic tool window that adapts to the current context of the IDE. It offers components to users that can be utilized to build an application. Most of them are related to UI. It is displayed as a sliding tree control that behaves much like Windows Explorer, but without grid or connection lines. Multiple segments of the Toolbox (tabs) can be expanded simultaneously, and the entire tree scrolls inside the Toolbox window.

Users simply pick up a component from the Toolbox and place it on the design surface, or paste it into the text editor. The following gestures can be used:

➤ Select a component in the Toolbox with a mouse click. Then move the mouse to the design surface and click to the appropriate location of the surface where you want to place the selected component.

➤ Drag a Toolbox component with the mouse to the design surface, and place it at the desired location.

➤ Double-click on a Toolbox component and it will be placed on the design surface at a default location.

There is a special item named Pointer (indicated with a small mouse pointer icon) in each tab or the Toolbox. You cannot drag it to the design surface. Click it if you previously selected a component but you changed your mind and don't want to place it on the design surface.

## Components in the Toolbox

The Toolbox always displays a set of components that can be used in the current context. If you are designing a WPF form, only those components appear on the Toolbox that can be added to WPF forms. When you are creating a web page, the appropriate ASP.NET and HTML controls are offered in the Toolbox, but no others (for example, WPF controls).

The current set of components is determined by the following factors:

➤ *Active document* — Each document (source code, form designers, UML diagrams, and so on) has an associated designer entity that provides the design surface with its built-in interactions. This designer can co-operate with the Toolbox and tell which components to offer to the user when any document (or any views belonging to the document) gets the focus.

➤ *Active solution* — The solution loaded into Visual Studio has a hierarchy that may contain components that can be put on the Toolbox. The designer behind the active document can negotiate with the Toolbox that certain components in the active solution also must be displayed.

Figure 5-34 shows an example of the Toolbox displayed for the WPF Designer, where the current solution contains several WPF user controls.

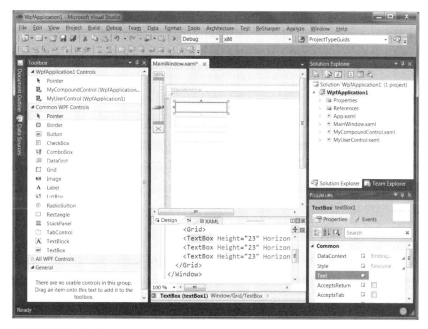

**FIGURE 5-34:** Toolbox components when designing a WPF form

In Figure 5-34, you can see four tabs, all of which are expanded, except the All WPF Controls tab (in the lower left of the screen). The Common WPF Controls tab and the All WPF Controls tab are displayed because the active document is a WPF form. The WpfApplication1 Controls tab is displayed because the active solution contains two WPF user controls (`MyCompoundControl` and `MyUserControl`) that also can be placed on a WPF form.

> *Most components displayed on Toolbox tabs are controls representing visual UI elements. The term "component" is generally used for building blocks that provide no UI, in contrast to controls. The collection of available controls also depends on the .NET Framework version your project targets. By default, Visual Studio 2010 projects target the .NET Framework 4 Client Profile. This reduces the size of deployment packages by not requiring the entire .NET Framework for installation. If your project requires a control that is not supported by the Client Profile, you can set your project to target .NET Framework 4 by editing the Application tab of project properties.*

There are several kinds of controls that can be displayed on the Toolbox. Right-click a tab or item in the Toolbox and turn on the Show All option in the context menu. The Toolbox displays all tabs that contain components for any designers in the Visual Studio IDE. You'll be surprised at how many of them are there! Figure 5-35 shows less than half of them.

Of course, when you expand tabs, only those controls are enabled that can be put to the active design surface. Turn off the Show All option to go back to the original state.

You can customize the Toolbox by rearranging items within a tab or adding custom tabs. Items that can be made available as Toolbox icons include components from the .NET Framework class library, COM components, controls for Windows Forms, WPF Forms and Web Forms, Silverlight, and HTML elements. You can also add text snippets to the Toolbox so that later you can insert them to a source code file.

## Using the Keyboard to Access Toolbox Functions

While most developers interact with the Toolbox through mouse gestures, you can use it with a keyboard exclusively. Press Ctrl+Alt+X to display the Toolbox and receive the keyboard focus. Use the up and down arrow keys to navigate to the control

| Toolbox |
| --- |
| ▷ Excel Controls |
| ▷ Word Controls |
| ▷ Windows Workflow v3.0 |
| ▷ Standard |
| ▷ Control Flow |
| ▷ Office Ribbon Controls |
| ▷ Common WPF Controls |
| ▷ SharePoint Controls |
| ▷ Windows Workflow v3.5 |
| ▷ Data |
| ▷ Flowchart |
| ▷ All Windows Forms |
| ▷ SharePoint Workflow |
| ▷ All WPF Controls |
| ▷ Validation |
| ▷ Messaging |
| ▷ Common Controls |
| ▷ Common Silverlight Controls |
| ▷ Navigation |
| ▷ Runtime |
| ▷ Containers |
| ▷ All Silverlight Controls |

**FIGURE 5-35:** Some of the many tabs on the Toolbox

you want to place on the design surface. Press the Ctrl key while using the up and down arrow keys and you can move among the tabs.

When you place the focus on the desired control, press Enter and the control is added to the design surface. The control immediately gets the focus, so you can use the arrow keys (or any other key combinations the designer supports) to change the location or the properties of the newly placed control.

You can use the Delete button to remove an item or an entire tab from the Toolbox, as explained later in this chapter.

## Customizing Toolbox Tabs

Components displayed in the sliding tree of the Toolbox are organized into tabs to form smaller groups. Each tab has a triangle symbol that can be used to collapse or expand the tab. The empty triangle represents the collapsed state of the tab; the full triangle shows the tab is expanded.

### Working with Tabs

A tab is a unit that can be customized separately from the others. You have a few options that can be accessed from the context menu when you right-click on a tab:

➤   By default, items in a tab are displayed in list view. Each control is represented by an icon and a short name, as shown in Figure 5-34. You can turn this option on or off by checking or unchecking the List View option. When it is turned off, controls in the tab are displayed as a set of icons, as shown in Figure 5-36.

➤   Controls within a tab are enumerated in the order they have been added. Select the Sort Items Alphabetically option to change this order. Even if you use the alphabetical order, the Pointer is always the top item in every tab.

➤   With the Move Up and Move Down commands, you can change the location of the tab within the sliding tree. Instead of the context menu, you can drag and drop the tab into a new location within the Toolbox.

➤   You can rename the tab.

➤   If you do not want to use a tab at all, you can remove it from the Toolbox with the Delete command. Because there is no undo operation to restore a removed tab, you must confirm your intention.

**FIGURE 5-36:** Items in the Common WPF Controls tab are displayed with List View mode turned off

### Rearranging Tab Items

You are free to rearrange items in the Toolbox:

➤   Click on any control in any tab, and keep the left mouse button down. You can drag the item to another location not only within the tab, but also to another tab. If you want to place the item into a tab that is not expanded yet, drag the item over the collapsed tab, wait about one second, and the tab is expanded. Drag the item to the desired location and drop it.

➤ With the Add Tab command (you can find it in the context menu of any tab or item), you can create a new tab. Type the name of the tab, and optionally drag it to a new location, and then place controls in it.

### Resetting the Toolbox

Any time you delete an item or a tab accidentally, or you get lost among tabs and controls after rearranging them, you can invoke the Reset Toolbox command that is available in item and tab context menus.

This command will reset the Toolbox to its default state. It will affect not only the tabs and controls belonging to the current designer (for example, WPF controls when your current document is a WPF Designer), but also all other designers.

## Adding Items to the Toolbox

There is a large ecosystem of Visual Studio Industry Partners, Independent Software Vendors (ISVs), community members, students, and hobbyists who create custom components. Most component vendors create installation kits that add controls to the Toolbox automatically. However, in many cases, you have only the binaries encapsulating controls, and you must add them manually to the Toolbox.

The Choose Toolbox Items dialog contains everything you need to add controls to the Toolbox. You can access this dialog from the Tools menu, or from the context menu of the Toolbox. Figure 5-37 shows this dialog displaying the WPF Components tab.

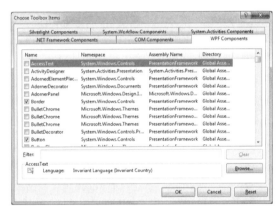

**FIGURE 5-37:** The Choose Toolbox Items dialog

This dialog has six tabs, each of which lists a well-defined set of components named by the tab:

➤ *.NET Framework Components* — This set includes Windows Forms, ASP.NET and mobile components available on your local computer.

➤ *COM Components* — This tab lists a set of installed and registered COM components contained on your computer.

➤ *WPF Components* — This tab lists components available for WPF application development.

➤ *Silverlight Components* — This set includes Silverlight controls and components contained on your computer.

➤ *System.Workflow Components, System.Activities Components* — These tabs lists components you can use in conjunction with the Workflow designer.

The main part of the dialog is the grid listing the components associated with the selected tab. You can identify the listed components according to name, namespace, and the declaring assembly's name. The Directory column also helps you to guess as to from where the specific assembly is loaded. Each item in the list contains a checkbox indicating if the item is displayed on the toolbar (checked) or not (unchecked).

The Filter text box under the list helps you to display only the components that match the filter string you type in. For example, if you type **Button** where you are on the WPF components tab, the list will contain every component having "Button" in its name, such as `Button`, `ButtonChrome`, `DialogButton`, `RadioButton`, and so on.

The Group box under the Filter text box displays some helpful information about the component. It shows you the icon representing the component and its language.

## Selecting a Component to Add

Use the Browse button to select a binary file representing a component that fits into the selected category. For example, in the COM Components category, you must select a file that contains a real COM component. If you want to add a file that does not fit in the selected category (for example, you select an assembly with Silverlight components in the System.Workflow Components tab), that will be refused.

Let's take a look at an example. Select the WPF Components tab, and click Browse. If you download the source code from this book's companion website (`www.wrox.com`), under the samples belonging to this chapter you will find a folder named `FluentRibbon`. Open this folder and select the `Fluent.dll` file. After you select the file, the IDE checks to see if it fits into the WPF category. `Fluent.dll` does, so the IDE then scans the assembly to find all WPF components and extracts the metadata information associated with them. The components found are added to the list and checked by default, as shown in Figure 5-38.

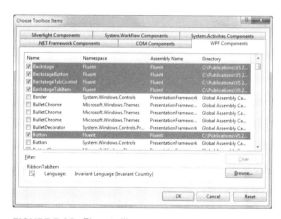

**FIGURE 5-38:** Fluent.dll components

The list may contain controls extracted from this new assembly that cannot be seen in the grid unless you scroll down. You can click on the column headers of the grid to order items by namespace or assembly name. Ordering generally helps you to arrange new controls into a continuous range in the grid. You can check or uncheck items individually.

## Blocked Components

Today, a majority of components are downloaded from the web. Because these components can arrive from untrusted sources, Visual Studio IDE does not allow loading them into its process space by default. If you try to add the `FluentBlocked.dll` (it is in the same folder as `Fluent.dll`) to the WPF Components tab, you will get a message, similar to, "The assembly 'Fluent, Version=...' could not be loaded. This assembly may have been downloaded from the web."

If you are sure that the downloaded component is coming from a trusted source, with a few manual steps, you can add it to the Toolbox:

1. Open Windows Explorer and go to the folder containing the component assembly.

2. Right-click on the assembly and view the file properties. At the bottom of the General tab, you see the Unblock button, as shown in Figure 5-39.

3. Click this button to resolve the block of this assembly, and then click OK.

4. Save your work in Visual Studio and restart it. Now, when you try to add this assembly to the Toolbox, it is not blocked any more.

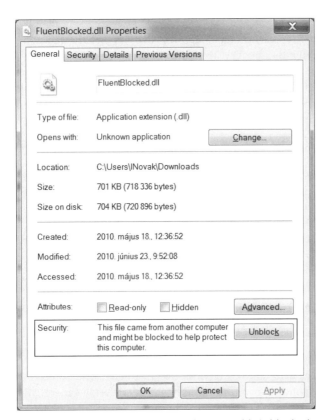

**FIGURE 5-39:** File properties show this assembly is blocked

## Adding Text Snippets to the Toolbox

When you use the code editor to edit any source files with text, you can drag selected text from the editor and drop it to the Toolbox. When you finish this operation, the text is put in the toolbar just as if it were a component. Its name is created from the text you've dragged to the Toolbox, and its icon indicates that it is a text snippet.

You can move, rename, and delete text snippet items just like any other Toolbar components. You can double-click a text snippet to insert it to the current caret position in the active text document, or drag it from the Toolbox and drop it to the text position where you want the snippet to insert.

## A Few More Points About Toolbox Customization

Extending Visual Studio with controls is definitely out of the scope of this book. There are many books that examine the aspects of custom control development. Some of them are about the hosting technology (such as WPF, Silverlight, or ASP.NET), while others are dedicated entirely to that topic. If you plan to develop your own custom components, look for the appropriate source of information depending on the technology for which you want to create components. These sources treat a number of topics related to Toolbox customization, including the following aspects related to Toolbox customization:

> ➤ You can assign icons and other kinds of metadata to your components that influence how they are displayed in the Toolbox.

> ➤ You can create deployment packages that integrate your components with the Toolbox.

> ➤ You can add licensing information to your components to restrict their usage to authorized users (customers and/or developers).

## VISUAL STUDIO GALLERY

Visual Studio 2010 was designed with extensibility in mind. Developers can add their own tools, custom controls, templates, and add-ins to the IDE to customize their workspace. This capability has been a part of Visual Studio since its first release. Hundreds of companies, hobbyists, and enthusiasts have been creating IDE extensions, but for a long time there was no common place to keep them.

At the end of February 2008, Microsoft launched the Visual Studio Gallery (`http://www .visualstudiogallery.com`) website that provides a catalog that showcases free and commercial products that complement or extend Visual Studio. The broad range of solutions you'll find in the gallery will give you a sense of the momentum Microsoft is seeing around Visual Studio Extensibility. Microsoft has a large and growing group of partners building businesses on the Visual Studio platform, and it also has a growing developer community focused on extending Visual Studio to create new tools.

Since it was launched (just a few months later than Visual Studio 2008), the Visual Studio Gallery has been growing as the one-stop shop for Visual Studio Extensions. Since that time, the Gallery gathered more than 1,600 extensions.

Chapter 4 describes how to upload your own Visual Studio Template to the Visual Studio Gallery. The following discussion provides a brief overview of the Gallery, focusing on how you can find products and integrate them into the IDE.

# Browsing the Visual Studio Gallery

You can visit the Gallery directly by navigating to the `http://www.visualstudiogallery.com` link or clicking on the Gallery tab when you are visiting the Visual Studio Development Center on MSDN. The homepage of the Gallery has been established so that you can easily browse among the extensions and find the ones you are interested in, as shown in Figure 5-40.

**FIGURE 5-40:** Visual Studio Gallery homepage

The left part of the page contains several options to filter and browse components listed in the main part of the page. By default, this list contains the latest ten contributions added to the Gallery, but by using the tabs above the list, you can easily navigate to see the highest ranked or most often visited components.

The one-click filtering options on the left side of the page make it easy to navigate to components that best fit your interest:

➤ *Categories* — Each component uploaded to Visual Studio Gallery is associated with one of the Tools, Controls, or Templates categories. *Tools* are extensions that add some functionality to the IDE. *Controls* are components that can be installed in the Visual Studio Toolbox. *Templates* are either project or item templates that appear in the New Project or Add New Item dialogs. By clicking on one of these categories, the appropriate components are displayed, and also the category is drilled down into further subcategories. For example, when you click Controls, you'll see several subcategories such as ASP.NET, SharePoint, Silverlight, WPF, and so on.

➤ *Visual Studio Versions* — Select the version of Visual Studio in which you want to use the component. The Gallery will list all the contributions registered as compatible with the selected version.

➤ *Cost Categories* — You can find three kinds of components on the Gallery according to how they affect your bank account. *Free* components can be used free of any charge, and most of them can be downloaded directly from the Gallery. The *Free Trial* category lets you access trial versions of paid components that are constrained in their usage either by time or functionality. *Paid* components are full versions that you cannot obtain directly from the Gallery. Instead, you are redirected to the website of the vendor where you can buy and download them.

➤ *Affiliation* — You can filter contributions according to their origins (vendor or author). You can choose from Microsoft, Visual Studio Industry Partners (VSIPs), or any other vendors.

➤ *Tags* — When components are uploaded, they are associated with a number of tags. Here you can select one from the most often visited tags to browse components uploaded with that tag.

These filters can be combined. For example, you can list all free WPF controls by selecting Controls, then clicking on the WPF subcategory, and choosing Free under Cost Categories. You will see a list of components according to the combination of these filter criteria, as shown in Figure 5-41.

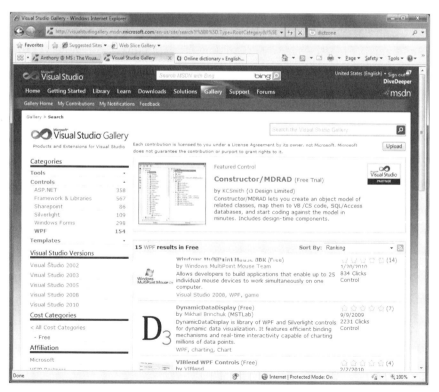

**FIGURE 5-41:** Using a combination of filters

By default, the list is sorted by ranking where the components with the highest rank are at the top of the list. You can change sorting at any time. Just select the appropriate item from the Sort By combo box.

Each component in the list contains a short description. You can click on the component name to navigate to its details page that provides you much more information. Should you click on the author's name or any of the component tags, the components by the selected author or the ones having the chosen tag are displayed, respectively.

The component details page helps you to decide whether the component is the one you are looking for. Each component can have a very detailed description (for example, product sheet, feature list, and so on) providing you the information to learn more about the component. You can see all reviews that visitors wrote about it and even follow the community discussions about the component. Figure 5-42 shows an example.

**FIGURE 5-42:** Details page of Visual Studio Color Theme Editor

## Downloading and Installing Components

Component authors and vendors can decide how you can download and install components. You can either download components directly from the Visual Studio Gallery (as indicated by the Download button in Figure 5-42), or you are redirected to the vendor's (author's) site for further instructions. In the latter case, you will find a Get Now button instead of Download.

The Visual Studio Gallery supports the new VSIX deployment kit format that was established especially for Visual Studio Extensions. When the selected component is available for direct installation, you can click the Download button to run or save the VSIX file representing the setup kit.

Visual Studio 2010 installs the Visual Studio Extension Installer utility that is associated with the .vsix extension. So, if you start the VSIX file downloaded from the Gallery, this utility starts and lets you carry on, or abort the installation, as shown in Figure 5-43.

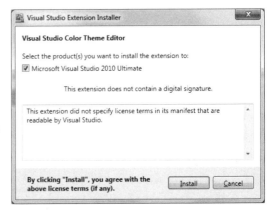

When the installation is complete, the utility warns you to restart all open Visual Studio instances in order for the new component to be successfully integrated into the IDE.

Later, if you would like to remove the component, you can use the Extension Manager dialog (Tools ➪ Extension Manager) to uninstall or disable it.

**FIGURE 5-43:** The startup screen of the Visual Studio Extension Installer utility

# Adding Your Own Contributions to the Gallery

Chapter 4 provides details about uploading Visual Studio project or item templates to the Gallery. The same simple process lets you add not only templates, but also tools or controls to the Gallery. This process entails the following three steps:

**1.** Select the category of your component (Tool, Control, or Template). This selection helps the repository engine to understand where to include your extension on the Gallery.

**2.** Select the way you want to share your component. You can either upload the VSIX installation kit directly to the Gallery (the details page will display the Download button in this case), or provide a link to a page with more specific information about the component and download instructions. When you decide to use a link, the details page will display the Get Now button.

**3.** Provide attributes and description for your component. This is where you tell the most important information about your component (such as its title, version, summary, thumbnail, and demo screenshot images, cost category, language, tags, supported Visual Studio versions, and a detailed description). After checking the "I agree to the contribution agreement" checkbox, your component gets uploaded to the repository, but stays unpublished.

You can review and edit the attributes of your uploaded components any time when you click the My Contributions link. The page lists your contributions and allows you to edit, publish, unpublish, or even to delete them, as shown in Figure 5-44.

**FIGURE 5-44:** You can review your contributions

This is the page where you can access visit and download statistics about your contributions.

## Working Together with the Community

The Gallery is a central site of the Visual Studio Extensibility community. You can help this community by sharing your experiences through component reviews and discussions. On the details page of any component, you can locate the Reviews tab where you can not only read what others share, but also can write your own reviews, as shown in Figure 5-45.

You can discuss issues about components by using the Discussions tab on the details page. Authors and vendors can enable or disable the discussion functionality when uploading their contributions. If you do not see the Discussion tab, it generally means the vendor has its own

**FIGURE 5-45:** You can write your own review about a component.

discussion forum outside of Visual Studio Gallery. Use the Get Now button to get to the vendor's page and find the appropriate forum there.

## SUMMARY

The Visual IDE was designed with many customization options in mind. It provides great window management features to allow arranging the tool windows and document windows on your workspace, and organizing them to fit the way you work. Visual Studio 2010 now provides enhanced document window management that supports both tabbed and floating documents, and multiple displays.

You can use similar flexibility to rearrange the IDE menu and toolbar items, as well as organize commands into your own menus and toolbars.

In addition to changing the visual properties of the IDE, you can influence the behavior of the environment and specific modules within the IDE. The Tools ➪ Options dialog is the central place where you can adjust these settings. The Export and Import Settings Wizard lets you store and reload these settings, and even share them among team members working together.

Visual Studio delivers more than a thousand commands available in the IDE. You do not need to use the mouse to invoke them through menu or toolbar items; you can associate keyboard shortcuts with them.

You can change the Start Page of Visual Studio. Although this extensibility option was already available in the first Visual Studio .NET version, Visual Studio 2010 delivers essential changes and lowers the barrier to entering to Start Page customization. With the help of the Custom Start Page Template, you can easily develop your own Start Pages.

Visual Studio Gallery provides a catalog that showcases free and commercial products that complement or extend Visual Studio. This site was launched just a few months later than Visual Studio 2008, and since that time, it has become the one-stop shop for Visual Studio Extensions. You can use this site to find extensions to help in your everyday work, and it provides a repository to share your contributions with the Visual Studio community.

Chapter 6 provides an overview of the extensibility options of Visual Studio. You will learn how to create your simple macros and add-ins to add new functionality to the IDE, and also dive deeper into advanced extensibility scenarios using the Visual Studio 2010 SDK.

# Visual Studio Extensibility

The Visual Studio development team continuously adds new features to this great tool from release to release. But, if you were to ask Visual Studio users if there are any features they miss, you would find only a few of them answering that they got everything. Should you ask them if they like functions and features as they are, or if they would modify them if there were a way, almost all of them would enumerate at least a dozen things to change.

Different developers like to use different approaches to development, and even change their way of working, depending on the customer or teammates they work with. You can imagine how complex it would be for the Visual Studio team to create a tool that satisfies everyone's needs. Instead of thinking about super-polished functions and features that ultimately solve all development and efficiency issues for all individuals, Visual Studio provides a great number of extensibility points to change how the IDE works, and allows adding new functionality created by third parties — including you.

Visual Studio is not just a development tool. It is a real development platform that you can customize and extend to turn it into your ultimate tool to use whether for your work or coding for fun.

This chapter provides an overview about Visual Studio extensibility to help you understand how the IDE works and how you can customize it either through configuration or programmatically. After reading this chapter, you will be familiar with the following:

➤ From a high-level view, the key elements in the Visual Studio architecture are the shell and the packages.

➤ Visual Studio provides a few extensibility options right out of the box, available immediately after you've installed it. These are customization, macros, and add-ins.

➤ For advanced scenarios (such as package development or extending the re-architected code editor of Visual Studio 2010), you definitely need the Visual Studio SDK, so you will learn about what it is and how to start using it.

This chapter goes a bit deeper than just learning about the basic concepts. You'll look at the following four different types of extensibility alternatives to show you that extending Visual Studio is within the reach of every .NET developer:

➤ Macro development is well known by everyone who has ever used Microsoft Word or other Office products. Visual Studio also supports macros in a very similar way. In this chapter, you'll learn about the structure of macros, and learn how to use Macro Explorer and Macros IDE through a few samples.

➤ Visual Studio add-ins provide a more sophisticated way to create new functionality for Visual Studio because developers can integrate commands and tool windows into the IDE to imitate those as if they were the original parts of the shell. You'll learn how add-ins integrate with Visual Studio and, you will develop a basic add-in to demonstrate those concepts.

➤ Visual Studio packages are the most powerful form of Visual Studio extensions. In this chapter, you'll create a very simple package that demonstrates how the most important concepts can be implemented with the *Managed Package Framework*.

➤ Visual Studio 2010 has a brand-new editor, completely written in managed code that leverages Windows Presentation Foundation (WPF) and .NET 4's Managed Extensibility Framework. The editor has been designed with extensibility in mind. You will see a few samples that demonstrate how easy it is to add custom components to the editor.

Although you will create very simple extensions in this chapter, understanding how they live symbiotically with Visual Studio and what their main concepts are will help you to decide which method to use in a certain scenario. This also provides you with starting points to create your own components.

## THE VISUAL STUDIO SHELL AND PACKAGES

Visual Studio was designed with extensibility in mind. To develop great extensions, it is very helpful to become familiar with the basic architecture that makes it possible to add your own functionality to the IDE.

Like almost all developers, you know that when you launch Visual Studio, the `devenv.exe` application is started. So, you may think that `devenv.exe` is actually Visual Studio. If you take a look at the properties of this file (you can find it under the `Common7\IDE` folder under the Visual Studio installation root), you will discover that the file size is about 1 MB. Can the functionality of Visual Studio fit in one megabyte? Can editors, designers, compilers, debuggers (and many tools) for C#, VB, and C++ all fit in this executable?

Of course, this file itself cannot be the whole Visual Studio package, because so many functions can hardly fit into one file. If you browse the installation folder structure, you find many files, including dozens of dynamic link library (DLL) files that most likely are part of Visual Studio. So, your assumption could be that Visual Studio is the `devenv.exe` file that loads a bunch of DLLs into memory. And, you may be saying to yourself, "Oh, creating an extension for Visual Studio must be writing a .DLL that somehow integrates with the IDE." From physical standpoint, this assumption is more or less correct. But, unfortunately, it does not reveal anything useful to get you started with extending Visual Studio.

From an architectural standpoint, Visual Studio has a key component called the *Shell* hosting other components called *packages*. What you perceive as the behavior of the IDE is actually a cooperation (or, perhaps, a symbiosis) of the Shell and hosted packages. The Shell provides the core services, including generic user interface (UI) functions such as window management and command handling, menus, hierarchy management, and so on. Packages add function-specific behavior to the Shell. For example, you can design forms with the Windows Forms Designer package, as shown in Figure 6-1.

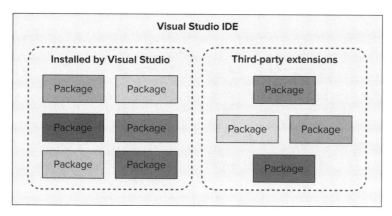

**FIGURE 6-1:**  The Shell hosts Packages

The majority of IDE functions are implemented in packages, including the C# or VB project types, testing features, the debugger, and many more — almost everything you take into account as Visual Studio. A majority of third-party extensions loaded into Visual Studio are also implemented in packages. Visual Studio handles all packages in the same way, independently of whether they are shipped with the IDE or installed by a third-party.

## Package Integration

Packages are COM objects, and the information about them is stored in the registry under the Visual Studio key.

You can imagine that complex packages like the C#, VB, F#, or C++ languages with all of their "accessories" could consume many system resources in terms of memory and CPU. If you do not use them, they do not press the CPU. But they might use memory if they sit within the Visual Studio process space. If you create a project using F#, you actually do not need services belonging to other languages, so why load them into the memory at all?

The architects of Visual Studio implemented the *package load* mechanism so that packages are loaded into memory the first time an event requiring the presence of the package is raised. These events can be one of the following:

➤ *Command activation* — The user (or some running code) activates a menu or toolbar command served by a package that has not yet been loaded. It doesn't matter if the user has clicked on a menu item or the running code has activated it with a "virtual click"; the result is the same.

➤ *Object or service request* — The Shell is about to use an object or a service in a package not yet loaded — for example, a tool window that should be displayed, or a service function that should be executed.

➤ *Context change* — The Shell can enter certain UI contexts. For example, when you start debugging a project, the Shell enters into the Debugging context. When a solution with a single project is loaded, the Shell enters into the SolutionHasSingleProject context. You can declare that a package should be loaded as the Shell enters a certain context. Visual Studio has a few predefined contexts, but you can also define your own.

So, if you do not need a package during the entire IDE session, it does not consume any memory. Should you click on a menu item activating a command sitting in a package that has not yet been loaded, the IDE will immediately load and initialize it. Should you ask for a tool window in a package not yet in memory, the IDE will start loading it.

This architecture is powerful. With packages, you can write new functionality for Visual Studio with almost the entire set of APIs and components used by the development team at Microsoft. The resulting binary is integrated into the Shell in the same way as any other packages created by Microsoft or other third parties.

 To create packages, install the Visual Studio Software Development Kit (VS SDK) available for free at the Microsoft Visual Studio Extensibility Development Center (http://msdn.com/vsx).

## EXTENSIBILITY OUT OF THE BOX

While the Visual Studio architecture is powerful (because it is designed with extensibility in mind), it would be complicated to extend Visual Studio if your only choice for creating extensions were developing packages. Of course, Visual Studio provides other mechanisms that support extension in much easier ways, enabling you to save time and the amount of work invested.

## Extending Visual Studio by Customization

Developers generally do not take into account customization and configuration as methods of extending applications — probably because none of them requires coding and building an artifact as in cases of traditional programming. However, they are great ways of adding new functionality to any application — and so it is in the case of Visual Studio.

The term "customization" here means that you can use some built-in UI to change the behavior of the application. "Configuration" means editing or adding some application-specific information. A very thin line separates these two concepts, so the term "customization" will be used here to cover both of them.

Many third-party tools (for example, documentation generators, refactoring tools, and so on) allow creating new functionality simply by customizing the tool, and Visual Studio also provides a few great ways. One of them is the capability to use code snippets to insert frequently used code patterns as you are editing the source.

Just because no traditional coding is required to customize Visual Studio, you should not underestimate the power of customization and configuration! Let's take a look at two short samples.

## Code Snippets Sample

You are not constrained to using only the snippets that ship with Visual Studio. You are also able (and encouraged) to develop your own. By creating a new snippet, you can add something new to the IDE — for example, a function that was not available before you developed it.

For example, you can create a simple C# snippet to add a file header comment with the following XML file when you save it with a `.snippet` extension, and then import it in the Code Snippet Manager:

```xml
<?xml version="1.0" encoding="utf-8"?>
<CodeSnippets xmlns="http://schemas.microsoft.com/VisualStudio/2005/CodeSnippet">
  <CodeSnippet Format="1.0">
    <Header>
      <Title>File Header Comment</Title>
      <Author>Istvan Novak (http://divedeeper.dotneteers.net)</Author>
      <Description>This snippet provides a file header comment</Description>
      <Keywords>
        <Keyword>File</Keyword>
        <Keyword>Header</Keyword>
        <Keyword>Comment</Keyword>
      </Keywords>
      <Shortcut>headcom</Shortcut>
    </Header>
    <Snippet>
      <Code Language="CSharp">
        <![CDATA[
        // ==============================================================
        // $FileName$
        //
        // $Description$
        //
        // Created by: NI
        // ==============================================================
        ]]>
      </Code>
```

```
      <Declarations>
        <Literal>
          <ID>FileName</ID>
          <ToolTip>Specify the name of the file</ToolTip>
          <Default>!FileName!</Default>
        </Literal>
        <Literal>
          <ID>Description</ID>
          <ToolTip>Provide a description of the file</ToolTip>
          <Default>!FileName!</Default>
        </Literal>
      </Declarations>
    </Snippet>
  </CodeSnippet>
</CodeSnippets>
```

When you import the file, the corresponding declaration gets a part of the available C# snippets. Figure 6-2 shows the dialog you see after importing the file.

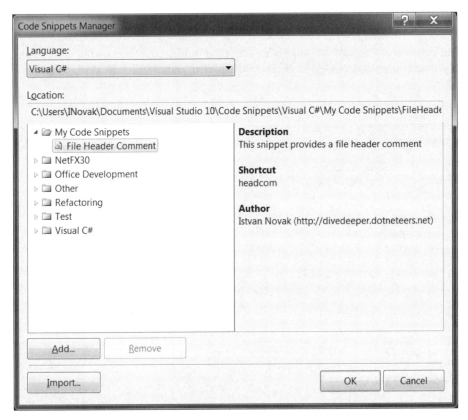

**FIGURE 6-2:** Code Snippet Manager with the new snippet definition

*Chapter 3 provides a more detailed description of how snippets can be used and created.*

## GhostDoc Sample

Many third-party tools also have been designed and implemented with extensibility in mind. One favorite is GhostDoc, which helps you to intelligently generate XML comments for source code elements like methods and properties. As shown in Figure 6-3, GhostDoc has a set of rules describing how to generate the comments for a certain source code object.

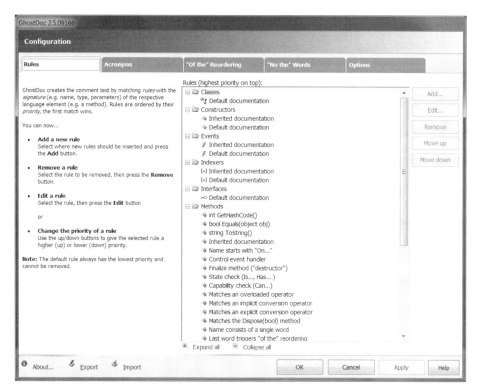

**FIGURE 6-3:** GhostDoc Rules configuration

When you select the "Default documentation" node in the "Constructors" category, and then click the Edit button, the dialog shown in Figure 6-4 appears, allowing you to edit the rules related to constructor comments. Figure 6-4 shows how the `<summary>` comment rule is set up for an instance constructor.

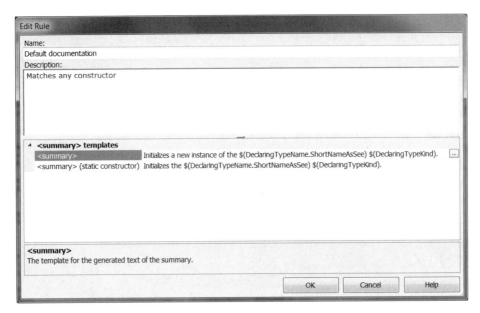

**FIGURE 6-4:** Instance Constructor Rules

Let's say that you have an uncommented constructor like this:

```
public SimplePackagePackage()
{
}
```

GhostDoc generates the following comment according to the rule:

```
/// <summary>
/// Initializes a new instance of the <see cref="SimplePackagePackage"/> class.
/// </summary>
public SimplePackagePackage()
{
}
```

## Using Macros to Automate Common Tasks

One of the key factors in the success of the Microsoft Office product family is the extensibility they provide via macros. Without knowing anything about the internal implementation of Office products, developers (as well as users from hobbyists to enthusiasts) can program macros with a simple Basic script using the *automation model* behind the scenes. The almost 20-year-old automation mechanism uses a simple (and great) idea. An object model is provided above the internal functions of the product, enabling the user to exploit them. The word "automation" comes from the fact that this object model allows writing simple scripts and programs to automate a sequence of tasks, instead of carrying out those tasks manually.

Visual Studio uses the same mechanism to utilize function values encapsulated in the product. A majority of the internal entities in the core services can be accessed through a COM-based automation object model. Just as is the case with Office applications, these entities can be used in macros that have their own user interfaces in Visual Studio — the Macro Explorer and the Macros IDE. Automation objects are not just used only for macros, but are heavily used in extensions, and as well as by add-ins and packages.

Macros provide the easiest way to extend Visual Studio — you don't even need to install the VS SDK. You can automate repetitive tasks in a few minutes by using the macro recording capabilities of Visual Studio. You can use macros in a very similar way to using them with Microsoft Office applications.

For a long time, while the .NET technology was not available, Visual Basic for Applications (VBA) was the programming language used for macro development. The .NET era introduced a new and really object-oriented Basic language (called Visual Basic .NET, or simply VB.NET) to the world, and Microsoft replaced the original VBA with a new version leveraging the constructs of VB.NET.

Macros access the Visual Studio automation object model and easily combine Visual Studio commands and objects to establish the desired behavior. To become a professional macro developer, you must know the object model behind the macros, as well as a few dozen patterns about using those objects. Visual Studio comes with a few macro samples to help you take a flying start. The best way to learn macro programming is to record macros and view recording results. You can extend this knowledge by borrowing coding patterns from the samples.

Although macros are great for task automation, they are not the right tools to create totally new functionality. When using macros, you should be aware of the fact that anyone can see the source code of your macro. Later in this chapter, you will learn more about macro development, and see a few samples.

For simple tasks, macros are powerful enough, and you can even create forms with the macros. However, they do not let you extend the UI or the services of Visual Studio. Generally, this constraint is why developers look for other options like add-ins and packages.

## Visual Studio Add-Ins

*Add-in*s are much more powerful than macros for developing Visual Studio extensions because you can access the Visual Studio automation objects and add new UI elements to the IDE (such as tool windows, menu and toolbar commands, and so on). An add-in is actually a COM object implementing two COM interfaces. They can integrate into the IDE so that you actually do not know that they are implemented as add-ins when you use them. The functions you add with an add-in look as if they were part of the IDE. If you write a macro, anyone can see the code you have written. An add-in is a compiled (managed or native) binary, so you can use the same techniques for guarding intellectual property as for any other managed or native binaries.

To deploy an add-in, simply create a setup project that produces an `.msi` file. Running this `.msi` file will do all the setup and registration tasks required for your add-in, and you can immediately start to use it with Visual Studio.

There is a project wizard in Visual Studio within the extensibility project types named Visual Studio Add-in. It guides you through the basic steps of creating a frame for a simple add-in. The wizard generates a great amount of code and comments to which you can add your own functionality. With the Visual Studio Add-in wizard, you can create add-ins with both managed and unmanaged code, but you should use managed code (Visual Basic or C#, according to your preference) unless you have no special reason for unmanaged development. Later in this chapter, you will learn how to use this wizard to create a simple add-in.

## EXTENSIONS WITH VISUAL STUDIO SDK

Visual Studio ships with a number of extensibility options out-of-the-box, but for advanced scenarios (such as creating Visual Studio packages or editor extensions), you need the Visual Studio Software Development Kit (VS SDK). This kit is free, and you can download it from the Microsoft Visual Studio Extensibility Development Center (`http://msdn.com/vsx`). When you visit this center, the download link is available right from the home page.

 *Note that there are separate versions of SDKs for the 2005, 2008, and 2010 versions of Visual Studio. Be sure to download the right one. Should you have more Visual Studio versions installed on your machine, you can download and install the right SDK for each of them, and they will work side-by-side. There are no separate SDKs that depend on the edition of your specific Visual Studio version, so the same SDK can be used for the Standard edition, as well as for the Professional or the Team System editions.*

Installing the VS SDK is very simple, so when you download the setup kit, you can immediately run the setup file. Follow the instructions on the screen and, in a few minutes, the VS SDK is ready to work with.

## The Full Power of Extensibility

After the installation of VS SDK, you will find many new files under the `VisualStudioIntegration` folder in the VS SDK root installation directory (which is `Visual Studio 2010 SDK` in your `Program Files` folder). Take a look at the content of `VisualStudioIntegration`. You will see that the `Common\Assemblies` folder collects dozens of interoperability and other useful assemblies. The VS SDK also installs a folder (`Common\Source\CSharp`) where you can find the source files of the most important tools and components of the kit, just like the Managed Package Framework source.

To use the core services of Visual Studio, you need to cooperate with a large number of COM objects (classes and interfaces). You have several options to do that, depending on the type of extension you are going to create. Figure 6-5 illustrates the stack of components working together to access those services.

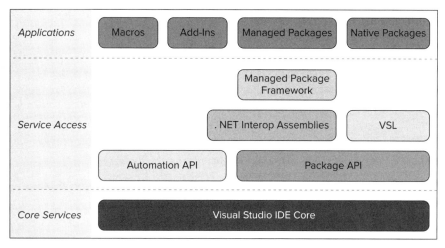

**FIGURE 6-5:** Extensibility components

Visual Studio extension artifacts can be developed as macros, add-ins, or packages. Although this book focuses on managed code development, both add-ins and packages can be developed with unmanaged (native) code (for example, by using C++).

Within Microsoft, a set of teams works on developing separate features of Visual Studio. There are teams creating packages for Visual Studio (which are actually extensions, even if you do not consider them as such because they ship and install together with the IDE). There are a few APIs that are used by the internal Microsoft teams from the beginning to access the core service functionality.

The Package API located directly above the Core Services shown in Figure 6-5 is one of the native APIs used by these teams. It is the same kind of Visual Studio API as, for example, the `Kernel32`
`.dll` and `User32.dll` used for the Windows operating systems. The Visual Studio team also created an Automation API over the Core Services, as shown in Figure 6-5. Both APIs use the COM technology, but while the Package API seems to be a flat API, automation objects compose a real object hierarchy. Although the scope of these two APIs has a relatively large intersection, there is functionality that can be accessed only by one of them.

## Visual Studio Package Development

For those who want to develop packages in the native way, the *Visual Studio Library* (*VSL*) provides the foundation on which to build. The VSL is a set of template-based C++ classes used to simplify the creation of packages in native C++. It relies on the *Active Template Library* (*ATL*) for its support of COM objects.

Developers using managed code cannot directly use COM-based APIs. The bridge between the two worlds is the set of interoperability (interop) assemblies. Interop assemblies help in the physical communication between COM and .NET. So, managed code developers can access the Automation API and the Package API, but this does not add value on the managed world side. Programmers must "manually" handle all the COM stuff related to life-cycle management, global unique identifiers (GUIDs), and so on.

*Managed Package Framework* (*MPF*) brings you a small library built on top of the interop assemblies. It implements the most important core types to develop packages in managed code by using VB, C#, or any other managed languages (including F# and the Iron family of languages). These core types deal with such concepts as packages, windows and tool windows, dialog pages, commands, menus, documents, and many more.

When creating managed packages, you typically build your code on the MPF types and interop assemblies. In many cases, you use both the automation objects and the Package API.

The interop assemblies, VSL, and the MPF are all parts of the VS SDK. Visual Studio installs only the Automation API, so you cannot develop your own packages out of the box.

## Editor Extensibility

Visual Studio 2010 is the first big movement to migrate the unmanaged code base of Visual Studio into managed code. The best evidence of this fact is the re-architected text editor that actually could be called a brand new editor. It is fully developed with managed code that leverages patterns frequently used in .NET programming.

The new editor uses WPF as its presentation technology, and it opens new opportunities over the simple features used before Visual Studio 2010. The development team designed the new editor with extensibility in mind and used the *Managed Extensibility Framework* (*MEF*) as the core technology to allow a straightforward and simple way of creating custom extensions. A great evidence of this architecture's usability is the fact that many editor features are physically implemented as extensions to a core functional set.

Following is a short list just to show you an example of this well-thought-out architecture:

➤ There is a fine control over editor *font properties*. It is possible to mix font faces, font styles, and sizes. You can alter the formatting of built-in languages, and even share the same formatting across different languages.

➤ A *line transformation* can be applied for each editor line that translates into vertical scaling and defining the space surrounding the line.

➤ There is a way to create *classifiers* that can be assigned to the specified editor content (for example, to the text in the Output window, or to the C# source in the code editor). Classifiers can have their own formatting.

➤ You can add *adornments* to the text that can be actually any piece of WPF `UIElement` definitions, including images, animations, and even video.

➤ If you do not like the current presentation of IntelliSense in the editor, you can change it.

From an architectural point of view, the new editor clearly separates the roles of objects working behind the scenes — and this is a big shift from the previous editor's implementation, which was poorly designed by means of object responsibilities and cooperation.

The editor separates the concept called *Text Model* from the presentation called *Text View Model*. The Text Model is responsible for handling the text buffer (a sequence of lines and characters) by using snapshots and versions to improve management of simultaneous (multi-thread) changes, and provides a clear way to track changes across versions. The Text View Model is responsible for formatting and rendering text, including a few dozen extensibility points to programmatically set up formatting and intercept rendering.

Later in this chapter, you will build a *classifier* to demonstrate the concepts introduced here.

## CREATING VISUAL STUDIO MACROS

This section dives a bit deeper into Visual Studio macro programming so that you can learn how to become an advanced macro developer.

From the standpoint of extensibility, macros are the lightest constructs used to add new functionality to Visual Studio. The good thing about using macros is that they are really simple to use in most scenarios when you want to automate tasks. The bad thing about using them is that you cannot use them to create new UIs integrated with the window management system of Visual Studio (just as you cannot add new services). So, if you want to achieve quick results and do not need to use a sophisticated UI, macros can be the perfect choice for you.

Macros are written in Visual Basic. Their syntax is very similar to that used with Office macros.

### Understanding the Structure of Macros

Macros are simple subroutines with no input parameters. Running a macro means running the code sitting in that subroutine. Macros are organized into *modules*. Every public subroutine with no parameters is taken into account as a macro that can be run.

The following code represents a very simple module with four methods:

```
Imports System
Imports EnvDTE
Imports EnvDTE80
Imports EnvDTE90
Imports System.Diagnostics
Imports System.Windows.Forms

Public Module SimpleMacros

    Public Sub SayHello()
        Call SayHelloWithGreetings("Hello from a macro")
    End Sub

    Public Sub SayHelloWithGreetings(ByVal greetings As String)
        MessageBox.Show(greetings)
    End Sub

    Public Function AskQuestion(ByVal question As String)
        Return MessageBox.Show(question, "question", MessageBoxButtons.YesNo, _
                    MessageBoxIcon.Question, MessageBoxDefaultButton.Button1, _
                    MessageBoxOptions.DefaultDesktopOnly, False)
```

```
        End Function

        Private Sub PrivateSayHello()
            Call SayHelloWithGreetings("Hello from a private subroutine")
        End Sub
    End Module
```

Of these methods, only `SayHello` is a valid macro. The others are not, because `SayHelloWithGreetings` has input parameters, `AskQuestion` is a function, and `PrivateSayHello` is not public.

Beside the modules, macros can use code sitting in classes. For example, you can move the functionality of the `SayHelloWithGreetings` method into a separate class:

```
Imports System
Imports EnvDTE
Imports EnvDTE80
Imports EnvDTE90
Imports System.Diagnostics
Imports System.Windows.Forms

Public Class Greetings

    Public Sub ShowGreetings(ByVal Greetings As String)
        MessageBox.Show(Greetings)
    End Sub

End Class
```

The `SayHello` method can be changed to use the `Greetings` class:

```
Imports System
Imports EnvDTE
Imports EnvDTE80
Imports EnvDTE90
Imports System.Diagnostics

Public Module SimpleMacros

    Public Sub SayHello()
        Dim greetings = New Greetings()
        greetings.ShowGreetings("Hello from a class")
    End Sub

End Module
```

Classes also can contain macros, but, of course, they cannot be instance methods. Rather, they use only shared (static, in C# terminology) methods with no input parameters and return values. So, if you put the `ShowSimpleGreetings` method into the previous `Greetings` class, it can be started as a macro:

```
Public Shared Sub ShowSimpleGreetings()
    MessageBox.Show("Greetings")
End Sub
```

Looking for the `Imports` statements in the previous snippets, you can see that namespaces are used with types declared in Visual Studio and .NET framework system assemblies (such as `EnvDTE` and `System.Windows.Forms`). Modules, classes, and references for the assemblies used are stored in a unit called a *macro project* that is physically a binary file with `.vsmacros` extension.

Visual Studio uses the macro project as the smallest unit of deployment. Storing all information in a single `.vsmacros` file makes deployment easy. If you want to extract the code from macro projects, you can export modules and classes into standard `.vb` files.

At the highest level, Visual Studio works with zero, one, or more macro projects put into a logical container called a *macro system*. It resembles a Visual Studio solution, but it is different. When the IDE is started, the macro system's projects are loaded independently of what kind of solution and projects are opened. The macro projects are not tied to any of your concrete projects. You can handle them as if they belonged to the IDE itself.

Projects of the macro system are totally independent from each other. You cannot make references among them like you can cross-reference projects in a Visual Studio solution.

## Using the Macro Explorer

If you want to have a look at the macro system, the easiest tool is the Macro Explorer window that can be accessed through the Tools ➪ Macros ➪ Macro Explorer menu function. As shown in Figure 6-6, this window displays a hierarchy of projects, modules, and classes, and, of course, macros in the system.

As you can see, the hierarchy contains the following two projects. (Both of them are installed with Visual Studio 2010.)

**FIGURE 6-6:** Macro system hierarchy in the Macro Explorer

➤ `MyMacros` is displayed in bold to illustrate that this project is set as the *recording project*. When you record a macro, it always will be put into the recording project.

➤ `Samples` is a great source for getting started with macro programming. It contains more than 50 working macros with basic explanations and comments. Examining the samples can help a lot toward understanding the philosophy of Visual Studio's automation model and solving common tasks.

If you expand the project nodes, you can see modules and classes belonging to that project. Classes and modules are not distinguished visually, but by expanding them, you can enumerate the macros they contain. In Figure 6-6, you see `MySamples` contains the `Greetings` class file with the `ShowSimpleGreetings` macro, as well as the `SimpleMacros` module with the `SayHello` macro from the earlier snippets.

Macro Explorer is not just a simple hierarchy view of macro projects and their items. You also can initiate actions from the context menus of items. Right-click on an item to reach its context menu, and select the action you would like to take.

Table 6-1 provides an overview of actions you can access from the quick menus.

**TABLE 6-1:** Actions Available in Macro Explorer

| ACTION | ITEM TYPE | DESCRIPTION |
|---|---|---|
| Load Macro Project . . . | Root | Adds a macro project to the macro system. You can select a .vsmacros file representing the project. The selected project will be added to macro system, and remains there after closing and restarting Visual Studio, unless you unload it. |
| Unload Macro Project | Project | Removes the project from the macro system. The remove operation does not delete the corresponding .vsmacros file, so later you'll be able to load it again. |
| New Macro Project | Root | While the Load Macro Project adds an existing .vsmacros file to the system, with this function you can create a new project with its own .vsmacros file. You must first select a macro template and set the name and path of the project file, as illustrated in Figure 6-7. You should accept the default path unless you have a good reason to put the project in another location. |
| Macros IDE | Root | Opens the Macros IDE, allowing you to edit macros in the project. |
| New Module | Project | Creates a new module and adds it to the selected project. You can select a module template and name your module, as shown in Figure 6-8. Remember that modules are not separate files. They are a logical part of the project file, so you cannot set a physical path to store them. |
| Set Recording Project | Project | Sets the project to be the one into which to save recorded macros. The project is displayed with bold typeface in the Macro Explorer window. |
| Edit | Module/Macro | Opens the Macros IDE and navigates to the selected module or macro so that you can start editing its content immediately. |

| ACTION | ITEM TYPE | DESCRIPTION |
|---|---|---|
| Rename | Module/Macro | Renames the selected module or macro. The Macro Explorer does not allow you to set an invalid name that does not comply with VB identifier syntax. |
| Delete | Module/Macro | After confirmation, deletes the macro or the module. Unlike unloading projects, deleting macros or modules physically removes the corresponding information from the `.vsmacros` file, so this operation cannot be undone. Use the Macros IDE to export affected modules or macros if you want to save the content before deletion. |
| New macro | Module | Adds a new macro to the selected module or class. In the case of modules, the new macro will be added as a `Public Sub`. In the case of classes, the new macro will be added as a `Shared Sub`. The new macro is named `Macro<N>`, where `<N>` represents the next available sequence number in the module. After adding the macro, the Macro IDE is shown with the focus set on the body of the new macro. |
| Run | Macro | Immediately runs the selected macro. |

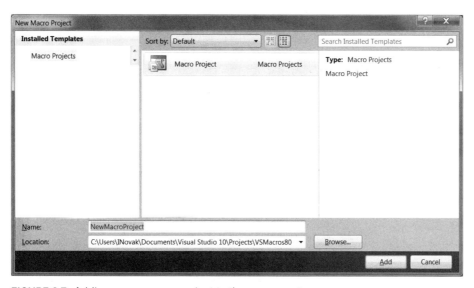

**FIGURE 6-7:** Adding a new macro project to the macro system

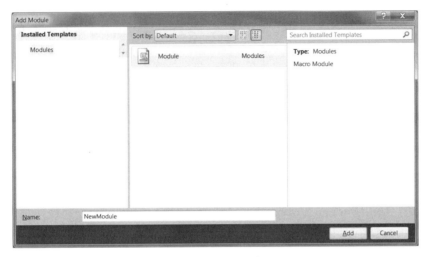

**FIGURE 6-8:** Adding a new module to a macro project

The actions summarized in Table 6-1 show you that the Macro Explorer is a central place for launching macros and displaying the macro system hierarchy, but not for editing them. When it is time to edit modules, classes, or macros, Macros IDE should be your tool.

## Using the Macros IDE

You can start Macros IDE indirectly from Macros Explorer by adding a new macro or editing an existing module or macro. By using the Tools ➪ Macros ➪ Macros IDE menu function, or using the Alt+F11 key sequence, you can start this separate IDE directly. The UI shown in Figure 6-9 resembles the Visual Basic development environment available in the Office applications, and also in Visual Studio.

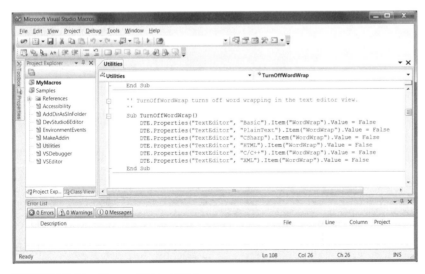

**FIGURE 6-9:** The Macros IDE in action

Even the structure of Macros IDE is very similar to Visual Studio IDE, so you may guess that it is a standalone application that can be loaded independently of Visual Studio. The macro system is a part of Visual Studio, and Macros IDE works with the projects composing the macro system. Even if it seems like a standalone application, it is a part of Visual Studio IDE.

## Using the Project Explorer and the Class View

The Project Explorer contains a hierarchical list of projects and modules just like Macro Explorer. However, here you cannot see macros in the list. The Project Explorer contains some other project-specific information not visible in the Macro Explorer, such as the list of referenced assemblies and a module called `EnvironmentEvents`. Figure 6-10 shows the Project Explorer displaying the referenced assemblies in the `Samples` project.

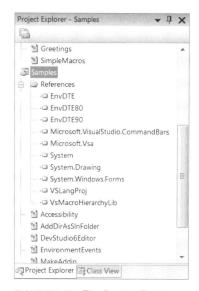

**FIGURE 6-10:** The Project Explorer in the Macros IDE

You may find it disturbing to have two separate UIs for displaying the structure of macro projects. The logic behind this approach is that you only need Macro Explorer to have a great overview about what macros you have, and, if you need any of them, you can immediately start from this tool window. The Project Explorer is built up very similarly to Solution Explorer. The view it provides is a development-time view where your main focus is to edit, try, and debug macros.

From the user experience point of view, the only thing that is a bit disturbing is that both the Macro Explorer and Project Explorer allow you to create new modules and macros. These two windows are synchronized, so any changes applied in one window will automatically appear in the other one.

Just as you can have a class view for your source code in Solution Explorer, you also have a Class View tool window in Macros IDE to see your code's structure. Figure 6-11 shows the `MyMacros` project with the methods of the `Greetings` class.

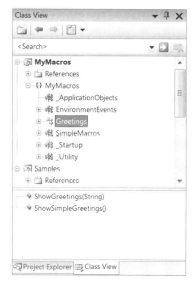

**FIGURE 6-11:** Class View in the Macros IDE

You can use the Class View for browsing your own modules, classes, and members, as well as objects in the referenced assemblies. You can see a few objects in Figure 6-11 that have names starting with an underscore (for example, `_ApplicationObject` and `_Startup`, `_Utility`). These are hidden modules that were created along with the macro project and are responsible for the run-time integration of macros with the Visual Studio IDE.

## Editing Projects and Macros

The Macros IDE provides a friendly environment to edit macro projects and individual macros. The UI and the logic are very similar to the user surface of Visual Studio, and functions work similarly, so it is easy to become familiar with this tool. However, there are a few things that work a bit differently than for Visual Studio projects. Let's take a look at the most important ones to make your macro-editing experience better.

In Macros IDE, you cannot add a new project to the macro system, and this function is available only from Macro Explorer. However, here you can edit any parts of the macros project, including the list of referenced assemblies and modules. You can also add new modules either by creating new ones, or adding an existing one.

As already discussed, the whole macro project is stored in a binary .vsmacros file. Adding an existing module to the macro project actually means that the content of an existing .vb file is imported into the .vsmacros file. Unlike in standard VB projects in Visual Studio where the source files can be edited externally, here editing the existing file you've added to the macro project does not affect your project, because a copy of the file content is merged into the project.

You can explicitly add a new module or a new class to a macro project. Actually, the term *module* has two meanings:

> The module is a part of a project (like a source file for a standard Visual Studio project). You can edit one module as one document in the Macros IDE code editor.

> The module is a language construct. To be more precise, it would be better use the term *module definition* to describe the language elements between the `Module` and `End Module` keywords.

The function names (Add New Module and Add New Class) suggest that you can put either a module definition or a class definition into a module. Do not treat this implicit suggestion as a constraint! You can put an unlimited number of module and class definitions into the same document, and classes even can be nested into modules.

Figure 6-12 shows the macro editor window within the Macros IDE. It resembles the experience you have with the VB editor in Visual Studio. You can open multiple documents (modules in your macro project) at the same time, and select your active document with tabs.

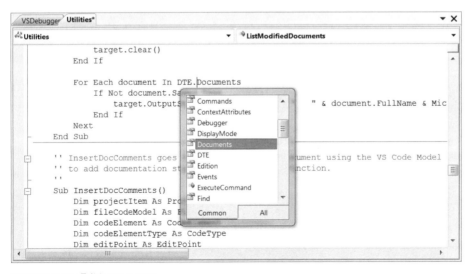

**FIGURE 6-12:** Editing a macro

The two combo boxes at the top of the editor area help you with quick navigation. The combo box on the left allows you to select a module or class definition, and the one on the right helps in selecting a member within that class or module. IntelliSense is available during macro editing, and code completion works as well.

You can also use the familiar editing functions like find and replace, bookmarks, block commenting, code outlining, and so on.

# Recording and Developing Macros

As mentioned previously, from a programming point of view, macros are actually subroutines written in VB. If you want to develop a macro, sooner or later you must create its code. It sounds easy, but as with any other kind of development, possessing the knowledge of the programming language is generally not enough to create applications. Also, a good understanding of the context of the programming language that should be used within is important.

And so it is with macro programming. The context where the VB language should be used is the Visual Studio IDE environment where services can be accessed through the automation model.

Earlier, you learned about how macros can be edited in the Macros IDE. Let's take a look at the basics to help you in getting started with creating macros.

## Learning by Macro Recording

The best way start discovering the elements of macro development is to record macros with the built-in recorder tool. Any time you do a repetitive task, you can record the steps required to replay the task. Replaying those steps is just one alternative! After you have finished recording those steps, you can immediately look at the macro body to see how your activities are represented in macros. This can help to shorten the learning process. First, try to observe shorter macros, and later you can examine longer ones.

The greatest thing about macro recording is that you are not obliged to accept the recorded macro as it is. You can change it, or simply cut parts and put them in other macros. When you discover how certain tasks are carried out, you can find out how you can parameterize commands, activities, and properties.

Let's see how macro recording works. After preparing for the task to record, you can click on Tools ⇨ Macros ⇨ Record TemporaryMacro, or press Ctrl+Shift+R. At this moment, macro recording starts. The recording toolbar appears on the screen (as shown in Figure 6-13), and a small icon is displayed on the status bar with the "Recording macro … " message, indicating that your activities are saved in a temporary macro.

**FIGURE 6-13:** Macro Recording toolbar

Following are the three buttons of the toolbar (from left to right):

➤ *Pause/Resume Recording* — Any time you want to temporarily pause macro recording (for example, if you've done something unintended and you want to return to a point to continue recording), you can use this button. When you are ready to go on, click on this button again to resume.

➤ *Stop Recording* — When you've finished recording, click this button and your macro will be saved into the `RecordingModule` of the current recording project into a macro named `TemporaryMacro`.

➤ *Cancel Recording* — Clicking this button cancels recording the macro without storing any data into `TemporaryMacro`.

After recording, you look at the freshly recorded macro, and, if you find it useful, you can save it either by moving it to another module, changing its name in the editor, or using the Tools ➪ Macros ➪ Save Temporary Macro menu item. Always save your macro, because the next recording will override the previous one.

Let's take a look at a very simple example in practice. Let's create a macro that inserts simple text into the source code.

1. Create a Visual C# console application project and name it `RecordingConsole`. When the project has been created, the `Program.cs` file is opened.

2. Move the cursor into the body of the `Main` method and enter a new line between the opening and closing braces.

3. Start macro recording by pressing Ctrl+Shift+R.

4. Type in the following text:

```
Console.WriteLine("Hello, world");
```

5. At the end of the line, press Enter, and then stop macro recording.

Now, you can go into the Macros IDE to edit the recorded macro. If you followed the instructions, you see a `TemporaryMacro` like this:

```
Option Strict Off
Option Explicit Off
Imports System
Imports EnvDTE
Imports EnvDTE80
Imports EnvDTE90
Imports System.Diagnostics

Public Module RecordingModule
    Sub TemporaryMacro()
        DTE.ActiveDocument.Selection.Text = "Console.WriteLine(""Hello, world"");"
        DTE.ActiveDocument.Selection.NewLine()
    End Sub
End Module
```

The recorder saves your activities done in Visual Studio IDE. Pressing the keyboard keys, clicking on menu or toolbar items, closing dialog boxes with OK, all generate information that will be persisted in the macro — and of course, typos and other unintended activities are also recorded. For example, the following macro shows the traces of correcting typos:

```
Public Module RecordingModule
    Sub TemporaryMacro()
```

```
          DTE.ActiveDocument.Selection.Indent(3)
          DTE.ActiveDocument.Selection.Text = "Console.WriteLine(""Hellow"
          DTE.ActiveDocument.Selection.DeleteLeft()
          DTE.ActiveDocument.Selection.Text = ", world"");"
          DTE.ActiveDocument.Selection.NewLine()
      End Sub
  End Module
```

Your recorded macro is immediately available in the Macros IDE and also in Macro Explorer, where you can run it!

 *Macro recording has an important limitation: It does not record any activities done within modal dialogs opened from commands. For example, when using the File ➪ New ➪ Project dialog, your settings typed there are not saved into the macro. The macro recorder only saves the fact that you've opened the dialog.*

## A Few Points About Macro Development

There are about a dozen of books published about Visual Studio macro development. The following discussion will not teach you every aspect, but rather highlight a few important things to help you to understand the entire macro development life cycle.

### Building and Running Macros

Macro projects must be built before running any macros within them. During the build process, the macro syntax and semantics are checked, just as with standard Visual Studio projects, and debug information can also be included to allow tracing and debugging macros. There is no partial build for modules or individual macros. If there is any build-time discoverable error that prevents the project from building successfully, no macro in that project can run. Macros IDE provides an error list accessible through the View ➪ Error List menu item (as shown in Figure 6-9) where you can check build issues.

There are several ways to run macros. You have already learned that you can start them from Macro Explorer. You can also run them from the Macros IDE, where you start them with or without debugging after moving the cursor to the name of the macro definition within the code editor. Visual Studio also allows you to customize your menus and toolbars with items running macros.

### Debugging a Macro

When you develop macros, you suffer from the same programming mistakes as with any other programming language, and the majority of these issues can be solved with the help of a debugger. The Macros IDE provides the same tools for debugging as the Visual Studio IDE, and you can use the same techniques to find and remove bugs as with other languages and project types.

Figure 6-14 shows debugging of a sample macro named `DecreaseTextEditorFontSize` that is located in the Accessibility module. In this figure, you see a breakpoint placed on the first statement line of the macro, and the current execution line that is the next line after the breakpoint. At the bottom of the screen, the Locals tool window lists the variables used in the macro where you can drill down to the internal values of the locally declared objects.

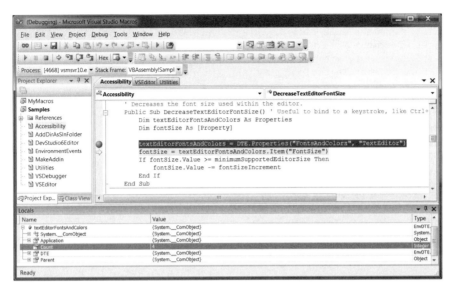

**FIGURE 6-14:** Debugging a macro

## Macro Deployment

Visual Studio provides a few templates for creating setup projects and installation kits for your applications. These kits can be used to copy the binaries and other content files, prepare shortcuts, register components, and so on. However, you cannot directly use them to create an install kit for a macro project.

Fortunately, macro projects are stored in binary `.vsmacros` files that represent the unit of deployment for macros. You can deploy a macro developed and tested on your machine by following these steps:

1. Discover where your macro project is stored on your source machine and copy it.

2. Check where Visual Studio stores macro projects on the destination machines, and paste them to the appropriate location.

3. Start Visual Studio 2010 and open the Macro Explorer.

4. Use the Load Macro Project function in the context menu of the Macros root node to add the freshly copied project file to the macro system.

After you follow these steps, the macros are ready to use on the destination machines. Generally, macros are stored in your user profile in the `Documents\Visual Studio 2010\Projects` folder, but this can be changed. To check where your macros are stored, open the Options dialog. Go to the Projects and Solutions category, and select the General tab. At the top of the dialog page, the "Visual Studio project location" contains the path you are looking for.

## Responding IDE Events

A great benefit of macro development is that macros can run to respond to Visual Studio IDE events. When you create a macro project, a module named `EnvironmentEvents` is also created that contains auto-generated code to access system events.

When you open this module, you can use the two combo boxes at the top of the code editor to generate event code-handling skeletons. From the left combo box, you can select the event category; from the right combo box, you can select the specific event in that category. For example, if you want to respond to an event when a solution is opened, select the `SolutionEvents` category from the left combo box, and the `Opened` event in the right one, as shown in Figure 6-15.

```
EnvironmentEvents                                          ▾ ✕
 SolutionEvents                    ▾    Opened                 ▾
 Public Module EnvironmentEvents

 Automatically generated code, do not modify

     Private Sub SolutionEvents_Opened() Handles SolutionEvents.Opened
         MessageBox.Show("A solution has been opened.")
     End Sub
 End Module
```

**FIGURE 6-15:** Adding a macro responding to a system event

You can put your macro code into the body of the generated event handler method. After building the macro, you can check that opening a solution triggers the event, popping up the message in the method body.

## Macro Samples

As discussed previously, recording macros and examining the `Samples` project can shorten your macro development learning curve. Let's take a look at a few code extracts and some explanations about their behavior. These samples intensively use the DTE automation model. Patterns used here also can support you when developing other kinds of extensibility components, such as add-ins and VSPackages.

### Accessing IDE Options

Macros often use Visual Studio IDE options for specific tasks. The `IncreaseTextEditorFontSize` and `DecreaseTextEditorFontSize` macros in the `Accessibility` module are good examples to demonstrate option usage.

```
Public Sub IncreaseTextEditorFontSize()
    Dim textEditorFontsAndColors As Properties

    textEditorFontsAndColors = DTE.Properties("FontsAndColors", "TextEditor")
    textEditorFontsAndColors.Item("FontSize").Value += fontSizeIncrement
End Sub

Public Sub DecreaseTextEditorFontSize()
    Dim textEditorFontsAndColors As Properties
```

```
        Dim fontSize As [Property]

        textEditorFontsAndColors = DTE.Properties("FontsAndColors", "TextEditor")
        fontSize = textEditorFontsAndColors.Item("FontSize")
        If fontSize.Value >= minimumSupportedEditorSize Then
            fontSize.Value -= fontSizeIncrement
        End If
    End Sub
```

The key to accessing IDE options is the `Properties` collection of the `DTE` object. This collection can be addressed with two indexes — the first being the name of the category, and the second being the name of the property page within that category. From the previous snippet, you can see that the `FontsAndColors` category defines the `TextEditor` property page.

First, you obtain an object representing that property page. The page holds a collection of objects, so go down to the one with the index of `FontSize`. Obviously, this is the size of the font used by the text editor.

> *Note that this produced an object and not a value. You can use the `Value` property of `fontSize` to read and change the real value behind that object.*

## Writing Output Messages

Macros can be very useful in outputting some project-related information that you cannot directly gain from the Visual Studio IDE. This information can be written to a pane in the output window.

The following sample can be found in the `VSDebugger` module and demonstrates how to write messages to an output pane:

```
Sub LastBreakReason()
    Dim outputWinPane As EnvDTE.OutputWindowPane

    outputWinPane = Utilities.GetOutputWindowPane("Debugger")
    Select Case DTE.Debugger.LastBreakReason
        Case dbgEventReason.dbgEventReasonBreakpoint
            outputWinPane.OutputString("Breakpoint hit" + vbCrLf)
        Case dbgEventReason.dbgEventReasonNone
            outputWinPane.OutputString("No reason" + vbCrLf)
        Case dbgEventReason.dbgEventReasonExceptionNotHandled
            outputWinPane.OutputString("Exception not handled by the debuggee" _
            + vbCrLf)
        Case dbgEventReason.dbgEventReasonExceptionThrown
            outputWinPane.OutputString("Exception thrown" + vbCrLf)
    End Select
End Sub
```

The output window displays a set of panes. The current pane can be selected in the "Show output from" combo box. When you want to write to a pane, the first task is to obtain a reference to an EvnDTE.OutputWindowPane object, and then you can call the OutputString method to display your message.

The Utilities class contains a method named GetOutputWindowPane that obtains the window pane object for you. As you can see from this method, you are not tied to using only the built-in output panes. You can also create custom window panes by specifying a unique name:

```
Function GetOutputWindowPane(ByVal Name As String,
    Optional ByVal show As Boolean = True) As OutputWindowPane
    Dim window As Window
    Dim outputWindow As OutputWindow
    Dim outputWindowPane As OutputWindowPane

    window = DTE.Windows.Item(EnvDTE.Constants.vsWindowKindOutput)
    If show Then window.Visible = True
    outputWindow = window.Object
    Try
        outputWindowPane = outputWindow.OutputWindowPanes.Item(Name)
    Catch e As System.Exception
        outputWindowPane = outputWindow.OutputWindowPanes.Add(Name)
    End Try
    outputWindowPane.Activate()
    Return outputWindowPane
End Function
```

The OutputWindow object is the one responsible for the output panes. The method's logic is straightforward. If it does not find the specified pane in the collection of existing window panes, it creates a new one and activates (displays) it.

## Traversing the Solution Hierarchy

With macros, you can traverse through the whole solution hierarchy, including the projects and their items in order to process them. The Utilities module implements a macro named ListProj that traverses through all items of the active project:

```
Sub ListProj()
    Dim project As Project
    Dim projectObjects As Object()
    Dim window As Window
    Dim target As Object

    window = DTE.Windows.Item(Constants.vsWindowKindCommandWindow)
    projectObjects = DTE.ActiveSolutionProjects
    If projectObjects.Length = 0 Then
        Exit Sub
    End If
    project = DTE.ActiveSolutionProjects(0)
    If (DTE.ActiveWindow Is window) Then
        target = window.Object
    Else
```

```
            target = GetOutputWindowPane("List Project")
            target.Clear()
        End If
        ListProjAux(project.ProjectItems(), 0, target)
    End Sub
```

`ListProj` accesses the active project through the `ActiveSolutionsProject` collection of the DTE object, and invokes `ListProjAux` to display items in that project.

There is another interesting feature that `ListProj` also implements. It checks if the macro is started from the Command window, and, in this case, it puts the output to that window; otherwise, it creates a "List Project" pane in the output window.

```
    Sub ListProjAux(ByVal projectItems As EnvDTE.ProjectItems, _
        ByVal level As Integer, ByVal outputWinPane As Object)
        Dim projectItem As EnvDTE.ProjectItem

        For Each projectItem In projectItems
            If projectItem.Collection Is projectItems Then
                Dim projectItems2 As EnvDTE.ProjectItems
                Dim notSubCollection As Boolean

                OutputItem(projectItem, level, outputWinPane)
                projectItems2 = projectItem.ProjectItems
                notSubCollection = projectItems2 Is Nothing
                If Not notSubCollection Then
                    ListProjAux(projectItems2, level + 1, outputWinPane)
                End If
            End If
        Next
    End Sub
```

`ListProjAux` is used recursively to display project items. Each item keeps a collection of nested project items that is used as a base of a recursive approach. The `OutputItem` method is called for every traversed item in order to display filename information.

```
    Sub OutputItem(ByVal projectItem As EnvDTE.ProjectItem, ByVal level As Integer, _
        ByVal outputWinPane As Object)
        Dim i As Integer = 0

        While (i < level)
            outputWinPane.OutputString("    ")
            i = i + 1
        End While
        outputWinPane.OutputString(projectItem.FileNames(1))
        outputWinPane.OutputString(Microsoft.VisualBasic.Constants.vbCrLf)
    End Sub
```

`OutputItem` first writes out indenting whitespace according to the nesting level, and then displays the item's full filename.

*Note that you can substitute* OutputItem *with your own custom method to process project items.*

### Dealing with User Input

The Interaction object type in the Microsoft.VisualBasic namespace contains a method named InputBox that can be easily used to collect user input, as the following sample macro shows:

```
Sub SaveView()
    Dim name As String

    name = InputBox("Enter the name you want to save as:", "Save window layout")
    If (name = "") Then
        MsgBox("Empty string, enter a valid name.")
    Else
        DTE.WindowConfigurations.Add(name)
    End If
End Sub
```

As its name suggests, InputBox pops up a modal dialog where you can enter an input string. You can specify a label for the input and a caption for the dialog. The SaveView macro uses this information to create a new window configuration item with the specified name and saves it the to the configuration settings.

By using the System.Windows.Forms namespace, you can create forms dynamically at run-time, and then show them. It may worth it to create simple modal dialogs, but if you need a more complex UI, you'd be better off working with Visual Studio add-ins.

## CREATING VISUAL STUDIO ADD-INS

As described earlier, Visual Studio has an extensibility point to integrate add-ins into the IDE. Add-ins are great tools to gain enhanced functionality. This section examines what add-ins are, and how you can use them. You will also build a small add-in to help you understand internal details through source code.

## Add-In Architecture

Add-ins are COM components that implement the following two COM interfaces:

➤ The IDTExtensibility2 interface is responsible for handling the life cycle of the add-in so that it can initialize and clean up after itself appropriately in the context of the IDE and the other add-ins.

➤ The IDTCommandTarget interface provides a way in which the add-in can handle commands the IDE routes to it.

COM components must be registered on the machine so that the IDE can work with them. Fortunately, the manual mechanism needed before with Visual Studio 2008 has been changed to enable you to more easily deploy your custom add-ins, without any explicit registration.

Add-ins can be developed both in managed and unmanaged code. While macros are deployed with source code, add-ins are deployed in binaries. This book only addresses how to use managed code.

The essential architecture is the same for native and managed implementations. The big difference is the way COM-specific code (that is, the COM interface implementation and automation model calls) is handled.

Add-ins can be loaded by Visual Studio at startup time or on-demand when the user explicitly asks it (using the Add-In Manager), or implicitly asks it (for example, activating a command owned by the add-in). Add-ins also can subscribe to IDE events (that is, to all events supported by the automation model), so that they can respond to system events of Visual Studio.

Add-ins can be written in command-line-safe mode so that they can be utilized when `devenv.exe` is started through the command line. Of course, command-line add-ins cannot pop up modal dialogs because they would block Visual Studio from running in command-line mode.

The integration architecture allows you to utilize the benefits of add-ins by not only using the automation model, but also by enabling the add-ins to work together with other add-ins. Proper design and documentation of your add-ins will let others use your add-in. When creating a new add-in, always separate its presentation layer from its service layer and allow the latter one to be used through commands.

## Creating a Simple Add-In

The easiest way to learn about the concepts described previously is to create an add-in and look into the source code details. The Visual Studio IDE provides a wizard to help you with the generation of a basic add-in that will come in handy for this endeavor.

### Using the Visual Studio Add-In Wizard

Use the File ⇨ New ⇨ Project menu item to select the Visual Studio Add-In project type. As shown in Figure 6-16, you will find it under the Other Project Types category in the Extensibility section.

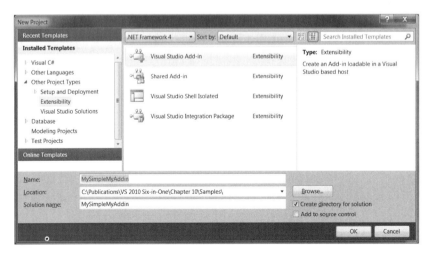

**FIGURE 6-16:** Selecting the Visual Studio Add-in project type

Set the name of the project to `MySimpleAddIn` and click the OK button. The Visual Studio Add-In Wizard starts and displays a welcome page. Click Next to go to the first information page, where you can select the programming language to use. As you see in Figure 6-17, you can select from four alternatives — C#, VB, managed C++, and native C++/ATL.

Select the "Create an Add-in using Visual C#" option and click Next. The second page of the wizard allows you to select a host application in which to embed your add-in. As shown in Figure 6-18, the add-in you create can be hosted by the Visual Studio 2010 IDE or the Macros IDE.

You can select both options on this page. In that case, your add-in will be integrated into both host applications. For right now, check only Microsoft Visual Studio 2010.

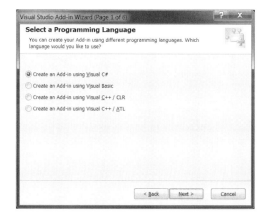

**FIGURE 6-17:** Selecting the programming language of the Add-in

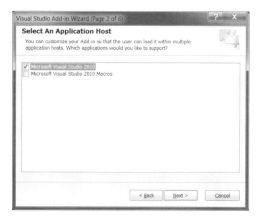

**FIGURE 6-18:** Selecting the application host

Click Next and you will then see the basic add-in information on the third wizard page. The information you set here is displayed in the Add-In Manager. Use the information shown in Figure 6-19 to set up the add-in.

Click Next to move on to the page where you set up a few add-in options, as shown in Figure 6-20.

**FIGURE 6-19:** Basic Add-in information page

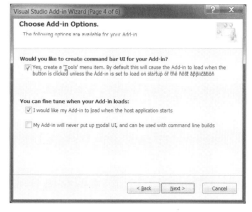

**FIGURE 6-20:** Add-in options page

Check the first option to create a menu item in the Tools menu for this add-in. When you select this menu item, a command is sent to your add-in, which can respond to this command. Check the second option to load it automatically when Visual Studio 2010 starts. Leave the third option unchecked, because this add-in will use a modal dialog (thus preventing it from being used with command-line builds).

Click the Next button and the wizard advances to the last information page, where you can generate text for the About dialog box, as shown in Figure 6-21. Since, for this example, you do not want to generate About information for this add-in, leave that option unchecked.

Click Next to move you to the last page that summarizes the information the wizard uses to generate the add-in. On this page, click Finish to start the source code generation. In a few seconds, the wizard creates a new project with the files summarized in Table 6-2.

**FIGURE 6-21:** Settings for the About dialog box

**TABLE 6-2:** Source Files of the Add-In Generated with the Wizard

| FILE | DESCRIPTION |
| --- | --- |
| AssemblyInfo.cs | Set of general assembly information attributes |
| Connect.cs | The declaration of the class responsible for the add-in integration with Visual Studio |
| MySimpleAddin - For Testing.AddIn | Configuration file for the add-in used for testing purposes |
| MySimpleAddin.AddIn | Configuration file for the add-in used for deployment |

The project generated by the wizard can be started immediately. However, you must make a small modification to the source code to demonstrate that the add-in really works. First, add a reference for the System.Windows.Forms assembly to the project. Then, open Connect.cs and add a new using clause to the file, as shown here:

```
using System.Windows.Forms;
```

Modify the body of the Exec method by adding the line with the MessageBox.Show call in the following code:

```
public void Exec(string commandName, vsCommandExecOption executeOption,
   ref object varIn, ref object varOut, ref bool handled)
```

```
  {
    handled = false;
    if (executeOption == vsCommandExecOption.vsCommandExecOptionDoDefault)
    {
      if (commandName == "MySimpleAddin.Connect.MySimpleAddin")
      {
        MessageBox.Show("Hello from MySimpleAddIn");
        handled = true;
        return;
      }
    }
  }
}
```

Let's try the add-in with Debug ⇨ Start Without Debugging or pressing Ctrl+F5. This action will start another instance of Visual Studio 2010 with the command representing the add-in in the Tools menu, as shown in Figure 6-22.

When you click on `MySimpleAddIn` menu item, the "Hello" message you added to the `Exec` method previously is popped up on the screen.

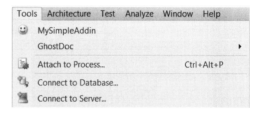

**FIGURE 6-22:** Add-in in the Tools menu

## The Connect Class

The lion's share of the work is done by the `Connect` class. Listing 6-1 shows the full content of this file. (Comments have been omitted for the sake of compactness.)

**LISTING 6-1: Connect.cs**

```
using System;
using Extensibility;
using EnvDTE;
using EnvDTE80;
using Microsoft.VisualStudio.CommandBars;
using System.Resources;
using System.Reflection;
using System.Globalization;
using System.Windows.Forms;

namespace MySimpleAddIn
{
  public class Connect : IDTExtensibility2, IDTCommandTarget
  {
    public Connect()
    {
    }

    public void OnConnection(object application, ext_ConnectMode connectMode,
      object addInInst, ref Array custom)
    {
```

*continues*

**LISTING 6-1** *(continued)*

```csharp
    _applicationObject = (DTE2)application;
    _addInInstance = (AddIn)addInInst;
    if (connectMode == ext_ConnectMode.ext_cm_UISetup)
    {
      object[] contextGUIDS = new object[] { };
      Commands2 commands = (Commands2)_applicationObject.Commands;
      string toolsMenuName = "Tools";

      Microsoft.VisualStudio.CommandBars.CommandBar menuBarCommandBar =
        ((Microsoft.VisualStudio.CommandBars.CommandBars)
        _applicationObject.CommandBars)["MenuBar"];

      CommandBarControl toolsControl = menuBarCommandBar.Controls[toolsMenuName];
      CommandBarPopup toolsPopup = (CommandBarPopup)toolsControl;

      try
      {
        Command command = commands.AddNamedCommand2(_addInInstance,
          "MySimpleAddIn",
          "MySimpleAddIn",
          "Executes the command for MySimpleAddIn",
          true,
          59,
          ref contextGUIDS,
          (int)vsCommandStatus.vsCommandStatusSupported +
            (int)vsCommandStatus.vsCommandStatusEnabled,
          (int)vsCommandStyle.vsCommandStylePictAndText,
          vsCommandControlType.vsCommandControlTypeButton);
        if ((command != null) && (toolsPopup != null))
        {
          command.AddControl(toolsPopup.CommandBar, 1);
        }
      }
      catch (System.ArgumentException)
      {
      }
    }
}

public void OnDisconnection(ext_DisconnectMode disconnectMode,
  ref Array custom)
{
}

public void OnAddInsUpdate(ref Array custom)
{
}

public void OnStartupComplete(ref Array custom)
{
}

public void OnBeginShutdown(ref Array custom)
{
```

```
      }

    public void QueryStatus(string commandName,
      vsCommandStatusTextWanted neededText,
      ref vsCommandStatus status,
      ref object commandText)
    {
      if (neededText == vsCommandStatusTextWanted.vsCommandStatusTextWantedNone)
      {
        if (commandName == "MySimpleAddIn.Connect.MySimpleAddIn")
        {
          status = (vsCommandStatus)vsCommandStatus.vsCommandStatusSupported |
            vsCommandStatus.vsCommandStatusEnabled;
          return;
        }
      }
    }

    public void Exec(string commandName, vsCommandExecOption executeOption,
      ref object varIn, ref object varOut, ref bool handled)
    {
      handled = false;
      if (executeOption == vsCommandExecOption.vsCommandExecOptionDoDefault)
      {
        if (commandName == "MySimpleAddIn.Connect.MySimpleAddIn")
        {
          MessageBox.Show("Hello from MySimpleAddIn");
          handled = true;
          return;
        }
      }
    }

    private DTE2 _applicationObject;
    private AddIn _addInInstance;
  }
}
```

Let's dive into its details of this code. To understand every bit, you must understand a lot of information about the command-handling mechanism of Visual Studio. Treating all those details would at least double the length of this chapter, so let's focus on a general overview of what the code does. If you want to look deeper behind the source code, use the reference documentation for the methods, parameters, and types.

The Connect class implements the IDTExtensibility2 and IDTCommandTarget interfaces. Both are COM dispatch interfaces, so, as a result, the Connect class is a COM object that can be integrated with Visual Studio 2010. IDTExtensibility2 is responsible for the IDE integration. IDTCommandTarget enables the IDE to send commands to the add-in. IDTExtensibility2 defines the methods summarized in Table 6-3. All methods have an array parameter named custom that can be used to pass data back to the caller.

**TABLE 6-3:** IDTExtensibility2 Members

| METHOD | DESCRIPTION |
| --- | --- |
| OnConnection | This event is raised when the add-in is loaded into the Visual Studio IDE. The `application` parameter points to the root object of the DTE automation model. `addInInst` refers to the `AddIn` instance in the automation model describing this add-in. The `connectMode` parameter defines the way in which the add-in is loaded into the IDE. Define this code to set up your add-in during connection time. |
| OnDisconnection | The Visual Studio IDE raises this event when the add-in is disconnected from the IDE. The `disconnectMode` parameter specifies the reason why the add-in has been disconnected. Use this method to put the add-in clean-up code here. |
| OnAddInsUpdate | This event is raised by the IDE when the add-in is loaded or unloaded in the IDE. You must define this method when you want to check dependencies among add-ins. For example, you want to ensure that all add-ins on which your add-in depends are loaded. |
| OnStartupComplete | This event is raised when Visual Studio finished the startup process. At this point, all add-ins are loaded into memory, so you can access them to finish your add-in initialization. You should put all the initialization code here that assumes any other add-ins or Visual Studio services are available. |
| OnBeginShutdown | The IDE sends this event to the add-in when Visual Studio starts the shutdown process. |

You can see in Listing 6-1 that only the `OnConnection` method defines behavior to initialize the add-in. All the other methods have empty bodies. `OnConnection` first stores the references to the automation model root in the `_applicationObject` field and the current add-in instance in the `_addinInstance` field, because they are used later. When the IDE loads the add-in to set up its user interface (signed with the `ext_cm_UISetup` connection mode), it triggers a few tasks implemented by this method:

➤ In a few steps, it obtains the reference to the Tools menu bar and stores it into the `toolsPopup` variable.

➤ It creates a new command with the `AddNamedCommand2` method passing the add-in instance and nine other parameters. It sets up the menu item UI for this command (names, icon, and visual properties) so that the command is enabled. As a result of the method call, when the menu item is clicked, the IDE routes this command to the add-in.

➤ It adds the menu item to the Tools menu bar.

The `IDTCommandTarget` interface defines two methods:

➤ The `QueryStatus` method is called by the Visual Studio IDE to check whether the add-in can understand the command (that is, knows what the command means and can execute it). The add-in also has a chance to retrieve the status of commands it supports (for example, enabled/disabled, visible/hidden). Also, this method is used by the IDE to allow the command to set its menu item and status bar text.

➤ The `Exec` method is called by the IDE when a command is about to execute and whether `QueryStatus` previously stated that the add-in supports that command.

In the previous implementation, `QueryStatus` responds to the event only when the IDE is asking for the command status (and not for command text information). It checks if the only command known by the add-in is called, and, in this case, returns a status saying, "I'm supporting the command, so you can execute it when the user clicks on the menu item, and also it is enabled on the UI."

`Exec` checks again if only the supported command is to execute. Then it shows the message box and signals that the command has been handled. The `handle` flag is important. Visual Studio can send the command to one or more add-ins (to all that support the command). If one command does not set the `handle` flag (it can leave `false` intentionally), the next add-in also has the chance to handle it.

## Managing and Loading Add-Ins

The Add-In Wizard generated two configuration files with the `.AddIn` extension and puts them in the project. One of them, `MySimpleAddIn.AddIn`, is put into the same directory as the `Connect.cs` file. The other one is put into your user profile under the `Documents\Visual Studio 10\Addins` folder. This configuration file is used by Visual Studio 2010 to obtain information about your add-in, and create the required information in the registry to load the related COM component.

Starting the add-in results in launching a second instance of Visual Studio with the add-in installed. Figure 6-23 shows the Debug properties of the project that cause this second instance to launch:

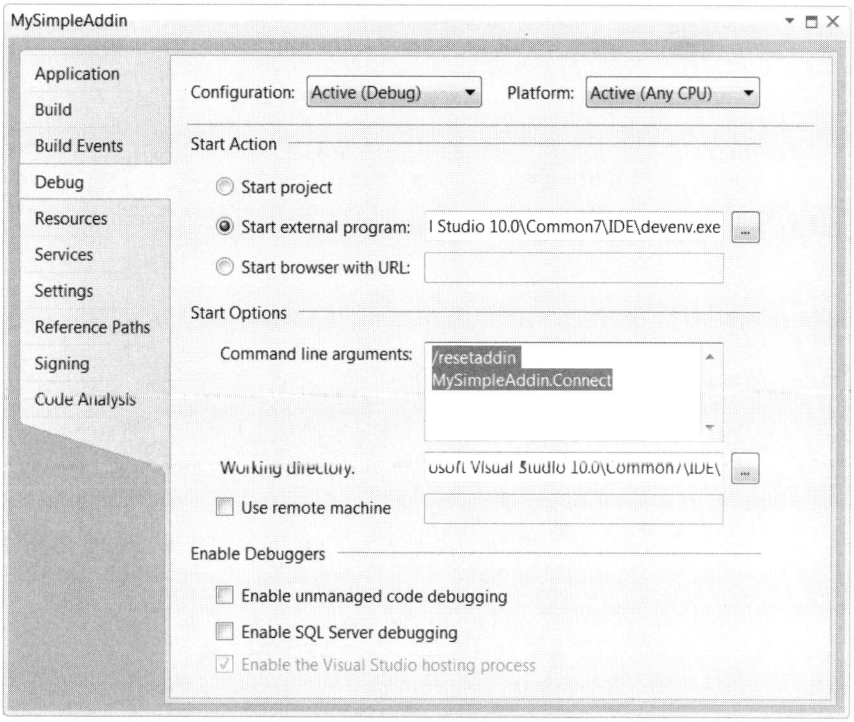

**FIGURE 6-23:** Debug properties of the add-in

You can see the `devenv.exe` is started with the `/resetaddin MySimpleAddIn.Connect` command line. This option set causes Visual Studio to reset all the settings for the add-in at startup time. Visual Studio then processes the `.AddIn` configuration files in the folders set up for add-in discovery. You can go to the Tools ⇨ Options dialog, and, in the Add-in/Macros security page of the Environment category, all these paths are listed.

Listing 6-2 shows what is in the `.AddIn` file used for testing.

**LISTING 6-2:** MySimpleAddIn — for Testing.AddIn

```xml
<?xml version="1.0" encoding="UTF-16" standalone="no"?>
<Extensibility xmlns="http://schemas.microsoft.com/AutomationExtensibility">
  <HostApplication>
    <Name>Microsoft Visual Studio</Name>
    <Version>10.0</Version>
  </HostApplication>
  <Addin>
    <FriendlyName>MySimpleAddIn</FriendlyName>
    <Description>Demonstrates how a simple add-in works</Description>
    <Assembly>
      C:\Publications\VS 2010 Six-in-One\Samples\Chapter~CA 6\MySimpleAddIn\
      MySimpleAddIn\bin\Project1.dll
    </Assembly>
    <FullClassName>MySimpleAddIn.Connect</FullClassName>
    <LoadBehavior>1</LoadBehavior>
    <CommandPreload>1</CommandPreload>
    <CommandLineSafe>0</CommandLineSafe>
  </Addin>
</Extensibility>
```

Visual Studio can read all the settings from here to register the COM information of the add-in. Table 6-4 summarizes the meaning of information nodes nested into the `<HostApplication>` and `<AddIn>` nodes. The schema defining the structure of `.AddIn` files contains other nodes, but they are not addressed here.

**TABLE 6-4:** Information Nodes in the .AddIn File

| NODE | DESCRIPTION |
| --- | --- |
| `<Name>` | Specifies the name of the application hosting the add-in. "Microsoft Visual Studio" means the main Visual Studio IDE, while "Microsoft Visual Studio Macros" stands for the Macros IDE. |
| `<Version>` | Sets the version of the host application. Visual Studio 2010 uses the value 10.0, while Visual Studio 2008 uses 9.0. |
| `<FriendlyName>` | This name is displayed in the Add-In Manager. |
| `<Description>` | This description appears in the Add-In Manager for the add-in. |
| `<Assembly>` | The name and full path of assembly encapsulating the add-in. |

| NODE | DESCRIPTION |
|------|-------------|
| `<FullClassName>` | This is the fully qualified name of the class implementing the add-in. Visual Studio uses this type to load the COM object, so naming your class in the code editor also requires changing the class name here. |
| `<LoadBehavior>` | This value determines whether or not the add-in is loaded at Visual Studio startup time. `0` specifies that the add-in must be started manually, because the IDE does not load it. `1` means the IDE loads the add-in at startup time. |
| `<CommandPreload>` | This flag specifies whether the add-in should be loaded to set up its UI at the first time when Visual Studio starts. The value of `1` means UI setup is requested; `0` means it is not necessary. |
| `<CommandLineSafe>` | Determines if the add-in can be loaded when Visual Studio is launched in command-line mode. 0 means that the add-in will display modal user interface and so may block `devenv.exe`. 1 means the add-in does not display UI. |

## Using the Automation Model

Visual Studio has its own automation model to access functionality through COM objects. The automation is provided through the *Development Tools Extensibility* (*DTE*) API that has been a part of Visual Studio (but not part of the VS SDK) for a long time. The key to the extensibility of Visual Studio is DTE. Even the first version of Visual Studio .NET (released in April, 2002) had an extensibility project type called Visual Studio Add-in that still remains in Visual Studio 2010.

Visual Studio macros and add-ins heavily use the automation object model of DTE, and packages also obtain value through the automation model. Having a good overview of this model and knowing where to look it up for certain tasks is a key to add-in development (as well as for macro programming).

The full graph of automation model hierarchy contains almost two hundred objects with many important methods and properties. This discussion does not examine all types, or even the most important ones. Instead of going into detail, this discussion provides starting points so that you will be able to discover the object model yourself.

Table 6-5 summarizes a functional grouping of object types, and recommends a few types and properties to start with. Here, "properties" refers to the ones belonging to the DTE object type.

**TABLE 6-5:** Functional Parts of the Automation Model

| FUNCTIONAL PART | DESCRIPTION |
|-----------------|-------------|
| Integrated Development Environment | Objects helping in the general management of the IDE. |
| | Properties include `AddIns`, `ActiveWindow`, `CommandBars`, `Commands`, `ContextAttributes`, `DisplayMode`, `Macros`, `MainWindow`, `Mode`, `SelectedItems`, `StatusBar`, `ToolWindows`, `WindowConfigurations`, and `Windows`. |

*continues*

**TABLE 6-5** *(continued)*

| FUNCTIONAL PART | DESCRIPTION |
|---|---|
| | Types include `AddIn`, `CommandBar`, `Command`, `Macros`, `OutputWindow`, `OutputWindowPanes`, `OutputWindowPane`, `SelectedItems`, `TaskList`, `TaskItems`, `TaskItem`, `ToolBox`, `ToolBoxTabs`, `ToolBoxTab`, `ToolBoxItems`, `ToolBoxItem`, `StatusBar`, and `Window`. |
| Solution model | Automation objects describing and managing the full project. hierarchy you can see in the Solution Explorer.<br><br>Properties include `ActiveSolutionProjects`, `Globals`, and `Solution`.<br><br>Types include `Globals`, `Solution`, `Projects`, `Project`, `ProjectItems`, and `ProjectItem`. |
| Document and Editor model | Object types managing the documents and text editors in the IDE.<br><br>Properties include `ActiveDocument`.<br><br>Types include `Document`, `TextDocument`, `TextSelection`, `TextPoint`, `EndPoint`, `TextRanges`, `TextRange`, and `VirtualPoint`. |
| Code model | Object types helping you to work with source code files. By using this type, you can access smaller parts of the source code.<br><br>Types include `CodeElements`, `CodeElement`, `FileCodeModel`, `CodeModel`, `CodeType`, `CodeNamespace`, `CodeStruct`, `CodeInterface`, `CodeClass`, `CodeEnum`, `CodeVariable`, `CodeDelegate`, `CodeProperty`, `CodeFunction`, and `CodeParameter`. |
| Debugger model | This part of the model allows you access to manage the debugger and debugging environment.<br><br>Properties include `Debugger`, and `Frame`.<br><br>Types include `BreakPoints`, `BreakPoint`, `Debugger`, `Expressions`, `Expression`, `Processes`, `Process`, `Programs`, `Program`, `Threads`, `Thread`, `StackFrames`, and `Stack`. |
| Build model | This part of the object model helps to manage build operations and configurations for projects and solutions.<br><br>Types include `SolutionBuild`, `BuildDependencies`, `BuildDependency`, `SolutionConfigurations`, `SolutionConfiguration`, `SolutionContexts`, and `SolutionContext`. |

| FUNCTIONAL PART | DESCRIPTION |
| --- | --- |
| IDE Events | Objects allowing access to events in the Visual Studio IDE. By subscribing to these events, you are able to respond to them. |
| | Properties include `Events`, `TaskListEvents`, `TextEditorEvents`, and `WindowEvents`. |
| | Types include `Events`, `BuildEvents`, `CommandEvents`, `DocumentEvents`, `DTEEvents`, `FindEvents`, `ProjectItemEvents`, `OutputWindowEvents`, `SelectionEvents`, `SolutionEvents`, and `ProjectItemsEvents`. |
| Miscellaneous types | Helper objects and objects not belonging to any of the previous categories. |
| | Properties include `ItemOperations`, `MacrosIDE`, `ObjectExtenders`, `Properties`, `SourceControl`, and `UndoContext`. |
| | Types include `ItemOperations`, `ObjectExtenders`, `Properties`, `Property`, `UndoContext`, `UIHierarchy`, `UIHierachyItems`, and `UIHierachyItem`. |

*The types and properties in Table 6-5 can be used as keywords to search MSDN to find the appropriate topic. If you want to see the full graph of automation objects, you should search MSDN with the "Automation Object Model Chart" expression. Select an item from the top of the result list. Visual Studio reference information pages are designed so that you can switch from any reference page to the right Visual Studio/.NET Framework version with a simple click. Should the page you clicked in the result list belong to a former Visual Studio version, you could switch to the Visual Studio 2010/.NET 4 version.*

## Going on with Add-In Development

Creating add-ins is the most popular form of developing Visual Studio extensions. When you surf the web for utilities and small tools to integrate with Visual Studio, a majority of the resulting hits are implemented as an add-in. This book merely scratches the surface of the topic.

To dive deeper into this kind of extensibility, you definitely need more knowledge and experience in the following areas:

➤ Using the DTE automation model

➤ Understanding the command and tool window architecture of Visual Studio

➤   Getting familiar with the most frequently used services of Visual Studio

➤   Deploying add-ins

 *If you want to get more information on add-in development, check out the book Professional Visual Studio Extensibility by Keyvan Nayyeri (Indianapolis: Wiley, 2008).*

If you feel you want even more than what is available with Visual Studio add-ins, and you want to create more complex extensions, Visual Studio packages will be your best friends.

# VISUAL STUDIO PACKAGES IN A NUTSHELL

The most powerful way to develop Visual Studio extensions is integrating *Visual Studio packages* (*VSPackages)* into the IDE. These packages are not limited to using the automation model, or only to a few core services, but can access the whole infrastructure of Visual Studio just like the packages created by the development team at Microsoft.

This book does not go into great detail about VSPackage development, but instead provides a general overview. To examine the most important concepts in the right context, let's build a very simple functional package just to scratch the surface.

## Creating a Package with a Simple Menu Command

A VSPackage is a class library containing the types responsible for the package infrastructure and functionality. In order for Visual Studio to recognize the compiled class library as a package, encapsulated types should have specific metadata information, and some additional steps are required after compilation. So, even if you could start building a package from an empty class library, it is much easier to use the VSPackage wizard installed with the VS SDK.

### Using the VSPackage Wizard

Start a new project with the File ➪ New ➪ Project menu function. The IDE displays the New File dialog to select the desired project type. You can find the *Visual Studio Integration Package* project type under the Other Project Types category in the `Extensibility` folder, as shown in Figure 6-24.

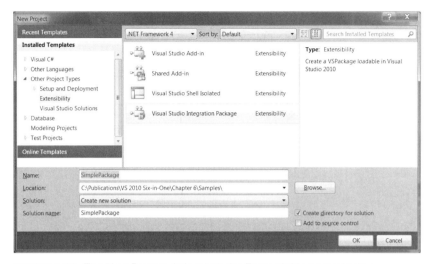

**FIGURE 6-24:** The New Project dialog with the Extensibility project types

 *If you do not find this project type (or many other project types) in the* Extensibility *folder, that means that the VS SDK is not (or not properly) installed on your machine. Install it according to the setup notes to go on with building the package.*

Name the package `SimplePackage` so that you can follow the code details later in this chapter. Click the OK button to start the Visual Studio Integration Package Wizard (which will be referred to as the VSPackage wizard), which welcomes you with the dialog shown in Figure 6-25.

**FIGURE 6-25:** The Welcome page of the VSPackage wizard

Click the Next button to continue specifying the package parameters, and you see the "Select a Programming Language" page of the wizard, as shown in Figure 6-26.

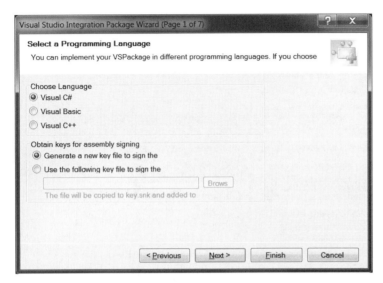

**FIGURE 6-26:** VSPackage wizard lets you select the programming language

Let's create the code in C#. Packages are strongly named assemblies, so you must sign the class library assembly with a key. For this project, let the wizard create the signing key. Click Next to get to the Basic VSPackage Information page, as shown in Figure 6-27.

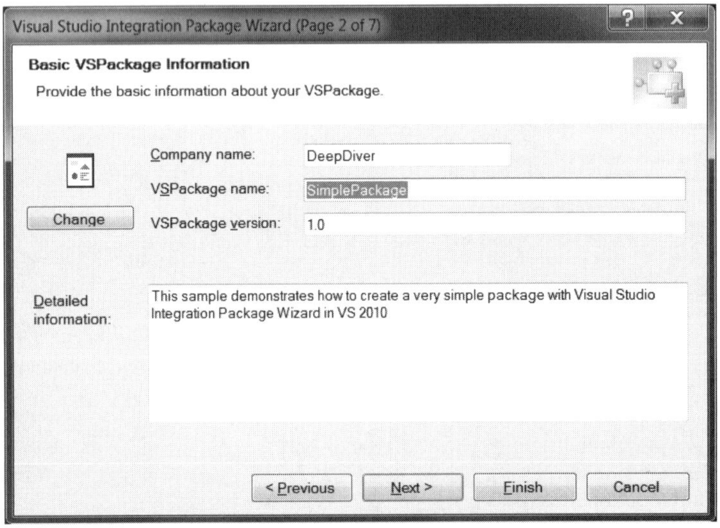

**FIGURE 6-27:** The wizard asks for the basic package information

The information you provide here will be used in the source code generated for the package, and will be displayed in the About dialog. The "Company name" will be used in the namespace of generated types, as well as the "VSPackage name," which also names the class representing the package in code. The "VSPackage version" is additional information to provide a way for distinguishing separate package releases. Text typed in the "Detailed information" field will be displayed in the About dialog, and can supply the user with more information than the name about what the package does.

When you click the Next button, the wizard moves you to the VSPackage Options page (Figure 6-28) to set a few more code-generation options.

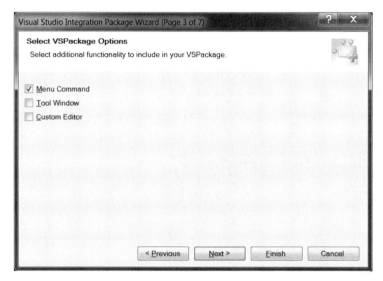

**FIGURE 6-28:** You can select a few code generation options

In this sample, you will create only a menu command that pops up a message on the screen, so you click the Menu Command option. If you selected the Tool Window option, the VSPackage wizard would create some more code for a simple tool window, and code to display it on the screen. For this exercise, leave that option and the Custom Editor option unchecked.

Click the Next button and the wizard goes to the page where you specify a few details about the menu command to create, as shown in Figure 6-29.

The command will be added to the Tools menu of Visual Studio, and in "Command name" field, you specify the text to be displayed for the menu item. According to the internal command-handling architecture, each command has an identifier. The Command ID field supplies a name for this identifier, and the VSPackage wizard will generate an ID value behind this name.

When you click Next, the wizard moves to the Select Test Project Options page, as shown in Figure 6-30.

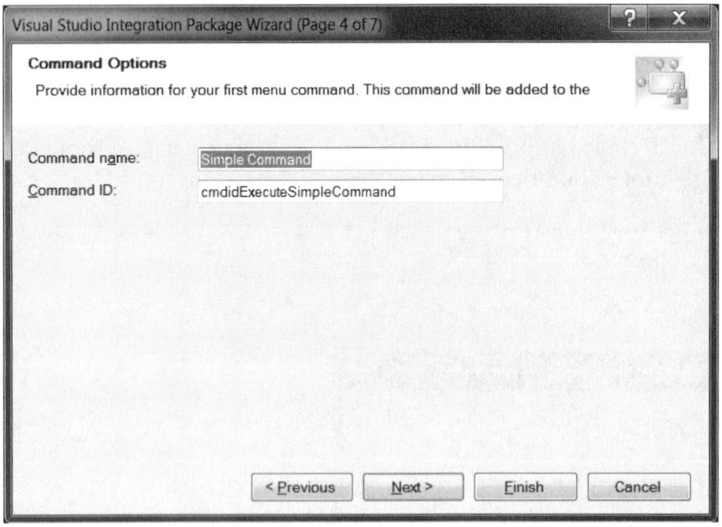

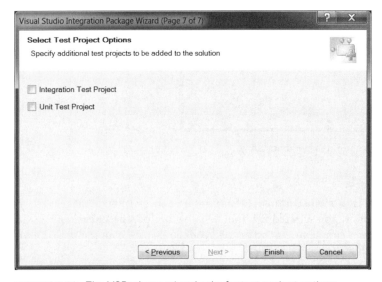

**FIGURE 6-29:** Command options are specified here

**FIGURE 6-30:** The VSPackage wizard asks for test project options

The wizard can create unit tests for the package to check if functional units of the package work properly. The wizard also can create an integration test project where packages are tested within the context of a Visual Studio instance.

For this example, you do not want to create any tests, so let's clear these options (by default, both are checked). Now, you have set all the parameters the wizard uses to produce the package project, so click the Finish button.

In a few seconds, the wizard generates the package project ready to build and run. With the Build ⇨ Rebuild Solution function, you can compile the package and carry out all other steps required to prepare the package to run within Visual Studio. So, let's rebuild it and start by pressing Ctrl + F5 (or selecting Debug ⇨ Start Without Debugging).

You might be surprised because a new instance of Visual Studio is started with "Experimental Instance" in its window caption. This is an instance of Visual Studio that hosts the `SimplePackage` component. The menu command implemented by this freshly generated package can be seen in the Tools menu, as shown in Figure 6-31.

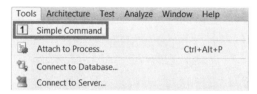

**FIGURE 6-31:** The menu command item appears in the Tools menu

## Source Code Structure

Nothing tells more about VSPackage than its source code, so let's look at what the VSPackage wizard generated for you. The wizard generated the code according to the parameters you specified, and it performed a lot of work in the background:

- ➤ It generated a class library project in C#.
- ➤ It added references to this project for the interoperability assemblies required to access Visual Studio functionality.
- ➤ It created resources used by the package and other resources used by the registration process.
- ➤ It added new MSBuild targets to the project to support the build and registration process of the package.
- ➤ It generated types responsible for implementing the package functionality.
- ➤ It set up the debug properties of the project to start Visual Studio Experimental Hive.

Table 6-6 summarizes the source files in the `SimplePackage` project.

**TABLE 6-6:** SimplePackage Source Files Generated by the VSPackage Wizard

| SOURCE FILE | DESCRIPTION |
| --- | --- |
| source.extension .vsixmanifest | The VSIX manifest file that plays vital role in the discovery and registration mechanism of Visual Studio extensions. |
| GlobalSupressions.cs | Attributes used to suppress messages coming from the static code analysis. |
| Guids.cs | GUID values used to identify the package and command objects within the package. |
| Key.snk | The signing key used to generate the strong name for the package assembly. |

*continues*

**TABLE 6-6** *(continued)*

| SOURCE FILE | DESCRIPTION |
| --- | --- |
| PkgCmdID.cs | Constants for identifying command values. |
| Resources.resx | A resource file to store your functional package resources — resources you use according to the functions you implement in the package. |
| SimplePackage.vsct | The *command table file* storing the definition of the menus and commands to be merged into the Visual Studio IDE during the registration process. |
| SimplePackage.cs | A class implementing the simple functionality of the package. |
| VSPackage.resx | A resource file to store package infrastructure resources — those resources that are used by Visual Studio to integrate your package into the IDE. |

The wizard added several assemblies to the class library project in addition the ones belonging to a class library by default. Their names start with the `Microsoft.VisualStudio` prefix, and most of them are interoperability assemblies having `Interop` in their names. These contain only proxy type definitions to access the core Visual Studio COM service interface and object types.

## Package Type Definition

Now, let's take a look at the source code of the package. The wizard added many useful comments to the generated source files. In the code extracts listed here, those comments have been cut out to make the listing shorter, and to improve the readability of the code. The indentations also have been changed a bit for the same purpose.

Listing 6-3 shows the source code of the most important file in the project named `SimplePackagePackage.cs`. This file implements the type representing the package.

**LISTING 6-3:** SimplePackagePackage.cs

```
using System;
using System.Diagnostics;
using System.Globalization;
using System.Runtime.InteropServices;
using System.ComponentModel.Design;
using Microsoft.Win32;
using Microsoft.VisualStudio.Shell.Interop;
using Microsoft.VisualStudio.OLE.Interop;
using Microsoft.VisualStudio.Shell;

namespace DeepDiver.SimplePackage
{
  [PackageRegistration(UseManagedResourcesOnly = true)]
  [InstalledProductRegistration(false, "#110", "#112", "1.0",
    IconResourceID = 400)]
```

```
[ProvideMenuResource("Menus.ctmenu", 1)]
[Guid(GuidList.guidSimplePackagePkgString)]
public sealed class SimplePackagePackage : Package
{
  public SimplePackagePackage()
  {
    Trace.WriteLine(string.Format(CultureInfo.CurrentCulture,
      "Entering constructor for: {0}", this.ToString()));
  }

  protected override void Initialize()
  {
    Trace.WriteLine(string.Format(CultureInfo.CurrentCulture,
      "Entering Initialize() of: {0}", this.ToString()));
    base.Initialize();
    OleMenuCommandService mcs = GetService(typeof(IMenuCommandService))
      as OleMenuCommandService;
    if (null != mcs)
    {
      CommandID menuCommandID = new CommandID(GuidList.guidSimplePackageCmdSet,
        (int)PkgCmdIDList.cmdidExecuteSimpleCommand);
      MenuCommand menuItem = new MenuCommand(MenuItemCallback, menuCommandID);
      mcs.AddCommand(menuItem);
    }
  }

  private void MenuItemCallback(object sender, EventArgs e)
  {
    IVsUIShell uiShell = (IVsUIShell)GetService(typeof(SVsUIShell));
    Guid clsid = Guid.Empty;
    int result;
    Microsoft.VisualStudio.ErrorHandler.ThrowOnFailure(uiShell.ShowMessageBox(
      0,
      ref clsid,
      "SimplePackage",
      string.Format(CultureInfo.CurrentCulture,
      "Inside {0}.MenuItemCallback()", this.ToString()),
      string.Empty,
      0,
      OLEMSGBUTTON.OLEMSGBUTTON_OK,
      OLEMSGDEFBUTTON.OLEMSGDEFBUTTON_FIRST,
      OLEMSGICON.OLEMSGICON_INFO,
      0,          // false
      out result));
  }
}
}
```

*Code file [SimplePackagePackage.cs] available for download at Wrox.com*

The SimplePackagePackage class becomes a working package by inheriting the behavior defined in the Package class of the Microsoft.VisualStudio.Shell namespace and by using the attributes decorating the class definition.

The `Package` base class implements the `IVsPackage` interface required by Visual Studio to take an object into account as a package. This interface provides a few methods managing the life cycle of a package and also offers methods to access package-related objects such as tool windows, options pages, and automation objects.

The overridden `Initialize` method is called after the package has been successfully sited in the Shell through the `IVsPackage` interface. This method must do all the initialization steps that require access to services provided by the Shell or other packages. Should you move this code to the package constructor, you probably would get a `NullReferenceException` because, at that point, all attempts to access the Shell would fail because the package is not yet sited, and actually has no contact with any Shell objects.

In this case, the `Initialize` method binds the single menu command provided by the package with its event handler method called `MenuItemCallback`:

```
protected override void Initialize()
{
  Trace.WriteLine(string.Format(CultureInfo.CurrentCulture,
    "Entering Initialize() of: {0}", this.ToString()));
  base.Initialize();

  // Add our command handlers for menu (commands must exist in the .vsct file)
  OleMenuCommandService mcs = GetService(typeof(IMenuCommandService))
    as OleMenuCommandService;
  if (null != mcs)
  {
    // Create the command for the menu item.
    CommandID menuCommandID = new CommandID(GuidList.guidSimplePackageCmdSet,
      (int)PkgCmdIDList.cmdidExecuteSimpleCommand);
    MenuCommand menuItem = new MenuCommand(MenuItemCallback, menuCommandID);
    mcs.AddCommand(menuItem);
  }
}
```

First, you call the `Initialize` method of the base class — `Package`, in this case. Look at the call of `GetService`. If you could select a method that is especially important when creating Visual Studio packages, probably the `GetService` method would be your choice. This method has one type parameter (call it service address) that retrieves a service object implementing the service interface specified by the address type.

You obtain an `OleMenuCommandService` instance that you can use to bind event handlers to *command objects*. So, you create a `CommandID` instance to address the command you put into the Tools menu, and then you instantiate a `MenuCommand` object to assign the `MenuItemCallback` method as a response for the command specified with the `CommandID` instance. The result of this short initialization code is that the package handles the event when the user clicks on the Simple Command menu item in the Tools menu by executing the `MenuItemCallback` method, which uses the `IVsUIShell` service to pop up a message box from within the IDE.

As mentioned, packages are COM objects that are registered with Visual Studio to support the on-demand loading mechanism and allow merging menus and toolbars into the user interface of the IDE. The information to be registered is created during the build process from attributes assigned to the package class:

```
[PackageRegistration(UseManagedResourcesOnly = true)]
[InstalledProductRegistration(false, "#110", "#112", "1.0", IconResourceID = 400)]
[ProvideMenuResource("Menus.ctmenu", 1)]
[Guid(GuidList.guidSimplePackagePkgString)]
public sealed class SimplePackagePackage : Package
{
  // ...
}
```

Table 6-7 summarizes the role of the attributes used by Visual Studio to integrate the package into the IDE.

**TABLE 6-7:** Attributes Decorating the Package Class

| ATTRIBUTE | DESCRIPTION |
| --- | --- |
| PackageRegistration | Adding this attribute to the class, the build process will handle it as a package, and looks for other attributes to prepare the package registration according to your intention. In this example, this attribute sets the UseManagedResourcesOnly flag to tell that all resources used by the package are described in the managed package, not in a satellite DLL. |
| InstalledProductRegistration | This attribute is responsible for providing information to be displayed in the Help ⇨ About dialog in the IDE. The constructor of this attribute takes parameters describing the resources holding the information to be displayed. These resources are defined in the VSPackage.resx file. |
| ProvideMenuResource | This attribute creates registry entries about menu and toolbar items provided by the package. Visual Studio uses the embedded resources here to merge the package menus into the Visual Studio menus. |
| Guid | Packages are COM objects, and so they must have a GUID uniquely identifying them. The Guid attribute is used by the .NET framework to assign this GUID value to a type. |

*For more information about the many other registration attributes, look up the VS SDK reference documentation to get more details about them.*

## The Command Table

The wizard generated a file named `SimplePackage.vsct`. This is an XML file, and the file extension refers to the acronym coming from the Visual Studio Command Table (VSCT) expression. The schema of the XML file defines the *command table* owned by the package.

The command table is transformed into a binary format during the build process, and is embedded into the package assembly as a resource. During the registration phase, the ID of this resource is put into the registry. When Visual Studio starts, it loads this binary resource information and merges it with the menus of the IDE, including toolbars and context menus. To avoid menu merges every time Visual Studio is launched, the IDE uses a cache mechanism, and carries out the merge process only once for each package.

Listing 6-4 shows the command table of the sample package. All comments placed into the generated file have been removed from this listing to save space. You should read those comments in the generated `.vsct` file because they will help you better understand the structure of the command table.

**LISTING 6-4: SimplePackage.vsct**

```xml
<?xml version="1.0" encoding="utf-8"?>
<CommandTable xmlns="http://schemas.microsoft.com/VisualStudio/~CA
  2005-10-18/CommandTable" xmlns:xs="http://www.w3.org/2001/XMLSchema">

  <Extern href="stdidcmd.h"/>
  <Extern href="vsshlids.h"/>
  <Extern href="msobtnid.h"/>

  <Commands package="guidSimplePackagePkg">
    <Groups>
      <Group guid="guidSimplePackageCmdSet" id="MyMenuGroup" priority="0x0600">
        <Parent guid="guidSHLMainMenu" id="IDM_VS_MENU_TOOLS"/>
      </Group>
    </Groups>

    <Buttons>
      <Button guid="guidSimplePackageCmdSet" id="cmdidExecuteSimpleCommand"
        priority="0x0100" type="Button">
        <Parent guid="guidSimplePackageCmdSet" id="MyMenuGroup" />
        <Icon guid="guidImages" id="bmpPic1" />
        <Strings>
          <CommandName>cmdidExecuteSimpleCommand</CommandName>
          <ButtonText>Simple Command</ButtonText>
        </Strings>
      </Button>
    </Buttons>

    <Bitmaps>
      <Bitmap guid="guidImages" href="Resources\Images_32bit.bmp"
        usedList="bmpPic1, bmpPic2, bmpPicSearch, bmpPicX, bmpPicArrows"/>
    </Bitmaps>
  </Commands>
```

```
    <Symbols>
      <GuidSymbol name="guidSimplePackagePkg"
        value="{f64159de-acd9-4208-b176-068fb137557c}" />
      <GuidSymbol name="guidSimplePackageCmdSet"
        value="{65a60456-eb59-4227-a8ec-d3f292cbd49f}">
        <IDSymbol name="MyMenuGroup" value="0x1020" />
        <IDSymbol name="cmdidExecuteSimpleCommand" value="0x0100" />
      </GuidSymbol>
      <GuidSymbol name="guidImages" value="{408845d6-7a42-48b8-8d1a-9f023317b71d}" >
        <IDSymbol name="bmpPic1" value="1" />
        <IDSymbol name="bmpPic2" value="2" />
        <IDSymbol name="bmpPicSearch" value="3" />
        <IDSymbol name="bmpPicX" value="4" />
        <IDSymbol name="bmpPicArrows" value="5" />
      </GuidSymbol>
    </Symbols>

  </CommandTable>
```

*Code file [SimplePackage.vsct] available for download at Wrox.com*

The .vsct file tells a lot about how Visual Studio is architected, how it solves the coupling of functions (commands), and user interface elements.

➤ Commands (actions to execute) are separated from the user interface element triggering the command. The same command can be assigned to different menus and toolbars. They will use the same action.

➤ Commands used together can be grouped and simply merged into existing menus by using the command group representation. It is much easier than coupling commands with hosting menus one-by-one.

➤ Elements are identified by symbols rather than using explicit values. This makes the coupling less error-prone. Values of symbols must be defined only once, and the VSCT compiler can check for mistyping.

The root element of a .vsct file is the CommandTable element. As you can see, all related elements are defined by the http://schemas.microsoft.com/VisualStudio/2005-10-18/CommandTable namespace. No doubt, the most important element is Commands, because this node defines commands, their initial layout, and behavior.

Any command in the Visual Studio IDE must belong to the IDE itself or to a package. To assign a command to the appropriate (owning) package, the package attribute of the Commands element must name the GUID of the corresponding package.

The Commands node can have a few child elements; each has a very specific role.

Group elements define *command groups*, each of which is a logical set of related commands that visually stand together. In the preceding .vsct file, you have a Group element that holds only a Button. A button represents a piece of a user interface element the user can interact with — in this case, a menu item that can be clicked. The Parent element defines the relationship between elements — for example, the Button element defined earlier is parented in the Group.

Toolbars and menus would be poor without icons to help the user associate a small image with the function. The Bitmap nodes allow defining the visual elements (icons) used in menus.

The `Symbols` section is a central place in the command table file where you can define the identifiers to be used in the other parts of the `.vsct` file. You can use the `GuidSymbol` element to define the "logical container GUID," and the nested `IDSymbol` elements to provide optional identifiers within the logical container. The name and the value attribute of these elements do exactly what you would expect — associate the symbol name with its value.

## Debugging the Package

Sooner or later, you find yourself debugging a package and searching for a bug. Debugging techniques are out of the scope of this book. However, the following discussion shows how can you debug your package and what is going on behind the scenes.

To debug or run a package, you should set it as the startup project. If your package is the only project is the solution, it is already marked as such. If you have more projects in the solution, you should mark any VSPackage project as the startup project.

Independently of whether you run a package with or without debugging, the Visual Studio Experimental Hive is started. You can check it on the project property pages on the Debug tab. Figure 6-32 shows it for the `SimplePackage` project.

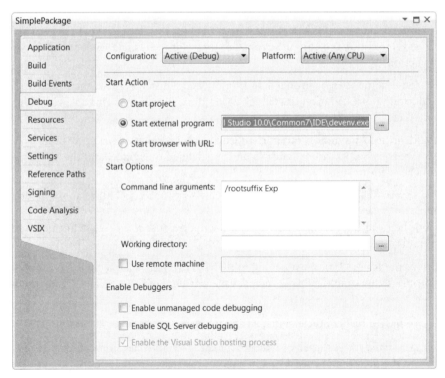

**FIGURE 6-32:** Debug properties of a package

You can see that `devenv.exe` is selected as the startup project, and it is launched with the `/rootsuffix Exp` command-line parameters. This command line starts the Experimental Hive.

When you start the project with Start Debugging (by pressing F5), Visual Studio attaches the debugger to the Experimental Hive instance, and so you can set breakpoints in Visual Studio. As your package running in the Experimental Hive reaches a breakpoint, you are taken back to the Debug view, as shown in Figure 6-33. In this case, a breakpoint was set within the `Initialize` method of the package class.

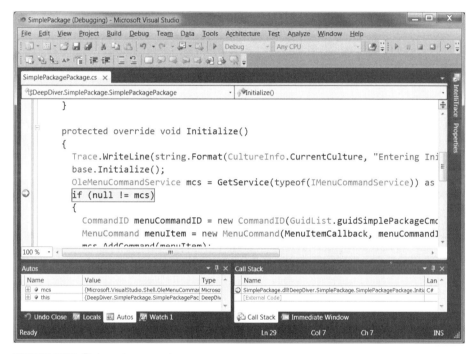

**FIGURE 6-33:** Debugging a package

You can use the same techniques for debugging a VSPackage as for any other application. All debugging features of Visual Studio are accessible. You can watch variables, evaluate expressions, set up conditional breakpoints, and so on.

## EXTENDING THE NEW EDITOR

The new code editor of Visual Studio 2010 is not just a piece of the Shell that is re-architected to leverage WPF technology and managed code. It is also a great subject of extensibility. Extending the behavior of the old code editor (built into Visual Studio 2005 or 2008) was painful because of the lack of documentation and complex interfaces.

This is no longer true for the new editor. Using the templates provided by the VS SDK, it takes just a few clicks to create a working skeleton of an extensible editor component.

# Extending the Editor with the Managed Extensibility Framework

The key technology enabling the creation of custom editor components new in .NET 4 is the *Managed Extensibility Framework* (MEF). The MEF is not a part of Visual Studio 2010. However, Visual Studio 2010 is one of the first Microsoft products that uses the MEF. The following discussion does not go into great detail about the MEF, but does provide a very brief overview to help you understand what it is and how it works.

Simply said, the MEF as a technology is intended to enable greater reuse of applications and components by turning today's statically compiled applications into dynamically composed ones.

Why is this dynamic composition so important? If you create applications from smaller independent parts, you can architect the application so that responsibilities are better divided. According to these responsibilities, you can separately test your parts, find bugs, and correct them. It is easier to handle these small parts individually than all of the pieces together, and (as you can imagine) it is easier to maintain them. However, the big issue is how to roll together these individual parts to form a whole application.

This is what the MEF does — parts declare their intention to work together with other pieces, and the MEF pulls all these parts together to form the application.

In the case of extending the Visual Studio 2010 Editor, the host application is Visual Studio, and the custom editor components are the parts to be composed dynamically with the editor within the IDE. The intention of parts for cooperation can be one of the following:

➤  A part can offer some functionality to be used by the host.

➤  A part wants to use some services implemented by the host.

➤  A combination of these two.

The MEF uses .NET attributes to express the intention for cooperation. These attributes can be found in the `System.ComponentModel.Composition` namespace.

## Using Export Attributes

The intention that a component offers a service to be consumed by other components is expressed with the `Export` attribute. For example, if you have an abstract service described with the `IGreetings` interface that contains a `SayHello` method, a custom part accessible from other MEF-aware components looks like this:

```
[Export(typeof(IGreetings))]
class SimpleGreeting : IGreetings
{
  public string SayHello()
  {
    return "Hello from Visual Studio 2010";
  }
}
```

The parameter of the Export attribute defines the contract the component satisfies. When the MEF composes the parts of the application, it uses this attribute to recognize that SimpleGreeting satisfies the IGreetings contract. When any other component or the host application queries the *composition container* for parts supporting the IGreetings contract, SimpleGreeting is also retrieved. Later in this chapter, you will see concrete examples of how to use Export to proffer parts implementing custom editor extensions.

## Accessing Services with Import Attribute

Generally, composable parts not only offer functions to other parts, but also intend to use services provided by other parts. This intention is expressed with the Import attribute.

Let's assume that you want to modify the SimpleGreeting component so that it can work together with an IContextInfo contract-aware component, like UserInfo in the following declaration:

```
[Export(typeof(IContextInfo))]
class UserInfo: IContextInfo
{
  public IDictionary<string, string> GetContextInfo()
  {
    return new Dictionary<string, string>
      { {"UserName", Environment.UserName } };
  }
}
```

The IContextInfo is a service from SimpleGreeting's point of view, and this is expressed like this:

```
[Export(typeof(IGreetings))]
class SimpleGreeting : IGreetings
{
  [Import(typeof(IContextInfo))]
  IContextInfo ContextInfo { get; set; }

  public string SayHello()
  {
    string userName;
    var props = ContextInfo.GetContextInfo();
    props.TryGetValue("UserName", out userName);
    return "Hello " + (userName ?? "<null>") + " from Visual Studio 2010";
  }
}
```

The Import attribute here is applied on the ContextInfo property, which is used in the SayHello method. The MEF takes care during the composition phase that ContextInfo will be set up and does not remain uninitialized.

The Visual Studio editor proffers about three dozen services that can be accessed using the pattern just described. Later in this chapter, you'll see a sample to learn how the editor's *classification type registry service* is consumed.

## Metadata Attributes

In many cases, it may be necessary to associate information with proffered or consumed services. Often, the information is used to explain the capabilities of a specific implementation of a common contract. Also, this information can be used to determine which implementation of a contract should be used during the composition phase.

Let's assume that you provided more than one service implementation for the earlier `IContextInfo` contract. How can the MEF decide which one should be used? If you do not support some other information helping the MEF in composition, it will not do the match-making between `IContextInfo` services and consumers.

The MEF allows attaching *metadata attributes* to services and consumers — to owners of `Export` and `Import` attributes. The Visual Studio editor uses these metadata attributes heavily for many purposes, including the following:

➤ Providing information that is displayed in the IDE about the editor extension (for example, in the Fonts and Colors options dialog)

➤ Determining the order in which competing components (that is, components implementing the same contract) should be applied

➤ Where user interface elements like *custom margins* should be placed in the IDE

➤ Assigning information to the components in order to provide a way to reference them from other components

Just as for `Export` and `Import` attributes, you will see concrete metadata attributes in the custom editor classifier sample later in this chapter.

# Editor Extensibility Points

The Visual Studio 2010 editor provides about a dozen extensibility points where developers can add their own components to change or extend the default behavior. Although this book does not examine editor extensions in detail, Table 6-8 lists the major extensibility points to help you imagine what sorts of options you have when thinking about altering the default behavior of the code editor.

**TABLE 6-8:** Major Editor Extensibility Points

| EXTENSIBILITY POINT | DESCRIPTION |
| --- | --- |
| Content type definition | The text behind the code editor is always associated with a *content type*. The content type determines how specific text should be handled in the editor. For example, different syntax coloring should be used for texts having "CSharp" content type than the ones having "Basic." Most editor extensions are associated with a content type to define where to use them. |
| | Content types form a hierarchy having the "text" type as the root. Content type extensibility means that developers can define their own content types, and put it into this hierarchy. |

| EXTENSIBILITY POINT | DESCRIPTION |
| --- | --- |
| Classifier provider | The parts (spans) of text in the editor can be classified to assign with some special formatting, such as syntax coloring used in C# or VB. A *classification provider* is a component that understands how certain parts of the text should be assigned with *classification types*. C# keywords and VB comments are both good examples of classification types.<br><br>Developers can create their customized providers to classify the text using either the built-in ones provided, or their own classification types. |
| Tagger providers | The parts (spans) of text can be associated with arbitrary data called a *text tag. Tagger providers* are extensions that can analyze the text and associate spans with tags. This mechanism is used by Visual Studio to display code errors and text markers.<br><br>Developers can create their own providers to add custom data (for example, some information used for refactoring) to text spans.<br><br>Tags are associated with the text behind the editor, and do not have a visible effect on rendering. However, tags are heavily used by *adornment providers*. |
| Adornments | The greatest new feature of editor extensibility is probably the support for adornments. These define visual effects that can be added either to the text displayed, or to the editor's text view itself. These adornments can be any WPF `UIElement` instances, so you can actually create any visual effect WPF supports (including shapes, animations, images, video, and so on).<br><br>Adornments are not just "eye candy" that simply add some sugar to your source code. They can be interactive, and developers can build actions into them. Using adornments, you can extend the text editor even with smart-tag-like elements and builders that make your code editing experience richer and more efficient than simply typing text. |
| Margins and scrollbars | Margins and scrollbars are the main view elements of the editor, in addition to the text view itself. The horizontal and vertical scrollbars of the editor and the line number margin are good examples. They are implemented through these extension points.<br><br>Developers can provide any number of margins in addition to the standard margins that appear around the text view, and locate them on any of the four sides of the text view area. |
| IntelliSense extensions | Visual Studio's IntelliSense is a general term for a group of features that provides information and completion for structured text. These features include statement completion, signature help, Quick Info, and smart tags. These features are implemented with a common architecture that contains such roles as broker, session, controller, source, and presenter. |

*continues*

**TABLE 6-8** *(continued)*

| EXTENSIBILITY POINT | DESCRIPTION |
| --- | --- |
| | Developers can define their own custom implementations for sources (through source providers), controllers, and presenters. For example, by creating a custom completion source provider and a presenter, you can change the list of completions offered on the screen, and even their presentation, if you prefer some enhanced view to the default list. |
| Mouse processors | You can add special handling for mouse input. Your own event processors can run before and/or after the default event handler, and so you can change how the editor responds to mouse interactions. |
| Drop handlers | You can customize the behavior of drag-and-drop operations through custom drop handlers. You can define your drop handler to handle specific formats (such as bitmaps, HTML, or CSV), or other custom formats. |

When you plan to create some functional editor enhancement, often it cannot be accomplished by creating a custom component for only one of the extension points outlined previously. You may have to create more small components working together. For example, if you have a programming library of your own, you may want to add functions to your editor that recognize types and members of this library in the code. Then you can add UI elements representing functions accelerating your coding tasks related to those types and members. This kind of enhancement may require adding custom components for the following extension points:

➤   Content type definitions representing the types and members of your programming library

➤   Classifiers for the types and members (probably a few separate classifiers, depending on how you group them functionally or visually)

➤   Adornments to represent types, members, and related actions

➤   Optional statement completions, smart tags, and mouse processors

To create full solutions, you may also have to use your editor extensions together with your own custom packages (for example, if you want to provide custom options pages or tool windows).

## Creating a Simple Classifier

Now, it is time to show how a few of the editor extensibility concepts just discussed can be put into practice. To illustrate how easy it is to create a custom editor component, let's create a classifier with Visual Studio's built-in template, and dig into the source code. After you understand how it works, you will modify the classifier so that it will highlight known file extensions (such as `.cs`, `.sln`, `.bmp`, and so on) in the editor.

The VS SDK installs a few project templates to create editor extensions. Use the File ➪ New ➪ Project function to start with an editor classifier. The project template can be found in the Extensibility category under Visual C# in the Installed Templates tab, as shown in Figure 6-34.

**FIGURE 6-34:** Creating an Editor Classifier project

Select your solution folder, set the project name to `FileAssocClassifier`, and then click OK. The new solution is generated in a few seconds, and the default classifier is ready to build and start. Start it with Debug ➪ Start Without Debugging, or by pressing Ctrl+F5.

Just as in the case of VSPackages, a new Visual Studio instance, the Experimental Hive, is started. Create a new text file by using the File ➪ New ➪ File function. The file opens in the document area of Visual Studio. Type some text into the file and you will immediately see the "magic" that the editor classifier created. The text will have a dark background and the font is underlined, as shown in Figure 6-35.

**FIGURE 6-35:** The default behavior of an editor classifier

What do you see? The template you used to create an editor classifier generates a simple classifier with one classification type named "ordinary," and declares that the full range of the text is classified as "ordinary." It also creates a *classification format* that sets the font color of "ordinary" to blue violet, and changes its style be underlined.

Table 6-9 lists the files comprising the classifier project.

**TABLE 6-9:** FileAssocClassifier Project Files

| FILE | DESCRIPTION |
|---|---|
| ClassificationFormat.cs | Type definition describing what kind of formatting should be used when the text with the matching classification is displayed. |
| ClassificationType.cs | Type definition representing the classification. |
| Classifier.cs | File with the classification provider and classifier definitions. |
| Classifier_large.png, Classifier_small.png | Bitmaps used to represent the classifier in the New Project dialog, in Extensions Manager, and on Visual Studio Gallery. |
| extension.vsmanifest | The VSIX manifest file used for the deployment of this component. |

## The Classification Type

The editor classifier template uses only one classification to describe the whole text in the editor as an instance of this classification. Listing 6-5 shows the source code of the static class responsible for defining this singleton classification type.

**LISTING 6-5: ClassifationType.cs**

```csharp
using System.ComponentModel.Composition;
using Microsoft.VisualStudio.Text.Classification;
using Microsoft.VisualStudio.Utilities;

namespace FileAssocClassifier
{
  internal static class OrdinaryClassificationDefinition
  {
    #region Type definition

    /// <summary>
    /// Defines the "ordinary" classification type.
    /// </summary>
    [Export(typeof(ClassificationTypeDefinition))]
    [Name("ordinary")]
    internal static ClassificationTypeDefinition OrdinaryClassificationType = null;

    #endregion
  }
}
```

*Code file [ClassificationType.cs] available for download at Wrox.com*

The `OrdinaryClassificationDefinition` class is a non-functional type definition, and it stands only for representing metadata for the classification type. The class is defined as static just as its only field `OrdinaryClassificationType`, which is decorated with the MEF attributes actually defining the "ordinary" classification.

```
[Export(typeof(ClassificationTypeDefinition))]
[Name("ordinary")]
```

The `Export` attribute uses the `ClassificationTypeDefinition` type as its parameter to sign the related member that satisfies the contract for a classification type. When composing the extensions with the editor, this is the contract from which the editor recognizes the classification type. The `Name` attribute is an MEF metadata attribute, and its value obviously is taken into account as the name of the classification type.

 *The preceding code would work if the class were instantiable and not static, because MEF would discover the classification type contract even in this case. However, making the class static signs the intention as "this is a metadata class, do not instantiate it."*

## The Classifier Provider and the Classifier

The key element of the classification is the *classifier* that bears the brunt of the work. The classifier is responsible for analyzing the text span provided by the editor for any classification types it recognizes. The editor uses the factory pattern to create the working instance of the classifier through a *classifier provider*. This pattern makes the classifier instantiation flexible, because appropriate classifier type is not hard-coded, but can be decided during run-time, and allows avoiding unnecessary instantiation of the classifier.

Both classes can be found in the `Classifier.cs` file shown in Listing 6-6.

**LISTING 6-6:** Classifier.cs

```
using System;
using System.Collections.Generic;
using System.ComponentModel.Composition;
using System.Windows.Media;
using Microsoft.VisualStudio.Text;
using Microsoft.VisualStudio.Text.Classification;
using Microsoft.VisualStudio.Utilities;

namespace FileAssocClassifier
{

  #region Provider definition
  /// <summary>
```

*continues*

**LISTING 6-6** *(continued)*

```csharp
/// This class causes a classifier to be added to the set of classifiers. Since
/// the content type is set to "text", this classifier applies to all text files
/// </summary>
[Export(typeof(IClassifierProvider))]
[ContentType("text")]
internal class OrdinaryClassifierProvider : IClassifierProvider
{

  /// <summary>
  /// Import the classification registry to be used for getting a reference
  /// to the custom classification type later.
  /// </summary>
  [Import]
  internal IClassificationTypeRegistryService ClassificationRegistry = null;

  //returns an instance of the classifier
  public IClassifier GetClassifier(ITextBuffer buffer)
  {
    return buffer.Properties.GetOrCreateSingletonProperty<OrdinaryClassifier>(
      delegate { return new OrdinaryClassifier(ClassificationRegistry); });
  }
}
#endregion //provider def

#region Classifier
/// <summary>
/// Classifier that classifies all text as an instance of the
/// OrdinaryClassifierType
/// </summary>
class OrdinaryClassifier : IClassifier
{
#pragma warning disable 67
    // This event gets raised if a non-text change would affect the classification
    // in some way,
    // for example typing /* would cause the classification to change in C#
    // without directly affecting the span.
    public event EventHandler<ClassificationChangedEventArgs>
      ClassificationChanged;
#pragma warning restore 67

    IClassificationType _classificationType;

    internal OrdinaryClassifier(IClassificationTypeRegistryService registry)
    {
      _classificationType = registry.GetClassificationType("ordinary");
    }

    /// <summary>
    /// This method scans the given SnapshotSpan for potential matches for this
    /// classification.
    /// In this instance, it classifies everything and returns each span as a
    /// new ClassificationSpan.
    /// </summary>
    /// <param name="trackingSpan">The span currently being classified</param>
```

```
    /// <returns>
    /// A list of ClassificationSpans that represent spans identified to be of
    /// this classification
    /// </returns>
    public IList<ClassificationSpan> GetClassificationSpans(SnapshotSpan span)
    {

        //create a list to hold the results
        List<ClassificationSpan> classifications = new List<ClassificationSpan>();
        classifications.Add(new ClassificationSpan(new SnapshotSpan(span.Snapshot,
 new Span(span.Start, span.Length)),
                                                    _classificationType));

        return classifications;
    }

    }
    #endregion //Classifier
}
```

*Code file [Classifier.cs] available for download at Wrox.com*

The OrdinaryClassifierProvider is in the role of the classifier provider, as its name suggests. The editor recognizes it as a provider from its definition:

```
[Export(typeof(IClassifierProvider))]
[ContentType("text")]
internal class OrdinaryClassifierProvider : IClassifierProvider
{
  // ...
}
```

The contract is defined by the IClassifierProvider type as the argument of the Export attribute, and the class also must implement this interface, because it contains the responsibilities of a classifier provider. The ContentType metadata attribute specifies that this provider is bound to the "text" content type. Because "text" is the root of the content types, this provider will be used for any text file, including C#, VB, XML, XAML, and so on.

The editor uses a *classification type registry* to store objects defining classifications. Because the classifier will use it, the provider must access this service. The following declaration provides that this service will be accessed through the ClassificationRegistry field:

```
[Import]
internal IClassificationTypeRegistryService ClassificationRegistry = null;
```

As you can see, this field is not initialized at instantiation time. This is where the MEF comes into the picture again. During the composition phase, the MEF will instantiate an OrdinaryClassifier Provider and will initialize the ClassificationRegistry field with the appropriate service instance.

When it is time to use the classifier, the editor first turns to the classifier provider by calling its GetClassifier method, passing the text buffer and the context information to this method.

The text buffer keeps track of its `Properties`, one of which is stored with the key `OrdinaryClassifier`, and the instance behind is the custom classifier. The `GetClassifier` method's body simply queries the properties of the text buffer for this instance, and, if that cannot be found, it simply instantiates it with the delegate specified.

```
return buffer.Properties.GetOrCreateSingletonProperty<OrdinaryClassifier>(
    delegate { return new OrdinaryClassifier(ClassificationRegistry); });
```

The first call to `GetOrCreateSingletonProperty` does the instantiation, and immediately stores the classifier instance among the properties. Any subsequent call will result in returning the classifier from the `Properties` collection.

 *Note that the classification type registry instance is passed to the classifier's constructor.*

Now, let's focus on the `OrdinaryClassifier` class that is responsible for classifying a span of text. This class implements the `IClassifier` interface defining the `ClassificationChanged` event and the `GetClassificationSpans` method. The key of the implementation is the method that takes an immutable span of text (as an instance of `SnapshotSpan`) and provides a list of `ClassificationSpan` objects describing spans that could be classified with the classifier.

The template's default implementation creates one element on the result list that is the full span of input text declared as one with the "ordinary" classification:

```
public IList<ClassificationSpan> GetClassificationSpans(SnapshotSpan span)
{
  List<ClassificationSpan> classifications = new List<ClassificationSpan>();
  classifications.Add(new ClassificationSpan(new SnapshotSpan(span.Snapshot,
    new Span(span.Start, span.Length)), _classificationType));
  return classifications;
}
```

The "ordinary" classification is represented by the `_classificationType` field initialized in the class constructor. The constructor uses the classification type registry instance you passed in the provider.

```
internal OrdinaryClassifier(IClassificationTypeRegistryService registry)
{
  _classificationType = registry.GetClassificationType("ordinary");
}
```

As you can see, the classifier is very simple. One more detail not yet mentioned is the `ClassificationChanged` event. This event is raised when a change outside of a certain text span could change the classification in the text span. A good example is when you type a C# comment block token (`/*`). All the text following this token might change the classification, because former language elements such as keywords and identifiers can become comments. Because this example is simple, this event is not addressed here.

## The Classification Format

The last element of the classifier pattern is the classification format defining how a certain classification should be formatted when the corresponding text is rendered in the editor view. This type is declared in the `ClassificationFormat.cs` file, as shown in Listing 6-7.

**LISTING 6-7:** ClassificationFormat.cs

```csharp
using System.ComponentModel.Composition;
using System.Windows.Media;
using Microsoft.VisualStudio.Text.Classification;
using Microsoft.VisualStudio.Utilities;

namespace FileAssocClassifier
{
  #region Format definition
  /// <summary>
  /// Defines an editor format for the OrdinaryClassification type that has a
  /// purple background and is underlined.
  /// </summary>
  [Export(typeof(EditorFormatDefinition))]
  [ClassificationType(ClassificationTypeNames = "ordinary")]
  [Name("OrdinaryText")]
  //this should be visible to the end user
  [UserVisible(true)]
  //set the priority to be after the default classifiers
  [Order(Before = Priority.Default)]
  internal sealed class OrdinaryFormat : ClassificationFormatDefinition
  {
    /// <summary>
    /// Defines the visual format for the "ordinary" classification type
    /// </summary>
    public OrdinaryFormat()
    {
      this.DisplayName = "Ordinary Text"; //human readable version of the name
      this.BackgroundColor = Colors.BlueViolet;
      this.TextDecorations = System.Windows.TextDecorations.Underline;
    }
  }
  #endregion //Format definition
}
```

*Code file [ClassificationFormat.cs] available for download at Wrox.com*

From the previous code snippets you have seen in this chapter, it may be obvious that the `Export` attribute with the `EditorFormatDefinition` type marks the class as one defining a classification format. The base class provides properties that can be set to change the default editor format for the corresponding classification.

The instance constructor simply sets the background color to blue violet, and adds underline to the font. If you examine the `ClassificationFormatDefinition` class, you will find other interesting properties such `BackgroundBrush`, `BackgroundOpacity`, `FontTypeFace`, `TextEffects`, and many more.

In addition to the `Export` attribute, you can see other metadata attributes that are important for defining the behavior of the classification format. Let's take a look at them.

The `ClassificationType` attribute binds the format definition with the classification. In this sample, it means that this format will be assigned only with the "ordinary" classification. The `Name` attribute assigns a name that can be used to refer to the format definition. The `DisplayName` attribute defines a name for the format that can be displayed at several places in the IDE. The `UserVisible` attribute allows displaying the format in the Options dialog in the Fonts and Colors tab, and lets the user change the format set programmatically.

Nothing prevents a span of text from having more than one classification at the same time. This is normal, because more classifiers work on the same text. The editor uses the corresponding classification formats in a certain order. The `Order` metadata attribute is used to define the place of the format in this chain. In this example, it is set so that this format will override the editor's default format.

Because the `UserVisible` attribute of the format definition is set to `true`, you can find and override the definition in the Fonts and Colors dialog, as shown in Figure 6-36.

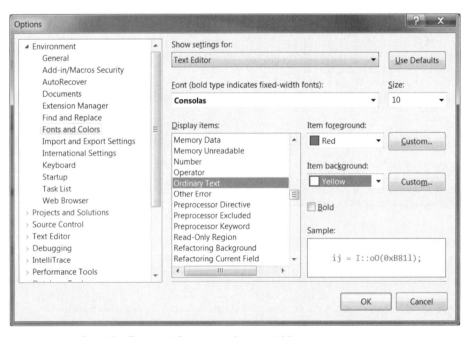

**FIGURE 6-36:** Classifier Format definition can be overridden

Now, when you create a new text file and type in some text, you can see that the colors set programmatically (black foreground and blue violet background) changed according to the Fonts and Colors dialog settings, as shown in Figure 6-37.

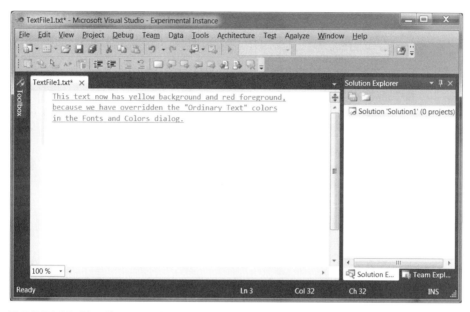

**FIGURE 6-37:** Classification colors changed

## Playing with the Classification

Now, you should have a basic understanding of classifiers. Let's modify the code so that the classifier recognizes known file extensions, and highlights them in the editor. To make this sample a bit more complex, let's use a separate format for extensions with text and non-text content.

First, let's define the classification types. Because you want to handle two classification formats, you need at least two classification types. Listing 6-8 shows how the ClassificationType.cs file is modified.

Available for
download on
Wrox.com

**LISTING 6-8:** The modified ClassificationType.cs file

```
using System.ComponentModel.Composition;
using Microsoft.VisualStudio.Text.Classification;
using Microsoft.VisualStudio.Utilities;

namespace FileAssocClassifier
{
  internal static class TextTypeFileAssocClassificationDefinition
  {
    [Export(typeof(ClassificationTypeDefinition))]
    [Name("textTypeFileAssoc")]
```

*continues*

**LISTING 6-8** *(continued)*

```
    internal static ClassificationTypeDefinition ClassificationType = null;
  }

  internal static class NonTextTypeFileAssocClassificationDefinition
  {
    [Export(typeof(ClassificationTypeDefinition))]
    [Name("nonTextTypeFileAssoc")]
    internal static ClassificationTypeDefinition ClassificationType = null;
  }
}
```

*Code file [ClassificationType.cs] available for download at Wrox.com*

As you can see, nothing special has been done here. The "ordinary" type definition has simply been dropped, and two new definitions created for the file associations with text and non-text types. To create a different visual appearance for these types, two classification formats should be specified, as shown in Listing 6-9.

**LISTING 6-9** The Modified ClassificationFormat.cs File

```
using System.ComponentModel.Composition;
using System.Windows.Media;
using Microsoft.VisualStudio.Text.Classification;
using Microsoft.VisualStudio.Utilities;

namespace FileAssocClassifier
{
  [Export(typeof(EditorFormatDefinition))]
  [ClassificationType(ClassificationTypeNames = "textTypeFileAssoc")]
  [Name("TextContentFormat")]
  [DisplayName("(Text Content)")]
  [UserVisible(true)]
  [Order(Before = Priority.Default)]
  internal sealed class TextContentFormat : ClassificationFormatDefinition
  {
    public TextContentFormat()
    {
      this.ForegroundColor = Colors.DarkGreen;
    }
  }

  [Export(typeof(EditorFormatDefinition))]
  [ClassificationType(ClassificationTypeNames = "nonTextTypeFileAssoc")]
  [Name("NonTextContentFormat")]
  [DisplayName("(Non-Text Content)")]
  [UserVisible(false)]
  [Order(Before = Priority.Default)]
  internal sealed class NonTextContentFormat : ClassificationFormatDefinition
  {
    public NonTextContentFormat()
    {
      this.ForegroundColor = Colors.DarkRed;
```

```
      this.TextDecorations = System.Windows.TextDecorations.OverLine;
    }
  }
}
```

*Code file [ClassificationFormat.cs] available for download at Wrox.com*

The two format definitions are very similar to each other. Actually, they differ in their names and in the text colors they use. You might notice one other slight difference — the `NonTextContentFormat` uses a `UserVisible` attribute with a `false` value, while `TextContentFormat` sets it to `true`. This is only for a demonstrative purpose to illustrate that `NonTextContentFormat` will not be displayed in the Fonts and Colors option dialog.

While the classification provider type actually remained the same, you must rewrite the classifier type, as shown in Listing 6-10.

**LISTING 6-10:** The Completely Changed Classifier.cs File

```
using System;
using System.Collections.Generic;
using System.ComponentModel.Composition;
using System.Windows.Media;
using Microsoft.VisualStudio.Text;
using Microsoft.VisualStudio.Text.Classification;
using Microsoft.VisualStudio.Utilities;
using Microsoft.Win32;
using System.Linq;

namespace FileAssocClassifier
{
  [Export(typeof(IClassifierProvider))]
  [ContentType("text")]
  internal class FileAssociationClassifierProvider : IClassifierProvider
  {
    [Import]
    internal IClassificationTypeRegistryService ClassificationRegistry;

    public IClassifier GetClassifier(ITextBuffer buffer)
    {
      return buffer.Properties.
        GetOrCreateSingletonProperty<FileAssociationClassifier>(
        delegate
        {
          return new FileAssociationClassifier(ClassificationRegistry);
        });
    }
  }

  class FileAssociationClassifier : IClassifier
  {
    public event EventHandler<ClassificationChangedEventArgs>
      ClassificationChanged;

    IClassificationType _textClassification;
```

*continues*

**LISTING 6-10** *(continued)*

```csharp
IClassificationType _nonTextClassification;
Dictionary<string, string> _fileAssociations =
    new Dictionary<string, string>();
int _maxAssocLength;

internal FileAssociationClassifier(IClassificationTypeRegistryService registry)
{
  _textClassification = registry.GetClassificationType("textTypeFileAssoc");
  _nonTextClassification =
    registry.GetClassificationType("nonTextTypeFileAssoc");
  foreach (var element in
    from item in
      (
        from name in Registry.ClassesRoot.GetSubKeyNames()
        where name.StartsWith(".")
        select new
        {
          Name = name,
          RegKey = Registry.ClassesRoot.OpenSubKey(name, false)
        }
      )
    select new
    {
      Key = item.Name.ToLower(),
      ContentType = (item.RegKey.GetValue("Content Type") ?? "").ToString()
    })
    _fileAssociations.Add(element.Key, element.ContentType);
  _maxAssocLength = _fileAssociations.Keys.Max(item => item.Length);
}

public IList<ClassificationSpan> GetClassificationSpans(SnapshotSpan span)
{
  var text = span.Snapshot.GetText(span);
  List<ClassificationSpan> classifications = new List<ClassificationSpan>();
  int searchOffset = 0;
  do
  {
    int wordStart = text.IndexOf(".", searchOffset);
    if (wordStart == -1 || wordStart >= text.Length - 1) break;
    var length = text.Length - wordStart;
    if (length > _maxAssocLength) length = _maxAssocLength;
    string keyFound = null;
    for (int i = length; i > 1; i--)
    {
      var toSearch = text.Substring(wordStart, i).ToLower();
      if (_fileAssociations.ContainsKey(toSearch))
      {
        keyFound = toSearch;
        break;
      }
    }
    if (keyFound == null)
    {
      searchOffset = wordStart + 1;
```

```
        }
        else
        {
          var classificationType = _fileAssociations[keyFound].StartsWith("text")
            ? _textClassification
            : _nonTextClassification;
          int wordLength = keyFound.Length;
          classifications.Add(new ClassificationSpan(
            new SnapshotSpan(span.Snapshot,
            new Span(wordStart + span.Start, wordLength)), classificationType));
          searchOffset = wordStart + wordLength;
        }
      }
    }
    while (true);
    return classifications;
  }
 }
}
```

*Code file [Classifier.cs] available for download at Wrox.com*

The classifier's constructor initializes the classification types and the dictionary of file associations. The `_fileAssociations` field stores file extensions with their content types. This container is initialized with a LINQ expression that looks up the registry and collects the interesting file extensions. Here you also store the maximum length of registered extensions, because it plays an important role in the algorithm recognizing the extensions in the text.

The lion's share of the work is done in the `GetClassificationSpans` method. First, it gets the text of the snapshot span, and then looks up all extensions.

There are many ways to do that. The algorithm used here seems a bit complicated; you may create a simpler solution. However, there are two important things to be keep in mind when programming the `GetClassificationSpan` method:

➤ The text spans returned must be ordered by their starting position and non-overlapping, in order to be displayed correctly in the editor.

➤ The algorithm must be efficient, because every keystroke triggers running it.

You may think efficiency is not so critical in this case, but that may not be the case. For example, in one sample run, the test machine had 690 file extensions, and the first algorithm was not quick enough. When the tester kept a key pressed, the editor started to clog up.

A better algorithm would start searching for the dot character incrementally. If it does not find the dot in the span, the work is done. If it is found, the algorithm extracts the maximum number of available characters following the dot — keeping in mind the length of the longest file extension. Then it looks up the extracted characters in the `_fileAssociations` dictionary. If that is not found, a shorter string is searched, unless the file extension to search for becomes empty. This is important, because, if you type something like **file.csxfg**, both `.c` and `.cs` are valid extensions, and, in this case, you would like to highlight the longer one, namely `.cs`.

After finding an extension, a new element is added to the classification span list with the appropriate type, depending on the content type stored as the value in the `_fileAssociations` dictionary, and the search goes on as long as there is any new extension to find.

Run the extension with Debug ➪ Start Without Debugging, and create a new text file. Type some text containing file extensions, using both text and non-text types. Figure 6-38 shows how the classifier works.

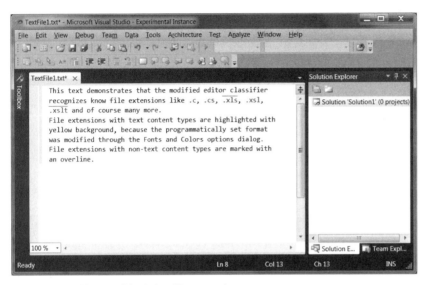

**FIGURE 6-38:** The modified classifier at work

You can also look up the Fonts and Colors options dialog to check that only the Text Content format is allowed for customization, as shown in Figure 6-39.

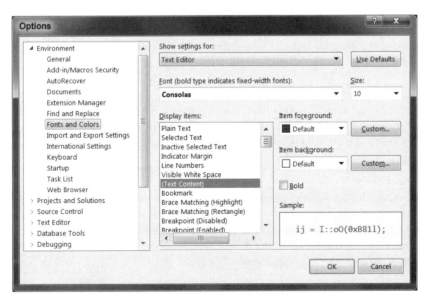

**FIGURE 6-39:** Text Content format is customizable

The `UserVisible` attribute of this format definition is used with the `true` parameter. Since this attribute of the non-text format definition was marked with `false`, that cannot be customized through this dialog.

## SUMMARY

Visual Studio is not only a tool but a real development platform you can customize and extend to turn it into your ultimate tool. From its first version, Visual Studio was designed with extensibility in mind, and you now have many options to change or enhance built-in functions, as well as creating new ones.

Although developers generally do not take into account customization and configuration as methods of extending applications, this is a real alternative. Many third-party tools (such refactoring tools, document generators, and so on) provide GUIs, configuration files to customize them in order to create new functionality. Code snippet management is a good example showing that Visual Studio itself also supports this option.

Macros provide the easiest way to extend Visual Studio. You can automate repetitive tasks in a few minutes by using the macro recording capabilities of Visual Studio. Macros access the Visual Studio automation object model, and easily combine the IDE commands and objects to establish the desired behavior. Although macros are great for task automation, they are not the right tools to create totally new functionality. When using macros, you should be aware of the fact that anyone can see the source code of your macro. Macros do not let you extend the UI or the services of Visual Studio.

Add-ins are much more powerful for developing Visual Studio extensions, because, in addition to accessing the Visual Studio automation objects, you can add new user interface elements to the IDE (such as tool windows, menu and toolbar commands, and so on). An add-in is actually a COM object implementing two COM interfaces. They can integrate into the IDE so that you actually do not know they are implemented as add-ins when you use them. The functions you add with an add-in look as if they were part of the IDE. An add-in is a compiled (managed or native) binary, so you can use the same intellectual property guarding techniques as for any other managed or native binaries.

While extensibility through macros and add-ins are built into Visual Studio out-of-the-box, by installing the VS SDK, you can use other options.

The most powerful way of developing Visual Studio extensions is to integrate Visual Studio packages into the IDE. These packages are not limited to using the automation model, or only to a few core services, but can access the whole infrastructure of Visual Studio just like the packages created by the development team at Microsoft. The VS SDK provides the Managed Package Framework to let you create VSPackages with managed code using either C# or VB. The VSPackage wizard helps you to create skeleton code for your packages in a few minutes.

Visual Studio 2010 has a brand-new code editor entirely written in managed code. This editor uses WPF as its presentation technology, and the development team designed it with extensibility in mind.

A great technology introduced in .NET 4, the Managed Extensibility Framework (MEF), is utilized to allow a straightforward and simple way of creating custom extensions. Writing editor components (such as classifiers, taggers, margins, adornments, IntelliSense presenters, and many more) is easy with the editor extensibility templates provided by the VS SDK.

Chapter 7 provides an overview about the .NET framework history. It includes the Windows development technologies used before .NET, and shows how the platform evolved until version 4 was released.

# PART II
# .NET 4

▶ **CHAPTER 7:** .NET Framework Version History

▶ **CHAPTER 8:** Modern UI Frameworks (WPF and Silverlight)

▶ **CHAPTER 9:** Windows Communication Framework (WCF)

▶ **CHAPTER 10:** Enhancements to the .NET Core Framework

▶ **CHAPTER 11:** Enhancements to the .NET Workflow Framework

▶ **CHAPTER 12:** Enhancements to the .NET Data Framework

▶ **CHAPTER 13:** Enhancements to the .NET Communications Framework

▶ **CHAPTER 14:** .NET Charting Components

# 7

# .NET Framework Version History

The .NET Framework represents one of the most important innovations in the history of software development. This chapter introduces you to the history of the .NET Framework, and takes you from the very beginning to the newest version.

First, you'll learn about some antecedents, focusing on Win32 programming in C, programming in C++, Visual Basic and Delphi, and COM programming. After that, you'll learn about the main goals of the .NET Framework.

This chapter describes the evolution of the .NET Framework, step by step, from version 1.0 to the newest version, 4.0. Also, you'll learn about the .NET Compact Framework, as well as .NET Micro Framework.

Finally, you'll learn about the .NET Framework architecture, including Common Language Run-time (CLR), Base Class Library (BCL), and the complete list of services of the architecture.

## BEFORE THE .NET FRAMEWORK

It is much easier to understand what led Microsoft professionals to the vision of the .NET Framework if you grasp a bit about the run-times used around 2000. During this period, developers had to use a lot of tools to develop a complex system. Some of them were chosen by way of preference and experience (for example, Delphi, Visual Basic, and C++), but others were selected just because they were all that was available on the market.

Let's take a look at some of those tools.

## Win/Win32 Programming in C

Before the age of the .NET Framework, the traditional programming language of Windows was C for a long time. The book *Programming Windows, Fifth Edition*, by Charles Petzold

(Redmond, WA: Microsoft Press, 1998), which primarily covered Windows APIs, was a key reference for developers.

The C language and its developer environment itself didn't help the programmers with their work. They had to deal with difficult syntaxes, manual memory handling, pointers, and so on. Despite the fact that C is a structured language, everything was missing that could have given it an object-oriented environment. The ancient Windows programs ran directly on the layer of the operating system, and directly used its services.

## C++ Programming

Upon first sight, C++ is an extension of the C language, providing a significant improvement compared to the C language — real object-oriented capabilities. But the object-oriented programming is not only a new environment or set of new tools; it's also a very new approach. An effective use of the new capabilities is impossible without understanding that deeply.

However, despite this new and effective object-oriented approach, C++ still didn't hide the Win32 API, and programmers still had to deal with memory handling, pointers, and syntax constructs.

The first steps to take advantage of C++ were the run-time engines (MFC, ATL, VCL, and so on). When an application was developed in one of these frameworks, the developers had to perform significant research before migrating an application to another framework.

The C++ frameworks offered static and dynamic translation:

➤ In the case of *static translation*, the run-time was physically bound to the EXE files.

➤ In the case of *dynamic translation*, the EXE file used an external DLL.

The DLLs of Microsoft's frameworks (for example, the DLL of MFC) were gradually added to the operating system.

The C++ frameworks were closer to the C language than to the object-oriented approach of C++. This has changed a lot. The functions of the Win32 API were increasingly available wrapped into object libraries. Despite the fact that C++ frameworks were greatly improved, C++ programming was still a difficult, painful experience.

## Programming in Visual Basic

Since 1998, more and more programmers have started to use Visual Basic (VB), primarily because of the release of Visual Studio 6.0. VB was very popular immediately from the beginning — thanks to its simplicity of creating complex user interfaces (UIs), COM/COM+ server components, and the accessing of data.

VB completely hid the Win32 API from the developers. (Unfortunately, most of them didn't even know what the Win32 API was.) To do that, VB needed a lot of tools, special classes, and VB-centric objects. The Win32 API was hidden by the msvbvm60.dll file, which refers to the Microsoft Visual Basic Virtual Machine, the run-time of VB programs. In VB, you had to use the Win32 API to access to the operating system's services. You could do that in VB, but this programming style is very far from what VB developers were used to.

The biggest problem with VB was that it appeared to be an object-oriented language, but, in reality, it was only "object-like." For example, although there are classes in VB, there is neither inheritance nor constructors.

## Programming in Delphi

Delphi is a very successful product from Borland. It has lots of users, similar to VB, and these users are still a very active community.

The programming language of this tool is Object Pascal, a real object-oriented language. Delphi provided components through an extensible IDE around Object Pascal. These had capabilities not only for developing thick and thin clients, but also for distributed systems and COM/COM+ components.

Delphi hid the Win32 API from the programmers with its own Visual Component Library (VCL) run-time. It doesn't require (in the VB sense) a run-time because its compiler-generated EXE files can be used independently (as if the run-time had been linked to the executable file).

When using the Win32API for Delphi, you could use most of Win32 API features immediately.

## COM Programming

Component Object Model (COM) programming was born as a solution for language-independent component reusability. COM cannot be referred to only in past tense, because it's still around, even in Microsoft's products, though with continuously decreasing intensity.

COM provides an architecture for developers that promises, "If you comply with the rules for creating COM classes, your code will be binary reusable."

One of the most important advantages of binary reusability is that the components can be reusable independently from the language they were developed in. Unfortunately, this reusability was not complete, because of the limitations of the developer tools.

In contrast, one of the most frequently mentioned disadvantages of COM programming is that it is missing real inheritance. Although COM provides some technologies for that, they are not easy to use.

However, COM provides a very important capability for developers — the transparency of the location of components. A component can even be in another process, or on another computer. If it's correctly installed (that is, marked into the registry), you don't have to deal the communication of processes and computers during the use of the component.

COM components also can be used as interfaces that are managed by the Microsoft Transaction Server (MTS), the ancestor of the COM+ run-time that is still a part of the Windows operating systems.

The common reference of COM and the .NET Framework often hides COM's pioneering role in the birth of the component-based approach and developer method. There is no question that COM is wrong, or that it is an already completely outdated technology, or that it was condemned to death from its birth! Moreover, COM originated the planning and developing method in which systems of binary reusable, flexible, and dynamically changeable components can be developed.

Generally, developers spend only 30 percent of their time creating code that belongs to some business function in the software under development. These business functions provide value directly to the end users, either on the UI, or in the expected operation of a function. In the other 70 percent of the time, developers develop code that is required for the execution of the software, but doesn't provide direct value to the business functions (for example, database transactions, communication framework of distributed systems, diagnostic logging, configuration management solutions, data encryption, and so on). Let's call them *infrastructure code*.

This rate of 30 percent-to-70 percent is also often similar in the number of code lines. It has effects not only during the development, but also during the other phases of the project (such as test and deployment).

How much better it would be to reverse this rate — 70 percent of your time was spent creating "useful" business code, and only 30 percent of your time was spent writing infrastructure code!

Of course, it is no coincidence that Microsoft also deemed this trend to be important. One of the most important goals of the development of the .NET Framework was to significantly reduce the quantity of infrastructure code written by the developers themselves.

## THE ORIGIN AND GOALS OF THE .NET FRAMEWORK

Microsoft released the first version of the .NET Framework in the middle of the year 2000, but the history of the .NET Framework goes back to the late 1990s. During the planning of the .NET Framework, software engineers became very excited because they wanted to create a brand new developer framework with a brand new approach, without the deficiencies and problems of the old platforms.

The basic properties of the .NET Framework have been based on the team's main goals as follows:

➤ *Independent run-time environment* — All .NET languages are equal. There are no running differences, for example, between VB.NET and C#. Actually, it doesn't matter which languages are used in the applications running on the framework. The execution is the same in all cases.

➤ *Clean, object-oriented basics* — Although the object-oriented paradigm was becoming more and more popular, Microsoft didn't offer any real object-oriented platform for developers before releasing the .NET Framework. The object-oriented basics appeared in the various available technologies, but they did not represent a real object-oriented platform (for example, they didn't offer real inheritance or polymorphism). One of the main goals of the .NET Framework was to be a real object-oriented environment in terms of run-time, architecture, and usability. The real object-oriented environment is no longer an external must or an accessory anymore, but rather a very strong foundation of the framework.

➤ *Full integration between the languages* — As mentioned previously, the .NET Framework can be used independently from programming languages. It also performs as an integration framework between these languages. Any components written on any .NET language can be used from any other components, and even written on any other .NET language. Moreover, components can be the ancestor of another component written on another .NET language, and this can be the ancestor of a third component written on a third language, and so on. As a part of the integration, there are no language borders in terms of exception handling and debugging.

➤ *Full interoperability with the existing programming paradigms* — The .NET framework has the capability to reuse existing dynamic link library (DLL), COM, or COM+ components. And it can also be done in the reverse order (that is, .NET components can be used from the old ones).

➤ *No more plumbing code required* — Before the .NET Framework, developers spent a lot of time and energy publishing the developed business functions in COM format, or using the existing COM components. In the .NET Framework, this step is no longer required. Developers can avoid the using of expressions GUID, IUnknown, BSTR, SAFEARRAY, and so on, mainly because the .NET Framework provides a layer above these things.

➤ *Simple deployment model* — After developing a new .NET component, there is no requirement to register it or any related binaries to the Windows Registry. Instead, the only thing developers must do is compile the component and copy it to a folder where they would like to run it. That means no more "DLL hell." Developers can use more than one different version of the same component.

➤ *Out-of-the-box base objects* — The .NET Framework contains hundreds of object types that help the developers in management of the low-level Windows APIs. These object types can be used the same way. It doesn't matter what .NET language developers use, and they don't need to understand the language-dependent object models. Moreover, these object types are organized into namespace hierarchies. Therefore, the functions can be found much easier and faster.

➤ *General security model* — The .NET Framework contains the security background itself. .NET applications can be executed in various security settings without any need to rewrite the application. During the execution, the framework verifies a lot of settings to prevent the unauthorized use of code or forbidden operations (for example, modifying or deleting files, editing registry entries, and so on).

## EVOLUTION OF THE .NET FRAMEWORK

Through the years, the .NET Framework has undergone quite an evolution, as shown in Figure 7-1.

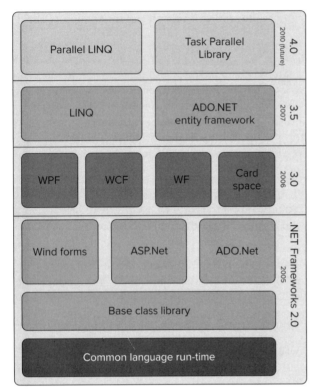

**FIGURE 7-1:** Evolution of the .NET Framework

Usually, all new releases of the .NET Framework provide a lot of new features and capabilities in every logical layer. In .NET Framework 1.1 and 2.0, the infrastructure services were extended and refined. Version 2.0 made the Windows Forms and ASP.NET technologies real architectural services. In practice, .NET 3.0 provided "only" architectural changes, as well as the next versions of the .NET Framework.

Table 7-1 shows the evolution of the .NET Framework. Each of these versions is described in a bit more detail in the sections following the table.

**TABLE 7-1:** .NET Framework Versions

| VERSION | RELEASE DATE | NEW FEATURES |
|---|---|---|
| .NET Framework 1.0 | | |
| .NET Framework 1.0 SP1 | March 19, 2002 | |
| .NET Framework 1.0 SP2 | August 7, 2002 | |
| .NET Framework 1.0 SP3 | September 9, 2004 | |

| VERSION | RELEASE DATE | NEW FEATURES |
| --- | --- | --- |
| .NET Framework 1.1 | July 10, 2003 | Support for mobile ASP.NET<br><br>Support for Open Database Connectivity (ODBC) and Oracle databases<br><br>.NET Compact Framework<br><br>Internet Protocol version 6 (IPv6) support |
| .NET Framework 1.1 SP1 | September 9, 2004 | |
| .NET Framework 2.0 | February 17, 2006 | 64-bit support<br><br>.NET Micro Framework<br><br>Language support for generics<br><br>Partial classes<br><br>Anonymous methods |
| .NET Framework 2.0 SP1 | November 19, 2007 | |
| .NET Framework 2.0 SP2 | January 16, 2009 | |
| .NET Framework 3.0 | November 21, 2006 | Windows Presentation Foundation (WPF)<br><br>Windows Communication Foundation (WCF)<br><br>Windows Workflow Foundation (WF)<br><br>CardSpace |
| .NET Framework 3.5 | November 9, 2007 | Entity Framework<br>LINQ<br>Extension methods<br>Expression trees |
| .NET Framework 3.5 SP1 | August 11, 2008 | |
| .NET Framework 4.0 | Announcement: September 29, 2008<br>Beta1: May 20, 2009<br><br>Beta2: October 19, 2009<br><br><br>RTM: April 12, 2010 | Parallel extensions<br><br>Support for IronRuby, IronPython, and F#<br><br>Inclusion of the Oslo modeling platform |

## .NET Framework 1.0

The first release of the .NET Framework was available for Windows 98, Me, NT 4.0, 2000, and XP. Because it was the first version of the .NET Framework, it had the power of the revolution of all the development.

One of the new approaches in the .NET Framework was the run-time and the execution of the applications. The typical levels of compiling and executing an application were the following:

1.  Write the code in any .NET language

2.  .NET compiler (`.DLL` or `.EXE`)

3.  .NET run-time (`mscoree.dll`)

    ➤   Class Loader

    ➤   Jitter

    ➤   Native assembly code

    ➤   Execution

4.  Windows APIs

Compiled binaries in the .NET Framework were called an *assembly*. The assembly contained not only intermediate language (IL) commands, but also metadata describing the interfaces of objects, version numbers, links to other objects, security settings, and so on.

## .NET Framework 1.1

Published on April 3, 2003, this was the first major .NET Framework upgrade. This was the first version of the .NET Framework that was included as part of the Windows operating system, shipping with Windows Server 2003.

Following were the main changes in version 1.1 from version 1.0:

➤   Provided built-in support for mobile ASP.NET controls as an elemental part of the .NET framework

➤   Enabled Code Access Security (CAS) in ASP.NET applications

➤   Enabled Windows Forms assemblies to execute in a semi-trusted manner from the Internet

➤   Provided built-in support for Open Database Connectivity (ODBC) and Oracle databases

➤   Introduced .NET Compact Framework, a version of the .NET Framework for small devices

➤   Provided support for Internet Protocol version 6 (IPv6)

➤   Introduced a lot of API changes

## .NET Framework 2.0

The next major version, .NET Framework 2.0, was released in the middle of February 2006 with Visual Studio 2005, Microsoft SQL Server 2005, and BizTalk 2006.

Without any Service Pack, Version 2.0 was the last version with support for Windows 98 and Windows Me. Version 2.0 with Service Pack 2 was the last version with official support for Windows 2000.

Following were the main changes in version 2.0:

➤ Included many API changes

➤ Included a new hosting API that gave a fine-grain control of multithreading, memory allocation, assembly loading, and more

➤ Provided full 64-bit support (both x64 and IA64)

➤ Provided language support for generics

➤ Improved ASP.NET web controls

➤ Introduced new data controls with declarative data binding

➤ Provided new personalization features for ASP.NET (themes, skins, and web parts)

➤ Introduced the .NET Micro Framework

➤ Included partial classes

➤ Included anonymous methods

➤ Included data tables

## .NET Framework 3.0

On November 21, 2006, .NET Framework 3.0 (codenamed WinFX) was released, and included some managed code APIs that are an integral part of the Windows Vista and Windows Server 2008 operating systems. It is also available for Windows XP SP2 and Windows Server 2003 as a download.

There are no major architectural changes included with this release, but .NET Framework 3.0 consists of four major new components:

➤ *Windows Presentation Foundation (WPF)* — A new user interface subsystem and API based on XML and vector graphics.

➤ *Windows Communication Foundation (WCF)* — A service-oriented messaging system that allows programs to interoperate locally or remotely, similar to web services.

➤ *Windows Workflow Foundation (WF)* — A service that allows for building task automation and integrated transactions using workflows.

➤ *Windows CardSpace* — This securely stores a person's digital identities and provides a unified interface for choosing the identity for a particular transaction (such as logging in to a website).

## .NET Framework 3.5

Version 3.5 of the .NET Framework was released on November 19, 2007, but it is not included with Windows Server 2008. As with .NET Framework 3.0, version 3.5 uses the Common Language Run-time (CLR) version 2.0. In addition, it installs .NET Framework 2.0 SP1 (which installs .NET

Framework 2.0 SP2 with 3.5 SP1) and .NET Framework 3.0 SP1 (which installs .NET Framework 3.0 SP2 with 3.5 SP1). These changes do not affect applications written for version 2.0, however.

The .NET Framework 3.5 Service Pack 1 was released on August 11, 2008. This release added new functionality and provided performance improvements, especially with WPF where 20 to 45 percent improvements were expected. Two new data service components were added — the ADO.NET Entity Framework and ADO.NET Data Services.

As with previous versions, a new .NET Compact Framework 3.5 was released with this update. Also, the source code of the Base Class Library in this version has been partially released (for debugging reference only) under the Microsoft Reference Source License.

Following were the changes since version 3.0:

- ➤ Included new language features
- ➤ Added support for expression trees and lambda methods
- ➤ Included extension methods
- ➤ Included expression trees to represent high-level source code at run-time
- ➤ Included anonymous types
- ➤ Included Language Integrated Query (LINQ to Objects, LINQ to XML, LINQ to SQL)
- ➤ Included paging support for ADO.NET
- ➤ Included an ADO.NET synchronization API to synchronize local caches and server-side data stores
- ➤ Included an asynchronous network I/O API
- ➤ Included a peer-to-peer networking stack
- ➤ Managed wrappers for Windows Management Instrumentation and Active Directory APIs
- ➤ Enhanced WCF and WF run-times
- ➤ Included support for HTTP pipelining and syndication feeds
- ➤ Included ASP.NET Ajax
- ➤ Included a new `System.CodeDom` namespace

## .NET Framework 4.0

Microsoft announced .NET Framework 4.0 on September 29, 2008. The Public Beta was released on May 20, 2009. Following were the most important focuses of this release:

- ➤ Parallel extensions to improve support for parallel computing
- ➤ Language innovations
- ➤ Full support for IronPython, IronRuby, and F#
- ➤ Support for a subset of the .NET Framework and ASP.NET with the "Server Core" variant of Windows Server 2008 R2

> ➤ Support for code contracts

> ➤ Inclusion of the Oslo modeling platform, along with the M programming language

On October 19, 2009, Microsoft released Beta 2 of the .NET Framework 4.0. At the same time, Microsoft announced the expected launch date of .NET Framework 4.0 as March 22, 2010.

In conjunction with .NET Framework 4.0, Microsoft will offer a set of enhancements, codenamed *Dublin*, for Windows Server 2008 application server capabilities. Dublin will extend IIS to be a "standard host" for applications that use either WCF or WF.

## .NET Compact Framework

In some circumstances, many of us are forced to use resource-constrained computing devices such as smart phones, PDAs, and so on. .NET Compact Framework (CF) a hardware-independent environment for running .NET applications on mobile devices. CF has the same architecture as the full CLR and managed code execution of the .NET Framework, but supports only a subset of the .NET classes, and contains a set of classes created especially for the CF.

## .NET Micro Framework

The .NET Micro Framework is designed for devices with very limited resources. It's very special because it can run with or without an operating system on the device. It has the following layers directly on the hardware:

> ➤ Hardware Abstraction Layer (HAL) that hides the hardware with an abstraction layer.

> ➤ Platform Abstraction Layer (PAL) that gives the basic functionality of the missing operating system.

> ➤ CLR, Libraries, and User Applications

The typical memory requirement of MF is 200-500 KB (the next smallest .NET implementation, .NET CF, needs around 12 MB), so it's very effective on remote controllers and other small devices.

Following is a short summary of .NET Micro Framework features:

> ➤ It has a very small memory footprint.

> ➤ It runs on the "metal" or on an existing operating system.

> ➤ It supports embedded peripherals and interconnects.

> ➤ It is optimized for low power consumption.

> ➤ It has multithreading support.

> ➤ Drivers can be written in C#.

## .NET FRAMEWORK ARCHITECTURE

The Microsoft .NET Center claims, "The .NET Framework is Microsoft's platform for building applications that have visually stunning user experiences, seamless and secure communication, and the ability to model a range of business processes."

Following are the components of the .NET Framework:

➤ *Common Language Run-time (CLR)* — This provides an abstraction layer over the operating system.

➤ *Base Class Libraries* — This is pre-built code for common low-level programming tasks.

➤ *Development frameworks and technologies* — These are reusable, customizable solutions for larger programming tasks.

Figure 7-2 shows the execution process of a typical .NET program, represented as the communication paths between the main components.

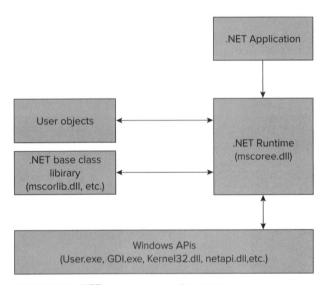

**FIGURE 7-2:** .NET program execution process

## Common Language Run-time (CLR)

As shown in Figure 7-3, the bottom layer of the .NET Framework is the CLR, which is directly responsible for executing the .NET applications. Following are the main parts of the CLR:

➤ *Common Type System (CTS)* — This defines the basic .NET types of the CLR. All of the type definitions, collaborations between them (for example, conversions), and metadata are defined here.

➤ *Common Language Specification* — The .NET languages do not support all of the types defined in the CTS by default. The Common Language Specification is the component that defines rules and subsets of types that help developers to use the .NET assemblies in all .NET languages.

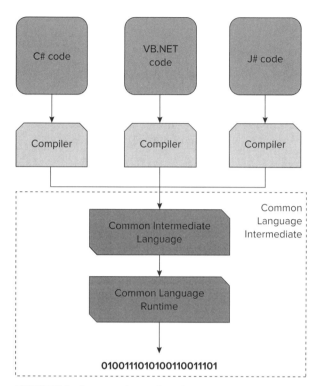

**FIGURE 7-3:** Common Layer Run-time

The most important part of the CLR is the `mscoree.dll` file that provides the following features:

- ➤ Finding the proper assembly
- ➤ Loading in the assembly
- ➤ Finding the proper type (with the help of the assembly's metadata)
- ➤ Translating the Microsoft Intermediate Language (MSIL) code

## Base Class Library

For the reasonable and efficient use of the functions of the CLR and Win32 APIs, developers need a lot of base objects wrapping the functions into well-usable objects by .NET languages. The main goal of the Base Class Library is to provide infrastructure services to the developers — services that provide a good and safe layer above the operating system's Win31 API.

The folder of base classes contains a lot of assemblies. The most important one is the `mscorlib.dll` file, which contains the most-used types and useful functions for general programming. Whatever .NET component you develop, in whatever architecture, you always use the `mscorlib.dll` assembly.

# Services of the .NET Architecture

The .NET Framework offers not only infrastructure, but also reliable architectural services for developers. These parts of the .NET Framework have significant value and content, helping with the development of multi-layered architectures. With them, you can build robust and scalable applications, while retaining the .NET Framework's simplicity and flexibility.

The services of the .NET Framework are so wide and large that an entire book could be written about each of them. However, the following sections provide a short summary of the most important components.

## ASP.NET

ASP.NET is for the development of web applications, with the capability of supporting various architectural layers — from the UI through the processes to the web service-based business functions. ASP.NET is one of the most complex parts of the .NET Framework.

## Windows Forms

The dialogs, forms, user messages, simple and composite UI elements, and so on, are required for all rich clients. The .NET Framework offers Windows Forms to achieve this goal. With the help of its object hierarchy, it's possible to manage the UI elements in a very easy way, and to create new visual components with a simple inheritance.

## Web Services

During the evolution of software technologies, the integration between platforms and systems was always very important. With the .NET Framework, the web services became really popular, as well as an easy-to-use technology in the integration between systems, even on different platforms.

## ADO.NET

ADO.NET is a set of .NET components that can be used to access data and data services. It's commonly used to access and modify data stored in relational databases, though it can also be used to access other structured data sources (via ADO.NET Providers).

## Workflow Foundation (WF)

Since the release of .NET Framework 3.0, Workflow Foundation (WF) has provided the base infrastructure of workflow definitions and execution. With the help of the WF, developers can define the following two types of workflows:

➤ *Sequence* — The steps of the process are in a time sequence.

➤ *State machine* — The process is a set of states, and the steps between these states are event-based ones.

The WF has the capabilities for being the base of both human and automated workflows.

### Windows Communication Framework (WCF)

Since the first release, the .NET Framework has contained special infrastructure services (for example, .NET remoting, web services, and message queue management) that provide communication between the components of distributed systems. Before WCF, developers had to decide during the implementation which service to use for a specific solution.

Released in .NET 3.0, WCF provides a unified solution for the communication between distributed components, and allows changes to the behavior and run-time properties of the communication channel, without recompiling the project.

### Windows Presentation Framework (WPF)

With Windows Vista, the concept of a computer graphics subsystem was totally redefined by Microsoft, and a brand new solution was created that maximizes the capabilities of graphic processors. In this context, WPF was released as a part of Vista and .NET Framework 3.0.

WPF includes a brand new UI concept and developer methodology. The WPF can physically separate the visual design and behavior, and allows programmers to write functional code, and designers to create the UI.

### CardSpace

The concept of *identity metasystems* is the unified platform of storing and handling digital IDs. The .NET Framework 3.0 CardSpace is an important part of this concept, providing a secure store method for using digital IDs.

Nowadays, everyone has countless digital IDs, (for example, the various website registrations). Of course, CardSpace not only stores these IDs, but also provides unified interfaces for the operations and transactions.

### Entity Framework

The ADO.NET in .NET Framework 3.5 significantly exceeds the former data-management methods. Former versions of ADO.NET raised an abstraction layer over the relational databases that provided unified methods for using the data stored in various database systems.

The Entity Framework brings this abstraction into the concept level. With the help of Object Relational Mapping (ORM) technologies, it provides a way to manage high-level entities instead of database tables and relations.

## MAIN BENEFITS OF THE .NET FRAMEWORK

Following are some of the main benefits offered by the .NET Framework:

> ➤ *Secure multi-language development platform* — .NET is a powerful and reliable technology for developers and IT professionals, because it provides enhanced capabilities in terms of the security, management, and updates, as well as in building, testing, and deploying reliable and secure software. .NET provides a real multi-language developer platform so

that developers can work in their preferred languages. The CLR provides support for the static languages (for example, VB and C#), but dynamic languages (for example, IronRuby and Managed JScript) are also supported.

➤ *Next-generation user experiences* — WPF provides a unified method for building rich applications with rich UIs. WPF offers support for two-dimensional and three-dimensional graphics for developers, hardware accelerated effects, scalability, interactive visualization, and excellent content readability. Moreover, designers can be the active part of the development process with the help of the file format, XAML.

➤ *Cross-browser, cross-platform, cross-device support* — Another tool for a rich UI in .NET is Silverlight, which helps developers with a cross-browser, cross-platform, cross-device plug-in for creating the next generation of rich, interactive applications.

➤ *Advanced web application development* — .NET offers a free, advanced technology for web development. ASP.NET can be the best tool in a developer's hand from small, personal websites to large, enterprise web applications. Moreover, ASP.NET Asynchronous JavaScript and XML (Ajax) enables developers to create more efficient, interactive, and rich web UIs that work on all of the popular browsers.

➤ *Secure and powerful web services* — WCF provides many capabilities for developing real distributed systems with extensible architecture, secure communication, messaging patterns, and so on.

➤ *Business processes* — As a part of the .NET Framework, WF can be used for developing powerful business processes in a more efficient way, thus improving productivity of both developers and end users.

➤ *Flexible data access options* — ADO.NET with Entity Framework and ADO.NET Data Services provide a rich set of components for developing distributed, data-centric applications. ADO.NET supports a lot of general development needs, including the creation of real multi-tier applications over databases. Entity Framework simplifies data access by providing a unified model for data from any database, and enables this model to reflect business requirements. ADO.NET Data Services provides a first-class infrastructure for the next wave of dynamic Internet applications by enabling web applications to expose data as REST-based data services that can be consumed by client applications in corporate networks and across the Internet.

## SUMMARY

This chapter provided you with a glimpse at the history and evolution of the .NET Framework was demonstrated. Early in the chapter, you learned about the most important predecessors of the .NET Framework, including Win/Win32 programming, C++ programming, Visual Basic programming, Delphi programming, and COM programming.

The .NET Framework evolved as a result of the deficiencies of previous developer tools and languages, and added a new architecture and a lot of new capabilities. The main goals of the .NET Framework were an independent run-time environment, clean, object-oriented basics, full integration between languages, full interoperability with existing programming paradigms, no requirements for plumbing code, a simple deployment model, out-of-the-box base objects, and a general security model.

Based on these goals, .NET Framework 1.0 was born in 2002. Since then, many new versions have been released, with more and more new capabilities answering to the newer and newer developer needs. This chapter took a brief look at all of the .NET Framework versions from 1.0 to the current 4.0, and discussed the main capabilities of each of them.

You also learned about the .NET Framework architecture and all of the .NET Framework services.

Chapter 8 begins a detailed look at the components of .NET Framework 4.0.

# 8

# Modern UI Frameworks (WPF and Silverlight)

Because software projects can allow less and less neglect when designing the user experience, new technologies are emerging to help create a new generation of applications. This chapter discusses the shift of focus in the software industry toward user experience (UX), and introduces you to Silverlight and Windows Presentation Foundation (WPF) — the two technologies that can help developer teams make this shift while enhancing development productivity, even for traditional line-of-business (LOB) applications.

## THE IMPORTANCE OF USER EXPERIENCE

Software development is changing. Ten years ago, the challenges developer teams faced were mostly technical. For example, it was very difficult to create a client-server application.

On the server side, functional SQL database servers already existed, but transferring data to the business logic required writing a lot of repetitive code. The most popular programming languages for the Microsoft platform were Visual Basic and C++ — neither of which was ideal for expressing complex business logic. Even Visual Basic 6.0 was not a real object-oriented language, and C++ was often too complex for the task at hand. When it came to performance though, C++ was the clear winner.

On the client side, things were slightly better. For a rich client, Visual Basic 6.0 was a good rapid application development (RAD) choice to display the user interface (UI), and, with decent tooling support, teams were fairly productive, too. However, there was a lot of repetitive coding required — displaying data, validating data, navigation between forms — all of which were mostly manual work, and prone to a lot of errors. Web applications were also difficult to create. A simple form validation required tons of code to highlight the field with the error, and repeat the entered data so that the user didn't have to.

The real challenge was the communication between client and server. The basics were already in place. You had socket support, and even some HTTP. You could send and receive messages. But what these messages contained, what their communication protocol was, how they encapsulated business entities, and how you could make sure that the message reached the recipient, all were entirely up to the development teams. Every team had its own way of accomplishing these tasks, and it was a mess. Only the largest companies could allow developing entire frameworks that coped with these problems.

This was the situation when .NET 1.0 came along in 2002. Visual Basic .NET (which was a huge departure from Visual Basic 6.0), and the new C# language, along with the Common Language Run-time (CLR) and it's Just In Time (JIT) compiler, retained the relative simplicity of Visual Basic, while approaching the performance of C++ code for most scenarios. Windows Forms was a big step forward from the Visual Basic 6 UI framework, and .NET had also improved client-server communication with an advanced network stack, and a remoting framework that allowed almost transparent calls between client and server. ASP.NET made a huge difference — it removed the spaghetti code of the old ASP framework, placing the logic in the code-behind, and having the HTML in a separate file.

The .NET framework was an excellent foundation to build upon. With further versions, you received more and more support for writing maintainable code, and common scenarios such as object-relational mapping (ORM) and workflow management were implemented by Microsoft and third parties.

Thanks to the reliable frameworks that cover more and more areas of typical software, developer productivity increased a lot. At the same time, the complexity of the business problems that software systems need to solve has been increasing at a much slower pace. The net result is that the effort required to create software solutions for the common business problems has decreased greatly during the last decade. This trend, and the amazing amount of computing power offered by today's hardware, allows the developer teams to turn their attention to the user.

Now, consider following trends:

➤ *The users' expectations regarding the usability, aesthetics, and responsiveness of the software they work with are increasing* — They see great examples on the web, on their phones, and grow conscious about how these applications look and behave. They begin to appreciate the joys of using a well-designed application, and they start to criticize the applications that were "good enough" a few years ago.

➤ *User experience (UX) is becoming a key differentiating factor when making decisions about purchasing a software system* — It has already happened in the consumer space (just think about the success of the Wii or the iPhone), and it is starting to happen in the business sector, in the case of line-of-business (LOB) software as well.

Software development is changing. Huge, well-designed platforms, frameworks, and tools make previously difficult development tasks a lot easier. In the meantime, there is an increasing business need for a great user experience. According to Microsoft researcher Bill Hill, there is a new target platform emerging: "It's homo sapiens version 1.0. It shipped about 100,000 years ago, there's no upgrade in sight, but it is the one that runs everything, right?" You must create software with the UX in mind first and foremost.

The second part of this chapter discusses two relatively new Microsoft technologies that can help developing software with a great UX: Microsoft Silverlight and WPF. But first, let's take a look at the people who can make it happen: designers and developers.

## DEVELOPERS ARE FROM VULCAN, DESIGNERS ARE FROM VENUS

If you have been to any developer conferences, or seen video recordings of sessions, you probably listened to one or more speaker showing off the latest and greatest tools for creating a website or a desktop application — and apologizing by saying, "As you can see, I am not a designer." Most developers proudly admit that they are not good with design. It is very rare that someone is a great developer and a great designer at the same time. This is not only because both professions take years to master, but also because they require diametrically opposite skills and ways of thinking.

If you are reading this book, you are probably a developer, as well. So, first, let's see what kind of thinking and skills make a developer great:

➤ *Developers think in extremes.* — This usually means yes or no, 0 or 1, true or false, pass or fail.

➤ *Developers value logic above all else (in their work).* — An application must behave in a logical manner. It must be built from logical components that cooperate logically. A software developer prefers that computers behave in a predictable way.

➤ *Developers strive to write code that always behaves the same under the same circumstances.* — Consistency is good. Surprises are almost always bad.

➤ *Developers are usually good at mathematics.* — Even if their areas of work do not require solving $n$-dimensional equations, chances are that they have received pretty good math grades in high school.

To sum up, developers think like a Vulcan from Star Trek (at least, when developing). Writing code is an engineering science, and although it is very creative, developers learned long ago that there are some ultimate laws they should not deviate from.

Interestingly, these skills are usually attributed to the left side of the brain. People with left-brain thinking are rational, analytical, logical, objective, and interested in the way things work, and how the parts are working together. Right-brain people, on the other hand, are intuitive, holistic, subjective, and are looking at the whole instead of the part. Yes, designers are usually right-brained people.

Table 8-1 shows a list of what functions are typically attributed to the left and right brain hemisphere. It almost seems as though designers come from Venus because of their sense of beauty and harmony.

**TABLE 8-1:** Functions of Left and Right Brain

| LEFT-BRAIN FUNCTIONS | RIGHT-BRAIN FUNCTIONS |
| --- | --- |
| Uses logic | Uses feeling |
| Detail oriented | "Big picture" oriented |
| Facts rule | Imagination rules |
| Words and language | Symbols and images |
| Present and past | Present and future |
| Math and science | Philosophy and religion |
| Can comprehend | Can "get it" (that is, meaning) |
| Knowing | Believes |
| Acknowledges | Appreciates |
| Order/pattern perception | Spatial perception |
| Knows object name | Knows object function |
| Reality based | Fantasy based |
| Forms strategies | Presents possibilities |
| Practical | Impetuous |
| Safe | Risk taking |

Source: http://www.viewzone.com/bicam.html

When looking at the way people think, scientists found that most people use one brain hemisphere a lot more than the other. Some are whole-brained in their thinking, but they are the minority.

If you accept that designers are right-brained and developers are left-brained, there is no wonder that members of the two professions have a hard time understanding each other. One reasons with logic, the other with feeling; one appreciates facts, the other possibilities; one looks at the details, the other at the big picture.

The car industry found out in the early twentieth century that you must merge form and function to be really successful. The car not only must work, but it must be a pleasure to drive, to look at, and to travel in. It is time for the software industry to follow the lead and get designers and developers to work together.

There are two Microsoft technologies that promise to bring forth this cooperation between designers and developers. WPF and Silverlight are both built from the ground up to allow for a never-before-seen level of designer-developer cooperation. Taking the old "separate presentation and functionality" software development mantra to a new level, Silverlight and WPF allow developers and designers to work separately. Developers ensure that data gets to the client and back to the server, and designers can independently create the data visualization and entry mechanisms for Homo Sapiens 1.0.

The rest of this chapter gives a quick overview of Silverlight and WPF. Because the basic concepts are almost the same for both technologies, Silverlight will be examined first. The second part of the chapter discusses the differences between Silverlight and WPF, and provides guidelines for choosing between the two. Finally, you will return to the designer-developer cooperation and learn about how these tools can help this cooperation become a reality.

## A NEW GENERATION OF PRESENTATION FRAMEWORKS

In 2001, Microsoft founder Bill Gates created a new team tasked with researching and developing a new presentation layer. .NET 1.0 wasn't even released at this point. At that time, there were at least four different, but overlapping, UI technologies within Microsoft: Windows Forms, GDI32, Visual Basic, and Internet Explorer's Trident rendering engine. The technology to be created by the new group was codenamed "Avalon."

 *You can learn more about the history and goals of Avalon in Chris Anderson's book,* Essential Windows Presentation Foundation *(Reading, MA: Addison-Wesley, 2007).*

The Avalon team aimed to merge the best of the web and the desktop, to integrate first-class multimedia with documents and UI, to streamline the designer-developer workflow, and to create a rich presentation platform that could utilize the increasing power of graphics hardware.

The first public appearance of Avalon was in 2003, at the Professional Developers Conference (PDC). Later, Avalon was renamed Windows Presentation Foundation (WPF), and it appeared in version 3.0 of the .NET Framework. WPF was still a novelty at the time. With limited (and buggy) support in Visual Studio 2005, and a nonexistent designer tool support, many were reluctant to climb the rather steep learning curve. Still, the most important thing was already there: a solid, well thought-out architecture and foundation that could be built upon. The pillars of WPF are the Extensible Application Markup Language (XAML), graphics processing unit (GPU) rendering, a layout system, data binding, styling, templating, animations, media, and document handling. Together, these formed an amazing toolset for building the rich applications most developers didn't even think they needed.

With the release of .NET Framework 3.5 and Visual Studio 2008, WPF gained some new features and performance enhancements, such as improved internationalization support and the capability to map two-dimensional elements onto a three-dimensional surface in an interactive manner.

However, the big feature push came with .NET Framework 3.5 SP1. Despite the Service Pack name, for WPF, this was more like a whole version step up. Client profile reduced the installation footprint to 25 MB for computers that didn't need the full .NET Framework. GPU-accelerated shaders allowed for interesting UI effects. DirectX integration allowed CAD software to have the context presented with Direct3D, as well as the controls and data display with WPF. An Office ribbon control was also added. Finally, Visual Studio 2008 could be used with WPF, as well as with Windows Forms.

In April 2007, Expression Blend 1.0 was released. Expression Blend (or simply "Blend") was designed to be the tool for the intermediary — the integrator who gets data, behavior, and presentation together. Blend alienated a lot of developers with its "designer-ish" look and feel, but with versions 2 and 3, it became an invaluable tool for anyone seriously working with WPF or Silverlight. Blend was the first "big" Microsoft application created in WPF. The largest WPF application is probably Visual Studio 2010. The entire UI of Visual Studio 2010 is created in WPF. Many of the performance and feature enhancements in WPF 4 were driven by the need of the Visual Studio team.

In the meantime, WPF's cousin, Silverlight (originally called WPF Everywhere, or WPF/E), began to take shape. The goal was to create a trimmed-down version of the Windows-only WPF, and take the same key principles over to the web, other operating systems, and devices.

Silverlight 1.0 was released in September 2007, and focused on media playback, utilizing some of the WPF XAML syntax, but programmable via the browser's JavaScript engine. The real revolution came with Silverlight 2.0, which launched one year later, in October 2008. In a mere 4 MB download, Silverlight 2.0 included a trimmed-down version of the full .NET Framework, dozens of controls, XAML and media support, deep zoom, and most of the WPF pillars mentioned previously.

Silverlight 3 came only nine months later, in July 2009, with H.264 video codec support, pixel shaders, limited GPU acceleration, perspective transform, out-of-browser support, touch support, and a brand new navigation framework, just to mention a few key enhancements. Silverlight is officially supported on Windows and Intel-based Mac OS X computers, in Firefox, Internet Explorer, and Safari.

Silverlight 4 launched in April 2010 (exactly 3 years after Silverlight 1 was introduced), and focuses on line-of-business (LOB) applications, media and advanced out-of-browser scenarios. A Linux version of Silverlight is also in the works. Novell's Mono project is developing Moonlight, an Open Source version of Silverlight. However, Moonlight was lagging behind as of this writing, still not having released Moonlight 3, which promises Silverlight 3 compatibility.

WPF 4.0 brings a handful of enhancements to the table. The entire text stack has been replaced to make text faster to render, and be sharper, more legible. New controls (such as a Silverlight-compatible Datagrid, Calendar, and DatePicker) have been added. Silverlight's Visual State Manager is now officially part of WPF. Touch and manipulation APIs to handle Windows 7's new multitouch capabilities are borrowed from the Surface SDK. WPF also borrowed Silverlight 3's GPU caching and layout rounding features, and added Pixel Shader 3 support.

Silverlight keeps running ahead with version 4. Out-of-browser applications get elevated support for Common Object Model (COM) interoperability, direct file access, and full network access. HTML hosting allows Silverlight applications to display HTML pages out-of-the-browser. Enhanced digital rights management (DRM) helps to keep Hollywood studios happy. Webcam and microphone support introduce new ways of interacting with your applications. Printing helps LOB scenarios. Styling and data binding enhancements eliminate the biggest pain points when comparing WPF and Silverlight.

In March 2010, Microsoft revealed its plans for its brand new mobile platform, Windows Phone 7. Windows Phone 7 is a clean start for Microsoft, leaving everything behind that Windows Mobile 6.5 had. Windows Phone 7 development will be done exclusively in managed code, either using Silverlight, or XNA (for graphics-heavy apps, mostly games). WP7's Silverlight is initially going to be a highly optimized version of Silverlight 3.

It is no secret that WPF and Silverlight are converging, and down the road, there may be a single codebase for the two. More and more scenarios are possible with both Silverlight and WPF. Later in this chapter, you will see some pointers on which one to choose.

## THE TEN PILLARS OF SILVERLIGHT

What may be most amazing about Silverlight and WPF is how the core concepts or pillars work together to create a whole that is much bigger than its parts. Although space does not permit the discussion in this chapter to go into any reasonable depth into either Silverlight or WPF, a good alternative is to examine Silverlight's features (or "pillars"), and give some pointers as to how these pillars can be combined. Hopefully, this will be enough to pique your interest and encourage you to look for more information.

Following are the ten pillars of Silverlight:

- ➤ *XAML* — This is the declaration language that describes the UI and resources.
- ➤ *Tools* — These are the tools of the trade.
- ➤ *Layout* — This involves putting controls on the screen in the right size, and in the right place.
- ➤ *Data binding* — This involves connecting the data and the UI.
- ➤ *Styles* — This involves changing the look of controls.
- ➤ *Templates* — This involves separating data, logic, and presentation.
- ➤ *Animations* — This is not just for eye candy. Animations and transitions can greatly enhance UX.
- ➤ *Media* — This involves creating a premium multimedia experience.
- ➤ *Networking* — This involves communication with the server and the cloud.
- ➤ *Others* — This includes features that may not be pillars, but that are important nevertheless.

Let's take a look at these in a bit more detail.

# XAML

To fully appreciate the relationship between XAML and Silverlight, a sample application would be most helpful.

 *Visual Studio 2010 allows you to create both Silverlight 3 and Silverlight 4 applications. However, out-of-the-box, only Silverlight 3 support is provided. To enable Silverlight 4 development, you must download and install "Silverlight 4 Tools for Visual Studio 2010" from* `http://www.silverlight.net/ getstarted`. *If you plan to follow the samples on your own computer, it is recommended that you perform this installation now.*

## Silverlight Hello World Application

Let's fire up Visual Studio 2010 and create your first Silverlight application. In the New Project dialog shown in Figure 8-1, choose Silverlight Application. (You can use the handy new template search function on the top right to find it quickly.)

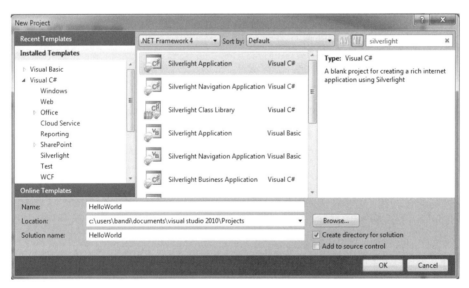

**FIGURE 8-1:** Creating a new Silverlight project in Visual Studio 2010

After providing the name and directory for the solution (call it `HelloWorld`), Visual Studio asks whether you want to "Host the Silverlight application in a new website." Keep the checkbox ticked, and ensure that the Silverlight Version is set to Silverlight 4. For now, don't enable WCF RIA Services (formerly known as .NET RIA Services).

After the project has been created, examine the Solution Explorer. There should be a new solution, with two projects. The first is the Silverlight project, containing two `.xaml` files (and `.xaml.cs` files behind them). The second project is the hosting website you asked the wizard to create. It contains the `HelloWorldTestPage.aspx` and the `HelloWorldTestPage.html` web pages, a `Silverlight.js` JavaScript library, the usual `Web.config`, and a `ClientBin` directory. If you build the solution now, you will see that the `ClientBin` folder has one item in it: the `HelloWorld.xap` file, which is the actual Silverlight application that gets downloaded and run in the browser. Figure 8-2 shows how the files are laid out for this sample Silverlight solution.

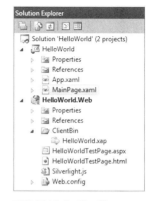

**FIGURE 8-2:** The file structure of a new Silverlight solution

You can also see that, after creating the solution, Visual Studio has opened up the `MainPage.xaml` file for editing, as shown in Figure 8-3. Just as with the split screen view of ASP.NET, you should see a split screen, with the empty Silverlight screen on top, and the XAML code at the bottom. If you don't have a split screen, click on the little horizontal line button at the bottom edge of the document editing window.

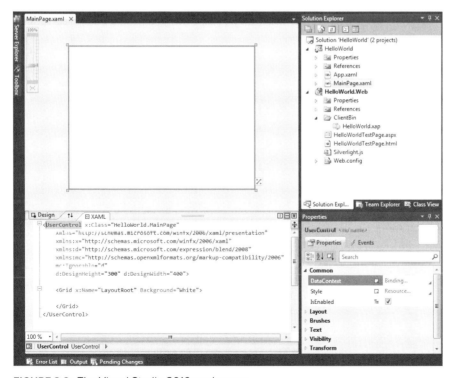

**FIGURE 8-3:** The Visual Studio 2010 workspace

So, what is XAML code? If you are familiar with XML, you can immediately see that XAML is basically XML. As a first approach, you can think of XAML as a way of serializing CLR object trees to XML. XAML has some additional syntax that helps with data binding, and other UI-related tasks.

Just like in the case of HTML, in Silverlight applications, XAML is mostly used to describe the UI of an application. Let's examine the contents of the `MainPage.xaml` file shown in Listing 8-1.

### LISTING 8-1: MainPage.xaml

```xml
<UserControl x:Class="HelloWorld.MainPage"
    xmlns="http://schemas.microsoft.com/winfx/2006/xaml/presentation"
    xmlns:x="http://schemas.microsoft.com/winfx/2006/xaml"
    xmlns:d="http://schemas.microsoft.com/expression/blend/2008"
    xmlns:mc="http://schemas.openxmlformats.org/markup-compatibility/2006"
    mc:Ignorable="d"
    d:DesignHeight="300" d:DesignWidth="400">

    <Grid x:Name="LayoutRoot" Background="White">

    </Grid>
</UserControl>
```

*Code file [MainPage.xaml] available for download at Wrox.com*

As with any XML file, you have one root element. In this case, this is a `UserControl`, with the type name and namespace `HelloWorld.MainPage`. There are a couple of XML namespaces also defined, including `xmlns:d`. This is a designer namespace, used by tools like Expression Blend and Visual Studio for specifying design-time properties such as the `d:DesignHeight` and `d:DesignWidth` properties of the `UserControl`. These properties do not play any role while running the application, but give a design-time width and height for the `UserControl` to use in the visual designer.

Within the `UserControl`, `MainPage.xaml` has a `Grid`. The `Grid` is a layout control. Its task is to arrange and display its children in rows and columns. The `Grid` has the name `LayoutRoot`, and has a white background color.

Change the XAML by inserting a `TextBlock` control in the `Grid`. The `MainPage.XAML` should now read as shown in Listing 8-2.

### LISTING 8-2: MainPage.xaml, with a Hello World TextBlock

```xml
<UserControl x:Class="HelloWorld.MainPage"
    xmlns="http://schemas.microsoft.com/winfx/2006/xaml/presentation"
    xmlns:x="http://schemas.microsoft.com/winfx/2006/xaml"
    xmlns:d="http://schemas.microsoft.com/expression/blend/2008"
    xmlns:mc="http://schemas.openxmlformats.org/markup-compatibility/2006"
    mc:Ignorable="d"
```

```
         d:DesignHeight="300" d:DesignWidth="400"

           xmlns:my="clr-namespace:HelloWorld">

         <Grid x:Name="LayoutRoot" Background="White">
           <TextBlock Text="Hello, World!" />
         </Grid>
       </UserControl>
```

*Code file [MainPage.xaml] available for download at Wrox.com*

As you would expect, the text "Hello, World!" now appears in the top-left corner. If you change the line with the TextBlock to include the HorizontalAlignment and VerticalAlignment properties, you can see that the text has moved to the center of the Grid.

```
         <Grid x:Name="LayoutRoot" Background="White">
           <TextBlock Text="Hello, World!"
                      HorizontalAlignment="Center" VerticalAlignment="Center" />
         </Grid>
```

Now, build and run the solution by pressing F5. If everything went well, you should see your first Silverlight application in the browser, as shown in Figure 8-4.

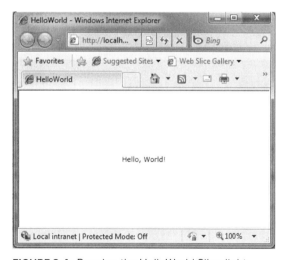

**FIGURE 8-4:** Running the HelloWorld Silverlight application

*Sample code in this chapter is available for download at this book's companion website* (www.wrox.com).

If you resize the browser, you will notice that the greeting text stays in the center, just as you would expect. Looking at the source code of the web page displayed in the browser reveals that the Silverlight plug-in is displayed via an HTML `<object>` tag. If the visitor does not have Silverlight plug-in installed, there is some HTML within the `<object>` tag that points to Microsoft's Silverlight download site. This HTML section can be customized as you wish — there are even some Search Engine Optimization (SEO) techniques that utilize this area (discussed later in this chapter). The most important parameter of the `<object>` tag is the "source" parameter that points to `"ClientBin/HelloWorld.xap"`. This is the compiled `HelloWorld` Silverlight application, automatically put within the `ClientBin` directory by the build process.

As you can see, XAML is a great way to describe the object hierarchy of the UI. XAML was designed to be the UI description language of WPF, but it is also used elsewhere in the .NET Framework, such as describing workflows in Workflow Foundation, or being the base language of XPS. When the WPF team (or, as it was called at the time, the Avalon team) designed XAML, they had the following goals in mind (among others):

➤ *XAML is based on XML* — This means that it is easily digestible for both computers and humans, and it is easy to validate.

➤ *XAML is Toolable* — When using design tools to create a UI, creating and interpreting XAML code is much easier than HTML because XAML does not allow non-closed tags. It is case-sensitive and is generally stricter. With XAML, you don't see the "Designer Generated Code — do not modify" warnings hidden in C# or Visual Basic files. You can easily modify the XAML, and the visual designer will immediately reflect your changes.

➤ *XAML can be both compiled and interpreted* — WPF compiles XAML, but it is also possible to load/create XAML on-the-fly, and load it into the application.

➤ *XAML is extensible* — You can define your own controls, or business classes, and have them within the XAML object hierarchy.

 *For more information on the goals of XAML, see* `http://blogs.windowsclient` `.net/rob_relyea/archive/2009/05/28/our-7-goals-for-xaml.aspx.` *For more information on the benefits of XAML, see* `http://blogs` `.windowsclient.net/rob_relyea/archive/2008/11/06/the-8-benefits-` `of-xaml-for-ui-and-beyond.aspx.`

## Adding Event Handlers

Having "Hello, World" in the middle of the browser window is nice, but for a real application, you probably want some interaction. Let's replace the `TextBlock` with a `Button` within the XAML:

```
<Grid x:Name="LayoutRoot" Background="White">
  <Button Content="Press me" HorizontalAlignment="Center"
      VerticalAlignment="Center" />
</Grid>
```

You may have noticed that while the `TextBlock` had a `Text` property, the `Button` has a `Content` property. The reason is that buttons are not restricted to display only text — they can display any Silverlight element or element tree. Remember how difficult it is to have anything other than an image and text on a button in Windows Forms? Remember how you must re-create the entire button logic, along with mouseover effects, click effects, event handlers in HTML and JavaScript if you want something more than just text or image within a button?

With Silverlight, this is very easy. Here is how you would put a video inside the button:

```
<Button HorizontalAlignment="Center" VerticalAlignment="Center">
  <Button.Content>
    <MediaElement Width="100" Height="75"
     Source="http://mschnlnine.vo.llnwd.net/d1/ch9/0/8/7/7/7/4/
        SL3Expression3Launch_ch9.wmv" />
  </Button.Content>
</Button>
```

The result appears in Figure 8-5.

**FIGURE 8-5:** Button with a video as its content

Notice that the `Content` property is not an attribute within the `<Button>` tag anymore. You moved it outside of the opening tag of the `Button` element, but it is still inside the `Button`. The `Button` is still fully functional with the video inside. It reacts when the mouse is hovered over it, when it is depressed, or when it is released.

*By the way, the referenced video is a fun little clip of how designers and developers can't get along, and how the Expression Studio and Silverlight can help them to change that.*

To actually capture the `Click` event, select the `Button`, and use the Property Browser. Activate the Events tab within the Property Browser, and locate the `Click` event handler. Note that you can even search for a property or event — this is very handy because there are tons of properties or events for most controls. Double-click on the empty drop-down next to the "Click" text, and a `Button_Click` event handler will be created for you within the code-behind file (`MainPage.xaml.cs`). The XAML file will have the wiring for the new event handler:

```
<Button HorizontalAlignment="Center" VerticalAlignment="Center"
  Click="Button_Click">
```

Just as in ASP.NET, Silverlight controls can have their own code-behind files. Let's have a look at the code-behind you just opened (Listing 8-3).

**LISTING 8-3: MainPage.xaml.cs**

```csharp
using System;
using System.Collections.Generic;
using System.Linq;
using System.Net;
using System.Windows;
using System.Windows.Controls;
using System.Windows.Documents;
using System.Windows.Input;
using System.Windows.Media;
using System.Windows.Media.Animation;
using System.Windows.Shapes;

namespace HelloWorld
{
  public partial class MainPage : UserControl
  {
    public MainPage()
    {
      InitializeComponent();
    }

    private void Button_Click(object sender, RoutedEventArgs e)
    {

    }
  }
}
```

*Code file [MainPage.xaml] available for download at Wrox.com*

The `MainPage` class is a partial class — the other part of the class is created from the `MainPage` `.xaml` file. (You can inspect it by right-clicking on the `InitializeComponent` call in the constructor, and selecting "Go To Definition" from the context menu.) The class is inherited from

UserControl. The constructor only has one instruction — it calls the InitializeComponent method, which builds up the control tree described in the XAML, and then creates and assigns the fields for the named elements (such as the LayoutRoot grid).

Let's put some logic within the Click event handler of the button:

```
private void Button_Click(object sender, RoutedEventArgs e)
{
   LayoutRoot.Background = new SolidColorBrush(Colors.Yellow);
}
```

Notice that you have not created a field or property called LayoutRoot — Visual Studio took care of that. The InitializeComponent method call found the proper element within the visual tree created from the XAML file, and assigned it to the LayoutRoot field.

If you run the application now, clicking the button should change the background of the entire application to yellow. If you come from an ASP.NET background, it is important to realize that there has been no postback — the event handler ran on the client, within the Silverlight plug-in itself.

## Code Versus XAML

As mentioned previously, XAML is basically an XML-based description of an object hierarchy. This means that what you can express in XAML, you should be able to express in C# or Visual Basic .NET as well. So, let's look the code-only equivalent of the MainPage user control shown in Listing 8-4.

**LISTING 8-4:** CodeOnly.xaml.cs

```
using System;
using System.Collections.Generic;
using System.Linq;
using System.Net;
using System.Windows;
using System.Windows.Controls;
using System.Windows.Documents;
using System.Windows.Input;
using System.Windows.Media;
using System.Windows.Media.Animation;
using System.Windows.Shapes;

namespace HelloWorld
{
  public partial class CodeOnly : UserControl
  {

    internal Grid LayoutRoot;

    public CodeOnly()
```

*continues*

**LISTING 8-4** *(continued)*

```
    {
        InitializeComponent();

        //Build the visual tree from code
        LayoutRoot = new Grid
        {
            Background = new SolidColorBrush(Colors.White)
        };

        var button = new Button
        {
            HorizontalAlignment = System.Windows.HorizontalAlignment.Center,
            VerticalAlignment = System.Windows.VerticalAlignment.Center,
            Content = new MediaElement
            {
                Width = 100,
                Height = 75,
                Source = new Uri(
"http://mschnlnine.vo.llnwd.net/d1/ch9/0/8/7/7/7/4/SL3Expression3Launch_ch9.wmv",
    UriKind.Absolute)
            }
        };

        button.Click += new RoutedEventHandler(button_Click);

        LayoutRoot.Children.Add(button);
        this.Content = LayoutRoot;
    }

    void button_Click(object sender, RoutedEventArgs e)
    {
        LayoutRoot.Background = new SolidColorBrush(Colors.Yellow);
    }
    }
}
```

*Code file [CodeOnly.xaml.cs] available for download at Wrox.com*

The LayoutRoot Grid is also removed from the CodeOnly.xaml file, leaving only the UserControl there, as shown in Listing 8-5.

**LISTING 8-5: CodeOnly.xaml**

```
<UserControl x:Class="HelloWorld.CodeOnly"
    xmlns="http://schemas.microsoft.com/winfx/2006/xaml/presentation"
    xmlns:x="http://schemas.microsoft.com/winfx/2006/xaml" />
```

*Code file [CodeOnly.xaml] available for download at Wrox.com*

To prove that the two methods are equal, open up the `App.xaml.cs` file, and find the `Application_Startup` method, where `RootVisual` is set to a new instance of the `MainPage` class. Replace this with the following:

```
private void Application_Startup(object sender, StartupEventArgs e)
{
  this.RootVisual = new CodeOnly();
}
```

If you run the application now, you will see exactly the same behavior. It seems like whatever you can do in XAML, you can do it in C# as well. The code approach is less readable, and more verbose, but certainly equivalent with the declarative.

But there is one very important exception: *Coding the UI effectively makes the designer-developer cooperation impossible.* There is no designer-friendly way to change the size or position of the button within `CodeOnly.xaml.cs`. There is no way a designer can add animations or change colors, replace controls without messing with your code — and probably neither of you want to do that.

So, the best practice is to keep everything you can in XAML. As you learn to appreciate the power of Silverlight and WPF, you will see that almost any design can be expressed in XAML. With proper architecture, the task of the developer is "simply" to acquire the data and send it back to the server, and the task of the designer is to display it and ensure that the user experience is fluid and fun to use. XAML, Visual Studio, and Expression Blend provide unparalleled basis for both developers and designers to do their ends of the work.

## Tools for Working with Silverlight (and WPF)

You may find it strange that tools are included as a pillar for Silverlight and WPF development. However, tooling is as important as the underlying technology — and, in the case of Silverlight and WPF, the tooling story is great with Visual Studio 2010 and Expression Blend. Knowing both of these tools is essential in achieving great productivity and fully harnessing the power of Silverlight and WPF.

First, there is Visual Studio 2010, arguably the best development tool out there. While Visual Studio 2008 was lacking big time with WPF, and especially Silverlight development (Silverlight 3 didn't even have a read-only visual XAML preview like Silverlight 2 had), Cider (the name of the Silverlight and WPF designer) really put its act together for Visual Studio 2010. Cider's main goal is to allow for RAD WPF and Silverlight development, thus, it focuses on things developers do — and completely ignores fancy things like animation, visual states, and even templates.

For these tasks, Microsoft has created Expression Design (a vector graphics drawing program), and especially Expression Blend. Blend is the tool for the interactive designer. It helps with creating the UI (including animations, wiring data, and business logic to the UI) and changing the look and feel of controls. Although Expression Blend gives access and even Intellisense for both XAML and C#/Visual Basic code, most of what the WPF and Silverlight platforms can do in terms of UI can be done in Blend without writing any code.

Take a look at Figure 8-6, which shows Visual Studio 2010 with the previous `HelloWorld` sample open.

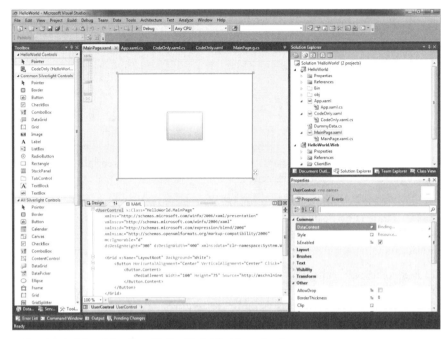

**FIGURE 8-6:** Visual Studio with the HelloWorld application

The central area displays the artboard on the top, and the XAML on the bottom. This split view is an excellent learning tool. Any change to the top area (like moving the button, changing colors, adding new controls, and so on) is immediately reflected on the bottom, and vice versa. If the XAML is changed, the end result can be seen on the top in a second. On the bottom right, the Property Browser has a very useful feature — the properties can be searched, as shown in Figure 8-7.

There is also a handy document outline window. Because XAML trees can get pretty huge, this helps finding the right element in the document.

For some developers, the dark, "designer-ish" look of Blend is a little scary. They may not feel at home with it. However, Blend is an indispensable tool for a developer who deals with XAML — unfortunately, some features that even gray

**FIGURE 8-7:** The VS2010 Property Browser

LOB applications need didn't make it to Visual Studio's Cider (such as `ItemTemplate` editing, which is discussed later in this chapter). The same `HelloWorld` application opened in Blend (preview for .NET 4) is shown in Figure 8-8.

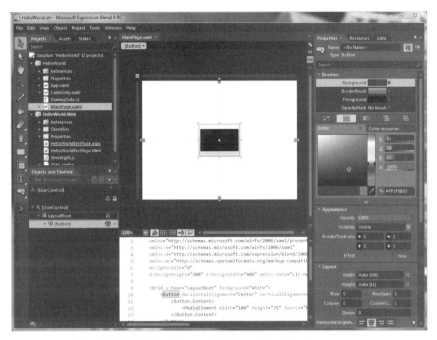

**FIGURE 8-8:** The HelloWorld application in Expression Blend

Again, the artboard and the split XAML view occupy most of the screen. The Property Editor panel looks fancier (and is easier to navigate because of the different value editors), and the numerical values can be changed by dragging over the property value display. The properties can be filtered in Blend, just like in Visual Studio. The toolbox is replaced by zooming, panning, manipulation tools, and basic controls — the rest of the controls can be found (and searched for) in the Assets panel. The Objects and Timeline panel is central for working in Blend. Unlike Cider's Document Outline, it is interactive, supports drag-and-drop for re-arranging controls, right-clicking for additional actions, and can be expanded with a timeline to create and edit animations.

## Layout

*Layout* means the way the controls are sized and placed on the screen. The Silverlight layout system is very flexible. It is easy to create layouts that automatically adapt to the following factors.

➤ Available screen size

➤ Number of items displayed

➤ Size of the displayed elements

➤ Magnification factor

Silverlight's layout strategy is different from what you may be used to in Windows Forms or ASP.NET. The key to understanding Silverlight's layout system is to understand the concept of containers.

There are two kinds of containers in Silverlight. `ContentControls` can have only one child. You can access the child of the `ContentControl` via the `Content` property. Examples for `ContentControl` descendants are `Button`, `Checkbox`, and `ScrollViewer`. You used the `Content` property of the `Button` earlier in the `HelloWorld` sample. But what if you want to place more than just one element within the `Button`?

The trick is that you can place a `Panel` as the `Content` of a `ContentControl`. `Panels` can have more than one child in the `Children` property. The `Grid` (which is a default panel when you create a new `UserControl` in Visual Studio) is an example of such a `Panel`. So, how do you place text next to the video in the button from the `HelloWorld` application?

```
<Button HorizontalAlignment="Center" VerticalAlignment="Center">
  <Button.Content>
    <StackPanel>
      <TextBlock Text="I am a button!" HorizontalAlignment="Center" Margin="5" />
      <MediaElement Width="100" Height="75"
          Source="http://mschnlnine.vo.llnwd.net/d1/ch9/0/8/7/7/7/4/
          SL3Expression3Launch_ch9.wmv" />
    </StackPanel>
  </Button.Content>
</Button>
```

The `Content` of `Button` is now a `StackPanel`. The `StackPanel` has two children — a centered `TextBlock`, and the `MediaElement` that plays the video. By default, the `StackPanel` arranges its children so that they are below each other. So, the `Button` described with the previous XAML looks like Figure 8-9.

**FIGURE 8-9:** Button with text and video

If you want to change the layout so that the text is to the left of the video, you must change the `StackPanel` itself, and add an `Orientation` attribute, as shown here:

```
<Button HorizontalAlignment="Center" VerticalAlignment="Center">
  <Button.Content>
    <StackPanel Orientation="Horizontal">
      <TextBlock Text="I am a button!" HorizontalAlignment="Center"
        VerticalAlignment="Center" Margin="5" />
```

```
        <MediaElement Width="100" Height="75"
    Source="http://mschnlnine.vo.llnwd.net/d1/ch9/0/8/7/7/7/4/
        SL3Expression3Launch_ch9.wmv" />
      </StackPanel>
    </Button.Content>
  </Button>
```

In this code snippet, the `TextBlock` has also received a new, `VerticalAlignment` attribute. If it is omitted, the `TextBlock` will have the same height as the `MediaElement` next to it, and thus, the text will be displayed on the top instead of in the middle.

This sample shows how Silverlight layout works. It is not the controls that determine where and how they will be displayed, but rather their containing control. The `StackPanel` arranges its children to be below each other (if the `Orientation` property is set to the default value of `Orientation.Vertical`), or the children can be next to each other (if the `Orientation` property is `Orientation.Horizontal`).

The actual layout algorithm is a little bit more complicated. The children have their say in what size they would prefer to be. This allows for adapting the layout to the size of the content. As the first step of the layout algorithm, starting from the top of the visual tree, Silverlight asks every element how big it would like to be ideally by calling the `MeasureOverride` method. Composite controls, such as `Panels` or `ContentContainers` calculate their answers by invoking the `MeasureOverride` method of their children.

In the second step, the `ArrangeOverride` method is called throughout the entire visual tree in a similar manner. In this case, the parents tell their children the actual amount of space available for them — and it is the responsibility of the children to fit in. If the available space is smaller than what the control ideally could fill, the controls can add a scroll bar, scale their content to a smaller size (such as an image or a video), or simply perform a crop. The ultimate limit for how big the root element can be is the size given to the HTML `<object>` tag — or, in the case of an out-of-browser (OOB) application, the size of the hosting window.

## Layout Containers in Silverlight

Layout containers in Silverlight include the following:

- ➤ Border
- ➤ Canvas
- ➤ StackPanel
- ➤ Grid
- ➤ Viewbox

### Border

`Border`s can have only one child. (But, as in the previous `Button` example, this can be another layout container.) As its name implies, `Border` puts a border around its content.

```
<Border HorizontalAlignment="Center" VerticalAlignment="Center"
  BorderBrush="Black" BorderThickness="3" CornerRadius="5">
  <TextBox Text="TextBox with a lot of text" Background="LightGray" />
</Border>
```

This code creates a `Border` around the `TextBox`. As you can see in Figure 8-10, the border has a thickness of 3 pixels, and its corners are also rounded with a radius of 5 pixels. But what is more interesting is that the size of the textbox and the border are both determined by the size of the text within the textbox. This is the result of the adaptive layout algorithm described earlier. During the layout phase, `Border` asks the `TextBox` to measure itself, and `TextBox` does so by measuring its own content elements — mainly the text and the decorators around it.

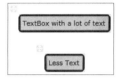

**FIGURE 8-10:** Border resizes around TextBox

Because `Border` does not have any specific size set (this is why the `HorizontalAlignment` and the `VerticalAlignment` properties are set), it sizes itself around its content, the `TextBox`. If you run the previous sample, you can see that if you change the text within the `TextBox`, the `Border` resizes itself accordingly.

You can also control the space between the borders of the `Border` and the `TextBox` by modifying the `Border`'s `Padding` property. The `Padding` property is defined on quite a few controls in Silverlight. For example, in a `TextBox`, `Padding` controls the space between the text and the bounds of the control.

## Canvas

`Canvas` is the simplest `Panel`, and it is the simplest layout container that can have more than one child. On a `Canvas`, you simply put items on absolute coordinates. The top-left corner is "0,0." `Canvas` allows its children to be of any size. If the children do not fit the `Canvas`, they are still shown outside the `Canvas`. (In WPF, you can clip the content to the bounds to the `Canvas` using the `ClipToBounds` property). The size of the `Canvas` itself does not depend on its children. This simplicity makes it the fastest layout control, and thus, the best choice, when adaptive layout is not needed.

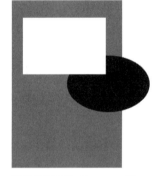

**FIGURE 8-11:** Canvas with Ellipse and Rectangle

The following code places a `Rectangle` and an `Ellipse` in the `Canvas`. The `Ellipse` extends outside the `Canvas`, as shown in Figure 8-11. The `Rectangle` is above the `Ellipse`, as it is later in the XAML. If you want to place the `Ellipse` above the `Rectangle`, you can use the `Canvas.ZIndex` property.

```
<Grid x:Name="LayoutRoot" Background="White">
  <Canvas Width="200" Height="300" Background="Gray" >
    <Ellipse Width="150" Height="100"
      Canvas.Left="100" Canvas.Top="100" Fill="Black" />
    <Rectangle Width="150" Height="100"
      Canvas.Left="20" Canvas.Top="33" Fill="White" />
  </Canvas>
</Grid>
```

Earlier, you learned that the controls are not responsible for their own placement. So, how is it that you can see left and top coordinates on the `Ellipse` and the `Rectangle` in the XAML? The trick is that these coordinates (`Canvas.Left` and `Canvas.Top`) are provided via a construct called *attached dependency properties*. Any child control of the `Canvas` in the visual tree can set these properties. Even though they are set within the children, handling these properties is still the responsibility of the `Canvas`, and the properties themselves are defined in the `Canvas`.

## StackPanel

As you've seen previously, `StackPanel` arranges its children either horizontally or vertically. Here is a slightly more complicated example:

```
<StackPanel Orientation="Horizontal" Background="Black">
  <StackPanel Orientation="Vertical">
    <Button Content="Button 1"/>
    <Button Content="Button 2" Width="100" />
    <Button Content="Button 3 with long text" />
  </StackPanel>
  <StackPanel Orientation="Horizontal" Background="Gray">
    <Button Content="Button 4"/>
    <Button Content="Button 5" Height="40" />
    <Button Content="Button 6 with long text" />
  </StackPanel>
</StackPanel>
```

This renders as shown in Figure 8-12.

The first, black `StackPanel` is set to a horizontal orientation, and has two more `StackPanels` as its children. Both children have three buttons — `StackPanel A` arranges them vertically, `StackPanel B` horizontally (this one has a gray background). In the case of the vertical `StackPanel`, its width is determined by the width of its biggest child — `Button 3`, which has the most text in it. The `StackPanel` resizes `Button 1` to fill the horizontal width of the panel. `Button 2` has a specified width, so it does not get resized by the `StackPanel`.

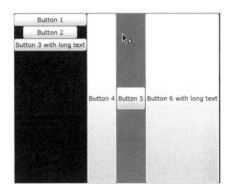

**FIGURE 8-12:** Three StackPanels

In the case of `StackPanels` with horizontal orientation, the panel dictates the height of its children. The gray `StackPanel`'s height is specified by the height of the outermost, black `StackPanel` — just like the height of `Button 4` and `Button 6`. The `Height` property of `Button 5` is set, so the setting takes precedence.

## Grid

`Grid` is the most complex, but also the most versatile layout control. It is somewhat similar to an HTML table. As the name implies, it allows its children to be placed in rows and columns. Following is an example. (Figure 8-13 shows the `Grid` in Visual Studio.)

```
<Grid x:Name="LayoutRoot" Background="Gray">
  <Grid.RowDefinitions>
    <RowDefinition Height="1*" />
```

```
        <RowDefinition Height="2*" />
    </Grid.RowDefinitions>
    <Grid.ColumnDefinitions>
        <ColumnDefinition Width="136" />
        <ColumnDefinition Width="264" />
    </Grid.ColumnDefinitions>
    <Ellipse Stroke="Black" StrokeThickness="1" Fill="White"  />
    <Ellipse Stroke="Black" StrokeThickness="3" Fill="White" Grid.Column="1"
     Margin="10,10,0,0" />
    <Ellipse Stroke="Black" StrokeThickness="5" Fill="White" Grid.Row="1"
     Grid.ColumnSpan="2" />
</Grid>
```

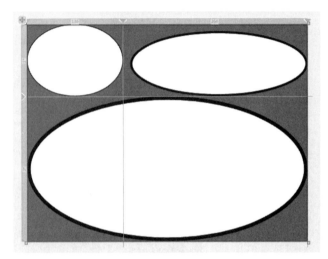

**FIGURE 8-13:** Grid as a layout container

This XAML snippet creates a Grid with gray background. The Grid has two rows: the second one is twice as big as the first one. This means that if the Grid is 300 pixels high, the first row will be 100 pixels, and the second 200 pixels high. The Grid also has two columns; they have a fixed size of 136 and 264 pixels. It is also possible to have a row or column auto-sized. In this case, the size of the content and the remaining space from the other rows or columns determine the size of the row or column.

The Grid has three Ellipses in it. The first one is in Column 0 and Row 0 (if no Grid.Row or Grid.Column attributes are specified, 0 is the default). The size of the first Ellipse is determined by the size of the top-left cell.

The Grid.Column="1" attribute of the second Ellipse puts it in the second column of the first row. This Ellipse also has a Margin of "10,10,0,0", meaning that the top and left margins are

10 pixels. The size of the second ellipse is also determined by the size of the top-right cell, minus the specified `Margin`.

The third `Ellipse` is placed in the second row. It also has a `ColumnSpan` attribute set to 2, so that it will occupy both cells in the second row.

If the intention is for the contents of a `Cell` to not occupy the entire available space, you must change the `HorizontalAlignment` and `VerticalAlignment` properties. These properties default to `Stretch`, but can also take on the value of `HorizontalAlignment.Left`, `HorizontalAlignment` `.Center`, `HorizontalAlignment.Right`, or `VerticalAlignment.Top`, `VerticalAlignment.Center`, `VerticalAlignment.Bottom`, respectively. In this case, you can use the `Margin` property to set the distance from the edges of the cell.

## Viewbox

`Viewbox` is a new addition to the Silverlight core framework. It was part of the Silverlight Toolkit before Silverlight 4.0. (Silverlight Toolkit is a set of Open Source controls developed by Microsoft that is not part of the Silverlight core platform.) Just like `Border`, `Viewbox` can have only one child. The goal of the `Viewbox` control is to provide resizing strategies if the content does not exactly fit in the available space.

The following sample has a `Grid` with four equally sized cells; every cell has a `Viewbox` in it. The most important property if a `Viewbox` is the `Stretch` property. The `Stretch` property defines how the content of the `Viewbox` is resized.

```
<Grid x:Name="LayoutRoot" Background="White">
  <Grid.RowDefinitions>
    <RowDefinition Height="150" />
    <RowDefinition Height="150" />
  </Grid.RowDefinitions>
  <Grid.ColumnDefinitions>
    <ColumnDefinition Width="200" />
    <ColumnDefinition Width="200" />
  </Grid.ColumnDefinitions>
  <Viewbox Stretch="None">
    <Button Content="Stretch:None" />
  </Viewbox>
  <Viewbox Stretch="Fill" Grid.Column="1">
    <Button Content="Stretch:Fill" />
  </Viewbox>
  <Viewbox Stretch="Uniform" Grid.Row="1">
    <Button Content="Stretch:Uniform" />
  </Viewbox>
  <Viewbox Stretch="UniformToFill" Grid.Column="1" Grid.Row="1">
    <Button Content="Stretch:UniformToFill" />
  </Viewbox>
</Grid>
```

Table 8-2 examines values for `Stretch`, and Figure 8-14 shows how the `Stretch` property works.

**TABLE 8-2**: Viewbox.Stretch Property

| STRETCH VALUE | VIEWBOX ACTION |
| --- | --- |
| None | The content does not get resized. `Viewbox` behaves like a `Border` with `BorderThickness = 0`. |
| Fill | The content fills the `Viewbox` entirely. If the aspect ratio (the width divided by the height) of the content is not the same as the aspect ratio of the `Viewbox`, the content may get distorted. |
| Uniform | The content is enlarged or reduced to fill as much of the `Viewbox` as possible while maintaining the aspect ratio. |
| UniformToFill | The content is enlarged or reduced to fill the entire `Viewbox`, while maintaining the aspect ratio. If the aspect ratio of the content and the `Viewbox` are not equal, some clipping will occur. |

## Custom Layout Panels

With creative nesting of the previously described layout panels, most common scenarios for a rectangular adaptive layout can be expressed. Still, if you need more, you can find some additional layout controls (such as `Accordion`, `LayoutTransformer`, `WrapPanel`, and `Expander`) in the Silverlight Toolkit. Because the layout model of Silverlight is completely open, you can also write your own panels. This book cannot go into detail, but the keys for writing your own layout containers are to inherit from `Panel` or `ContentControl`, and override the `ArrangeOverride` and `MeasureOverride` methods.

**FIGURE 8-14:**  Viewbox with StretchMode None, Fill, Uniform, and UniformToFill

# Data Binding

Data binding is used to connect elements of the UI to data, or other UI elements. Silverlight's data binding works in cooperation with styles, templates, layouts, and even animation. Data binding allows for two-way synchronization and validation, and automatically ensures that the UI and the underlying data are consistent. You can use data binding techniques for data display and data entry as well. Data binding is a key element in making the separation between the UI and the logic possible.

## Simple Data Binding

The simplest form of data binding is when you connect a single UI element to a data property. Listing 8-6 shows a `Clock` application using data binding. Listing 8-7 shows the `ClockViewModel.cs` file.

**LISTING 8-6:** ClockSample.xaml

```xaml
<UserControl x:Class="DatabindingDemo.ClockSample"
  xmlns="http://schemas.microsoft.com/winfx/2006/xaml/presentation"
  xmlns:x="http://schemas.microsoft.com/winfx/2006/xaml"
  xmlns:d="http://schemas.microsoft.com/expression/blend/2008"
  xmlns:mc="http://schemas.openxmlformats.org/markup-compatibility/2006"
  xmlns:local="clr-namespace:DatabindingDemo"
  mc:Ignorable="d"
  d:DesignHeight="300" d:DesignWidth="400"
  xmlns:dataInput="clr-namespace:System.Windows.Controls;assembly=
      System.Windows.Controls.Data.Input">
  <UserControl.DataContext>
    <local:ClockViewModel />
  </UserControl.DataContext>

  <Grid x:Name="LayoutRoot" Background="White">
    <TextBlock Text="{Binding Path=CurrentTime}"
     HorizontalAlignment="Center" VerticalAlignment="Center" />
  </Grid>
</UserControl>
```

*Code file [ClockSample.xaml] available for download at Wrox.com*

**LISTING 8-7:** ClockViewModel.cs

```csharp
using System;
using System.ComponentModel;
using System.Windows.Threading;

namespace DatabindingDemo
{
  public class ClockViewModel : INotifyPropertyChanged
  {
    private DispatcherTimer timer;
    public ClockViewModel()
    {
      timer = new DispatcherTimer();
      timer.Interval = TimeSpan.FromSeconds(1);
      timer.Tick += timer_Tick;
      timer.Start();
    }

    void timer_Tick(object sender, EventArgs e)
    {
      NotifyPropertyChanged("CurrentTime");
    }

    private void NotifyPropertyChanged(string propertyName)
```

*continues*

**LISTING 8-7** *(continued)*

```
    {
      if (PropertyChanged != null)
        PropertyChanged(this, new PropertyChangedEventArgs(propertyName));
    }

    public DateTime CurrentTime
    {
      get { return DateTime.Now; }
    }

    public event PropertyChangedEventHandler PropertyChanged;
  }
}
```

*Code file [ClockViewModel.cs] available for download at Wrox.com*

At first, the `Clock` sample application seems to be a bit overcomplicated. After all, you could have simply created a timer in the code-behind, and updated the context of the `TextBlock` whenever the timer fires. However, with complex master-detail relationships and multiple objects, the advantages of the separate data object and data binding become obvious.

 *There is also a popular architecture pattern, called* Model-View-ViewModel (MVVM) *that relies heavily on the data binding. MVVM allows for UI logic testability and complete separation of the UI and the application logic. Discussing MVVM in depth is beyond the scope of this book, but you can find some pointers at the end of this chapter. If you are planning to develop serious applications with Silverlight or WPF, you should definitely get yourself acquainted with the pattern.*

Remember how XAML is nothing but a way to describe an object hierarchy? Here, you use this XAML feature to create an instance of the `ClockViewModel` class, and assign it to the `DataContext` property of the `UserControl`. The XML namespace `local` refers to the assembly that contains the `ClockViewModel`. When the XAML is executed by the Silverlight run-time, the `ClockViewModel` object is created, which, in turn, starts its timer.

The `DataContext` property is inherited down the visual tree (but it can be changed on any element). This means that the `LayoutRoot` grid and its children also have their `DataContext` set to the same `ClockViewModel` instance. The `DataContext` is also inherited by the `TextBlock` that is used to display the time.

The `Text` property of the `TextBlock` contains a data binding expression: `Text="{Binding Path=CurrentTime}"`. This connects the `Text` property to the `CurrentTime` property of the `DataContext`. At every tick of the timer, the `PropertyChanged` event is fired. The `INotifyPropertyChanged` interface (which only defines the `PropertyChanged` event) is how the Silverlight run-time learns about changes in the data binding source objects. Firing the `PropertyChanged` event instructs the Silverlight run-time to update all properties that have been bound to the data object property in question. From this point on, the display is automatic and handled by the Silverlight run-time.

The `{Binding}` clause within XAML has several additional options to make data binding more powerful. Following are some of the most important ones:

➤ `Converter` — This allows you to create custom display logic and to convert any entered data to something a backing field can more easily understand. (For example, if you want to display and enter a property of a size as "24x48" in a `TextBox`, you can implement the `IValueConverter` interface and write the converter code.)

➤ `Mode` — This can be set to `OneTime` (does not do further updates), `OneWay` (default), and `TwoWay`.

➤ `Source` — This specifies the data source for the binding. `Source` can be omitted, and, in this case, the `DataContext` will be the source object, just like in the earlier `Clock` sample.

➤ `Path` — This can be omitted as a shorthand. The binding expression in the `Clock` sample can also be written as `Text="{Binding CurrentTime}"`.

## Data Binding Between Two UI Elements

You can also data-bind two UI elements. Here is a small sample that binds a `TextBox` to a `Slider`:

```
<Slider HorizontalAlignment="Center" x:Name="slider1" Width="100"
  Margin="0,109,0,0" VerticalAlignment="Top" />
<TextBox HorizontalAlignment="Center" VerticalAlignment="Center"
  Text="{Binding Path=Value, Mode=TwoWay, ElementName=slider1,
  ValidatesOnException=True}" Width="40" />
```

As you can see, you have a two-way binding here. You can move the `Slider`, and the `TextBox` automatically updates. Similarly, you can enter a number in the `TextBox`, and the `Slider` updates. This automatic binding is done via dependency properties instead of the `INotifyPropertyChanged` interface, which is more suited for business data objects. Dependency properties are essentially control properties that can participate in data binding, styling, and animation, and are managed by the Silverlight (or WPF) run-time.

The binding update is triggered when the `TextBox` loses focus. (You can use the Tab key for this.) The input controls in Silverlight are prepared to display validation errors. If the value entered in the `TextBox` is invalid (for example, it contains a letter), an exception will be raised. Because you set the `ValidatesOnExceptions` property of the `Binding` to `True`, the exception actually appears as a user-friendly notification, as shown in Figure 8-15. Further binding validation options include `ValidatesOnDataErrors` and `ValidatesOnNotifyDataErrors`.

**FIGURE 8-15:** TextBox showing a Validation error

## Data Binding to a List of Objects

Most of the time, the task is to display multiple objects at the same time — for example, in a ListBox, DataGrid, or even a DropDownList. Suppose the application has to list the authors of this book. The Author object is very simple:

```
public class Author
{
  public string Name { get; set; }
  public string Chapters { get; set; }
}
```

To display a list of Author objects in a DataGrid, simply declare a DataGrid in XAML (DataGrid is part of the Silverlight Toolkit, so you will have to install Silverlight Toolkit from http://silverlight.codeplex.com, and add a project reference to the System.Windows.Controls namespace):

```
<data:DataGrid Name="myGrid" />
```

And, in the code-behind, assign the ItemsSource property of the DataGrid like this:

```
myGrid.ItemsSource = authors;
```

If authors is of type IEnumerable<Author> (or something similar, like a List<Author>), and it has any data, the Author objects will be displayed as shown in Figure 8-16.

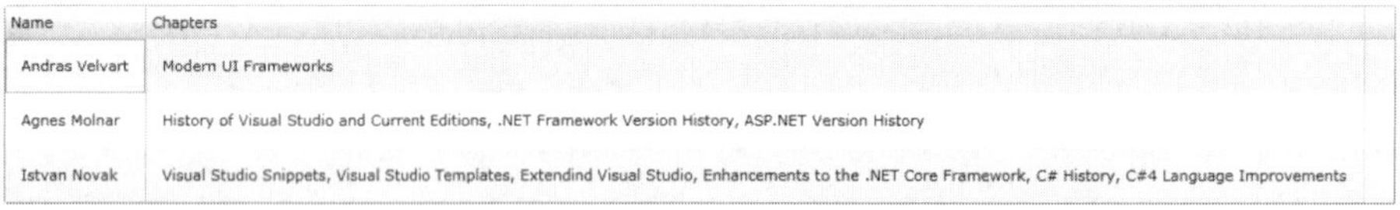

| Name | Chapters |
|---|---|
| Andras Velvart | Modern UI Frameworks |
| Agnes Molnar | History of Visual Studio and Current Editions, .NET Framework Version History, ASP.NET Version History |
| Istvan Novak | Visual Studio Snippets, Visual Studio Templates, Extendind Visual Studio, Enhancements to the .NET Core Framework, C# History, C#4 Language Improvements |

**FIGURE 8-16:** Displaying Author objects in a DataGrid

Notice that the DataGrid object was intelligent enough to determine the columns of the Grid based on the Author object. Of course, this behavior can be overridden with the AutoGenerateColumns property. DataGrid is an extremely powerful control, with features like grouping, sorting, filtering, rearranging columns, templating, in-place editing, and validation, just to name a few.

The important thing to note here is that Silverlight and WPF data binding works directly with the displayed objects. There is no need to explicitly create ListItems and put references to the contained object in Tags, or find the selected item via an indexed array. The developer can keep working with the objects of the business domain, and the XAML will take care of the display.

If a new Author is added to the list, the UI is expected to immediately show it. For simplicity's sake, create a simple Button that adds a new author to the authors list:

```
<Button Content="Add new author" Click="AddAuthor_Click" />
```

The event handler looks like this:

```
private void AddAuthor_Click(object sender, RoutedEventArgs e)
{
  authors.Add(new Author {
                     Name = "New Author",
                     Chapters = "New Author Chapters"
                 });
}
```

However, clicking the Button does not update the DataGrid. Setting the ItemsSource property of the DataGrid to null, and then back to the authors field, works, but this is a downright ugly solution. There surely must be a better way.

The better way is the INotifyCollectionChanged interface. Just like INotifypropertyChanged can get your property changes to show up in the UI, the INotifyCollectionChanged interface helps with automatically propagating changes to a list in the UI. The simplest way to take advantage of the INotifyCollectionChanged interface is to use the built-in ObservableCollection<Author> instead of List<Author>. Now, pressing the Button adds a new item to the list, which immediately shows up in the DataGrid. Listing 8-8 shows the entire DatabindingList.cs file.

**LISTING 8-8:  DatabindingList.cs**

```
using System.Windows;
using System.Windows.Controls;
using System.Collections.ObjectModel;

namespace DatabindingDemo
{
  public partial class ListDatabinding : UserControl
  {
    private ObservableCollection<Author> authors;

    public ListDatabinding()
    {
      InitializeComponent();
      authors = new ObservableCollection<Author>
      {
        new Author { Name = "Andras Velvart", Chapters = "Modern UI Frameworks" },
        new Author { Name = "Agnes Molnar",
          Chapters = "History of Visual Studio and Current Editions,
              .NET Framework Version History,
              ASP.NET Version History" },
        new Author { Name = "Istvan Novak",
          Chapters = "Visual Studio Snippets, Visual Studio Templates,
              Extendind Visual Studio, Enhancements to the
              .NET Core Framework, C# History,
              C#4 Language Improvements" }
```

*continues*

**LISTING 8-8** *(continued)*

```
      //Other authors...
    };

    myGrid.ItemsSource = authors;
  }

  private void AddAuthor_Click(object sender, RoutedEventArgs e)
  {
    authors.Add(new Author { Name = "New Author",
                 Chapters = "New Author Chapters" });
  }
}

public class Author
{
  public string Name { get; set; }
  public string Chapters { get; set; }
}
}
```

## Master-Detail Data Binding

It is easy to create a master-detail interface using UI-to-UI binding. Listing 8-9 shows the entire XAML code that extends the previous sample with a detail panel.

**LISTING 8-9:** ListDatabinding.xaml

```xml
<UserControl x:Class="DatabindingDemo.ListDatabinding"
  xmlns="http://schemas.microsoft.com/winfx/2006/xaml/presentation"
  xmlns:x="http://schemas.microsoft.com/winfx/2006/xaml"
  xmlns:d="http://schemas.microsoft.com/expression/blend/2008"
  xmlns:mc="http://schemas.openxmlformats.org/markup-compatibility/2006"
  mc:Ignorable="d"
  d:DesignHeight="300" d:DesignWidth="400"
  xmlns:data="clr-namespace:System.Windows.Controls;assembly=
       System.Windows.Controls.Data">

  <UserControl.Resources>
    <!-- Give TextBlocks a bit more space-->
    <Style TargetType="TextBlock">
      <Setter Property="Padding" Value="8,8,8,8" />
    </Style>
  </UserControl.Resources>

  <Grid x:Name="LayoutRoot" Background="White">
    <StackPanel>
      <TextBlock HorizontalAlignment="Center" Text="Book Authors" />
      <Button Content="Add new author" Click="AddAuthor_Click" />
      <data:DataGrid Name="myGrid" />
      <!-- The details panel -->
```

```
<Border CornerRadius="10" BorderBrush="Black"
  BorderThickness="1" Margin="10">
  <StackPanel DataContext="{Binding ElementName=myGrid, Path=SelectedItem}">
    <TextBlock HorizontalAlignment="Center"
      Text="{Binding Path=Name, StringFormat=Name: \{0\}}"
      FontWeight="Bold"  />
    <TextBlock HorizontalAlignment="Center"
      Text="{Binding Path=Chapters, StringFormat=Chapter: \{0\}}"
      TextWrapping="Wrap" />
  </StackPanel>
</Border>
    </StackPanel>
  </Grid>
</UserControl>
```

*Code file [ListDatabinding.xaml] available for download at Wrox.com*

The code-behind has not changed at all. Running this sample and selecting a row in the `DataGrid` displays the details of the selected author in a nice rounded border, as shown in Figure 8-17.

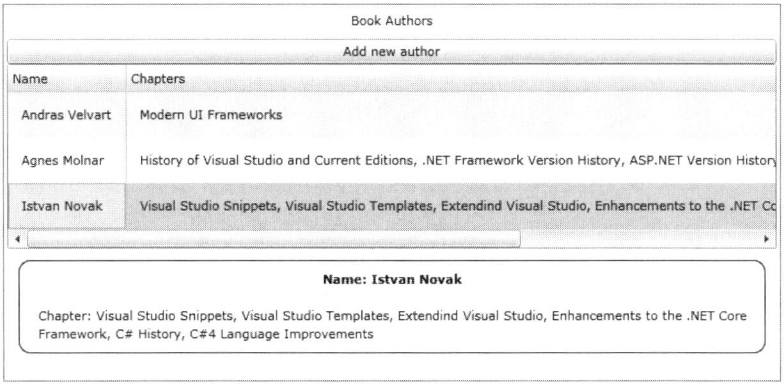

**FIGURE 8-17:** Typical master-details UI

So, how does the details panel work? The root of the details panel is a `Border`. The `DataContext` of the `Border` is bound to the `SelectedItem` property of the `DataGrid`, which (as its name implies) points to the currently selected item in the `DataGrid`. If the `DataGrid` displays objects of the `Author` type, the `SelectedItem` will also contain an instance of the `Author` type (or `null`, if nothing is selected).

The trick here is to again utilize the inheriting nature of the `DataContext` property. If the `Border`'s `DataContext` is set to the selected `Author`, then all its descendants in the visual tree will have the same `DataContext`. Consequently, the two `TextBlocks` will also display the `Name` and `Chapter` properties of the selected `Author`. Note that the bindings have a very handy `StringFormat` binding that uses the same `String.Format` formatter syntax as the core run-time.

# Styles

You have already seen how you can change the look of controls via the `Background`, `Stroke`, and other properties. For example, you can change how a `TextBlock` looks and behaves with the following XAML:

```
<TextBlock Text="I am stylish, am I not?" HorizontalAlignment="Center"
    VerticalAlignment="Center" FontFamily="Comic Sans MS"
    FontSize="20" FontStyle="Italic"
    FontWeight="Bold" TextTrimming="WordEllipsis" Width="199">
    <TextBlock.Foreground>
        <LinearGradientBrush EndPoint="0.5,1" StartPoint="0.5,0">
            <GradientStop Color="Black" Offset="0" />
            <GradientStop Color="Gray" Offset="1" />
        </LinearGradientBrush>
    </TextBlock.Foreground>
    <TextBlock.Effect>
        <BlurEffect Radius="2" />
    </TextBlock.Effect>
</TextBlock>
```

When rendered, this XAML looks like Figure 8-18.

When the styles are specified within the element, they are called *inline styles*. There are several problems with inline styles. The first problem is that they are verbose, and make it difficult to read the XAML and concentrate on the actual control tree. The second one is that they cannot be reused easily — you must repeat the styles for every control. The third problem is that if you want to change the look and feel of the entire application, there is no one central place where you can do it.

*I am stylish, am I...*

**FIGURE 8-18:** Text with style

Luckily, the Silverlight styling features go way beyond inline styles or property setters. You can create resources that contain brushes, styles, templates, or even entire objects. Resources can be local to a control, or they can be placed into an external file. Listing 8-10 extracts some of the styles to a resource within the parent `UserControl`.

**LISTING 8-10:** Font, Blur Effect, and Foreground Brush Extracted to a UserControl Resource

```
<UserControl x:Class="Styles.MainPage"
    xmlns="http://schemas.microsoft.com/winfx/2006/xaml/presentation"
    xmlns:x="http://schemas.microsoft.com/winfx/2006/xaml"
    xmlns:d="http://schemas.microsoft.com/expression/blend/2008"
    xmlns:mc="http://schemas.openxmlformats.org/markup-compatibility/2006"
    mc:Ignorable="d"
    d:DesignHeight="300" d:DesignWidth="400" FontStretch="Normal">
    <UserControl.Resources>
        <FontFamily x:Key="FontFamily1">Comic Sans MS</FontFamily>
        <BlurEffect x:Key="Effect1" Radius="2" />
        <LinearGradientBrush x:Key="ForegroundBrush" EndPoint="0.5,1"
            StartPoint="0.5,0">
            <GradientStop Color="Black" Offset="0" />
```

```xml
            <GradientStop Color="Gray" Offset="1" />
        </LinearGradientBrush>
    </UserControl.Resources>

    <Grid x:Name="LayoutRoot" Background="White">
        <TextBlock Text="I am stylish, am I not?" HorizontalAlignment="Center"
          VerticalAlignment="Center" FontFamily="{StaticResource FontFamily1}"
          FontSize="20" FontStyle="Italic" FontWeight="Bold"
          TextTrimming="WordEllipsis" Width="199"
          Effect="{StaticResource Effect1}"
          Foreground="{StaticResource ForegroundBrush}">
        </TextBlock>
    </Grid>
</UserControl>
```

Now, you can reuse the resources in any other control. For example, the resource with the key `ForeGroundBrush` can be reused in another `TextBlock`, or even to specify the stroke brush of a `Rectangle`:

```xml
<Rectangle Fill="White" Height="63" Width="121"
  Stroke="{StaticResource ForegroundBrush}" StrokeThickness="5"/>
```

Of course, the `Rectangle` can only refer to the resource — if it is within the same `UserControl`. If you want to reuse the resource throughout your entire project, you can create a new resource dictionary and move it there, or make it truly global by putting it into the `App.xaml` resource directory.

Still, even with resources, if you want all your `TextBlocks` to look the same, you must set all the important properties to the proper resources. Styles to the rescue! A *style* is nothing more than a set of property setters. For example, you can collect the properties of the `TextBlock` into a style:

```xml
<Style x:Key="TextBlockStyle1" TargetType="TextBlock">
  <Setter Property="Foreground" Value="{StaticResource ForegroundBrush}" />
  <Setter Property="Effect" Value="{StaticResource Effect1}" />
  <Setter Property="FontFamily" Value="{StaticResource FontFamily1}" />
  <Setter Property="TextTrimming" Value="WordEllipsis" />
  <Setter Property="FontSize" Value="20" />
  <Setter Property="FontStyle" Value="Italic" />
  <Setter Property="FontWeight" Value="Bold" />
</Style>
```

The Style definition is placed inside a resource dictionary — either within the `UserControl`, or an external one (such as the `App.xaml`). Using the previous style, the `TextBlock` definition is reduced to the following:

```xml
<TextBlock Text="I am stylish, am I not?" HorizontalAlignment="Center"
  VerticalAlignment="Center" Width="199"
  Style="{StaticResource TextBlockStyle1}" />
```

Just like with HTML, instead of named styles, you can define a default style for a control since Silverlight 4. If you want to make all `TextBlocks` have the same default style, just remove the `x:Key` attribute from the `Style` definition:

```
<Style TargetType="TextBlock">
  . . .
</Style>
```

Now, you can also remove the `Style` resource reference from the `TextBlock`, and still have exactly the same result as the first sample. Of course, just like with HTML cascading styles, the default styles can be overridden by providing implicit values, or within another resource dictionary.

Using `BasedOn` styles, the previous style can be decomposed to two styles:

```
<Style TargetType="TextBlock" x:Key="TextBlockFontSetterStyle">
  <Setter Property="FontFamily" Value="{StaticResource FontFamily1}" />
  <Setter Property="FontSize" Value="20" />
  <Setter Property="FontStyle" Value="Italic" />
  <Setter Property="FontWeight" Value="Bold" />
</Style>
<Style TargetType="TextBlock" BasedOn="{StaticResource TextBlockFontSetterStyle}">
  <Setter Property="Foreground" Value="{StaticResource ForegroundBrush}" />
  <Setter Property="Effect" Value="{StaticResource Effect1}" />
  <Setter Property="TextTrimming" Value="WordEllipsis" />
</Style>
```

## Templates

Separating logic and presentation is a key design principle for Silverlight and WPF. Styles are perfect for making small changes to one or more controls, such as setting colors, fonts, and so on. Templates allow the designer to go further, and replace the entire visual tree of a control, or change how data is displayed or laid out in a `ListBox`.

 *While Visual Studio 2010 has no support for editing templates described in this section, this is one of those areas where Blend really shines. You should use Blend for template-related tasks.*

### Control Templates

*Control templates* redefine the template or visual tree for a control. Listing 8-11 shows a very simple `ControlTemplate` for a `Button`.

**LISTING 8-11:** ButtonTemplating.xaml

```xaml
<UserControl x:Class="TemplateDemos.ButtonTemplating"
    xmlns="http://schemas.microsoft.com/winfx/2006/xaml/presentation"
    xmlns:x="http://schemas.microsoft.com/winfx/2006/xaml"
    xmlns:d="http://schemas.microsoft.com/expression/blend/2008"
    xmlns:mc="http://schemas.openxmlformats.org/markup-compatibility/2006"
    mc:Ignorable="d"
    d:DesignHeight="300" d:DesignWidth="400">
    <UserControl.Resources>
        <ControlTemplate x:Key="ButtonControlTemplate1" TargetType="Button">
            <Grid>
                <Ellipse Fill="White" Stroke="Black"/>
                <ContentPresenter Margin="10" Content="{TemplateBinding Content}"/>
            </Grid>
        </ControlTemplate>
    </UserControl.Resources>

    <Grid x:Name="LayoutRoot" Background="White">
        <Button Content="Button" HorizontalAlignment="Center"
         VerticalAlignment="Center"
         Template="{StaticResource ButtonControlTemplate1}" />
        <Button Content="Button with looong text" HorizontalAlignment="Center"
         VerticalAlignment="Top" Template="{StaticResource ButtonControlTemplate1}"
         Margin="0,79,0,0" />

    </Grid>
</UserControl>
```

*Code file [ButtonTemplating.xaml] available for download at Wrox.com*

The `ControlTemplate` is stored as a resource; thus, it can be moved into an external resource dictionary. The template itself is very simple. It contains of a `Grid`, an `Ellipse` that fills the `Grid`, and a `ContentPresenter` control. The latter uses `TemplateBinding` to bind itself to the `Content` property of the `Button`. This technique can be used to wire up the internals of a control to the settings and properties that the control's user (the developer or designer) sets.

Thanks to the amazing adaptive layout capabilities of Silverlight and WPF, the previous `Button` already resizes itself to the size of the content. Since there is no explicit size set for the `Grid`, it takes on the size of its biggest child, the `ContentPresenter` — which is the size of the content set in the `Button`'s properties, plus a 10-pixel margin in every direction. In the next step, the `Ellipse` gets sized to the `Grid`, and, thus, the entire button is sized according to the size of the content, as shown in Figure 8-19.

**FIGURE 8-19:** Templating a Button

Even though the entire visual tree has been completely replaced, the new `Button` works as expected. `Click` events fire (as they should), but there is no visual indicator of clicking the mouse, or even hovering over the `Button`.

To allow complete separation between logic and appearance, Silverlight introduced the concept of *visual states*, which are basically sets of changes to the properties within the template, controlled by the control's logic. Visual states can define animations (for example, the size of the button can pulse while the mouse is over it), transitions (for example, smoothly change the background color when mouse is hovered), or just plain property setters (for example, make the border wider when the button is focused).

Visual states are controlled by the VisualStateManager. To transition between two states from within your code, you can use the GotoState method, as shown here:

```
VisualStateManager.GoToState(control, stateName, useTransitions);
```

This moves the control control to the state specified by the string parameter stateName. The useTransitions parameter is Boolean — setting it to false skips the transition animations between the states.

So, the logic determines the transitions between states. But how do you define the states themselves? Listing 8-12 shows an example that has transitions and property setters.

**LISTING 8-12:** ButtonTemplating.xaml

```xml
<UserControl x:Class="TemplateDemos.ButtonTemplating"
  xmlns="http://schemas.microsoft.com/winfx/2006/xaml/presentation"
  xmlns:x="http://schemas.microsoft.com/winfx/2006/xaml"
  xmlns:d="http://schemas.microsoft.com/expression/blend/2008"
  xmlns:mc="http://schemas.openxmlformats.org/markup-compatibility/2006"
  mc:Ignorable="d"
  d:DesignHeight="300" d:DesignWidth="400">
  <UserControl.Resources>
    <ControlTemplate x:Key="ButtonControlTemplate1" TargetType="Button">
      <Grid>
        <VisualStateManager.VisualStateGroups>
          <VisualStateGroup x:Name="CommonStates">
            <VisualStateGroup.Transitions>
              <VisualTransition GeneratedDuration="0:0:0.3"/>
            </VisualStateGroup.Transitions>
            <VisualState x:Name="Normal"/>
            <VisualState x:Name="Pressed">
              <Storyboard>
                <ColorAnimationUsingKeyFrames
                 Storyboard.TargetProperty="(Shape.Fill).(SolidColorBrush.Color)"
                  Storyboard.TargetName="ellipse">
                  <EasingColorKeyFrame KeyTime="0" Value="#FFF9FF00"/>
                </ColorAnimationUsingKeyFrames>
              </Storyboard>
            </VisualState>
            <VisualState x:Name="Disabled"/>
            <VisualState x:Name="MouseOver">
              <Storyboard>
                <ColorAnimationUsingKeyFrames
                 Storyboard.TargetProperty="(Shape.Fill).(SolidColorBrush.Color)"
                  Storyboard.TargetName="ellipse">
                  <EasingColorKeyFrame KeyTime="0" Value="#FFFDFFB3"/>
                </ColorAnimationUsingKeyFrames>
```

```xml
              </Storyboard>
            </VisualState>
          </VisualStateGroup>
          <VisualStateGroup x:Name="FocusStates">
            <VisualState x:Name="Unfocused"/>
            <VisualState x:Name="Focused">
              <Storyboard>
                <DoubleAnimationUsingKeyFrames
                  Storyboard.TargetProperty="(Shape.StrokeThickness)"
                  Storyboard.TargetName="ellipse">
                  <EasingDoubleKeyFrame KeyTime="0" Value="2"/>
                </DoubleAnimationUsingKeyFrames>
              </Storyboard>
            </VisualState>
          </VisualStateGroup>
        </VisualStateManager.VisualStateGroups>
        <Ellipse x:Name="ellipse" Fill="White" Stroke="Black"/>
        <ContentPresenter Margin="10" Content="{TemplateBinding Content}"/>
      </Grid>
    </ControlTemplate>
  </UserControl.Resources>

  <Grid x:Name="LayoutRoot" Background="White">
    <Button Content="Button" HorizontalAlignment="Center"
      VerticalAlignment="Center"
      Template="{StaticResource ButtonControlTemplate1}" />
    <Button Content="Button with looong text" HorizontalAlignment="Center"
      VerticalAlignment="Top" Template="{StaticResource
      ButtonControlTemplate1}" Margin="0,79,0,0" />
  </Grid>
</UserControl>
```

*Code file [ButtonTemplating.xaml] available for download at Wrox.com*

This is the same sample as shown previously, with the added visual state features. The visual states are grouped in `VisualStateGroups`. There are two `VisualStateGroups` for a `Button`: `CommonStates` (`Normal`, `Pressed`, `Disabled`, and `MouseOver`) and `FocusedStates` (`Focused` and `Unfocused`). There is also an implicit `Base` state that essentially represents the visual tree as set within the `ControlTemplate`.

Only one state can be active at a certain time within a `VisualStateGroup`. Note that `Pressed` also implies `MouseOver`, so there is no contradiction here — but the designer may have to copy some settings from `MouseOver` to `Pressed` if the two states change different properties, in order to keep the consistency of the "feel."

While there can be only one active state within a `VisualStateGroup`, the `VisualStateGroups` themselves are independent. A `Button` can be in the `Focused` and the `MouseOver` states at the same time. If the two states change the same properties over the `Base` state, the resulting behavior is undefined. Luckily, Blend warns about this, as shown in Figure 8-20.

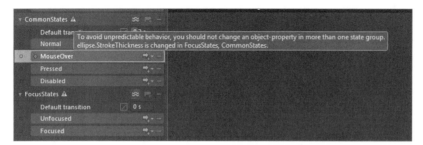

**FIGURE 8-20:** Blend warns about conflicting Visual State settings.

Here is the code snippet again for the Focused state:

```
<VisualState x:Name="Focused">
  <Storyboard>
    <DoubleAnimationUsingKeyFrames
        Storyboard.TargetProperty="(Shape.StrokeThickness)"
        Storyboard.TargetName="ellipse">
      <EasingDoubleKeyFrame KeyTime="0" Value="2"/>
    </DoubleAnimationUsingKeyFrames>
  </Storyboard>
</VisualState>
```

This code snippet simply sets the StrokeThickness property for the Ellipse within the Button to 2, in the Focused state. The properties themselves are set via Storyboards. A Storyboard is an animation feature, so it may seem like an overkill for simply setting properties, but Storyboards allow for advanced (and, if misused, very annoying) features — such as pulsating the color of the button within the MouseOver state indefinitely.

The XAML for the MouseOver and Pressed states look pretty similar to the previous one. The difference is that there is a transition defined for the entire state group:

```
<VisualStateGroup.Transitions>
  <VisualTransition GeneratedDuration="0:0:0.3"/>
</VisualStateGroup.Transitions>
```

This instructs Silverlight that when the properties change within the VisualStateGroup, the change should occur as a smooth linear animation, and last 0.3 seconds. Easings can also be applied to make the transition non-linear, or even bouncy. Visual states can also have more specific transitions. Separate transitions can be defined for entering or exiting a state, or even between two specific states.

 *Visual states can also be used to represent the states of a user control, or even an entire application.*

A `Style` can also be defined to apply this template to all `Buttons`. After all, the `ControlTemplate` is nothing more than a property, and properties can be set from styles:

```
<Style TargetType="Button">
  <Setter Property="Template" Value="{StaticResource ButtonControlTemplate1}"/>
</Style>
```

After including this code snippet in the `Resources` part of the `UserControl` (or an external resource file, along with the referenced `ButtonControlTemplate1` resource), the `Template` attributes of the `Buttons` can be removed. The style applies for all `Buttons`, so the look and feel of your little application will stay the same, with the additional benefit of new buttons automatically skinned similarly.

## Templates for Data Binding

Templates are cool for re-skinning controls, but where they really shine is data binding. For example, apart from its control template, a `ListBox` has three more templates to define:

➤ `ItemTemplate` — This defines how a `ListBox` item should look.

➤ `ItemsPanel` — This defines the layout panel that contains the items.

➤ `ItemContainerStyle` —Although it is not strictly a template, the style (and, therefore, the template) of the `ListItems` can be changed via `ItemContainerStyle`.

Suppose you want to list the authors from the earlier data binding sample in a nice horizontal `Listbox`. The code-behind is the same as the `Author` sample was earlier (`ListDatabinding.cs`) — the only difference is that this time the items will be displayed in a `ListBox`, so the `ItemsSource` of the `ListBox` called `myListBox` must be set at the end of the constructor.

```
myListBox.ItemsSource = authors;
```

The XAML is pretty simple so far, as shown in Listing 8-13.

**Available for download on Wrox.com**

**LISTING 8-13: DatabindingTemplates.xaml**

```
<UserControl x:Class="TemplateDemos.DatabindingTemplates"
    xmlns="http://schemas.microsoft.com/winfx/2006/xaml/presentation"
    xmlns:x="http://schemas.microsoft.com/winfx/2006/xaml"
    xmlns:d="http://schemas.microsoft.com/expression/blend/2000"
    xmlns:mc="http://schemas.openxmlformats.org/markup-compatibility/2006"
    mc:Ignorable="d"
    d:DesignHeight="300" d:DesignWidth="400">

  <Grid x:Name="LayoutRoot" Background="White">
    <ListBox x:Name="myListBox" Height="88" Margin="8,8,8,0"
      VerticalAlignment="Top"/>

  </Grid>
</UserControl>
```

*Code file [DatabindingTemplates.xaml] available for download at Wrox.com*

However, running the code results in a rather disappointing screen display, as shown in Figure 8-21.

What happened? The ListBox had no idea what to display for each Author, so it called (via the ContentPresenter control) the ToString() method for each Author object, and displayed all of the results below each other. To display the Authors themselves, the ItemTemplate must be defined. Listing 8-14 shows one way to do it.

**FIGURE 8-21:** First try at binding to a ListBox

Available for download on Wrox.com

**LISTING 8-14:** DatabindingTemplates.xaml

```xaml
<UserControl x:Class="TemplateDemos.DatabindingTemplates"
    xmlns="http://schemas.microsoft.com/winfx/2006/xaml/presentation"
    xmlns:x="http://schemas.microsoft.com/winfx/2006/xaml"
    xmlns:d="http://schemas.microsoft.com/expression/blend/2008"
    xmlns:mc="http://schemas.openxmlformats.org/markup-compatibility/2006"
    mc:Ignorable="d"
    d:DesignHeight="300" d:DesignWidth="400">
  <UserControl.Resources>
    <DataTemplate x:Key="AuthorTemplate">
      <StackPanel Width="100">
        <TextBlock Text="{Binding Name}" x:Name="tbName" />
        <TextBlock Text="{Binding Chapters}" TextTrimming="WordEllipsis" />
      </StackPanel>
    </DataTemplate>
  </UserControl.Resources>

  <Grid x:Name="LayoutRoot" Background="White">
    <ListBox x:Name="myListBox" Height="160" Margin="8,8,8,0"
        VerticalAlignment="Top"
        ItemTemplate="{StaticResource AuthorTemplate}"/>
  </Grid>
</UserControl>
```

*Code file [DatabindingTemplates.xaml] available for download at Wrox.com*

Just as in the case of a ControlTemplate, a visual tree is defined within the DataTemplate. In this case, a 100-pixel-wide StackPanel hosts two TextBlocks, one for the Name, and the other for the Chapter property. This visual tree is created for every item in the ListBox, with the DataContext of the DataTemplates set to the current Author. Running the code now gets a slightly better result, as shown in Figure 8-22.

**FIGURE 8-22:** Using DataTemplates in a ListBox

The items look okay now, but they are still arranged vertically. This is where ItemsPanelTemplate helps. If nothing is defined, the ListBox uses a VirtualizingStackPanel to arrange its items. VirtualizingStackPanel is like a StackPanel, except that it performs better with high item-count scenarios by creating the visual tree only for those items that are visible in the current scroll window. By redefining the `ItemsPanelTemplate`, the default `VirtualizingStackPanel` can be replaced with any container item — such as a `WrapPanel`, or even a `RadialPanel` that arranges the items in a circle. However, for this example, a `StackPanel` with a horizontal layout will do.

```xml
<UserControl.Resources>
  <DataTemplate x:Key="AuthorTemplate">
    <StackPanel Width="100">
      <TextBlock Text="{Binding Name}" x:Name="tbName" />
      <TextBlock Text="{Binding Chapters}" TextTrimming="WordEllipsis" />
    </StackPanel>
  </DataTemplate>
  <ItemsPanelTemplate x:Key="ItemsPanelTemplate1">
    <StackPanel Orientation="Horizontal"/>
  </ItemsPanelTemplate>
</UserControl.Resources>
```

And to reference the newly created `ItemsPanelTemplate`, the declaration of the `ListBox` changes to the following:

```xml
<ListBox x:Name="myListBox" Height="160" Margin="8,8,8,0" VerticalAlignment="Top"
    ItemTemplate="{StaticResource AuthorTemplate}"
    ItemsPanel="{StaticResource ItemsPanelTemplate1}"/>
```

The result can be seen on Figure 8-23.

The selected item still retains the default selection border. This is where the `ItemsContainer` style comes into the scene. The default style defines the following `VisualStateGroups`:

**FIGURE 8-23:** Using ItemsPanelTemplate to place items horizontally

➤ `CommonStates` for mouseover and disabled

➤ `FocusStates` for focused/unfocused look

➤ `LayoutStates` for adding fancy transitions when an item is loaded or unloaded (that is, removed)

➤ `SelectionStates` for handling selections

The sample to demonstrate `ItemContainerStyle` rotates the selected item 180 degrees with a little bouncy effect. It is fun, but not something to use in a business application. Listing 8-15 shows the final XAML illustrating `ItemTemplate`, `ItemsPanelTemplate`, and `ItemContainerStyle`.

**LISTING 8-15:** DatabindingTemplates.xaml

```xml
<UserControl x:Class="TemplateDemos.DatabindingTemplates"
    xmlns="http://schemas.microsoft.com/winfx/2006/xaml/presentation"
    xmlns:x="http://schemas.microsoft.com/winfx/2006/xaml"
```

*continues*

**LISTING 8-15** *(continued)*

```xml
    xmlns:d="http://schemas.microsoft.com/expression/blend/2008"
    xmlns:mc="http://schemas.openxmlformats.org/markup-compatibility/2006"
    mc:Ignorable="d"
    d:DesignHeight="300" d:DesignWidth="400">
<UserControl.Resources>
  <DataTemplate x:Key="AuthorTemplate">
    <StackPanel Width="100">
      <TextBlock Text="{Binding Name}" x:Name="tbName" />
      <TextBlock Text="{Binding Chapters}" TextTrimming="WordEllipsis" />
    </StackPanel>
  </DataTemplate>
  <ItemsPanelTemplate x:Key="ItemsPanelTemplate1">
    <StackPanel Orientation="Horizontal"/>
  </ItemsPanelTemplate>
  <Style x:Key="ListBoxItemStyle1" TargetType="ListBoxItem">
    <Setter Property="Padding" Value="3"/>
    <Setter Property="HorizontalContentAlignment" Value="Left"/>
    <Setter Property="VerticalContentAlignment" Value="Top"/>
    <Setter Property="Background" Value="Transparent"/>
    <Setter Property="BorderThickness" Value="1"/>
    <Setter Property="TabNavigation" Value="Local"/>
    <Setter Property="Template">
      <Setter.Value>
        <ControlTemplate TargetType="ListBoxItem">
          <Grid Background="{TemplateBinding Background}">
            <VisualStateManager.VisualStateGroups>
              <VisualStateGroup x:Name="SelectionStates">
                <VisualStateGroup.Transitions>
                  <VisualTransition GeneratedDuration="0:0:0.5">
                    <VisualTransition.GeneratedEasingFunction>
                      <ElasticEase EasingMode="EaseOut"/>
                    </VisualTransition.GeneratedEasingFunction>
                  </VisualTransition>
                </VisualStateGroup.Transitions>
                <VisualState x:Name="Unselected"/>
                <VisualState x:Name="Selected">
                  <Storyboard>
                    <DoubleAnimationUsingKeyFrames Storyboard.TargetProperty=
"(UIElement.RenderTransform).(TransformGroup.Children)[2].
    (RotateTransform.Angle)"
Storyboard.TargetName="contentPresenter">
                      <EasingDoubleKeyFrame KeyTime="0" Value="180"/>
                    </DoubleAnimationUsingKeyFrames>
                  </Storyboard>
                </VisualState>
              </VisualStateGroup>
            </VisualStateManager.VisualStateGroups>
            <ContentPresenter x:Name="contentPresenter"
              ContentTemplate="{TemplateBinding ContentTemplate}"
              Content="{TemplateBinding Content}"
              HorizontalAlignment="{TemplateBinding HorizontalContentAlignment}"
```

```
              Margin="{TemplateBinding Padding}"
              RenderTransformOrigin="0.5,0.5">
              <ContentPresenter.RenderTransform>
                <TransformGroup>
                  <ScaleTransform/>
                  <SkewTransform/>
                  <RotateTransform/>
                  <TranslateTransform/>
                </TransformGroup>
              </ContentPresenter.RenderTransform>
            </ContentPresenter>
          </Grid>
        </ControlTemplate>
      </Setter.Value>
    </Setter>
  </Style>
</UserControl.Resources>

<Grid x:Name="LayoutRoot" Background="White">
  <ListBox x:Name="myListBox" Height="55" Margin="8,8,8,0"
VerticalAlignment="Top" ItemTemplate="{StaticResource AuthorTemplate}"
ItemsPanel="{StaticResource ItemsPanelTemplate1}"
ItemContainerStyle="{StaticResource ListBoxItemStyle1}"/>

</Grid>
</UserControl>
```

*Code file [DatabindingTemplates.xaml] available for download at Wrox.com*

The running application looks like Figure 8-24. Notice how the code-behind stayed the same, but the look and feel of the application has completely changed.

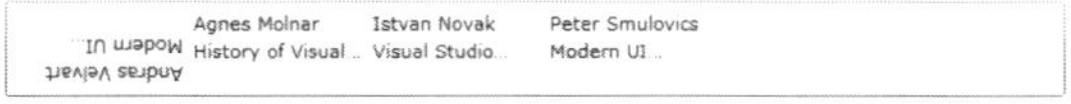

**FIGURE 8-24:** The Selected Item is now displayed upside down

## Animations

Although animations are often considered useless eye candy and unnecessary bling, when designed by professionals and in a discrete manner, animations play a vital part in enhancing the overall user experience of a product. In the real world, transitions don't happen instantaneously (with a few exceptions, such as in the case of turning on a lamp). They have speed, acceleration and deceleration. Animations and transitions can also help direct the attention of the user, explain why things happen (for example, when you minimize a window to the taskbar, the short animation shows where the window disappeared to), and generally make the virtual experience feel smoother and better by bringing it closer to the real world.

In Silverlight, animations are technically nothing more than a gradual change of properties over time. Silverlight (and WPF) animations are time-based instead of frame-based. This means that if an animation is set to last 2 seconds, it will take exactly 2 seconds, even if the computer is very busy, and can only display a few frames while the animation runs. In addition to the fact that a time-based animation is more predictable, it also allows the Silverlight run-time to continuously adapt to the computer's performance by skipping or interpolating animation frames.

## Storyboards and Animations

The best tool for creating complex animations is Blend. However, to understand how animations work, it is enough to start with a simple example in XAML, as shown in Listing 8-16.

**LISTING 8-16:** BouncingCircle.xaml

```xaml
<UserControl
    xmlns="http://schemas.microsoft.com/winfx/2006/xaml/presentation"
    xmlns:x="http://schemas.microsoft.com/winfx/2006/xaml"
    xmlns:d="http://schemas.microsoft.com/expression/blend/2008"
    xmlns:mc="http://schemas.openxmlformats.org/markup-compatibility/2006"
    mc:Ignorable="d"
    xmlns:i="clr-namespace:System.Windows.Interactivity;assembly=
        System.Windows.Interactivity"
    xmlns:im="clr-
     namespace:Microsoft.Expression.Interactivity.Media;
     assembly=Microsoft.Expression.Interactions"
    x:Class="AnimationDemo.BouncingCircle"
    d:DesignHeight="300" d:DesignWidth="400">

    <UserControl.Resources>
      <Storyboard x:Name="Storyboard1">
        <DoubleAnimation Storyboard.TargetProperty="(Canvas.Left)"
          Storyboard.TargetName="ellipse" To="320" />
        <DoubleAnimation Storyboard.TargetProperty="(Canvas.Top)"
          Storyboard.TargetName="ellipse" To="230" />
      </Storyboard>
    </UserControl.Resources>
    <Canvas x:Name="LayoutRoot">
      <!-- This Action launches the storyboard when the left mouse button
           is pressed in the Canvas -->
      <i:Interaction.Triggers>
        <i:EventTrigger EventName="MouseLeftButtonDown">
          <im:ControlStoryboardAction Storyboard="{StaticResource Storyboard1}"/>
        </i:EventTrigger>
      </i:Interaction.Triggers>
      <Ellipse x:Name="ellipse" Fill="Black" Height="50" Canvas.Left="20"
        Canvas.Top="20" Width="50" />
    </Canvas>
</UserControl>
```

*Code file [BouncingCircle.xaml] available for download at Wrox.com*

This code generates the animation as illustrated in Figure 8-25. To start the animation, you need to click on the ellipse. The click is handled by a `ControlStoryboardAction`. The Action requires the `Microsoft.Expression.Interactions` assembly, which you can add via the Add Reference dialog, on the .NET tab. The assembly is part of the Blend SDK. If you do not have Blend or the

Blend SDK installed, you can still launch the Storyboard from code-behind by adding `Storyboard1.Begin();` to the end of the constructor. You'll learn more about triggers, actions and behaviors later in this chapter.

The root animation entity is called a `Storyboard`. The `Storyboard` has one or more child `Animations` that, in turn, animate a single property on a single element. In the previous sample, `Storyboard1` has two animations that control the `Canvas.Left` and `Canvas.Top` properties of the `Ellipse`. A single `Storyboard` can have child animations that affect properties of different elements.

**FIGURE 8-25:** Simple animation

Child animations share the same clock. This means that starting the animations happens simultaneously. A `Storyboard` can also be repeated, reversed, seeked, paused, or the common clock's speed can be changed (via the `SpeedRatio` property), thus making the entire `Storyboard` run slower or faster.

Animations can change properties of any type. However, they only work with dependency properties. There are different animations for different property types:

➤   `DoubleAnimation` for animating double properties (such as position and opacity).

➤   `ColorAnimation` for animating colors (`Brushes`).

➤   `PointAnimation` for `Points`.

➤   `ObjectAnimation` for changing properties of other types. `ObjectAnimation` does not support interpolation, though, because you cannot only set 30 percent of the `Visibility` property to `Collapsed`.

Another important aspect of Silverlight and WPF animations is that the `From` property can be omitted. In this case, the value will navigate from its current value to the specified `To` value. This feature helps a lot in situations when an animation must start before another one is finished — as in the case of a panel sliding out when hovered over, and sliding in when the mouse leaves it. Without relative animations, extra code would have to be written to stop the panel from jumping when the mouse is moved off it before it fully opens.

To make animations even more natural, Silverlight has keyframe and easing functionality. *Keyframes* help in cases when a simple value-to-value animation is not enough, and several, precisely controlled in-between points are needed. Keyframes can also be used for discrete jumps between values, without interpolation.

*Easings* can make an animation slow down, bounce, or even behave spring-like. For example, by adding `BounceEase` easing function to the previous `Canvas.Top` animation, you can achieve the bouncing ball effect, as shown in Figure 8-26. Here is the part of the XAML that has changed:

```
<DoubleAnimation Storyboard.TargetProperty="(Canvas.Top)"
  Storyboard.TargetName="ellipse" To="230" >
  <DoubleAnimation.EasingFunction>
```

```
         <BounceEase EasingMode="EaseOut" Bounces="4"/>
      </DoubleAnimation.EasingFunction>
   </DoubleAnimation>
```

Easings can be applied to the beginning of the animation
(EaseIn), end (EaseOut) of the animation, or to both
(EaseInOut). There are a lot of built-in easings available for
Silverlight. Figure 8-27 shows how they appear in Blend. Just
like the built-in layout containers, these cover most of what
a "normal" application needs. However, if these don't satisfy
the needs of the designer, new easings can easily be created by
inheriting from the EasingFunctionBase class.

**FIGURE 8-26:** BounceEase applied to
the animation

## Transformations

*Transformations* allow moving, rotating, scaling (changing the size), and
skewing any UI element. Silverlight 3 also introduced a PlaneProjection
transform that can rotate two-dimensional elements in three-dimension.

The animation sample shown earlier is created for easy understanding,
but is not ideal in terms of performance. The reason for this is that the
bouncing circle sample animates the Canvas.Left and Canvas.Top
properties. This, in turn, triggers a recalculation of the layout for the
Canvas and the Ellipse.

Even though it is probably not noticeable in the sample, layout recalculation
is an expensive operation — the affected part of the visual tree must be
traversed with the MeasureOverride and ArrangeOverride methods. It
is easy to imagine that in the case of a complicated scene, this will take
considerable amount of time, making the animation jerky.

Here is the revised Storyboard of the bouncing circle sample, using
TranslateTransform to move the Ellipse:

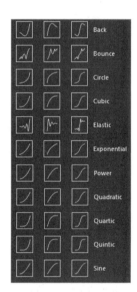

**FIGURE 8-27:** Built-in
animation easings in
Blend

```
<UserControl.Resources>
  <Storyboard x:Name="Storyboard1">
    <DoubleAnimation Storyboard.TargetProperty="X"
      Storyboard.TargetName="ellipseTranslate" To="320" />
    <DoubleAnimation Storyboard.TargetProperty="Y"
      Storyboard.TargetName="ellipseTranslate" To="230" >
      <DoubleAnimation.EasingFunction>
        <BounceEase EasingMode="EaseOut"/>
      </DoubleAnimation.EasingFunction>
    </DoubleAnimation>
  </Storyboard>
</UserControl.Resources>
```

The animations refer to the element `ellipseTranslate`, which is defined within the `Ellipse` tag:

```
<Ellipse x:Name="ellipse" Fill="Black" Height="50"
  Canvas.Left="20" Canvas.Top="20" Width="50" >
  <Ellipse.RenderTransform>
    <TranslateTransform x:Name="ellipseTranslate" />
  </Ellipse.RenderTransform>
</Ellipse>
```

Changing the size, position, rotation, or other transform properties via Silverlight's render transformations does not trigger a layout recalculation. This results in much less work for the CPU to do; therefore, more complex animations can be performed before the performance starts to degrade. WPF has the notion of *layout transformations* that do affect the layout — this can be very useful in certain cases. For Silverlight, the Silverlight Toolkit has a `LayoutTransformer` that does pretty much the same thing.

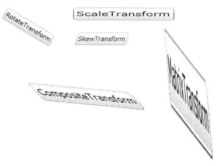

Figure 8-28 shows the available transformations in Silverlight, except `TranslateTransform`, which simply relocates the element.

**FIGURE 8-28:** Render transformations in Silverlight

# Media

Media in Silverlight includes playing back audio and video files, access to the microphone and the webcam on the computer, DRM, and Deep Zoom. This section describes the basics of Silverlight media.

## Audio and Video Playback

Just playing an audio or video file is very simple when using the `MediaElement` control. When compiled and run, this code plays back a Designer-versus-Developer video from Channel9:

```
<UserControl x:Class="MediaDemos.MainPage"
    xmlns="http://schemas.microsoft.com/winfx/2006/xaml/presentation"
    xmlns:x="http://schemas.microsoft.com/winfx/2006/xaml"
    xmlns:d="http://schemas.microsoft.com/expression/blend/2008"
    xmlns:mc="http://schemas.openxmlformats.org/markup-compatibility/2006"
    mc:Ignorable="d"
    d:DesignHeight="300" d:DesignWidth="400">

  <Grid x:Name="LayoutRoot" Background="White">
    <MediaElement Source="http://mschnlnine.vo.llnwd.net/d1/ch9/0/8/7/7/7/4/
        SL3Expression3Launch_ch9.wmv"
        Stretch="Uniform" />
  </Grid>
</UserControl>
```

The `MediaElement` can play both audio and video files. It supports a number of delivery methods (including progressive download, Windows Media Streaming over HTTP, ASX, Server Side Playlist, or a custom `MediaStreamSource`, where the developer can implement his or her own way of delivering content to a decoder).

As for the encoding format, Windows Media Audio (WMA) Standard and Professional, as well as Windows Media Video 7, 8, and 9, are supported from the Microsoft codec family. For audio, MP3 is also supported, and Silverlight can handle H.264 (which is the most widespread high-quality online video format) as well.

 *For a complete reference of supported delivery methods, containers, and codecs, check the Silverlight SDK documentation.*

`MediaElement` can `Play`, `Pause`, and `Seek` media, or `Stop` playing it. It fires events to track playing status, buffering, and current position within the media file. It is also possible to change the `Volume`. The `Stretch` property behaves exactly as in the case of `Viewbox`.

`MediaElement` is a rectangular UI element. Silverlight has a `VideoBrush` that can be associated with a `MediaElement` using the `SourceName` property. If a `VideoBrush` is used to fill an element, or even as the `Stroke` of a shape, the video will play within the element. Here is an interesting effect when the `VideoBrush` is used as the `Foreground` brush for a `TextBlock`:

```
<UserControl.Resources>
  <VideoBrush x:Key="myVideoBrush"
    SourceName="myMediaElement" Stretch="UniformToFill"/>
</UserControl.Resources>
<Grid x:Name="LayoutRoot" Background="White">
  <MediaElement Visibility="Collapsed" x:Name="myMediaElement"
    Source="http://mschnlnine.vo.llnwd.net/d1/ch9/0/8/7/7/7/4/
    SL3Expression3Launch_ch9.wmv"
    Stretch="Uniform" />
  <TextBlock Text="Text with a VideoBrush"
    Foreground="{StaticResource myVideoBrush}"
    FontFamily="Arial Black" FontWeight="Bold"
    FontSize="72" />
</Grid>
```

Figure 8-29 shows the output.

# Text with a VideoBrush

**FIGURE 8-29:** Text with a VideoBrush

Another sample that shows off the power of the `VideoBrush` is the video puzzle game that can be reached at `http://demo.themsteam.com/videopuzzle/`. Figure 8-30 shows the game.

**FIGURE 8-30:** The Silverlight Video puzzle developed by MS Team LLC. (Copyright 2004-2008, MS Team LLC)

## Deep Zoom

Silverlight's unique Deep Zoom capability (it is not available in WPF) enables visitors to browse through hundreds of high-resolution images very quickly and smoothly. "High resolution" here means giga- or even terrapixels. The new Bing Maps (Figures 8-31 and 8-32) uses Deep Zoom to provide a smooth zooming experience, starting from the whole World, and zooming in to a level where license plates and people's faces could be recognized if they weren't blurred for privacy reasons.

**FIGURE 8-31:** The Earth on Bing maps

**FIGURE 8-32:** Bing Maps after zooming in to Streetside view

Deep Zoom is based on the Seadragon technology acquired by Microsoft. A key attribute of the technology is that the performance and required bandwidth only depends on the amount of pixels on the screen, not on the size of the images displayed. Seadragon performs its magic by creating small tiles of the images at different resolutions, and utilizing advanced heuristics that only downloads the required tiles of those images that are on the screen.

Deep Zoom (or rather, the `MultiScaleImage` control) can also handle lots of `SubImages` at the same time. Approximately 1,000 images is where the performance starts to degrade with Silverlight 3. These `SubImages` can be moved around the viewport, faded out, and filtered with code, thus creating a truly unique experience for finding and browsing images on the web. Figure 8-33 shows an example.

**FIGURE 8-33:** Zoomery (www.zoomery.com) displaying 223 images out of a 5,684-image database, using Deep Zoom.

## Smooth Streaming

*Smooth streaming* (or *adaptive streaming*) is one of the most interesting delivery methods for video on the web. As the bandwidth available at people's homes grows bigger and bigger, user demand for really high-quality video increases. Silverlight aims to be the best solution for high-quality online video.

There are several problems with online video today that smooth streaming set out to solve. One such problem is network bandwidth. While HD quality video can be transmitted on 2-3 megabits per second, and a lot of Internet connections exceed this bandwidth, there are tons of broadband connections out there that are slower. If the available bandwidth is not enough for the stream being played, there are constant interruptions while buffering occurs. Also, the actual bandwidth between the player and the media server can vary greatly — the media server can be overwhelmed, or the end user may have a fraction of his or her previous bandwidth when others on the same network (same household, for example) are also downloading huge files.

Another important factor that contributes to the end user's playback experience is the computing power of the computer used. Decoding and displaying HD video is a very computationally intensive task — the color value of millions of pixels must be calculated at least 30 times per second. Any time the computer is not up to this task (for example, the CPU is busy with something else, or the computer was not powerful enough to begin with), the glitch is noticeable.

It is also difficult to seek within a movie. Certain players using progressive download don't even allow seeking to the end of the movie, until the entire file has been downloaded. This not only frustrates the user, but wastes the bandwidth of the content provider, as well if the user only wants to see the last five minutes.

To solve these problems, content producers encode the video for different bandwidths. However, in order to choose the optimal bandwidth, the user must know a lot of technical details, and maybe switch between the "high bandwidth" and "low bandwidth" versions manually several times during a movie.

Smooth streaming also requires the content to be encoded with multiple bitrates. The big advantage is that smooth streaming continuously monitors the available bandwidth and the CPU load — and, if any of those factors indicate that a slower bandwidth version is needed, the smooth streaming player automatically and seamlessly switches to the lower-quality version. The end result is that users get the best possible continuous playback, even during rough bandwidth and CPU conditions.

Another advantage is that buffering is virtually eliminated. When a movie starts, or a seek is performed, the player automatically switches to the lowest possible bitrate. This makes seeking pretty much instantaneous — finding the right spot in the movie is just like doing it with a DVD player. After the movie has been playing for a few seconds with the low quality, the heuristics automatically increase the quality as long as the network and the CPU can handle it.

In the case of a live broadcast, smooth streaming users can pause and rewind the live video, while retaining the previously mentioned advantages. Live encoding is, however, much more difficult than encoding for a video-on-demand service. Expression Encoder 4 can perform live smooth streaming, but you will need a 6-8 core CPU to perform live encoding, and even then you have to switch off a lot of quality optimizations and limit the broadcast to just a few bandwidths. The best bet today is to have a dedicated hardware encoder.

*To experience smooth streaming yourself, go to* `http://www.iis.net/media/` `experiencesmoothstreaming.`

## Webcam and Microphone Access

Silverlight 4 introduced a much-requested feature: webcam and microphone access. A simple `Webcam` application has the XAML file shown in Listing 8-17 and the `.cs` file shown in Listing 8-18.

**LISTING 8-17:** Webcam.xaml

```xaml
<UserControl x:Class="MediaDemos.Webcam"
    xmlns="http://schemas.microsoft.com/winfx/2006/xaml/presentation"
    xmlns:x="http://schemas.microsoft.com/winfx/2006/xaml"
    xmlns:d="http://schemas.microsoft.com/expression/blend/2008"
    xmlns:mc="http://schemas.openxmlformats.org/markup-compatibility/2006"
    mc:Ignorable="d"
    d:DesignHeight="300" d:DesignWidth="400">

    <Grid x:Name="LayoutRoot" Background="White">
      <Button Content="Enable Camera" Click="Button_Click" />
      <Ellipse x:Name="ellipse" Stroke="Black" StrokeThickness="1" />
    </Grid>
</UserControl>
```

*Code file [Webcam.xaml] available for download at Wrox.com*

**LISTING 8-18:** Webcam.cs

```csharp
using System.Windows;
using System.Windows.Controls;
using System.Windows.Media;

namespace MediaDemos
{
  public partial class Webcam : UserControl
  {

    private VideoBrush webcamBrush;

    public Webcam()
```

```
  {
    InitializeComponent();
  }

  private void Button_Click(object sender, RoutedEventArgs e)
  {
    if (!CaptureDeviceConfiguration.RequestDeviceAccess())
    {
      MessageBox.Show("In that case, I won't show anything for you");
      return;
    }

    var videoDevice = CaptureDeviceConfiguration.GetDefaultVideoCaptureDevice();
    var cs = new CaptureSource();
    cs.VideoCaptureDevice = videoDevice;
    webcamBrush = new VideoBrush();
    webcamBrush.SetSource(cs);
    ellipse.Fill = webcamBrush;
    cs.Start();
  }
 }
}
```

*Code file [Webcam.cs] available for download at Wrox.com*

Figure 8-34 shows how running the application uncovers the face of yours truly.

To start using the webcam, the user must allow access to the capture devices. For privacy reasons, access can only be requested from a user-initiated action. Thus, you need a button and have its `Click` event handled. If the request is successful, the default video device is used, and a `CaptureSource` object is set up. Finally, a `VideoBrush` is created with the `CaptureSource` object, and capturing is started.

Silverlight can also enumerate all the video and audio capture devices on the system with the `CaptureDeviceConfiguration` `.GetAvailableVideoCaptureDevices` and `GetAvailableAudioCaptureDevices` methods. The result of these method calls can be presented to the user, who can choose the video or audio capture device to use.

**FIGURE 8-34:** Testing out the Webcam application

Silverlight also allows access to the captured video and audio data via the `VideoSink` and `AudioSink` abstract classes. Inheriting from these classes and overriding the `OnSample` method or the `OnSamples` method gets the raw video and audio data. Silverlight does not provide any built-in feature to encode or transfer the captured media — it is up to the developer to create this functionality.

# Networking

Because Silverlight is a client-side technology that (mostly) lives in the browser, it must connect to the server (or the cloud) for data to work with. Silverlight offers a range of communication tools — from low-level sockets, through HTTP connections, to WCF and WCF RIA Services. These networking stacks work similar to what .NET developers are used to from the "big" framework. However, there are two key differences because of the lightweight, sandboxed, and browser-based nature of Silverlight.

The first difference is *security*. By default, Silverlight (just like Flash or JavaScript) only allows connections back to the server it was downloaded from. The reason for this restriction is to mitigate threats like denial of service (DoS) attacks, domain name server (DNS) attacks, reverse-tunnel attacks, cross-site attacks, and so on. If a server wants to allow a Silverlight (or Flash) application to use its resources, it can have a policy file that controls the access. Silverlight also takes Flash's `crossdomain.xml` files into account, therefore making those sites available to Silverlight that have only been allowed to be accessed via the Flash `crossdomain.xml` file. Policy files can also be used by socket connections, but, in this case, the policy files will be downloaded from a different socket port.

The second important difference between standard .NET and Silverlight network access is that in Silverlight, *every server communication is asynchronous*. This may seem a bit restrictive, but synchronous server communication would block the UI thread most of the time, stopping animations or even freezing the browser — so a background thread and callback mechanism would have to be created for most cases anyway.

## Communicating via HTTP

Apart from the familiar `WebClient` class, there are two completely separate network stacks for HTTP communication: `BrowserHttpStack` and `ClientHttpStack`.

As the name implies, `BrowserHttpStack` utilizes the hosting browser to make HTTP calls to the web. This means that browser restrictions (such as maximum number of connections to a given server, cookies, and so on) are in effect for the browser stack. Also, the browser stack only allows `GET` and `POST` for the HTTP method — `PUT` or any other verbs are result in a `NotSupportedException`. To create a `WebRequest` object that uses the browser stack, use the `WebRequestCreator.BrowserHttp` class:

```
WebRequest rq = WebRequestCreator.BrowserHttp.Create(new Uri
    ("http://www.response.hu"));
```

`ClientHttpStack` (introduced in Silverlight 3) allows customizing response status codes, request methods, authentication, bodies and headers, and sending HTTP XML requests such as messages to SOAP and REST services. `ClientHttpStack` also allows manipulation of cookies. Creating a `WebRequest` for the client stack is very similar to how the `WebRequest` for the browser stack is created:

```
WebRequest rq = WebRequestCreator.ClientHttp.Create(new Uri
    ("http://www.response.hu"));
```

## WCF

Silverlight supports connecting to Windows Communication Foundation (WCF) endpoints. Note that Silverlight (at least as of version 3) only supports `BasicHttpBinding` and `PollingDuplexHttpBinding`. Connecting a Silverlight application to a WCF service is similar to what you are used to within Visual Studio, as shown in Figure 8-35.

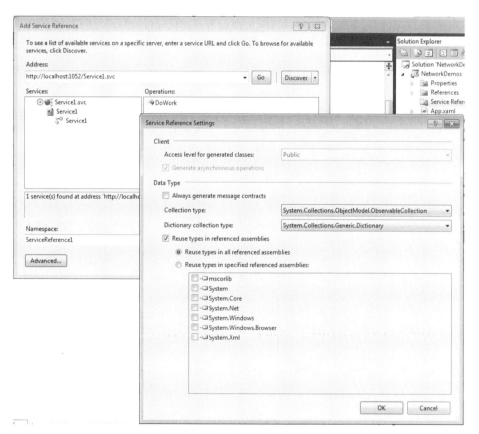

**FIGURE 8-35:** Consuming a WCF Service in Silverlight

As with other Silverlight networking methods, WCF only provides asynchronous calls to the server. Here is a very simple WCF service call:

```
var sc = new ServiceReference1.Service1Client();
sc.DoWorkCompleted += (obj, args) => { MessageBox.Show
    ("Do work completed!"); };
sc.DoWorkAsync();
```

## WCF RIA Services

WCF RIA Services (formerly called .NET RIA Services) builds on top of WCF, and aims to make data transfer between a .NET server and a Silverlight client as transparent as possible. WCF RIA Services addresses common CRUD (Create-Read-Update-Delete) scenarios while retaining type safety through all the layers. Middle-tier entities have corresponding client-side code generated, along with domain contexts that allow transparent access to server data through Language Integrated Query (LINQ). Service methods can also be invoked. The middle tier can connect to any database provider, including Entity Framework, LINQ-To-SQL, and POCO (Plain Old CLR Objects). RIA Services can transfer the client-side LINQ query to the server, and translate it to T-SQL for the database layer.

> *Essentially, it is possible to write LINQ queries using Intellisense in Silverlight to access the database layer, without breaking the architectural integrity, or introducing hand-composed SQL queries that pose serious security problems.*

A common problem with client-server scenarios is that part of the application logic (such as validation) must be duplicated. The validation should run on the client for immediate feedback to the user — but also on the server to ensure that the validation cannot be skipped with a malicious client. WCF RIA Services addresses this situation by using attributes and code sharing. This is possible because the same framework runs on the client and the server (but the Silverlight client does not have all the .NET libraries, of course), thus source code can be shared.

WCF RIA Services also integrates with the pluggable ASP.NET membership-provider models. This makes it easy to add a Silverlight application to an existing website with authentication, authorization, and profile requirements, or re-use the proven ASP.NET membership infrastructure — including the management tools — for the Silverlight application.

> *If you want to learn more about WCF RIA Services, visit Brad Abrams' blog at* http://blogs.msdn.com/brada, *or look for the WCF RIA Services section in* www.silverlight.net *for tutorials, videos, and in-depth articles.*

# Other Features

There are a lot of Silverlight features not yet examined. However, because this chapter is just an introduction to WPF and Silverlight, these features will only get a few paragraphs of coverage, despite the fact that entire chapters (or even books) could be written about some of them.

## Out-of-Browser (OOB) Applications

Silverlight applications mostly live in the browser as plug-ins. However, Silverlight supports taking applications out of the browser, and onto the desktop. Installing out-of-browser (OOB) applications is always a user-initiated process — either by right-clicking the Silverlight application and choosing "Install <appname> Application onto this computer," or by clicking on a developer-created piece of UI that calls the `Application.Install` method. Either way, the user is prompted whether he or she really wants to install the application, and whether the installer should create a shortcut on the desktop or the Start menu.

By default, the OOB applications run within the same sandbox as in the browser, so no user account control (UAC) prompts are necessary. OOB applications work on OS X as well, so here is a great way to create OS X desktop applications without even owning a Mac!

Some features are only available in OOB mode. These include the `WebBrowser` control and the `HtmlBrush` class. The `WebBrowser` is a full-featured web browser that can be used as a rectangular frame within the Silverlight application, and display any web page or HTML content (including websites that have other Silverlight, or even Flash, plug-ins). The `HTMLBrush` is similar to `VideoBrush`. When attached to a `WebBrowser` control, it can be used as a brush for any UI element. However, while the `WebBrowser` control remains interactive and accepts keyboard and mouse input, the `VideoBrush` loses the interactivity.

OOB applications can also be installed with elevated privileges. (Figure 8-36 shows OOB settings in Visual Studio 2010.) Elevated privileges eliminate the need from cross-domain policy files, and allow reading from or sending information to any website; give access to files and directories within the `My Documents` folder; and allow a level of COM interoperability, so that Office automation can be done.

**FIGURE 8-36:** Silverlight OOB Settings in Visual Studio

## Printing

Printing is by far Silverlight 4's most requested feature. Printing in Silverlight is based on a callback model:

```
PrintDocument pd = new PrintDocument();
pd.DocumentName = "My Silverlight document";
pd.PrintPage += (obj, args) =>
{
  args.PageVisual = LayoutRoot; args.HasMorePages = false;
};

pd.Print();
```

In the `PrintPage` event handler, a `UIElement` element can be defined that will be rasterized and sent to the printer. The `UIElement` does not necessarily have to be in the visual tree; it can be constructed on-the-fly, and in-memory. The `HasMorePages` property tells the print engine whether there will be more pages to print — if so, the `PrintPage` event handler gets called again for the next page.

## Bitmap Effects

*Bitmap effects* (or *shader effects*, or *shaders*) originate from computer graphics and gaming, and are usually tied to graphics processors (GPUs). In Silverlight, the same language can be used to create shaders: High level Shader Language 2.0 (HLSL2.0). However, adding shaders to a Silverlight application comes with a performance penalty. Even though the shader program gets "JIT-ed" and is run on all available processor cores, it still can slow down the application considerably. (WPF 4 supports HLSL 3.0, and can run the shaders on the GPU.)

Silverlight has two built-in shader effects: `Blur` and `DropShadow`. Both have properties that allow fine-tuning them, and, along with the capability to create custom effects using HLSL2.0, they can really add to the visual appeal of an application — again, when not overused.

## Local Messaging

If several Silverlight applications or plug-ins are running on the same computer, local messaging enables communication between the Silverlight applications — even if they are not running on the same web page or the same browser or even if some of them are running OOB. Local messaging works with named message channels, and has a fairly simple API.

For sending messages, create a `LocalMessageSender` object with the name of the messaging channel, and call its `SendAsync(string)` method. For receiving messages, a `LocalMessageReceiver` object must be created the same way, and the `MessageReceived` event is fired when a message arrives. The receiver can also return a reply using the `MessageReceivedEventArgs.Response` property that the sender can receive in the `SendAsyncCompleted` event. If a bidirectional communication is required, the two applications can set up two communication channels — one for each direction.

## GPU Acceleration

Silverlight 3 and later versions support limited GPU acceleration. GPU acceleration can be turned on for the entire plug-in via the `<object>` tag in the HTML file that hosts the plug-in, by adding the following parameter:

```
<param name="enableGPUAcceleration" value="true" />
```

On Mac OS X, GPU acceleration only works in full screen because of technical limitations. Another requirement is having a DirectX9-compatible video card or and OpenGL2-compatible card for the Mac.

GPU acceleration can only help in certain situations. Unlike WPF (where GPU composition is the default), Silverlight doesn't try to be very clever on when and where to use the GPU. Instead, the developer must mark the `UIElement` by setting the `CacheMode` property to `BitmapCache`.

The key to understanding how GPU acceleration works in Silverlight is that it is nothing more than transferring the rendered bitmap for the specified `UIElement` into the memory of the graphics card, and doing the rest of the composition there. GPU acceleration can help when the pixels of the rendered `UIElement` (along with its children) are rarely changing and, thus, the cache does not need to be invalidated after.

Composition on the GPU can offload the work of translation, scale, rectangular clipping, or rotation animations and alpha blending to the GPU, thus freeing the CPU to do other tasks, and increasing the performance of the entire application. Silverlight also has special mechanisms in place for GPU-accelerating video, making full-screen HD video possible even with today's high-resolution monitors. GPU can help accelerate perspective transforms, but in Silverlight 4, pixel shader effects are still performed by the CPU.

 For a more in-depth look at Silverlight's GPU Acceleration, read the András Velvárt blog post at `http://dotneteers.net/blogs/vbandi/archive/2009/07/30/discovering-silverlight-3-deep-dive-into-gpu-acceleration.aspx`.

## Isolated Storage

*Isolated storage* is a local storage on the user's computer that can be used as a local cache, store user preferences, or any other data. Every application has a quota of 1 MB per application, which increases to 25 MB when the application is installed as an OOB application. The quota can be increased if needed with user consent. Even though the physical storage on the computer where the isolated storage files are stored is hidden, the actual content is not obfuscated, thus it is not suitable for storing private data such as passwords. However, additional encryption can be applied to the files that can help with storing sensitive data.

Isolated storage can be thought of as a virtual file system, even a complete tree of directories and files. It also allows for storing settings in a key-value combination via the application-scoped `IsolatedStorageSettings.ApplicationSettings` or the site-scoped `IsolatedStorageSettings.SiteSettings`.

## Navigation and Search Engine Optimization

As Silverlight (and other RIA technologies) merge the web with the desktop experience, some important usability questions arise. The way you use web and desktop applications is different. Do you want to enable the back and forward buttons in the browser for Silverlight? How can you bookmark the current status of an application (such as the currently displayed item in a web shop) or send the link over to a friend? What about search engines? How will they index the content and drive traffic to the site?

Whether to choose a desktop-like or a web-like experience (or merge the two) is, of course, up to the UX designer. But, if deep linking and back button support is needed, Silverlight's built-in Navigation Framework can help.

Visual Studio 2010 includes an application template called Silverlight Navigation Application. Creating a project based on this template results in an application with a few pages (Home and About). Clicking on the navigation links behaves just like clicking on a browser link — the program switches to another "page," and the URL changes (for example, the About page's URL adds a "#/ About" text to the end).

The important difference between this and the conventional browser navigation is that the page does not get reloaded — the Silverlight application keeps running, and no intermediate white page is shown, as is the case between two HTML pages. Back and forward buttons work in the navigation application, just like bookmarking and deep linking. The key to the navigation API is the `System.Windows.Controls.Frame` class. `Frame` loads and hosts `Pages`, handles navigation, and can integrate with the browser's history. There are also facilities to extract information from the query string (`NavigationContext`), and URL mapping (`UriMapper` class).

What about Search Engine Optimalization (SEO)? It is not too practical to build up a full website using Silverlight if search engines cannot read the information and, therefore, visitors won't come to the site. The two-sentence version of the SEO trick is to build a "mirror" page in ASP.NET that feeds from the same database, and outputs the relevant content and navigation within the fallback part of the Silverlight's `<object>` tag in the HTML hosting page. The ASP.NET application can also dynamically generate the `robots.txt` and sitemap XML file to direct the search engines' spider to the right content. This approach also helps when the user does not (or cannot) have Silverlight installed, but needs to access the content of the site.

 *To see the Silverlight SEO for yourself, go to your favorite search engine, and search for "silverlight store mouse." The results will take you to a Silverlight web shop that demonstrates the SEO techniques described here.*

# WINDOWS PRESENTATION FOUNDATION

While Silverlight is a trimmed down, smaller version of WPF and the .NET Framework, WPF aims to be complete. In Silverlight, there is usually only one way to do things; WPF offers several different approaches to the same problem.

The HelloWorld application in WPF looks very similar to the Silverlight version at the beginning of this chapter. Listing 8-19 shows the XAML for the WPF version:

**LISTING 8-19: MainWindow.xaml**

```
<Window x:Class="WpfHelloWorld.MainWindow"
        xmlns="http://schemas.microsoft.com/winfx/2006/xaml/presentation"
        xmlns:x="http://schemas.microsoft.com/winfx/2006/xaml"
        Title="MainWindow" Height="350" Width="525">
  <Grid>
    <TextBlock Text="Hello, World!" HorizontalAlignment="Center"
      VerticalAlignment="Center" />
  </Grid>
</Window>
```

*Code file [MainWindow.xaml] available for download at Wrox.com*

The Grid control and its TextBlock content are exactly the same as in the Silverlight version. Even the XAML namespaces are the same. The only difference is with the root element; with WPF, it is Window.

The other key difference occurs when running the application. Instead of a browser and a plug-in, you get a full desktop application, as shown in Figure 8-37.

WPF applications can also run within the browser. This is called *XBAP deployment*. However, running a WPF application in the browser requires the entire .NET Framework to

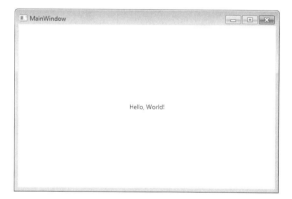

**FIGURE 8-37**: The WPFHelloWorld application

be installed on the user's computer, and, thus, only works in Windows (while Silverlight works on other platforms, and only needs the Silverlight plug-in).

To create an XBAP application, you must choose WPF Browser Application in the New Project dialog of Visual Studio 2010, as shown in Figure 8-38.

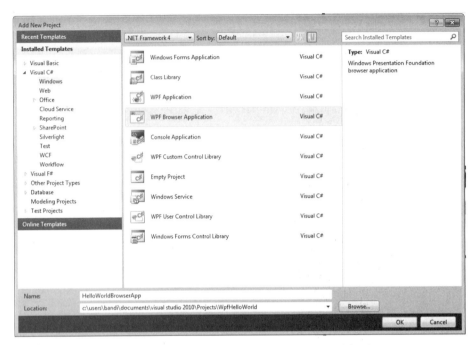

**FIGURE 8-38:** Creating a WPF Browser (XBAP) Application in Visual Studio

Figure 8-39 shows what a `HelloWorld` WPF XBAP application looks like in the browser.

**FIGURE 8-39:** An XBAP application in the Browser

WPF 4 also introduced running XBAP applications in full-trust mode, and access to the HTML Document Object Model (DOM) via the `BrowserInteropHelper` class.

As you can see from the previous sample, the key principles and pillars of Silverlight also apply to WPF. The most important features that Silverlight has and WPF does not (at least in version 4) are smooth streaming, Deep Zoom, easy webcam and microphone access, and, of course, cross-platform compatibility.

## WPF Features not Available in Silverlight

This section introduces some of the unique WPF features not found in Silverlight. This examination is by no means complete, because the WPF platform is a lot more comprehensive than Silverlight. Rather, this discussion merely provides just a subjective selection.

### Rich Document Presentation with Flow Documents

*Flow documents* allow displaying rich document content in an adaptive way. Flow documents can adapt to changes in view window size and font size to suit many different viewing scenarios. In Figure 8-40, you can how see the SDK viewer demo from the MSDN Library (http://msdn .microsoft.com/en-us/library/aa972141.aspx) adapts.

**FIGURE 8-40:** In a narrow window, FlowDocument displays one column; in a wider window two columns; and in a wide window with big font size it reverts back to one column

The children of the `FlowDocument` class are usually paragraphs, lists, sections, tables, and so on. A `FlowDocument` can also contain any WPF `UIElement`, such as buttons, images, or even media players.

When a `FlowDocument` is placed within a `FlowDocumentReader`, UI for paging, search, changing viewing mode, and zooming content are also displayed. Of course, these features can be customized or even turned off. Here is a simple `FlowDocument` XAML code snippet:

```
<FlowDocumentReader>
  <FlowDocument>
    <Paragraph>Hello, World!</Paragraph>
    <Paragraph>This is the Flow Document demo.</Paragraph>
    <Paragraph>
      This is an inline calendar:
      <Calendar />
      And the text goes on here...
    </Paragraph>
  </FlowDocument>
</FlowDocumentReader>
```

Figure 8-41 shows this code running.

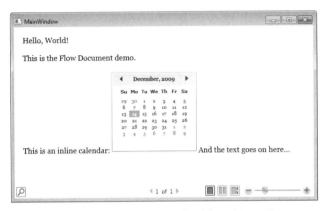

**FIGURE 8-41:** FlowDocument sample with an interactive Calendar control inline

Combined with the new font-rendering capabilities of WPF 4, flow documents can provide an excellent reading experience.

## Additional Layout Containers and Controls

While `WrapPanel` has made its way into the Silverlight Toolkit, and `Viewbox` is now in the core Silverlight run-time, WPF still has a few more layout containers up its sleeve — `ListView`, `DockPanel`, and `UniformGrid`.

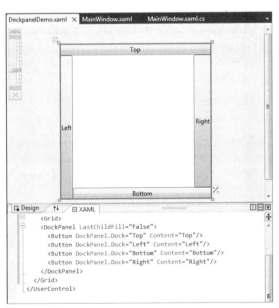

`ListView` allows listing its items in a list or grid (or custom) layout, displaying its items similarly to Windows Explorer.

`DockPanel`'s children have a `DockPanel.Dock` attached property that instructs `DockPanel` where to dock the specified child. The order of the children is important, because docking the next child happens in the remaining area of the `DockPanel`. For example, if the first child is docked to the top, and the next one to the left, the first occupies the entire width of the top part. Thus, the second can only occupy the entire height of the remaining area of the `DockPanel`. The `DockPanel`'s `LastChildFill` property indicates whether the last child should fill the entire remaining area. Figure 8-42 shows `DockPanel` within the Visual Studio 2010 Designer.

**FIGURE 8-42:** DockPanel in Visual Studio

UniformGrid is used to display more similar items in a grid-like layout. UniformGrid tries to determine the optimal number of rows and columns for a given number of items, and size them uniformly. The number of rows or columns can also be specified via the Rows and Columns properties. Figure 8-43 shows how a UniformGrid arranges 5 or 35 buttons.

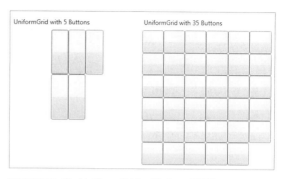

**FIGURE 8-43:** UniformGrid with 5 and 35 buttons

WPF also supports menu and toolbar functionality through the Menu, ToolBar, ToolBarPanel, and ToolBarTray controls. Another interesting interoperability scenario is made possible through the WindowsFormsHost control that can host any Windows Forms control within WPF. This mixing of technologies is also possible from the other direction — a Windows Forms application can host a WPF control via the ElementHost control.

## Windows 7 integration

WPF 4 introduces several new features to take advantage of Windows Vista and Windows 7, such as Aero glass, multitouch, and integration with Windows 7's new taskbar.

### Aero Glass

To make parts of the WPF window look "glassy," the application must access some unmanaged API. Microsoft's Adam Nathan has blogged about how to enable Aero glass functionality at http://blogs.msdn.com/adam_nathan/archive/2006/05/04/589686.aspx. Using his GlassHelper class, you can get the result displayed in Figure 8-44.

### Touch

Touch and multitouch are supported via the manipulation API. Any UIElement can have its IsManipulationEnabled property set to True. This allows the UIElement

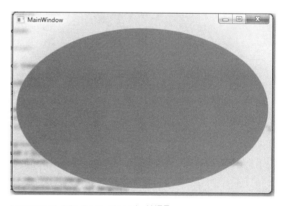

**FIGURE 8-44:** Aero glass in WPF

to receive manipulation events, such as ManipulationStarted, ManipulationStarting, ManipulationDelta, ManipulationCompleted, and ManipulationInertiaStarting. Handling these events and changing the manipulated element's translate, scale, and rotation transforms accordingly allows for surface-like moving, rotating, and scaling. In fact, the most complex control in the Surface SDK, the ScatterView control that encapsulates the "classic" element rotation, as well as tossing functionality, is also available in the Microsoft Surface Toolkit for Windows Touch touch-enabled WPF applications.

## Taskbar Integration

To access the new Windows 7 shell's features (such as jump lists, progress bar, overlay icons, thumbnail toolbars, and so on), you must reference the `System.Windows.Shell` namespace. For example, the following code adds a new `JumpList` item that starts the application with a special command-line parameter:

```
var jl = new JumpList();
jl.ShowFrequentCategory = true;
jl.ShowRecentCategory = true;

var jt = new JumpTask();
jt.CustomCategory = "My Jumplist items";
jt.Description = "My item's description";
jt.Title = "My Jumplist item";
jt.Arguments = "/startedfromjumplist";
jt.ApplicationPath = System.Reflection.Assembly.GetExecutingAssembly().
    GetName().CodeBase;
jl.JumpItems.Add(jt);
jl.Apply();
```

To create icon overlays and thumbnail buttons, the `Window.TaskbarItemInfo` property can be used, as shown in Listing 8-20.

Available for
download on
Wrox.com

**LISTING 8-20:** MainWindow.xaml for Win 7 Feature Demos

```xaml
<Window x:Class="Win7FeatureDemo.MainWindow"
        xmlns="http://schemas.microsoft.com/winfx/2006/xaml/presentation"
        xmlns:x="http://schemas.microsoft.com/winfx/2006/xaml"
        Title="MainWindow" Height="350" Width="525">
  <Window.TaskbarItemInfo>
    <TaskbarItemInfo x:Name="Button1" Overlay="rectangle.bmp"
        Description="Button1">
      <TaskbarItemInfo.ThumbButtonInfos>
        <ThumbButtonInfo x:Name="ThumbButton1" Click="ThumbButtonInfo_Click"
            ImageSource="ellipse.bmp" Description="I am a thumb button!" />
      </TaskbarItemInfo.ThumbButtonInfos>
    </TaskbarItemInfo>
  </Window.TaskbarItemInfo>
  <Grid>
    <Ellipse IsManipulationEnabled="True" HorizontalAlignment="Stretch"
      VerticalAlignment="Stretch" Fill="Gray" />
  </Grid>
</Window>
```

*Code file [MainWindow.xaml] available for download at Wrox.com*

When running this application, the taskbar looks like what is shown on Figure 8-45. The rectangle is the icon overlay, and the little black-and-white face on the thumbnail is the ThumButton. There can be more than one thumb button. For example, Windows Media Player uses thumb buttons to allow quick access to previous, next, and pause functionality.

Programs performing long-running operations and running on Windows 7 can indicate the status of their progress on the taskbar. This allows the user to determine the status of the operation without bringing the application to the front, just by looking at the taskbar.

**FIGURE 8-45:** Icon Overlay and Thumb Button

To use this feature in your application, set the TaskbarItemInfo.ProgressValue to a value between 0 and 1, and TaskbarItemInfo.ProgressState to Normal. The ProgressState can also be set to Indeterminate (to display an indeterminate animation), Error (to make the progress bar red, indicating an error in the progress), None (to clear any progress bar display), and Paused (to make the progress bar yellow).

## A Different Control Templating Model

WPF only introduced Silverlight's Visual State Manager (VSM) in WPF 4. Because of this, WPF controls are based on a different templating model than Silverlight ones. Here is a snippet from the template of a WPF TextBox:

```
<Setter Property="Template">
  <Setter.Value>
    <ControlTemplate TargetType="{x:Type TextBox}">
      <Microsoft_Windows_Themes:ListBoxChrome x:Name="Bd"
        SnapsToDevicePixels="true" Background="{TemplateBinding Background}"
        BorderBrush="{TemplateBinding BorderBrush}"
        BorderThickness="{TemplateBinding BorderThickness}"
        RenderFocused="{TemplateBinding IsKeyboardFocusWithin}"
        RenderMouseOver="{TemplateBinding IsMouseOver}">
        <ScrollViewer x:Name="PART_ContentHost"
          SnapsToDevicePixels="{TemplateBinding SnapsToDevicePixels}"/>
      </Microsoft_Windows_Themes:ListBoxChrome>
      <ControlTemplate.Triggers>
        <Trigger Property="IsEnabled" Value="false">
          <Setter Property="Background" TargetName="Bd"
            Value="{DynamicResource {x:Static SystemColors.ControlBrushKey}}"/>
          <Setter Property="Foreground"
            Value="{DynamicResource {x:Static SystemColors.GrayTextBrushKey}}"/>
        </Trigger>
      </ControlTemplate.Triggers>
    </ControlTemplate>
  </Setter.Value>
</Setter>
```

There are several interesting things in this template. One is that the look and feel of WPF controls are coherent with the current Windows theme. The other one is that instead of visual states, the template operates with triggers. For example, the `IsEnabled` property automatically triggers two setters to change the colors accordingly — in the VSM model, you had a state group controlled by the logic.

Similarly, the mouse hover states can be expressed as property triggers based on the `IsMouseOver` property. The WPF 4 controls also implement the VSM states for Silverlight compatibility, but the default control states are based on the trigger model.

### VisualBrush

`VisualBrush` is very much like the Silverlight `VideoBrush` introduced earlier, but instead of video, its source can be any WPF control. This allows for cool effects, like the ever-so-popular reflection effect, with minimal performance overhead.

### WPF 3D

WPF sports a fairly sophisticated three-dimensional engine that is integrated with the rest of the visual tree that is sophisticated for a UI framework — don't try to write your next CAD or Quake game using WPF 3D. WPF 3D supports models, lights, materials, and cameras. Two-dimensional elements can also be mapped to three-dimensional models.

For example, it is possible to put a `DataGrid` on a sphere, and it will stay interactive. However, three-dimension in WPF does not support three-dimensional primitives like spheres, cubes, or teapots — only the most basic three-dimensional building block, a triangle, is supported. Therefore, creating even the simplest three-dimensional scene is quite a lot of work. There is no simple access to the third dimension, like the perspective transform of Silverlight.

## CHOOSING BETWEEN WPF AND SILVERLIGHT

With WPF being able to run in the browser with the XBAP deployment model, and Silverlight running OOB, even with elevated trust since version 4, the number of requirements that only one or the other technology can satisfy is rapidly decreasing. Still, when creating a new project in Visual Studio, you must make a distinct decision on which project type to choose.

Table 8-3 shows some scenarios when one or the other technology is clearly a better choice as of WPF4 and Silverlight 4 Beta versions.

**TABLE 8-3:** Silverlight and WPF Scenarios

| SILVERLIGHT RECOMMENDED | WPF RECOMMENDED |
| --- | --- |
| The application is to be run inside the browser. | Windows is the target platform. |
| The application is to be run on non-Windows operating systems or even mobile devices. | Tight Windows 7 integration is required (such as taskbar, jump lists, and so on). |

| SILVERLIGHT RECOMMENDED | WPF RECOMMENDED |
|---|---|
| Silverlight-specific media functionality is used (such as smooth streaming or Deep Zoom). | Access to the full .NET Framework is needed. |
| You don't need any WPF-specific functionality. | Access to the full computer is needed (such as in the case of a CD burner application). |
| The web deployment model is preferred. | You must integrate with native code where Silverlight's COM interop is not enough. |
| | Basic three-dimensional or DirectX integration is needed. |
| | Displaying complex documents is required. |
| | You need the full, no-compromise .NET Framework. |

To sum up, if Silverlight satisfies your needs, go for it, because your application will run on more platforms and will be easier to migrate to mobile or even WPF in the long run. But, if you only need to run on Windows, and need the full power of WPF and the .NET Framework, along with native code integration and hardware access, jump onto the WPF bus without hesitation. Whichever path you take, you most certainly will have a fun and fruitful ride with these exciting technologies!

# DESIGNER - DEVELOPER COOPERATION IN SILVERLIGHT AND WPF

This chapter started by describing the importance of UX, and the idea that designers and developers must work together in order to achieve a great UX. After looking at the most important pillars (features) of Silverlight and WPF, it is time to return to that thought and investigate how Visual Studio 2010 and Expression Blend can help designers and developers to cooperate and create great applications together.

The key to a successful designer developer workflow is total separation between logic, data, and UI. As illustrated earlier, Silverlight and WPF do a great job as a platform in this regard. Let's see how the tools and some architectural considerations can support the cooperation.

## A Common Solution Format

Visual Studio and Expression Blend share a common solution file format. This means that a project created with Visual Studio 2010 can be opened with Expression Blend 4, and vice versa. The people working on the project can be sure that they are using exactly the same project, editing the same files, and seeing what the other team sees. Of course, it is good practice to use a source control in order to do check-ins, and avoid editing the same physical file. Subversion or Team Foundation Server both work great — Team Foundation Server is even integrated into Blend to help with source control.

Even if there is only a single person working on a project, both Visual Studio and Expression Blend offer hooks to easily switch to the other tool, and continue working there. For example, right-clicking an XAML file in the Solution Explorer of Visual Studio offers the option to open the XAML (and the entire solution) in Blend — and similarly, Blend can open the project in Visual Studio, as shown in Figure 8-46. If a project is already open in the other tool, switching between the two tools with Alt+Tab prompts for loading the changes.

## Blendability

Even though Blend can use the same project as Visual Studio, it does not automatically mean that the project is editable in Blend. For example, there may be a user control or a data object that accesses the server for some data in its constructor. Because the server may not be available in design time, but property accessors and bindings are run when initializing the visual designer, this will result in an error, even if running the project works perfectly. Both Blend and Visual Studio 2010 display useful error information in this case, as shown in Figure 8-47 and Figure 8-48.

**FIGURE 8-46:** Right-clicking on a file in Blend offers to open the solution in Visual Studio

---

> ⚠ Exception was thrown on "BrokenUserControl": Cannot create an instance of "BrokenUserControl". Click here to hide detail.
>
> An Unhandled Exception has occurred
>
> ***Something wrong has happened***
>
> at DevignerDemos.BrokenUserControl..ctor() in c:\users\bandi\documents\visual studio 2010\Projects \DevignerDemos\DevignerDemos\BrokenUserControl.xaml.cs:line 20
>
> Click here for help debugging common load failures

**FIGURE 8-47:** Design time error in Visual Studio

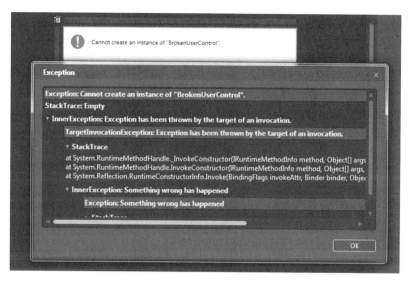

**FIGURE 8-48:** Design time error in Expression Blend

The designer surface will become read-only until the problem is corrected. While the XAML can still be edited, this effectively renders the designer unable to work with the project. Ensuring that the visual designers and Blend always work is called *blendability*. There are other cases when run-time and design time behave differently. For example, neither Blend nor Cider call the constructor of the UserControl currently displayed. Therefore, some properties may not be set in design mode.

To differentiate between design time and run-time, developers can use the DesignerProperties .IsInDesignMode Boolean property. If this value is true, the design code can be switched to a design-time behavior, and provide dummy data in the data object, instead of trying to reach a live database. This dummy data can be used by the designer to set up bindings in a what-you-see-is-what-you-get (WYSIWYG) manner.

## Design Time Sample Data in Blend

Designers do not have to rely on developers to create sample data for their bindings or to experiment with different ways of presenting data. Blend offers a feature called *sample data*. This is essentially an XML "database" that can be created visually in Blend, and used as a data-binding source with simple drag-and-drop operations.

The cool thing about sample data is that the number of records can be changed very easily, and there are tons of built-in sample data types that create random lorem ipsum text, company names, person names, prices, email addresses, images, and so on. Figure 8-49 shows how design-time data is used in Blend to create a list of chairs with designer's names and prices.

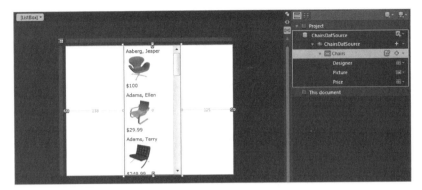

**FIGURE 8-49:** Using sample data in Blend

The sample data can also be used as a real data source for simple applications or parts of an application that display some data but do not need server functionality. The sample "database" can be set up, and then the randomly generated data can be changed manually.

## SketchFlow

SketchFlow is a dynamic prototyping tool, built into Expression Blend (Figure 8-50). *Dynamic prototypes* are much more than wireframes that most developer shops use to mock-up screens. Prototypes are interactive, can contain sample (or even live) data, and have the navigation functionality in place.

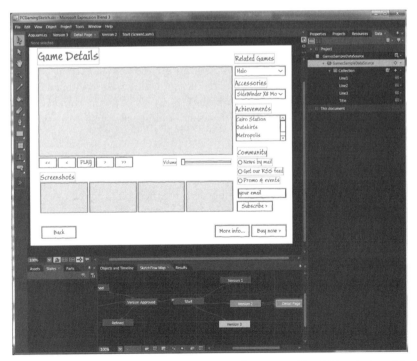

**FIGURE 8-50:** Editing SketchFlow prototypes in Expression Blend. The design of the UI intentionally looks like a paper drawing to direct the attention to the content and layout, instead of the subtle things like shades of color and precise placement.

The big advantage of dynamic prototypes is that it allows the end user to role-play his or her day using the prototype and give immediate feedback if some information is not displayed or hard to reach. Dynamic prototypes are cheap to create and modify, and, thus, allow experimenting with different approaches to the UI. Once accepted by the client, prototypes can also serve as part of the developer's specification, showing the general layout, fields to display, and interactivity to implement in a self-explaining way.

SketchFlow is available for both WPF and Silverlight, and uses the styling and templating features of these platforms to achieve its sketchy look. End users can view the sketches in the SketchFlow Player. The SketchFlow Player also allows the customer to provide feedback by adding textual comments, and drawing on the sketch UI with the mouse.

## Triggers, Actions, and Behaviors

Triggers and actions can be thought of as reusable, customizable, designer-friendly event handlers.

An action is a piece of .NET code that does something — changes a property, starts a Storyboard, moves something around, plays a sound, opens a link — basically anything a piece of code can do. Actions can also have parameters that further enhance their reusability.

A trigger is the "event" that activates the action. The built-in triggers include EventTrigger (fires when a specific event occurs), TimerTrigger (fires at specific intervals), and KeyTrigger (fires when a specified key is pressed). There are other triggers available in the Expression Blend Gallery (such as the MouseGestureTrigger that fires when the mouse is moved in a pre-specified way, or a double-click trigger).

To apply an action to a piece of UI in Blend, the action can be dragged from the Assets panel to the "Objects and Timeline" panel, or the UI element itself on the design surface. A trigger is automatically added, but its parameters can be changed, or the entire trigger replaced in the property inspector for the action.

Actions and triggers are attached to a Dependency Object by default. If a trigger or action only makes sense on a specific element (such as an action that selects the next or previous item in a ListBox), the action can be constrained when specifying the generic base class, and Blend will not allow using it on the wrong element.

Behaviors are useful when simple triggers actions are not enough. Just like an action, it is attached to a target element (AssociatedObject), and provides two methods to override — OnAttached and OnDetached. In these methods, the event handlers can be hooked up to the AssociatedObject, and, basically, any other functionality can be coded up. A good Behavior example is the MouseDragElementBehavior that makes the associated object "draggable" without any further code — obviously it handles the MouseLeftButtonDown, MouseMove, and MouseLeftButtonUp events in one single package.

There is no limit to what actions and behaviors can do. You can find a whole physics engine embedded in behaviors that move UI elements around and handle gravity and collision, and one of the built-in Blend samples is a breakout-style game called "Beehive," where the entire logic of the game is coded using triggers, actions, and behaviors.

# Model-View-ViewModel Pattern

Even though `Behaviors` can be used to do amazing things, it is probably not be the best architectural pattern to follow for building applications that need total designer-developer separation. An emerging pattern, called Model-View-ViewModel (MVVM) seems to be the ideal solution. Blend itself has been built with MVVM, as well as tons of other complex WPF or Silverlight projects.

MVVM may sound familiar — it has a lot to do with the Model-View-Controller (MVC) pattern. MVVM is designed to take full advantage of the advanced data-binding capabilities of WPF and Silverlight. Following are the goals of the MVVM pattern:

➤  Separate logic and data from presentation

➤  Make the UI logic testable by itself

➤  Avoid spreading UI logic into too many, hard-to-find places (such as event handlers of user controls)

Following are the main components of MVVM:

➤  *Model* — The Model represents business data (such as books, authors, orders, and so on). In some implementations, the Model also "knows" how to send itself back to the server, or retrieve additional model objects.

➤  *View* — The View is essentially the UI. In the case of WPF and Silverlight, it is the XAML code. MVVM purists insist on no code-behind for the View — UI-specific coding should be done with behaviors. However, sometimes it is more efficient and cost-effective to put some code in the code-behind, but you have to know and understand the rules to see when to break them.

➤  *ViewModel* — The ViewModel is the data that represents the View. It connects the View with the Model, while storing the status of the View (such as whether the user has logged in). The ViewModel is wired to the View via data binding — the ViewModel is set as the `DataContext` in XAML. The View can inform the ViewModel of events via a loose commanding mechanism. For example, if the user clicks the "Delete record" button, a corresponding command is invoked.

There are a lot of different MVVM approaches and implementations to be found on the web — probably too many to decide which one to use. Some only work with WPF, some prefer Silverlight, and some work with both. They all have their strengths and weaknesses. Following are some recommendations, but feel free to find (or even create) your own preferred frameworks:

➤  Laurent Bugnion's MVVM Light Toolkit (`http://www.galasoft.ch/mvvm/getstarted`)

➤  Microsoft's Patterns and Practices Group develops Prism, that also helps with composite applications (`http://msdn.microsoft.com/en-us/library/dd458809.aspx?rssCatalogv2.1`)

➤  Caliburn (`http://www.codeplex.com/caliburn`) with additional UI patterns

➤  Silverlight FX (`http://projects.nikhilk.net/SilverlightFX`) also goes beyond MVVM

## SUMMARY

In this chapter, you learned about how the focus of software development is shifting from technical problems to the user experience (UX). The key to building applications with a modern UX is to bring together the developer with the designer — the Designer with capital "D," who is not just good with graphics tools, but is able to design a usable, productive, and enjoyable UI for the customer's problem at hand.

Silverlight and WPF are two technologies can bring the worlds of the designer and developer closer, through the power XAML, layout, data binding, styling, templating, media, and the Expression Blend and Visual Studio 2010 tools.

Chapter 9 takes a closer look at Windows Communication Foundation (WCF).

# Windows Communication Foundation (WCF)

Based on the Service Oriented Architecture (SOA), Windows Communication Foundation (WCF) is a framework used to design applications with the capability to inter-communicate. WCF was initially named "Indigo," and was introduced as part of .NET Framework 3.0 in 2006. According to MSDN (http://msdn.microsoft.com/en-us/library/ms735119.aspx.), "Windows Communication Foundation (WCF) is Microsoft's unified programming model for building service-oriented applications. It enables developers to build secure, reliable, transacted solutions that integrate across platforms and interoperate with existing investments."

SOA is an architectural paradigm where you have a collection of loosely coupled and extensible services, with each service having the capability to be modified independently of one another in such a way that the integration of the services remains intact. WCF is a framework from Microsoft that facilitates designing and developing SOA applications within the managed environment.

This chapter takes a look at how WCF fits into the greater .NET toolset, as well as the basics of SOA using WCF. In this chapter, you will learn how to implement a WCF service using Visual Studio 2010.

Before digging into the details, let's do a quick review of WCF in comparison to ASMX Web Services.

## WCF VERSUS ASMX WEB SERVICES

One of the most common descriptions of WCF is to say that it is web service. Although you can use WCF to create web services that match the traditional model of web services, there are a lot more possibilities with WCF.

It is important to consider the way that WCF and ASMX Web Services are related, because both are currently supported in the .NET development stack. A common analogy is used to describe the overall differences between WCF and ASMX Web Services is to metaphorically consider them as an aircraft. ASMX Web Services are the Cessna of services, with a simple configuration interface, and a limited number of options. They are something easy for anyone to grasp and understand. On the other hand, WCF Services are like commercial jets. They have a lot more options, configuration settings, switches, and knobs available, but with that comes a steeper learning curve and time investment.

WCF will not necessarily replace ASMX Web Services because of the simple setup process to configure ASMX Web Services. But, when looking at more robust or secure communications between applications, WCF will become the solution of choice.

## A QUICK LOOK AT SOA

SOA is a very popular architectural paradigm that enables an excellent integration of loosely coupled distributed applications and services over a network. Web services and similar application services are an example of SOA implementations. Service-oriented designs will typically be characterized by providing the following:

➤ Platform independence

➤ Loose coupling

➤ Location transparency and reduced cost of maintenance

➤ Support for seamless updates over time

➤ Easier maintenance and seamless deployment

When implementing a solution using SOA, the resulting solution will contain the following elements:

➤ Service

➤ Service provider

➤ Service consumer(s)

➤ Service registry

➤ Service contract

➤ Service proxy

➤ Service lease

➤ Message

➤ Service description

➤ Advertising and discovery

Let's take a look at each of these in a bit more detail.

# Service

A *service* may be defined as an implementation of a stateless, well-defined, self-contained, independent business functionality that has the capability of accepting one or multiple requests and returning one or multiple responses using a well-defined, standard interface. A service is independent of the technology on which it is implemented; so the interface to the service should be platform-independent. A service should also have the capability to be dynamically discovered and called at run-time.

# Service Provider

The *service provider* is a network-addressable entity that provides the service. This would typically be the hosted Internet/intranet location that is hosting the specific service solution for the consumer(s).

# Service Consumer(s)

The *service consumer* is the entity that consumes (or uses) the services provided by the service provider by locating the service in the service registry, binding to the service, and then executing the service methods. It is very common for multiple service consumers to be within a specific service-oriented application.

An example of this would be individual workstation clients that consume web services data provided through a single service provider.

# Service Registry

The *service registry* is a network-based repository of published services. This registry is used by the service consumers at run-time to locate a service and bind to it.

The advantages of using a service registry include the following:

➤ Scalability

➤ Loose coupling

➤ Hot updates

➤ Dynamic service lookup

Using a service registry rather than hard-coding service provider locations allows for a more dynamic service environment, widespread service distribution, and redundancy.

# Service Contract

The *service contract* is a specification that denotes how the service consumer will interact with the service provider for a particular service. A service contract defines the various types of communications, message formats, and input/output data specifications for all interactions.

## Service Proxy

The *service proxy* is a reference to the service at the service consumer's end. It is provided by the service provider to facilitate the service method calls.

## Service Lease

The *service lease* is a predefined duration that denotes the lifetime of a service. This implies a time after which the service will no longer be valid. Note that, as and when this time period elapses, the service consumer should request the service registry to grant a fresh, new service lease so that the service consumer can regain access to the service and execute the service methods.

## Message

Service providers and service consumers communicate through the use of *messages*. So, messages are the medium of communication between service providers (that is, the providers of the services) and service consumers (that is, the consumers of the services). Note that such messages are in predefined XML format.

The service contract(s) discussed previously are used to define the specific formats of the individual messages transferred between the client and server.

## Service Description

The *service description* is a specification that contains the necessary information to invoke a service. Such information may include the parameters, the constraints, and the policies that define how the service should be invoked.

This is a more detailed overview of the actual service contract that defines all interactions. Typically, this would be in the form of a published document or specification that shows example service communications and provides information for easy discovery. A common example here would be something similar to the "Test" page that .NET automatically generates for ASMX Web Services.

## Advertising and Discovery

*Advertising* and *discovery* are two of the most essential properties in SOA. While the former relates to the capability of a service to publish its description so as to be located by the service consumers, the latter relates to the capability of the service consumers to discover the published services from the service registry, and then invoke them as needed.

## BUILDING BLOCKS OF THE WCF ARCHITECTURE

As mentioned, WCF is a framework from Microsoft used to design and implement applications that can have the capability to inter-communicate. Unification of the existing .NET technologies, support for cross-platform interoperability, security, service-oriented development, and reliability are some of the key advantages of designing applications using WCF. WCF runs on top of .NET's

Common Language Run-time (CLR), and helps you build service-oriented applications by leveraging the benefits of .NET's managed environment.

WCF provides a great platform for unifying Microsoft's distributing technologies (web services, remoting, COM+, and so on) under one umbrella. The three most important concepts related to WCF architecture include services, clients, and messages. This section examines the building blocks of the WCF architecture, as shown in Figure 9-1.

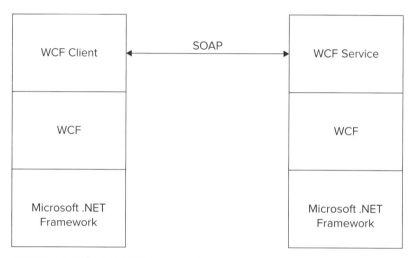

**FIGURE 9-1:** WCF and .NET Framework

You can have three contracts in WCF — a *service contract*, a *data contract*, and a *message contract*. Any WCF `Service` class implements at least one service contract — an interface that is used to define the operations that are exposed by the WCF `Service` class. Such operations may also include data operations — exposed using data contracts.

Actually, a WCF `Service` class is just like any other class, except that it is marked with the `ServiceContract` attribute. Individual methods within the `Service` class are marked with an `OperationContract` attribute that defines it as an externally visible operation of the service. A message contract may be defined in a way that allows you to change the format of the messages. Note that the `ServiceContract`, `DataContract`, and other related attributes are defined in the `System.ServiceModel` namespace.

Given the use of the `OperationContract` attribute, it is possible to have methods within a `Service` class that are not marked with the attribute. This will hide the method from consumption within a WCF service. Keep in mind that, for DLL references and so on, the access modifier of the method will still control the availability to external callers.

In WCF, a *binding* denotes how a particular service can communicate with other services of its kind, and also with other clients. Each service can be made available via one or more binding at any given time.

Table 9-1 shows the predefined, built-in bindings in WCF.

**TABLE 9-1:** WCF Predefined, Built-in Bindings

| BINDING | PURPOSE |
| --- | --- |
| basicHttpBinding | This binding is used to provide backward compatibility support for ASMX-based clients. This binding uses Simple Object Access Protocol (SOAP) 1.1 messages, and is used when a WCF service must communicate to non-WCF based system. |
| wsHttpBinding | This binding sends SOAP 1.2 messages and implements WS* specifications to support security, reliability, ordered delivery, and transactions. |
| netTCPBinding | This binding sends SOAP 1.2 messages and uses binary encoding and optimized communications between WCF clients and services on a Windows network. This binding can only be used when working with WCF-to-WCF communication, but is the fastest communications process possible. This can be used to replace COM+ and .NET remoting models. |
| netNamedPipeBinding | This binding provides secure, reliable named pipe communications between WCF services and WCF clients that are stored on the same machine. This communication should be used for communications between processes that exist on the same server. |
| netPeerTcpBinding | This binding is used to set up peer-to-peer communications, for full information. (See the MSDN article at http://technet.microsoft.com/en-us/library/bb726971.aspx.) |
| msmqIntegrationBinding | This binding is used to enable applications to send and receive messages using Microsoft Message Queuing (MSMQ), and allows integration with applications already using MSMQ. |
| wsDualHttpBinding | This binding is used to allow two-way communications between a client and service. Although similar in nature to wsHttpBinding, this method exposes the client's IP address to the service, and requires that the client be reachable via a public URI. |
| wsFederationHttpBinding | This binding provides a communication system that allows for seamless passing of identities between systems by implementing support for the WS-Federation protocol. |
| netMsmqBinding | This binding provides a method to allow an application the capability to send messages via an MSMQ queue. This allows for disconnected message communication and various options for security. |

*Endpoints* in WCF are used to associate a service contract with its address. *Channels* are actually a bridge between a service and its client. Following are the types of supported channels in WCF:

➤ Simplex Input

➤ Simplex Output

➤ Request-reply

➤ Duplex

To help put the concept of endpoints and channels into perspective, let's use a common problem to describe the functionality provided by endpoints and channels.

Let's say you are going on a trip where you are driving to a destination. To get to your end destination, you would follow a simple process. You would get into your vehicle and take the necessary roads/highways to get to the final destination.

Using this scenario as an example, the location that you are going to is the endpoint, your vehicle is the request being sent, and the roads are the channel in which the message is communicated. An endpoint is simply a physical address that a user can call (for example, `http://www.mydomain.com/service/svc/get`), and the channel is responsible for the reception and transmission of the data between the client and the endpoint.

## GETTING STARTED WITH WCF

A typical WCF implementation would have a *WCF service* and a *WCF client*. The WCF client would consume the services provided by the WCF service. A WCF service is based on three concepts — address, binding, and contract. And, as mentioned, a WCF service and a WCF client communicate using messages, as shown in Figure 9-2.

**FIGURE 9-2:** WCF Service and WCF Client

This section examines how you can get started using WCF in your applications. You will implement a simple WCF service and then use ASP.NET Ajax to consume the service.

The service that is created will be used to provide employee information to the ASP.NET web application.

# Creating the WCF Service

Note that a WCF service contains the following:

➤ A Service class

➤ A hosting environment

➤ One or more endpoints

The Service class is written using a language targeted at the managed environment of the .NET CLR. The *hosting environment* is the environment inside the context of which the WCF service would execute. The endpoints enable the clients or the service consumers to access the WCF service.

WCF services can be hosted in a couple of different ways — via Internet Information Services (IIS), similar to that of ASMX services, or as individual process hosts within a standard executable.

There are two templates that you can choose from to create WCF services: the Visual Studio WCF Service Library template and the Visual Studio Service Application template.

Let's first use the Visual Studio WCF Service Library template to create a WCF Service. To do this, follow these steps:

1. Open Visual Studio 2010.

2. Click on File ➪ New ➪ Project.

3. Select WCF Service Application from the list of the templates displayed, as shown in Figure 9-3.

4. Provide a name for your project and click OK to save.

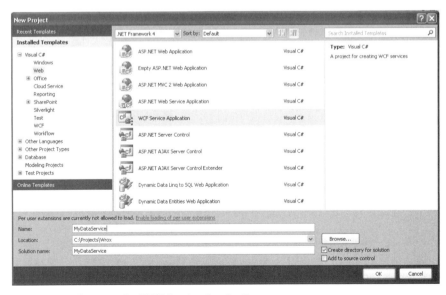

**FIGURE 9-3:** Creating the WCF Service Application

A WCF Service Application project is then created. At first glance, the `Service` class looks as follows:

```
using System;
namespace MyDataService
{
    // NOTE: You can use the "Rename" command on the "Refactor" menu to change
    // the class name "Service1" in code, svc and config file together.
    public class Service1 : IService1
    {
        public string GetData(int value)
        {
            return string.Format("You entered: {0}", value);
        }

        public CompositeType GetDataUsingDataContract(CompositeType composite)
        {
            if (composite == null)
            {
                throw new ArgumentNullException("composite");
            }
            if (composite.BoolValue)
            {
                composite.StringValue += "Suffix";
            }
            return composite;
        }
    }
}
```

The `Service` class in the previous code snippet implements the interface `IService1`, as shown here:

```
using System.Runtime.Serialization;
using System.ServiceModel;
namespace MyDataService
{
    // NOTE: You can use the "Rename" command on the "Refactor" menu
    // to change the interface name "IService1" in both code
    // and config file together.
    [ServiceContract]
    public interface IService1
    {

        [OperationContract]
        string GetData(int value);

        [OperationContract]
        CompositeType GetDataUsingDataContract(CompositeType composite);

        // TODO: Add your service operations here
    }

    // Use a data contract as illustrated in the sample below
    // to add composite types to service operations.
```

```
[DataContract]
public class CompositeType
{
    bool boolValue = true;
    string stringValue = "Hello ";

    [DataMember]
    public bool BoolValue
    {
        get { return boolValue; }
        set { boolValue = value; }
    }

    [DataMember]
    public string StringValue
    {
        get { return stringValue; }
        set { stringValue = value; }
    }
}
}
```

## Creating the Service Interface

Any WCF `Service` class implements at least one service contract. In this example, the service contract that the `Service` class would implement is `IEmployeeDataService`.

Right-click on the project in the Solution Explorer and create a new file called `EmployeeDataService.cs`. Place the following code there:

```
[ServiceContract]
public interface IEmployeeDataService
{
    List<String> GetData();
    [OperationContract]
    List<String> GetEmployeeList();
}
```

This is the service contract that will be extended by a `Service` class you will create later. Note that there are two method declarations in this interface — the `GetData()` method and the `GetEmployeeList()` method. While the former is not marked with the `OperationContract` attribute, the latter is. This implies that, of these two methods, only the `GetEmployeeList()` method will be exposed for client-callable operations. This is because any method that isn't marked with the `OperationContract` attribute is not included in the service contract.

Given the use of interfaces to define a service, since the `GetData` method is not needed for service implementation, it would most often be a best practice to omit the method from the interface definition to prevent any service implementers from creating methods that are not needed.

## Creating the Service Class

The Service class in this example is EmployeeDataService. It implements the interface
IEmployeeDataService. Open the EmployeeDataService.cs file and place the following code
beneath the service contract created earlier:

```
public class EmployeeDataService : IEmployeeDataService
    {
        public List<String> GetData()
        {
            List<String> lstEmployee = new List<string>();
            lstEmployee.Add("Joydip");
            lstEmployee.Add("Peter");
            lstEmployee.Add("Michael");
            lstEmployee.Add("Sandry");
            lstEmployee.Add("Albert");
            lstEmployee.Add("Russell");
            return lstEmployee;
        }

        public List<String> GetEmployeeList()
        {
            List<String> lstEmployee = new List<string>();
            lstEmployee.Add("Joydip");
            lstEmployee.Add("Peter");
            lstEmployee.Add("Michael");
            lstEmployee.Add("Sandry");
            lstEmployee.Add("Albert");
            lstEmployee.Add("Russell");
            return lstEmployee;
        }
    }
```

Here's how the complete source code of the EmployeeDataService.cs file should look:

```
using System.ServiceModel;
using System.Collections.Generic;
using System;

namespace MyDataService
{
    [ServiceContract]
    public interface IEmployeeDataService
    {
        List<String> GetData();
        [OperationContract]
        List<String> GetEmployeeList();
    }

    public class EmployeeDataService : IEmployeeDataService
    {
        public List<String> GetData()
```

```
        {
            List<String> lstEmployee = new List<string>();
            lstEmployee.Add("Joydip");
            lstEmployee.Add("Peter");
            lstEmployee.Add("Michael");
            lstEmployee.Add("Sandry");
            lstEmployee.Add("Albert");
            lstEmployee.Add("Russell");
            return lstEmployee;
        }

        public List<String> GetEmployeeList()
        {
            List<String> lstEmployee = new List<string>();
            lstEmployee.Add("Joydip");
            lstEmployee.Add("Peter");
            lstEmployee.Add("Michael");
            lstEmployee.Add("Sandry");
            lstEmployee.Add("Albert");
            lstEmployee.Add("Russell");
            return lstEmployee;
        }
    }
}
```

It is important to note that, in this example, the interface and concrete implementations were completed in the same file within the same assembly. In many cases, this might not be the situation. The concrete service implementation might be in another file or in an entirely different project.

## Defining Data Contracts

Similar to service contracts, you can also define data contracts. If the operations defined as part of the service contract return simple types (that is, primitive types), you do not need to declare a data contract. However, data contracts are required if the service contract defines operations that return instances of complex types.

As an example, if the GetEmployeeList() method were to return an instance of a class type, you must define a data contract. Data contracts are used to define how in-memory types can be converted to a serializable format so that the data can be transmitted across the wire. A data contract is defined using the [DataContract] attribute, which can be applied to a struct or class. Individual members of a data contract are then defined using the DataMember attribute.

Data contracts in WCF are defined using the DataContract attribute. Here is an example:

```
using System.Runtime.Serialization;
[DataContract]
class EmployeeData
{
[DataMember] public int employeeID {get; set;}
[DataMember] public String firstName {get; set;}
[DataMember] public String lastName {get; set;}
}
```

In this example, the `EmployeeData` class is defined as a data contract, and each of the members within the class is offered as a `DataMember`. If you have a property that is calculated or otherwise shouldn't be passed across the communication wire, you can omit the `DataMember` attribute.

## Specifying the Binding Information

Now that you have created the service contract, data contract, and the service implementation, you must specify the binding information for the service to make it accessible by service consumers or clients. In order for a WCF service to be accessed by the clients, the service must expose at least one endpoint. An endpoint denotes the address, binding, and contract information for the service.

To specify the binding information for the service, open the `App.Config` file and insert the following code inside the `<system.serviceModel>` tags:

```
<system.serviceModel>
    <bindings>
      <basicHttpBinding>
        <binding name="BasicHttpBinding_IEmployeeDataService"
               closeTimeout="00:01:00"
          openTimeout="00:01:00" receiveTimeout="00:10:00" sendTimeout="00:01:00"
          allowCookies="false" bypassProxyOnLocal="false"
               hostNameComparisonMode="StrongWildcard"
          maxBufferSize="65536" maxBufferPoolSize="524288"
               maxReceivedMessageSize="65536"
          messageEncoding="Text" textEncoding="utf-8" transferMode="Buffered"
          useDefaultWebProxy="true">
          <readerQuotas maxDepth="32" maxStringContentLength="8192"
               maxArrayLength="16384"
            maxBytesPerRead="4096" maxNameTableCharCount="16384" />
          <security mode="None">
            <transport clientCredentialType="None" proxyCredentialType="None"
               realm="" />
            <message clientCredentialType="UserName" algorithmSuite="Default" />
          </security>
        </binding>
      </basicHttpBinding>
    </bindings>
    <client>
      <endpoint address="http://myserver/MyDataService/Service1.svc"
          binding="basicHttpBinding"
               bindingConfiguration="BasicHttpBinding_IEmployeeDataService"
          contract="IEmployeeDataService"
               name="BasicHttpBinding_IEmployeeDataService" />
    </client>
  </system.serviceModel>
```

This creates a `basicHttpBinding` for the example service specifying many additional properties on the binding (such as the `openTimeout`, `receiveTimeout`, sending timeout, `bufferSize`, and maximum message size). Additional configuration on the binding specifies that no security is being used for the transport. The endpoint is defined with an address that represents where the svc file will be hosted by IIS, notes that the endpoint should use the configuration defined earlier in the configuration, and that the contract for the service is IEmployeeDataService.

This declarative method for defining service endpoints is not the only way to configure your service. It is also possible to configure a service programmatically using the .NET API methods to creating the service host, endpoint, and binding. A simpler implementation using this method is as follows:

```
public static void Main()
{
ServiceHost serviceHost = new ServiceHost
    (typeof(MyDataService.EmployeeDataService));
serviceHost.AddEndpoint
    (typeof(MyDataService.EmployeeDataService),
    new BasicHttpBinding(),
    "http://myserver/MyDataService/Service1.svc");
serviceHost.Open();
Console.Writeline("Press the ENTER key to stop the service");
Console.Readline();
s.Close();
}
```

## Hosting the WCF Service

A WCF service can be hosted using IIS, or by using Windows Activation Service (WAS). To host your WCF service in IIS, you must simply create a virtual directory, and make it point to the directory where your service is located. WCF services hosted in IIS can be accessed using SOAP over HTTP.

Here's what you can specify in the App.Config file in the hosting application to access your WCF service hosted in IIS:

```
<?xml version="1.0" encoding="utf-8" ?>
<configuration>
  <system.serviceModel>
    <behaviors>
      <serviceBehaviors>
        <behavior>
          <serviceMetadata httpGetEnabled ="true"/>
        </behavior>
      </serviceBehaviors>
    </behaviors>
    <protocolMapping>
      <add binding="wsHttpBinding" scheme ="http"/>
    </protocolMapping>
  </system.serviceModel>
</configuration>
```

This configuration information notes that it is possible for the service to publish metadata information using the Get method of the HTTP protocol. The second section maps the HTTP protocol to the wsHttpBinding. Note that your endpoint configurations must still be completed and have been omitted from this example for brevity.

Just like with the configuration of bindings and endpoints, you can use the APIs to set up the service host. Similar to the previous example, the following assumes that all bindings and endpoints have been properly configured:

```
using System;
using System.ServiceModel;
namespace MyHostingApp
{
    class Program
    {
        static void Main()
        {
            ServiceHost serviceHost = new
                ServiceHost(typeof(MyDataService.EmployeeDataService));
            serviceHost.Open();
            Console.WriteLine("Press the ENTER to stop the service");
            Console.ReadLine();
            serviceHost.Close();
        }
    }
}
```

## Creating the Service Proxy

To create a WCF client, all you must do is create a proxy that can be used to connect to a particular endpoint on the service, and then call the operations via the proxy created earlier. You can use the command-line tool called `svcutil` to create a WCF service proxy, as shown here:

```
svcutil http://localhost/MyDataService/Service1.svc/out:MyDataServiceProxy.cs
```

When you execute the `svcutil` command-line tool with the parameters shown in Figure 9-4, the tool generates a client configuration file, and a proxy class for the WCF service would be generated in the output path specified.

**FIGURE 9-4:** Generating the service proxy

The proxy class looks like this:

```
   System.CodeDom.Compiler.GeneratedCodeAttribute("System.ServiceModel", "4.0.0.0")]
[System.ServiceModel.ServiceContractAttribute
      (ConfigurationName="IEmployeeDataService")]
public interface IEmployeeDataService
{    [System.ServiceModel.OperationContractAttribute
           (Action="http://tempuri.org/IEmployeeDataService/GetEmployeeList",
           ReplyAction="http://tempuri.org/IEmployeeDataService/
           GetEmployeeListResponse")]
    string[] GetEmployeeList();
}
[System.CodeDom.Compiler.GeneratedCodeAttribute("System.ServiceModel", "4.0.0.0")]
public interface IEmployeeDataServiceChannel : IEmployeeDataService,
      System.ServiceModel.IClientChannel
{
}
[System.Diagnostics.DebuggerStepThroughAttribute()]
[System.CodeDom.Compiler.GeneratedCodeAttribute("System.ServiceModel", "4.0.0.0")]
public partial class EmployeeDataServiceClient :
      System.ServiceModel.ClientBase<IEmployeeDataService>, IEmployeeDataService
{
    public EmployeeDataServiceClient()
    {
    }
       public EmployeeDataServiceClient(string endpointConfigurationName) :
           base(endpointConfigurationName)
    {
    }
       public EmployeeDataServiceClient(string endpointConfigurationName,
             string remoteAddress) :
           base(endpointConfigurationName, remoteAddress)
    {
    }
       public EmployeeDataServiceClient(string endpointConfigurationName,
             System.ServiceModel.EndpointAddress remoteAddress) :
           base(endpointConfigurationName, remoteAddress)
    {
    }
       public EmployeeDataServiceClient
           (System.ServiceModel.Channels.Binding binding,
           System.ServiceModel.EndpointAddress remoteAddress) :
           base(binding, remoteAddress)
    {
    }
       public string[] GetEmployeeList()
    {
       return base.Channel.GetEmployeeList();
    }
}
```

Similar to the way that ASMX web service proxy classes are created, it is typically *not* necessary to modify the methods that are automatically generated by the svcutil application. You will notice that the created proxy class will contain methods for each OperationContract defined within the ServiceContract.

Now that you have properly created the proxy class, it is time to create the client that will use the proxy to consume the service.

## Creating the Service Client — The Service Consumer

Let's create a WCF service client that will use the WCF service proxy class created earlier to connect to the WCF service and invoke its exposed operations. The WCF service client simply must instantiate the WCF service proxy, and then use this instance to call the `GetEmployeeList()` method. The returned employee names are stored in a string list and displayed on the console.

```
using System;
namespace MyDataServiceClient
{
    class Program
    {
        static void Main()
        {
            EmployeeDataServiceClient client = new EmployeeDataServiceClient();
            string[] lstEmployee = client.GetEmployeeList();
            Console.WriteLine("Displaying the Employee Names:\n");
            for (int index = 0; index < lstEmployee.Length; index++)
                Console.WriteLine(lstEmployee[index].ToString());
            Console.Read();
            client.Close();
        }
    }
}
```

You must be sure that you also add all configuration items to the application configuration as output from the `svcutil` application. It is important to note here that, when working with the auto-generated proxy classes, specifics of the WCF implementation are not needed, and coding can be done just as in any other application.

When you execute the application, the output is similar to what is shown in Figure 9-5.

**FIGURE 9-5:** Displaying the Employee Names

# WORKING WITH AN AJAX-ENABLED WCF SERVICE

You can easily create an Ajax-enabled WCF service using Visual Studio 2010 that will allows you to call a WCF service using client-side JavaScript. To create one, you right-click on the Solution Explorer, navigate to Add ➪ New Project, and then select "AJAX enabled WCF Service" from the list of the project templates displayed. Your Ajax-enabled WCF service would initially look like this:

```
using System.ServiceModel;
using System.ServiceModel.Activation;
namespace MyDataService
{
    [ServiceContract(Namespace = "")]
    [AspNetCompatibilityRequirements(RequirementsMode =
        AspNetCompatibilityRequirementsMode.Allowed)]
    public class MyAjaxEnabledService
    {
        // To use HTTP GET, add [WebGet] attribute. (Default ResponseFormat
        // is WebMessageFormat.Json)
        // To create an operation that returns XML,
        //     add [WebGet(ResponseFormat=WebMessageFormat.Xml)],
        //     and include the following line in the operation body:
        //         WebOperationContext.Current.OutgoingResponse.ContentType =
        //         "text/xml";
        [OperationContract]
        public void DoWork()
        {
            // Add your operation implementation here
            return;
        }

        // Add more operations here and mark them with [OperationContract]
    }
}
```

You must replace the default operation called DoWork() with your custom method. In the case of this example, you see a different implementation of the ServiceContract and OperationContract attributes where they are applied directly to a class and its methods, rather than to an interface that later has a concrete implementation. From this, you can start to see some of the flexibility provided with the WCF system.

When you create a new Ajax-enabled WCF service, Visual Studio 2010 also automatically inserts the necessary configuration information in your application's web.config file. The default additions to the configuration file will look similar to the following:

```
<system.serviceModel>
    <serviceHostingEnvironment aspNetCompatibilityEnabled="true" />
    <services>
        <service name="MyDataService.MyAjaxEnabledService">
            <endpoint address="" behaviorConfiguration=
```

```
            "MyDataService.MyAjaxEnabledServiceAspNetAjaxBehavior"
          binding="webHttpBinding" contract="MyDataService.MyAjaxEnabledService" />
      </service>
    </services>
    <behaviors>
      <endpointBehaviors>
        <behavior name="MyDataService.MyAjaxEnabledServiceAspNetAjaxBehavior">
          <enableWebScript />
        </behavior>
      </endpointBehaviors>
      <serviceBehaviors>
        <behavior name="">
          <serviceMetadata httpGetEnabled="true" />
          <serviceDebug includeExceptionDetailInFaults="false" />
        </behavior>
      </serviceBehaviors>
    </behaviors>
  </system.serviceModel>
```

You can see from this example that a service is defined, and the service endpoint is set up with a base address using the webHttpBinding and the specific service contract defined by the application.

Consuming this service is easy — just drag and drop a ScriptManager control in your web form and specify the service reference path, as shown here:

```
<asp:ScriptManager ID="ScriptManager1" runat="server">
        <Services>
            <asp:ServiceReference Path="~/MyAjaxEnabledService.svc" />
        </Services>
</asp:ScriptManager>
```

With this completed, you can now reference the service by name within JavaScript for you application. For example, if MyAjaxEnabledService contained a method for GetWeatherInformation that returned a string, you could use the following code to display the information to the user.

```
<script type="text/javascript">
function GetWeather()
{
    MyAjaxEnabledService.GetWeatherInformation(onSuccess);
}

function onSuccess(result)
{
    document.getElementById('myelement').value = result;
}
</script>
```

As you can see, this is very simple because the ScriptManager has completed most of the heavy lifting and created function calls with callbacks and other forms of management.

# REST AND WCF

Representational State Transfer (REST) is a style of accepting requests where information is put into the URI for the request. The basic advantages of RESTful services are simplicity, support for caching endpoints, and support for interoperability. Also, REST is lightweight when compared to SOAP, because it doesn't need too much XML markup code.

Note that REST is, in itself, a combination of standards, including the following:

➤  HTTP

➤  URL

➤  HTML

➤  XML

WCF provides excellent support for designing and implementing REST-based services through the use of a new binding called `WebHttpBinding`. Support for REST-based services is was initially provided in the 3.5 release of WCF.

Following is an example that illustrates how you can use WCF to implement RESTful services in your applications:

```
[ServiceContract]
interface IEmployeeDataService
{
[OperationContract]
[WebGet]
int GetEmployeeID(string employeeName);
}
```

It is simple to add the `[WebGet]` attribute to your method to make it available via a REST format. WCF 4.0 provides greater control over the structure/format of the URL structure by expanding the `WebGet` attribute to allow for a `UriTemplate` to be specified.

For example, to define a `UriTemplate` for subtraction with two values being passed, you could use something similar to the following:

```
[WebGet(UriTemplate = "Sub?x={x}&y={y}")]
```

If you are creating a WCF service that should be accepting values via a HTTP `Post` request, you would use the `WebInvoke` attribute rather than the `WebGet`. Both attributes are contained in the `System.ServiceModel.Web` namespace.

# IMPLEMENTING A WCF SERVICE DECLARATIVELY

A *declarative WCF service* is one that you can implement using a configuration-based, flexible, extensible model. You typically use XML to store a declarative WCF service. Declarative services are those that are defined declaratively in XAML. You can define what you would want your service to do, rather than how it is to be done. Also, you can define the service operations and even the implementation of the service operations declaratively.

## Defining the Service Contract

Consider the following service contract implemented programmatically:

```
public interface IWCFService
{
  String GetAddress(String customerID);
}
```

You can now use declarative programming in WCF .NET 4 and define the same service contract, as shown in the following code snippet:

```
<ServiceContract Name="IWCFService">
 <OperationContract Name="GetAddress">
  <OperationArgument Name="input" Type="p:String" />
  <OperationArgument Direction="Out" Name="Result"
   Type="p:String" />
  </OperationContract>
</ServiceContract>
```

Note that the `<ServiceContract>` element shown in this code snippet is used to specify the name of the service contract. The `<OperationContract>` element is used to expose one or more operations. In essence, it is used to specify one or more operations that are exposed by the service.

Now, you can have parameters for your operations, right? The `GetAddress()` method accepts a string argument — the `customerID`. The method returns the address of the customer represented by the `customerID` passed as parameter to the method.

To represent the parameters or arguments of an operation, you must use the `<OperationArgument>` element. Essentially, you would have one service contract element with one or more operation contracts, with the operation contracts, in turn, having one or more operation argument elements. Note that the direction attribute denotes whether the argument is an input or an output.

Once you have defined the service contract, you must define how the contract would be projected — that is, what protocols should the consumers of the service contract use, and so on. Here is how you can do this for the service contract defined earlier:

```
<Service.KnownProjections>
  <SoapContractProjection x:Name="IWCFServiceSoapProjection">
   <ServiceContract x:Name="IWCFService">
    <OperationContract Name="GetAddress" x:Name="GetAddress">
     <OperationArgument Name="customerID" Type="p:String" />
     <OperationArgument Direction="Out" Name="Result"
      Type="p:String" />
     </OperationContract>
    </ServiceContract>
   </SoapContractProjection>
  </Service.KnownProjections>
```

## Hosting the Service

To host the declarative service created earlier in this section, you can use the following code:

```
class Program
{
   static Service service;
    static void Main()
   {
      using (TextReader textReader = File.OpenText("IWCFService.xml"))
      {
         service = (Service)XamlServices.Load(textReader);
      }
      Uri address = new Uri("http://localhost:8000/IWCFService");
      WorkflowServiceHost host = new WorkflowServiceHost (service, address);
      try
      {
         host.Open();
         Console.WriteLine("Service started...press any key to stop...");
         Console.ReadLine();
      }
      catch (Exception ex)
      {
         Console.WriteLine("Error occured: "+ex.Message);
      }
      finally
      {
         host.Close();
      }
   }
}
```

Note in the previous code snippet that the XAML file called `IWCFService.xml` is loaded using the `File.OpenText()` method. Next, an instance of `WorkflowServiceHost` is created, and it is used to start the service by making a call to the `Open()` method. Note that the `WorkflowServiceHost` class extends the `ServiceHostBase` class, and can be used to host workflow-based services. You can use this class to configure and expose a workflow as a service so that it can be consumed by clients.

## Implementing the Service Logic Declaratively

The following code snippet illustrates how you can implement the service logic in XAML declaratively for the service created earlier:

```
<?xml version="1.0" encoding="utf-8" ?>
<Service
 xmlns="clr-namespace:System.ServiceModel;
   assembly=System.WorkflowServiceModel"
 xmlns:wsm="clr-namespace:System.WorkflowServiceModel;
   assembly=System.WorkflowServiceModel"
 xmlns:wsma="clr-namespace:System.WorkflowServiceModel.
   Activities;assembly=System.WorkflowServiceModel"
 xmlns:wm="clr-namespace:System.WorkflowModel;
```

```
  assembly=System.WorkflowModel"
xmlns:wma="clr-namespace:System.WorkflowModel.
  Activities;assembly=System.WorkflowModel.Activities"
xmlns:b="clr-namespace:BasicService;assembly=BasicService"
xmlns:s="clr-namespace:System;assembly=mscorlib"
xmlns:ss="clr-namespace:System.ServiceModel;
  assembly=System.ServiceModel"
xmlns:sss="clr-namespace:System.ServiceModel.Security;
  assembly=System.ServiceModel"
xmlns:sx="clr-namespace:System.Xml;
  assembly=System.Runtime.Serialization"
xmlns:p="http://schemas.microsoft.com/netfx/2008/
   xaml/schema"xmlns:p1="http://tempuri.org"
xmlns:x="http://schemas.microsoft.com/winfx/2006/xaml"
xmlns:x2="http://schemas.microsoft.com/netfx/2008/xaml"
xmlns:con="http://schemas.contoso.com/order/2008">
<Service.KnownProjections>
 <SoapContractProjection x:Name="IWCFServiceSoapProjection">
  <ServiceContract x:Name="IWCFServiceContract">
   <OperationContract Name="GetMessage" x:Name="GetMessage">
    <OperationArgument Name="customerID" Type="p:String" />
    <OperationArgument Direction="Out" Name="Result"
     Type="p:String" />
    </OperationContract>
   </ServiceContract>
  </SoapContractProjection>
 </Service.KnownProjections>
 <Service.Implementation>
  <WorkflowServiceImplementation Name="WCFService"
   xmlns="clr-namespace:System.WorkflowServiceModel;
    assembly=System.WorkflowServiceModel">
   <WorkflowServiceImplementation.Body>
    <ServiceOperation OperationContract="{x2:Reference
     IWCFService.GetMessage}" CanCreateInstance="true"
     xmlns="clr-namespace:System.WorkflowServiceModel.
      Activities;assembly=System.WorkflowServiceModel">
     <ServiceOperation.Body>
      <DynamicActivityAction
        xmlns="clr-namespace:System.WorkflowModel;
        assembly=System.WorkflowModel">
      <DynamicActivityAction.InVariables>
        <Variable x:Name="customerID" x:TypeArguments="p:String" />
      </DynamicActivityAction.InVariables>
      <DynamicActivityAction.OutVariables>
        <Variable x:Name="Result"
         x:TypeArguments="p:String" />
      </DynamicActivityAction.OutVariables>
      <wma:Assign x:TypeArguments="p:String" To="out
       [Result]" Value="Result" />
      </DynamicActivityAction>
     </ServiceOperation.Body>
    </ServiceOperation>
   </WorkflowServiceImplementation.Body>
  </WorkflowServiceImplementation>
```

```
    </Service.Implementation>
    <Service.Endpoints>
     <Endpoint Uri="http://localhost:8080/GetMessage">
       <Endpoint.Binding>
        <ss:BasicHttpBinding />
       </Endpoint.Binding>
       <Endpoint.ContractProjection>
        <SoapContractProjection>
         <SoapContractProjection.Contract>
          <ServiceContract x:Name="IWCFService">
           <OperationContract Name="GetMessage"
            x:Name="IWCFService.GetMessage">
           <OperationArgument Name="customerID" Type="p:String" />
           <OperationArgument Name="Result"
            Type="p:String" Direction="Out" />
           </OperationContract>
          </ServiceContract>
         </SoapContractProjection.Contract>
        </SoapContractProjection>
       </Endpoint.ContractProjection>
      </Endpoint>
     </Service.Endpoints>
    </Service>
```

## SUMMARY

Windows Communication Foundation (WCF) is a framework from Microsoft that provides a simplified approach to designing and implementing applications that can inter-communicate. It provides a seamless integration of a number of enterprise technologies under a single umbrella. This chapter looked at the fundamentals of WCF, as well as how you can implement a WCF service and then consume it.

Chapter 10 focuses on enhancements to the .NET core framework, items mostly contained only inside the System namespace.

# 10

# Enhancements to the .NET Core Framework

Changes in a release of a new .NET Framework version may affect the core run-time engine (including Common Language Run-time and the Common Type System), the Base Class Library (BCL), Framework services (such as ASP.NET, WPF, WCF and so on), and connected tools and utilities.

While changes in .NET 3.0, 3.5, and 3.5 SP1 targeted mainly the Framework services part and the BCL, the .NET 4 release touched the Common Language Run-time (CLR) significantly and added brand new services (and related BCL types) to shift toward new programming paradigms. This chapter and the following ones (closing with Chapter 21) detail all the new technologies, paradigms, services, and tools that are new in .NET 4.

This chapter covers fundamental enhancements and improvements to the core .NET Framework. You can use them in your managed applications independently of whether you are using Windows Forms, ASP.NET, Windows Presentation Foundation (WPF), Windows Workflow Foundation (WF), Windows Communication Foundation (WCF), Silverlight, Azure, SQL Server, SharePoint, or whatever other technology you use with .NET.

Here's what you'll discover in this chapter:

> *Changes in the CLR* — This .NET framework version got a new CLR that has many great enhancements. Now a native process is able to host more CLR versions side-by-side. As an important improvement to Component Object Model (COM) interoperability and version resiliency, the CLR can handle type equivalence. Programming language changes in this version are primarily about dynamic capabilities, based on a new component called Dynamic Language Run-time (DLR).

> *Parallel computing* — Using the Task Parallel Library (TPL) and Parallel Language Integrated Query (PLINQ), you can turn your sequential algorithms into concurrent ones without having to write tremendous plumbing code for threading infrastructure.

When you can split your algorithm into tasks that can run parallel, TPL undertakes the challenge to execute them concurrently, while entirely hiding low-level constructs (such as threads, semaphores, locks, and so on) from you.

➤ *Code contracts* — Contracts allow you to express preconditions, postconditions, and object invariants in your code for run-time checking, static analysis, and documentation.

➤ *Managed Extensibility Framework (MEF)* — .NET 4 contains a new technology that allows you to shift your statically compiled applications into dynamically composed ones. With MEF, you have a flexible plug-in system where the composition is based on declarative syntax, practically free from any plumbing code.

## CHANGES IN COMMON LANGUAGE RUN-TIME

Admittedly the soul of the .NET Framework is the CLR. At the beginning of the .NET history, each of the .NET 1.0, .NET 1.1, and .NET 2.0 versions had their own CLRs. The .NET 3.0, .NET 3.5, and .NET 3.5 SP1 Framework versions used CLR 2.0, because these versions were about extending the BCL and adding architecture services (like WF, WCF, WPF, and Cardspace) to the framework.

After almost five years, .NET 4 ships with a new CLR, consistently having the version number 4.0. In this section, you will learn the following important core features of CLR 4.0:

➤ Now a native process is able to host more CLR versions side-by-side.

➤ DLR is an organic part of the .NET Framework.

➤ A type equivalence feature implemented in the CLR helps deploying applications accessing COM objects without deploying Primary Interop Assemblies (PIAs).

 *This section contains sample code using the C# 4.0 syntax, mainly the feature called* dynamic binding, *but also named and optional parameters. You may not be familiar with these syntax elements. Chapter 25 gives you a detailed overview of them with many useful code snippets.*

*You can go on reading this chapter without being aware of these constructs, because they are intuitive enough. If you find something in the source code where you suspect a syntax error or a typo, note that it's probably not an error but rather the use of C# 4.0 syntax.*

## In-Process Side-By-Side Execution

The CLR development team at Microsoft invested a lot of resources to provide compatibility among CLRs, so that each new version would be highly compatible with the old versions. Theoretically, each new version of the .NET Framework could have been developed so that it was completely compatible with older versions, and a concrete CLR could run applications developed with any of the preceding versions. In this way, old .NET Framework versions could be seamlessly updated to a newer one so that only one (the latest) version is installed on a computer, while being able to run the applications originally targeting an old framework version.

## Understanding Side-By-Side Execution

This approach has serious limitations. Aiming at full compatibility would mean that any design issues, naming mistakes, or paradigm decisions should stay in the framework forever. This simply does not work, because it is a very strict limitation for future innovations! *Full compatibility* means not only that all source code will compile with all new framework versions, but also all documented and undocumented behaviors remain the same. It would mean, for example, that even if you have multiple CPU cores in your machine, any existing framework implementation would not be allowed to leverage on this capability implicitly, because of backward compatibility issues, as .NET Framework 1.0 BCL was designed with single CPU core in mind.

The CLR team avoided the "one-CLR-rules" scenario and designed the .NET Framework from the very first version with the capability to run separate versions side-by-side on the same computer. This is a good approach from the point of view that it prevents the "innovation bottleneck." However, the side-by-side scenario opens up an important question of which CLR version an application or a component should use from the ones installed on the machine.

## Issues Before CLR 4.0

.NET Framework was designed to run the application using the CLR with which it was built. Well, this idea works well for managed applications. The CLR loads into the process space of the application, and that simply works. However, when the original CLR is not present, the application must run with another version of the CLR that is automatically the latest version installed on the computer.

There are issues with managed COM components used by native applications (like Word, Excel, Outlook, or other applications expecting COM extensions). If the native application tries to load two managed COM components with separate CLRs, it simply cannot be done. Only one CLR version can be loaded into an operating system process, which always happens to be the latest installed on the machine.

## .NET 4 Changes in CLR Hosting

CLR 4.0 provides a new approach to side-by-side hosting. The installation of a new .NET Framework has no effect on existing applications. Managed applications and the add ins they load run against the version of the .NET Framework with which they were built and tested. In contrast to the preceding versions, the applications do not automatically use the latest .NET Framework installed on the machine, unless explicitly directed to do so.

Native applications now can host managed COM components built and tested with separate CLRs. The process can host more CLR versions side-by-side, and so each COM component can run with the CLR version with which it was registered.

Using .NET 4, the situation presented earlier with the Excel add-in developed by Agnes goes away. While the appropriate .NET Frameworks are installed on the customer's machines, Excel's process will host all the CLRs required for running the set of add-ins. Microsoft promises to keep this feature in all new .NET Framework versions.

# DLR Integration

Most developers are familiar with the fact that types and operations are strictly checked during the compilation process. The compiler generates Microsoft Intermediate Language (MSIL) code that explicitly carries out those operations by invoking methods.

There are programming languages that behave adversely — for example, the *dynamic languages*. The compiler makes only a few checks upon types and their operations. The majority of them are postponed to the execution of the corresponding operation at run-time. In addition to the dynamic languages, there are *script languages* and *object models* (for example, COM objects over the Microsoft Office functionality, the DTE object model in Visual Studio, the HTML DOM in Internet Explorer, and so on) that also check operations at run-time.

For a long time, .NET was unable to handle the interoperability between static and dynamic languages in a straightforward and easy-to-use way. It simply did not fit into the compiling approach, and the CLR itself was designed entirely with a static type system in mind.

## Expression Trees in .NET 3.5

.NET Framework 3.5 added a little twist that targeted dynamism. Related to LINQ query expressions, a new feature was added to the language compilers — the capability to create expression trees.

*Expression trees* are data structures representing expressions that can be evaluated at run-time. The compiler supports creating code that assembles an expression tree instead of compiling instructions to calculate the expression value. For example, the developer can declare a lambda expression like this:

```
Expression<Func<int, bool>> exprTree = value => value > 42;
```

Behind the scenes, the compiler creates MSIL instructions representing the following code:

```
ParameterExpression valueParam = Expression.Parameter(typeof(int), "value");
ConstantExpression fortyTwo = Expression.Constant(42, typeof(int));
BinaryExpression valueGreaterThanFortyTwo =
  Expression.LessThan(valueParam, fortyTwo);
Expression<Func<int, bool>> exprTree =
  Expression.Lambda<Func<int, bool>>(
    valueGreaterThanFortyTwo,
    new ParameterExpression[] { valueParam });
```

At run-time, an expression tree can be evaluated with concrete parameter values. For example, you can print out the result like this:

```
Console.WriteLine(exprTree.Compile().Invoke(25));
```

This "small" compiler feature in .NET 3.5 was an important step toward supporting dynamic language integration. The compiler creates code to represent an operation, and allows the run-time to determine how to carry out the operation. This feature makes it possible to translate a LINQ query expression into a SQL query to be executed at the database backend.

## DLR to the Rescue

.NET 4 has a set of services that add dynamic programming capabilities to the CLR and allow interoperation between .NET objects and dynamic languages. The DLR solves the problem of dynamically typed languages like Python and Ruby not easily running directly on top of the CLR (because the CLR is primarily designed for statically typed languages). The DLR has the services to help plug this hole and allow dynamically typed languages to run on top of the CLR (by working through the DLR).

Following are the main advantages of the DLR:

➤ *The DLR helps language implementers port their dynamic languages to .NET.* — With the traditional approach, language implementers needed to emit code (of course, in addition to implementing lexers, parsers, semantic analysis, and so on). Virtual machines allowed the languages to emit a higher-level intermediate language instead of fully optimized machine code. With the DLR, they do not need to emit code. Instead, they can produce an abstract semantic tree (.NET expression trees) and some run-time helpers if needed. The DLR and CLR do the rest of the work of running the operation represented by the semantic tree.

➤ *Languages implemented using the DLR still benefit from improvements in the CLR.* — The CLR is designed to support a wide variety of programming languages, and it contains shared services to this purpose such as garbage collection, just-in-time (JIT) compilation, a sandboxed security model, and many more. When a new CLR version is released (for example, with performance improvements), languages automatically benefit from these enhancements.

➤ *In the DLR, Microsoft provides common language interoperability with fast dynamic invocations.* — The interoperability is based on common protocol for objects implemented in one language to be used by other languages. *Dynamic typing* means that the object can decide (at run-time) if it supports a particular operation with the specified parameters or not. The DLR enables dynamic objects to participate in this protocol for negotiating how to perform abstract operations on any object. The DLR also provides a *call site caching mechanism* that allows fast dynamic invocations without the performance penalties of the CLR's reflection model.

➤ *Applications can use any language supporting the DLR hosting model.* — The DLR provides multiple script run-time environments per `AppDomain`, as well as remote script run-times in other `AppDomains`. Host applications can execute script files or snippets of code in the context of those bindings — by injecting variables into the context, and extracting variable values after executing the code.

Figure 10-1 shows how strongly typed and dynamic languages can use the DLR.

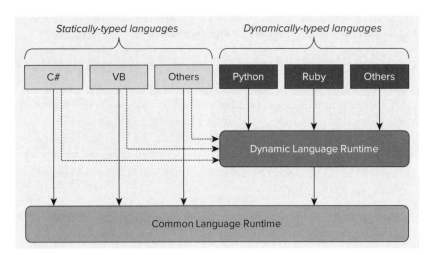

**FIGURE 10-1:** Utilizing the DLR

Strongly typed languages (such as Visual Basic and C#) use the CLR directly to execute applications. Dynamically typed languages (such as Python and Ruby) can't easily run directly on top of the CLR, because the CLR is primarily designed for statically typed languages. The DLR provides this missing layer for dynamically typed languages, and also helps statically typed languages access objects and services developed in a dynamic way.

Following are the fundamental services of the DLR (of course, there are others):

➤ *Call sites* — These provide a caching mechanism per operation in dynamic code. Every time you execute an operation such as MyOp(A, B), the DLR would have to analyze what MyOp means with A and B as operation parameters. For example, when MyOp is addition, A is a floating-point number, and B is an integer, MyOp(A, B) results in a floating-point number representing A+B. Without having a cache, the analysis could take much longer than the A+B operation itself. With caching, this performance penalty can be significantly reduced.

➤ *Expression trees* — These are the extensions of expression trees introduced in .NET 3.5 with LINQ providers. They are key players in the lowering of the bar for porting (dynamic) languages to .NET, and so are absolutely one of the core pillars of the DLR. Expression trees are compiled (the DLR ships this compiler as a part of its services), and the result is a delegate for invoking the code represented by the tree.

➤ *Dynamic object interoperability* — As a core principle of dynamic operations, objects receive messages describing operations with their actual parameters. Dynamic object interoperability is about providing service types to create objects that can translate these messages to explicit operations.

Depending on the physical type of the object to be accessed dynamically, separate communication models can be used. For example, to access CLR-hosted objects, some mechanism built over .NET reflection can be used. For COM objects, the standard COM IDispatch-based mechanism can be applicable. For other types of object provider environments, some other run-time binding could work. This kind of job is the responsibility of run-time binders. Figure 10-2 shows an architectural overview of how languages, DLR services, and run-time environments work together.

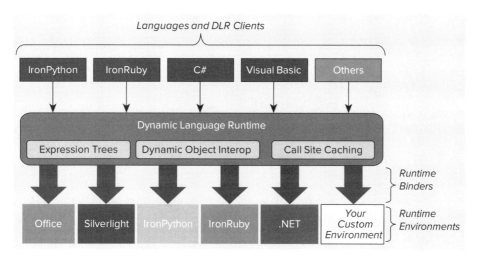

**FIGURE 10-2:** DLR high-level architecture diagram

The DLR encourages you to interact with dynamic languages and also to create your own dynamic objects. In the remaining discussion of the DLR, you'll learn how easy these tasks are — by going through examples.

## Invoking IronPython Code Example

In this example, you write a very simple IronPython program and access it from a C# console application. It will be very simple, so you should be able to understand it without any Python background. To use IronPython, you must download and install the run-time from the Downloads tab of the IronPython project's home page on CodePlex at `http://ironpython.codeplex.com`.

Create a new C# console application project and name it `IronPythonRunner`. Use the Browse tab of the Add reference dialog to navigate to the IronPython run-time's installation folder, and add the selected assemblies shown in Figure 10-3 to the project.

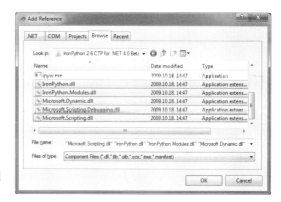

**FIGURE 10-3:** IronPython run-time assemblies

> *You will find this folder directly under your operating system's* Program Files *folder (on 64-bit systems, under the* Program Files (x86) *folder) in a folder with an* IronPython *prefix.*

Add a new text file item and name it Calculate.py, where .py is the standard extension for IronPython program files. This file should be in the same folder from where the console application is started, so set the Build Action property of Calculate.py to Content, and the "Copy to Output Directory" property to Copy Always.

Enter the following short program into the Calculate.py file:

```
def Add(A, B):
    return A + B
```

This small Python code snippet adds A and B, and retrieves the result of this operation. What is less obvious if you're not familiar with Python is that A and B can be any objects, and the operation will be successful while the "+" operator is defined on their types.

Copy the code in Listing 10-1 into the Program.cs file to invoke the Python code snippet.

**LISTING 10-1:** Program.cs File of IronPythonRunner

```csharp
using System;
using IronPython.Hosting;

namespace IronPythonRunner
{
  class Program
  {
    static void Main(string[] args)
    {
      var ipy = Python.CreateRuntime();
      dynamic calculator = ipy.UseFile("Calculate.py");
      Console.WriteLine(calculator.Add("Welcome in IronPython on ",
          DateTime.Now.ToShortDateString()));
      for (int i = 1; i < 4; i++)
        for (int j = 5; j < 8; j++)
          Console.WriteLine("{0} + {1} = {2}", i, j,
            calculator.Add(i, j));
    }
  }
}
```

*Code file [Program.cs] available for download at Wrox.com*

The code is really simple. The `Python` object located in the `Python.Hosting` namespace is responsible for managing the run-time environment. You can obtain a reference for an object (named `calculator` in this C# context) to access the operations defined by the `Calculate.py` mini-program:

```
var ipy = Python.CreateRuntime();
dynamic calculator = ipy.UseFile("Calculate.py");
```

You can invoke the `Add` operation defined in the Python code snippet through the `calculator` object:

```
calculator.Add("Welcome in IronPython on ",
DateTime.Now.ToShortDateString())calculator.Add(i, j)
```

As a benefit of dynamic behavior, you can pass two strings or two integers to `Add`, and it dynamically maps the call to string concatenation or integer addition, respectively. Of course, there are many other type combinations accepted by `Add`. Figure 10-4 shows the output of the console application.

**FIGURE 10-4:** Output of the application

 *The IronPython run-time comes with a brief language tutorial. Open the* `Tutorial\Tutorial.htm` *file under the installation folder, and play with the language by modifying the* `Calculate.py` *and* `Program.cs` *files.*

## ExpandoObject Example

The DLR defines an interesting type called `ExpandoObject` in the `System.Dynamic` namespace. This is a great type to demonstrate the power of the DLR when used together with C# 4.0, which now supports dynamic operations (operations resolved at run-time). Instead of telling you what this type is about, let's first see an example.

Create a C# console application and name it `ExpandoObjectDemo`. Listing 10-2 shows the code to copy into the `Program.cs` file.

**LISTING 10-2:** Program.cs File of ExpandoObjectDemo

```
using System;
using System.Dynamic;

namespace ExpandoObjectDemo
{
  class Program
  {
    static void Main(string[] args)
    {
      dynamic customer = new ExpandoObject();
      customer.Id = 116;
      customer.Name = "John Doe";
      Console.WriteLine("Customer: ({0}), {1}",
        customer.Id, customer.Name);

      dynamic address = new ExpandoObject();
      address.Id = "SHIP";
      address.Line1 = "xxxx 7th Street";
      address.Line2 = "My Great Company";
      address.City = "Los Angeles";
      address.State = "CA";
      Console.WriteLine("Address type and State: ({0}), {1}",
        address.Id, address.State);
    }
  }
}
```

*Code file [Program.cs] available for download at Wrox.com*

Reading this code, the first question developers might ask is, "Does this code compile at all?" This example creates two `ExpandoObject` instances. The first time it is used as a `Customer` object with `Id` and `Name` properties; the second time as an `Address` object with properties such as `Id`, `Line1`, `State`, and so on. Is this object so flexible?

The answer is that the preceding code compiles and runs without errors or warnings, because of the dynamic behavior of `ExpandoObject`. Moreover, the following code snippet is also valid. You could insert it into Listing 10-2.

```
dynamic triangle = new ExpandoObject();
triangle.A = new { X = 0, Y = 0, Z = 0 };
triangle.B = new { X = 100, Y = 100, Z = 0 };
triangle.C = new { X = 0, Y = 100, Z = 100 };
```

`ExpandoObject` is a dynamic "jolly joker" whose members can be dynamically added and removed at run-time. The only public member defined by this type is its default constructor, and, of course, it inherits public methods from `System.Object`. Figure 10-5 shows all of them as shown in the IntelliSense list when editing your code.

The key to this behavior is the `dynamic` type used to declare the variables referencing `ExpandoObject` instances. This is a new type in C# that instructs the compiler to treat all operations on the referenced object dynamically, using the DLR.

```
class Program
{
  static void Main(string[] args)
  {
    object customer = new ExpandoObject();
    customer.
  }                    Equals
}                      GetHashCode
                       GetType
                       ToString
```

**FIGURE 10-5:** ExpandoObject public members in IntelliSense

For the statements setting `ExpandoObject` properties, instead of compiling MSIL instructions directly to set those properties, the compiler emits code that sends messages to the object, such as, "Set the property named `Id` to 116." (Regardless, MSIL property setter instructions could not be emitted because an `ExpandoObject` does not have an `Id` property.)

The DLR sends the message to the object at run-time, and that stores the name and value of property in a dictionary. When the `Id` property is about to read, a "Get the value of the property named `Id`" message is sent to the `ExpandoObject`, and that uses its dictionary to look up and retrieve the value.

## DynamicObject Example

The DLR provides you with utility types you can use to create your own dynamic objects. At run-time, a dynamic operation is dispatched to the target object with the following steps:

1. If the target is a COM object, the operation is dispatched dynamically through the COM `IDispatch` interface.

2. If the target object type implements the `IDynamicMetaObjectProvider` interface of the `System.Dynamic` namespace, that interface is used, and the target itself is asked to perform the operation.

3. Otherwise, the target is a standard .NET object, and the operation will be dispatched using reflection on its type, and a C# "run-time binder" that implements a C# lookup and overload resolution semantics at run-time.

The `IDynamicMetaObjectProvider` interface contains about a dozen methods to implement. The DLR provides the `DynamicObject` type to implement this interface as a base class for your dynamic objects.

Let's create a simple dynamic class to resolve environment variables with property syntax. For example, you do not have to write something like this:

```
Environment.GetVariable("Path")
```

Instead, you can use a dynamic shortcut such as this:

```
envObject.Path
```

Start with a C# console application, and name it `DynamicObjectDemo`. Add a new class item file with the name `DynamicEnvironment.cs` to the project. Listing 10-3 shows the code you should copy to this file.

**LISTING 10-3: DynamicEnvironment.cs**

```
using System;
using System.Dynamic;

namespace DynamicObjectDemo
{
  public class DynamicEnvironment: DynamicObject
  {
    private EnvironmentVariableTarget _TargetEnv;
    private bool _IgnoreMissingProperty;

    public DynamicEnvironment(
      EnvironmentVariableTarget targetEnv = EnvironmentVariableTarget.User,
      bool ignoreMissingProperty = false)
    {
      _TargetEnv = targetEnv;
      _IgnoreMissingProperty = ignoreMissingProperty;
    }

    public override bool TryGetMember(GetMemberBinder binder, out object result)
    {
      result = Environment.GetEnvironmentVariable(binder.Name, _TargetEnv);
      return result != null || _IgnoreMissingProperty;
    }
  }
}
```

*Code file [DynamicEnvironment.cs] available for download at Wrox.com*

The constructor allows you to pass an optional `EnvironmentVariableTarget` to set if you want to bind the object to the machine or to the user environment. The `ignoreMissingProperty` parameter's `true` value allows you to retrieve a `null` value for non-existing environment variables instead of raising run-time exception.

The property name resolution is handled by the overridden `TryGetMember` method. It accepts two parameters. The `binder` represents the operation message sent by the DLR. In this case, it holds the name of the property to resolve. The `result` should be set to the object to be retrieved from the operation, and, in this case, it will be the value of the property. The return value of the method is set to `true` if the operation message can be handled by this method; otherwise it is `false`.

The logic of the method is simple. If the property name refers to an existing environment variable, the resolution is successful, and retrieves the variable value; otherwise, it retrieves `null`, or fails, depending on the value of `_IgnoreMissingProperty`.

Listing 10-4 shows the `Program.cs` file demonstrating `DynamicEnvironment`.

**LISTING 10-4:** Program.cs File of DynamicObjectDemo

```csharp
using System;

namespace DynamicObjectDemo
{
  class Program
  {
    static void Main(string[] args)
    {
      dynamic env = new DynamicEnvironment(ignoreMissingProperty: true);
      Console.WriteLine(env.Path);
      Console.WriteLine(env.Temp);
      Console.WriteLine(env.NonExisting ?? "<null>");
    }
  }
}
```

*Code file [Program.cs] available for download at Wrox.com*

This program runs as expected. Because there is no environment variable with name `NonExisting`, the third output line will be "`<null>`". Set the `ignoreMissingProperty` value to `false` to ask `DynamicEnvironment` to raise an exception when an unknown property is used. Running the program now will raise a `RuntimeBinderException` (shown in Figure 10-6) telling you that `NonExisting` property could not be resolved.

**FIGURE 10-6:** RuntimeBinderException raised

 *This example is very simple, and not really robust. For example, it cannot resolve USERNAME or MACHINENAME, because those are not available through the Environment.GetEnvironmentvariable method. Play with this example and try to make it more useful by extending it with the missing features!*

## Type Equivalence

.NET 4 has greatly improved COM interoperability. From the CLR's point of view, the most important feature is type equivalence. It is required to deploy applications without deploying PIAs for the COM components with which the application cooperates. This feature is implemented at the

CLR level, and, in addition to the support for "No-PIA Deployment," it also provides the capability for you to create applications with loose type-coupling and version resiliency.

To interoperate with a certain COM interface, you must use a .NET type wrapping the functionality of that interface. Building these wrapper types manually is very laborious, especially when you have hundreds of COM interfaces (for example, in the case of using the Microsoft Office automation model). PIAs are .NET assemblies generated from COM interfaces to facilitate strongly typed interoperability. For large object models, the related PIAs are large as well, so these assemblies can easily bloat the size of your application. They can also cause versioning issues when they are distributed independently of your application.

The No-PIA feature allows you to continue to use PIAs at design time without having them around at run-time. Instead, the C# compiler will append the small part of the PIA that a program actually uses directly to its assembly. At run-time, the PIA does not have to be loaded.

## No-PIA Example Featuring Type Equivalence

Let's create a simple example to help understand the concept of type equivalence. This application will create a Word document and insert some text and a table into it.

Start Visual Studio 2010 and create a new C# Console Application project with the name `TypeEquivalenceDemo`. Add a new C# Class Library project with the name `WordHelper` to the solution, and a reference to this project from `TypeEquivalenceDemo`.

This example will use Word automation, so you must add a reference for the `Microsoft.Office.Interop.Word` interoperability assembly (PIA for Word) to both projects. When using the Add Reference dialog, you may see more instances of this assembly. Select one with the version number `12.0.0.0`. When you select the referenced assembly in Solution Explorer, you can see its Embed Interop Types property set to `true`, as shown in Figure 10-7.

**FIGURE 10-7:** Embed Interop Types is set to True

This property value is the key to using the No-PIA feature. During build time, the compiler examines the `Microsoft.Office.Interop.Word` assembly, collects all types directly or indirectly touched by the callers, and bakes them into the application assemblies.

Rename the `Class1.cs` in `WordHelper` to `TableHelper.cs` and copy the code in Listing 10-5 into this file.

**LISTING 10-5:** TableHelper.cs

```csharp
using System;
using Word = Microsoft.Office.Interop.Word;

namespace WordHelper
{
  public static class TableHelper
  {
    public static void InsertTable(Word.Application wordApp, int rows, int columns)
    {
      wordApp.ActiveDocument.Tables.Add(
      Range: wordApp.Selection.Range,
      NumRows: rows,
      NumColumns: columns,
      DefaultTableBehavior: Word.WdDefaultTableBehavior.wdWord9TableBehavior,
      AutoFitBehavior: Word.WdAutoFitBehavior.wdAutoFitFixed);
    }

    public static Type WordType
    {
      get { return typeof(Word.Application); }
    }
  }
}
```

*Code file [TableHelper.cs] available for download at Wrox.com*

Change the content of the Program.cs file in the TypeEquivalenceDemo project to the one you see in Listing 10-6.

**LISTING 10-6:** Program.cs

```csharp
using System;
using WordHelper;
using Word = Microsoft.Office.Interop.Word;

namespace TypeEquivalenceDemo
{
  class Program
  {
    static void Main(string[] args)
    {
      var word = new Word.Application();
      word.Visible = true;
      word.Documents.Add();
      word.Selection.TypeText(Text: "This is a table");
      TableHelper.InsertTable(word, 3, 2);
      Console.WriteLine("Equality: {0}",
        typeof(Word.Application) == TableHelper.WordType);
```

*continues*

**LISTING 10-6** *(continued)*

```
        Console.WriteLine("Equivalence: {0}",
          typeof(Word.Application).IsEquivalentTo(TableHelper.WordType));
      }
    }
  }
```

*Code file [Program.cs] available for download at Wrox.com*

When you run this application, it does exactly what you assume according to the source code — it creates a Word document and inserts the "This is a table" text, followed by a table of three rows and two columns. The interesting thing is how this task is done. Because of the No-PIA mode, a few types are added to both the `TypeEquivalenceDemo` and `WordHelper` assemblies representing Word interoperability types in the `Microsoft.Office.Interop.Word` assembly. Such a type is `Word.Application`.

But, if there are two `Word.Application` type declarations (created by the compiler) in two separate assemblies, the .NET Framework's Common Type System handles them as separate, unrelated types. In this case, how do you pass a `Word.Application` instance defined in the `TypeEquivalenceDemo` assembly when calling `TableHelper.InsertTable` that is defined in the `WordHelper` assembly and expecting a `Word.Application` type also defined there?

## Equivalence Instead of Equality

Accomplishing the aforementioned task would not be possible in any CLR prior to CLR 4.0. But, it's available in CLR 4.0, because of the type equivalence feature. Behind the scenes, you can run the following line of code:

```
    TableHelper.InsertTable(word, 3, 2);
```

This results in the following code compiling:

```
    TableHelper.InsertTable((Word.Application)word, 3, 2);
```

In this code, the `Word.Application` cast uses the type generated in the `WordHelper` assembly. The type equivalence feature means that the CLR is able to successfully carry out the specified cast.

The last two statements of the `Main` method in Listing 10-6 compare the two `Word.Application` types for equality (using the "equals" operator) and for equivalence (using the `Type.IsEquivalentTo` method). The first comparison results in `false`, and the second results in `true`, as shown in Figure 10-8.

**FIGURE 10-8:** Results of equality comparisons

### Equivalence in the CLR

As discussed previously, CLR 4.0 supports embedding type information for COM types directly into managed assemblies, instead of obtaining that type information from interoperability assemblies. The compiler generates concise code, and the embedded type information includes only the types and members that are actually used by the managed assembly. Because of this behavior, two assemblies might have very different views of the same COM type. Each assembly has a different System.Type object to represent its view of that COM type.

From the CLR's perspective, type equivalence means a COM object that is passed from one assembly to another can be cast to the appropriate managed type in the receiving assembly.

The CLR supports equivalence only for COM types, and, as a limitation, only for interfaces, structures, enumerations, and delegates. So, classes are not subject to this behavior. Two COM types are taken into account as equivalent ones, where the following criteria are met:

> The types are both interfaces or both structures or both enumerations or both delegates.

> Both types are COM import types.

>> If they are interfaces, they should be decorated with the ComImportAttribute and GuidAttribute attributes.

>> The assemblies in which they are defined (that are generally two separate ones) have either the ImportedFromTypeLibAttribute or the PrimaryInteropAssembly Attribute attribute.

> The GuidAttribute values of these types are equal.

During the build process, the compiler detects if a type is used in a context where type equivalence is assumed. In this case, it checks if the criteria are met. In cases when there are issues, the compiler raises appropriate error messages.

The compiler decorates the compiled type declarations with the TypeIdentifierAttribute and the CompilerGeneratedAttribute attributes.

 *As of this writing, the Beta 2 version of the .NET Framework and Visual Studio 2010 are available. There are some contradictions between the MSDN documentation and the real operation of type equivalence, mainly about the role of the TypeIdentifierAttribute. The criteria described previously are subject to change. Check the current MSDN documentation for "Type Equivalence and Embedded Interop Types."*

## PARALLEL COMPUTING

In the last 15 years, computer CPUs evolved quite fast, and, according to Moore's law, their computing capacity was doubled every 18 months. This was especially eye-catching for graphics cards and GPUs, where the performance improvements exceeded even Moore's law. For a long time, this amazing progress has been achieved by increasing the clock speed of CPUs, and, of course, processor architectures evolved also.

This increase of clock speed meant that performance of applications also increased (almost linearly), without the need to change the software architecture.

## The Challenge of Many-core Shift

In accordance with Moore's law, the tendency to double the number of transistors placed on a unit of chip surface continues. However, this is not true for the CPU clock speed! Every further increase of clock speed implicates more caloric to dissipate, and cooling processors is becoming a big issue for manufacturers. Also, there are some hard physical limits — light isn't getting any faster.

Although the speed of CPUs cannot be increased significantly, the number of transistors per unit of area still can be. Manufacturers will put two or four CPU cores in the chip with the same area they used to put only one before. So, even if the clock speed of CPUs cannot be improved according to Moore's law, their processing capacities can!

Figure 10-9 shows an example of Windows Task Manager displaying 128 fully loaded CPU cores in a single computer. It's not a trick — it's a real server machine!

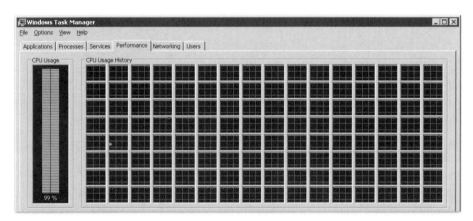

**FIGURE 10-9:** 128 CPU cores in a server computer

And here is another interesting fact: Microsoft's Windows 7 can be scaled up to 256 CPU cores. The *many-core shift* is not about the future; it's already here!

## Software: The Weakest Link

Improving the computing capacity by increasing the number of CPU cores can be utilized quite well with web applications. The architecture of web servers easily allows assigning separate user requests to separate processors. Developers do not have to do any very special coding to allow the web to server scale up when adding new cores. However, putting a bottleneck in the database layer of web applications can put the brakes on scaling.

Even if you do not have this kind of a database bottleneck, there is one thing that cannot be solved without changing architecture. Although you may have a large number of processors, the response time of one user request cannot be decreased below a certain threshold. If the algorithm serving the user request runs sequentially (it can run only on a single thread), even having a hundred CPUs can't reduce the response time below that threshold.

The advantages of multiple (many-core) CPUs cannot be utilized in the case of desktop applications, where the architectural constraints allow only sequential execution. Of course, having multiple cores means that multiple applications can run in parallel, but that won't help to decrease the running time of slow sequential applications. These kinds of applications can't benefit from putting two, four, or even more CPU cores into the desktop machine.

So, it's often not worth it to use multiple cores with applications designed and implemented with "sequential-style." The multi-core shift opens new horizons — but requires software architected with enabling parallelism in order to achieve the potential performance benefits.

From this aspect, a majority of today's software is the weakest link.

## Issues with Multi-Threading

Today, if you want to develop an application supporting concurrent execution of certain parts of algorithms, you cannot avoid directly using threads. Managing multiple threads is definitely challenging. You're faced with several tasks to be solved correctly in order to build a properly running and bug-free application. Multiple threads introduce situations where you have to handle variable and resource synchronization, flow control that utilizes data structures designed with sequential usage in mind, race-conditions, deadlocks, live-locks, and many more.

The literature discussing concurrent programming is vast, handles all aspects, and even suggests design patterns for certain problem contexts — but it does not simplify multi-threading. Even if you find a simple principle or pattern to transform a sequential task into a parallel one, you still must cope with a few more difficulties, including the following:

➤ The aspect of parallelism will spread through the entire task. You must find the principle to split the sequential task into smaller independent parallelizable parts. You must wrap these parts into threads, and take care of managing common resources, synchronizing their access. The flow control among tasks should be managed carefully — for example, at the end, tasks should wait while each of them finishes its work.

➤ In the final code that enables your algorithm to benefit from parallelism, the real business code (that is, the code implementing the business functionality) will be mixed up with the code originating from the parallel aspect. The latter can significantly balloon the size of business code by a number of code lines. Any further change in the code requires extra development resources, because the entire code is longer. You have a greater likelihood to be lost in the code, or touch a part of the infrastructure code, instead of the business code.

➤ Testing this code is more challenging and resource-wasting. To keep the level of test code coverage at a certain point, you definitely must write more unit test cases. The correctness of parallelism infrastructure (for example, avoiding race conditions) also requires additional test cases.

After development, these multi-threaded applications generate more work during their support phase. If it happens that the application does not work according to the requirements, or some bugs are caught (for example, a suspect of race condition), parallelism adds some extra tasks to troubleshooting, including the following:

➤ You must guess as to whether the issue is in the design or in the implementation.

➤ Debuggers and tracing tools do not provide enough help to step through multi-thread programs. Just think about placing a breakpoint in a code line used by several threads! Sometimes it is not easy to tell the debugger that you want to stop only when a certain thread reaches that breakpoint.

Once you have a few years of experience with concurrent programming, you may be able to avoid some common pitfalls. Unfortunately, many developers do not have this kind of background.

# The Microsoft Approach

There are many approaches to help the shift from sequentially running applications toward parallel ones. These include specialized programming languages, pattern libraries, and tools examining the code and restructuring it, parallelism-aware compilers, and so on.

Microsoft has a different approach that is based on the "rule of 80/20." Its own solution (called *Parallel Computing Platform*) provides a technology efficiently targeting the issues coming from the use of multiple CPU cores. Instead of the sophistication in threading models, or automating parallelism and hiding it from developers, this uses a declarative approach. It provides a simple model to allow developers to explicitly declare that certain parts of their programs can be executed in parallel. The platform takes care of the implementation.

The Parallel Computing Platform builds on the following simple design goals:

➤ Developers should be freed from the complexity of parallel coding tasks to focus on solving business issues, and so their productivity could improve.

➤ The process of creating properly working, maintainable, and scalable parallel applications must be significantly simplified.

➤ Expectations both from native and managed code developers must be taken into account.

These are three main pillars (features) of this approach:

➤ High-level parallel programming concepts and abstractions allow leveraging values of parallel programming with minimal change in existing code.

➤ The approach lowers the entry barriers developers need to start dealing with parallel programming.

➤ The approach provides tools that, in addition to expressing parallelism, ensure great support (debugging, profiling, and so on) for developers.

## Tools, Programming Models, Run-times

Microsoft ships fundamental elements of its Parallel Computing Platform with .NET 4 and Visual Studio 2010. Figure 10-10 shows the stack of these elements.

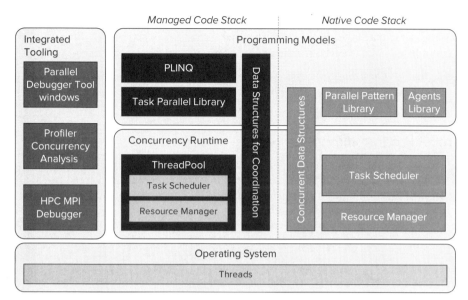

**FIGURE 10-10:** Stack of Parallel Computing Platform elements

The two main blocks (represented by Programming Models and Concurrency Run-time) are shipped with .NET Framework and with the Visual C++ 2010 Run-time, while the Integrated Tools are the part of Visual Studio 2010. As you can see, there are separate (but very similar) stacks for managed code (in the middle part of Figure 10-10) and native code (the right part of the figure). This discussion addresses only the managed stack.

Contrary to the thread-based model developers have used for a long time, the new programming model is declarative. Developers can split up their algorithms and longer code into smaller tasks, and can declare control flow among them. For example, they can declare that certain tasks can run concurrently, while others should run in a certain, well-defined order. Executing tasks according to the defined control flow is the responsibility of the run-time. Thread management, synchronization, and recovery from exceptions are all done by the run-time.

Following are key components of the Managed Code stack:

➤ *Task Parallel Library* (TPL) — This is the run-time element providing this functionality with its high-level programming concepts.

➤ *Parallel Language Integrated Query* (PLINQ) — This utilizes TPL for data parallelism. Standard LINQ expressions can be easily marked for concurrent execution (even a degree of parallelism can be set up), and so data can be processed in a multithreaded fashion without knowing anything about threads or TPL concepts.

➤ The *Concurrency Run-time* — This is responsible for translating the concept using tasks into threading. It uses the *ThreadPool* as its fundamental tool to manage .NET Framework-level and operating system-level threads.

➤ *Task Scheduler* — Having thousands of tasks that can run simultaneously does not mean that thousands of threads will be started. The Task Scheduler is responsible for assigning tasks to threads, taking into account the degree of parallelism that can be achieved.

➤ *Data Structures for Coordination* — This includes high-performance collection classes that are lock-free and thread-safe, and also includes other lightweight objects for synchronization and lazy initialization.

## Overview of Parallel Programming Architecture

While Figure 10-10 is a very good overview of the Parallel Computing Platform's elements, it does not reflect how the intentions of developers are manifested in parallel execution. Figure 10-11 provides another view of the architecture that helps you understand the role of specific elements.

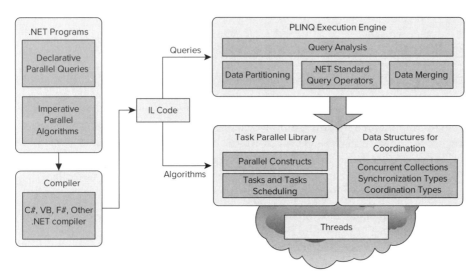

**FIGURE 10-11:** Parallel Programming Architecture

Your applications developed with the .NET 4 Framework may contain code parts that you intend to run in parallel. You can write PLINQ queries that are query expression declarations extended with small instructions signifying them for parallel execution. Also, you can write imperative algorithms where you explicitly declare the parts (called *tasks*) that can run concurrently.

At the end of the day, parallel constructs are executed by threads. The TPL provides the constructs and task scheduling. Data structures for coordination provide you with concrete types (such as `ConcurrentBag`, `ConcurrentQueue`, `Barrier`, `CountdownEvent`, and many more) to help you in resource management and synchronization of your tasks.

Using any of the .NET compilers, the resulting intermediate-language code will target either the TPL layer (imperative algorithms) or use the PLINQ Execution Engine (declarative queries). Parallel query expressions will use the TPL layer during query execution.

# Parallel LINQ

LINQ expressions are great for shifting imperative data processing algorithms to declarative ones. Instead of requiring the developer to lay down the algorithm in the form of cycles, filters, or result aggregations using standard programming language instructions, a query expression is used to define the developer's intention.

PLINQ is a new technology that allows executing LINQ expressions concurrently in machines with more CPU cores. The main purpose of PLINQ is to enable speedup of query execution on in-memory data through more efficient use of system resources, especially on multicore hardware. "Speedup" in this context means the difference in execution time between a query's sequential execution, and its execution either wholly or in part in parallel mode. Later in this chapter, you will learn that using PLINQ is really easy.

Figure 10-11 shows you what PLINQ adds to the execution of standard LINQ expressions. Parallel execution is based on partitioning the original data among multiple tasks so that they are able to run parallel with the least overhead of locking and other coordination. The standard .NET query operators are implemented in the PLINQ execution engine so that they support parallelism. After the query has been carried out on each partition, the partial results should be merged into the final aggregated result.

## The LoremIpsumQuery Example

PLINQ does a great job of transforming sequential queries into parallel ones. The best way to demonstrate this is to show you an example that clearly points out the benefits of PLINQ against imperative programming. When downloading the source code for Chapter 10 from this book's companion web site (www.wrox.com), you will find a sample named LoremIpsumQuery that is used here to introduce PLINQ benefits.

LoremIpsumQuery is a small WPF application that allows you to query word occurrences in texts generated by the Lorem Ipsum generator (http://www.lipsum.com), and shows statistics indicating the distribution of a specified word. The program works on 32 pre-generated text files, each of them containing more than 10,000 words generated. The input database consolidates the generated text into single-line records with two fields defining the index of the generated text file (called book) and the word in the file. This database is the LIRecords.txt file containing the single-line records in tab-separated entries.

The result of the queries is represented by an IEnumerable<LIResult>, where LIResult is a simple structure composed from two integer fields, Book and WordCount. Figure 10-12 shows the application querying statistics for the word "ipsum."

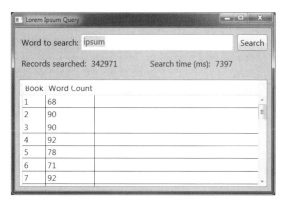

**FIGURE 10-12:** Sample screenshot of LoremIpsumQuery

Without LINQ, you could program the query by simply iterating through records and counting the occurrences of the specified word in a book using a `Dictionary` object. Listing 10-7 shows one possible implementation.

**LISTING 10-7: Manual Query Definition**

```
private IEnumerable<LIResult> ManualQuery(string wordToSearch)
{
  var result = new Dictionary<int, LIResult>();
  foreach (var record in LIRecords)
  {
    if (String.Compare(record.Word, wordToSearch, true) == 0)
    {
      LIResult book;
      if (result.TryGetValue(record.Book, out book))
        book.WordCount++;
      else
        result.Add(record.Book, new LIResult(record.Book, 1));
    }
  }
  return result.Values;
}
```

*Code file [MainWindow.xaml.cs] available for download at Wrox.com*

This code is not complex, but reading it, you need time to guess what it does. The implementation using LINQ is much more straightforward, and immediately tells you what the intention of the query is. Listing 10-8 shows the LINQ implementation.

**LISTING 10-8: Query Definition with LINQ**

```
private IEnumerable<LIResult> UsingLinq(string wordToSearch)
{
  return from record in LIRecords
         where String.Compare(record.Word, wordToSearch, true) == 0
         group record by record.Book into book
         select new LIResult(book.Key, book.Count());
}
```

*Code file [MainWindow.xaml.cs] available for download at Wrox.com*

The LINQ solution is great, but it is still sequential, and so it uses only one CPU core. For a moment, let's forget that you have PLINQ. The manual query in Listing 10-7 can be transformed into a multithread query using the threading architecture built into .NET.

There are several strategies to do that, and Listing 10-9 shows one of them. The basic idea of this parallel algorithm is to partition the work according to the number of CPU cores in your machine.

Each thread picks up one record from the database, and processes the partial result locally in the thread. When a thread finishes its job (that is, there are no more records to process), it merges the partial result into the aggregated one.

**LISTING 10-9:** Parallel Query Implemented Manually

```
private IEnumerable<LIResult> ManualParallelQuery(string wordToSearch)
{
  var result = new Dictionary<int, LIResult>();
  int partitionsCount = Environment.ProcessorCount;
  int remainingCount = partitionsCount;
  IEnumerator<LIRecord> enumerator = LIRecords.GetEnumerator();
  // --- Resource protection block for enumerator
  try
  {
    // --- Synchronization of partitions
    using (var done = new ManualResetEvent(false))
    {
      // --- Each partition has its own thread
      for (int i = 0; i < partitionsCount; i++)
      {
        ThreadPool.QueueUserWorkItem((obj) =>
        {
          var partialResult = new Dictionary<int, LIResult>();
          while (true)
          {
            LIRecord record;
            // --- Lock (inefficient) to access the next element
            lock (enumerator)
            {
              if (!enumerator.MoveNext()) break;
              record = enumerator.Current;
            }
            if (String.Compare(record.Word, wordToSearch, true) == 0)
            {
              LIResult book;
              // --- Lock (indefficient) to aggregate result
              lock (partialResult)
              {
                if (partialResult.TryGetValue(record.Book, out book))
                  book.WordCount++;
                else
                  partialResult.Add(record.Book,
                    new LIResult(record.Book, 1));
              }
            }
          }
          // --- Merge partial result to the aggregated result
          lock (result)
```

*continues*

**LISTING 10-9** *(continued)*

```
          {
            foreach (var item in partialResult.Values)
            {
              LIResult book;
              if (result.TryGetValue(item.Book, out book))
                book.WordCount += item.WordCount;
              else
                result.Add(item.Book, item);
            }
          }
          // --- Sign that job is ready when last partition finished
          if (Interlocked.Decrement(ref remainingCount) == 0) done.Set();
        });
      }
      // --- Wait for partitions to finish their job
      done.WaitOne();
    }
  }
  finally
  {
    enumerator.Dispose();
  }
  return result.Values;
}
```

*Code file [MainWindow.xaml.cs] available for download at Wrox.com*

The first thing you notice is that this code is really complex, and, despite the comments, understanding it is not really easy. Only a little part of this code deals with the real calculation logic. All other parts are required to synchronize threads, and coordinate resource access.

With PLINQ, this coding nightmare is as simple as the LINQ implementation. Listing 10-10 shows the code, which removes all the pain points from the manual parallel query implementation.

**LISTING 10-10: Query Definition with PLINQ**

```
private IEnumerable<LIResult> UsingParallelLinq(string wordToSearch)
{
  return from record in LIRecords.AsParallel()
         where String.Compare(record.Word, wordToSearch, true) == 0
         group record by record.Book into book
         select new LIResult(book.Key, book.Count());
}
```

*Code file [MainWindow.xaml.cs] available for download at Wrox.com*

This query definition is almost the same as the PLINQ solution in Listing 10-8. The only difference is the `AsParallel()` method that tells operations on `LIRecords` can be executed using multiple CPU cores. This simple extension causes the Parallel LINQ provider to plan the execution so that the whole query is divided into independent chunks capable of running concurrently, and merges the partial results together forming the final result. Behind the scenes, PLINQ has many strategies to execute the query. Sometimes it requires more than one pass to produce the results.

## Comparing LoremIpsumQuery Implementations

Table 10-1 shows a comparison of the four approaches used in `LoremIpsumQuery`. The table contains the execution times and the performance ratio (in percentages) related to the imperative query in Listing 10-7.

**TABLE 10-1:** Query Implementations

| IMPLEMENTATION TYPE | EXECUTION TIME (IN MS) | PERFORMANCE |
|---|---|---|
| Imperative query | 7.386 | 100 percent |
| Query declaration with LINQ | 7.580 | 97 percent |
| Imperative multi-thread query | 12.985 | 57 percent |
| Query declaration with PLINQ | 2.171 | 340 percent |

This table indicates that LINQ produces almost the same result (3 percent slower) as that of the manual imperative query implementation. Results also show that the manual multithread strategy used in Listing 10-9 was counterproductive. Instead of accelerating the query, the inefficient locking solution made is slower than the original one.

The last row of the table clearly shows that PLINQ really did a great job. The machine it was running on had four CPU cores, and a real 340 percent performance. PLINQ has a definitely better strategy that was used in Listing 10-9!

## Influencing PLINQ Behavior

The `AsParallel()` method transforming a sequential query into a parallel one retrieves a `ParallelQuery<TSource>` object, where `TSource` represents the type of object on which to execute the query. `ParallelQuery<TSource>` defines standard query operators as extension methods, and so the compiler uses them to replace the `where`, `select`, `group by`, `orderby`, and other clauses with those methods (with full accordance of the C# language specification of query expressions).

There are a few extension methods having a `With` prefix that can be used to influence how a parallel query is executed. Table 10-2 describes these methods.

**TABLE 10-2:** Extension Methods Influencing PLINQ Behavior

| METHOD | DESCRIPTION |
| --- | --- |
| WithDegreeOfParallelism | Sets the degree of parallelism to use in a query. *Degree of parallelism* is the maximum number of concurrently executing tasks that will be used to process the query. The method accepts one integer parameter that sets this degree. As of this writing, it is not documented how the query works when this value is greater than the number of CPU cores. |
| WithExecutionMode | Sets the execution mode of the query. The method accepts a `ParallelExecutionMode` enumeration parameter that has two values with the following meaning:<br><br>`Default` — By default, the system will use algorithms for queries that are ripe for parallelism, and will avoid algorithms with high overheads that will likely result in slowdowns for parallel execution.<br><br>`ForceParallelism` — Parallelizes the entire query, even if that means using high-overhead algorithms. PLINQ is designed to exploit opportunities for parallelization. However, not all queries benefit from parallel execution. For example, when a query contains a single user delegate that does very little work, the query will usually run faster sequentially. This is because the overhead involved in enabling parallelizing execution is more expensive than the speedup that is obtained. |
| WithMergeOptions | Sets the merge options for this query, which specify how the query will buffer output. The method accepts a `ParallelMergeOptions` enumeration parameter that has the following four values:<br><br>`Default` — Use the default merge type, which is `AutoBuffered`.<br><br>`NotBuffered` — This option causes each processed element to be returned from each thread as soon as it is produced. This behavior is analogous to "streaming" the output. If the `AsOrdered()` operator (described later) is present in the query, `NotBuffered` preserves the order of the source elements. Although `NotBuffered` starts yielding results as soon as they are available, the total time to produce all the results might still be longer than using one of the other merge options.<br><br>`AutoBuffered` — This option causes the query to collect elements into a buffer, and then periodically yield the buffer contents all at once to the consuming thread. This is analogous to yielding the source data in "chunks," instead of using the "streaming" behavior of `NotBuffered`. `AutoBuffered` may take longer than `NotBuffered` to make the first element available on the consuming thread. |

| METHOD | DESCRIPTION |
|--------|-------------|
| | `FullyBuffered` — This option causes the output of the whole query to be buffered before any of the elements are yielded. When you use this option, it can take longer before the first element is available on the consuming thread, but the complete results might still be produced faster than by using the other options. |
| `WithCancellation` | Sets the `CancellationToken` to associate with the query. `CancellationToken` is a new concept in .NET 4. Its role is to propagate notifications that operations should be cancelled. The token accepted by this method is used by LINQ to recognize that the operation encapsulating this query is cancelled. |

To restrict the query in Listing 10-10 to use up to three threads, you can write the following code:

```
return from record in LIRecords.AsParallel().WithDegreeOfParallelism(3)
       where String.Compare(record.Word, wordToSearch, true) == 0
       group record by record.Book into book
       select new LIResult(book.Key, book.Count());
```

In PLINQ, the goal is to maximize performance, while maintaining correctness. A query should run as fast as possible, but still produce the correct results. In some cases, correctness requires the order of the source sequence to be preserved. However, ordering can be computationally expensive. Let's assume that you have the following query:

```
var animalQuery = (from animal in animals.AsParallel()
                   where animal.Age > 10
                   select animal)
                      .Take(100);
```

Despite the intention that you would like to get the first 100 animals over the age of 10 years, this query does not necessarily produce what you expect. Because of the parallel execution, it instead retrieves some set of 100 animals that meet the condition.

You can change this behavior with the `AsOrdered()` operator to meet the original expectation:

```
var animalQuery = (from animal in animals.AsParallel().AsOrdered()
                   where animal.Age > 10
                   select animal)
                      .Take(100);
```

When order preservation is no longer required, use `AsUnordered()` to turn it off. It could be useful when composing queries, as shown in this example:

```
var animalQuery = (from animal in animals.AsParallel().AsOrdered()
                   where animal.Age > 10
```

```
                          select animal)
                        .Take(100);
    var filteredResult = from animal in animalQuery.AsUnordered()
                         where animal.LivesInWater == true
                         select animal
```

You do not have to use `AsOrdered()` for a sequence produced by order-imposing operators, because PLINQ preserves their ordering. So, operators such as `OrderBy()` and `ThenBy()` are treated as if they were followed by a call to `AsOrdered()`.

Sometimes you want to combine PLINQ queries with sequential ones, for preserving order or for performance reasons. You can transform a parallel query into a sequential one with the `AsSequential()` operator. For example, the following query is composed from a parallel one retrieving an ordered set, followed by a sequential one retrieving the first three elements:

```
    var custInvoices = from invoice in invoices.AsParallel()
                       orderby invoices.CustomerID
                       select new
                       {
                         Details = invoice.InvoiceDetails,
                         Date = invoide.DeliveryDate,
                         Total = invoice.Total
                       };
    var topThreeInvoice = custInvoices.AsSequential().Take(3);
```

Because `custInvoices` is a parallel query, `topThreeInvoice` also would be a parallel one by default. Getting the first three elements sequentially is definitely faster than using a parallel query.

> *There were great presentations about parallel computing at Microsoft's Professional Developers Conference (PDC) 2009. If you would like to understand how PLINQ works behind the scenes, the "PLINQ: LINQ, but Faster" presentation provides you with interesting details. You can watch or download the session video from* `http://microsoftpdc.com/Sessions/FT21`.

## Task Parallel Library

After so many years of the thread-oriented multitasking in .NET, TPL is a real revolution. The mission of TPL is to help you parallelize your code so that you can focus on the work your code is designed to accomplish — in other words, TPL is to turn your time spent on building multi-threading infrastructure into creating valuable business functions.

TPL is a set of public types and APIs in the `System.Threading` and `System.Threading.Tasks` namespaces that allows a great shift to code based on a high-level concept called *tasks*. Without enumerating a list of features, a few code snippets can convince you of the power of TPL. Here is the first snippet:

```
Parallel.Invoke(
    () => TaskA(),
    () => TaskB(),
    () => TaskC());
```

The static `Invoke` method of the `Parallel` class takes three tasks represented by `TaskA`, `TaskB`, and `TaskC`, and invokes them to run concurrently. `Invoke` also waits until each task completes, and then passes back the control. Remember the code in Listing 10-9 where 90 percent of the code was the multithreading infrastructure? Here, you won't find any infrastructure code! This snippet contains only declarative code, and is as concise as it can be.

Each argument of `Invoke` is turned into a `Task` object that can be found in the `System.Threading .Tasks` namespace. `Task` is the basic unit of code that is scheduled to be executed by a thread.

The next code snippet should also tell its intention to you:

```
Parallel.For(0, 10, counter =>
    {
        var rnd = new Random((int)(DateTime.Now.Ticks + counter));
        Console.WriteLine("Task {0} started.", counter);
        Thread.Sleep(100 + rnd.Next(20));
        Console.WriteLine("Task {0} finished.", counter);
    });
```

`Parallel.For` defines a `for` cycle where the body of the cycle is a set of independent tasks having a `counter` parameter. Because these tasks are independent, they can be executed in parallel.

When you put this code snippet into a console application and run it, you can clearly see that the tasks forming the cycle body run independently. Figure 10-13 shows a sample.

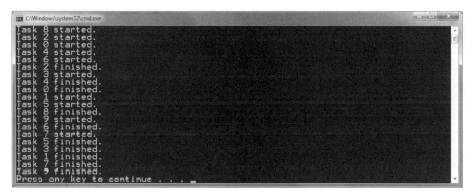

**FIGURE 10-13:** Sample of running the Parallel.For code snippet

This screenshot was taken on a quad-core computer where the default degree of parallelism is four, according to the number of cores, so TPL runs up to four threads that can be active at the same time. From this screenshot, you can see that the first five rows are `started` messages, as if five threads were run at the same time. This is because the `Thread.Sleep()` calls in the middle of the tasks allow the scheduler to start other threads. Sleeping threads are treated as passive ones.

## The Parallel Class

Probably the best point at which to start with parallel programming with the .NET Framework is the `Parallel` class. Using the 80/20 rule metaphor, this class possesses the 20 percent of all parallel functionality that helps you transform your sequential application into a parallel one, while achieving the 80 percent of possible performance gain. You can see how easy it is to use the `Parallel.Invoke` or `Parallel.For` method. The aim of the `Parallel` class is to provide support for parallel loops and regions, and it is supported by three methods having many overloads:

➤ `Parallel.Invoke` — Executes a set of actions (methods with no input parameters and no return value) in parallel

➤ `Parallel.For` — Executes a `for` loop, in which iteration may run in parallel

➤ `Parallel.Foreach` — Executes a `foreach` operation on a strongly typed collection (implementing `IEnumerable<T>`) in which iterations may run in parallel

Let's dive into these methods a bit deeper.

Each method has one or more overloads accepting a parameter with type `ParallelOptions`. The role of this class is to provide a few options influencing the execution of the specified parallel operation. These options can be accessed through the properties of the class:

➤ `CancellationToken` — This sets the token that can be used to check if the operation must be cancelled.

➤ `MaxDegreeOfParallelism` — This limits the number of concurrent operations run by `Parallel` method calls that are passed this `ParallelOptions` instance to the set value, if it is positive. If this property is `-1`, then there is no limit placed on the number of concurrently running operations.

➤ `TaskScheduler` — This allows you to associate a task scheduler with this `ParallelOptions` instance (or get the current scheduler). Setting this property to `null` indicates that the current scheduler should be used.

### Parallel.Invoke

The `Invoke` method has only two overloads. One of the method signatures accepts only actions, while the other allows specifying `ParallelOptions`. Listing 10-11 shows the `Program.cs` file of a console application demonstrating these method overloads.

**Available for download on Wrox.com**

**LISTING 10-11: Program.cs Demonstrating Parallel.Invoke Overloads**

```
using System;
using System.Threading.Tasks;

namespace ParallelInvoke
```

```
{
  class Program
  {
    static void Main(string[] args)
    {
      Console.WriteLine("*** Invoke with default ParallelOptions");
      var start = DateTime.Now;
      Parallel.Invoke(
        () => { CPUWastingAction("Task A", start); },
        () => { CPUWastingAction("Task B", start); },
        () => { CPUWastingAction("Task C", start); },
        () => { CPUWastingAction("Task D", start); }
        );
      Console.WriteLine();
      Console.WriteLine("*** Invoke with manual ParallelOptions");
      var maxTwoCPUs = new ParallelOptions { MaxDegreeOfParallelism = 2 };
      start = DateTime.Now;
      Parallel.Invoke(maxTwoCPUs,
        () => { CPUWastingAction("Task A", start); },
        () => { CPUWastingAction("Task B", start); },
        () => { CPUWastingAction("Task C", start); },
        () => { CPUWastingAction("Task D", start); }
        );
    }

    static void CPUWastingAction(string message, DateTime start)
    {
      Console.WriteLine("{0,6:0} {1} started",
        (DateTime.Now - start).TotalMilliseconds, message);
      long sum = 0;
      for (int i = 0; i < 10000000; i++)
      {
        if (Environment.ProcessorCount > 0)
        {
          sum += i;
        }
      }
      Console.WriteLine("{0,6:0} {1} finished",
        (DateTime.Now - start).TotalMilliseconds, message);
    }
  }
}
```

*Code file [Program.cs] available for download at Wrox.com*

The first `Invoke` call uses the default options, while the second one passes a `ParallelOptions` instance, setting it up so that up to two concurrent operations can be executed at the same time. For demonstration purposes, the `CPUWastingAction` method is invoked, which runs a cycle just for consuming CPU resources to emulate a long computation. Having a look at Figure 10-14, you can recognize the degree of parallelism changing.

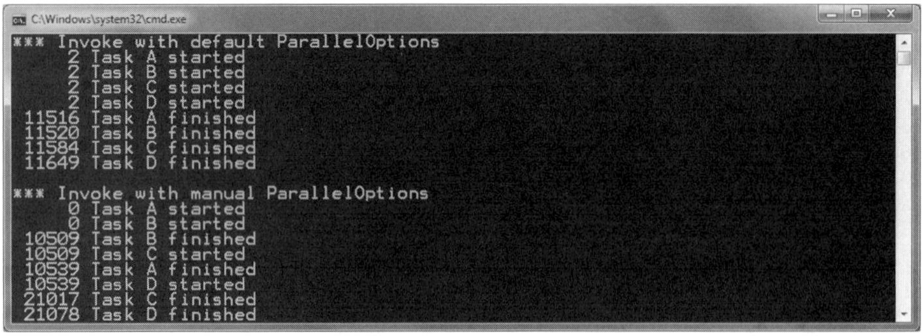

**FIGURE 10-14:** Parallel.Invoke calls with different degrees of parallelism

The numbers before task messages are the time in milliseconds elapsed from the start of the `Invoke` call. The first `Invoke` started all the four parallel tasks (the demo was run on a quad-core machine). The second `Invoke` call started only two tasks (because of the maximum degree of parallelism specified), and the other two had to wait while a thread became free for the task.

## Parallel.For

While `Parallel.Invoke` has only two overloads, `Parallel.For` offers a dozen methods that fall into two categories: `For` and the generic `For<TLocal>` method. `For` has the following overloads:

```
ParallelLoopResult For(int fromInclusive, int toExclusive, Action<int> body);

ParallelLoopResult For(int fromInclusive, int toExclusive,
  Action<int, ParallelLoopState> body);

ParallelLoopResult For(int fromInclusive, int toExclusive,
    ParallelOptions options,
  Action<int> body);

ParallelLoopResult For(int fromInclusive, int toExclusive, ParallelOptions options,
  Action<int, ParallelLoopState> body);

ParallelLoopResult For(long fromInclusive, long toExclusive, Action<long> body);

ParallelLoopResult For(long fromInclusive, long toExclusive,
  Action<long, ParallelLoopState> body);

ParallelLoopResult For(long fromInclusive, long toExclusive,
    ParallelOptions options,
  Action<long> body);

ParallelLoopResult For(long fromInclusive, long toExclusive,
    ParallelOptions options,
  Action<long, ParallelLoopState> body);
```

As you see, the first four methods use `int` parameters, while the second four mirror them with `long` arguments.

The cycle iterates from the `fromInclusive` value to the one before `toExclusive`. When you use the values 0 and 3, the iteration body will be executed for 0, 1, and 2, but not for 3. When you set `fromInclusive` greater than or equal to `toExclusive`, the cycle won't execute the body.

Just as in the case of `Parallel.Invoke`, you can use a `ParallelOptions` instance during the execution.

You can run two kinds of bodies with the `For` method. The first, represented by an `Action<int>` or `Action<long>` instance, simply takes the iteration counter that can be used in the bodies. When your logic requires that, in certain conditions, you break the cycle, use the `Action<int, ParallelLoopState>` or `Action<long, ParallelLoopState>` instances. In this case, the body code will get a `ParallelLoopState` instance, letting you break a cycle, or be aware of the fact that one of the body methods has already requested a break.

`ParallelLoopState` instances will be created by the `Parallel.For` method for each thread. You must not instantiate this class, or pass an instance among the threads. Within the iteration body you are allowed to call the loop state instance's `Stop` or `Break` method, or read its properties. Table 10-3 describes the semantics of `ParallelLoopState` members.

**TABLE 10-3:** ParallelLoopState Members

| MEMBER | DESCRIPTION |
| --- | --- |
| Break | This method communicates that the parallel loop should cease execution (at the system's earliest convenience) of iterations beyond the current iteration. |
| | You may use `Break` to communicate to the loop that no other iterations after the current iteration need to be run. For example, if `Break` is called from the third iteration of a `for` loop iterating in parallel from 0 to 10, all iterations less than 3 should still be run, but the iterations from 4 through to 10 are not necessary. |
| | The loop does not start iterations with indices greater than the index of iteration invoking `Break`, but does not abort iterations already started. It may happen that any iteration with an index that is not assumed to run after `Break` has already been started. |
| | Instead, the `LowestBreakIteration` property is set to the iteration index calling `Break`. Iterations already started can check for this property to decide whether to break the cycle or not. |
| | More iterations can call `Break`. In this case, `LowestBreakIteration` is set to the current iteration's index, if that index is less than the current value of `LowestBreakIteration`. |

*continues*

**TABLE 10-3** *(continued)*

| MEMBER | DESCRIPTION |
|---|---|
| Stop | This method communicates that the parallel loop should cease execution at the system's earliest convenience. |
| | You may use Stop to communicate to the loop that no other iterations need to be run. Invoking Stop will halt starting new iterations. However, it does not abort iterations already started. Instead, it sets the IsStopped property to true. |
| IsExceptional | This property tells whether any iteration of the loop has thrown an exception that went unhandled by that iteration. |
| IsStopped | The true value of this property indicates that one of the iterations has called Stop. |
| LowestBreakIteration | This property retrieves a Nullable<long> value that represents the lowest iteration of the loop from which Break was called. If no iteration of the loop called Break, it will return null. |
| ShouldExitCurrentIteration | The true value of this property indicates that the current iteration of the loop should exit based on requests made by this or other iterations. It may be either because a Stop was invoked, or a Break, where the breaking iteration's index was less than the current iteration index. |

Each method retrieves a ParallelLoopResult instance that provides a completion status on the execution of the loop. The IsCompleted property of the structure tells you whether the loop has finished, or interrupted before all iterations could run. The LowestBreakIteration property tells you the index of the lowest iteration from which Break was called.

Let's demonstrate these concepts with a simple example searching for a specific byte in an array of blobs. Listing 10-12 shows the source code of the Program.cs file in the example's console application.

**LISTING 10-12:** Program.cs Demonstrating Parallel.For with ParallelLoopState

```csharp
using System;
using System.Threading.Tasks;

namespace ParallelFor
{
  class Program
  {
    static void Main(string[] args)
    {
      const int ByteSeries = 100000;
      const int BlobSize = 100;
```

```
const byte ToSearch = 123;
byte[][] DumpInfo = new byte[ByteSeries][];

Parallel.For(0, ByteSeries, index =>
  {
    var blob = new byte[BlobSize];
    new Random((int)DateTime.Now.Ticks).NextBytes(blob);
    lock (DumpInfo) { DumpInfo[index] = blob; }
  });

Parallel.For(0, ByteSeries, (index, state) =>
  {
    if (state.ShouldExitCurrentIteration) return;

    Console.WriteLine("Search in blob #{0}", index);
    foreach (byte b in DumpInfo[index])
    {
      if (b == ToSearch)
      {
        Console.WriteLine("Halt request in #{0}", index);
        state.Stop();
        break;
      }
    }
  });
Console.WriteLine("Press Enter to exit...");
Console.ReadLine();
    }
  }
}
```

*Code file [Program.cs] available for download at Wrox.com*

The DumpInfo two-dimensional array holds 100,000 blobs, each of them having a size of 100 bytes. The first Parallel.For loop initializes the blobs with random bytes, and this loop does not use ParallelLoopState. The second Parallel.For loop iterates through blobs and searches for a byte with a value of 123. In the iteration body, state represents the ParallelLoopState instance. When 123 is found, the Stop method signs the loop is about to be halted. Because, at the entry of the iteration body the ShouldExitCurrentIteration property is checked, any iteration bodies starting after Stop will immediately return without searching the blob. Figure 10-15 shows an output of this example.

**FIGURE 10-15:** Output of the Parallel.For example

A consequence of iterations running concurrently is that the `Stop` request may occur in many iteration bodies, in even more than the maximum degree of parallelism! This output was generated on a quad-core machine, and shows that five iterations invoked `Stop` while the whole loop halted.

In the example, you could use `IsStopped` instead of `ShouldExistCurrentIteration` without changing the behavior.

## Parallel.For<TLocal>

The `Parallel.For<TLocal>` method allows the loop to pass data (an instance of `TLocal` type) among the iteration bodies. The method has the following overloads:

```
ParallelLoopResult For<TLocal>(int fromInclusive, int toExclusive,
  Func<TLocal> localInit, Func<int, ParallelLoopState, TLocal, TLocal> body,
  Action<TLocal> localFinally);

ParallelLoopResult For<TLocal>(long fromInclusive, long toExclusive,
  Func<TLocal> localInit, Func<long, ParallelLoopState, TLocal, TLocal> body,
  Action<TLocal> localFinally);

ParallelLoopResult For<TLocal>(int fromInclusive, int toExclusive,
  ParellelOptions options, Func<TLocal> localInit,
  Func<int, ParallelLoopState, TLocal, TLocal> body, Action<TLocal> localFinally);

ParallelLoopResult For<TLocal>(long fromInclusive, long toExclusive,
  ParallelOptions options, Func<TLocal> localInit,
  Func<long, ParallelLoopState, TLocal, TLocal> body, Action<TLocal> localFinally);
```

The semantics of `fromInculsive`, `toExclusive` and `options` are exactly the same as in the case of `For`. However, the iteration body handling is extended with a thread-local state-variable instance. You must pass three delegates (`localInit`, `body`, and `localFinally`) to the methods with the following meaning:

➤ `localInit` — This delegate represents a function retrieving an instance of `TLocal`. This is called exactly once for each thread, before any iterations would run on that thread. You must use this method to set up the initial value of the `TLocal` instance.

➤ `body` — This delegate does the iteration. In addition to the iteration index and the `ParallelLoopState` instance, it accepts the `TLocal` instance of the thread running the current iteration. Your iteration should do its work, and retrieve a `TLocal` instance to be passed to the next iteration that will run on the same thread.

➤ `localFinally` — This delegate is called exactly once for each thread, passing the last state of the thread's `TLocal` state-variable. This is the best place to consolidate thread-level results into an accumulated loop result. Of course, this delegate is called after all iterations running on the current thread are completed.

An example tells the story much more clearly. Let's modify the algorithm in Listing 10-12 so that all occurrences of the byte value searched are counted and the blob with the lowest index containing that value is also recorded. Listing 10-13 shows the modified code.

**LISTING 10-13:** Program.cs Demonstrating Parallel.For<TLocal>

```csharp
using System;
using System.Threading.Tasks;

namespace ParallelForTLocal
{
  class Program
  {
    static void Main(string[] args)
    {
      const int ByteSeries = 100000;
      const int BlobSize = 100;
      const byte ToSearch = 123;
      byte[][] DumpInfo = new byte[ByteSeries][];

      Parallel.For(0, ByteSeries, index =>
      {
        var blob = new byte[BlobSize];
        new Random((int)DateTime.Now.Ticks).NextBytes(blob);
        lock (DumpInfo) { DumpInfo[index] = blob; }
      });

      var result = new SearchInfo { FirstBlobNo = ByteSeries };

      Parallel.For<SearchInfo>(0, ByteSeries,
        // --- Thread-level initializer
        () => new SearchInfo { FirstBlobNo = ByteSeries },

        // --- Iteration body
        (index, state, searchInfo) =>
        {
          var counter = 0;
          foreach (byte b in DumpInfo[index])
            if (b == ToSearch) counter++;
          if (counter > 0)
          {
            searchInfo.Count += counter;
            if (searchInfo.FirstBlobNo > index)
              searchInfo.FirstBlobNo = index;
          }
          return searchInfo;
        },

        // --- Thread-level finalizer
        (searchInfo) =>
        {
          lock (result)
          {
            result.Count += searchInfo.Count;
            if (searchInfo.FirstBlobNo < result.FirstBlobNo)
```

*continues*

**LISTING 10-13** *(continued)*

```
                {
                  result.FirstBlobNo = searchInfo.FirstBlobNo;
                }
              }
            });

        Console.WriteLine("Value {0} found {1} times, first in DumpInfo[{2}]",
          ToSearch, result.Count, result.FirstBlobNo);
        Console.WriteLine("Press Enter to exit...");
        Console.ReadLine();
      }
    }

    class SearchInfo
    {
      public int FirstBlobNo { get; set; }
      public int Count { get; set; }
    }
  }
```

*Code file [Program.cs] available for download at Wrox.com*

In the code, `SearchInfo` represents the `TLocal` instance passed to the iteration bodies. The `Parallel.For<SearchInfo>` call takes three delegates implemented as lambda functions (each is marked with a comment). The first delegate initializes this `SearchInfo` instance. The second delegate is the iteration body. When the byte value searched is found in the current blob, the `SearchInfo` instance is modified accordingly. Notice that this delegate returns the modified (if there were any modifications) version of this instance; and it will be passed to the next iteration on the same thread.

When a thread finishes, the thread-level `SearchInfo` instance's `Count` property shows the number of byte value matches, while `FirstBlobNo` is the lowest iteration index that has a matching byte — and these property values are for the iterations running on that thread.

The third delegate is about consolidating the thread local results into the accumulated result, which is displayed at the end.

 *The* `Parallel.For<SearchInfo>()` *could be used without the* `<SearchInfo>` *generic parameter, because the C# compiler could infer the type from the delegates passed as arguments. However, it is a good practice to indicate it, especially when you are using lambda functions for delegates, because it helps reading and understanding.*

## Parallel.ForEach

The `Parallel.ForEach` method is very similar to the `Parallel.For` method. It allows executing iteration bodies concurrently. The `ForEach` method also resembles `For`, because it has two main branches. `ForEach<TSource>` provides the functionality similar to `For`, while `ForEach<TSource, TLocal>` implements the construct allowing communication among iteration bodies.

However, there is an essential difference between `For` and `ForEach`. While `For` iterates through a range of integral values (`int` or `long`), `ForEach` iterates through elements of an `IEnumerable<TSource>`. The `ForEach` method has more overloads than `For` — actually, each variant of `For` has the matching variant of `ForEach`. Consider the following method signatures of `For`:

```
ParallelLoopResult For(int fromInclusive, int toExclusive, ParallelOptions options,
    Action<int, ParallelLoopState> body);

ParallelLoopResult For<TLocal>(int fromInclusive, int toExclusive,
        ParallelOptions options,
    Func<TLocal> localInit, Func<int, ParallelLoopState, TLocal, TLocal> body,
    Action<TLocal> localFinally);
```

You can find the matching versions of `ForEach` overloads as shown in the following code snippet:

```
ParallelLoopResult ForEach<TSource>(IEnumerable<TSource> source,
        ParallelOptions parallelOptions, Action<TSource, ParallelLoopState> body)

ParallelLoopResult ForEach<TSource, TLocal>(IEnumerable<TSource> source,
        ParallelOptions parallelOptions, Func<TLocal> localInit,
        Func<TSource, ParallelLoopState, TLocal, TLocal> body,
        Action<TLocal> localFinally)
```

The semantics for how the `ParallelLoopState` value, the `localInit`, `body`, and `localFinally` delegates are used is exactly the same as introduced earlier when treating the `For` methods. A slight difference is that the `body` delegate takes an instance of `TSource` instead of an iteration index. There are method overloads where you can pass both a `TSource` instance and a `long` index to the body delegate with the following signature:

```
Func<TSource, ParallelLoopState, long, TLocal, TLocal> body
```

When you think about how to implement a parallel `For` or `ForEach` cycle, you'll recognize that the work should somehow be partitioned, so that it may be distributed among the CPU cores (or threads). It's very easy to partition a range of integers as represented by the `fromInclusive` and `toExclusive` parameters. However, partitioning an `IEnumerable<T>` is more difficult, because its length is unknown, and it can be traversed only sequentially.

The TPL uses an abstraction represented by the `Partioner<T>` for partitioning strategies of `IEnumerable<T>` collections. In several scenarios, when the data in the collection is orderable (for example, items in a `Dictionary` can be ordered by item keys), partitioning should be done with ordering. The `OrderingPartitioner<T>` class is an abstraction for this.

`ForEach` has overloads where the `source` parameter of the methods can be represented by a `Partitioner<T>` or `OrderedPartitioner<T>`, instead of `IEnumerable<T>`.

## Working with Tasks

The `Parallel` class provides uniquely simple declarative units of work to be run concurrently. The `Invoke` method and loops are really useful in many situations, but there are scenarios where algorithms cannot be composed so easily. This is where tasks come into the picture.

The name "Task Parallel Library" obviously refers to a *task* as the most important abstraction in the approach to parallelism. Developers using traditional multi-threading have to think in "path of execution" when programming parallel algorithms. A majority of their efforts tend to be spent on organizing a large amount of plumbing code wrapping around relatively small amount of real code related to the algorithm itself. The mission of tasks is to free developers from the "path of execution" thinking, and change their mindset toward the "unit of work" paradigm.

"Unit of work" means that algorithms are gradually decomposed into smaller pieces (*units*) that run their bodies sequentially. Dependencies among these units are mapped, so that units available for parallel working could be discovered. Figure 10-16 shows an example for this decomposition.

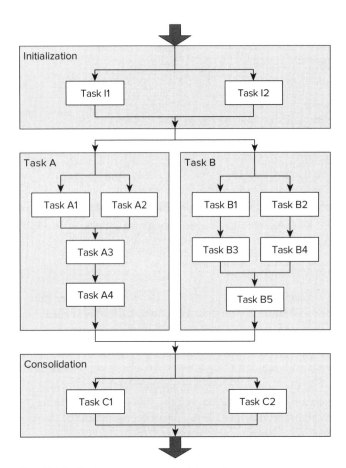

**FIGURE 10-16:** Decomposing a task to units

The algorithm shown in Figure 10-16 can be decomposed to an Initialization task at the beginning and Consolidation task at the end. The body of the algorithm uses two calculations, Task A and Task B, that are independent and their partial results are combined to the final result in the Consolidation task. These high-level tasks are individually split into smaller units. Arrows show the control flow among them.

When you see this net of tasks, you simply find those that can run parallel. It's obvious that Task A and Task B can run side-by-side, but even within them (just as in Initialization and in Consolidation), you can easily discover the units that are good candidates for concurrent execution (such as Task I1 and Task I2, Task A1 and Task A2, and the others).

The concept of a task in TPL allows you to make the same kind of decomposition programmatically.

> *Sometimes it is not obvious how to transform a sequential algorithm into a parallel one, especially in cases when sequential algorithms contain loops where iterations depend on the preceding one. If you do not have the appropriate background in algorithm theory, you can use the web to search for parallel solutions. Once you have a concurrent version of an algorithm, you can use the "unit of work" approach to describe it with TPL.*

### Creating and Starting Tasks

The TPL is very strong in describing tasks and control flow. Listing 10-14 demonstrates this statement by programmatically defining the task visualized in Figure 10-16. You will get a detailed explanation about this code and the concepts used within, but before getting to that, examine the code listing thoroughly, compare it with Figure 10-16, and try to understand it. You'll see it's intuitive.

**LISTING 10-14: Describing Tasks in Figure 10-15 with TPL**

Available for
download on
Wrox.com

```
using System;
using System.Threading.Tasks;

namespace DecompositionSample
{
  class Program
  {
    static void Main(string[] args)
    {
      // --- Initialization
      var taskInitialization = Task.Factory.StartNew(() =>
        {
          Console.WriteLine("Prepare to run 'Initialization'");
```

*continues*

**LISTING 10-14** *(continued)*

```
      var taskI1 = Task.Factory.StartNew(() =>
        { Console.WriteLine("  Executing 'Task I1'"); },
        TaskCreationOptions.AttachedToParent);
      var taskI2 = Task.Factory.StartNew(() =>
      { Console.WriteLine("  Executing 'Task I2'"); },
        TaskCreationOptions.AttachedToParent);
    });
  taskInitialization.Wait();
  Console.WriteLine("'Initialization' finished.");

  // --- Task A and Task B running concurrently
  var taskA = Task.Factory.StartNew(() =>
  {
    // --- Describe the control flow of Task A
    Console.WriteLine("Prepare to run 'Task A'");
    var taskA1 = Task.Factory.StartNew(() =>
    { Console.WriteLine("  Executing 'Task A1'"); },
      TaskCreationOptions.AttachedToParent);
    var taskA2 = Task.Factory.StartNew(() =>
    { Console.WriteLine("  Executing 'Task A2'"); },
      TaskCreationOptions.AttachedToParent);
    Task.WaitAll(taskA1, taskA2);
    Task.Factory.StartNew(() =>
    { Console.WriteLine("  Executing 'Task A3'"); },
      TaskCreationOptions.AttachedToParent).Wait();
    Task.Factory.StartNew(() =>
    { Console.WriteLine("  Executing 'Task A4'"); },
      TaskCreationOptions.AttachedToParent);
  });
  var taskB = new Task(() =>
  {
    // --- Describe the control flow of Task B
    Console.WriteLine("Prepare to run 'Task B'");
    var taskB1 = Task.Factory.StartNew(() =>
    { Console.WriteLine("  Executing 'Task B1'"); },
      TaskCreationOptions.AttachedToParent);
    var taskB2 = Task.Factory.StartNew(() =>
    { Console.WriteLine("  Executing 'Task B2'"); },
      TaskCreationOptions.AttachedToParent);
    var taskB3 = taskB1.ContinueWith((task) =>
    { Console.WriteLine("  Executing 'Task B3'"); });
    var taskB4 = taskB2.ContinueWith((task) =>
    { Console.WriteLine("  Executing 'Task B4'"); });
    Task.WaitAll(taskB3, taskB4);
    Task.Factory.StartNew(() =>
    { Console.WriteLine("  Executing 'Task B5'"); },
      TaskCreationOptions.AttachedToParent);
  });
```

```
        taskB.Start();
        Task.WaitAll(taskA, taskB);
        Console.WriteLine("'Task A' and 'Task B' finished.");

        // --- Consolidation
        var taskConsolidation = Task.Factory.StartNew(() =>
        {
          Console.WriteLine("Prepare to run Task Consolidation");
          var taskC1 = Task.Factory.StartNew(() =>
          { Console.WriteLine("  Executing 'Task C1'"); },
            TaskCreationOptions.AttachedToParent);
          var taskC2 = Task.Factory.StartNew(() =>
          { Console.WriteLine("  Executing 'Task C2'"); },
            TaskCreationOptions.AttachedToParent);
        });
        taskConsolidation.Wait();
        Console.WriteLine("'Consolidation' finished.");
        Console.WriteLine("Press Enter to exit...");
        Console.ReadLine();
      }
    }
  }
```

*Code file [Program.cs] available for download at Wrox.com*

When you run this code, it generates output similar to Figure 10-17.

**FIGURE 10-17:** Output of running the code of Listing 10-14

In Figure 10-17, you can see that Task A and Task B run concurrently, because child tasks belonging to Task A and Task B are combed. According to the control flow definition, the last running child of Task A is Task A4, and the last running child of Task B is Task B5.

Now, let's dive into the details of the code.

The most important type in this declaration is the `Task` class. An instance of this class can be used to represent a task, or its static `Factory` property can be used to instantiate tasks. With a few exceptions in the sample code, all the tasks are instantiated with the `Task.Factory.StartNew()` method:

```
var taskA = Task.Factory.StartNew(() =>
{
  Console.WriteLine("Prepare to run 'Task A'");
  // ...
});
```

`StartNew` takes an `Action` as its input parameter (the code uses lambda expressions to represent these `Action` instances), creates a `Task` instance, and immediately starts it. This method has a few overrides accepting other parameters like a `CancellationToken`, a `TaskScheduler`, or a `TaskCreationOptions` instance — these overrides mirror the variety of `Task` constructors.

Instantiating and starting a task can be separated into two steps:

```
var taskB = new Task(() =>
{
  Console.WriteLine("Prepare to run 'Task B'");
  // ...
});
taskB.Start();
```

## Defining Control Flow

TPL uses the concept of *parent task* and *child tasks* to describe a task hierarchy. "Hierarchy" means that a parent task is terminated only when all children complete their activities. You can attach a task to its parent by passing `TaskCreationOptions.AttachedToParent` to the construction method instantiating a task:

```
var taskA = Task.Factory.StartNew(() =>
{
  // ...
  var taskA1 = Task.Factory.StartNew(() =>
  { Console.WriteLine("  Executing 'Task A1'"); },
    TaskCreationOptions.AttachedToParent);
  // ...
}
```

`TaskCreationOptions` also has two other flags influencing how the scheduler should handle the related task (`PreferFairness` and `LongRunnning`), and those can be combined with `AttachedToParent`.

It is very important to use the `AttachedToParent` value to mark a child task. Should you miss this markup, the task will be a simple task created within the body of another task. In this case, the wrapping task can be finished without waiting for the finalization of the task created in its body. Listing 10-15 shows a sample where this parent-child relation is not set up.

**LISTING 10-15:** Tasks without Parent-Child Relationship

```
using System;
using System.Threading;
using System.Threading.Tasks;

namespace DecompositionSample
{
  class Program
  {
    static void Main(string[] args)
    {
      var taskInitialization = Task.Factory.StartNew(() =>
        {
          Console.WriteLine("Prepare to run 'Initialization'");
          var taskI1 = Task.Factory.StartNew(() =>
            {
              Thread.Sleep(100);
              Console.WriteLine("  Executing 'Task I1'");
            });
          var taskI2 = Task.Factory.StartNew(() =>
            {
              Thread.Sleep(100);
              Console.WriteLine("  Executing 'Task I2'");
            });
        });
      taskInitialization.Wait();
      Console.WriteLine("'Initialization' finished.");
      Thread.Sleep(1000);
      Console.WriteLine("Press Enter to exit...");
      Console.ReadLine();
    }
  }
}
```

When you run this code, you can see that `taskInitialization` is finished before `taskI1` and `taskI2`. Figure 10-18 shows this scenario.

**FIGURE 10-18:** Main tasks finishes before its subtasks

Moreover, if you omit the last `Thread.Sleep(1000)` statement from the code, you will not see `taskI1` and `taskI2` execute, because the main task terminates, and the application closes while the two incomplete tasks are waiting.

At a certain point, concurrently running tasks must meet before going on. For example, both Task A and Task B must be finished before Consolidation can run; or finishing both Task A1 and

Task A2 is a prerequisite before Task A3 is allowed to run. These scenarios can be handled by the `Wait` method of a `Task` instance, or the static `WaitAll` and `WaitAny` methods. For example, before Consolidation can run, the following code is used:

```
var taskA = Task.Factory.StartNew(() => { ... });
var taskB = new Task(() => { ... });
taskB.Start();
Task.WaitAll(taskA, taskB);
```

Task 3 uses the `Wait` method before Task 4 is run:

```
Task.Factory.StartNew(() =>
{ Console.WriteLine("  Executing 'Task A3'"); },
  TaskCreationOptions.AttachedToParent).Wait();
Task.Factory.StartNew(() =>
{ Console.WriteLine("  Executing 'Task A4'"); },
  TaskCreationOptions.AttachedToParent);
```

Looking back at Listing 10-14 you can see that neither the Initialization nor the Consolidations tasks have an explicit `Wait` or `WaitAll` for their concurrently running Task I1, Task I2 and TaskC1, Task C2 pairs. Because they are child tasks, their parents will implicitly wait for their completion.

The sequential relationship between tasks (or among a chain of tasks) can be handled with the `ContinueWith` method. For example, the synchronization between B1 and B3 is described in this way:

```
var taskB1 = Task.Factory.StartNew(() =>
{ Console.WriteLine("  Executing 'Task B1'"); },
  TaskCreationOptions.AttachedToParent);
// ...
var taskB3 = taskB1.ContinueWith((task) =>
{ Console.WriteLine("  Executing 'Task B3'"); });
```

Of course, you could use `Wait` instead of `ContinueWith`:

```
var taskB1 = Task.Factory.StartNew(() => { ... });
// ...
taskB1.Wait();
var taskB3 = Task.Factory.StartNew(() => { ... });
```

However, `ContinueWith` has a few advantages. First of all, it's declarative against the imperative approach represented by `Wait`. You can pass the preceding task to `ContinueWith`, and that provides you more control, because your continuation logic can utilize the result and status of that task. Although you can explicitly use the status of the preceding task with the `Wait` pattern, it is a static approach, because you must know that task at compile-time. `ContinueWith` allows you to assemble a chain (or net) of your tasks at run-time.

## Tasks with Results

In many cases, tasks are to compute a certain value or even a complex structure — for example a customer account report. You can use the `Task<TResult>` type for this purpose. `Task<TResult>` is derived from Task, so you can substitute a Task instance with a Task<Result> instance anywhere. Of course, the delegates representing task bodies must be instances of Func<TResult> instead of instances of Action, because they must retrieve a TResult. This computed value (object) can be queried through the Task<TResult>.Result instance property.

Result has a nice behavior. If the task is not finished, Result will wait for the completion before retrieving the property value. Be aware that Result does not start the task, so, in case of a non-running task, you should wait infinitely for its Result.

Listing 10-16 shows a short example demonstrating Task<Result> concepts.

**LISTING 10-16: Using Task<Result>**

```csharp
using System;
using System.Threading;
using System.Threading.Tasks;

namespace TasksWithResults
{
  class Program
  {
    static void Main(string[] args)
    {
      var task1 = Task.Factory.StartNew<int>(() =>
        {
          int result = 0;
          for (int i = 0; i < 10000000; i++) result += i + i%10;
          return result;
        });
      var task2 = Task.Factory.StartNew<double>(() =>
        {
          double result = Math.PI;
          for (int i = 0; i < 10; i++)
          {
            Thread.Sleep(10);
            result *= (i+1.1)*Math.E;
          }
          return result;
        });
      var task3 = Task.Factory.StartNew<string>(() => "The result is: ");
      Console.WriteLine(task3.Result + (task1.Result + task2.Result));
      Console.WriteLine("Press Enter to exit...");
      Console.ReadLine();     }
  }
}
```

*Code file [Program.cs] available for download at Wrox.com*

The three task instances (task1, task2, and task3) are used to calculate a string used by the Console.WriteLine call in the last statement. They do dummy calculations, but these are good for demonstration purposes. All tasks are started right after their instantiation. When the control flow reaches the `Console.WriteLine` call, there is a high likelihood that `task1` and `task3` finish, but `task2` does not (because it has a `Thread.Sleep(10)` call within). However, you do not have to handle this situation. The `Result` properties will take care that each particular factor gets calculated before the final result is computed.

## Executing Tasks

After you have started tasks, TPL takes care of executing them. At the end of the day, each task is executed on a working thread with the help of the `System.Threading.ThreadPool` and `System.Threading.TaskScheduler` classes. TPL does not create a thread for each task. It uses a lighter mechanism to provide concurrency.

It may be easier to understand the essence of this mechanism through a simple example. Let's assume that a console application creates two tasks, Task 1 and Task 2, in this order. Later, when Task 2 runs, it creates three more tasks, namely Task 2A, Task 2B, and Task 2C, also in this order.

The CLR uses its own thread pool to delegate user work items to worker threads. These items are added to the Global Queue of the CLR Thread Pool with the static `QueueUserWorkItem` method of the `ThreadPool` class. When a working thread becomes available, it gets the next work item waiting in this queue. After processing the item, the working thread becomes available again to process another work item.

TPL wraps tasks into work items so that each working thread implements its own thread-local queue. So, when Task 1 and Task 2 are started, they are put into the Global Queue as work items. Let's assume that Task 1 is delegated to Working Thread #1 (denoted as WT#1) and Task 2 to Working Thread #N (denoted as WT#N). Figure 10-19 shows this scenario.

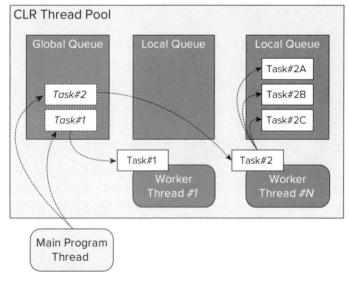

**FIGURE 10-19:**  Working threads have their own local queue

Now, when Task 2 creates new tasks, those go into the local queue of WT#N, and not into the Global Queue. Let's assume that WT#N first finishes with processing Task 2, and then, a bit later, WT#1 with processing Task 1. The working threads do not stop at this point and so they do not become available for other work items! Figure 10-20 shows what happens next.

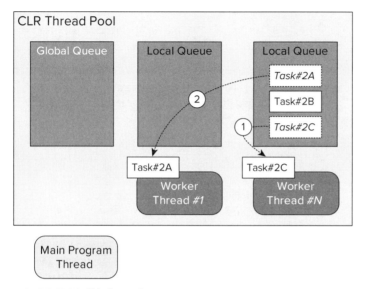

**FIGURE 10-20:** Work-stealing

Now, the Local Queue of WT#N is not empty; there are three tasks waiting for execution. The thread picks up Task 2C from the queue (as if the queue were a stack) and starts executing it. But Task 2C is the latest task created, and it was put to the Local Queue after Task 2A and 2C! Why does WT#N take this one and not Task 2A? The reason is performance — because Task 2C was created later then task 2A, there is a greater likelihood that more resources of Task 2C are cached into the memory than resources for Task 2A.

When WT#1 finishes (a bit later than WT#N), it sees its Local Queue is empty. However, it also looks at other Local Queues and discovers that WT#N has two tasks in its queue. WT#1 picks up ("steals") Task 2A from the Local Queue of WT#N and starts executing it. This is called *work-stealing* with TPL terminology. "Stolen" tasks are picked up from the beginning of the queue, intentionally, because of performance reasons.

Should WT#N finish Task 2C earlier than WT#1 finishes Task 2A, WT#N would grab Task 2B for execution; otherwise, WT#1 would steal it.

## Task-Related Types

There are several types that can help you with task-related activities; most of them can be found in the System.Threading.Tasks namespace. Table 10-4 lists them with a brief description of their functionality.

**TABLE 10-4:** Concurrent Collection Classes

| TYPE NAME | DESCRIPTION |
|---|---|
| `Task` | This class represents an asynchronous operation, and implements the abstraction of "task" as discussed earlier in this chapter. |
| `Task<TResult>` | This class represents a `Task` that retrieves a result of type `TResult`. |
| `TaskCancelledException` | This exception class can be used to communicate that a task is cancelled. Through its `Task` property, you can access the cancelled task instance. If no task is assigned to the exception, `Task` is `null`. |
| `TaskCompletionSource<TResult>` | This type acts as the producer for a `Task<TResult>` and its completion, without bounding the class instance to a delegate. <br><br> You can use this class to create your own asynchronous operation that provides the interface of a `Task<Result>` instance for the consumers. The `Task` property retrieves the `Task<Result>` instance for the consumers, which hides the asynchrony used internally. There are a few methods (such as `SetResult`, `SetException`, `SetCancelled`, and a few more) that communicate the status of the asynchrony mechanism back to the `Task` property. |
| `TaskFactory, TaskFactory<Result>` | These classes provide support for creating and scheduling `Task` objects. Their methods such as `StartNew`, `ContinueWhenAll`, `ContinueWhenAny`, `FromAsync` (and their generic forms) provide you a notation for task instantiation, which lets you feel as if you're using task-specific declarative language. |
| `TaskScheduler` | This class represents a scheduler object responsible for the low-level work of queuing tasks onto threads. |

## Coordination Data Structures

.NET Framework 4.0 introduces several new types that are useful in parallel programming. These types are heavily used by the TPL and the PLINQ execution engine. They are not for internal use only. Moreover, you are encouraged to build them into your concurrent algorithms.

These types can be grouped into the following categories:

➤ *Concurrent Collection Classes* — The collection classes in the `System.Collections.Concurrent` namespace provide thread-safe add and remove operations with sophisticated locking mechanisms.

➤ *Synchronization Primitives* — The `System.Threading` namespace has new synchronization primitives that enable fine-grained concurrency and faster performance by avoiding expensive locking mechanisms found in legacy multithreading code.

➤ *Lazy Initialization Classes* — These classes help you to wrap your custom types into "lazy" classes that allow you to postpone the memory and resource allocation for an object until it is needed.

➤ *Cancellation Primitives* — One of the most difficult things with multiple-threads is the proper cancellation of them. Cancellation primitives help you to simplify this scenario.

## Concurrent Collection classes

Collection classes introduced in .NET Framework 1.0 and 2.0 require user code to take any locks when it accesses items. This behavior has been changed with the new concurrent collection classes, which do not require any user code. You simply use their methods, and can be sure that no concurrent issues (such as race conditions or deadlocks) will occur.

Earlier in this chapter, the `LorumIpsumQuery` sample showed you that an inefficient locking pattern may lead to poor performance. The concurrent collection classes can significantly improve performance over types generally used with your own locking-scheme (such as `ArrayList` and `List<T>`) in scenarios where multiple threads add, insert, modify, and remove items from a collection. These new classes are optimized for these scenarios, and provide thread-safe add and remove operations that avoid locks wherever possible, and use fine-grained locking where locks are necessary.

Table 10-5 lists these new concurrent collection classes.

**TABLE 10-5:** Concurrent Collection Classes

| TYPE NAME | DESCRIPTION |
| --- | --- |
| `BlockingCollection<T>` | This class provides blocking and bounding capabilities for thread-safe collections. `BlockingCollection<T>` allows removal attempts from the collection to block until data is available to be removed. |
| | Also, you can use `BlockingCollection<T>` to enforce an upper-bound on the number of data elements allowed in the collection. Addition attempts to the collection may then block until space is available to store the added items. |

*continues*

**TABLE 10-5** *(continued)*

| TYPE NAME | DESCRIPTION |
|---|---|
| ConcurrentBag<T> | This class represents a thread-safe, unordered collection of objects. You can use ConcurrentBag<T> where the same thread will be both producing and consuming data stored in the bag, because ConcurrentBag<T> performance is optimized for these scenarios. |
| ConcurrentDictionary<TKey, TValue> | This class represents a thread-safe collection of key-value pairs that can be accessed by multiple threads concurrently. You can use the class instead of Dictionary<TKey, TValue> easily, because it implements the same semantics. The internal implementation of this class provides a much better scaling for multiple threads in both for small and large size dictionaries than you can achieve with Dictionary<TKey, TValue>. |
| ConcurrentQueue<T> | This class represents a thread-safe First-In-First-Out (FIFO) collection. |
| ConcurrentStack<T> | This class represents a thread-safe Last-In-First-Out (LIFO) collection. |

Except ConcurrentDictionary<TKey, TValue>, all other classes implement the IProducer ConsumerCollection<T> interface, which represents a collection that allows for thread-safe adding and removing of data.

## Synchronization Primitives

The System.Threading namespace contains new types that avoid expensive locking mechanisms found in legacy multithreading code. Most of these types are lightweight, and enable fine-grained concurrency and faster performance than predecessors in the .NET Framework.

Table 10-6 lists these new synchronization primitives.

**TABLE 10-6:** Synchronization Primitives

| TYPE NAME | DESCRIPTION |
|---|---|
| Barrier | This class is new, and it does not have a predecessor in the previous .NET Framework versions. Barrier enables multiple tasks to cooperatively work on an algorithm in parallel through multiple phases. <br><br> You can use this class to manage a group of tasks to cooperate by moving through a series of phases, where each in the group signals it has arrived at the Barrier in a given phase, and implicitly waits for all others to arrive. |

| TYPE NAME | DESCRIPTION |
|---|---|
| | A real-life example is when company cars are driven across the U.S. from Seattle to Miami. The drivers do not drive in a convoy, but agree on several points (let's say Denver and Houston) where they wait for each other. When everyone arrives at these barriers, they start the next section of the route.<br><br>The same `Barrier` instance can be used for multiple phases. |
| `CountdownEvent` | This class represents a synchronization primitive that is signaled when its count reaches zero.<br><br>You can use this class in fork-and-join scenarios, because it provides an easy rendezvous mechanism.<br><br>`CountdownEvent` allows a thread to wait until one or more threads finish some other operation. An instance of this class is initialized with an integral count, typically greater than 0. Threads can block waiting on the event until the count reaches 0, at which point the `CountdownEvent` will be set. The count is decremented using `CountdownEvent`'s `Decrement` method, which is typically called by a worker thread completing a unit of work being tracked by the event. |
| `ManualResetEventSlim` | This type is a slimmed down and lighter-weight version of its predecessor, `ManualResetEvent`, and can be used to notify one or more waiting threads that an event has occurred.<br><br>The price of slimming is that you can use an instance of `ManualResetEventSlim` only for intra-process communication. |
| `SemaphoreSlim` | This lightweight class can be used to limit the number of threads that can access a resource or pool of resources concurrently. It has a predecessor named `Semaphore` that was introduced by .NET Framework 2.0. However, while `Semaphore` leverages on Windows kernel semaphores, `SemaphoreSlim` does not. |
| `SpinLock, SpinWait` | These synchronization primitives enable a thread to wait. They can improve performance when the wait time is expected to be short, by avoiding expensive sleeping and blocking operations.<br><br>`SpinLock` is a mutual-exclusion lock primitive that causes the thread that is trying to acquire the lock to wait in a loop (or spin) for a period of time before yielding its quantum. `SpinLock` is a value type, for performance reasons, so if you need to pass a `SpinLock` instance around, it should be passed by reference, rather than by value.<br><br>`SpinWait` is a small, lightweight type that will spin for a specified time and eventually put the thread into a wait state if the spin count is exceeded. `SpinWait` is a value type; its members are not thread-safe. If multiple threads must spin, each should use its own instance of `SpinWait`. |

These synchronization primitives play an important role in TPL implementation. They are heavily used, and significantly contribute to the great performance of TPL.

## Lazy Initialization Classes

Postponing initialization of type members until they are needed is a frequently used programming pattern. It is especially useful when initialization is expensive by means of consumed CPU cycles, memory, or other resources. Lazy initialization classes listed in Table 10-7 can help you in these scenarios.

**TABLE 10-7:** Lazy Initialization Types

| TYPE NAME | DESCRIPTION |
| --- | --- |
| `System.Lazy<T>` | This class provides support for lazy initialization of a `T` instance. When you create an instance of `Lazy<T>`, it does not instantiate `T`. You can access the instance behind `Lazy<T>` using its `Value` property. |
| | Lazy initialization occurs the first time the `Lazy<T>` `.Value` property is accessed, or the `Lazy<T>` `.ToString` method is called. |
| `System.Threading.LazyInitializer` | This static class provides lazy initialization routines. With .NET Framework 4.0, you can use a few overloads of the `EnsureInitialized` method. In the future, the class may be extended with more helper methods. |
| | In scenarios where you must lazy-initialize a large number of objects, you might decide that wrapping each object in a `Lazy<T>` requires too much memory, or too many computing resources. Or, you might have stringent requirements about how lazy initialization is exposed. In such cases, you can use the static `EnsureInitialized` methods to lazy-initialize each object without wrapping it in an instance of `Lazy<T>`. |
| `System.Threading.ThreadLocal<T>` | This class provides thread-local storage of data with type `T`. Although this class uses lazy initialization in its implementation, "laziness" isn't its main functionality. By providing an instance of `ThreadLocal<T>`, you can be sure that the T instance accessed through the `Value` property is shared within the thread it was created. |
| | Its role is similar as the role of the `ThreadStatic` attribute used to decorate static fields in order to have thread-local behavior. However, `ThreadLocal<T>` provides better performance. |

## Cancellation Primitives

If you have ever tried to solve the cancellation of a work carried out by several threads running in parallel, you know how complex it could be, especially for blocking calls. TPL provides a few types that simplify the complexity of cancellation. The primitives listed in Table 10-8 can be used in your parallel applications using tasks, PLINQ expression, or `Parallel` loops.

**TABLE 10-8:** Cancellation Primitives

| TYPE NAME | DESCRIPTION |
| --- | --- |
| CancellationToken | This structure propagates notification that operations should be cancelled. You can pass an instance of `CancellationToken` to blocking calls such as `BlockingCollection.Add(...)`, `BlockingCollection.Take(...)`, `ManualResetEventSlim.Wait(...)`, `Task.Wait(...)`, and `Task.WaitAll(...)`. These methods have overloads that accept a `CancellationToken` instance, and finish their operation when a cancellation occurs. |
| CancellationTokenSource | This class signals to a `CancellationToken` that is should be cancelled. You can use this class as a conductor in cooperative cancellation scenarios. You can pass the `Token` property of a `CancellationTokenSource` instance to methods accepting it. When the `Cancel` method is called, all instances having the token belonging to this `CancellationTokenSource` instance will be notified. |

# CODE CONTRACTS

Modern software architecture uses layers and components with exact boundaries and well-defined responsibilities. Without this kind of approach, it is difficult to write testable software with good quality. The cooperation among these components is generally defined by *contracts*. For many developers, contracts are the definitions of interfaces (interface classes) and related data transfer objects or entities the components use to define the communication surface. For example, let's assume that you develop warehouse stock management software where one of the interface classes is `WarehouseService` and a related entity is `Order`:

```
public class WarehouseService
{
  public void QueueOrder(Order order)
  {
    // ...
  }
}

public class Order
```

```
{
    public string CustomerName { get; set; }
    public int ProductId { get; set; }
    public int Quantity { get; set; }
}
```

Unfortunately, these two classes leave many issues. When you see their definitions and want to use them, you must ask the architect (or even the developer) some questions about these classes to use them successfully. Here are a few questions you may ask:

➤   What happens if a `null` value is passed to the `QueueOrder` method? You may assume, it raises an `ArgumentNullException`, but you cannot be sure.

➤   What if the `CustomeName` property in the `Order` instance is `null`, or an empty string? Is the order valid in this case?

➤   What if the `Quantity` property of `Order` is negative? Does it mean that actually a product is returned to the warehouse? Can this value be zero?

These questions would not be necessary if there were a way to describe the behavior of the `QueueOrder` method in such an unambiguous way as the signature of the method. Actually, the answers to these questions should be the part of the contract defining the `WarehouseService` behavior.

This is where a new .NET Framework feature, programming with *code contracts*, comes into the picture. The basic idea behind code contracts is that classes and methods should explicitly state what they require, and what they guarantee if those requirements are met. This practice was first introduced by Bertrand Meyer with the Eiffel programming language, and Microsoft Research also has a project called Spec#, that covers a formal language for API contracts (influenced by Eiffel, JML, and AsmL languages). These contracts are not only human-readable but can also be picked up by tooling that can perform run-time checking or static verification, or perhaps include them in generated documentation.

## Understanding the Code Contracts System

There are two basic parts that are involved in using code contracts in the .NET Framework 4.0. The first part is the *code contract library*. Contracts are encoded using static method calls defined in the `Contract` class of the `System.Diagnostics.Contracts` namespace. Contracts are declarative, and these static calls at the beginning of your methods can be thought of as part of the method signature. For example, the `QueueOrder` method treated earlier could be extended with a few declarative contracts:

```
public void QueueOrder(Order order)
{
    Contract.Requires(order != null);
    Contract.Requires(order.Quantity > 0);
    // ...
}
```

Generally, in the .NET Framework, attributes are used to express declarative elements for types and members. However, code contracts are methods, and not attributes, because attributes are very limited in what they can express. Just think about how to describe order != null with attributes.

The second part of the code contract system is the *set of tools* that adds a great value to the code contract library. This set contains three tools that can be accessed from a command line and can also be integrated with Visual Studio 2010:

➤ Ccrewrite.exe — This tool modifies the MSIL instructions of an assembly to place the contract checks into the physical code stream. With the library, you declare your contracts at the beginning of the method. This is the tool that enables run-time checking of contracts to help you debug your code. Without it, contracts are simply documentation, and shouldn't be compiled into your binary.

➤ Cccheck.exe — This tool examines code without executing it, and tries to prove that all of the contracts are satisfied. There are attributes in the contract library that let you specify which assemblies, types, or members should be checked.

➤ Ccrefgen.exe — This tool creates separate contract reference assemblies that contain only the contracts. The rewriter and static checker will then make use of any contract assemblies when they are doing their instrumentation and analysis.

While the code contract library is a part of .NET Framework 4.0, tools are not. You can download them from the Code Contracts site on DevLabs (http://msdn.microsoft.com/en-us/devlabs/dd491992.aspx).

 *As of this writing, Code Contract Tools come with Academic License. It is not clear what kind of license you will need to use the tools with the final version of Visual Studio 2010.*

## Declaring Code Contracts

Code contracts can be used to define three types of conditions:

➤ *Preconditions* — These express what program state is required for a method to run successfully.

➤ *Postconditions* — These tell you what you can rely upon at the completion of the method.

➤ *Object invariants* — These are guarantees about conditions that will always be true for an object.

Because code contracts are used primarily to help find bugs in code, they are conditionally compiled when you define the symbol CONTRACTS_FULL. This means that, without this symbol, your contracts will not be checked at run-time. If you want to ensure that code contracts do not change your business logic, all conditions that are checked must be side-effect free.

Code contracts will result in code running within the encapsulating method, and so contracts are inherited. If you have a class, let's say `MyClass`, code contracts defined and checked there will also be checked in direct or indirect descendants of `MyClass`.

## Preconditions

*Preconditions* describe a particular condition that must be true upon entry to the method (checking the method input). In other words, preconditions are contracts on the state of the world when a method is invoked.

Preconditions are expressed using `Contract.Requires` or `Contract.Requires<TException>` methods. Here are a few examples:

```
Contract.Requires(customer.Name != null);
Contract.Requires(order.TotalAmount >= 0, "Amount cannot be a negative number");

Contract.Requires<ArgumentNullException>(customer.Name != null);
Contract.Requires<ArgumentException>(order.ItemID.Length == 6,
  "ID must be exacly 6 characters");
```

The arguments of `Requires` are a predicate defining the precondition, and an optional message to use at run-time when the condition is not met. There is an important restriction on the predicate — all members mentioned in preconditions must be at least as accessible as the method itself. When you use the generic form of `Requires<TException>`, a `TException` is raised at run-time if the precondition is evaluated to `false`.

> `Requires<TException>` *is always compiled (even if you do not use the* `CONTRACTS_FULL` *symbol), so use of this method entails a hard dependency on the tools. You should decide if you want that before using this method.*

Your legacy code (any code written before .NET 4) may contain many preconditions by means of checking method inputs. Tools also can use `if` statements and recognize them as legacy forms of code contracts, if you help with the `EndContractBlock` method call, as the sample shows:

```
public void QueueOrder(Order order)
{
  if (order == null)
    throw new ArgumentNullException("order");
  if (order.CustomerName == null)
    throw new ArgumentNullException("order.CustomerName");
  Contract.EndContractBlock();
  if (order.CustomerName.Length == 0)
    order.CustomerName = "<noname>";
  // ...
}
```

In this case, tools (for instance Cccheck.exe) take the first two if statements into account as a negated precondition, but not the third one, because it is preceded by the Contract.EndContractBlock method. However, this form of precondition is highly restricted. It must be written as shown here. There are no else clauses, and the body of the then clause must be a single throw statement.

## Postconditions

*Postconditions* are contracts on the state of a method when it terminates. In other words, the condition is checked just prior to exiting a method. Unlike preconditions, members with less visibility may be mentioned in a postcondition. There are two kinds of postconditions:

➤ *Normal* — These express a condition that must hold on normal termination of the method.

➤ *Exceptional* — These express a condition when a particular exception is raised by the method, as a part of its contract.

These conditions can be described by the Contract.Ensures and Contract.EnsuresOnThrow <TException>, respectively. In the latter case, TException is the type of exception thrown (the exception can also be a subtype of TException). Here are a few examples:

```
Contract.Ensures(order.CustomerID != 0);
Contract.EnsuresOnThrow<ArgumentException>(!transactionCompleted);
```

Because of the nature of postconditions, it is normal to make conditions for the return value or output values of a method. The Contract class provides several special methods that may be used to access these values. There is no language element in C# or Visual Basic to refer to the return value, so you can refer to it in a postcondition with the Contract.Result<T> method, where T is the type of the return value. For example, you can express that the returned integer should be between 100 and 200:

```
Contract.Ensures(Contract.Result<int>() >= 100 && Contract.Result<int>() <= 200);
```

Output parameters may not be set before the code contract line where they are used in a postcondition; otherwise, the compiler would raise an error. To avoid this situation, you can use the Contract.ValueAtReturn<T>(out T t) method, where T is the type of the output value. For example, you can express that the output string cannot be longer than 64 characters:

```
public void HashText(string text, out string hash)
{
  Contract.Ensures(Contract.ValueAtReturn<string>(out hash).Length <= 64);
  //
}
```

 You can also use the Contract.OldValue<T> *method to refer to a pre-state in a postcondition, and two quantifiers* (Contract.Exists<T>, Contract .ForAll<T>) *are also supported. You can read details of using them in the reference documentation of the* Contract *class.*

## Object Invariants

*Object invariants* are object-wide contracts about a condition that is guaranteed to always hold. They can be thought of as postconditions on every single public member of the object.

Because invariants characterize the object type, related contracts should be put into a separate method. This method must not have any parameters, and should return `void`. You can use any name for this method (a suggested practice is to use the `ObjectInvariant` name), and it must be marked with the `ContractInvariantMethod` attribute. Here is an example:

```
public class Stock
{
  public int ProductId { get; set; }
  public int InStock { get; set; }
  // ...
  [ContractInvariantMethod]
  protected void ObjectInvariant()
  {
    Contract.Invariant(InStock >= 0);
    // ...
  }
}
```

As you can see, individual invariants within invariant methods are specified using the `Contract.Invariant` method. The method can contain no other code than a sequence of calls to `Contract.Invariant`.

## Interface Contracts

Many design patterns use *interfaces* as contracts among communicating components, and obviously that is the place where code contracts should be put. However, many programming languages (including C# and Visual Basic) do not allow putting method bodies into the interface definition. Writing contracts for interface methods requires creating a separate contract class to hold them, and linking the contract class with the interface by a pair of attributes.

The contract class must exactly mirror the signatures of members, as the following example shows:

```
[ContractClass(typeof(IStockHandlerContract))]
interface IStockHandler
{
  void AddToStock(int amount);
  int CurrentStock { get; }
}

[ContractClassFor(typeof(IStockHandler))]
sealed class IStockHandlerContract : IStockHandler
{
  void IStockHandler.AddToStock(int amount)
  {
    Contract.Requires(amount >= 0);
  }

  int IStockHandler.CurrentStock
  {
    get
```

```
    {
      Contract.Ensures(Contract.Result<int>() >= 0);
      return default(int);
    }
  }
}
```

The original interface must be marked with the `ContractClass` attribute pointing to the class describing the code contracts, and this class must point back to the interface type with the `ContractClassFor` attribute. The contract class is expected to use explicit implementation of the contracted interface. Within the members, you can describe code contracts just as if they belonged to the class.

The contract class is intended to be used only for contract checks. It is always a good practice to declare it as an internal sealed class. For non-`void` methods and properties, the contract class must return values; otherwise, the code would not compile. The best practice is to return a dummy value with the `default` operator.

## Code Contract Tools in Visual Studio

As mentioned earlier, Code Contract tools are not the part of either .NET Framework 4.0 or Visual Studio 2010. They can be downloaded from the Code Contracts site on DevLabs (`http://msdn.microsoft.com/en-us/devlabs/dd491992.aspx`). After downloading, you can immediately install the tools. It is very easy, and takes only a few minutes.

The next time you start Visual Studio 2010, you will see a new Code Contracts property page accessible by right-clicking on Properties in the Solution Explorer when a project node is selected. Figure 10-21 shows this new page.

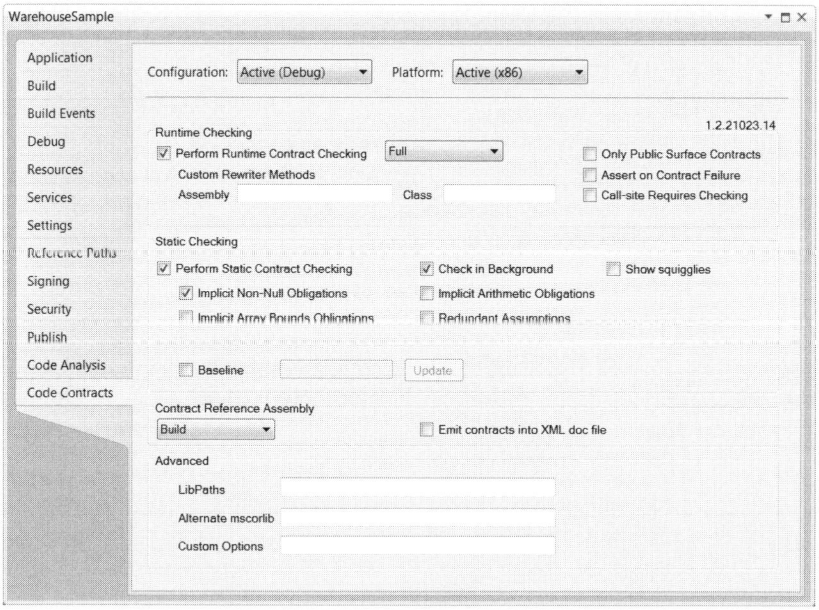

**FIGURE 10-21:** Code Contracts property page

Without going through all options available in the property page, here are the most important settings you may use:

➤ You can turn on or off run-time checking (Ccrewite.exe), and tune checks with a few knobs.

➤ You can turn on or off static checking (Cccheck.exe) and define what kind of checks to carry on. When static checking is turned on, Cccheck.exe will run as a part of your build, and will generate warnings and errors related to code contracts (or the lack of them).

➤ You can also create contract reference assemblies with Ccrefgen.exe as the part of the build process.

The static code checker utility is very useful. It helps to highlight issues in your code that may lead to bugs — you can even use it with your legacy code.

## Run-time Behavior

Code contracts and related tools can be used in several ways:

➤ You can use the Contract class for documentation purposes only.

➤ With the tools, you can perform static code analysis and use code contracts to respond to the issues coming from the analysis.

➤ You can create full contracts for your fundamental types and methods (even for all of them) and use the contracts during the debug build process.

➤ You may find code contracts so important and useful that you want to also use them in the production releases.

While, in the first two cases, code contracts are "decorations" only, in the latter two cases, code contracts should influence the run-time behavior of types they are attached to.

When you turn on run-time checking (set the Perform Runtime Contract Checking checkbox shown in Figure 10-21), Ccrewite.exe will change the MSIL code of the types with code contracts in the assemblies generated by the compiler.

By default, Contract methods are not compiled into the final code, except Contract.Requires <TException>, and so they do not influence the run-time behavior of the code. However, when the run-time checking is turned on, Ccrewite.exe examines code contracts in your code and makes a lot of changes in the final code:

➤ Code representing preconditions is placed at the entry of the related methods directly before the method body.

➤ Code contracts for postconditions are declared in the code at the beginning of members. The code for checking postconditions is moved to the exit section of the method, after the result, and all output variables are already calculated.

➤ Object invariants are checked at the end of each public method. If an invariant calls a public method in the same class, then the invariant check is disabled and checked only at the end of the outermost method call to that class. This also happens if the class is re-entered because of a call to a method on another class.

When a condition is not met, the run-time will raise a `ContractException`. The `Contract` class has a `ContractFailed` event you can subscribe to in order to be notified about contract violations. This event allows you to access a `ContractFailedEventArgs` instance that tells you everything about the context of failure.

 *If you are interested in the changes* `Ccrewrite.exe` *makes with your code, use the .NET Reflector utility that allows you to disassemble the code after it has been instrumented by* `Ccrewrite.exe`.

## MANAGED EXTENSIBILITY FRAMEWORK

The Managed Extensibility Framework (MEF) is a new technology that is being shipped as a part of .NET Framework 4.0, and you can consider it as a new part of the BCL. MEF as a technology is intended to enable greater reuse of applications and components by turning today's statically compiled applications into dynamically composed ones.

This section addresses the following topics:

➤ The challenge of dynamic software composition

➤ A simple example to demonstrate what the shift to dynamically composed applications means

➤ The basic concepts of MEF illustrated with code snippets

➤ Directions you should follow to dive deeper into MEF

### The Challenge

The mission of MEF is to solve the old problem of maintaining a piece of statically compiled software that continuously changes (let's say it "evolves") during its lifetime. Writing package software or enterprise applications — with all mandatory dances such as unit and user acceptance testing, documentation, and so on — is generally the easiest (and almost the most amusing) part.

Should the time to extend (or change) the software come, the amusement is over. Even if you do not have problems coming from the architecture — that is, functions that were changed or added still work perfectly — you still must compile and deploy the application. Quite often, that means removing the previous software version from client and server machines, and then installing the new software.

Separating a statically compiled application into smaller physical units (*assemblies*) can help this situation, especially when these smaller units are loaded dynamically. Using a tool for configuration (for example, a file describing which components to load) and creating a plug-in model definitely helps you.

The situation gets more and more complex if you have several configurations of the application that should be deployed differently to client machines. From the efforts point of view, it means that developers spend approximately 20 percent of their effort developing the original application and about 80 percent maintaining it through the years. If you could turn at least a part of that painful 80 percent into something more useful (for example, investing in creating better business value or an improved user experience), both your customers and your boss would be happier, and probably you would be better paid. That is where MEF comes into the picture.

## Dynamic Composition

Why is this dynamic composition so important? If you create applications from smaller independent components, you can architect the application so that responsibilities are better divided, and boundaries are more obvious. According to these responsibilities, you can test your components separately, find bugs, and correct them. It is easier to handle these small parts individually than all the pieces together, and it is easier to maintain them. However, the question is how do you roll together these individual parts to form an entire application?

Well, this is what MEF does — parts declare their intention to work together with other parts, and MEF pulls all of them together to form the application. Instead of a monolithic and statically compiled piece of software, you could have a dynamically composed one, where you could even have the possibility to "drop into" a new part (such as inserting a new LEGO brick to an existing composition). One of the first Microsoft applications that utilizes MEF is Visual Studio 2010, where the code editor is actually built with MEF.

## The Open/Closed Principle

You may think the design methodologies of dynamically composed and statically compiled applications are very different. You cannot say one of them is easier while the other is more complex. They are simply different. However, there is a primary design principle from the aspect of dynamism that should be your guiding star.

This is the *Open/Closed Principle* that is credited to Bertrand Meyer in his book *Object Oriented Software Construction* (Upper Saddle River, New Jersey: Prentice-Hall, 2000). This principle says that you should create your software entities (components) so that they are open for extensibility, but closed for modifications. It can be translated so that if you create software entities, you should create objects so that they possess the opportunity to be extended without changing their source code.

One example of applying this principle is when you create a base class with virtual methods as extensibility points. When it's time to modify the behavior, you keep the base class untouched, and write a derived class overriding the virtual methods.

The reason behind this principle is that modifying the source code of an existing (even tested) component introduces risks with a relatively high mitigation cost. You can introduce new bugs, change the expected logic, or even break existing interfaces. The Open/Closed Principle actually says that you can modify a system without changing existing code. Instead, you add new (and, of course, tested) code.

For applications composed dynamically from smaller parts, this principle suggests creating software components that do not allow changing their source code, but allow loading parts that change the behavior.

## A Simple MEF Example

The best way to grasp the concept of how MEF can respond to the challenge of dynamic software composition is to create a short example.

Start Visual Studio and create a C# console application with the name `MefGreetings`. This application will be a refactored form of the "Hello, World" example with extensibility in mind. You are going to create a separate component responsible for greeting the user. Add two code files to the project, and name them `IGreetings.cs` and `SimpleGreeting.cs`. Copy the source code from Listing 10-17 to `IGreeting.cs`, and from Listing 10-18 to `SimpleGreeting.cs`.

**LISTING 10-17:** IGreetings.cs

```
namespace MefGreetings
{
  interface IGreetings
  {
    string SayHello();
  }
}
```

*Code file [IGreetings.cs] available for download at Wrox.com*

**LISTING 10-18:** SimpleGreeting.cs

```
namespace MefGreetings
{
  class SimpleGreeting : IGreetings
  {
    public string SayHello()
    {
      return "Hello from Visual Studio 2010";
    }
  }
}
```

*Code file [SimpleGreeting.cs] available for download at Wrox.com*

Change the `Program.cs` file as shown in Listing 10-19, and the example application is ready to build and run.

**LISTING 10-19: Program.cs**

```
using System;

namespace MefGreetings
{
  class Program
  {
    static void Main(string[] args)
    {
      var greetings = new SimpleGreeting();
      Console.WriteLine(greetings.SayHello());
    }
  }
}
```

*Code file [Program.cs] available for download at Wrox.com*

Run the application, and it does exactly what you expect — it displays the "Hello from Visual Studio 2010" message. Despite of the refactoring of the application, the SimpleGreeting and Program are still tightly coupled. Although, the greeting text is decoupled from the console class through the IGreetings interface, the SimpleGreeting class is directly instantiated. Now, let's turn your application to a "MEFish" one!

## Getting MEF into the Game

To utilize MEF, add a reference to the System.ComponentModel.Composition assembly, because MEF types and attributes are declared here. You are going to turn this application to a dynamically composed one in few simple steps.

Decorate the SimpleGreeting class with the Export attribute. This attribute will signify that SimpleGreeting is a composable part that has a service offered to the external world. The attribute has a typeof(IGreetings) parameter, which is the identifier of the contract SimpleGreeting is about to export. Listing 10-20 shows SimpleGreetings.cs after this change.

**LISTING 10-20: SimpleGreeting with the Export Attribute**

```
using System.ComponentModel.Composition;

namespace MefGreetings
{
  [Export(typeof(IGreetings))]
  class SimpleGreeting : IGreetings
  {
    public string SayHello()
    {
      return "Hello from Visual Studio 2010";
    }
  }
}
```

*Code file [SimpleGreetings.cs] available for download at Wrox.com*

In the `Main` method, you must tell the application that a component implementing the `IGreetings` service contract should be used instead of instantiating the `SimpleGreetings` class. With MEF, it is a few lines of code, as shown in Listing 10-21.

**LISTING 10-21: Composing the Application From Parts**

```csharp
using System;
using System.Reflection;
using System.ComponentModel.Composition.Hosting;
using System.ComponentModel.Composition;

namespace MefGreetings
{
  class Program
  {
    [Import]
    private IGreetings Greetings { get; set; }

    static void Main(string[] args)
    {
      var program = new Program();
      program.Run();
    }

    private void Run()
    {
      var catalog = new AssemblyCatalog(Assembly.GetExecutingAssembly());
      var container = new CompositionContainer(catalog);
      container.ComposeParts(this);

      Console.WriteLine(Greetings.SayHello());
    }
  }
}
```

*Code file [Program.cs] available for download at Wrox.com*

When you run this code, you can see that it still displays the "Hello from Visual Studio 2010" message. Let's see how this program works!

To access the component (an instance of `SimpleGreeting`), a private property named `Greeting` is set up with the `Import` attribute. Any time the program wants to use a service of the component, this property can be used to invoke the functionality. The `Run` method shows how to use it:

```csharp
Console.WriteLine(Greetings.SayHello());
```

But, as you see, there is no code in the application that explicitly initializes the `Greetings` property. So, you might expect a `NullReferenceException` when running the program, although it does not happen. MEF takes care of binding the `Greeting` property with a component instance via the three "magic" lines in the `Run` method:

```
var catalog = new AssemblyCatalog(Assembly.GetExecutingAssembly());
var container = new CompositionContainer(catalog);
container.ComposeParts(this);
```

The first line creates an *assembly catalog* using the current console application's assembly. In MEF, a catalog is a collection of composable parts that can be composed with a host to form an application. An assembly catalog contains all parts that can be found in the specified assembly. In this example, `SimpleGreeting` is a part that can be found in the catalog represented by an assembly.

The second line instantiates a *composition container* using the assembly catalog. This container is a matchmaker. It looks in the catalogs for the parts offering services (this is what the `Export` attribute marks), and for those that are requesting services (the `Import` attribute signifies that fact). The container uses its own logic to match the offers with the requests. The third line calling the `ComposeParts` method does this match-making.

As a result, the composition container creates a `SimpleGreeting` instance and assigns it to the `Greetings` property. So, calling the `SayHello` method does not raise an exception. It works and writes out the message.

## Multiple Parts

Add another part implementing the `IGreetings` service contract to the application by creating a new class with the `UserGreeting` name. Copy the source code in Listing 10-22 into the file.

**LISTING 10-22:** UserGreeting.cs

```csharp
using System;
using System.ComponentModel.Composition;

namespace MefGreetings
{
  [Export(typeof(IGreetings))]
  class UserGreeting: IGreetings
  {
    public string SayHello()
    {
      return "Hello " + Environment.UserName;
    }
  }
}
```

---

*Code file [UserGreetings.cs] available for download at Wrox.com*

When you build and run the application, it stops working with a `ChangeRejectedException`. What could be wrong? You have not actually changed anything, just added a new class! Well, that new class is the source of the problem. When the composition container wants to make matches, it is faced with the issue of having two components implementing the IGreetings contract. One of them is SimpleGreeting; the other is the new UserGreeting class. Which one is the one to bind with the Greetings property having the Import attribute? The composition container cannot decide, and that's why it raises an exception.

Change the application logic so that all components supporting the IGreetings interface can write their messages. Modify the Greetings property to allow it to handle a collection of parts implementing IGreeting:

```
[ImportMany]
private IEnumerable<IGreetings> Greetings { get; set; }
```

The ImportMany attribute expresses this intention. Note the IEnumerable<IGreetings> type of this property! It allows MEF to retrieve a collection of parts, and you can allow all of them to write out their messages:

```
foreach (var grt in Greetings)
{
  Console.WriteLine(grt.SayHello());
}
```

With this change the application can run, and, this time, two messages are put to the console.

## Using Host Services

Up until now, in the example, only the host application accessed the services of the "plugged-in" components. In the real world, components would also use the services of the host application. With a few modifications, you can change the application to reflect this situation.

Create a new file named IContextInfo.cs with the source code in Listing 10-23.

**LISTING 10-23: IContextInfo.cs**

```
using System.Collections.Generic;

namespace MefGreetings
{
  public interface IContextInfo
  {
    IDictionary<string, string> GetContextInfo();
  }
}
```

*Code file [IContextInfo.cs] available for download at Wrox.com*

The GetContextInfo method provides a dictionary of key and value pairs where — just for the sake of simplicity — keys and values are both strings. Create a type named AppInfo that implements this contract, and mark it with the Export attribute, as shown in Listing 10-24.

**LISTING 10-24: AppInfo.cs**

```
using System;
using System.Collections.Generic;
using System.ComponentModel.Composition;

namespace MefGreetings
{
  [Export(typeof(IContextInfo))]
  class AppInfo : IContextInfo
  {
    public IDictionary<string, string> GetContextInfo()
    {
      return new Dictionary<string, string>
      {
        { "UserName", Environment.UserName },
        { "MachineName", Environment.MachineName }
      };
    }
  }
}
```

*Code file [AppInfo.cs] available for download at Wrox.com*

AppInfo is a service object in the application that can be accessed through the IContextInfo contract identity. Listing 10-25 shows how the UserGreeting class should be modified to utilize this contract.

**LISTING 10-25: The Modified UserGreeting.cs File**

```
using System;
using System.ComponentModel.Composition;

namespace MefGreetings
{
  [Export(typeof(IGreetings))]
  class UserGreeting: IGreetings
  {
    [Import]
    IContextInfo ContextInfo { get; set; }

    public string SayHello()
    {
      string userName;
      var props = ContextInfo.GetContextInfo();
      props.TryGetValue("UserName", out userName);
      return "Hello " + userName ?? "<None>";
    }
  }
}
```

*Code file [UserGreeting.cs] available for download at Wrox.com*

The `UserGreeting` class does not know where it gets an `IContextInfo`-aware service object from. If you decorate the `ContextInfo` property with the `Import` attribute, the composition container binds the right object to the property.

When you build and run the application, it will work as you expect — binding the application and its dynamic parts, as shown in Figure 10-22.

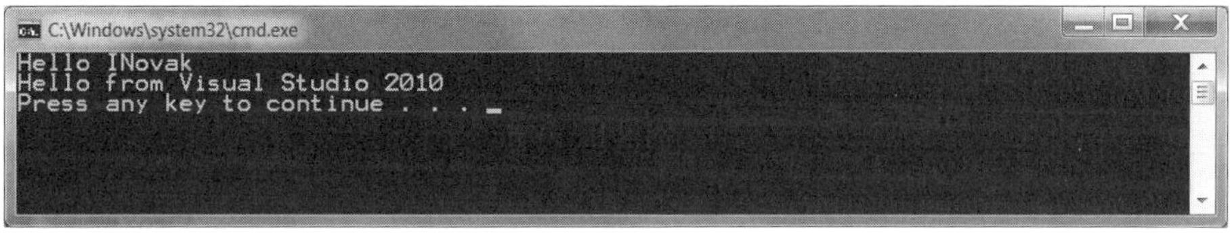

**FIGURE 10-22:** Application with dynamic parts

This simple example has shown just a taste of how MEF helps in composing applications. To understand what's behind the scenes, it's time to dive a bit deeper into MEF concepts.

# Basic MEF Concepts

As you have just seen, programming with MEF is easy. However, architecting your applications so that they can easily leverage the potential that MEF provides requires an understanding of the primary concepts.

The fundamental concept of MEF is *parts*. An application is built of parts. During construction, you do the following:

➤ *Export* the services parts offer to be utilized by other parts

➤ *Import* the services your parts intend to use

➤ *Compose* the parts so that they provide the functionality you want to achieve

## Parts and Contracts

Parts export services other parts may need, and optionally import services offered by other parts. MEF's default discovery mechanism to identify parts is based on standard .NET attributes defined in the `System.ComponentModel.Composition` namespace. Parts are decorated with the `Export` or `Import` attributes. To be recognized as a part, the corresponding entity should contain at least one export. Entities containing only imports are not taken into account as parts.

The loosely coupled nature of dynamic applications works with the idea that parts do not depend directly on one another. The thing that determines this dependency between parts is called a *contract*. Parts explicitly mark their intentions to be bound with other parts using contracts. Exported parts say, "Hey, I implement the contract named Foo. If there is anyone wanting to use Foo, here I am." Parts having `Import` attributes say, "In order to work, I need a part supporting the contract named Foo. Is there anyone who could provide an implementation for me?"

Contracts are identified by two properties: a *contract name* and a *contract type* (that is a System.Type instance). To match an exported and an imported contract, both the name and the type must be equal. The mechanism discovering parts can infer the name and the type of the contract where the Export and Import attributes are used. For example, let's say that you define the import like this:

```
[Import]
IContextInfo ContextInfo { get; set; }
```

The name of the contract becomes the full name of the IContextInfo type (MefGreetings.IContextInfo), while its type will be inferred from the type of the property and becomes IContextInfo.

> You can play with the contract matching mechanism. Try to decorate the SimpleGreeting, UserGreeting *classes with the following combinations of their Export attributes:*
>
> ```
> [Export]
>
> [Export("IGreetings", typeof(IGreetings))]
> [Export("MefGreetings.IGreetings", typeof(IGreetings))]
> ```
>
> *Build and run the* MefGreetings *sample to understand how they work! In addition, you can play with the* ContextInfo *property's* Import *attribute of the* UserGreeting *class.*

As a convention, wherever possible, use only types in contract definitions.

## Exports and Imports

By now, you can see that the Export attribute can be used to mark an entity as a part. As a great design feature of MEF, an Export attribute can decorate an entire class, a field, or a property, and, moreover, a method of a class. At first, it is not obvious why it is useful, so let's have a look at each of these cases.

When you apply Export for an entire class, the exported object is an instance of that class. However, if you do not own the source code of a class (for example, it is in a third-party assembly), and you cannot mark it as a part, this approach does not work.

In this case, you can decorate a field or a property with Export. Have a look at the following code snippet:

```
public class DalParameters
{
  [Export("MaxRowsToRetrieve")]
  public static int MaxRows = 1000;

  [Export("CustomerTable")]
```

```
        public string CustomerTable
        {
          get { return "Customer_"; }
        }
    }
```

The `DalParameters` class has two imported parts represented by the static `MaxRows` field and the `CustomerTable` instance property. Their corresponding types (`int` and `string`) are intrinsic CLR types, so there is no way to add an `Export` attribute to the class representing them. Using named contracts, you can import these parts:

```
[Import("MaxRowsToRetrieve")]
public int MaxRows { get; private set; }

[Import("CustomerTable")]
public string CustomerTableName { get; private set; }
```

If `Export` is applied on fields or properties, MEF uses the value of the property or field at composition time. This approach has several benefits:

➤   You can have one or more related exports within the same type.

➤   You can import sealed types, CLR intrinsic, and third-party types.

➤   You can decouple the export from how the export was created.

Moreover, MEF goes beyond properties and fields — you can export methods! In this case, methods are exported as delegates indicated by the contract type.

Assume that you have a `Customer` class with string properties of `Name` and `State`. You can define a part that can filter customers:

```
public class CustomerFilter
{
  [Export("CustomerFilter", typeof(Func<Customer, bool>))]
  bool LivesInCA(Customer customer)
  {
    return customer.State == "CA";
  }
}
```

Note that the `Export` attribute explicitly declares the delegate type representing the contract. Without it, MEF would not be able to infer the type of the delegate as the default contract type. You can bind this part to a service wanting to filter customers easily:

```
[Export]
class CustomerProcessor
{
  [Import("CustomerFilter")]
  Func<Customer, bool> Filter { get; set; }

  public void ProcessCustomers(IEnumerabe<Customer> customers)
```

```
    {
      foreach (var customer in customers.Where(Filter))
      {
        Console.WriteLine(customer.Name);
      }
    }
  }
}
```

This time, the contract was specified with the name `CustomerFilter` and type of `Func<Customer, bool>`. Because `Func<Customer, bool>` is a type that might be used frequently, it is more specific to use a distinguishing name for the contract. MEF is capable of inferring the contract type from the delegate property definition, and so you must declare only the contract name in the `Import` attribute.

Right now, there is a limitation in the framework — method exports cannot have more than four arguments.

Method exports provide you with an opportunity you cannot get with other exports — lightweight code generation. With the .NET Framework, you can generate types and methods on-the-fly, and call these methods from the exported one.

You can decorate fields and properties with the `Import` attribute — the examples showed how easy it is. At composition time, MEF takes care of setting the values of those properties and fields. You are not obliged to use the `public` modifier. You can also signify the members with the other modifiers, and so you can use private fields and methods. However, do not forget about the fact that, at the end of the day, MEF must be able to set the member values. It has a few consequences you must take into account when designing your components:

➤    In medium or partial trust environments, non-public members cannot be set by MEF.

➤    If you use read-only properties (a property with only the `get` accessor), MEF has no way to set the property value, and composition will fail.

## Composition Containers and Catalogs

Exported and imported parts must meet to be composed into a working application. This role is undertaken by the *composition container*. Its name tells exactly what it is assumed to do. It is a container, because it contains composable parts that declare their intention to share services (exports) with other components and their willingness to consume services (imports) provided by other parts. The composition container is the matchmaker that binds together parts selling services with parts buying them.

The composition container is the entity with which you must interact to control the composition process, or query composition information (for example, a list of parts implementing a certain contract).

You can add parts directly to the composition container. For example, the parts building up the `MefGreetings` sample could be composed together with the following code:

```
var container = new CompositionContainer();
container.ComposeParts(this,
  new SimpleGreeting(),
  new UserGreeting(),
  new AppInfo());
```

There is a significant issue with this solution — it's static. This approach explicitly enumerates the parts composing the application. It uses types that should be known at compile time, and lacks dynamic discovery of parts.

Instead, the `MefGreetings` sample builds up the composition container utilizing a catalog:

```
var catalog = new AssemblyCatalog(Assembly.GetExecutingAssembly());
var container = new CompositionContainer(catalog);
container.ComposeParts(this);
```

A catalog in MEF is an abstraction of an inventory that contains parts. The great thing about a catalog is the fact that it has dynamic behavior. Its content is established at run-time, and so it can be used for dynamic discovery. For example, the `AssemblyCatalog` used in the code snippet is an inventory for all composable parts contained in a concrete physical assembly.

MEF is shipped with a number of catalogs out-of-the-box. Table 10-9 describes them.

**TABLE 10-9:** MEF Catalogs

| TYPE NAME | DESCRIPTION |
| --- | --- |
| TypeCatalog | This catalog is a container for types. During the discovery, all exports are collected that are exploited by the types in the catalog. You can use this catalog when you know exactly the types providing exports — for example, when you create unit tests. |
| AssemblyCatalog | This catalog discovers all exports in a specified assembly. You can use this catalog when you know which assemblies contain exports. With AssemblyCatalog, you can put dynamism into your application. You can separate the static (not affected by changes) and dynamic (subject to changes) partitions of the application into different assemblies. Creating an AssemblyCatalog on the dynamic partition allows you better change management. |
| DirectoryCatalog | This catalog discovers all the exports in all the assemblies in a directory. You can set an absolute or a relative path when creating a DirectoryCatalog. If you specify a relative path, it is relative to the base directory of the current AppDomain. With this catalog, you can add enormous flexibility to an application! Just drop an assembly into the folder of the catalog, restart your application, and It can immediately use the exports in the newly dropped assembly. |
| AggregateCatalog | As the name of this type suggests, it combines multiple catalogs into a single catalog. A common pattern is that you aggregate several DirectoryCatalog instances to aggregate all folders where you allow/expect extension assemblies into a combined catalog. (Visual Studio 2010 internally utilizes this.) |

MEF allows you to create your own catalogs. For example, when you store parts in a database, you can create a `DatabaseCatalog` type to discover them.

## Parts and Metadata

In many cases, you must associate information with exports, to provide a more granulated control over the composition mechanism. Here is a short list of reasons why this control can be important:

➤ Contracts can have capabilities that certain implementations provide, while others do not. For example, a part can work only when the computer running the application has specific software installed (for example, Microsoft Word).

➤ A part intends to tell some information about itself that is used by its potential consumers. For example, a part implementing a new user control may tell its host window that it must be docked at the bottom.

➤ A part can tell information about itself that determines how its services are processed on the consumer side. Assume your part represents a step in a pipeline handled by a processor. The processor executes those steps in a specific order, and so you must assign the correct order information to your part.

MEF allows attaching metadata to the exports. This information can be used by the composition engine during the matchmaking, and is accessible by the consumers of parts so that they may utilize this data.

The `ExportMetaData` attribute provides the easiest way to add this information to a part. For example, you can sign that your component is able to be involved in a database transaction:

```
[Export(typeof(IDatabaseTask))]
[ExportMetadata("SupportsTransaction", true)]
[ExportMetadata("PMC", "Remove_Customer")]
public class RemoveCustomerTask: IDatabaseTask
{
  // ...
}


[Export(typeof(IDatabaseTask))]
[ExportMetadata("SupportsTransaction", false)]
public class CalculateBonusTask: IDatabaseTask
{
  // ...
}
```

The parameters of `ExportMetadata` are name and value pairs. You can attach as many metadata attributes to an export as you need. However, as you can see, this kind of metadata is weakly typed. MEF allows you to attach strongly typed metadata to exports — moreover, it encourages you to do so. You can create your own metadata attributes. The following code snippet is an example of using this feature:

```
[MetadataAttribute]
[AttributeUsage(AttributeTargets.Class, AllowMultiple=false)]
public class DalMetadataAttribute: Attribute
```

```
    {
      public bool SupportsTransaction { get; set; }
      public bool AllowsNestedTransaction { get; set; }
    }
```

Create your own attribute and decorate it with `MetadataAttribute`. Add properties to the attribute to represent the strongly typed information to which you intend to attach exports. Now, you can attach this attribute to the export:

```
[Export(typeof(IDatabaseTask))]
[DalMetadata(SupportsTransaction = true, AllowsNestedTransaction = false)]
public class RemoveCustomerTask: IDatabaseTask
{
  // ...
}
```

You can derive the metadata attribute from `ExportAttribute` and, in this case, you have a more compact form to describe your export:

```
[MetadataAttribute]
[AttributeUsage(AttributeTargets.Class, AllowMultiple=false)]
public class DalExportAttribute: ExportAttribute
{
  public DalExportAttribute(): base(typeof(IDatabaseTask)) { }
  public bool SupportsTransaction { get; set; }
  public bool AllowsNestedTransaction { get; set; }
}

// ...

[DalExport(SupportsTransaction = true, AllowsNestedTransaction = false)]
public class RemoveCustomerTask: IDatabaseTask
{
  // ...
}
```

Metadata attached to exports can be queried and used during composition and later, when a part is about to be used.

## Composition

Parts only declare their intention to be exported. *Composition* is the mechanism that makes the matching among the parts. This matchmaking is triggered by any of the parts — primarily by the MEF host — either explicitly or implicitly.

When you have a large number of parts with complex connections among them — by means of exports and imports — the composition process can be expensive. The default composition container is frugal with these costs, and joins only the dependencies of the part triggering the matchmaking process.

## Explicit and Implicit Composition

Earlier, in Listing 10-21, explicit composition was used:

```
class Program
{
  [ImportMany]
  private IEnumerable<IGreetings> Greetings { get; set; }

  // ...

  private void Run()
  {
    var catalog = new AssemblyCatalog(Assembly.GetExecutingAssembly());
    var container = new CompositionContainer(catalog);
    container.ComposeParts(this);
    // ...
  }
}
```

The `ComposeParts` call on a container explicitly triggered the composition for the current `Program` instance, and, as a result, the `Greetings` property's value was set — in MEF terms, "the import was satisfied."

You could have used implicit composition by querying the composition container for a specific part:

```
class Program
{
  // ...

  private void Run()
  {
    var catalog = new AssemblyCatalog(Assembly.GetExecutingAssembly());
    var container = new CompositionContainer(catalog);
    var greetings = container.GetExportedValues<IGreetings>();
    // ...
  }
}
```

In this pattern, the `Program` class does not have the `Greetings` imported property, instead, the `GetExportedValues<>` generic method is used to retrieve all parts implementing the `IGreetings` contract.

As these small examples show, the matchmaking can be started with a concrete part (explicit composition) or with a contract type (implicit composition). During this process, the dependencies of the initiating contract or part are resolved. If necessary, this resolution traverses through the graph of all direct and indirect dependencies.

## Part Instantiation

When exports and imports are resolved, the composition container may need to create new object instances for a variety of reasons:

➤ An entire class is an exported part, and an import referencing a related contract must be satisfied. In this case, the exported class is instantiated, and this instance is assigned to the import.

➤ A property (or field) of a class is exported. To satisfy a related import, this class is instantiated, and then the appropriate property's value (or field value) is assigned to the import.

➤ A method of a class is exported. In this case, the hosting class is created, and a delegate to the exported method is assigned to the import.

Of course, if exported parts are members of static classes, no instantiation takes place.

Because this instantiation occurs behind the scenes, you do not have the same control, as in the case when you are the one who explicitly creates those instances. By default, MEF uses the default constructor of the class (the constructor with no parameters). If there is no default constructor, MEF looks for exactly one constructor decorated with the ImportingConstructor attribute. If there is such a constructor, its parameters are taken into account as imports. MEF satisfies those imports, and uses them as parameters with which to call the constructor. If there is no such constructor, MEF raises an exception, because it cannot create an instance.

Earlier, in Listing 10-25, the import of an IContextInfo part was implemented in this way:

```
[Export(typeof(IGreetings))]
class UserGreeting: IGreetings
{
  [Import]
  IContextInfo ContextInfo { get; set; }

  public string SayHello()
  {
    string userName;
    var props = ContextInfo.GetContextInfo();
    props.TryGetValue("UserName", out userName);
    return "Hello " + userName ?? "<None>";
  }
}
```

With ImportingConstructor, it also could be done as follows:

```
[Export(typeof(IGreetings))]
class UserGreeting: IGreetings
{
  IContextInfo ContextInfo { get; set; }

  [ImportingConstructor]
  public UserGreeting(IContextInfo contextInfo)
  {
    ContextInfo = contextInfo;
  }

  public string SayHello()
  {
    // ... Omitted for the sake of brevity
  }
}
```

You may wonder why it is useful to have two constructs for the same task. Well, there is an important difference between the `Import` property and `ImportingConstructor` approach.

When you use the `Import` property, first the declaring class is instantiated with the default constructor, and then MEF assigns the imported value to the property. This means that you cannot use the property's value in the constructor body. Contrast this to instantiating the class with an `ImportingConstructor`. This means you are able to use the imported values, because those are passed as constructor parameters.

## Lazy Instantiation

As you learned earlier, during composition of a part, an import will trigger the instantiation of a part (or parts) that expose the necessary exports required for the original requested part. In the case of imported properties and fields, this means that their values are set before they are used. In many situations, it may happen that the properties are not used at all, or are used later after their original construction. If the instantiation of property values is expensive (takes a relatively long time, consumes many CPU cycles, holds a large amount of resources, and so on), it is a good approach to delay this instantiation — and prevent the recursive composition down the graph.

MEF supports a feature called *lazy instantiation*. To use it, all you must do is to import a type `System.Lazy<T>` instead of `T` directly. For example, the `UserGreetings` class in Listing 10-25 could be implemented with lazy instantiation:

```
[Export(typeof(IGreetings))]
class UserGreeting : IGreetings
{
  [Import]
  Lazy<IContextInfo> ContextInfo { get; set; }

  public string SayHello()
  {
    string userName;
    var props = ContextInfo.Value.GetContextInfo();
    props.TryGetValue("UserName", out userName);
    return "Hello " + userName ?? "<None>";
  }
}
```

As you can see from the `SayHello` method, in this case, the imported part behind `ContextInfo` is accessed through the `Value` property. The actual instantiation of the part is carried out when `Value` is first queried, and subsequent queries use that cached instance.

## Import Notification

There are situations where you need an explicit notification about the fact that all imports have been satisfied and you can safely use them (such a situation is known as *recompostion*, and will be discussed shortly). In this case, you must implement the `IPartImportsSatisfiedNotification` interface that has only one method named `OnImportsSatisfied`.

The next code snippet is an example about dynamically pumping data into a WPF window's data grid:

```
[Export]
public partial class WindowWithDataGrid : Window,
  IPartImportsSatisfiedNotification
{
  [Import]
  ICustomerList CustomerRepository { get; set; }

  public ListingsWindow()
  {
    InitializeComponent();
  }

  public void OnImportsSatisfied()
  {
    Dispatcher.Invoke(new Action(() =>
    {
      dataGrid.ItemsSource = CustomerRepository.GetAllCustomers();
    }
    ));
  }
}
```

`WindowWithDataGrid` is an exported part, and when it is assigned to an import by MEF, the default constructor is called. At that moment, `CustomerRepository` is a `null` reference, because MEF has not yet satisfied this import. As soon as it is done, the `OnImportsSatisifed` method is called that sets the grid's `ItemSource` on the main UI thread with the help of the `Dispatcher` class.

## Recomposition

Many applications are designed to dynamically change at run-time. For example, you can download a new component from a web site, and that component goes functional without restarting your application. Or, a rule system can be extended by components describing new or changed rules just by dropping an assembly to a folder holding the rule repository.

MEF was designed with these scenarios in mind, and it is prepared to handle them. This concept is called *recomposition*, which is changing values of imports after the initial composition.

Depending on your application logic, recomposition can be explicit (you explicitly tell MEF to recompose bindings among parts), or event-driven (a catalog recognizes changes — for example, a new assembly has been copied to a watched folder). You can imagine that parts supporting recomposition may need to be implemented differently from those that support only an initial composition. To let MEF know your component can handle recomposition, you can set the `AllowRecomposition` property of the `Import` attribute to `true`. The `WindowWithDataGrid` sample you've seen earlier is a great candidate to demonstrate this:

```
[Export]
public partial class WindowWithDataGrid : Window,
  IPartImportsSatisfiedNotification
```

```
  {
    [Import(AllowRecomposition=true)]
    ICustomerList CustomerRepository { get; set; }

    public ListingsWindow()
    {
      InitializeComponent();
    }

    public void OnImportsSatisfied()
    {
      Dispatcher.Invoke(new Action(() =>
      {
        dataGrid.ItemsSource = CustomerRepository.GetAllCustomers();
      }
      ));
    }
  }
}
```

When you have more imports in your exported part, you can restrict recomposition to a subset of them by setting `AllowRecomposition` to `true` only for the relevant imports. Just as for the initial composition, the `OnImportSatisfied` method of `IPartImportSatisfiedNotification` will be fired every time a recomposition occurs. In the previous sample, this notification causes the data grid be refreshed.

When you prepare your application to support this type of dynamic behavior, you must be aware of the following facts:

➤ When recomposition occurs, imported properties and fields are replaced. For arrays and collections, that means, instead of updating the existing array or collection, it is replaced with a new array or collection instance.

➤ Recomposition is not supported with the `ImportingConstructor` pattern.

As a best practice, it is worth designing your exported parts with recomposition in mind, even if you do not allow this behavior. It will adorn your application with flexibility.

## Part lifetime

Once an application ships, the authors of that application won't have control over the set of parts. After deployment, third-party extensions also come into play. So, it's very important that you understand a part's lifetime, and its implications.

MEF parts are living in a composition container. This container is the owner entity of these parts, and is responsible for instantiating and disposing of them. This control is never transferred to any actor requesting the part from the container, or working with it indirectly (through an import). Both developers of exported parts, and developers of consumers importing that specific part, should be able to control the part's lifecycle by means of "shareability." When an exported part is shared, at most, one instance of that part may exist per container. If an export is non-shared, each request for that specific part is served by a new instance.

Exported parts can control their shareability with the `PartCreationPolicy` attribute that takes an argument with the type of `CreationPolicy`, as shown in the following example:

```
[PartCreationPolicy(CreationPolicy.NonShared)]
[Export(typeof(IGreetings))]
public class MyNonSharedGreeting: IGreetings
{
  // ...
}
```

The `CreationPolicy` enumeration has three values. `Shared` and `NonShared` have the meaning as discussed earlier, and `Any` means the part author allows the part to be used as either `Shared` or `NonShared`. The attribute in the sample declares that every request for the `MyNonSharedGreeting` part should retrieve a new instance of this part.

Imports can also constrain the creation policy of parts used to supply the import values. The `Import` and `ImportMany` attributes have a property called `RequiredCreationPolicy`, and you can specify its value from the `CreationPolicy` enumeration type, as shown in the following example:

```
[Export]
class Program
{
  [ImportMany(RequiredCreationPolicy = CreationPolicy.NonShared)]
  private IEnumerable<IGreetings> Greetings { get; set; }
}
```

The behavior of the composition container is determined by the part creation policies of the export and the related imports. Table 10-10 summarizes this behavior.

**TABLE 10-10:** Part Creation Behavior

| IMPORT BEHAVIOR | PART: ANY | PART: SHARED | PART: NONSHARED |
| --- | --- | --- | --- |
| Any | Shared | Shared | Non-shared |
| Shared | Shared | Shared | No match |
| NonShared | Non-shared | No match | Non-shared |

When any of the import and export part creation policies are set to `Shared` while the other is set to `NonShared`, the composition container does not make a match between the exported part and the import.

The composition container that is responsible for creating parts holds references for shared parts and for all non-shared parts that implement `IDisposable`, or are used in an import configured to allow recomposition. When the container is disposed, all references to parts held by the container will be cleaned up. For parts implementing `IDisposable`, the `Dispose` method is called.

Non-shared parts that do not have references in the container are not disposed together with the container. Continuously requesting non-shared parts from the container may lead to memory issues, so you must use them very carefully.

## Accessing Metadata

You can decorate exported parts with metadata attributes holding additional custom properties about the part. This metadata is used by the composition container for implicit filtering — to decide whether an import matches the export or not. You can also access this metadata and utilize it in the program control logic.

Let's assume you develop parts implementing the `ILoggerTask` contract:

```
interface ILoggerTask
{
  void WriteLog(LogItemType type, object message);
}
```

You want to be able to filter parts according to the log entry item type they accept, and you also want to know if they support transactional behavior or not. You also would like to assign names to the parts for diagnostic purposes. When these exported parts are ready, they look like these sample classes:

```
[LogChannelExport(ItemType = LogItemType.Error, IsTransactional = false)]
[ExportMetadata("Name", "Local Errors")]
public class LocalErrorsChannel: ILoggerTask
{
  public void WriteLog(LogItemType type, object message) { /* .. */ }
}

[LogChannelExport(ItemType = LogItemType.All, IsTransactional = true)]
[ExportMetadata("Name", "All Log Messages")]
public class GeneralLogChannel : ILoggerTask
{
  public void WriteLog(LogItemType type, object message) { /* .. */ }
}

[Export(typeof(ILoggerTask))]
[ExportMetadata("Name", "Simple Channel")]
public class SimpleChannel : ILoggerTask
{
  public void WriteLog(LogItemType type, object message) { /* .. */ }
}
```

The export definitions use both weakly typed metadata specified with the `ExportMetadata` attribute and strongly typed metadata defined by the `LogChannelExport` attribute:

```
[MetadataAttribute]
[AttributeUsage(AttributeTargets.Class, AllowMultiple = false)]
public class LogChannelExportAttribute: ExportAttribute
```

```
  {
    public LogChannelExportAttribute() : base(typeof(ILoggerTask)) { }
    public bool IsTransactional { get; set; }
    public LogItemType ItemType { get; set; }
  }
```

You can access the metadata of your parts in a weakly typed fashion with the following Import pattern:

```
[ImportMany]
public Lazy<ILoggerTask, IDictionary<string, object>>[]
  AllChannelsWithMetadata { get; set; }
```

The second generic argument of the Lazy<,> type allows you access the part metadata properties through the Metadata collection:

```
foreach (var item in AllChannelsWithMetadata)
{
  Console.WriteLine("{0} {1}", item.Metadata["Name"],
    item.Metadata.ContainsKey("ItemType")
    ? item.Metadata["ItemType"] : "<none>");
}
```

When you intend to access the metadata in a strongly typed fashion, or you want to use it for implicit filtering, you must use a separate approach. You define a *metadata view interface* with read-only properties matching with your metadata property names, as shown in the following example:

```
public interface ILogChannelProperties
{
  LogItemType ItemType { get; }
  [DefaultValue(false)]
  string Name { get; }
  [DefaultValue(false)]
  bool IsTransactional { get; }
}
```

As you can see, this metadata view contains all properties. While ItemType and IsTransactional were assigned to the exported part in a strongly typed manner, Name was used in a weakly typed way. In the Import definitions, use the following pattern:

```
[ImportMany]
public Lazy<ILoggerTask, ILogChannelProperties>[] Channels { get; set; }
```

The second type argument of the Lazy<,> type provides you access to the metadata through view properties:

```
foreach (var item in Channels)
{
  Console.WriteLine("{0}: {1}", item.Metadata.Name, item.Metadata.ItemType);
}
```

The metadata view interface also provides a way for the composition container to perform implicit filtering. The `ILogChannelProperties` type contains three read-only properties. The container checks if the exported parts define a metadata property for those that are defined by the view. If they do, the import is satisfied; otherwise, it is not.

If you want to avoid filtering by a metadata view property, you can do so by decorating it with the `DefaultValue(false)` attribute. You can see the `ILogChannelProperties` view defines implicit filtering only for the `ItemType` property. From the three parts implementing the `ILoggerTask` contract (`LocalErrorsChannel`, `GeneralLogChannel`, `SimpleChannel`), the `Channels` property container contains only two. The `SimpleChannel` part is implicitly filtered out, because it does not have an `ItemType` metadata property.

## A Few More Points on MEF

From the concepts and patterns introduced in this section you can see that MEF provides you with sophisticated tools for composing your application from smaller and pluggable parts. Under the covers, MEF provides many more features and design principles to enable you to tailor it to your custom need. Following are a few of them (without the need for completeness) to give you further direction to dive in deeper into MEF:

➤ MEF itself was designed with extensibility in mind. All elements in MEF (parts, catalogs, and composition containers) can be tailored to your custom needs. The `Export` and `Import` attributes and all related notations are a concrete implementation — called the *Attributed Programming Model* — of an abstract mechanism. Instead of using attributes, you can create your own programming model — for example, utilizing configuration files — to represent exports and imports.

➤ From the examples presented earlier, you can see only some very simple ways to query the composition container for parts. You can look up the reference documentation of `GetExport`, `GetExportedValue`, `GetExportedValueOrDefault`, and related methods in the `CompositionContainer` class to obtain more information about other ways to query the container.

➤ You can have much more control handling changes (even dynamically) in catalogs. More information and samples can be obtained through the `CompositionBatch` and `PartCreator<>` types. You can event write your own dynamic catalogs triggering the change of context and recomposing your application — for example, responding to the event when the network becomes unavailable or an online connection is restored.

➤ Although the samples in this chapter used only console applications, you can use MEF in all application or component types, including Windows Forms or WPF applications, ASP.NET, or ASP.NET MVC web sites.

➤ MEF is also available for Silverlight 3 and Silverlight 4 applications.

 *The MEF run-time is part of .NET Framework 4.0. The MEF samples and tools are not. They can be found on CodePlex, primarily in the MEF (*http://MEF .codeplex.com*) and MEFContrib (*http://MEFContrib.codeplex.com*) projects.*

# SUMMARY

.NET Framework 4.0 contains fundamental enhancements to the core functionality related to the preceding version. In this chapter, you learned about those features that you can use independently of whether you are using Windows Forms, ASP.NET, WPF, WF, WCF, Silverlight, or any other .NET technology.

After almost five years, .NET 4 ships with a new CLR that has important new core improvements. In CLR 4.0, a native process is able to host more CLR versions side-by-side. .NET 4 supports deploying applications accessing COM objects without deploying PIAs, and it is possible through a new CLR feature called type equivalence.

.NET 4 has a set of services that add dynamic programming capabilities to the CLR, and allow interoperation between .NET objects and dynamic languages. DLR allows dynamically typed languages like Python and Ruby to run on top of the CLR. DLR is also the base of the new dynamic features in C# and Visual Basic.

The many-core shift (using CPUs with multiple cores) has already happened. However, today, software is the weakest link, because most applications are designed to run sequentially. Microsoft provides a great technology in .NET 4 that efficiently targets issues coming from the use of multiple CPU cores. Instead of the sophistication in threading models, or automating parallelism, and hiding it from developers, this uses a declarative approach built on TPL. It allows developers to explicitly declare that certain parts of their program can be executed in parallel. The platform takes care of the implementation.

Now, LINQ is also multi-core enabled. PLINQ queries can use all CPUs in your computer concurrently to execute in-memory queries that were previously carried out sequentially.

Modern software architecture uses the concept of contracts to describe responsibilities of components and communication through boundaries. The most frequently used .NET programming languages (such as C# and Visual Basic) do not give you tools beyond type and interface definitions. Code contracts in .NET 4 provide a contract library to describe preconditions, postconditions, and object invariants. Related tools allow you static code analysis, contract document generation, and instrumenting your code with run-time contract checks.

The MEF ships with .NET 4. This new technology helps you to shift statically compiled applications into dynamically composed ones. You can signify your components that export services offered to other parts, and sign the intention to use imported services provided by other parts or a host application. MEF uses the concept of a composition container that makes the matching among your parts in run-time. With MEF, you can easily implement scenarios where parts of your applications or services can be easily changed without following the "remove/reinstall" deployment pattern.

In Chapter 11, you will learn about the enhancements of the .NET Workflow Framework (WF 4.0), which is not just an updated version of WF 3.5, but has been totally redesigned and rewritten.

# 11

# Enhancements to the .NET Workflow Framework

In the "good old days" of application programming, the imperative approach ruled the world of software development. Today, you can find a number of other paradigms as replacements (or augmentations) to the traditional imperative model. The .NET family of languages is moving toward functional programming support (not only F#, but also C# and Visual Basic). The .NET run-time supports the declarative approach from the beginning — just think about attributes decorating types, members, and parameters. There are also several tools helping developers to apply aspect-oriented programming.

From the release of .NET 3.0 in 2006, workflow-based development appeared in the palette of paradigms supported by the framework — and, of course, by Visual Studio. The Windows Workflow Foundation (WF) was the run-time library that put workflows into the hands of developers. In contrast to the traditional imperative approach, this new paradigm manages work coordination and operations differently:

➤ Workflows use a declarative model of writing applications by linking together building blocks called *activities* rather than line-by-line coding.

➤ Workflows usually have a visual counterpart that allows a flowchart-like description of their logic.

➤ Instead of keeping units of work in memory, workflows can handle long-running work by persisting themselves to a durable storage (such as a database) when idle, and by loading them again once there is some work to be performed.

➤ Business rules for workflows can be defined separately from other code (infrastructure code, UI code, and so on), making it easier to modify them.

Since its first release, WF went through a number of essential changes. The new version (Workflow Foundation 4.0, or simply WF 4.0) saw enormous changes relative to the previous versions — actually, it was totally redesigned and rewritten.

There are so many great things in WF 4.0 that there is no reason to focus only on new features. This chapter provides a detailed overview about the new workflow framework, and points out the main differences when treating concrete features. This overview covers the following topics:

➤ *An introduction to WF 4.0* — You will learn about the basics of the new workflow designer workspace in the IDE. To experience a few activities and the use of this new design surface, you will build a simple workflow using input and output arguments.

➤ *Flowcharts and coded workflows* — While WF 3.5 offered sequential and state machine workflows, WF 4.0 uses only one kind of workflow. However, with the `Flowchart` activity, you can create flowchart-like workflows where you can create a flow of activities by connecting elements. This section of the chapter introduces you to this feature, and also teaches you how to create workflows from code.

➤ *Workflow architecture* — In this section of the chapter, you learn about the essential concepts behind WF 4.0, such as workflow instances, hosts, activities, and extensions. This section also helps you understand the major differences between WF 3.5 and WF 4.0 programming models.

➤ *Workflow activity library* — You will learn about 40 built-in activities shipped with .NET 4. Most of them are totally new, while others already existed in WF 3.0 and WF 3.5. In this section, you'll see an overview of all WF 4.0 built-in activities.

➤ *Using the compensation transaction model* — In this section, you will create a sample application to learn about the transaction and error-handling activities of WF 4.0.

➤ *Persistence and human interactions* — Many workflows implement human interactions, such as providing additional data or making decisions. In this section, you learn about the features of WF 4.0 used to manage these interactions with the help of persistence.

➤ *Workflow services* — WF 4.0 leverages Windows Communication Foundation (WCF) features, and provides a great design-time and run-time support for web service based workflows. In this section, you learn the basics of creating and using workflow services.

## AN INTRODUCTION TO WF 4.0

With the multi-targeting feature of Visual Studio, you can create not only WF 4.0 applications, but also WF 3.0 or WF 3.5 workflows. WF 4.0 is a completely new design; it has been totally rewritten. However, you can still take advantage of your knowledge of previous versions of WF (including concepts), but you cannot directly use code from applications with versions prior to WF 4.0.

The primary concept (that is, you can assemble a workflow from building blocks called activities) has not changed, but designers, tools, and the internal architecture have been improved significantly.

If you have WF 3.0 or WF 3.5 code, you can still maintain that code in Visual Studio 2010, but WF 3.0 and 3.5 activities (and other services) are not interchangeable with WF 4.0. If you have custom activities created in previous WF versions, those can be reused — generally without any modifications — in WF 4.0 with the help of the `Interop` activity.

## The Workflow Design Surface

As a part of the redesign process, the WF team at Microsoft listened to the feedback related to the WF 3.5 designer, and created a new designer with a much better user experience than the former one. The improvement is so great that it can hardly be explained in words. Figure 11-1 shows the Visual Studio environment you can use to develop workflows.

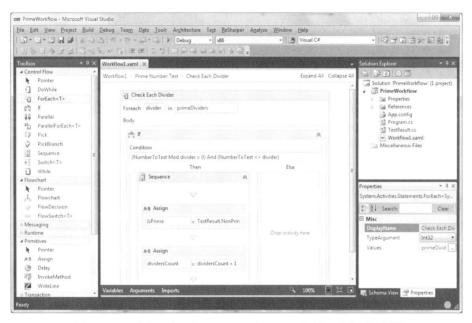

**FIGURE 11-1:** The new workflow development environment in Visual Studio 2010

The main part of the workspace is occupied by the designer surface. At the top, you see a navigation bar that allows you to zoom in and out among the levels of workflow hierarchy. You can nest activities into workflows and into compound activities and establish a workflow with several logical layers. In Figure 11-1, you see the details of a `ForEach` activity of a bigger workflow containing other elements.

At the bottom of the design surface, you see a command bar where you can edit Arguments, Variables, and Imports, as well as zoom within the design surface. The activities you can build into your workflows are located in the Toolbox on the left side. The new workflow design surface is based on WPF technology, and, as you can see, the Properties window in the lower right is similar to the one used by the WPF designer.

Contrast this screenshot with Figure 11-2 that shows the WF 3.5 designer workspace. The old designer is built on the same concepts as Windows Forms, and it uses GDI+ technology.

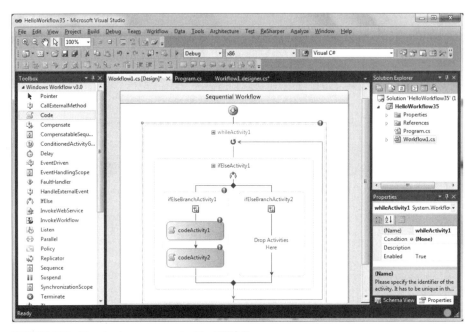

**FIGURE 11-2:** The designer supported by WF 3.5

Compared to Figure 11-1, you can see that the old designer used a different layout approach that resembled a flowchart, rather than the new one that is closer to a component diagram. Another eye-catching difference is the grouping of controls in the Toolbox. Although, you can customize the Toolbox content and group controls into tabs by yourself, the WF 4.0 design surface offers you a predefined grouping, in contrast to WF 3.5, where controls were poured into one tab.

## The Hello Workflow Application

To discover a few nice features of WF 4.0, let's build a simple "Hello, World" style application using the Workflow Console Application template so that the application can accept a string parameter to display. Navigate to File ➪ New ➪ Project, and select the Workflow subcategory under C#. Take care that .NET Framework 4 is selected as the target framework (as shown in Figure 11-3); otherwise, you create a WF 3.0 or WF 3.5 application. Select the Workflow Console Application, name the project `HelloWorkflow`, and click OK.

**FIGURE 11-3:** New project with the Workflow Console Application template

The newly created project skeleton is very similar to a standard console application, but you can find two additional files added to the project. An `App.config` file is prepared to indicate that your project requires WF 4.0. The `Workflow1.xaml` file is an empty workflow that is started in the `Main` method of `Program.cs`.

 *With WF 3.0 and WF 3.5, the workflow is defined in a `.cs` file having a `.designer.cs` file in the back, similar to Windows Forms applications. WF 4.0 uses a simple `.xaml` file without any code-behind file to declare a workflow.*

From the Toolbox, drag a `Sequence` activity to the design surface where it says "Drop Activity here." You can find this component in the Control Flow category. This activity will be responsible for creating a sequence of other child activities you will add soon. In the Properties window, change the `DisplayName` property to "Hello Workflow".

## Adding an Input Argument

This workflow accepts an input parameter, but you still must define it. At the bottom of the designer surface, locate the Arguments link. Click it to display the pane to add the input argument the workflow expects. Create a new argument with the name `Message`. Specify its direction as In, and leave the default `String`

**FIGURE 11-4:** The Arguments pane showing the Message workflow argument

argument type. The Arguments pane in Figure 11-4 shows this argument.

## Adding Activities to the Workflow

Now, drag three `WriteLine` activities (you can find them in the Primitives category) into the drop area of the `Sequence` activity. Each of them has a `Text` property displayed in the design surface (and also available in the Properties window). Set the `Text` property of the first `WriteLine` activity to the "The workflow has started" string, and the `Text` of the third one to "The workflow has finished". Include the opening and closing quotes in the `Text` property values! `Text` expects an expression, and here you specify literal text constants delimited by quotes.

Set the second `WriteLine` activity to `"Message: " + Message`. This activity will display the `Message` workflow argument you pass before starting the workflow instance. When you are typing the `Text` property, IntelliSense is working, and you can select the argument from the displayed continuation list.

> *When setting up the `Text` properties, you can see that both the designer surface and the Properties window display the "Enter a VB expression" hint, although, you work with a C# project. Before you think it is a bug, you should know that all expressions in WF 4.0 use the Visual Basic syntax.*
>
> *These expressions do not compile into Microsoft Intermediate Language (MSIL) code when you build your project. They are evaluated at run-time by the workflow activities using them. This is why the expression syntax is independent of the programming language implementing the workflow — and it is the Visual Basic syntax.*

The finished workflow should look like Figure 11-5.

At this point, your workflow is ready to run. Start it by pressing Ctrl+F5. It displays the following output:

```
The workflow has started
Message:
The workflow has finished
```

## Passing Input Arguments to the Workflow

You can see from the second line that the workflow used the default `Message` argument (empty string), because the application had not set a concrete value. Let's change `Program.cs` to specify a concrete argument.

Open the `Program.cs` file and look into the `Main` method:

**FIGURE 11-5:** The finished workflow in the design surface

```
static void Main(string[] args)
{
    WorkflowInvoker.Invoke(new Workflow1());
}
```

The code is really simple. The static `WorkflowInvoker` class provides an `Invoke` method to start a `Workflow1` instance. Now, change the `Main` method to the one shown in Listing 11-1 to pass the `Message` argument.

**LISTING 11-1:** Program.cs (HelloWorkflow)

```csharp
using System;
using System.Collections.Generic;
using System.Activities;

namespace HelloWorkflow
{
  class Program
  {
    static void Main(string[] args)
    {
      var arguments = new Dictionary<string, object>
        {
          {"Message", "Hello from WF 4.0"}
        };
      WorkflowInvoker.Invoke(new Workflow1(), arguments);
    }
  }
}
```

*Code file [Program.cs] available for download at Wrox.com*

Arguments are passed to the workflow in a `Dictionary` object holding name-and-value pairs. The workflow will match the workflow arguments by their names. The dictionary of `arguments` is passed to the `Invoke` method.

When you run the modified application, it produces the output you expect:

```
The workflow has started
Message: Hello from WF 4.0
The workflow has finished
```

## Adding an Output Argument

Workflows can return output arguments that can be used by host applications. For example, output of a workflow can be passed to another workflow. Let's modify the "Hello Workflow" application so that it creates an output argument composed from the message written to the console by the second `WriteLine` activity and the current time.

Click the Arguments link and add a second string argument named `Result`. The direction of this argument should be Out, as shown in Figure 11-6,

| Name | Direction | Argument type | Default value |
|---|---|---|---|
| Message | In | String | Enter a VB expression |
| Result | Out | String | Default value not supported |
| Create Argument | | | |

| Variables | Arguments | Imports | | ⚲ 100% |

**FIGURE 11-6:** Define the Result output parameter

## Adding a Variable

The output message will be generated in two steps. First, the message part is composed before executing the WriteLine activity. Second, the timestamp is added. Workflow variables are the constructs you can use to store values and use them within the workflow. You can take a workflow variable for a workflow into account just like a local method variable for the declaring method.

Select the "Hello Workflow" sequence, click the Variables link in the design surface, and add a new variable. Name it temp and leave its type of String. The Scope of the variable will be set to "Hello Workflow," which means that this variable is available within this activity. Figure 11-7 shows how the Variables pane should look after adding temp.

**FIGURE 11-7:** Define the temp workflow variable

## Creating the Output Value

Add an Assign activity (found in the Primitives category) between the first and second WriteLine activity. On the design surface, it displays two text boxes — the first one names the target variable to store the expression represented by the second one. In the Property window, these text boxes are covered by the To and Value properties, respectively.

Set the first text box (To property) to temp, and the second one (Value property) to "Message: " + Message. Now, the value of temp contains the message the second WriteLine activity is about to display, so set its Text property to temp. Add another Assign activity between the second and third WriteLine and set the To and Value properties to temp and temp + " (" + DateTime.Now.ToString("HH:mm:ss") + ")", respectively.

Add a third Assign activity after the third WriteLine and set it to assign the value of temp to the Result output argument. Now the workflow should look like the design surface shown in Figure 11-8.

**FIGURE 11-8:** The modified workflow

## Extracting the Workflow Output

This workflow produces the output you would expect, but somehow it should be extracted from the workflow. Modify the Main method in the Program.cs file as shown in Listing 11-2.

**LISTING 11-2:** The Modified Program.cs File (HelloWorkflow)

```
using System;
using System.Collections.Generic;
using System.Activities;

namespace HelloWorkflow
{
```

```csharp
class Program
{
  static void Main(string[] args)
  {
    var arguments = new Dictionary<string, object>
      {
        {"Message", "Hello from WF 4.0"}
      };
    IDictionary<string, object> output =
      WorkflowInvoker.Invoke(new Workflow1(), arguments);
    Console.WriteLine("Workflow output:");
    Console.WriteLine(output["Result"]);
  }
}
```

*Code file [Program.cs] available for download at Wrox.com*

The output arguments of the workflow are returned in an `IDictionary<string, object>` instance, so you can easily access arguments by their names. When you run the application by pressing Ctrl+F5, you see the following output:

```
The workflow has started
Message: Hello from WF 4.0
The workflow has finished
Workflow output:
Message: Hello from WF 4.0 (08:15:54)
```

 *You could implement this workflow without using variables at all. You could assign values directly to the* `Result` *output argument. However, choosing this way demonstrated variables that are essential concepts in WF 4.0.*

The `Workflow1.xaml` file is a declarative description of the workflow. Right-click the design surface and invoke the View Code command (or simply press F7) to see the XAML code behind the designer, as shown in Listing 11-3.

**LISTING 11-3:** Workflow1.xaml (Code View)

```xml
<Activity mc1:Ignorable="sap" x:Class="HelloWorkflow.Workflow1"
  xmlns="http://schemas.microsoft.com/netfx/2009/xaml/activities"
  xmlns:mc="clr-namespace:Microsoft.CSharp;assembly=System"
  xmlns:mc1="http://schemas.openxmlformats.org/markup-compatibility/2006"
  xmlns:mcr="clr-namespace:Microsoft.CSharp.RuntimeBinder;
    assembly=Microsoft.CSharp"
  xmlns:mv="clr-namespace:Microsoft.VisualBasic;assembly=System"
  xmlns:mva="clr-namespace:Microsoft.VisualBasic.Activities;
    assembly=System.Activities"
  xmlns:s="clr-namespace:System;assembly=mscorlib"
```

*continues*

**LISTING 11-3** *(continued)*

```xml
  xmlns:s1="clr-namespace:System;assembly=System"
  xmlns:s2="clr-namespace:System;assembly=System.Xml"
  xmlns:s3="clr-namespace:System;assembly=System.Core"
  xmlns:s4="clr-namespace:System;assembly=System.ServiceModel"
  xmlns:sa="clr-namespace:System.Activities;assembly=System.Activities"
  xmlns:sad="clr-namespace:System.Activities.Debugger;
    assembly=System.Activities"
  xmlns:sap="http://schemas.microsoft.com/netfx/2009/xaml/
    activities/presentation"
  xmlns:scg="clr-namespace:System.Collections.Generic;assembly=System"
  xmlns:scg1="clr-namespace:System.Collections.Generic;
    assembly=System.ServiceModel"
  xmlns:scg2="clr-namespace:System.Collections.Generic;assembly=System.Core"
  xmlns:scg3="clr-namespace:System.Collections.Generic;assembly=mscorlib"
  xmlns:sd="clr-namespace:System.Data;assembly=System.Data"
  xmlns:sl="clr-namespace:System.Linq;assembly=System.Core"
  xmlns:ss="clr-namespace:System.Security;assembly=System.Core"
  xmlns:ss1="clr-namespace:System.Security;assembly=mscorlib"
  xmlns:st="clr-namespace:System.Text;assembly=mscorlib"
  xmlns:x="http://schemas.microsoft.com/winfx/2006/xaml">
  <x:Members>
    <x:Property Name="Message" Type="InArgument(x:String)" />
    <x:Property Name="Result" Type="OutArgument(x:String)" />
  </x:Members>
  <sap:VirtualizedContainerService.HintSize>
    304,721
  </sap:VirtualizedContainerService.HintSize>
  <mva:VisualBasic.Settings>
    Assembly references and imported namespaces for internal implementation
  </mva:VisualBasic.Settings>
  <Sequence DisplayName="Hello Workflow"
    sad:XamlDebuggerXmlReader.FileName="C:\Publications\VS 2010 Six-in-One\
    Chapter 11\Samples\HelloWorkflow\HelloWorkflow\Workflow1.xaml"
    sap:VirtualizedContainerService.HintSize="264,681">
    <Sequence.Variables>
      <Variable x:TypeArguments="x:String" Name="temp" />
    </Sequence.Variables>
    <sap:WorkflowViewStateService.ViewState>
      <scg3:Dictionary x:TypeArguments="x:String, x:Object">
        <x:Boolean x:Key="IsExpanded">True</x:Boolean>
      </scg3:Dictionary>
    </sap:WorkflowViewStateService.ViewState>
    <WriteLine sap:VirtualizedContainerService.HintSize="242,61"
      Text="The workflow has started" />
    <Assign sap:VirtualizedContainerService.HintSize="242,58">
      <Assign.To>
        <OutArgument x:TypeArguments="x:String">[temp]</OutArgument>
      </Assign.To>
      <Assign.Value>
        <InArgument x:TypeArguments="x:String">["Message: " + Message]</InArgument>
      </Assign.Value>
    </Assign>
    <WriteLine sap:VirtualizedContainerService.HintSize="242,61" Text="[temp]" />
```

```
      <Assign sap:VirtualizedContainerService.HintSize="242,58">
        <Assign.To>
          <OutArgument x:TypeArguments="x:String">[temp]</OutArgument>
        </Assign.To>
        <Assign.Value>
          <InArgument x:TypeArguments="x:String">[temp + " (" +
            DateTime.Now.ToString("HH:mm:ss") + ")"]</InArgument>
        </Assign.Value>
      </Assign>
      <WriteLine sap:VirtualizedContainerService.HintSize="242,61"
        Text="The workflow has finished" />
      <Assign sap:VirtualizedContainerService.HintSize="242,58">
        <Assign.To>
          <OutArgument x:TypeArguments="x:String">[Result]</OutArgument>
        </Assign.To>
        <Assign.Value>
          <InArgument x:TypeArguments="x:String">[temp]</InArgument>
        </Assign.Value>
      </Assign>
    </Sequence>
  </Activity>
```

The root element of the XAML description is the `<Activity>` element that defines about two dozen namespaces used in the rest of the declaration. You can recognize the workflow arguments nested into the `<x:Members>` node. It is also easy to identify the `Sequence`, `WriteLine`, and `Assign` activities with their properties.

The XAML description also contains elements and attributes defining the visual properties used by the designer to arrange the workflow layout on the design surface. For example, occurrences of the `sap:VirtualizedContainerService.HintSize` attribute tell the size of the bounding rectangle belonging to a layout element. You can also find the `<sap:WorkflowViewStateService.ViewState>` element nested into `<Sequence>`, indicating that this activity is expanded on the screen.

## CREATING FLOWCHARTS AND CODED WORKFLOWS

With previous WF versions, you could create two basic kinds of workflows:

➤  *Sequential workflows* — The control flow of a workflow starts from the first activity and executes other activities in the defined sequence. Activities can include control flow activities such as `IfElse`, `Parallel`, `While`, and so on, but there is no way to use something like a `Goto` activity to change the sequential order. When the last activity in the sequence is finished, the workflow completes.

➤  *State-machine workflows* — The control flow follows the transitions of a state-machine. As the current state changes, the activities assigned to the specific transition are executed. When a final state is reached, the workflow completes.

WF 4.0 does not make such a separation among workflows. It provides a composite activity called `Sequence`. With the nested child activities, it offers you the same model as a sequential workflow in versions prior to WF 4.0. However, it does not provide an activity like "StateMachine" to support the other model. Instead, you can use a composite activity named `Flowchart`. You can nest child activities into `Flowchart` and connect them together to form a flow.

# Flowcharts in WF 4.0

Now, let's create a flowchart-based workflow that checks whether an integer number is a prime number. Although this is not a typical application of a workflow, this example can be helpful when learning about the `Flowchart` activity.

Create a new Workflow Console Application and name it `PrimeWorkflow`. Add a new code file to the project, name it `TestResult.cs`, and define the following enumerated type:

```
namespace PrimeWorkflow
{
  public enum TestResult
  {
    NotTested,
    Prime,
    NonPrime
  }
}
```

The algorithm will return `NotTested` if the input argument is greater than 1 billion. If it is less, `Prime` or `NonPrime` will be returned according to the test. Build the project right now — it will be important in a future step.

The check is very simple. Let's try to divide the number with a few prime numbers (from 2 to 31). If the number can be divided with the prime number without a remainder, it cannot be a prime number. For demonstration purposes, the workflow will be extended to count the number of different primes that divide the argument, and it will display a few messages according this counter.

## Adding a Flowchart to the Workflow

Open the `Workflow1.xaml` file and drag a `Flowchart` activity (located in the Flowchart tab) to the design surface. This activity will display a simple Start state representing the entry point of this activity.

Add an `Int32` input argument to the workflow and name it `NumberToTest`. Add an output argument, and name it `IsPrime`. Click the Argument Type column and, in the drop-down list, select "Browse for Types." A new dialog pops up. Expand the `<Current project>` node and its children unless you find the `TestResult` node, then select it and close the dialog. If you had not built the project earlier, you would not be able to find the `TestResult` type there.

The algorithm will use two variables. Add the `dividersCount` variable with a type of `Int32`, and another one, `primeDividers`, with the type of `Int32[]`. For the latter variable, select the "Array of [T]" from the Variable type column, and then select `Int32` from the dialog that pops up.

## Adding a FlowDecision Activity

Drag a `FlowDecision` activity to the `Flowchart` beneath the `Start` point. Set its properties to the following values:

➤ Condition: `NumberToTest > 1000000000`

➤ FalseLabel: `Testable`

➤ TrueLabel: `Too big to test`

Drop two `Assign` activities to the `Flowchart` and set their corresponding properties to these values:

➤ (First activity) `To: IsPrime; Value: TestResult.NotTested`

➤ (Second activity) `To: IsPrime; Value: TestResult.Prime`

Now, you can draw the flows among the `Start` point, the `FlowDecision`, and the two `Assign` activities. When you move the mouse over the `Start` point, four handles will appear on each side of this activity. Move the mouse to the handle beneath the `Start` point, click the mouse, and drag the line over the `FlowDecision` activity. When the handles belonging to `FlowDecision` appear, release the mouse button over one of these handles. An arrow will be drawn connecting the `Start` point with the `FlowDecision`. This is how you can draw the connection among activities dropped to the design surface of a `Flowchart`.

When you move the mouse over the `FlowDecision`, the handles display their own labels (you set them through the `FalseLabel` and `TrueLabel` properties earlier). Connect the `Too big to test` label with the first `Assign` activity, and then the `Testable` label with the second `Assign` activity.

Figure 11-9 shows the `Flowchart` activity. Your drawing should have a similar topology.

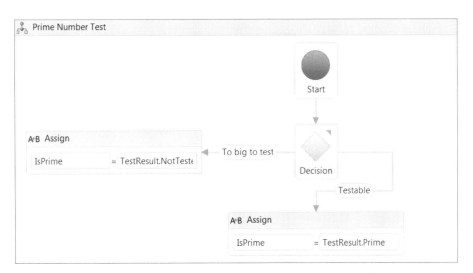

**FIGURE 11-9:** FlowDescision is connected with the Start point and the two Assign activities

Now, add two more `Assign` activities and three more `WriteLine` activities to the `Flowchart`. Table 11-1 summarizes how their properties should be set up.

**TABLE 11-1:** Activity Properties

| ACTIVITY | PROPERTY VALUES |
| --- | --- |
| Assign | DisplayName: `Init Primes Array` |
| | To: `primeDividers` |
| | Value: `{2, 3, 5, 7, 11, 13, 17, 19, 23, 29, 31}` |

*continues*

**TABLE 11-1** *(continued)*

| ACTIVITY | PROPERTY VALUES |
|---|---|
| Assign | DisplayName: Reset Counter |
| | To: dividersCount |
| | Value: 0 |
| WriteLine | Text: "This number has only one prime divider!" |
| WrileLine | Text: "This number must be a prime number!" |
| WriteLine | Text: "This number has several prime dividers!" |

## Adding a ForEach<T> Activity

Add a ForEach<T> activity to the design surface. This activity iterates through a collection of elements. The T type parameter represents the type of elements in the collection. By default, it is System.Int32, and now you need exactly this type. Set the DisplayName property of this activity to "Check Each Divider".

Connect the Assign activity at the Testable branch of the FlowDecision to Init Prime Arrays, then this activity to Reset Counter and then this one to Check Each Divider. The topology of the workflow should look like Figure 11-10.

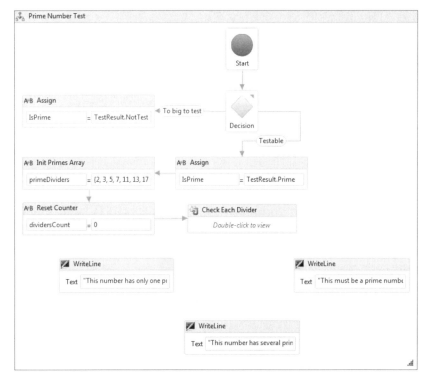

**FIGURE 11-10:** More activities added to the workflow

Now, double-click the `Check Each Divider` activity to edit its properties and nested activities. The design surface changes and zooms into this activity. At the top of the design pane, you can see the Workflow → Prime Number Test → Check Each Divider path indicating where you are in the current workflow.

In the text box near to the `ForEach` label, set the cycle variable name to `divider`, then the collection expression in the next text box to `primeDividers`. (You can set this latter field through the `Values` property as well.) As a result, this activity will iterate through the elements of `primeDividers` and makes the current value accessible through the `divider` variable in body activities.

Drag an `If` activity to the body of the `ForEach` and set the `Condition` to `(NumberToTest Mod divider = 0) And (NumberToTest <> divider)`. This condition will check if `NumberToTest` can be divided with the current `divider`, and this number is not the `divider` itself (in this latter case, `NumberToTest` is a prime number).

Drag a `Sequence` to the `Then` branch of the `If` activity, and add two `Assign` activities to its body with the following properties:

➤ (First activity) To: `IsPrime`; Value: `TestResult.NonPrime`

➤ (Second Activity) To: `dividersCount`; Value: `dividersCount + 1`

The `Check Each Divider` activity now should look like Figure 11-11. This activity will observe when `NumberToTest` is not a prime number, and it counts the number of its different prime dividers.

**FIGURE 11-11:** The Check Each Divider activity

## Adding a FlowSwitch Activity

Go back to the `Prime Number Test` activity (click the related link, which is labeled Flowchart, at the top of the designer pane). Drag a `FlowSwitch` activity from the Toolbox and drop it somewhere into the empty place among the `Check Each Divider` and the `WriteLine` activities. This activity is a representation of a `switch` statement in C# (Case in Visual Basic). In the popup that appears, leave the default value `Int32`, then set its `Expression` property to `dividersCount`. This activity will branch according to the current value of this expression.

Connect `Switch` to the `WriteLine` where text is "This number must be a prime Number." Click the connection arrow and look at its properties. Uncheck the `IsDefaultCase` property and set `Case` to 0. Now, Connect the `Switch` to the `WriteLine` activity saying "This number has only one prime divider!" and set the link's `Case` property to 1. And, finally, connect the `Switch` to the third `WriteLine` activity and, in this case, leave the `IsDefaultCase` property checked. As a result, if the `dividersCount` variable is different from 0 and 1, this branch — this `WriteLine` activity — is executed. Figure 11-12 shows the completed workflow.

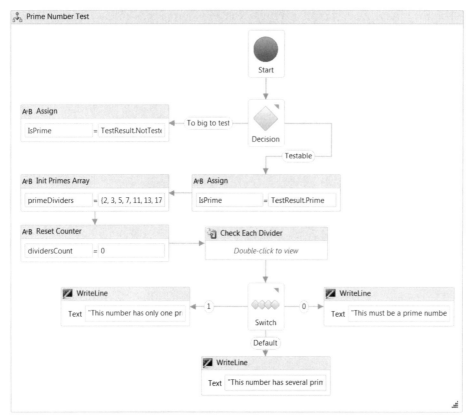

**FIGURE 11-12:** The completed workflow

## Running the Flowchart Workflow

Change the `Program.cs` file of the `PrimeWorkflow` project as shown in Listing 11-4.

---

**LISTING 11-4: Program.cs (PrimeWorkflow)**

```
using System;
using System.Activities;
using System.Collections.Generic;

namespace PrimeWorkflow
{

  class Program
  {
    static void Main(string[] args)
    {
      var arguments = new Dictionary<string, object>
        {
```

```
          {"NumberToTest", 24}
        };
      IDictionary<string, object> output =
        WorkflowInvoker.Invoke(new Workflow1(), arguments);
      Console.WriteLine("Test result for {0}: {1}",
        arguments["NumberToTest"],
        output["IsPrime"]);
    }
  }
}
```

*Code file [Program.cs] available for download at Wrox.com*

As you can see from this listing, flowchart workflows are managed exactly the same way as sequential workflows are. From the outside, you cannot notice any difference; you do not see how the workflow is internally implemented.

Run the application by pressing Ctrl+F5, and you see the output:

```
This number has several prime dividers!
Test result for 24: NonPrime
```

When you run the workflow with the `"NumberToTest"` argument set to 7, 4, and 459, you'll see the following output:

```
This must be a prime number!
Test result for 7: Prime

This number has only one prime divider!
Test result for 4: NonPrime

This number has several prime dividers!
Test result for 459: NonPrime
```

## Code-Only Workflows

Earlier, you learned that WF 4.0 describes workflows with XAML. When the run-time behind WF 4.0 reads a XAML workflow, it is represented in memory as a tree of object instances. The workflow execution uses this in-memory set of objects. The XAML file is a declarative description of the object set representing the workflow. You can produce this object set without XAML using only code — just as you can assemble a WPF form with code instead of the XAML markup.

In this section, you will learn about this kind of workflow declaration by reproducing the "Hello Workflow" application in pure code without using the workflow designer.

Create a new C# console application project (ensure that you are using .NET Framework 4.0) and name it `CodedHelloWorkflow`. Add a reference to the `System.Activities` assembly that contains the WF 4.0 types the coded workflow application is going to use. Copy the code in Listing 11-5 to `Program.cs`.

**LISTING 11-5:** Program.cs (CodedHelloWorkflow)

```csharp
using System;
using System.Activities;
using System.Activities.Statements;
using System.Collections.Generic;

namespace CodedHelloWorkflow
{
  class Program
  {
    static void Main(string[] args)
    {
      var arguments = new Dictionary<string, object>
        {
          {"Message", "Hello from WF 4.0"}
        };
      IDictionary<string, object> output =
        WorkflowInvoker.Invoke(new HelloWorkflow(), arguments);
      Console.WriteLine("Workflow output:");
      Console.WriteLine(output["Result"]);
    }
  }

  internal class HelloWorkflow : Activity
  {
    public InArgument<String> Message { get; set; }
    public OutArgument<String> Result { get; set; }

    public HelloWorkflow()
    {
      var temp = new Variable<string>("temp");
      Implementation = () =>
        new Sequence
        {
          DisplayName = "Hello Workflow",
          Variables = { temp },
          Activities =
            {
              new WriteLine { Text = "The workflow has started" },
              new Assign<string>
              {
                To = new OutArgument<String>(temp),
                Value = new InArgument<string>(ctx => "Message: " +
                  Message.Get(ctx))
              },
              new WriteLine { Text = new InArgument<string>(ctx =>
                temp.Get(ctx)) },
              new Assign<string>
              {
                To = new OutArgument<String>(temp),
                Value = new InArgument<string>(ctx => temp.Get(ctx) +
                  " (" + DateTime.Now.ToString("HH:mm:ss") + ")")
              },
```

```
                    new WriteLine { Text = "The workflow has finished"},
                    new Assign<string>
                    {
                      To = new OutArgument<string>(ctx => Result.Get(ctx)),
                      Value = new InArgument<string>(ctx => temp.Get(ctx))
                    },
                  }
              };
          }
        }
      }
```

*Code file [Program.cs] available for download at Wrox.com*

When you run this application, you see that it produces similar output to `HelloWorkflow`. When you take a look at the `Main` method, you can see that here the `Invoke` method instantiates an internal workflow class named `HelloWorkflow`. Input arguments are passed, while output arguments are extracted exactly the same way as in the graphically designed workflow.

It may be surprising, but the workflow itself is an activity — that is why `HelloWorkflow` derives from the `Activity` class:

```
internal class HelloWorkflow : Activity
{
  // ...
}
```

The activities the workflow is assumed to execute are defined in a declarative fashion. Look at the constructor of the class:

```
public HelloWorkflow()
{
  var temp = new Variable<string>("temp");
  Implementation = () =>
    new Sequence
    {
      // ...
    }
}
```

The `Implementation` property is a type of `Func<Activity>` and the lambda expression used here declares the `Sequence` activity with all nested activities. Because it is just a declaration, creating this lambda expression is a cheap operation. When the workflow is about to be executed, the method represented by the lambda expression behind `Implementation` is called.

## Declaring Workflow Arguments

Workflow arguments are declared as simple read-write properties:

```
public InArgument<String> Message { get; set; }
public OutArgument<String> Result { get; set; }
```

Obviously, the generic `InArgument<>` and `OutArgument<>` types define the input and output arguments, respectively. The type parameters tell the type of the arguments — in this case, both of them are strings. When you run the workflow, the `HelloWorkflow` class is instantiated, and input arguments are matched with the appropriate property by the names in the dictionary passed to the `Invoke` method.

 *Try to pass a wrong argument name in the* Main *method — for example,* Msg *instead of* Message. *You'll receive a* System.ArgumentException *with the message, "The values provided for the root activity's arguments did not satisfy the root activity's requirements."*

## Declaring Variables

The `HelloWorkflow` constructor defines the `temp` local variable that is used as a workflow variable:

```
var temp = new Variable<string>("temp");
```

Although it contains string data, it is not declared as a native string variable, but rather as `Variable<string>`. The `"temp"` argument used here tells the name of the variable. You may wonder why this kind of workaround is required instead of using a native variable.

The reason is that workflow instances can be persisted to storage when they are idle (for example, waiting for user input). In this case, their state represented by their variables should be persisted. Without going into detail, this persistence requires that workflow variables can be referenced. The `Variable` generic type provides this requirement. The .NET reflection does not provide a way to retrieve local variable information for a method, so the `"temp"` name passed to the argument helps the workflow run-time to manage the distinction of variables.

## Building Activities

The `Sequence` activity is defined like this:

```
new Sequence
{
  DisplayName = "Hello Workflow",
  Variables = { temp },
  Activities =
    {
      // ...
    }
}
```

The `DisplayName` property is the one you can set in the Properties window when using the workflow designer. The `Variables` container contains those `Variable<>` instances that are taken into account as variables constituting the state of a workflow instance. The `Activities` container enumerates the nested activities of `Sequence` to execute in the order as they are listed.

## Using Expressions

The properties of `WriteLine` and `Assign` are a great representation of using arguments and variables in expressions. You can see strange constructs using the `Get` method of workflow arguments and variables like these:

```
To = new OutArgument<String>(temp)
// ...
Value = new InArgument<string>(ctx => "Message: " + Message.Get(ctx))
// ...
Text = new InArgument<string>(ctx => temp.Get(ctx))
```

To get the actual data from a `Variable` instance, you must use the `Get` method. The workflow itself does not store any data elements; you must obtain the data from the context of a concrete workflow instance. This is why the lambda expressions are used in the earlier code snippets. The `ctx` expression parameter is an instance of the `ActivityContext` class. You must pass the context to the `Get` method of the `Variable` instance to extract the value of the variable.

The properties of the `Activity` class are actually workflow parameters that can be represented by `InArgument<T>` or `OutArgument<T>` instances. The `Text` property of `WriteLine` and `Value` property of `Assign` are input arguments, while the `To` property of `Assign` is an output argument.

Be sure to put the entire expression into the constructor of `InArgument` or `OutArgument`. If you'd write the following

```
Value = "Message: " + new InArgument<string>(ctx => Message.Get(ctx))
```

instead of the following

```
Value = new InArgument<string>(ctx => "Message: " + Message.Get(ctx))
```

the output would be

```
Message: System.Activities.InArgument`1[System.String]
```

instead of

```
Message: Hello from WF 4.0
```

## WORKFLOW ARCHITECTURE

By now, you have seen several examples of using the workflow designer to create a workflow, and you have also learned that you can define code-only workflows. Several concepts were also mentioned, such as workflow instances, activities, variables, arguments, workflow persistence, and so on.

This section provides an overview of the workflow architecture so that you can understand how these concepts fit into the entire picture. Figure 11-13 shows an overview of this architecture with its essential elements.

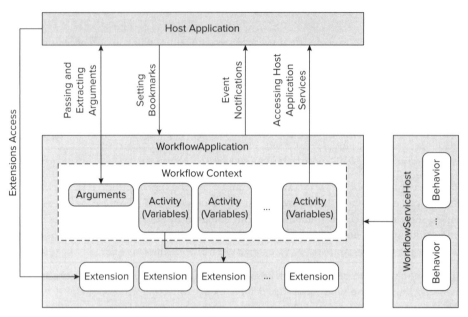

**FIGURE 11-13:** Overview of workflow architecture

## WorkflowApplication and Hosts

The `WorkflowApplication` class of the `System.Activity` namespace is a core element of the workflow architecture. This class provides a host for a single workflow instance. It is a proxy to the actual workflow instance that is managed by the workflow run-time. Each workflow instance is put into a separate `WorkflowApplication` instance. When running workflow instances, it may get idle — for example, while waiting for user input. A `WorkflowApplication` takes care of persisting the workflow instance, unloading it from the memory, and later reloading and resuming it.

A `WorkflowApplication` must be instantiated, set up, and executed within a host application. It can be a simple console application (the examples treated thus far have demonstrated this), a Windows Forms or WPF application, a Windows service, and any other form of executable artifacts. The host application should not only create the `WorkflowApplication` instance, but also have to set up its context (including arguments), create and configure extensions, and start it.

In many cases, a workflow should start as a response to a specific message received from the network, or from another process. When the workflow is completed, the response message should be transferred back to the sender. WF 4.0 provides a `WorkflowServiceHost` class that listens for WCF messages to process them. When a message arrives, it instantiates and starts a `WorkflowApplication` instance hosting the requested workflow instance.

During the lifecycle of a workflow, the host application can communicate with the workflow.

➤ It can pass input arguments to the workflow, and retrieve output arguments produced by the workflow. The earlier samples showed you several examples handling arguments.

➤ The host application can access extensions (you will learn about this concept later) belonging to the workflow. In addition to other features, extensions provide a way to pass data from the host to the workflow (or back), and they can be accessed by any activities in the workflow.

➤ The workflow generates events (for example, when it starts, gets idle, or completes). The host application can respond to these events. For example, when a workflow completes, it can notify the user or clean up UI resources.

➤ The workflow can get into an idle state when it is expected to wait for the user (for example, the user must make a decision). The host application can resume the workflow when the expected user interaction (for example, the user made the decision) is done. This mechanism is handled with bookmarks that specify a resume point and pass data (for example, the decision of the user) to the workflow.

➤ The workflow has the opportunity to access host application services.

Although there might be multiple instances of a workflow executing simultaneously (for example, one instance for each request), they do not interact with each other. There is no mechanism within the workflow to communicate with other instances, and an instance is unaware of the fact that other instances may exist.

## Activities

A workflow (and so a `WorkflowApplication`) executes a single activity. This activity can be a composite activity encapsulating a collection of other activities, so a workflow actually executes a tree (or set) of activities. In the earlier samples, you saw examples of activities such as `WriteLine`, `Assign`, `Sequence`, `Flowchart`, `ForEach`, and so on.

WF 4.0 provides a large set of predefined activities. The whole framework was designed with extensibility in mind, so you can easily add your own custom activities to the existing ones. The developer community also provides activity components, so, before developing activity components, check whether you can use existing ones.

One of the key features of WF 4.0 is the explicit definition of arguments and variables. In the earlier samples, you saw that workflows and activities can have arguments, and that activities can define and use variables. Arguments are used just like variables, except they can be passed into and out of a workflow or an activity. Like workflows, activities are stateless. Their state is maintained by the workflow context through arguments and variables. Of course, activities can access them.

Activities are derived directly or indirectly from the abstract `Activity` class of the `System.Activities` namespace and form a tree of object types. Table 11-2 summarizes the most important abstract `Activity` classes that are used by concrete activity components.

**TABLE 11-2:** Abstract Activity Classes

| CLASS | DESCRIPTION |
|-------|-------------|
| `Activity` | The root class of the activity hierarchy. Its main responsibility is to provide an activity instance (and so workflow instance) identification, and support composite activity creation. |
| `NativeActivity` | This class is a base class for custom activities that implement execution logic using the `Execute(ActivityExecutionContext)` method, which has full access to the run-time's features. |
| `CodeActivity` | This class is a base class for creating a custom activity with imperative behavior defined with the `Execute(CodeActivityContext)` method, which gives access to variable and argument resolution and extensions. |
| `AsyncCodeActivity` | This class is a base class for asynchronous operations, and manages code activity execution from start to completion through the `BeginExecute` and `EndExcute` methods. |
| `ActivityWithResult` | These classes retrieve the value or type of an activity output argument. This argument can be accessed through the `Result` property. |

All classes in Table 11-2 derive directly from `Activity`. All activities except `Activity` have derived generic classes with results, such as, `NativeActivity<TResult>`, `CodeActivity<TResult>`, `AsyncCodeActivity<TResult>`, and `ActivityWithResult<TResult>`, respectively. They all have a `Result` property that retrieves an output argument with a type of `TResult`.

## Extensions

Extensions are object instances that can be accessed by both workflow activities and the host application. Extensions provide services to all the activities used in a workflow. Generally, these extensions are created and configured by the host and added to the `WorkflowApplication` instance managing the workflow. A typical application of extensions is sharing data among activities. For example, when several activities in a workflow use a database, the connection string information can be shared among activities through an extension. Extensions can be used to inject information into workflows (that is, can be used to implement the Dependency Injection design pattern for workflows). Connection string sharing is an example.

Extension classes do not have to be derived from a specific class like activities have to; any class can be an extension.

➤   `InstanceStore` (declared in the `System.Runtime.Persistence` namespace) is used to persist the current state of the workflow and retrieve it from the store when needed. This extension plays a key role in the scalability of workflows. The workflow state can be persisted to a store, and the workflow instance can be unloaded from the memory while it is idle. If there is a massive amount of workflow instances, WF 4.0 can save system resources by sweeping out inactive workflows from memory and provide resources for active workflows only.

➤ PersintenceParticipant (declared in the System.Activities.Persistence namespace) derived classes can take part in the persistence process. In addition to the arguments and variables, these extensions can collect a dictionary of values that also should be persisted.

➤ TrackingParticipant (declared in the System.Activities.Tracking namespace) derived classes can access the workflow-tracking infrastructure and access tracking records.

## Workflow Activity Model Changes

The WF programming model has been totally redesigned to make it both simpler and more robust. The key change in this model is that Activity is the core base type in the programming model, and it represents both workflows and activities. The model becomes fully declarative. Remember the CodedHelloWorkflow sample where the workflow declaration was about setting up activities and properties using object and collection initializers with lambda expressions.

With WF 3.5, you had to create a WorkflowRuntime instance to invoke a workflow. In WF 4.0, you can simply create a workflow instance (that is, an Activity-derived instance) and execute it. This behavior simplifies unit testing and application scenarios where you do not want to go through the trouble of setting up a specific environment.

To demonstrate how the WF 4.0 programming model has changed, let's compare two simple workflows, one of them written with WF 3.5 and the other one with WF 4.0. Both workflows define a custom activity that receives a string in its Message argument and displays it on the console.

In this section, only a part of the source code is listed, but you can download the full source code from the book's website at www.wrox.com.

### SimpleHelloWF35

This sample project has been created with the Sequential Workflow Console Application project using .NET Framework 3.5 — and so, it uses WF 3.5. The project contains a custom activity named CustomWriteLineWF35. The designer of this activity is shown in Figure 11-14.

The code declaring this custom activity is shown in Listing 11-6.

**FIGURE 11-14:** The CustomWriteLineWF35 activity in design view

**Available for download on Wrox.com**

**LISTING: 11-6:  CustomWriteLineWF35.cs**

```
using System;
using System.ComponentModel;
using System.Workflow.ComponentModel;
using System.Workflow.Activities;

namespace SimpleHelloWF35
{
```

*continues*

**LISTING 11-6** *(continued)*

```csharp
public partial class CustomWriteLineWF35 : SequenceActivity
{
  public CustomWriteLineWF35()
  {
    InitializeComponent();
  }

  public static DependencyProperty MessageProperty =
    DependencyProperty.Register("Message", typeof(string),
    typeof(CustomWriteLineWF35));
  [DescriptionAttribute("Message")]
  [BrowsableAttribute(true)]
  [DesignerSerializationVisibilityAttribute(
    DesignerSerializationVisibility.Visible)]
  public string Message
  {
    get
    {
      return ((string)(GetValue(MessageProperty)));
    }
    set
    {
      SetValue(MessageProperty, value);
    }
  }

  private void codeActivity1_ExecuteCode(object sender, EventArgs e)
  {
    Console.WriteLine(Message);
  }
}
```

*Code file [CustomWriteLineWF35.cs] available for download at Wrox.com*

The largest part of this code defines the Message property using a DependencyProperty. In order for this code to write a message to the console, a CodeActivity is used, and its ExecuteCode event handler method writes the message to the console.

The workflow uses this custom activity shown in Figure 11-15.

The code representing this workflow is two C# files with about 70 lines.

The Program.cs file that runs this workflow is shown in Listing 11-7.

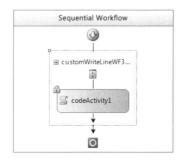

**FIGURE 11-15:** The SimpleHelloWF35 workflow

**LISTING 11-7:** Program.cs (SimpleHelloWF35)

```csharp
using System;
using System.Threading;
using System.Workflow.Runtime;

namespace SimpleHelloWF35
{
  class Program
  {
    static void Main(string[] args)
    {
      using (var workflowRuntime = new WorkflowRuntime())
      {
        var waitHandle = new AutoResetEvent(false);
        workflowRuntime.WorkflowCompleted += (sender, e) => waitHandle.Set();
        workflowRuntime.WorkflowTerminated += (sender, e) =>
        {
          Console.WriteLine(e.Exception.Message);
          waitHandle.Set();
        };
        var instance = workflowRuntime.CreateWorkflow(typeof(Workflow1));
        instance.Start();
        waitHandle.WaitOne();
      }
    }
  }
}
```

*Code file [Program.cs] available for download at Wrox.com*

From this listing, you can see the compulsory dances with the `WorkflowRuntime` instance and the `AutoResetEvent` to start the workflow and wait for its completion.

## SimpleHelloWF4

The second project is created from the Workflow Console Application template with .NET Framework 4.0, and so it uses WF 4.0. In contrast to the `SimpleHelloWF35` application, the custom activity writing to the console does not require a design surface, its code shown in Listing 11-8 is really simple.

**LISTING 11-8:** CustomWriteLineWF4.cs

```csharp
using System;
using System.Activities;

namespace SimpleHelloWF4
{
  public sealed class CustomWriteLineWF4 : CodeActivity
```

*continues*

**LISTING 11-8** *(continued)*

```
    {
       public InArgument<string> Message { get; set; }

       protected override void Execute(CodeActivityContext context)
       {
          Console.WriteLine(context.GetValue(Message));
       }
    }
 }
```

*Code file [CustomWriteLineWF4.cs] available for download at Wrox.com*

Compare the declaration of the `Message` input argument with the implementation in Listing 11-6. The declaration used by WF 4.0 is short and very intuitive. Also, the custom activity itself is a `CodeActivity`. Its `Execute` method is an overridden virtual method and not an event handler method as used in Listing 11-6.

The definition of this workflow uses a simple XAML file that is about 18 lines long, as shown in Listing 11-9. Remember, the WF 3.5 solution used about 70 lines in C#.

**Available for download on Wrox.com**

**LISTING 11-9:** Workflow1.xaml (SimpleHelloWF4)

```
<Activity mc:Ignorable="sap"
  x:Class="SimpleHelloWF4.Workflow1"
  sap:VirtualizedContainerService.HintSize="240,240"
  mva:VisualBasic.Settings="Assembly references and imported namespaces
    for internal implementation"
  xmlns="http://schemas.microsoft.com/netfx/2009/xaml/activities"
  xmlns:local="clr-namespace:SimpleHelloWF4"
  xmlns:mc="http://schemas.openxmlformats.org/markup-compatibility/2006"
  xmlns:mva="clr-namespace:Microsoft.VisualBasic.Activities;
    assembly=System.Activities"
  xmlns:sad="clr-namespace:System.Activities.Debugger;assembly=System.Activities"
  xmlns:sap="http://schemas.microsoft.com/netfx/2009/xaml/activities/presentation"
  xmlns:x="http://schemas.microsoft.com/winfx/2006/xaml">
  <local:CustomWriteLineWF4
    sad:XamlDebuggerXmlReader.FileName="C:\Publications\VS 2010 Six-in-One\
      Chapter 11\Samples\SimpleHelloWF4\SimpleHelloWF4\Workflow1.xaml"
    sap:VirtualizedContainerService.HintSize="200,200"
    Message="Hello from WF 4.0" />
</Activity>
```

*Code file [Workflow1.xaml] available for download at Wrox.com*

The `Program.cs` file of this project is very simple, as shown in Listing 11-10.

**LISTING 11-10:** Program.cs (SimpleHelloWF4)

```csharp
using System.Activities;

namespace SimpleHelloWF4
{

  class Program
  {
    static void Main(string[] args)
    {
      WorkflowInvoker.Invoke(new Workflow1());
    }
  }
}
```

*Code file [Program.cs] available for download at Wrox.com*

Here, the `WorkflowInvoker` static class does everything in contrast to Listing 11-7. You can find this kind of simplicity almost everywhere in the WF 4.0 programming model.

As you see, the programming style used is very different from the one applied in WF 3.5 — and makes your programs shorter, easier to test (the shorter they are, the more testable they are), and very straightforward.

## WORKFLOW ACTIVITY LIBRARY

You can choose from a wide variety of predefined activities when designing your workflows. The Toolbox offers about 40 activities by default, and you can add more activities using the "Choose items" command from the Toolbox context menu.

This section provides an overview of these predefined activities. Most of them can be found in the `System.Activities.Statements`, `System.Activities`, and `System.ServiceModel.Activities` namespaces.

You have already seen that workflows and activities have a common root class, the `System.Activities.Activity` class. As a consequence of this great design, activities (like workflows) can have input and output arguments. These arguments can be set (and their value can be get) through public properties of classes representing activities. While previous sections of this chapter used the term "arguments," this section will use the term "properties" to point out that arguments are represented in code with properties.

Some activities are simple ones executing a well-defined operation. The majority of these are composite activities encapsulating other activities. Generally, you can access these constituting activities in code through the `Body` property of their parents.

All activities are new in WF 4.0, because all of them have been redesigned and rewritten. This section provides a short overview of each of them. However, there are WF 4.0 activities with matching semantics of a particular WF 3.5 activity. The overview indicates this functional matching.

## Primitive Activities

These activities provide you with primitive operations such as assignment, method invocation, delay, output messages, and so on.

Table 11-3 summarizes the primitive activities you can find in the activity library.

**TABLE 11-3:** Primitive Activities

| ACTIVITY | DESCRIPTION |
| --- | --- |
| Assign | This activity sets workflow argument or variable values from within a workflow. Use the `To` property to define the argument or variable to set, and the `Value` property to specify the value. |
| Assign\<T\> | This is the generic form of the `Assign` activity. You can specify the type of argument or variable to set. |
| Delay | This activity creates a timer for a specific duration. When the activity's timer expires, the `Delay` activity completes its execution. You can use the `Duration` property to set the `TimeSpan` of the timer. |
| InvokeMethod | This activity calls a public method of a specified object or type. You can use the `TargetType`, `TargetObject` and `MethodName` properties to set up the object and method to invoke. You can pass `GenericTypeArguments` and `Parameters` to the method. Set the `RunAsynchronously` flag to `true` to run the method in a background thread. |
| WriteLine | This activity writes a specified string to a specified `TextWriter` object. Use the `Text` property to set the string to write to the output. Leave the `TextWriter` property empty if you want to write the string to the default output; otherwise, set it to the intended `TextWriter` object. |

Except for `Delay`, all activities in Table 11-3 are new. In WF 3.5 you can implement the other activities simply by defining `CodeActivity` instances.

In WF 4.0 you can easily define your own primitive activities by creating new activities inheriting from `System.Activity.CodeActivity`.

## Flow Control Activities

All activities belonging to this category are composite activities nesting child activities in their body. The parent activity has a predefined control flow determining how child activities are executed.

Table 11-4 summarizes the flow control activities defined in WF 4.0, describing their semantics.

**TABLE 11-4:** Flow Control Activities

| ACTIVITY | DESCRIPTION |
| --- | --- |
| DoWhile | This class represents a looping activity that executes contained activities at least once, until a condition is no longer true.<br><br>First, the body activity of DoWhile is executed, and then the Condition property is checked. While this condition is met, the body is executed cyclically. |
| ForEach<T> | This activity executes its body activity action once for each value provided in the Values collection. T defines the type of the values provided in the Values collection. |
| If | This activity models an If-Then-Else statement with a Boolean Condition. When it is evaluated to true, the activity set in the Then property is executed; otherwise, the activity set in the Else property is carried out. You can leave either Then or Else empty.<br><br>This property is semantically the same as IfElse in WF 3.5. |
| Parallel | This activity executes all child activities simultaneously and asynchronously. The activity operates by simultaneously scheduling each Activity in its Branches collection at the start. It completes when all of its Branches complete, or when its CompletionCondition property evaluates to true. While all the Activity objects run asynchronously, they do not execute on separate threads, so each successive activity only executes when the previously scheduled activity completes or goes idle. If none of the child activities of this activity go idle, this activity executes them in the same way as a Sequence activity (see more about this later in this table) does.<br><br>This activity has the same name as the Parallel activity in WF 3.5, but semantically is different. |
| ParallelForEach<T> | This activity enumerates the elements of a collection and executes an embedded statement for each element of the Values collection in parallel. You can imagine it as using the Parallel activity where the Branches property is set up dynamically according to the body of the corresponding ForEach<T> activity. All the execution semantics treated for Parallel are the same for this activity. |
| Pick | This activity behaves similarly to Switch (see more on this later in this table) in that it executes only one of several activities in response to events. The Branches property contains a collection of PickBranch events. Only one of these PickBranch activities is executed — the first one that signs that its trigger event has been fired. Other PickBranch activities are ignored. |

*continues*

**TABLE 11-4** *(continued)*

| ACTIVITY | DESCRIPTION |
|---|---|
| PickBranch | This activity is a potential path of execution within a `Pick` activity. A `PickBranch` contains a `Trigger` and an `Action`. At the beginning of a `Pick` element's execution, all the trigger activities from all `PickBranch` elements are scheduled. When the first trigger activity completes, the corresponding action activity is scheduled, and all other trigger activities are canceled. |
| Sequence | This activity executes a set of child activities according to a single, defined ordering. The `Activities` collection defines the activities to be executed. They are carried out in the order they are added to the collection. When the last activity in the collection completes, the `Sequence` activity completes. |
| | In WF 3.5 the `Sequence` activity has the same semantics as in WF 4.0. |
| Switch<T> | This activity selects one choice from a number of activities to execute, based on the value of a given expression of the type specified in this object's type specifier. Each case in the `Cases` dictionary consists of a value (serving as the key for the dictionary) and an activity (serving as the value for the dictionary). The `Expression` property of `Switch` is evaluated and compared against the keys in the `Cases` dictionary. If a match is found, the corresponding activity is executed. |
| While | This activity executes a contained workflow element while a condition evaluates to `true`. First, the `Condition` property is evaluated, and if it's `true`, the `Body` of the activity is executed. This cycle goes on while the condition is met. |
| | The `While` activity in WF 3.5 has the same semantics as in WF 4.0. |

# Workflow Run-Time Activities

There are a few activities influencing the behavior of the workflow run-time. These activities are described in Table 11-5.

**TABLE 11-5:** Workflow Run-Time Activities

| ACTIVITY | DESCRIPTION |
|---|---|
| Persist | Persistence is a key issue related to long-running workflows and, of course, to scalability. You can create extensions that persist your own custom information in addition to the default workflow state (including arguments and variables). You may have reasons to persist the workflow information at certain points when the run-time would not save this information automatically (for example, if your business logic requires it). |
| | This activity requests the run-time to persist the workflow instance. |

| ACTIVITY | DESCRIPTION |
|---|---|
| TerminateWorkflow | In many workflows (especially the ones with human interaction) there may be some exceptional branches that require terminating your workflow, either with success or failure.<br><br>This activity terminates the running workflow instance, raises the `Completed` event in the host, and reports error information. Once the workflow is terminated, it cannot be resumed.<br><br>In WF 3.5 you can use the `Terminate` activity with the same semantics. |
| Interop | This activity manages the execution of an activity developed in WF 3.0 or WF 3.5 (`System.Workflow.ComponentModel.Activity` derived type) within a WF 4.0 workflow. The `Interop` activity will not appear in the workflow designer Toolbox unless the workflow's project has its Target Framework setting set to .NET Framework 4, (generally, the default setting is .NET Framework 4 Client Profile). Use the `ActivityProperties` and `ActivityType` properties of the `Interop` class to parameterize the WF 3.0 or WF 3.5 activity to execute. |

## Flowchart-Specific Activities

As you have seen earlier, WF 4.0 supports creating flowchart-like workflows. Other composite activities such as `Sequence`, `Foreach<T>`, `Parallel`, `Pick`, and so on, declare simple control flow strategy. For example, a `Sequence` activity executes nested activities in the order they are added to the `Activities` collection.

In contrast, `Flowchart` allows you to drop several activities to the design surface and draw connections describing the control flow among the nested activities.

Table 11-6 describes the activities that allow you to create flowchart-like workflows.

**TABLE 11-6:** Flowchart-Specific Activities

| ACTIVITY | DESCRIPTION |
|---|---|
| Flowchart | This activity models workflows using the familiar flowchart paradigm. It uses the `Nodes` collection to describe all activities within the flowchart. This collection contains `FlowNode` instances. The `StartNode` property describes the first activity in the workflow, and each `FlowNode` instance is capable of defining the next activity to execute. |
| FlowNode | This class is the abstract base class for all the different node types that can be contained within a `Flowchart` activity. You can develop your own flowchart-aware activities inheriting from this class. |

*continues*

**TABLE 11-6** *(continued)*

| ACTIVITY | DESCRIPTION |
|---|---|
| FlowStep | This class is a `FlowNode`-derived class that executes a specified `Action` and has a `Next` pointer to the `FlowNode` to be executed as the next step of the workflow. When you drop a non-`FlowNode` activity to the design surface of a `Flowchart`, that activity is wrapped into a `FlowStep` instance. |
| FlowDecision | This activity is a specialized `FlowNode` that provides the capability to model a conditional node with two outcomes. The condition is evaluated by the workflow run-time, and its `true` or `false` outcome determines the next action to take. |
| FlowSwitch<T> | This activity is a specialized `FlowNode` that allows modeling a switch construct, with one expression and one outcome for each match. The expression is evaluated by the workflow run-time and the outcome determines the next action to take. |

Of course, you can nest any other activities into a `Flowchart` activity. However, `FlowNode`-derived activities such as `FlowDecision` and `FlowSwitch<T>` can be used only within a `Flowchart`.

## Error-Handling Activities

Most workflows can (must) handle errors and exceptions either as a standard branch of a process (for example, an item is out of stock), or as an occasional event (for example, the inventory system is temporarily out of order). The error-handling activities help you define how certain errors and exceptions should be managed in your workflows.

While WF 3.5 used fault handlers, WF 4.0 uses the `try-catch-finally` exception-handling pattern.

Table 11-7 describes the activities you can use.

**TABLE 11-7:** Error-Handling Activities

| ACTIVITY | DESCRIPTION |
|---|---|
| TryCatch | This activity contains a `Try` activity to be executed by the workflow run-time within an exception handling block. It contains a `Catches` collection composed from `Catch` elements that describe exception-handling branches. The `Finally` property defines workflow element to be executed when the `Try` and any necessary activities in the `Catches` collection complete execution. |
| Throw | This activity throws an exception. |
| Rethrow | This activity throws a previously thrown exception from within a `Catch` activity. It can only be used within a `Catch` block of a `TryCatch` activity. |

Later in this chapter, you will see an example that demonstrates how to use these activities.

# Transaction-Handling Activities

One of the key success factors of modern workflow applications is the capability to manage long-running transactions. *Long-running transactions* are those transactions where you cannot use either the begin-commit-rollback pattern generally implemented by database management systems, or the two-phase commit pattern used by distributed systems. There might be many reasons why these patterns can't be applied, the most frequent being that one (or more) of the parties involved in the transaction do not support any of the two previously described patterns.

WF 4.0 uses a transaction model named *compensating transaction*. This model does not ensure atomicity (that is, your transaction is either entirely executed or rolled back to the starting point as if nothing happened). Instead, it provides that the transaction is either entirely done (committed) or, in the case when it cannot be entirely committed, changes are compensated.

A common example is when you register for a conference and separately book an airline ticket and hotel. If everything's okay, all fees are withdrawn from your credit card account. If the conference is cancelled, your registration fee is returned, and, in many cases, other fees are also put back to your account. However, if you buy tickets with special conditions or you cancel your hotel too close to the check-in date, a part of the fee is withheld as a cancellation fee. In this case, your original transaction is not rolled back — you do not get all your money back, only a part of it. You are compensated, albeit partially.

Table 11-8 describes the activities WF 4.0 uses to implement the compensating transaction model.

**TABLE 11-8:** Transaction-Handling Activities

| ACTIVITY | DESCRIPTION |
| --- | --- |
| CompensableActivity | This activity is the core compensation activity in WF 4.0. Any activities that perform work that may need to be compensated are placed into the Body of a CompensableActivity. It also allows the developer to optionally specify a compensation and confirmation activity to schedule appropriate business logic in the event of errors or successful completion of the Body. Compensation and confirmation of a CompensableActivity is invoked by using the CompensationToken returned by the CompensableActivity. |
| | If the Body activity is cancelled before it has completed, the CancellationHandler activity is executed. The CompensationHandler activity is executed when subsequent workflow activities fail and the workflow is aborted, and it is used to undo the work of the Body activity if the Body has completed. |
| | The ConfirmationHandler activity is executed when the activity has been confirmed. By default, confirmation happens automatically when the workflow instance has completed. |

*continues*

**TABLE 11-8** *(continued)*

| ACTIVITY | DESCRIPTION |
| --- | --- |
| CancellationScope | This activity associates cancellation logic with the main path of execution. The work that may need to be cancelled is placed into the Body of a CancellationScope. The CancellationHandler property contains the activity that is executed in the event of cancellation. |
| Compensate | This activity can be used to explicitly invoke the compensation handler of a CompensableActivity. When the Target property is specified, the Compensate activity explicitly invokes the compensation handler of the target CompensableActivity. When Target is not specified, the Compensate activity invokes the default compensation for any child CompensableActivity activities in the reverse order of successful completion. |
| Confirm | This activity can be used to explicitly invoke the confirmation handler of a CompensableActivity. When the Target property is specified, the Confirm activity explicitly invokes the confirmation handler of the target CompensableActivity. When Target is not specified, the Confirm activity executes the default confirmation for any child CompensableActivity activities in the reverse order of successful completion. |

Later in this chapter, you will learn more about the compensating transaction model used by WF 4.0 through a sample.

## Collection-Handling Activities

WF 4.0 provides some predefined activities that enable you to manipulate collections in your workflow. You can declare collection arguments and variables, as the following declarations show:

```
Variable<ICollection<Customer>> customerList =
  new Variable<ICollection<Customer>>();
// ...
InArgument<ICollection<Order>> Orders { get; set; }
```

There are several primitive activities allowing you to work with collections. All of them have a type parameter defining the type of elements in the collection, and a Collection property containing a reference to the collection argument or variable that is the subject of the operation. The Item property — where the operation has this argument — specifies the collection item used by the operation.

Table 11-9 summarizes these collection-handling activities.

**TABLE 11-9:** Collection-Handling Activities

| ACTIVITY | DESCRIPTION |
|---|---|
| AddToCollection<T> | Adds an item to the specified collection. |
| ClearCollection<T> | Clears a specified collection of all items. |
| ExistsInCollection<T> | Indicates whether a given item is present in a given collection. Its Result property is true if the item is in the collection; otherwise, it is false. |
| RemoveFromCollection<T> | Removes an item from a specified collection. Its Result property is true if the item has been removed from the collection (because it was present in the collection); otherwise, it is false. |

## Messaging Activities

Most workflows involve different people and systems having well-defined roles in a workflow. Often, the whole business workflow (a business process) is divided technically into smaller ones composing the entire process. For example, from your point of view, the whole process of ordering a book from a web shop is one business workflow that completes when you receive the book. From the web shop point of view, this process must be divided into smaller workflows (order placement, shipment scheduling, payment collection, delivery, and so on), and, generally, third-party service providers are also involved.

When you create distributed workflows (either simple or complex ones), those workflows must communicate. In many cases, workflows are built on inhomogeneous back-end systems (ERP, CRM, inventory, enterprise directory, and so on) that provide services for the business processes. WF 4.0 provides a more sophisticated model for inter-workflow communication and accessing external services than WF 3.5 had. It seamlessly integrates with Windows Communication Foundations (WCF), and provides more activities than WF 3.5.

Table 11-10 summarizes the built-in messaging activities of WF 4.0.

**TABLE 11-10:** Messaging Activities

| ACTIVITY | DESCRIPTION |
|---|---|
| Send | This activity sends a message to a service. It has about a dozen of properties to set up the message to send, including Content, EndPointAddress, ServiceContractName, OperationName, and many others. |
| Receive | This activity receives a message. When the message has arrived, it can be accessed through the Content property. |

*continues*

**TABLE 11-10** *(continued)*

| ACTIVITY | DESCRIPTION |
|---|---|
| SendReply | This activity sends the reply message as part of a request/response message exchange pattern on the service side. |
| ReceiveReply | This activity receives a message as part of a request/response message exchange pattern. |
| CorrelationScope | This activity provides implicit message correlation-management services for child messaging activities. Through a CorrelationHandle instance messages, such a request and the related response can be correlated. For example, when the CorrelationScope contains a Send and a ReceiveReply activity, the workflow will correlate the response message with the correct workflow instance. |
| InitializeCorrelation | This activity initializes correlation without sending or receiving a message. Typically, correlation is initialized by sending or receiving a message. If correlation must be initialized before a message is sent or received, this activity can be used to initialize the correlation. |
| TransactedReceiveScope | This activity enables you to flow a transaction into a workflow or dispatcher-created server-side transactions. This wasn't possible in WF 3.5. You could have transactions on the client, and you could have transactions on the server, but they would not be able to cooperate. With the TransactedReceiveScope activity, WF 4.0 provides a great solution. |

 *Using messaging in workflows requires a deep understanding of messaging patterns and WCF. It is definitely out of the scope of this chapter to dive into this topic deeper. In this chapter, you'll find an example demonstrating the* WorkflowServiceHost *class, where a few messaging activities will be used.*

*Microsoft has released many samples for demonstrating messaging in WF 4.0. You can download these samples from* http://www.microsoft.com/downloads/details.aspx?FamilyID=35ec8682-d5fd-4bc3-a51a-d8ad115a 8792&displaylang=en, *or you can search for "WCF WF Samples .NET 4" on MSDN.*

While most of the activities treated by now are contained in the System.Activities and System.Activities.Statements namespaces, messaging activities are declared within the System.ServiceModel.Activities namespace.

# USING THE COMPENSATING TRANSACTION MODEL

Although Table 11-8 summarizes the activities related to transaction handling, it's difficult to imagine how the compensating transaction pattern works in practice. Because it is an essential part of WF 4.0, understanding the concepts behind it helps you develop more robust workflows.

Let's create an example that helps you understand how this pattern works with WF 4.0. This example also demonstrates error-handling concepts through a TryCatch activity.

## The ConferenceWorkflow Example

This example will demonstrate a very simplified case of a conference registration when you also arrange travelling and book a hotel reservation.

Create a new Workflow Console Application, and name it ConferenceWorkflow. Drag and drop a TryCatch activity to the design surface of Workflow1, and then a Sequence activity to the Try block. Set its DisplayName property to Conference Preparations. Add a WriteLine activity to Conference Preparations with the Text property set to "Conference preparations started." Click the "Add an activity" link of the Finally block, and drop a WriteLine there with the "Conference preparations completed" text. Click the Conference Preparations link of the Try block.

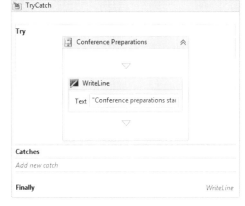

Figure 11-16 shows the workflow you've created.

**FIGURE 11-16:** The TryCatch activity of the ConferenceWorkflow example

As you would expect, when you run this workflow by pressing Ctrl+F5, it generates the following output:

```
Conference preparations started
Conference preparations completed
```

Add a Parallel activity to Conference Preparations below WriteLine and set its DisplayName to "Registration and Travelling." Drop two Compensable activities to the Parallel activity and set their DisplayName to "Registration" and "Travelling," respectively. Add a Sequence property to the body of Registration, and another one to the body of Travelling, respectively. Drop a WriteLine to the Sequence in Registration with Text and set it to "(Body) Pay $1.500 registration fee." Add a Delay after this WriteLine with its Duration set to TimeSpan.FromSeconds(2).

Add a WriteLine to the Sequence in Travelling with Text set to "(Body) Pay $1.000 for travelling and hotel", and then a Delay with Duration set to TimeSpan.FromSeconds(1).

Now, the Registration and Travelling activities should look like Figure 11-17.

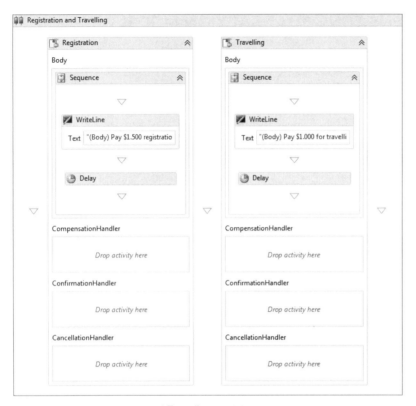

**FIGURE 11-17:** Registration and Travelling activity

Now the workflow generates the following output when you run it:

```
Conference preparations started
(Body) Pay $1.000 for travelling and hotel
(Body) Pay $1.500 registration fee
Conference preparations completed
```

## Implementing Cancellation, Confirmation, and Compensation

As you can see in Figure 11-17, the CompensableActivity instances (Registration, Travelling) have three sections with no actions specified yet. The CancellationHandler is executed when the Body action is cancelled. The CompensationHandler is executed when the Body action is successfully executed, but any subsequent errors or exceptions prevent the workflow from completing successfully. The ConfirmationHandler is executed when the workflow completes.

### CANCELLATION IS NOT A FAILURE

Do not mix the concepts of cancellation and failure! "Failure" means that some error happened, or an exception is raised. "Cancellation" means that an activity has been scheduled to run, but it was cancelled before it was completed. For example the `Parallel` and `ParallelForEach<T>` activities schedule the activities in their body to run. Every time when a branch completes, these activities evaluate their `CompletionCondition` property. If this shows `true`, all the branches scheduled, but not run, are cancelled.

Of course, failures can be caught and handled, so that they will cause activities to be cancelled.

Add six `WriteLine` activities to the empty handler sections with their `Text` property set according to Table 11-11, respectively.

**TABLE 11-11:** Text Properties of WriteLine Activities

| ACTIVITY | DESCRIPTION |
| --- | --- |
| `CompensationHandler (Registration)` | "(Compensation) $1.500 registration fee paid back" |
| `CompensationHandler (Travelling)` | "(Compensation) $800 travelling and hotel fee paid back" |
| `ConfirmationHandler (Registration)` | "(Confirmation) See you in Vegas!" |
| `ConfirmationHandler (Travelling)` | "(Confirmation) Enjoy your flight!" |
| `CancellationHandler (Registration)` | "(Cancellation) Your registration has not been done" |
| `CancellationHandler (Travelling)` | "(Cancellation) Your hotel reservation has not been done" |

Run the workflow by pressing Ctrl+F5. All `CompensableActivity` bodies run, and the workflow completes successfully, so there is no surprise that the following output is displayed:

```
Conference preparations started
(Body) Pay $1.000 for travelling and hotel
(Body) Pay $1.500 registration fee
Conference preparations completed
(Confirmation) See you in Vegas!
(Confirmation) Enjoy your flight!
```

However, one thing in the output is worth mentioning. Note, that the confirmation messages are preceded with the "Conference preparations started" message coming from the `Finally` block of the `TryCatch` activity. Confirmation handlers run only after all workflow activities completed successfully.

## Cancellation

Let's see how cancellation works by setting the `CompletionCondition` property of the `Registration` and `Travelling` activity to `True`. When you run the workflow, it produces the following output:

```
Conference preparations started
(Body) Pay $1.000 for travelling and hotel
(Body) Pay $1.500 registration fee
(Cancellation) Your registration has not been done
Conference preparations completed
(Confirmation) Enjoy your flight!
```

This output shows that the `Registration` activity is cancelled and `Travelling` is confirmed. How can that be? Both the `Registration` and the `Travelling` activities have a `Delay` activity that suspends them for a while. Travelling resumes after one second and that branch completes at this point. The `CompletionCondition` of the `Parallel` activity is evaluated to `true`, so `Registration` (it is still suspended) is cancelled. When you change the `Delay` activities so that `Travelling` resumes slower, you get the following output:

```
Conference preparations started
(Body) Pay $1.000 for travelling and hotel
(Body) Pay $1.500 registration fee
(Cancellation) Your hotel reservation has not been done
Conference preparations completed
(Confirmation) See you in Vegas!
```

## Compensation

Compensation is not as easy to implement as cancellation because the failure triggering the compensation happens at a point in the workflow where you are outside of `CompensableActivity` to compensate. You do not even have information about what activities within that `CompensableActivity` are cancelled. Generally, however, a cancelled action does not need compensation (although, in certain cases, it might).

The key to establishing the right compensation model for a concrete workflow is the `CompensationToken` type. A `CompensationToken` instance can be set as a result of a `CompensableActivity`. By checking these tokens, you can make decisions about what activities need to be compensated (and how).

Let's modify the `ConferenceWorkflow` example to use `CompensationToken` instances.

Add two variables with the `TryCatch` scope. Name them `registrationToken` and `travellingToken`, and set their types to `System.Activities.Statements.CompensationToken`. (Select "Browse for Types" from the Variable Type column and drill down to the `CompensationToken` type in the `System.Activities` assembly). Select the `Registration` and then the `Travelling` activities, and set their `Result` property to `registrationToken` and `travellingToken`, respectively.

Drop a `Throw` activity into the `Conference Preparations Sequence` after the `Registration` and `Travelling` activity. Set its `Exception` property to `New System.InvalidOperationException()`. This activity will raise an exception.

 *Here, the* `System.InvalidOperationException` *is used just for demonstration purposes to mimic a business exception. In real workflows, always define your own exception types and raise them to signal failures your workflow is prepared to handle.*

Now, click the "Add new catch" link in the `Catches` section of the `TryCatch` activity, then set the `Exception` field to `System.InvalidOperationException` by browsing for this type. This will catch the exception you raise with the `Throw` activity. Drop a `Sequence` activity to this `Catch` block, and then add two `If` activities to this `Sequence`. Set the `Condition` properties of the two `If` activities to `Not registrationToken Is Nothing` and to `Not travellingToken Is Nothing`, respectively. Add one `Compensate` activities to the `Then` blocks, and set their `Target` property to `registrationToken` and `travellingToken`, respectively.

The `Catches` block of `TryCatch` should be similar to the one shown in Figure 11-18.

Set the `Duration` property of the `Delay` activities embedded into `Registration` and `Travelling`, so that the one for the `Registration` is 2 seconds, the one for `Travelling` is 1 second. Run the application, and you receive the following output:

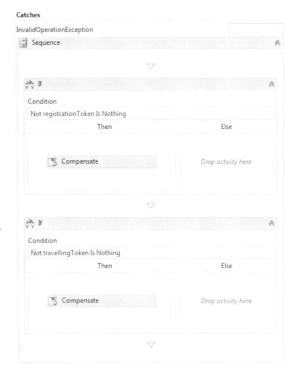

**FIGURE 11-18:** The Catches block after adding Compensate activities

```
Conference preparations started
(Body) Pay $1.000 for travelling and hotel
(Body) Pay $1.500 registration fee
(Cancellation) Your registration has not been done
(Compensation) $800 travelling and hotel fee paid back
Conference preparations completed
```

What happened?

Because the `CompletionCondition` property of the `Conference Preparations` activity is set to `True`, the `Travelling` activity finishes before `Registration` and causes it to be cancelled.

Because `Travelling` completes and its `Result` property is set to `travellingToken`, the token will be assigned a concrete `CompensationToken` instance. `Registration` is cancelled, so although its `Result` property is set to `registrationToken`, this variable remains `null` (`Nothing` in Visual Basic).

The exception raised by the `Throw` activity is caught, but because only `travellingToken` has a non-`null` value, only the related `Compensate` activity will be executed. The `travellingToken` variable holds the information about the related `CompensableActivity`, and because it is set as the `Target` property of `Compensate`, the appropriate compensation handler is invoked. If you modify the `Delay` activities so that `Registration` finishes first, the output will change:

```
Conference preparations started
(Body) Pay $1.000 for travelling and hotel
(Body) Pay $1.500 registration fee
(Cancellation) Your hotel reservation has not been done
(Compensation) $1.500 registration fee paid back
Conference preparations completed
```

 *This workflow is quite far away from being complete or correct. It does not handle many issues that you must manage in real workflows. However, it shows you the WF 4.0 implementation of the compensating transaction pattern. Play with this example and try to modify it to reflect real-world situations.*

## PERSISTENCE AND HUMAN INTERACTIONS

In a real business environment, workflows are not as simple as in the examples you've seen thus far in this chapter:

➤   In most cases, there are thousands of workflow instances running in an hour (or even in a minute).

➤   Although many workflows are automated, there are almost always human interactions — human decisions — involved in workflows.

➤   Workflows are distributed. Several activities are done by external systems, or by humans working with their special applications.

By now, all the examples used `WorkflowApplication` instances kept in the operational memory of the computer where the workflow application ran. Imagine what would happen if hundreds of thousands of workflow instances were kept in memory! If humans are involved in the workflows, maybe most of the running workflows were sitting and waiting for human interaction.

In this section, you will learn how WF 4.0 copes with the situations similar to these. The related concepts are presented through a sample project named `DomainNameWorkflow` that you can download from the book's companion website (`www.wrox.com`).

## The DomainNameWorkflow Project

The project demonstrating these concepts is simple. In the real world, it would be more complex. It is a WPF application that demonstrates two human roles. First, it allows customers placing domain name requests. Second, a decision-maker at the service provider company can approve or deny

this request. The application uses a back-end database to store domain name requests.

Of course, using one client application for demonstrating two separate roles is not very realistic, but it's easy enough to follow. When you use the application, its user interface looks like Figure 11-19.

The main part of Figure 11-19 is occupied by a list box displaying the domain name requests having been placed. Each item of the list shows the name ant the status of the request that can be one of the `New`, `Approved`, or `Denied` values.

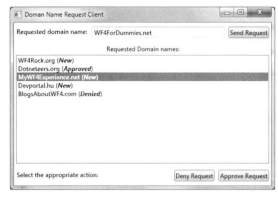

**FIGURE 11-19:** Domain Name Request workflow in action

The top of the form contains the controls used by the customer to place a domain name request. The two buttons at the bottom are used by the decision-maker to either approve or deny the request.

### The Structure of the Project

The WPF application is represented by the `RequestClient` project that has only a few files, as summarized in Table 11-12.

**TABLE 11-12:** RequestClient Project Files

| FILE | DESCRIPTION |
|---|---|
| ApproveDomainNameRequest.cs | A `CodeActivity` saving the status (`Approved` or `Denied`) back to the database. |
| CreateDomainNameRequest.cs | A `CodeActivity` saving a new domain name request into the database. |
| ProcessDomainNameRequest.cs | The main workflow of the entire domain name request procedure. |
| WaitForApproval.cs | An activity waiting for the approval of a placed domain name request. |
| App.config | The application configuration file storing connection string information to back-end databases. |

*continues*

**TABLE 11-12** *(continued)*

| FILE | DESCRIPTION |
|---|---|
| `App.xaml, App.xaml.cs` | The main file of the WPF application, and its code-behind file. |
| `DNRequest.edmx, DNRequest.Designer.cs` | The ADO .NET entity data model of the request database. |
| `MainWindow.xaml, MainWindow.xaml.cs` | The main form of the application and its code-behind file. |
| `RequestClientProxy.cs` | A proxy class allowing the workflow instance access to the main form's functions. |

The project stores two kinds of data in its back-end database. While it waits for the request approval, the states of workflow instances representing new requests are persisted into the database with the built-in `SqlWorkflowInstanceStore` extension. When a workflow instance completes, the related information is removed from the database. The requests are also stored in a user table (`DNRequest`). This table persists the request data even after the related workflow instance completes.

## The Main Workflow

The main workflow of the domain request process is implemented as a code-only workflow. It contains only a few activities constituting a sequence, as shown in Listing 11-11.

**LISTING 11-11:** ProcessDomainNameRequest.cs

```
using System.Activities;
using System.Activities.Statements;
using DomainNameDAL;

namespace RequestClient.Activities
{
  public sealed class ProcessDomainNameRequest: Activity
  {
    public InArgument<string> DomainName { get; set; }
    public ProcessDomainNameRequest()
    {
      var request = new Variable<DNRequest>("request");
      var status = new Variable<string>("status");
      Implementation =
        () =>
        new Sequence
        {
          DisplayName = "Process Domain Name Request",
          Variables =
            {
              request,
```

```
                  status
               },
           Activities =
             {
               new CreateDomainNameRequest
               {
                 DomainName = new InArgument<string>(ctx => DomainName.Get(ctx)),
                 Request = new OutArgument<DNRequest>(ctx => request.Get(ctx))
               },
               new InvokeMethod
               {
                 TargetType = typeof (RequestClientProxy),
                 MethodName = "AddDNRequestToList",
                 Parameters =
                   {
                     new InArgument<DNRequest>(ctx => request.Get(ctx))
                   }
               },
               new WaitForApproval
               {
                 BookmarkName = "ApproveRequest",
                 Status = new OutArgument<string>(ctx => status.Get(ctx))
               },
               new InvokeMethod
               {
                 TargetType = typeof (RequestClientProxy),
                 MethodName = "UpdateDNRequest",
                 Parameters =
                   {
                     new InArgument<int>(ctx => request.Get(ctx).RequestID),
                     new InArgument<string>(ctx => status.Get(ctx))
                   }
               }
             }
           };
     }
   }
}
```

---

*Code file [ProcessDomainNameRequest.cs] available for download at Wrox.com*

This workflow is instantiated and started when the customer clicks the Send Request button (see Figure 11-19). It invokes the following activities:

1. The `CreateDomainNameRequest` wraps the request into a `DNRequest` record, and saves it into the database.

2. The first `InvokeMethod` activity calls the `AddDNRequestToList` method that appends the new request into the list of request (that is, the list in the middle of Figure 11-19).

3. The `WaitForApproval` activity suspends the current workflow instance and forces the workflow run-time to persist it to the database. After the decision-maker approves or

denies the request, the workflow instance is reloaded from the database, and the workflow is resumed.

**4.** The second `InvokeMethod` activity calls the `UpdateDNRequest` method that updates the state of the request in the list.

## Preparing the Workflow Database

The workflow will save its state in a SQL Server database using the `SqlWorkflowInstanceStore` built-in extension. This extension assumes that you set up the expected database schema (tables, views, and stored procedures). You must access a SQL Server database where you have rights to create a database. The easiest way is to install SQL Server 2008 Express on your computer.

Open the Server Explorer (View ➪ Server Explorer). Right-click on Data Connections and invoke the Create New SQL Server Database. Specify the server name you intend to use, and the database name (use, for example, `DomainNameData`). Figure 11-20 shows the dialog to set up the new database information.

Open the `SqlWorkflowInstanceStoreSchema.sql` file. (You can locate it in the `SqlScripts` folder of the `RequestClient` project.) In the code editor, right-click and start the `Execute SQL` command. Specify the database login parameters, and, in the Connection Properties tab, type **DomainNameData** (or the name of the database you've created) into the "Connect to database" field, and then click Connect. When the script completes, in Server Explorer, you can check the tables, views, and stored procedures created.

**FIGURE 11-20:** The Create New SQL Server Database dialog

In addition to the tables the script created, the `DomainNameWorkflow` will use a custom table (`DNRequest`) to store entity state information about domain name requests. Run the `DNRequest.sql` script (it's also located in the `SqlScripts` folder) with the `Execute SQL` command to create this table.

## Storing a New Request into the Database

When the user clicks the Send Request button, the first step of the workflow saves it into the `DNRequest` table of the database. This step is executed by an instance of the `CreateDomainNameRequest` activity, as shown in Listing 11-12.

**LISTING 11-12: CreateDomainNameRequest.cs**

```
using System.Activities;
using DomainNameDAL;

namespace RequestClient.Activities
```

```
{
  public sealed class CreateDomainNameRequest: CodeActivity
  {
    public InArgument<string> DomainName { get; set; }
    public OutArgument<DNRequest> Request { get; set; }

    protected override void Execute(CodeActivityContext context)
    {
      using (var dataContext = new DomainNameDataEntities())
      {
        var request = new DNRequest
        {
          WorkflowID = context.WorkflowInstanceId,
          RequestedName = DomainName.Get(context),
          Status = "New"
        };
        dataContext.AddToDNRequest(request);
        dataContext.SaveChanges();
        Request.Set(context, request);
      }
    }
  }
}
```

*Code file [CreateDomainNameRequest.cs] available for download at Wrox.com*

This activity is a `CodeActivity`, and its `Execute` method does the job. It accepts an input argument with `DomainName` of the requested domain, and it returns back a `DNRequest` entity representing the request. The record is created and stored with the Entity Framework 4.0, where the related data context and the `DNRequest` entity are defined in `DNRequest.edmx`.

There is an especially important code line in Listing 11-12:

```
WorkflowID = context.WorkflowInstanceId
```

It saves the identifier of the current workflow instance into the `WorkflowID` field of the `DNRequest` record. The instance identifier is a GUID, and, later in this example, it will be used to resume the appropriate workflow instance when someone approves or denies the domain name request.

## Communicating with the Host Application

Two steps in the workflow are simple `InvokeMethod` activities that update the user interface. The first is run as soon as the request is queued; the second, when it is approved or denied. The workflow somehow must communicate with the UI. It sounds easy, but there are two issues to solve:

➤ The workflow instance must know the main window of the application (that is a singleton) in order to communicate with it.

➤ Any UI updates should happen in the UI thread.

There are several alternatives for solving the first issue. In this example, this is it is done by a static class named `RequestClientProxy` that forwards requests to the main application window. Listing 11-13 shows the implementation of this class.

**LISTING 11-13: RequestClientProxy.cs**

```
using DomainNameDAL;

namespace RequestClient
{
  public static class RequestClientProxy
  {
    public static MainWindow AppInstance { get; set; }

    public static void AddDNRequestToList(DNRequest request)
    {
      AppInstance.AddDNRequestToList(request);
    }

    public static void UpdateDNRequest(int requestId, string status)
    {
      AppInstance.UpdateDNRequest(requestId, status);
    }
  }
}
```

*Code file [RequestClientProxy.cs] available for download at Wrox.com*

As you can see, the `AppInstance` property of this class accepts an instance of the main window, and both method calls (`AddDNRequestToList` and `UpdateDNRequest`) are forwarded to that instance. The following extract from `MainWindow.xaml.cs` shows how these methods are implemented:

```
public partial class MainWindow
{
  public ObservableCollection<DNRequest> Requests { get; set; }
  // ...
  private void Window_Loaded(object sender, RoutedEventArgs e)
  {
    // ...
    RequestClientProxy.AppInstance = this;
    // ...
  }

  public void AddDNRequestToList(DNRequest request)
  {
    Dispatcher.BeginInvoke(
      new Action(() => Requests.Add(request)));
  }

  public void UpdateDNRequest(int requestId, string status)
```

```
        {
          Dispatcher.BeginInvoke(new Action(
            () =>
              {
                for (var i = 0; i < Requests.Count; i++)
                {
                  if (Requests[i].RequestID != requestId) continue;
                  var request = Requests[i];
                  request.Status = status;
                  Requests[i] = request;
                  RequestList.SelectedIndex = i;
                  RequestList.Focus();
                  break;
                }
              }));
      }
      // ...
    }
```

The `Window_Loaded` event handler method sets the `AppInstance` property of the `RequestClientProxy` to the window instance created by the application. The methods updating the UI use the `Dispatcher.BeginInvoke` method, because the `AddDNRequestToList` and `UpdateDNRequest` methods are called from the threads of the workflow instances and not from the UI thread.

## Suspending the Workflow Instance

The most exciting part of the workflow is where its execution is suspended unless the appropriate user makes the decision about the requested domain name. In a simple application, you could implement it as a method call that is blocked until the user specifies the required input. But in the world of workflows, that's an improper solution.

This request workflow simply suspends the workflow instance, sweeps it out from memory, and releases resources held by the instance — and, of course, persists the workflow so that it could be resumed later. This step in the workflow is defined with the `WaitForApproval` custom activity:

```
new WaitForApproval
{
  BookmarkName = "ApproveRequest",
  Status = new OutArgument<string>(ctx => status.Get(ctx))
}
```

Suspending and resuming a workflow instance is done with a concept called a *bookmark*. A bookmark is a point in the workflow to remember. The `WaitForApproval` activity allows the workflow developer to set the name of this bookmark (`BookmarkName` property). However, it could even be hard-coded into the activity. The `Status` output argument will retrieve the expected user input when that is provided and the workflow is resumed.

Listing 11-14 shows the definition of `WaitForApproval`.

**LISTING 11-14: WaitForApproval.cs**

```csharp
using System.Activities;

namespace RequestClient.Activities
{
  public class WaitForApproval: NativeActivity
  {
    public string BookmarkName { get; set; }
    public OutArgument<string> Status { get; set; }

    protected override void Execute(NativeActivityContext context)
    {
      context.CreateBookmark(BookmarkName,
        (ctx, bookmark, obj) => Status.Set(ctx, obj.ToString()));
    }

    protected override bool CanInduceIdle { get { return true; } }
  }
}
```

*Code file [WaitForApproval.cs] available for download at Wrox.com*

This simple definition does a lot behind the scenes. The CanInduceIdle property's value is set to true. This setting is very important, because it allows the workflow to enter the idle state while waiting for the bookmark to resume.

The Execute method calls the context's CreateBookmark method, passing the bookmark name and a delegate to call when the bookmark is resumed. This delegate — here it is implemented with a lambda expression — accepts three parameters. The first, ctx, is a NativeActivityContext. Bookmark is a Bookmark object (not used here), and obj is an object representing the user input. When the workflow is resumed, the input provided by the user is passed and here the delegate receives it in obj. As you can see, this object is simply stored into the output parameter of this activity.

## Configuring SqlWorkflowInstanceStore

Executing the WaitForApproval method causes the workflow instance not only to be suspended, but also persisted. This is done with the SqlWorkflowInstanceStore object that is a special built-in workflow extension. (You can look at it as a plug-in component for the workflow.) Activities can check if a certain extension is assigned with the workflow, and they can use the services of the extensions.

SqlWorkflowInstanceStore is derived from InstanceStore defined in the System.Runtime .DurableInstancing namespace. You can derive your own persistence class from InstanceStore to save the workflow state to another durable storage (for example, into an XML file).

The following extract from MainWindow.xaml.cs shows how the InstanceStore is prepared, configured, and used:

```
public partial class MainWindow
{
  public ObservableCollection<DNRequest> Requests { get; set; }
  private string _PersistenceConnStr;
  private InstanceStore InstanceStore { get; set; }

  public MainWindow()
  {
    InitializeComponent();
  }

  private void Window_Loaded(object sender, RoutedEventArgs e)
  {
    var config = ConfigurationManager.
      OpenExeConfiguration(ConfigurationUserLevel.None);
    _PersistenceConnStr = ((ConnectionStringsSection)config.
      GetSection("connectionStrings")).
      ConnectionStrings["Persistence"].ConnectionString;
    InstanceStore = new SqlWorkflowInstanceStore(_PersistenceConnStr);

    var view = InstanceStore.Execute(InstanceStore.CreateInstanceHandle(),
      new CreateWorkflowOwnerCommand(),
      TimeSpan.FromSeconds(30));
    InstanceStore.DefaultInstanceOwner = view.InstanceOwner;
    // ...
    RequestClientProxy.AppInstance = this;
    // ...
  }

  private void OnRequestButtonClick(object sender, RoutedEventArgs e)
  {
    var parameters = new Dictionary<string, object>
                       {
                         {"DomainName", DomainNameBox.Text}
                       };
    DomainNameBox.Text = string.Empty;
    var wkf = new WorkflowApplication (new ProcessDomainNameRequest(),
      parameters);
    ConfigureWorkflow(wkf);
    wkf.Run();
  }

  private void ConfigureWorkflow(WorkflowApplication wkf)
  {
    wkf.InstanceStore = InstanceStore;
    wkf.PersistableIdle = e => PersistableIdleAction.Unload;
  }

  // ...
}
```

The `Window_Loaded` method is responsible for preparing a `SqlWorkflowInstanceStore` object that is to be used by all workflow instances. `Window_Loaded` first queries the application configuration file to obtain the connection string used by the SQL database, and passes it to the newly created

`SqlWorkflowInstanceStore` instance, which is immediately stored in the `InstanceStore` field. The next statement registers the application as a workflow service host, which acts as a lock owner in the persistence database.

The `OnRequestButtonClick` event handler method creates a new workflow instance and passes the workflow parameters. However, before calling the `Run` method that synchronously executes the workflow, it calls the `ConfigureWorkflow` method to pass the prepared `InstanceStore` extension to this workflow instance:

```
wkf.InstanceStore = InstanceStore;
wkf.PersistableIdle = e => PersistableIdleAction.Unload;
```

The `PersistableIdle` event property is called by the workflow when it is about to be persisted. You can add your own custom persistence actions here. This delegate simply returns a `PersistableIdleAction.Unload`. It causes the workflow to be unloaded from memory (and release resources) after its state has been persisted.

You can check the effects of these settings. Figure 11-19 shows three domain name requests in `New` state, so they are waiting for approval. The persistence database stores the state information about these workflow instances. You can easily query them, as shown in Figure 11-21.

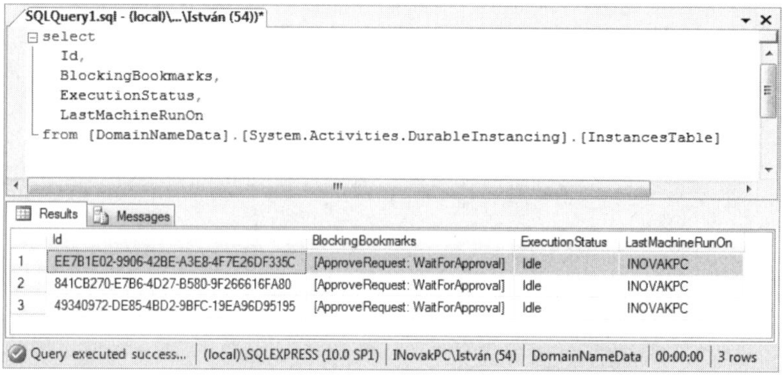

**FIGURE 11-21:** Querying the workflow persistence database

The query result shows that all the three workflow instances are in an idle state and their blocking bookmark is the `ApproveRequest` bookmark of the `WaitForApproval` activity. There are two important things this figure should implicitly suggest to you.

➤ The `LastMachineRunOn` column tells the name of the last computer on which this workflow instance had run before it went idle. WF 4.0 entirely supports resuming a workflow instance on another machine than the one on which it was frozen. For example, you could run a separate client application on another machine for approving requests.

➤ The column name `BlockingBookmarks` implicitly tells that you can have more than one bookmark for a workflow instance. A workflow can have several activities running in parallel, and each of them may have a bookmark.

## Resuming the Workflow Instance

When there is a decision about the domain name request, the workflow can be resumed. This example demonstrates that, in the real world, you can encapsulate a child workflow (or even more child workflows) into a parent workflow. The approval part is implemented as a child workflow that has only a simple activity named `ApproveDomainNameRequest`. This activity is implemented as shown in Listing 11-15.

**LISTING 11-15:** ApproveDomainNameRequest.cs

```
using System.Activities;
using DomainNameDAL;
using System.Linq;

namespace RequestClient.Activities
{
  class ApproveDomainNameRequest: CodeActivity
  {
    public InArgument<string> Status { get; set; }
    public InArgument<int> RequestId { get; set; }

    protected override void Execute(CodeActivityContext context)
    {
      var requestId = RequestId.Get(context);
      using (var dataContext = new DomainNameDataEntities())
      {
        var request = dataContext.DNRequest.
          First(rq => rq.RequestID == requestId);
        request.Status = Status.Get(context);
        dataContext.SaveChanges();
      }
    }
  }
}
```

*Code file [ApproveDomainNameRequest.cs] available for download at Wrox.com*

This activity uses the `DNRequest` entity to store the new state of the request that is passed to this activity through the `Status` input argument. To update the appropriate request, the identifier of the request also should be passed.

The most interesting part of the code is located in the `MainWindow.xaml.cs` file, as the following extract shows:

```
public partial class MainWindow
{
  private void OnApproveButtonClick(object sender, RoutedEventArgs e)
  {
    ChangeRequestStatus("Approved");
  }

  private void OnDenyButtonClick(object sender, RoutedEventArgs e)
```

```
    {
      ChangeRequestStatus("Denied");
    }

    private void ChangeRequestStatus(string newStatus)
    {
      var request = RequestList.SelectedItem as DNRequest;
      if (request == null) return;
      var parameters = new Dictionary<string, object>
                          {
                            {"Status", newStatus},
                            {"RequestId", request.RequestID}
                          };
      var wkf = new WorkflowApplication(new ApproveDomainNameRequest(), parameters);
      ConfigureWorkflow(wkf);
      wkf.Run();
      var toResumeWkf = new WorkflowApplication(new ProcessDomainNameRequest());
      ConfigureWorkflow(toResumeWkf);
      toResumeWkf.Load(request.WorkflowID);
      toResumeWkf.ResumeBookmark("ApproveRequest", newStatus);
    }
  }
```

The work is done in the `ChangeRequestStatus` method that accepts the status sting (`"Approved"` or `"Denied"`) as an input parameter. From the currently selected list box item, it obtains the identifier of the request and starts the `ApproveDomainNameRequest` workflow that saves the status back to the database. After the approval, the idle workflow must be resumed. First, a new instance of the workflow is created, but instead of starting it with the `Run` method, something different happens. The `Load` method is called with the identifier of the workflow instance. (This is why a `DNRequest` entity stores a `WorkflowID` field.) It retrieves the status of the instance from the database.

The key is the `ResumeBookmark` method that specifies the bookmark to resume, and passes the status of the request that is used by the `WaitForApproval` activity.

As a result, the main workflow is resumed, and the `InvokeMethod` activity following `WaitForApproval` runs and updates the UI with the new request state.

## Workflow Tracking

The workflow run-time provides you with special built-in extensions that you can use to track a workflow's execution. These are very useful for both diagnostics and the recording of an audit trail. In this section, you will examine WF 4.0 tracking extensions through an enhanced version of `DomainNameWorkflow`. This project is named `DomainNameWorkflowTracking`, and its source code is among the others that you can download from this book's companion website (www.wrox.com). Before turning to the source code of this project, let's explore an overview of the tracking pattern used by WF 4.0.

### Tracking Records

The workflow run-time raises tracking events when something changes in the state of a workflow instance. You can also add your own events to a workflow. Events are represented by classes derived from the `TrackingRecord` abstract class of the `System.Activities.Tracking` namespace. Table 11-13 summarizes these classes.

**TABLE 11-13:** TrackingRecord Derived Types

| TYPE | DESCRIPTION |
| --- | --- |
| `ActivityStateRecord` | This class describes a tracking record for an activity. The workflow run-time creates a record when the state of a specific activity in a workflow instance changes. |
| `ActivityScheduledRecord` | This class represents a tracking record of an activity being scheduled for execution. |
| `WorkflowInstanceRecord` | This class describes a tracking record for a workflow instance. The run-time creates a record when the state of workflow instance changes. This class has several derived classes associated with special workflow instance events, such as aborting, suspending, terminating an instance, or observing unhandled exception. |
| `BookmarkResumptionRecord` | This class contains tracking information about a resumed bookmark. |
| `CustomTrackingRecord` | This class contains activity-specific or user-defined tracking information. Its three built-in derived classes include `InteropTrackingRecord`, `ReceiveMessageRecord`, and `SendMessageRecord`. |

Tracking records contain useful information about the event; you can access them through their properties. You can also create your own `TrackingRecord` derived classes. Use `CustomTrackingRecord` as the base class for events belonging to your custom activities.

## Participating in the Tracking Process

The run-time uses special extensions inherited from the `TrackingParticipant` abstract class of the `System.Activities.Tracking` namespace to allow catching of the tracking events. Add one or more extensions to a workflow instance, and those are notified when a tracking event happens. Then your extensions can process the tracking records generated by the events.

WF 4.0 implements only one built-in tracking participant. It is `EtwTrackingParticipant` that emits an Event Tracking for Windows (ETW) event to an ETW session that contains the data from the tracking record.

When you add a tracking participant extension to a workflow instance, you can assign it with a tracking profile. The profile tells the run-time the set of events the participant is interested in. The tracking profile is assembled by several tracking queries that help the developer to set up a profile. For example, the participant's profile can define a query saying that it is interested only in activity state changes where the state is either "New" or "Closed." The run-time won't forward any other kind of events to the participant.

Later in this chapter, you will see a concrete example of creating a tracking profile with the help of tracking queries.

## Persisting Tracking Information

So, now you have enough information to dive into the source code. Open the source code of the `DomainNameWorkflowTracking` project so that you can examine it. This project has exactly the same functionality as `DomainNameWorkflow`, except that it implements a tracking participant that stores tracking event information in a SQL Server database table.

In order for you to see how this sample works, run the `DNRequestTracking.sql` script file in the `SqlScripts` folder against the `DomainNameData` database. Open the file, right-click, and start Execute SQL. When the Connect dialog appears, click Options, select the `DomainNameData` database in the Connection Properties tab, and click Connect.

This script creates a table called `DNRequestTracking`, and the `DNRequest.edmx` file defines the entity to manipulate this table.

The key type of this application is `DNRequestTrackingParticipant` that implements a custom tracking participant, as shown in Listing 11-16.

**LISTING 11-16: DNRequestTrackingParticipant.cs**

```csharp
using System;
using System.Activities.Tracking;

namespace RequestClient.Extensions
{
  internal class DNRequestTrackingParticipant: TrackingParticipant
  {
    protected override void Track(TrackingRecord record, TimeSpan timeout)
    {
      using (var dataContext = new DomainNameDataEntities())
      {
        var wtr = record as WorkflowInstanceRecord;
        if (wtr != null)
        {
          var tr = new DNRequestTracking
          {
            WorkflowID = wtr.InstanceId,
            Type = "W",
            EventDate = DateTime.UtcNow,
            Data = wtr.State
          };
          dataContext.AddToDNRequestTracking(tr);
        }
        var brtr = record as BookmarkResumptionRecord;
        if (brtr != null)
```

```
        {
          var tr = new DNRequestTracking
          {
            WorkflowID = brtr.InstanceId,
            Type = "B",
            EventDate = DateTime.UtcNow,
            Data = brtr.BookmarkName
          };
          dataContext.AddToDNRequestTracking(tr);
        }
        var astr = record as ActivityStateRecord;
        if (astr != null)
        {
          var tr = new DNRequestTracking
          {
            WorkflowID = astr.InstanceId,
            Type = "A",
            EventDate = DateTime.UtcNow,
            Data = astr.Activity.Name + "(" + astr.State + ")"
          };
          dataContext.AddToDNRequestTracking(tr);
        }
        var ctr = record as CustomTrackingRecord;
        if (ctr != null)
        {
          var tr = new DNRequestTracking
          {
            WorkflowID = ctr.InstanceId,
            Type = "C",
            EventDate = DateTime.UtcNow,
            Data = ctr.Data["Message"].ToString()
          };
          dataContext.AddToDNRequestTracking(tr);
        }
        dataContext.SaveChanges();
      }
    }
  }
}
```

*Code file [DNRequestTrackingParticipant.cs] available for download at Wrox.com*

Although the source code for this class seems long, its functionality and logic is easy to understand. The DNRequestTrackingParticipant class is derived from the TrackingParticipant class. The overridden Track method accepts two arguments:

➤  record is a TrackingRecord holding the properties of event raised.

➤  timeout is a TimeSpan to define the maximum time span that can be spent in this method body. Theoretically, you should implement this method to meet this timeout expectation.

The body of Track checks the type of the TrackingRecord passed, initializes, and then saves a DNRequestTracking entity accordingly.

## Configuring the Tracking Participant

Before using the `DNRequestTrackingParticipant` extension, you must configure it, and also add it to the workflow instance that is assumed to use it. The following extract from `MainWindow.xaml.cs` shows how you can do this:

```csharp
public partial class MainWindow
{
  // ...
  private DNRequestTrackingParticipant _TrackingParticipant;

  private void Window_Loaded(object sender, RoutedEventArgs e)
  {
    // ...
    InitTrackingParticipant();
    // ...
  }

  private void InitTrackingParticipant()
  {
    var profile =
      new TrackingProfile
      {
        Name = "DNRequestTrackingProfile",
        Queries =
          {
            new WorkflowInstanceQuery {States = { "*" } },
            new BookmarkResumptionQuery { Name = "*" },
            new ActivityStateQuery
            {
              ActivityName = "*",
              States = { "*" }
            },
            new CustomTrackingQuery
            {
              Name = "*",
              ActivityName = "*"
            }
          }
      };
    _TrackingParticipant =
      new DNRequestTrackingParticipant { TrackingProfile = profile };
  }

  private void ConfigureWorkflow(WorkflowApplication wkf)
  {
    wkf.InstanceStore = InstanceStore;
    wkf.PersistableIdle = e => PersistableIdleAction.Unload;
    wkf.Extensions.Add(_TrackingParticipant);
  }
}
```

When the application's main window is loaded, the `InitTrackingParticipant` method creates a `TrackingProfile` and passes it to the newly created `DNRequestTrackingParticipant` instance. As you can see, the `TrackingProfile` is composed from four `TrackingQuery`-derived instances (`WorkflowInstanceQuery`, `BookmarkResumptionQuery`, `ActivityStateQuery` and `CustomTrackingQuery`). The queries use properties to set up filters for specific tracking record instances. The profile with the settings in the listing accepts any tracking records.

The last line in `ConfigureWorkflow` adds the newly created tracking participant extension to the workflow instance. Remember, `ConfigureWorkflow` is called when a new workflow instance is created, but before it is started. If the last line were not in this method, the workflow instance would not use the tracking participant.

## Custom Tracking Events

In addition to the tracking events raised by the run-time, you can also define other tracking points and events in your custom activities. The `ApproveDomainNameRequest` and `CreateDomainNameRequest` activities have been extended with a custom tracking event. Listing 11-17 shows how it is implemented for `ApproveDomainNameRequest`.

Available for download on Wrox.com

**LISTING 11-17:** ApproveDomainNameRequest.cs

```csharp
using System.Activities;
using System.Activities.Tracking;
using System.Linq;

namespace RequestClient.Activities
{
  class ApproveDomainNameRequest: CodeActivity
  {
    public InArgument<string> Status { get; set; }
    public InArgument<int> RequestId { get; set; }

    protected override void Execute(CodeActivityContext context)
    {
      var requestId = RequestId.Get(context);
      using (var dataContext = new DomainNameDataEntities())
      {
        var request = dataContext.DNRequest.
          First(rq => rq.RequestID == requestId);
        request.Status = Status.Get(context);
        dataContext.SaveChanges();
        // --- Custom tracking point
        var userRecord =
          new CustomTrackingRecord("Custom")
          {
            Data = { { "Message", "DNRequest updated" } }
          };
        context.Track(userRecord);
      }
    }
  }
}
```

*Code file [ApproveDomainNameRequest.cs] available for download at Wrox.com*

The Data property of the CustomTrackingRecord instance is a dictionary of key and value pairs. Here a "Message" key is passed. When the tracking participant persists a CustomTrackingRecord (see Listing 11-16), it extracts the value belonging to the "Message" key.

## Running the DomainNameWorkflowTracking Application

Now, you can try this tracking participant to see how it works. Run the application, send a request for a domain name (let's say WF4Rocks.org), and approve this request. Close the application and run the following query against the database:

```
SELECT WorkflowID, [Type], [Data]
  FROM [DomainNameData].[dbo].[DNRequestTracking]
```

This query produces results similar to the following:

```
WorkflowID                               Type Data
---------------------------------------- ---- -----------------------------------
6DA4292C-F675-4714-AEA6-23D9D5287C72 W    Started
6DA4292C-F675-4714-AEA6-23D9D5287C72 A    ProcessDomainNameRequest(Executing)
6DA4292C-F675-4714-AEA6-23D9D5287C72 A    Process Domain Name Request(Executing)
6DA4292C-F675-4714-AEA6-23D9D5287C72 A    CreateDomainNameRequest(Executing)
6DA4292C-F675-4714-AEA6-23D9D5287C72 C    DNRequest created
6DA4292C-F675-4714-AEA6-23D9D5287C72 A    CreateDomainNameRequest(Closed)
6DA4292C-F675-4714-AEA6-23D9D5287C72 A    InvokeMethod(Executing)
6DA4292C-F675-4714-AEA6-23D9D5287C72 A    InvokeMethod(Closed)
6DA4292C-F675-4714-AEA6-23D9D5287C72 A    WaitForApproval(Executing)
6DA4292C-F675-4714-AEA6-23D9D5287C72 W    Idle
6DA4292C-F675-4714-AEA6-23D9D5287C72 W    Unloaded
6DA4292C-F675-4714-AEA6-23D9D5287C72 W    Resumed
6DA4292C-F675-4714-AEA6-23D9D5287C72 B    ApproveRequest
9E3BB17D-2B43-4EA6-A9A4-1623B2D51FEF W    Started
6DA4292C-F675-4714-AEA6-23D9D5287C72 A    WaitForApproval(Closed)
9E3BB17D-2B43-4EA6-A9A4-1623B2D51FEF A    ApproveDomainNameRequest(Executing)
6DA4292C-F675-4714-AEA6-23D9D5287C72 A    InvokeMethod(Executing)
9E3BB17D-2B43-4EA6-A9A4-1623B2D51FEF C    DNRequest updated
6DA4292C-F675-4714-AEA6-23D9D5287C72 A    InvokeMethod(Closed)
9E3BB17D-2B43-4EA6-A9A4-1623B2D51FEF A    ApproveDomainNameRequest(Closed)
6DA4292C-F675-4714-AEA6-23D9D5287C72 A    Process Domain Name Request(Closed)
6DA4292C-F675-4714-AEA6-23D9D5287C72 A    ProcessDomainNameRequest(Closed)
9E3BB17D-2B43-4EA6-A9A4-1623B2D51FEF W    Completed
9E3BB17D-2B43-4EA6-A9A4-1623B2D51FEF W    Deleted
6DA4292C-F675-4714-AEA6-23D9D5287C72 W    Completed
6DA4292C-F675-4714-AEA6-23D9D5287C72 W    Deleted
```

In the list, you can see the workflow instance and activity state changes. You can also see two different WorkflowID values. The one beginning with 6 belongs to the workflow started when you clicked the Send Request button; the other one is triggered by the Approve button.

## WORKFLOW SERVICES

Earlier in this chapter, you learned how to host a workflow within a console application, or within a WPF application. Workflows also can be hosted in a web service, which provides an ideal way to expose workflow solutions to clients. WF 4.0 leverages WCF features and provides a great design-time and run-time support for web service based workflows. In this section, you will learn the basics of creating and using workflow services.

## Creating a Workflow Service

WF 4.0 has a very strong integration with WCF. As you learned earlier, there are several activities handling WCF messages and managing important techniques such as message correlation. Workflow services are the result of marrying workflows with WCF web services.

Create a new project with the WCF Service Workflow Application template and name the project `SimpleWorkflowService`. Figure 11-22 shows that you can find this template within the Workflow category in the New Project dialog.

**FIGURE 11-22:** Select the WCF Workflow Service Application template

The project is a special WCF web service that hosts a workflow. (You'll recognize the `Web.config` file). The serviced workflow is defined in the `Service1.xamlx` file, and when you open it, you can see a small `Sequence` activity already prepared for you. Figure 11-23 shows the designer surface, and you can see that the workflow service contains a `Receive` and a `Send` activity.

Workflow services do not have input and output arguments. You won't find the Arguments link at the bottom of the designer surface. Of course, workflow services can have inputs and outputs, but those are not implemented as `InArgument` or `OutArgument` instances. A workflow services receives messages. It extracts the input parameters and processes them according to the required functionality. When the result is prepared, it uses messages to send back the result to the caller.

**FIGURE 11-23:** The basic workflow created by the template

You can handle input and output parameters of workflow services in two ways:

➤ They can be standard WCF message classes with the `MessageContract` (and related) attributes.

➤ You can handle them as individual parameters.

In this example, you are going to use parameters. The input and output parameters are stored in workflow variables, so first declare them. When you click the Variables link in the designer, the Variables pane shows two variables named `handle` and `data`. Do not touch `handle`, but rename `data` to `operand`. Add a new `Int32` variable, and name it `result`. Figure 11-24 shows the Variables pane with these declarations.

| Name | Variable type | Scope | Default |
|---|---|---|---|
| handle | CorrelationHandle | Sequential Service | Handle cannot be initialized |
| operand | Int32 | Sequential Service | Enter a VB expression |
| result | Int32 | Sequential Service | Enter a VB expression |
| Create Variable | | | |

| Variables | Imports | | 🔍 100% ▢ ▣ ▣ |

**FIGURE 11-24:** Workflow service variables

Rename the `OperationName` property of `ReceiveRequest` to `GetSquare` and click the View Message link beside Content. Select the Parameters option and add a new `Operand` parameter as an `Int32` to the grid, assign it to the `operand` variable as Figure 11-25 shows, and click OK.

Now, click the View Message link of the `SendResponse` activity and select the Parameters option. Define `Result` as a new `Int32` parameter. Assign it to the `result` variable, as shown in Figure 11-26.

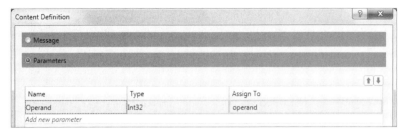

**FIGURE 11-25:** Define the input parameter of the workflow service

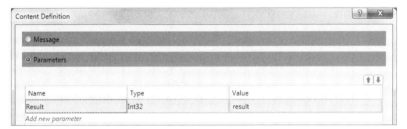

**FIGURE 11-26:** Define the output parameter of the workflow service

The workflow service now can receive input parameters and send back the result. Add an `Assign` activity between the `Receive` and `Send` activities to declare the processing step. Set its `To` property to `result`, and its `Value` property to `operand*operand`.

This simple service is ready to run! Set `Service1.xamlx` as the start page and run the project by pressing Ctrl+F5. The WCF Test client application starts. Double-click on the `GetSquare` method in the tree view, specify an operand value (let's say 123), and click the Invoke button. The Response pane displays the result. Figure 11-27 shows the XML request and response data.

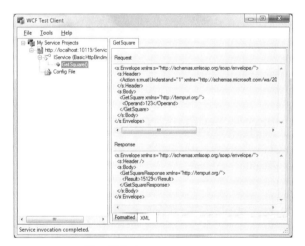

**FIGURE 11-27:** The WCF Test Client in action

## Using WorkflowServiceHost

In many cases, you may host workflow services in your special web applications, maybe in Windows services. You are not obliged to use the WCF Workflow Service Application template. You can place the workflow services in any other kind of host applications.

WF 4.0 provides you the `WorkflowServiceHost` class in the `System.ServiceModel.Activities` namespace so that you can easily exploit your workflows through web service interfaces. WCF workflow services also utilize `WorkflowServiceHost`.

In this section, you will learn how to use `WorkflowServiceHost`. Instead of creating an application from scratch, you will examine a prebuilt sample named `DomainNameWorkflowWithHost`. As you may guess from the name, this sample is a modified version of the `DomainNameWorkflowTracking` application, and you can find this project in the source code that you can download from this book's companion website (www.wrox.com). The application modifies the original workflow so that instead of manual domain name request approval, it uses a web service. This web service will be hosted by the same client application that is used to create requests.

Start Visual Studio 2010 with Administrator privileges (that is, using the "Run as administrator" command).

 *Because of the enhanced security in Windows Vista and Windows 7, your application might not work. The workflow may generate an exception that indicates you do not have access to the specified port. You have two alternatives to resolve this situation. First, you can run Visual Studio with administrative privileges. Second, you can grant your Windows login access to the desired ports. To do this, start a command window with administrator privileges and execute the following command:*

```
netsh http add urlacl url=http://+:8765/ user=Domain\UserName
```

*The 8765 port here is the one used in this sample application.*

## Changing the Main Workflow

The domain name request workflow is defined in the `ProcessDomainNameRequest` activity. The previous version of this workflow had the four activities in a sequence:

```
public ProcessDomainNameRequest()
{
  // ...
  Implementation =
    () =>
    new Sequence
    {
      DisplayName = "Process Domain Name Request",
      Variables = { ... },
      Activities =
        {
          new CreateDomainNameRequest { ... },
          new InvokeMethod { ... },
```

```
            new WaitForApproval { ... },
            new InvokeMethod { ... }
        }
    };
}
```

The `WaitForApproval` activity was used to wait while the user approves the request. This activity has been replaced to send a message to the hosted workflow that processes the request and sends back the approval message. Listing 11-18 shows how the `ProcessDomainNameRequest` class has been changed.

---

**LISTING 11-18:** ProcessDomainNameRequest.cs (extract)

```csharp
using System;
using System.Activities;
using System.Activities.Statements;
using System.ServiceModel;
using System.ServiceModel.Activities;

namespace RequestClient.Activities
{
  public sealed class ProcessDomainNameRequest: Activity
  {
    public InArgument<string> DomainName { get; set; }
    public ProcessDomainNameRequest()
    {
      var request = new Variable<DNRequest>("request");
      var status = new Variable<string>("status");
      var send = new Send
      {
        OperationName = "Approve",
        ServiceContractName = "ApproveDNRequest",
        Content = new SendParametersContent
        {
          Parameters =
          {
            { "request", new InArgument<DNRequest>(ctx => request.Get(ctx)) }
          }
        },
        EndpointAddress = new InArgument<Uri>
          (env => new Uri("http://localhost:8765/ApproveDNRequest")),
        Endpoint = new Endpoint
        {
          Binding = new BasicHttpBinding()
        }
      }; // Define the SendRequest workflow
      Implementation =
        () =>
        new Sequence
        {
          DisplayName = "Process Domain Name Request",
          Variables = { request, status },
```

*continues*

**LISTING 11-18** *(continued)*

```
            Activities =
            {
                // --- Not changed, body omitted for clarity
                new CreateDomainNameRequest { ... },
                // --- Not changed, body omitted for clarity
                new InvokeMethod { ... },
                // --- WaitForApproval removed
                new CorrelationScope
                {
                    Body = new Sequence
                    {
                        Activities =
                        {
                            send,
                            new ReceiveReply
                            {
                                Request = send,
                                Content = new ReceiveParametersContent
                                {
                                    Parameters = {{"status", new OutArgument<string>(status)}}
                                }
                            }
                        }
                    }
                },
                // --- Not changed, body omitted for clarity
                new InvokeMethod { ... }
            }
        };
    }
  }
}
```

*Code file [ProcessDomainNameRequest.cs] available for download at Wrox.com*

The `WaitForApproval` activity has been replaced with a `CorrelationScope` activity. It sends a message defined in the `send` activity, and waits while the correlated response comes back from the approval workflow. Then, it puts the value of the "status" element of the response into the `status` workflow variable (it is used by subsequent activities).

The request message is defined by a `Send` activity. It is instantiated before the `Implementation` part of the workflow, because it must be passed to be the first activity in the sequence of the `CorrelationScope`. The `ServiceContractName` and the `OperationName` specified here must be exactly the same as used at the service side (examined in more detail later) so that the service can understand the message. The requested domain name is passed in the `"request"` message parameter (its value is taken from the `request` variable).

The `Send` activity sets up the service endpoint address and the bindings to access the approval service.

## The Approval Workflow

The `WorkflowServiceHost` will host the `ApprovementWorkflow` activity that listens to incoming requests, makes the decision about approving or denying the domain name, and sends back the result in a message. Listing 11-19 shows the source code of this activity.

**LISTING 11-19:** ApprovementWorkflow.cs

```csharp
using System;
using System.Activities;
using System.Activities.Statements;
using System.ServiceModel.Activities;

namespace RequestClient.Activities
{
  public class ApprovementWorkflow: Activity
  {
    public ApprovementWorkflow()
    {
      var request = new Variable<DNRequest>("request");
      var status = new Variable<string>("status");
      var receive = new Receive
      {
        OperationName = "Approve",
        ServiceContractName = "ApproveDNRequest",
        CanCreateInstance = true,
        Content = new ReceiveParametersContent
        {
          Parameters = { {"request", new OutArgument<DNRequest>(request)} }
        }
      };

      Implementation =
        () =>
        new Sequence
          {
            DisplayName = "Approvement Workflow",
            Variables = { request, status },
            Activities =
              {
                receive,
                new Delay { Duration = TimeSpan.FromSeconds(10) },
                new ApproveDomainNameRequest
                  {
                    Request = new InArgument<DNRequest>(ctx => request.Get(ctx)),
                    Status = new OutArgument<string>(ctx => status.Get(ctx))
                  },
                new SendReply
                  {
                    Request = receive,
                    Content = new SendParametersContent
```

*continues*

**LISTING 11-19** *(continued)*

```
                    {
                        Parameters = { {"status", new InArgument<string>(status)} }
                    }
                }
            }
        };
    }
  }
}
```

*Code file [ApprovementWorkflow.cs] available for download at Wrox.com*

Here, a `Receive` activity is instantiated that sets up its `ServiceContractName` name and `OperationName` properties to the same as used by the `Send` activity in Listing 11-18. The `CanCreateInstance` property is set to `true`, indicating that a new workflow instance is created to process the message if the message does not correlate to an existing workflow instance. These settings provide that the approval workflow receives the message sent by the client. It extracts the `"request"` message parameter and puts it into the `request` variable.

The workflow is simple. After it receives the request message, it delays for 10 seconds, emulating a long process. Then the `ApproveDomainNameRequest` activity is invoked to approve or deny the domain name. The result is sent back to the caller by the `SendReply` activity.

You can see that `SendReply` sets its `Request` property to the message received. It is the key of the correlation mechanism. When sending the response message back to the caller, `SendReply` extracts the correlation information from the received message and puts it into the response. The caller side will use this information to correlate the appropriate request with the matching response.

You can also see that the `Receive` activity does not specify either a service endpoint address or a binding. The activity obtains these settings from the hosting `WorkflowServiceHost` instance.

The `ApproveDomainNameRequest`'s logic is very simple. It approves all domain names ending with `".org"` and denies any other requests. Listing 11-20 shows the source code of this activity.

**LISTING 11-20: ApproveDomainNameRequest.cs**

```
using System.Activities;
using System.Activities.Tracking;
using System.Linq;

namespace RequestClient.Activities
{
  class ApproveDomainNameRequest: CodeActivity
  {
    public InArgument<DNRequest> Request { get; set; }
    public OutArgument<string> Status { get; set; }

    protected override void Execute(CodeActivityContext context)
```

```
    {
      using (var dataContext = new DomainNameDataEntities())
      {
        var requestId = Request.Get(context).RequestID;
        var request = dataContext.DNRequest.
          First(rq => rq.RequestID == requestId);
        request.Status = request.RequestedName.EndsWith(".org")
          ? "Approved" : "Denied" ;
        dataContext.SaveChanges();
        Status.Set(context, request.Status);
        var userRecord =
          new CustomTrackingRecord("Custom")
          {
            Data = { { "Message", "DNRequest updated" } }
          };
        context.Track(userRecord);
      }
    }
  }
}
```

*Code file [ApproveDomainNameRequest.cs] available for download at Wrox.com*

## Configuring WorkflowServiceHost

The last step to put the things together is creating and configuring the `WorkflowServiceHost` instance encapsulating the `ApprovementWorkflow`. It is done in the `Window_Loaded` method of the main window where `InitServiceHost` is called:

```
public partial class MainWindow
{
  // ...
  private WorkflowServiceHost _ApproveWorkflowHost;
  // ...

  private void Window_Loaded(object sender, RoutedEventArgs e)
  {
    // ...
    InitServiceHost();
    // ...
  }

  private void Window_Unloaded(object sender, RoutedEventArgs e)
  {
    _ApproveWorkflowHost.Close();
  }

  private void InitServiceHost()
  {
    var approveService =
      new WorkflowService
        {
          Name = "ApproveDNRequest",
```

```
                    Body = new ApprovementWorkflow(),
                    Endpoints =
                        {
                            new Endpoint
                                {
                                    ServiceContractName = "ApproveDNRequest",
                                    AddressUri = new Uri("http://localhost:8765/ApproveDNRequest"),
                                    Binding = new BasicHttpBinding(),
                                }
                        }
                };
            _ApproveWorkflowHost = new WorkflowServiceHost(approveService);
            var trackingBehavior = new DNRequestTrackingBehavior();
            _ApproveWorkflowHost.Description.Behaviors.Add(trackingBehavior);
            _ApproveWorkflowHost.Open();
        }
    }
```

The `InitServiceHost` method creates an instance of `WorkflowService`, and this instance is passed to the constructor of `WorkflowServiceHost`. The `WorkflowService` instance creates a new `ApprovementWorkflow` as the `Body` of the host, and encapsulates the service endpoints the host is listening to. The code configuring the host does not stop here. The `WorkflowServiceHost` is extended with a `DNRequestTrackingBehaivor`.

As the last step of the configuration, the `Open` method starts the host. It listens to messages and processes them unless the application is closed. In this case, the `Window_Unloaded` event handler method closes the host and stops it from responding to any more messages.

## Workflow Behaviors

You can add behaviors to the `WorkflowServiceHost` class when you configure the host instance. In the previous versions of the `DomainNameWorkflow`, you instantiated a workflow instance programmatically as a response for a button's `Click` event, and you were able to add extensions (for example, the `DNRequestTrackingParticipant`) to that instance. The `WorkflowServiceHost` does not allow you direct instantiation, so another mechanism is required to inject extensions into the workflow instances.

This is where behaviors enter into the picture. Where a `WorkflowServiceHost` instantiates a new workflow, it goes through all its defined behaviors, generates and configures the associated extension, and then adds it to the workflow instance before that is started.

The `DomainNameWorkflowWithHost` project uses the `DNRequestTrackingBehavior` to extend the workflows with the following:

```
    var trackingBehavior = new DNRequestTrackingBehavior();
    _ApproveWorkflowHost.Description.Behaviors.Add(trackingBehavior);
```

This behavior allows the approval workflow to use the same tracking extension as the request workflow. Listing 11-21 shows the definition of this tracking behavior.

**LISTING 11-21:** DNRequestTrackingBehavior Definition

```
internal sealed class DNRequestTrackingBehavior: IServiceBehavior
{
  public void ApplyDispatchBehavior(ServiceDescription serviceDescription,
    ServiceHostBase serviceHostBase)
  {
    var workflowServiceHost = serviceHostBase as WorkflowServiceHost;
    if (workflowServiceHost == null) return;
    var tracker = new DNRequestTrackingParticipant();
    workflowServiceHost.WorkflowExtensions.Add(tracker);
  }

  public void AddBindingParameters(ServiceDescription serviceDescription,
    ServiceHostBase serviceHostBase,
    Collection<ServiceEndpoint> endpoints,
    BindingParameterCollection bindingParameters)
  {
  }

  public void Validate(ServiceDescription serviceDescription,
    ServiceHostBase serviceHostBase)
  {
  }
}
```

*Code file [DNRequestTrackingParticipant.cs] available for download at Wrox.com*

The class implements the `IServiceBehavior` interface of the `System.ServiceModel.Description` namespace. This interface can be found in the `System.ServiceModel.dll` assembly, so it is the part of WCF. This behavior uses only the `ApplyDispatchBehavior` method that explicitly adds a `DNRequestTrackingParticipant` to the `WorkflowExtensions` collection of the service host. The host will inject this extension into any new workflow instances.

## Running the Application

The application is ready to run. When you start it, you can add new requests. Because the approval process takes about 10 seconds, it takes about 10 seconds while a new request goes to either Approved or Denied state. Figure 11-28 shows the application in action.

You can try to send more than one request. Later, when you query the `DNRequestTracking` table, you can observe that each approval workflow takes a separate workflow instance, and workflow instances processing overlapping requests also overlap.

**FIGURE 11-28:** The application in action

## SUMMARY

WF 4.0 is not just a simple enhancement of WF 3.5. It has been totally redesigned and rewritten. It now uses a XAML description of workflows, and provides a WPF-based designer that can handle larger workflows than its predecessor.

WF 4.0 uses a new architecture where workflows and activities have a common root object (System.Activities.Activity). With this model, you can describe sequential and flowchart-like workflows, or even mix them. The activity library shipped with .NET Framework 4.0 contains about 40 new activities, and you can also develop your own custom activities easily.

WF 4.0 provides a great support for the compensating transaction model, and allows you to create workflow services in a few minutes. The workflow model is extensible. You can create extensions for workflow persistence and tracking, and also inject your own custom extensions to workflows.

Chapter 12 focuses on enhancements to the .NET Data Framework, including Language Integrated Query (LINQ), Entity Framework, and the Entity Data Source Control.

# 12

# Enhancements to the .NET Data Framework

This chapter focuses on enhancements to the .NET Data Framework. The .NET Data Framework is an important component of the .NET Framework because it provides the key pieces of functionality to get, manipulate, and update data to various data persistence stores. Microsoft has added a vast amount of functionality in this space, starting with the .NET 3.0 release and with the introduction of Language Integrated Query (LINQ). In this chapter, you will learn about the following:

- ➤ Language Integrated Query (LINQ)
- ➤ Parallel LINQ (PLINQ)
- ➤ Entity Framework
- ➤ Entity Data Source Control

## LANGUAGE INTEGRATED QUERY (LINQ)

As mentioned, LINQ is a query translation pipeline that was introduced as part of the .NET Framework 3.0.

According to Microsoft, "The LINQ Project is a codename for a set of extensions to the .NET Framework that encompasses language-integrated query, set, and transform operations. It extends C# and Visual Basic with native language syntax for queries and provides class libraries to take advantage of these capabilities."

LINQ provides an Object Relational Mapping (ORM) among business objects and the underlying data source(s) in your application. LINQ allows you to integrate your queries right into the object model. In essence, it provides a simplified framework for accessing relational data in an object-oriented way. LINQ queries are strongly typed, and you can detect errors in your queries at compile time itself. You can also debug your LINQ queries easily.

In addition to the benefits of LINQ when used as an ORM tool, LINQ can also be beneficial when using any in-memory operations working with arrays or collections for searching, filtering, and ordering of records.

 *Note that any language targeted at the Common Language Run-time (CLR) has built-in support for LINQ. So, you can use C#, F#, and Visual Basic (VB) 9 to write your LINQ queries.*

## LINQ Operators

An *operator* is a symbol that works on an *operand* to perform a specific operation. There are a number of operators in LINQ to facilitate query operations.

The `System.Query.Sequence` static class in the `System.Query` namespace is comprised of a set of static methods. These methods, commonly known as *standard query operators*, are of the following two types:

➤ Standard query operators for `IEnumerable(T)` operate on objects that implement the `IEnumerable(T)` interface

➤ Standard query operators for `IQueryable(T)` operate on objects that implement the `IQueryable(T)` interface

Table 12-1 shows the LINQ operators and their categories.

**TABLE 12-1:** LINQ Operators

| OPERATOR TYPE | OPERATORS |
| --- | --- |
| Aggregation | Aggregate |
| | Average |
| | Count |
| | LongCount |
| | Max |
| | Min |
| | Sum |
| Conversion | Cast |
| | OfType |
| | ToArray |
| | ToDictionary |
| | ToList |
| | ToLookup |
| | ToSequence |

| OPERATOR TYPE | OPERATORS |
| --- | --- |
| Element | DefaultIfEmpty |
| | ElementAt |
| | ElementAtOrDefault |
| | First |
| | FirstOrDefault |
| | Last |
| | LastOrDefault |
| | Single |
| | SingleOrDefault |
| Equality | EqualAll |
| Generation | Empty |
| | Range |
| | Repeat |
| Grouping | GroupBy |
| Joining | GroupJoin |
| | Join |
| Ordering | OrderBy |
| | ThenBy |
| | OrderByDescending |
| | ThenByDescending |
| | Reverse |
| Partitioning | Skip |
| | SkipWhile |
| | Take |
| | TakeWhile |
| Quantifying | All |
| | Any |
| | Contains |
| Restriction | Where |
| Selection | Select |
| | SelectMany |

*continues*

**TABLE 12.1** *(continued)*

| OPERATOR TYPE | OPERATORS |
|---|---|
| Set | Concat |
| | Distinct |
| | Except |
| | Intersect |
| | Union |

Using LINQ, you can easily query and organize items in a list, filter for a specific list item or items, or even transpose objects into other objects. The following samples show a few of these concepts:

```
String[] cities = {"London", "New York", "New Delhi", "Tokyo", "Paris"};
//Sort items by name
var sortedResults = from x in cities
                    orderby x
                    select x;
//Find cities that start with New
var newCities = from x in cities
                where x.StartsWith("New")
                select x;

//output results
Console.WriteLine("Sorted")
foreach (var city in sortedResults)
Console.WriteLine(city);
Console.Writeline("Filtered")
foreach (var city in newCities)
Console.WriteLine(city);
```

From these examples you can see that the basic structure of a LINQ query starts with `from __ in __`. You define an alias to represent an item in the collection being queried. In these examples, x was used to represent an individual city. For the rest of the LINQ query, Visual Studio provides full IntelliSense support for the properties and methods made available by the queried object. The next portion of the sample queries are either a limiting `where` clause or a `orderby` clause used to re-order the lists.

This is just taste of the power of LINQ and how it can simplify actions when working with objects in memory.

## LINQ Implementations

LINQ has been implemented to work against a number of data and object sources. The most common implementations include the following.

➤   LINQ to Objects

➤   LINQ to XML

➤   LINQ to DataSet

➤ LINQ to SQL

➤ LINQ to Entities

## LINQ to Objects

LINQ to Objects is an implementation of LINQ that can be used to query the in-memory objects or in-memory collections of objects. Note that such objects or collections of such objects should be of type `T:System.Collections.IEnumerable` or `T:System.Collections.Generic`.

Let's take a look at how you can use LINQ to Objects to query an in-memory collection of objects. Consider the following class:

```
public class Product
{
public int ProductID { get; set; }
public string ProductName { get; set; }
public string ProductType { get; set; }
public int Quantity { get; set; }
}
```

The following code snippet illustrates how you can populate a generic `List` of type `Product` and return it:

```
static List<Product> PopulateData()
        {
            List<Product> products = new List<Product>();
            products.Add(new Product { ProductID = 1, ProductName =
                "Lenovo", ProductType = "Laptop", Quantity = 100 });
            products.Add(new Product { ProductID = 2, ProductName =
                "Compaq", ProductType = "Laptop", Quantity = 150 });
            products.Add(new Product { ProductID = 3, ProductName =
                "DELL", ProductType = "Laptop", Quantity = 200 });
            products.Add(new Product { ProductID = 4, ProductName =
                "HCL", ProductType = "Laptop", Quantity = 150 });
            products.Add(new Product { ProductID = 5, ProductName =
                "Acer", ProductType = "Laptop", Quantity = 200 });
            return products;
        }
```

You could then use LINQ to Objects to order this listing based on the product name and then output the list for review:

```
            List<Product> products = PopulateData();
            var sortedResults = from x in products
                                orderby x.ProductName
                                select x;
            foreach (var p in sortedResults)
            {
                Console.WriteLine(p.ProductName);
            }
```

As you can see here, this is a simple extension to the previous example using LINQ against the array of strings. This time, the alias of x allows access to the individual properties of the class, which can then be used to filter, order, or otherwise process the collection.

## LINQ to XML

Previously known as XLINQ, LINQ to XML is an API that can be used to query data from XML data sources. It can be used to map your LINQ queries to XML data sources.

The following code snippet shows an XML document called `Products.xml`:

```xml
<?xml version="1.0" encoding="utf-8" ?>
<Products>
  <Product>
    <ProductID>1</ProductID>
    <ProductName>Lenovo</ProductName>
    <ProductType>Laptop</ProductType>
    <Quantity>100</Quantity>
  </Product>
  <Product>
    <ProductID>2</ProductID>
    <ProductName>Compaq</ProductName>
    <ProductType>Laptop</ProductType>
    <Quantity>150</Quantity>
  </Product>
  <Product>
    <ProductID>3</ProductID>
    <ProductName>DELL</ProductName>
    <ProductType>Laptop</ProductType>
    <Quantity>200</Quantity>
  </Product>
  <Product>
    <ProductID>4</ProductID>
    <ProductName>HCL</ProductName>
    <ProductType>Laptop</ProductType>
    <Quantity>150</Quantity>
  </Product>
  <Product>
    <ProductID>5</ProductID>
    <ProductName>Acer</ProductName>
    <ProductType>Laptop</ProductType>
    <Quantity>200</Quantity>
  </Product>
</Products>
```

Using LINQ to XML, it is possible for you to load and query this document like any other object. This provides for a simple interface for working with XML documents without the need for XPATH and other techniques.

The following snippet loads the XML document and shows items with a `Quantity` greater than `150`:

```
XDocument productDocument = XDocument.Load("myFile.xml");
var result = from x in productDocument.Descendants("Products");
                where (int)x.Element("Quantity") > 150
                select (string)x.Element("ProductType") + " " +
                    (string)x.Element("ProductName");
foreach(string element in result)
    Console.WriteLine(element);
```

This example might look at bit complex at first, but if you look at the multiple components, it should be easy to digest. The first line of the code is used to load the static file `myFile.xml` into an `XDocument` object. The `XDocument` object allows LINQ to query the input XML.

The second line of code is a three-part LINQ query. The first line defines the individual element alias of `x` and instructs the query to work with the `Descendents` of `"Products"`. This ensures that the rest of the query will operate on each individual product node within the document.

The third line of code defines the `where` clause using the `Element` method to retrieve the `Quantity` element, and converts it to an integer then ensures that it is greater than `150`. The conversion to integer is needed because the type of the element is not known.

The fourth line of code then defines the result of the query, which is the `ProductType`, followed by a space, and then the `ProductName`. This results in an array of strings that indicate the matching elements.

The final lines of code are used to output the results.

In the case of working with documents that include attributes, you can use the `Attribute` method to get access to specific attributes, as shown in the previous example. If you need to walk up or down a complex document structure, you can chain together calls to the `Element` method.

Consider the following example:

```
x.Element("MyElement").Element("MyChild")
```

This would get access to the `"MyChild"` node contained within the `MyElement` node of the document.

## LINQ to DataSet

LINQ to DataSet is a LINQ implementation that you can use to query data from `DataSet` or `DataTable` instances. For example, assume that you have the following code that loads information to a `DataTable`:

```
static DataTable PopulateData()
    {
        DataTable products = new DataTable();
        products.Columns.Add("ProductID", typeof(Int32));
        products.Columns.Add("ProductName", typeof(String));
        products.Columns.Add("ProductType", typeof(String));
        products.Columns.Add("Quantity", typeof(Int32));
        products.Rows.Add(1, "Lenovo", "Laptop", 100);
        products.Rows.Add(1, "Compaq", "Laptop", 150);
        products.Rows.Add(1, "DELL", "Laptop", 200);
        products.Rows.Add(1, "HCL", "Laptop", 150);
        products.Rows.Add(1, "Acer", "Laptop", 200);
        products.Rows.Add(1, "Test", "TV", 200);
        return products;
    }
```

By using LINQ to DataSet, you can query this `DataTable` to return only the `Laptops` using the following snippet:

```
var queryableDs = PopulateData().AsEnumerable();
var result = from record in queryableDs
                where record["ProductType] == "Laptop"
```

```
                            select record;
               foreach (var product in result)
                    Console.WriteLine(product["ProductName"]);
```

The process to query a `DataTable`/`DataSet` is slightly different because of the need to call
`AsEnumerable()` to get the results to a format that can be interacted with by the LINQ system. In
the previous example, the first two lines are divided out to more accurately illustrate this concept.
However, it would be perfectly valid to do `PopulateData().AsEnumerable()` after the `in` keyword
in the first line of the LINQ statement.

For the remainder of the LINQ statement, the syntax should be familiar because you use the
standard array accessors to get access to individual fields — first you have the `where` clause to select
product type, then a `select` that returns the entire object.

## LINQ to SQL

Previously known as DLINQ, LINQ to SQL is an implementation of LINQ that can be used to
query data from SQL Server databases. It is just like any other ORM tool that can be used to
retrieve data from SQL Server databases.

To work with LINQ to SQL, you must create a `DataContext`. A `DataContext` is actually a
gateway to LINQ to SQL queries. It accepts the LINQ queries as input, and then processes those
queries to produce corresponding SQL statements.

To create a `DataContext` in LINQ to SQL, follow these steps:

1. Right-click on the project in the Solution Explorer and select Add ⇨ New Item.

2. From the list of the templates displayed, select "LINQ to SQL Classes," as shown
   in Figure 12-1.

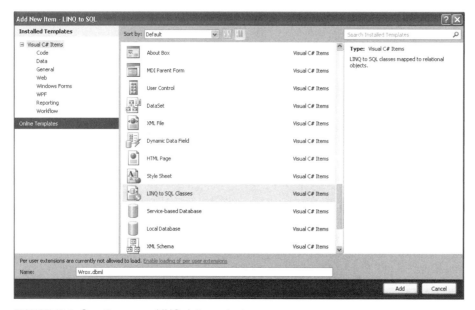

**FIGURE 12-1:** Creating a new LINQ data context

**3.** Provide a name to the `DataContext` and click OK.

**4.** Drag and drop the table(s) you need (in this example, it's the `Product` table of the `AdventureWorks` database, as shown in Figure 12-2).

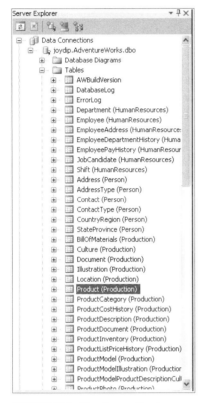

**FIGURE 12-2:** The Server Explorer

Once the `DataContext` has been created, you can use LINQ to query data, as shown in the following code snippet:

```
WroxDataContext dataContext = new WroxDataContext();
var result = from p in dataContext.Products select p;
foreach (var v in result)
    Console.WriteLine(v.Name);
```

Working with LINQ from a SQL context is very simple because the generated data context is strongly typed, just as if you were working with manually created objects. So, all query functions can be completed as if public properties existed for each column within the database.

One important item to note that is specific to LINQ to SQL is that the query itself is *not* actually executed until you start the enumeration of the results. So, if you have a LINQ statement followed by ten lines of code before you work with the results, the execution of the database query will be delayed until the time of query. Also, given this behavior, each iteration of results will result in a new database query being executed.

In the following example, the entire contents of the Products table is returned twice, once for each foreach statement:

```
WroxDataContext dataContext = new WroxDataContext();
            var result = from p in dataContext.Products select p;
            foreach (var v in result)
                Console.WriteLine(v.Name);
            foreach (var v in result)
                Console.WriteLine(v.Name);
```

You can get around this limitation by converting the results to a list or an array. This will execute the query and put the results in memory. The following example only executes the query once:

```
WroxDataContext dataContext = new WroxDataContext();
            var result = from p in dataContext.Products select p;
            var list = result.ToList();
            foreach (var v in list)
                Console.WriteLine(v.Name);
            foreach (var v in list)
                Console.WriteLine(v.Name);
```

The final thing to note here is that, because of the deferred execution model of LINQ to SQL, it is possible to perform a complex, conditional query, and ensure that the actual execution contains the proper data.

For example, consider the following:

```
var result = from p in dataContext.products select p;
if(orderbyProduct) //Variable declared elsewhere
    result - from r in result orderby r.ProductName select r;
if(onlyActive) //Variable declared elsewhere
    result = from r in result where r.Active select r;
foreach(var item in result)
    Console.WriteLine(item.Name)
```

If you did not consider deferred execution when looking at this example, it would be assumed that three different database queries would be completed. However, given the way that LINQ filters, the database query is executed once, during the foreach loop. This allows you to actually build out a dynamic filter/order condition. This can be especially helpful when working with an advanced search or other configurable search process.

## PARALLEL LINQ (PLINQ)

Parallel LINQ (PLINQ), which is part of the Parallel Extensions Library, is a concurrency execution engine that is used to execute LINQ queries. It was previously known as Parallel Framework Extensions (PFX), and is a managed concurrency library. According to MSDN (http://msdn .microsoft.com/en-us/magazine/cc163329.aspx), "PLINQ is a query execution engine that accepts any LINQ-to-Objects or LINQ-to-XML query and automatically utilizes multiple processors or cores for execution when they are available."

PLINQ is composed of the following:

➤ *Task Parallel Library (TPL)* — This is a task parallelism component.

➤ *Parallel LINQ (PLINQ)* — This is a concurrency execution engine built on top of the managed environment of the CLR.

Following is an example of a typical PLINQ query:

```
var myList = Enumerable.Range(1, 50);
var result = from i in myList.AsParallel() where i <= 10 select i;
   foreach (var x in result)
      {
          Console.WriteLine(x);
      }
```

The `AsParallel()` extension method is defined as follows:

```
public static class System.Linq.ParallelEnumerable {
    public static IParallelEnumerable<T> AsParallel<T>(
        this IEnumerable<T> source);
//Other Standard Query Operators
}
```

# ENTITY FRAMEWORK

The Entity Framework is an extended ORM from Microsoft that is used to reduce the impedance mismatch between the relational and the object model in an application. It makes this possible through the Entity Data Model (EDM), an extended Entity Relational Model that allows you to work with domain-specific properties, rather than being concerned about how the data is actually represented and stored in the underlying database.

The Entity Framework is called an *extended ORM* because it provides the following additional features over and above an ORM:

➤ Change tracking

➤ Entity inheritance

## Entity Framework Architecture

Following are the architectural components of the Entity Framework:

➤ The Entity Data Model (EDM)

➤ LINQ to Entities

➤ Entity Client

➤ Object Services

➤ Entity SQL

## The Entity Data Model

The EDM is an Entity Relationship Model in the Entity Framework, and has the following three layers:

➤ *The Conceptual or the C-Space Layer* — This is modeled using Conceptual Schema Definition Language (CSDL), and is used to define the entities and their relationships. You can query data from this layer using Entity SQL (which will be discussed shortly).

➤ *The Conceptual-Storage or the C-S Mapping Layer* — This is modeled using Mapping Specification Language (MSL), and is used to map the conceptual layer to the logical layer.

➤ *The Logical or the Storage Layer or the S-Space* — This is modeled using Store Schema Definition Language (SSDL), and is used to represent the storage schema of the underlying database in use.

Accordingly, the EDM uses .CSDL, .MSL, or .SSDL files to represent each of these layers.

You can create an EDM using the Entity Data Model Wizard included with Visual Studio 2010. To do this, follow these steps:

**1.** Right-click on the project in the Solution Explorer and click on Add ➪ New Item.

**2.** From the list of the templates displayed, select ADO.NET Entity Data Model, as shown in Figure 12-3. Click Add.

**FIGURE 12-3:** Creating a new ADO.NET Entity Data Model

**3.** The Entity Data Model Wizard is shown next. Select "Generate from database," as shown in Figure 12-4. Click Next.

**4.** Now, specify the connection properties, as shown in Figure 12-5. Click Next.

FIGURE 12-4: The Entity Data Model Wizard

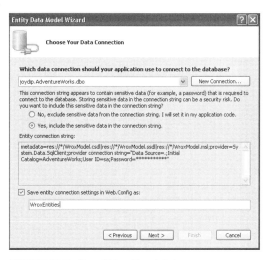

FIGURE 12-5: Specifying the database connection properties

5. Next, select the database objects you need in your model, as shown in Figure 12-6. Click Finish.

FIGURE 12-6: Select the database objects

The EDM is then created and saved in a file having an extension of .dbml.

Listing 12-1 shows what a portion of a typical EDM would look like in its XML view. Note that all additional properties have been removed from the EDM example.

---

**LISTING 12-1: EDM in XML**

```xml
<?xml version="1.0" encoding="utf-8"?>
<edmx:Edmx Version="2.0" xmlns:edmx="http://schemas.microsoft.com/ado/
    2008/10/edmx">
  <!-- EF Runtime content -->
  <edmx:Runtime>
    <!-- SSDL content -->
    <edmx:StorageModels>
      <Schema Namespace="WroxModel.Store" Alias=
          "Self" Provider="System.Data.SqlClient"
          ProviderManifestToken="2008" xmlns:store=
          "http://schemas.microsoft.com/ado/2007/12/edm/
          EntityStoreSchemaGenerator" xmlns="http://schemas.microsoft.com/
          ado/2009/02/edm/ssdl">
        <EntityContainer Name="WroxModelStoreContainer">
          <EntitySet Name="Product" EntityType=
              "WroxModel.Store.Product" store:Type=
              "Tables" Schema="Production" />
        </EntityContainer>
        <EntityType Name="Product">
          <Key>
            <PropertyRef Name="ProductID" />
          </Key>
          <Property Name="ProductID" Type="int" Nullable="false"
              StoreGeneratedPattern="Identity" />
          <Property Name="ModifiedDate" Type="datetime" Nullable="false" />
        </EntityType>
      </Schema>
    </edmx:StorageModels>
    <!-- CSDL content -->
    <edmx:ConceptualModels>
      <Schema Namespace="WroxModel" Alias="Self"
          xmlns:annotation=
          "http://schemas.microsoft.com/ado/2009/02/edm/annotation"
      xmlns="http://schemas.microsoft.com/ado/2008/09/edm">
        <EntityContainer Name="WroxEntities" annotation:LazyLoadingEnabled="true">
          <EntitySet Name="Products" EntityType="WroxModel.Product" />
        </EntityContainer>
        <EntityType Name="Product">
          <Key>
            <PropertyRef Name="ProductID" />
          </Key>
          <Property Name="ProductID" Type="Int32" Nullable="false"
              annotation:StoreGeneratedPattern="Identity" />
        </EntityType>
      </Schema>
    </edmx:ConceptualModels>
    <!-- C-S mapping content -->
    <edmx:Mappings>
```

```
    <Mapping Space="C-S" xmlns=
        "http://schemas.microsoft.com/ado/2008/09/mapping/cs">
      <EntityContainerMapping StorageEntityContainer="WroxModelStoreContainer"
          CdmEntityContainer="WroxEntities">
        <EntitySetMapping Name="Products"><EntityTypeMapping TypeName=
            "WroxModel.Product"><MappingFragment StoreEntitySet="Product">
          <ScalarProperty Name="ProductID" ColumnName="ProductID" />
        </MappingFragment></EntityTypeMapping></EntitySetMapping>
      </EntityContainerMapping>
    </Mapping>
  </edmx:Mappings>
</edmx:Runtime>
<!-- EF Designer content (DO NOT EDIT MANUALLY BELOW HERE) -->
<Designer xmlns="http://schemas.microsoft.com/ado/2008/10/edmx">
  <Connection>
    <DesignerInfoPropertySet>
      <DesignerProperty Name="MetadataArtifactProcessing" Value=
          "EmbedInOutputAssembly" />
    </DesignerInfoPropertySet>
  </Connection>
  <Options>
    <DesignerInfoPropertySet>
      <DesignerProperty Name="ValidateOnBuild" Value="true" />
      <DesignerProperty Name="EnablePluralization" Value="True" />
      <DesignerProperty Name="IncludeForeignKeysInModel" Value="True" />
    </DesignerInfoPropertySet>
  </Options>
  <!-- Diagram content (shape and connector positions) -->
  <Diagrams>
    <Diagram Name="WroxModel" ZoomLevel="73">
      <EntityTypeShape EntityType="WroxModel.Product" Width=
          "2.625" PointX="0.75" PointY="0.75" Height=
          "5.0436002604166656" IsExpanded=
          "true" /></Diagram></Diagrams>
  </Designer>
</edmx:Edmx>
```

## LINQ to Entities

The LINQ to Entities implementation of LINQ is an API that you can use to query data exposed by the EDM in a strongly typed way.

The following code snippet is an example of a LINQ to Entities query:

```
WroxModel.WroxEntities context = new WroxModel.WroxEntities();
    var result = from product in context.Products
            select product;
    foreach (var p in result)
Console.WriteLine (p.ProductName);
```

As you can see from this example, once the EDM is created, the process to query the entities is just the same as other types of LINQ queries.

## Entity Client

Entity Client is a provider that acts as a gateway to entity-level queries in the Entity Framework. You can use this provider to write your queries using Entity SQL, and perform CRUD (Create, Read, Update, Delete) operations on the data exposed by the EDM.

## Entity SQL

Like T-SQL, Entity SQL is a data store-independent, text-based query language that you can use to perform CRUD operations on data exposed by the EDM. It is not strongly typed like LINQ, but you can use it to compose or build your own dynamic queries, and then execute them.

The following code snippet illustrates how you can use Entity SQL in your application:

```
using (EntityConnection entityConnection =
        new EntityConnection("Name=WroxEntities"))
    {
        try
        {
            entityConnection.Open();
            EntityCommand entityCommand = entityConnection.CreateCommand();
            entityCommand.CommandText = "WroxEntities.AddNewProduct";
            entityCommand.CommandType = CommandType.StoredProcedure;
            entityCommand.Parameters.AddWithValue("ProductID", 2);
            entityCommand.Parameters.AddWithValue("ProductName", "DELL");
            entityCommand.Parameters.AddWithValue("ProductType", "Laptop");
            entityCommand.Parameters.AddWithValue("Quantity", 150);
            entityCommand.ExecuteNonQuery();
        }
        catch (Exception ex)
        {
            Console.WriteLine("Error: "+ex.ToString());
        }
    }
```

## Object Services

Object Services is an API that allows you to work with your entities exposed by the EDM as in-memory objects, or a collection of in-memory objects. You can use this API to query data from any data source. Also, the Object Services Layer provides the following features:

➤ Change tracking and identity resolution

➤ Lazy loading

➤ Inheritance

➤ Optimistic concurrency

You can also use the Object Services API to query data exposed by the EDM using Entity SQL or LINQ to Entities.

The following code snippet shows how you can use Object Services to retrieve data exposed by the EDM:

```
using (ObjectContext context = new ObjectContext("Name=WroxEntities"))
    {
        var result = from p in context.CreateQuery<WroxModel.Product>
            ("WroxEntities.Product") select p;
        foreach (WroxModel.Product product in result)
        {
            Console.WriteLine(product.ProductName);
        }
    }
```

## THE ENTITY DATA SOURCE CONTROL

The Entity Data Source control is a new data source control introduced in Visual Studio 2008 Beta 1. It is now available as part of Visual Studio 2010, and can be used to retrieve data exposed by the EDM.

Following is an example of how the Entity Data Source control looks in markup code:

```
<asp:EntityDataSource ID="EntityDataSource1" runat="server"
    ConnectionString="name=WroxEntities" DefaultContainerName=
    "WroxEntities" EntitySetName="Product"> </asp:EntityDataSource>
```

## CHOOSING BETWEEN LINQ TO ENTITIES AND LINQ TO SQL

Both the Entity Framework and LINQ to SQL provide ORM functionality. Deciding which of the two is more appropriate for you can be a complicated decision-making process that depends on your specific implementation.

For example, LINQ to SQL is a solution that is designed to go against Microsoft SQL Server directly. If your needs require communication with another data store, the Entity Framework is a much more appropriate solution.

The Entity Framework also supports much more complex data mapping and query processes. For example, LINQ to SQL provides a one-to-one mapping of tables, views, and stored procedures. The Entity Framework has the capability to handle many-to-many relationships and other more complex situations, or it allows for a single class to map to data within multiple tables.

You might consider LINQ to SQL as the predecessor (or "little brother") to the more robust and powerful Entity Framework. Various online sources indicate that Microsoft is recommending the Entity Framework as the "going forward" technology.

## SUMMARY

This chapter provided an overview of enhancements to the .NET Data Framework. Two ORM technologies, LINQ to SQL and Entity Framework, were discussed and appropriate applications provided for each. A broader overview of the LINQ was provided with several examples.

Chapter 13 takes a look into the enhancements that have been introduced to .NET Communication Foundation.

# 13

# Enhancements to the .NET Communication Framework

You learned about the details of Windows Communication Foundation (WCF) in Chapter 9, which provided an overview of what WCF is and how it can be leveraged. Given how new WCF is, major improvements and enhancements have been added, with major functionality added in both the .NET 3.5 and .NET 4 releases, all of which have occurred shortly after the initial WCF release with .NET 3.0.

This chapter focuses on the changes that have been introduced, and provides readers who have used older versions of WCF with some insight into new functionality that results from these new implementations.

## ENHANCEMENTS IN WCF FRAMEWORK 3.5

The WCF Framework was first introduced in 2006 as part of .NET Framework 3.0. As part of the .NET 3.5 release, a lot of effort was put forth to make WCF the true "going-forward" technology for building out solutions created with a focus on Service Oriented Architecture (SOA). So, key additions with .NET 3.5 included the following:

- ➤ Support for Ajax-enabled WCF services
- ➤ Improved support for WCS standards
- ➤ A new WCF designer
- ➤ New WCF Tools (`WcfSvcHost` and `WcfTestClient`)
- ➤ Support for REST-based WCF services
- ➤ Support for WCF and Windows Forms (WF) interactivity

These enhancements to WCF expanded the usability of WCF to include working with Ajax-enabled web applications, as well as providing diagnostic tools to help developers more quickly diagnose and resolve configuration and setup issues with their WCF services.

One great addition to WCF with the .NET 3.5 release was the addition of the UserNamePasswordValidator class contained in the System.IdentityModel.Selectors namespace. With this class, it is possible for developers to extend an implementation of this class to specify their own user-verification systems. The following example "WroxValidator" class validates that the calling user provided a username of user and a password of password1!:

```
using System;
using System.IdentityModel.Selectors;
using System.IdentityModel.Tokens;
using System.ServiceModel;
namespace Wrox
{
    public class WroxValidator : UserNamePasswordValidator
    {
        public override void Validate(String userName, String password)
        {
            if (!userName.Equals("user")) || !password.Equals("password1!"))
            {
                throw new SecurityTokenException("User Name and/or
                    Password incorrect...!");
            }
        }
    }
}
```

From a programming perspective, this is simple: Inherit from the UserNamePasswordValidator class and override the Validate method. The only note here is that, rather than having a Boolean return value, if a user fails validation, you must throw an exception. The proper exception type to throw is SecurityTokenException.

Once a custom validator has been configured, you can update the service behavior to require a service credential, and then specify your specific type for validation. Following is an example configuration that defines basic transport level security and utilizes the custom WroxValidator created previously:

```
<?xml version="1.0" encoding="utf-8" ?>
<configuration>
  <system.web>
    <compilation debug="true" />
  </system.web>
  <system.serviceModel>
    <services>
      <bindings>
        <wsHttpBinding>
          <binding name="WroxAuthentication">
```

```
            <security mode="Transport">
              <transport clientCredentialType="Basic" />
            </security>
          </binding>
        </wsHttpBinding>
      </bindings>

      <behaviors>
        <serviceBehaviors>
          <behavior name="WroxValidator.ServiceBehavior">
            <serviceCredentials>
              <userNameAuthentication
              userNamePasswordValidationMode="Custom"
              customUserNamePasswordValidatorType="Wrox.WroxValidator, Wrox"/>
            </serviceCredentials>
          </behavior>
        </serviceBehaviors>
      </behaviors>
    </system.serviceModel>
  </configuration>
```

# ENHANCEMENTS IN WCF FRAMEWORK 4.0

Although a certain amount of time elapsed between the release of .NET 3.5 and 4.0, another round of major enhancements was added to WCF with this release. Following is a quick list of the items that are discussed throughout the remainder of this chapter:

➤ Simplified configuration

➤ Standard endpoints

➤ Discovery

➤ REST improvements

➤ Routing service

## Simplified Configuration

Configuration in WCF 4.0 is much simpler compared to its earlier counterparts. In WCF 3.x, you needed to specify the endpoints, behavior, and so on, for the service host. With WCF 4.0, default endpoints, binding information, and behavior are provided by default. In essence, WCF 4.0 eliminates the need for any WCF configuration when you are implementing a particular WCF service.

A few standard endpoints and default binding/behavior configurations are created for any WCF service in WCF 4.0. This makes it easy to get started with WCF, because the tedious configuration details of WCF 3.x are no longer required.

Consider the following WCF service:

```
using System;
using System.ServiceModel;
namespace WroxService
{
    [ServiceContract]
    public interface ITestService
    {
        [OperationContract]
        String DisplayMessage();
    }

    public class TestService : ITestService
    {
        public String DisplayMessage()
        {
            return "Hello World!";
        }
    }
}
```

In WCF 4.0, you can use `ServiceHost` to host the WCF service without the need for any configuration information whatsoever. Following is all the code you need to host your WCF service and display the address, binding, and contract information:

```
using System.ServiceModel;
using System;
using System.ServiceModel.Description;
namespace WroxClient
{
    class Program
    {
        static void Main(string[] args)
        {
            ServiceHost serviceHost = new ServiceHost
                (typeof(WroxService.TestService));
                serviceHost.AddServiceEndpoint
                (typeof(WroxService.TestService),
                new BasicHttpBinding(),
                "http://localhost:1607/
                TestService.svc");
            serviceHost.Open();
            foreach (ServiceEndpoint serviceEndpoint
                in serviceHost.Description.Endpoints)
              Console.WriteLine("Address: {0}, Binding: {1},
                Contract: {2}", serviceEndpoint.Address,
                serviceEndpoint.Binding.Name,
                serviceEndpoint.Contract.Name);
            Console.ReadLine();
```

```
                    serviceHost.Close();
                }
        }
    }
```

You can refer to the examples in Chapter 9 of this book for an example of the long-hand configuration setup that is needed to configure WCF prior to the 4.0 release.

Client consumption configuration has also been greatly simplified, with the following items being the only necessary configuration:

```
<?xml version="1.0" encoding="utf-8" ?>
<configuration>
 <system.serviceModel>
    <behaviors>
      <serviceBehaviors>
        <behavior>
          <serviceMetadata httpGetEnabled ="true"/>
        </behavior>
      </serviceBehaviors>
    </behaviors>
 </system.serviceModel>
</configuration>
```

This configures everything using the default configuration, which uses a `BasicHttpBinding`. If you need to do any further configuration, or use a more secure binding protocol (such as `wsHttpBinding`), you only need to add an additional `protocolMapping` code to your configuration, similar to the following:

```
<?xml version="1.0" encoding="utf-8" ?>
<configuration>
 <system.serviceModel>
    <behaviors>
      <serviceBehaviors>
        <behavior>
          <serviceMetadata httpGetEnabled ="true"/>
        </behavior>
      </serviceBehaviors>
    </behaviors>
    <protocolMapping>
      <add binding="wsHttpBinding" scheme ="http"/>
    </protocolMapping>
 </system.serviceModel>
</configuration>
```

## Standard Endpoints

*Standard endpoints* are items provided by the .NET framework that can be used to more quickly configure standard endpoints for common application functions. Table 13-1 shows the standard endpoints for WCF 4.0.

**TABLE 13-1:** Standard Endpoints in WCF 4.0

| STANDARD ENDPOINT | PURPOSE |
|---|---|
| announcementEndpoint | This endpoint has a fixed contract. It is only necessary to specify the binding and the address. |
| discoveryEndpoint | This endpoint is used to set up WCF discovery messages. |
| mexEndpoint | This endpoint is used to allow metadata exchange for your service. |
| workflowControlEndpoint | This endpoint is used to allow for the calling of control operations on a Windows Workflow instance. |
| webHttpEndpoint | This endpoint automatically adds a fixed webHttpBinding for the application with the webHttpBehavior. |
| webScriptEndpoint | This endpoint sets up a WCF service to allow calling from an Ajax-enabled web application. |
| udpAnnouncementEndpoint | This endpoint is used to send announcements over a User Datagram Protocol (UDP) binding. |
| udpDiscoveryEndpoint | This endpoint is used to send discovery messages over a UDP binding. |

You can use any of the endpoints shown in Table 13-1 by referencing them in the `<configuration>` element using the endpoint name. Following is an example:

```
<configuration>
  <system.serviceModel>
    <services>
      <service name="WroxService">
        <endpoint kind="basicHttpBinding" contract="IMyService"/>
        <endpoint kind="mexEndpoint" address="mex" />
      </service>
    </services>
  </system.serviceModel>
</configuration>
```

## Discovery

There are two modes of operation:

➤ *Ad-hoc mode* — In this mode, there is no centralized server, and all service announcements and client requests are sent in a multicast manner.

➤ *Managed mode* — In this mode, you have a centralized server. Such a server is known as a *discovery proxy*, where the services are published centrally, and the clients who need to consume such published services connect to this to retrieve the necessary information.

You can just add the standard `"udpDiscoveryEndpoint"` endpoint and also enable the `<serviceDiscovery>` behavior to enable service discovery in the ad-hoc mode. Here is an example:

```
<configuration>
    <system.serviceModel>
      <services>
        <service name="TestService">
          <endpoint binding="wsHttpBinding" contract="ITestService" />
          <!-- add a standard UDP discovery endpoint-->
          <endpoint name="udpDiscovery" kind="udpDiscoveryEndpoint"/>
        </service>
      </services>
      <behaviors>
        <serviceBehaviors>
        <behavior name="TestService.MyServiceBehavior">
          <!-- To avoid disclosing metadata information, set the
               value below to false and remove the metadata
               endpoint above before deployment -->
          <serviceMetadata httpGetEnabled="true"/>
          <!-- To receive exception details in faults for debugging
               purposes, set the value below to true.  Set to false
               before deployment to avoid disclosing exception
               information -->
          <serviceDebug includeExceptionDetailInFaults="false"/>
          <serviceDiscovery />
          </behavior>
        </serviceBehaviors>
        </behaviors>
    </system.serviceModel>
</configuration>
```

Note in the previous code snippet how a new `EndPoint` has been added to discover the service. Also, the `ServiceDiscovery` behavior has been added. You can use the `DiscoveryClient` class to discover your service and invoke one of its methods.

You must create an instance of the `DiscoveryClient` class and pass `UdpDiscoveryEndPoint` to the constructor of this class as a parameter to discover the service. Once the endpoint has been discovered, the discovered endpoint address can then be used to invoke the service. The following code snippet illustrates this:

```
using System;
using System.ServiceModel;
using System.ServiceModel.Discovery;
namespace WroxConsoleApplication
{
    class Program
    {
        static void Main(string[] args)
        {
            DiscoveryClient discoverclient = new DiscoveryClient(new
                UdpDiscoveryEndpoint());
            FindResponse findResponse = discoverclient.Find(new
```

```
                    FindCriteria(typeof(ITestService)));
                EndpointAddress endpointAddress =
                    findResponse.Endpoints[0].Address;
                MyServiceClient serviceClient = new MyServiceClient(new
                    WSHttpBinding(), endpointAddress);
                Console.WriteLine(serviceClient.DisplayMessage());
            }
        }
    }
```

WCF 4.0 also enables you to configure services to announce their endpoints as soon as they are started. Here is how you can configure your service to announce endpoints at start time:

```
<configuration>
  <system.serviceModel>
    <services>
      <service name="TestService">
        <endpoint binding="wsHttpBinding" contract="ITestService"/>
        <endpoint kind="udpDiscoveryEndpoint"/>
      </service>
    </services>
    <behaviors>
      <serviceBehaviors>
        <behavior>
          <serviceDiscovery>
            <announcementEndpoints>
              <endpoint kind="udpAnnouncementEndpoint"/>
            </announcementEndpoints>
          </serviceDiscovery>
        </behavior>
      </serviceBehaviors>
    </behaviors>
  </system.serviceModel>
</configuration>
```

## REST Improvements

WCF 4.0 comes with improved support for REST-based features. You now have support for an automatic Help page that describes the REST-based services available for the service consumers or clients. This feature is turned on by default, though you can also manually configure the property, as shown in the following code listing:

```
<configuration>
  <system.serviceModel>
    <serviceHostingEnvironment aspNetCompatibilityEnabled="true" />
    <behaviors>
      <endpointBehaviors>
        <behavior name="WroxTestHelpBehavior">
          <webHttp helpEnabled="true" />
        </behavior>
      </endpointBehaviors>
    </behaviors>
```

```
            <services>
              <service name="WroxSampleWCFService">
                <endpoint behaviorConfiguration="WroxTestHelpBehavior"
                          binding="webHttpBinding"
                          contract="WroxSampleWCFService" />
              </service>
            </services>
          </system.serviceModel>
        </configuration>
```

WCF 4.0 also comes with support for HTTP caching using the `AspNetCacheProfile` attribute. Note that the `AspNetCacheProfile` support actually uses the standard ASP.NET output caching mechanism to provide you with caching features in your WCF service.

To use this attribute, you should add a reference to the `System.ServiceModel.Web.Caching` namespace. You can apply this attribute in a `WebGet` operation, and specify the cache duration of your choice. The following code snippet can be used in your service contract method to make use of this feature:

```
using System.ServiceModel.Web.Caching;
[OperationContract]
[WebGet]
[AspNetCacheProfile("WroxCache")]
String GetProductName();
```

Accordingly, you should set the cache profile in your application's `web.config` file, as shown here:

```
<caching>
 <outputCacheSettings>
    <outputCacheProfiles>
       <add name="WroxCache" duration="60" varyByParam="format"/>
    </outputCacheProfiles>
 </outputCacheSettings>
</caching>
```

This functionality allows you to significantly reduce the load on a web server for standard web `Get` requests. It is not possible to cache requests when used with a HTTP `Post` submission process. Similar to the output cache configuration of ASP.NET, you use the `varyByParams` option to configure the specific parameters that will cause different cache keys to be created.

# Routing Service

Routing is a feature in WCF 4.0 that is used to determine how a message should be forwarded, and when a request from the client comes in. Filters determine how the routing service redirects the requests that come in from the client to a particular WCF service. These filters are mapped with the corresponding WCF service endpoints using a routing table. Following are the available filter types:

➤   Action

➤   Address

➤   AddressPrefix

➤  And

➤  Custom

➤  Endpoint

➤  MatchAll

➤  XPath

In WCF 4.0, you have the `RoutingService` class that you can use to implement generic WCF routing mechanisms in your application. Following is how the `RoutingService` class looks:

```
[ServiceBehavior(AddressFilterMode = AddressFilterMode.Any,
    InstanceContextMode = InstanceContextMode.PerSession,
    UseSynchronizationContext = false, ValidateMustUnderstand = false)]
public sealed class RoutingService : ISimplexDatagramRouter, ISimplexSessionRouter,
    IRequestReplyRouter, IDuplexSessionRouter
{
    ... // implementation omitted
}
```

Hosting a `RoutingService` is as simple as hosting a WCF service. You must simply create an instance of the `ServiceHost`, and then specify the `RoutingService` for the service type. Here is an example:

```
public static void Main()
{
    ServiceHost serviceHost = new ServiceHost(typeof(RoutingService));
        try
        {
            serviceHost.Open();
            Console.WriteLine("Routing Service started...");
            Console.WriteLine("Press <ENTER> to stop the Routing Service.");
            Console.ReadLine();
            serviceHost.Close();
        }
        catch (CommunicationException ce)
        {
            Console.WriteLine(ce.Message);
            serviceHost.Abort();
        }
}
```

Once the `RoutingService` has been started by making a call to the `Open()` method on the `ServiceHost` instance, it can route messages as needed. Following is an example of a typical configuration you would use to specify the routing information for your routing service:

```
<?xml version="1.0" encoding="utf-8" ?>
<configuration>
 <system.serviceModel>
    <services>
       <service name="System.ServiceModel.Routing.RoutingService"
```

```
              behaviorConfiguration="TestBehavior">
        <host>
          <baseAddresses>
            <add baseAddress="http://localhost:1809/TestService"/>
          </baseAddresses>
        </host>
        <endpoint
                  address=""
                  binding="wsHttpBinding" name="TestRoutingEndpoint"
                    contract="System.ServiceModel.Routing.
                    IRequestReplyRouter"/>
      </service>
    </services>
    <behaviors>
      <serviceBehaviors>
        <behavior name="TestBehavior">
          <serviceMetadata httpGetEnabled="True"/>
          <serviceDebug includeExceptionDetailInFaults="True"/>
          <routing routingTableName="ServiceRouterTable"/>
          <!--The Router Table Contains Entries for services-->
        </behavior>
      </serviceBehaviors>
    </behaviors>

    <!--Define Services Here-->
    <client>
      <endpoint
      name="WroxService" binding="wsHttpBinding"
      address="http://localhost:2709/Services/WroxService.svc"
      contract="*">
      </endpoint>
    </client>
    <!--Routing Defination-->
    <routing>
      <!--Filter For Detecting Messages Headers to redirect-->
      <filters>
        <filter name="TestFilter" filterType="MatchAll"/>
      </filters>
      <!--Define Routing Table, This will Map the service with Filter-->
      <routingTables>
        <table name="ServiceRouterTable">
          <entries>
            <add filterName="TestFilter" endpointName="WroxService"/>
          </entries>
        </table>
      </routingTables>
    </routing>
  </system.serviceModel>
</configuration>
```

Note that the routing service shown in the previous code snippet is hosted at `http://localhost:1809/TestService`. It uses `wsHttpBinding`.

## SUMMARY

This chapter provided an introduction to major changes that have been introduced in Windows Communication Foundation (WCF). In this chapter, you learned about enhanced support for RESTful application development, discovery improvements, and methods to make developing and using WCF easier for both the novice and experienced programmer.

Chapter 14 takes a close look at .NET charting components.

# 14

# .NET Charting Components

In Chapter 8, you learned why the overall user experience is important for your applications. If the users of your software can handle it intuitively and easily, they will have a positive experience. If the application is tedious and laborious to work with, or it does not give the expected feedback, users won't use it — or, at least, they won't be happy.

For applications that work with numbers (or with a large set of numbers), the experience users perceive is more important. Charts are great tools for improving this experience. Displaying charts for a certain set of numbers offers a nicer experience than a simple table of data, and, in one look, charts will convey the same information than can be represented in a complex table.

For a long time, no chart controls were shipped with Visual Studio. If you wanted to use them, you had to buy one from a user interface (UI) component vendor, or download an Open Source component with the appropriate license. Visual Studio 2010 and .NET 4 change all this. Two kinds of sophisticated chart controls are the part of the framework — one for Windows Forms applications, and one for ASP.NET Web applications.

The two chart controls share the same concepts, and they differ only in technology-dependent features. This chapter focuses on using the Windows Forms chart control, and Chapter 16 examines the ASP.NET charting improvements.

In this chapter, you will learn the following things about charts:

> *Creating charts* — You will create a simple chart, customize it, and bind data from a Language Integrated Query (LINQ) expression.

> *Using charts* — The Chart control supports more than 30 types of charts, and more than a hundred properties that can be used to customize them. You'll learn about the most important chart elements and their customization opportunities.

> *Advanced chart manipulations* — Utilizing some more advanced features of the Chart control requires more than setting up properties at design time. You will learn about these advanced features, including annotations and data manipulations.

# CREATING CHARTS

.NET Framework 4.0 has a great charting solution for Windows Forms applications. Types related to charting components can be found in the `System.Windows.Forms.DataVisualization` assembly in the `System.Windows.Forms.DataVisualization.Charting` namespace. The most important type is the `Chart` control shown in Figure 14-1, which can be dragged from the Toolbox to your forms. As you can see, this control is located under the Data tab in the Toolbox.

**FIGURE 14-1:** Windows Forms Chart control in the Toolbox

Adding a simple chart to your application generally entails the following three steps:

1. Prepare the data you want to visualize with the chart.

2. Design and set up the visual properties of the chart.

3. Bind your data to the chart.

Let's start this discussion by jumping ahead to Step 2 so that you can use manually entered data to get a better overview of the chart's visual elements. After you are familiar with how to set up chart properties, the discussion will take you back to Step 1 to add programmatically computed data to the chart.

## Creating a Simple Chart

Working with a Windows Forms chart is easy, because most of the design can be done visually by setting up various chart properties. To see this in action, create a C# Windows Forms application and name it `ProcessInfoChart`. Rename `Form1.cs` to `MainForm.cs`. Click OK on the dialog that appears when you have changed the forms name. Set the `Text` property of `MainWindow` to "Process Information Chart."

### Adding a Chart Control to a Form

Drag a `Chart` control to the design surface of `MainWindow` and set its `Dock` property to `Fill`. The chart is immediately shown with sample design time data so that you can immediately check its visual properties. If you run the application at this point, the chart will be empty.

Turn on the Categorized view in the Properties window and scroll down to the Chart category, as shown in Figure 14-2. Here, you can find those collection properties that are, in most cases, the starting points of chart setup activities.

### Manually Adding Data to the Chart

Often, you create chart data programmatically as a result of calculation or report generation. However, when you design the chart

**FIGURE 14-2:** Chart properties

and set up its visual properties, it is very useful to check how your data would look. To do this, you can manually add your sample data to the chart.

The smallest unit of data in a chart is the *data point*. Data points are organized into *series*, and a chart can show one or more series. Let's set up a single series containing five data points.

In the Property window, click the Series collection and click the ellipsis button. The Series Collection Editor opens with Series1 shown on the left side and the Series1 properties on the right side of the dialog. Scroll down to the Data category in the property grid, and click the Points collection, as shown in Figure 14-3.

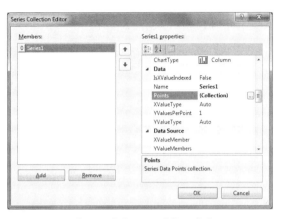

**FIGURE 14-3:** Series Collection Editor dialog

This property holds the data points belonging to the series. Click the ellipsis button to open the DataPoint Collection Editor, which is empty when it opens. Click the Add button five times to create five data points for the series.

As you add data points, the design surface of the chart is automatically updated to display the points. Data points are indexed from 0 to 4. Select the point with index 0, and scroll down to the Data categories in the property grid, as shown in Figure 14-4. Set XValue to 0 and YValues to 1. As the name suggests, you can have multiple Y values for a data point. You'll learn about using these later in this chapter. However, for now, just set this to the single value of 1.

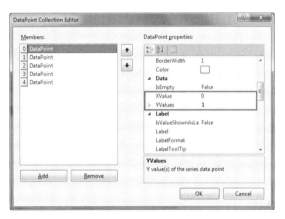

**FIGURE 14-4:** DataPoint Collection Editor dialog

Repeat the setting of the XValue and YValues property pairs for the other DataPoint instances in ascending order of their indices. Use the values from 1 to 4 for XValue and 2 to 5 for YValues. As you set the data points, the chart updates its design-time view.

At this point, you've set up the charts with real data that will be displayed when you run the application, as shown in Figure 14-5. Close all open editors and press Ctrl + F5 to start the chart application.

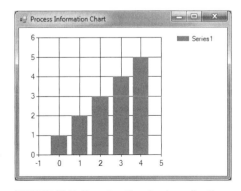

**FIGURE 14-5:** Running the chart application

As you resize the application window, the chart automatically updates its view to the new window size. Close the application.

## Adding a New Chart Area

In the form designer, select the chart and again display the Series Collection Editor (which, as you recall, is the `Series` property under the Chart category). This time, add a new series in this editor with the Add button, and set up five data points (use the DataPoints Collection Editor). This time, use the range from 0 to 4 for `XValue` and the decreasing range from 5 to 1 for `YValues`.

When you run the application again, you'll see two data series displayed in the chart, as shown in Figure 14-6.

A chart can contain one or more *chart areas* that can be used to simultaneously display several views of the data behind the chart. For example, you can display the series in Figure 14-6 in separate chart areas.

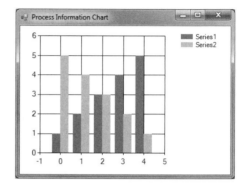

**FIGURE 14-6:** Two series displayed in the chart

In the form designer, select the chart and launch the ChartArea Collection Editor by clicking the ellipsis button belonging to the `ChartAreas` property under the Chart category. Use the Add button to add a new chart area, (which will be named `ChartArea2`), and close the editor. You'll notice that the design area of the chart is split into two vertical panes. The chart you've prepared before went to the upper pane, while the bottom pane stays empty. The empty area is reserved for `ChartArea2`, but right now, that does not contain any data to display.

Go to the Series Collection Editor again. Select `Series2` and set its `ChartArea` property (you can find it under the Chart category) to `ChartArea2`. Now, your second area also contains a view with data. When you run your application, as shown in Figure 14-7, you can see that the two series are displayed in separate chart areas.

Your chart is simple and nice, but does not tell anything about what you can see in it.

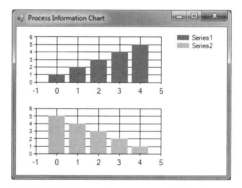

**FIGURE 14-7:** Two chart areas with their own series

## Setting up Titles and Legends

Adding a title to a chart can help the user understand what data he or she sees there. The `Chart` control allows you to add one or more titles to the chart that can be assigned to either the chart, or one of its chart areas. Setting up chart titles is very simple.

Launch the Title Collection Editor by clicking the ellipsis button belonging to the `Titles` property under the Chart category. Use the Add button to create a new Title, and then set its `Text` property — you'll find it with name "(Text)" right under the Appearance category — to

`My Secret Data`. Expand the `Font` property and set `Size` to 12. You can immediately see the newly created title in the design view, located at the top of the chart.

Now, add two more titles and set their `Text` properties to `Increasing Trend` and `Decreasing Trend`, respectively. Select `Title2`, and scroll down to the Docking category in the property grid. Here you find five properties that determine where the title is displayed and how it is aligned.

Set the `DockedToChartArea` to `ChartArea1`. The "Increasing Trend" is displayed within the first chart area. Set the `IsDockedInsideChartArea` to `False` and the title moves outside of the chart area, docked at the top. Change the `Docking` property to `Bottom`, and the title moves below the chart area.

Change `Title3` similarly as `Title2`, but set `DockedToChartArea` to `ChartArea2` in this case. When you run the application, you will see all the three titles in the chart, as shown in Figure 14-8.

When you create a chart, a legend is automatically added to it. You can see this legend in Figure 14-8 at the top-right area of the window containing `Series1` and `Series2`. The default legend is docked to the chart, but you can attach legends to chart areas.

Start the Legend Collection Editor by clicking the ellipsis button belonging to the `Legends` property under the Chart category, and click the Add button to create

**FIGURE 14-8:** Titles assigned to the chart

a new Legend. The new `Legend2` is also docked to the chart, and is placed on the left side of the existing `Legend1`. Right now, no series is associated with the legend, so it is empty, as its placeholder indicates on the design surface. Close the Legend Collection Editor, and go to Edit Chart Series.

Select `Series1`, scroll down to the Chart category, and set the `Name` property to `Revenue`. Changing the series name immediately updates the legend using the new name instead of `Series1`. Similarly, rename `Series2` to `Cost`. You can attach a series to a legend to be displayed there. By default,

all series are attached to `Legend1`. Scroll down to the Legend property of `Cost` (you'll find in under the Legend category) and change it to `Legend2`. Now, the `Cost` series is moved from the first legend to the new one, as the designer surface immediately reflects.

Now, go back to edit `Legends`. A legend has a set of properties under the Docking category that determine how those displayed in the chart control. Select `Legend1` and scroll down to the Docking property category. Set the `DockedToChartArea` to `ChartArea1`. Change the same property for `Legend2` to `ChartArea2`, and also set the `IsDockedInsideChartArea` to `False`. This set of actions moves each legend to the right of its chart area, as shown in Figure 14-9.

**FIGURE 14-9:** Each chart area has its own legend

## Adding a Three-Dimensional Effect to the Chart

In many cases, a three-dimensional effect may offer a trendier look to your charts. With the `Chart` control, it's very easy to change your chart to have this modern look.

Launch the ChartArea Collection Editor and select `ChartArea1`. At the top of the property grid, find the `Area3DStyle` property, and extend it to access its sub-properties. Change the `(Enable3D)` property to `True`, set `PointDepth` to `40`, `PointGapDepth` to `10` and `WallWidth` to `0`.

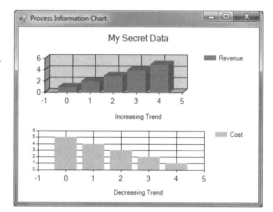

**FIGURE 14-10:** Three-dimensional effect added to the chart

The first chart area displays the data in a three-dimensional fashion. When you build and run your application, you can check it, as shown in Figure 14-10.

Now, your chart seems to give more information to the user than its first version, when only data points could be seen. There are many other customization opportunities for the chart. You can change how chart axes look, or you can add labels and annotations to the chart element. Of course, alignments, fonts, colors, and gradients can be adjusted for each element. Later in this chapter, you will learn more about these customization options.

Now, let's turn to programmatically adding data to the chart.

# Adding Data to the Chart Programmatically

By now, in the sample application, all data points have been set up manually. In real applications, data is generated at run-time; series and data points are set up according to results of calculations or reports.

The `Chart` control supports two models to set up data points at run-time:

➤ You can use the appropriate chart properties to add data points one-by-one in a program. This is the traditional imperative approach.

➤ You can bind a data source to the chart, and declare how series and data points should be extracted from the data source. This approach is the declarative approach. You can easily bind data coming from databases, LINQ expressions, or in-memory objects — without having to program any cycle to create and set data points.

This section provides a short overview of these approaches.

## Adding Data Points Programmatically

The data you've added manually can also be created programmatically.

Start the Series Collection Editor to clear the data points you've added. Select the Revenue series. Go to the Points property and click the ellipsis button to display the DataPoints Collection Editor. Select all data points (click the first DataPoint, and then click the last DataPoint while pressing the Shift key), and click Remove. Repeat the same action for the Cost series.

In the design surface, select the MainForm and click the Events button in the Properties window to list the form events. Double-click on Load to create an event handler method to run when the form is loaded. You'll use this method to set up data points. Listing 14-1 shows the full source code of MainForm.cs (the unused using clauses have been removed).

**LISTING 14-1:** MainForm.cs of ProcessInfoChart

```csharp
using System;
using System.Windows.Forms;
using System.Windows.Forms.DataVisualization.Charting;

namespace ProcessInfoChart
{
  public partial class MainForm : Form
  {
    public MainForm()
    {
      InitializeComponent();
    }

    private void MainForm_Load(object sender, EventArgs e)
    {
      var revnSeries = chart1.Series["Revenue"];
      var costSeries = chart1.Series["Cost"];
      for (int i = 0; i < 5; i++)
      {
        revnSeries.Points.Add(new DataPoint(i, i + 1));
        costSeries.Points.Add(new DataPoint(i, 5-i));
      }
    }
  }
}
```

*Code file [MainForm.cs] available for download at Wrox.com*

You can access a series through the Series property of the chart. You can then index either by the series name or its position. In the sample, the name is used. The data points of the series can be manipulated through the Points property. In the list, new DataPoint instances are added with the XValue and YValues properties specified in the constructor.

When you build and run the application, you'll see that the chart looks the same as shown in Figure 14-10.

## Binding a Data Source to the Chart

A more natural (and simpler) method is to bind the chart to a data source. Let's bind the chart to the result of a LINQ expression that retrieves the top ten processes by means of consumed memory. Add a new code file to the `ProcessInfoChart` project with name `ProcessInfo.cs`. Listing 14-2 shows the content you should copy into this file.

**LISTING 14-2: ProcessInfo.cs**

```
using System.Collections.Generic;
using System.Diagnostics;
using System.Linq;

namespace ProcessInfoChart
{
  public class ProcessInfo
  {
    public string Name { get; set; }
    public long WorkingSet { get; set; }
    public long PeakWorkingSet { get; set; }
  }

  public class ProcessList
  {
    public static IEnumerable<ProcessInfo> GetTopWorkingSet(int topN)
    {
      return (from process in Process.GetProcesses()
              orderby process.WorkingSet64 descending
              select new ProcessInfo
                {
                  Name = process.ProcessName,
                  WorkingSet = process.WorkingSet64,
                  PeakWorkingSet = process.PeakWorkingSet64
                }
             ).Take(topN);
    }
  }
}
```

*Code file [ProcessInfo.cs] available for download at Wrox.com*

One instance of the `ProcessInfo` class describes a data point in the chart. The `ProcessList` static class encapsulates the `GetTopWorkingSet` method that returns a collection of data points representing the processes.

The next step is creating a data source with Visual Studio. Build the project so that later you can select `ProcessInfo` as the type of data source object.

Select `chart1` in the design surface of `MainForm` and scroll down to the Data category in the Properties window. Click the `DataSource` property. Click the arrow to the right of the property value. In the drop-down list, click the Add Project Data Source link to start setting up a data source.

When the Data Source Configuration Wizard appears, choose the Object data source type and click Next. Expand `ProcessInfoChart`. Mark the `ProcessInfo` class as shown in Figure 14-11.

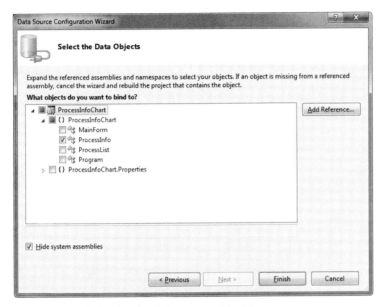

**FIGURE 14-11:** Selecting the data source object type

Click Finish. The wizard generates the `processInfoBindingSource` object for you, and sets it as the data source of the chart. Of course, this object does not yet know the real data, but knows the "shape" of the data that is represented by the `ProcessInfo` type. In order to display chart data, you must declare how to extract series from the data source.

Start the Series Collection Editor to set up data source binding information for each series. Select `Revenue` and rename it by changing the `Name` property to `Working Set`. Scroll down to the DataSource category and set the `XValueMember` property to `Name`, and set `YValueMembers` to `WorkingSet`. You can select these values from the drop-down list, as shown in Figure 14-12.

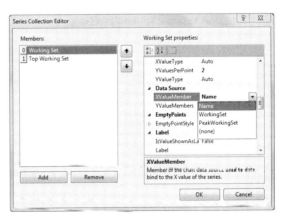

**FIGURE 14-12:** You can use drop-down list to select value members

Change the `Cost` series name to `Top Working Set`. Set `XValueMember` to `Name` and `YValueMembers` to `PeakWorkingSet`.

The chart application contains false titles, so it's time to fix them. Start the Titles Collection editor and change the (Text) properties of `Title1`, `Title2`, and `Title3` to `Process Information Charts`, `Top 10 Processes by Working Set`, and `Top 10 Processes by Peak Working Set`, respectively.

At this point, the chart's visual properties are set up. The only thing that remains is to bind the data coming from the `ProcessList.GetTopWorkingSet()` method to the chart. It's simple. In the `MainForm_Load` event, you can set up this binding as shown in Listing 14-3.

### LISTING 14-3: MainForm.cs Modified for Data Binding

```
using System;
using System.Windows.Forms;
using System.Windows.Forms.DataVisualization.Charting;

namespace ProcessInfoChart
{
  public partial class MainForm : Form
  {
    public MainForm()
    {
      InitializeComponent();
    }

    private void MainForm_Load(object sender, EventArgs e)
    {
      processInfoBindingSource.DataSource = ProcessList.GetTopWorkingSet(10);
    }
  }
}
```

*Code file [MainForm.cs] available for download at Wrox.com*

Build and run the application to see the results. Figure 14-13 shows the chart with the two chart areas showing process information.

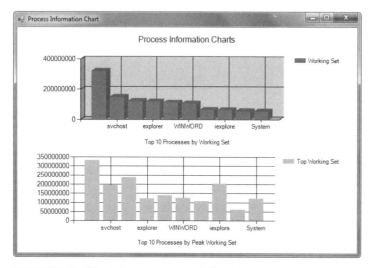

**FIGURE 14-13:** Chart showing process information

When you see this chart, you'll note a few issues. For example, only every second process name is displayed, and chart areas have different sizes. Later in this chapter, you will make more changes and customizations with charts, and will discover the answers for these issues.

## Adding Charts to WPF Applications

Unfortunately, Microsoft did not package a Windows Presentation Foundation (WPF) chart control with .NET Framework 4.0. However, that does not mean you must surrender using the `Chart` control in WPF applications. Let's create a simple WPF application using a Windows Forms chart.

Start a new WPF Application project and name it `WpfSimpleChart`. Add a reference to the `WindowsFormsIntegration` assembly. The main windows of this application will host a Windows Forms user control, so change the `MainWindow.xaml` file as shown in Listing 14-4.

**LISTING 14-4:** MainWindow.xaml

```xml
<Window x:Class="WpfSimpleChart.MainWindow"
        xmlns="http://schemas.microsoft.com/winfx/2006/xaml/presentation"
        xmlns:x="http://schemas.microsoft.com/winfx/2006/xaml"
        Title="MainWindow" Height="350" Width="525" Loaded="Window_Loaded">
  <DockPanel>
    <WindowsFormsHost HorizontalAlignment="Stretch" Name="ChartHost"
      VerticalAlignment="Stretch" />
  </DockPanel>
</Window>
```

*Code file [MainWindow.xaml] available for download at Wrox.com*

The `WindowsFormHost` control named `ChartHost` will embed the user control encapsulating the chart. This user control will be assigned to the host control in the `Window_Loaded` event.

Create a new Windows Forms User Control and name it `SimpleChart`. Drag a `Chart` control from the Toolbox to the design surface of the user control, and keep its default `chart1` name. Set the `Dock` property of `chart1` to `Fill`, and you'll see the user control resembles the one shown in Figure 14-14.

You do not need to set any other properties of the chart manually. Go to the code view of `SimpleChart.cs` and copy the initialization code shown in Listing 14-5.

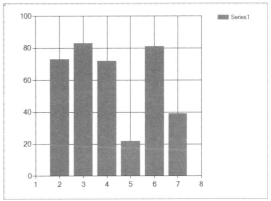

**FIGURE 14-14:** Chart control at design time

**LISTING 14-5:** SimpleChart.cs

```csharp
using System.Drawing;
using System.Windows.Forms;
using System.Windows.Forms.DataVisualization.Charting;
using System;

namespace WpfSimpleChart
{
  public partial class SimpleChart : UserControl
  {
    public SimpleChart()
    {
      InitializeComponent();
      SetupChart();
    }

    private void SetupChart()
    {
      var title = new Title("This is a Windows Forms chart in WPF");
      title.Font = new System.Drawing.Font("Calibri", 18F, FontStyle.Bold);
      chart1.Titles.Add(title);
      var datapoints = chart1.Series[0].Points;
      for (int i = 0; i <= 10; i++)
        datapoints.Add(new DataPoint(i,
          Math.Pow(Math.Abs(5-i), 2.5)));
    }
  }
}
```

*Code file [SimpleChart.cs] available for download at Wrox.com*

The initialization code sets up five data points in the chart and adds a title. When you instantiate SimpleChart, it will show up in the chart. The last step to allow this chart to be displayed in a WPF window is to embed it into the ChartHost control. Listing 14-6 shows you how easy it is.

**LISTING 14-6:** MainWindow.xaml.cs

```csharp
using System.Windows;

namespace WpfSimpleChart
{
  public partial class MainWindow : Window
  {
    public MainWindow()
    {
      InitializeComponent();
```

```
    }

    private void Window_Loaded(object sender, RoutedEventArgs e)
    {
      ChartHost.Child = new SimpleChart();
    }
  }
}
```

*Code file [MainWindow.xaml.cs] available for download at Wrox.com*

Your chart is now hosted in the WPF `MainWindow`, and your application is ready to run.
Figure 14-15 shows that it works as expected.

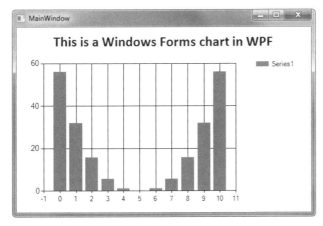

**FIGURE 14-15:** Chart hosted in a WPF window

 *Although the chart is hosted in a WPF window, it uses GDI+ technology to render the chart. Right now, Microsoft does not ship a WPF chart with Visual Studio 2010. When you need to use one, you can buy one from your preferred UI control vendor or examine free WPF chart solutions.*

## USING CHART CONTROLS

Earlier in this chapter, you read an overview of chart creation, and you became familiar with a few chart elements (such as chart areas, series, data points, titles, and so on). Now, let's dive deeper into the use of chart controls.

# Elements of a Chart

A chart has many elements, each playing a specific role in rendering the final view of the chart. Table 14-1 describes various chart elements, as shown in Figure 14-16.

**TABLE 14-1:** Chart Elements

| ELEMENT | DESCRIPTION |
| --- | --- |
| Chart picture | This is the entire image that is produced, and corresponds to the root `Chart` class. |
| Series | This is a related group of data points. Each series has an associated chart type. The number of series that a chart can display, as well as how it displays the series, depends on the chart type you specify. This element corresponds to the `Series` class. |
| Chart area | This is a rectangular area that is used to draw the series, labels, axes, grid lines, tick marks, and so on. Depending on the chart type, multiple series can be plotted in one chart area. This element corresponds to the `ChartArea` class. |
| Plot area | This is the rectangular area in a chart area that is used to plot the chart series and grid lines. Labels, tick marks, and axes titles are drawn outside of the plotting area, but inside the chart area. The plot area can be set using the `InnerPlotPosition` property of the hosting `ChartArea`. |
| Title | This is a title on the chart picture. You can add any number of titles to a chart picture. This element corresponds to the `Title` class, an item in the chart's `Titles` collection. |
| Axis label | This is a label on an axis. It is generated automatically if no custom labels are supplied. This element corresponds to the `Label` class. |
| Axis title | This is the title of an axis, which describes what the axis represents. |
| Legend | This is a legend for the chart picture. There can be more than one legend in a chart picture. This element corresponds to an item in the chart's `Legends` collection. |
| Grid lines | These are the horizontal and vertical grid lines, which usually occur in conjunction with tick marks. This element corresponds to the `Grid` class. |
| Tick marks | These are marks on the axes, which usually occur in conjunction with grid lines. This element corresponds to the `TickMark` class. |
| Data label | This is a label that describes a data point. |

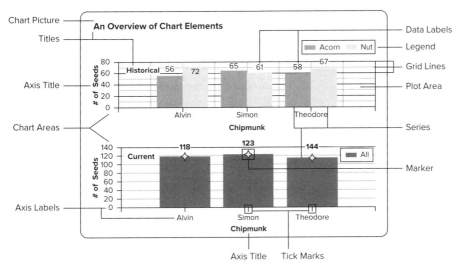

**FIGURE 14-16:** Overview of chart elements

## The Chart Class

The Chart class is a Windows Forms control class. When you intend to add charting functionality to your applications, you must add one or more Chart controls to your forms, and set up their properties. The Chart control has dozens of properties, many of which are the common Windows Forms control properties (such as the ones in the Behavior, Design, and Layout categories), while others influence the appearance of chart elements.

The Chart class has a few properties that you can use to set up the data and the structure of the chart, they can be found under the Chart and Data categories. Table 14-2 describes them.

**TABLE 14-2:** Properties Defining the Structure and Data of a Chart

| PROPERTY | DESCRIPTION |
| --- | --- |
| Annotations | You can add annotations to the chart or to the data points in the chart. The chart control comes with 13 types of annotations, including lines, arrows, texts, rectangles, borders, and many more. |
| ChartAreas | Each chart may contain one or more chart areas. A chart area is a rectangular area where you can plot a specific chart type for one or more data series belonging to a chart. Earlier in this chapter, Figure 14-6 showed a chart with one chart area displaying the two data series of the chart. Figure 14-7 showed how these series were assigned to separate chart areas. |

*continues*

**TABLE 14-2** *(continued)*

| PROPERTY | DESCRIPTION |
|---|---|
| Legends | Each chart can have zero, one, or more legends that may belong either to the chart, or to a specific chart area. Earlier in this chapter, Figure 14-8 showed a single legend assigned with the chart. Figure 14-9 showed how this legend was split into two, each associated with one chart area. |
| Series | Series are sets of data points from which the entire data content of the chart is composed. One chart may have one or more series. Each series can be assigned to exactly one chart area, and can be shown in one legend or without a legend. The series also should be assigned to exactly one chart area. |
| Titles | Titles are text decorations that can belong either to the chart, or to one of the chart areas. You can add an unlimited number of titles to the chart, and you can dock, align, and position them relatively to the chart or chart area to which they belong. |
| DataSource | You can bind the chart to a data source, just like any other data-aware controls. The `DataSource` property defines the source from which the chart obtains its data. |

Figure 14-17 shows a simplified Unified Modeling Language (UML) class diagram of the entities related to the `Chart` class. This figure helps you visualize the relations among the entities described in Table 14-2.

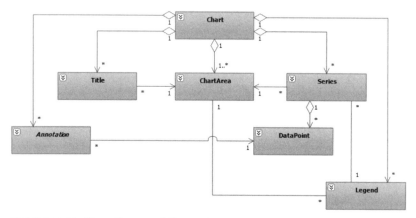

**FIGURE 14-17:** Class diagram of Chart-related entities

# Chart Types

The `Chart` control can display more than 30 types of charts. Some of them are general-purpose chart types — like Column, Bar, and Area charts — but there are a few of them that have special applications — such as Stock, Polar, or Radar charts. You can set the chart type separately for each series, and one series has exactly one chart type.

The `ChartType` property of a `Series` instance holds the chart type defining how the specific series should be displayed. It gets its value from the `SeriesChartType` enumeration. One chart area may contain one or more series, and each series within a chart area may use separate chart types.

However, not all chart types are compatible with each other — they cannot be shown in the same chart area. If you try to use incompatible chart types together, you will get the following error messages:

➤ In design mode, the chart disappears and the following message is displayed in the chart placeholder: "Chart Preview is not available. An action that you have performed has caused failure in Chart Preview."

➤ At run-time, an `InvalidOperationException` is raised with the following message: "The chart area contains incompatible chart types."

When you add data points to a series, each `DataPoint` instance may have exactly one X value (defined by the `XValue` property) and one or more Y values (defined by the `YValues` property). Earlier in this chapter, you saw samples that utilized only one Y value per data point, but there are chart types (for example Range, Bubble, Candlestick, and Stock charts) that require more (two or four) Y values.

`Series` has a property named `YValuesPerPoint` with a default value of 1. When you select the chart type, this value will be automatically updated to the required number of Y values for the selected chart type. When you declare a data point manually, you can set a comma-separated list of double values in the `YValues` property of a `DataPoint`. If you set the values programmatically, `YValues` is represented as a double array (`double[]`, in C#), so you can use an array to set this property.

`Series` and their `DataPoint` instances have custom properties that vary with chart types. For example, column and bar charts have a `DrawStyle` property defining how the column or bar should be drawn (flat, cylinder, emboss, and so on).

Let's take a closer look at chart types, and how you should set up data points depending on the chart type used for a specific series.

## Column and Bar Charts

The most frequently used charts are *column charts* representing each value as a column. This is the default type for a series. Figure 14-18 shows a column chart with two series.

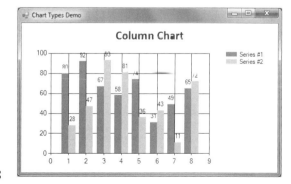

**FIGURE 14-18:** Column chart example

When you use more than one series in a column chart, you can display them with a *stacked column chart*. This kind of chart is very good when you combine data values from sub-values represented by separate series. For example, when you have sales numbers for two or more products represented by data series, the stacked column chart can also display the sum of sales numbers, as shown in Figure 14-19.

Stacked column charts have a custom property with the name `StackedGroupName`. You can use this property to set which series should be put in a common stack. Series having the same

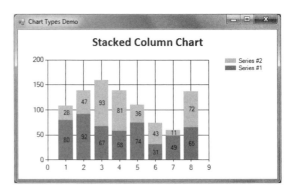

**FIGURE 14-19:**  Stacked column chart example

`StackedGroupName` are collected to form one stack. For example, when you have eight series, you can form three stacks holding three, three, and two data points, respectively.

Another option is to use a *100 percent stacked column* chart. It works with the same logic as the stacked column chart, but the sum of data points in one stack are normalized to 100 percent, and data points are displayed as percentages. Figure 14-20 shows the same data as in Figure 14-19, but with a 100 percent stacked chart.

*Bar chart*s are very similar to column charts, but they permute the X and Y axes. Figure 14-21 shows how the column chart in Figure 14-18 looks when you transform it to a bar chart.

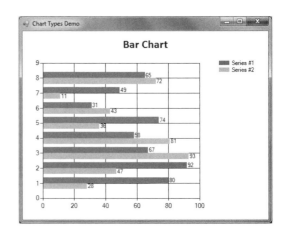

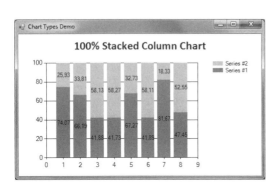

**FIGURE 14-20:**  100 percent stacked column chart example

**FIGURE 14-21:**  Bar chart example

Bar charts can also be stacked just as column charts. You can select a *stacked bar chart* and a *100 percent stacked bar chart* as the chart type for your series.

## Line Charts

*Line charts* are also very popular because they can express trends, and also suggest how you have interpolated values. A line chart simply connects data points with straight lines, as shown in Figure 14-22.

In Figure 14-22 you have data points only with integer X-coordinates from 1 to 8, but you can easily interpolate Y values for non-existing data points. For example, the Y value for X = 1.5 is about 40, as you see from the chart, and it is 37.5 when you calculate it.

Another kind of line chart is called a *spline chart*. This chart is similar to a line chart, except that it connects the different data points using splines instead of straight lines. Spline charts are compatible with line charts, and that means you can add line and spline charts to the same chart area. Figure 14-23 shows an example of merging a line and a spline chart.

Spline charts are also good for visual interpolation. Because, unlike line charts, they do not have breaks at the data points; when you look at a spline chart, you have a feeling that you have lots of data points instead of merely a few ones.

## Point Charts

*Point charts* are very simple. They show data points by drawing a visible marker having a center point with (X, Y) coordinates coming from the data point. When you use point charts instead of line charts or column charts, they do not provide you with the same "visual value" as lines or columns, as shown in Figure 14-24.

Point charts are more useful in situations when your data has two orthogonal dimensions, and so can be plotted as a set of points in a two-dimensional coordinate system. For example, you can use a point chart to show how a group

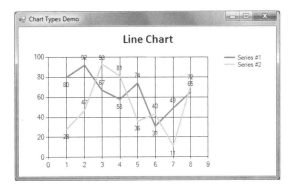

**FIGURE 14-22:** Line chart example

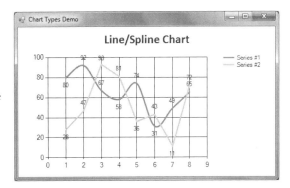

**FIGURE 14-23:** A line chart and a spline chart in the same chart area

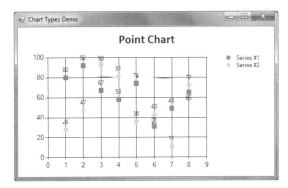

**FIGURE 14-24:** Point chart example

of people solved two tasks. The X-axis shows the result of task #1, while the Y-axis reflects the result of task #2. Figure 14-25 shows a point chart demonstrating this scenario.

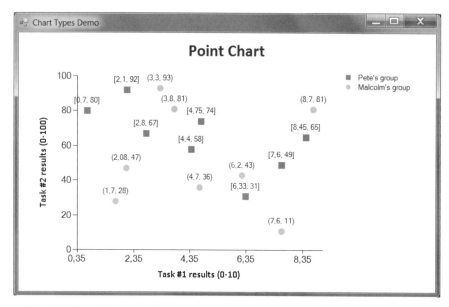

**FIGURE 14-25:** Point chart with two-dimensional data points

## Area Charts

An *area chart* graphically displays quantitative data. It is based on the line chart. The area between axis and line are commonly emphasized with colors, textures, and hatchings. Commonly, you use an area chart to compare two or more quantities. Figure 14-26 shows an example of an area chart with two series.

You have two kinds of area charts: one based on a line chart, and the other based on a spline chart (which is named SplineArea). While putting more series to a line chart generally does not deteriorate the view of individual series, putting more series on the same area chart can debase

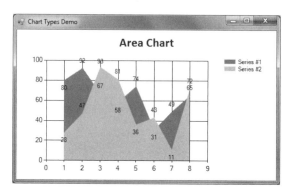

**FIGURE 14-26:** Area chart with two series

the value of the chart. In Figure 14-26, Series #2 enshrouds a large portion of Series #1. You can use transparent coloring to get rid of this situation. Figure 14-27 shows another view of the area chart with a spline-based area and semi-transparent coloring.

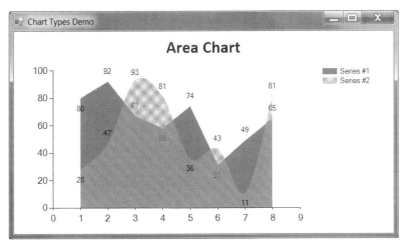

**FIGURE 14-27:** Area chart with semi-transparent coloring

Just as you can stack column and bar charts, you can stack area charts. Figure 14-28 shows a *stacked area chart.* You can also use *100 percent stacked area chart*s.

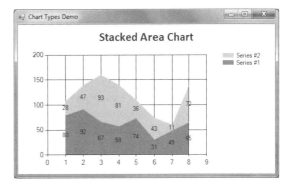

**FIGURE 14-28:** Stacked area chart example

## Pie and Doughnut Charts

A *pie chart* is a circular chart divided into sectors, illustrating percentages. In a pie chart, the arc length of each sector (and, consequently, its central angle and area) is proportional to the quantity it represents. The pie chart is perhaps the most ubiquitous statistical chart in the business world and in the mass media. Pie charts can be an effective way of displaying information, in particular if the intent is to compare the size of a slice with the whole pie, rather than comparing the slices among each other.

When you display a pie chart, you generally put only one series in a chart area. Although you can put more series in a pie chart, the Chart control will render only the first series. Figure 14-29 shows a pie chart example. When you display pie charts, the legend contains the explanation for the data points, and not for the series, as reflected in Figure 14-29.

*Doughnut charts* provide a very similar view to pie charts. They have a hole in the pie, and thus resemble a doughnut. Both pie and doughnut charts can be spectacular in three-dimensional

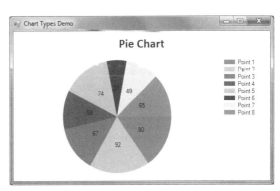

**FIGURE 14-29:** Pie chart example

views. You can even put more emphasis on certain slices by rotating the chart, or by exploding the related data point. Figure 14-30 shows a doughnut chart in a three-dimensional view.

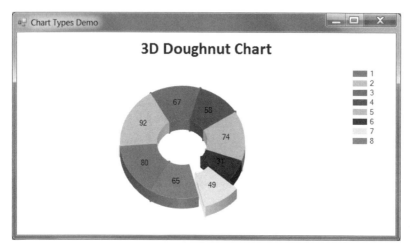

**FIGURE 14-30:** A three-dimensional doughnut chart example

## Range Charts

As their name suggests, *range charts* can display data points representing ranges ("from" and "to" values). If you change a chart type to one of the range charts, the YValuePerPoints property of the corresponding Series instance changes to 2. This property value indicates that you must provide two numbers for the YValues properties of data points in the series.

You can use four different types of range charts. You can use *range column charts* and *range bar charts* (as shown in Figure 14-31) that are very similar to column and bar charts, except that columns and bars are not drawn from the zero point of the Y axis to the data point's Y value, but rather between the two YValues provided.

You can also display range charts based on line charts (the name "range chart" covers this idea) or spline charts (as shown in Figure 14-32), which are called *spline range charts*.

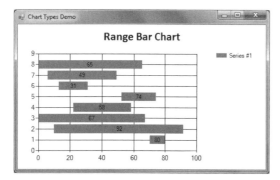

**FIGURE 14-31:**  Range bar chart example

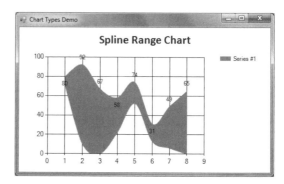

**FIGURE 14-32:**  Spline range chart example

Just like area charts, using multiple series with range charts and spline range charts can result in series covering each other, so you must be careful with them, or use semi-transparent coloring.

## Special Chart Types

The Chart control implements a few chart types for special purposes (for example, statistical and financial scenarios). Let's take a look at a few of them.

*Step line charts* are special forms of line charts that use horizontal and vertical lines to connect data points, resulting in a step-like progression. Figure 14-33 shows an example of a step line chart.

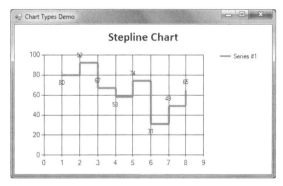

**FIGURE 14-33:** Step line chart example

A *candlestick chart* is a style of bar chart used primarily to describe, over time, price movements of a security (finance), derivative, or currency. It is a combination of a line chart and a bar chart, in that each bar represents the range of price movement over a given time interval. It is most often used in technical analysis of equity and currency price patterns.

The candlestick chart type uses four Y values (high, low, open, and close values) related to stock information. The size of the line is determined by the high and low values, while the size of the bar is determined by the open and close values. The open and close bars are displayed using different colors. The color used depends on whether the stock's price has gone up or down. Figure 14-34 shows an example of a candlestick chart.

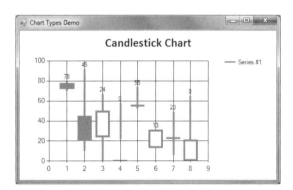

**FIGURE 14-34:** Candlestick chart example

When specifying Y values for data points, be careful, because you can specify inconsistent Y values for a data point. For example, in Figure 14-34 the data point with X value of 4 has lower open and close values than the low value, and, obviously, it cannot be so in reality.

A candlestick chart is actually a special form of a *stock chart*. A stock chart uses the same four Y values (high, low, open and close), but the markers for open and close values can be lines, triangles, or candlestick bars. Figure 14-35 shows a stock chart with data points customized so that you can see all available styles for markers.

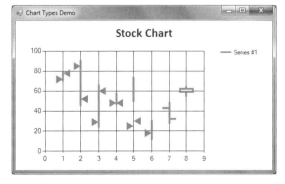

**FIGURE 14-35:** Stock chart example

You can customize the stock chart so that you can enable or disable open and closing price values. The data point with X value of 6 is displayed with a disabled close value.

The *polar chart* type is a circular graph on which data points are displayed using the angle, and the distance from the center point — according to the polar coordinate system. The X axis is located on the boundaries of the circle, and the Y axis connects the center of the circle with the X axis. Figure 14-36 shows an example of this chart type.

The *radar chart* is used to display multivariate data in the form of a two-dimensional chart of three or more quantitative variables represented on axes starting from the same point. The relative position and angle of the axes is typically uninformative. It is also known as *web chart*, *spider chart*, and *star chart*. Unlike most other chart types, the radar chart type uses the circumference of the chart as the X axis. Figure 14-37 shows you an example of this chart type.

## More About Custom Properties

Most chart types have a few custom properties you can use to customize chart rendering. When you set the `ChartType` property of a `Series` instance, you'll find a `CustomProperties` category that holds special properties interpreted in the context of the selected chart type. In Figure 14-38 you can see the custom properties of a column chart (on the left) and a stock chart (on the right) side by side.

If a custom property is applicable to both the chart's `Series` and `DataPoint` objects, any custom property that is set for a series is applied to all data points contained within that series. Data points belonging to the series inherit these custom properties, but you can change them on

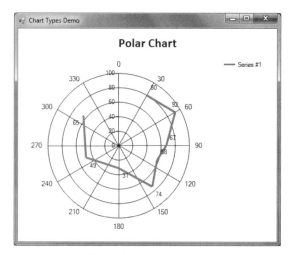

**FIGURE 14-36:** Polar chart example

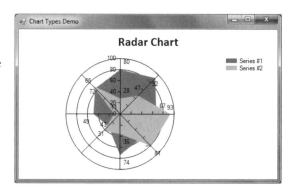

**FIGURE 14-37:** Radar chart example

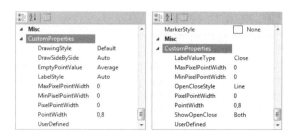

**FIGURE 14-38:** Custom properties of a column chart and a stock chart

a data-point basis. Custom properties that apply to `DataPoint` objects have a higher priority than those that apply to `Series` objects. If the same custom property is set for a `Series` object and one of its `DataPoint` objects, the setting for the `DataPoint` object takes precedence.

For example, this feature was used when creating Figure 14-35, where a few data points have different rendering style from the others.

*There are many properties and custom properties you can use to tailor chart types to your needs. You can read more about them in the MSDN documentation of the* Chart *control at* http://msdn.microsoft.com/en-us/library/ dd489233(VS.100).aspx.

## Chart Coordinate System

The Chart control uses a coordinate system to position titles, legends, annotations, and chart areas in the chart picture. To do this, it uses each element's Position property. The chart coordinate system has the following characteristics:

➤   The chart coordinate system has its origin (0, 0) in the upper-left corner of the chart picture.

➤   In the (X, Y) coordinates, the X value points to the horizontal axis, and the Y value points to the vertical axis.

The unit of measure is a percentage of the chart picture's width and height. Coordinate values must be between 0 and 100. Relative coordinates ensure that objects remain relative to one another when the chart is resized.

A chart area positions each of its elements using a similar coordinate system. Coordinates (0, 0) represent the upper-left corner of the chart area, and coordinates (100, 100) represent the lower-right corner of the chart area. When a legend is docked to a chart area, it is positioned using the chart area's coordinate system.

Understanding how the coordinate system works is especially useful when you want to implement custom drawing or user interactions (for example, mouse hit testing). To perform custom drawing using GDI+ functions in your code, you must convert the relative coordinates to absolute pixel coordinates. The ChartGraphics class contains methods for absolute-to-relative and relative-to-absolute conversion of PointF, RectangleF, and SizeF structures. To demonstrate these concepts, you can change the WpfSimpleChart sample program to add custom drawings.

Open the WpfSimpleChart project, and then open the SimpleChart.cs user control in design view. In the Properties window, add an event handler method for the PostPaint event, and write the method body as shown in Listing 14-7.

**Available for download on Wrox.com**

**LISTING 14-7: SimpleChart.cs (chart1_PostPaint Method Added)**

```
using System.Drawing;
using System.Windows.Forms;
using System.Windows.Forms.DataVisualization.Charting;
using System;

namespace WpfSimpleChart
{
  public partial class SimpleChart : UserControl
```

*continues*

**LISTING 14-7** *(continued)*

```
{
  public SimpleChart()
  {
    InitializeComponent();
    SetupChart();
  }

  private void SetupChart()
  {
    var title = new Title("This is a Windows Forms chart in WPF");
    title.Font = new System.Drawing.Font("Calibri", 18F, FontStyle.Bold);
    chart1.Titles.Add(title);
    var datapoints = chart1.Series[0].Points;
    for (int i = 0; i <= 10; i++)
      datapoints.Add(new DataPoint(i,
        Math.Pow(Math.Abs(5-i), 2.5)));
  }

  private void chart1_PostPaint(object sender, ChartPaintEventArgs e)
  {
    // --- Uncomment this code to see how custom paint works
    if (e.ChartElement is ChartArea)
    {
      var chartArea = e.ChartElement as ChartArea;
      var areaRect = new RectangleF(10.0F, 10.0F, 80.0F, 80.0F);
      var absAreaRect = e.ChartGraphics.GetAbsoluteRectangle(areaRect);
      var rect = new Rectangle((int)absAreaRect.X, (int)absAreaRect.Y,
        (int)absAreaRect.Width, (int)absAreaRect.Height);
      e.ChartGraphics.Graphics.DrawRectangle(System.Drawing.Pens.Red, rect);
    }
    else if (e.ChartElement is Series)
    {
      var series = e.ChartElement as Series;
      foreach (DataPoint point in series.Points)
      {
        var position = new PointF();
        position.X = (float)e.ChartGraphics.GetPositionFromAxis(
          "ChartArea1", AxisName.X, point.XValue);
        position.Y = (float)e.ChartGraphics.GetPositionFromAxis(
          "ChartArea1", AxisName.Y, point.YValues[0]);
        position = e.ChartGraphics.GetAbsolutePoint(position);
        for (int rad = 5; rad <= 35; rad += 10)
        {
          e.ChartGraphics.Graphics.DrawEllipse(System.Drawing.Pens.Purple,
            position.X - rad / 2, position.Y - rad / 2, rad, rad);
        }
      }
    }
  }
}
```

*Code file [SimpleChart.cs] available for download at Wrox.com*

This code draws a bounding rectangle around the chart area defined by the `areaRect` rectangle and leaves 10 percent padding within the chart area. The `GetAbsoluteRectangle` method of the `ChartGraphics` class is used to translate relative coordinates to absolute ones stored in `absAreaRect`.

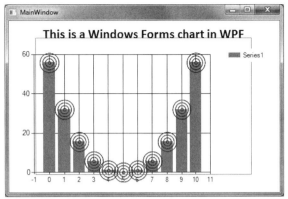

The cycle that iterates through data points draws concentric circles around data points. This cycle uses the `GetPositionFromAxis` method to translate the X value and Y value of a data point to absolute coordinates.

**FIGURE 14-39:** Custom drawings

When you build and run the application, you can see the result of custom drawing, as shown in Figure 14-39.

## Three-Dimensional Charts

As you have seen, the `Chart` control supports displaying three-dimensional charts. The `ChartArea` class has a property named `Area3DStyle` with the type of `ChartArea3DStyle`. This is the property you can use to set up and customize how the specific chart area should display a three-dimensional chart. Figure 14-40 shows how the properties in `ChartArea.Area3DStyle` correspond to the appearance of the three-dimensional chart area.

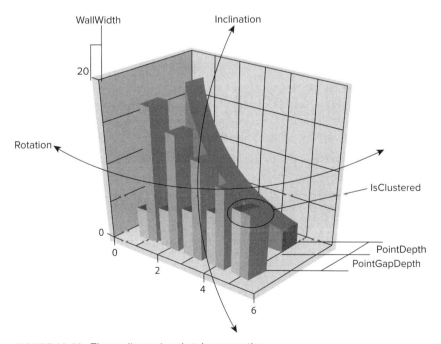

**FIGURE 14-40:** Three-dimensional style properties

Table 14-3 summarizes the properties you can use to customize the three-dimensional view.

**TABLE 14-3:** ChartArea3DStyle Properties

| PROPERTY | DESCRIPTION |
| --- | --- |
| Enable3D | Gets or sets a flag that toggles the three-dimensional rendering on and off for a chart area. |
| Inclination | Gets or sets the angle of rotation around the horizontal axes for three-dimensional chart areas. |
| IsClustered | Gets or sets a flag that determines whether the data series for a bar or column chart are clustered (that is, displayed along distinct rows). For example, in Figure 14-40, you can see three series. Two of them use a column chart, the third one uses a spline area chart. The IsClustered flag is set to true, and so the two column charts share the same cluster. Should you set this flag to false, you would see the chart as shown in Figure 14-41. |
| IsRightAngleAxes | Gets or sets a flag that determines whether a chart area is displayed using an isometric projection. Isometric views are not actually three-dimensional, because the displayed angles of rotation may not match the actual angles of rotation around the vertical and horizontal axes. The actual angles are controlled using the Rotation and Inclination properties, respectively. |
| LightStyle | Gets or sets the style of lighting for a three-dimensional chart area. Use the LightStyle.None value when you want no lighting to be applied. LightStyle.Simplistic provides you with a simple lightening where the hue of all chart area elements is fixed. When LightStyle.Realistic is applied, the hue of all chart area elements changes, depending on the amount of rotation. |
| Perspective | Gets or sets the percent of perspective for a three-dimensional chart area. The allowable range is 0 to 100 percent, and the default is 0 percent. If you set the Perspective property, the IsRightAngleAxes property will be automatically set to false, because these properties are mutually exclusive. |
| PointDepth | Gets or sets the depth of data points displayed in a three-dimensional chart area. The PointDepth property can be applied to the depth of bar, column, line, pie, and spline chart data points only. If you set this property for other chart types (for example, bubble and point charts) that cannot have their point depths "stretched," it will reserve extra space for the data points, but will not increase their depths. |
| PointGapDepth | Gets or sets the distance between series rows in a three-dimensional chart area. The unit of measurement is expressed as a percentage of the distance between data points in one row. |
| Rotation | Gets or sets the angle of rotation around the vertical axes for three-dimensional chart areas. |
| WallWidth | Gets or sets the width of the walls displayed in a three-dimensional chart area. The allowable range is 0 to 30 pixels. |

The three-dimensional chart coordinate system has the added Z coordinate (X, Y, Z). It is also a percentage of the chart area's depth. The chart area's back wall has a Z value of 0, and the front end of the chart area has a Z value of 100.

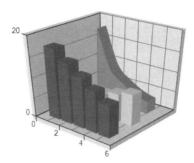

**FIGURE 14-41:** Three-dimensional chart rendered with IsClustered set to false

## Appearance of Chart Elements

In the `Chart` control, you can customize the appearance of all chart elements using their appearance properties. Each chart element contains a rich set of appearance properties, which enables you to control the `Chart` control's appearance to very fine granularities. The best way to know what you can control in an element is to look into the Appearance category in the Properties window. Table 14-4 describes the properties that can be used for most line-type elements.

**TABLE 14-4:** Properties Influencing the Appearance of Line-Type Elements

| PROPERTY | DESCRIPTION |
| --- | --- |
| LineColor, BorderColor | Gets or sets the line color of a line (border). |
| LineDashStyle, BorderDashStyle | Gets or sets the line style of a line (border). |
| LineWidth, BorderWidth | Gets or sets the line (border) width. |
| StartCap | Gets or sets a style for the cap at the start of a line. |
| EndCap | Gets or sets a style for the cap at the end of the line. |
| ShadowColor | Gets or sets the color of a line's shadow. |
| ShadowOffset | Gets or sets the size of a line's shadow. |

Table 14-5 summarizes the properties that can be used with surfaces, including data points, markers, and annotations. Of course, if surfaces have lines or borders, they also have properties shown in Table 14-4.

**TABLE 14-5:** Properties Determining the Appearance of Line-Type Elements

| PROPERTY | DESCRIPTION |
| --- | --- |
| BackGradientStyle | Gets or sets the background gradient style. |
| BackHatchStyle | Gets or sets the background hatching style. |
| BackImage | Gets or sets the background image. |
| BackImageAlignment | Gets or sets the alignment of the background image, which is used with the `Unscaled` drawing mode. |

*continues*

**TABLE 14-5** *(continued)*

| PROPERTY | DESCRIPTION |
|---|---|
| BackImageTransparentColor | Gets or sets a color that will be replaced with a transparent color when the background image is drawn. |
| BackImageWrapMode | Gets or sets the drawing mode of the background image. |
| BackSecondaryColor | Gets or sets the secondary background color. This property is used when the background uses a gradient style. |

You can control text elements with additional properties summarized in Table 14-6.

**TABLE 14-6:** Properties Controlling Text Element Appearance

| PROPERTY | DESCRIPTION |
|---|---|
| Font | Gets or sets the font for the text. |
| ForeColor | Gets or sets the color of the text element. |
| ShadowColor | Gets or sets the color of the text shadow. This property can be set to any valid ARGB (alpha, red, green, blue) value. The alpha value can be used to achieve a "realistic" shadowing effect. |
| ShadowOffset | Gets or sets the shadow offset, in pixels, of the text. |
| TextOrientation | Gets or sets the orientation of the text. |
| TextStyle | Gets or sets the style of the text. The five possible styles are TextStyle .Default, TextStyle.Shadow, TextStyle.Emboss, TextStyle.Embed, and TextStyle.Frame. |

There are many other properties determining the appearance of chart elements. Most of them are refreshed in the design view as soon as you set or change them. Sometimes, the easiest way to find out what they do is to try them in design mode. If you are not sure what they are for, position to the specific property in the Properties window and press F1 to obtain the help for them.

Instead of setting series and data point colors individually, you can use `Palette` objects that define a set of colors. The `Chart.Palette` property defines a set of default colors to use for series and data points. The `Series.Palette` property likewise defines a set of default colors to use for its data points. Use these properties to give your series and data points a specific look. To specify a custom palette for the `Chart` control, use the `Chart.PaletteCustomColors` property. This property takes precedence over `Chart.Palette`. Likewise, to specify a custom palette for a series, use the `Series .PaletteCustomColors` property.

The `Chart` control can smooth the sharp color gradients by using anti-aliasing. This makes the chart image much more pleasing to the viewer's eyes. To do this, set the `Chart.AntiAliasing` property to `AntiAliasingStyles.Text`, `AntiAliasingStyles.Graphics`, or `AntiAliasingStyles.All`.

When shadows are displayed for any chart element, you can also smooth the shadows by setting the `Chart.IsSoftShadows` property to `True`.

Figure 14-42 shows the effect of anti-aliasing with a zoom factor of two.

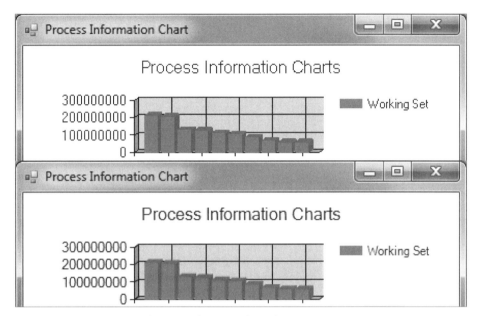

**FIGURE 14-42:** Using anti-aliasing with text and graphics

The top part of the figure turns all antialiasing options off, while the bottom part turns them on.

## Axes and Related Chart Elements

You can customize the appearance and behavior of axes belonging to your chart. A `ChartArea` instance contains a property called `Axes` that is an array of `Axis`. The definition of `Axes` suggests that you can read and write this property, but you should use it as read-only. You can index the element of `Axes` with the `AxisName` enumeration, which has the values summarized in Table 14-7.

**TABLE 14-7:** Values of the AxisName Enumeration

| VALUE | DESCRIPTION | POSITION FOR BAR AND STACKED BAR CHARTS | OTHER CHARTS |
|---|---|---|---|
| X | Primary X-axis | Left vertical axis | Bottom horizontal axis |
| Y | Primary Y-axis | Bottom horizontal axis | Left vertical axis |
| X1 | Secondary X-axis | Right vertical axis | Top horizontal axis |
| Y1 | Secondary Y-axis | Top horizontal axis | Right vertical axis |

There are a few charts (polar, pie, doughnut, and radar) where polar-like axes are used. Of course, their axis positions are different than those indicated in Table 14-6.

An `Axis` can be customized with dozens of properties. Table 14-8 describes the most frequently used ones.

**TABLE 14-8:** Axis Properties

| PROPERTY | DESCRIPTION |
| --- | --- |
| ArrowStyle | Gets or sets the arrow style of a two-dimensional axis. This style is not applied to three-dimensional chart areas. The possible styles are defined with the values of the `AxisArrowStyle` enumeration (`None`, `Triangle`, `SharpTriangle`, `Lines`). |
| InterlacedColor | Gets or sets the color of interlaced strip lines. |
| IsInterlaced | Gets or sets a flag that determines if interlaced strip lines are displayed for an axis. |
| StripLines | Gets a `StripLinesCollection` object that holds the strip lines for an axis. Strip lines are used to draw rectangular strips across a `ChartArea` object, and are always drawn across the entire area. |
| MajorGrid | Gets or sets a `Grid` object used to set the major grid line properties for an axis. Major grid lines are always drawn in conjunction with a data point. That is, they will occur at the same point along an axis as a data point, for categorical axis tick marks. For value axes, major grid lines by default are drawn wherever labels occur. |
| MajorTickMark | Gets or sets a `TickMark` object used to set the major tick mark properties of an axis. Major tick marks are always drawn in conjunction with a data point. Categorical axis tick marks will occur at the same point along an axis as a data point. For value axes, major tick marks are drawn by default wherever labels occur. |
| MinorGrid | Gets or sets a `Grid` object used to specify the minor grid line attributes of an axis. Minor grid lines are drawn in between the major grid lines. |
| MinorTickMark | Gets or sets a `TickMark` object used to set the minor tick mark properties of an axis. |
| Interval | Gets or sets the interval of an axis. This property determines how often the labels, major tick marks, and grid lines associated with the axis are drawn. |
| IntervalAutoMode | Gets or sets a flag that determines if a fixed number of intervals is used on the axis, or if the number of intervals depends on the axis size. You can use the values of the `IntervalAutoMode` enumeration (`FixedCount`, `VariableCount`). |

| PROPERTY | DESCRIPTION |
|---|---|
| IntervalOffset | Gets or sets the interval offset of an axis. This value is used as the interval offset of the labels of an axis, as well as the major tick marks and grid lines associated with the axis. |
| IntervalOffsetType | This property determines the interval offset type of an axis, and is used for the interval offset type of the labels, major tick marks, or major grid lines of an axis. |
| IntervalType | This property determines the interval type of an axis, and is used for the interval type of the labels, major tick marks, or major grid lines of an axis. |
| CustomLabels | Gets a CustomLabelsCollection object used to store CustomLabel objects. |
| IsLabelAutoFit | Gets or sets a flag that determines whether axis labels are automatically fitted. |
| LabelAutoFitMinFontSize | Gets or sets the minimum font size that can be used by the label auto-fitting algorithm. |
| LabelAutoFitMaxFontSize | Gets or sets the maximum font size that can be used by the label auto-fitting algorithm. |
| LabelAutoFitStyle | Gets or sets the allowable label changes that can be made to enable the label to be fit along an axis. |
| LabelStyle | Specifies the style, formatting, and so forth, of axis labels. |
| | If the IsLabelAutoFit property is true, the font size, font angle, and the use of offset labels are determined automatically. If you set any one of the LabelStyle.Font.Size, Angle, or IsStaggered properties, the IsLabelAutoFit property will be set to false. |
| MaximumAutoSize | Gets or sets the maximum size of the axis, measured as a percentage of the chart area. This value is used by the automatic layout algorithm. |
| Enabled | Gets or sets a value that indicates whether an axis is enabled. |
| | If an axis is not enabled, the axis, along with its attributes (tick marks, strip lines, labels, and so forth), will not be displayed. If an axis is enabled, the axis, along with all its attributes (tick marks, strip lines, labels, and so forth), will be displayed, regardless of whether or not it is being used to plot a Series. |
| | If a value of Auto is used, an axis may or may not be displayed, depending on whether it is being used to plot a Series. The axes that are used to plot data are determined by the XAxisType and YAxisType property settings. |

*continues*

**TABLE 14-8** *(continued)*

| PROPERTY | DESCRIPTION |
|---|---|
| Crossing | Setting this property for a primary axis will determine where the other primary axis crosses it, and, similarly, setting it for a secondary axis will determine where the other secondary axis crosses it. For example, setting the `Crossing` property of the primary X-axis determines where the primary Y-axis will cross it. |
| IsLogarithmic | Gets or sets a flag that indicates whether the axis is logarithmic. Zeros or negative data values are not allowed on logarithmic charts. |
| IsMarginVisible | Gets or sets a flag that determines whether to add a margin to the axis. |
| IsReversed | Gets or sets a flag that indicates whether the axis is reversed. If set to reversed, the values on the axis are in reversed sort order, and the direction of values on the axis is flipped. |
| IsStartedFromZero | Gets or sets a flag that indicates whether the minimum value of the axis will be automatically set to zero if all data point values are positive. If there are negative data point values, the minimum value of the data points will be used. |
| LogarithmBase | Gets or sets a value for the logarithm base for the logarithmic axis. |
| Minimum | Gets or sets the minimum value of an axis. Note that, if you set this value explicitly, the X-values of data elements must be taken into account. If all data points have X-values of zero, the `Chart` control will assume the first data point occurs at zero. Also, if the `Minimum` value is explicitly set, the `IsStartedFromZero` property will be ignored. The `Minimum` value must be less than the `Maximum` value. |
| Maximum | Gets or sets the maximum value of an axis. |
| ScaleBreakStyle | Gets or sets the axis scale break style. Scale breaks are intentional discontinuities on the Y-axis that are most often used to redistribute the data points in a series on a chart. This feature improves readability when there are large differences between the high and low values of the data in one series being plotted. Scale breaks are not drawn for differences between data in multiple series. |
| TextOrientation | Gets or sets the orientation of the text in the axis title. This property takes its value from the `TextOrientation` enumeration (`Auto`, `Horizontal`, `Rotated90`, `Rotated270`, `Stacked`). |
| Title | Gets or sets the title of the axis. |
| TitleAlignment | Gets or sets the alignment of an axis title. This property takes its value from the `StringAlignment` enumeration (`Near`, `Center`, `Far`). |
| TitleFont | Gets or sets the title font properties of an axis. |
| TitleForeColor | Gets or sets the text color of an `Axis` object title. You can use any valid ARGB (alpha, red, green, blue) color. |

Most properties can be used very easily. When you change their values, the design surface refreshes immediately, and so you can check the effect of changes. However, there are a few properties that need further explanation.

## Strip Lines

*Strip lines* are used to draw rectangular strips across a `ChartArea` object, and are always drawn across the entire area. You can draw unlimited numbers of strip lines in a chart area. Listing 14-8 shows an example of setting up strip lines.

**LISTING 14-8:** Windows Forms Code Setting Up Strip Lines

```
using System;
using System.Windows.Forms;
using System.Windows.Forms.DataVisualization.Charting;
using System.Drawing;

namespace StripLinesSample
{
  public partial class Form1 : Form
  {
    public Form1()
    {
      InitializeComponent();
    }

    private void Form1_Load(object sender, EventArgs e)
    {
      // --- Set up data points
      var series = chart1.Series[0];
      series.Color = Color.Red;
      series.BorderColor = Color.DimGray;
      series.BorderWidth = 2;
      for (int i = 0; i < 6; i++)
      {
        series.Points.Add(new DataPoint(10 * i + 10, 5 * i + 5));
      }

      // --- Set up X-axis
      var xAxis = chart1.ChartAreas[0].Axes[(int)AxisName.X];
      xAxis.MinorGrid.Enabled = true;
      xAxis.MinorGrid.Interval = 5;
      xAxis.MinorTickMark.Enabled = true;
      xAxis.MinorTickMark.Interval = 5;

      // --- Set up strip line #1
      var stripLine1 = new StripLine();
      stripLine1.BackColor = Color.LightSalmon;
      stripLine1.Interval = 10;
      stripLine1.IntervalOffset = 6;
      stripLine1.StripWidth = 3;
      stripLine1.Text = "#1";
```

*continues*

**LISTING 14-8** *(continued)*

```
        stripLine1.TextOrientation = TextOrientation.Horizontal;

        // --- Set up strip line #2
        var stripLine2 = new StripLine();
        stripLine2.BackColor = Color.LightSteelBlue;
        stripLine2.Interval = 10;
        stripLine2.IntervalOffset = 1;
        stripLine2.StripWidth = 3;
        stripLine2.Text = "#2";

        xAxis.StripLines.Add(stripLine1);
        xAxis.StripLines.Add(stripLine2);
    }
  }
}
```

*Code file [Form1.cs] available for download at Wrox.com*

This listing demonstrates how to set up axis and strip line properties. The `Form1_Load` event handler method starts with setting up the series colors, and creates six data points. Then it obtains a reference for the primary X-axis with the following variable declaration:

```
var xAxis = chart1.ChartAreas[0].Axes[(int)AxisName.X];
```

With setting up `MinorGrid` and `MinorTickMark` properties, a secondary gridline is added to the X-axis. You can recognize the minor grid lines shown in Figure 14-43.

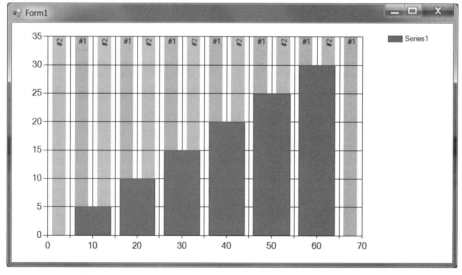

**FIGURE 14-43:** Grid lines and strip lines

The sample sets up two strip lines that are also shown in Figure 14-43. In the code, a few properties are used to set up the characteristics of strip lines. BackColor defines their color. Interval sets the frequency the strip lines are drawn along the axis. IntervalOffset sets the position of the first strip line; StripWidth defines the width of strip line to be drawn. You can set a Text for the strip line that is shown near to the secondary X-axis at the top of the plot area.

## Custom Axis Labels

Axis labels are automatically created when you set up data points, they are coming from either the XValue property of the data point, or according to the XValueMember binding property specified for the series.

You can add custom labels to any axis that can substitute the default labels, or can be additions. The CustomLabels property of an Axis instance holds CustomLabel objects that describe how a custom axis label should be displayed.

Custom labels are displayed in rows that can be indexed from 0 to 10. This index can be accessed through the RowIndex property. Index value 0 is the label closest to the axis, while value 10 signs the farthest label row. When you add any custom label in row 0, the default labels are not displayed. You can also set FromPosition and ToPosition values to define where to put the label on the specified axis.

Listing 14-9 shows a small application's code that changes the default custom labels and sets up a few additional ones.

**LISTING 14-9:** Adding Custom Labels to an Axis

```
using System;
using System.Drawing;
using System.Windows.Forms;
using System.Windows.Forms.DataVisualization.Charting;

namespace CustomLabelSample
{
  public partial class Form1 : Form
  {
    public Form1()
    {
      InitializeComponent();
    }

    private void Form1_Load(object sender, EventArgs e)
    {
      // --- Obtain X-axis
      var xAxis = chart1.ChartAreas[0].Axes[(int)AxisName.X];

      // --- Set up data points
      var series = chart1.Series[0];
      for (int i = 0; i < 6; i++)
      {
        series.Points.Add(new DataPoint(10 * i + 10, 5 * i + 5));
        // --- Custom label for data points
        var label = new CustomLabel(10*i, 10*i + 20, "#" + i, 0,
```

*continues*

**LISTING 14-9** *(continued)*

```
        LabelMarkStyle.None);
      xAxis.CustomLabels.Add(label);
    }

    // --- Further custom labels
    var lowerLabel = new CustomLabel(0, 30, "Lower part", 1,
      LabelMarkStyle.LineSideMark);
    lowerLabel.ForeColor = Color.Red;
    xAxis.CustomLabels.Add(lowerLabel);

    var upperLabel = new CustomLabel(30, 70, "Upper part", 1,
      LabelMarkStyle.LineSideMark);
    upperLabel.ForeColor = Color.Green;
    xAxis.CustomLabels.Add(upperLabel);

    var domainLabel = new CustomLabel(0, 70, "Entire domain", 3,
      LabelMarkStyle.None);
    domainLabel.ForeColor = Color.Blue;
    xAxis.CustomLabels.Add(domainLabel);
    }
  }
}
```

*Code file [Form1.cs] available for download at Wrox.com*

The `CustomLabel` constructor takes five arguments. The first two set the `FromPosition` and `ToPosition` values, and the third specifies the text of the label. The fourth parameter sets the `RowIndex` of the label, while the fifth defines how label marks should be drawn. Figure 14-44 shows the chart with the specified custom labels.

You can see from Listing 14-9 that, in the cycle creating the data points, all default labels are changed with custom ones. When you want to replace default labels, you should add custom labels with `RowIndex` 0.

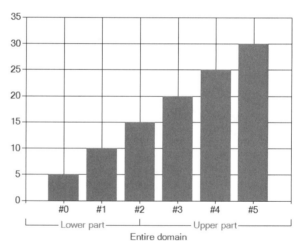

**FIGURE 14-44:** Custom labels

## Data Points

You can add a lot of customizations to your data points. You can even set each data point in your chart to have a different style. Customization is much more than just setting colors, borders, fonts, and styles. Listing 14-10 shows you the code of a simple application that decorates four data points with different adornments.

**LISTING 14-10:** Data Point Customization

```csharp
using System;
using System.Drawing;
using System.Windows.Forms;
using System.Windows.Forms.DataVisualization.Charting;

namespace DataPointSample
{
  public partial class Form1 : Form
  {
    public Form1()
    {
      InitializeComponent();
    }

    private void Form1_Load(object sender, EventArgs e)
    {
      var series = chart1.Series[0];

      var dp1 = new DataPoint(0.0, 15.0);
      dp1.BorderColor = Color.Black;
      dp1.BorderWidth = 3;
      dp1.Color = Color.LightGreen;
      series.Points.Add(dp1);

      var dp2 = new DataPoint(1.0, 10.0);
      dp2.Color = Color.Red;
      dp2.CustomProperties = "DrawingStyle=Cylinder";
      dp2.MarkerStyle = MarkerStyle.Diamond;
      dp2.MarkerSize = 20;
      dp2.MarkerColor = Color.PaleGoldenrod;
      dp2.MarkerBorderColor = Color.Black;
      series.Points.Add(dp2);

      var dp3 = new DataPoint(2.0, 20.0);
      dp3.BackHatchStyle = ChartHatchStyle.DiagonalBrick;
      dp3.BackSecondaryColor = Color.DarkBlue;
      dp3.AxisLabel = "Pos: #VALX";
      series.Points.Add(dp3);

      var dp4 = new DataPoint(3.0, 10.0);
      dp4.CustomProperties = "DrawingStyle=Wedge";
      dp4.Font = new Font("Calibri", 18F);
      dp4.Label = "[#VALX, #VAL]";
      series.Points.Add(dp4);
    }
  }
}
```

*Code file [Form1.cs] available for download at Wrox.com*

Figure 14-45 shows how the customized data points are displayed in a bar chart.

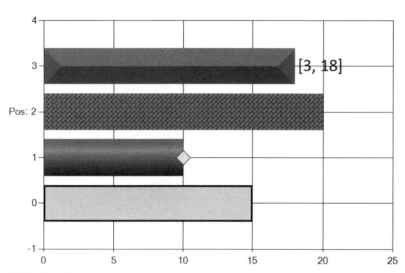

**FIGURE 14-45:** Customized data points

The code adds four data points (dp1, dp2, dp3, and dp4) to the single series of the chart. The dp1 point is customized so that only the border and the bar's color are changed. The second data point (dp2) changes its drawing style by setting the DrawingStyle custom property to the value Cylinder, and it also adds a diamond-shape marker.

The label of a data point can be simply customized by changing the AxisLabel property as dp3 does. The label can use tokens that are replaced by their values at run-time. The #VALX token represents the XValue of the data point. You can see in Figure 14-45 that dp3 has an axis label (Pos: 2) with a different format than the other data points. When you edit the AxisLabel property, it provides you a keyword editor (shown in Figure 14-46) that helps you with inserting these special tokens.

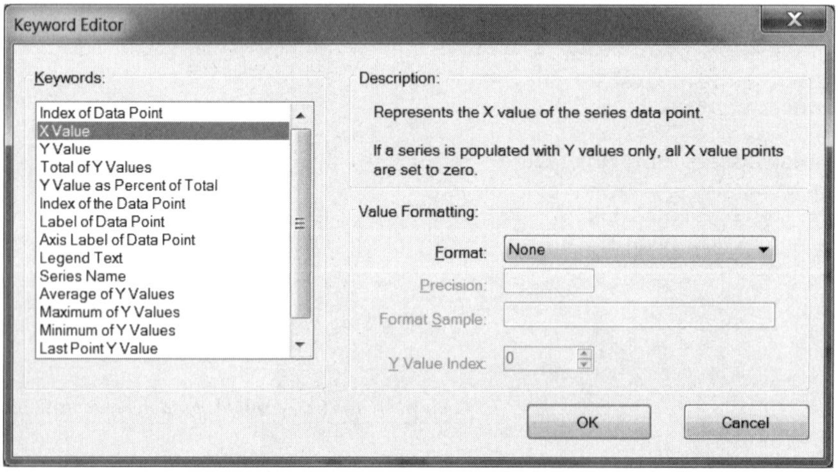

**FIGURE 14-46:** Keyword editor

The fourth data point adds a custom label to the data point. The `Label` property can use the same tokens as used for the `AxisLabel` property.

# ADVANCED CHART MANIPULATION

By now, you've learned to create great charts with the new `Chart` control, and you are familiar with chart elements and most customization options. The `Chart` control has many properties you can use to change its visual properties and behavior, and they are generally very simple to use. The `Chart` control's designer is a great tool to use to understand the meaning and effects of setting those properties to specific values, because changes are immediately reflected in the design surface. You can also write simple and straightforward programs to set these properties from code.

For most cases, when you intend to use the `Chart` control, what you've learned is enough to encapsulate spectacular charts into your applications. However, there are some more advanced features of the `Chart` control, so let's look at some of them.

## Annotations

The great advantage of charts over the use of tables is that they could provide a better representation of data — especially when you deal with dozens or hundreds of numbers — and they can catch your eye in a moment, unlike tables. A few words, arrows, or other decorations can be invaluable to help you focus on the essential data visualized by the chart.

Chart annotations allow you to create these small decorations. The `Chart` control has a collection property named `Annotations`, and you can add an unlimited number of `Annotation` instances to it.

### Annotation Types

There are several annotation types shipped with the `Chart` control. They form a type hierarchy with `Annotation` class as a root. Table 14-9 summarizes these classes, and describes their most essential properties.

**TABLE 14-9:** Annotation Types

| ANNOTATION TYPE | DESCRIPTION |
|---|---|
| Annotation | This abstract class defines properties and methods common to all annotations. By default, annotations are positioned using relative coordinates, with (0, 0) representing the top-left corner, and (100, 100) representing the bottom-right corner of the chart image. It is also possible to switch from this relative coordinate system to a system that uses axis values. With an axis coordinate system, X and Y (which represent the position of the top-left corner of an annotation) are set using X axis and Y axis values, instead of values that range from 0 to 100. |

*continues*

**TABLE 14-9** *(continued)*

| ANNOTATION TYPE | DESCRIPTION |
|---|---|
| LineAnnotation | This represents a line annotation. You can use the `StartCap` and `EndCap` properties to set the cap styles for the line's ends. |
| HorizontalLineAnnotation | This represents a horizontal line annotation, and derives from `LineAnnotation`. |
| VerticalLineAnnotation | This represents a vertical line annotation, and derives from `LineAnnotation`. |
| TextAnnotation | This represents a text annotation. Use the `Text` property to define the text you would like to show in the annotation. You can use data point value tokens such as `#VALX`, `#VAL`, `#TOTAL`, and so on. (Listing 14-10 and the related comments treat them.) The `IsMultiline` property can get or set the flag indicating whether the annotation text is multi-line. |
| RectangleAnnotation | This represents a rectangle with text annotation, and derives from `TextAnnotation`. It allows you to enclose the text in a rectangle, and provides about a dozen properties to customize the rectangle border and fill area. |
| EllipseAnnotation | This represents an ellipse with text annotation, and derives from `TextAnnotation`. It allows you to enclose the text in an ellipse, and provides about a dozen properties to customize the ellipse border and fill area. |
| ArrowAnnotation | This represents an arrow annotation. Arrow annotations can be used to connect to points on the chart, or to highlight a single chart area. You can define the style and size of the arrow with the `ArrowStyle` and `ArrowSize` properties, respectively. |
| Border3DAnnotation | This represents an annotation with a three-dimensional border, and derives from `RectangleAnnotation`. Use the `BorderSkin` compound property to set the attributes of the border. |
| CalloutAnnotation | This represents a callout with text annotation, and derives from `TextAnnotation`. You can set the style of the callout line anchor cap and the annotation callout style with the `CalloutAnchorCap` and `CalloutStyle` properties, respectively. |
| PolylineAnnotation | This represents a polyline annotation. You can use the `StartCap` and `EndCap` properties to set the cap styles for the polyline's ends. There are two properties to set the path points of a polyline annotation. `GraphicsPath` can be used only at run-time, and `GraphicsPathPoints` is available only at design-time. |

| ANNOTATION TYPE | DESCRIPTION |
|---|---|
| PolygonAnnotation | This represents a polygon annotation, and derives from PolyLineAnnotation. You can use the standard properties to set the fill area of the polygon. |
| ImageAnnotation | This represents an image annotation. The Image property tells the name of the image to be used. ImageWrapMode sets the drawing mode of the images. You can use the ImageTransparentColor property to define a color that will be replaced with a transparent color when the image is drawn. |
| AnnotationGroup | This represents a group of annotations, and implements the *composite design pattern*. Add the nested decorations to the Annotations collection property. |

Figure 14-47 shows a simple chart with a few annotations.

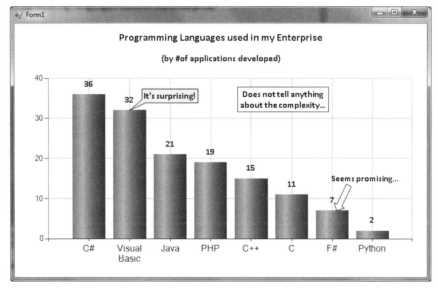

**FIGURE 14-47:** Chart decorated with annotations

There are four annotations in this figure. There is a RectangleAnnotation for the chart area with the "Does not tell. . ." text within it. The other three annotations are anchored to data points. The Visual Basic data point holds a CalloutAnnotation while the F# data point has two of them — an ArrowAnnotation and a TextAnnotation.

## Anchoring Annotations

Annotations can belong to the chart area, or be anchored with one of the data points. There are two ways to use axis values when you specify the position and size of an annotation:

➤ Set the AxisX, AxisY, or both of these annotation properties to the AxisX and AxisY property values of a ChartArea object.

➤ Use the AnchorDataPoint property to anchor the annotation to a data point. In this case, its positioning is automatically calculated. At design time, the Property grid lets you select the data point from those you have already added to the chart series.

Table 14-10 describes a set of properties starting with the Anchor prefix that define how the annotation should be anchored.

**TABLE 14-10:** Anchor Properties

| PROPERTY | DESCRIPTION |
|---|---|
| AnchorAlignment | Gets or sets the alignment of an annotation to the anchor point. The annotation must be anchored by either using the AnchorDataPoint property, or by setting the AnchorX and AnchorY properties. Its X and Y properties must be set to NaN (NotSet in design mode). |
| AnchorDataPoint | Gets or sets the data point to which an annotation is anchored. The annotation is anchored to the X and Y values of the specified data point, and automatically uses the same axes coordinates as the data point. |
| | To automatically position the annotation relative to the anchor point, ensure that its X and Y properties are set to NaN. The AnchorAlignment property can be used to change the automatic position alignment of the annotation to the anchor point. The AnchorOffsetX and AnchorOffsetY properties may be used to add extra spacing. |
| | When you use this property, ensure that the AnchorX and AnchorY properties are set to Double.NaN, because they have precedence. Set this value to a null reference (Nothing in Visual Basic) to disable annotation anchoring to a data point. |
| AnchorOffsetX | Gets or sets the offset from the anchor point for the X position of an annotation. |
| AnchorOffsetY | Gets or sets the offset from the anchor point for the Y position of an annotation. |
| AnchorX | Gets or sets the X coordinate to which the annotation is anchored. To automatically position an annotation relative to an anchor point, ensure that its X property is set to NaN. The AnchorAlignment property can be used to change the automatic position alignment of the annotation to the anchor point. The AnchorOffsetX and AnchorOffsetY properties may be used to add extra spacing. Set this value to NaN to disable annotation anchoring to the value. |
| | This property has a higher priority than the AnchorDataPoint property. |
| AnchorY | Gets or sets the Y coordinate to which the annotation is anchored. |

## Moving Annotations

By default, annotations are fixed to the chart area. Because they use a relative coordinate system, you can resize the chart and the annotations also resize, keeping their relative positions.

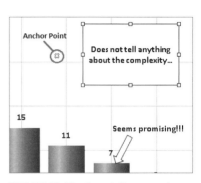

With a few properties, you can allow the user to select, resize, and move annotations with the mouse. This is a great feature, because you can create applications that allow adding and placing of annotations in your chart at run-time.

Figure 14-48 shows how a `RectangleAnnotation` in Figure 14-47 has been selected, resized, and moved.

**FIGURE 14-48:** Annotations can be selected, resized and moved

In Figure 14-48, you can see that the anchor point can be separately moved from the annotation. Once the user has finished moving the annotation, you can write code to query the anchor properties in Table 14-9, and you can save the design.

Table 14-11 describes the properties influencing how the user can interact with annotations at run-time.

**TABLE 14-11:** Anchor Properties

| PROPERTY | DESCRIPTION |
| --- | --- |
| AllowAnchorMoving | Specifies whether the end user is allowed to move the annotation anchor using a mouse. |
| AllowMoving | Specifies whether the end user is allowed to move an annotation using a mouse. |
| AllowPathEditing | Specifies whether the end user is allowed to move the points of a polygon annotation using a mouse. |
| AllowResizing | Specifies whether the end user is allowed to resize an annotation using a mouse. |
| AllowSelecting | Specifies whether the end user is allowed to select an annotation using a mouse. |
| AllowTextEditing | Specifies whether the text in an annotation may be edited when the end user double-clicks the text. |

If you plan to resize the annotation or edit polyline paths, you must also set `AllowSelecting` to `true`.

Table 14-12 describes several events for the `Chart` class to handle user actions related to annotations.

**TABLE 14-12:** Class Events Handling Annotations

| EVENT | DESCRIPTION |
|---|---|
| AnnotationPlaced | Occurs when the end-user places an annotation on the chart. |
| AnnotationPositionChanged | Occurs when the annotation position is changed. |
| AnnotationPositionChanging | Occurs when the annotation position is about to change. This event uses the `AnnotationPositionChangingEventArgs` argument that allows checking the new position before the change is committed. |
| AnnotationSelectionChanged | Occurs when a selection of the annotation is changed. |
| AnnotationTextChanged | Occurs when the annotation text is changed. |

All events except `AnnotationPositionChanging` accept `EventArgs` arguments. The `sender` object passed to the event handler holds a reference to the affected annotation instance.

## Binding Data to Series

Earlier in this chapter, you saw examples (Listing 14-2 and Listing 14-3) that used the chart's `DataSource` property to bind data from a LINQ expression. The `DataSource` property accepts many types as data sources for binding, including the following:

➤ `DataView`

➤ Data Readers (SQL, OleDB).

➤ `DataSet`

➤ Arrays

➤ Lists

➤ `SqlCommand/OleDbCommand`

➤ `SqlDataAdapter/OleDbDataAdapter`

➤ All `IEnumerable` objects

You can bind data to a series by setting the `XValueMember` and `YValueMember` properties. Data binding also can be used to bind information coming from the data source to other properties of a `Chart` instance. Go to the Data property category of the chart and expand the `(DataBinding)` property to see what chart properties can be bound to a data source.

*Data binding is a general technology in the .NET framework that has several flavors. For example, Windows Forms, ASP.NET, and WPF technologies have a slightly different implementation for data binding — according to the differences in the base technologies behind them.*

*The* Chart *control treated in this chapter uses the Windows Forms technology. To see a detailed description of Windows Forms data binding in .NET 4, visit the MSDN page at* http://msdn.microsoft.com/en-us/library/ ef2xyb33(VS.100).aspx.

While, at design-time, you can bind data to the chart only through the DataSource property, the Chart control has a few methods that allow you more control over this mechanism. Table 14-13 describes these methods.

**TABLE 14-13:** Data-Binding Methods of the Chart Control

| METHOD | DESCRIPTION |
|---|---|
| DataBind | This method binds the Chart control to the specified data source. |
| | In cases where a data source is set to a chart, and no other data operations are required, the DataBind method does not have to be explicitly called. In these cases, the Chart itself will bind the data to the data source prior to being rendered. |
| DataBindTable | This method automatically creates and binds series data to the specified data table, and optionally populates X-values. Each column of the table becomes a Y-value for a series, with one series per column. The X-value field of the series can also be provided. |
| DataBindCrossTable | Data binds a chart to the table, with one series created per unique value in a given column. |

You can modify the ProcessInfoChart sample to use DataBindTable method instead of the DataSource property set up at design-time. Change the code in MainForm.cs to that shown in Listing 14-11.

**LISTING 14-11:** MainForm.cs Using the DataBindTable Method

```
using System;
using System.Windows.Forms;
using System.Windows.Forms.DataVisualization.Charting;
using System.Collections.Generic;

namespace ProcessInfoChart
```

*continues*

**LISTING 14-11** *(continued)*

```
{
  public partial class MainForm : Form
  {
    public MainForm()
    {
      InitializeComponent();
    }

    private void MainForm_Load(object sender, EventArgs e)
    {
      chart1.DataSource = null;
      var processes = new List<ProcessInfo>(ProcessList.GetTopWorkingSet(10));
      chart1.Series.Clear();
      chart1.DataBindTable(processes, "Name");
      chart1.Series[1].ChartArea = "ChartArea2";
      chart1.Series[1].Legend = "Legend2";
    }
  }
}
```

*Code file [MainForm.cs] available for download at Wrox.com*

Because `DataBindTable` creates a new series, the code first clears the `Series` collection, and then up to `Series[1]` to use the second chart area and the related legend.

You can directly bind data through the `Series.Points` property. (It has a type of `DataPoint Collection`.) Table 14-14 describes the data-binding methods available for a `DataPointCollection` instance.

**TABLE 14-14:** Data-binding Methods of DataPointCollection

| METHOD | DESCRIPTION |
|---|---|
| DataBind | Data binds the X-value, Y-value(s), and property values of the data points (such as `Tooltip` or `LabelStyle`) to the data source. |
| DataBindXY | Data binds the X-value and Y-value(s) of the data points in the collection to the specified columns of the specified data sources. |
| DataBindY | Data binds the Y-value(s) of the data points to the specified columns of the specified data source. |

You can modify the `ProcessInfoChart` sample to use the `DataBindXY` method of the series. Change the code in `MainForm.cs` to that shown in Listing 14-12.

**LISTING 14-12:** MainForm.cs Using the DataBindXY Method

```csharp
using System;
using System.Windows.Forms;
using System.Windows.Forms.DataVisualization.Charting;
using System.Collections.Generic;

namespace ProcessInfoChart
{
  public partial class MainForm : Form
  {
    public MainForm()
    {
      InitializeComponent();
    }

    private void MainForm_Load(object sender, EventArgs e)
    {
      chart1.DataSource = null;
      var processes = new List<ProcessInfo>(ProcessList.GetTopWorkingSet(10));
      var series1 = chart1.Series[0];
      series1.Points.DataBindXY(processes, "Name", processes, "WorkingSet");
      var series2 = chart1.Series[1];
      series2.Points.DataBindXY(processes, "Name", processes, "PeakWorkingSet");
    }
  }
}
```

*Code file [MainForm.cs] available for download at Wrox.com*

*Methods in Table 14-13 and Table 14-14 have several restrictions on the data source types they can accept. They also have several advantages and disadvantages. You can check them out in the MSDN documentation at* http://msdn.microsoft.com/ en-us/library/dd456766(VS.100).aspx.

## The DataManipulator class

The Chart control has a property named DataManipulator that exposes an instance of a class also called DataManipulator. You can use this class to perform data-manipulation operations at run-time. These operations include copying values, filtering, grouping and sorting data, exporting data to a DataSet object, and applying a financial formula to data.

You can download the source code for the DataManipulatorSample application to check out how the data manipulations treated in this section can be implemented. This application contains a simple chart with two chart areas. The primary area is generally the input the DataManipulator class works with, while the secondary area displays the results. The code snippets shown in this section are extracted from the MainForm.cs file of the source code; most of them are simple menu item event handler methods.

*In this section, you will find an overview of* DataManipulator *features. There are a few more features not treated here. For more details, see the* DataManipulator *documentation in MSDN at* http://msdn.microsoft.com/en-us/library/ system.windows.forms.datavisualization.charting.datamanipulator_ members(VS.100).aspx.

## Filtering Data

DataManipulator supports the following three kinds of filtering:

➤ You can filter for the top *N* values in a series.

➤ You can filter out data points matching a very simple condition.

➤ You can create your own data point filter class to apply more complex criteria.

You can use the FilterTopN method for getting the top *N* values from a series, as the following code snippet shows:

```
private void FilterTop10MenuItem_Click(object sender, EventArgs e)
{
  chart1.DataManipulator.FilterSetEmptyPoints = true;
  chart1.DataManipulator.FilterTopN(10, "Series1", "Series2");
}
```

The first argument of FilterTopN is the number of data points to filter. The other two string parameters name the input and output series, respectively. Setting the FilterSetEmptyPoints to true causes the DataManipulator to create empty points for those data points that are left from Series1 as a result of filtering. Running this application displays the results in the secondary area, as shown in Figure 14-49.

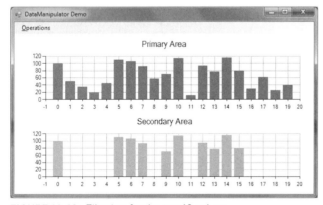

**FIGURE 14-49:** Filtering for the top 10 values

There is another method called `Filter` where you can use a `CompareMethod` enumeration to define the operation to use for filtering. Be aware of the fact that the condition is defined for those data points that should be omitted from the result set. The following snippet demonstrates this:

```
private void FilterLessThan50MenuItem_Click(object sender, EventArgs e)
{
  chart1.DataManipulator.FilterSetEmptyPoints = true;
  chart1.DataManipulator.Filter(CompareMethod.MoreThan, 50.0,
    "Series1", "Series2");
}
```

The intention is to display only those data points in the result that have a Y value less than 50, so you must use the `CompareMethod.MoreThan` enumeration value to reflect this reverse logic.

When you need more complex filtering logic (for example, criteria not supported by the `Compare Method` enumeration), you can create a data point filter class and pass that class to the `Filter` method. A data point filter class must implement the `IDataPointFilter` interface, as the following code snippet shows:

```
private class BetweenFilter : IDataPointFilter
{
  private double lowerValue;
  private double upperValue;

  public BetweenFilter(double lower, double upper)
  {
    lowerValue = lower;
    upperValue = upper;
  }

  bool IDataPointFilter.FilterDataPoint(DataPoint point, Series series,
    int pointIndex)
  {
    return point.YValues[0] > upperValue || point.YValues[0] < lowerValue;
  }
}
```

The `BetweenFilter` class implements a data point filter that will put those data points into the result set that are within the specified range. The `FilterDataPoint` method retrieves `true` if the data point should be omitted from the result set, otherwise, it is `false`. As you can see, the reverse condition is applied in this method — the condition defines the data point that should be omitted from the result set.

You can use the data point filter class as shown in the following code snippet:

```
private void CustomFilterMenuItem_Click(object sender, EventArgs e)
{
  chart1.DataManipulator.FilterSetEmptyPoints = true;
  chart1.DataManipulator.Filter(new BetweenFilter(10.0, 60.0),
    "Series1", "Series2");
}
```

## Sorting Data

The DataManipulator provides a Sort method that orders your data points in ascending or descending order. Ordering uses the Y value data of the specified series by default, and orders the Series.Points collection accordingly. However, ordering your data points does not change the X values of your data points. For most chart types, you will not see that the data points are ordered! The chart output remains the same because rendering uses only the X value and Y value properties of a data point, and ignores their physical order within the Series.Points collection.

To cope with this situation, you must align the data points so that their X values reflect the sort position. The following code extract shows how you can implement sorting:

```
private void SortDataMenuItem_Click(object sender, EventArgs e)
{
  var series2 = chart1.Series[1];
  chart1.DataManipulator.Sort(PointSortOrder.Descending, series2);
  AlignSeries(series2);
}
// ...
private void AlignSeries(Series series)
{
  for (int i = 0; i < series.Points.Count; i++)
  {
    series.Points[i].XValue = i;
    series.Points[i].IsEmpty = false;
  }
}
```

After calling the Sort method, the AlignSeries method resets the X values of the series. Because Series.Points contains data points in descending order, aligning the X values will cause the secondary chart to be displayed correctly, as shown in Figure 14-50.

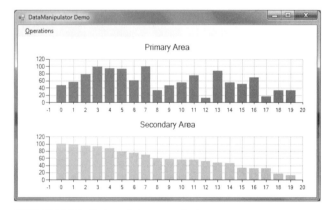

**FIGURE 14-50:** Data points are sorted

## Copying Values

You can easily copy series data to another series with the `CopySeriesValues` method. However, you must ensure that source and destination data series are aligned — that is, they have the same number of data points and the same data in their corresponding X values. Here is a short code extract to demonstrate this:

```
private void CopyValuesMenuItem_Click(object sender, EventArgs e)
{
  AlignSeries(chart1.Series[1]);
  chart1.DataManipulator.CopySeriesValues("Series1:Y", "Series2:Y");
  chart1.Invalidate();
}
```

The `DataManipulatorSample` application contains filtering functions that may change the number of data points during these operations. The `AlignSeries` method ensures that `Series2` will be aligned to `Series1` — this is the same method used for data sorting. The input strings address the Y values to be copied from `Series1` to `Series2`.

You can play with copying values. In the design surface, change the chart type of `Series2` to `SplineRange`, and modify the `CopySeriesValues` call:

```
chart1.DataManipulator.CopySeriesValues("Series1:Y", "Series2:Y2");
```

Now, the code copies the Y values of `Series1` to the Y2 values (second Y value) of `Series2`. Because a `SplineRange` chart uses two Y values, you now have real range values in the secondary area, as shown in Figure 14-51.

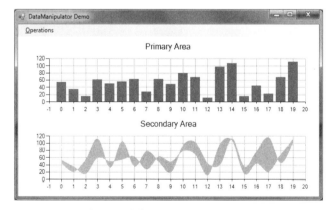

**FIGURE 14-51:** Copying Y2 values

 *Do not forget to change the* `CopySeriesValue` *call's arguments back to the original values, and also reset the chart type of* `Series2` *to* `Column`.

### Export Data to a DataSet Object

A great feature of `DataManipulator` is that it can export chart data to a `DataSet` object. You can use this feature for saving chart data, or passing it to other controls that work with `DataSet` instances.

The `DataManipulatorSample` application demonstrates this feature by passing the exported `DataSet` to a form that displays a `DataGridView` object. The following code implements this task:

```
private void ExportToDataSetMenuItem_Click(object sender, EventArgs e)
{
  var dataSet = chart1.DataManipulator.ExportSeriesValues();
  var exportForm = new ExportedDataForm(dataSet);
  exportForm.ShowDialog();
}
```

The essential work is done by the `ExportSeriesValues` method that produces a `DataSet` instance holding all chart data. Each series is put in a separate table within the data set. The `ExportedDataForm` class gets this data in its constructor and sets up the `ExportedDataGrid` object:

```
public partial class ExportedDataForm : Form
{
  public ExportedDataForm()
  {
    InitializeComponent();
  }

  public ExportedDataForm(DataSet dataSet): this()
  {
    ExportedDataGrid.DataSource = dataSet;
    ExportedDataGrid.DataMember = "Series1";
  }
}
```

The `ExportedDataGrid` object can display only one table at a time. The code sets it through the `DataMember` property to `Series1`.

### Apply Statistical Formula to Data

Through the `Statistics` property of the `DataManipulator` class, you can access statistical operations such as mean, covariance, correlation calculations, and many more. The following code snippet shows how to calculate and display the correlation value between `Series1` and `Series2`:

```
private void ApplyStaticticsMenuItem_Click(object sender, EventArgs e)
{
  var corrValue = chart1.DataManipulator.Statistics.
    Correlation("Series1", "Series2");
  MessageBox.Show(String.Format("Correlation between the series is: {0}",
    corrValue));
}
```

*Statistical operations generally result in scalar values, or very simple structures. Check out the MSDN documentation of the* StatisticFormula *class (this is the type behind the* Statistics *property) for operations you can use with chart data at* http://msdn.microsoft.com/en-us/library/system.windows.forms .datavisualization.charting.statisticformula_members(VS.100).aspx.

## Apply Financial Formula to Data

To perform financial analysis on one or more Series objects, use the FinancialFormula method of the DataManipulator class. FinancialFormula has many overloads, all of them having the same parameter structure:

➤ *Formula name* — Specify the type of the formula here with a FinancialFormula enumeration value. The number of parameters, input, and output, as well as the requirements for each parameter, change based on the formula you choose here.

➤ *Parameters* — Some formulas require parameters, and some enable you to optionally supply them. A few formulas do not use parameters. If a formula takes multiple parameters, specify them as a comma-separated string (for example, "3, 5").

➤ *Input values* — Specify in a comma-separated string the names of instantiated Series objects to which you wish to apply the formula.

➤ *Optional output values* — Specify in a comma-separated string the name of instantiated Series objects to which you want to save the output. If you do not specify output values, the formula stores the first output value in the first listed input value, and so on. In this case, the method throws an exception if the number of input values is less than the number of output values.

The following code snippet calculates a moving average from Series1, and puts the results in Series2:

```
private void ApplyFormulaMenuItem_Click(object sender, EventArgs e)
{
   chart1.DataManipulator.FinancialFormula(
      FinancialFormula.MovingAverage,
      "5",
      "Series1",
      "Series2");
}
```

The second argument, 5, defines the number of samples to use to calculate the moving average. Figure 14-52 shows the result of the operation.

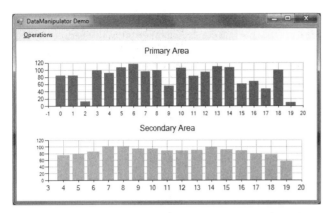

**FIGURE 14-52:** Applying a moving average financial formula

You can see that the secondary area does not contain data points for the 0-3 range of X values. When you use a formula that involves moving averages, the formula ignores the starting data points until it has enough data points to calculate the moving average. In this case, if you want to calculate a five-day moving average, the formula ignores the first four data points, since there are not enough data points to calculate a five-day moving average until the fifth day.

You can change this kind of operation by setting the DataManipulator's StartFromFirst property. By default, it is set to false. However, if StartFromFirst is set to true, the formula calculates the moving average for the beginning points, even though there are not enough data points yet. This gives you the advantage of having one moving average for each input data point in the series.

*For detailed information about financial formulas supported by the* DataManipulator *class, visit the MSDN page at* http://msdn.microsoft.com/en-us/library/dd489253(VS.100).aspx.

## More Chart Manipulations

You can do a few more things with charts in your application. Here is a short list of these opportunities without the need of completeness. URLs in parentheses are links to the related MSDN documentation with more details.

➤ *Chart data serialization* — You can convert your charts into a format that you can save or transmit. You typically use this to save chart properties, but you can also use it to retrieve data and load it into an existing chart control. (http://msdn.microsoft.com/en-us/library/dd456693(VS.100).aspx)

➤ *Chart printing* — In the Chart control for Windows Forms, you can print the chart picture. (http://msdn.microsoft.com/en-us/library/dd456718(VS.100).aspx)

➤ *Chart interactivity* — In the `Chart` control for Windows Forms, you use mouse events and the `HitTest` method to enable chart interactivity. You can also use cursors, scrolling, and zooming. (`http://msdn.microsoft.com/en-us/library/dd456772(VS.100).aspx`)

➤ *Customize chart drawing* — In the `Chart` control, you can use events to customize chart behavior, such as performing custom drawing with the `PrePaint` and `PostPaint` event handler methods. (`http://msdn.microsoft.com/en-us/library/dd456617(VS.100).aspx`)

## SUMMARY

Using charts in your application can significantly improve the user experience. For a long time, no chart controls were shipped with Visual Studio. If you wanted to use them, you had to buy one from a UI component vendor, or download one Open Source component with the appropriate license. Visual Studio 2010 changes this situation. It provides you a great Windows Forms `Chart` control that you can simply drag from the Toolbox to your forms.

You can easily set up the `Chart` control through the dozens of properties it exploits. It has a great design-time support — when you change a property, the design-time view changes accordingly.

You can choose from more than 30 chart types, and customize them through general and chart type specific properties. The `Chart` control supports data binding and many manipulations, including filtering, sorting values, and applying financial formulas.

Chapter 15 begins the discussion of ASP.NET 4 with an overview of the evolution of this important environment.

# PART III
# ASP.NET 4.0

▶ **CHAPTER 15:** ASP.NET Version History

▶ **CHAPTER 16:** ASP.NET Charting Controls

▶ **CHAPTER 17:** ASP.NET Dynamic Data

▶ **CHAPTER 18:** ASP.NET Model-View-Controller (MVC)

▶ **CHAPTER 19:** ASP.NET Ajax Improvements

▶ **CHAPTER 20:** Ajax Control Toolkit, jQuery, and More

# 15

# ASP.NET Version History

As the first chapter of the ASP.NET part of the book, this chapter traces the history of ASP.NET, and provides information on all the different versions that have evolved through the years. To understand the evolution of ASP.NET, a good starting point might be where it all began — the birth of the World Wide Web.

## DEVELOPMENT OF THE WEB AND WEB DEVELOPMENT

Today, most people are unable to imagine their everyday lives without cell phones and the Internet. But life was very different even just a few years ago, when neither the Internet nor cell phones were around. Effective long-distance communication has always been important. Some people may remember stories about letters wandering weeks or months en route from the sender to the recipient, sometimes being carried by homing pigeons or stagecoaches. Even the dissemination of news and messages was a difficult thing to do efficiently — cave paintings, posters, newspapers, town criers, and so on, all attempted to spread the news and information to all people.

Ancient civilizations had their own unique ways of communicating with one another. The first concept of an "Information Highway" in Europe was conceived by a surgeon who wanted to create a process to teach and share new medical techniques in the Middle Ages. Unfortunately, the concept was thought of as blasphemy by the Church, and the surgeon was beheaded for witchery.

In the modern ages, Tim Berners-Lee, an independent contractor of the European Organization for Nuclear Research (CERN), was the first person who built an early software project (ENQUIRE) that was similar to today's World Wide Web.

A few years later, he realized that physicists needed to share data around the world. After some unsuccessful attempts, he finally got support from his CERN bosses, Mike Sendall and Robert Cailliau. They began to implement a new system on a NeXT workstation that finally got the name World Wide Web (WWW).

The birth of the WWW as a publicly available service on the Internet occurred on August 6, 1991, the day when Berners-Lee posted a short message about his project on a newsgroup:

> *"The WorldWideWeb (WWW) project aims to allow all links to be made to any information anywhere. [. . .] The WWW project was started to allow high energy physicists to share data, news, and documentation. We are very interested in spreading the web to other areas, and having gateway servers for other data. Collaborators welcome!"*

Since then, the WWW has been one of the fastest evolving industries in history. More and more easy-to-use web developer software tools have been born with better and better developer efficiency, as well as the WYSIWYG (what you see is what you get) experience. Moreover, with these tools, knowledge about Hypertext Markup Language (HTML) or any other programming language is not required for creating basic web pages. (But, of course, it is generally recommended for professional results.)

The next generation of web development tools uses the strong growth in Microsoft .NET, Java, or other similar technologies to utilize the web as a way to run applications online. Instead of running executable code on a local computer, users interact with online applications to consume content, create new content, or use some services. They are now able to interact with applications from any location around the world, instead of being tied to a specific computer or workstation for their application environment.

## ENTER ASP

The standardized markup language for developing web pages has been HTML. The original goal of this markup language was to make available to developers those parts of simple page documents that can point to other pages (hyperlink). The first version of HTML contained only a few elements (for example, headings, quotations, and lists), but over time, a lot of elements have been added, including frames, images, formatting and font styles, and so on.

HTML has evolved a lot in another area, too. Instead of the need to create constant, unchanged documents, there were more and more frequently changing HTML pages that required dynamic changes to their content.

The two available ways to achieve this goal were client-side and server-side solutions. But client-side scripting has some problems with that, one of them being that the server must send the entire content to the client to be processed. Another main issue is that there is no guarantee that all clients can process the content received from the server.

For these reasons, server-side solutions became much more popular. The server-side engines send the ready HTML code to the client, but the content of this HTML is dynamic, meaning that it can change from one request to another. Eventually, the purpose of the server-side engines was to generate HTML code and send it to the clients as an answer to their requests.

Active Server Pages (ASP), which is also known as Classic ASP, is Microsoft's answer to these new requirements. Overall, ASP is not a programming language, but rather a programming framework. It's a special programming method embedded in HTML pages. During the processing of the ASP page, the web engine parses the content of the page. It displays the HTML code parts and runs the embedded ASP scripts. Finally, IIS sends the code made from the HTML and ASP result to the client.

Following is an example:

```
<HTML>
<HEAD><TITLE>Visual Studio 2010 Welcome Page</TITLE></HEAD>
<BODY>
<%  Response.Write("<h1>Hello Visual Studio 2010!</h1>")  %>
</BODY>
</HTML>
```

The language of most ASP pages is JScript or VBScript, but other third-party active scripting languages have evolved as well (for example, PerlScript).

## ENTER ASP.NET

ASP was a good solution for server-side active scripting, but it experiences a problem. The presentation and content are mixed together. In 1997, Microsoft began realizing how to solve this problem. The task of developing the new model was given to two young professionals, Mark Anders (a manager of IIS team) and Scott Guthrie (who joined Microsoft in 1997, and is currently the Corporate Vice President of .NET Developer Platform).

Guthrie offered the following description of the birth of ASP.NET:

> *"We actually started the ASP.NET project in late 1997 and early 1998. At the time, ASP was still relatively new, and we initially weren't sure whether there was anything left to do in the web space. (Little did we know!) We then spent a lot of time talking with developers and customers using ASP, and quickly realized that there were a lot of things left to resolve.*

> *"Some specific issues/requests came up again and again from customers — provide the ability to write much cleaner code that provided good code/content separation (rather than mixing code up in the HTML), provide the ability to write applications using a variety of coding languages (and not just VBScript and JScript), deliver a more robust execution environment (avoiding memory leaks and crashes that could bring down the server), provide a much cleaner configuration/code deployment model, deliver a built-in security architecture, enable built-in output caching support to improve scalability, and more.*

> *"A colleague of mine (Anders) and I spent about two months brainstorming ideas about how we could build a programming model that delivered all of this. Eventually, we decided we needed to put together a prototype to try out the concepts, and I ended up coding it up over the Christmas and New Year's holiday in 1997/1998 (I was a hardcore geek then.) We showed off the prototype to a lot of people within the company, built a lot of excitement, and got the go-ahead to build a team to deliver it."*

The name of the initial prototype was "XSP." Guthrie explained in a 2007 interview that, "People would always ask what the 'X' stood for. At the time, it really didn't stand for anything. XML started with that; XSLT started with that. Everything cool seemed to start with an 'X,' so that's what we originally named it."

The first initial prototype of XSP used Java, but it was soon decided to try to build it on the top of the .NET Common Language Run-time (CLR) because of its benefits. Guthrie said in an interview with the *New York Times* that this decision was an extremely huge risk, because the success of the new XSP platform would be dependent on the success of the CLR that was still in its infancy. So, the first real target of CLR was the XSP team in the Microsoft itself.

With this decision, the XSP prototype was re-developed in C# (known internally as "Project Cool") that was also kept secret from the public. At the same time, it was renamed to "ASP+" because this new platform was seen as the successor of ASP, and the easy migration from ASP was an important goal of the project.

The first demonstration of ASP+ was at the ASP Connections Conference in Phoenix on May 2, 2000, by Anders. The very first public demonstration was made at the Professional Developer Conference (PDC) on July 11, 2000, in Orlando, Florida. In Bill Gates' keynote presentation, ASP+ was demonstrated with COBOL, but support of other languages (Visal Basic .NET and C#) was also announced. Python and Perl support was announced as part of third-party interoperability tools.

The final name of ASP.NET was decided when the ".NET" branding was introduced by Microsoft in the second half of 2000. Anders explained:

> *"The .NET initiative is really about a number of factors. It's about delivering software as a service; it's about XML and web services and really enhancing the Internet in terms of what it can do ... we really wanted to bring its name more in line with the rest of the platform pieces that make up the .NET framework."*

According to Microsoft's official ASP.NET website, "Microsoft ASP.NET is a free technology that allows programmers to create dynamic web applications. ASP.NET can be used to create anything from small, personal websites through to large, enterprise-class web applications. All you need to get started with ASP.NET is the free .NET Framework and the free Visual Web Developer."

One of ASP.NET's main goals was to simplify the learning path of developers from Windows application development to web development.

**BETTER THAN THE CLASSIC**

Following are main improvements offered by ASP.NET over Classic ASP:

➤ ASP.NET enables faster developing and is less error-prone.

➤ It separates business logic and presentation by using the code-behind development method.

➤ With compiled code, applications run faster with less design-time and develop-time errors.

➤ Run-time error handling can be significantly improved by `try-catch` blocks in the code.

➤ With the wide set of controls and class libraries, applications can be built very rapidly. User-defined controls allow creating and using web templates (such as menus). Moreover, most of these controls can be built visually with most editors.

➤ ASP.NET pages can be coded in the languages of VB.NET, C#, J#, and so on, because ASP.NET leverages the multi-language capabilities of .NET Framework CLR.

➤ ASP.NET offers metaphors similar to Microsoft Windows applications (for example, controls and events).

➤ ASP.NET is capable of caching the parts of the page or the whole page, to improve performance.

➤ Session state can be saved to a Microsoft SQL Server database, or in a separate process. That way, session values are kept after a reset of the web server, or when the ASP.NET worker process is recycled.

➤ Depending on the site configuration, all ASP.NET controls have generated valid HTML 4.0, XHTML 1.0, or XHTML 1.1 output since version 2.0.

## ASP.NET VERSION HISTORY

Through the years, the various versions of ASP.NET have provided new features and functionalities. Before reading about the version history of ASP.NET, take a look at the summary capsules of ASP.NET shown in Table 15-1 for each of the versions to be examined in this chapter.

**TABLE 15-1:** ASP.NET Versions

| VERSION | DATE | NEW FEATURES |
| --- | --- | --- |
| ASP.NET 1.0 | January 16, 2002 | Standard object-oriented features were supported<br><br>Early-binding and type safety<br><br>Use of dynamic link library (DLL) class libraries and other features of the web server |
| ASP.NET 1.1 | April 24, 2003 | Support of mobile devices<br><br>Automatic input validation |
| ASP.NET 2.0 | November 7, 2005 | Support for 64-bit processors<br><br>New data controls (`GridView`, `FormView`, `DetailsView`)<br><br>Declarative data access techniques (`SqlDataSource`, `ObjectDataSource`, `XmlDataSource`)<br><br>Navigation controls<br><br>Master pages<br><br>Login controls<br><br>Themes and skins<br><br>Web parts<br><br>Personalization services<br><br>Pre-compilation<br><br>Localization<br><br>Provider class model |
| ASP.NET 3.0 | November 21, 2006 | Windows Communication Foundation<br><br>Windows Cardspace |
| ASP.NET 3.5 | November 19, 2007 | New data controls (`ListView`, `DataPager`)<br><br>ASP.NET Ajax<br><br>Support for HTTP pipelining and syndication feeds<br><br>Windows Communication Foundation (WCF) support for RSS, JSON, POX, and partial trust<br><br>Other .NET Framework 3.5 features, for example LINQ |

| VERSION | DATE | NEW FEATURES |
|---|---|---|
| ASP.NET 3.5 SP1 | August 11, 2008 | ASP.NET dynamic data |
| | | Controlling browser history in ASP.NET Ajax |
| | | Capability to combine more JavaScript files into a single file |
| | | New namespaces |
| ASP.NET 4.0 | 2010 | ASP.NET Web Forms Framework |
| | | ASP.NET Model-View-Controller (MVC) Framework |

## ASP.NET 1.0

Microsoft had been developing the first version of ASP.NET for four years, and released a series of beta versions in 2000 and 2001. Also, dozens of books promoted by Microsoft had been written about ASP.NET before the first version. Finally, ASP.NET 1.0 was released on January 16, 2002, as part of the .NET Framework 1.0.

Following were the main features of ASP.NET 1.0:

➤ The standard object-oriented features were supported (inheritance, polymorphism, and so on)

➤ Early-binding and type safety were possible, with no more need to use `Server .CreateObject(...)`.

➤ Developers could use DLL class libraries and other features of the web server to build more robust applications, while not only rendering HTML pages, but also doing much more (for example, exception handling).

## ASP.NET 1.1

ASP.NET 1.1 was released on April 24, 2003, together with Windows Server 2003 and Visual Studio .NET 2003.

This version focused on improving support of mobile devices. The other important improvement was automatic input validation.

## ASP.NET 2.0

ASP.NET 2.0 (codenamed "Whidbey") was released on November 7, 2005, with Visual Studio 2005, Visual Web Developer Express, and SQL Server 2005.

This version offered several important improvements, including the following:

➤ Support for 64-bit processors

➤ New data controls

➤ New techniques for declarative data access

➤ Navigation controls

➤ Master pages

➤ Login controls

➤ Themes and skins

➤ Web parts

➤ Personalization services

➤ Full pre-compilation

➤ New localization technique

➤ Provider class model

Let's take a look at each of these in a bit more detail.

## Support for 64-Bit Processors

Obviously, 64-bit architecture processors can handle more memory and larger files than 32-bit CPUs. The 64-bit architecture allows systems to address up to 1 TB (1,000 GB) of memory, while the 32-bit CPUs can handle only 4 GB of memory. Most benefits of 64-bit processors are unnoticed without a 64-bit operating system, software, and drivers that are able to take advantage of the 64-bit CPU features.

The version 2.0 of ASP.NET was capable of supporting 64-bit architectures, with all of their benefits.

## New Data Controls

New data controls introduced in this version included the following:

➤ `GridView` — Displays the values of a data source in a table where columns represent the fields, and rows represent the records. The `GridView` control enables the users to select, sort, and edit the items.

➤ `FormView` — Displays the values of a single record from a data source using user-defined templates. The `FormView` control allows the users to edit, delete, and insert records.

➤ `DetailsView` — Displays the values of a single record from a data source in a table, where the rows represent the fields of the record. The `DetailsView` control allows the users to edit, delete, and insert records.

## New Techniques for Declarative Data Access

Following are the new techniques for declarative data access introduced in this version:

➤ `SqlDataSource` — This is for using a SQL database as the data source in data-bound controls.

> ➤ `ObjectDataSource` — This is for using business objects as the data source in data-bound controls of multi-tier web application architectures.

> ➤ `XmlDataSource` — This represents an XML data source to data-bound controls.

## Navigation Controls

The ASP.NET navigation controls can be used to enhance the user experience, as well as to help with consistent site navigation and finding information around the site. As the sites grow and contain more and more content, and this content is moved around in the site, it becomes more and more difficult to manage all of the links.

With the help of ASP.NET site navigation, you are able to store links to all pages of the site in a central location, and display these links in lists or navigation menus on all of your pages in the same way, including a web server navigation control.

Following are the navigation features introduced in ASP.NET 2.0:

> ➤ Site maps

> ➤ ASP.NET controls

> ➤ Programmatic controls

> ➤ Access rules

> ➤ Custom site map providers

## Master Pages

In ASP.NET, not only can you create consistent navigation for your sites but also a consistent layout with the help of master pages. Master pages define the look and feel, as well as the behavior of the pages in the application. You can create content pages that contain the content you want to display separated from master pages, and assign the proper master page to them. When users request a page, the content from the page will merge with the layout of the master page to produce output.

## Login Controls

With the help of the ASP.NET login controls, you can build a robust login solution for your web applications without writing any program code. Login controls can be integrated with ASP.NET membership and forms authentication by default to help automate user authentication.

## Themes and Skins

Themes allow you to define the look of pages by way of a property settings collection. These settings can be consistently applied to the pages of a web application, to the entire web application, or to all web applications of the server. Themes are the collection of the following elements:

> ➤ Skins

> ➤ Cascading style sheets (CSS)

> ➤ Images

> ➤ Other resources

The themes assign a set of personalization styles and attributes to the site elements to be customized, including control properties, page stylesheets, images, templates, and so on.

A special directory is used to store all themes for a website or for the web server.

All themes contain at least one skin. Skin files contain property settings for controls such as `Label`, `TextBox`, `Button`, or `Calendar`. Control skin settings are similar to the control markup, but contain only the properties.

Following are the types of control skins:

➤ *Default skin* — When a theme is applied to a page, all of its controls of the same type will use the default skin defined by the theme. For example, if you create a `TextBox` default skin, all `TextBox` controls on your page will use this default skin.

➤ *Named skin* — When a control skin has a `SkinID` property set, it's a named skin. These are not automatically applied to the controls with the same type. You must explicitly assign the named skin to the controls. This can be done by setting the control's `SkinID` property. In that way, you're able to set different skins for different instances of the same control.

## Web Parts

Web parts are units of a page that contain an integrated set of controls and information as a unit and enable users to build their pages out of web parts (like using building blocks) and modify properties of the web parts directly from a browser. Web parts can be shared (which means that their appearance and behavior is the same for all users) or personalized (which means a user can modify properties in his or her personal view of the page).

The main benefit of the ASP.NET web parts is that the end users are able to personalize and edit the web pages without needing the help of a developer or administrator. Moreover, web parts can be exported from a site and imported to another application, so the quantity of configuration tasks can be also reduced.

One other powerful capability of the web parts is their connectivity. Users can set connections between them, so, for example, the child web part can display the details of the item chosen on the parent web part.

These capabilities make the ASP.NET web parts very powerful, and capable of being the base of various ASP.NET-based server applications (for example, SharePoint).

## Personalization Services

ASP.NET has a lot of personalization features available for all authenticated users, including the following:

➤ *User profiles* — ASP.NET user profiles are persistent collections of information fields about the individual user. These allow you to manage user properties without creating and maintaining a custom database.

➤ *Themes* — Themes allow you to define the look of pages by way of a property settings collection.

➤ *Custom error pages* — ASP.NET provides various ways to display user-friendly messages in case an error occurs. You can trap errors either on the page or application level.

With personalization features, your application defines its own collection of personalized data, and the ASP.NET run-time parses and compiles that. Personalized data is completely transparent to end users.

## Full Pre-Compilation

When users request a page for the first time, ASP.NET web pages and code files are compiled dynamically. Then, the compiled resources will be cached, so that the next request to the same page is quick and efficient.

The pre-compilation of full sites is also available in ASP.NET.

This provides many benefits for the users, including the following:

➤ The response is faster.

➤ The compile-time bugs and errors can be identified early.

➤ The source code doesn't need to be deployed to the production server.

## Localization

By using localization, you can customize your application for a given culture and locale. ASP.NET 2.0 improved the localization process, and had a lot of new features that included the following:

➤ The auto-detection of the HTTP header field (`Accept-Language`) by the browser configures the set of languages preferred in the response to the request.

➤ Resources can be accessed programmatically.

➤ `RESX` or `RESOURCE` files are compiled and linked into run-time assemblies.

➤ Controls and their properties can be tied to the resources in a declarative way.

➤ The creation of resources has design-time support.

The most important benefit of using multilingual web applications with language-separated site structures is that you need much less maintenance during the site's lifecycle.

## Provider Class Model

As stated on MSDN, "A *provider* is a software module that provides a uniform interface between a service and a data source." The main goals during the design of the ASP.NET 2.0 provider model were flexibility and extensibility, and providing a simple way to write custom providers.

Following were the default providers in ASP.NET 2.0:

➤ Membership provider

➤ Role management provider

➤ Site map provider

➤ Profile provider

- ➤ Session state provider

- ➤ Web events provider

- ➤ Web parts personalization provider

- ➤ Protected configuration provider

# ASP.NET 3.0

ASP.NET 3.0 (which was released on November 21, 2006, with .NET Framework 3.0) contained some brand new basic components:

- ➤ Windows Communication Foundation (WCF)

- ➤ Windows Presentation Foundation (WPF)

- ➤ Windows Workflow Foundation (WF)

From the perspective of ASP.NET, the most important new components in .NET Framework 3.0 were WCF and Windows CardSpace (WCS).

## Windows Communication Foundation (WCF)

WCF (codenamed "Indigo") is a standardized, service-oriented communication infrastructure on the top of web services protocols that enables connecting to other services, even on platforms other than the .NET Framework. WCF provides a standard programming model to developers, so they can use the same environment whether they are developing web services or .NET remote applications. Basically, developers can create Service-Oriented Architectures (SOA) by using WCF, but WCF is capable of communicating with binary information or XML, as well as realizing peer-to-peer communication.

WCF is a real framework, with a lot of benefits that include the following:

- ➤ Security

- ➤ Transaction management

- ➤ Secure message transfer

- ➤ Logging

- ➤ Trace

- ➤ Performance counters

In WCF, there are two roles: the *service* provides one or more end points, and the *clients* connect to this service, send requests to, and get responses from that.

All endpoints contain three basic things:

- ➤ *Address* — The URL of the endpoint where clients can connect

- ➤ *Binding* — The mode of the communication (for example, HTTP, TCP/IP, and so on)

- ➤ *Contract* — The interface that defines the supported operations of the service

### Windows CardSpace (WCS)

WCS is a new, secure, and comfortable way of managing identities, instead of the classic username-password method. Following are the main benefits of using WCS:

➤ It provides a simple way of creating and maintaining digital authentication.

➤ It can be also a local authentication provider that can generate secure personal tokens.

WCS-based solutions are one of the most modern browser-based applications and web services.

# ASP.NET 3.5

ASP.NET 3.5 was released on November 19, 2007. It was released with Visual Studio 2008 and Windows Server 2008, and its main new features were the following:

➤ New data controls

➤ ASP.NET Ajax

➤ Support for HTTP pipelining and syndication feeds

➤ WCF Support for RSS, JSON, POX and Partial Trust

## New Data Controls

Following were new data controls introduced with this version of ASP.NET:

➤ `ListView` — The ASP.NET `ListView` control binds and displays the items of a connected data source. You can define views and custom templates and styles, with the capability of displaying individual items or groups of them. Users can edit, insert, and delete data, as well as sort and page through displayed data.

➤ `DataPager` — The `DataPager` control provides paging functionality for ASP.NET data controls that implement the `IPageableItemContainer` interface (for example `ListView`).

## ASP.NET Ajax

Ajax (Asynchronous JavaScript and XML) is a web development technique used to build interactive web applications. Ajax web applications can be more interactive, usable, and faster. They don't require the user to reload the full page after sending or receiving small data pieces from the database server.

Ajax is the combination of the following techniques:

➤ XHTML (or HTML) and CSS

➤ DOM

➤ `XMLHttpRequest`

➤ XML

ASP.NET Ajax is Microsoft's free framework to give Ajax capabilities to the developers both on the server and client sites. It contains the following components:

➤ ASP.NET Ajax Extensions with client-side JavaScript packages

➤ Server-side ASP.NET Ajax

➤ ASP.NET Ajax Control Toolkit

➤ jQuery Library

With these components, developers can create their applications through either client-side or server-side development, or a combination of both. On the client side, you have the Microsoft Ajax Library, which includes the following:

➤ Visual and non-visual components, behaviors

➤ Browser compatibility

➤ Networking

➤ Core services

On the server side, you have ASP.NET Ajax Extensions, which include the following:

➤ Script support

➤ Web services

➤ Server controls

## Support for HTTP Pipelining and Syndication Feeds

After caching an ASP.NET request by IIS, a web server assigns a unique token based on the authentication model (Windows, Basic or Digest) to that. This token is alive during the session and is tied with the whole worker process.

The account used in the request depends on the impersonation configured in the ASP.NET application. The default setting is that the impersonation is disabled, but, in this case, the thread runs under the default account of the worker process, which is not good, because it opens up a lot of attack capabilities.

The ASP.NET worker process has one main task. It hands the request over to the HTTP pipeline, which is a chain of managed objects activated by creating a new instance of the `HttpRuntime` class.

## WCF Support for RSS, JSON, POX, and Partial Trust

Instead of running a WCF application in full trusted environments, version 3.5 of ASP.NET enables WCF applications also to run in partial trusted environments. Because WCF applications can be deployed to medium trust IIS environments, shared hosting became available, too.

Thanks to the extensible model of WCF, a lot of web standards (such as RSS, JSON and POX) are also supported in ASP.NET 3.5.

## ASP.NET 3.5 SP1

Version 3.5 SP1 of ASP.NET was released on August 11, 2008, together with the Visual Studio 2008 Service Pack 1. New features included the following:

➤ Incorporation of ASP.NET dynamic data

➤ Support for managing the browser history from the ASP.NET Ajax applications

➤ The capability to combine multiple JavaScript files into a single file so that downloading can be faster

➤ New namespaces (`System.Web.Abstraction, System.Web.Routing`)

## ASP.NET 4.0

When Visual Studio 2010 and .NET 4 arrived, ASP.NET developers were provided with two mature frameworks for building web applications — the ASP.NET Web Forms framework and the ASP.NET Model-View-Controller (MVC) framework. Both build on top of the core ASP.NET run-time, and both are getting some new features to start the next decade.

### Web Forms Framework

ASP.NET Web Forms Framework enables quick-and-easy development of web applications. Web Forms are similar to Windows Forms because they have similar properties, methods, and events, but the web user interface (UI) elements also can render themselves to the markup language requested by the client.

Following are the main enhancements of the Web Forms in ASP.NET 4.0:

➤ Capability to set metatags

➤ Closer work with browsers on the client side

➤ Support for ASP.NET routing in Web Forms

➤ More control of view state

➤ More control of automatically generated IDs

➤ More control of the HTML generated by `FormView` and `ListView`

➤ Data source controls filtering

➤ Selected rows can be persisted in data controls

### MVC Framework

The MVC pattern is very popular in architectures of modern applications. As shown in Figure 15-1, applications with MVC architecture can be separated into the following three main layers:

➤ *Model* — This layer implements the business logic for the application's data domain.

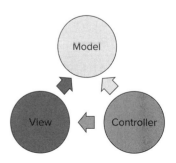

**FIGURE 15-1:** MVC architecture

➤ *View* — This layer displays the application's UI.

➤ *Controller* — This layer controls user interaction, works with the Model, and selects the appropriate View to render and display the UI.

The first MVC version in ASP.NET was released as an add-on framework for ASP.NET 3.5 SP1. The second release of ASP.NET MVC is shipped with Visual Studio 2010. It focuses on better developer productivity, and providing the infrastructure for handling large, enterprise web developer projects.

MVC 2 is included in ASP.NET 4 Beta 2 and includes the following new features and capabilities:

➤ *Areas* — With the help of areas, controllers and views can be grouped to building subsets of a large application. You can implement each area as a separate ASP.NET MVC project so that the complexity of the application can be easier to maintain.

➤ *Data Annotation Attribute validation support* — This lets you add validation logic to a model by adding metadata attributes to a class property. This provides a metadata-driven validation of user inputs.

➤ *Templated helpers* — These help you associate display and edit templates with data types. With the help of them, you can reduce the amount of typing of HTML code.

➤ *Dynamic data* — Dynamic data simplifies the creation of data-driven web applications by discovering the LINQ-to-SQL or Entity Framework data model, and determining the appropriate rendering method of the UI.

Following are the main benefits of the MVC architecture:

➤ It's capable of building strongly layered applications so that business functions can be separated from data accessing and displaying.

➤ Web applications with MVC architecture are easy to maintain.

➤ Creating unit tests for the application is easy.

One more important benefit of ASP.NET 4.0 that is particularly liked by many professional developers is the capability in ASP.NET 4.0 to create pages optimized for search engines. *Search Engine Optimization (SEO)* is the process of site and page optimization for search engines that results in higher relevance and ranking.

ASP.NET 4.0 provides some new capabilities designed to improve your sites and pages for SEO. The most relevant new capabilities are the support of manipulating the metadata headers and search engine friendly routing.

## SUMMARY

As you have seen in this chapter, ASP.NET has experienced a huge amount of improvement over the last eight years. It has evolved from a basic web development language to a very powerful, modern, and impressive environment.

In Chapter 16, you'll learn more about charting controls in ASP.NET.

# 16

# ASP.NET Charting Controls

For a long time, no `Chart` controls were shipped with Visual Studio. If you wanted to use them, you had to buy one from a user interface (UI) component vendor, or download Open Source charting components with the appropriate license. With Visual Studio 2010 and .NET Framework 4.0, Microsoft ships two `Chart` controls — one for Windows Forms applications, and another one for ASP.NET applications. In Chapter 14, you learned about the features of the Windows Forms `Chart` control.

Although ASP.NET and Windows Forms are very different in their UI principles, the two `Chart` controls share the same concepts. After you have learned one of them, you can start using the other one in a few minutes.

With Visual Studio 2010, you can drag a `Chart` control directly from the Toolbox to your design surface. You can easily set up both `Chart` controls through the dozens of properties they exploit. Charts have great design-time support. When you change a property, the design-time view changes accordingly.

You can choose from more than 30 chart types and customize them through general and chart type-specific properties. The `Chart` control supports data binding and many manipulations, including filtering, sorting values, and applying financial formulas.

Most concepts of the Windows Forms `Chart` control treated in Chapter 14 are the same for the ASP.NET `Chart` control, including the chart elements and their structure, most property and method names, chart types, three-dimensional chart handling, customization, data manipulations, and many more. If you have skipped Chapter 15, you can still understand how to use the ASP.NET `Chart` control. However, you won't have the overview of charting concepts that you would after reading that chapter.

In this chapter, you will learn about the specific features and behaviors for the ASP.NET `Chart` control:

➤ *Creating charts* — You will learn about the basic steps of creating ASP.NET charts, handling postback events, and binding your data to a chart.

➤ *Rendering ASP.NET charts* — Although, when using Windows Forms charts, you do not have to deal with their rendering, because of the distributed nature of web applications, with ASP.NET charts, you have several rendering options. You will learn about them in this chapter.

➤ *Chart state management* — State management is a fundamental concept for all web applications. In this chapter, you will learn how the ASP.NET `Chart` control implements this concept.

➤ *User interactivity* — A chart itself is "only" a static figure conveying to you a thousand words. Adding interactivity to a chart improves the user experience your customers can have when facing their data. In this chapter, you'll discover how you can use the ASP.NET `Chart` control to provide interactivity for the user.

> *In this chapter, you will build and analyze simple ASP.NET Web Application projects. Most code samples in this chapter can be found in the* `PetShopCharts` *sample ASP.NET application. You can download the source code files from the book's download site at www.wrox.com. The focus is on the ASP.NET* `Chart` *control and not on ASP.NET development in general. You do not need to set up Internet Information Services (IIS) on your computer. All samples work with the ASP.NET Development Server installed with Visual Studio 2010. You'll be able to build these samples even if you're a novice web developer.*

## CREATING CHARTS

Chapter 14 examined many details surrounding the creation and use of Windows Forms `Chart` controls, and discussed how to use them to create simple applications. Although the ASP.NET `Chart` control shares the same concepts as the Windows Forms control, you must follow different guidelines when creating charts in web applications — because of the distributed nature of the web. In this section, you create a few samples to learn how to start using charts in ASP.NET.

## Adding a Chart Control to a Page

Create a new ASP.NET Empty Web Application and name it `SimpleAspNetChart`. Add a new Web Form item with the name `Default.aspx`. It becomes the default startup page of the application. Use the Source view of `Default.aspx` page by clicking the Source tab at the bottom of the document window — unless you are not already in this view. On the Toolbox, expand the Data tab, drag a

Chart control, and drop it between the `<div>` and `</div>` HTML tags. The chart automatically creates `Series` and `ChartArea` elements, as you can see in Listing 16-1.

**LISTING 16-1:** Default.aspx after Adding the Chart Control

```
<%@ Page Language="C#" AutoEventWireup="true" CodeBehind=
"Default.aspx.cs"
Inherits="SimpleAspNetChart.Default" %>

<%@ Register assembly="System.Web.DataVisualization, Version=4.0.0.0,
Culture=neutral, PublicKeyToken=31bf3856ad364e35"
namespace="System.Web.UI.DataVisualization.Charting"
tagprefix="asp" %>

<!DOCTYPE html PUBLIC "-//W3C//DTD XHTML 1.0 Transitional//EN"
"http://www.w3.org/TR/xhtml1/DTD/xhtml1-transitional.dtd">

<html xmlns="http://www.w3.org/1999/xhtml">
<head runat="server">
    <title></title>
</head>
<body>
    <form id="form1" runat="server">
    <div>
      <asp:Chart ID="Chart1" runat="server">
        <Series>
          <asp:Series Name="Series1">
          </asp:Series>
        </Series>
        <ChartAreas>
          <asp:ChartArea Name="ChartArea1">
          </asp:ChartArea>
        </ChartAreas>
      </asp:Chart>
    </div>
    </form>
</body>
</html>
```

As the `<%@ Register %>` directive shows, the Chart control can be found in the `System.Web`
`.DataVisualization` assembly.

When you turn to Design view, you can see the chart displays sample data. But when you run the application, only an empty chart is displayed. You can add data points to the chart in the Design view by editing the `Points` property of `Series1` in the Series Collection Editor or manually typing data points in the Source view.

```
<asp:Chart ID="Chart1" runat="server" Width="490px">
  <Series>
    <asp:Series Name="Series1">
```

```
        <Points>
          <asp:DataPoint XValue = "0" YValues = "15" />
          <asp:DataPoint XValue = "1" YValues = "20" />
          <asp:DataPoint XValue = "2" YValues = "28" />
          <asp:DataPoint XValue = "3" YValues = "13" />
          <asp:DataPoint XValue = "4" YValues = "7" />
        </Points>
        </asp:Series>
      </Series>
    <ChartAreas>
      <asp:ChartArea Name="ChartArea1">
      </asp:ChartArea>
    </ChartAreas>
  </asp:Chart>
```

Now, when you run the application, you can see a chart containing five data points, as shown in Figure 16-1.

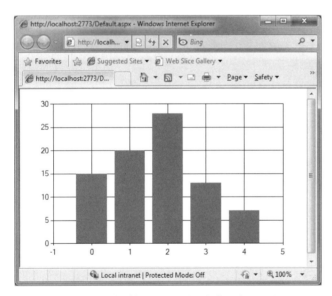

**FIGURE 16-1:** A simple Chart control with five data points

*You can set up data points in the ASP.NET* Chart *control exactly as you do it with the Windows Forms control. Select the* Chart *control in the Design view, and, in the Properties window, scroll down to the* Series *property that can be found under the Chart category. Click the ellipsis button of the* Series *property to display the Series Collection Editor, and find the* Points *property for* Series1.

Of course, you can set up a `Chart` from code. You can carry out the initialization in the `Page_Load` event, as Listing 16-2 shows.

**LISTING 16-2:** Default.aspx.cs with Simple Chart Initialization Codeusing System;

```
using System.Drawing;
using System.Web.UI.DataVisualization.Charting;

namespace SimpleAspNetChart
{
  public partial class Default : System.Web.UI.Page
  {
    protected void Page_Load(object sender, EventArgs e)
    {
      // --- Set up chart title
      var title = new Title("This is an ASP.NET Chart control");
      title.Font = new System.Drawing.Font("Calibri", 24F, FontStyle.Bold);
      Chart1.Titles.Add(title);

      // --- Set up chart type
      var series1 = Chart1.Series[0];
      series1.Points.Clear();
      series1.ChartType = SeriesChartType.SplineRange;

      // --- Create data points
      for (int i = 0; i <= 10; i++)
        Chart1.Series[0].Points.Add(new DataPoint(i,
          Math.Pow(Math.Abs(5 - i), 2.5)));
    }
  }
}
```

The ASP.NET `Chart` control and all related types can be found in the `System.Web.UI` `.DataVisualization.Charting` namespace. The `Page_Load` event handler method sets up the chart title and the `Series1` chart type to `SplineRange` and then creates data points using a simple formula.

Because you create data points programmatically in the `Page_Load` event, you should remove the previously added data points from `Default.aspx`. You can also change the size of the chart.

```
<body>
  <form id="form1" runat="server">
    <div>
      <asp:Chart ID="Chart1" runat="server" Height="400px" Width="600px">
        <Series>
          <asp:Series Name="Series1">
          </asp:Series>
        </Series>
        <ChartAreas>
          <asp:ChartArea Name="ChartArea1">
          </asp:ChartArea>
        </ChartAreas>
```

```
        </asp:Chart>
      </div>
    </form>
</body>
```

Figure 16-2 shows the chart created with this code.

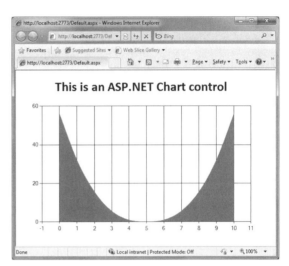

# Setting up Charts in an Event Handler Method

Just as with other controls, charts can be set up in event handler methods. Let's change the formula in Listing 16-2 so that the user can specify the number of points to display and the exponent used in the `Math.Pow` function. Listing 16-3 shows how the `Default.aspx` file is changed to provide input fields for these two arguments.

**FIGURE 16-2:** Chart control initialized in code-behind

---

**LISTING 16-3:** Default.aspx with New Input Fields for User-Specified Arguments

```
<%@ Page Language="C#" AutoEventWireup="true" CodeBehind="Default.aspx.cs"
    Inherits="SimpleAspNetChart.Default" %>

<%@ Register assembly="System.Web.DataVisualization, Version=4.0.0.0,
    Culture=neutral, PublicKeyToken=31bf3856ad364e35"
    namespace="System.Web.UI.DataVisualization.Charting"
    tagprefix="asp" %>

<html xmlns="http://www.w3.org/1999/xhtml">
<head runat="server">
    <title></title>
</head>
<body>
    <form id="form1" runat="server">
    <div>
      Number of data points:
      <asp:TextBox ID="PointsNumBox" runat="server"></asp:TextBox>
      <br />
      Exponent in formula:
      <asp:TextBox ID="ExponentBox" runat="server"></asp:TextBox>
      <br /><br />
      <asp:Button ID="DrawChartButton" runat="server"
            Text="Draw the Chart!" onclick="DrawChartButton_Click" />
      <br />
      <asp:Chart ID="Chart1" runat="server" Height="400px" Width="600px">
        <Series>
          <asp:Series Name="Series1">
          </asp:Series>
        </Series>
```

```
          <ChartAreas>
            <asp:ChartArea Name="ChartArea1">
            </asp:ChartArea>
          </ChartAreas>
          <Titles>
            <asp:Title Font="Calibri, 24pt" Name="Title1">
            </asp:Title>
          </Titles>
        </asp:Chart>
      </div>
    </form>
  </body>
</html>
```

*Code file [Default.aspx] available for download at Wrox.com*

The two input parameters are represented by the `PointsNumBox` and `ExponentBox` controls. When the user clicks `DrawChartButton`, the `DrawChartButton_Click` event handler method is executed, and it sets up the chart's data points, as Listing 16-4 shows.

**LISTING 16-4:** Default.aspx.cs Implementing the DrawChartButton_Click Handler

```csharp
using System;
using System.Drawing;
using System.Web.UI.DataVisualization.Charting;

namespace SimpleAspNetChart
{
  public partial class Default : System.Web.UI.Page
  {
    protected void Page_Load(object sender, EventArgs e)
    {
      var series1 = Chart1.Series[0];
      series1.ChartType = SeriesChartType.SplineRange;
      SetTitleForInvalidState();
    }

    protected void DrawChartButton_Click(object sender, EventArgs e)
    {
      // --- Process input parameters
      int numberOfPoints;
      double exponent;
      if (!Int32.TryParse(PointsNumBox.Text, out numberOfPoints) ||
          !Double.TryParse(ExponentBox.Text, out exponent))
      {
        SetTitleForInvalidState();
        return;
      }
      // --- Create data points
      for (int i = 0; i < numberOfPoints; i++)
        Chart1.Series[0].Points.Add(new DataPoint(i,
          Math.Pow(Math.Abs(numberOfPoints / 2 - i), exponent)));
```

*continues*

**LISTING 16-4** *(continued)*

```
    // --- Set title
    var title = Chart1.Titles[0];
    title.Text = String.Format("{0} points with exponent {1}",
      numberOfPoints, exponent);
    title.ForeColor = Color.Black;
  }

  private void SetTitleForInvalidState()
  {
    var title = Chart1.Titles[0];
    title.Text = "No valid chart data specified yet...";
    title.ForeColor = Color.Maroon;
  }
 }
}
```

*Code file [Default.aspx.cs] available for download at Wrox.com*

DrawChartButton_Click checks if the input parameters can be parsed as numbers. If they cannot, the chart title is modified to signal this fact; otherwise, data points are calculated and the chart title is changed. Figure 16-3 shows the chart after the DrawChartButton_Click event handler has been executed.

## Binding Data to the Chart

Most charts use data points as result of a report or query against a database. ASP.NET controls support the standard .NET data binding mechanism, and the Chart control also utilizes this to provide you with a convenient and easy way to set up your data points. In Chapter 14, you built a simple data-bound chart using a LINQ expression, and also saw an overview of several data binding methods supported by the Chart control.

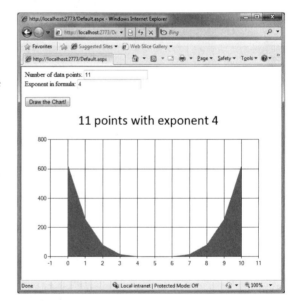

**FIGURE 16-3:** Chart after the "Draw the Chart!" button was clicked

The ASP.NET Chart control supports the same mechanisms as the Windows Forms Chart control. This section examines another data binding sample utilizing the Chart.DataBindCrossTable method that provides a great support to obtain data points for multi-series charts.

Download the PetShopCharts sample application and open its solution file in Visual Studio 2010. Open the DataBindCrossTable.aspx file in Code view. This page connects to a Microsoft Access database representing the Enterprise Resource Planning (ERP) system of a company managing a network of small pet shops, and creates a sales history chart. Listing 16-5 shows how the page binds the sales information coming from the database to the chart.

**LISTING 16-5:** DataBindCrossTable.aspx.cs

```csharp
using System;
using System.Data.OleDb;
using System.Data;
using System.Web.UI.DataVisualization.Charting;

namespace PetShopCharts
{
  public partial class DataBindCrossTable : System.Web.UI.Page
  {
    protected void Page_Load(object sender, EventArgs e)
    {
      var connection = Helpers.Utility.GetChartDataConnection(this);
      var commandStr = "SELECT Period, Total, Category from SalesByYearAndPetKind";
      var command = new OleDbCommand(commandStr, connection);
      command.Connection.Open();
      var reader = command.ExecuteReader(CommandBehavior.CloseConnection);
      Chart1.DataBindCrossTable(
          reader,
          "Category",
          "Period",
          "Total",
          "");
      reader.Close();
      connection.Close();
      foreach (var series in Chart1.Series)
      {
        series.ChartType = SeriesChartType.Spline;
        series.BorderWidth = 4;
      }
    }
  }
}
```

*Code file [DataBindCrossTable.aspx.cs] available for download at Wrox.com*

The page uses the standard pattern to set up a connection to an Access database and prepares a `reader` object to execute a query. The `GetChartDataConnection` method of the `Helpers.Utility` static class is responsible for preparing this connection, and its source code is very short:

```csharp
public static OleDbConnection GetChartDataConnection(Page page)
{
  string fileNameString = page.MapPath(".") + "\\App_Data\\PetShopData.mdb";
  string myConnectionString = "PROVIDER=Microsoft.Jet.OLEDB.4.0;Data Source="
    + fileNameString;
  return new OleDbConnection(myConnectionString);
}
```

The lion's share of the work is done by the `DataBindCrossTable` method:

```
Chart1.DataBindCrossTable(
  reader,
  "Category",
  "Period",
  "Total",
  "");
```

This method reads the content represented by the `reader` object and groups the records into a series according to the field name passed in the second argument. The third and fourth arguments define the fields providing the values for the `XValue` and `YValues` properties of data points, respectively. The fifth argument allows setting up data bindings for any other data point properties. So, this sample creates separate data series according to the `Category` field using `Period` as the X value and `Total` as the Y value of data points.

Because `DataBindCrossTable` creates a new series, you must define the visual properties of these newly instantiated series. This is why the `DataBindCrossTable` invocation is followed by a `foreach` cycle:

```
foreach (var series in Chart1.Series)
{
  series.ChartType = SeriesChartType.Spline;
  series.BorderWidth = 4;
}
```

The `DataBindCrossTable.aspx` file contains several other visual properties for the chart, but those do not influence data binding. When you run the application and navigate to the sample page, you can see that five series are created as a result of the `DataBindCrossTable` call, as shown in Figure 16-4.

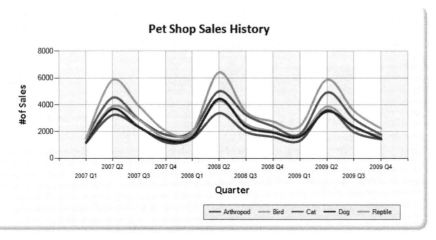

**FIGURE 16-4:** Chart created with DataBindCrossTable

# RENDERING ASP.NET CHARTS

Thus far, you have learned how to create simple ASP.NET charts using the designer, how to set up data points manually and programmatically, and how to bind information coming from a database to your chart.

Although when using Windows Forms charts you do not have to deal with the rendering of charts, because of the distributed nature of web applications, with ASP.NET charts, you have several rendering options. This section examines a few scenarios and how to choose the appropriate rendering option in a certain scenario.

There is no HTML tag for describing a chart or any of the chart elements. When you run the page that generates the output shown in Figure 16-4, very simple HTML content is generated, as Listing 16-6 shows.

**LISTING 16-6:** Output HTML Content for Figure 16-4

```
<!DOCTYPE html PUBLIC "-//W3C//DTD XHTML 1.0 Transitional//EN"
  "http://www.w3.org/TR/xhtml1/DTD/xhtml1-transitional.dtd">

<html xmlns="http://www.w3.org/1999/xhtml">
<head>
  <title>
    Data binding with the DataBindCrossTable method
  </title>
</head>
<body>
  <form method="post" action="DataBindCrossTable.aspx" id="form1">
    <div class="aspNetHidden">
      <input type="hidden" name="__VIEWSTATE" id="__VIEWSTATE"
        value="/wEPDwUJNDI2M..." />
    </div>
    <div>
      <img id="Chart1" src="/ChartImg.axd?i=chart_7cf32..." alt=""
        style="height:400px;width:800px;border-width:0px;" />
    </div>
  </form>
</body>
</html>
```

The chart is represented by an image as the `<img>` HTML tag signs it. The source of the image is a URL, like this:

```
="/ChartImg.axd?i=chart_7cf323be4363473f9b87dbb136452ccd_0.png&
  g=751de08f64274dc0a8e4ab40b116ae51
```

The chart images are managed by an `HttpHandler` that is accessed with the `/ChartImg.axd` address. The `i` and `g` request arguments identify the image to be retrieved. The ASP.NET `Chart` control has several properties to define how chart images are rendered. You can find them under the

Image category in the Properties window, as shown in Figure 16-5.

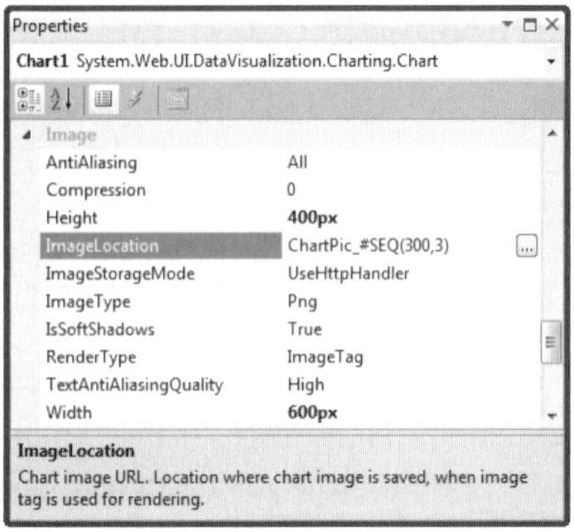

# Image URL Rendering

By default, the `RenderType` property of a `Chart` control is set to `ImageTag` (as Figure 16-5 shows). The `ImageLocation` and `ImageStorageMode` properties determine how images are stored and retrieved when the HTML page is about to display them. `ImageStorageMode` is set to `UseHttpHandler` by default, but you can change it to use `UseImageLocation` to specify a folder where the generated chart images should be put.

You can also define the type of image used for the chart picture by setting up the `ImageType` property to one of the `Bmp`, `Jpeg`, `Png` (this is the default), or `Emf` values. When you select the `Jpeg` format, you can also set the `Compression` property to a value between 0 and 100, where 0 provides the best picture quality and 100 the worst.

**FIGURE 16-5:** Chart properties for image handling

## Changing Image Location

When you render a chart picture as an image, it is automatically saved to a file. The `ImageLocation` property determines the absolute or relative location and name of this file, and the file extension is automatically added, depending on the image type specified.

Open the `SimpleAspNetChart` project again to play with the image rendering options. Create a new folder under the project root in Solution Explorer and name it `ChartImages`. Change the `ImageStorageMode` property to `UseImageLocation`. This will cause the image to be stored in a well-defined folder on the web server. Set the `ImageLocation` property to `/ChartImages/ChartPic_#SEQ(4,3)`. This value tells the chart control the location of where the rendered chart picture files should be stored. The `#SEQ(4,3)` formatter instructs the chart to create a sequential number as the part of the chart picture filename, where 4 is the maximum sequential number and 3 is the image file time to live (in seconds).

Start the application by pressing Ctrl+F5 and click the "Draw the Chart!" button three times with different input parameters. Without closing the application, go back to Visual Studio. In the Solution Explorer, right-click on the `ChartImages` folder and then click the Open Folder command in Windows Explorer. You can see all chart images rendered since the application was launched, as shown in Figure 16-6.

You can recognize the four chart pictures already rendered. The first holds only a chart title. Now, click the "Draw the Chart!" button again with a new set of parameters and look back to the `ChartImages` folder. It still has four image files, but the first picture was overridden with the file representing the last chart — as a result of 4 in `#SEQ(4,3)`. You can see the folder content in Figure 16-7.

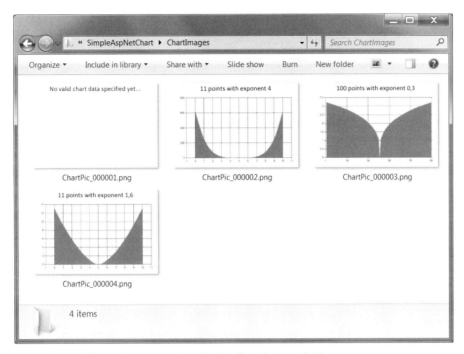

**FIGURE 16-6:** Chart pictures rendered in the ChartImages folder

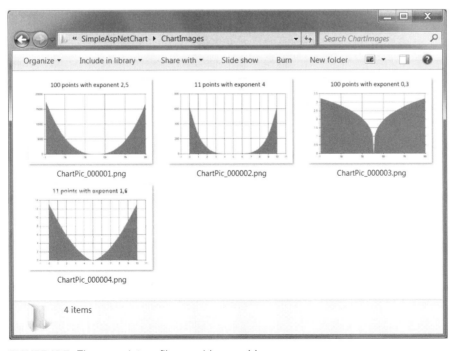

**FIGURE 16-7:** The new picture file overrides an old one.

When you look at the HTML source of the chart's page, you can see that now the `<img>` tag uses a direct reference to the picture file:

```
<img id="Chart1" src="/ChartImages/ChartPic_000001.png?06b79a20-fae8-47f7-
    a1c2-2e55a3c9b3d9" alt="" style="height:400px;width:600px;border-width:0px;" />
```

## Changing the Image File Format

You can change `ImageType` property to define the file type of the image to be rendered for the chart. This property takes its value from the `ChartImageType` enumeration. You do not have too many options, and there is no way to select any subtype for a selected image type. Table 16-1 summarizes the types you can choose from, and gives you several hints for which scenarios to use them in.

**TABLE 16-1:** ImageType Property Values

| IMAGETYPE VALUE | DESCRIPTION |
| --- | --- |
| BMP | This is an uncompressed `BMP` format with 32-bit pixel depth. An image with 600x400 pixels takes about 938 KB. This format requires much more bandwidth than the others to transfer the picture over the network. However, on the server side, it may require fewer CPU cycles to render than the others, because of the lack of compression. |
| | Use this format only when you explicitly need a `BMP` format on the client — or on the server side for further processing. |
| JPEG | The well-known `JPEG` format produces a high picture quality by default. You can use the `Compression` property to define the `JPEG` compression value (between 0 and 100, where 0 provides the best picture quality, 100 the worst). For the 600x400 pixels picture shown in Figure 16-3, it provides the size of 58 KB and 15 KB with `Compression` set to 0 and 80, respectively. This format can produce the smallest files in size — for the price of quality degradation. |
| | You can effectively use this format for charts with few colors and large areas having the same color and tone. |
| PNG | As the default format for chart images, the `PNG` format is the best in most scenarios. It provides a lossless compression for chart images, and so it keeps their quality high with a relatively small size. The compression algorithm used by `PNG` is especially great for chart-like bitmaps, and often produces smaller files than `JPEG`. |
| | The picture in Figure 16-3 produces a `PNG` file with a size of 18 KB. In contrast, the `JPEG` file takes 58 KB. Unless you have some special reason, use the `PNG` format type. |

| IMAGETYPE VALUE | DESCRIPTION |
|---|---|
| EMF | This format produces images with the Enhanced Metadata Format (EMF). This format records the graphical primitives used to draw a picture, and so it is a vector format combined with the capability to also store bitmaps. Pictures with this format often have the smallest size, mainly for line charts. However, the same EMF files can be displayed differently, depending on the browser type or other application opening the files, unlike the other formats. |

If you have situations where it's difficult to choose the appropriate file type, define test scenarios, execute, and evaluate them. Using the default Png format works in most scenarios.

## Using Charts with Legacy Web Sites

Often, you must integrate your web pages into legacy websites. You can embed your charts created with the ASP.NET Chart control in the same way as any other ASP.NET pages. One solution is to use the HTML <iframe> tag that defines an inline frame that contains another document.

The PetChartsSample project has a sample page named HtmlPageWithIFrame.html that represents a legacy website's page. The source code of the page is really simple, as Listing 16-7 shows.

Available for
download on
Wrox.com

**LISTING 16-7:** HtmlPageWithIFrame.html

```html
<html>
  <head>
    <title>Leagcy HTML Page using an IFRAME tag</title>
  </head>
  <body>
    <h3>
      This sample demonstrates how to use the ASP.NET Chart control
      within an &lt;iframe&gt; tag of an existing  Legacy web page.
    </h3>
    <iframe style="WIDTH: 800px; HEIGHT: 400px" marginWidth="0"
      marginHeight="0" src="DataBindCrossTable.aspx" frameBorder="YES"
      width="800" height="400"
      scrolling="no" />
    <iframe style="WIDTH: 200px; HEIGHT: 400px" marginWidth="10"
      marginHeight="0" src="LegacyHtmlPage.htm" frameBorder="NO"
      width="800" height="400"
      scrolling="no" />
  </body>
</html>
```

*Code file [HtmlPageWithIFrame.html] available for download at Wrox.com*

The page contains two `<iframe>` tags. The first encapsulates the `DataBindCrossTable.aspx` page that produces the chart shown in Figure 16-4. You do not have to change that page at all to embed the chart into a legacy website. The second `<iframe>` embeds another HTML page from the same legacy site. Figure 16-8 shows what you see when displaying the `HtmlPageWithIFrame.htm` page.

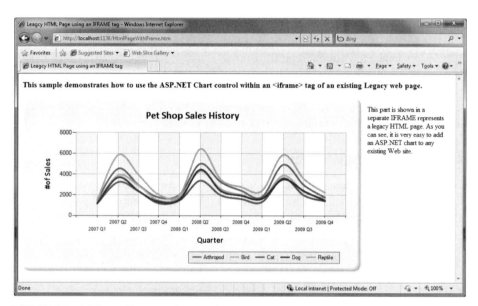

**FIGURE 16-8:** Adding a Chart to a legacy site

## Binary Stream Rendering

When binary streaming is used, the chart image is sent directly to the client. When the browser requests the image of the chart, it does this in the same manner as when it requests a static image from the web server. This is particularly useful when the chart image is frequently modified at run-time, or when a web form is used. The binary stream rendering method is fast because it does not require any disk space or security rights for writing data to the temporary image files.

You can implement binary chart streaming easily with two pages:

➤ *First page* — A page that creates the `Chart` control. This is a simple `.aspx` page, where the `Chart` control's `RenderType` property is set to `BinaryStreaming`. On this page, all HTML tags are removed, leaving only the `Chart` definition in XML. Of course, you can still use code-behind to initialize the chart dynamically.

➤ *Second page* — Another page that makes reference to the first page with the `Chart` control. This page contains an `<img>` tag (or an `<asp:Image>` element) with its `src` (or `ImageUrl`) attribute set to the name of the first page.

Open the `PetShopCharts` project, were you can find an example for binary rendering. The `Chart` control is defined in the `DogSalesChart.aspx` file, as shown in Listing 16-8.

**LISTING 16-8:** DogSalesChart.aspx

```
<%@ Page Language="C#" AutoEventWireup="true" CodeBehind="DogSalesChart.aspx.cs"
    Inherits="PetShopCharts.DogSalesData" %>

<asp:chart id="Chart1" runat="server" height="500px" width="800px"
    rendertype="BinaryStreaming" BackColor="Khaki" BackGradientStyle="DiagonalLeft"
    BackSecondaryColor="DarkGoldenrod">
    <ChartAreas>
        <asp:ChartArea Name="ChartArea1">
            <AxisY Title="Sales Number" TitleFont="Calibri, 14.25pt, style=Bold">
                <MinorGrid Enabled="True" Interval="100" LineColor="Silver" />
            </AxisY>
            <AxisX Interval="1" IsLabelAutoFit="False" LabelAutoFitMaxFontSize="12"
                LabelAutoFitMinFontSize="12" >
                <MajorGrid LineColor="Silver" />
                <LabelStyle Font="Calibri, 12pt, style=Bold" />
            </AxisX>
        </asp:ChartArea>
    </ChartAreas>
    <Legends>
        <asp:Legend BackColor="PapayaWhip" BorderColor="DimGray"
            DockedToChartArea="ChartArea1" Name="Legend1">
        </asp:Legend>
    </Legends>
</asp:chart>
```

*Code file [DogSalesChart.aspx] available for download at Wrox.com*

As you see, this chart does not contain any HTML elements, only the `<asp:Chart>` element.
Fortunately, the designer still supports editing all the chart properties just as if it were embedded in
a usual `.aspx` page. The `RenderType` property of the chart is set to `BinaryStream`.

The `DogSalesChart.aspx.cs` contains the logic that obtains chart data with the `DataBindCrossTable`
methods using the same pattern as shown in Listing 16-6. The code-behind file uses the `region` page
parameter to query the sales statistics for the specified region, as the following code extract shows:

```
protected void Page_Load(object sender, EventArgs e)
{
    var region = Request["region"];
    var connection = Helpers.Utility.GetChartDataConnection(this);
    var commandStr = "SELECT PetName, Total, ShopName from DogSalesData where" +
        " Region = '" + region + "',";
    var command = new OleDbCommand(commandStr, connection);
    // ...
}
```

Listing 16-9 shows the `BinaryStreamRendering.aspx` file that references `DogSalesChart.aspx`.

**LISTING 16-9:** BinaryStreamRendering.asxp

```
<%@ Page Language="C#" AutoEventWireup="true"
  CodeBehind="BinaryStreamRendering.aspx.cs"
  Inherits="PetShopCharts.BinaryStreamRendering" %>

<!DOCTYPE html PUBLIC "-//W3C//DTD XHTML 1.0 Transitional//EN"
  "http://www.w3.org/TR/xhtml1/DTD/xhtml1-transitional.dtd">

<html xmlns="http://www.w3.org/1999/xhtml">
  <head runat="server">
    <title>Sales Data through binary stream rendering</title>
  </head>
  <body>
    <form id="form1" runat="server">
    <table>
      <tr>
        <td colspan=2>
          <h2>Dog Sales in the Western Region</h2>
          <asp:Image ID="ImageWest"
            ImageUrl="DogSalesChart.aspx?region=West"
            runat="server" Height="500px" Width="800px" />
        </td>
      </tr>
      <tr>
        <td>
          <h4>Dog Sales in the Eastern Region</h4>
          <asp:Image ID="ImageEast"
            ImageUrl="DogSalesChart.aspx?region=East"
            runat="server" Height="250px" Width="400px" />
        </td>
        <td>
          <h4>Dog Sales in the Northern Region</h4>
          <asp:Image ID="ImageNorth"
            ImageUrl="DogSalesChart.aspx?region=North"
            runat="server" Height="250px" Width="400px" />
        </td>
      </tr>
    </table>
    </form>
  </body>
</html>
```

*Code file [BinaryStreamRendering.aspx] available for download at Wrox.com*

This file contains three `<asp:Image>` elements referencing `DogSalesChart.aspx`, with three different region settings. Of course, you can set any other parameters of the `Image` element. The second and third images display the original image in half size. Figure 16-9 shows a part of the `BinaryStreamRendering.aspx` page as you see it in the browser.

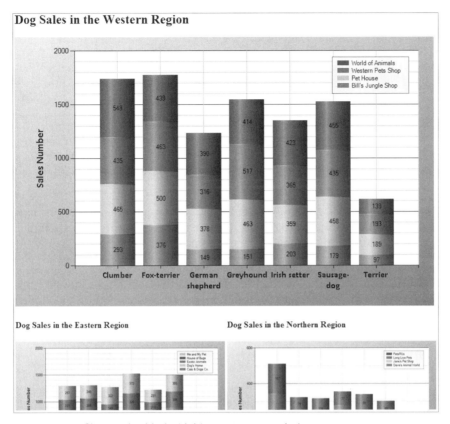

**FIGURE 16-9:** Chart embedded with binary stream rendering

The binary stream rendering is another simple solution to embed chart images into a legacy website. You do not have to touch the `.aspx` page. You create the referencing page with an HTML `<img>` tag. Listing 16-10 shows an example.

**LISTING 16-10:** BinaryStreamRendering.htm

```
<!DOCTYPE html PUBLIC "-//W3C//DTD XHTML 1.0 Transitional//EN"
    "http://www.w3.org/TR/xhtml1/DTD/xhtml1-transitional.dtd">
<html xmlns="http://www.w3.org/1999/xhtml">
  <head>
    <title>Chart in a legacy web site with binary streaming</title>
  </head>
  <body>
    <h2>Dog Sales in the Southern Region</h2>
    <img src="DogSalesChart.aspx?region=South" height="500px" width="800px"
      alt="Southern Region" />
  </body>
</html>
```

*Code file [BinaryStreamRendering.htm] available for download at Wrox.com*

## CHART STATE MANAGEMENT

View state is used by the ASP.NET page framework to automatically save the page and its control values prior to rendering the page, and state management is accomplished using view state. When an ASP.NET page is processed, the current state of the page and its controls are converted into a string and saved in the page as a hidden field with a __VIEWSTATE name. When the page is posted back to the server (such as through a postback event when a server-side control is clicked), the page parses the view state string at page initialization, and restores property information in the page.

Charts generally obtain their data from persisted information — for example, from a file or a database — and their state information is not necessarily stored in the view state string. By default, the Chart control does not use view state. Its EnableViewState property is set to false.

However, there are situations when using the view state provides better performance. If you expect many postbacks to the page with a chart, and the chart data is expensive to reproduce, using the view state can help you to be frugal with system resources and provide a better response time. Also, you can benefit from state management when you create the chart information on-the-fly.

When using state management, you should consider the increase in the amount of data sent from the server to the client. Using state management on appearance settings causes a relatively small increase in network traffic, while using state management on several hundred or thousand data points causes a large increase in network traffic.

This section examines a few chart samples to demonstrate state management.

## Saving Chart State

When you work with chart data that is expensive to produce (or is unrepeatable) and you expect postbacks to the chart page, one possible way to persist the data between postbacks is enabling chart state management. There is a sample in the PetShopCharts project representing this scenario.

The BasicChartStateManagement.aspx page generates a random series in the Page_Load method, as shown in Figure 16-10.

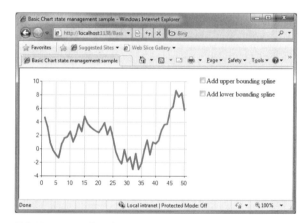

**FIGURE 16-10:** Random series on the BasicChartState Management.aspx page

The page contains two checkboxes that allow you to add or remove an upper and a lower bounding spline series to the chart as soon as you check or uncheck them. Every time you change the Checked property of any checkbox control, a postback occurs. If you cannot save the state of the chart between postbacks, you lose the random series generated in the Page_Load method.

Listing 16-11 shows the code-behind file for the page that allows you to store series information in the page's view state.

**LISTING 16-11:** BasicChartStateManagement.aspx.cs

```
using System;
using System.Web.UI.DataVisualization.Charting;

namespace PetShopCharts
{
  public partial class BasicChartStateManagement : System.Web.UI.Page
  {
    protected void Form_Init(object sender, EventArgs e)
    {
      Chart1.EnableViewState = true;
    }

    protected void Page_Load(object sender, EventArgs e)
    {
      if (!IsPostBack)
        GenerateRandomData(Chart1.Series[0]);
      if (UpperSpline.Checked)
        AddNewSeries("UpperSpline", 5.0);
      else RemoveSeries("UpperSpline");
      if (LowerSpline.Checked)
        AddNewSeries("LowerSpline", -5.0);
      else RemoveSeries("LowerSpline");
    }

    private void GenerateRandomData(Series series)
    {
      const double MaxStep = 5.0;
      series.Points.Clear();
      var rand = new Random((int)DateTime.Now.Ticks);
      var lastValue = 5.0;
      for (int i = 0; i < 50; i++)
      {
        series.Points.AddXY(i + 1, lastValue);
        lastValue += MaxStep * rand.NextDouble() - MaxStep/2;
        series.Points[i].YValues[0] = lastValue;
      }
    }

    private void AddNewSeries(string name, double distance)
    {
      RemoveSeries(name);
      var baseSeries = Chart1.Series["Default"];
      var newSeries = new Series(name);
      newSeries.ChartType = SeriesChartType.Spline;
      newSeries.BorderWidth = baseSeries.BorderWidth;
      Chart1.Series.Add(newSeries);
      foreach (var point in baseSeries.Points)
      {
        newSeries.Points.AddXY(point.XValue, point.YValues[0] + distance);
      }
    }
```

*continues*

**LISTING 16-11** *(continued)*

```
    private void RemoveSeries(string name)
    {
      var index = Chart1.Series.IndexOf(name);
      if (index >= 0) Chart1.Series.RemoveAt(index);
    }
  }
}
```

*Code file [BasicChartStateManagement.aspx.cs] available for download at Wrox.com*

The key to the solution is the `Form_Init` method that turns on chart state management by setting the `EnableViewState` property to `true`. The `Page_Load` method checks whether the current request for the page is a postback. If it is the first call, the random series is generated. After the default series is either generated or loaded from the view state, the upper and lower splines are drawn according to the state of checkboxes.

When a bounding spline is selected, the `AddNewSeries` method can iterate through the data points of the existing series and create the points for the selected bounding series. Figure 16-11 shows what happens when you check both splines. As you can see, the line enclosed between the upper and lower lines is exactly the same as the one drawn in Figure 16-10.

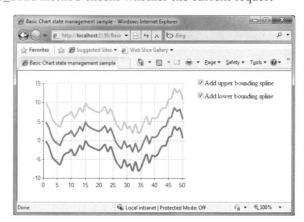

**FIGURE 16-11:** The chart preserves its state between postbacks.

The HTML page generated for this chart (excluding the chart picture) is about 16 KB when state management is turned on, and about 3 KB when turned off. The difference is 13 KB, and this space is used by 150 data points (3 series and 50 data points in each).

## Advanced Chart State Management

The `BasicChartStateManagement.aspx` page saves more state information than required, because it saves the state of the additional series that can be calculated (and it's cheap) from the data generated for the base series. If there were a way you could tell the chart to save only the base series, you could save resources reserved by about a hundred data points. This is especially important when your chart contains more — let's says a few hundred or thousand — data points.

### Chart Serialization Basics

The `Chart` control is designed to provide you with flexibility in its state management. You can set the `ViewStateContent` property of the chart to influence what kind of data is to be saved into the view state. The values of `ViewStateContent` are taken from the `SerializationContents` enumeration. Table 16-2 summarizes the enumeration values you can use.

**TABLE 16-2:** SerializationContents Values

| VALUE | DESCRIPTION |
| --- | --- |
| Default | Serialize all chart content with non-default property values. This includes appearance properties, series and their data points, axis minimums/maximums, and so forth. |
| Data | Serialize data values from all chart series. This does not include appearance properties. |
| Appearance | Serialize all appearance properties (such as color or line style) if they have non-default values. |
| All | Serialize all chart information. This includes all appearance properties and data point values. |

The Chart control has a Serializer property with a ChartSerializer object instance behind it. Using the properties of ChartSerializer, you can control how the chart data is serialized. By setting the SerializableContent property, you can exactly set the string value representing the chart's view state.

## Using Serialization in State Management

In the PetShopCharts project, you can find the AdvancedChartStateManagement.aspx page that demonstrates these view state serialization concepts. The UI of the page is exactly the same as for the BasicChartStateManagement.aspx page. Listing 16-12 shows the source code of the code-behind file. A few methods have not changed, and their body is omitted for the sake of brevity.

**LISTING 16-12:** AdvancedChartStateManagement.aspx.cs

Available for download on Wrox.com

```csharp
using System;
using System.Web.UI.DataVisualization.Charting;
using System.IO;

namespace PetShopCharts
{
  public partial class AdvancedChartStateManagement : System.Web.UI.Page
  {
    protected void Form_Init(object sender, EventArgs e)
    {
      Chart1.EnableViewState = true;
    }

    protected void Page_Load(object sender, EventArgs e)
    {
      var content = SerializationContents.Default;
      if (!IsPostBack)
```

*continues*

**LISTING 16-12** *(continued)*

```
      {
        GenerateRandomData(Chart1.Series[0]);
        var sw = new StringWriter();
        Chart1.Serializer.Content = content;
        Chart1.Serializer.Save(sw);
        Chart1.ViewStateData = sw.ToString();
      }
      else
      {
        var sr = new StringReader(Chart1.ViewStateData);
        Chart1.Serializer.Content = content;
        Chart1.Serializer.Load(sr);
      }

      if (UpperSpline.Checked)
        AddNewSeries("UpperSpline", 5.0);
      else RemoveSeries("UpperSpline");
      if (LowerSpline.Checked)
        AddNewSeries("LowerSpline", -5.0);
      else RemoveSeries("LowerSpline");
    }

    private void GenerateRandomData(Series series)
    {
      // --- No change
    }

    private void AddNewSeries(string name, double distance)
    {
      // --- No change
    }

    private void RemoveSeries(string name)
    {
      // --- No change
    }
  }
}
```

*Code file [AdvancedChartStateManagement.aspx.cs] available for download at Wrox.com*

The Page_Load method is the one that has changed to implement this advanced view state management. It starts with setting the content variable to SerializationContents.Default that will be used later to define what chart properties should be serialized. If the page is about to be loaded the first time, the base series data points are generated and immediately saved into the Chart's view state:

```
GenerateRandomData(Chart1.Series[0]);
var sw = new StringWriter();
```

```
Chart1.Serializer.Content = content;
Chart1.Serializer.Save(sw);
Chart1.ViewStateData = sw.ToString();
```

The `Serializer` property provides you with additional properties and methods to create the view state data. The `Save` method serializes all chart content with non-default property values (as a result of setting the `Content` property to `SerializationContents.Default` through the `content` variable). Setting the `ViewStateData` property tells the chart that all important state information has been already created. The chart does not serialize its state information, but accepts the content of `ViewStateData` as its state to be persisted.

At this time, only the default series has data points, and so no other data points get serialized.

When the `Page_Load` method is called as a result of a postback, the view state data of the base series is deserialized from the `ViewStateData` property of the chart:

```
var sr = new StringReader(Chart1.ViewStateData);
Chart1.Serializer.Content = content;
Chart1.Serializer.Load(sr);
```

The last section of `Page_Load` creates the additional series from the base series data that either was just generated or reloaded from the view state.

As a result of this tuning, the size of the generated HTML page decreases from 13 KB to about 8 KB.

## Playing with the Serialization Content

Listing 16-12 sets the `Content` property of the chart's `Serializer` to `SerializationContents` `.Default`, and so not only the data, but also the appearance information is saved for the default series generated in the `Page_Load` method.

Change the first line of the method to the following so that only series data would be saved:

```
var content = SerializationContents.Data;
```

When you run the page and set any of the additional series to be displayed, the result will not be exactly what you expect, as Figure 16-12 shows.

The base series is shown as a column chart instead of a line chart. The cause of this behavior is simple. The `ChartType` property of the base series was not serialized because the content was set to `Data`, and so no appearance information was saved in the view state. When the base series gets deserialized, the `ChartType` property is set to `Column`, because this is its default value.

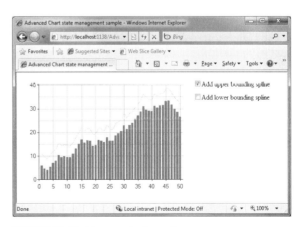

**FIGURE 16-12:** Unexpected result

You can fix this issue by setting the missing series properties right after deserializing the view state:

```
protected void Page_Load(object sender, EventArgs e)
{
  var content = SerializationContents.Data;
  if (!IsPostBack)
  {
    // ...
  }
  else
  {
    var sr = new StringReader(Chart1.ViewStateData);
    Chart1.Serializer.Content = content;
    Chart1.Serializer.Load(sr);
    // --- Add this:
    Chart1.Series["Default"].ChartType = SeriesChartType.Line;
    Chart1.Series["Default"].BorderWidth = 4;
  }
  // ...
}
```

Although you can do this, it makes your code less readable.

# USER INTERACTIVITY

A well-designed chart helps you visualize data to analyze the past, to display present or future trends, and to understand the background of certain behaviors or phenomena. The chart itself is "only" a static figure telling you a thousand words. Adding interactivity to a chart improves the user experience your customers can have when faced with their data.

The Chart control was designed with interactivity in mind. This section examines a few ways that help you add interactivity to your chart.

## Using Tooltips

The simplest interaction you can add to a chart is providing tooltips for data points and legend items. As you move the mouse over any data point or legend item, a tooltip is displayed.

The TooltipValuesSample.aspx page in PetChartsSample demonstrates how easy it is to set up tooltips. This chart allows you to run arthropod sales statistics against the pet shop database by selecting a region. When you move the mouse over a data point, a tooltip is displayed, as shown in Figure 16-13. Moving the mouse over legend items also displays a tooltip.

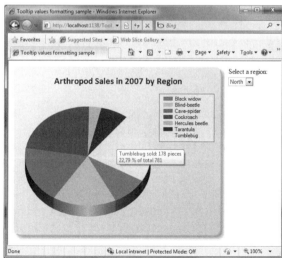

**FIGURE 16-13:** Displaying a tooltip for data points

Listing 16-13 shows the code enabling the chart data to be displayed with tooltips.

**LISTING 16-13: TooltipValuesSample.aspx.cs**

```csharp
using System;
using System.Data;
using System.Data.OleDb;
using System.Web.UI.DataVisualization.Charting;

namespace PetShopCharts
{
  public partial class TooltipValuesSample : System.Web.UI.Page
  {
    protected void Page_Load(object sender, EventArgs e)
    {
      var region = RegionList.SelectedValue;
      var connection = Helpers.Utility.GetChartDataConnection(this);
      var commandStr = "SELECT PetName, Total from PetSalesFor2007 where" +
        " Region = '" + region + "' and Kind=5;"; // --- Arthropods
      var command = new OleDbCommand(commandStr, connection);
      command.Connection.Open();
      var reader = command.ExecuteReader(CommandBehavior.CloseConnection);
      var points = Chart1.Series[0].Points;
      points.DataBindXY(reader, "PetName", reader, "Total");

      // --- Set legend texts
      foreach (var point in points)
      {
        point.LegendText = point.AxisLabel;
        point.AxisLabel = "";
      }
      reader.Close();
      connection.Close();

      // --- Set up series
      var series = Chart1.Series[0];
      series.ToolTip = "#LEGENDTEXT sold: #VAL{D} pieces\n" +
        "#PERCENT of total #TOTAL";
      series.LegendToolTip = "#PERCENT";
    }
  }
}
```

Code file [TooltipValuesSample.aspx.cs] available for download at Wrox.com

The Page_Load method uses a data reader object to obtain the sales statistics from the database. This time, the data points are bound to the chart with the Series.Points.DataBindXY method. The cycle following the DataBindXY call sets the legend text for data points, and removes their axis labels.

The most important statements of this sample are at the end of the method body setting the ToolTip and LegendToolTip properties. The tokens in the property values (starting with a # character) are substituted with the concrete values at run-time.

When the server renders the chart image, it assigns a `<map>` element to the `<img>` tag, as the following short extract shows:

```
<img id="Chart1" src="/ChartImg.axd?i=chart_4bfd..." alt=""
  usemap="#Chart1ImageMap" style="height:400px;width:500px;border-width:0px;" />
<map name="Chart1ImageMap" id="Chart1ImageMap">
  <area shape="poly" coords="176,207,241,309,241,..." title=""
  alt="Blind-beetle sold: 127 pieces
16,26 % of total 781" />
<!-- ... -->
</map>
```

## Handling Clicks on Data Points

The `Chart` control makes it very easy to respond to events when you click on a data point or a legend item. The `ClickOnDataPointsSample.aspx` page shows you how to do that. It improves the `TooltipValuesSample.aspx` page so that when you click on one of the doughnut chart slices, the slides are exploded. There are only a few changes in the code-behind file related to Listing 16-13. These modifications are shown in Listing 16-14.

**LISTING 16-14:** ClickOnDataPointsSample.aspx.cs

```
using System;
using System.Data;
using System.Data.OleDb;
using System.Web.UI.WebControls;

namespace PetShopCharts
{
  public partial class ClickOnDataPointsSample : System.Web.UI.Page
  {
    protected void Page_Load(object sender, EventArgs e)
    {
      // ...
      // --- Added to the Page_Load method
      series.PostBackValue = "#INDEX";
      series.LegendPostBackValue = "#INDEX";
      if (!IsPostBack)
      {
        series.Points[0].CustomProperties += "Exploded=true";
      }
    }

    protected void Chart1_Click(object sender, ImageMapEventArgs e)
    {
      int pointIndex = int.Parse(e.PostBackValue);
      var series = Chart1.Series[0];
      if (pointIndex >= 0 && pointIndex < series.Points.Count)
```

```
    {
        series.Points[pointIndex].CustomProperties += "Exploded=true";
    }
  }
 }
}
```

*Code file [ClickOnDataPointsSample.aspx.cs] available for download at Wrox.com*

Setting either the `PostBackValue` or the `LegendPostBackValue` property of a series instance will initiate a postback when any of the series' data points (or any legend item associated with the series) is clicked. The code in Listing 16-14 sets these property values to `#INDEX` so that the data point index is posted back when the click event occurs. The chart's `OnClick` event is set to `Chart1_Click` that parses the postback value to obtain the index of the data point clicked, and sets the `Exploded` custom property of the slice clicked to `true`. Figure 16-14 shows what happens when you click on the Tumblebug slice.

You can also click on the legend items to explode the appropriate data point slice.

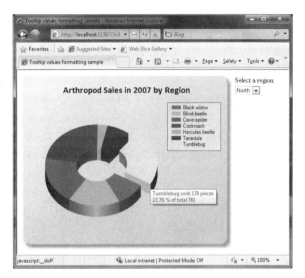

**FIGURE 16-14:** A slice of the doughnut chart is clicked

## Interactivity With Ajax

Ajax (Asynchronous JavaScript and XML) is a group of interrelated web development techniques used on the client-side to create interactive web applications. With Ajax, web applications can retrieve data from the server asynchronously in the background without interfering with the display and behavior of the existing page.

This section explores how easy it is to combine a chart's interactivity features with Ajax to improve the user experience.

*This chapter is definitely not about Ajax and related techniques. You can read a more detailed overview about Ajax and its improvements in .NET Framework 4.0 in Chapter 19. Chapter 20 introduces you to the Ajax Control Toolkit. This chapter only examines a few examples that may whet your appetite, but definitely won't present you with the full menu Ajax offers.*

## Handling Click Events

With Ajax, you can post-back a message to the web page in a separate asynchronous communication channel using an `XMLHttpRequest` object at the background. When the page processes the request, it sends back the results, and only a well-defined part of the page is refreshed according to the results returned. This communication is asynchronous, so it does not prevent the user from interacting with the page.

The `PetShopCharts` project contains a page named `AjaxClickEvent` that allows you to click any point on the chart and refresh the chart's subtitle with information about what has been clicked. Figure 16-15 shows how the subtitle changes when you click on the third data point in the second series.

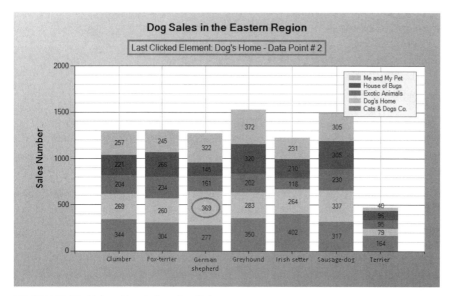

**FIGURE 16-15:** Using Ajax to handle click events

To allow using Ajax communication on your page, you must add an `<asp:ScriptManager>` and an `<asp:UpdatePanel>` control to your page:

```
<%@ Page Language="C#" AutoEventWireup="true" CodeBehind="AjaxClickEvent.aspx.cs"
  Inherits="PetShopCharts.AjaxClickEvent" %>

<!DOCTYPE html PUBLIC "-//W3C//DTD XHTML 1.0 Transitional//EN"
  "http://www.w3.org/TR/xhtml1/DTD/xhtml1-transitional.dtd">

<html xmlns="http://www.w3.org/1999/xhtml">
<head runat="server">
  <title>Ajax Click event sample</title>
</head>
<body>
```

```
    <form id="form1" runat="server">
      <div>
        <asp:ScriptManager ID="ScriptManager1" runat="server" />
        <asp:UpdatePanel ID="UpdatePanel1" runat="server">
          <ContentTemplate>
            <asp:Chart ...>
              <!-- Chart details omitted -->
            </asp:Chart>
          </ContentTemplate>
        </asp:UpdatePanel>
      </div>
    </form>
  </body>
</html>
```

The ScriptManager is responsible for managing ASP.NET Ajax script libraries and script files, partial-page rendering, and client proxy class generation for web and application services. The UpdatePanel control enables a section of a page to be partially rendered without a postback. The <ContentTemplate> element encapsulates the page section updated by the UpdatePanel.

Listing 16-15 shows how the Ajax controls work together with the page in an asynchronous manner.

**Available for download on Wrox.com**

### LISTING 16-15: AjaxClickEvent.aspx.cs

```csharp
using System;
using System.Data;
using System.Data.OleDb;
using System.Web.UI;
using System.Web.UI.DataVisualization.Charting;
using System.Web.UI.WebControls;

namespace PetShopCharts
{
  public partial class AjaxClickEvent : System.Web.UI.Page
  {
    protected void Page_Load(object sender, EventArgs e)
    {
      // --- Initialize chart from database
      var connection = Helpers.Utility.GetChartDataConnection(this);
      var commandStr = "SELECT PetName, Total, ShopName from DogSalesData " +
        "where Region = 'East';";
      var command = new OleDbCommand(commandStr, connection);
      command.Connection.Open();
      var reader = command.ExecuteReader(CommandBehavior.CloseConnection);
      Chart1.DataBindCrossTable(reader, "ShopName", "PetName", "Total", "");
      reader.Close();
      connection.Close();
      foreach (var series in Chart1.Series)
      {
        series.ChartType = SeriesChartType.StackedColumn;
        series.IsValueShownAsLabel = true;
      }
```

*continues*

**LISTING 16-15** *(continued)*

```
    // --- Set up Ajax event handling
    Chart1.Click += new ImageMapEventHandler(Chart1_Click);
    foreach (Series series in this.Chart1.Series)
    {
      series.PostBackValue = "Series:" + series.Name + ", #INDEX";
    }
    Chart1.Attributes["onclick"] =
      ClientScript.GetPostBackEventReference(this.Chart1, "@").
      Replace("'@'", "'Chart:' +_getCoord(event)");
    Chart1.Style[HtmlTextWriterStyle.Position] = "relative";
    ClientScript.RegisterClientScriptBlock(
        typeof(Chart),
        "Chart",
        @"function _getCoord(event){if(typeof(event.x)=='undefined')" +
        "{return event.layerX+', '+event.layerY;}" +
        "return event.x+','+event.y;}",
        true);
  }

  protected void Chart1_Click(object sender, ImageMapEventArgs e)
  {
    Chart1.Titles["MessageTitle"].Text = "Nothing";
    string[] input = e.PostBackValue.Split(':');
    if (input.Length == 2)
    {
      string[] seriesData = input[1].Split(',');
      if (input[0].Equals("Series"))
      {
        Chart1.Titles["MessageTitle"].Text = "Last Clicked Element: " +
          seriesData[0] + " - Data Point #" + seriesData[1];
      }
      else if (input[0].Equals("Chart"))
      {
        var hit = this.Chart1.HitTest(
          Int32.Parse(seriesData[0]),
          Int32.Parse(seriesData[1]));
        if (hit != null)
        {
          Chart1.Titles["MessageTitle"].Text =
            "Last Clicked Element: " + hit.ChartElementType.ToString();
        }
      }
    }
  }
}
```

*Code file [AjaxClickEvent.aspx.cs] available for download at Wrox.com*

After the `Page_Load` method adds data points using the `DataBindCrossTable` method, it sets up Ajax event handling with the following steps:

**1.** Subscribes to the `Chart1_Click` event handler method.

**2.** Sets the postback values of each series sending back the series name and index.

**3.** Sets the `Chart` control's `onclick` event to do a postback using the `_getCoord` JavaScript function in its arguments.

**4.** Injects the `_getCoord` JavaScript function into the scripts of the page.

As a result of this setup, any time the user clicks on any chart element, an asynchronous postback occurs that will activate the `Chart1_Click` event handler at the server side. This receives an `ImageMapEventArgs` instance and uses its `PostBackValue` property to parse which chart element was clicked.

If a data point was clicked, `PostBackMessage` contains the series name and the data point number. If the any other chart element was clicked, `PostBackMessage` holds its coordinates. In this case, the chart's `HitTest` method tells which chart element was hit.

At the end, the chart's subtitle is updated at the server side and the chart control encapsulated within the `UpdatePanel` is sent back asynchronously. At the browser side, the image representing the chart is updated, while the rest of the page (that is, the rest of the HTML document model) remains intact.

 *When you run the sample, open the source code of the page. You can see the chart's* onclick *event (in the* <img> *tag representing the chart), the* _getCoord *function, and the* __doPostBack *calls of* <area> *tags with the appropriate postback values.*

## Triggering Chart Events

By default, any postback control inside an `UpdatePanel` control causes an asynchronous postback and refreshes the panel's content. However, you can also configure other controls on the page to refresh an `UpdatePanel` control.

You do this by defining a trigger for the `UpdatePanel` control. A trigger is a binding that specifies which postback control and event cause a panel to update. When the specified event of the trigger control is raised (for example, a button's `Click` event), the update panel is refreshed.

This mechanism is very useful for charts. Clicking a data point or a legend item in a `Chart` control can trigger updating other parts of the page — for example, it can refresh a table telling you details about the data point you've clicked.

The `AjaxTriggerSample` page in the `PetShopCharts` project utilizes this mechanism to display two related charts. The first stacked column chart shows details about year 2009's sales statistics, where data is organized into series by regions. When you click any of the data points in this chart, the second chart is updated asynchronously by a trigger to show sales detail drill-downs. Figure 16-16 shows these charts in action.

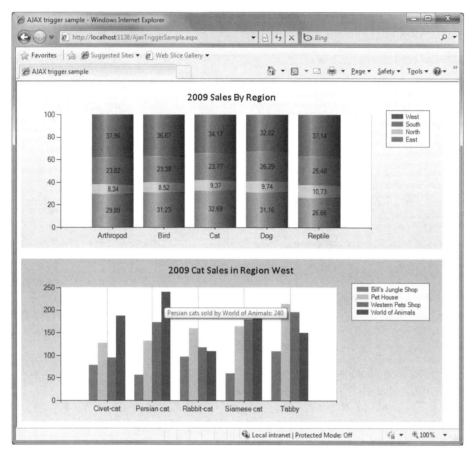

**FIGURE 16-16:** Charts of the AjaxTriggerSample page

To achieve the result you see in Figure 16-16, you must wrap the second chart into an `UpdatePanel` and define an `AsynchPostBackTrigger` for it, as shown in Listing 16-16. The `Chart` controls' details are omitted from this listing for the sake of readability.

**LISTING 16-16:** AjaxTriggerSample.asxp

```
<%@ Page Language="C#" AutoEventWireup="true"
   CodeBehind="AjaxTriggerSample.aspx.cs"
   Inherits="PetShopCharts.AjaxTriggerSample" %>

<!DOCTYPE html PUBLIC "-//W3C//DTD XHTML 1.0 Transitional//EN"
   "http://www.w3.org/TR/xhtml1/DTD/xhtml1-transitional.dtd">
<html xmlns="http://www.w3.org/1999/xhtml">
<head runat="server">
  <title>AJAX trigger sample</title>
</head>
```

```
<body>
  <form id="form1" runat="server">
  <div>
    <asp:ScriptManager ID="ScriptManager1" runat="server" />
    <asp:Chart ID="Chart1" runat="server"
      OnClick="Chart1_Click" ...>
      <!-- Chart details omitted -->
    </asp:Chart>
    <br />
    <br />
    <asp:UpdatePanel ID="UpdatePanel1" runat="server">
      <ContentTemplate>
        <asp:Chart ID="Chart2" runat="server" BackColor="LightSkyBlue" ...>
          <!-- Chart details omitted -->
        </asp:Chart>
      </ContentTemplate>
      <Triggers>
        <asp:AsyncPostBackTrigger ControlID="Chart1" />
      </Triggers>
    </asp:UpdatePanel>
  </div>
  </form>
</body>
</html>
```

*Code file [AjaxTriggerSample.aspx] available for download at Wrox.com*

The `ControlID` attribute of `AsynchPostBackTrigger` defined in the `<Triggers>` element enables `Chart1` to be a trigger for the wrapping `UpdatePanel` control. The code-behind file of the page (in Listing 16-17) shows how `Chart1` triggers the update of `Chart2`.

**LISTING 16-17:** AjaxTriggerSample.aspx.cs

```
using System;
using System.Data;
using System.Data.OleDb;
using System.Web.UI.DataVisualization.Charting;
using System.Web.UI.WebControls;

namespace PetShopCharts
{
  public partial class AjaxTriggerSample : System.Web.UI.Page
  {
    protected void Page_Load(object sender, EventArgs e)
    {
      var connection = Helpers.Utility.GetChartDataConnection(this);
      var commandStr = "SELECT Region, KindName, Total from SalesByYearAndRegion"
        + " where Year=2009";
      var command = new OleDbCommand(commandStr, connection);
      command.Connection.Open();
      var reader = command.ExecuteReader(CommandBehavior.CloseConnection);
```

*continues*

**LISTING 16-17** *(continued)*

```
    Chart1.DataBindCrossTable(reader, "Region", "Kindname", "Total", "");
    reader.Close();
    connection.Close();
    foreach (var series in Chart1.Series)
    {
      series.ChartType = SeriesChartType.StackedColumn100;
      series.CustomProperties = "DrawingStyle=Cylinder";
      series.IsValueShownAsLabel = true;
      series.PostBackValue = "#AXISLABEL;" + series.Name;
      series.ToolTip = "#AXISLABELs sold in " + series.Name + ": #VAL{D}";
    }
  }

  protected void Chart1_Click(object sender, ImageMapEventArgs e)
  {
    var pars = e.PostBackValue.Split(';');
    var connection = Helpers.Utility.GetChartDataConnection(this);
    var commandStr = "SELECT Petname, ShopName, Total "
      + "from YearlyAccumulatedSales "
      + "where Year=2009 and "
      + "KindName='" + pars[0] + "' and "
      + "Region='" + pars[1] + "';";
    var command = new OleDbCommand(commandStr, connection);
    command.Connection.Open();
    var reader = command.ExecuteReader(CommandBehavior.CloseConnection);
    Chart2.DataBindCrossTable(reader, "ShopName", "PetName", "Total", "");
    reader.Close();
    connection.Close();
    Chart2.Titles[0].Text = "2009 " + pars[0] + " Sales in Region " + pars[1];
    foreach (var series in Chart2.Series)
    {
      series.ChartType = SeriesChartType.Column;
      series.ToolTip = "#AXISLABELs sold by " + series.Name + ": #VAL{D}";
    }
  }
}
```

*Code file [AjaxTriggerSample.aspx.cs] available for download at Wrox.com*

The Page_Load event initializes a chart series with the DataBindCrossTable method that creates a series for each region. The foreach cycle following the data binding part is responsible for setting up the visual series properties, and PostBackValue, which is the key in this scenario. The following assignment sets the postback value so that the axis label and the series name is passed back when the user click a data point:

```
series.PostBackValue = "#AXISLABEL;" + series.Name;
```

When you comment out this line and run the sample, no postback happens, because setting PostBackValue triggers rendering postback scripts.

So, when the user clicks a data point, the Chart1_Click event handler method is invoked as a result of the asynchronous postback. It obtains the PostBackValue sent by Chart1 as a property of its ImageMapEventArgs parameter. Chart1_Click splits this value into two parts that will be used as input parameters for the query being carried out as the data source of Chart2. After binding the query results to Chart2, the foreach cycle sets up the series' properties.

This kind of master-detail chart solution is very powerful. If it takes time (let's say a few seconds) while the second chart gets updated, you can use an Ajax UpdateProgress control. While the chart is being updated, the user is not prevented from examining the first chart. Of course, you can use any controls instead of the second chart, and with this mechanism, you can also cascade more controls in a master-detail scenario.

## Real Time Charts

The asynchronous nature of Ajax is a great candidate for displaying real-time charts where data is queried periodically, and a chart is updated with the new data regularly. The AjaxRealTimeSample page of the PetShopCharts project demonstrates this scenario.

The page contains a chart that displays real-time stock exchange data of fictitious indexes so that the information is refreshed every second. Figure 16-17 shows the chart after several asynchronous refreshes.

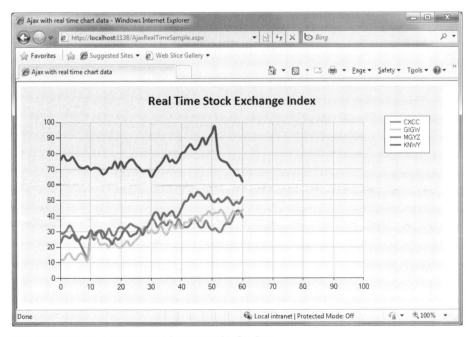

**FIGURE 16-17:** Real-time chart after several refreshes

The page uses an Ajax `Timer` control that periodically executes asynchronous postback to the page. Listing 16-18 shows how the page is defined using the Ajax controls. The `<asp:Chart>` details are omitted for the sake of brevity.

**LISTING 16-18:** AjaxRealTimeSample.aspx

```
<%@ Page Language="C#" AutoEventWireup="true"
    CodeBehind="AjaxRealTimeSample.aspx.cs"
  Inherits="PetShopCharts.AjaxRealTimeSample" %>

<!DOCTYPE html PUBLIC "-//W3C//DTD XHTML 1.0 Transitional//EN"
    "http://www.w3.org/TR/xhtml1/DTD/xhtml1-transitional.dtd">
<html xmlns="http://www.w3.org/1999/xhtml">
<head runat="server">
  <title>Ajax with real time chart data</title>
</head>
<body>
  <form id="form1" runat="server">
  <div>
    <asp:ScriptManager ID="ScriptManager1" runat="server" />
    <asp:UpdatePanel ID="UpdatePanel1" runat="server">
      <ContentTemplate>
        <asp:Chart ID="Chart1" runat="server" ...
          EnableViewState="True">
          <!-- Chart details omitted -->
        </asp:Chart>
        <asp:Timer ID="Timer1" runat="server" Interval="1000"
          OnTick="Timer1_Tick" />
      </ContentTemplate>
    </asp:UpdatePanel>
  </div>
  </form>
</body>
</html>
```

*Code file [AjaxRealTimeSample.aspx] available for download at Wrox.com*

The `Timer` control is in the same `UpdatePanel` as the chart, so, after each `OnTick` event, the chart will be updated. The `Timer` control's `Interval` property is set to 1,000 milliseconds, so the chart is refreshed in every second. The real-time chart works so that every `OnTick` event creates new data points and appends these to the existing ones. Because `OnTick` generates postbacks, the chart state should be saved between them, so the `EnableViewState` property of the chart is set to `true`.

Listing 16-19 shows how the `Page_Load` method and the `Timer1_Tick` event handler method work together to form the solution.

**LISTING 16-19:** AjaxRealTimeSample.aspx.cs

```csharp
using System;

namespace PetShopCharts
{
  public partial class AjaxRealTimeSample : System.Web.UI.Page
  {
    const int NewPoints = 10;
    const int MaxPoints = 100;
    const int LowerBound = 10;
    const int UpperBound = 100;
    const int StepBack = 20;
    const int SingleStep = 5;

    protected void Page_Load(object sender, EventArgs e)
    {
      if (!IsPostBack)
      {
        var rand = new Random((int)DateTime.Now.Millisecond);
        foreach (var series in Chart1.Series)
        {
          series.Points.AddXY(0, rand.Next(LowerBound, UpperBound));
        }
        Timer1_Tick(this, EventArgs.Empty);
      }
    }

    protected void Timer1_Tick(object sender, EventArgs e)
    {
      var rand = new Random((int)DateTime.Now.Ticks);
      foreach (var series in Chart1.Series)
      {
        var lastYValue = series.Points[series.Points.Count - 1].YValues[0];
        var lastXValue = series.Points[series.Points.Count - 1].XValue + 1;
        for (int index = 0; index < NewPoints; index++)
        {
          lastYValue += rand.Next(1 - SingleStep, SingleStep);
          if (lastYValue >= UpperBound)
            lastYValue -= StepBack;
          else if (lastYValue <= LowerBound)
            lastYValue += StepBack;
          series.Points.AddXY(lastXValue++, lastYValue);
        }
      }
      // --- Remove points from the left chart side if number of
      // --- points exceeds the maximum number.
      while (this.Chart1.Series[0].Points.Count > MaxPoints)
      {
        foreach (var series in this.Chart1.Series)
```

*continues*

**LISTING 16-19** *(continued)*

```
            series.Points.RemoveAt(0);
        }
        // --- Adjust scale
        double axisMinimum = Chart1.Series[0].Points[0].XValue - 1.0;
        if (axisMinimum < 0.0) axisMinimum = 0.0;
        Chart1.ChartAreas[0].AxisX.Minimum = axisMinimum;
        Chart1.ChartAreas[0].AxisX.Maximum = axisMinimum + MaxPoints;
    }
  }
}
```

*Code file [AjaxRealTimeSample.aspx.cs] available for download at Wrox.com*

The page class defines a few constant values used during the data generation. The `Page_Load` event takes care of generating the initial random data points for the series — each of which represents a specific stock exchange index. When `Page_Load` is executed the first time, it also calls `Timer1_Tick` to generate the first set of data points.

The whole data-generation logic is implemented in the `Timer1_Tick` method. It is not enough to generate new data points. The method also should take care of removing obsolete data — for example, data points shifting out of the chart's time window. If the method did not remove the old data, after a while, there would be too many data points. They would require extra time to render and consume too much network bandwidth because of transferring the chart's view state through the network.

After new data points are generated, `Timer1_Click` removes the obsolete data (it keeps open a time window for 100 data points) with the following simple cycle:

```
while (this.Chart1.Series[0].Points.Count > MaxPoints)
{
  foreach (var series in this.Chart1.Series)
    series.Points.RemoveAt(0);
}
```

The `XValue` property of data points is continuously increasing as new information is generated. It is not enough to delete old data points, but the X-axis also should be kept in synch with data points. The last few lines of `Timer1_Click` are responsible for this:

```
double axisMinimum = Chart1.Series[0].Points[0].XValue - 1.0;
if (axisMinimum < 0.0) axisMinimum = 0.0;
Chart1.ChartAreas[0].AxisX.Minimum = axisMinimum;
Chart1.ChartAreas[0].AxisX.Maximum = axisMinimum + MaxPoints;
```

Figure 16-18 shows how the X-axis is shifted after about a half minute.

**FIGURE 16-18:** Axis minimum and maximum values are modified.

## A Few More Points on User Interactivity

This section has just scratched the surface of user interactivity opportunities. There are many other alternatives that enable coding interactions with charts. Here is a short list of them:

➤ You can use Ajax controls such as `UpdateProgress`, `ScriptManager`, and `ScriptManagerProxy` for advanced scenarios.

➤ You can customize legend items, and respond to events when legend items are clicked.

➤ You can use JavaScript code and binary image streaming combined with Ajax to show other charts in tooltips and overlay panels.

➤ You can capture mouse events with client-side scripts.

It is worth exploring these opportunities on your own, because they may help you to create more attractive charts with fascinating user experiences.

## SUMMARY

The ASP.NET `Chart` control shipped with .NET Framework 4.0 and Visual Studio 2010 shares the charting concepts with the Windows Forms `Chart` control (detailed in Chapter 14). You can easily set up the ASP.NET `Chart` control through the dozens of properties it exploits. Charts have a great design-time support; when you change a property, the design-time view changes accordingly. You can choose from more than 30 chart types, and customize them through general and chart type-specific properties. The `Chart` control supports data binding and many manipulations, including filtering, sorting values, and applying financial formulas.

Because of the distributed nature of the web, you have several options to render charts. You can use them as images (with a number of format and storage options) or as binary streams. Chart controls can be easily integrated with legacy websites.

The Chart control has a smart state management implementation that lets you fine-tune which chart properties (and how) to save into the view state. With a few lines of code, you can balance among performance, used processing capacity, and network bandwidth, and establish solutions that are frugal with resources.

The Chart control has great user interactivity support, starting with handling tooltips, to using sophisticated asynchronous and real-time charting solutions with Ajax.

Chapter 17 provides an overview about the new Dynamic Data feature of ASP.NET 4.0, and you will learn how to create a functional data-driven web application leveraging the Dynamic Data framework.

# 17

# ASP.NET Dynamic Data

To create a functional data-driven web application, you must combine many complex components. ASP.NET Dynamic Data was introduced in ASP.NET 3.5 SP1, and ASP.NET 4 improved its features. It offers an excellent starting point for creating data-driven web applications following some simple steps.

This chapter examines ASP.NET Dynamic Data and the possibilities it offers to create data-driven web applications from an existing data model. This chapter starts with a simple data model and then upgrades to a more complex data model to show the most interesting features offered by Dynamic Data. You will also find many step-by-step instructions and examples throughout the chapter.

## CREATING A NEW DYNAMIC DATA WEB SITE

By taking advantage of ASP.NET Dynamic Data, it is possible to create a *data-driven* website with little or no coding. Also, once you create a Dynamic Data web application, you can customize its behavior to fit particular requirements. In real-world data-driven websites, you must always add some code to tailor a Dynamic Data application. Therefore, it is very important to learn the most common customization features offered by Dynamic Data's powerful framework and its *scaffolding mechanism*.

### Working Against a Data Model

A Dynamic Data web application requires one of the following registered data contexts:

> ➤ A LINQ to SQL class

> ➤ An ADO.NET Entity Framework class

Visual Studio 2010 provides the Dynamic Data Web Site template, which allows you to create an ASP.NET Dynamic Data website. However, the first step is to have a data model prepared for a functional data-driven website.

You can work with a single table to help understand the basic *CRUD* (short for Create, Read, Update, and Delete) operations automatically generated based on a very simple data model, working with a LINQ to SQL class. Then, you can work with a more complex data model with many tables and different kinds of relationships between them. Figure 17-1 shows the structure of a very simple Game table.

It has an auto-increment primary key, GameId, and two fields:

➤ Name

➤ ReleaseDate

### Game

| | Column Name | Condensed Type | Nullable |
|---|---|---|---|
| 🔑 | GameId | int | No |
| | Name | nvarchar(50) | No |
| | ReleaseDate | date | Yes |

**FIGURE 17-1:** A simple table named Game

The Game table is part of the RetroGames SQL Server 2008 database. You can create a new database with a similar table in order to run this example. The goal is to understand the basic structure of an ASP.NET Dynamic Data website.

## Creating the Website Using a Template

Once you have created the aforementioned table, follow these steps to create a Dynamic Data website using a website template:

1. Create a new website in Visual Studio 2010. Select File ➪ New ➪ Web Site in the main menu (or press Shift + Alt + N).

2. Select Visual C# under Installed Templates and "Dynamic Data LINQ to SQL Web Site" in the New Web Site dialog box. Select File System in the "Web location" combo box and enter **RetroGamesWeb1** as the solution's name.

*The default folder in which Visual Studio 2010 creates the folder for the solution that contains the new website in the file system is the* Visual Studio 2010\WebSites *folder in your* Documents *folder. Considering the example, if your* Documents *folder is* C:\Users\Gaston\Documents, *the IDE will create the new website structure in* C:\Users\Gaston\Documents\Visual Studio 2010\WebSites\RetroGamesWeb1.

3. Click OK, and Visual Studio will generate a new website based on the specified template, with dozens of files organized in many folders, as shown in Figure 17-2.

In this case, you are working with a LINQ to SQL model. However, it is very important to remember that you can also use an ADO.NET Entity Framework model if you choose "Dynamic Data Entities Web Site" in the New Web Site dialog box.

## Adding the Data Model and Registering the Data Context

Now, it is necessary to add the link to the data that the Dynamic Data framework must consider to generate the website. To do this, you must do the following:

➤ Create a data context, or the classes that represent database entities.

➤ Register the aforementioned data context with Dynamic Data. This way, the framework will be able to use it.

First, in this case, follow these steps to create a copy of the database file in the project. However, in other cases, you may wish to use other methods to link the database.

**1.** Right-click on the `App_Data` folder in the Solution Explorer and select Add Existing Item in the context menu that appears. A file selection dialog box will appear.

**2.** Select Data Files in the file type combo box. (It shows Web Files by default.)

**3.** Navigate to the folder that contains the SQL Server database file (`RetroGames.mdf`), select it, and click Add. It will appear in the `App_Data` folder, as shown in Figure 17-3. Additionally, you will be able to access it through Data Connections in the Server Explorer.

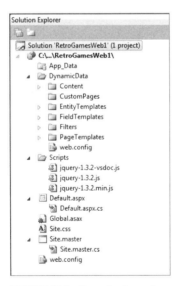

**FIGURE 17-2:** Organization of files in folders

**FIGURE 17-3:** Adding the SQL Server database file to the App_Data folder

Now, follow these steps to create a data model using LINQ to SQL:

**1.** Right-click on the project's name (`C:\...\RetroGamesWeb1\`) in the Solution Explorer and select Add ASP.NET Folder ➪ App_Code in the context menu that appears. The IDE will add an `App_Code` folder in the website, as shown in Figure 17-4.

**FIGURE 17-4:** App_Code folder added

2. Right-click on the new `App_Code` folder in the Solution Explorer and select Add New Item in the context menu that appears. A template selection dialog box will appear.

3. Select "LINQ to SQL Classes for Visual C#" under Installed Templates.

4. Enter the name for the database model, **RetroGames.dbml**, and click Add. The IDE will display the Object Relational Designer (O/R Designer) for `App_Code/RetroGames.dbml`.

5. Go to Server Explorer. Expand the database file node under Data Connections and then the Tables node. Drag the `Game` table into the O/R Designer's left panel. It will appear as an entity with the same name, as shown in Figure 17-5.

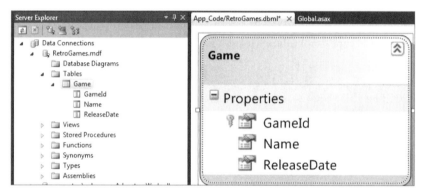

**FIGURE 17-5:** Entity appearing in O/R Designer

After following the aforementioned steps, the `App_Code/Retrogrames.dbml` node in the Solution Explorer will contain two files:

➤ `RetroGames.dbml.layout`

➤ `RetroGames.designer.cs`

The `RetroGames.designer.cs` file contains the definition for the `RetroGamesDataContext` class, an implementation of `System.Data.Linq.DataContext` that represents the database:

```
[global::System.Data.Linq.Mapping.DatabaseAttribute(Name="RetroGames")]
public partial class RetroGamesDataContext : System.Data.Linq.DataContext
```

Its parameterless constructor reads the connection string from the `Web.config` XML configuration file:

```
public RetroGamesDataContext() :
        base(global::System.Configuration.ConfigurationManager.ConnectionStrings
    ["RetroGamesConnectionString"].ConnectionString, mappingSource)

{
    OnCreated();
}
```

The RetroGamesConnectionString parameter is defined in the following Web.config XML lines:

```
<?xml version="1.0"?>
<configuration>

  <connectionStrings>
    <add name="RetroGamesConnectionString" connectionString=
        "Data Source=.\SQLEXPRESS;AttachDbFilename=|DataDirectory|
        \RetroGames.mdf;Integrated Security=
        True;User Instance=True"
      providerName="System.Data.SqlClient" />
  </connectionStrings>
```

Additionally, the RetroGames.designer.cs file contains the definition for the entity classes (that is, the tables previously dropped into the O/R Designer). In this case, it is just one entity class, Game, which is an implementation of INotifyPropertyChanging and INotifyPropertyChanged:

```
[global::System.Data.Linq.Mapping.TableAttribute(Name="dbo.Games")]
public partial class Game : INotifyPropertyChanging, INotifyPropertyChanged
```

Finally, follow these steps to register the data context with Dynamic Data.

1. Open the Global.asax file.

2. Find the following commented lines in the RegisterRoutes static method:

```
public static void RegisterRoutes(RouteCollection routes) {
    //                      IMPORTANT: DATA MODEL REGISTRATION
    // Uncomment this line to register a LINQ to SQL model for
    // ASP.NET Dynamic Data.
    // Set ScaffoldAllTables = true only if you are sure that you
    // want all tables in the
    // data model to support a scaffold (i.e. templates) view.
    // To control scaffolding for
    // individual tables, create a partial class for the table and apply the
    // [ScaffoldTable(true)] attribute to the partial class.
    // Note: Make sure that you change "YourDataContextType" to the name
    // of the data context
    // class in your application.
    // DefaultModel.RegisterContext(typeof(YourDataContextType),
    // new ContextConfiguration() { ScaffoldAllTables = false });
```

3. Uncomment the previously bolded code that registers the data context based on a LINQ to SQL model. Replace YourDataContextType with the name of the implementation of System.Data.Linq.DataContext that represents the database (in this case, RetroGamesDataContext). Also, enable automatic scaffolding for the data model assigning true to ScaffoldAllTables instead of the default false value. The following snippet shows the new uncommented code:

```
DefaultModel.RegisterContext(typeof(RetroGamesDataContext),
    new ContextConfiguration() { ScaffoldAllTables = true });
```

4. Save the changes to the Global.asax file.

*It is very important to understand that it is not convenient to enable scaffolding in all cases because it can pose a security risk — the resulting website will expose all the tables in the data model for the CRUD operations. Therefore, you should understand how Dynamic Data works with a simple model, and then you can use it in a more complex scenario, considering the necessary customizations. The forthcoming examples are focused on the core Dynamic Data features and don't explain the potential security risks. However, you should take that into account before deploying a website generated with the Dynamic Data framework.*

If you don't want to make all tables viewable by using Dynamic Data, you can set the `ScaffoldTableAttribute` to `true` in each partial class that represents the table that you want to be displayed. Another alternative is to set the `ScaffoldTableAttribute` to `false` in each partial class that represents the table that you don't want to be part of the Dynamic Data website.

For example, if you have many tables and you don't want the `Game` table to be part of the Dynamic Data website, you must include the following namespace in the `RetroGames.designer.cs` file:

```
using System.ComponentModel.DataAnnotations;
```

Then, you can set the `false` value to the `ScaffoldTableAttribute` adding the following boldfaced line before the `Game` public partial class definition:

```
[global::System.Data.Linq.Mapping.TableAttribute(Name="dbo.Game")]
[ScaffoldTable(false)]
public partial class Game : INotifyPropertyChanging, INotifyPropertyChanged
```

However, the code for `RetroGames.designer.cs` is automatically generated by the O/R Designer. If the model changes in the future, you could lose the changes made to this file. Therefore, there is another alternative — create a partial class, use an attribute to define an associated class to define metadata, and keep it in a different file. This way, you can refresh the code generated by the O/R Designer and the metadata information will be safe in a different file. You will learn how to define an associated class to define metadata in an independent file later in this chapter.

## Displaying Data from Existing Tables

So far, you've just made very small changes to the code provided by the template. Therefore, the Dynamic Data website will use the built-in data validation, as well as provide default CRUD operations and scaffolding behavior.

Follow these steps to display data from the `Game` table and test the simple Dynamic Data website:

**1.** Right-click on the `Default.aspx` page in the Solution Explorer and select "View in Browser" in the context menu that appears. Your default web browser will display a page with the list of tables available in the data model — in this case, the `Game` table (`Games` hyperlink), as shown in Figure 17-6.

Favorites
Dynamic Data Site
Page
Safety
Tools
DYNAMIC DATA SITE
Back to home page
My tables
Table Name
Games

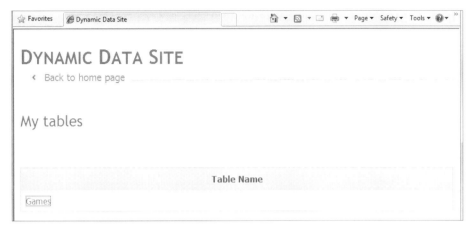

**FIGURE 17-6:** List of available tables

2. Now, click the hyperlink for the desired table listed under "My tables" (`Games` for the `Game` table). The web browser will display a page (`http://localhost:2952/RetroGamesWeb1/Games/List.aspx`) with the data from the selected table. It will provide buttons on the left, with three operations for each record — Edit, Delete, and Details. Additionally, an "Insert new item" button will appear at the bottom of the page, as shown in Figure 17-7.

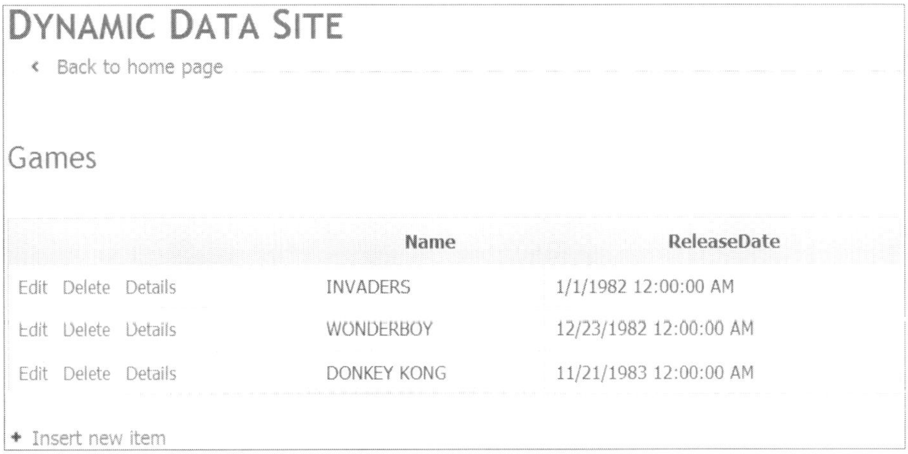

DYNAMIC DATA SITE
Back to home page
Games
Name
ReleaseDate
Edit Delete Details
INVADERS
1/1/1982 12:00:00 AM
Edit Delete Details
WONDERBOY
12/23/1982 12:00:00 AM
Edit Delete Details
DONKEY KONG
11/21/1983 12:00:00 AM
Insert new item

**FIGURE 17-7:** Table options and "Insert new item" button

3. Click the Details button for one of the records and the web browser will display a new page (`http://localhost:2952/RetroGamesWeb1/Games/Details.aspx?GameId=1`) with

the corresponding entry of the table using a detailed view, and offering the Edit and Delete operations at the bottom, as shown in Figure 17-8.

You can go back to the previous grid view of the data from the selected table by clicking on "Show all items" (a link to `http://localhost:2952/RetroGamesWeb1/Games/List.aspx`) at the bottom of the page.

If the table has too many records to display in just one page, the page that displays the data from the table will automatically split the grid into many pages, and provide page numbers to navigate through them, as shown in Figure 17-9.

**FIGURE 17-8:** Details view

**FIGURE 17-9:** Page navigation tools

You can also sort the data in the grid by clicking on the desired field name's column header. This works by calling a JavaScript postback for the `GridView` control that is displaying the data from the table. If you click on the `Name` column header, the following JavaScript code is executed:

```
javascript:__doPostBack('ctl00$ContentPlaceHolder1$GridView1','Sort$Name')
```

> *By following a few steps, you can create a Dynamic Data website capable of navigating the records from existing tables and buttons for CRUD operations. This kind of rapid web application is also useful in a development environment when it is necessary to query and populate tables in a database.*

## Creating Simple CRUD Applications

Go back to the detailed list view for the `Game` table (`Games` link) and click the "Insert new item" button at the bottom of the web page. The web browser will display a new page (http://localhost:2952/RetroGamesWeb1/ Games/Insert.aspx) with data entry fields. You can enter data for each field and click the Insert button to add a new record, as shown in Figure 17-10.

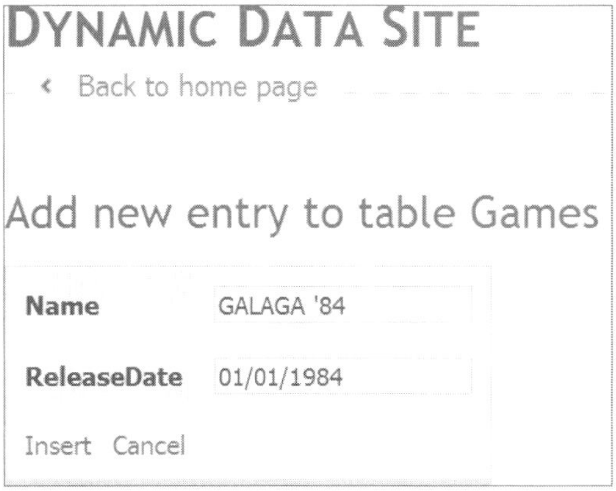

Once you insert the new record or cancel the addition, the web browser will go back to the detailed list view for the table.

The Insert button works by calling a JavaScript postback for the FormView control that is displaying the field names and edit controls for the new record. For example, in the aforementioned case, the following JavaScript code will be executed:

**FIGURE 17-10:** Page with fields for adding data

```
javascript:WebForm_DoPostBackWithOptions
    (new WebForm_PostBackOptions
    ("ctl00$ContentPlaceHolder1$FormView1$ctl02",
    "", true, "", "", false, true))
```

Now, click the Edit button at the left of one of the records. The web browser will display a new page (http://localhost:2952/RetroGamesWeb1/ Games/Edit.aspx?GameId=1) with data edition fields. You can edit the data for each field and click the Update button to commit the changes to the database table, as shown in Figure 17-11.

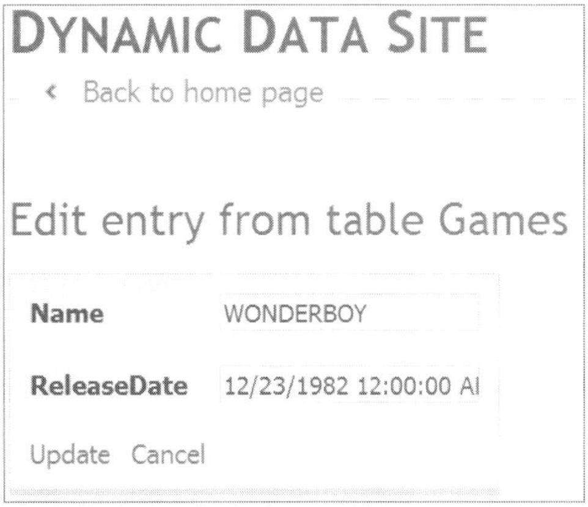

Once you update the record or cancel the edition, the web browser will go back to the detailed list view for the table. Remember that you can also access the record edition page by clicking Edit while displaying the details for the record.

The Update button also works by calling a JavaScript postback for the FormView control that is displaying the field names and edit controls for the record being edited.

**FIGURE 17-11:** Page with fields for editing data

Now, click the Delete button at the left of one of the records. The web browser will display a dialog box asking for a confirmation in order to proceed with the removal. If you click OK, the record will be deleted from the table, and the web browser will go back to the detailed list view for the table. The Delete button also works by calling a JavaScript postback.

## Understanding the Default URLs

Table 17-1 shows the relative URLs for each of the CRUD operations for the Game table, considering http://localhost:2952/RetroGamesWeb1 as the website main's location for this case.

**TABLE 17-1:** Default Relative URLs for the Different Operations on the Game Table

| OPERATION | RELATIVE URL |
|---|---|
| Create (insert a new record) | Games/Insert.aspx |
| Update (edit an existing record) | Games/Edit.aspx?GameId=GameIdToEdit |
| View details | Games/Details.aspx?GameId=GameIdToView |
| List (show all the record from the table) | Games/List.aspx |

As you can see in Table 17-1, the URLs are composed of the entity name (Games for the Game table), followed by the operation's name. If the operation requires a record, it adds the primary key to identify the record as a parameter, and it names the parameter with the primary key field's name (for example, GameId).

Therefore, if you add a Manufacturer table, using the same templates, you will be able to edit the data for the manufacturer with the ManufacturerId = 50 entering the following URL in your web browser:

```
http://localhost:2952/RetroGamesWeb1/Manufacturers/Edit.aspx?ManufacturerId=50
```

You will also be able to list all the records for this new table by entering the following URL in your web browser:

```
http://localhost:2952/RetroGamesWeb1/Manufacturers/List.aspx
```

 *As you can see, the Dynamic Data website exposes a lot of information about the underlying database model in the URLs. Therefore, as previously explained, it is very important to consider security issues before publishing an ASP.NET website using the Dynamic Data framework.*

The Global.asax file contains the route definition that enables the previously explained *separate-page mode*, where different pages perform the List, Detail, Insert, and Update tasks. The following lines (inside the RegisterRoutes static method) define the dynamic data route with a table, followed by an action as a pattern for the four possible actions:

```
routes.Add(new DynamicDataRoute("{table}/{action}.aspx") {
    Constraints = new RouteValueDictionary(new { action =
        "List|Details|Edit|Insert" }),
    Model = DefaultModel
});
```

The code in the `Application_Start` method in the `Global.asax` file calls the `RegisterRoutes` method when the Dynamic Data web application starts, as shown in the following lines:

```
void Application_Start(object sender, EventArgs e) {
    RegisterRoutes(RouteTable.Routes);
}
```

A `DynamicDataRoute` instance (`System.Web.DynamicData.DynamicDataRoute`) represents a route that is used by ASP.NET Dynamic Data.

## Customizing Dynamic Data's URL Routing

You can change the default URL routing. You can do it by editing the previously shown lines for the `RegisterRoutes` static method, in order to replace the pattern for the dynamic data route. For example, if you want the route to show the action followed by the table, the following lines will produce the results shown in Table 17-2.

```
routes.Add(new DynamicDataRoute("{action}/{table}.aspx") {
    Constraints = new RouteValueDictionary(new { action =
        "List|Details|Edit|Insert" }),
    Model = DefaultModel
});
```

**TABLE 17-2:** New Relative URLs for the Different Operations on the Game Table

| OPERATION | RELATIVE URL |
|---|---|
| Create (insert a new record) | `Insert/Games.aspx` |
| Update (edit an existing record) | `Edit/Games.aspx?GameId=GameIdToEdit` |
| View details | `Details/Games.aspx?GameId=GameIdToView` |
| List (show all the record from the table) | `List/Games.aspx` |

Another alternative provided by the Dynamic Data templates is the *combined-page mode*, where a single page performs the List, Detail, Insert, and Update tasks. To enable this mode, comment the previously shown lines that added the dynamic routes and uncomment the route definitions in the separate-page mode section. Listing 17-1 shows the resulting code in the `RegisterRoutes` static method, defining two dynamic routes with the table, followed by the `ListDetails.aspx` page and the following actions for each new `DynamicDataRoute` instance:

➤   `PageAction.List`

➤   `PageAction.Details`

**LISTING 17-1: Code for the Combined-Page Mode in the Global.asax File**

```
public static void RegisterRoutes(RouteCollection routes) {
    DefaultModel.RegisterContext(typeof(RetroGamesDataContext),
        new ContextConfiguration() { ScaffoldAllTables =
        true });
    // Original URL routing
    //routes.Add(new DynamicDataRoute("{table}/{action}.aspx") {
    //     Constraints = new RouteValueDictionary(new { action =
    //         "List|Details|Edit|Insert" }),
    //     Model = DefaultModel
    //});

    // Customized URL routing
    //routes.Add(new DynamicDataRoute("{action}/{table}.aspx")
    //{
    //     Constraints = new RouteValueDictionary(new { action =
    //         "List|Details|Edit|Insert" }),
    //     Model = DefaultModel
    //});

    // Combined-page mode
    routes.Add(new DynamicDataRoute("{table}/ListDetails.aspx")
    {
        Action = PageAction.List,
        ViewName = "ListDetails",
        Model = DefaultModel
    });

    routes.Add(new DynamicDataRoute("{table}/ListDetails.aspx")
    {
        Action = PageAction.Details,
        ViewName = "ListDetails",
        Model = DefaultModel
    });
}
```

*Code file [RetroGamesWeb1/Global.asax] available for download at Wrox.com*

After making the aforementioned changes, all the operations work on the same URL,
`http://localhost:2952/RetroGamesWeb1/Games/ListDetails.aspx`.

Notice that `ListDetails` is the combination of List and Details. The template page is different than
the List template used in the previous cases.

## Performing CRUD Operations on the Same Page

The behavior of the Dynamic Data website will be slightly different because all the CRUD
operations are going to run on the same page. Thus, a new selection mechanism is available to
choose the active record, and different buttons provide access to the different operations.

Follow these steps to display data from the Game table and test the new behavior of the Dynamic Data website:

1.  Display the Default.aspx page in your default web browser.

2.  Click the hyperlink for the desired table listed under "My tables" (Games for the Game table). Now, the web browser displays the page that will allow you to perform all the operations, including listing the data from the selected table, http://localhost:2952/ RetroGamesWeb1/Games/ListDetails.aspx. The first row appears with a yellow background, the selected record, and the detailed view for this selected record will appear at the bottom of the page. It will provide buttons on the left with three operations for each record — Edit, Delete, and Select. There is no need to show a Details button, because the detailed view is already visible for the selected record. Also, three buttons will appear at the bottom of the detailed view for the selected record — Edit, Delete, and New — as shown in Figure 17-12.

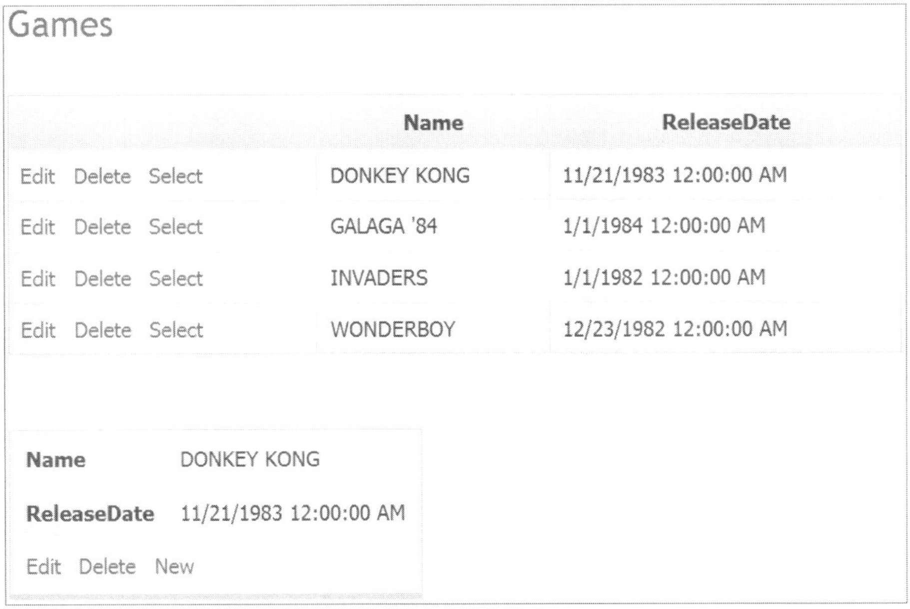

**Games**

| | | | Name | ReleaseDate |
|---|---|---|---|---|
| Edit | Delete | Select | DONKEY KONG | 11/21/1983 12:00:00 AM |
| Edit | Delete | Select | GALAGA '84 | 1/1/1984 12:00:00 AM |
| Edit | Delete | Select | INVADERS | 1/1/1982 12:00:00 AM |
| Edit | Delete | Select | WONDERBOY | 12/23/1982 12:00:00 AM |

| | |
|---|---|
| **Name** | DONKEY KONG |
| **ReleaseDate** | 11/21/1983 12:00:00 AM |
| Edit  Delete  New | |

**FIGURE 17-12:** Detailed view with three buttons

3.  Click the Select button for a different row. The corresponding record appears with a yellow background and its detailed view will appear at the bottom of the page. It works by calling a JavaScript postback for the GridView control that is displaying the data from the table:

```
javascript:__doPostBack('ctl00$ContentPlaceHolder1$GridView1','Select$1')
```

**4.** Click the Edit button at the left of one of the rows. The grid will enable an in-place editing of the record and will provide Update and Cancel buttons, as shown in Figure 17-13.

| | Name | ReleaseDate |
|---|---|---|
| Edit  Delete  Select | DONKEY KONG | 11/21/1983 12:00:00 AM |
| Update  Cancel | GALAGA '84 NEW EDIT | 1/1/1984 12:00:00 AM |

**FIGURE 17-13:** Update and Cancel buttons

**5.** Click the Edit button at the bottom of the page. This button enables the capability to update each field using the detailed view instead of the aforementioned in-place editing, as shown in Figure 17-14.

| | | |
|---|---|---|
| Edit  Delete  Select | GALAGA '84 | |
| Edit  Delete  Select | INVADERS | |
| Edit  Delete  Select | WONDERBOY | |

| | |
|---|---|
| **Name** | GALAGA '84 NEW EDIT |
| **ReleaseDate** | 1/1/1984 12:00:00 AM |
| Update  Cancel | |

**FIGURE 17-14:** Updating fields through the detailed view

> *By commenting and uncommenting a few lines of code, you can provide in-line editing capabilities and perform all the operations in a single page working with the combined-page mode. You can select the desired Dynamic Data's URL routing according to the applications' requirements.*

# Creating a Dynamic Data Application for Master-Detail Relationships

So far, you have learned about the basics for Dynamic Data with a single table. Before diving deeper into Dynamic Data's templates structure, let's move to a more complex data model, with many tables and different kinds of relationships between them.

Figure 17-15 shows the structure of the following new tables related to the Game table:

➤   GameCategory

➤   Gender

➤   Player

➤   PlayerScore

Also, the Game table has a new Boolean field, Played, and a GameCategoryId that represents a many-to-one relationship with GameCategory.

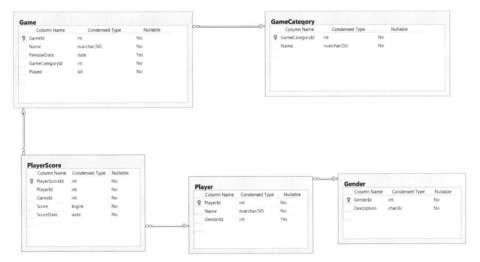

**FIGURE 17-15:** Structure of new tables

Each game must have a category. Each time a game is played by a player, the score is saved in the PlayerScore table. Each player must have a gender (male or female, defined in the Gender table).

The five tables are part of a new version of the RetroGames SQL Server 2008 database. You can create a new database with a similar structure to run this example. The goal is to use a data model with many kinds of relationships in an ASP.NET Dynamic Data website.

Follow the previously described steps to create a new ASP.NET Dynamic Data LINQ to SQL website with the new data model. Use RetroGamesWeb2 as the solution's name. Remember to add the data model and to register the data context. The O/R Designer's left panel will display the five entities and their relationships, as shown in Figure 17-16.

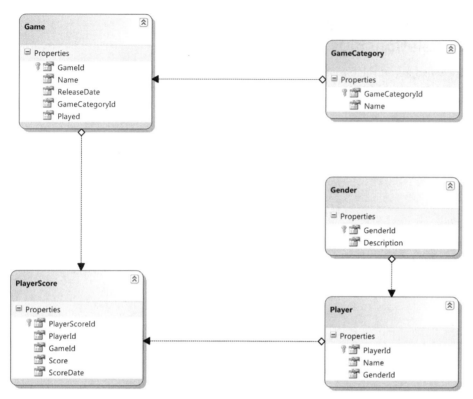

**FIGURE 17-16:** Entities and their relationships

## Filtering Data from Many Related Tables

As happened with the previous database, you just made very small changes to the code provided by the template. However, in this case, there are many complex relationships that the Dynamic Data must decode to provide really useful CRUD operations and scaffolding behavior.

Follow these steps to display data from the different related tables and test the default filters offered by a more complex Dynamic Data website:

1.  Display the `Default.aspx` page in your default web browser. It will display a page with the list of tables available in the data model — in this case, the five tables, as shown in Figure 17-17.

2.  Now, click the `Games` hyperlink under "My tables" (`Games` for the `Game` table). The web browser will display the `Games/List.aspx` page with the data from the selected table. In this case, it also shows the Name for the `GameCategory` and a "View PlayerScores" button for each row. Because the Played field is of the Boolean type (`bit` type in SQL Server), it uses a checkbox to display its value. Also, it displays two filter combo boxes, `Played` and `GameCategory`, as shown in Figure 17-18.

## My tables

| Table Name |
| --- |
| GameCategories |
| Games |
| Genders |
| Players |
| PlayerScores |

**FIGURE 17-17:** List of tables

## Games

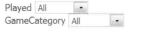

Played  All
GameCategory  All

| | | | Name | ReleaseDate | Played | PlayerScores | GameCategory |
| --- | --- | --- | --- | --- | --- | --- | --- |
| Edit | Delete | Details | INVADERS | 1/1/1982 12:00:00 AM | ☑ | View PlayerScores | Space |
| Edit | Delete | Details | WONDERBOY | 12/23/1982 12:00:00 AM | ☐ | View PlayerScores | Arcade |
| Edit | Delete | Details | DONKEY KONG | 11/21/1983 12:00:00 AM | ☐ | View PlayerScores | Arcade |
| Edit | Delete | Details | GALAGA '84 | 1/1/1984 12:00:00 AM | ☐ | View PlayerScores | Space |

✦ Insert new item

**FIGURE 17-18:** Page with data from a selected table

*The default behavior of Dynamic Data is to add filters to Boolean fields, enumerations, and each foreign key. However, you can also customize the default templates to add more filters.*

**3.** Select a GameCategory in the corresponding combo box at the top of the grid, and the grid will be updated to display the games that correspond to the selected category. You can also click a `GameCategory` link in a row and the detailed view for this entity will display a View Games link to show all the games that correspond to the this category, as shown in Figure 17-19 and Figure 17-20. In fact, by clicking the View Games link, the website shows the list with a `GameCategory` filter applied, `Games/List.aspx?GameCategoryId=1`.

**FIGURE 17-19:** Selecting a game category

**FIGURE 17-20:** Viewing all games in a selected game category

4. Now, click on "View PlayerScores" in one row and the detailed view for this entity will display the scores registered for many players for this game. Both the `Game` and the `Player` columns will show links to their corresponding detailed views, as shown in Figure 17-21. This way, the Dynamic Data framework is capable of creating web pages for a table with many relationships, such as `PlayerScores`.

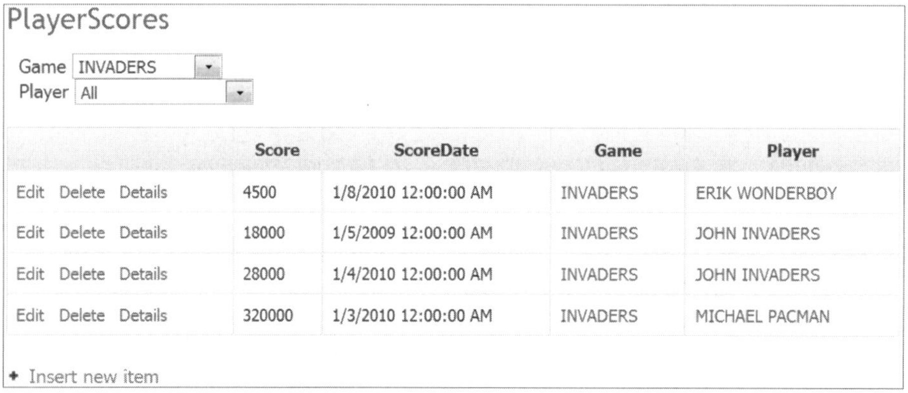

## PlayerScores

Game INVADERS
Player All

| | | | Score | ScoreDate | Game | Player |
|---|---|---|---|---|---|---|
| Edit | Delete | Details | 4500 | 1/8/2010 12:00:00 AM | INVADERS | ERIK WONDERBOY |
| Edit | Delete | Details | 18000 | 1/5/2009 12:00:00 AM | INVADERS | JOHN INVADERS |
| Edit | Delete | Details | 28000 | 1/4/2010 12:00:00 AM | INVADERS | JOHN INVADERS |
| Edit | Delete | Details | 320000 | 1/3/2010 12:00:00 AM | INVADERS | MICHAEL PACMAN |

✦ Insert new item

**FIGURE 17-21:** Detailed view

**5.** Click the "Insert new item" button at the bottom of the web page. The web browser will display a new page with data entry fields. The Game and the Player fields are going to be represented by combo boxes that allow you to choose from the available values in the corresponding tables. In this case, because the button was clicked while displaying the scores registered for a specific game, the Game will show it as the default value for the Game field. You can enter data for each field and click the Insert button to add a new record, and choose the values for the foreign keys using the combo boxes, as shown in Figure 17-22.

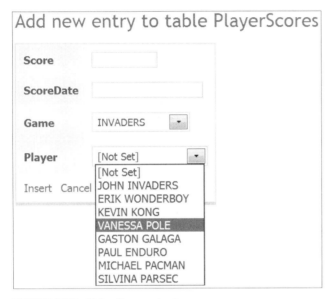

**FIGURE 17-22:** Using the combo boxes

 *By following a few steps, you can create a Dynamic Data website capable of navigating the records from tables with many complex one-to-many relationships and buttons for CRUD operations. The default templates use combo boxes to allow the user to select data from related tables, and offer a very simple navigation scheme.*

## Performing Complex CRUD Operations on the Same Page

You can also follow the previously described steps to switch to the combined-page mode.

In this case, the in-line editing capabilities will also display combo boxes for the Game and the Player fields in the grid, as shown in Figure 17-23.

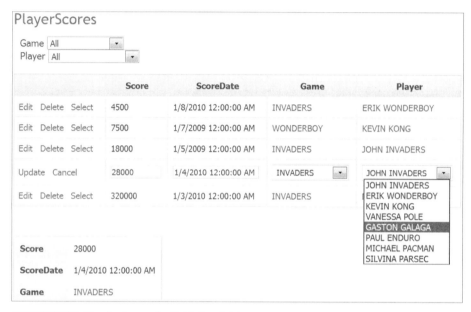

**FIGURE 17-23:** Combo boxes for fields in a table

# WORKING TO MODIFY IMPLEMENTATION TO FIT BUSINESS NEEDS

So far, you have been working with the default behavior offered by the Dynamic Data framework and its associated templates. In real-world situations, you must usually modify the implementation to fit business needs. Thus, let's dive deeper into Dynamic Data's structure to understand the different pieces that make it possible to generate this kind of web application.

## Understanding Dynamic Data's Structure

Figure 17-24 shows all the folders and files that compose the resulting Dynamic Data website. Table 17-3 describes the files at the root level and Table 17-4 describes the sub-folders inside the DynamicData folder.

**TABLE 17-3:** Root Level Files in an ASP.NET Dynamic Data Website

| FILE | DESCRIPTION |
| --- | --- |
| Default.aspx | This ASP.NET page displays the tables and views registered in the associated meta-model. As previously explained, each table or view appears rendered as a HyperLink control, and when the user clicks on it, the selected table lists its contents. |
| Global.asax | This registers an instance of the MetaModel class (System.Web .DynamicData.MetaModel), representing one or multiple databases, and adds routes to the RouteCollection object as previously described. |
| Site.css | This is the cascading style sheet (CSS) used by all the Dynamic Data page templates and controls. |
| Site.master | This is the master page for the website. Both Default.aspx and all the Dynamic Data page templates use this master page. |
| Web.config | This is the XML-based configuration file for the website. |

**TABLE 17-4:** Folders Found Inside the DynamicData Folder in an ASP.NET Dynamic Data Website

| FOLDER | DESCRIPTION |
| --- | --- |
| Content | This contains the Images sub-folder and the GridViewPager control. The Images sub-folder contains all the GIF images used as icons in the page control responsible for allowing the user to switch between multiple pages. |
| CustomPages | This folder is empty by default. It allows defining custom page templates used to override the default page templates found in the PageTemplates folder for a specific table. |
| EntityTemplates | This contains the entity templates that are responsible for creating the UI to view, edit, and insert data. |
| FieldTemplates | This contains the user controls used to create the UI to view and edit the data for each different field type. |
| Filters | This contains the user controls used to create the UI to filter the data rows being displayed. As previously explained, there are three filter templates. |
| PageTemplates | This contains the page templates that create the UI for all the operations supported by Dynamic Data. This folder contains the page templates that you were using during the different examples; Details.aspx; Edit. aspx, Insert.aspx, List.aspx, and ListDetails.aspx. As previously discussed, the URL routing defined in the Global.asax file defines which page to call for each action. |

The `System.Web.DynamicData` namespace and assembly contains the classes that provide the core functionality for the Dynamic Data framework, extensibility features, and customization capabilities. The tag prefix `asp:` is registered for this namespace. For example, the following lines define a `Sytem.Web.DynamicData.DynamicDataManager` using `asp:DynamicDataManager`:

```
<asp:DynamicDataManager ID="DynamicDataManager1" runat="server"
      AutoLoadForeignKeys="true">
   <DataControls>
      <asp:DataControlReference ControlID="FormView1" />
      <asp:DataControlReference ControlID="GridView1" />
   </DataControls>
</asp:DynamicDataManager>
```

To make it possible to work with the Dynamic Data framework, both the `DetailsView` and `GridView` controls have been extended to display fields by using templates instead of hard-coded rules. Both the `FormView` and `ListView` controls also implement a similar behavior by using a `DynamicControl` object (`System.Web.DynamicData.DynamicControl`) in their templates and specifying which field to display in the row. The Dynamic Data framework builds the UI for all these controls considering the specified templates.

The default validation considers the metadata read in the data model (including the data types and their limitations) as the number of characters for a `char`-style column and the `null` acceptance.

## Customizing the Look and Feel

The `Site.css` file contains the definitions for the styles used by the Dynamic Data page template and controls. Thus, you can use it to change the look and feel for the pages and control when a style is involved.

For example, the default style for a row selected in a grid (used in the combined-page mode) is the following:

```
.DDSelected
{
    background-color: #fdffb8;
}
```

The following new version applies a black border color with a double style and uses a bold font to emphasize the selected row:

```
.DDSelected
{
    background-color: #fdffb8;
    border-color: Black;
    border-style: double;
    font-weight: bold;
}
```

Figure 17-25 shows the results of this change.

**FIGURE 17-24:** Folders and files of the website

| | Name | ReleaseDate | Played | PlayerScores | GameCategory |
|---|---|---|---|---|---|
| **Games** | | | | | |
| Played All ▾ | | | | | |
| GameCategory All ▾ | | | | | |
| **Edit Delete Select** | **INVADERS** | **1/1/1982 12:00:00 AM** | ☑ | **View PlayerScores** | **Space** |
| Edit Delete Select | WONDERBOY | 12/23/1982 12:00:00 AM | ☐ | View PlayerScores | Arcade |

**FIGURE 17-25:** Changing the default style

You can also check the `CssClass` used by a specific control in a template. For example, the following code corresponds to the `ForeignKey.ascx` filter template, in the `DynamicData/Filters` folder. It uses the `DDFilter` CSS class.

```
<%@ Control Language="C#" CodeFile="ForeignKey.ascx.cs"
    Inherits="ForeignKeyFilter" %>

<asp:DropDownList runat="server" ID="DropDownList1" AutoPostBack="True"
    CssClass="DDFilter"
    OnSelectedIndexChanged="DropDownList1_SelectedIndexChanged">
    <asp:ListItem Text="All" Value="" />
</asp:DropDownList>
```

The default definition for this class is as follows:

```
.DDFilter
{
    font: .95em Tahoma, Arial, Sans-serif;
    color:#666;
}
```

The following new version for the code that defines the aforementioned class in the `Site.css` file applies an aqua background color and uses a bold font to emphasize the combo box:

```
.DDFilter
{
    font: .95em Tahoma, Arial, Sans-serif;
    color:#666;
    font-weight: bold;
    background-color: Aqua;
}
```

 *You can check the `CssClass` used by the different controls in the templates and make the necessary changes to adapt the look and feel of the website to your needs.*

The default title and header for all the pages that compose a Dynamic Data website is `Dynamic Data Site`, and this is defined in the `Site.master` file. You can change this file to customize the title and the header.

For example, Listing 17-2 shows a customized version of the file with `Retro-gamers championship` as the new title and header. The code that was changed appears in bold.

**LISTING 17-2: A New Title and Header in the Site.master File**

```
<%@ Master Language="C#" CodeFile="Site.master.cs" Inherits="Site" %>

<!DOCTYPE html PUBLIC "-//W3C//DTD XHTML 1.0 Transitional//
    EN" "http://www.w3.org/TR/xhtml1/DTD/
    xhtml1-transitional.dtd">

<html xmlns="http://www.w3.org/1999/xhtml">
<head runat="server">
    <title>Retro-gamers championship</title>
    <link href="~/Site.css" rel="stylesheet" type="text/css" />
    <asp:ContentPlaceHolder id="head" runat="server">
    </asp:ContentPlaceHolder>
</head>
<body>
    <h1 class="DDMainHeader">Retro-gamers championship</h1>
    <div class="DDNavigation">
        <a runat="server" href="~/"><img alt="Back to home page"
            runat="server" src="DynamicData/Content/Images/back.gif"
            />Back to home page</a>
    </div>

    <form id="form1" runat="server">
    <div>
        <%-- TODO: Enable partial rendering by setting the
            EnablePartialRendering attribute to "true" to
            provide a smoother browsing experience.
            Leaving partial rendering disabled will provide a better
            debugging experience while the application is
            in development. --%>
        <asp:ScriptManager ID="ScriptManager1" runat="server"
            EnablePartialRendering="false"/>

        <asp:ContentPlaceHolder id="ContentPlaceHolder1" runat="server">
        </asp:ContentPlaceHolder>
    </div>
    </form>
</body>
</html>
```

*Code file [RetroGamesWeb2/Site.master] available for download at Wrox.com*

Also, the default title before displaying the available tables and views is My Tables, and this is defined in the Default.aspx file. You can change this file to customize this header.

For example, Listing 17-3 shows a customized version of the file with Click on the desired entity name as the new header. The code that was changed appears in bold.

**LISTING 17-3:  A New Header in the Default.aspx File**

```
<%@ Page Language="C#" MasterPageFile="~/Site.master"
     CodeFile="Default.aspx.cs" Inherits="_Default" %>

<asp:Content ID="headContent" ContentPlaceHolderID="head" Runat="Server">
</asp:Content>

<asp:Content ID="Content1" ContentPlaceHolderID="ContentPlaceHolder1"
        Runat="Server">
    <asp:ScriptManagerProxy ID="ScriptManagerProxy1" runat="server" />

    <h2 class="DDSubHeader">Click on the desired entity name</h2>

    <br /><br />

    <asp:GridView ID="Menu1" runat="server" AutoGenerateColumns="false"
        CssClass="DDGridView" RowStyle-CssClass="td"
            HeaderStyle-CssClass="th" CellPadding="6">
        <Columns>
            <asp:TemplateField HeaderText="Table Name" SortExpression="TableName">
                <ItemTemplate>
                    <asp:DynamicHyperLink ID="HyperLink1" runat="server">
                        <%# Eval("DisplayName") %></asp:DynamicHyperLink>
                </ItemTemplate>
            </asp:TemplateField>
        </Columns>
    </asp:GridView>
</asp:Content>
```

*Code file [RetroGamesWeb2/Default.aspx] available for download at Wrox.com*

Of course, you will surely want to customize the CSS styles used for each element. Figure 17-26 shows the results of the changes in the two files.

## Working with Page Templates

In the example just shown, the web browser is using the ListDetails.aspx page template to display the combined-page mode with in-line editing capabilities. You can make the necessary changes to this page template, found in the DynamicData/PageTemplates folder.

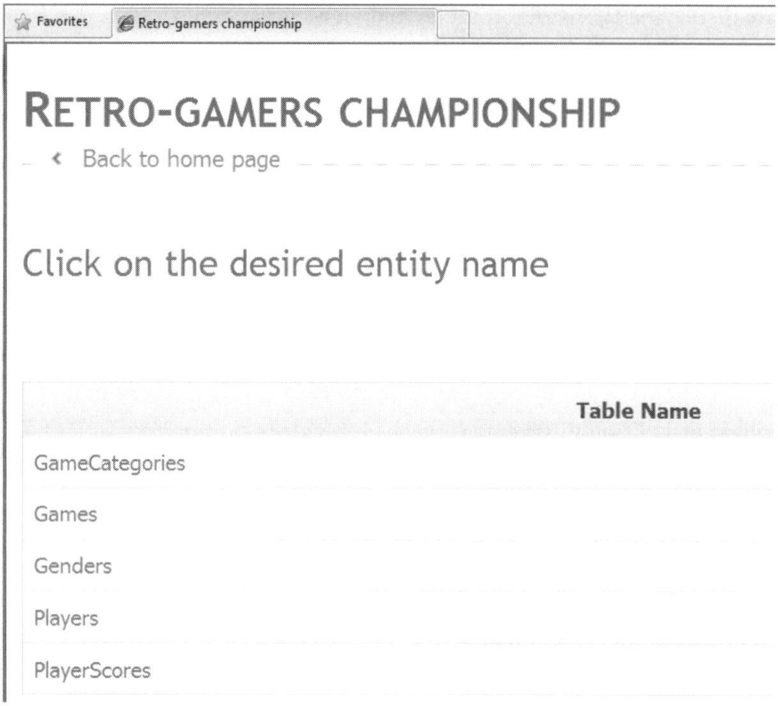

**FIGURE 17-26:** Page with new title and header

For example, you can make the necessary changes to use alternating background colors by following these steps:

1. Open the `Site.css` file.

2. Add a new style to define an aqua background color for an alternating row style, `tars`:

```
table.DDGridView .tars
{
    background-color: Aqua;
}
```

3. Now, open the `ListDetails.aspx` page template and switch to the Design view.

4. Click on the grid control, `asp:GridView#GridView1`. Go to its properties and enter **tars** in Styles ⇨ AlternatingRowStyle ⇨ CssClass. This way, the `GridView` will apply the previously defined style to alternate styles in the different rows. The design view will display an aqua background alternating in the different rows of the grid, as shown in Figure 17-27.

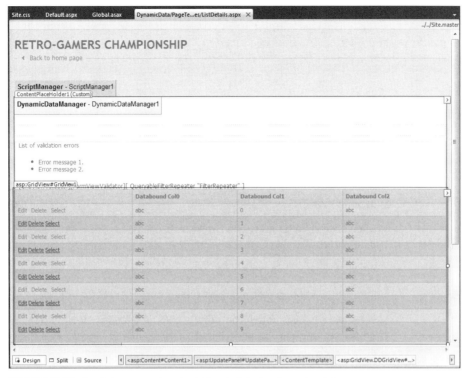

**FIGURE 17-27:** Applying a previously defined style to alternate styles

Figure 17-28 shows the results of applying the new CSS style in the grid when the website displays the data from the `PlayerScores` table.

## PlayerScores

Game **All**
Player **All**

| | Score | ScoreDate | Game | Player |
|---|---|---|---|---|
| Edit Delete Select | 4500 | 1/8/2010 12:00:00 AM | INVADERS | ERIK WONDERBOY |
| Edit Delete Select | 7500 | 1/7/2009 12:00:00 AM | WONDERBOY | KEVIN KONG |
| Edit Delete Select | 18000 | 1/5/2009 12:00:00 AM | INVADERS | JOHN INVADERS |
| Edit Delete Select | 28000 | 1/4/2010 12:00:00 AM | INVADERS | JOHN INVADERS |
| Edit Delete Select | 320000 | 1/3/2010 12:00:00 AM | INVADERS | MICHAEL PACMAN |

**FIGURE 17-28:** Applying the new CSS style in the grid

*It is possible to edit the other page templates to customize the presentation of the different controls and their behavior as explained in the previous example. However, it is very important to keep the necessary basic structure to make it possible for these templates to work with the Dynamic Data framework.*

Table 17-5 describes the five page templates provided by Dynamic Data.

**TABLE 17-5:** Page Templates

| FILE | DESCRIPTION |
|------|-------------|
| Details.aspx | Shows the detailed view of a single record. It uses a `DetailsView` control. |
| Edit.aspx | Allows the user to edit a single record. It uses a `DetailsView` control. |
| Insert.aspx | Lets the user insert a new record. It uses a `DetailsView` control. |
| List.aspx | Displays a list of records from a table using a grid and provides combo boxes to allow users to filter data. It uses `GridView`, `GridViewPager`, and `DropDownList` controls. |
| ListDetails.aspx | Displays a list of records from a table using a grid, provides combo boxes to allow users to filter data and enables in-line editing and visualization of details in the same page. It uses `GridView`, `GridViewPager`, and `DropDownList` controls. |

## Working with Field Templates

ASP.NET Dynamic Data uses field templates to render the data in the data-bound controls. They are user controls derived from the `FieldTemplateUserControl` class (`System.Web .DynamicData.FieldTemplateUserControl`) that maps fields in the data-bound controls to data types in the data model. The Dynamic Data framework infers the data type for the related field at run-time, and then it checks for the appropriate field template to render the data in the data-bound control.

The field template to be used in each case depends on the data type and the mode — display, edit, or insert. Some field templates provide a specific edit or insert template different than the one used for the display mode. For example, the `DateTime.ascx` template is used for displaying a `DateTime` data type. However, when editing or inserting, the `DateTime_Edit.ascx` is used.

You can make the necessary changes to an existing field template, found in the `DynamicData/FieldTemplates` folder. For example, you can change the default CSS class for the `DataTime` field template when it is running in the edit mode by following these steps:

**1.** Open the `Site.css` file.

**2.** Add a new style to define an aqua background color for the control, `DDTextBoxEdit`:

```
.DDTextBoxEdit
{
    background-color: #0000FF;
    color: #FFFFFF;
    font-weight: bold;
}
```

**3.** Now, open the `DateTime_Edit.ascx` field template and replace `CssClass="DDTextBoxEdit"` with `CssClass="DDTextBoxEdit"`, as shown in Listing 17-4. This way, the textbox displayed when editing a `DateTime` data type will apply the previously defined style to use a different background. You can check it by editing a row from the `Game` table, as shown in Figure 17-29.

**FIGURE 17-29:** Editing a row

Available for download on Wrox.com

**LISTING 17-4: A Customized DateTime_Edit.ascx.**

```
<%@ Control Language="C#" CodeFile="DateTime_Edit.ascx.cs"
    Inherits="DateTime_EditField" %>

<asp:TextBox ID="TextBox1" runat="server" CssClass="DDTextBoxEdit"
    Text='<%# FieldValueEditString %>' Columns="20"></asp:TextBox>

<asp:RequiredFieldValidator runat="server" ID="RequiredFieldValidator1"
    CssClass="DDControl DDValidator" ControlToValidate="TextBox1"
    Display="Dynamic" Enabled="false" />
<asp:RegularExpressionValidator runat="server"
    ID="RegularExpressionValidator1" CssClass=
    "DDControl DDValidator" ControlToValidate="TextBox1"
    Display="Dynamic" Enabled="false" />
<asp:DynamicValidator runat="server" ID="DynamicValidator1"
    CssClass="DDControl DDValidator" ControlToValidate=
    "TextBox1" Display="Dynamic" />
<asp:CustomValidator runat="server" ID="DateValidator" CssClass="DDControl
    DDValidator" ControlToValidate="TextBox1" Display="Dynamic"
    EnableClientScript="false" Enabled="false"
    OnServerValidate="DateValidator_ServerValidate" />
```

*Code file [RetroGamesWeb2/FieldTemplates/DateTime_Edit.ascx] available for download at Wrox.com*

Table 17-6 describes the 18 field templates provided by Dynamic Data.

**TABLE 17-6:** Field Templates

| FILE | DESCRIPTION |
|------|-------------|
| Boolean.ascx | Uses a `CheckBox` control to display Boolean data. |
| Boolean_Edit.ascx | Uses a `CheckBox` control to enable users to edit a Boolean value. |
| Children.ascx | Uses a `HyperLink` control to display the fields that have a one-to-many relationship, and offers a redirection to the relation entity detailed view. |
| Children_Insert.ascx | This control has the functionality to prevent the insertion of a child field value while the field is being added. |
| DateTime.ascx | Uses a `Literal` control to display `DataTime` data. |
| DateTime_Edit.ascx | Uses a `TextBox` control to enable users to edit a `DataTime` value. It supports the `Regex` class. |
| Decimal_Edit.ascx | Uses a `TextBox` control to enable users to edit decimal and numeric values. It supports the `Regex` class. |
| Enumeration.ascx | Displays enumeration values. |
| Enumeration_Edit.ascx | Uses a `DropDownList` control to enable users to select from a list of enumeration values in a combo box. |
| ForeignKey.ascx | Uses a `HyperLink` control to display the fields that have a many-to-one relationship and offers a redirection to the relation entity detailed view. |
| ForeignKey_Edit.ascx | Uses a `DropDownList` control to enable users to edit fields that have a many-to-one relationship, selecting from a list of related values in a combo box. |
| Integer_Edit.ascx | Uses a `TextBox` control to enable users to edit integer values. It supports the `Regex` class. |
| Multiline_Edit.ascx | Uses a `TextBox` control (with its `MultiLine` property set to `true`) to enable users to edit a text block. It also renders a `RegularExpressionValidator` control when the data model defines a `RegularExpression` attribute. |
| ManyToMany.ascx | Displays many-to-many fields, when the table is a pure join one and the application's data model is based on ADO.NET Entity Framework. LINQ to SQL doesn't support many-to-many relationships. |

| FILE | DESCRIPTION |
|---|---|
| `ManyToMany_Edit.ascx` | Enables users to edit fields that have a many-to-many relationship in a pure join table and the application's data model is based on ADO. NET Entity Framework. LINQ to SQL doesn't support many-to-many relationships. |
| `Text.ascx` | Uses a `Literal` control to display string and many numeric data types. |
| `Text_Edit.ascx` | Uses a `TextBox` control (with its `TextMode` property set to `SingleLine`) to enable users to edit single-line text. It also renders a `RegularExpressionValidator` control when the data model defines a `RegularExpression` attribute. The `MaxLength` property for the `TextBox` control is enforced according to the maximum length defined in the field in the data model. |
| `Url.ascx` | Uses a `HyperLink` control to display URLs. |

By default, Dynamic Data uses the edit-mode field templates for the insert mode when is doesn't find a user control defined with the `_Insert.ascx` suffix.

## Working with Entity Templates

*Entity templates* are user controls that allow you to customize the layout for a table. They are user controls derived from the `EntityTemplateUserControl` class (`System.Web.DynamicData. EntityTemplateUserControl`). The default entity templates display the fields in a two-column table — one column for the field names, and the other for the field values.

Dynamic Data provides three entity templates, found in the `DynamicData/EntityTemplates` folder. They are included in the page templates that define the different operations, as shown in Table 17-7.

**TABLE 17-7:** Entity Templates

| FILE | INCLUDED IN THE PAGE TEMPLATE |
|---|---|
| `Default.ascx` | `Details.aspx` |
| `Default_Edit.ascx` | `Update.aspx` |
| `Default_Insert.ascx` | `Insert.aspx` |

The combined-page mode `ListDetails.aspx` page template will also use the three entity templates.

The entity templates use the previously explained field templates to display the fields. The page templates display the corresponding entity template using the `DynamicEntity` control and replacing it with the appropriate entity template at run-time.

If you want to display the fields with a different organization, you can define a new entity template for the desired table. Follow these steps to create a new customized entity template for the Game table:

1. Right-click on the EntityTemplates sub-folder located in the DynamicData folder, and select Add New Item in the context menu that appears. A template selection dialog box will appear.

2. Select "Web User Control for Visual C#" under Installed Templates and activate the "Place code in separate file" checkbox.

3. Enter the name for the entity set representing the table (Games.ascx), and click Add.

> *By default, the entity set representing the table will have a plural form because both LINQ to SQL and ADO.NET Entity Framework pluralize the generated object names. For example,* Games *represents the* Game *table. However, it is always convenient to check the data model for the name of the entity set representing the table.*

4. Enter the markup shown in Listing 17-5 in the Games.ascx file. This markup creates a new layout of the Game table displaying its field names and values.

5. Open the class file for the page (Games.ascx.cs) and replace the base class from UserControl to System.Web.DynamicData.EntityTemplateUserControl, as shown in the following definition:

```
public partial class DynamicData_EntityTemplates_Games :
    System.Web.DynamicData.EntityTemplateUserControl
```

**LISTING 17-5:** A Customized Entity Template, Games.ascx.

```
<%@ Control Language="C#" AutoEventWireup="true" CodeFile="Games.ascx.cs"
    Inherits="DynamicData_EntityTemplates_Games" %>
<tr>
  <td class="DDLightHeader">
      <asp:Label ID="Label1" runat="server" Text="Name" />
  </td>
  <td>
    <asp:DynamicControl ID="DynamicControl1" runat="server"
        DataField="Name" />
  </td>
  <td class="DDLightHeader">
    <asp:Label ID="Label3" runat="server"
        Text="Game's category" />
  </td>
  <td>
    <asp:DynamicControl ID="DynamicControl4" runat="server"
```

```
          DataField="GameCategory" />
    </td>
  </tr>
  <tr>
    <td class="DDLightHeader">
      <asp:Label ID="Label2" runat="server" Text="Release date" />
    </td>
    <td>
      <asp:DynamicControl ID="DynamicControl3" runat="server"
          DataField="ReleaseDate" />
    </td>
  </tr>
  <tr>
    <td class="DDLightHeader">
      <asp:Label ID="Label4" runat="server" Text="Was it played?" />
    </td>
    <td>
      <asp:DynamicControl ID="DynamicControl5" runat="server"
          DataField="Played" />
    </td>
  </tr>
```

*Code file [RetroGamesWeb2/DynamicData/EntityTemplates/Games.ascx] available for download at Wrox.com*

Now, when you select a record from the Games entity set, the layout for its detailed view at the bottom of the grid will be as shown in Figure 17-30 because it will use the previously defined Games.ascx entity template to display its field names and values.

The markup code shown in Listing 17-5 is very easy to understand. It defines a Label control for each field and a DynamicControl control to render the field using the corresponding field template at run-time.

**FIGURE 17-30:** New layout in detailed view

The following lines defined the label and the dynamic control for the Played field. In this case, the label displays the text Was it played? instead of the default field name:

```
<td class="DDLightHeader">
  <asp:Label ID="Label4" runat="server" Text="Was it played?" />
</td>
<td>
  <asp:DynamicControl ID="DynamicControl5" runat="server"
      DataField="Played" />
</td>
```

The `Game` table has a foreign key, `GameCategoryId`. However, you don't want to display the numeric value; you want to show the value of the `Name` field in the related `GameCategory` table. Therefore, you must specify `GameCategory`, the foreign table, for the `DataField` property, instead of `GameCategoryId`, as shown in the following lines:

```
<td class="DDLightHeader">
  <asp:Label ID="Label3" runat="server"
      Text="Game's category" />
</td>
<td>
  <asp:DynamicControl ID="DynamicControl4" runat="server"
      DataField="GameCategory" />
</td>
```

## Working with Filter Templates

ASP.NET Dynamic Data uses filter templates to render the UI for data filtering. They are user controls derived from the `QueryableFilterUserControl` class (`System.Web.DynamicData` `.QueryableFilterUserControl`). As previously described, data filtering allows the user to display the rows based on a value in a selected column, using a `DropDownList` control. Dynamic Data provides three filter templates, found in the `DynamicData/Filters` folder, as shown in Table 17-8.

**TABLE 17-8:** Filter Templates

| FILE | DESCRIPTION |
| --- | --- |
| `Boolean.ascx` | Displays the following values: `All`, `True`, and `False`. |
| `Enumeration.ascx` | Displays the string representations of the enumeration values. It also offers the `All` value to remove the filter. |
| `ForeignKeys.ascx` | Displays the values from the related table. It also offers the `All` value to remove the filter. |

If the associated field value accepts nulls, all the filters also provide a `[Not set]` value.

If you want to display `Yes` and `No` instead of `True` and `False` for the Boolean filters in a Dynamic Data website, you can make a few changes to the default filter template.

Follow these steps to customize the `Boolean.ascx` filter template:

**1.** Listing 17-6 shows the code for `Boolean.ascx`. Add the `Label` control writing the boldfaced line of code. This way, the text (yes/no/all filter) will appear before the field name and the combo box (`DropDownList` control).

**2.** Open the class file for the page (`Boolean.ascx.cs`) and replace the following two lines that add the `Yes` and `No` elements to the `DropDownList` control, `DropDownList1`, in the `Page_Init` method, with the boldfaced ones shown in Listing 17-7:

```
DropDownList1.Items.Add(new ListItem("Yes", Boolean.TrueString));
DropDownList1.Items.Add(new ListItem("No", Boolean.FalseString));
```

**LISTING 17-6: A Customized Filter Template, Boolean.ascx**

```
<%@ Control Language="C#" CodeFile="Boolean.ascx.cs" Inherits="BooleanFilter" %>

<asp:Label ID="Label1" runat="server" Text=" (yes/no/all filter) " ></asp:Label>
<asp:DropDownList runat="server" ID="DropDownList1" AutoPostBack=
        "True" CssClass="DDFilter"
    OnSelectedIndexChanged="DropDownList1_SelectedIndexChanged">
</asp:DropDownList>
```

*Code file [RetroGamesWeb2/DynamicData/Filters/Boolean.ascx] available for download at Wrox.com*

**LISTING 17-7: The New Code for the Page_Init Method in the Customized Filter Template, Boolean.ascx.cs**

```
protected void Page_Init(object sender, EventArgs e) {
    if (!Column.ColumnType.Equals(typeof(bool))) {
        throw new InvalidOperationException(String.Format("A boolean
            filter was loaded for column '{0}' but the column has
            an incompatible type '{1}'.", Column.Name,
            Column.ColumnType));
    }

    if (!Page.IsPostBack) {
        DropDownList1.Items.Add(new ListItem("All", String.Empty));
        if (!Column.IsRequired) {
            DropDownList1.Items.Add(new ListItem("[Not Set]", NullValueString));
        }
        DropDownList1.Items.Add(new ListItem("Yes", Boolean.TrueString));
        DropDownList1.Items.Add(new ListItem("No", Boolean.FalseString));
        // Set the initial value if there is one
        string initialValue = DefaultValue;
        if (!String.IsNullOrEmpty(initialValue)) {
            DropDownList1.SelectedValue = initialValue;
        }
    }
}
```

*Code file [RetroGamesWeb2/DynamicData/Filters/Boolean.ascx.cs] available for download at Wrox.com*

Now, when you display the data from the `Game` table that contains the `Played` Boolean field, its filter displays `Yes` and `No` options, and it displays more information to the user about its filtering possibilities, as shown in Figure 17-31.

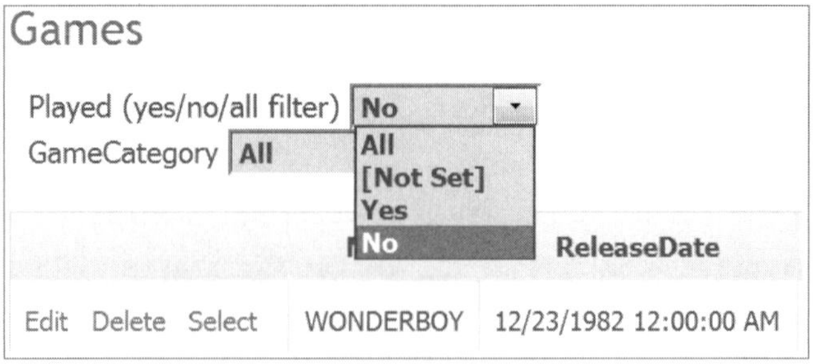

## Creating Custom Pages

Sometimes, a custom entity template

**FIGURE 17-31:** Display after filter has been applied

isn't enough, and it is necessary to create a custom page template for a specific table. Dynamic Data provides the `DynamicData/CustomPages` folder that allows you to create a sub-folder with the entity set names in order to hold their custom page templates.

Follow these steps to create a customized `ListDetails.aspx` page template for the `Player` table (`Players` entity set):

1. Create a new sub-folder, `Players`, in the `CustomPages` sub-folder, located in the `DynamicData` folder.

2. Now, copy the `ListDetails.aspx` page template found in the `PageTemplates` sub-folder to the new `Players` sub-folder.

3. Open the previously copied page template, `DynamicData/CustomPages/Players/ListDetails.aspx`, and switch to the Design view.

4. Click on the grid control, `asp:GridView#GridView1`. Go to its properties and enter **100** in Paging ⇨ PageSize. This way, the `GridView` will display 100 rows per page for the Player table.

5. Switch to the Source view. Add a new label before the label that displays the table name:

```
<h2 class="DDSubHeader">
    <asp:Label ID="Label1" runat="server" Text="Hall of fame"></asp:Label>
</h2>
```

6. Add another label before the `DetailsPanel Panel` control:

```
<h2 class="DDSubHeader">
    <asp:Label ID="Label3" runat="server" Text="Details for the
        selected player:"></asp:Label>
</h2>
```

Now, when you select the `Player` table, Dynamic Data will use the customized `ListDetails.aspx` page template in the combined-page mode, and the previously added labels will appear, as shown in Figure 17-32.

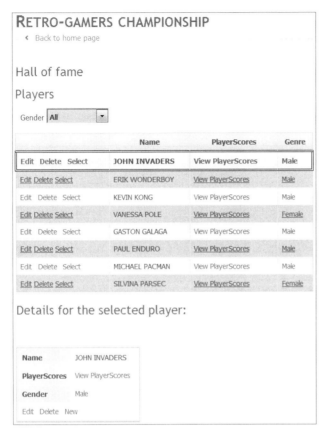

**FIGURE 17-32:** Customized template with labels added

*In this simple example, the new customized page added just two labels. However, you can combine your ASP.NET experience with the different customization possibilities offered by Dynamic Data in order to create data-driven web applications prepared to fit even the most complex business needs.*

## Customizing Validations

The default Dynamic Data validation considers the metadata and includes the following three rules:

➤ Required fields

➤ Maximum field length

➤ Type enforcement

You can include additional validation information in the data model by creating validation methods and by using `System.ComponentModel.DataAnnotations` attributes. You can also create your own customized attributes.

However, you must also add specific validation code overriding the `OnValidate` method or handling the `Validate` event to enforce more complex business rules that involve multiple fields.

It is possible to include additional validation information to the `RetroGames.designer.cs` file. However, it is more convenient to create a new partial class to keep this information safe from the code generated by the O/R Designer.

Follow these steps to create a new class that adds a simple range validation for the `Score` field in the `PlayerScore` table:

1. Create a new class in the `App_Code` folder. Use the name of the entity that needs metadata information, `PlayerScore.cs`.

2. Add the following two `using` declarations:

   ```
   using System.ComponentModel;
   using System.ComponentModel.DataAnnotations;
   ```

3. Add the `partial` keyword to the class definition and remove its constructor.

4. Add a new class with the entity name (`PlayerScore`) as a prefix and `MetaData` as a suffix — in this case, `PlayerScoreMetaData`.

5. Add a new public object property to the `PlayerScoreMetaData` class for each field found in the `PlayerScore` entity. Listing 17-8 shows the new `PlayerScoreMetaData` class with the public object properties.

6. Add a `MetadataType` attribute to the partial class (`PlayerScore`) that represents the extension of the entity class. Specify the metadata definition class `PlayerScoreMetaData`, as shown in the following line:

   ```
   [MetadataType(typeof(PlayerScoreMetaData))]
   ```

7. Add the following lines before the `Score` property definition. Listing 17-8 shows the complete property definition in `PlayerScore.cs` with the new line:

   ```
   [Range(1, 100000000,
           ErrorMessage = "Value for {0} must be between {1} and {2}.")]
   ```

---

**LISTING 17-8: The Code for the Score Property Definition with the Range Validation**

```
using System;
using System.Collections.Generic;
using System.Linq;
using System.Web;
// Added
using System.ComponentModel;
using System.ComponentModel.DataAnnotations;
```

```
[MetadataType(typeof(PlayerScoreMetaData))]
public partial class PlayerScore
{

}

public class PlayerScoreMetaData
{
    public object PlayerScoreId { get; set; }
    public object PlayerId { get; set; }
    public object GameId { get; set; }
    [Range(1, 100000000,
        ErrorMessage = "Value for {0} must be between {1} and {2}.")]
    public object Score { get; set; }
    public object ScoreDate { get; set; }
    public object Game { get; set; }
    public object Player { get; set; }
}
```

*Code file [RetroGamesWeb2/App_Code/PlayerScore.cs] available for download at Wrox.com*

Now, if you try to insert a new record in the
PlayerScore table and enter an out-of-range
score value, the validation text specified will
appear at the right side of the field's value, as
shown in Figure 17-33.

The new metadata code applied the
RangeAttribute (System.ComponentModel
.DataAnnotations.RangeAttribute) to
the Score property. This way, it specifies a
minimum, 1, and maximum value, 100000000,

**FIGURE 17-33:** Validation text being displayed

for this property. If the value of the property is not within the minimum and maximum values, the
code raises a validation exception considering the ErrorMessage string.

You can also apply a RangeAttribute with the RangeAttribute(Type, String, String)
constructor, as shown in the following line for a Decimal field:

```
[Range(typeof(Decimal),"200", "15000")]
```

*It is very important to master data model validations in order to take full
advantage of Dynamic Data capabilities. The previously shown example is just a
simple case of a range validation. You will usually need to combine many
different kinds of validations in complex models.*

## SUMMARY

There are many other advanced topics related to ASP.NET Dynamic Data. This chapter just scratched the surface of the features offered by its powerful templates and framework. This chapter also discussed many of the customization possibilities offered by ASP.NET Dynamic Data and how it relates to other ASP.NET components and the data models.

Following are some key points from this chapter:

➤ You can create a data-driven application following many simple steps using the Dynamic Data templates.

➤ You can create simple and complex CRUD applications based on Dynamic Data.

➤ You must create a robust data model to take full advantage of Dynamic Data's features.

➤ You must combine Dynamic Data's features with the validation capabilities offered by the underlying data model.

➤ You can work with customized templates for fields, entities, and filters.

➤ You have the capability of defining CSS styles to customize the look and feel of the rendered web pages.

➤ You can create custom pages for specific entities when the templates aren't enough.

Chapter 18 takes a look at the ASP.NET Model View Controller (MVC).

# 18

# ASP.NET Model View Controller (MVC)

In Chapter 17, you read about the ASP.NET Dynamic Data feature, which became mature with .NET Framework 4. This chapter introduces the ASP.NET Model-View-Controller (MVC) technology that recently reached its 2.0 version, which is a built-in component of Visual Studio 2010. ASP.NET MVC 1.0 was an out-of-band release for Visual Studio 2008. Although the MVC team made ASP.NET MVC 2 available for Visual Studio 2008, too, the version shipping with Visual Studio 2010 utilizes several new features that are released with the ASP.NET 4.0 platform.

After reading this chapter, you will be familiar with the following:

> *Introduction to MVC* — You will learn about MVC and similar design patterns to understand how ASP.NET MVC differs from the ASP.NET Web Forms approach.

> *Creating an MVC 2 application* — You will create a very simple web application with MVC 2, and learn about the structure of MVC web projects. In contrast to the file-based request routing, MVC uses a different routing model. As you progress through the example, you will learn about the new routing approach.

> *Adding new MVC 2 pages* — You will extend the simple web site with a few pages using the cornerstones of MVC applications: models, views, and controllers.

> *Customization in MVC 2* — MVC was designed with easy extensibility and customization in mind. Here you will discover that customizing your controllers and the way views render the user interface (UI) is incredibly simple.

> *Routing details* — One of the keys to MVC's simplicity is the routing model it uses. You will learn more about the routing model in this chapter.

> *Testing with MVC 2* — MVC has been designed and implemented with Test Driven Development (TDD) in mind. In this chapter, you will learn how to refactor an MVC application's architecture to support unit testing.

You do not need any previous experience with ASP.NET MVC to understand MVC 2. This chapter provides enough detail to dive into this topic.

## INTRODUCTION TO MVC

MVC is an architectural pattern frequently used in software development. The roots of this pattern go back to 1979, when Trygve Reenskaug described this pattern during his work on SmallTalk-80 at Xerox Palo Alto Research Center (PARC).

The MVC pattern helps to separate the data (model), the application logic (controller), and the UI (view) concerns from each other, which leads to properly decoupled components within the application.

One of the advantages of this decoupling is that it makes the application more testable, and, thus, helps developers to implement an application with the TDD approach. Of course, if you are not a fan of TDD, or you are following another development method, using TDD with ASP.NET MVC is not mandatory. It is a great option, however, because ASP.NET MVC itself is implemented with TDD in mind. This is evidenced by the fact that the source code (which is Open Source) contains thousands of unit tests.

The *model* is domain-specific data on which the user and the application operate. These are mostly Plain Old CLR Object (POCO) classes without any additional behavior. These classes are used to transport input from the user through one or more views to the application to process, or to display some data (for example, in a tabular form) for the user.

The application logic (also called the *domain* or *business logic*) is the application code that adds functionality or behavior to the model. A domain logic function usually takes parameters from the user, or takes a model filled with data. After receiving the model, the data usually goes through some kind of validation procedure. If everything is valid, the data gets processed, and the user gets back another model representing the result. Keeping these things moving according to the application logic is the responsibility of the *controller*.

The *view* is a representation of the UI, which is an HTML page in an ASP.NET MVC application. The view provides the surface to display the model (a model can have several views to show the model in different forms), and also allows the user to interact with the data. For example, a model provides a user name, email address, and password; and a registration form represents a related view.

Figure 18-1 shows how the previously described components interact with each other.

As you can see from Figure 18-1, the view can reference the model directly, but the model has no knowledge about views using it. The model and the view do not know anything about controllers manipulating them.

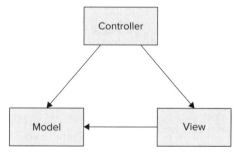

**FIGURE 18-1:** MVC component interaction

# Similar Design Patterns

MVC is not the only design pattern that solves the software engineering problem of decoupling the data from the UI and from the user interaction logic. There are several other design patterns that are very similar to MVC. Let's take a look at two other frequently used design patterns.

## Model-View-Presenter

The Model-View-Presenter (MVP) pattern is a derivative pattern of MVC. MVP is a user interface design pattern, and its goal is to help the automated testing of the presentation layer.

In MVC, the controller controls the view and operates on the data, and the view does not know about entities controlling it. In MVP, the view itself holds a reference to a presenter (which is the controller's counterpart in MVP), and when an interaction happens in the view, it delegates the handling of that interaction to its presenter.

Microsoft implemented the MVP pattern in the Web Client Software Factory, which can be found at `http://www.codeplex.com/websf`.

## Model-View-ViewModel

The Model-View-ViewModel (MVVM) pattern originates from Microsoft and is based on Martin Fowler's Presentation Model design pattern. However, this pattern was established by Microsoft, primarily for Windows Presentation Foundation (WPF) when it was in its early design phase. Today, WPF 4.0 and Microsoft Silverlight 4.0 also have their own components that help developers use this pattern in their applications.

The model in MVVM has the same role as in MVC. View is also the same as in the MVC pattern. ViewModel can be also matched to the controller in MVC, but with "extras." The ViewModel is responsible for binding and converting the data from the model to the view through WPF's sophisticated data binding subsystem. The ViewModel exposes commands to the view, which can be bound to UI controls (for example, to buttons). When the user clicks the button, a command is triggered that is executed in the ViewModel.

# Microsoft and the Web Platform

Microsoft's first approach to the web platform was the classic Active Server Pages (ASP) in 1996. It was like VBScript for the web. Because of the way VBScript was architected, there was no type checking, just run-time type determination.

When the Microsoft .NET Framework 1.0 was released in 2002, it brought something totally new to the web developers: ASP.NET 1.0. One of the great things about ASP.NET was that web developers were able to choose their favorite programming language to implement a web application. ASP.NET leveraged the dynamic compilation feature of the .NET Framework and provided a full set of controls ready for rapid development.

ASP.NET 1.0 was implemented an event-based model to the web platform, which was very similar to the one familiar to desktop application developers. Web applications should be stateless by the nature of how HTTP request-responses work, but ASP.NET 1.0 brought a "not-so-stateless" hybrid model with its ViewState feature. ViewState was used to carry the state back and forth between the client's browser and the web server.

Although it provided a lot of web platform features that were previously not available for developers, ASP.NET 1.0 had some drawbacks. The view was the `aspx` page, and the controller was the code-behind file for the page. You could not call it really *decoupled*. Because of this, testing the code — at least the UI tier — was a real challenge. The huge size of the ViewState for a complex page could become very frustrating in cases where you had a strong customer requirement stating that you had to provide a fast response from an application.

When ASP.NET 2.0 was released in 2005, it was not just a new version of the framework. Developers noticed a lot of rework, and it was clearly visible that Microsoft (which had learned from feedback) modified and extended the platform in a great way. A full-blown web part framework had been added, with all controls rendered in XHTML 1.1 compliant HTML. Adaptive rendering supported device- or browser-specific output for the same control. Developers got a full suite of security classes that helped to implement user authentication and role-based authorization for web applications.

Microsoft ASP.NET MVC 1.0 was launched in December 2007 in a form of a Community Technology Preview (CTP). Until it was released to manufacturing (RTM) in March 2009, Microsoft released five preview releases, one Beta release, and two Release Candidates (RCs). Many developers thought MVC 1.0 was not mature enough for enterprise application development, because it was missing some frequently used features, one of the most important of which was client-side validation.

The developer team actively listened to feedback from the community and engineered the framework to address the community needs. In 2010 (almost exactly one year later), ASP.NET MVC 2 was released, together with .NET Framework 4 and a complete toolset for MVC development in Visual Studio 2010.

 *ASP.NET MVC 2 is Open Source — just as MVC 1.0. You can download the source code from* `http://aspnet.codeplex.com`.

## What Is Microsoft ASP.NET MVC 2?

For developers creating software for the Microsoft ASP.NET platform — and who are not familiar with the MVC design pattern — one obvious question is, "What's in this for me?" Answering this question mostly begins with a sort of comparison.

ASP.NET MVC is not a replacement for ASP.NET Web Forms; it's a brand-new thing. Microsoft does not plan to cancel the development and support for Web Forms. These two technologies will be maintained near to each other, and they share a common base ASP.NET architecture and services.

Web Forms is suitable for Rapid Application Development (RAD) scenarios where developers either do not have the knowledge of how to output XHTML-compliant HTML by hand, or they are not required to do so. One thing is for sure. When going with Web Forms, the heavy lifting of input gathering and output creation will be done for the developer by the framework, and he or she will not have to think about that. Web Forms will provide a stateful UI solution.

 *One introductory video (*`http://www.asp.net/mvc/videos/why-aspnet-mvc-3-minute-overview-video-for-decision-makers`*) uses the motorbike (MVC) versus car (Web Forms) comparison for describing how MVC relates to Web Forms. It says that Web Forms have a lot of abstraction levels over the technology (HTML) used to render them, while MVC is "closer to the metal and is a much more hands-on experience."*

ASP.NET MVC 2 overcomes some limitations of Web Forms and provides other ways to deal with code complexity, such as separation of concerns, extensibility, and mapping requests to methods instead of files. MVC 2 brings several new design patterns, development methodologies, and components on board to help web developers be more productive.

MVC is used in conjunction with several technologies (best practices), as well as with a few design patterns. In this chapter, you will develop a sample application that utilizes some of them. So, let's take a look at some of them.

 *From here on in this chapter, the term "MVC" is used instead of ASP.NET MVC 2. The terms "MVC 1.0" or "MVC 2" are used to highlight the version-specific context.*

## Test Driven Development (TDD)

TDD is not a testing methodology. It has nothing to do with your test team. TDD is an approach; it is about how you write your code.

For TDD, you need a Unit Testing Framework such as MbUnit, xUnit, nUnit, or you can use the great built in framework provided by Microsoft as part of Visual Studio 2010.

Another often-used component of successful TDD is a mocking framework that helps you to mock your different classes and layers (such as a controller class or a data access layer). Mock objects simulate the functionality and behavior of a given class, but you are in control. TDD is often used to create fake data persistence classes to be able to execute unit tests that need data persistence functionality without connecting to a real data store (like a relational database or a set of XML files).

Keep in mind that developing with TDD is different from regular software development. To understand this, take a look at the steps of the usual development process shown in Figure 18-2.

During regular development, you write your code based on some kind of specification, and afterward, you write your unit and integration tests to see whether the application functionality runs without errors and meets the functional requirements.

In TDD, the process works differently, as you can see in Figure 18-3.

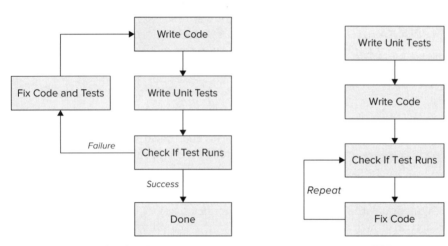

**FIGURE 18-2:** Regular development steps          **FIGURE 18-3:** TDD steps

First, you write your unit tests for a function within the application, generating empty application classes and stub methods — and, of course, the tests will fail if you run them, because, at the moment, there is no implementation behind. The second step is to implement the functionality within the tests, and if everything is in its place, you'll see green lights in your test manager, which means that your code fulfills the requirements of the tests you wrote before.

Whenever you add new functionality to the application, you must write the unit tests first and then repeat the same procedure.

As discussed in Chapter 2, Visual Studio 2010 helps using the TDD pattern with its new "Generate Code from Usage" feature.

## Interface-Based Development

Another good practice is *interface-based development*. It's especially useful when developing with TDD, or implementing a decoupled system where you want to separate the definition of an entity from its implementation. The key to this separation is (wherever it's required and possible) is to encapsulate definitions into interfaces.

Interface-based development results in more maintainable, reusable, and testable code. In real-world scenarios, when you develop with interface-based design, you can develop a large portion of the application with the interface definitions without writing any concrete code. Listing 18-1 shows an example of using an interface in a fictitious banking system.

LISTING 18-1: Interface Definitions for a Banking System

```
public interface IAccountingService
{
  IAccountDetails GetAccountDetails(ICustomer customer);
  ITransaction TransferMoney(ICustomer sender,
                             ICustomer receiver,
                             ITransferDetails details);
}

public interface IAccountDetails
{
  // Account detail properties
}

public interface ICustomer
{
  // Customer properties
}

public interface ITransferDetails
{
  // Transfer details
}

public interface ITransaction
{
  // Transaction data
}
```

As you see, with interfaces, you can describe functionality without sticking it to the implementation details of concrete classes. Both input arguments and results are handled with interfaces. This design makes it possible to have different `IAccountService` implementations for different banking systems, but with the same functionality.

## Repository Design Pattern

Most applications have a need to store and retrieve data from some kind of data store, which is usually a relational database management system (RDBMS) such as SQL Server, Oracle, or DB2.

The *Repository Design Pattern* acts as a mediator between the relational store and your applications logic. By using well-designed repository classes, it's the developers choice where and how to store the data. Repository Design Pattern adds another level of decoupling to your system by encapsulating the data store-specific implementation details into its own classes.

Listing 18-2 shows a book repository interface with functions defined for finding, retrieving, and storing book data.

**LISTING 18-2:** IBookRepository Interface Definition

```
using System.Linq;

namespace AcmeDomain
{
  public interface IBookRepository
  {
    IQueryable<IBook> GetBooks();
    IBook GetBookById(int id);
    IBook CreateBook();
    void InsertBook(IBook book);
    void SaveBook(IBook book);
    void DeleteBook(int id);
  }
}
```

As you see in Listing 18-2, the IBookRepository interface defines the operations that can be performed on a Book entity, and it does not contain any persistence technology implementation details.

Listing 18-3 shows an extract from an implementation of the BookRepository class that uses .NET Entity Framework as its persistence technology. The advantage of this design is that this class can be swapped, for example, to a LINQ to SQL implementation later.

**LISTING 18-3:** BookRepository Concrete Implementation

```
using System;
using System.Linq;
using AcmeDomain;

namespace AcmeLibrary.Models
{
  public class BookRepository: IBookRepository
  {
    public IBook GetBookById(int id)
    {
      // --- Method body omitted
    }

    public void InsertBook(IBook book)
    {
      var newBook = book as Book;
      if (newBook == null)
        throw new ArgumentException("AcmeLibrary.Model.Book expected.", "book");
      using (var context = new AcmeLibraryDataEntities())
      {
        context.AddToBooks(newBook);
```

```
            context.SaveChanges();
        }
    }

    // --- Other methods omitted from this listing
    }
}
```

The `BookRepository` class implements the operations defined in the `IBookRepository` interface.

## Dependency Injection

*Dependency Injection (DI)* is an architectural pattern that helps keep components decoupled within the system, and provides a unified access to it. The DI pattern is not new. Implementations have been around for a long time in the Java platform, and some of them have been ported and new ones have been written for the .NET Framework (for example, Ninject, Spring.Net, Castle/Windsor, Unity, and Structured Map). Throughout this chapter, you will use Microsoft's Unity component.

> *Dependency Injection is sometimes called* Inversion of Control (IoC). *There are community discussions about which naming is better, because IoC is a more generic pattern than DI. Throughout this chapter, DI is used, because it reflects the intention of the pattern better than IoC.*

As its name says, DI is changing the way that different classes and interfaces are controlled, as well as how they are instantiated and accessed. The instantiation is not done by the function that is currently executing. Instead, instantiation is carried out by an external component (from the perspective of the executing code) — the container.

When you ask for a concrete instance from a DI container, you get an instance where dependencies (for example, references to a parent instance, or other linked instances) are resolved by the container.

There are different injection techniques that can be used by a DI container to inject dependencies of an entity:

➤ *Constructor Injection* — The entity gets the dependent objects in its constructor parameter or parameters (assuming it has more than one dependent object). Some or all parameters of a constructor are injected by the DI container when the given class is instantiated (and so its constructor is executed).

➤ *Property (Setter) Injection* — The entity gets its dependent object (or objects) through a property (or through several properties).

➤ *Method Call Injection* — The dependent objects of an entity are set by one or more methods calls where the dependencies are passed in method parameters. This kind of injection is frequently used in the initialization of parent-child class hierarchies.

A DI container behaves like a registry of interface-class associations, named class instances. Before using the container to resolve a specific interface, you must first register that interface with a concrete implementation.

## Service Locator Pattern

The *Service Locator Pattern* centralizes distributed service object lookups, provides a centralized point of control, and may act as a cache that eliminates redundant lookups. It used in software development to encapsulate the processes involved in obtaining a service with a strong abstraction layer.

In a decoupled system, you do not always have the knowledge of the environment in which your code will run, or you may want to create a component that must be able to run in several environments. For example, you may need a component that can be used both in a web application and also in a Windows service. In the latter case, you don't have access to a valid `HttpApplication` instance, but you can have a dependency on some interface implementation like an `IEmailSenderService`.

A Service Locator implementation provides a singleton instance of itself, and it requires only a one-time registration of the DI container that holds the registry data.

Listing 18-4 shows how a service can be resolved when using a `ServiceLocator` implementation for Unity.

**LISTING 18-4:** BookService Class Using ServiceLocator to Resolve Another Service

```
public class BookService
{
  public SendMailAboutNewBooks ()
  {
    var emailSenderService = ServiceLocator.Current.
      GetInstance<IEmailSenderService>();
  }
}
```

# Extensibility in MVC

The MVC framework was designed with extensibility in mind. The design patterns play an important role in the extensibility features of MVC. With these features, you can customize the whole framework to your taste.

Internally, MVC is built as a coherent set of independent components that can be replaced by other components. You have a default implementation of MVC components that you can use with your application. However, if you need something more sophisticated than the default implementation, you have two options:

➤   You can inherit from the classes representing MVC components and implement your own components with more control — or on the contrary, simplify them (for example, using default values).

> ➤ All components in the framework derive from abstract base classes or implement interfaces. You can replace the original components to create your own ones deriving from the appropriate abstract classes or implementing the interfaces.

You have many extension points in MVC. Instead of discussing them separately, you will meet them later in this chapter in the context where they are used.

## CREATING AN MVC 2 APPLICATION

Visual Studio 2010 ships with MVC 2 out-of-the-box. You can start developing an MVC 2 application with the File ➪ New ➪ Project command. The New Project dialog contains two templates (ASP.NET MVC 2 Web Application and ASP.NET MVC 2 Empty Web Application) for both the C# and Visual Basic languages. Figure 18-4 shows these templates. (You can display them by typing **MVC** into the search box of the dialog.)

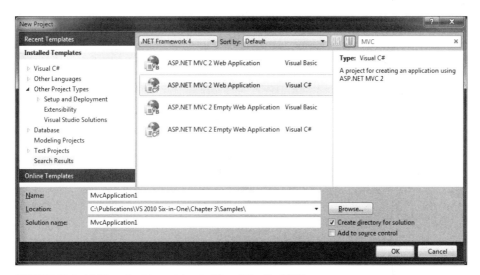

**FIGURE 18-4:** MVC project templates in Visual Studio 2010

In this chapter, you will learn about MVC application development through a sample called AcmeLibrary. In this section, you will create this project and learn how its structure supports the MVC pattern. You will also discover how the model, view, and controller work together to establish the expected behavior.

Display the New Project dialog (File ➪ New ➪ Project) and select the ASP.NET MVC 2 Web Application template that can be found under Visual C# in the Web category. Set the name of the project to AcmeLibrary and click OK.

Visual Studio displays a dialog shown in Figure 18-5 that asks whether you would like to create a unit test project for this application. As mentioned earlier, MVC leverages the TDD approach, and this dialog emphasizes this intention. In this example, you will not create unit tests, so select the second option in the dialog (as shown in Figure 18-5) and click OK.

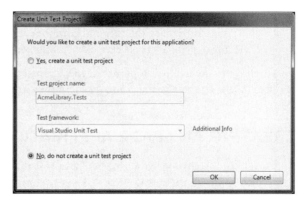

**FIGURE 18-5:** The Create Unit Test Project dialog

In a few seconds, Visual Studio 2010 creates the project skeleton that immediately can be built and run. Use the Debug ⇨ Start Without Debugging command (or press Ctrl+F5) to build and run the `AcmeLibrary` application. The ASP.NET Development Server starts and displays the home page of `AchmeLibrary`, as shown in Figure 18-6.

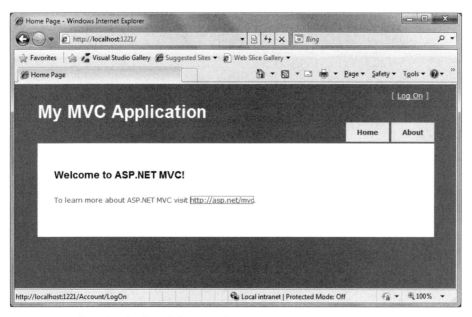

**FIGURE 18-6:** Running the AcmeLibrary application

As you can see in Figure 18-6, the application provides a link from the Home page to an About page and also has a Log On link. Close the application page in the web browser and go back to Visual Studio.

## The Project Structure

When you created the `AcmeLibrary` project, Visual Studio generated several folders and files. You can follow this structure in the Solution Explorer tool window, as shown in Figure 18-7.

The first important folder from the web application's perspective is the `Content` folder. It contains the cascading style sheet (CSS) files for the application. Usually, an `Images` folder under `Content` holds the images utilized in the web site. You can change the overall design of your site by modifying `Site.css` file or changing it to another CSS file (and, of course, replacing `Site.css` references in the appropriate master pages).

The second important folder is the `Scripts` folder. It contains about a dozen JavaScript files used by the project. It is worth mentioning that the project created for you has built-in support for jQuery client-side scripting, and includes a jQuery validation plug-in to support model validation in HTML forms without an additional round-trip to the server.

As their names suggest, the three other folders (`Controllers`, `Models`, and `View`) are closely related to the MVC pattern. The `Controllers` folder contains the classes that play the controller role in project. Figure 18-7 shows that Visual Studio created two controllers, one for the Home page (`HomeController.cs`) and another one for the About page (`AccountController.cs`).

**FIGURE 18-7:** Solution Structure

The `Views` folder is the container for all classes playing the view role in the MVC pattern. Classes representing views and their helper types are grouped into subfolders. The `Account` subfolder holds views related to the logon and account-handling functionality; `Home` encapsulates the views related the About and Home pages. (This one is in the `Index.aspx` file, and later this name will be explained.) The `Shared` folder holds helper pages and type, such as the `Error.aspx`, `LogOnUserControl.ascx` and `Site.Master` files.

 *When you look at the* `.aspx`, `.ascx`, *and* `.master` *files, you can recognize that they do not have corresponding code-behind files in contrast to the files with similar extensions in ASP.NET web projects. Many functions handled by the code-behind files in ASP.NET projects (such as, for example, collecting form data, validation, and navigation) are managed in a totally different way in ASP.NET MVC, with no need for a code-behind file.*

The `Models` folder is a container for files defining model types in the MVC pattern. The Home page and About page do not reference any model class — or you could even say they use an empty model with no properties or operations. The `AccountModel.cs` file in this folder contains model classes for the account-handling functions.

The `Models`, `Controllers`, and `Views` folders are not just for simply organizing files in the project. They provide role-specific context menu functions. For example, when you right-click the `Controllers` folder and, in the context menu, click the Add submenu, you can see the "Controller ..." command, as shown in Figure 18-8. This command allows you to add a new controller class to your website.

**FIGURE 18-8:** Controller-specific context menu commands

Similarly, you will find a "View ..." command under the Add submenu when you right-click the `Views` folder. If you rename the folders, you can still build your application, but it won't run (or at least not as you expect). You also will lose the folder-specific commands in the context menus. Keep the folder names as they are.

The `Global.asax` file and the `Web.config` file play the same role in MVC 2 as in the traditional ASP.NET web projects.

## How Does it Work?

When you create a web application with ASP.NET, at the end of the day, requests are mapped to `.aspx` files (or simply to HTML files). For example, when the request is represented by the `http://MySuperWebSite.org/KnowledgeBase/WindowsIssues.aspx` URL, the `WindowsIssues.aspx` file under the `KnowledgeBase` folder will be rendered to generate the HTML output shown in the browser.

The MVC framework resolves requests differently. Let's look at the `Site.Master` file located in the `Shared` subfolder under `Views`. Listing 18-5 shows this file. (Line breaks and a few comments after `</div>` tags are inserted for the better readability.)

**LISTING 18-5:** Site.Master

```
<%@ Master Language="C#" Inherits="System.Web.Mvc.ViewMasterPage" %>

<!DOCTYPE html PUBLIC "-//W3C//DTD XHTML 1.0 Strict//EN"
  "http://www.w3.org/TR/xhtml1/DTD/xhtml1-strict.dtd">
<html xmlns="http://www.w3.org/1999/xhtml">

<head runat="server">
  <title>
    <asp:ContentPlaceHolder ID="TitleContent" runat="server" />
  </title>
  <link href="../../Content/Site.css" rel="stylesheet" type="text/css" />
</head>

<body>
  <div class="page">
    <div id="header">
```

```
            <div id="title">
              <h1>
                My MVC Application
              </h1>
            </div> <!-- Title -->
            <div id="logindisplay">
              <% Html.RenderPartial("LogOnUserControl"); %>
            </div>
            <div id="menucontainer">
              <ul id="menu">
                <li><%: Html.ActionLink("Home", "Index", "Home")%></li>
                <li><%: Html.ActionLink("About", "About", "Home")%></li>
              </ul>
            </div>
          </div> <!-- Header -->
          <div id="main">
            <asp:ContentPlaceHolder ID="MainContent" runat="server" />
            <div id="footer">
            </div>
          </div>
        </div> <!-- Page -->
    </body>
    </html>
```

*Code file [Site.Master] available for download at Wrox.com*

While an ASP.NET web project master page inherits from the code-behind class that derives directly from the System.Web.UI.MasterPage type, this page (as you see here in the <%@ Master %> tag) inherits from the System.Web.Mvc.ViewMasterPage class that derives from System.Web.UI .MasterPage. The structure of the page is very similar to master pages in ASP.NET web projects.

The Site.Master page contains a <div> tag with the menucontainer identifier, which seems weird:

```
<div id="menucontainer">
  <ul id="menu">
    <li><%: Html.ActionLink("Home", "Index", "Home")%></li>
    <li><%: Html.ActionLink("About", "About", "Home")%></li>
  </ul>
</div>
```

These few lines represent the rectangular Home and About menu items shown in Figure 18-6. An ASP.NET master page uses web controls to represent the menu, like this:

```
<asp:Menu ID="NavigationMenu" runat="server" CssClass="menu"
  EnableViewState="false"
  IncludeStyleBlock="false" Orientation="Horizontal">
  <Items>
    <asp:MenuItem NavigateUrl="~/Default.aspx" Text="Home"/>
    <asp:MenuItem NavigateUrl="~/About.aspx" Text="About"/>
  </Items>
</asp:Menu>
```

The main difference between the two representations is not about using ASP.NET controls or plain HTML, but the way the user is directed to the link. When you look after the HTML code fragment that the navigation menus render, you will see difference. The following HTML snippet is rendered by the ASP.NET master page:

```
<ul class="level1">
  <li><a class="level1" href="Default.aspx">Home</a></li>
  <li><a class="level1" href="About.aspx">About</a></li>
</ul>
```

The HTML snippet for the MVC master page is different:

```
<ul id="menu">
  <li><a href="/">Home</a></li>
  <li><a href="/Home/About">About</a></li>
</ul>
```

While the ASP.NET master page uses filenames in the requests belonging to the link, the MVC master page uses folder names.

To understand what is happening in an MVC application, let's examine the lifecycle of the request from the beginning. To use this technology efficiently, you must know how the MVC platform works. ASP.NET MVC 2 is based on the routing component of ASP.NET, which became available with .NET Framework 3.5 SP1. The routing component is responsible for mapping an incoming HTTP request to a controller's action within the application.

Figure 18-9 provides a high-level overview of the lifecycle of an HTTP request that comes from a user's browser.

The request goes through the routing component and reaches a `Controller`. The `Controller` invokes the appropriate actions and retrieves an `ActionResult` sent back to the user.

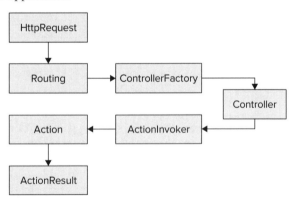

**FIGURE 18-9:** High-level view of an HTTP request's lifecycle

## Routing

Request handling within MVC applications is based on routing information provided by the developer during the initialization of the application. Listing 18-6 shows how this initial setup is done in the `Global.asax.cs` file.

Available for download on Wrox.com

**LISTING 18-6: Global.asax.cs**

```
using System;
using System.Collections.Generic;
using System.Linq;
```

```
using System.Web;
using System.Web.Mvc;
using System.Web.Routing;

namespace AcmeLibrary
{
  // Note: For instructions on enabling IIS6 or IIS7 classic mode,
  // visit http://go.microsoft.com/?LinkId=9394801

  public class MvcApplication : System.Web.HttpApplication
  {
    public static void RegisterRoutes(RouteCollection routes)
    {
      routes.IgnoreRoute("{resource}.axd/{*pathInfo}");
      routes.MapRoute(
          "Default", // Route name
          "{controller}/{action}/{id}", // URL with parameters
          new // Parameter defaults
          {
            controller = "Home",
            action = "Index",
            id = UrlParameter.Optional
          }
      );
    }

    protected void Application_Start()
    {
      AreaRegistration.RegisterAllAreas();
      RegisterRoutes(RouteTable.Routes);
    }
  }
}
```

*Code file [Global.asax.cs] available for download at Wrox.com*

When the web application starts, the `Application_Start` method is called that registers areas and then invokes the `RegisterRoutes` method that sets up the routing table.

There are two different kinds of routes:

➤ You can specify a route that should be ignored by the MVC framework, and use the default ASP.NET request routing instead. The URL pattern used in the call of the `IgnoreRoute` method says that request for files with `.axd` extensions should not be handled by the MVC routing.

➤ You can map a route to a controller's action within the application. An *action* is the executable code within a controller class processing the input from the incoming request and generating an action result. The call of the `MapRoute` method sets the pattern for the default route, and also specifies the default parameters for the default controller, action, and ID to be used in the case when the request would not specify them.

IgnoreRoute and MapRoute are extension methods for the RouteCollection class and provided by the MVC framework. Figure 18-10 show how an HTTP request is forwarded to the entity responsible for processing it after the request is sent from a client's browser through the routing component.

The first entry point within IIS for the request is the UrlRoutingModule, provided by ASP.NET. Its task is to forward the request to the UrlRoutingHandler. The UrlRoutingHandler checks the incoming URL within its RouteCollection and, if a match is found, it forwards the request to the appropriate handler.

The IgnoreRoute method creates a route associated with the StopRoutingHandler,

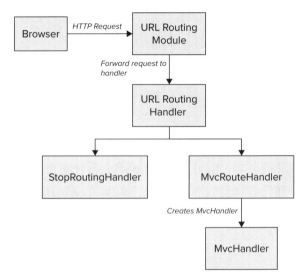

**FIGURE 18-10:** HTTP request flow in MVC

which means that ASP.NET stops processing that URL and forwards it to the other handlers registered with IIS.

The MapRoute method creates a route associated with the MvcHandler, which is the first real entry point to an MVC application. From this point, you can use a RequestContext instance to all data required to fulfill the request. RequestContext contains the current HttpContext and the matched RouteData.

Now, with this short explanation, you can see how the menu links in the HTML representation of AcmeLibrary's Home and About menu items work:

```
<ul id="menu">
  <li><a href="/">Home</a></li>
  <li><a href="/Home/About">About</a></li>
</ul>
```

When the request is for "/" (for example, the URL is "http://AcmeLibrary.com/"), no controller and no action name is provided, so the default "Home" controller is used with the default "Index" action. The ControllerFactory component shown in Figure 18-9 resolves the "Home" name to the HomeController class, and the ActionInvoker component resolves the "Index" name to the Index public method.

When the request is for "/Home/About" (for example, the URL is "http://AcmeLibrary.com/Home/About"), the "Home" controller is used with the "About" action that is mapped to the About public method of the HomeController class.

## The Controller Class

Let's have a look at the `HomeController` class that holds the code responsible for executing the `Index` and `About` actions. Listing 18-7 shows the source code of this class, which is surprisingly compact.

**LISTING 18-7:** HomeController.cs

```
using System;
using System.Collections.Generic;
using System.Linq;
using System.Web;
using System.Web.Mvc;

namespace AcmeLibrary.Controllers
{
  [HandleError]
  public class HomeController : Controller
  {
    public ActionResult Index()
    {
      ViewData["Message"] = "Welcome to ASP.NET MVC!";
      return View();
    }

    public ActionResult About()
    {
      return View();
    }
  }
}
```

*Code file [HomeController.cs] available for download at Wrox.com*

`HomeController` derives from the `Controller` class of the `System.Web.Mvc` namespace. The `HandleErrorAttribute` decorating this class declares that this controller should handle errors in the default way by redirecting them to the `Error.aspx` page.

The two public methods, `Index` and `About`, represent the actions and return an `ActionResult` instance. Both methods call the `View` method that retrieves a `ViewResult` instance — where `ViewResult` inherits from `ActionResult`.

The `View` method returns the view that matches the action result name from the `Views` subfolder that, in turn, matches the controller name. So, in this case, `View` returns an instance pointing to the `Views/Home/Index.aspx` or `Views/Home/About.aspx` for the `Index` and `About` actions, respectively. The `ViewData` member set in the `Index` method is a dictionary — its type is `ViewDataDictionary` — that holds entries with a string key and a `System.Object` value. The `Index` method sets the entry with the `Message` key to the welcome string.

When the action method retrieves the `ActionResult` instance, the controller interprets the result and decides what activity to take. In the case of the `Index` and `About` actions, the result is a `ViewResult` instance, so the controller navigates to the view implicitly or explicitly named by this result.

## The View

The `Index` and `About` views defined in the `Index.aspx` and `About.aspx` pages in the `Views/Home` folder are really simple, as shown in Listing 18-8 and Listing 18-9.

**LISTING 18-8: Index.aspx**

```
<%@ Page Language="C#" MasterPageFile="~/Views/Shared/Site.Master"
    Inherits="System.Web.Mvc.ViewPage" %>

<asp:Content ID="Content1" ContentPlaceHolderID="TitleContent" runat="server">
  Home Page
</asp:Content>

<asp:Content ID="Content2" ContentPlaceHolderID="MainContent" runat="server">
  <h2><%: ViewData["Message"] %></h2>
  <p>
    To learn more about ASP.NET MVC visit
    <a href="http://asp.net/mvc"
       title="ASP.NET MVC Website">http://asp.net/mvc</a>.
  </p>
</asp:Content>
```

*Code file [Index.aspx] available for download at Wrox.com*

**LISTING 18-9: About.aspx**

```
<%@ Page Language="C#" MasterPageFile="~/Views/Shared/Site.Master"
    Inherits="System.Web.Mvc.ViewPage" %>

<asp:Content ID="aboutTitle" ContentPlaceHolderID="TitleContent" runat="server">
  About Us
</asp:Content>

<asp:Content ID="aboutContent" ContentPlaceHolderID="MainContent" runat="server">
  <h2>About</h2>
  <p>
    Put content here.
  </p>
</asp:Content>
```

*Code file [About.aspx] available for download at Wrox.com*

As you can see, both pages provide the `<asp:Content>` tags that match with the appropriate `<asp:ContentPlaceHolder>` tags in the master page (`Site.Master`). `Index.aspx` in Listing 18-8 uses the `ViewData` member to extract the "Message" property encapsulated into the view.

> ### AUTO-ENCODING SYNTAX
>
> You may recognize a new `<%: ... %>` syntax element in Listing 18-8 rendering the `ViewData["Message"]` expression. This syntax automatically HTML-encodes the expression specified in its body. Automatic encoding is a method that dramatically reduces the risk of cross-site scripting (XSS) vulnerabilities.
>
> This syntax is new in .NET 4. As mentioned earlier in this chapter, ASP.NET MVC 2 can be used together with .NET 3.5 (in Visual Studio 2010 and in Visual Studio 2010), but, in this case, you cannot use the auto-encoding syntax. You should use the old `<%= ... %>` element.

## ADDING NEW MVC 2 PAGES

The `AcmeLibrary` application created with the ASP.NET MVC 2 Web Application project template does not provide any real functions yet. In this section, you add functions to the application that allow you to list and edit books. The application will persist all information in a SQL Server database. The components you create here are a great demonstration of MVC's strength. You can establish a clear architecture with short and simple source code.

## Create a Database

The `AcmeLibrary` application will manage a list of books that are stored in a database. So, first you must create this database and define its structure.

In Solution Explorer, right-click the `App_Data` folder. In the context menu, select the Add ⇨ New Item command. When the dialog appears, select the SQL Server Database item in the Data category, and set its name to `AcmeLibraryData.mdf`, as shown in Figure 18-11.

**FIGURE 18-11:** Adding a new database to the project

Double-click the new `AcmeLibraryData.mdf` file in Solution Explorer to display the Server Explorer tool window. Then, right-click the Tables node and select the Add New Table command. Add the fields shown in Figure 18-12 to the table. Set the Id field as the primary key of the table and set its `(Is Identity)` property in the Column Properties tab to `Yes`.

When you are finished, press Ctrl+S to save the table, and name it `Book`.

## Create a Model

Now, you must add a model for the `Book` table. Select the `Models` folder in Solution Explorer, and, with the Add ➪ New Item command in its context menu, add a new ADO.NET Entity Data Model item with `AcmeLibraryModel.edmx` name to the folder. When you click OK in the Add New Item dialog, the Entity Data Model Wizard starts with the "Choose Model Contents" page. Select the Generate from database option and click Next.

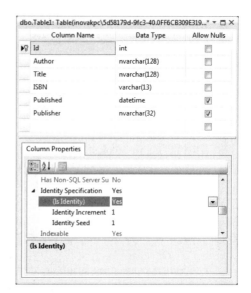

**FIGURE 18-12:** Add a new table to the database

In the "Choose your data" connection page, select `AcmeLibraryData.mdf` from the connection combo box. Select the "Save entity connection settings in Web.Config as" checkbox and type **AcmeLibraryDataEntities** in the text box below the checkbox. Click Next to move to the next wizard page.

In the Choose Your Database Objects page (shown in Figure 18-13), select the `Book` table and check both checkboxes below the database objects' list. Set the Model Namespace to `AcmeLibraryDataModel` and click Finish.

The ADO.NET entity model is created for you. Build your project so that the ASP.NET MVC 2 tools can observe the new classes in the model.

**FIGURE 18-13:** The Choose Your Database Objects page

*Providing a detailed overview about Entity Framework 4.0 (EF 4.0 — the `AcmeLibraryModel.edmx` file generates code using this framework) is beyond the scope of this chapter. The examples used here are intuitive enough so that you can understand them with no EF 4.0 experience, assuming you have used .NET data access technologies such as ADO.NET or LINQ to SQL before.*

*If you are novice using EF 4, you will find great resources in MSDN when you search for "Beginner's Guide to the ADO.NET Entity Framework."*

## Listing Books

You now have a database and have defined a model using EF 4.0. To display a list of books, you need a view that represents this list, and also a controller connecting the model and the view. Reading the letters in "MVC" from left to right, you may think the next step is to create a view, and then you can start building a controller. Although that can be done, creating a controller first has some advantages over the "create-view-first" approach.

When dealing with books, you probably want to have views (pages) provide functions like adding a new book to the list, or modifying the attributes of an existing book. In most cases, you want the links (buttons or other kind of UI elements) to these functions to be available from the page displaying the list of books, which means that those pages would have a shared controller with actions such as Create, Edit, Delete, and so on.

So, let's create the controller responsible for manipulating books.

### Creating the BookController Class

Select the `Controllers` folder in Solution Explorer. Right-click, and choose Add ⇨ Controller from the context menu. The Add Controller dialog pops up, as shown in Figure 18-14.

Type **BookController** into the Controller Name text box and set the checkbox to add actions to the controller for `Book` operations such as Create, Edit, Delete, and Details.

**FIGURE 18-14:** The Add Controller dialog

If you leave the checkbox empty, the controller is generated only with a single `Index` action. Listing 18-10 shows the source code of the `BookController` class.

**LISTING 18-10:** BookController.cs

```csharp
using System;
using System.Collections.Generic;
using System.Linq;
using System.Web;
using System.Web.Mvc;
using AcmeLibrary.Models;

namespace AcmeLibrary.Controllers
{
  public class BookController : Controller
  {
    public ActionResult Index()
    {
      return View();
    }

    public ActionResult Details(int id)
    {
      return View();
    }

    public ActionResult Create()
    {
      return View();
    }

    [HttpPost]
    public ActionResult Create(FormCollection collection)
    {
      try
      {
        // TODO: Add insert logic here
        return RedirectToAction("Index");
      }
      catch
      {
        return View();
      }
    }

    public ActionResult Edit(int id)
    {
      return View();
    }

    [HttpPost]
    public ActionResult Edit(int id, FormCollection collection)
    {
      try
```

```
        {
          // TODO: Add update logic here
          return RedirectToAction("Index");
        }
        catch
        {
          return View();
        }
      }

      public ActionResult Delete(int id)
      {
        return View();
      }

      [HttpPost]
      public ActionResult Delete(int id, FormCollection collection)
      {
        try
        {
          // TODO: Add delete logic here
          return RedirectToAction("Index");
        }
        catch
        {
          return View();
        }
      }
    }
  }
```

*Code file [BookController.cs] available for download at Wrox.com*

 *For the sake of brevity and improved readability, this listing omits action header comments. The original source code contains header comments for each action, telling you the request URL to access it.*

Notice that there are three actions — Create, Edit, and Delete — that have overloaded methods decorated with HttpPost attribute and accepting a FormCollection parameter. The HttpPost attribute is used to restrict an action method so that the method handles only HTTP POST requests. The FormCollection instance represents a form value provider. When the user fills in a form (for example, the one required to create a new Book instance), it is passed to the actions handling them as a FormCollection.

The BookController class is just an empty skeleton that does not integrate actions with the model or with the appropriate views.

Add the following `using` clause to the existing `using` clauses in the file header:

```
using AcmeLibrary.Models;
```

Integrate the `Index` action with the model by changing its body to the following code:

```
public ActionResult Index()
{
  var context = new AcmeLibraryDataEntities();
  var books = context.Books;
  return View(books);
}
```

This code retrieves all books and passes data to the `View` method that interprets the `books` collection as the model.

## Creating the Index View

Although the `Index` action accesses the model, there is no view yet that displays the list of books. The MVC 2 tools integrated with Visual Studio 2010 makes it very simple to create a new view.

Open the `BookController.cs` file if it's closed, and click into the body of the `Index` method to place the caret cursor there. Right-click the code editor and select the Add View command from the context menu.

 *There is a small bug in the RTM version of Visual Studio 2010. In some cases, it pops up context menus so that you must scroll (even if there is enough space on the screen). To access the Add View command, you must scroll up to the top of the context menu.*

The Add View dialog pops up, allowing you to specify parameters for the new view to create. Figure 18-15 shows this dialog in action.

Set the View Name to **Index**. Check the "Create a strongly-typed view" option and select `AcmeLibrary.Models.Book` from the "View data class" combo box. The "View content" combo box allows you to set the type of the view you want to generate. You can choose from the following items:

➤ *Create* — A view to enter data for a new item.

➤ *Delete* — A view to confirm a deletion of an item.

➤ *Details* — A view to browse the details (attributes) of an item.

**FIGURE 18-15:** The Add View dialog

➤ *Edit* — A view to edit the details (attributes) of an item.

➤ *Empty* — An empty view that you must manually edit after its skeleton has been generated.

➤ *List* — A view listing the model items in a collection.

Select List, because you are going to create a view that lists books in the database.

The "Select master page" checkbox allows you to define the master page attributes (that is, which master page to use, and the identifier of the content placeholder the view will be nested in). Leave the checkbox checked, and also leave the master page attributes with their default values.

You can check the "Create a partial view (.ascx)" checkbox to create a view as an ASP.NET user control, but for now, uncheck this option.

When you click the Add button, the view is generated for you, and it is automatically put into the Book folder under Views, according to the controller action. Listing 18-11 shows the generated source code of the view.

**LISTING 18-11:** Book/Index.aspx

```
<%@ Page Title="" Language="C#" MasterPageFile="~/Views/Shared/Site.Master"
  Inherits="System.Web.Mvc.ViewPage<IEnumerable<AcmeLibrary.Models.Book>>" %>

<asp:Content ID="Content1" ContentPlaceHolderID="TitleContent" runat="server">
  Index
</asp:Content>
<asp:Content ID="Content2" ContentPlaceHolderID="MainContent" runat="server">
  <h2>
    Index
  </h2>
  <table>
    <tr>
      <th></th>
      <th>Id</th>
      <th>Author</th>
      <th>Title</th>
      <th>ISBN</th>
      <th>Published</th>
      <th>Publisher</th>
    </tr>
    <% foreach (var item in Model)
      { %>
    <tr>
      <td>
        <%: Html.ActionLink("Edit", "Edit", new { id=item.Id }) %>
        |
        <%: Html.ActionLink("Details", "Details", new { id=item.Id })%>
        |
        <%: Html.ActionLink("Delete", "Delete", new { id=item.Id })%>
      </td>
      <td><%: item.Id %> </td>
      <td><%: item.Author %></td>
      <td><%: item.Title %></td>
```

*continues*

**LISTING 18-11** *(continued)*

```
        <td><%: item.ISBN %></td>
        <td><%: String.Format("{0:g}", item.Published) %></td>
        <td><%: item.Publisher %></td>
    </tr>
    <% } %>
  </table>
  <p>
    <%: Html.ActionLink("Create New", "Create") %>
  </p>
</asp:Content>
```

*Code file [Book/Index.aspx] available for download at Wrox.com*

As you can see, the code is very simple. The list is represented by an HTML `<table>`, where the first column contains links for the available actions like Edit, Details, and Delete.

Select the `AcmeLibrary` project in Solution Explorer. Build and run the project by pressing Ctrl+F5. When the application starts, it goes to the home page. Append the `Book/Index` request path to the current URL in your browser's address line to navigate to the list of books. Figure 18-16 shows the page with an empty list of books.

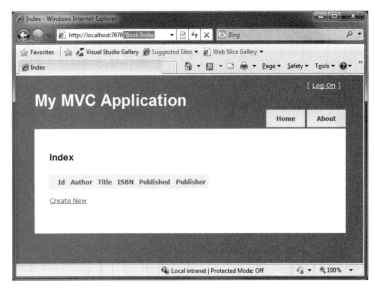

**FIGURE 18-16:** The empty list of books

The page is currently not available from the home page of the application, but you can easily put a link there by modifying the `Site.Master` file. Insert the following line between the two existing links in the `<ul id="menu">` tag:

```
<li><%: Html.ActionLink("Book", "Index", "Book")%></li>
```

Using the Server Explorer, open the `Book` table with the Show Table Data context menu command, and add a few records to the table. Build and run your application and click the Book link. Your browser navigates to the `Book/Index` pages and lists the books you've recently added directly to the `Book` table, as shown in Figure 18-17.

**FIGURE 18-17:** The list of books can be accessed through a link

When you try to click to any of the Edit, Details, Delete, or Create New links, you'll receive a server error because the views of actions represented by these links have not yet been implemented.

# Adding Book Actions

Creating the controller actions and views for manipulating books is really simple and straightforward — thanks to the great tools and architecture behind MVC 2. First, let's create the `Details` action.

## Adding the Details View

The `Details` action displays the attributes of the model instance, and does not provide controls to edit them. Change the body of the `Details` method in the `BookController` class to the following code:

```
public ActionResult Details(int id)
{
    var context = new AcmeLibraryDataEntities();
```

```
    var book = context.Books.First(b => b.Id == id);
    return View(book);
}
```

This code created an `AcmeLibraryDataEntities` context and used it to query the `Book` instance having the identifier received by the `Details` method. This identifier comes from the third parameter of the `ActionLink` representing the action in the `Index.aspx` file:

```
<%: Html.ActionLink("Details", "Details", new { id=item.Id })%>
```

The `Details` action retrieves a view encapsulating the `Book` instance with the specified identifier. Right-click the body of the `Details` method in the code editor, and start the Add View context menu command. Configure the Add View dialog as shown in Figure 18-18.

The content of the dialog is very similar to the one used for creation of the Index view (shown in Figure 18-15), but this time, the name of the view is set to Details, and the "View content" combo is set to the Details type. Click Add, and the `Details.aspx` page is generated in the `Views/Book` folder. The source code of this new view is simple, as shown in Listing 18-12.

**FIGURE 18-18:** Creating the Details view

**LISTING 18-12:** Book/Details.aspx

```
<%@ Page Title="" Language="C#" MasterPageFile="~/Views/Shared/Site.Master"
    Inherits="System.Web.Mvc.ViewPage<AcmeLibrary.Models.Book>" %>

<asp:Content ID="Content1" ContentPlaceHolderID="TitleContent" runat="server">
    Details
</asp:Content>
<asp:Content ID="Content2" ContentPlaceHolderID="MainContent" runat="server">
    <h2>
        Details
    </h2>
    <fieldset>
        <legend>Fields</legend>
        <div class="display-label">Id</div>
        <div class="display-field"><%: Model.Id %></div>
        <div class="display-label">Author</div>
        <div class="display-field"><%: Model.Author %></div>
        <div class="display-label">Title</div>
        <div class="display-field"><%: Model.Title %></div>
        <div class="display-label">ISBN</div>
        <div class="display-field"><%: Model.ISBN %></div>
        <div class="display-label">Published</div>
```

```
    <div class="display-field">
      <%: String.Format("{0:g}", Model.Published) %></div>
    <div class="display-label">Publisher</div>
    <div class="display-field"><%: Model.Publisher %></div>
  </fieldset>
  <p>
    <%: Html.ActionLink("Edit", "Edit", new { id=Model.Id }) %>
    |
    <%: Html.ActionLink("Back to List", "Index") %>
  </p>
</asp:Content>
```

*Code file [Book/Details.aspx] available for download at Wrox.com*

Build the project and start it by pressing Ctrl+F5. From the home page, navigate to the list of books, and click on the Details link of any book displayed in the list. The page with the book attributes appears in your browser, as shown in Figure 18-19.

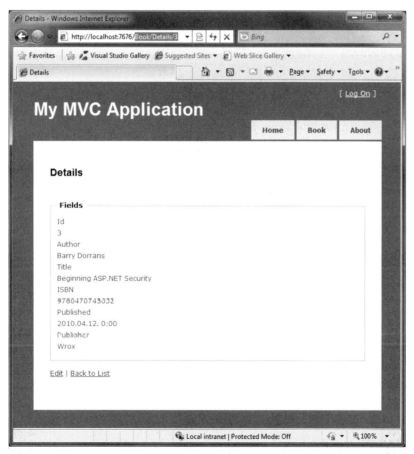

**FIGURE 18-19:** The details of a book

Notice the /Book/Details/3 request string in the URL of the page. The identifier at the end of the request is received by the Details action method.

## Adding the Edit View

From the controller's point of view, editing a book requires two actions:

➤ When the user selects the Edit link of a book in the list, the book information should be read from the database and displayed in a view that allows editing.

➤ When the user has edited the book's properties, the information submitted should be saved into the database.

The two Edit methods of the BookController class are dedicated to these actions:

```
public ActionResult Edit(int id)
{
  // ...
}

[HttpPost]
public ActionResult Edit(int id, FormCollection collection)
{
  // ...
}
```

The first Edit method is called when the Edit link of a book is clicked; the second is invoked when the edited book information is submitted. Both methods receive the identifier of the book; the second method receives a FormCollection instance containing the new values for book properties.

Notice the HttpPost attribute decorating the second Edit method. When the form with edited book information is submitted, an HTTP POST is used, and the routing algorithm will forward the request to this Edit method.

Now, implement these methods with the following code:

```
public ActionResult Edit(int id)
{
  var context = new AcmeLibraryDataEntities();
  var book = context.Books.First(b => b.Id == id);
  TempData["context"] = context;
  TempData["book"] = book;
  return View(book);
}

[HttpPost]
public ActionResult Edit(int id, FormCollection collection)
{
  try
  {
    var context = TempData["context"] as AcmeLibraryDataEntities;
    var book = TempData["book"] as Book;
    if (context != null && book != null)
```

```
      {
        book.Author = collection["Author"];
        book.Title = collection["Title"];
        book.ISBN = collection["ISBN"];
        DateTime published;
        if (DateTime.TryParse(collection["Published"], out published))
        {
          book.Published = published;
        }
        book.Publisher = collection["Publisher"];
        context.SaveChanges();
        context.Dispose();
      }
      return RedirectToAction("Index");
    }
    catch
    {
      return View();
    }
  }
}
```

The first method reads the selected book from the database — exactly the same way as the `Details` method does — and passes it to the view returned. However, it stores the `context` and `book` variables into the `TempData` collection so that those can be retrieved in the second edit method. The reason behind this activity is that the `context` and the `book` instances can be reused later when saving the information back to the database.

The second method extracts the `context` and the `book` information from the `TempData` collection and changes each book property according to the values stored in the collection passed to the method. The data context is notified every time a book property is set, so the `SaveChanges` method recognizes that the book instance should be saved back to the database, and persists it. You do not need the context instance any more for this operation, so it is disposed. After the successful save operation, the user is redirected to the page with the list of books.

You still need to create the Edit view. Use the Add View context menu command from the code editor within any of the Edit methods. This time, name the view **Edit**, and select the Edit content type in the View content dialog. Listing 18-13 shows the source code of the new view created in the `Book` folder.

**LISTING 18-13: Book/Edit.aspx**

```
<%@ Page Title="" Language="C#" MasterPageFile="~/Views/Shared/Site.Master"
   Inherits="System.Web.Mvc.ViewPage<AcmeLibrary.Models.Book>" %>

<asp:Content ID="Content1" ContentPlaceHolderID="TitleContent" runat="server">
  Edit
</asp:Content>
<asp:Content ID="Content2" ContentPlaceHolderID="MainContent" runat="server">
  <h2>
    Edit
  </h2>
```

*continues*

**LISTING 18-13** *(continued)*

```
<% using (Html.BeginForm())
   {%>
<%: Html.ValidationSummary(true) %>
<fieldset>
  <legend>Fields</legend>
  <div class="editor-label">
    <%: Html.LabelFor(model => model.Id) %>
  </div>
  <div class="editor-field">
    <%: Html.TextBoxFor(model => model.Id) %>
    <%: Html.ValidationMessageFor(model => model.Id) %>
  </div>
  <div class="editor-label">
    <%: Html.LabelFor(model => model.Author) %>
  </div>
  <div class="editor-field">
    <%: Html.TextBoxFor(model => model.Author) %>
    <%: Html.ValidationMessageFor(model => model.Author) %>
  </div>
  <div class="editor-label">
    <%: Html.LabelFor(model => model.Title) %>
  </div>
  <div class="editor-field">
    <%: Html.TextBoxFor(model => model.Title) %>
    <%: Html.ValidationMessageFor(model => model.Title) %>
  </div>
  <div class="editor-label">
    <%: Html.LabelFor(model => model.ISBN) %>
  </div>
  <div class="editor-field">
    <%: Html.TextBoxFor(model => model.ISBN) %>
    <%: Html.ValidationMessageFor(model => model.ISBN) %>
  </div>
  <div class="editor-label">
    <%: Html.LabelFor(model => model.Published) %>
  </div>
  <div class="editor-field">
    <%: Html.TextBoxFor(model => model.Published,
      String.Format("{0:g}", Model.Published)) %>
    <%: Html.ValidationMessageFor(model => model.Published) %>
  </div>
  <div class="editor-label">
    <%: Html.LabelFor(model => model.Publisher) %>
  </div>
  <div class="editor-field">
    <%: Html.TextBoxFor(model => model.Publisher) %>
    <%: Html.ValidationMessageFor(model => model.Publisher) %>
  </div>
  <p>
    <input type="submit" value="Save" />
  </p>
</fieldset>
```

```
  <% } %>
  <div>
    <%: Html.ActionLink("Back to List", "Index") %>
  </div>
</asp:Content>
```

*Code file [Book/Edit.aspx] available for download at Wrox.com*

The Edit view is as simple as the Details and List views discussed previously. Each attribute of the book has three associated HTML tags: one for the label, another one for the input field to edit the attribute, and a third one to validate the field content. You will learn about field validation later in this chapter.

The Id field is bound to an Identity column in the database, so its value is automatically generated at the SQL Server side. You do not need this field, so you can remove the associated HTML tags from the view. Also, you can rename the <legend> tag from "Fields" to "Book Attributes."

Figure 18-20 shows the Edit view in action after running your application and selecting the Edit link of a book from the list.

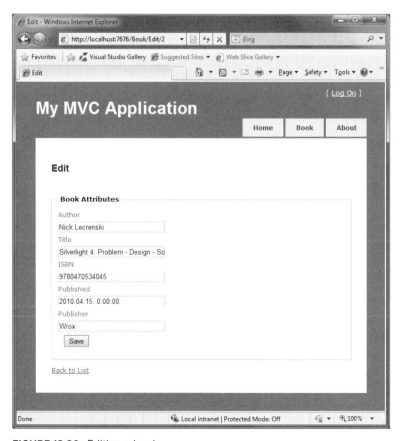

**FIGURE 18-20:** Editing a book

## Adding the Create View

Similar to the Edit view, the Create view has also two actions in the controller class:

```
public ActionResult Create()
{
  // ...
}

[HttpPost]
public ActionResult Create(FormCollection collection)
{
  // ...
}
```

Their semantics resemble the Edit actions. The first method is called when you are about to provide the view for editing a new `Book` entity. The second is invoked when the new `Book` instance is to be saved into the database. You can use the following code to define the body of these action methods:

```
public ActionResult Create()
{
  var context = new AcmeLibraryDataEntities();
  var book = new Book
             {
               Author = "(Author)",
               Title = "(Title)",
               ISBN = "(ISBN)"
             };
  context.AddToBooks(book);
  TempData["context"] = context;
  TempData["book"] = book;
  return View(book);
}

[HttpPost]
public ActionResult Create(FormCollection collection)
{
  return Edit(-1, collection);
}
```

You can see that the implementation of `Create` action methods is very similar to the `Edit` methods. Actually, the second `Create` method reuses the appropriate `Edit` method, passing the `collection` and -1 as a placeholder of the id parameter that is unused within `Edit`.

The first `Create` method simply creates a new `Book` instance, initializes a few fields, and adds it to the context. The `context` and `book` variables are put into the `TempData` collection as they are utilized in the `Edit` method called from the second `Create` method.

You could probably now guess how to generate the Create view. Use the Add View context menu command while your cursor is within one of the `Create` methods. Name the view **Create** and choose Create in the "View content" combo box. The code for the Create view will be almost exactly the same as for Edit (as shown in Listing 18-13). However, the `value` attribute of the Submit button is set to "Create" (it's "Save" in the `Edit.aspx` file).

Remove the HTML tags related to the `Id` field and change the `<legend>` tag to "New Book Attributes." You can now run your application. Click the Create New link at the bottom of the book list and edit the attributes of a new book, as shown in Figure 18-21.

**FIGURE 18-21:** Create a new book

When you click the Create button, the new book will be added to the list of books.

## Adding the Delete View

Now that you have worked with the Create and Edit views, there is no surprise that the `BookController` class has two `Delete` actions. Copy the following code into the `Delete` action methods:

```
public ActionResult Delete(int id)
{
  var context = new AcmeLibraryDataEntities();
  var book = context.Books.First(b => b.Id == id);
  TempData["context"] = context;
```

```
    TempData["book"] = book;
    return View(book);
}

[HttpPost]
public ActionResult Delete(int id, FormCollection collection)
{
    try
    {
        var context = TempData["context"] as AcmeLibraryDataEntities;
        var book = TempData["book"] as Book;
        if (context != null && book != null)
        {
            context.DeleteObject(book);
            context.SaveChanges();
            context.Dispose();
        }
        return RedirectToAction("Index");
    }
    catch
    {
        return View();
    }
}
```

The first `Delete` action is used when the book information is about to be shown in a view where the user can confirm the delete operation. The second `Delete` action is invoked when the operation is confirmed. Now, you can most likely figure out how these methods work without any further explanation.

Use the Add View command invoked from within one of the `Delete` methods and use Delete both for the view name and for the View content selection. The structure of the generated `Delete.aspx` file resembles to the `Details.aspx` file. You do not need to display all book attributes in the confirmation page. Let's keep only the Author, Title, and ISBN fields. Remove the HTML tags associated with other fields. Your Delete view should look like the code in Listing 18-14.

---

**LISTING 18-14:** Book/Delete.aspx

```
<%@ Page Title="" Language="C#" MasterPageFile="~/Views/Shared/Site.Master"
    Inherits="System.Web.Mvc.ViewPage<AcmeLibrary.Models.Book>" %>

<asp:Content ID="Content1" ContentPlaceHolderID="TitleContent" runat="server">
    Delete
</asp:Content>
<asp:Content ID="Content2" ContentPlaceHolderID="MainContent" runat="server">
    <h2>
        Delete
    </h2>
    <h3>
        Are you sure you want to delete this book?
    </h3>
    <fieldset>
        <legend>Fields</legend>
        <div class="display-label">Author</div>
```

```
     <div class="display-field"><%: Model.Author %></div>
     <div class="display-label">Title</div>
     <div class="display-field"><%: Model.Title %></div>
     <div class="display-label">ISBN</div>
     <div class="display-field"><%: Model.ISBN %></div>
   </fieldset>
   <% using (Html.BeginForm())
      { %>
   <p>
     <input type="submit" value="Delete" />
     |
     <%: Html.ActionLink("Back to List", "Index") %>
   </p>
   <% } %>
</asp:Content>
```

*Code file [Book/Delete.aspx] available for download at Wrox.com*

Build and run `AcmeLibrary` and create a few fake books. In the book list, click the Delete link of a fake book. You will see a confirmation screen similar to Figure 18-22.

**FIGURE 18-22:** Confirm the delete operation

Click the Delete button and the book will be deleted immediately.

## CUSTOMIZATION IN MVC 2

Thus far, you have learned that the MVC 2 tools shipped with Visual Studio 2010 (such as the Add Controller and Add View commands) help you to create functional web pages in a few minutes. MVC provides many customization opportunities to tailor your web site's UI and behavior to fit your needs. This section examines a few features that make this customization possible.

## Model Binding

The `BookController` class's `Edit` action used the following code to write back the edited book data to the database:

```
[HttpPost]
public ActionResult Edit(int id, FormCollection collection)
{
  try
  {
    var context = TempData["context"] as AcmeLibraryDataEntities;
    var book = TempData["book"] as Book;
    if (context != null && book != null)
    {
      book.Author = collection["Author"];
      book.Title = collection["Title"];
      book.ISBN = collection["ISBN"];
      DateTime published;
      if (DateTime.TryParse(collection["Published"], out published))
      {
        book.Published = published;
      }
      book.Publisher = collection["Publisher"];
      context.SaveChanges();
      context.Dispose();
    }
    return RedirectToAction("Index");
  }
  catch
  {
    return View();
  }
}
```

The largest part of this code converts the form properties stored in `collection` into the `book` variable. MVC has a mechanism called *model binding* that can populate model attributes by matching key/value pairs with the names of properties on a concrete .NET type. With model binding, you can shorten the previous code and remove the need of dealing with each property in a `Book` instance:

```
[HttpPost]
public ActionResult Edit(int id, FormCollection collection)
{
  try
```

```
    {
      var context = TempData["context"] as AcmeLibraryDataEntities;
      var book = TempData["book"] as Book;
      if (context != null && book != null)
      {
        UpdateModel(book, collection.ToValueProvider());
        context.SaveChanges();
        context.Dispose();
      }
      return RedirectToAction("Index");
    }
    catch
    {
      return View();
    }
  }
```

The `UpdateModel` method has several overloads. The one used in the example updates the `book` variable (representing the model) from the controller's value provider. The `FormCollection` instance passed to the method can be converted to a value provider with the `ToValueProvider` method. All the mechanic work is done by this simple method call — like parsing the string form of properties, and converting them to the appropriate types (such as handling the `DateTime` value of the `Published` property).

With model binding, you can go even further. Let's see the original implementation of the `Create` actions in the controller:

```
public ActionResult Create()
{
  var context = new AcmeLibraryDataEntities();
  var book = new Book
            {
                Author = "(Author)",
                Title = "(Title)",
                ISBN = "(ISBN)"
            };
  context.AddToBooks(book);
  TempData["context"] = context;
  TempData["book"] = book;
  return View(book);
}

[HttpPost]
public ActionResult Create(FormCollection collection)
{
  return Edit(-1, collection);
}
```

The first `Create` method instantiated an `AcmeLibraryDataEntities` context so that the second `Create` method can simply call the `Edit` action. This context creation is not really required by the time the Create view is displayed, because it will have an active role only in the second `Create` method.

Let's change the implementation of these methods:

```
public ActionResult Create()
{
  var book = new Book
              {
                Author = "(Author)",
                Title = "(Title)",
                ISBN = "(ISBN)"
              };
  return View(book);
}


[HttpPost]
public ActionResult Create(Book newBook)
{
  try
  {
    using (var context = new AcmeLibraryDataEntities())
    {
      context.AddToBooks(newBook);
      context.SaveChanges();
    }
    return RedirectToAction("Index");
  }
  catch
  {
    return View();
  }
}
```

Now, the first `Create` method creates a `Book` instance just to set a few default values. Look at the signature of the second method. It has been changed so that now it accepts a `Book` instance. Knowing that the `Create` action method is being invoked via an HTTP POST request, and that `Book` is a .NET type that is totally unknown to HTTP, how can an HTTP request and routing handle the method call and supply a `Book` instance?

The answer again lies with the model binding. The incoming data is parsed and used to populate the method action parameters. With this solution, the `Create` actions look more natural, and they do not need the entity context be passed through `TempData`.

Using the model binding feature, you can change the actions of the entire `BookController` class, as shown in Listing 18-15.

**LISTING 18-15: Updated BookController class**

```
using System.Linq;
using System.Web.Mvc;
using AcmeLibrary.Models;

namespace AcmeLibrary.Controllers
```

```
{
  public class BookController : Controller
  {
    public ActionResult Index()
    {
      var context = new AcmeLibraryDataEntities();
      var books = context.Books;
      return View(books);
    }

    public ActionResult Details(int id)
    {
      var context = new AcmeLibraryDataEntities();
      var book = context.Books.First(b => b.Id == id);
      return View(book);
    }

    public ActionResult Create()
    {
      var book = new Book
                 {
                   Author = "(Author)",
                   Title = "(Title)",
                   ISBN = "(ISBN)"
                 };
      return View(book);
    }

    [HttpPost]
    public ActionResult Create(Book newBook)
    {
      try
      {
        using (var context = new AcmeLibraryDataEntities())
        {
          context.AddToBooks(newBook);
          context.SaveChanges();
        }
        return RedirectToAction("Index");
      }
      catch
      {
        return View(newBook);
      }
    }

    public ActionResult Edit(int id)
    {
      using (var context = new AcmeLibraryDataEntities())
      {
        var book = context.Books.First(b => b.Id == id);
        context.Detach(book);
```

*continues*

**LISTING 18-15** *(continued)*

```
      return View(book);
    }
  }


  [HttpPost]
  public ActionResult Edit(Book editedBook)
  {
    try
    {
      using (var context = new AcmeLibraryDataEntities())
      {
        context.Books.Attach(editedBook);
        context.Books.ApplyOriginalValues(
          new Book { Id = editedBook.Id });
        context.SaveChanges();
      }
      return RedirectToAction("Index");
    }
    catch
    {
      return View(editedBook);
    }
  }


  public ActionResult Delete(int id)
  {
    return Edit(id);
  }


  [HttpPost]
  public ActionResult Delete(Book bookToDelete)
  {
    try
    {
      using (var context = new AcmeLibraryDataEntities())
      {
        context.Books.Attach(bookToDelete);
        context.Books.DeleteObject(bookToDelete);
        context.SaveChanges();
      }
      return RedirectToAction("Index");
    }
    catch
    {
      return View(bookToDelete);
    }
  }
}
}
```

*Code file [BookController.cs] available for download at Wrox.com*

# Validation

There is a serious issue with the AcmeLibrary application — *validation*. When you create a new book and leave the title or ISBN information empty when clicking the Create button, you will see validation messages to the right of the invalid fields. However, when you edit an existing book, something different happens. If you set an invalid field value and save the book, the invalid field's value is reverted to its original value without any notification. Try to set an ISBN number longer than 13 characters, and you'll be given an exception.

It's time to deal with validation. In MVC, the model is validated according to its metadata. The model (for example, the Book) has implicit metadata such as the type and nullability of a property used during the validation. For example, the Published property of the Book class is a DateTime. So, you cannot type any kind of string data into the text box representing this property, only data that can be parsed as DateTime.

The implicit metadata information is rarely enough for providing full validation for model objects. For example, the ISBN number used in AcmeLibrary should be exactly 13 characters long, and each character can be only a decimal digit. The MVC engine is not aware of this fact unless you declare it.

## Validation Attributes

The .NET base class library has a namespace called System.ComponentModel.DataAnnotations that includes attributes you can use to define validation rules declaratively. For a moment, forget that the Book class is automatically generated from the ADO.NET entity model. If you created it manually, you could decorate its properties with data annotation attributes, as shown in Listing 18-16.

**LISTING 18-16:** Data Annotation Attributes Applied for the Book class

```
public class Book
{
  public int Id { get; set; }

  [Required(ErrorMessage = "Please provide the author(s) name")]
  public string Author { get; set; }

  [Required(ErrorMessage = "Please provide a title")]
  public string Title { get; set; }

  [RegularExpression(@"[0-9]{13}$",
    ErrorMessage = " This must be exactly 13 digits")]
  public string ISBN { get; set; }

  public DateTime Published { get; set; }

  public string Publisher { get; set; }
}
```

Table 18-1 summarizes the attributes that the `System.ComponentModel.DataAnnotations` namespace provides you for validation.

**TABLE 18-1:** Validation Attributes

| ATTRIBUTE | DESCRIPTION |
| --- | --- |
| `RequiredAttribute` | This attribute specifies that when a field on a form is validated, the field must contain a value. A validation exception is raised if the property is `null`, contains an empty string (" "), or contains only white-space characters.<br><br>In the case of strings, by setting the `AllowEmptyStrings` property to `true`, you can tell the attribute that empty is a valid value. By default, this property is `false`. |
| `StringLengthAttribute` | This attribute can be used to validate the length of a string. You can specify `MinimumLength` and `MaximumLength` values, too.<br><br>The error message of this attribute supports localization also. Its default value is "`The field {0} must be a string with a maximum length of {1}`". The first placeholder is the name of the field in most cases; the second one is the maximum length of the field. The same rule applies to the minimum-length error message. |
| `RangeAttribute` | This attribute can be used to validate a numeric value to be within a range. The value itself does not have to be numeric, but it must be convertible to a numeric value via a `TypeConverter`. If these conditions are met, then the attribute will do the automatic type conversion during validation. For the type conversion, you can give the type of the value in the `OperandType` property. |
| `RegularExpressionAttribute` | This attribute can be used to match the value of the property against a regular expression. It can include formatted phone number validation, for example, but the possibilities are limitless because of the nature of regular expressions. |
| `DataTypeAttribute` | This attribute is not a real validation attribute, but derives from `ValidationAttribute`. This attribute can be used to specify what kind of data the given property holds internally (for example, when the .NET type of the property is string). |

| ATTRIBUTE | DESCRIPTION |
|-----------|-------------|
| | Following are the valid data types, the members of the `DataType` enumeration: |
| | `DateTime` |
| | `Date` |
| | `Time` |
| | `Duration` |
| | `PhoneNumber` |
| | `Currency` |
| | `Text` |
| | `Html` |
| | `MultilineText` |
| | `EmailAddress` |
| | `Password` |
| | `Url` |
| | `ImageUrl` |
| | `Custom` |
| | If `Custom` is specified as a `DataType`, then the `CustomDataType` property should be set to the name of the type. |
| `CustomValidationAttribute` | This attribute is used to perform custom validation. The `IsValid` method is invoked to perform validation. It then redirects the call to the method that is identified by the `Method` property, which, in turn, performs the actual validation. |
| | The attribute can be applied to types, properties, fields, methods, and method parameters. When it is applied to a property, the attribute is invoked whenever a value is assigned to that property. When it is applied to a method, the attribute is invoked whenever the program calls that method. When it is applied to a method parameter, the attribute is invoked before the method is called. |

## Extending the Model with Validation Metadata

The Book class is automatically generated by the ADO.NET Entity model class. You could theoretically decorate the model classes with the attributes in Table 18-1, but when you change the model, these attributes will be lost.

Automatic code generation is a frequently used technique in software development, and many Visual Studio item types also use this technique. MVC is prepared for this situation, and allows you to assign metadata to model classes through an associated metadata provider class.

Add a new code file to the Models folder and name it BookMetadata.cs. Listing 18-17 shows the code you should put into this new file.

**LISTING 18-17:** BookMetadata.cs

```csharp
using System;
using System.ComponentModel.DataAnnotations;

namespace AcmeLibrary.Models
{
  [MetadataType(typeof(BookMetadata))]
  public partial class Book
  {
    // --- Augmentation of the Book class in the model
  }

  public class BookMetadata
  {
    public int Id { get; set; }

    [Required(ErrorMessage = "Please provide the author(s) name")]
    public string Author { get; set; }

    [Required(ErrorMessage = "Please provide a title")]
    public string Title { get; set; }

    [RegularExpression(@"[0-9]{13}$",
      ErrorMessage = "ISBN must be exactly 13 digits")]
    public string ISBN { get; set; }

    public DateTime Published { get; set; }

    public string Publisher { get; set; }
  }
}
```

*Code file [BookMetadata.cs] available for download at Wrox.com*

The partial Book class in Listing 18-17 is the same class as generated by the ADO.NET entity model file (AcmeLibraryModel.edmx). Thanks to the partial definition, the code fragment in this listing decorates this class with a `MetadataType` attribute telling that `BookMetadata` contains data annotation attributes for `Book`. `BookMetadata` defines placeholder properties having the same name and type as the ones in `Book`. As a result of this definition, attributes decorating the `BookMetadata` properties are considered by the MVC framework as if those attributes were added directly to `Book` properties.

## Preparing the Controller for Validation

The current implementations of controller actions execute the related database transactions and let the database operation raise an exception. This approach is not correct for the following reasons:

➤ There is no use wasting resources on database operations if the properties are invalid. This check can be done before talking to the database.

➤ It might be that the database transactions are alright, because the action does not hurt the consistency of data. However, the current state of the model — the set of its properties — may hurt business rules.

You can check the validity of the model before executing the action expecting valid data. The key is the `ModelState` property of the controller that is a `ModelStateDictionary` instance. Using the `IsValid` property of `ModelState`, you can avoid starting an operation with invalid data. For example, you can modify the `Create` action to avoid creating a new book with wrong data:

```
[HttpPost]
public ActionResult Create(Book newBook)
{
  if (ModelState.IsValid)
  {
    try
    {
      using (var context = new AcmeLibraryDataEntities())
      {
        context.AddToBooks(newBook);
        context.SaveChanges();
      }
      return RedirectToAction("Index");
    }
    catch (Exception)
    {
      return View(newBook);
    }
  }
  return View(newBook);
}
```

The `ModelState` property contains a detailed state describing model properties and related validation errors based on the data annotations and implicit metadata belonging to the model class. If your controller has more business rules to check, you can do further validation checks.

For example, when the publication date cannot be ahead of the current calendar date by more than 180 days, you can add the following check to the `Create` method:

```
[HttpPost]
public ActionResult Create(Book newBook)
{
  if (newBook.Published != null &&
    (newBook.Published.Value - DateTime.Now).TotalDays > 180)
  {
    ModelState.AddModelError("Published",
      "A future publication date cannot be ahead more than 180 days");
  }
  if (ModelState.IsValid)
  {
    try
    {
      using (var context = new AcmeLibraryDataEntities())
      {
        context.AddToBooks(newBook);
        context.SaveChanges();
      }
      return RedirectToAction("Index");
    }
    catch (Exception)
    {
      return View(newBook);
    }
  }
  return View(newBook);
}
```

As you see, the validation check precedes checking for `ModelState.IsValid`.

## Displaying Validation Issues

By default, the view generated with the Add View command contains a placeholder for a validation summary, as the following code extract (`Create.aspx`) shows:

```
<asp:Content ID="Content2" ContentPlaceHolderID="MainContent" runat="server">
  <h2>Create</h2>
  <% using (Html.BeginForm())
     {%>
  <%: Html.ValidationSummary(true) %>
  <fieldset>
    <legend>New Book Attributes</legend>
    <div class="editor-label">
      <%: Html.LabelFor(model => model.Author) %>
    </div>
    <!-- ... -->
  </fieldset>
  <% } %>
```

```
        <div>
          <%: Html.ActionLink("Back to List", "Index") %>
        </div>
    </asp:Content>
```

The `true` argument passed to `Html.ValidationSummary` prevents the validation errors belonging to model properties from being displayed. Change it to `false` and add optional message to display validation information summary:

```
<%: Html.ValidationSummary(false, "There are some invalid input data:") %>
```

Now, when you build and run `AcmeLibrary`, you can see how the `Create` action works when you provide invalid book properties. Figure 18-23 shows several validation errors.

**Create**

There are some invalid input data:

- Please provide a title
- ISBN must be exactly 13 digits
- A future publication date cannot be ahead more than 180 days

**New Book Attributes**

Author
(Author)

Title
Please provide a title

ISBN
12345    ISBN must be exactly 13 digits

Published
2011.12.31    A future publication date cannot be ahead more than 180 days

Publisher

Create

Back to List

**FIGURE 18-23:** Validation errors shown in the Create view

You see that invalid properties are marked with a shaded background, and a message that is repeated in the validation summary.

## Managing Business Rules

The check for the future publication date you have added recently is a rule that should also be checked for the `Edit` action. One option is to copy and paste the validation code into the `Edit` method. However, when you have many rules to check, you can become confused and forget about checking each rule at both in the Create and Edit actions. The best solution is to raise validation to the model level.

There are several ways to solve this, depending on the architecture pattern — and style — you intend to use in your application. Here is one solution that adds a validation method to the Book entity class:

Add a new file named BookValidation.cs to the Models folder. Extend the Book entity class with a Validate method, as shown in Listing 18-18.

**LISTING 18-18:** BookValidation.cs

```
using System;
using System.Web.Mvc;

namespace AcmeLibrary.Models
{
  public partial class Book
  {
    public void Validate(ModelStateDictionary modelState)
    {
      if (Published != null &&
        (Published.Value - DateTime.Now).TotalDays > 180)
      {
        modelState.AddModelError("Published",
          "A future publication date cannot be ahead more than 180 days");
      }
    }
  }
}
```

*Code file [BookValidation.cs] available for download at Wrox.com*

This code is really simple, and now you can invoke Validate in the Create and Edit actions:

```
[HttpPost]
public ActionResult Create(Book newBook)
{
  newBook.Validate(ModelState);
  if (ModelState.IsValid)
  {
    // ...
  }
  return View(newBook);
}

[HttpPost]
public ActionResult Edit(Book editedBook)
```

```
{
  editedBook.Validate(ModelState);
  if (ModelState.IsValid)
  {
    // ...
  }
  return View(editedBook);
}
```

## Client-Side Validation

In many cases, most of the simple validation rules can be checked at the client side without a round-trip to the server. It's very easy to use JavaScript-based client-side validation with MVC 2. When you created the ASP.NET MVC 2 web application, the required JavaScript files were copied into the `Scripts` folder. You can easily add client-side validation support to your views. For example, you can modify the main content of the `Create.aspx` file, as the following code extract shows:

```
<asp:Content ID="Content2" ContentPlaceHolderID="MainContent" runat="server">
  <script src="/Scripts/MicrosoftAjax.js" type="text/javascript"></script>
  <script src="/Scripts/MicrosoftMvcValidation.js" type="text/javascript"></script>
  <% Html.EnableClientValidation(); %>
  <h2>Create</h2>
  <% using (Html.BeginForm())
     {%>
  <%: Html.ValidationSummary(false, "There are some invalid input data:") %>
  <fieldset>
    <legend>New Book Attributes</legend>
    <div class="editor-label">
      <%: Html.LabelFor(model => model.Author) %>
    </div>
    <!-- Other fields are omitted from this listing -->
  </fieldset>
  <% } %>
  <div>
    <%: Html.ActionLink("Back to List", "Index") %>
  </div>
</asp:Content>
```

You must add only the two `<script>` tags and use the `<% Html.EnableClientValidation %>` tag. The next time you run the application, model rules defined by the `Book` metadata are validated at the client side.

However, there are two important things you should be aware of when using the client side validation:

➤ The custom validation code you implemented explicitly at the server side (for example, the rule checking of future publication dates) is not checked — and so its failure is not indicated — at the client side. When client-side validation rules succeed, then the model data is sent to the server, and the server-side validation happens there.

> ➤ Even if you implement all validation at the client side, you must not trust only client-side validation. Robust business logic should check all business rules at the server (service) side as well.

# UI Customization

The Add View command (available in the context menu of the code editor, or from the Solution Explorer) helps you to generate a view in a few seconds. This view may be short, simple, and easy to work with, but not necessarily the one you would like to put into the live version of your application. The ASP.NET MVC 2 Framework provides you many ways to define the UI according to your style and using the standard design of your company or your customers.

In the `Views/Shared` folder, you can see that the `Site.Master` page and the `Content` folder hold the `Site.css` file. You can use the same techniques as for any other ASP.NET application to change your application's general outlook by changing/adding master files and CSS files. Because of the perspicuous structure of these files, a practiced web designer can create awesome and attractive web sites for your MVC 2 application.

However, there are some other ways you can easily customize the views in your application.

## Using Templated Helpers

MVC 2 has a new feature called *templated helpers*, probably the most important new feature for developer productivity. Earlier in this chapter, in the source code listings of views, you saw several rendering tags that were not explained there, such as the following ones:

```
<% using (Html.BeginForm()) {%>

<%: Html.LabelFor(model => model.Author) %>

<%: Html.TextBoxFor(model => model.Title) %>
<%: Html.ValidationMessageFor(model => model.Title) %>

<%: Html.ActionLink("Back to List", "Index") %>
```

The magical `Html` object that the `LabelFor`, `TextBoxFor`, and other methods are invoked on is defined in the `System.Web.Mvc.ViewPage` class the views derive from. Its type is `HtmlHelper`, which has many methods and extension methods (defined in about a dozen classes). With these extensions, you can get rid of creating HTML tags on your own. Actually, these `HtmlHelper` methods help you with the following services:

> ➤ They know how to generate HTML output for native or compound HTML controls, including their attributes.

> ➤ They can query the metadata belonging to your model, and use this information when generating the code for the view.

These methods work a bit trickier than they look. For example, the `LabelFor` method accepts a function that projects a model to a property. In the previous code snippet, a lambda expression is used to project `model` to `model.Author`. The value of this expression is retrieved as a LINQ `Expression` (defined in the `System.Linq.Expressions` namespace) and not as a simple reference to the property value. The `Expression` class is a special class (it is beyond the scope of these book to explain why), and it provides access to the metadata of properties.

So, the `LabelFor` method can access the metadata of properties and render the HTML output according to it.

*The views generated for the* `AcmeLibrary` *project are strongly typed views. Their* `<@Page>` *tag has an* `Inherits` *attribute with the value* `System.Web.Mvc .ViewPage<AcmeLibrary.Models.Book>`. *The type parameter of the* `ViewPage` *determines the type of the model the view works with, and that's how the model's metadata can be accessed.*

## Display and Edit Templates

There are two major template types within MVC: *display templates* and *edit templates*. `HtmlHelper` provides a separate set of methods available at model and at property levels to help the rendering of these templates.

These helper methods for model properties are available in two flavors. One accepts a string literal that contains the name of the property, and another one accepts an expression, as you have already seen with the `LabelFor` method. The following code snippet shows the different versions of the `Display` method rendering the `Title` property:

```
<%: Html.Display ("Title") %>
<%: Html.DisplayFor (model => model.Title) %>
```

When you're using the string literal based `Display` method, it looks for the given property in your model class, and also in the `ViewData` property belonging to the view instance.

If you want to output the editor for the same property, you can use the `Editor` method as follows:

```
<%= Html.Editor ("Title") %>
<%= Html.EditorFor (model => model.Title) %>
```

You have helper methods to display a read-only representation view or an editor view for the entire model. These are the `DisplayForModel` and `EditorForModel` methods.

```
<%= Html.DisplayForModel () %>
<%= Html.EditorForModel () %>
```

For example, you can change the `Edit.aspx` file in the `Views/Book` folder for a shorter version using the `EditorForModel` method:

```
<%@ Page Title="" Language="C#" MasterPageFile="~/Views/Shared/Site.Master"
Inherits="System.Web.Mvc.ViewPage<AcmeLibrary.Models.Book>" %>

<asp:Content ID="Content1" ContentPlaceHolderID="TitleContent" runat="server">
  Edit
</asp:Content>
<asp:Content ID="Content2" ContentPlaceHolderID="MainContent" runat="server">
  <h2>
    Edit
  </h2>
  <% using (Html.BeginForm()) {%>
  <%: Html.ValidationSummary(true) %>
  <fieldset>
    <legend>Fields</legend>
    <%: Html.EditorForModel() %>
    <p>
      <input type="submit" value="Save" />
    </p>
  </fieldset>
  <% } %>
  <div>
    <%: Html.ActionLink("Back to List", "Index") %>
  </div>
</asp:Content>
```

When you build and run `AcmeLibrary`, the rendered editor page is almost the same as the one you saw in Figure 18-20. However, in the latter case, you can edit the `Id` field as well. It's very easy to correct this behavior. Add the `HiddenInput` attribute to the `Id` property of the `BookMetadata` class:

```
// --- Add this using clause
using System.Web.Mvc;

namespace AcmeLibrary.Models
{
  // ...
  public class BookMetadata
  {
    [HiddenInput]
    public int Id { get; set; }
    // ...
  }
}
```

This attribute results in the view rendering the `Id` property in a label, so you cannot edit it. You can easily hide the `Id` (even from displaying it) by changing the `HiddenInput` attribute:

```
[HiddenInput(DisplayValue = false)]
public int Id { get; set; }
```

What is happening behind the scenes?

ASP.NET MVC 2 ships with a default set of code-only templates for different data types. Template rendering is that part of MVC where the metadata associated with model controls the HTML output.

Each property is rendered with two parts: a label and a field. The default templates assign predefined CSS classes to the HTML tags, and it makes much easier to put together a website with great design. Listing 18-19 shows the HTML content rendered from Edit.aspx.

---

**LISTING 18-19:** HTML Rendered from Edit.aspx

```
<h2>Edit</h2>
<form action="/Book/Edit/3" method="post">
  <fieldset>
    <legend>Fields</legend>
    <input id="Id" name="Id" type="hidden" value="3" />
    <div class="editor-label"><label for="Author">Author</label></div>
    <div class="editor-field">
      <input class="text-box single-line" id="Author" name="Author"
        type="text" value="Barry Dorrans" />
    </div>
    <div class="editor-label"><label for="Title">Title</label></div>
    <div class="editor-field">
      <input class="text-box single-line" id="Title" name="Title"
        type="text" value="Beginning ASP.NET Security" />
    </div>
    <div class="editor-label"><label for="ISBN">ISBN</label></div>
    <div class="editor-field"><input class="text-box single-line"
      id="ISBN" name="ISBN" type="text" value="9780470743652" />
    </div>
    <div class="editor-label">
      <label for="Published">Published</label>
    </div>
    <div class="editor-field">
      <input class="text-box single-line" id="Published"
        name="Published" type="text" value="2010.04.12. 0:00:00" />
    </div>
    <div class="editor-label">
      <label for="Publisher">Publisher</label>
    </div>
    <div class="editor-field">
      <input class="text-box single-line"
        id="Publisher" name="Publisher" type="text" value="Wrox" />
    </div>
    <p><input type="submit" value="Save" /></p>
  </fieldset>
</form>
<div>
  <a href="/Book">Back to List</a>
</div>
```

You can clearly recognize the class attributes such as `editor-label`, `editor-field`, `text-box`, `single-line`, and so on.

## Metadata Attributes

Earlier in this chapter in Table 18-1, you saw a few data annotation attributes that provide validation metadata to a model. MVC provides data annotations that provide metadata for rendering a view. MVC 2 introduced many new metadata types. Figure 18-24 shows two data annotation hierarchies. The left side shows annotations in MVC 1.0, and the right side shows them in MVC 2.

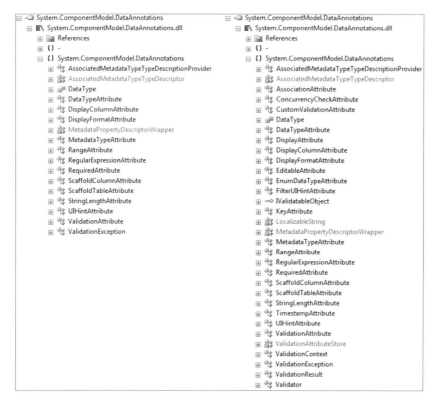

**FIGURE 18-24:** Data annotations in MVC and MVC 2

Let's take a look at the most important attributes decorating a model.

### DisplayColumnAttribute

This attribute can be used on properties represented by .NET classes or child models. (You could even call them *compound properties*.) When MVC renders a property with this attribute, it will display the given property values of the class behind the property. Let's take a look at an example in the form of a partial model code snippet:

```
public class MoneyTransfer
{
  // other model properties

  [DisplayColumn ("FullName")]
  public Person Customer { get; set; }
}

public class Person
{
  public string FirstName { get; set; }
  public string LastName { get; set; }
  public string FullName
  {
    get { return FirstName + " " + LastName; }
  }
}
```

When you create a view for `MoneyTransfer`, the `Customer` property will display the `FullName` of the related `Person` instance.

### DisplayFormatAttribute

This attribute allows you to control how the given property is formatted during the rendering process. Possible uses include `Date`, `DateTime`, `Time`, and `Currency` formatting. This attribute supports the standard .NET formatting characters and placeholders.

If a `DataTypeAttribute` also decorates a specific property, `DisplayFormat` is overridden by `DataTypeAttribute`. In real-world scenarios, these two attributes are rarely used with the same model properties.

### ScaffoldColumnAttribute

If you add this attribute to a property with the value of `false`, the model level template render helper within MVC will not render the given property.

 Scaffolding *is the mechanism for generating web page templates based on database schemas. ASP.NET Dynamic Data uses scaffolding to generate a Web-based UI that lets a user view and update a database. This class uses the* `Scaffold` *property to enable scaffolding in a Dynamic Data Web Site. Scaffolding enhances the ASP.NET page framework by dynamically displaying pages based on the data model with no physical pages required. You can find more details about scaffolding in Chapter 17.*

### UIHintAttribute

When the template is rendered for a model, the type of the property or the decorating `DataTypeAttribute` determines the HTML control used to represent the property. In many cases, it does not provide enough control over rendering. The `UIHintAttribute` allows specifying the template or user control to display a data field (model property).

Later in this chapter, you will see an example of using this attribute.

## DisplayAttribute

This is a general-purpose attribute that lets you specify localizable strings for types and members of entities used in models. `DisplayAttribute` has a single default constructor, and several properties. These properties are summarized in Table 18-2.

**TABLE 18-2:** DisplayAttribute Properties

| PROPERTY | DESCRIPTION |
| --- | --- |
| AutoGenerateField | Sets a value that indicates whether the UI should be generated automatically in order to display this field. |
| AutoGenerateFilter | Sets a value that indicates whether a filtering UI is automatically displayed for this field. |
| Description | Sets a value that is used to display a description in the UI. This property is typically used as a tooltip or description UI element that is bound to the member using this attribute. |
| GroupName | Sets a value that is used to group fields in the UI. |
| Name | Sets a value that is used for display in the UI. The name is typically used as the field label for a UI element that is bound to the property that is annotated with this attribute. |
| Order | Sets the order weight of the column. Columns are sorted in increasing order based on the order value. Columns without this attribute have an order value of 0. Negative values are valid and can be used to position a column before all non-negative columns. If an order is not specified, presentation layers should consider using the value 10,000. This value lets explicitly ordered fields be displayed before and after the fields that do not have a specified order. |
| Prompt | Sets a value that will be used to set the watermark for prompts in the UI. |
| ResourceType | Gets or sets the type that contains the resources for the ShortName, Name, Prompt, and Description properties. If this value is null, the ShortName, Name, Prompt, and Description properties are assumed to be literal, non-localized strings. If this value is not null, the string properties are assumed to be the names of public static properties that return the actual string value. |
| ShortName | Gets or sets a value that is used for the grid column label. |

Although all properties in Table 18-2 have getter and setter accessors, do not use the properties to access values behind them. Instead, use the appropriate `Get` method suffixed with the property name. For example, you can access the value of the `Description` property with the `GetDescription` method. The only exceptions are `ResourceType` and `ShortName`, where you can use both accessors.

### HiddenInputAttribute

By adding this attribute to a property, you can tell the default template rendering helper to render the property in edit mode as an `<input>` HTML tag with hidden type. Or, if you set its `DisplayValue` property to `false`, it will not render anything in display mode.

### DisplayNameAttribute

This attribute is not a data annotation. It is a member of the `System.ComponentModel` namespace and it is used by .NET UI frameworks since .NET 2.0. MVC also utilizes this attribute during rendering the views. You can define labels of properties with it. For example, you can change the default `"Author"` label with the following code snippet:

```
public class BookMetadata
{
  // ...
  [DisplayName("Author(s) name:")]
  public string Author { get; set; }
  // ...
}
```

## Custom Templates

The Add View command you used to generate view classes uses default templates that are very useful for creating a simple application. However, you, your company, or your customer probably have different conventions for creating a website, including design, layout, behavior, and many other things. You can write your own templates to customize the exact rendering of all your data types. Handling them is very easy, because these templates are partial views stored within your project.

Table 18-3 summarizes the locations where your templates can be stored.

**TABLE 18-3:** Custom Template Locations

| LOCATION | DESCRIPTION |
| --- | --- |
| /Views/Shared/Displaytemplates | This folder holds all the shared templates used by the display helpers. Shared templates can be used by any controller defined in your MVC 2 project. |
| /Views/Shared/EditorTemplates | This folder contains the shared templates used by the editor helpers. |

*continues*

**TABLE 18-3** *(continued)*

| LOCATION | DESCRIPTION |
|---|---|
| /Views/*Controller*/<br>    DisplayTemplates | This folder holds controller-specific templates used by the *Controller* tag in the path is the name of the controller the templates belong to. |
| /Views/*Controller*/EditorTemplates | This folder contains the controller-specific templates used by the editor helpers. |

To demonstrate how easy UI customization is with templates, let's change AcmeLibrary. You have probably noticed that sometimes the title information and author names do not fit into the textbox displayed in the Edit view. You can change the rendering of these textboxes, and this could be useful for other controllers as well.

Create a new folder under Views/Shared and name it EditorTemplates. This is the location to place the editor templates shared among views. Add a new MVC 2 View User Control item into this folder (with the Add ⇨ New Item command in the context menu), and name it LongerText.ascx. Type the very short source code shown in Listing 18-20 into this file.

**LISTING 18-20: LongerText.ascx**

```
<%@ Control Language="C#" Inherits="System.Web.Mvc.ViewUserControl<string>" %>
<%: Html.TextBox(String.Empty, Model, new { style="width: 240pt"}) %>
```

*Code file [LongerText.cs] available for download at Wrox.com*

The user control is derived from the ViewUserControl<> class of the System.Web.Mvc namespace, and it is a strongly typed view using string, as the type parameter of the class indicates. Here the TextBox helper method is used to render the HTML output. The second parameter, Model, is the object representing the property used as the model for this user control. Now, the first parameter is an empty string, signaling that the Model directly holds the information to show. But you could use a non-empty string here to name a specific property to be used by the control. The third parameter is an anonymous object instance that instructs the Htm.TextBox method to render the input control with the specified style attribute that is used to set the width of the textbox.

Create an EditorTemplates folder under Views/Book to create a template for displaying the Publisher field as a drop-down list. Any templates in this folder can be used only by the BookController class. Add a new MVC 2 View User Control into this folder with the name Publisher.ascx, and copy the code shown in Listing 18-21 into this file.

**LISTING 18-21: Publisher.ascx**

```
<%@ Control Language="C#" Inherits="System.Web.Mvc.ViewUserControl<string>" %>
<%: Html.DropDownList("", new SelectList(new []
    {
      new {name="Self-Published"},
      new {name="Wrox" },
      new {name="Wiley"},
      new {name="(unknown)"}
    },
    "name", "name",
    Model),
    "Select a publisher") %>
```

*Code file [Publisher.ascx] available for download at Wrox.com*

This user control uses the DropDownList helper method. It passes an instance of SelectList initialized with a collection of objects to be shown in the lists. The two "name" literals passed to the SelectList constructor signal that both the identifier of a list item and its displayed content is the value of the name property.

You must tell the template generator that these custom templates should be used when generating the Edit view for the BookController class. It is very easy; you simply add UIHint attributes to the BookMetadata class. You can also add several DisplayName properties to change the label of the properties.

Listing 18-22 shows how to change the BookMetadata class.

**LISTING 18-22: BookMetadata.cs (extract)**

```
public class BookMetadata
{
  [HiddenInput(DisplayValue = false)]
  public int Id { get; set; }

  [Required(ErrorMessage = "Please provide the author(s) name")]
  [DisplayName("Author(s) name:")]
  [UIHint("LongerText")]
  public string Author { get; set; }

  [Required(ErrorMessage = "Please provide a title")]
  [DisplayName("Title of the book:")]
  [UIHint("LongerText")]
  public string Title { get; set; }

  [RegularExpression(@"[0-9]{13}$",
    ErrorMessage = "ISBN must be exactly 13 digits")]
  [DisplayName("ISBN-13:")]
  public string ISBN { get; set; }
```

*continues*

**LISTING 18-22** *(continued)*

```
[DisplayName("Date of publication:")]
public DateTime Published { get; set; }

[DisplayName("Published by:")]
[UIHint("Publisher")]
public string Publisher { get; set; }
}
```

*Code file [BookMetadata.cs] available for download at Wrox.com*

Build and run the `AcmeLibrary` project and select a book to edit. You can immediately see the changes, as shown in Figure 18-25.

The Publisher field now uses a drop-down list. The Author and Title properties have a longer textbox, and all properties have new labels.

## View Engines

The *view engine* is the component that is responsible for rendering the content of a view. Out of the box, Microsoft ASP.NET MVC 2 provides a Web Forms-based view engine implementation. However, this does not mean that using Web Form-esque is the only way to represent your views.

MVC uses the `IViewEngine` interface to define the responsibilities of a view engine, and its default implementation is `WebFormViewEngine` (both types are in the `System.Web.Mvc` namespace). So, if you are familiar with ASP.NET development, constructing the views for an MVC application will be easy.

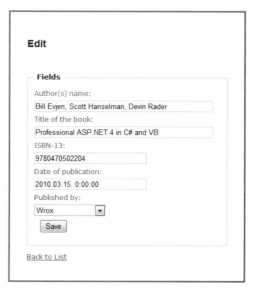

**FIGURE 18-25:** The Edit view using custom templates

The definition of the `IViewEngine` interface is as follows:

```
namespace System.Web.Mvc
{
  public interface IViewEngine
  {
    ViewEngineResult FindPartialView(
      ControllerContext controllerContext,
      string partialViewName,
      bool useCache);

    ViewEngineResult FindView(
```

```
        ControllerContext controllerContext,
        string viewName,
        string masterName,
        bool useCache);

    void ReleaseView(
        ControllerContext controllerContext,
        IView view);
    }
}
```

The default `WebFormViewEngine` implementation derives from the `VirtualPathProviderViewEngine` abstract class that is an ASP.NET-based implementation, but is not Web Forms-specific. This class is using ASP.NET's virtual path provider-based support for view discovery.

There are other alternative view engine implementations you can use with MVC, as shown in Table 18-4.

**TABLE 18-4:** Alternative View Engines

| VIEW ENGINE | DESCRIPTION |
|---|---|
| Spark View Engine | The Spark View Engine is a full-blown view engine with its own text template engine behind it. The goal of this engine is to reduce the clutter in your views, and provide a cleaner HTML. (See `http://dev.dejardin.org`.) |
| Brail View Engine | This view engine is a .NET port from MonoRail. The template language used for this engine is Boo. The reason behind this is that, when using the MonoRail framework, you can write your code in Boo, too, so you don't have to learn a new template language for authoring your views. <br><br> This project is available within the popular `MVCContrib` project on CodePlex at `http://mvccontrib.codeplex.com`. |
| Sharp Tiles View Engine | This view engine uses a JavaServer Pages Standard Tag Library (JSTL) syntax-based template engine. In this way, it brings the JSTL syntax to ASP.NET MVC applications. (See `http://sharptiles.org`.) |
| NHaml View Engine | This view engine is a .NET port of the popular Haml view engine available on Rails. The design goal of this markup language is to make it possible to write clean XHTML-compatible HTML without the inline usage of code blocks. (See `http://code.google.com/p/nhaml`.) |
| NDjango View Engine | Django (which is the base of the .NET implementation of this engine) is a template language for Python developers. NDjango is the .NET port and out-of-the-box it has a view engine implementation for ASP.NET MVC. (See `http://ndjango.org`.) |

As you can see, you have plenty of choices to author your views, and it almost does not matter what developer background you have. With the different available view engines, you probably will find one that you can use to begin to work with.

## ROUTING DETAILS

The routing component is the soul of the MVC framework. It provides an intuitive way of mapping requests to controller classes and action methods. Its implementation is very sophisticated, letting you declaratively control how action methods are executed, and allowing you to handle aspects such as authorization, request and result filtering. As with all components in the MVC framework, routing is also extensible.

This section provides important details about routing.

## Controller Factory

Earlier in this chapter during the discussion of the routing algorithm (take another look at Figure 18-9 and Figure 18-10), you learned that, after MvcHandler receives a request, it needs to look for a controller that is associated with the RouteData of the request. To achieve this task, the handler extracts the mandatory "controller" parameter from the associated RouteData and uses the Controller Factory component that knows how to instantiate the controller.

The Controller Factory's responsibility is described by the IControllerFactory interface:

```
namespace System.Web.Mvc
{
  using System.Web.Routing;

  public interface IControllerFactory
  {
      IController CreateController(
        RequestContext requestContext,
        string controllerName);

      void ReleaseController(IController controller);
  }
}
```

As you see, the interface has only two methods: CreateController (which instantiates) and ReleaseController (which destroys the controller). Of course, in the MVC framework, you have a default implementation, the DefaultControllerFactory class. This class uses reflection-based type resolution by searching the default namespaces for a class that has the given name with the Controller suffix and implements the IController interface.

Because the Controller Factory is the component that knows how to instantiate a specific controller, in TDD scenarios, you can use a factory that is capable of injecting the appropriate domain model (data access) layer into your controllers.

In the examples for this chapter, all controllers (HomeController, AboutController, and BookController) are defined in the same assembly and in the same namespace, so the MVC engine can easily find the appropriate controller class by names such as "Home", "About," and "Book." However, you may have controllers in external assemblies where the classes are in a separate namespaces. So, how can the name of the controller be resolved?

The Controller Factory can handle this scenario. You have a few ways to declare the external namespaces where the DefaultControllerFactory searches for the controller classes. One place is to describe the external namespace definition is the MapRoute method (remember, the RegisterRoutes method utilizes MapRoute in the Global.asax.cs file), as shown here:

```
routes.MapRoute(
  "RouteWithNamespaceTag",
  "/{controller}/{action}",
  new
  {
    controller = "ControllerInExternalAssembly",
    action = "Index"
  },
  new[]
  {
    "MyApp.ExternalControllers.Controllers"
  }
);
```

The DefaultControllerFactory implementation looks for controller types in an application-level namespace registry within the ControllerBuilder class. The previous namespace can be added to the namespace registry with the following statement:

```
ControllerBuilder.Current.DefaultNamespaces.
  Add("MyApp.ExternalControllers.Controllers");
```

## Influencing the Execution Flow

After the controller type is resolved and the controller instance is created, the DefaultControllerFactory invokes the Execute method of the controller.

The responsibility of a controller is defined by the IController interface. MVC defines a ControllerBase abstract class to be the base class for all MVC controllers, and derives the Controller class from it. Controller provides methods that respond to HTTP requests sent to an ASP.NET MVC web site.

The action execution logic is much more flexible than simply invoking the Execute method, as shown in Figure 18-26.

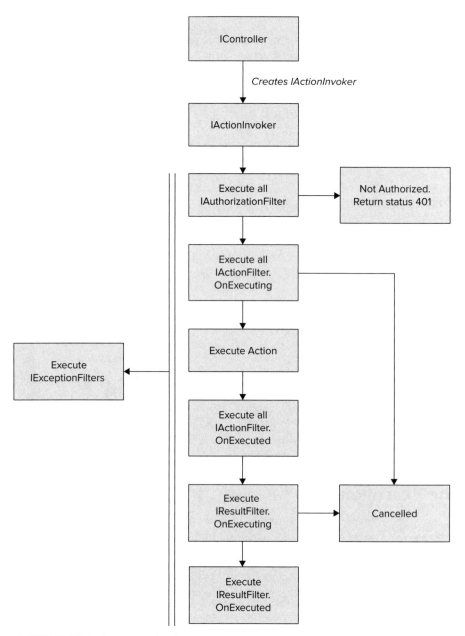

**FIGURE 18-26:** Action execution flow

MVC 2 makes this flow extensible. It allows you to influence the flow in an aspect-oriented manner. You can use .NET attributes to inject these aspects into your code.

# Authorization

Before executing any action, the controller check attributes implementing the
`IAuthorizationFilter` interface:

```
public interface IAuthorizationFilter
{
  void OnAuthorization(AuthorizationContext filterContext);
}
```

If the invocation of `OnAuthorization` signals that authorization fails, an `HttpUnauthorizedResult`
is set for the current context, and the further execution is interrupted. There are a few
attributes implementing `IAuthorizationFilter`. Let's take a look at a few of them. Of course,
you can create your own `IAuthorizationFilter` attributes.

## AuthorizationAttribute

By default, any user can execute an action. However, you can restrict the scope of authorized
users by decorating an action with the `AuthorizeAttribute`:

```
[Authorize(Users="Joe, Zana", Roles="Admins, Managers")]
public ActionResult CheckAccount ()
{
}
```

This example shows how easy it is to use this attribute. You can define the users allowed to execute
an action by their user name or the names of roles they are in. `CheckAccount` can be executed by all
users that are named `Joe` or `Zana`, or all users having at least one of the `Admins` and `Managers` roles.

`AuthorizeAttribute` allows authorization based on the logged-in user's name or role membership.
This attribute can be applied at class or method level; multiple definitions are allowed at one place.

## ChildActionOnlyAttribute

You can create an action whose sole purpose is to be invoked from other actions as a child action.
In this case, it doesn't make sense for anyone to invoke that action directly through an HTTP
request. The `ChildActionOnlyAttribute` blocks an action's execution if it is not a child action of
another action. This means that, from a URL, this action is not callable, but it's callable during the
rendering of a view through the `HtmlHelper` class's `Action` or `RenderAction` methods.

```
[ChildActionOnly]
public ActionResult RenderSiteStatistics ()
{
}
```

If someone does navigate to a URL that maps to `RenderSiteStatistics`, the filter will block the
request by throwing an `InvalidOperationException`, saying, "The action 'RenderSiteStatistics' is
accessible only by a child request."

## RequireHttpsAttribute

This attribute checks the current HTTP request's `IsSecureConnection` property, and only allows the action to execute it when the request was done through a secure connection (such as the HTTPS protocol).

```
[RequireHttps]
public ActionResult LoginUser (string username, string clearTextPassword)
{
}
```

## ValidateAntiForgeryTokenAttribute

This attribute checks the presence of a specially formatted cookie and hidden form field's value. If all the required data is there and is valid, the action can be executed.

This attribute tries to prevent an action from getting executed during a cross-site scripting (XSS) attack. `ValidateAntiForgeryAttribute` should be only applied to an action that is allowed to execute during an HTTP POST request. As a prerequisite, a call must be made to the `HtmlHelper` class's `AntiForgeryToken` method, which puts the required data into the action's result.

```
[HttpPost]
[ValidateAntiForgeryToken]
public ActionResult XSSProtectedAction ()
{
}
```

The related view should look like this:

```
<% using(Html.BeginForm()) { %>
  <%: Html.AntiForgeryToken() %>
  <!-- Form field definitions -->
<% } %>
```

This view will be rendered something like the following HTML fragment:

```
<form action="/Book/Edit" method="post" >
  <input name="__RequestVerificationToken" type="hidden" value="Ac/
    +BHd54K-/as67G..." />
  <!-- Form field definitions -->
</form>
```

## ValidateInputAttribute

If you want to disable validation either for a specific action method or across a specific controller, you can use the `ValidateInputAttribute`:

```
[ValidateInput (EnableValidation=false)]
public ActionResult ThisMethodCanNotContainDangerousRequestData ()
{
}
```

Unfortunately, to use `ValidateInputAttribute` with .NET 4, you must also make a further configuration change. To successfully disable request validation, you must add the following to your `web.config` file:

```
<configuration>
  <system.web>
    <httpRuntime requestValidationMode="2.0"/>
  </system.web>
</configuration>
```

This is because the request processing pipeline was changed in .NET 4.

## Action and Result Filtering

When the user is authorized to execute an action (all attributes implementing `IAuthorizationFilter` allowed to go on with the execution), the real action execution is wrapped by objects implementing `IActionFilter`:

```
public interface IActionFilter
{
  void OnActionExecuting(ActionExecutingContext filterContext);
  void OnActionExecuted(ActionExecutedContext filterContext);
}
```

The objects implementing these two interface methods should be attributes decorating the action method. The MVC framework provides the abstract `ActionFilterAttribute` class to derive your own filter attributes.

First, all `OnActionExecuting` methods are called. This method receives the execution context information as its argument. It can return an `ActionResult` or a `null` value if the filter does not want to alter the result. A `Cancel` property is defined in the `ActionExecutingContext` class so that the method can flag the cancellation of the action to prevent it from being executed.

If the filter does not cancel the action and an exception is raised, the body of the action method is executed.

After the execution of the action, the `OnActionExecuted` method is invoked — in the reverse order as `OnActionExecuting` methods were called. At this point of execution, there is some kind of `ActionResult` available.

Before returning the result to the user, the next step of the processing pipeline is to use the `IResultFilter` interface:

```
public interface IResultFilter
{
  void OnResultExecuting(ResultExecutingContext filterContext);
  void OnResultExecuted(ResultExecutedContext filterContext);
}
```

You can use the `ActionFilterAttribute` class to derive your own result filtering attributes, just as in the case of action filtering. The execution logic of `OnResultExecuting` and `OnResultExecuted` methods is exactly the same as the logic for `OnActionExecuting` and `OnActionExecuted`. The `Cancel` property or the `ResultExecutingContext` passed to these methods can be set to `true` to prevent the other filters in the row from being invoked.

Both the `OnActionExecuted` and `OnResultExecuted` methods can receive the exception thrown by the action, and they can process them.

## Exception Filtering

If an exception was thrown during the execution, it's available for examination in the `OnActionExecuted` and `OnResultExecuted` methods. If an exception can be handled, the `ExceptionHandled` property of the executing context can be set to `true`. If it does not happen, the exception will be propagated up in the execution chain.

If there is an unhandled exception raised during the action, the `IExceptionFilter` interface gets the role:

```
public interface IExceptionFilter
{
  void OnException(ExceptionContext filterContext);
}
```

The framework invokes the `OnException` method of all attributes implementing `IExceptionFilter`. The MVC framework provides you the `HandleErrorAttribute` class with the default behavior of redirecting you to an error page that displays the exception raised. Of course, you may create your own exception filters if you need them.

## ActionResult

You have already met the `ViewResult` class, which is the one generally retrieved by action methods in the `BookController` class. There are a plethora of classes representing the results (outcomes) of actions. All these classes inherit the abstract `ActionResult` class having the following simple definition:

```
public abstract class ActionResult
{
  public abstract void ExecuteResult(ControllerContext context);
}
```

MVC 2 ships with about a dozen classes deriving from `ActionResult`, as shown in Table 18-5.

**TABLE 18-5:** ActionResult Derived Classes

| TYPE | DESCRIPTION |
| --- | --- |
| EmptyResult | This class represents a result instructing the controller to take no action. Returning an EmptyResult.Instance from your action is like returning a null from a method. In this case, nothing will be written into the HTTP response. You may have several reasons to use this type. For example, it can be a result of a security-related action where you don't want to expose anything to the end user. |
| HttpUnauthorizedResult | This class represents the result of an unauthorized HTTP request. If you return a new instance of this class, it will end up in an HTTP status 401 message (which is the standard status code for unauthorized access). Usually, this result is returned from a class implementing the IAuthorizationFilter interface. |
| ContentResult | This class represents a user-defined content type that is the result of an action method. You can have arbitrary content and set it through the Content, ContentType, and ContentEncoding properties. |
| JavaScriptResult | The name of the class speaks for itself, as it retrieves JavaScript content. You can use its Script property to set the script to return. |
| JsonResult | This class is suitable to serialize a .NET class for client-side script consumption (for example, as a result of an Ajax call). With the properties this class provides, you can be in total control of how the data should be serialized to the client. This class has a property named JsonRequestBehavior that, by default, denies the execution of an action for the HTTP GET verb. If you want to allow an action to return JavaScript Object Notation (JSON) content for a GET request, you should set this property to JsonRequestBehavior.AllowGet. |
| RedirectResult | This result can be used to redirect the user to another URL at the end of the action. One of the examples is when you have finished editing a book selection and you're redirecting the user to the Book list view. |
| RedirectToRouteResult | This result is similar to RedirectResult, but instead of a hard-coded URL, you can refer to one of the registered routes within the application. |

*continues*

**TABLE 18-5** *(continued)*

| TYPE | DESCRIPTION |
|------|-------------|
| `FileResult` | This type is an abstract class and serves as a base class for returning a HTTP response with the `Content-Disposition` HTTP header value. |
| `FileContentResult` | This `FileResult` derived class can supply a `byte` array, and that array will be written as a file into the response stream. |
| `FilePathResult` | This `FileResult` derived class can provide a server-side filename with an absolute path, and the contents of the file will be written into the response stream. |
| `FileStreamResult` | This `FileResult` derived class can supply an opened `Stream` object, and that stream will be written into the response stream. The content of the stream will be written in 4,096-byte long chunks. |
| `ViewResultBase` | This abstract class serves as a base class for returning rendered HTML content to the user. |
| `PartialViewResult` | This result type is returning a partial view to the user. It derives from `ViewResultBase`. |
| `ViewResult` | This class represents the most commonly used `ActionResult` type. It returns the complete rendered HTML pages to the user. |

## TESTING WITH MVC 2

As mentioned earlier in this chapter, MVC 2 was designed and implemented with TDD in mind. This chapter would not be complete if you could not see how great MVC is when combined with TDD.

Of course, it is beyond the scope of this book to thoroughly examine TDD. However, you can learn how to create unit tests in conjunction with MVC, and this is the most important step if you want to deal with TDD.

In this section, you'll learn about a version of `AcmeLibrary` that has been refactored to support unit testing. You do not have to carry out every step to change the application; you can download the source code from the book's companion web site (`www.wrox.com`).

## Refactoring AcmeLibrary

A good testing approach is where you can test the concerns (the model, the view, and the controller) separately from each other. When testing an MVC application, the most challenging part is the controller.

The model generally can be tested separately from other parts of the application — with the well-known unit testing techniques — because it is independent from the view and from the controller. The view is just plain UI, and the only logic behind it is the one that simply binds the element of the model to the elements of the UI.

However, testing a controller is tougher, because it has a dependency on the underlying model that generally uses some kind of persistence. If you want to test a controller separately from the model, your model must be mocked, and there also must be a way to inject a model into the controller. When your live application runs, the controller gets the real model instance; when it is unit tested, a fake model can be injected into it.

Using a fake model is important from the TDD perspective. Even if you do not have your model implemented, you must be able to test a controller — and that is where you are going to use the fake model.

## What Needs to Be Changed?

There are several ways to satisfy controller testing requirements, and one possibility is demonstrated here. This approach applies the following refactoring steps on the `AcmeLibrary` MVC web application to support writing unit tests for the `BookController` class:

➤ The application uses the interface-based development pattern to define the responsibilities of the model (`Book`) as an interface (`IBook`).

➤ With the help of the repository pattern, the model operations executed by the `BookController` class have been extracted into a repository interface (`IBookRepository`).

➤ The `BookController` class has been refactored so that it can accept an injected model.

➤ A new unit test project has been added to the solution.

➤ The classes defining the domain model of the `AcmeLibrary` application (entity interface, repository interface) have been moved to a separate assembly that can be referenced by both the web application's assembly and from the unit test's assembly.

➤ A fake model class (fake repository) has been defined for unit test purposes.

➤ A few unit test method has been coded.

You may think that these steps generate a lot of work. Yes that's true — however, it's not so much. But there are a few arguments that are worth mentioning:

➤ If you start designing and implementing your MVC application with testing in mind, you do not need to change the application. You can build it right in the proper way.

➤ With refactoring tools, you can automate most of the refactoring work. For example, you can extract the model and repository interfaces from the current implementation classes.

➤ Tests applied from the beginning of the implementation give you confidence and mitigate the risk of bugs discovered too late — assuming they run successfully, and bugs discovered are fixed.

So, let's see how these changes have been applied to the `AcmeLibrary` application.

## New Project Structure

The `AcmeLibrary` solution treated by now in this chapter contains only one project — the one created as an ASP.NET MVC 2 web application. It has been changed to include two more projects, as shown in Figure 18-27.

Most of the code still remains in the `AcmeLibrary` project, but the interfaces representing the domain model (`IBook` and `IBookRepository`) have been extracted into a separate `AcmeDomain` assembly. The `AcmeLibraryTest` project is a container for unit tests.

**FIGURE 18-27:** The new AcmeLibrary solution structure

 *When you create a new ASP.NET MVC 2 project, Visual Studio lets you create a test project immediately, as shown earlier in Figure 18-5.*

## Setting Up the Domain Model

The `AcmeLibrary` application works with `Book` as the most important entity. `BookController` defines the interaction logic and also invokes the persistence services provided by the `AcmeLibraryDataEntities` class generated from the entity model. To separate the `BookController` class from the persistence services — using the Repository Pattern — the `IBookResository` interface has been extracted, as shown in Listing 18-23.

**LISTING 18-23: IBookRepository.cs**

```
using System.Linq;

namespace AcmeDomain
{
  public interface IBookRepository
  {
    IQueryable<IBook> GetBooks();
    IBook GetBookById(int id);
    IBook CreateBook();
    void InsertBook(IBook book);
    void SaveBook(IBook book);
    void DeleteBook(int id);
  }
}
```

*Code file [IBookRepository.cs] available for download at Wrox.com*

This interface defines operations used by the action methods in BookController. This definition is simple. Only two things require further explanation:

➤   The Book class is defined in the AcmeLibrary project (and it is automatically generated), so it cannot be moved to a separate assembly. A great solution could be to extract an abstract BookBase class from Book, but that does not work because Book must be derived from EntityObject. So, the properties of a book are represented as an IBook interface.

➤   The GetBooks method retrieves an IQueryable<IBook> instance to leverage the query composition features of LINQ.

Listing 18-24 shows the IBook interface representing the main entity used by the repository.

**LISTING 18-24: IBook.cs**

```
using System;
using System.Collections.Generic;

namespace AcmeDomain
{
  public interface IBook
  {
    // --- Attributes
    int Id { get; set; }
    string Author { get; set; }
    string Title { get; set; }
    string ISBN { get; set; }
    DateTime? Published { get; set; }
    string Publisher { get; set; }

    // --- Entity operations
    IDictionary<string, object> Validate();
  }
}
```

*Code file [IBook.cs] available for download at Wrox.com*

Notice the Validate method that can be used to check the integrity of an IBook instance.

## Implementing the Repository

The data persistence operations can easily be refactored from the BookController class. The BookRepository class in the Models folder implements the IBookRepository interface, as the code extract in Listing 18-25 shows.

**LISTING 18-25:** BookRepository.cs (extract)

```csharp
using System;
using System.Linq;
using AcmeDomain;

namespace AcmeLibrary.Models
{
    public IBook GetBookById(int id)
    {
      using (var context = new AcmeLibraryDataEntities())
      {
        var book = context.Books.First(b => b.Id == id);
        if (book != null) context.Detach(book);
        return book;
      }
    }

    public void InsertBook(IBook book)
    {
      var newBook = book as Book;
      if (newBook == null)
        throw new ArgumentException("AcmeLibrary.Model.Book expected.", "book");
      using (var context = new AcmeLibraryDataEntities())
      {
        context.AddToBooks(newBook);
        context.SaveChanges();
      }
    }
    // --- Other methods are omitted from this listing
  }
}
```

*Code file [BookRepository.cs] available for download at Wrox.com*

The BookController class does not consume BookRepository directly. Instead, it uses the repository interface, as the shown in the code extract in Listing 18-26.

**LISTING 18-26:** BookController.cs (extract)

```csharp
using System;
using System.Web.Mvc;
using AcmeDomain;
using AcmeLibrary.Models;

namespace AcmeLibrary.Controllers
{
  public class BookController : Controller
```

```csharp
{
  private readonly IBookRepository _BookRepository;

  public BookController()
  {
    _BookRepository = ServiceLocator.GetInstance(
      typeof(IBookRepository)) as IBookRepository;
  }

  public BookController(IBookRepository repository)
  {
    _BookRepository = repository;
  }

  public ActionResult Index()
  {
    return View(_BookRepository.GetBooks());
  }

  [HttpPost]
  public ActionResult Create(Book newBook)
  {
    ValidateBook(newBook);
    if (ModelState.IsValid)
    {
      try
      {
        _BookRepository.InsertBook(newBook);
        return RedirectToAction("Index");
      }
      catch (Exception)
      {
        return View(newBook);
      }
    }
    return View(newBook);
  }

  private void ValidateBook(IBook book)
  {
    var result = book.Validate();
    if (result == null) return;
    foreach (var item in result)
    {
      ModelState.AddModelError(item.Key, item.Value.ToString());
    }
  }
  // --- Other methods are omitted from this listing
}
}
```

*Code file [BookController.cs] available for download at Wrox.com*

The class utilizes the _BookRepository field to store a reference to the IBookRepository used in persistence operations. The default constructor uses the ServiceLocator static class to inject the appropriate repository instance into the controller. There is another constructor where you can inject a custom repository instance into BookController.

The BookRepository class is injected into BookController in the Application_Start method of the Global.asax.cs file:

```
protected void Application_Start()
{
  ServiceLocator.RegisterInstance<IBookRepository>(
    typeof(BookRepository));
  AreaRegistration.RegisterAllAreas();
  RegisterRoutes(RouteTable.Routes);
}
```

> *The ServiceLocator class is a very lightweight implementation of the Service Locator pattern. (Its source code is available for download at www.wrox.com.) It does not use a Dependency Injection container behind it, just for the sake of simplicity. In real life, it is always worth it to use a Dependency Injection container, because it adds a lot of value as you extend your application.*
>
> *You can also implement a different pattern. You may leave the default constructor of the BookController class and create a custom controller factory that injects the repository instance into the controller.*

### Attaching Book to IBook

In the domain model, the IBook interface represents the properties and validation behavior of a book. The real persistence model is defined by the AcmeLibraryModel.edmx file that automatically generates the Book class. Listing 18-27 shows how to declare that the automatically generated Book is an implementation of IBook.

**LISTING 18-27:** BookValidation.cs

```
using System;
using System.Collections.Generic;
using AcmeDomain;

namespace AcmeLibrary.Models
{
  public partial class Book: IBook
  {
    public IDictionary<string, object> Validate()
    {
      return Published == null ||
```

```
                (Published.Value - DateTime.Now).TotalDays <= 180
                  ? null
                  : new Dictionary<string, object>
                  {
                    { "Published",
                      "A future publication date cannot be ahead more than 180 days"}
                  };
          }
        }
      }
```

<hr />

*Code file [BookValidation.cs] available for download at Wrox.com*

This file contains a partial class definition, so the Book class fragment here is merged with the fragment defined by the AcmeLibraryModel.edmx.cs file. Because of the specification of partial classes in C#, you can "inject" the IBook interface implementation into Book. The IBook properties are already implemented by Book. This file adds the definition of the Validate method.

## Creating and Running Unit Tests

The structural changes of AcmeLibrary make it easy to create unit tests for the BookController class. You can create a fake repository that emulates the behavior of the persistence layer (BookRepository). There are several solutions for implementing such a fake class. Listing 18-28 shows a simple solution persisting books in memory.

**LISTING 18-28:** TestBookRepository.cs

```csharp
using System.Collections.Generic;
using System.Linq;
using AcmeDomain;
using AcmeLibrary.Models;

namespace AcmeLibraryTest
{
  public class TestBookRepository: IBookRepository
  {
    private static readonly Dictionary<int, Book> _Books =
      new Dictionary<int, Book>();

    public static void Reset()
    {
      _Books.Clear();
    }

    public IQueryable<IBook> GetBooks()
    {
      return _Books.Values.AsQueryable();
    }

    public IBook GetBookById(int id)
```

*continues*

**LISTING 18-28** *(continued)*

```
    {
      Book book;
      return _Books.TryGetValue(id, out book)? book : null;
    }

    public IBook CreateBook()
    {
      return new Book();
    }

    public void InsertBook(IBook book)
    {
      book.Id = _Books.Count + 1;
      _Books.Add(book.Id, book as Book);
    }

    public void SaveBook(IBook book)
    {
      _Books[book.Id] = book as Book;
    }

    public void DeleteBook(int id)
    {
      _Books.Remove(id);
    }
  }
}
```

*Code file [TestBookRepository.cs] available for download at Wrox.com*

As you see, this in-memory implementation is very simple. It uses a `Dictionary<,>` instance where the identifier of a book is used as the key, and a `Book` instance as the value. Because this dictionary is static, you can share the repository among unit tests instantiating the `TestBookRepository` class.

Listing 18-29 shows an extract from the `BookControllerTest.cs` file implementing a few unit tests.

**LISTING 18-29: BookControllerTest.cs (Extract)**

```
  [TestClass]
public class BookControllerTest
{
  [ClassInitialize()]
  public static void MyClassInitialize(TestContext testContext)
  {
    TestBookRepository.Reset();
    ServiceLocator.RegisterInstance<IBookRepository>(
```

```
        typeof(TestBookRepository));
  }

  [TestMethod]
  public void InsertValidBooksOk()
  {
    for (int i = 1; i <= 10; i++)
    {
    var book = new Book
               {
                 Author = "Author" + i,
                 Title = "Title" + i,
                 ISBN = "0123456789012",
                 Published = new DateTime(1998, 1, 1),
                 Publisher = "Wrox"
               };
    var bc = new BookController();
    var result = bc.Create(book) as RedirectToRouteResult;
    Assert.IsNotNull(result);
    Assert.AreEqual(result.RouteValues["action"], "Index");
    }
    var list = new BookController().Index() as ViewResult;
    Assert.IsNotNull(list);
    var model = list.ViewData.Model as IEnumerable<IBook>;
    Assert.AreEqual(model.Count(), 10);
  }
}
```

*Code file [BookControllerTest.cs] available for download at Wrox.com*

The `MyClassInitialize` method injects the `TestBookRepository` class into `BookController`, so when you instantiate a `BookController`, the test repository is used.

The `InsertValidBooksOk` test method emulates the insertion of ten books. After each insertion, it checks whether the result of the action is a `RedirectToRouteResult`, forwarding the user to the "Index" — this is the sign of proper operation. When all books are inserted, it checks that the book list contains exactly ten elements.

The test project contains another test case (not listed here) to check what happens when a book with a wrong publishing date is about to be inserted.

With the Test ⇨ Run ⇨ "All Tests in Solution" command, you can run all `AcmeLibrary` unit test cases. The checkmarks (as shown in Figure 18-28) indicate successful test cases.

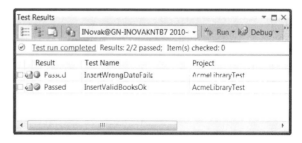

**FIGURE 18-28:** Successful test cases

*In real life, you should create many more unit tests. You should cover all normal and expected exceptional cases for each action. You can play with the downloaded source code and create more tests.*

# A FEW MORE POINTS ON MVC 2

By now, you have learned about the most important things regarding ASP.NET MVC. You know how to create and customize applications, and you also have a good understanding about how to prepare your projects to support testing scenarios. However, MVC 2 has so many great features that this chapter is not long enough to cover everything. Following are a few more exciting capabilities of the framework.

## Areas

An ASP.NET MVC project organizes source files into folders — one for models, another one for controllers, and another folder for views, and so on. If you have dozens of them, you can feel that your development environment is getting messy. It becomes quite difficult to keep track of how each item relates to a specific area of application functionality.

To reduce this difficulty, ASP.NET MVC lets you organize your project into *areas*, where each area represents a functional group of your application (for example, reporting, site administration, social functions, asset management, and so on).

## Metadata Providers

MVC heavily uses metadata associated with your models. If the data annotations attributes defined in the `System.ComponentModel.DataAnnotations` namespace don't meet your needs, you can create your own custom metadata provider by creating a class that inherits from one of the `ModelMetadataProvider`, `AssociatedMetadataProvider`, or `DataAnnotationsModelMetadataProvider` classes.

## Value Providers

ASP.NET MVC has a concept called *value providers* to help you extract data coming from different sources into model properties. You can implement your own `IValueProvider` interface-based implementation to create a custom value provider, or use one of the following value providers available out-of-the-box:

- ➤ `QueryStringValueProvider` — This value provider extracts values from the query string part of the incoming URL.

- ➤ `RouteDataValueProvider` — This value provider extracts values from the route data of the matched route.

> ➤ `FormValueProvider` — This value provider extracts values from the form fields of a HTML form. Obviously, this can work only for HTTP `POST` actions.

> ➤ `HttpFileCollectionValueProvider` — This value provider extracts values from a posted forms submitted file collection, the values from `INPUT` type `FILE` tags.

## Model Binders

When your controller is about to invoke one of its action methods and is trying to find suitable values for the method's parameters, it uses value providers and model binders. While value providers represent the supply of data items available to your controller, model binders are responsible for taking all these data items and trying to map them onto whatever type of parameter your method takes.

You can create your own model binders by implementing the `IModelBinder` interface, or using (reusing) one of the available model binders (`ByteArrayModelBinder`, `LinqBinaryModelBinder`, or `HttpPostedFileBaseModelBinder`).

## Child Actions

MVC 2 has a new concept called a *child action*, which is an action that can be invoked from inside a view, utilizing the `Html.RenderAction` helper method. `RenderAction` retrieves a result, and this is rendered inside the view that invoked it.

Child actions are very useful for componentizing your application. With their help, you can create reusable widgets with application logic.

## Asynchronous Controllers

By the nature of IIS, when a request arrives, it is processed by a thread picked up from the thread pool. Until the request is processed, the associated thread is blocked. Long-running requests may cause the thread pool to run out of available threads, and incoming requests to be queued. An asynchronous controller (that is, a controller derived from the `AsynchController` class) resolves this situation by using two separate methods for each action:

> ➤ The first method receives the input and then launches the body belonging to the action asynchronously on a separate thread.

> ➤ The second method (callback method) is invoked automatically by the MVC framework when the asynchronous operation started by the first method completes. This method takes care of sending the response back to the caller of the action.

## SUMMARY

In this chapter, you learned about the Model-View-Controller (MVC) design pattern, and saw how Microsoft implemented it based on its ASP.NET 4.0 platform. The first version of ASP.NET MVC was an out-of-band release for Visual Studio 2008, but it is an out-of-the-box feature in Visual

Studio 2010 — with the name MVC 2. Simultaneously, you can use MVC 2 in Visual Studio 2008 with .NET 3.5 SP1.

MVC 2 comes with great tooling that helps you easily create controllers and views using predefined templates. When you have your model class ready, you can create controller and view skeletons in a few seconds. MVC uses its own routing model to resolve requests to public action methods in controller classes — in contrast to ASP.NET Web Forms, which resolves requests to files.

MVC was designed with customization and extensibility in mind. With a few changes, you can totally change the outlook of your MVC application's UI, and you can easily customize the templates used for rendering views. With templated helpers, you can get rid of the nitty-gritty details of rendering HTML markup. There are many extensibility points in MVC that you can utilize to improve your application's architecture with injecting aspects (cross-cutting concerns).

MVC fully supports the TDD approach; it also has been implemented with TDD.

In Chapter 19, you will learn about the Asynchronous JavaScript and XML (Ajax) technology, and its improvements shipped with Visual Studio 2010 and .NET 4 Framework.

# 19

# ASP.NET Ajax Improvements

If you hit the Wikipedia website and search for the term "Ajax," you will find that it may refer to more than 50 things in mythology, sports, vehicles, fiction, and music. The name itself is not new (Homer first mentioned it in his *Iliad)*. However, as we use it today in the scope of IT, the term characterizes this decade's revolution in the history of web programming.

In its current context, the term "Ajax" (which is actually an acronym for *Asynchronous JavaScript and XML*) was coined by Jesse James Garrett in 2005. It refers not to a *single technology*, but rather to a *group of technologies* that existed well before the dawn of Web 2.0 and rich internet applications (RIAs). Nevertheless, new interactive web applications have incorporated these technologies into a single programming approach, and with that came the need for a better user experience.

Because the overall user experience is one of the features that can help to make a website unique and to beat the competition, over the last few years, AJAX-enabled websites have become so mainstream that even the word "Ajax" now appears in the English language. This chapter provides details about how Ajax works under the hood, and how you can use ASP.NET to control it with a high-level programming approach.

After reading this chapter, you will be familiar with the following:

➤ *Using the ASP.NET Ajax server controls* — Originally, ASP.NET targeted server-side developers, and so it is not a surprise that, although Ajax is primarily a client-side technology, Microsoft added full support for it also on the server side. If you are a server-side developer, this chapter explains how you can use ASP.NET web controls to add Ajax functionality to your pages.

➤ *Using the Microsoft Ajax Library* — If you want to utilize the full power of Ajax, whether you like it or not, you must write JavaScript code, and Microsoft helps you with a fully featured JavaScript library. This chapter guides you through the Microsoft Ajax Library, and you will learn how you can access Document Object Model (DOM) elements, handle events, and use declarative data binding on the client side, even for server-side data.

If you (like many other web developer all over the world) are primarily creating managed code for web applications, you probably enjoy the .NET environment, and try to keep yourself away from JavaScript. This chapter helps you recognize similar concepts on the client, and make you feel comfortable in JavaScript.

# UNDERSTANDING AJAX

Imagine an e-commerce website where you can browse the products on the Product Catalog page, and you can click on a big fancy Buy button that drops the current item into your basket. The product list is displayed on the left, and the content of the basket (with the total amount due for the purchase) is displayed on the right side of the page. From a user's perspective, there are two expectations from this page — all pieces of the page must be always up to date, and it must work fast. From the developer's point of view, it is important that the server be notified every time a user clicks on the Buy button, so the basket management cannot be completely performed on the client side.

Let's see what happens in the background. When the user clicks on the Buy button, the browser sends a request to the web server that processes the request, updates the user's basket in the database, and creates the HTML response. The HTML response is then transmitted back to the client, and is displayed in the browser. This is called a *round-trip*, and you can see that, depending on the network latency and the application complexity, it may take a long time.

The more important thing is that, while the browser waits for a response, the user interface (UI) is locked, so the user cannot do anything else but watch the hourglass and the progress bar. What's more, after the response is received by the browser, the whole page is refreshed (to update the content of the basket) and scrolled to the top.

As you can see in Figure 19-1, the user and the browser are completely synchronized with the server. While the server processes the request, the user waits, and while the user works on the page, the server waits. These long wait states and the loss of the scroll context result in a very poor user experience.

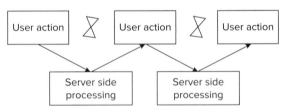

**FIGURE 19-1:** Synchronous user interface

If you could decouple the client and the server, and let them work asynchronously, the user experience could be much better, as shown in Figure 19-2. While the server processes a previous Buy request, the user would be able to browse other products.

However, this approach completely differs from the classic use of the web — you do not want to send a URL to the server and you do not

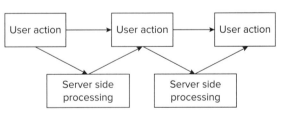

**FIGURE 19-2:** Asynchronous user interface

want to refresh the whole page. You just want to send the selected product's ID, expect an HTML fragment as a response, and update only the corresponding part of the page. Because browsers were not originally designed for this type of architecture, web developers called out for a new hero, and `XMLHttpRequest` was born.

## The XMLHttpRequest Object

The user interface created by the engineers of the Outlook web Access for Microsoft Exchange Server 2000 faced the same challenge, and the engineers decided to create a new object called `XMLHTTPRequest` that could be accessed via ActiveX from Internet Explorer 5.0. Later, the Gecko layout engine implemented a native JavaScript object called the `XMLHttpRequest` that followed the original Microsoft implementation. However, neither the name nor the syntax was 100 percent the same, which resulted in a serious incompatibility problem among various browser versions that still persists today. The solution to the problem was discovered in many Ajax wrapper libraries over the years.

The `XMLHttpRequest` object acts as a mini-browser in the browser. It can send HTTP requests to the server and asynchronously receive the responses, and all that can be driven and handled in JavaScript.

The following code example shows the use of the `XMLHttpRequest` object on a page that displays the current time of the server, while other parts of the page are not updated. First, you create the server-side component as an ASPX page that returns the current server time in a HTML fragment:

Available for download on Wrox.com

```
<%@ Page Language="C#" %>
<script runat="server">
  protected void Page_Load( object sender, EventArgs e )
  {
    // Simulate server side processing.
    System.Threading.Thread.Sleep( 1500 );

    this.Response.Clear();
    this.Response.Write(
      "<b>Server time is " + DateTime.Now.ToLongTimeString() + "</*b>" );
    this.Response.Expires = -1; // Disable client cache.
    this.Response.End();
  }
</script>
```

*Code file [1-XMLHttpRequest\Time.aspx] available for download at Wrox.com*

Then, you create a simple HTML page that contains a button:

Available for download on Wrox.com

```
<!DOCTYPE html PUBLIC "-//W3C//DTD XHTML 1.0 Transitional//EN"
  "http://www.w3.org/TR/xhtml1/DTD/xhtml1-transitional.dtd">
<html xmlns="http://www.w3.org/1999/xhtml">
<head>
  <title>XMLHttpRequest sample</title>
  <script type="text/javascript">
    var oXmlHttp;

    function getServerTime()
```

```
      {
        oXmlHttp = new XMLHttpRequest();
        oXmlHttp.open( "GET", "time.aspx" );
        oXmlHttp.onreadystatechange = onStateChanged;
        oXmlHttp.send();
        document.getElementById("divResult").innerHTML +=
          "Request sent...<br />";
      }

      function onStateChanged()
      {
        if (oXmlHttp.readyState == 4)  // 4 = READYSTATE_COMPLETE
        {
          if( oXmlHttp.status == 200 )  // 200 = HTTP_OK
          {
            document.getElementById("divResult").innerHTML +=
              "Response from server: " +
              oXmlHttp.responseText + "<br />";
          }
        }
      }
    </script>
  </head>
  <body>
    <h1>XMLHttpRequest sample</h1>
    <input type="button"
           value="Get server time" onclick="getServerTime()" />
    <div id="divResult" />
  </body>
</html>
```

---

*Code file [1-XMLHttpRequest\Default.htm] available for download at Wrox.com*

When the user clicks on the "Get server time" button, the getServerTime JavaScript function is called, which initializes the XMLHttpRequest object and sends an asynchronous GET request to time.aspx. The readyState property of the oXmlHttp object continuously signals the current state of the round-trip, and, whenever it changes, the onStateChanged method is called. In this event handler, the response is displayed only if the whole response is received without error.

This sample does not seem to be at all complicated, but it is not cross-browser. If you code the same functionality cross-browser in pure JavaScript, the result is at least three times longer (or more). In practice, it is not uncommon for multiple parts of the page to use Ajax in more complex scenarios and implement them with raw JavaScript, and this would be very time-consuming work. The need for productivity brought Ajax libraries into life.

## ASP.NET and Ajax

The calendar showed June 2005, and most of the ASP.NET team was focused on delivering ASP.NET 2.0 and Visual Studio 2005. A small group was founded inside the team and started to work on a new project codenamed "Atlas." The goal of Atlas was to add the Ajax functionality to the ASP.NET architecture, and support asynchronous UI programming on the server, as well as the client side.

The initial release of Atlas was in January 2007 under the brand of ASP.NET AJAX, and was released as an extension to ASP.NET 2.0. The next major milestone was version 3.5 that was released as part of ASP.NET 3.5, and received designer support in Visual Studio 2008. ASP.NET 4.0 contains ASP.NET Ajax 4.0, and the Visual Studio 2010 integrated development environment (IDE) adds some nice designer features to help with client-side development.

 *The ASP.NET team continually publishes previews of the next version of ASP.NET Ajax that you can access at* http://aspnet.codeplex.com. *As of this writing, a Beta version is available for download.*

ASP.NET Ajax has the following pillars:

➤ *ASP.NET Ajax Extensions* — This is a server-side framework that adds new Ajax functionality to existing server-side code with new web controls such as the `ScriptManager`, the `UpdatePanel`, and the `UpdateProgress`.

➤ *Microsoft Ajax Library* — This is a client-side JavaScript framework that does not depend on ASP.NET on the server, so it can be used with other server-side technologies. Using (or even modifying) the Library source code for free is permitted by the New BSD License.

➤ *ASP.NET Ajax Control Toolkit* — This is an Open Source project built on top of the Microsoft Ajax Library that provides more than 40 reusable controls and control extenders. It is a joint effort between Microsoft and the community, and new controls are continually added to the Toolkit.

➤ *Visual Studio* — This provides design-time support and project templates to create Ajax components and Ajax-enabled web applications in a productive manner.

The ASP.NET Ajax technology was designed to be cross-browser and a *Browser Compatibility Layer* ensures that this goal is achieved by every component built on top of it. ASP.NET Ajax supports Internet Explorer 6.0+, Mozilla Firefox 1.5+, Opera 9.0+, Safari 2.0+, and Google Chrome.

## USING THE ASP.NET AJAX SERVER CONTROLS

Ajax can drastically boost the user experience of most web applications — that is, Ajax is friendly with the end users. However, when you try to implement it with the XMLHttpRequest object and pure JavaScript, you find that it is completely different from what you are used to on server side — that is, Ajax is not so friendly with the developers.

If you have chosen ASP.NET (because you liked the higher abstraction level it gives you to create a server-side web application) and Visual Studio (because you liked its productivity features), using the XMLHttpRequest object makes you feel like being thrown back to the Stone Age. Microsoft felt that pain, and created the *ASP.NET Ajax Extensions* component (that later became an integral part of ASP.NET) to provide the same high-level control-centric approach for the basic (but most common) Ajax scenarios in ASP.NET.

The ASP.NET Ajax Extensions contains a set of server-side controls that contain not only server code, but also script code that runs on the client. However, you probably do not even notice that, because the scripts are "automagically" managed by the run-time and the controls — you use these controls just like any other web control in the designer and code behind.

The flagship is the `ScriptManager` control that is responsible for managing script resources for client components, partial page rendering, localization, web services, and can even manage your custom scripts. You must drop the `ScriptManager` control onto the page in order to use Ajax features on the page.

The most notable control in the set is the `UpdatePanel` that enables you to refresh selected parts of the page. You can take almost any existing ASP.NET control, embed it into an `UpdatePanel`, and it will work asynchronously. As a server-side developer, you do not have to worry about client side scripts; it will just work for most scenarios.

If you want to notify the user that an asynchronous request is currently running in the background, you can use the `UpdateProgress` control. The `UpdateProgress` contains a placeholder that you can fill with a static message or a progress image, and it will be automatically displayed when the associated `UpdatePanel` control executes a request in the background.

Sometimes you want to send the whole page or content of an `UpdatePanel` to the server at defined intervals. You can use the `Timer` control that triggers an event on the client that you can process on the server.

To see a simple scenario with these controls, create an ASPX page with a `GridView` and a `SqlDataSource` control that retrieves records from the `Customer` table of the `Northwind` database. Enable the sorting and paging for the `GridView` and set the `PageSize` to 30 to display so many items on the page that the user must scroll down to access the pager and go to the next page.

```
<asp:GridView runat="server"
    DataSourceID="NorthwindDS"
    AllowPaging="True" PageSize="30"
    AllowSorting="True" />

<asp:SqlDataSource ID="NorthwindDS" runat="server"
    ConnectionString="<%$ ConnectionStrings:Northwind %>"
    SelectCommand="SELECT [CompanyName], [ContactName] FROM [Customers]" />
```

*Code file [2-ServerControls\Default.aspx] available for download at Wrox.com*

If you compile and try this in a browser, you find that it works as expected — the records are displayed on pages and you can sort them. However, every time you click on a column header or a page number, the whole page is refreshed. You will notice the quick flicker and that you lose your scroll context.

Let's use the `UpdatePanel` to Ajax-enable this page!

Your first step should always be to drag the `ScriptManager` from the Ajax Extensions group of the Toolbox, and drop it onto the top of the page. Without the `ScriptManager`, the magic will not happen, so do not forget it! Next, drag the `UpdatePanel` from the same group of the Toolbox and drop it onto the page. Then, select the `GridView` and the `SqlDataSource` control, and move it into the grey content placeholder of the `UpdatePanel`. If you prefer to do it in markup, here is the code that the designer generates:

```
<asp:ScriptManager runat="server" />

<asp:UpdatePanel runat="server" id="up">
  <ContentTemplate>
    <asp:GridView runat="server"
      DataSourceID="NorthwindDS"
      AllowPaging="True" PageSize="30"
      AllowSorting="True" />

    <asp:SqlDataSource ID="NorthwindDS" runat="server"
      ConnectionString="<%$ ConnectionStrings:Northwind %>"
      SelectCommand="SELECT [CompanyName], [ContactName] FROM [Customers]" />
  </ContentTemplate>
</asp:UpdatePanel>
```

*Code file [2-ServerControls\Default.aspx] available for download at Wrox.com*

As you can see, there is nothing special in it. The `UpdatePanel` is a standard server-side control with a `ContentTemplate` child element that can contain any additional controls, and those controls are automatically Ajax-enabled by the `UpdatePanel`. You can build and try it in a browser, and you will see the much more user-friendly behavior of the page.

To further enhance the user experience, you can drop an `UpdateProgress` control onto the page and enter any text as its content. Then, do not forget to go to the Properties window and set the `AssociatedUpdatePanelD` property to point to the previously used `UpdatePanel`, or do the same in markup like this:

```
<asp:UpdateProgress runat="server" AssociatedUpdatePanelID="up">
  <ProgressTemplate>
    Refreshing...
  </ProgressTemplate>
</asp:UpdateProgress>
```

*Code file [2-ServerControls\Default.aspx] available for download at Wrox.com*

However, if you try it now, the `UpdateProgress` is not displayed, because the response from the server returns quickly. You can simulate network latency or slow response rendering by adding the following sleep to the `Page_Load` event handler on the server:

```
protected void Page_Load(object sender, EventArgs e)
{
  System.Threading.Thread.Sleep( 3000 );
}
```

*Code file [2-ServerControls\Default.aspx] available for download at Wrox.com*

You can even set the `DisplayAfter` property of the `UpdateProgress` to 0 to force to display its content immediately when an asynchronous request begins.

This is the basic use of the `ScriptManager`, the `UpdatePanel`, and the `UpdateProgress` controls. However, all these controls have additional properties (not covered here) that enable you to address more complex scenarios with them (such as calling web services or connecting multiple `UpdatePanel`s to each other). Because they are standard ASP.NET web controls, you can modify their properties, subscribe to their events, and call their methods from code behind. Additionally, these controls rely heavily on client scripts, and the client framework is written with extensibility in mind, so you can handle events or modify properties on the client side as well.

## Refactoring the Framework Libraries

Let's change focus for a moment and look into the rendered HTML code that is sent to the client in the previous example. If you compare the markup of the original page in the View Source dialog of the browser with the Ajax-enabled version, you can clearly see that a bunch of `<script>` tags are added to the page. These script references are added automatically by the `ScriptManager` control.

In previous versions of the Framework, the default behavior of the `ScriptManager` was to automatically add references to the Microsoft Ajax Library, and although the `ScriptManager` can be very handy even if you do not use the client-side Library, you had no opt-out of this feature. Because the Library was implemented in monolithic (and relatively large) JavaScript files, the side effect was a significantly larger page size, even if the application did not use the client library.

In the new 4.0 version, both of these pain points are addressed. The Microsoft Ajax Library is now implemented in the form of *split script* files, and you can choose which subset of the framework your code relies on. You can fine-tune the `ScriptManager` via its new `MicrosoftAjaxMode` property. This property can have one of the following values:

➤ `Enabled` — All scripts of the Microsoft Ajax Library are included. For compatibility reasons, this is the default behavior.

➤ `Disabled` — If you do not use the Microsoft Ajax Library, you can set the `MicrosoftAjaxMode` property to `Disabled`, and the `ScriptManager` will not render any script reference into the page.

➤ `Explicit` — If you set the `MicrosoftAjaxMode` property to `Explicit`, you must manually add all references. Because dependencies are not automatically resolved, you must ensure that you include all scripts that have dependencies to each other in the order they reference each other.

In `Explicit` mode, the following script names are available:

➤ `MicrosoftAjaxCore.js`

➤ `MicrosoftAjaxComponentModel.js`

➤ `MicrosoftAjaxSerialization.js`

➤ `MicrosoftAjaxGlobalization.js`

➤ `MicrosoftAjaxHistory.js`

- ➤ `MicrosoftAjaxNetwork.js`

- ➤ `MicrosoftAjaxWebForms.js`

- ➤ `MicrosoftAjaxWebServices.js`

- ➤ `MicrosoftAjaxApplicationServices.js`

- ➤ `MicrosoftAjaxTemplates.js` (new for ASP.NET Ajax 4)

- ➤ `MicrosoftAjaxAdoNet.js` (new for ASP.NET Ajax 4)

Figure 19-3 shows the dependencies between the split script files.

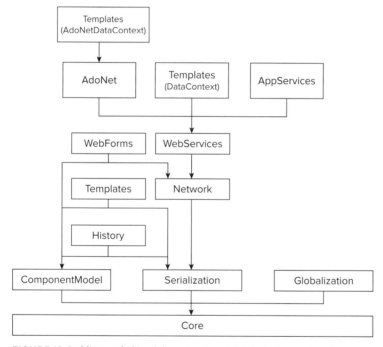

**FIGURE 19-3:** Microsoft Ajax Library scripts and their dependencies

As an example, if you would like to call the `TimeService.asmx` web service, but you do not use templates, globalization, history, and so on, then you can configure the `ScriptManager` like this:

```
<asp:ScriptManager ID="ScriptManager1" runat="server"
  EnablePartialRendering="False"
  MicrosoftAjaxMode="Explicit">
  <CompositeScript>
    <Scripts>
      <asp:ScriptReference Name="MicrosoftAjaxCore.js" />
      <asp:ScriptReference Name="MicrosoftAjaxSerialization.js" />
      <asp:ScriptReference Name="MicrosoftAjaxNetwork.js" />
      <asp:ScriptReference Name="MicrosoftAjaxWebServices.js" />
    </Scripts>
```

```
    </CompositeScript>
    <Services>
      <asp:ServiceReference Path="TimeService.asmx" />
    </Services>
  </asp:ScriptManager>
```

Microsoft recommends the use of split script files only for those developers who are concerned about the performance of their web applications. If you do, you can also see in this code an example of how to further optimize your website performance by using the `CompositeScript` element to merge the selected split script files into a single composite file to minimize the number of requests from the browser to the server.

## Using the Microsoft CDN

As previously discussed, if you use the client-side features of ASP.NET Ajax, you introduce a dependency on the JavaScript files of the Ajax Library. Although the Microsoft Ajax Library is published under the New BSD License that allows even the modification of the source code, most applications and developers do not take advantage of this opportunity, and use the script files because they are provided by Microsoft.

If you have more than one web application referencing the Ajax Library, or you access websites on the Internet that are built using ASP.NET Ajax, your browser will download the same JavaScript files from every domain, and maintain a client-side cache for them independently from each other. If you and many other sites are using the same script files, then why not share and reference them from a single common location? However, if you set up a single server and connect millions of clients to it, it will be overloaded, and the overall client experience will be significantly worse. This is where the Ajax *Content Delivery Network (CDN)* comes into the picture.

A CDN is a system of strategically placed "edge cache" servers containing copies of the same data to maximize bandwidth for access to the data from clients. The system is architected so that the clients access a copy of the data near the clients, thus minimizing the network latency without causing a bottleneck on a single central server. That means that a web page can reference a resource on a well-known external domain name, and the request is routed to the nearest replica of that content without the browser noticing the redirection. If you have a resource that you publish on a CDN, you no longer must worry about network latency and local bandwidth, even if you have clients all over the world.

Microsoft decided to publish the JavaScript files of the Microsoft Ajax Library, the *jQuery Library,* and the *jQuery Validation Library* to its own CDN. Applications that are built on top of these libraries no longer must host their script files on their own servers, but can reference them via the `ajax.microsoft.com` domain. Currently, Microsoft Ajax version 0911 (beta), jQuery version 1.3.2, and jQuery Validate version 1.5.5 are available this way. Because more and more web applications (not only that are built with ASP.NET, but also with PHP or other technologies) will reference these files on that CDN location, the browser will more likely already have a copy of those files in its cache when the user accesses a new website.

To use the Microsoft Ajax CDN, all you must do is change your script references to point to `http://ajax.microsoft.com`, as shown in the following example. (The `0911` here means the November 2009 beta, the latest version available as of the writing this chapter.)

```
<script type="text/javascript"
        src="http://ajax.microsoft.com/ajax/beta/0911/MicrosoftAjax.js"></script>
```

Note that you can also use the debug version of the scripts by adding a `debug.js` suffix to the end of the URL:

```
<script type="text/javascript"
        src="http://ajax.microsoft.com/ajax/beta/0911/
             MicrosoftAjax.debug.js"></script>
```

> *The full list of the files, along with the corresponding URLs, is available at* `http://www.asp.net/ajax/cdn`.

If your application references the script files via the `ScriptManager` control, you can add the `EnableCdn="true"` attribute, which forces the application to download *all* script files (including those that are used by the Web Forms infrastructure) from the Microsoft CDN.

Following are the advantages of using the Microsoft CDN:

➤ The client request is processed much faster. Because it is targeting a server in another domain, the browser can parallelize the requests.

➤ The files might not even need to be downloaded, because they are cached on the client across multiple websites.

➤ You no longer have to pay for the bandwidth of these files because the CDN is operated by Microsoft.

Following are the disadvantages of using the Microsoft CDN:

➤ By using the Microsoft CDN, you are introducing an external dependency into your application architecture. Although it is very unlikely that the Microsoft CDN will be temporarily down (or will be permanently shut down), if that happens, your application will be unusable.

➤ The external domain must be accessible by the clients, even if your application targets the intranet. The good news is that the script files can be easily cached on your local proxy server, so you can still minimize the external bandwidth usage.

➤ Because it is a `microsoft.com` domain, all cookies you received from other Microsoft sites are sent to the Microsoft CDN as well. Although you cannot know what these cookies actually do, they may allow tracking the users, and that might raise privacy issues. (Note that other players in this business face the same issue.)

> *Before you decide to use the Microsoft CDN, be sure to read the five-page Terms of Use agreement at* `http://www.asp.net/ajaxlibrary/CDNTermsOfUse.ashx`.

As you can see from this examination, the risks of using the Microsoft CDN are highly exceeded by its advantages. Because more and more applications will be built on top of it, you can expect a much better end-user experience.

## USING THE MICROSOFT AJAX LIBRARY

Now that you are familiar with the JavaScript files that constitute the Microsoft Ajax Library, let's get a quick overview of what features you already had in the 3.5 version, and then a glimpse at the details of the enhancements you receive in ASP.NET 4.0.

The heart of the Microsoft Ajax Library is a component officially called *Core Services*, which is a set of JavaScript functions that simulates object-oriented programming (OOP) on the client. The word "simulate" is used here because JavaScript is not an object-oriented language. However, thanks to this component, you can create namespaces, classes, interfaces, enums, and you have inheritance, event handling, reflection, and so on.

Core Services is implemented in the `MicrosoftAjax.js` file, so you must import it into your page, as shown here:

Available for
download on
Wrox.com

```
<script type="text/javascript" src="MicrosoftAjax.js"></script>
```

*Code file [3-AjaxLibrary\01-Basics.htm] available for download at Wrox.com*

After importing this script file, you can create your own namespace:

Available for
download on
Wrox.com

```
Type.registerNamespace('Book');
```

*Code file [3-AjaxLibrary\01-Basics.htm] available for download at Wrox.com*

The syntax may seem strange at first, but don't forget that you are still in JavaScript, and your hands are tied by the language. The syntax of a class declaration is more unusual to a server-side developer, although it is a well-known JavaScript approach.

First, you create a function that is essentially the constructor of your class:

Available for
download on
Wrox.com

```
Book.MessageBox = function(initialMessage)
{
    this._message = initialMessage;
}
```

*Code file [3-AjaxLibrary\01-Basics.htm] available for download at Wrox.com*

After that, you use the `prototype` syntax to create your class members. Unfortunately, there are no properties in JavaScript (at least not in the sense that you have in .NET with getter and setter methods). Therefore, all class members are implemented as methods. However, the recommended naming convention is to use the `get_` and `set_` prefix for property getters and setters. You can implement your `MessageBox` class with a `message` property and a `show` function like this:

```
Book.MessageBox.prototype =
{
  get_message: function()
  {
    return this._message;
  },

  set_message: function(value)
  {
    this._message = value;
  },

  show: function()
  {
    alert(this._message);
  }
}
```

*Code file [3-AjaxLibrary\01-Basics.htm] available for download at Wrox.com*

The last step is to register this class to the *Microsoft Ajax run-time*. Without this step, you are able to instantiate your class and call its methods, but you cannot inherit from this class. If your class implements an interface such as `Sys.IDisposable`, or inherits from a base class, you can specify that also in the `registerClass` function call.

```
Book.MessageBox.registerClass('Book.MessageBox');
```

*Code file [3-AjaxLibrary\01-Basics.htm] available for download at Wrox.com*

Now, you have a `MessageBox` class in your `Book` namespace, and you are free to use it anywhere in your code to display a pop-up message to the user:

```
var msgBox = new Book.MessageBox('Hello World!');
msgBox.show();
```

*Code file [3-AjaxLibrary\01-Basics.htm] available for download at Wrox.com*

Built on top of this type system, the Core Services component also contains a set of classes that extend the built-in JavaScript `Array`, `Boolean`, `Date`, `Error`, `Number`, `Object`, and `String` types. The most notable is probably the `String` class extension that gives you methods with which you are already familiar on the server-side: `endsWith`, `format`, `localeFormat`, `startsWith`, `trim`, trimStart, and trimEnd. The String.format method supports the same placeholder syntax in JavaScript that you can use in C#:

```
var name = 'John Doe';
var today = new Date();
var message = String.format('Hello {0}, have a nice {1:dddd}!', name, today);
var msgBox = new Book.MessageBox(message);
```

*Code file [3-AjaxLibrary\01-Basics.htm] available for download at Wrox.com*

For more complex scenarios, you can even switch to the Sys.StringBuilder class, and call its append or appendLine methods.

If you try the previous example, you probably get the name of the day displayed in English. However, the Microsoft Ajax Library fully supports script localization and globalization via the Sys.CultureInfo class that is used by the localeFormat method added to the Date, Number and String types.

Core Services also extends the debugging and error-handling capabilities on the client. With the Sys.Debug class, you can trace messages, use assertions, or even break into the debugger. To standardize error handling, the Sys namespace contains a set of predefined exception types, and the Error class is extended with static methods to raise these types with minimal coding.

For example if you want to throw a Sys.InvalidOperationException if the show method is called without setting the message to display, you can use the Error.invalidOperation method:

```
show: function()
{
  if (this._message === undefined)
  {
    throw Error.invalidOperation("The 'message' must be set
        before calling 'show'.");
  }
  alert(this._message);
}
```

*Code file [3-AjaxLibrary\01-Basics.htm] available for download at Wrox.com*

In addition to the Core Services, the Microsoft Ajax Library contains a *Networking Layer* that is responsible for hiding the details of asynchronous requests and serialization. If you want to download a file that contains JavaScript Object Notation (JSON) data from the server, you no longer have to use the down-level XMLHttpRequest object. You can build your browser-agnostic logic on top of the Sys.Net.WebRequest class like this:

```
var request = new Sys.Net.WebRequest();
request.set_url('authors.txt');
request.add_completed(function(executor)
{
```

```
            var authors = eval('(' + executor.get_responseData() + ')');
            // Process the authors array here...
        });
        request.invoke();
```

You probably want to allow the user to manually initiate this request (by clicking on a button, for example) and display the result on the page. That means you need access to the DOM of the page. By using the Microsoft Ajax Library, you can access DOM elements and manage events with browser-independent code. The Component Services layer of the library allows you to create non-visual components, behaviors, and controls in a structured and standardized way.

To access a DOM element, you can use the `$get` function that is a shortcut for the static `getElementById` method of the `Sys.UI.DomElement` class. The `Sys.UI.DomElement` is essentially a wrapper around the raw DOM element, and you can read or write any of its properties via this wrapper.

Another often-used shortcut is the `$addHandler` function that points to the `addHandler` method of the `Sys.UI.DomEvent` class. This method provides a standard way to subscribe an event handler to an event exposed by a DOM element.

For example, if you want to refactor the previous code to send the `WebRequest` when the user clicks on a button and display the results on the page, you need an HTML `input` and a `div` element:

```
<input id="btnGet" type="button" value="Display author" />
<div id="divResult" />
```

You can get a reference to the `btnGet` button and subscribe to its click event in the `pageLoad` method with the `btnGetClick` event handler:

```
$addHandler($get('btnGet'), "click", btnGetClick);
```

In the `btnGetClick` function, you can send the request to the server and display the results on the `divResult` placeholder via its `innerHTML` property:

```
function btnGetClick()
{
    var request = new Sys.Net.WebRequest();
    request.set_url('authors.txt');
    request.add_completed(function(executor)
    {
```

```
        var authors = eval('(' + executor.get_responseData() + ')');
        var msg = String.format('This sample is written by {0} {1}.',
                authors[0].FirstName, authors[0].LastName);
        $get('divResult').innerHTML = msg;
    });
    request.invoke();
}
```

*Code file [3-AjaxLibrary\01-Basics.htm] available for download at Wrox.com*

If you want to manage events, it is important to know the order of the client life-cycle events. The full page life cycle is out of the scope of this book. However, let's touch on this topic because there are some minor (but important) changes in this area.

The first event that is fired is the `init` event of the `Sys.Application` class that is raised after all scripts have been loaded, but before any objects are created. This event is raised only one time when the page is first rendered, and gives you a point in the life cycle to add your custom component to the page. To handle this event, you must subscribe to it with the `Sys.Application.add_init` method.

If you are not a component developer, you should use the `load` event that is raised after all scripts have been loaded, and all objects are created and initialized. You do not have to explicitly bind a handler to this event. Instead, you can create a function with the reserved name `pageLoad`. In ASP.NET 4, you can also use the `Sys.onReady` function to register a function that is called when the DOM is ready and when all required resources have been loaded.

In earlier versions of the Ajax Library, if you wanted the `pageLoad` method to be called before the `window.onload` event was raised, you had to manually call the `Sys.Application.initialize` method at the bottom of the page. From ASP.NET 4.0, this call is no longer required, because the `pageLoad` method is called immediately after the DOM content is finished loading and before the `window.onload` event.

## Working with DOM Elements

Earlier in this chapter, you saw examples of how to use the `$get` function to get a reference to a DOM element by its ID. While the `$get` function is very useful, modern Web 2.0 applications more and more often need more flexibility over how DOM elements are selected. The Microsoft Ajax Library 4 introduces a new helper function (named `Sys.get`) that allows selecting elements not only by their IDs, but also by their names or CSS classes. `Sys.get` is also capable of returning references to Ajax Library components.

The `Sys.get` function expects two parameters:

➤ `selector` — This is used to define what you are looking for.

➤ `context` — This is essentially the scope of the search.

If you omit the second parameter, the function searches the entire DOM.

The format (or, to be more precise, the first character of the `selector` parameter) determines how the function performs the search. The `selector` can be in one of the following formats:

➤ `$componentname` — If you use the `$` prefix, the function will look for a component (for example, `DataView`) with the specified name. In this case, the `Sys.get` function behaves like the `$find` method.

➤ `#id` — If you use the `#` prefix, the method will behave like the `$get` function. Internally, the `$get` function delegates the call to the `Sys.get` function, and adds the `#` prefix to the ID.

➤ `.class` — If you use the `.` prefix, the function will search for an element with the specified CSS class.

➤ `elementname` — If you do not use a prefix, the `Sys.get` function will return an element with the specified name (for example, `<div>`).

For example, to create a static unordered list of continents on a page, you would use the following:

```
<ul id="continents" class="list">
  <li class="item">Asia</li>
  <li class="item">Africa</li>
  <li class="item">North America</li>
  <li class="item">South America</li>
  <li class="item">Antarctica</li>
  <li class="item">Europe</li>
  <li class="item">Australia</li>
</ul>
```

*Code file [3-AjaxLibrary\02-Selector.htm] available for download at Wrox.com*

To get a reference to the first element in the document with the ID of `"continents"`, you can use the following function call:

```
Sys.get('#continents')
```

*Code file [3-AjaxLibrary\02-Selector.htm] available for download at Wrox.com*

At first, it seems a bit longer than using `$get`, but you will quickly get used to it, because this function is much more powerful. For example, you can get the first element that has the `"item"` CSS class attached to it:

```
Sys.get('.item')
```

*Code file [3-AjaxLibrary\02-Selector.htm] available for download at Wrox.com*

Or, you can get the first `li` element in the document:

```
Sys.get('li')
```

*Code file [3-AjaxLibrary\02-Selector.htm] available for download at Wrox.com*

You can also use the `context` parameter to scope the search, and get the first element within a parent element that has the ID of `"continents"`:

```
Sys.get('li', Sys.get('#continents'))
```

*Code file [3-AjaxLibrary\02-Selector.htm] available for download at Wrox.com*

As you may have noticed, the method always returns a single element (the first match), and not an element set. Another thing to note is that the different types of searches (by component name, by ID, by class, or by element name) are not combined in a single selector. Both may seem to be a very strict limitation of the `Sys.get` method, especially if you are familiar with the capabilities of the jQuery Library. The good news is that, if the jQuery Library is loaded into the page, and the selector is not in one of the previously mentioned formats, the call will be automatically forwarded to jQuery. That means that you do not have to know whether the Microsoft Ajax Library or the jQuery Library resolves the query; you just use any syntax you want, and you work with the results.

Continuing the previous example, if you have jQuery, you can get not only the first, but also the last continent with `Sys.get`:

```
Sys.get('#continents .item:last')
```

*Code file [3-AjaxLibrary\02-Selector.htm] available for download at Wrox.com*

Or you can also get the fourth continent:

```
Sys.get('#continents .item:eq(3)')
```

*Code file [3-AjaxLibrary\02-Selector.htm] available for download at Wrox.com*

Or you can even get the first `"America"` continent:

```
Sys.get('#continents .item:contains("America")')
```

*Code file [3-AjaxLibrary\02-Selector.htm] available for download at Wrox.com*

As you can see, jQuery integrates pretty well with the Microsoft Ajax Library. As a result, you can use the advantages of both worlds in your application.

## The Script Loader

Earlier in this chapter, you saw how Microsoft split up the JavaScript files loaded by the `ScriptManager` to optimize the page load time. The same *split script files* can also be used in pure client-side code if you are using the Microsoft Ajax Library in the browser and no ASP.NET Ajax on the server. However, in this case, it is your responsibility to ensure that all the required files are loaded before you want to use them, and also that they are loaded in the correct order. This is where the new *Script Loader* can make your life easier.

Because the Microsoft Ajax Library consists of JavaScript files, the natural way of incorporating them into a web page is by using the declarative `script` tag in the page header:

```
<script type="text/javascript" src="MicrosoftAjax.js"></script>
```

However, JavaScript enables you to download external script files with imperative code, and the Script Loader of the Microsoft Ajax Library wraps this functionality and extends it with additional features. The Script Loader is implemented in the `Sys.loader` type that resides in the very small (11 KB) `Start.js` file. The `Start.js` file is designed to be a bootstrapper for the whole Library, and that is the only script file you have to reference in a `script` tag. Because the Microsoft Ajax Library is available via the Microsoft Ajax CDN, you can also load it from there:

```
<script src="http://ajax.microsoft.com/ajax/beta/0911/Start.js"
        type="text/javascript"></script>
```

After the `Script.js` file is downloaded and parsed on the client, you can use the `Sys.require` method to define on which standard script files your code depends. For example, if you need history and jQuery support, you can load them like this:

```
<script src="Start.js" type="text/javascript"></script>
<script type="text/javascript">
  Sys.require(
    [Sys.scripts.History, Sys.scripts.jQuery],
    function()
    {
      // History and jQuery available here
    }
  );
</script>
```

The `Sys.require` method accepts three parameters, but, in most cases, you will probably call it with only two. In the first parameter, you can define the *features* that should be loaded. Table 19-1 shows the available split script file features, and you can use the `Sys.scripts` (which acts like an enum) value to reference them.

**TABLE 19-1:** Available Split Script Files

| SCRIPT FILE NAME | SYS.SCRIPTS VALUE |
|---|---|
| MicrosoftAjaxAdoNet.js | AdoNet |
| MicrosoftAjaxApplicationServices.js | ApplicationServices |
| MicrosoftAjaxComponentModel.js | ComponentModel |
| MicrosoftAjaxCore.js | Core |
| MicrosoftAjaxDataContext.js | DataContext |
| MicrosoftAjaxGlobalization.js | Globalization |
| MicrosoftAjaxHistory.js | History |
| MicrosoftAjaxNetwork.js | Network |
| MicrosoftAjaxSerialization.js | Serialization |
| MicrosoftAjaxTemplates.js | Templates |
| MicrosoftAjaxWebServices.js | WebServices |
| jquery-1.3.2.min.js | jQuery |
| jquery.validate.min.js | jQueryValidate |

Features may also include *components*. So, for example, if you use the `DataView` and the `Watermark` components on the page, you do not have to know which script files contain them. You just load them via a single `Sys.require` call:

```
Sys.require([Sys.components.dataView, Sys.components.watermark]);
```

Because the `Sys.require` function loads the scripts asynchronously, you may find the second parameter useful, which is a callback that is called when all the features are available.

The Script Loader relies on metadata about every feature defined in the `Start.js` file via the `Sys.loader.defineScripts` method. Because you can also use this method to describe your custom script files, it is worth taking a look at how Microsoft did it (code fragment from `Start.js`):

```
loader.defineScripts
(
  {
    releaseUrl: "%/MicrosoftAjax" + "{0}.js",
    debugUrl: "%/MicrosoftAjax" + "{0}.debug.js",
    executionDependencies: ["Core"]
  },
  [
    {
      name: "Core",
      executionDependencies: null,
      isLoaded: !!window.Type
```

```
        },
        {
          name: "Serialization",
          isLoaded: !!Sys.Serialization
        },
        {
          name: "Network",
          executionDependencies: ["Serialization"],
          isLoaded: !!(Sys.Net && Sys.Net.WebRequest)
        },
        {
          name: "WebServices",
          executionDependencies: ["Network"],
          isLoaded: !!(Sys.Net && Sys.Net.WebServiceProxy)
        }
        // Additional lines omitted for clarity [...]
      ]
    );
```

As you can see, the metadata description does not follow the object-oriented approach. Instead, it uses JavaScript literals to minimize to code needed. The second parameter of the function contains the set of scripts to define with custom metadata, and the first parameter contains a default set of properties that are applied to each defined script.

With every script, you can set the following properties:

➤ A unique name used to identify the script. The name is automatically added to the Sys. scripts collection as an alias, and you can use it to reference the script.

➤ A releaseUrl and a debugUrl that point to the minified and the verbose versions of the file. The loader automatically uses the correct version based on the URL of itself (Start .js or Start.debug.js), and the Sys.debug property. In addition to that, if you load the Start.js file from the Microsoft Ajax CDN, the subsequent files are also downloaded from the CDN instead of your server — except jQuery and jQuery Validate, which are always downloaded from the CDN. The % token is replaced with the value of the Sys.loader .basePath property, and the {0} token is replaced with the name of the script.

➤ A Boolean expression (in the isLoaded property) can be used to test if the script is already successfully loaded.

➤ A list of other scripts that should be loaded before the current script is loaded (dependencies property) or before the current script is executed (executionDependencies property).

➤ A list of other scripts (in the contains property) built into the script file. This is only used by composite scripts.

➤ Plugins, components, and behaviors that are implemented in the script.

Note the executionDependencies property, because this gives the real power to the Loader. Because the Loader has information about the script dependencies, you no longer have to worry about them! You just reference a feature, and you can be sure that all the required script files will be loaded at the time you want to use it.

Because you only need the dependencies to be satisfied at run-time (that is what the executionDependencies are used for), the Loader can even parallelize the download of the files. If you want to ensure that the dependencies are already available when the script file is loaded, you must force the Loader to switch to serial downloading, and use the dependencies property just like the jQuery and jQuery Validate Library do (code snippet copied from Start.debug.js):

```
loader.defineScripts(
  null,
  [
    {
      name: "jQuery",
      releaseUrl: ajaxPath + "jquery/jquery-1.3.2.min.js",
      debugUrl: ajaxPath + "jquery/jquery-1.3.2.js",
      isLoaded: !!window.jQuery
    },
    {
      name: "jQueryValidate",
      releaseUrl: ajaxPath + "jquery.validate/1.5.5/jquery.validate.min.js",
      debugUrl: ajaxPath + "jquery.validate/1.5.5/jquery.validate.js",
      dependencies: ["jQuery"],
      isLoaded: !!(window.jQuery && jQuery.fn.validate)
    }
  ]
);
```

Because you are already familiar with the concept of the split script files, you know that this granular approach can reduce the total byte size of the scripts downloaded to the client. On the other hand, if there are quite a lot of individual files that should be downloaded, the separate HTTP connections may cause a notable delay at page load time, and may degrade the overall performance. Many JavaScript experts recommend using fewer (but larger) scripts files to minimize the overhead added by the HTTP transport. As always, you must balance between the two approaches based on your unique needs.

If you use *script combining* on the server, you can use the contains property in the metadata to inform the Script Loader that a single file contains multiple features, like Microsoft does with the MicrosoftAjax.js (code snippet copied from Start.debug.js):

```
{
  name: "MicrosoftAjax",
  releaseUrl: "%/MicrosoftAjax.js",
  debugUrl: "%/MicrosoftAjax.debug.js",
  executionDependencies: null,
  contains: ["Core", "ComponentModel", "History",
            "Serialization", "Network",
            "WebServices", "Globalization"]
}
```

If you have a page that requires the Core, the ComponentModel, the History, the Serialization, the Network, the WebServices, and also the Globalization features, and you reference all of them in a single Sys.require call. The Script Loader realizes that it is better to download the same content in a single composite script, and downloads only MicrosoftAjax.js, instead of downloading seven individual files. This script-combining feature is managed automatically by the Loader; all you have to do is to describe the composite scripts with the `contains` property for your custom scripts.

Note the following two things with script combining:

➤ The Script Loader is a client-side component. It can download only what is already available on the server. It is still your responsibility to combine and publish the composite scripts on the server.

➤ The Loader chooses the composite script file only if all the scripts that it contains are required on the page, and only if you load them with a single `Sys.require` call.

You can use composite scripts and single scripts mixed in a page. If you have a single `Sys.require` call with the seven components mentioned earlier, plus the jQuery Library, the Loader will download the composite script with a single HTTP request, and the jQuery Library with another request.

The Script Loader also supports loading scripts on demand. You can use the `script` tag or `Sys.require` calls to load the scripts required by most of your users at page load time, and *delay loading* those scripts that are needed for specific features and a smaller number of users. For example, if you have a Print button on the page, you can use its event handler to download the script files required for the print functionality with the `Sys.loader.loadScripts` function. This will definitely cause a small delay for those users who clicked the Print button (but only the first time, because the browser will cache the script file), but will provide better page load time for all users.

As you have probably already realized, the Script Loader is a really smart component. It supports script dependencies, composite scripts, parallel download, lazy loading, the Microsoft Ajax CDN, and so on. All the features of the Script Loader are available not only for the Microsoft Ajax Library and the jQuery Library, but also for your custom scripts. However, if you want to integrate your own scripts, you should take a look at the `Sys.loader.registerScript` function, and the recommended implementation pattern that supports this architecture.

## Client-Side Data Binding with Templates

Let's suppose you have an object array, and your task is to display the objects in an unordered list on the page. For this example, let's consider an array of country data in a local variable named `countries`. You can fill this array from the server or initialize it locally:

```
var countries = [
    { Name: 'Austria', Code: 'at', Capital: 'Vienna' },
    { Name: 'Hungary', Code: 'hu', Capital: 'Budapest' },
    { Name: 'United States', Code: 'us', Capital: 'Washington, D.C.' }
    // ...
];
```

*Code file [3-AjaxLibrary\03-MixCodeAndMarkup.htm] available for download at Wrox.com*

You can also have a set of image files that are named by the country code and contain the flags of the countries. To complete the task, you must render HTML markup of the unordered list

(<ul>...</ul> tags), the list items (<li>...</li>), the country name in bold (<b>...</*b>), and the flag image (<img...>). Because you have an array, you can write a for loop and iterate through all items in the array, and generate the HTML markup by concatenating the HTML tags and the country data, and, finally, display the result string in the innerHTML of a div:

```
var s = '<ul>';
for (var i = 0; i < countries.length; i++)
{
    s += '<li><b>';
    s += countries[i].Name;
    s += '</*b> - ';
    s += countries[i].Capital;
    s += ' <img src="../images/';
    s += countries[i].Code;
    s += '.gif" /></li>';
}
s += '</ul>';
$get('divResult').innerHTML = s;
```

*Code file [3-AjaxLibrary\03-MixCodeAndMarkup.htm] available for download at Wrox.com*

Although this code is fairly simple, it is neither short nor easy to maintain. If you must change the design or restructure your page, you cannot do that only in a CSS style sheet or in the HTML markup — you must modify the code. This also means that a JavaScript developer is required every time, even if the modification is minor and related to the design, and not to the logic of the page. Writing or maintaining this kind of code is a fully manual task. Your developer environment can give you IntelliSense and syntax highlighting, but you have a fairly good chance that you will not get any designer support for it.

The root of the problem lies in mixing the code and the design. You have already seen this problem on the server side with classic ASP. It is solved by the separation of code and markup in ASP.NET, and an additional layer of abstraction was also introduced with data binding. Unfortunately, the HTML markup and the JavaScript language do not support this declarative approach. But, thanks to the new client-side DataView control and the Sys.Binding class, you can transform your data to HTML markup with imperative (and also in declarative) code in ASP.NET 4.0.

## Using the DataView Control

The coding nightmare of client-side data binding is solved by adding template functionality to the Microsoft Ajax Library in the form of the Sys.UI.DataView class. The DataView class acts as a client control, and behaves similarly to the server-side ListView control — it can have a data source, multiple templates, rendering, and user action events, and is capable of displaying either a single record or multiple records. Because you are used to it on server side, this control can be configured in declarative markup on the client, or can also be instantiated in JavaScript code.

To use the Microsoft Ajax templating engine on your page, you must first load the MicrosoftAjax Templates.js file that itself relies on Serialization, ComponentModel, and the Core script files — so do not forget to add them as well, and be careful with the order of the script references:

```
<script type="text/javascript" src="MicrosoftAjaxCore.js"></script>
<script type="text/javascript" src="MicrosoftAjaxComponentModel.js"></script>
<script type="text/javascript" src="MicrosoftAjaxSerialization.js"></script>
<script type="text/javascript" src="MicrosoftAjaxTemplates.js"></script>
```

*Code file [3-AjaxLibrary\04-DataViewDeclarative.htm] available for download at Wrox.com*

With the `DataView` control, you can solve the previously described task to display the countries and their flags in an unordered list in the following way:

```
<body xmlns:sys="javascript:Sys" xmlns:dv="javascript:Sys.UI.DataView">
  <ul
    class="sys-template"
    sys:attach="dv"
    dv:data="{{ countries }}" >
    <li>
      {{ Name }} ({{ Capital }})
      <img sys:src="{{ '../images/' + Code + '.gif' }}" />
    </li>
  </ul>
</body>
```

*Code file [3-AjaxLibrary\04-DataViewDeclarative.htm] available for download at Wrox.com*

This code may seem a bit familiar and also a bit strange at first. You can recognize the standard XHTML tags (body, ul, li, img) and their attributes (class, src). However, you probably have not seen the sys: and dv: prefixes before. Don't forget that this code is essentially XML, so you can add any new prefixes with their namespace declarations just when they are needed. In this code, the sys and the dv namespaces are declared at the body level — and this is the recommended practice.

The sys:attach system attribute is recognized by the templating engine, and means that an instance of the `DataView` class (referenced with the dv alias) should be attached to the current XHTML element (ul). `DataView` will automatically repeat the child element of the current element (in this case, the li tag) and its content as many times as required by the data source. Therefore, for simple scenarios, you do not have to explicitly mark an item placeholder or an item template.

Because the `DataView` will take care of rendering the HTML markup, the elements that the `DataView` is attached to should not be displayed by the browser. That is specified by hiding the ul element with the sys-template CSS class that contains only the following setting:

```
<style type="text/css">
  .sys-template
  {
    display: none;
  }
</style>
```

*Code file [3-AjaxLibrary\04-DataViewDeclarative.htm] available for download at Wrox.com*

Although, theoretically, you could choose any name for this CSS class, the sys-template is not only a naming convention, it is mandated by the template engine.

Any attribute that begins with the dv: prefix sets a property of the DataView control. The data property is set to the bound data that is to be rendered by the control. (It is very similar to the DataSource property of server-side controls.)

Within the template, you can use the {{ }} syntax to mark the placeholders where the values should be rendered. Between the double curly braces, you can write any expression that can be evaluated in JavaScript. The expression will be evaluated in the context of the data item. As a result, you can directly refer to any properties of the current record in the data source. You can add the {{ }} expression directly to the markup without wrapping it into an HTML tag, but you can also bound to an attribute of a tag. If you bound to an HTML attribute, you must prepend the sys: prefix to it, as you can see at the sys:src attribute of the img tag in the previous example.

For an ASP.NET developer, the {{ Name }} expression is very similar to the <%# Eval('Name') %> server-side expression. However, later in this chapter, you will see that the client version is more powerful because it imitates the more mature data-binding features of *Windows Presentation Foundation (WPF)*.

This declarative markup renders a bulleted list in the browser, as shown in Figure 19-4.

- Austria (Vienna) ▤
- Australia (Canberra) ▧
- Brasil (Brasilia) ▧
- Croatia (Zagreb) ▤
- Spain (Madrid) ▤
- Finland (Helsinki) ✚
- Greece (Athens) ▤
- Hungary (Budapest) ▤
- Sweden (Stockholm) ▤
- Slovakia (Bratislava) ▧
- United Kingdom (London) ▧
- United States (Washington, D.C.) ▤

**FIGURE 19-4:** Bulleted list rendered by the DataView control

The previous code shows the declarative way of using the DataView control. If you want to strictly separate the markup and the logic, you have the option of creating the DataView imperatively from code. In this case, you can clean up the markup and remove all the DataView-related settings:

```
<body xmlns:sys="javascript:Sys">
  <ul class="sys-template">
    <li>
      {{ Name }} ({{ Capital }})
      <img sys:src="{{ '../images/' + Code + '.gif' }}" />
    </li>
  </ul>
</body>
```

*Code file [3-AjaxLibrary\04-DataViewDeclarative.htm] available for download at Wrox.com*

The DataView can be instantiated, configured, and attached with a single line of code — for example, in the pageLoad event handler:

```
function pageLoad()
{
  Sys.create.dataView("ul",
  {
    data: countries
  });
}
```

*Code file [3-AjaxLibrary\05-DataViewFromCode.htm] available for download at Wrox.com*

The `Sys.create.dataView` method attaches a new `DataView` instance to the specified element. To specify an element, you use a *selector* that can point to an HTML element (in this case, the single `ul` tag), an ID, or a CSS class. To refer to an ID, use the `"#"` prefix (for example, `"#myid"`). To select elements by their CSS class, use the `"."` prefix (for example, `".myclass"`) in the selector. Furthermore, if you loaded the jQuery Library into the page, you could use the full jQuery selector syntax. In the second parameter, this method allows you to configure the `DataView` — in this case, only the `data` property is set.

## Using Pseudo-Columns in a Template

In addition to the properties of the records in the data source, the template engine provides two additional *pseudo-columns* that you can access in your data-binding expressions. The first one is `$index` that contains the zero-based numerical index of your current record, and the second one is `$dataItem` that is basically the current record rendered.

The following code shows an example of how to use these pseudo-columns:

Available for download on Wrox.com

```
<body xmlns:sys="javascript:Sys" xmlns:dv="javascript:Sys.UI.DataView">
  <ul
    class="sys-template"
    sys:attach="dv"
    dv:data="{{ countries }}" >
    <li sys:class-altRow="{{ $index % 2 == 1 }}">
      {{ Name }} ({{ Capital }})
      <img sys:src="{{ '../images/' + Code + '.gif' }}" />
      <a sys:href="{{ getUrl($dataItem) }}">Open webpage</a>
    </li>
  </ul>
</body>
```

*Code file [3-AjaxLibrary\06-DataViewPseudoColumns.htm] available for download at Wrox.com*

This code uses the `$index` pseudo-column to conditionally apply the `.altRow` CSS class to every second list item. The syntax to accomplish this is again strange — you must use the `sys:class-` attribute (yes, the ending dash is part of the attribute name) and append the name of your CSS class after the dash. After that, it is up to you to define the CSS class in your style sheet.

Available for download on Wrox.com

```
<style type="text/css">
  .altRow
  {
    background-color: rgb(252,254,203);
  }
</style>
```

*Code file [3-AjaxLibrary\06-DataViewPseudoColumns.htm] available for download at Wrox.com*

If you want to modify a single CSS property, and not apply a complete stylesheet class, you can do that with the `sys:style-` attribute (again, the dash is part of the attribute name). For example, to change the font size of a span based on the position of the item in the `DataView`, you can use the `sys:style-font-size` attribute:

```
<span sys:class-altRow="{{ $index % 2 == 1 }}"
      sys:style-font-size="{{ $index * 2 + 'pt' }}">
  {{ Capital }}
</span>
```

*Code file [3-AjaxLibrary\06-DataViewPseudoColumns.htm] available for download at Wrox.com*

Another practical use of the `$index` attribute is to set the client `id` attribute of an HTML tag with unique values, as shown in the following example:

```
<input type="button" sys:id="{{ 'btn' + $index }}" ... />
```

The `$dataItem` pseudo-column is used to pass the current record to the custom `getUrl` function that is responsible for calculating the URL of the "Open web page" link. The `getUrl` function receives the complete record. Therefore, you can access any properties of the current country within the function:

```
function getUrl(country)
{
  return String.format("http://www.{0}.{1}", country.Capital, country.Code);
}
```

*Code file [3-AjaxLibrary\06-DataViewPseudoColumns.htm] available for download at Wrox.com*

Both the `$index` and the `$dataItem` are basically shortcuts to access the most important properties of a variable called `$context`. In addition to the `index` and the `dataItem`, the `$context` variable provides additional useful properties and methods. For example, you can use the `containerElement`, the `nodes`, and the `template` properties, and the `get` method, to retrieve information about the rendered markup, or the `data` property to access all records in the data source.

The following example shows how you can display the next country for every record with the `$context` variable:

```
The next country is {{ getNextCountry($context) }}
function getNextCountry(context)
{
  if( context.index + 1 < context.data.length )
  {
    return context.data[ context.index + 1 ].Name;
  }
}
```

*Code file [3-AjaxLibrary\06-DataViewPseudoColumns.htm] available for download at Wrox.com*

You can also query or set properties of the current HTML element in an expression using the `$element` variable.

If you combine all these tricks into a single page, you will get the result shown in Figure 19-5.

- ▪ ▭
- ▪ ....▪▪ ......▪▪▪▪▪▪ ".....
- ▪ ▪▪▪ ▪▭▪ ......▪▪▪▪▪ — ▪▪ .......
- ▪ Croatia (Zagreb) ▭ · <u>Open webpage #4</u> — The next country is Spain
- ▪ Spain (Madrid) ▭ · <u>Open webpage #5</u> — The next country is Finland
- ▪ Finland (Helsinki) ✚ · <u>Open webpage #6</u> — The next country is Greece
- ▪ Greece (Athens) ▤ · <u>Open webpage #7</u> — The next country is Hungary
- ▪ Hungary (Budapest) ▭ · <u>Open webpage #8</u> — The next country is Sweden
- ▪ Sweden (Stockholm) ▤ · <u>Open webpage #9</u> — The next country is Slovakia
- ▪ Slovakia (Bratislava) ▪ · <u>Open webpage #10</u> — The next country is United Kingdom
- ▪ United Kingdom (London) ▦ · <u>Open webpage #11</u> — The next country is United States
- ▪ United States (Washington, D.C.) ▪ · <u>Open webpage #12</u> — The next country is undefined

**FIGURE 19-5:** Result of using pseudo columns in a template

## Running Code Inside a Template

It sometimes happens that the declarative syntax is not powerful enough to express the required functionality. In this case, you have no other option than adding some code to the template. One of the most-required scenarios is to render or not render a specific element based on a return value of a JavaScript expression. This is where the sys:if attribute comes into the picture.

In one of the previous examples, you saw how to display a value from the next record in the current template by calling a custom function (getNextCountry). Using the sys:if attribute, you can implement the same functionality without the external function:

```
<span sys:if="$index + 1 !== $context.data.length" />
    The next country is {{ $context.data[ $index + 1 ].Name }}.
</span>
```

*Code file [3-AjaxLibrary\07-DataViewConditionals.htm] available for download at Wrox.com*

Here you can see how to use the $index and $context pseudo-columns to access the next record. The new part is the sys:if attribute that can contain arbitrary code that will be evaluated every time a data item is rendered. If you add the sys:if attribute to an HTML element, that tag will be rendered only if the specified JavaScript expression evaluates to true. In this example, a span is rendered for every record except the last one.

Another common scenario is to render a tag only for the first record, or before the first record. The following code snippet renders a drop-down list box with the countries and a default "Select a country" item before the first record:

```
<select
    class="sys-template"
    sys:attach="dv"
```

```
  dv:data="{{ countries }}">
  <option sys:if="$index == 0" value="" selected="selected">
    Select a country
  </option>
  <option sys:value="{{ Code }}">{{ Name }}</option>
</select>
```

*Code file [3-AjaxLibrary\07-DataViewConditionals.htm] available for download at Wrox.com*

The sys:if attribute can also be used to render a separator item between the data items. In the following example, the list bullets are turned off, and a horizontal rule is rendered between the countries:

Available for download on Wrox.com

```
<ul
  class="sys-template"
  sys:attach="dv"
  dv:data="{{ countries }}"
  style="list-style-type: none" >
  <li>
    <hr sys:if="$index !== 0" />
    {{ Name }} ({{ Capital }})
  </li>
</ul>
```

*Code file [3-AjaxLibrary\07-DataViewConditionals.htm] available for download at Wrox.com*

Figure 19-6 shows the rendered page.

Select a country ▾

Austria (Vienna) ☰ · Open webpage #1 — The next country is Australia.

Australia (Canberra) ▦ · Open webpage #2 — The next country is Brasil.

Brasil (Brasilia) ▦ · Open webpage #3 — The next country is Croatia.

Croatia (Zagreb) ☰ · Open webpage #4 — The next country is Spain.

Spain (Madrid) ⬌ · Open webpage #5 — The next country is Finland.

Finland (Helsinki) ╬ · Open webpage #6 — The next country is Greece.

Greece (Athens) ☰ · Open webpage #7 — The next country is Hungary.

Hungary (Budapest) ☰ · Open webpage #8 — The next country is Sweden.

Sweden (Stockholm) ▤ · Open webpage #9 — The next country is Slovakia.

Slovakia (Bratislava) ▦ · Open webpage #10 — The next country is United Kingdom.

United Kingdom (London) ▦ · Open webpage #11 — The next country is United States.

United States (Washington, D.C.) ▦ · Open webpage #12

**FIGURE 19-6:** Using conditional expressions

Although the `sys:if` attribute allows you to execute any code, its primary purpose is to allow you to evaluate an expression that should return with a `true` or a `false` value. If you want to execute some custom code before or after an item is rendered, you can do that in the `sys:codebefore` and in the `sys:codeafter` attributes.

 *The* `sys:if`, `sys:codebefore`, *and* `sys:codeafter` *attributes provide great flexibility to the template engine. However, be careful, because the result is that the declarative template skeleton gets mixed with imperative code.*

## Adding Interaction with Events Inside the Template

All the examples you have seen rendered the data for the user, and the user could do nothing else except read it. In addition to reading the data, probably the most-often performed user action is to select a record, and then do something with it. Fortunately, the `DataView` control supports user events and the `Select` event natively.

Events are raised when the user clicks on an HTML tag rendered by the template. To specify the name of the command, you can use the `sys:command` attribute on any HTML tag you want to support events. The `Select` command is handled specially, because it works without setting any additional properties, and the `DataView` control provides property wrapper methods to retrieve the selected item.

In the following example, you can see the previous country example refactored, so the user is able to select a single country, and then click on the "Get country details" link that displays additional information about the selected country in a pop-up window, as shown in Figure 19-7.

Available for
download on
Wrox.com

```
<body xmlns:sys="javascript:Sys" xmlns:dv="javascript:Sys.UI.DataView">
  <ul
    id="countryList"
    class="sys-template"
    sys:attach="dv"
    dv:data="{{ countries }}"
    dv:initialselectedindex="7"
    dv:selecteditemclass="selected">
    <li sys:command="Select" style="cursor: pointer">
      {{ Name }} ({{ Capital }})
    </li>
  </ul>
  <a href="#" onclick="getDetails()">Get country details</a>
</body>
```

*Code file [3-AjaxLibrary\08-DataViewSelectCommand.htm] available for download at Wrox.com*

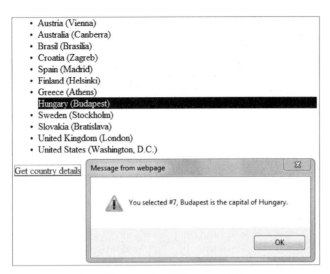

**FIGURE 19-7:** Handling events within a template

As you can see, the same unordered list is used as before. The only difference is that now the user can click on any item to select it. This selectability feature is added to the `li` element with the `sys:command="Select"` attribute, and the cursor is changed with the `style` attribute to provide a visual clue for the user.

The `DataView` is able to automatically add a CSS class to the currently selected element if the name of this class is defined in the `selectedItemClass` property. You can use this CSS class to highlight the selected data item. Note that even if you move the `sys:command` and the `style` attributes to a child element inside the template, the `selectedItemClass` will be added to the whole list item. That means that although you can raise the `Select` event from any part of the data item, only the whole data item can be selected, not parts of it.

This code also shows that you can specify the item selected when the control is first rendered by setting its zero-based index in the `dv:initialselectedindex` property.

After the user successfully selects a record, he or she can click on the "Get country details" link that calls the `getDetails` custom JavaScript function. Note that this function call is outside the template, and, because no context parameters are passed to the function, the selection information must be queried from the `DataView`.

The following code snippet shows the implementation of the `getDetails` method:

```
function getDetails()
{
    var dv = $find("countryList");
    var country = dv.get_selectedData();
    var msg = String.format("You selected #{0}, {1} is the capital of {2}.",
                            dv.get_selectedIndex(),
```

```
                              country.Capital,
                              country.Name);
      alert(msg);
}
```

Here you can see how you can use the $find function to get a reference to an existing DataView instance by specifying the unique id of the wrapping HTML element. After you have a Sys. UI.DataView instance in the dv variable, you can query its selectedData and selectedIndex properties via their getter methods using the get_ naming convention. These are writable properties. Therefore, by calling their set_ methods, you can change the selection in the DataView.

Just like server-side controls, the DataView control supports multiple commands on a single data item. The way you implement this is the same that you're used to on the server side. Declare a generic event handler method on the control level; then, when you raise the event inside the template, you specify the command name and a command argument. These two parameters are passed to your event handler and help you determine where the user clicked.

The following code snippet shows how you can raise multiple events from a single data item:

```
<ul
  id="countryList"
  class="sys-template"
  sys:attach="dv"
  dv:data="{{ countries }}"
  dv:initialselectedindex="7"
  dv:selecteditemclass="selected"
  dv:oncommand="{{ onCommand }}">
  <li>
    <span sys:command="Select" style="cursor: pointer">
      {{ Name }}
    </span>
    ({{ Capital }})
    <img
      style="cursor: pointer"
      sys:alt="{{ 'Flag of ' + Name }}"
      sys:src="{{ '../images/' + Code + '.gif' }}"
      sys:command="ShowFlag"
      sys:commandargument="{{ $dataItem }}" />
  </li>
</ul>
<img id="imgLargerFlag" />
```

This code renders an unordered list of country names, capitals, and a small image that displays the flag of the country. The sys:command attribute is added to the country name and the image, so the user is able to click on these elements, but not on the capital. When the user clicks on the country name, the built-in Select command is raised. As a result, the selected list item is highlighted with the selected class specified in the dv:selecteditemclass property.

However, when the user clicks on the image, the custom `onCommand` event handler function (that is assigned in the `dv:oncommand` attribute) is called, and the `ShowFlag` command name and the current data item are passed to it as a command argument. Here you can see how this custom event handler is implemented:

```
function onCommand(sender, e)
{
  switch(e.get_commandName())
  {
    case "Select":
      // Let the DataView handle selection.
      return;
    case "ShowFlag":
      var country = e.get_commandArgument();
      var img = $get("imgLargeFlag");
      img.src = String.format("../images/flag_{0}.gif", country.Code);
      img.alt = country.Name;
  }
}
```

*Code file [3-AjaxLibrary\09-DataViewCustomCommand.htm] available for download at Wrox.com*

This method is called when the user clicks on a country name or a flag thumbnail. That means this method is called even for the built-in `Select` command, so you must write your code to prepare to handle multiple types of events. Just like on the server side, the event handler receives two parameters: the `sender` that contains a reference to the `DataView` control, and the `e` that contains event specific parameters. The `e` is of type `Sys.CommandEventArgs` that inherits from `Sys.CancelEventArgs`, and has the following properties:

➤ `cancel`

➤ `commandName`

➤ `commandArgument`

➤ `commandSource`

If you set the `cancel` property to `true` (via its `set_cancel` wrapper method) in the `"Select"` case branch, you can prevent the default behavior, and the clicked item will not be selected and highlighted. The `commandName` and `commandArgument` behave just like their server-side counterparts. You can get the values you set with the `sys:command` and `sys:commandargument` attributes. The `commandSource` contains a reference to a `Sys.UI.DomElement` that wraps the HTML element that is clicked by the user.

In this example, if the user clicks on a country name or a thumbnail image, the `onCommand` event handler is called for both cases. In the event handler, the command name is queried, and custom code is executed only for the `ShowFlag` event. In this case, you get the current record (that is passed as `$dataItem` in the `commandArgument` property) and use its values to display the large flag in the `imgLargeFlag` image outside the `DataView`.

In addition to the `command` event, the `DataView` raises additional events while the content is being rendered:

➤ The `fetchSucceeded` and the `fetchFailed` events are raised when the `DataView` successfully loaded the source data, or if the loading failed.

➤ The `itemRendering` and `itemRendered` events are raised before and after each item is rendered.

➤ The rendering and rendered events are raised before and after the whole dataset is rendered in the control.

## Using External Templates

By default, the template engine repeats the first child item of the HTML element to which the `DataView` is attached. For most cases, this is a very convenient behavior. However, sometimes you may want to add a non-data-bound first item, or a header, or even a footer item manually.

On the server side, this problem is solved with the `itemplaceholder` and the `itemtemplate` properties of the `ListView` control, and you can find similar concepts on the client side as well. You can mark an HTML element within your `DataView` as an item placeholder, and you can mark an external element as an item template. The `DataView` will repeat the external element as many times as required by the data source, and will substitute the item placeholder with it.

The following example generates an unordered list with manual header and footer items. Figure 19-8 shows the rendered page.

Available for download on Wrox.com

```
<ul
   sys:attach="dv"
   dv:data="{{ countries }}"
   dv:itemplaceholder="#itemPlaceholder"
   dv:itemtemplate="#itemTemplate">
   <li><a href="Add.aspx">Click here to add a new country to the list</a></li>
   <li id="itemPlaceholder"></li>
   <li><a href="More.aspx">More...</a></li>
</ul>
<div id="itemTemplate" class="sys-template">
   <li>
      {{ Name }} ({{{ Capital }}})
   </li>
</div>
</ul>
```

*Code file [3-AjaxLibrary\10-ExternalTemplates.htm] available for download at Wrox.com*

The item template is defined in an external `div` container, its child item is repeated (when the `DataView` is rendered), and, finally, the result overwrites the placeholder in the `DataView`. It is worth pointing out that if you use external templates, the `sys-template` class should not be attached to the host element of the `DataView` but rather to the external template container.

In this example, the `DataView` is attached to the `ul` element, and the `itemplaceholder` and `itemtemplate` properties are used to point to the placeholder and the template. You can utilize the *selector syntax* for both properties by using the # sign to point to an HTML element.

Select a country ▾

- Click here to add a new country to the list
- Austria (Vienna)
- Australia (Canberra)
- Brasil (Brasilia)
- Croatia (Zagreb)
- Spain (Madrid)
- Finland (Helsinki)
- Greece (Athens)
- Hungary (Budapest)
- Sweden (Stockholm)
- Slovakia (Bratislava)
- United Kingdom (London)
- United States (Washington, D.C.)
- More...

**FIGURE 19-8:** Creating header and footer items with external templates

# Advanced Data-Binding Scenarios

Earlier in this chapter, you learned about the templating engine of the Microsoft Ajax Library, and learned how to display data on the client. All the examples demonstrated *one-time, one-way bindings*. That means the template was evaluated only once, and the data was rendered on the client when the page loaded, or when an event was raised. But when the data was modified by a client-side script, the page was not updated. Fortunately, the Microsoft Ajax Library supports not only one-way, one-time bindings, but it is also capable of building a continuous connection between the data source and the controls on the UI.

## Live Binding

If one-time binding does not suit your needs because you want to automatically update the UI when the data changes, then you must switch to *live binding*. Live binding requires that the template engine be notified when a value of a variable or a property changes. When the template engine receives these notifications, it refreshes the rendered markup.

The only problem is that the JavaScript language itself does not natively support raising notifications when a value changes. Therefore, a manual workaround is needed.

If you already looked into the Ajax Library or created custom client components, you have probably met the `raisePropertyChanged` method of the `Sys.Component` class. You can invoke this method in a property set accessor to raise the `propertyChanged` event. However, your class will have this event only if it inherits from the `Sys.Component`, `Sys.UI.Behavior`, or the `Sys.UI.Control` base class. With this approach, if you have a simple object array bound to a `DataView` control, you would have to wrap it inside a component to build your code using the `propertyChanged` event.

Fortunately, a new class in Microsoft Ajax Library 4, `Sys.Observer`, drastically makes your life easier by fully implementing the *observer pattern*. The primary purpose of this class is to make any object *observable* by providing helper methods to modify the object. If you use these methods, the `Sys.Observer` class will take care of raising all the notification events.

To make the previous `countries` collection observable, all you have to do is call the `Sys.Observer.makeObservable` method:

**Available for download on Wrox.com**

```
Sys.Observer.makeObservable(countries);
```

*Code file [3-AjaxLibrary\11-LiveBinding.htm] available for download at Wrox.com*

The `makeObserver` function adds a bunch of new methods to the target object that can be used to modify it in an observable manner. If the object is an array, additional array modification methods are added as well.

For example, you can add a new item to the array so that subscribers will be notified about it by calling the `insert` method:

**Available for download on Wrox.com**

```
countries.insert(0, { Name: 'Switzerland', Capital: 'Bern' });
```

*Code file [3-AjaxLibrary\11-LiveBinding.htm] available for download at Wrox.com*

Also, you can remove the first item from the collection by calling the `removeAt` method:

```
countries.removeAt(0);
```

You can also call the original functions of the `Sys.Observer` class, but, in this case, you must pass the observable target as well:

```
Sys.Observer.removeAt(countries,0);
```

It is also possible to modify a property of the target object with the `setValue` method. However, if you modify multiple properties and you do not want to raise the `propertyChanged` event until all the properties are updated (for example, to avoid UI flickering and displaying partially updated records), you can suspend the notification, and then send them all when you are done:

```
countries.beginUpdate();
Sys.Observer.setValue(countries[0], 'Name', 'Österreich');
Sys.Observer.setValue(countries[0], 'Capital', 'Wien');
Sys.Observer.setValue(countries[5], 'Name', 'Suomi');
Sys.Observer.setValue(countries[7], 'Name', 'Magyarország');
countries.endUpdate();
```

The `DataView` control is smart enough to recognize if a data source is observable, and is capable of handling the collection or property changed event automatically. Still, you must slightly modify your data-binding syntax to indicate which parts of the template should be updated when the data source changes:

```
<ul
  class="sys-template"
  sys:attach="dv"
  dv:data="{{ countries }}" >
  <li>
    <span>{ binding Name }</span>
    <span>{ binding Capital }</span>
  </li>
</ul>
```

As you can see in this example, you must use the `binding` markup extension, and then the name of the property you want to display. These placeholders will be automatically updated when the source data changes. However, note that you must always modify your data source via the `Sys.Observer` methods. If you modify the data source directly, without going through the interface, notification events will not be raised.

## Top-Level Binding

The live-binding syntax supports not only specifying the name of the property you want to bind to, but also additional optional parameters. One of the additional parameters is the `source` that points to the object that property should be bounded to the target control. Using the `source` parameter allows you to create *top-level bindings*, which means that you can define data-binding expressions outside of a `DataView`.

You can create a global object, and you can bind one of its properties to a `span`. What's more, if you make your global object observable and use the live binding syntax, updates are immediately displayed on the UI:

```
<head>
  <script type="text/javascript">
    var country = { Name: 'Magyarország', Code: 'hu', Capital: 'Budapest' };
    Sys.Observer.makeObservable(country);

    function translate()
    {
      Sys.Observer.setValue(country, 'Name', 'Hungary');
    }
  </script>
</head>
<body xmlns:sys="javascript:Sys">
  The country of the day is
  <span sys:innertext="{ binding Name, source={{ country }} }"></span>
  <a href="#" onclick="translate()">Translate name</a>
</body>
```

*Code file [3-AjaxLibrary\12-TopLevelBinding.htm] available for download at Wrox.com*

You can also point the `source` property to the `window` object to access global variables:

```
var today = new Date().format('D');
<span sys:innertext="{ binding today, source={{ window }} }"></span>
```

*Code file [3-AjaxLibrary\12-TopLevelBinding.htm] available for download at Wrox.com*

After clicking the "Translate name" link, the page gets updated, and the image shown in Figure 19-9 is rendered.

Today is Thursday, 10 December 2009 and the country of the day is Hungary Translate name

**FIGURE 19-9:** Using top-level binding

## Two-Way Binding

It often happens that you not only want to display data on the UI, but also want to enable the user to change the data, and you want to write it back to the data source. Fortunately, the live binding syntax supports *two-way data binding*, which means that you do not have to write code to implement this feature. You can express it declaratively. The behavior can be set on the `mode` parameter of the binding expression using the `Sys.BindingMode` enumeration:

```
<input type="text" sys:value="{ binding Name, source={{ data }}, mode=oneWay }"/>
```

Remember that the default behavior is for `Sys.BindingMode.auto` to use two-way binding if the target is an `input`, `select`, or `textarea` element, or a component that implements the `Sys.INotifyPropertyChanged` interface; otherwise it is *one-way*. Because you most likely create input controls to query input from the user, and you need two-way binding for that, in most cases, you will not change the default, which means that you can omit the `mode` parameter.

Using two-way data binding, you can load the value of a textbox into a global variable (`username`) and then display the global variable with a `span`:

Available for
download on
Wrox.com

```
Please enter your name:
<input type="text"
  sys:value="{ binding username, source={{ window }} }" />
<br />
Hello
<span sys:innertext="{ binding username, source={{ window }} }"></span>
```

*Code file [3-AjaxLibrary\13-TwoWayBinding.htm] available for download at Wrox.com*

Two-way data binding also opens the door for many useful data-binding scenarios. For example, you can bind a UI element's property to another UI element's property. In the following example, you can see a textbox and a checkbox, and the `checked` property of the checkbox is bound directly to the `disabled` property of the textbox, so the user must clear the checkbox to enable editing:

Available for
download on
Wrox.com

```
<input type="text"
  id="txt"
  sys:value="{ binding username, source={{ window }} }"
  sys:disabled="{ binding checked, source={{ chk }} }" />
<input type="checkbox" id="chk" />
<label for="chk">Disable editing</label>
```

*Code file [3-AjaxLibrary\13-TwoWayBinding.htm] available for download at Wrox.com*

The entered name is displayed on the page when the user navigates away from the textbox (the input control loses focus), as shown in Figure 19-10.

**FIGURE 19-10:** Binding properties to each other

## Custom Converters

If you are familiar with Windows Presentation Foundation (WPF), you have probably realized the similarities between the WPF data-binding syntax and the live binding in the Ajax Library. Another common point is the concept of *converters*.

If you have a data source and you want to bind its value to a UI element's property, it can happen that they have different types. If it happens anywhere else in code and not in a declarative expression, you would probably cast your data value to the property's type, or call a helper function to resolve the data type mismatch. The concept of converters helps you to implement this functionality in a standardized way with a maximum level of code reuse.

In addition to the `source` and the `mode` parameters, the live binding syntax lets you specify a *convert* and a *convert back function*. The convert function is called when the data flows from the data source to the UI element, and the convert back function is called when the UI element's property value is loaded back to the data source. Both functions receive two parameters — the value that is about to be converted, and a `Sys.Binding` instance that you can use to query any information about the source and the target of the binding. Although this feature also works with global functions, it is recommended that you implement the converter methods as members of the `Sys.converters` object.

The following markup renders a textbox and a disabled button. The goal is to enable the button only if the user enters "I Accept."

```
If you accept the agreement please type "I Accept" here:
<input type="text"
   sys:value="{ binding disabled,
                source={{ btn }},
                mode=oneWayToSource,
                convertBack=disableConverter,
                expectedResult=I Accept }" />
<br />
<input type="button"
   id="btn"
   value="Submit registration" />
```

*Code file [3-AjaxLibrary\14-Converters.htm] available for download at Wrox.com*

As you can see from the syntax, the button's `disabled` property (*source*) is bound to the value of the textbox (*target*). By default, the live binding would be two-way, but the behavior is changed to `oneWayToSource`, because you probably do not want to display the value of the `disabled` property (`true` or `false`) in the textbox. This way, you ensure that the data flows only from the textbox to the button.

However, there is still a type mismatch between the string `value` and the Boolean `disabled` properties. Therefore, a custom converter function called `disableConverter` is created. This is configured as a `convertBack` method, so the template engine will call it when the value of the target (textbox) is transferred to the source (button) — and that is exactly what is needed now. The `disableConverter` function is implemented with nothing special about this situation, so you can easily reuse it anywhere else in your code.

```
Sys.converters.disableConverter = function(value, binding)
{
   return (value !== binding.expectedResult);
}
```

*Code file [3-AjaxLibrary\14-Converters.htm] available for download at Wrox.com*

Figure 19-11 shows the result page.

One thing to note is that the "I Accept" value is not hard-coded into the converter, but rather it is passed as a parameter. You can add additional parameters to your binding syntax, and all of them will be added as *expando properties*

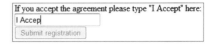

**FIGURE 19-11:** The button is disabled with live binding

to the `Sys.Binding` instance. You do not have to register these additional properties. Just configure them in the binding expression, and the converter will receive their values. Just be careful, because a typo (even in casing) can create additional properties, and your converter will fail to work.

If you must convert a value when it is transferred from the data source to the UI element, you can write a similar function (the signature is the same), but you must change the binding expression to use the `convert` keyword instead of the `convertBack`.

The templating engine provides strong support for converters. However, there is currently no built-in converter in the Microsoft Ajax Library.

## Master-Detail Binding

The `DataView` control and the live binding feature of the Microsoft Ajax Library supports *master-detail* scenarios. In a master-detail scenario, you define two DataView controls and connect them to each other. When the user selects a record in the master `DataView` that shows only some top-level fields from the record, the details `DataView` is automatically updated to display the additional fields. As you may guess, this feature heavily relies on the `select` command in the master view, and the trick is how you define the data source of the details view.

The following example displays the list of countries, and when the user selects a country, the name, the capital, and the flag of the country is displayed below the list.

```
Please select a country:
<ul
  id="master"
  class="sys-template"
  sys:attach="dv"
  dv:data="{{ countries }}"
  dv:selecteditemclass="selected" >
  <li sys:command="Select" style="cursor: pointer">
    {{ Name }}
    (<span>{ binding Capital }</span>)
  </li>
</ul>
<div
  class="sys-template"
  sys:attach="dv"
  dv:data="{ binding selectedData,
            source={{ $find('master') }} }">
  <img
    sys:src="{ binding Code,
              convert=stringConverter,
              format=../images/flag_{0}.gif }"
    sys:alt="{{ Name }}"
    style="float: left; margin-right: 10px; "/>
  <h2>{{ Name }}</h2>
  <label for="txtCapital">Capital:</label>
  <input type="text" id="txtCapital"
    sys:value="{ binding Capital }" />
</div>
```

*Code file [3-AjaxLibrary\15-MasterDetail.htm] available for download at Wrox.com*

In Figure 19-12, you can see what is rendered by the browser after the user clicks on the United States record.

Let's analyze this code step by step. The master view is the HTML `ul` element, and the details view is the `div` underneath. Both HTML elements have the `DataView` attached, because the `DataView` is able to display a single record and also multiple records. In the master view, the `select` command is implemented with the default behavior without any custom event handler. Only the `selecteditemclass` property is defined to highlight the selected country on the UI.

FIGURE 19-12: Master-detail view

As you saw before, when the user selects a record, its data item is loaded into the `selectedData` property of the `DataView`. This is the value the details view is bound to by using the `$find` method to get the `Sys.UI.DataView` instance attached to the master HTML element, and use it as the data source object. If you want to write more compact code, you can express the same by using the `$` prefix and the ID of the HTML element:

```
dv:data="{ binding selectedData, source={{ $master }} }"
```

*Code file [3-AjaxLibrary\15-MasterDetail.htm] available for download at Wrox.com*

The `selectedData` property will contain a country record. Therefore, you can bind to its `Name`, `Capital`, and `Code` properties. This code also utilizes a custom `stringConverter` to get the flag image URL based on the country code using the `String.format` method:

```
Sys.converters.stringConverter = function(value, binding)
{
    return String.format(binding.format, value);
}
```

*Code file [3-AjaxLibrary\15-MasterDetail.htm] available for download at Wrox.com*

Because live binding is used, the changes to the `selectedData` property are propagated to the details view that will refresh itself automatically. In addition to that, because the data is bound to an `input` element in the details view, and that is, by default, a two-way binding, if the user changes the capital name in the textbox, the new value appears in the master view after the textbox loses the focus. Note that this can happen because the master and the details view essentially use the same data source, the `countries` object array.

## Working with Server-Side Data

Earlier, you saw examples of how to use the client-side `DataView` control to display and manage data that comes from a local data source. However, in real-world scenarios, the data is stored on the server, so you must add additional steps to download it to the client, and then upload the changes back to the server. The Microsoft Ajax Library fully supports interoperating with web services, Ajax-enabled WCF services, and ADO.NET Data Services on the server.

To port the country example to the server, first create a `Country` class in C# that encapsulates all country-related data:

```csharp
public class Country
{
    public string Name;
    public string Code;
    public string Capital;

    public Country()
    {}

    public Country( string name, string code, string capital)
    {
        this.Name = name;
        this.Code = code;
        this.Capital = capital;
    }
}
```

*Code file [App_Code\Country.cs] available for download at Wrox.com*

Then, create a new ASMX web service called `CountryService` with a `private static countries` list, and initialize it with country data:

```csharp
[WebService( Namespace = "http://balassy.spaces.live.com/Samples/" )]
[System.Web.Script.Services.ScriptService]
public class CountryService : System.Web.Services.WebService
{
    private static List<Country> countries = new List<Country>()
    {
        new Country( "Austria", "at", "Vienna" ),
        new Country( "Australia", "au", "Canberra" ),
        new Country( "Brasil", "br", "Brasília" )
        // Add more countries here...
    };
}
```

*Code file [App_Code\CountryService.cs] available for download at Wrox.com*

You may notice that the `ScriptService` attribute is added to the web service class. This attribute is required if you want to access the web service from JavaScript, and, actually, that is all you have to add to your code to Ajax-enable your web service.

Finally, add the web service methods you want to publish for your clients.

```csharp
[WebMethod]
public Country[] GetCountriesByName()
{
    return this.GetCountries( "Name", true );
```

```
    }

    [WebMethod]
    public Country[] GetCountries( string orderby, bool asc )
    {
      Func<Country, string> keySelector;
      switch( orderby )
      {
        case "Name":
          keySelector = new Func<Country, string>( c => c.Name );
          break;
        case "Code":
          keySelector = new Func<Country, string>( c => c.Code );
          break;
        case "Capital":
          keySelector = new Func<Country, string>( c => c.Capital );
          break;
        default:
          keySelector = new Func<Country, string>( c => c.Name );
          break;
      }
      IEnumerable<Country> result = asc ?
        CountryService.countries.OrderBy( keySelector ) :
        CountryService.countries.OrderByDescending( keySelector );
      return result.ToArray();
    }
```

*Code file [App_Code\CountryService.cs] available for download at Wrox.com*

In this scenario, two methods are added to the service class, and both return the list of countries. The GetCountries is a universal method that allows the client to specify the sorting and direction of the result array. The GetCountriesByName is simpler, because it does not accept any parameters and always returns the countries ordered by their names.

At this point, you can just press Ctrl+F5 in Visual Studio and test your web service in the browser. Note that Visual Studio opens the CountryService.asmx URI directly, and a test page is generated automatically. On the test page, you can find a link (CountryService.asmx?WSDL) to the *Service Description* required by the service clients to build their client side proxies.

However, if you want to call this web service from JavaScript, the ASP.NET run-time can generate for you a fully featured client-side proxy in JavaScript on-the-fly. To get this proxy, all you have to do is change the URI to CountryService.asmx/jsdebug. By adding /jsdebug, you get the more readable debug version of the proxy; by adding /js you can get the minified release version.

It worth stopping for a moment and exploring the generated script proxy that contains two classes:

```
...
CountryService.registerClass('CountryService',Sys.Net.WebServiceProxy);
...
Country.registerClass('Country');
...
```

Because the server-side `Country` class is used in the web service interface, a similar class is also generated for the client. To call the web service, you get a class called `CountryService` that derives from the `Sys.Net.WebServiceProxy` base class.

Now, that you have a fully featured proxy class that hides the details of the web service SOAP call, you can display the countries on the client. First, create a `DataView` without specifying the data source:

```
<ul
  id="countryList"
  class="sys-template"
  sys:attach="dv"
  <li>
    {{ Name }} ({{ Capital }})
  </li>
</ul>
```

*Code file [4-ServerSideData\1-WebService.htm] available for download at Wrox.com*

To access the proxy class, add a script reference to the `/js` or `/jsdebug` URL:

```
<script type="text/javascript" src="CountryService.asmx/jsdebug"></script>
```

*Code file [4-ServerSideData\1-WebService.htm] available for download at Wrox.com*

With the proxy class, call the web service when the page is fully loaded. Before that, take a moment to reconsider what is happening under the hood.

The only way to initiate an HTTP request from the client is to use the `XMLHttpRequest` object in the browser, and that is what the `Sys.Net.WebServiceProxy` class uses as well. However, the `XMLHttpRequest` calls are asynchronous. Therefore, all service proxy methods accept a success and a failure callback method reference. That means that, although the `GetCountriesByName` method does not have any parameter on the server, when you call it on the client, you must pass at least a success callback reference to process the results:

```
function pageLoad()
{
  CountryService.GetCountriesByName(onSuccess);
}

function onSuccess(results)
{
  $find('countryList').set_data(results);
}
```

*Code file [4-ServerSideData\1-WebService.htm] available for download at Wrox.com*

The success callback receives the return value of the web method as a parameter. Because you know that it is the country list you want to display, you can get the `DataView` component by using the `$find` method, and set the `data` property of it.

And that's all! With only two lines of code, you called a SOAP web service from JavaScript and displayed the results with a declarative template. It's not complicated at all, right?

Sure it's not. Nevertheless, it is a so often used scenario that every line counts, and, therefore, the DataView control provides direct support for it. You can strip out the `<script>` tag, the web service call, and the success callback, and configure the web service URI directly on the DataView.

Available for
download on
Wrox.com

```
<ul
  class="sys-template"
  sys:attach="dv"
  dv:autofetch="true"
  dv:dataprovider="../Services/CountryService.asmx"
  dv:fetchoperation="GetCountriesByName"
  <li>
    {{ Name }} ({{{ Capital }}})
  </li>
</ul>
```

*Code file [4-ServerSideData\2-DataFromService.htm] available for download at Wrox.com*

The `dataProvider` property of the `DataView` class can point to a JSON Web Service URI, or to an instance of a `Sys.Net.WebServiceProxy` object, or to any class that implements the `Sys.Data`
`.IDataProvider` interface. In the `fetchOperation` property, you can define the name of the web method that you want to call. By setting the `autoFetch` property to `true`, you can ensure that you do not have to update the `DataView` manually. It will retrieve the data immediately from the data source when the page loads, or when the `dataProvider` or the `fetchOperation` property is changed.

If you want to call a web method that expects parameters, you must set the `fetchParameters` property as well:

Sort by: Capital ▼

- Greece (Athens)
- Brasil (Brasilia)
- Slovakia (Bratislava)
- Hungary (Budapest)
- Australia (Canberra)
- Finland (Helsinki)
- United Kingdom (London)
- Spain (Madrid)
- Sweden (Stockholm)
- Austria (Vienna)
- United States (Washington, D.C.)
- Croatia (Zagreb)

**FIGURE 19-13:** The user can select the order of the records

Available for
download on
Wrox.com

```
<ul
  id="countryList"
  class="sys-template"
  sys:attach="dv"
  dv:autofetch="true"
  dv:dataprovider="../Services/CountryService.asmx"
  dv:fetchoperation="GetCountries"
  dv:fetchparameters="{{ { orderby: 'Capital', asc: false } }}"
  <li>
    {{ Name }} ({{{ Capital }}})
  </li>
</ul>
```

*Code file [4-ServerSideData\3-DataFromServiceWithParameters.htm] available for download at Wrox.com*

Of course, you can even let the user select the ordering of the countries, as shown in Figure 19-13.

First, provide a drop-down list box, and display the available orderings:

```
<select onchange="onSort(this.value)">
  <option value="Name">Name</option>
  <option value="Capital">Capital</option>
</select>
```

*Code file [4-ServerSideData\4-DataFromServiceWithParametersBinding1.htm] available for download at Wrox.com*

The `onSort` event handler is called when the user selects a new value from the list. Here you can update the `fetchParameters`, and then re-fetch the data from the server:

```
function onSort(orderby)
{
  var dv = $find("countryList");
  dv.get_fetchParameters().orderby = orderby;
  dv.fetchData();
}
```

*Code file [4-ServerSideData\4-DataFromServiceWithParametersBinding1.htm] available for download at Wrox.com*

As you can see, it is very easy to call a web service and display the results on the client with templates. This covers a large portion of server-side data scenarios, though it is often required for the modified data to be uploaded to the server.

## Updating the Data on the Server

If you want to implement a read-write scenario, you must delegate all data management to the new `Sys.Data.DataContext` class. This class encapsulates everything required to retrieve the data from the server, track changes on the client, and then load the modified data back to the server. `DataContext` implements the `IDataProvider` interface, which means that you can use a `DataContext` instance directly as a data source for your `DataView` controls:

```
<ul
  class="sys-template"
  sys:attach="dv"
  dv:autofetch="true"
  dv:dataprovider="{{ dataContext }}"
  dv:fetchoperation="GetCountriesByName"
  <li>
    {{ Name }} ({{ Capital }})
  </li>
</ul>
```

*Code file [4-ServerSideData\6-DataContextRead.htm] available for download at Wrox.com*

As you can see, the `dataProvider` property does not point to the web service directly any more. Instead, it is wrapped by a `DataContext` instance that is created when the page loads. (You will see that in a minute.)

You may notice that, although the service URI is encapsulated by the DataContext, the name of the web method is still defined on the DataView instance. If you find this a bit confusing, you are not alone, and this will likely change in the next previews or the RTM release.

The only thing missing is the DataContext instance. The DataContext resides in the MicrosoftAjaxDataContext.js file, and, because that relies on a bunch of other files, it is best to use the new Script Loader to load the required files in the right order:

```
<script src="Start.debug.js" type="text/javascript"></script>
<script type="text/javascript">
  var dataContext;
  Sys.require([Sys.components.dataView, Sys.components.dataContext]);
  Sys.onReady(function()
    {
      dataContext = Sys.create.dataContext(
        { serviceUri: "../Services/CountryService.asmx" }
      );
    }
  );
</script>
```

*Code file [4-ServerSideData\6-DataContextRead.htm] available for download at Wrox.com*

After the required scripts are downloaded and initialized, a new Sys.Data.DataContext instance is created, and its serviceUri property is set to the web service URI.

If you test the code you have at this point, you will not notice any change in the browser. The data is downloaded and displayed on the page; nothing fancy so far. However, if you change your DataView and provide input controls for the users, you can utilize the benefits of the DataContext class.

So, first rewrite the DataView template to display textboxes instead of static texts, and use live bindings that are, by default, two-way to notify the data source — in this case, the DataContext — if the data is modified by the user:

```
<div
  id="countryList"
  class="sys-template"
  sys:attach="dv"
  dv:autofetch="true"
  dv:dataprovider="{{ dataContext }}"
  dv:fetchoperation="GetCountriesByName">
  <div>
    Name:
    <input type="text" sys:value="{ binding Name }" />
    Capital:
    <input type="text" sys:value="{ binding Capital }" />
  </div>
</div>
```

*Code file [4-ServerSideData\7-DataContextReadWrite.htm] available for download at Wrox.com*

The browser will render textboxes as shown in Figure 19-14.

| | | | |
|---|---|---|---|
| Name: | Australia | Capital: | Canberra |
| Name: | Austria | Capital: | Vienna |
| Name: | Brasil | Capital: | Brasília |
| Name: | Croatia | Capital: | Zagreb |
| Name: | Finland | Capital: | Helsinki |
| Name: | Greece | Capital: | Athens |
| Name: | Hungary | Capital: | Budapest |
| Name: | Slovakia | Capital: | Bratislava |
| Name: | Spain | Capital: | Madrid |
| Name: | Sweden | Capital: | Stockholm |
| Name: | United Kingdom | Capital: | London |
| Name: | United States | Capital: | Washington, D.C. |

[ Save changes ] [ Refresh from server ]

**FIGURE 19-14:** Using two-way binding to update data

To support updates, you must set the name of the update web method in the `saveOperation` property:

Available for download on Wrox.com

```
dataContext = Sys.create.dataContext(
  {
    serviceUri: "../Services/CountryService.asmx",
    saveOperation: "UpdateCountries"
  }
);
```

*Code file [4-ServerSideData\7-DataContextReadWrite.htm] available for download at Wrox.com*

In this case, the `UpdateCountries` web method is used for updating countries. However, its signature is still not known. The `DataContext` automatically takes care of all change tracking in the background by using the `Sys.Observer` class and is able to provide a *changeset* that contains only the inserted, modified, and updated items. If you want to send this changeset to the server, you can call the `saveChanges` method that will call the `saveOperation` web method. The only question is, exactly what is posted by the client to the server?

Add a button to the GUI to let the user post the changes back to the server:

Available for download on Wrox.com

```
<input type="button" value="Save changes"
  onclick="dataContext.saveChanges()" />
```

*Code file [4-ServerSideData\7-DataContextReadWrite.htm] available for download at Wrox.com*

At this point, you can run the page in the browser, modify any record, and then click on the "Save changes" button to initiate an update in the background, which will obviously fail, because you still do not have the web method on the server. However, you can use *Fiddler* or *Firebug* to examine the body of this POST request.

For example, if you change "United Kingdom" to "UK," and "United States" to "US," the `DataContext` will send the following JSON data to the server (the code has been broken into more lines to make it more readable):

```
{
  "changeSet":
  [
    {
      "action":1,
      "item":
      {
        "__type":"Country",
        "Name":"UK",
        "Code":"uk",
        "Capital":"London"
      }
    },
    {
      "action":1,
      "item":
      {
        "__type":"Country",
        "Name":"US",
        "Code":"us",
        "Capital":"Washington, D.C."
      }
    }
  ]
}
```

The client sends a single `changeSet` object to the server that is an array of change objects. Every change object has two properties:

➤ `action` — This property describes what happened to the specified item. This property has one of the following `Sys.Data.ChangeOperationType` values: `insert` (0), `update` (1) or `remove` (2).

➤ `item` — This property carries the modified records. As you can see, there is no explicit identity or previous value column. It is up to you to determine on the server which was the original item and how the properties are changed.

Actually, the changeset contains `Sys.Data.ChangeOperation` instances that can have more properties, but, in this scenario, only the `action` and the `item` properties are used.

Now that you know what is sent by the client, you can prepare to receive it on the server. First, mirror the `ChangeOperationType` enum in C#:

```
public enum ChangeOperationType { insert, update, remove }
```

*Code file [App_Code\Change.cs] available for download at Wrox.com*

Then, create a generic `Change` class to mimic the change records sent by the client, with an `action` and an `item` property:

```
public class Change<T>
{
  public ChangeOperationType action;
  public T item;
}
```

*Code file [App_Code\Change.cs] available for download at Wrox.com*

Now, you have everything to implement the `UpdateCountries` method that is set as the `saveOperation` for the `DataContext`:

```
[WebMethod]
public void UpdateCountries( List<Change<Country>> changeSet )
{
  foreach( Change<Country> change in changeSet )
  {
    switch( change.action )
    {
      case ChangeOperationType.insert:
        // Implement insert here...
        break;
      case ChangeOperationType.update:
        this.UpdateCountry( change.item );
        break;
      case ChangeOperationType.remove:
        // Implement remove here...
        break;
    }
  }
}
```

*Code file [App_Code\CountryService.cs] available for download at Wrox.com*

Because the client sends an array, you can use a generic list as a method parameter, iterate through all the records, and examine what happened with them. The previous code snippet implements only the update operation case branch, because the client supports only updating so far. Updating a country is delegated to the private `UpdateCountry` method:

```
private void UpdateCountry( Country newCountry )
{
  Country oldCountry = CountryService.countries.Where(
    c => c.Code == newCountry.Code ).First();
  oldCountry.Name = newCountry.Name;
  oldCountry.Capital = newCountry.Capital;
}
```

*Code file [App_Code\CountryService.cs] available for download at Wrox.com*

Remember, the server-side "data store" is implemented as a private static list in the `CountryService.countries` field. So, in this simple case, it is very easy to persist the changes. In real-world scenarios, you would probably do some database operation here.

In addition to updating, the `DataContext` also supports tracking insertions and deletions. To add a new item on the client, you can call the `insertEntity` method, and the `removeEntity` method to remove one. In these cases, the changeset will contain `Sys.Data.ChangeOperationType.insert` and `Sys.Data.ChangeOperationType.remove` actions. `DataContext` also supports identity generation for insertions with its `getIdentityMethod` and `getNewIdentityMethod` properties.

It is often requested that the client be able to refresh the data from the server, and you can complete this by calling the `fetchData` method of the `DataView` object — for example, in a `click` event handler of a button:

```
<input type="button" value="Refresh from server"
   onclick="$find('countryList').fetchData(
            null,
            null,
            Sys.Data.MergeOption.overwriteChanges)" />
```

*Code file [4-ServerSideData\7-DataContextReadWrite.cs] available for download at Wrox.com*

The `DataView` forwards this call to the `DataContext`, which also has a `fetchData` method, because it implements the `Sys.Data.IDataProvider` interface.

However, because the data on the client is already being tracked for changes, it is important to define how the data on the client and the data from the server should be merged. This is what you can set with a `Sys.Data.MergeOption` value in the third parameter. If you set `MergeOption.appendOnly`, then unsaved changes are preserved on the client, and will not be overwritten with the data from the server. If you set `MergeOption.overwriteChanges`, then values obtained from the server will overwrite the values on the client.

As you can see, the `DataContext` is a very complex object with very convenient usage. You can use it even in simpler client-only scenarios. Just pass your object to it via its `trackData` method, and the full power of the change tracking engine is added to your object.

## Working with ADO.NET Data Services

Earlier, you saw how easy is to access a web service on the server, even from JavaScript, because script proxy generation and JSON serialization is automatically provided by the run-time. However, it may happen that you need a more lightweight, more flexible, and fully RESTful interface, and Microsoft recommends *ADO.NET Data Services* (formerly codenamed *Astoria*) for this purpose. ADO.NET Data Services has some specialties on the server, and the Microsoft Ajax Library contains classes to support these features.

The `Sys.Data.AdoNetServiceProxy` is a low-level class that inherits from `Sys.Net.WebServiceProxy`, implements the `Sys.Data.IDataProvider` interface, and provides methods and properties for interacting with ADO.NET Data Services. It supports the query, insert, update, and remove REST operations, and also optimistic concurrency. Although you can use the `WebServiceProxy` class to call an ADO.NET Data Service, it is much more convenient with this class, because it manages the HTTP commands and the HTTP headers automatically. Under the hood, it uses the `Sys.Data.AdoNetQueryBuilder` class for creating data service queries. However, if you want, you can use this class directly from your code.

If you have a read-write scenario, you can use the `Sys.Data.AdoNetDataContext` class that relies on `AdoNetServiceProxy`, inherits from `DataContext`, and provides support for ADO.NET-specific features (such as identity management, hierarchical data, links between entity sets, and optimistic concurrency).

## Retrieving Cross-Domain Data

Now that you have learned how to use Ajax and JavaScript to query data asynchronously from the server, you are probably tempted to try to use this technology with the numerous data sources already available all over the web. Why not? All these web service calls rely on the underlying `XMLHttpRequest` object (that is essentially a mini-browser), so theoretically it should work. However, in practice, it probably won't, and the reason is security.

Every modern user agent enforces a security concept called the *Same Origin Policy* that was originally designed for Netscape Navigator 2.0, and since then, all major browsers have adopted it. The Same Origin Policy is a protection mechanism that helps to isolate web applications coming from different domains.

From the Ajax perspective, the policy means that a script running on a page can connect with `XMLHttpRequest` only to its originating server (with the same protocol, domain name, and port) and cannot connect to other servers on the network. In practice, it means that, if you host a page, the script running on it will not be able to connect to web services offered by Google, Microsoft, Flickr, Twitter, and so on, because they reside in other domains.

Fortunately (or unfortunately if you see it from the end-user's or the security expert's point of view), there are ways to bypass the Same Origin Policy. For example, if you add a `<script>` tag to the `<head>` of your HTML page, you can load an external JavaScript from another domain, and that will behave as an exception from the policy. The question is how to use this trick to simulate cross-domain Ajax requests that return a value.

In most cases, regular Ajax requests return a JSON value such as this:

```
{ firstName: 'György', lastName: 'Balássy' }
```

However, if you return this object structure in a script that is loaded with a `<script>` tag in the header, the JSON expression will be evaluated, but there is no way to pass the result to the caller. Luckily, the downloaded script can contain not only a static object, but also a function call:

```
MyCallback({ firstName: 'György', lastName: 'Balássy' });
```

This expression is also evaluated. Thus, if there is a `MyCallback` function on the page, it will be called, and the JSON object is passed to it as an input parameter. To make this trick work, the server must know the name of the callback function already available on the page, and the client is responsible for passing this prefix as an input parameter of the call itself.

This extension of the JSON format is called *JSONP* (which stands for "JSON with padding,") or simply "cross-domain JSON." As you can see, JSONP is really simple (it doesn't even require an `XMLHttpRequest` call), but because it bypasses the Same Origin Policy, it can also be extremely dangerous. On the other hand, it breaks a really painful limit of Web 2.0 applications, so it is not a surprise that the Microsoft Ajax Library fully supports JSONP.

In the next example, you will see how you can incorporate Twitter into your web page with JSONP and the Microsoft Ajax Library. After importing the `MicrosoftAjax.js` and the `MicrosoftAjaxTemplates.js` files, create a `DataView` that will display the Tweets of a given user:

Available for download on Wrox.com

```
<ul
  id="dvResults"
  class="sys-template"
  sys:attach="dv">
  <li>
    <b>{{ text }}</*b>
    <br />
    {{ created_at }}
  </li>
</ul>
```

*Code file [4-ServerSideData\8-JSONP.htm] available for download at Wrox.com*

You can even create an input textbox and a button to ask the user for a Twitter account to query:

Available for download on Wrox.com

```
<input type="text" id="txtUserName" />
<input type="button" value="Get tweets" onclick="getTweets();" />
```

*Code file [4-ServerSideData\8-JSONP.htm] available for download at Wrox.com*

When the user clicks on the button, the following `getTweets` function is called:

Available for download on Wrox.com

```
function getTweets()
{
  var userName = $get('txtUserName').value;
  var uri =
    String.format("http://twitter.com/status/user_timeline/{0}.json?count=5",
      encodeURI(userName));
  Sys.Net.WebServiceProxy.invoke(uri, null, true, null, onComplete);
}
```

*Code file [4-ServerSideData\8-JSONP.htm] available for download at Wrox.com*

In this function, the username is first read from the textbox, then the Twitter service URI is constructed. Next, the static `invoke` method of the `WebServiceProxy` class is called with the service URI and the callback method. The third `true` parameter means that the service should be called with an HTTP GET request.

After the successful web service call, the Ajax Library calls the specified callback function `onComplete`, in which you can set the result data as the data source of the `DataView`:

```
function onComplete(results)
{
    $find('dvResults').set_data(results);
}
```

*Code file [4-ServerSideData\8-JSONP.htm] available for download at Wrox.co*

The `DataView` is rendered by the browser, as you can see in Figure 19-15.

That's very straightforward — but, wait a minute, how is the callback function required by JSONP passed to the web service?

The `Sys.Net.WebServiceProxy` class has two properties that support switching from JSON to JSONP, but, for most cases, you do not have to set them manually:

**FIGURE 19-15:** Using JSONP to query Twitter

➤ By setting the `enableJsonp` property to `true`, you can indicate that the web service supports JSONP, and the `WebServiceProxy` should use JSONP instead of JSON. The default value of this property is `false`. However, the `invoke` method examines the service URI and defaults to JSONP when it detects a cross-domain request.

➤ In the `jsonpCallbackParameter`, you can set the name of the query string variable that is expected by the web service to contain the name of the callback function. The default value is `"callback"` that is appropriate for most JSONP web services. However, if your web service differs from the de facto standard, you can override the default here.

You can use Fiddler to examine the communication between the client and the remote server to see how these properties work. The request contains the following headers (in addition to others that are omitted here for clarity):

```
GET /status/user_timeline/wrox.json?count=3&callback=Sys._jsonp1 HTTP/1.1
Host: twitter.com
```

As you can see, the `WebServiceProxy` class automatically added the `callback` parameter and generated an internal callback function called `Sys._jsonp1`. As expected, the response contains a call for this function, and the result JSON object array is passed as an input parameter:

```
HTTP/1.0 200 OK
Content-Type: application/json; charset=utf-8

Sys._jsonp1( JSON object array omitted );
```

The auto-generated `Sys._jsonp1` will then pass the service result to the `onComplete` callback function, where it is displayed with the `DataView`.

From this example, you can see that the Microsoft Ajax Library supports cross-domain requests with JSONP, and the transition is completely transparent.

## SUMMARY

Ajax has played an important role in web user experience, and revolutionized web applications by making them more responsive and more interactive. Unfortunately, the technologies that are covered by this umbrella name are not so developer-friendly, and you must incorporate helper libraries to implement Ajax-based features effectively.

The .NET Framework provides full support to Ajax-enable your existing applications, and you can use the well-known web control architecture to add Ajax features to your website. The `ServerManager` control hides all the details of script management, and just by wrapping a part of your page with an `UpdatePanel` control, you can make it refresh itself asynchronously.

If you are familiar with the basic concepts of JavaScript, and want to write browser-agnostic (but short) code, you can write your client-side code on top of the Microsoft Ajax Library. This Library not only contains a browser compatibility layer, but also adds OOP-like features to the JavaScript language. The new `DataView` control, the client-side data-binding feature, and the templating engine echo the similar functions long existing on the server.

As you saw in this chapter, the Microsoft Ajax Library hides the browser-specific details for basic client-side programming tasks. However, to be more productive, additional libraries can be built on top of this layer. The Microsoft Ajax Toolkit and the jQuery Libraries are integrated with the Microsoft Ajax Library, and, in Chapter 20, you will learn how to use them to perform client-side programming on a higher abstraction layer.

# 20

# ASP.NET Ajax Control Toolkit and jQuery

In Chapter 19, you learned about the new Ajax improvements and saw several examples of using the ASP.NET Ajax Library. You also read about jQuery library and used jQuery in a few samples.

Ajax and jQuery are primarily client-side technologies. They are built on JavaScript. If you do not have any server-side technologies, but rather just a simple web server with standard HTTP/HTTPS protocol, you can still use both of them. However, most applications work with information, and the nature of these applications is that they store and handle data at the server side — somewhere in the Internet cloud — and not at the client.

This chapter dives deeper into the ASP.NET Ajax Control Toolkit and the jQuery technology. These are two important pieces of the full toolset that you can use together with your ASP.NET applications to improve the user experience.

This chapter covers the following main topics:

➤ *First look at the Ajax Control Toolkit* — You are going to change an ASP.NET Web Application using "flickering" postbacks to an improved one using the Ajax Control Toolkit.

➤ *Using the Controls of the Toolkit* — This section provides a detailed overview of most server-side controls and extenders shipped with the Toolkit. You learn more about them through many small samples.

➤ *The jQuery library* — In this section, you will learn about the jQuery JavaScript library that is designed to make it easier to navigate a document, select document object model (DOM) elements, create animations, handle events, and develop Ajax applications.

*Chapter 19 provides a very good overview of using the ASP.NET Ajax Library, and includes many examples and code snippets. It also explains the basic concepts of Ajax. If you are new to Ajax programming, or you are not an experienced developer in this field, it's highly recommended that you read Chapter 19 to fully understand concepts treated here.*

## FIRST LOOK AT THE AJAX CONTROL TOOLKIT

The ASP.NET Ajax Control Toolkit contains a rich set of ASP.NET server-side controls that you can use to build highly responsive and interactive Ajax-enabled Web applications. It is often referred to as simply the Ajax Control Toolkit, and this chapter often refers to it simply as the "Toolkit."

The Toolkit contains more than 40 frequently used controls, including the `AutoCompleteExtender`, `CollapsiblePanelExtender`, `ComboBox`, `MaskedEditExtender`, `Accordion`, and many more. Most of them add simple, but powerful, functionality to your websites, and improve the user experience, all of which increases the value of the user experience. Although, at the end of the day, JavaScript is used at the client side, the controls in the Toolkit remove the majority of JavaScript-related programming challenges from your task list.

Using the Ajax Control Toolkit, you can build Ajax-enabled ASP.NET Web Forms applications by dragging and dropping controls from the Visual Studio Toolbox onto a Web Forms page and then using them just like other ASP.NET server-side controls.

The ASP.NET Ajax Control Toolkit started its life as an Open Source project in May 2006, and it is still a very active project. You can find it on CodePlex (`http://www.codeplex.com/AjaxControlToolkit`). It is a joint effort between Microsoft and the ASP.NET Ajax community. Controls provided by the project are built on top of the Microsoft ASP.NET Ajax framework. The Toolkit was designed to support not only Internet Explorer, but also Firefox, Safari, Opera, and Google Chrome. Most controls work seamlessly and independently of the browser you use. However, there are a few compatibility issues. The project team tracks them and provides service releases on a regular basis.

## Installing the Ajax Control Toolkit

You can download the latest version of the ASP.NET Ajax Control Toolkit from its home on CodePlex by clicking on the Downloads tab. As of this writing, the freshest version was the ASP.NET Ajax Library Beta 0911 (released on November 18, 2009). As the name of download indicates, this is not only the Ajax Control Toolkit, but also the ASP.NET Ajax Library that now includes all the ASP.NET Web Forms server controls that were included in the original Ajax Control Toolkit.

When you download and extract the library, you can find the Ajax Control Toolkit in the `AjaxNetLibrary\WebForms` folder under the root where you extracted the downloaded file. You will also find there the `Release` subfolder with the `AjaxControlToolkit.dll` file, as shown in

Figure 20-1. The `Debug` folder also contains the Debug build of this assembly.

You can easily integrate the Toolkit with Visual Studio by adding the controls to the Toolbox. Open an ASP.NET Web Application project in Visual Studio 2010, or create an ASP.NET Empty Web Application project. Add a new Web Form to it and name it, for example, `Default.aspx`.

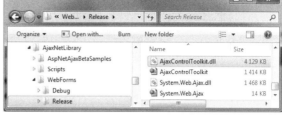

**FIGURE 20-1:** Ajax Control Toolkit in the folder structure of ASP.NET Ajax Library

Open an `.aspx` file (for example, `Default .aspx`) so that you can display Visual Studio's Toolbox. Right-click on any toolbox tab (for example, the AJAX Extensions tab) and run the Add Tab command. A new empty tab appears. Name it "Ajax Control Toolkit." This tab is just a placeholder for controls, since it does not yet contain any controls. Right-click on this tab and run the Choose Items command.

When the Choose Toolbox Items dialog appears, select the .NET Frameworks Components tab. Click the Browse button and select the `AjaxControlToolkit.dll` from the `Release` folder shown in Figure 20-1. Visual Studio will warn you that you are going to add a file downloaded from a network location, and it can potentially harm your computer. Confirm that you really want to load it. The new controls found in the `AjaxControlToolkit.dll` will be selected in the dialog, and marked to be added to the tab. Close the dialog by clicking the OK button, and Visual Studio adds all the controls found in the assembly to the tab, as shown in Figure 20-2.

Of course, in Figure 20-2 you can see only a part of the controls added. The Ajax Control Toolkit provides more than 40 controls you can add to your web pages.

**FIGURE 20-2:** Ajax Control Toolkit tab with the newly added controls

## Controls Installed with the Toolkit

When you look at the names of controls, you find two kinds:

➤ *Standard controls* — These have a simple name, such as `Rating`, `Accordion`, `Editor`, `TabContainer`, and so on. These are simple controls that work just like any other standard ASP.NET controls. You can drag them from the Toolbox onto an ASP.NET page in either Design view or Source view.

➤ *Control extenders* — These can be easily recognized because their names ends with "Extender" by convention (with only a few exceptions). As the names suggest, a control extender extends the functionality of an existing control. For example, the `ConfirmButtonExtender` extends the standard ASP.NET `Button` control. It changes the `Button` control's behavior so that the `Button` displays a confirmation dialog when you click it.

### Upgrading to a New Version

If you have already installed an older version of the Toolkit, or you have downloaded a new one and you want to change your projects using this latter version, you can avoid annoying versioning issues with a few recommended steps:

**1.** Open the ASP.NET web project (or solution) you intend to upgrade and remove all references to the `AjaxControlToolkit.dll` assembly.

**2.** Right-click on the project in Solution Explorer, and run the Open Folder command from Windows Explorer. When the Explorer opens, go into the `bin` folder and delete `AjaxControlTookit.dll`.

**3.** Add a new `Dummy.aspx` file to your project. Go to the Toolbox and right-click the Ajax Control Toolkit tab. Run the Delete Tab command to remove all Toolkit controls previously added.

**4.** Follow the steps described earlier to add the controls of the new Toolkit version to the Toolbox again.

**5.** Temporarily drag a simple control (for example, `ComboBox`) from the Ajax Control Toolkit tab to `Dummy.aspx`. Visual Studio will add the reference to the `AjaxControlToolkit` assembly (of course, to the new version you have just installed).

**6.** Delete `Dummy.aspx`.

If you have more than one ASP.NET Web Application project in your solution, repeat these steps for each project. Of course, you must remove the Ajax Control Toolkit tab from the Toolbox and then add the new controls only once.

## Creating a Simple Web Application with the Toolkit

The best way to get started with the Toolkit is to create a simple application. In this section, you will change the `FindAnExpertDemo` sample project that you can download from this book's companion website (www.wrox.com).

### The FindAnExpertDemo Project

`FindAnExpertDemo` is a very simple ASP.NET application that displays information about selected experts. You have two drop-down lists on the page. The first allows you to select an expertise. The second drop-down list is filled up with names of people who have the selected expertise. As you select one of them, a photo and a short description of the expert is displayed. Figure 20-3 shows this application at work.

**FIGURE 20-3:** A Screenshot of FindAnExpertDemo

Every time you select a new expertise from the first drop-down list, a postback is initiated to fill the list with experts who have the selected expertise.

Start Visual Studio 2010 and open the `FindAnExpertDemo` project. The user interface (UI) of the application is very simple. It uses only a few standard ASP.NET controls, as shown in Listing 20-1.

**LISTING 20-1:  Default.aspx of the FindAnExpertDemo Project**

```
<%@ Page Language="C#" AutoEventWireup="true" CodeBehind="Default.aspx.cs"
    Inherits="FindAnExpertDemo.Default" %>

<!DOCTYPE html PUBLIC "-//W3C//DTD XHTML 1.0 Transitional//EN"
    "http://www.w3.org/TR/xhtml1/DTD/xhtml1-transitional.dtd">
<html xmlns="http://www.w3.org/1999/xhtml">
<head runat="server">
  <title>Find an Expert Demo</title>
</head>
<body>
  <form id="form1" runat="server">
  <div>
    <table>
      <tr>
        <td>
          Select an expertise:
        </td>
        <td>
          <asp:DropDownList ID="ExpertiseList" runat="server" AutoPostBack="true"
            OnSelectedIndexChanged="ExpertiseList_SelectedIndexChanged">
          </asp:DropDownList>
        </td>
      </tr>
      <tr>
        <td>
          Select the expert:
        </td>
        <td>
          <asp:DropDownList ID="ExpertList" runat="server" AutoPostBack="true"
            OnSelectedIndexChanged="ExpertList_SelectedIndexChanged">
          </asp:DropDownList>
        </td>
      </tr>
    </table>
    <br />
    <table>
      <tr>
        <td>
          <asp:Label ID="Description" runat="server" Text=""></asp:Label>
        </td>
        <td>
          <asp:Image ID="Photo" runat="server" />
```

*continues*

**LISTING 20-1** *(continued)*

```
            </td>
          </tr>
        </table>
      </div>
    </form>
  </body>
</html>
```

*Code file [Default.aspx] available for download at Wrox.com*

The content of the drop-down lists is read from a database through the `DataAccess` class, which has the blueprint shown in Listing 20-2. You can examine the method bodies omitted from the listing by opening the `DataAccess.cs` file.

**LISTING 20-2: DataAccess.cs (Code Extract)**

```csharp
using System.Collections.Generic;
using System.Data;
using System.Data.OleDb;
using System.Web;

namespace FindAnExpertDemo
{
  public class Expertise
  {
    public int Id { get; set; }
    public string Name { get; set; }
  }

  public class Expert
  {
    public int Id { get; set; }
    public string Name { get; set; }
    public int ExpertiseId { get; set; }
    public string Description { get; set; }
    public string Photo { get; set; }
  }

  public class DataAccess
  {
    private HttpServerUtility _Server;

    public DataAccess(HttpServerUtility server)
    {
      _Server = server;
    }
```

```csharp
    public IEnumerable<Expertise> GetExpertiseList()
    {
      // ...
    }

    public IEnumerable<Expert> GetExpertList(string expertise)
    {
      // ...
    }

    private OleDbConnection GetDataConnection()
    {
      // ...
    }
  }
}
```

*Code file [DataAccess.cs] available for download at Wrox.com*

The UI logic can be found in the `Default.aspx.cs` file. This logic is very simple. Only three event handler methods are defined, as shown in Listing 20-3.

**LISTING 20-3: Default.aspx.cs**

```csharp
using System;
using System.Collections.Generic;
using System.Web.UI.WebControls;

namespace FindAnExpertDemo
{
  public partial class Default : System.Web.UI.Page
  {
    protected void Page_Load(object sender, EventArgs e)
    {
      if (!IsPostBack)
      {
        var da = new DataAccess(Server);
        foreach (var item in da.GetExpertiseList())
        {
          ExpertiseList.Items.Add(new ListItem(item.Name, item.Id.ToString()));
        }
        Photo.Visible = false;
        if (ExpertiseList.Items.Count > 0)
        {
          ExpertiseList.SelectedIndex = 0;
          ExpertiseList_SelectedIndexChanged(ExpertiseList, EventArgs.Empty);
        }
      }
    }
```

*continues*

**LISTING 20-3** *(continued)*

```
protected void ExpertiseList_SelectedIndexChanged(object sender, EventArgs e)
{
  var experts = new Dictionary<int, Expert>();
  ExpertList.Items.Clear();
  experts.Clear();
  var da = new DataAccess(Server);
  foreach (var item in da.GetExpertList(ExpertiseList.SelectedValue))
  {
    ExpertList.Items.Add(new ListItem(item.Name, item.Id.ToString()));
    experts.Add(item.Id, item);
  }
  Session["Experts"] = experts;
  if (ExpertList.Items.Count > 0)
  {
    ExpertList.SelectedIndex = 0;
    ExpertList_SelectedIndexChanged(ExpertList, EventArgs.Empty);
  }
}

protected void ExpertList_SelectedIndexChanged(object sender, EventArgs e)
{
  var experts = Session["Experts"] as Dictionary<int, Expert>;
  Expert expert;
  if (experts.TryGetValue(Int32.Parse(ExpertList.SelectedValue),
    out expert))
  {
    Description.Text = expert.Description;
    Photo.ImageUrl = "/Photos/" + expert.Photo + ".png";
    Photo.Visible = true;
  }
}
```

*Code file [Default.aspx.cs] available for download at Wrox.com*

## Improving FindAnExpertDemo with Ajax Control Toolkit

There are a few issues with the FindAnExpertDemo solution. The first is that every time you select an item from the expertise or expert drop-downs, a page postback occurs and the page flickers. The second is that you do not have a value similar to "Select an expertise" or "Select an expert" in the drop-downs.

You can use the Ajax Control Toolkit to solve these issues. The Toolkit contains a control named CascadingDropDown that can be attached to an ASP.NET DropDownList control to get automatic population of a set of DropDownList controls. CascadingDropDown also enables a common scenario in which the contents of one list depend on the selection of another list, and does so without having to embed the entire data set in the page, or transfer it to the client.

## Adding a ToolkitScriptManager to the Page

When you work with Ajax in ASP.NET, you must add a `ScripManager` object to your page that is responsible for managing script libraries and script files, partial-page rendering, and client proxy class generation for web and application services. If you try to use `ScriptManager` with the Ajax Control Toolkit, you'll get some error messages that depend on what kind of control you use from the Toolkit.

You should use the `ToolkitScripManager` object (you can drag it from the Ajax Control Toolkit tab to your page) instead of `ScriptManager`. The `ToolkitScriptManager` class derives from `ScriptManager` and enables the automatic combination of multiple script files in the corresponding web page.

So, drag and drop the `ToolkitScriptManager` control from the Toolbox to your page somewhere within the `<form>` element. After you drop it the source code should look like this:

```
<body>
    <form id="form1" runat="server">
    <asp:ToolkitScriptManager ID="ToolkitScriptManager1" runat="server" />
    <!-- ... -->
    </form>
</body>
```

 *If you simply type the* `ToolkitScriptManager` *declaration, the project will not contain the necessary references, and you will get an error about the unknown control.*

## Adding CascadingDropDown Extenders

There are two drop-down lists on the page, so you must add a `CascadingDropDown` extender for each of them. You can add these controls anywhere within the form. Let's add it directly before the closing `</form>` element:

```
<form id="form1" runat="server">
<asp:ToolkitScriptManager ID="ToolkitScriptManager1" runat="server" />
<!-- Form content comes here... -->
<asp:CascadingDropDown ID="ccdExpertise" runat="server"
  TargetControlID="ExpertiseList"
  Category="Expertise"
  PromptText="Please select an Expertise"
  LoadingText="Loading..."
  ServicePath="ExpertiseService.asmx"
  ServiceMethod="GetDropDownContent" />
<asp:CascadingDropDown ID="ccdExpert" runat="server"
  TargetControlID="ExpertList"
  Category="Expert"
  ParentControlID="ExpertiseList"
```

```
              PromptText="Please select an Expert"
              LoadingText="Loading..."
              ServicePath="ExpertiseService.asmx"
              ServiceMethod="GetDropDownContent" />
          </form>
```

As can you see from this code snippet, there are many properties used by `CascadingDropDown`. `TargetControlID` tells the extender which `DropDownList` to extend. The `PrompText` property tells the control what text to use for the default item in the list representing that no real item is selected. While the control's content is being loaded, the text defined by `LoadingText` is displayed in the control.

The content of the `DropDownList` may hold different content depending on the UI logic. For example, at the beginning of a use case, it may contain vehicle categories, or later concrete car models. `Category` is the logical name of the content the `DropDownList` should be populated with.

The second extender with the `ccdExpert` identifier contains a property name `ParentControlID`. This represents the identifier of the `DropDownList` that is used as the parent control. As the parent's selected value changes, this control is re-populated according to the value selected in the parent control. For example, in the `FindAnExpertDemo`, when the user changes the `Expertise` drop-down list to "Visual Basic," the `Expert` drop-down list is populated with the name of Visual Basic experts.

The `CascadingDropDown` extender uses ASP.NET web services to populate the content of the attached `DropDownList`. The `ServicePath` property refers to the web service responsible for the population, while `ServiceMethod` holds the name of the method to be called. This method should have the following signature:

```
public CascadingDropDownNameValue[] ServiceMethodName(string knownCategoryValues,
    string category);
```

The `knownCategoryValues` argument contains an empty string when the service method is called for a `DropDownList` that is not parented (its `ParentControlID` is not set), or a combination of the parent control's `Category` property and its selected value. The `category` argument is set for the control's `Category` property. For example, when the `ExpertiseList` control is populated, `knownCategoryValues` is an empty string, while category is set to "Expertise." When you select "Visual Basic" in the `ExpertiseList` control, the service method is called to populate the `ExpertList` control with `knownCategoryValues` set to `Expertise;1` and category to `Expert`.

## Adding the ExpertiseService Class to the Project

So, in order for you to populate the lists, add a new web service item to the project and name it `ExpertiseService`. Listing 20-4 shows the code you should copy into this new web service file.

**LISTING 20-4: ExpertiseService.asmx.cs**

```
using System;
using System.Collections.Generic;
using System.Collections.Specialized;
using System.Web.Script.Services;
```

```
using System.Web.Services;
using AjaxControlToolkit;

namespace FindAnExpertDemo
{
  [ScriptService]
  public class ExpertiseService : WebService
  {
    [WebMethod]
    public CascadingDropDownNameValue[] GetDropDownContent(
      string knownCategoryValues,
      string category)
    {
      var result = new List<CascadingDropDownNameValue>();
      var da = new DataAccess(Server);
      if (category.Equals("Expertise"))
      {
        foreach (var item in da.GetExpertiseList())
        {
          result.Add(
            new CascadingDropDownNameValue(item.Name, item.Id.ToString()));
        }
      }
      else if (category.Equals("Expert"))
      {
        var values = CascadingDropDown.
          ParseKnownCategoryValuesString(knownCategoryValues);
        foreach (var item in da.GetExpertList(values["Expertise"]))
        {
          result.Add(
            new CascadingDropDownNameValue(item.Name,
              String.Format("{0}${1}${2}",
              item.Id, item.Photo, item.Description)));
        }
      }
      return result.ToArray();
    }
  }
}
```

*Code file [ExpertiseService.asmx.cs] available for download at Wrox.com*

The web service class is decorated with the ScriptService attribute, indicating that ExpertiseService can be invoked from scripts. The interesting thing is that both CascadingDropDown controls use the GetDropDownContent service method. The category argument is used to branch according to the control to be populated. Both controls use the DataAccess component introduced in Listing 20-2.

When the ExpertList control is populated, you must query only the experts possessing the expertise represented by the selected value of the ExpertiseList drop-down. The ParseKnownCategoryValuesString method helps in with creating the StringDictionary held by the values variable. When you select "Visual Basic" in ExpertiseList, the Expertise;1 is put into this dictionary so that you can address it with Expertise to retrieve the value 1.

## Discovering the Effect of CascadingDropDown

You are almost ready to try the effect of `CascadingDropDown` extenders. Because you do not need to make an explicit postback when the `ExpertiseList` control is populated with values or its selection is changed, the code-behind file of `Default.aspx` gets very simple. This time, the code is not ready to respond when you select a concrete expert, so the body of the `ExpertList_SelectedIndexChanged` method should be commented out. Listing 20-5 shows the file after these modifications.

**LISTING 20-5: Default.aspx.cs Modified**

```
using System;
using System.Collections.Generic;
using System.Web.UI.WebControls;

namespace FindAnExpertDemo
{
  public partial class Default : System.Web.UI.Page
  {
    protected void Page_Load(object sender, EventArgs e)
    {
      if (!IsPostBack)
      {
        Photo.Visible = false;
      }
    }

    protected void ExpertList_SelectedIndexChanged(object sender, EventArgs e)
    {
      //var experts = Session["Experts"] as Dictionary<int, Expert>;
      //Expert expert;
      //if (experts.TryGetValue(Int32.Parse(ExpertList.SelectedValue),
      //  out expert))
      //{
      //  Description.Text = expert.Description;
      //  Photo.ImageUrl = "/Photos/" + expert.Photo + ".png";
      //  Photo.Visible = true;
      //}
    }
  }
}
```

*Code file [Default.aspx.cs] available for download at Wrox.com*

Of course, you must change the declaration of the `ExpertiseList` control in the `Default.aspx` file so that it won't make any more explicit postbacks:

```
<table>
  <tr>
    <td>Select an expertise:</td>
    <td><asp:DropDownList ID="ExpertiseList" runat="server" /></td>
  </tr>
```

```
<tr>
  <td>Select the expert:</td>
  <td>
    <asp:DropDownList ID="ExpertList" runat="server" AutoPostBack="true"
      OnSelectedIndexChanged="ExpertList_SelectedIndexChanged" />
  </td>
</tr>
</table>
```

The `CascadingDropDown` attached to the `ExpertList` control initiates a postback as soon as you select an item. For security purposes, it is verified that arguments to postback or callback events originate from the server control that originally rendered them. In the case of `CascadingDropDown` control, this verification would fail unless you turn off event validation:

```
<%@ Page Language="C#" AutoEventWireup="true" CodeBehind="Default.aspx.cs"
  Inherits="FindAnExpertDemo.Default" EnableEventValidation="false" %>
```

 *Setting the* `EnableEventValidation` *property to* `false` *is not recommended because of security reasons. However, to be able to use the* `CascadingDropDown` *extender in Ajax Control Toolkit Beta 0911, this is the easiest way to allow a postback from the extender. Hopefully, this issue will be solved in one of the next releases.*

Now, you can build and run the modified application. Do not forget to set `Default.aspx` as the startup page. As shown in Figure 20-4, when you start the application, you see both drop-down lists contain the "Please Select an . . ." value, and the second list is disabled, because before you can select an expert, you must select an expertise.

**FIGURE 20-4:** CascadingDropDown controls in action

When you select a real item in the expertise list, the expert list is populated accordingly, as shown in Figure 20-5.

When you select an item, the postback is executed. But because the `ExpertList_SelectedIndexChanged` method's body is commented out, nothing is changed on the page as a result of the postback. This postback could also be done asynchronously using the `UpdatePanel` control, which is part of the standard ASP.NET Ajax Extensions and not part of the Toolkit.

**FIGURE 20-5.** The expert list is populated according the selected expertise.

## Using an UpdatePanel

There is a `<table>` element in `Default.aspx` that holds a `Label` and an `Image` control to show the description and the photo of the selected expert, respectively. You can wrap this table into an `UpdateTable` control and define a trigger for it so that any events related to the `ExpertList` control will be handled asynchronously. These events also will refresh the content within the `UpdatePanel`. Listing 20-6 shows the full source of the `Default.aspx` file after adding the `UpdatePanel`.

**LISTING 20-6:** Default.aspx Modified with an UpdatePanel Control

```
<%@ Page Language="C#" AutoEventWireup="true" CodeBehind="Default.aspx.cs"
  Inherits="FindAnExpertDemo.Default" EnableEventValidation="false" %>

<%@ Register Assembly="AjaxControlToolkit" Namespace="AjaxControlToolkit"
  TagPrefix="asp" %>
<!DOCTYPE html PUBLIC "-//W3C//DTD XHTML 1.0 Transitional//EN"
  "http://www.w3.org/TR/xhtml1/DTD/xhtml1-transitional.dtd">
<html xmlns="http://www.w3.org/1999/xhtml">
<head runat="server">
  <title>Find an Expert Demo</title>
</head>
<body>
  <form id="form1" runat="server">
  <asp:ToolkitScriptManager ID="ToolkitScriptManager1" runat="server" />
  <div>
    <table>
      <tr>
        <td>Select an expertise:</td>
        <td><asp:DropDownList ID="ExpertiseList" runat="server" /></td>
      </tr>
      <tr>
        <td>Select the expert:</td>
        <td>
          <asp:DropDownList ID="ExpertList" runat="server" AutoPostBack="true"
            OnSelectedIndexChanged="ExpertList_SelectedIndexChanged" />
        </td>
      </tr>
    </table>
    <br />
    <asp:UpdatePanel ID="UpdatePanel1" runat="server">
      <ContentTemplate>
        <table>
          <tr>
            <td>
              <asp:Label ID="Description" runat="server" Text=""></asp:Label>
            </td>
            <td><asp:Image ID="Photo" runat="server" /></td>
          </tr>
        </table>
      </ContentTemplate>
      <Triggers>
        <asp:AsyncPostBackTrigger ControlID="ExpertList" />
      </Triggers>
    </asp:UpdatePanel>
  </div>
  <asp:CascadingDropDown ID="ccdExpertise" runat="server"
    TargetControlID="ExpertiseList"
    Category="Expertise" PromptText="Please select an Expertise"
```

```
      LoadingText="Loading..."
      ServicePath="ExpertiseService.asmx" ServiceMethod="GetGetDropDownContent" />
    <asp:CascadingDropDown ID="ccdExpert" runat="server" TargetControlID="ExpertList"
      Category="Expert" ParentControlID="ExpertiseList"
      PromptText="Please select an Expert"
      LoadingText="Loading..." ServicePath="ExpertiseService.asmx"
      ServiceMethod="GetGetDropDownContent" />
  </form>
</body>
</html>
```

*Code file [Default.aspx] available for download at Wrox.com*

The `<Triggers>` element within the `UpdatePanel` contains an `AsynchPostBackTrigger` attached to the `ExpertList` control. When the user selects an expert from the list, an asynchronous postback is sent to the server that can set the description and the photo of the expert. As soon as the asynchronous call is completed, the controls within the update panel are refreshed with the description text and photo. Of course, you must write the body of the `ExpertList_ SelectedIndexChanged` event handler method, as shown in Listing 20-7.

**LISTING 20-7:** Default.aspx.cs After Handling the ExpertList Events

```
using System;

namespace FindAnExpertDemo
{
  public partial class Default : System.Web.UI.Page
  {
    protected void Page_Load(object sender, EventArgs e)
    {
      if (!IsPostBack)
      {
        Photo.Visible = false;
      }
    }

    protected void ExpertList_SelectedIndexChanged(object sender, EventArgs e)
    {
      var fields = ExpertList.SelectedValue.Split('$');
      Description.Text = fields[2];
      Photo.ImageUrl = "/Photos/" + fields[1] + ".png";
      Photo.Visible = true;
    }
  }
}
```

*Code file [Default.aspx.cs] available for download at Wrox.com*

The body of `ExpertList_SelectedIndexChanged` is short, and it uses a simple serialization trick. In the `ExpertiseService.asmx.cs` file, the information about experts was added to the `ExpertList` control as a part of its value:

```
foreach (var item in da.GetExpertList(values["Expertise"]))
{
  result.Add(
    new CascadingDropDownNameValue(item.Name,
      String.Format("{0}${1}${2}",
      item.Id, item.Photo, item.Description)));
}
```

The content of the selected item's value is split, and the `Description` and `Photo` controls are set according to the value fields.

Now, build and run the `FindAnExpertDemo` application. As you can see, it provides you the same functionality as the original implementation, but there is no flickering when you change the selection of any drop-down lists.

The application's code preserved the original architecture (there is still a separate data access layer), and the UI code became shorter and turned many imperative elements into declarations.

## USING THE CONTROLS OF THE TOOLKIT

When you look at the Toolbox, you can count more than 40 controls on the Ajax Control Toolkit tab. Earlier, you examined the `CascadingDropDown` extender that can be attached to ASP.NET `DropDownList` controls. There are many other useful controls that improve the user experience of your websites and provide a simple programming model. This section provides a detailed overview of most of them.

Table 20-1 summarizes the controls shipped with the Beta 0911 version of the Ajax Control Toolkit. As you have seen, there are server controls in the Toolkit that can be used individually, and extender controls that extend the functionality of other controls to which they are attached. Extender controls are marked with an italic font in Table 20-1.

**TABLE 20-1:** Controls Shipped with Ajax Control Toolkit Beta 0911

| CONTROL | DESCRIPTION |
| --- | --- |
| Accordion | This control lets you define multiple panes and display them one at a time. The `Accordion` control contains one or more `AccordionPane` controls. Each `AccordionPane` control has a template for its header and its content. The selected pane is automatically persisted across postbacks. |
| *AlwaysVisibleControlExtender* | This control extends any ASP.NET control and lets you pin it to the page so that it appears to float over the background body content when it is scrolled or resized. The extender keeps the position of the control a specified distance from the horizontal and vertical sides. |

| CONTROL | DESCRIPTION |
| --- | --- |
| *AnimationExtender* | This class lets you use a powerful animation framework with existing pages in an easy, declarative fashion. It plays animations whenever a specific event like OnLoad, OnClick, OnMouseOver, or OnMouseOut is raised by the target control. |
| AsyncFileUpload | This is an ASP.NET Ajax control that allows you asynchronously upload files to the server. The file-uploading results can be checked both in the server and client sides. |
| *AutoCompleteExtender* | This control extends any ASP.NET TextBox control. It associates that control with a pop-up panel to display words that begin with the prefix that is entered into the text box. When the user has entered more characters than a specified minimum length, a popup displays words or phrases that start with that value. |
| *CalendarExtender* | This control enables you to display date picker when focus is moved to an input element. |
| | This extender can be attached to any ASP.NET TextBox control. It provides client-side date-picking functionality with customizable date format and UI in a pop-up control. You can interact with the calendar by clicking on a day to set the date, or the "Today" link to set the current date. |
| *CascadingDropDown* | This is an extender that can be attached to an ASP.NET DropDownList control to get automatic population of a set of DropDownList controls. Each time the selection of one the DropDownList controls changes, the CascadingDropDown makes a call to a specified web service to retrieve the list of values for the next DropDownList in the set. |
| *CollapsiblePanelExtender* | This extender adds collapsible sections to a web page. CollapsiblePanelExtender targets any ASP.NET Panel control. You specify which control or controls on the page should act as the open and close controllers for the panel. Alternatively, the panel can be set to automatically expand and collapse when the mouse cursor moves in or out of it. |

*continues*

**TABLE 20-1** *(continued)*

| CONTROL | DESCRIPTION |
|---|---|
| `ColorPickerExtender` | This extender enables you to display a pop-up color picker when the focus is moved to an input element. You can attach the `ColorPickerExtender` to any ASP.NET `TextBox` control. It provides client-side color-picking functionality with UI in a pop-up control. Optionally, you can specify a button to display the color-picker popup and a control that previews a color from the color palette. |
| ComboBox | This is a control that, like `AutoCompleteExtender`, combines the flexibility of a `TextBox` with a list of options that users are able to choose from. It borrows many of its properties, behaviors, and naming conventions from the Windows Forms `ComboBox` control, and is derived from the same base class as the `ListBox`, `BulletedList`, and `DropDownList` web controls. |
| `ConfirmButtonExtender` | This extender catches clicks on a button (or on any instance of a type that is derived from `Button`) and displays a message to the user. If the user clicks OK, the button or link functions normally. If the user does not click OK, the click event is trapped and the button does not perform its default submit behavior. Optionally, you can specify client script to execute when the buttons are clicked in the confirm dialog box. |
| `DragPanelExtender` | This extender allows users to easily add "draggability" to their controls. The `DragPanelExtender` targets any ASP.NET `Panel` and takes an additional parameter that signifies the control to use as the "drag handle." Once initialized, the user can freely drag the panel around the web page using the drag handle. |
| `DropDownExtender` | This extender can be attached to almost any ASP.NET control to provide a SharePoint-style drop-down menu. The displayed menu is merely another panel or control. In the previous sample, the drop-down is a `Panel` that contains `LinkButtons`. The drop-down is activated by left- or right-clicking the attached control. If the behavior is attached to a `Hyperlink` or `LinkButton`, clicking on the link itself will operate normally. |

| CONTROL | DESCRIPTION |
|---|---|
| *DropShadowExtender* | This extender applies a drop shadow to an ASP.NET `Panel` control. The extender allows you to specify how wide the shadow is, how opaque it is, and whether the shadow should have rounded corners. For pages that let the user move or resize the panel, the `DropShadowExtender` has a mode that will resize and reposition the shadow to match the target panel at run-time. |
| *DynamicPopulateExtender* | This extender replaces the contents of a control with the result of a web service or page method call. The method call returns a string of HTML that is inserted as a child of the target element. |
| *FilteredTextBoxExtender* | This is an extender that lets users enter only characters that you define into a text box or that prevents users from entering characters that you specify. |
| *HoverMenuExtender* | This is an extender that can be attached to any ASP.NET `WebControl`, and will associate that control with a pop-up panel to display additional content. When the user moves the mouse cursor over the main control, two things happen.<br><br>The pop-up panel is displayed at a position specified by the page developer (at the left, right, top, or bottom of the main control).<br><br>Optionally, a CSS style is applied to the control to specify it as "hot." |
| `Editor` | This control allows you to easily create and edit HTML content. Various buttons in the toolbar are used for content editing. You can see generated HTML markup and a preview document. |
| *ListSearchExtender* | This extender lets you search for items in a `ListBox` or `DropDownList` by typing. The extender performs an incremental search within the `ListBox` based on what has been typed so far. The prompt message that is displayed when you click the list can be customized, along with its CSS class and position. |

*continues*

**TABLE 20-1** *(continued)*

| CONTROL | DESCRIPTION |
| --- | --- |
| *MaskedEditExtender* | This extender attaches to a `TextBox` control to restrict the kind of text that can be entered. `MaskedEditExtender` applies a "mask" to the input that permits only certain types of characters to be entered. The supported data formats are `Number`, `Date`, `Time`, and `DateTime`. `MaskedEditExtender` uses the culture settings specified in the `CultureName` property. If none is specified, the culture setting will be the same as the page. |
| *ModalPopupExtender* | This extender allows you to display content in an element that mimics a modal dialog box, which prevents the user from interacting with the rest of the page. The modal content can contain any hierarchy of controls. It is displayed above a background (in z-order) that can have a custom style applied to it. |
| *MultiHandleSliderExtender* | This extender provides a feature-rich extension to a regular `Textbox` control. It allows you to choose a single value, or multiple values in a range, through a graphical slider interface. It supports one handle, dual handles, or any number of handles bound to the values of `TextBox` or `Label` controls. It also provides options for read-only access, custom graphic styling, hover and drag handle styles, as well as mouse and keyboard support for accessibility. |
| *MutuallyExclusiveCheckBoxExtender* | This extender can be attached to any `CheckBox` control. By adding a number of checkboxes to the same "Key," only one checkbox with the specified key can be checked at a time. This extender is useful when a number of choices are available, but only one can be chosen (similar to a radio button). The use of checkboxes, however, allows you to choose to uncheck a value, which is normally not possible with radio buttons. This also provides a more consistent and expected interface than using JavaScript to allow the de-selection of a `RadioButton` item. |

| CONTROL | DESCRIPTION |
|---------|-------------|
| *NoBot* | This control attempts to provide CAPTCHA-like bot/spam prevention without requiring any user interaction. This approach is easier to bypass than an implementation that requires actual human intervention, but NoBot has the benefit of being completely invisible. NoBot is probably most relevant for low-traffic sites where blog/comment spam is a problem and 100 percent effectiveness is not required. |
| *NumericUpDownExtender* | This is an extender that can be attached to a TextBox control to add "up" and "down" buttons that increment and decrement the value in the TextBox. The increment and decrement can be simple +1/-1 arithmetic. They can cycle through a provided list of values (like the months of the year), or they can call a web service to determine the next value. Page authors can also provide custom images to be used instead of the default up/down button graphics. |
| *PagingBulletedListExtender* | This extender can be attached to a BulletedList control and provide client-side sorted paging. It is very flexible and lets you specify either the number of characters used in the heading indices, or the maximum number of items to display per index. |
| *PasswordStrength* | This is an extender that can be attached to a TextBox control used for the entry of passwords. The PasswordStrength extender shows the strength of the password in the TextBox, and updates itself as the user types the password. The indicator can display the strength of the password as a text message or with a progress bar indicator. |
| *PopupControlExtender* | This extender can be attached to any control in order to open a pop-up window that displays additional content. This pop-up window will probably be interactive, and will probably be within an Ajax UpdatePanel, so it will be able to perform complex server-based processing (including postbacks) without affecting the rest of the page. The pop-up window can contain any content, including ASP.NET server controls, HTML elements, and so on. |

*continues*

**TABLE 20-1** *(continued)*

| CONTROL | DESCRIPTION |
|---|---|
| Rating | This control provides an intuitive rating experience that allows users to select the number of stars that represents their ratings. The page designer can specify the initial rating, the maximum rating to allow, the alignment and direction of the stars, and custom styles for the different states a star can have. Rating also supports a ClientCallBack event that allows custom code to run after the user has rated something. |
| ReorderList | This control implements a bulleted, data-bound list with items that can be reordered interactively. To reorder the items in the list, the user simply drags the item's control bar to its new location. Graphical feedback is shown where the item will be placed as it is dragged by the user. The data source is updated after the item is dropped in its new location. |
| ResizableControlExtender | This is an extender that attaches to any element on a web page, and allows the user to resize that control with a handle that attaches to lower-right corner of the control. The resize handle lets the user resize the element as if it were a window. The appearance of the resize handle can be specified by the page designer with a CSS style. |
| RoundedCornersExtender | This extender applies rounded corners to existing elements. To accomplish this, it inserts elements before and after the element that is selected, so the overall height of the element will change slightly. You can choose which corners of the target panel should be rounded by setting the Corners property. |
| SeaDragon | This control can be used for interactively viewing images. Use your mouse to pan and zoom around the image. |
| SliderExtender | This extender allows upgrading a TextBox to a graphical slider that allows the user to choose a numeric value from a finite range. The Slider's orientation can be horizontal or vertical, and it can also act as a "discrete" slider, allowing only a specified number of values within its range. |

| CONTROL | DESCRIPTION |
|---|---|
| *SlideShowExtender* | This is an extender that targets image controls. You can provide it with buttons to hit Previous, Next, and Play. You can configure the slide show to play automatically on render, allow it loop through the images in a round-robin fashion, and also set the interval for slide transitions. You can use a page method to supply images to the slide show or use a web service. |
| TabContainer | This is a control that creates a set of tabs that can be used to organize page content. A TabContainer is a host for a number of TabPanel controls. |
| *TextBoxWatermarkExtender* | This extender can be attached to a TextBox control to get "watermark" behavior. When a watermarked TextBox is empty, it displays a message to the user with a custom CSS style. Once the user has typed some text into the TextBox, the watermarked appearance goes away. The typical purpose of a watermark is to provide more information to the user about the TextBox itself without cluttering up the rest of the page. |
| *ToggleButtonExtender* | This extender can be attached to a CheckBox control. ToggleButtonExtender enables the use of custom images to show the state of the CheckBox. The behavior of the CheckBox is unaffected. |
| *UpdatePanelAnimationExtender* | This is a simple extender that allows you to utilize the powerful animation framework with existing pages in an easy, declarative fashion. It is used to play animations both while an UpdatePanel is updating, and after it has finished updating. |
| *ValidationCalloutExtender* | This extender enhances the functionality of existing ASP.NET validators. To use this control, add an input field and a validator control as you normally would, and attach a ValidationCalloutExtender to it. |

As you can see from Table 20-1, most controls in the Ajax Control Toolkit are extenders that can be attached to an existing ASP.NET control. Later in this section you'll learn about most new Ajax server-side controls, and then you will learn more about extenders.

## New Server Controls

The AjaxControlToolkit.dll adds several ASP.NET controls to the Toolbox. Most of them are very simple and intuitive to use. However, they have many properties and methods you can use.

An examination of all of them would not fit into this chapter. Instead of showing all the nitty-gritty details, this section focuses on getting started with these controls, and helps you to discover them on your own.

The best way to become familiar with the new server controls is to learn them through example. You can download the `ActControlSamples` project from this book's companion website (www.wrox.com) and try the samples introduced here.

## The ComboBox Control

The `ComboBox` control of the Toolkit is very similar to the `ComboBox` control you can use with Windows Forms. But, of course, you can use it with ASP.NET applications. It can be described as a `DropDownList` that can be typed directly into like a `TextBox`. The semantics of `ComboBox` are also very similar to an ASP.NET `DropDownList`.

**FIGURE 20-6:** ComboBoxSample.aspx page

Open the `ActControlSamples` project. There you'll find a page named `ComboBoxSample.aspx`. This page contains a `DropDownList` control to set the `AutoCompleteMode` property of the other two `ComboBox` controls on the page. The first `ComboBox` instance is initialized in the `.aspx` file; the second picks up values from a database. When you run the sample, you see the page shown in Figure 20-6.

Listing 20-8 shows the source code of the UI.

**LISTING 20-8:** ComboBoxSample.aspx

```
<%@ Page Language="C#" AutoEventWireup="true"
   CodeBehind="ComboBoxSample.aspx.cs"
   Inherits="ActControlSamples.ComboBoxSample" %>

<%@ Register Assembly="AjaxControlToolkit" Namespace="AjaxControlToolkit"
   TagPrefix="asp" %>
<!DOCTYPE html PUBLIC "-//W3C//DTD XHTML 1.0 Transitional//EN"
   "http://www.w3.org/TR/xhtml1/DTD/xhtml1-transitional.dtd">
<html xmlns="http://www.w3.org/1999/xhtml">
<head runat="server">
  <title>Ajax ComboBox sample</title>
</head>
<body>
  <form id="form1" runat="server">
  <asp:ToolkitScriptManager ID="ToolkitScriptManager1" runat="server" />
  <div>
    <p>
      Select <code>AutoCompleteMode</code> value from this
```

```
          <code>DropDownList</code>:</p>
      <asp:UpdatePanel ID="UpdatePanel1" runat="server">
        <ContentTemplate>
          <asp:DropDownList ID="AutoCompleteModeList" runat="server"
            AutoPostBack="true"
            OnSelectedIndexChanged="AutoCompleteModeList_SelectedIndexChanged">
            <asp:ListItem Value="None" />
            <asp:ListItem Value="Append" />
            <asp:ListItem Value="Suggest" />
            <asp:ListItem Value="SuggestAppend" />
          </asp:DropDownList>
          <p>
            Simple <code>ComboBox</code> filled with numbers:</p>
          <asp:ComboBox ID="SimpleComboBox" runat="server"
            AutoPostBack="true"
            OnSelectedIndexChanged="SimpleComboBox_SelectedIndexChanged"
            OnItemInserted="SimpleComboBox_ItemInserted"
            OnItemInserting="SimpleComboBox_ItemInserting">
            <asp:ListItem Value="0">Please select a value</asp:ListItem>
            <asp:ListItem Value="1">One</asp:ListItem>
            <asp:ListItem Value="2">Two</asp:ListItem>
            <asp:ListItem Value="3">Three</asp:ListItem>
            <asp:ListItem Value="4">Four</asp:ListItem>
          </asp:ComboBox>
           
          <asp:Label ID="SimpleComboLabel" runat="server" Text="" /><br />
        </ContentTemplate>
      </asp:UpdatePanel>
      <p>
        <code>ComboBox</code> filled from a database:</p>
      <asp:ComboBox ID="DataBoundComboBox" runat="server"
        AutoPostBack="True"
        OnSelectedIndexChanged="DataBoundComboBox_SelectedIndexChanged"
        DataSourceID="ExpertDataSource"
        DataTextField="Name"
        DataValueField="ID"
        MaxLength="0">
      </asp:ComboBox>
      <asp:AccessDataSource ID="ExpertDataSource" runat="server"
        DataFile="~/App_Data/ExpertData.mdb"
        SelectCommand="SELECT * FROM [Expertise]">
      </asp:AccessDataSource>     
      <asp:Label ID="DataBoundComboLabel" runat="server" Text="" /><br />
    </div>
  </form>
</body>
</html>
```

*Code file [ComboBoxSample.aspx] available for download at Wrox.com*

You can encapsulate the ComboBox controls into an UpdatePanel. However, it is not required to make them work. You can see that the SimpleComboBox is wrapped in an UpdatePanel, while

DataBoundComboBox is not. The two ComboBox instances raise a few events that let you examine how they work. Both of them respond to the SelectedIndexChanged event, and display the current selection. Listing 20-9 shows the code behind the UI.

**LISTING 20-9:** ComboBoxSample.aspx.cs

```csharp
using System;
using System.Data;
using System.Data.OleDb;
using System.Web.UI.WebControls;
using AjaxControlToolkit;

namespace ActControlSamples
{
  public partial class ComboBoxSample : System.Web.UI.Page
  {
    protected void Page_Load(object sender, EventArgs e)
    {
    }

    protected void AutoCompleteModeList_SelectedIndexChanged(object sender,
      EventArgs e)
    {
      var autoComplete = (ComboBoxAutoCompleteMode)Enum.Parse(
        typeof(ComboBoxAutoCompleteMode),
        AutoCompleteModeList.SelectedValue);
      SimpleComboBox.AutoCompleteMode = autoComplete;
      DataBoundComboBox.AutoCompleteMode = autoComplete;
    }

    protected void SimpleComboBox_SelectedIndexChanged(object sender, EventArgs e)
    {
      SimpleComboLabel.Text = String.Format("{0}: {1}",
        SimpleComboBox.SelectedValue, SimpleComboBox.SelectedItem);
    }

    protected void SimpleComboBox_ItemInserted(object sender,
      ComboBoxItemInsertEventArgs e)
    {
      SimpleComboLabel.Text = String.Format("{0}: {1}",
        SimpleComboBox.SelectedValue, SimpleComboBox.SelectedItem);
    }

    protected void SimpleComboBox_ItemInserting(object sender,
      ComboBoxItemInsertEventArgs e)
    {
      if (e.Item.Text.StartsWith("Q"))
      {
        e.Cancel = true;
        return;
      }
```

```
        if (e.Item.Text.StartsWith("E"))
          e.InsertLocation = ComboBoxItemInsertLocation.OrdinalText;
        else if (e.Item.Text.StartsWith("N"))
        {
          e.InsertLocation = ComboBoxItemInsertLocation.Append;
          e.Item.Value = SimpleComboBox.Items.Count.ToString();
        }
      }

    protected void DataBoundComboBox_SelectedIndexChanged(object sender,
      EventArgs e)
    {
      DataBoundComboLabel.Text = String.Format("{0}: {1}",
        DataBoundComboBox.SelectedValue, DataBoundComboBox.SelectedItem);
      }
    }
  }
```

---

*Code file [ComboBoxSample.aspx.cs] available for download at Wrox.com*

The `AutoCompleteModeList` allows you to select the value of the `AutoCompleteMode` property. This determines how the `ComboBox` automatically completes the text that is typed into it:

➤ When `Suggest` is specified, the `ComboBox` will show the list, highlight the first matched item, and, if necessary, scroll the list to show the highlighted item.

➤ When `Append` is specified, the `ComboBox` will append the remainder of the first matched item to the user-typed text, and highlight the appended text.

➤ When `SuggestAppend` is specified, both of these behaviors are applied.

➤ When `None` (the default value) is specified, the `ComboBox`'s auto-complete behaviors are disabled.

Figure 20-7 shows how the `SimpleComboBox` behaves when the `SuggestAppend` mode is selected.

The most interesting method in Listing 20-9 is `SimpleComboBox_ItemInserting` that is invoked when a text value is about to be inserted into the combo box. This method cancels the insertion for any text starting with the letter Q. By default, the new text is appended at the end of the list. But this code changes this behavior so that, when you insert a text starting with E, it will be inserted into the list according the new text's ordinal (alphabetical) position.

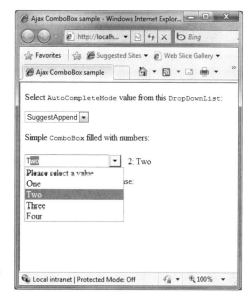

**FIGURE 20-7:** ComboBox using AutoCompleteMode set to SuggestAppend

The new text is inserted with the same value as the text. However, you can change it. `SimpleComboBox_ItemInserting` changes this logic so that, for any text starting with N, the value will be changed to an integer sequential number. In Figure 20-8, you can see the results.

Type the following text into the first `ComboBox` and enter each by pressing Tab (use this order): **Five, Quarter, Six, Seven, Eight, Nine**. "Quarter" starts with Q, so it is not inserted at all. All numbers are appended at the end of the list, except "Eight" because it starts with E. All numbers have the same value and text (check the text of the label to the right of the combo) except "Nine," because it starts with N.

There are a few other properties of `ComboBox` you can use to change the control's behavior. Table 20-2 summarizes them.

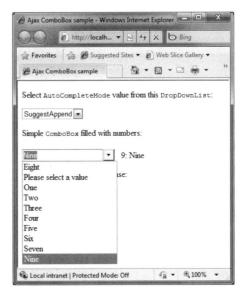

**FIGURE 20-8:** Checking the insertion logic of SimpleComboBox

**TABLE 20-2:** ComboBox Properties

| PROPERTY | DESCRIPTION |
|---|---|
| `DropDownStyle` | Determines whether the user is allowed to enter text that does not match an item in the list, and whether the list is always displayed. If `DropDownList` is specified, users are not allowed to enter text that does not match an item in the list. When `DropDown` (the default value) is specified, any text is allowed. If `Simple` is specified, any text is allowed and the list is always displayed, regardless of the `AutoCompleteMode` property value. |
| `CaseSensitive` | Specifies whether user-typed text is matched to items in the list in a case-sensitive manner. The default is `false`. |
| `RenderMode` | Specifies whether the `ComboBox` is rendered as an `Inline` or `Block` level HTML element. The default is `Inline`. |
| `ItemInsertLocation` | Determines whether to `Append` or `Prepend` new items when they are inserted into the list, or whether to insert them in an `Ordinal` manner (alphabetically) based on the item `Text` or `Value`. The default is `Append`. |
| `ListItemHoverCssClass` | When specified, replaces the default styles applied to highlighted items in the list with a custom CSS class. |

## The TabContainer Control

You can use the `TabContainer` control to organize a page into several panels. A `TabContainer` is a host for a number of `TabPanel` controls. The `ActControlSamples` project contains a `TabContainerSample` page that provides a similar view of experts, as you've built it in the `FindAnExpertDemo` project. Figure 20-9 and Figure 20-10 shows the two tabs of the `TabContainer` used by the page.

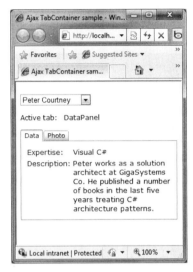

FIGURE 20-9: The Data tab of TabContainerSample.aspx

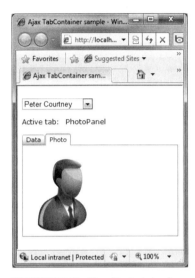

FIGURE 20-10: The Photo tab of TabContainerSample.aspx

Open the `TabContainerSample.aspx` page to look at its details. The page uses `UpdatePanel` control to refresh the `TabContainer` content triggered by the selection changes in the drop-down list you can see at the top of Figure 20-9. Listing 20-10 shows the structure of the `TabContainer` control.

**LISTING 20-10: TabContainerSample.asxp (Code Extract)**

```
<asp:TabContainer ID="TabContainer1" runat="server"
  AutoPostBack="true"
  onactivetabchanged="TabContainer1_ActiveTabChanged">
  <asp:TabPanel ID="DataPanel" HeaderText="Data" runat="server">
    <ContentTemplate>
      <table>
        <tr valign="top">
          <td>Expertise:</td>
          <td>
            <asp:Label ID="ExpertiseLabel" runat="server" Text="" />
          </td>
        </tr>
        <tr valign="top">
          <td>Description:</td>
```

*continues*

**LISTING 20-10** *(continued)*

```
              <td>
                <asp:Label ID="DescriptionLabel" runat="server" Text="" />
              </td>
            </tr>
          </table>
        </ContentTemplate>
      </asp:TabPanel>
      <asp:TabPanel ID="PhotoPanel" HeaderText="Photo" runat="server">
        <ContentTemplate>
          <br />
          <asp:Image ID="Photo" runat="server"
            Height="128px" Width="128px" />
          <br />
        </ContentTemplate>
      </asp:TabPanel>
    </asp:TabContainer>
```

*Code file [TabContainerSample.aspx] available for download at Wrox.com*

You can embed zero, one, or more `TabPanel` control instances into a `TabContainer`. Each `TabPanel` can define a number of child controls within its `<ContentTemplate>` element. You can also catch the event when the active tab has been changed. Listing 20-11 shows the code belonging to `TabContainerSample.aspx`.

**LISTING 20-11: TabContainerSample.aspx.cs**

```
using System;
using System.Web.UI;
using System.Web.UI.WebControls;

namespace ActControlSamples
{
  public partial class TabContainerSample : System.Web.UI.Page
  {
    protected void Page_Load(object sender, EventArgs e)
    {
    }

    protected void ExpertList_SelectedIndexChanged(object sender, EventArgs e)
    {
      var fields = ExpertList.SelectedValue.Split('$');
      var expLabel =
        Page.FindControl("TabContainer1$DataPanel$ExpertiseLabel") as Label;
      expLabel.Text = fields[0];
      var descrLabel =
        Page.FindControl("TabContainer1$DataPanel$DescriptionLabel") as Label;
      descrLabel.Text = fields[1];
      var photo =
        Page.FindControl("TabContainer1$PhotoPanel$Photo") as Image;
      photo.ImageUrl = "/Photos/" + fields[2] +".png";
```

```
      }

      protected void TabContainer1_ActiveTabChanged(object sender, EventArgs e)
      {
        ActiveTabLabel.Text = TabContainer1.ActiveTab.ID;
      }

      protected void ExpertList_DataBound(object sender, EventArgs e)
      {
        ExpertList_SelectedIndexChanged(ExpertList, EventArgs.Empty);
        TabContainer1_ActiveTabChanged(ExpertList, EventArgs.Empty);
      }
    }
  }
```

*Code file [TabContainerSample.aspx.cs] available for download at Wrox.com*

The `ExpertList_SelectedIndexChanged` event handler method splits the `SelectedValue` string that contains the expert data, (such as `Expertise`, `Description`, and `Photo`) separated by dollar signs, and sets the appropriate label and image control properties with these values. Note that the controls within `TabPanes` cannot be accessed directly, because they do not have member fields within the class representing the page. You can address them with the `Page.FindControl` method. For example, the control with the identifier `Photo` within the `PhotoPanel` tab can be accessed with the address `TabContainer1$PhotoPanel$Photo`.

The `TabContainer1_ActiveTabChanged` event handler displays the identifier of the selected tab. The `ExpertList` control is a data-bound control. As soon as its content is read and set up, the `ExpertList_DataBound` method is called, and the information within the `TabContainer` is refreshed.

Although Listing 20-10 does not show it, the `TabContainer` and the label displaying the active tab is wrapped with an `UpdatePanel`, so all event handling happens asynchronously.

The `TabContainer` control contains several interesting properties summarized in Table 20-3.

**TABLE 20-3:** TabContainer Properties

| PROPERTY | DESCRIPTION |
| --- | --- |
| ActiveTabChanged | This event is fired on the server side when a tab is changed after a postback. |
| OnClientActiveTabChanged | The name of a JavaScript function to attach to the client-side `tabChanged` event. |
| CssClass | A CSS class override used to define a custom look and feel for the tabs. |
| ActiveTabIndex | The index of the `TabPanel` to show. |
| Height | Sets the height of the body of the tabs (does not include the `TabPanel` headers). |

*continues*

**TABLE 20-3** *(continued)*

| PROPERTY | DESCRIPTION |
|---|---|
| Width | Sets the width of the body of the tabs. |
| ScrollBars | Sets the mode to display scrollbars in the body of the TabContainer. The values are taken from the ScrollBars enumerated type (None, Horizontal, Vertical, Both, Auto). |
| TabStripPlacement | Tells whether to render the tabs on top of the container or below (Top, Bottom). |

The TabPanel controls can be customized through the properties described in Table 20-4.

**TABLE 20-4:** TabPanel Properties

| PROPERTY | DESCRIPTION |
|---|---|
| Enabled | This flag tell whether to display the Tab for the TabPanel by default. This can be changed on the client. |
| OnClientClick | The name of a JavaScript function to attach to the client-side click event of the tab. |
| HeaderText | The text to display in the tab. |
| HeaderTemplate | A single-instance template to use to render the header. |
| ContentTemplate | A single-instance template to use to render the body. |

## The Accordion Control

The Accordion control lets you define multiple panes and display them one at a time. It is like having several CollapsiblePanelExtender controls, where only one can be expanded at a time. The Accordion control contains one or more AccordionPane controls. Each AccordionPane control has a template for its header and its content. The control can also be data-bound.

It's very easy to create an Accordion control. The AccordionSample.aspx page of the ActControlSamples project is a good demonstration of an Accordion control with three AcordionPanes. Listing 20-12 shows the control's definition.

**LISTING 20-12: AccordionSample.aspx (Code Extract)**

```
<asp:Accordion ID="Accordion1" runat="server"
  Width="300px"
  HeaderCssClass="header"
  HeaderSelectedCssClass="selectedheader"
```

```
    ContentCssClass="content"
    AutoSize="None">
    <Panes>
      <asp:AccordionPane ID="AccordionPane1" runat="server">
        <Header>Expert #1</Header>
        <Content>
          This expert has been chief programmer at several enterprise
          projects building business applications with Visual Basic.
          He's especially strong in developing middleware components.
        </Content>
      </asp:AccordionPane>
      <asp:AccordionPane ID="AccordionPane2" runat="server">
        <Header>Expert #2</Header>
        <Content>
          He works as a solution architect at GigaSystems Co. He
          published a number of books in the last five years treating
          C# architecture patterns.
        </Content>
      </asp:AccordionPane>
      <asp:AccordionPane ID="AccordionPane3" runat="server">
        <Header>Expert #3</Header>
        <Content>
          She started her own company named VBToTheTop in 2003 and now
          she's a well-known mentor for Visual Basic developers
          working in Europe.
        </Content>
      </asp:AccordionPane>
    </Panes>
  </asp:Accordion>
```

*Code file [AccordionSample.aspx] available for download at Wrox.com*

By default, the `Accordion` control does not assign any specific styles to the elements of the control. And, without styles, the control works, but when you see it in a web page, you would not think it is interactive at all. Figure 20-11 shows how the control looks like with its default style.

You can set up the `HeaderCssClass`, `HeaderSelectedCssClass`, and `ContentCssClass` properties to provide a more attractive (and intuitive) look for the control, as shown in Figure 20-12.

When you click one of the headers, the control provides a smooth animation to show the content behind the clicked header. The `TransitionDuration` property allows setting the length of time to use to transition between `Accordion` panes in milliseconds; the default value is 250. You can set the `FramesPerSecond` property to define the number of steps per second in the transition animations; the default value is 30. With the `FadeTransitions` flag, you can influence whether to fade the accordion panes when transitioning.

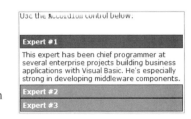

**FIGURE 20-11:** The default style of the Accordion control

**FIGURE 20-12:** Providing custom style for the Accordion control

You will find another page named `AccordionWithDataSample.aspx` in the sample project that demonstrates how easy it is to bind an `Accordion` control with a data source. Listing 20-13 shows the full source code of this file.

**LISTING 20-13:** AccordionWithDataSample.aspx

```
<%@ Page Language="C#" AutoEventWireup="true"
   CodeBehind="AccordionWithDataSample.aspx.cs"
   Inherits="ActControlSamples.AccordionSample" %>

<%@ Register Assembly="AjaxControlToolkit" Namespace="AjaxControlToolkit"
   TagPrefix="asp" %>
<!DOCTYPE html PUBLIC "-//W3C//DTD XHTML 1.0 Transitional//EN"
   "http://www.w3.org/TR/xhtml1/DTD/xhtml1-transitional.dtd">
<html xmlns="http://www.w3.org/1999/xhtml">
<head runat="server">
  <title>Ajax Accordion control sample</title>
  <link rel="Stylesheet" href="/Styles/Accordion.css" />
</head>
<body style="font-family:verdana;font-size:12px">
  <form id="form1" runat="server">
  <asp:ToolkitScriptManager ID="ToolkitScriptManager1" runat="server" />
  <div>
    <p>
      Select experts to list in the <code>Accordion</code> control</p>
    <asp:DropDownList ID="ExpertiseList" runat="server"
      AutoPostBack="true"
      DataSourceID="ExpertiseDataSource"
      DataTextField="Name" DataValueField="ID">
    </asp:DropDownList>
    <br /><br />
    <asp:AccessDataSource ID="ExpertiseDataSource" runat="server"
      DataFile="~/App_Data/ExpertData.mdb"
      SelectCommand="SELECT [ID], [Name] FROM [Expertise]"></asp:AccessDataSource>
    <asp:AccessDataSource ID="ExpertDataSource" runat="server"
      DataFile="~/App_Data/ExpertData.mdb"
      SelectCommand="SELECT * FROM [Expert] WHERE ([Expertise] = ?)">
      <SelectParameters>
        <asp:ControlParameter ControlID="ExpertiseList"
          Name="Expertise" PropertyName="SelectedValue"
          Type="Int16" />
      </SelectParameters>
    </asp:AccessDataSource>
    <asp:UpdatePanel ID="UpdatePanel1" runat="server" >
      <ContentTemplate>
    <asp:Accordion ID="Accordion1" runat="server"
      Width="300px"
      HeaderCssClass="header"
      HeaderSelectedCssClass="selectedheader"
      ContentCssClass="content"
      AutoSize="None"
```

```
            DataSourceID="ExpertDataSource">
            <HeaderTemplate>
              <asp:Label ID="Label1" runat="server"
                Text='<%# HttpUtility.HtmlEncode(Convert.ToString(Eval("Name"))) %>' />
            </HeaderTemplate>
            <ContentTemplate>
              <table>
                <tr>
                  <td>
                    <asp:Label ID="Label1" runat="server"
                      Text='<%# HttpUtility.HtmlEncode(Convert.ToString(
                        Eval("Description"))) %>' />
                  </td>
                  <td>
                    <asp:Image ID="Image1" runat="server" Width="128px" Height="128px"
                      ImageUrl='<%# "/Photos/" + HttpUtility.HtmlEncode(
                        Convert.ToString(Eval("Photo"))) + ".png" %>' />
                  </td>
                </tr>
              </table>
            </ContentTemplate>
          </asp:Accordion>
          </ContentTemplate>
          <Triggers>
            <asp:AsyncPostBackTrigger ControlID="ExpertiseList" />
          </Triggers>
        </asp:UpdatePanel>
      </div>
      </form>
  </body>
</html>
```

*Code file [AccordionWithDataSample.aspx] available for download at Wrox.com*

This file defines two data sources: one for the `ExpertiseList` control, and one for the `Accordion`. These data sources are bound, so, when you select a new item in the `ExpertiseList`, the `Accordion`'s data source is refreshed with the experts having the specified expertise — with no extra coding. The `DataSourceID` property of the `Accordion` is set to this data source. However, you must explicitly call the `DataBind` method:

```
protected void Page_Load(object sender, EventArgs e)
{
    Accordion1.DataBind();
}
```

The data is displayed according to the `HeaderTemplate` and `ContentTemplate` definitions. Figure 20-13 shows the page in action.

**FIGURE 20-13:** Accordion control using data binding

The control has several other properties not examined here, yet which are also very useful when customizing the `Accordion` control. Table 20-5 describes them.

**TABLE 20-5:** Accordion Properties

| PROPERTY | DESCRIPTION |
|---|---|
| AutoSize | This value specifies how to restrict the layout of the Accordion control: <br><br> None — The control grows and shrinks without restriction. <br><br> Limit — The `Accordion` control never grows larger than the value specified by its `Height` property. This causes the content to scroll if the content is too long to be displayed in the allotted space. <br><br> Fill — The control is a fixed size, as specified in its `Height` property. This causes the content to expand or shrink if the content does not fit exactly into the allotted space. |
| RequireOpenedPane | This value specifies that the currently opened pane does not close when its header is clicked (which ensures one pane is always open). The default is `true`. |
| SuppressHeaderPostbacks | This flag specifies whether the client-side click handlers of elements inside a header are called. This is useful when you want to include hyperlinks in the headers for accessibility. |

## The AsyncFileUpload Control

The standard ASP.NET `FileUpload` control does not work within an Ajax `UpdatePanel`. If you want to place it in an update panel, then a postback trigger is also required to upload the file. The Toolkit's `AsyncFileUpload` control allows you to upload the file in an asynchronous manner, and it works with `UpdatePanel`. A great advantage of this control is that it uploads the file without any postback, and provides both client-side and server-side events.

The control provides different coloring options for file uploads. For example, it can have a green background when the file is uploaded successfully and a red one when upload fails. You can also show a "progress" image while file uploading is in progress.

You can find the `AsyncFileUploadSample.aspx` page in the `ActControlSamples` project to examine how this control works. This page contains client-side scripts, as shown in Listing 20-14.

**LISTING 20-14:** AsynchFileUploadSample.aspx

```
<%@ Page Language="C#" AutoEventWireup="true"
    CodeBehind="AsynchFileUploadSample.aspx.cs"
    Inherits="ActControlSamples.AsynchFileUploadSample" %>
```

```
<%@ Register Assembly="AjaxControlToolkit" Namespace="AjaxControlToolkit"
  TagPrefix="asp" %>
<!DOCTYPE html PUBLIC "-//W3C//DTD XHTML 1.0 Transitional//EN"
  "http://www.w3.org/TR/xhtml1/DTD/xhtml1-transitional.dtd">
<html xmlns="http://www.w3.org/1999/xhtml">
<head runat="server">
  <title>Ajax AsynchFileUpload control sample</title>
  <script type="text/javascript" language="javascript">
    function onStartUpload(sender, args) {
      document.getElementById('StatusLabel').innerText =
        'File is being uploaded.';
    }

    function onUploadError(sender, args)
    {
      var fileName = args.get_fileName();
      var errorMessage = args.get_errorMessage();
      document.getElementById('StatusLabel').innerHTML = fileName +
        " <span style='color:red;'>" + errorMessage + "</span>";
    }

    function onUploadComplete(sender, args)
    {
      var fileName = args.get_fileName();
      var contentType = args.get_contentType();
      var text = fileName + " is uploaded.<br/>Size: " +
      args.get_length() + " bytes";
      if (contentType.length > 0)
      {
        text += ", content type: '" + contentType + "'.";
      }
      document.getElementById('StatusLabel').innerHTML = text;
    }
  </script>
</head>
<body style="font-family: verdana; font-size: 12px">
  <form id="form1" runat="server">
  <asp:ToolkitScriptManager ID="ToolkitScriptManager1" runat="server" />
  <div>
    <p>
      Select a file to upload</p>
    <asp:UpdatePanel ID="UpdatePanel1" runat="server">
      <ContentTemplate>
        <asp:AsyncFileUpload ID="AsyncFileUpload1" runat="server"
          Width="400px"
          OnClientUploadError="onUploadError"
          OnClientUploadStarted="onStartUpload"
          OnClientUploadComplete="onUploadComplete"
          CompleteBackColor="Lime"
          UploaderStyle="Traditional" ErrorBackColor="#FF5050"
          ThrobberID="Throbber"
          OnUploadedComplete="AsyncFileUpload1_UploadedComplete"
          UploadingBackColor="LightBlue" />
```

*continues*

**LISTING 20-14** *(continued)*

```
            <asp:Label ID="Throbber" runat="server" Style="display: none">
                <img src="Images/UploadIndicator.gif" align="absmiddle"
                    alt="loading" />
            </asp:Label>
            <br />
            <br />
            <asp:Label ID="StatusLabel" runat="server" />
        </ContentTemplate>
      </asp:UpdatePanel>
    </div>
    </form>
</body>
</html>
```

*Code file [AsynchFileUploadSample.aspx] available for download at Wrox.com*

The `AsyncFileUpload` control in the page sets up several properties. Table 20-6 summarizes the properties you can use with the control.

**TABLE 20-6:** AsyncFileUpload Properties

| PROPERTY | DESCRIPTION |
| --- | --- |
| CompleteBackColor | The control's background color to set when upload has completed. |
| ContentType | Gets the MIME content type of a file sent by a client. |
| ErrorBackColor | The control's background color to set when an upload error occurs. |
| FileContent | Gets a `Stream` object that points to an uploaded file to prepare for reading the contents of the file. |
| FileName | Gets the name of a file on a client to upload using the control. |
| HasFile | Gets a flag indicating whether the control contains a file. |
| OnClientUploadComplete | The name of a JavaScript function executed on the client side after the file is successfully uploaded. |
| OnClientUploadError | The name of a JavaScript function executed on the client side if the file uploading failed. |
| OnClientUploadStarted | The name of a JavaScript function executed on the client side on the file uploading started. |
| PostedFile | Gets an `HttpPostedFile` object that provides access to the uploaded file. |

| PROPERTY | DESCRIPTION |
|---|---|
| ThrobberID | The ID of the control that is shown while the file is uploading. |
| UploaderStyle | The control's appearance style (Traditional or Modern). |
| UploadingBackColor | The control's background color when uploading is in progress. The default value is White. |
| Width | The control's width. |

The control in Listing 20-14 uses a multi-frame GIF image to signal the progress of the update. This image is bound to the AsyncFileUpload control through the ThrobberID property:

```
<asp:AsyncFileUpload ID="AsyncFileUpload1" runat="server" ...
  ThrobberID="Throbber" ... />
<asp:Label ID="Throbber" runat="server" Style="display: none">
  <img src="Images/UploadIndicator.gif" align="absmiddle" alt="loading" />
</asp:Label>
```

The onStartUpload, onUploadError and onUploadComplete JavaScript functions are associated with the client event properties. You can call the get_fileName, get_errorMessage, get_contentType, get_length, and get_path methods of the args event parameter to access the corresponding properties of the file uploaded. For example, onUploadComplete uses this to display information about the file:

```
function onUploadComplete(sender, args)
{
  var fileName = args.get_fileName();
  var contentType = args.get_contentType();
  var text = fileName + " is uploaded.<br/>Size: " +
  args.get_length() + " bytes";
  if (contentType.length > 0)
  {
    text += ", content type: '" + contentType + "'.";
  }
  document.getElementById('StatusLabel').innerHTML = text;
}
```

Figure 20-14 shows an example how file information is displayed when the control successfully completes the upload process.

When there is any problem during the upload, the onUploadError client function displays the status, as shown in Figure 20-15.

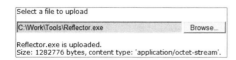

**FIGURE 20-14:** A file has been successfully uploaded.

**FIGURE 20-15:** The file upload failed.

The `AsyncFileUpload` control sends a postback to the page when the file upload is successfully completed. You can respond to this event and save the file, as shown in Listing 20-15.

LISTING 20-15: AsynchFileUpload.aspx.cs

```
using System;
using System.IO;
using AjaxControlToolkit;

namespace ActControlSamples
{
  public partial class AsynchFileUploadSample : System.Web.UI.Page
  {
    protected void Page_Load(object sender, EventArgs e)
    {
    }

    protected void AsyncFileUpload1_UploadedComplete(object sender,
      AsyncFileUploadEventArgs e)
    {
      if (AsyncFileUpload1.HasFile)
      {
        string strPath = MapPath("~/Uploads/") + Path.GetFileName(e.filename);
        AsyncFileUpload1.SaveAs(strPath);
      }
    }
  }
}
```

*Code file [AsynchFileUpload.aspx.cs] available for download at Wrox.com*

 *Although the `AsyncFileUpload` control is very easy to use, there are some issues with it. Once the file is uploaded, there is no way to clear the content of file upload control. There is no way to cancel the upload or to monitor the progress of uploading. Uploading starts as soon as you select the file. It stores the files in the session.*

## The Editor Control

The `Editor` control of the Ajax Control Toolkit (formerly named `HtmlEditor`) provides rich editor functionality to easily create and edit HTML content. With the editor, you can use many formatting functions, including fonts, color, indentations, bulleted and numbered lists, hyperlinks, and many more. The functions can be accessed through toolbar items and keyboard shortcuts. The control provides a view of the generated HTML markup and a preview of the edited document.

The `EditorSample.aspx` page of the sample project provides an example of using the `Editor` control. You can edit your content in the editor, and, by clicking the Submit button, you can post it back to display the content on the page. Figure 20-16 shows this example in action.

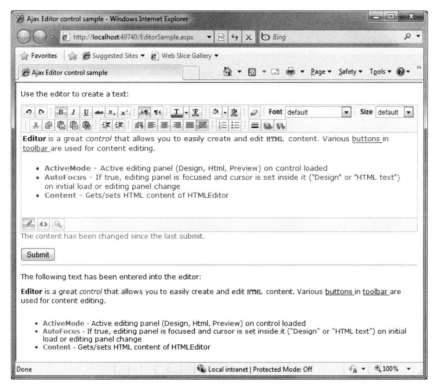

**FIGURE 20-16:** EditorSample.aspx in action

Although you can see a complex UI with toolbars and lots of buttons, the source code declaring the page is really simple, as shown in Listing 20-16.

**LISTING 20-16:** EditorSample.aspx

```
<%@ Page Language="C#" AutoEventWireup="true" CodeBehind="EditorSample.aspx.cs"
  Inherits="ActControlSamples.EditorSample" %>

<%@ Register Assembly="AjaxControlToolkit"
  Namespace="AjaxControlToolkit.HTMLEditor"
  TagPrefix="asp" %>
<%@ Register Assembly="AjaxControlToolkit" Namespace="AjaxControlToolkit"
  TagPrefix="asp" %>
```

*continues*

**LISTING 20-16** *(continued)*

```
<!DOCTYPE html PUBLIC "-//W3C//DTD XHTML 1.0 Transitional//EN"
    "http://www.w3.org/TR/xhtml1/DTD/xhtml1-transitional.dtd">
<html xmlns="http://www.w3.org/1999/xhtml">
<head runat="server">
  <title>Ajax Editor control sample</title>
</head>
<body style="font-family:verdana;font-size:12px">
  <form id="form1" runat="server">
  <asp:ToolkitScriptManager ID="ToolkitScriptManager1" runat="server" />
  <div>
    <asp:UpdatePanel ID="UpdatePanel1" runat="server">
      <ContentTemplate>
        <p>Use the editor to create a text:</p>
        <asp:Editor ID="Editor1" runat="server"
          OnContentChanged="Editor1_ContentChanged" />
        <asp:Label ID="ChangedLabel" runat="server" ForeColor="Red"
          Text="The content has been changed since the last submit."
          Visible="False" />
        <br />
        <br />
        <asp:Button id="SubmitButton" runat="server"
          Text="Submit"
          Onclick="SubmitButton_Click" />
         
        <hr />
        <p>The following text has been entered into the editor:</p>
        <asp:Literal id="EditorContentLiteral" Runat="server" />
      </ContentTemplate>
    </asp:UpdatePanel>
  </div>
  </form>
</body>
</html>
```

*Code file [EditorSample.aspx] available for download at Wrox.com*

As you see from the code, the only real property set after dragging the Editor control from the Toolbox to the page is OnContentChanged. The logic of the page checks if the content has changed since the last time it was submitted, and signals it on the screen with the ChangedLabel control.

Not only is the UI definition simple, but the code behind the UI is simple as well, as shown in Listing 20-17.

**LISTING 20-17: EditorSample.aspx.cs**

```
using System;

namespace ActControlSamples
{
  public partial class EditorSample : System.Web.UI.Page
```

```
  {
    protected void Page_Load(object sender, EventArgs e)
    {
    }

    protected void SubmitButton_Click(object sender, EventArgs e)
    {
      EditorContentLiteral.Text = Editor1.Content;
      var changed = Session["EditorContentChanged"];
      if (changed != null)
        ChangedLabel.Visible = (bool)changed;
      Session["EditorContentChanged"] = false;
    }

    protected void Editor1_ContentChanged(object sender, EventArgs e)
    {
      Session["EditorContentChanged"] = true;
    }
  }
}
```

*Code file [EditorSample.aspx.cs] available for download at Wrox.com*

The control does not need any special initialization, so the `Page_Load` method is empty. Both the `SubmitButton_Click` and the `Editor1_ContentChanged` methods are fired when the page is posted back as a result of clicking the Submit button. First, the `Editor1_ContentChanged` runs then `SubmitButton_Click`.

The HTML content of the editor is accessed through the `Content` property. Because it is an HTML string, you can directly assign it to the `Text` property of the `EditorContentLiteral` control. The `Session` stores whether or not the content was changed from the last submit, and `ChangedLabel` visibility is set accordingly.

Table 20-7 summarizes the properties you can use with the `Editor` control.

**TABLE 20-7:** Editor Properties

| PROPERTY | DESCRIPTION |
| --- | --- |
| ActiveMode | Sets the active editing panel (Design, Html, Preview) to use when the control is loaded. The default is Design. |
| AutoFocus | If this flag is set to true, the editing panel is focused and the cursor is set inside it (Design or HTML view) on initial load or editing panel change. |
| Content | Gets or sets the HTML content of the Editor. |
| CssClass | A CSS class override that is used to define a custom look and feel for the Editor. |

*continues*

**TABLE 20-7** *(continued)*

| PROPERTY | DESCRIPTION |
|---|---|
| DesignPanelCssPath | Sets the path of additional CSS file used for `Editor`'s content rendering in `Design` panel. If not set, the default CSS file is used, which is embedded as a `WebResource` and is a part of the Toolkit assembly. |
| DocumentCssPath | Sets the path of CSS file used for `Editor`'s content rendering in `Design` and `Preview` panels. If not set, the default CSS file is used, which is embedded as a `WebResource` and is a part of the Toolkit assembly. |
| Height | Sets the height of the body of the `Editor`. |
| HtmlPanelCssClass | A CSS class override used to define a custom look for the `Editor`'s HTML mode panel. |
| IgnoreTab | If this flag is set to `true`, Tab key navigation is suppressed inside the `Editor` control. |
| InitialCleanUp | If `true`, the `Editor`'s content is cleaned up on initial load. Microsoft Word-specific tags are removed. |
| NoScript | If `true`, JavaScript code is suppressed in `Editor`'s content. |
| NoUnicode | If `true`, all Unicode characters in HTML content are replaced with `&#code;`. |
| OnClientActiveModeChanged | This is the client-side script that executes after active mode (editing panel) has changed. |
| OnClientBeforeActiveModeChanged | The client-side script that executes before active mode (editing panel) has changed. |
| SuppressTabInDesignMode | If `true`, no white spaces are inserted on Tab key press in `Design` mode. The default Tab key navigation is processing in this case. |
| Width | Sets the width of the body of the editor. |

The richness of functionality that the `Editor` control provides may be an issue when you want to constrain the available formatting options. You have no properties to enable or disable specific editor features. However, it does not mean that you cannot solve this issue. You can derive a new custom ASP.NET control from `Editor`, customize it, and use this derived editor in your pages.

The `ActControlSamples` project contains an example of this customization. There is a page named `CutomEditorSample.aspx` that is an exact copy of `EditorSample.aspx` you've seen earlier — it uses an `Editor`-derived class instead of the original control. Listing 20-18 shows how easy is to carry out the customization.

**LISTING 20-18:** CustomEditor.cs

```csharp
using AjaxControlToolkit.HTMLEditor;
using ToolbarButton = AjaxControlToolkit.HTMLEditor.ToolbarButton;


namespace ActControlSamples
{
  public class CustomEditor : Editor
  {
    protected override void FillTopToolbar()
    {
      TopToolbar.Buttons.Add(new ToolbarButton.Undo());
      TopToolbar.Buttons.Add(new ToolbarButton.Redo());
      TopToolbar.Buttons.Add(new ToolbarButton.HorizontalSeparator());
      TopToolbar.Buttons.Add(new ToolbarButton.Bold());
      TopToolbar.Buttons.Add(new ToolbarButton.Italic());
      TopToolbar.Buttons.Add(new ToolbarButton.Underline());
      TopToolbar.Buttons.Add(new ToolbarButton.StrikeThrough());
      TopToolbar.Buttons.Add(new ToolbarButton.SubScript());
      TopToolbar.Buttons.Add(new ToolbarButton.SuperScript());
      TopToolbar.Buttons.Add(new ToolbarButton.HorizontalSeparator());
      TopToolbar.Buttons.Add(new ToolbarButton.Cut());
      TopToolbar.Buttons.Add(new ToolbarButton.Copy());
      TopToolbar.Buttons.Add(new ToolbarButton.PasteText());
    }

    protected override void FillBottomToolbar()
    {
    }
  }
}
```

*Code file [CustomEditor.cs] available for download at Wrox.com*

The `AjaxControlToolkit.HTMLEditor` `.ToolbarButton` class has several nested classes representing editor buttons on the toolbar. With overriding of the `FillTopToolbar` and `FillBottomToolbar` methods, you can define your own buttons — and so you can constrain the functionality of your editor.

The `CustomEditor` class keeps the bottom toolbar empty, and so allows you to use only the `Design` edit panel. The top toolbar contains only font formatting buttons. Figure 20-17 shows this custom editor in action.

**FIGURE 20-17:** Customized Editor control in action

# Control Extenders

A majority of controls in the Ajax Control Toolkit are extenders. They cannot be used as individual controls. They are always attached to another ASP.NET control to add value by extending that control's behavior. This section examines almost all extender controls in the Toolkit.

All extenders have a `TargetControlID` property that can be used to identify the control to which the extender is attached. Consider the following example:

```
<asp:Button ID="DisableButton" runat="server"
  Text="Disable this CheckBox"
  OnClick="DisableButton_Click" />
<asp:ConfirmButtonExtender ID="ConfirmButtonExtender1" runat="server"
  TargetControlID="DisableButton"
  ConfirmText="Are you sure you want to do that?" />
```

This structure implicitly tells you that an extender can have exactly one control to which it is attached. However, a control may have zero, one, or more extenders extending it.

 *Most of extenders have many more properties than introduced and demonstrated in this section's samples. For a complete reference of properties visit the Ajax Control Toolkit Sample site (`http://www.asp.net/ajax/ajaxcontroltoolkit/samples`).*

## Button and Checkbox Extenders

Two extenders can be attached to `CheckBox` controls:

➤ `ToggleButtonExtender` enables the use of custom images to show the state of the `CheckBox` without affecting the attached `CheckBox`'s behavior.

➤ With `MutuallyExclusiveCheckBoxExtender`, you can add a number of checkboxes to the same "Key," and only one `CheckBox` with the specified key can be checked at a time.

The third control, `ConfirmButtonExtender`, catches clicks on a button (or on any instance of a type that is derived from `Button`, such as a `LinkButton`) and displays a message to the user. If the user clicks OK, the button or link functions normally.

The `ButtonExtendersSample.aspx` page in the sample project demonstrates these concepts. Figure 20-18 shows the example page in action.

Each checkbox in the page has an attached `ToggleButtonExtender`. A `ConfirmButtonExtender` close to the top of the page disables or enables

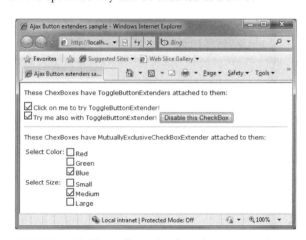

**FIGURE 20-18:** ButtonExtendersSample.aspx in action

the checkbox on its left side. The six checkboxes at the bottom part form two groups with attached MutuallyExclusiveCheckBoxExtender instances. All controls in the page are wrapped with an UpdatePanel. The code defining the UI part above the horizontal bar is shown in Listing 20-19.

**LISTING 20-19:** ButtonExtendersSample.aspx (Code Extract, Part 1)

```
<asp:CheckBox ID="CheckBox1" Checked="true"
   Text="Click on me to try ToggleButtonExtender!"
   runat="server" />
<asp:ToggleButtonExtender ID="ToggleExt1" runat="server"
   TargetControlID="CheckBox1"
   ImageWidth="16" ImageHeight="16"
   CheckedImageUrl="Images/Checked.png"
   CheckedImageOverUrl="Images/Checked-Hovered.png"
   DisabledCheckedImageUrl="Images/Checked-Disabled.png"
   CheckedImageAlternateText="Checked"
   UncheckedImageUrl="Images/Unchecked.png"
   UncheckedImageOverUrl="Images/Unchecked-Hovered.png"
   DisabledUncheckedImageUrl="Images/Unchecked-Disabled.png"
   UncheckedImageAlternateText="UnChecked" />
<asp:CheckBox ID="CheckBox2" Checked="true"
   Text="Try me also with ToggleButtonExtender!"
   runat="server" />
<asp:ToggleButtonExtender ID="ToggleExt2" runat="server"
   TargetControlID="CheckBox2"
   ImageWidth="16" ImageHeight="16"
   CheckedImageUrl="Images/Checked.png"
   CheckedImageOverUrl="Images/Checked-Hovered.png"
   DisabledCheckedImageUrl="Images/Checked-Disabled.png"
   CheckedImageAlternateText="Checked"
   UncheckedImageUrl="Images/Unchecked.png"
   UncheckedImageOverUrl="Images/Unchecked-Hovered.png"
   DisabledUncheckedImageUrl="Images/Unchecked-Disabled.png"
   UncheckedImageAlternateText="UnChecked" />
<asp:Button ID="DisableButton" runat="server"
   Text="Disable this CheckBox"
   OnClick="DisableButton_Click" />
<asp:ConfirmButtonExtender ID="ConfirmButtonExtender1" runat="server"
   TargetControlID="DisableButton"
   ConfirmText="Are you sure you want to do that?"
   ConfirmOnFormSubmit="true" />
```

*Code file [ButtonExtendersSample.aspx] available for download at Wrox.com*

As you see, you can define images for all CheckBox state combinations. Unfortunately, when you want to declare more ToggleButtonExtender instances, you must set all the image-related properties separately for each extender. With ImageHeight and ImageWidth, you define the height and width, respectively, of the image that will be displayed.

The definition of the ConfirmButtonExtender is much shorter. You can initialize the ConfirmText property to tell the extender the text to show in the confirmation message.

You can also define a JavaScript function with the `OnClientCancel` property to run when the user cancels the confirmation. Setting the `ConfirmOnFormSubmit` property to `true` can be useful if the page contains ASP.NET validator controls, and the confirm dialog box should be displayed only after all validation checks pass. You can also set up the `DisplayModalPopupID` so that the `ConfirmButtonExtender` works together with a `ModalPopupExtender` control. (You will learn about this later in this chapter.)

The code defining the checkboxes at the bottom part of the page forming the `Color` and `Size` groups is shown in Listing 20-20.

**LISTING 20-20: ButtonExtendersSample.aspx (Code Extract, Part 2)**

```
<table>
  <tr>
    <td valign="top">Select Color:</td>
    <td>
      <asp:Panel ID="ColorPanel" runat="server">
        <asp:CheckBox ID="Red" runat="server" Text="Red" />
        <asp:MutuallyExclusiveCheckBoxExtender
          ID="MutExt1" runat="server" TargetControlID="Red"
          Key="Color" />
        <asp:CheckBox ID="Green" runat="server" Text="Green" />
        <asp:MutuallyExclusiveCheckBoxExtender
          ID="MutExt2" runat="server" TargetControlID="Green"
          Key="Color" />
        <asp:CheckBox ID="Blue" runat="server" Text="Blue" />
        <asp:MutuallyExclusiveCheckBoxExtender
          ID="MutExt3" runat="server" TargetControlID="Blue"
          Key="Color" />
      </asp:Panel>
    </td>
  </tr>
  <tr>
    <td valign="top">Select Size:</td>
    <td>
      <asp:Panel ID="SizePanel" runat="server">
        <asp:CheckBox ID="Small" runat="server" Text="Small" />
        <asp:MutuallyExclusiveCheckBoxExtender
          ID="MutExt4" runat="server" TargetControlID="Small"
          Key="Size" />
        <asp:CheckBox ID="Medium" runat="server" Text="Medium" />
        <asp:MutuallyExclusiveCheckBoxExtender
          ID="MutExt5" runat="server" TargetControlID="Medium"
          Key="Size" />
        <asp:CheckBox ID="Large" runat="server" Text="Large" />
        <asp:MutuallyExclusiveCheckBoxExtender
          ID="MutExt6" runat="server" TargetControlID="Large"
          Key="Size" />
      </asp:Panel>
    </td>
  </tr>
</table>
```

*Code file [ButtonExtendersSample.aspx] available for download at Wrox.com*

The Key property of the MutuallyExclusiveCheckBoxExtender names the logical group to which the attached CheckBox instance belongs. The extender takes care that only one checkbox in that logical group (the one checked the last time) can remain checked.

There is a simple logic behind the .aspx file, as shown in Listing 20-21.

**LISTING 20-21:** ButtonExtendersSample.aspx.cs

```csharp
using System;
using System.Web.UI.WebControls;
using AjaxControlToolkit;

namespace ActControlSamples
{
  public partial class ButtonExtendersSample : System.Web.UI.Page
  {
    protected void Page_Load(object sender, EventArgs e)
    {
      CreateToggleButtonExtender(Red, ColorPanel);
      CreateToggleButtonExtender(Green, ColorPanel);
      CreateToggleButtonExtender(Blue, ColorPanel);
      CreateToggleButtonExtender(Small, SizePanel);
      CreateToggleButtonExtender(Medium, SizePanel);
      CreateToggleButtonExtender(Large, SizePanel);
    }

    protected void DisableButton_Click(object sender, EventArgs e)
    {
      CheckBox2.Enabled = !CheckBox2.Enabled;
      DisableButton.Text =
        (CheckBox2.Enabled ? "Disable" : "Enable") + " this CheckBox";
    }

    private void CreateToggleButtonExtender(CheckBox checkBox, Panel panel)
    {
      var ext = new ToggleButtonExtender();
      ext.TargetControlID = checkBox.ID;
      ext.ImageWidth = ToggleExt1.ImageWidth;
      ext.ImageHeight = ToggleExt1.ImageHeight;
      ext.CheckedImageUrl = ToggleExt1.CheckedImageUrl;
      ext.CheckedImageOverUrl = ToggleExt1.CheckedImageOverUrl;
      ext.DisabledCheckedImageUrl = ToggleExt1.DisabledCheckedImageUrl;
      ext.UncheckedImageUrl = ToggleExt1.UncheckedImageUrl;
      ext.UncheckedImageOverUrl = ToggleExt1.UncheckedImageOverUrl;
      ext.DisabledUncheckedImageUrl = ToggleExt1.DisabledUncheckedImageUrl;
      panel.Controls.Add(ext);
    }
  }
}
```

*Code file [ButtonExtendersSample.aspx.cs] available for download at Wrox.com*

The majority of this logic is about attaching `ToggleButtonExtender` instances to the checkboxes organized into the `Color` and `Size` logical groups. Without this code, you must create six `<asp:ToggleButtonExtender>` elements with their ten properties (nine of them having the same values) in the `.aspx` file. That would be laborious and error-prone. The `CreateToggleButtonExtender` method solves this problem by copying the properties of `ToggleExt1` when `Page_Load` runs.

## TextBox Extenders

Ajax Control Toolkit implements ten extenders that can be attached to `TextBox` controls. These extenders can improve the user experience with filling in data forms. Using them, you can transform your simple (and maybe boring) data entry pages to sexy ones. You can find the following `TextBox`-related extenders in the Toolkit:

- ➤ The `AutoCompleteExtender` provides a pop-up panel to display words that begin with the prefix that is entered into the text box. When the user has entered more characters than a specified minimum length, a popup displays words or phrases that start with that value.

- ➤ `CalendarExtender` provides client-side date-picking functionality with customizable date format and UI in a pop-up control.

- ➤ `ColorPickerExtender` enables you to display a pop-up color picker when the focus is moved to an input element. It provides client-side color-picking functionality with a UI in a pop-up control.

- ➤ `FilteredTextBoxExtender` lets users enter into a text box only characters that you define, or prevents users from entering characters that you specify.

- ➤ `MaskedEditExtender` applies a "mask" to the input that permits only certain types of characters/text to be entered. The supported data formats are `Number`, `Date`, `Time`, and `DateTime`.

- ➤ `MultiHandleSliderExtender` allows you to choose a single value, or multiple values in a range, through a graphical slider interface. It supports one handle, dual handles, or any number of handles bound to the values of `TextBox` or `Label` controls.

- ➤ `NumericUpDownExtender` adds "up" and "down" buttons that increment and decrement the value in the `TextBox`. The increment and decrement can be simple +1/-1 arithmetic. They can cycle through a provided list of values (like the months of the year), or they can call a web service to determine the next value.

- ➤ The `PasswordStrength` extender shows the strength of the password in the `TextBox` and updates itself as the user types the password. The indicator can display the strength of the password as a text message, or with a progress bar indicator.

➤ `SliderExtender` allows upgrading a `TextBox` to a graphical slider that enables the user to choose a numeric value from a finite range. The `Slider`'s orientation can be horizontal or vertical, and it can also act as a "discrete" slider, allowing only a specified number of values within its range.

➤ The `TextBoxWatermarkExtender` provides "watermark" behavior for the attached `TextBox`. When a watermarked `TextBox` is empty, it displays a message to the user with a custom CSS style.

The `TextBoxExtendersSample.aspx` page of the `ActControlSamples` project shows you examples of how to use the `TextBox` extenders just described. This sample allows you to fill in a fictitious registration page, as shown in Figure 20-19.

**FIGURE 20-19:** TextBoxExtendersSample.aspx

 *This sample does not demonstrate the use of the* `AutoCompleteExtender` *control. You can find a great video about it at* http://www.asp.net/learn/ajax-videos/video-122.aspx.

The Full Name field is defined in the code as shown here:

```
<tr>
  <td>Full Name:</td>
  <td>
    <asp:TextBox ID="FullName" runat="server" />
    <asp:TextBoxWatermarkExtender ID="WmExt" TargetControlID="FullName"
      WatermarkText="&lt;your name&gt;"
      WatermarkCssClass="watermarked"
      runat="server" />
  </td>
</tr>
```

As you can see in Figure 20-19, the text specified in the `WatermarkText` attribute is shown when the `FullName` text box does not have the focus. You can also specify the CSS class to be used for the watermark (`WatermarkCssClass` property) that uses a simple CSS entry in this sample:

```
<style type="text/css">
  .watermarked { color: Gray }
</style>
```

The Requested Login Name field uses a `FilteredTextBoxExtender` that accepts letters, numbers, and the dot character:

```
<tr>
  <td>Requested Login Name:</td>
  <td>
    <asp:TextBox ID="LoginName" runat="server" />
    <asp:FilteredTextBoxExtender ID="FtbExt" TargetControlID="LoginName"
      FilterType="Custom, Numbers, LowercaseLetters, UppercaseLetters"
      ValidChars="."
      runat="server" />
  </td>
</tr>
```

The `FilterType` property defines the keys that should be accepted by the control. You can enumerate one or more of the `Custom`, `Numbers`, `LowercaseLetters`, and `UppercaseLetters` values. When `Custom` is defined, you can set additional characters to accept in the `ValidChars` property.

The Password and Confirm Password fields are each attached to a `PasswordStrenghth` extender. The only difference between them is that Password displays all characters you type in, while Confirm Password hides them. The Password field is defined with the following code:

```
<tr>
  <td>Password:</td>
  <td>
    <asp:TextBox ID="Password" runat="server" />
    <asp:PasswordStrength ID="PwStrength" TargetControlID="Password"
      DisplayPosition="RightSide"
      StrengthIndicatorType="Text"
      PreferredPasswordLength="10"
      PrefixText="Strength:"
      MinimumNumericCharacters="1"
      MinimumSymbolCharacters="1"
      RequiresUpperAndLowerCaseCharacters="false"
      TextStrengthDescriptions="Very Poor;Weak;Average;Strong;Excellent"
      CalculationWeightings="50;15;15;20"
      runat="server" />
  </td>
</tr>
```

Most properties have very intuitive names, and they tell what they are used for. `TextStrengthDescriptions` contains a semicolon-separated list of descriptions to be used for the password strength levels. `CalculationWeightings` lists semicolon-separated numeric values used to determine the weighting of a strength characteristic. There must be 4 values specified that must total 100. The format is `A;B;C;D`, where A equals the length weighting, B equals the numeric weighting, C equals the casing weighting, and D equals the symbol weighting. Figure 20-20 shows you the run-time behavior of the `PasswordStrength` extender.

| Password: | ItsWeak | Strength:Weak |
| Password: | Its100%VeryStrong | Strength:Excellent |

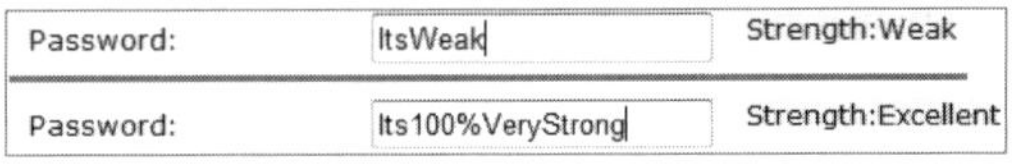

**FIGURE 20-20:** The PasswordStrength extender in action

The Birth Date field uses a `CalendarExtender` that is displayed when you click the button to the right of the text box. Its behavior is defined with this code:

```
<tr>
  <td>Birth Date:</td>
  <td>
    <asp:TextBox ID="BirthDate" runat="server" />
    <asp:Button ID="PopupButton" runat="server" Height="24" Width="28"
      Text="..." />
    <asp:CalendarExtender ID="CalExt" TargetControlID="BirthDate"
      Format="MMMM d, yyyy"
      PopupButtonID="PopupButton"
      runat="server" />
  </td>
</tr>
```

With the `PopupButtonID` property, you can define the control that pops up the calendar pane. When you leave it empty, the calendar pane is displayed on the page as soon as the attached `TextBox` receives the focus. Figure 20-21 shows the `CalendarExtender` control in action.

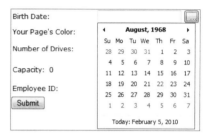

**FIGURE 20-21:** CalendarExtender in action

The Your Page's Color field uses a `ColorPickerExtender` so that, while the user moves the mouse over the color palette, the background of the field's label is set to show the color under the mouse pointer. Figure 20-22 shows this.

This behavior is defined with the following code snippet where the `SampleControlID` property binds the color under the mouse pointer to the field label:

**FIGURE 20-22:** ColorPickerExtender in action

```
<tr>
  <td>
    <asp:Panel ID="SamplePanel" runat="server">
      Your Page's Color:
    </asp:Panel>
  </td>
  <td>
    <asp:TextBox ID="PageColor" runat="server" />
    <asp:ColorPickerExtender ID="CpExt" TargetControlID="PageColor"
      SampleControlID="SamplePanel"
      runat="server" />
  </td>
</tr>
```

The Number of Drives field demonstrates how to attach a `NumericUpDownExtender` to a `TextBox`:

```
<tr>
  <td>Number of Drives:</td>
  <td>
    <asp:TextBox ID="DriveNumber" runat="server" />
    <asp:NumericUpDownExtender ID="NumExt" TargetControlID="DriveNumber"
      Width="40"
      Minimum="0"
      Maximum="3"
      runat="server" />
  </td>
</tr>
```

The extender adds up and down buttons to the right of the `TextBox`, and lets you move the values between 0 and 3. With the `RefValue` properties, you can define non-numeric values as a semicolon-separated list. `NumericUpDownExtender` also can use web services to provide the subsequent values when clicking the up or down buttons. You can also provide your own buttons with the `TargetButtonDownID` and `TargetButtonUpID` properties.

The Capacity field's `TexBox` is attached to a `SliderExtender` that lets you choose a value between 0 and 500. The extender binds the current slider value to a label control, as shown in Figure 20-23.

**FIGURE 20-23:** Using the SliderExtender control

The following very simple code sets up this behavior:

```
<tr>
  <td>Capacity: 
    <asp:Label ID="SliderValue" runat="server" Text=""/>
  </td>
  <td>
    <asp:TextBox ID="Capacity" runat="server" /> 
    <asp:SliderExtender ID="SliderExt" TargetControlID="Capacity"
      Minimum="0"
      Maximum="500"
      BoundControlID="SliderValue"
      EnableHandleAnimation="true"
      runat="server" />
  </td>
</tr>
```

*There is another slider extender,* `MultiHandleSliderExtender`, *that (as its name suggests) allows you to use more than one handle. The* `TextBoxExtendersSample.aspx` *does not contain any demonstration of this control. You can find a demo and more information about this slider extender at* `http://www.asp.net/AJAX/AjaxControlToolkit/Samples/ MultiHandleSlider/MultiHandleSlider.aspx`.

The Employee ID field demonstrates the use of the `MaskedEditExtender` control. The following code sets up this extender to allow typing only employee IDs with `LLL-99-99` format, where `L` stands for letters and `9` for numbers:

```
<tr>
  <td>Employee ID:</td>
  <td>
    <asp:TextBox ID="EmpID" runat="server" />
    <asp:MaskedEditExtender ID="MeExt" TargetControlID="EmpID"
      Mask="LLL-99-99"
      ErrorTooltipEnabled="True"
      runat="server" />
  </td>
</tr>
```

This extender has many properties you can use for culture-specific format settings. Look at the reference of this extender to discover the large set of properties you can use to customize it.

## List Extenders

There are three extenders in the Ajax Control Toolkit that can be attached to ASP.NET list controls:

➤ `CascadingDropDown` can be attached to an ASP.NET `DropDownList` control to get automatic population of a set of `DropDownList` controls. When you modified the `FindAnExpertDemo` sample application, you learned a lot about using this extender.

➤ `ListSearchExtender` lets you search for items in a `ListBox` or `DropDownList` by typing. The extender performs an incremental search within the `ListBox` based on what has been typed so far.

➤ `PagingBulletedListExtender` can be attached to a `BulletedList` control and provide client-side sorted paging. It is very flexible, and lets you specify either the number of characters used in the heading indices, or the maximum number of items to display per index.

The `ListExtendersSample.aspx` page demonstrates the use of the latter two extenders. This sample binds the list of experts from the database you've already used several times in the listings appearing in this chapter. Figure 20-24 shows this page in action.

Listing 20-22 shows the definition of the UI shown in Figure 20-24.

**FIGURE 20-24:** The ListExtendersSample .aspx page in action

**LISTING 20-22: ListExtendersSample.aspx**

```
<%@ Page Language="C#" AutoEventWireup="true"
  CodeBehind="ListExtendersSample.aspx.cs"
  Inherits="ActControlSamples.ListExtendersSample" %>

<%@ Register Assembly="AjaxControlToolkit" Namespace="AjaxControlToolkit"
  TagPrefix="act" %>
<!DOCTYPE html PUBLIC "-//W3C//DTD XHTML 1.0 Transitional//EN"
  "http://www.w3.org/TR/xhtml1/DTD/xhtml1-transitional.dtd">
<html xmlns="http://www.w3.org/1999/xhtml">
<head runat="server">
  <title>Ajax List extenders sample</title>
  <style type="text/css">
    .searchprompt { color: red; font-size: 10px; }
    .selectedIndex { background-color: Yellow; }
  </style>
</head>
<body style="font-family: verdana; font-size: 12px">
  <form id="form1" runat="server">
  <act:ToolkitScriptManager ID="ToolkitScriptManager1" runat="server" />
  <div>
    <p>
      This list box is attached to a ListSearchExtender:</p>
    <br />
    <asp:ListBox ID="ExpertList" runat="server"
      DataSourceID="AccessDataSource1"
      DataTextField="Name"
      DataValueField="ID"
      Rows="8" />
    <asp:AccessDataSource ID="AccessDataSource1" runat="server"
      DataFile="~/App_Data/ExpertData.mdb"
      SelectCommand="SELECT [ID], [Name] FROM [Expert]" />
    <act:ListSearchExtender ID="ListSearchExtender1"
      TargetControlID="ExpertList"
      PromptText="Type to search"
      PromptCssClass="searchprompt"
      PromptPosition="Bottom"
      runat="server" />
    <br />
    <br />
    <hr />
    <p>The following list is decorated with PgingBuletedListExtender.</p>
    <asp:BulletedList ID="BulletedExpertList" runat="server"
      DataSourceID="AccessDataSource1"
      DataTextField="Name"
      DataValueField="ID" />
    <act:PagingBulletedListExtender ID="PagingExt"
      TargetControlID="BulletedExpertList"
      ClientSort="True"
      IndexSize="1"
      Separator=" | "
```

```
            SelectIndexCssClass="selectedIndex"
            runat="server" />
    </div>
    </form>
</body>
</html>
```

*Code file [ListExtendersSample.aspx] available for download at Wrox.com*

The `PrompText` property of the `ListSearchExtender` control sets the message to display when the `ListBox` or `DropDownList` is given focus (as you see in Figure 20-24). The `PromptText` is replaced by the search text typed by the user. You can set the location of the prompt with `PromptPosition`.

The `PagingBulletedListExtender` can sort the items you provide at the client side (assuming those are not sorted at the server side) by setting `ClientSort` to `True`. The extender can work so that you either set the `IndexSize` property or `MaxItemPerPage`. The first defines the number of characters in the index headings; the second sets the maximum number of items per page. With `Separator`, you can specify a string to separate links to pages.

## Panel Extenders

Following are extenders in the Ajax Control Toolkit that can be attached to panels to provide nice visual effects:

➤ `CollapsiblePanelExtender` adds collapsible sections to a web page. This extender targets any ASP.NET `Panel` control. You specify which control or controls on the page should act as the open and close controllers for the panel.

➤ The `DragPanelExtender` targets any ASP.NET `Panel` and takes an additional parameter that signifies the control to use as the "drag handle." Once initialized, the user can freely drag the panel around the web page using the drag handle.

➤ `DropShadowExtender` applies a drop shadow to an ASP.NET `Panel` control. The extender allows you to specify how wide the shadow is, how opaque it is, and whether the shadow should have rounded corners. For pages that let the user move or resize the panel, the `DropShadowExtender` has a mode that will resize and reposition the shadow to match the target panel at run-time.

Figure 20-25 shows how these extenders are used in the `PanelExtendersSample.aspx` page.

This page contains two main panels. At the top of the page, you can see a panel attached to a `CollapsiblePanelExtender`. As you see, this panel also has a shadow, because a

**FIGURE 20-25:** PanelExtendersSample.aspx in action

`DropShadowExtender` is also attached to the control. The second rectangular panel is decorated with a `DragPanelExtender`. In Figure 20-25, it is moved from its original position to a new location partially overlapping with the collapsible panel.

Listing 20-23 shows the code of the page.

**LISTING 20-23: PanelExtendersSample.aspx**

```
<%@ Page Language="C#" AutoEventWireup="true"
  CodeBehind="PanelExtenders.aspx.cs"
  Inherits="ActControlSamples.PanelExtenders" %>

<%@ Register Assembly="AjaxControlToolkit"
  Namespace="AjaxControlToolkit" TagPrefix="asp" %>
<!DOCTYPE html PUBLIC "-//W3C//DTD XHTML 1.0 Transitional//EN"
  "http://www.w3.org/TR/xhtml1/DTD/xhtml1-transitional.dtd">

<html xmlns="http://www.w3.org/1999/xhtml">
<head runat="server">
  <title>Ajax Panel extenders sample</title>
</head>
<body style="font-family: verdana; font-size: 12px">
  <form id="form1" runat="server">
  <asp:ToolkitScriptManager ID="ToolkitScriptManager1" runat="server" />
  <div>
    <asp:Panel ID="Panel2" runat="server" Height="30px">
      <div style="padding: 5px; cursor: pointer; vertical-align: middle;">
        <div style="float: left;">Dynamics in C#?</div>
        <div style="float: left; margin-left: 20px;">
          <asp:Label ID="Label1" runat="server">(Show Details...)</asp:Label>
        </div>
        <div style="float: right; vertical-align: middle;">
          <asp:ImageButton ID="Image1" runat="server"
            ImageUrl="~/Images/ShowDetails.png"
            AlternateText="(Show Details...)" />
        </div>
      </div>
    </asp:Panel>
    <asp:Panel ID="CSharpPanel" runat="server"
      Style="padding: 12px; background-color: Yellow"
      Height="0">
      <p>
        For a long time, C# could not compete with the flexibility of
        these languages and tools. But, that is no longer the case.
      </p>
    </asp:Panel>
    <asp:CollapsiblePanelExtender ID="cpeDemo" runat="Server"
      TargetControlID="CSharpPanel"
      ExpandControlID="Panel2"
      CollapseControlID="Panel2"
      Collapsed="True"
      TextLabelID="Label1"
      ImageControlID="Image1"
```

```
          ExpandedText="(Hide Details...)"
          CollapsedText="(Show Details...)"
          ExpandedImage="~/Images/HideDetails.png"
          CollapsedImage="~/Images/ShowDetails.png"
          SuppressPostBack="true" />
      <asp:DropShadowExtender ID="DropShadowExtender1" runat="server"
        TargetControlID="CSharpPanel"
        Width="8"
        Rounded="true"
        Radius="6"
        Opacity=".25"
        TrackPosition="true" />
      <br />
      <hr />
      <div style="height: 300px; width: 250px; float: left; padding: 5px;" >
        <asp:Panel ID="DraggablePanel" runat="server" Width="250px"
          style="z-index: 20;">
          <asp:Panel ID="HandlePanel" runat="server" Width="100%" Height="20px"
            BorderStyle="Dotted" BorderWidth="1px" BorderColor="black">
            <div style="cursor:move">Drag Me</div>
          </asp:Panel>
          <asp:Panel ID="InfoPanel" runat="server" Width="100%" Height="200px"
            Style="overflow:auto; padding: 8px" BackColor="#4B4BCC"
            ForeColor="whitesmoke" BorderWidth="2px" BorderColor="black"
            BorderStyle="Solid" >
            <div>
              <p>
                The new version of C# provides dynamic binding as a unified
                approach to selecting and carrying out operations dynamically.
                Operations can be uniformly applied on various objects
                independently of whether a specific object comes from COM
                (through interoperability), IronRuby, IronPython, the HTML
                DOM, or from any other dynamic context.
              </p>
            </div>
          </asp:Panel>
        </asp:Panel>
      </div>
      <div style="clear: both;"></div>
      <asp:DragPanelExtender ID="DragPanelExtender1" runat="server"
        TargetControlID="DraggablePanel"
        DragHandleID="HandlePanel" />
    </div>
    </form>
  </body>
</html>
```

*Code file [PanelExtendersSample.aspx] available for download at Wrox.com*

You can set separate controls to expand and collapse the panel through the `ExpandControlID` and `CollapseControlID` properties of the `CollapsiblePanelExtender`, respectively. You can also specify the text and images for the states of the panel with the `ExpandedText`, `CollapsedText`, `ExpandedImage`, and `CollapsedImage` properties. When you set the `SuppressPostBack` property to `True`, no postbacks are initiated when you expand or collapse the panel.

The `DropShadowExtender` has a few properties to specify how the shadow should be applied for the panel. `Width` lets you set the size of the shadow, which can be `Rounded` with the specified `Radius`. Shadow `Opacity` also can be set. When your panel is movable or resizable, setting the `TrackPosition` to `True` will cause the shadow to follow the panel.

`DragPanelExtender` requires only specifying the `DragHandleID` property that points to the control that serves as the handle to move the panel.

## Popup Extenders

Two extender controls help you to display pop-up panels (or other pop-up controls) on the page:

➤ `PopupControlExtender` can be attached to any control in order to open a pop-up window that displays additional content. This pop-up window will probably be interactive and will probably be within an Ajax `UpdatePanel`, so it will be capable performing complex server-based processing (including postbacks) without affecting the rest of the page.

➤ `ModalPopupExtender` allows you to display content in an element that mimics a modal dialog box, which prevents the user from interacting with the rest of the page.

When you open the `ActControlsSample` project, the `PopupExtenderSample.aspx` page shows you how you can use these controls. This sample uses a `PopupControlExtender` to display a `ListBox` filled up with expert names. This is bound to a `TextBox` so that, when it receives the focus, the `ListBox` is immediately popped up. Figure 20-26 shows you this situation.

Selecting an item from the `ListBox` will close the pop-up panel and use the selected expert's name to create the `TextBox`'s content. When you click the Send Message button, a modal pop-up panel is displayed, allowing you to confirm message sending, as shown in Figure 20-27.

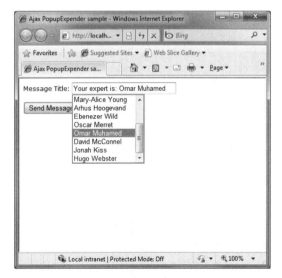

**FIGURE 20-26:** The ListBox is automatically popped up when the TextBox receives the focus

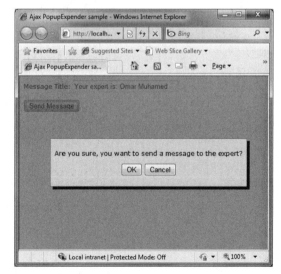

**FIGURE 20-27:** Modal pop-up panel in the page

Listing 20-24 shows the source code of `PopupExtendersSample.aspx`.

**LISTING 20-24: PopupExtendersSample.aspx**

```
<%@ Page Language="C#" AutoEventWireup="true"
  CodeBehind="PopupExtenderSample.aspx.cs"
  Inherits="ActControlSamples.PopupExtenderSample" %>

<%@ Register Assembly="AjaxControlToolkit" Namespace="AjaxControlToolkit"
  TagPrefix="asp" %>
<!DOCTYPE html PUBLIC "-//W3C//DTD XHTML 1.0 Transitional//EN"
  "http://www.w3.org/TR/xhtml1/DTD/xhtml1-transitional.dtd">
<html xmlns="http://www.w3.org/1999/xhtml">
<head runat="server">
  <title>Ajax PopupExpender sample</title>
  <style type="text/css">
    .modalBackground
    {
      background-color:Gray;
      filter:alpha(opacity=70);
      opacity:0.7;
    }
  </style>
</head>
<body style="font-family: verdana; font-size: 12px">
  <form id="form1" runat="server">
  <asp:ToolkitScriptManager ID="ToolkitScriptManager1" runat="server" />
  <div>
    <asp:UpdatePanel runat="server" ID="up2">
      <ContentTemplate>
        Message Title:
        <asp:TextBox ID="MessageTextBox" runat="server" Width="200"
          AutoComplete="off" />
        <br />
        <br />
        <asp:Panel ID="ExpertPanel" runat="server" CssClass="popupControl">
          <div style="border: 1px outset white; width: 140px">
            <asp:ListBox ID="ExpertList" runat="server" Width="140px"
              DataSourceID="ExpertDataSource"
              DataTextField="Name"
              DataValueField="Name"
              AutoPostBack="True"
              Rows="0"
              OnSelectedIndexChanged="ExpertList_SelectedIndexChanged" />
            <asp:AccessDataSource ID="ExpertDataSource" runat="server"
              DataFile="~/App_Data/ExpertData.mdb"
              SelectCommand="SELECT [ID], [Name] FROM [Expert]" />
            <asp:PopupControlExtender ID="ExpertPopupExt" runat="server"
              TargetControlID="MessageTextBox"
              PopupControlID="ExpertPanel"
              CommitProperty="value"
```

*continues*

**LISTING 20-24** *(continued)*

```
                Position="Bottom"
                CommitScript="e.value = 'Your expert is: ' + e.value;" />
          </div>
      </asp:Panel>
      <asp:Button ID="SendButton" runat="server" Text="Send Message" />
        
      <asp:Label ID="MessageStatus" runat="server" Text="" />
      <asp:Panel ID="PopupPanel" runat="server"
        Style="display:none; padding: 8px; background-color: #DDDDDD;
         border : solid 1px Gray; color: Black">
        <p>Are you sure, you want to send a message to the expert?</p>
        <div>
          <p style="text-align: center;">
            <asp:Button ID="OkButton" runat="server" Text="OK"
              OnClick="OkButton_Click"
              UseSubmitBehavior="False"/>
            <asp:Button ID="CancelButton" runat="server" Text="Cancel"
              OnClick="CancelButton_Click"
              UseSubmitBehavior="False"/>
          </p>
        </div>
      </asp:Panel>
      <asp:ModalPopupExtender ID="ModalPopupExtender" runat="server"
        TargetControlID="SendButton"
        PopupControlID="PopupPanel"
        BackgroundCssClass="modalBackground"
        OkControlID="OkButton"
        CancelControlID="CancelButton"
        DropShadow="true" />
    </ContentTemplate>
  </asp:UpdatePanel>
 </div>
 </form>
</body>
</html>
```

*Code file [PopupExtendersSample.aspx] available for download at Wrox.com*

The `PopupControlExtender`'s `TargetControlID` property points to `MessageTextBox` — to the control that pops up the panel when receiving the focus. Its `PopupControlID` property refers to the control to be popped up. `CommitProperty` specifies the property on the control being extended that should be set with the result of the popup. `CommitScript` specifies additional script to run after setting the result of the popup. In this case, these properties result in the host `TextBox` being set to the "Your Expert is . . ." text when you select an item from the popup `ListBox`.

The `ModalPopupExtender` control binds the panel to also show up with its `PopupControlID` property. It specifies the controls representing the OK and Cancel buttons with the `OkControlID` and `CancelControlID` properties, respectively.

The `PopupControlExtender` does not know when to hide the panel popped up. You must manually signal that event. Listing 20-25 shows the code behind the UI.

**LISTING 20-25:** PopupExtendersSample.aspx.cs

```
using System;

namespace ActControlSamples
{
  public partial class PopupExtenderSample : System.Web.UI.Page
  {
    protected void Page_Load(object sender, EventArgs e)
    {
    }

    protected void ExpertList_SelectedIndexChanged(object sender, EventArgs e)
    {
      ExpertPopupExt.Commit(ExpertList.SelectedValue);
      MessageStatus.Text = "";
    }

    protected void OkButton_Click(object sender, EventArgs e)
    {
      MessageStatus.Text = "Message sent.";
    }

    protected void CancelButton_Click(object sender, EventArgs e)
    {
      MessageStatus.Text = "Message sending cancelled.";
    }
  }
}
```

*Code file [PopupExtendersSample.aspx.cs] available for download at Wrox.com*

`ExpertList_SelectedIndexChanged` responds to the event when you select an expert from the list. You must call the `Commit` method of the `PopupControlExtender` with the value to commit — in this case, the name of the expert. You can also respond to the event when the modal pop-up panel's buttons are clicked. The previous code uses them to set a label telling you the result of the modal pop-up dialog.

## The ValidatorCalloutExtender Control

The `ValidatorCalloutExtender` adds nice callouts to your controls having validators. The great thing is that you do not have to change anything with your existing forms; just add `ValidatorCalloutExtender` instances to them. The `ValidatorCallout ExtenderSample.aspx` page of the `ActControlSamples` project demonstrates how easy is to do that. Figure 20-28 shows this sample in action.

**FIGURE 20-28:** ValidatorCalloutExtenderSample.aspx in action

This page has two validator controls, one for the Full Name field and another one for the Confirm Password field. Listing 20-26 shows an extract of the page definition.

**LISTING 20-26:** ValidatorCalloutExtenderSample.aspx (Code Extract)

```
<table>
  <tr>
    <td>Full Name:</td>
    <td>
      <asp:TextBox ID="FullName" runat="server" />
      <asp:TextBoxWatermarkExtender ID="WmExt" TargetControlID="FullName"
        WatermarkText="&lt;your name&gt;"
        WatermarkCssClass="watermarked"
        runat="server" />
      <asp:RequiredFieldValidator ID="RequiredFieldValidator1" runat="server"
        ErrorMessage="Full name is required."
        ControlToValidate="FullName" Display="Dynamic" />
      <asp:ValidatorCalloutExtender runat="Server" ID="ReqValExt"
        TargetControlID="RequiredFieldValidator1"
        HighlightCssClass="validatorCalloutHighlight" />
    </td>
  </tr>
  <tr>
    <!-- Password field omitted -->
  </tr>
  <tr>
    <td>Confirm Password:</td>
    <td>
      <asp:TextBox ID="Password2" runat="server" TextMode="Password" />
      <!-- PasswordStrength control omitted -->
      <asp:CompareValidator ID="CompareValidator1" runat="server"
        ErrorMessage="The two password fields must be equal!"
        ControlToCompare="Password"
        ControlToValidate="Password2" Display="Dynamic" />
      <asp:ValidatorCalloutExtender runat="Server" ID="CompareValExt"
        TargetControlID="CompareValidator1"
        HighlightCssClass="validatorCalloutHighlight"
        CloseImageUrl="~/Images/Close.png"
        WarningIconImageUrl="~/Images/Warning.png"/>
    </td>
  </tr>
</table>
```

*Code file [ValidatorCalloutExtendersSample.aspx] available for download at Wrox.com*

You must specify the validator control in the `TargetControlID` property of `ValidatorCalloutExtender` — and not the control to which the validator is attached. With the `HighlightCssClass` property, you can set the style to apply to the callout when that is shown. You can also change the images used to display the warning sign and the close glyph of the callout with the `WarningIconImageUrl` and `CloseImageUrl` properties, respectively.

# Animations

While the Ajax Control Toolkit primarily focuses on providing great Ajax controls and extenders, it also includes a powerful animation framework that you can use to add awesome visual effects on your pages.

Although the animations are implemented in JavaScript and you can easily use them from client-side code, the Toolkit provides several classes to make it very easy to use the animation framework without writing any JavaScript. You can declare animations via XML markup.

Extenders with animation support (such as `AnimationExtender` and `UpdatePanelExtender`) expose various events (such as `OnClick`) that can be associated with a generic XML animation declaration.

The `AnimationSample.aspx` page of the `ActControlSamples` project demonstrates the basic concepts of using the `AnimationExtender` class with animation markup. When you run this page, you will find six images that are animated when you move the mouse over them. When you move the mouse away from them, they are reset to their original look with reverse animations. Figure 20-29 shows this sample in action, when the mouse is dragged over the second image and that is resized with the animation framework.

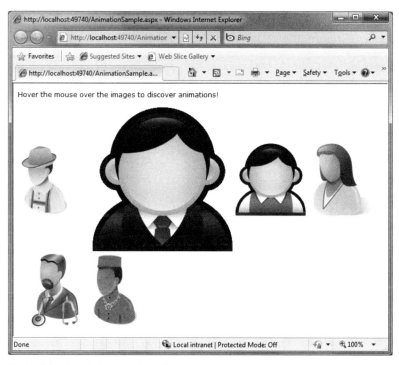

**FIGURE 20-29:** AnimationSample.aspx in action

All images have an `AnimationExtender` attached to them. This extender contains the XML markup that describes the animation. The leftmost image and the related animation are declared with this code:

```
<asp:Image ID="Image1" runat="server" Width="128" Height="128"
  ImageUrl="~/Photos/Arhus.png" />
<!-- ... -->
<asp:AnimationExtender ID="AnimExt1" runat="server"
  TargetControlID="Image1">
  <Animations>
    <OnMouseOver>
      <FadeOut Duration=".5" Fps="20" />
    </OnMouseOver>
    <OnMouseOut>
      <FadeIn Duration=".5" Fps="20" />
    </OnMouseOut>
  </Animations>
</asp:AnimationExtender>
```

The `<Animations>` element is the root of the XML markup. It contains animation description for two events: `OnMouseOver` is triggered when the user moves the mouse over the attached control, and `OnMouseOut` animation is started when the mouse leaves that control. `FadeOut` and `FadeIn` are simple animations, and they do exactly what their names suggest. The `Duration` attribute specifies the length in seconds of the animation, while `Fps` defines the number of frames to be created in one second.

You can use other animation primitives. For example, the second image from the left is resized with the following code:

```
<asp:Image ID="Image2" runat="server" Width="128" Height="128"
  ImageUrl="~/Photos/Chiang.png" />
<!-- ... -->
<asp:AnimationExtender ID="AnimExt2" runat="server"
  TargetControlID="Image2">
  <Animations>
    <OnMouseOver>
      <Resize Width="256" Height="256" />
    </OnMouseOver>
    <OnMouseOut>
      <Resize Width="128" Height="128" />
    </OnMouseOut>
  </Animations>
</asp:AnimationExtender>
```

You can trigger animations with several events. These are summarized in Table 20-8.

**TABLE 20-8:** Events Triggering Animations

| EVENT | DESCRIPTION |
|---|---|
| OnLoad | The animation is played as soon as the page is loaded. |
| OnClick | The animation is played when the target control is clicked. |
| OnMouseOver | The animation is triggered to play when the mouse moves over the target control. |
| OnMouseOut | The animation is started when the mouse moves out of the target control. |
| OnHoverOver | An animation similar to the one for OnMouseOver, except it will stop the OnHoverOut animation before it plays. |
| OnHoverOut | An animation similar to the one for OnMouseOut, except it will stop the OnHoverOver animation before it plays. |

Within the events, you can use simple animation primitives or composite animation declarations. You can use the `<Parallel>` and `<Sequence>` composition elements to allow the declared animation primitives run in parallel or in their specified sequence, respectively. The third image demonstrates using fade and resize animation primitives fired in parallel.

```
<asp:Image ID="Image3" runat="server" Width="128" Height="128"
  ImageUrl="~/Photos/Jonah.png" />
<!-- ... -->
<asp:AnimationExtender ID="AnimExt3" runat="server"
  TargetControlID="Image3">
  <Animations>
    <OnMouseOver>
      <Parallel>
        <FadeOut Duration=".5" Fps="20" />
        <Resize Width="256" Height="256" />
      </Parallel>
    </OnMouseOver>
    <OnMouseOut>
      <Parallel>
        <FadeIn Duration=".5" Fps="20" />
        <Resize Width="128" Height="128" />
      </Parallel>
    </OnMouseOut>
  </Animations>
</asp:AnimationExtender>
```

You can check the animation of the fourth image in the `AnimationSample.aspx` file. It replaces the `<Parallel>` composition element with `<Sequence>`. You can use many other animations besides the fade and resize animations, as shown in Table 20-9.

**TABLE 20-9:** Animations

| ANIMATION | DESCRIPTION |
|---|---|
| Condition | This is used as a control structure to play a specific child animation, depending on the result of executing the `conditionScript`. If the `conditionScript` evaluated to `true`, the first child animation is played. If it evaluates to `false`, the second child animation is played (although nothing is played if the second animation is not present). |
| Case | This animation is used as a control structure to play a specific child animation, depending on the result of executing the `selectScript`, which should evaluate to the index of the child animation to play. If the provided index is outside the bounds of the child animations (or if nothing was returned), then it will not play anything. |
| FadeIn | This animation performs a fade in from the current opacity to the `maximumOpacity`. |
| FadeOut | This animation performs a fade out from the current opacity to the `minimumOpacity`. |
| Pulse | This animation fades an element in and out repeatedly to create a pulsating effect. The `iterations` determine how many pulses there will be. The `duration` property defines the length of each fade in or fade out, not the length of the animation as a whole. |
| Interpolated | This animation assigns a range of values between `startValue` and `endValue` to the designated property. |
| Color | This animation transitions the value of a property between two colors (although it does ignore the alpha channel). The colors must be seven-character hex strings (such as `#33AA44`). |
| Length | This is identical to `Interpolated`, except that it adds a unit to the value before assigning it to the property. |
| Move | This animation is used to move the target element. If the `relative` flag is set to `true`, then it treats the `horizontal` and `vertical` properties as offsets to move the element. If the `relative` flag is `false`, then it will treat the `horizontal` and `vertical` properties as coordinates on the page where the target element should be moved. |
| Resize | This animation changes the size of the target from its current values to the specified `width` and `height`. |
| Scale | This animation scales the size of the target element by the given `scaleFactor`. If `scaleFont` is `true`, the size of the font will also scale with the element. If `center` is `true`, then the element's center will not move as it is scaled. |

You can use actions as animation primitives. For example, with the `EnableAction` primitive, you can disable or enable other animation actions (events) while an animation is in progress. For example, the fifth image (the first in the second row) does not allow you to carry out any other actions on it while the animations are not entirely played:

```
<asp:Image ID="Image5" runat="server" Width="128" Height="128"
  ImageUrl="~/Photos/Ebenezer.png" />
<!-- ... -->
<asp:AnimationExtender ID="AnimExt5" runat="server"
  TargetControlID="Image5">
  <Animations>
    <OnHoverOver>
      <Sequence>
        <EnableAction Enabled="false" />
        <Resize Width="256" Height="256" />
        <EnableAction Enabled="true" />
      </Sequence>
    </OnHoverOver>
    <OnHoverOut>
      <Sequence>
        <EnableAction Enabled="false" />
        <Resize Width="128" Height="128" />
        <EnableAction Enabled="true" />
      </Sequence>
    </OnHoverOut>
  </Animations>
</asp:AnimationExtender>
```

You can also use other actions, as described in Table 20-10.

**TABLE 20-10:** Animation Actions

| ANIMATION | DESCRIPTION |
|---|---|
| EnableAction | This action changes whether or not the target is disabled. |
| HideAction | This action simply hides the target from view (by setting its style's `display` attribute to "none"). |
| StyleAction | This action is used to set a particular attribute of the target's style. |
| OpacityAction | This action will set the opacity of the target. |
| ScriptAction | The action is used to execute arbitrary JavaScript code. |

The `AnimationExtender` can describe animations that can be executed on other targets than the control attached to the extender through the `TargetControlID` property. You can set the `AnimationTarget` property of any primitives to involve other controls into the animation.

For example, the sixth image carries out animations on the first image with the following declarations:

```
<asp:Image ID="Image6" runat="server" Width="128" Height="128"
  ImageUrl="~/Photos/Omar.png" />
<!-- ... -->
<asp:AnimationExtender ID="AnimExt6" runat="server"
  TargetControlID="Image6">
  <Animations>
    <OnMouseOver>
      <FadeOut AnimationTarget="Image1" Duration=".5" Fps="20" />
    </OnMouseOver>
    <OnMouseOut>
      <FadeIn AnimationTarget="Image1" Duration=".5" Fps="20" />
    </OnMouseOut>
  </Animations>
</asp:AnimationExtender>
```

In addition to the `AnimationExtender` control, you can use the `UpdatePanelAnimationExtender` control. This latter one is a non-visual control, so it has different events that trigger animations. The `OnUpdating` event starts the animation when the `UpdatePanel` begins updating; `OnUpdated` plays the animation after the `UpdatePanel` has finished updating (but only if the `UpdatePanel` was changed).

 *You can find detailed reference information about using Ajax Control Toolkit animations at* `http://www.asp.net/AJAX/AjaxControlToolkit/Samples/ Walkthrough/AnimationReference.aspx`.

## THE JQUERY LIBRARY

In addition to the Ajax Control Toolkit, jQuery — a lightweight, cross-browser, JavaScript library — is another great tool for improving the user experience of your ASP.NET websites. This library emphasizes interaction between JavaScript and HTML, because jQuery is designed to make it easier to navigate a document, select DOM elements, create animations, handle events, and develop Ajax applications. It was released in January 2006 by John Resig, and is now used by many big websites. jQuery is one of the most popular JavaScript libraries in use today.

jQuery makes JavaScript code easier and quicker to write. The library provides helper functions that dramatically increase your productivity while decreasing your frustration. The resulting code is easier to read and more robust because the higher level of abstraction hides a number of checks and error-handling procedures. As you have already seen in Chapter 19, jQuery works together seamlessly with the ASP.NET Ajax Library.

This section describes jQuery. You can find the samples treated here in the `jQuerySamples` project that can be downloaded from the book's companion website (`www.wrox.com`).

## "Hello, World" with jQuery

To get closer to jQuery, let's have a look at how a "Hello, World" sample can be written with this library. Listing 20-27 shows a sample where you can click a link to get a message popped up on the screen.

**LISTING 20-27:** jQueryHello.htm

```html
<!DOCTYPE html PUBLIC "-//W3C//DTD XHTML 1.0 Transitional//EN"
    "http://www.w3.org/TR/xhtml1/DTD/xhtml1-transitional.dtd">
<html xmlns="http://www.w3.org/1999/xhtml">
<head>
    <title>Hello from jQuery sample</title>
    <script type="text/javascript"
        src="http://ajax.microsoft.com/ajax/beta/0911/Start.js"></script>
  <script type="text/javascript">
    Sys.require(
      [Sys.scripts.Templates, Sys.scripts.jQuery]
    );
  </script>
    <script type="text/javascript">
      function pageLoad() {
        $('a').click(function (event) {
          alert("Hello from jQuery!");
          event.preventDefault();
        });
      }
    </script>
</head>
<body>
    <a href="">Click here for a welcome message!</a>
</body>
</html>
```

*Code file [jQueryHello.htm] available for download at Wrox.com*

The sample uses the script loader mechanism you learned about in Chapter 19. The body of this HTML file contains a link (<a> element). When the page is loaded, the `pageLoad` function runs and defines the code to handle the event when the link is clicked.

The `$('a')` represents the `jQuery` function with the `'a'` expression (the `$` function is an alias for `jQuery`). The `jQuery` function is the root of jQuery library, defined as follows:

```javascript
var jQuery = window.jQuery = window.$ = function( selector, context ) {
    return new jQuery.fn.init( selector, context );
};
```

So, `$('a')` takes a selector and returns a wrapped array of HTML elements, called a *wrapped set*. In this case, it will return the DOM object represented by the <a> element in the page. The `click` method of the `jQuery` object takes a callback to a function to be called when the object behind the selector is clicked.

As a result, the following code runs when you click the link:

```
alert("Hello from jQuery!");
event.preventDefault();
```

The `alert` method displays the "Hello" message. The `event.preventDefault()` function is also called to prevent the default event handler method from running.

The previous script could be written in a more verbose form like this:

```
function pageLoad() {
    jQuery('a').click(onClick);
}
function onClick(event) {
    alert("Hello from jQuery!");
    event.preventDefault();
}
```

## jQuery Library and jQuery Object

The word "query" in the library's name tells exactly its essence. It refers to running queries over the DOM of the page. Your tools to query and find elements within the DOM are quite limited when you are using the standard methods of the document's DOM elements. For example, you can obtain the element by its identifier:

```
var elem = document.getElementById("dataTable");
```

Unlike in ASP.NET, in the HTML DOM, multiple elements can share the same ID. If a set of elements match the identifier passed, then method `getElementById` would only return the first matching element, while `getElementsByName` would return the whole collection.

jQuery is much more powerful. It provides an amazing interface for selecting DOM elements in a fashion that resembles querying data in SQL rather than obtaining elements by identifiers. The root object of the library (also named `jQuery`) is not just for querying DOM objects. It has functionality that goes far beyond this:

➤ jQuery is chainable. The `jQuery` object itself, as well as most of the functions and filters, return a `jQuery` object. The returned object contains the original wrapped set as modified by the function itself.

➤ jQuery provides an abstract eventing model that allows cross-browser compatibility. You can trigger events programmatically, and you have about a dozen helper methods to simplify the binding of handlers to common events.

➤ Through the jQuery object, you can access the built-in engine for visual effects. In the library, you find an effective engine for building custom animations, plus a few facilities for quickly implementing common effects such as fading and sliding.

➤ jQuery has strong Ajax support (based on the ajax function), through which you can control all aspects of a web request.

➤ Most nontrivial JavaScript code uses some kind of client-side cache. You do not have to create your own, because jQuery provides one.

## Selectors and Filters

Just as the WHERE clause is the key for a SQL statement to select records matching specified conditions, selectors and filters are the essence of jQuery to access DOM elements. With selectors, you can position to specific elements in the DOM. Filters specify additional conditions to include or exclude the element in the wrapped set as the result of the jQuery operation.

The jQuerySelectors.htm file in the jQuerySamples project contains several sample queries. This file contains a table with bulleted lists in each cell, as shown in Figure 20-30.

Each button at the bottom of the page represents an operation based on a jQuery wrapped set. For example, the "First Album to Red" button changes the first <li> item in the page to have a red color with the following script:

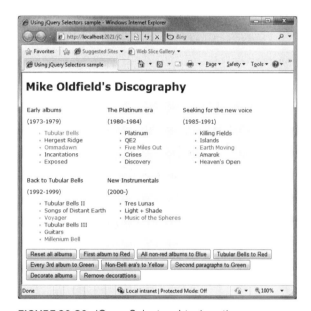

**FIGURE 20-30:** jQuerySelectors.htm in action

```
function firstToRed() {
  $("li:first").addClass("red");
}
```

In this sample, li is a selector ("select all li elements in the page"), and :first is a filter ("select the first item from the selector"). The combination of them results in "select the first li item in the page." The addClass is a jQuery method that adds the specified CSS class to the items in the wrapped set.

There are several selectors, as shown in Table 20-11.

**TABLE 20-11:** Selectors Supported by jQuery

| SELECTOR | DESCRIPTION |
| --- | --- |
| `#id` | Returns the first element, if any, in the DOM with a matching `id` attribute. |
| `element` | Returns all elements with a matching `element` name. |
| `.class` | Returns all elements with a matching CSS `class`. |
| `*` | Returns all elements in the page. |
| `selector1, ..., selectorN` | Applies all given basic selectors, and returns the combined results. |
| `parent > child` | Given a selector, returns the collection of all child elements that match the child selector. |
| `ancestor descendant` | Given an ancestor selector, returns the collection of all descendant elements that match the descendant selector. The descendant does not have to be a child of the ancestor. It can be a grandchild or even a more derived element in the hierarchy. |
| `prev + next` | Given a selector, returns the collection of all sibling elements that match the `next` selector and are located next to the `prev` selector. |
| `prev ~ sibling` | Given a selector, returns the collection of all sibling elements that match the `sibling` selector and follows the `prev` selector. |

Most queries selectors are composed with filters. Table 20-12 summarizes the filters you can use in jQuery.

**TABLE 20-12:** Filters in jQuery

| FILTER | DESCRIPTION |
| --- | --- |
| `:first` | Returns the first element of the selected collection of elements. |
| `:last` | Returns the last element of the selected collection of elements. |
| `:not(selector)` | Filters out all elements matching the specified `selector`. |
| `:even` | Returns all even elements in the selected collection. |
| `:odd` | Returns all odd elements in the selected collection. |
| `:nth-child(expr)` | Returns all child elements of any parent that match the given expression. The expression can be an index or a math sequence (for example, 4n+3), including standard sequences (such as odd and even). |

| FILTER | DESCRIPTION |
|---|---|
| `:first-child` | Returns all elements that are the first child of their parent. |
| `:last-child` | Returns all elements that are the last child of their parent. |
| `:only-child` | Returns all elements that are the only child of their parent. |
| `:contains(text)` | Returns all elements that contain the specified text. |
| `:empty` | Returns all elements with no children. (Text is considered a child node.) |
| `:has(selector)` | Returns all elements that contain at least one element that matches the given selector. |
| `:parent` | Returns all elements that have at least one child. (Text is considered a child node.) |
| `:hidden` | Returns all elements that are currently hidden from view. Input elements of type "hidden" are added to the list. |
| `:visible` | Returns all elements that are currently visible. |

Let's take a look at a few examples. The `jQuerySelectors.htm` file has a sample that marks all albums containing "Tubular Bells" in their titles. This operation is carried out with the following code snippet:

```
function markTubularBells() {
    $("ul li:contains('Tubular Bells')").attr("class", "item red");
}
```

This query takes all `ul` elements and then all of their `li` descendants that contain "Tubular Bells" in their text. The `attr` method sets their class attribute to `"item red"` that changes their font color to red. Because `li` elements are always descendants of `ul` elements, you could simply write the query as follows:

```
$("li:contains('Tubular Bells')")
```

Because of the parent-child relationship between `ul` and `li`, the following expression also works:

```
$("ul > li:contains('Tubular Bells')")
```

The `:nth-child` filter is very powerful. You can mark every third album within an era represented by a table cell with the following function:

```
function thirdToGreen() {
    $("li:nth-child(3n)").attr("class", "item green");
}
```

Here the `3n` argument of `:nth-child` refers to "every third."

You can combine selectors and filters. For example, you can set the background of table cells that do not have any albums with "Bells" in the album name with the following code:

```
function bckToYellow() {
    $("td:not(:contains('Bells'))").attr("class", "yellowBack");
}
```

Here, the td selector selects all table cells. The :contains('Bells') filter select those that have "Bells" somewhere in their text, and the :not filters out the ones that match with the :contains('Bells') expression. The affected table cells have a yellow background.

Another interesting query expression is implemented behind the "Second paragraphs to Green" button. It sets the color of the second paragraphs in the table cells (the paragraphs containing the years) only when there is "19" in the paragraph text. The code behind the function is very simple:

```
function secondParagraph() {
    $("p+p:contains('19')").attr("class", "green");
}
```

The first p in the query selects all paragraphs (<p> elements). The +p expression selects the next sibling paragraphs. The :contains('19') expression filters out only those that contain 19 in their text. Let's say that you insert some non-paragraph text between the <p> elements, like this:

```
<td valign="top">
  <p>Early albums</p>
  <h3>very early</h3>
  <p>(1973-1979)</p>
  <ul id="earlyAlbums" class="list">
    <li class="item">Tubular Bells</li>
    <li class="item">Hergest Ridge</li>
    <li class="item">Ommadawn</li>
    <li class="item">Incantations</li>
    <li class="item">Exposed</li>
  </ul>
</td>
```

The p+p expression will not match the "(1973-1979)" paragraph because it not subsequent with "Early albums." However, p~p would match with it.

You can also filter by attribute values adding power to the query capabilities. Table 20-13 summarizes the attribute filters supported by jQuery.

**TABLE 20-13:** Attribute Filters Supported by jQuery

| ATTRIBUTE FILTER | DESCRIPTION |
|---|---|
| [attribute] | Returns all elements that have the specified attribute. |
| [attribute = value] | Returns all elements that have the specified attribute set to the specified value. |
| [attribute != value] | Returns all elements whose specified attribute (if present) has a value different from the given one. |

| ATTRIBUTE FILTER | DESCRIPTION |
|---|---|
| `[attribute^=value]` | Returns all elements whose specified attribute (if present) begins with the specified value. |
| `[attribute$=value]` | Returns all elements whose specified attribute (if present) ends with the specified value. |
| `[attribute*=value]` | Returns all elements whose specified attribute (if present) contains the specified value. |

The "All non-red albums to Blue" button uses attribute filtering to mark the albums that do not have the "red" class in their style:

```
function nonRedToBlue() {
  $("li:not([class*='red'])").attr("class", "item blue");
}
```

*Data form processing* is a common activity in web application development. You can use the selectors and filters to access form elements. For example, you can access all buttons in a form with the following query:

```
$("form input[type=button]")
```

This query gets all `<input>` elements within the `<form>` that have their `type` attribute set to "`button`". jQuery helps accessing form elements by defining form filters (pseudo-filters), which are summarized in Table 20-14.

**TABLE 20-14:** Form Filters in jQuery

| FILTER | DESCRIPTION |
|---|---|
| `:input` | Returns all elements that have a role in collecting input data, including `textarea` and drop-down lists. |
| `:text` | Returns all input elements whose type attribute is `text`. |
| `:password` | Returns all input elements whose type attribute is `password`. |
| `:checkbox` | Returns all input elements whose type attribute is `checkbox`. |
| `:radio` | Returns all input elements whose type attribute is `radio`. |
| `:submit` | Returns all input elements whose type attribute is `submit`. |
| `:reset` | Returns all input elements whose type attribute is `reset`. |

*continues*

**TABLE 20-14** *(continued)*

| FILTER | DESCRIPTION |
|---|---|
| :image | Returns all input elements whose type attribute is image. |
| :button | Returns all input elements whose type attribute is button. |
| :file | Returns all input elements whose type attribute is file. |
| :hidden | Returns all input elements whose type attribute is hidden. |
| :enabled | Returns all input elements that are currently enabled. |
| :disabled | Returns all input elements that are currently disabled. |
| :checked | Returns all checkbox or radio elements that are currently checked. |
| :selected | Returns all list elements that are currently selected. |

The last four pseudo-filters in Table 20-14 are very convenient, because you can grab all input elements in a page that are enabled or disabled. You can also easily get all checkboxes and radio buttons checked, as well as list items currently selected.

## Chaining and Utility Functions

One of the best features of jQuery is its chainability, which is possible because the jQuery object itself (as well as most of the functions and filters) returns a jQuery object. The returned object contains the original wrapped set as modified by the function itself. In the previous sample, you saw example of chained expressions — for example, the .attr method has been used to set the specific attributes of all elements in a wrapped set.

You can use chaining to make complex queries more readable by cascading them. For example, consider the following expressions:

```
$("td:not(:contains('Bells'))")
// ...
$("li:nth-child(3n)")
```

This is how they would appear in chained form:

```
$("td").not(":contains('Bells')")
// ...
$("li").filter(":nth-child(3n)")
```

You can access the DOM items in wrapped sets, and you can process them easily with the help of a few utility functions summarized in Table 20-15.

**TABLE 20-15:** Utility Functions Provided by jQuery

| UTILITY FUNCTIONS | DESCRIPTION |
| --- | --- |
| each(callback) | Loops over the content of the wrapped set and executes the specified callback function. |
| length | Property that returns the number of elements in the wrapped set. |
| eq(position) | Reduces the wrapped set to the single element at the specified position. |
| get() | Returns the content of the wrapped set as an array of DOM elements. |
| get(index) | Returns the DOM elements at the specified position in the wrapped set. |
| index(element) | Returns the 0-based index in the wrapped set of the specified DOM element, if any. |

The each() function is very useful, because you can iterate through the items in the wrapped set. The "Decorate albums" and "Remove decorations" buttons use this function:

```
function decorateAlbums() {
  $("li:not(:contains('***'))").each(function (i) {
    this.title = this.innerText;
    this.innerText = "*** " + this.innerText + " (" + i + ")";
  });
}

function removeDecorations() {
  $("li:contains('***')").each(function (i) {
    this.innerText = this.title;
  });
}
```

The difference between each() and a manual JavaScript loop is that each() automatically maps the this object to the element in the collection being processed. The callback function receives an optional integer parameter that is the (0-based) index of the iteration. In the previous code snippet, this index number is used to create the decoration text for the album.

Later in this section you will learn about a number of methods that can be used with wrapper sets.

## Eventing Model and Event Handlers

jQuery provides an abstract eventing model that allows cross-browser compatibility. Instead of handling browser-specific events, jQuery offers a set of events that work seamlessly with all widespread browsers, including Internet Explorer, Firefox, Safari, and Google Chrome. You can bind event-handler methods to jQuery events, or trigger them with helper methods.

All events have helper functions to bind handlers to the specific event, and most of them also have helpers to trigger those events. Table 20-16 summarizes these events, and names the binding functions and trigger methods.

**TABLE 20-16:** jQuery Events, Binding Helpers, and Triggers

| EVENT | BINDING FUNCTION | TRIGGER METHOD | EVENT FIRED WHEN. . . |
|---|---|---|---|
| beforeunload | | | A browser window is unloaded or closed by the user. |
| blur | blur(fn) | blur() | An element loses focus because either the user clicked outside of it or tabbed away. |
| change | change(fn) | change() | The element loses focus and its value has been modified since it gained focus. |
| click | click(fn) | click() | The user clicks on the element. |
| dblclick | dblclick(fn) | dblclick() | The user double-clicks on the element. |
| error | error(fn) | error() | The window object signals that an error has occurred — usually a JavaScript error has been detected. |
| focus | focus(fn) | focus() | An element receives focus either via the mouse or tab navigation. |
| keydown | keydown(fn) | keydown() | A key is pressed. |
| keypress | keypress(fn) | keypress() | A key is pressed and released. A keypress is defined as a successive keydown and keyup events. |
| keyup | keyup(fn) | keyup() | A key is released. This event follows keypress. |
| load | | | The element and all of its content has finished loading. |
| mousedown | | | A mouse button is pressed. |
| mouseenter | | | The mouse enters in the area of an element. |
| mouseleave | | | The mouse leaves the area of an element. |
| mousemove | | | The mouse is moved while it is over an element. |
| mouseout | | | The mouse is moved out of an element. Unlike mouseleave, this event also fires when the mouse moves into or out of child elements. |

| EVENT | BINDING FUNCTION | TRIGGER METHOD | EVENT FIRED WHEN... |
|---|---|---|---|
| mouseover | | | The mouse is moved onto an element. Unlike mouseenter, this event also fires when the mouse moves into or out from child elements. |
| mouseup | | | The mouse button is released. This event follows mousedown. |
| resize | | | An element is resized. |
| scroll | | | An element is scrolled. |
| select | select(fn) | select() | The user selects some text in a text field. |
| submit | submit(fn) | submit() | A form is submitted. |
| unload | | | A browser window is unloaded. |

As you see from Table 20-16, there are events you cannot programmatically trigger or bind an event handler method to.

The jQueryEventHandling.htm page in the jQuerySamples project demonstrates these concepts. The page contains six images. When you click them, they display a pop-up message telling you the name behind the image. When you move the mouse onto the images, their background is changed. Figure 20-31 shows this simple page in action when the mouse is moved onto the first image in the second row.

The code that causes this behavior is simple. It binds events with their handlers in the pageLoad method:

```
function pageLoad() {
  $("img").click(function (event) {
    alert("This is " + this.alt + ".");
    event.preventDefault();
  });

  $("img").mouseenter(function (event) {
    event.currentTarget.className = "faded";
  });
```

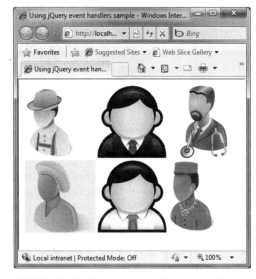

**FIGURE 20-31**: jQueryEventHandling.htm in action

```
    $("img").mouseleave(function (event) {
      event.currentTarget.className = "";
      if (event.currentTarget.id == "img6") {
        $("#img1").click();
      }
    });
  }
```

You can recognize the `click(fn)`, `mouseenter(fn)`, and `mouseleave(fn)` binding functions. As you can see from the code, there is a little twist in the `mouseleave` event. When the mouse leaves the sixth image, it triggers the click event of the first image.

In addition to the helper methods, you can bind handlers to the corresponding events in a more sophisticated way. Table 20-17 summarizes the jQuery functions you can use to bind and unbind event handlers to wrapped set items.

**TABLE 20-17:** Functions Binding and Unbinding Event Handlers

| METHOD | DESCRIPTION |
| --- | --- |
| bind | Associates the given function to one or more events for each element contained in the wrapped set. |
| die | This function removes a live event handler from all current and future elements of the wrapped set. This means that if a new DOM element is added that matches the conditions of the wrapped set, the element will be automatically unbound from the handler. |
| live | This function binds the specified event handler to all current and future elements of the wrapped set. This means that if a new DOM element is added that matches the conditions of the wrapped set, the element will be automatically bound to the handler. |
| one | Works like bind, except that any event handler is automatically removed after it has been run once. |
| trigger | Triggers the given event for each element in the wrapped set. |
| triggerHandler | Triggers the given event on one element in the wrapped set and cancels the default browser actions. |
| unbind | Removes bound events from each element in the wrapped set. |

These methods have several parameters. For example, the `bind` method has three of them:

```
bind(eventName, eventData, eventHandler)
```

The first argument of bind is a string that names the event to handle (for instance, "click", "mouseenter", and so on). The second argument represents any input data coming with the event. The third argument is the JavaScript function to bind the event to.

## Visual Effects and Animations

In most web applications, client-side scripting is used to improve the user experience by adding simple effects and animations. The jQuery library has a simple, but powerful, built-in engine for visual effects. The jQueryVisualEffects.htm page demonstrates how easy it is to use the jQuery visual effects. This page uses the same six images you saw in Figure 20-31, but this time, the pageLoad method sets up the event handlers to use the slideToggle effect:

```
function pageLoad() {
  $("img").mouseenter(function (event) {
    $("#" + event.currentTarget.id).slideToggle("slow");
  });

  $("img").mouseleave(function (event) {
    $("#" + event.currentTarget.id).slideToggle("slow");
  });
}
```

Table 20-18 summarizes the visual effects supported by jQuery.

**TABLE 20-18:** Visual Effects

| EFFECT | DESCRIPTION |
| --- | --- |
| animate | Performs a custom animation of a set of CSS properties. |
| fadeIn | Displays the matched elements by fading them to opaque. |
| fadeOut | Hides the matched elements by fading them to transparent. |
| fadeTo | Adjusts the opacity of the matched elements. |
| hide | Hides the matched elements. |
| show | Displays the matched elements. |
| slideDown | Displays the matched elements with a sliding motion. |
| slideToggle | Displays or hides the matched elements with a sliding motion. |
| slideUp | Hides the matched elements with a sliding motion. |
| stop | Stops the currently running animation on the matched elements. |
| toggle | Binds two or more handlers to the matched elements, to be executed on alternate clicks. |

Most effect methods take one or more arguments describing the effect. Generally, the first argument is the time of the animiation specified in milliseconds or literally such as `"slow"` or `"fast"`. All effect methods take an optional callback argument invoked when the animation is completed.

 *For more detail on animations and visual effects, see the jQuery reference and tutorial at* http://api.jquery.com/category/effects/. *You will also find examples there to help you better understand how a specific effect works.*

## jQuery Ajax Features

In jQuery, you can easily leverage the Ajax infrastructure and carry out asynchronous postbacks. The key of this behavior is the `ajax` function through which you can control all aspects of a web request. The jQueryAjax.htm page demonstrates how easy is to call a web service with this method. The page has a link, and when you click on it, it initiates the asynchronous postback. When the call is completed, the result is displayed, as shown in Figure 20-32.

The `ajax` method is called as the following code snippet shows:

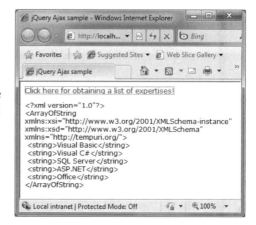

**FIGURE 20-32:** Calling a Web service from jQuery

```
function pageLoad() {
  $('a').click(callAjax)
}

function callAjax(event) {
  $.ajax(
    {
      type: "POST",
      url: "/ExpertiseService.asmx/GetExpertises",
      data: "",
      success: function (response) {
      $("#result")[0].innerText = response.xml;
    }
  });
  event.preventDefault();
}
```

You can see that the `success` parameter defines the function to run when the web service call completed. This method simply copies the XML result into a literal text field in the page.

The web service at the back-end is also very simple, as Listing 20-28 shows.

**LISTING 20-28:** ExpertiseService.asmx

```
using System.Web.Script.Services;
using System.Web.Services;

namespace jQuerySamples
{
  [ScriptService]
  public class ExpertiseService : System.Web.Services.WebService
  {
    [WebMethod]
    public string[] GetExpertises()
    {
      return new string[]
      {
        "Visual Basic",
        "Visual C#",
        "SQL Server",
        "ASP.NET",
        "Office"
      };
    }
  }
}
```

*Code file [ExpertiseService.asmx] available for download at Wrox.com*

## SUMMARY

The ASP.NET Ajax Control Toolkit and the jQuery technology are two great pieces of the full toolset you can use together with your ASP.NET applications to improve the user experience.

The Ajax Control Toolkit provides you with more than 40 server-side controls. Most of them are extenders that can be attached to existing server-side controls to extend (improve) their functionality. There are also new controls that can be used individually. You can use the Toolkit from scratch to build your websites and pages, but it is also very easy to add these controls to existing pages.

The jQuery library makes JavaScript code easier and quicker to write. The library provides helper functions that dramatically increase your productivity, while decreasing your frustration. In addition to accessing HTML DOM elements, jQuery offers you browser-independent event-handling mechanism, visual effects, and Ajax infrastructure support.

Chapter 21 provides a brief overview of the history of the Visual Basic programming language, including its roots, and its main characteristics.

# PART IV
# VB.NET

▶ **CHAPTER 21:** History of Visual Basic

▶ **CHAPTER 22:** Visual Basic 10.0 Language Improvements

# 21

# History of Visual Basic

The Visual Basic programming language has been changed a lot over the course of the past decade. However, the language dialect that developers use today with the "Visual" prefix was born when the .NET Framework was released in February 2002. The roots of the Basic language go back to 1964.

In recent years, many reports have been published about the popularity of programming languages, and Visual Basic was ranked in the top five most popular in each of them. There were years when surveys showed Visual Basic as the first or second most popular one. In the .NET platform, Visual Basic is used by about 60 percent of developers as the primary programming language.

This chapter provides a brief overview of the history of the Visual Basic programming language. The discussions in this chapter assume that you are familiar with the fundamental constructs of the language and that you have already used it. If you are not a Visual Basic developer, this chapter also helps to provide you with context.

This chapter covers the following topics:

- ➤ The roots of the Visual Basic language
- ➤ A brief history of the language used in the 1990s
- ➤ The main characteristic of Visual Basic.NET (7.0) introduced with .NET 1.0
- ➤ A brief overview of features in Visual Basic 2005 (8.0) and Visual Basic 2008 (9.0)

In the past, every major Visual Studio release introduced a new version of the Visual Basic and C# languages, following the main course of improvements in the .NET Framework. The same holds true for Visual Studio 2010, which introduces Visual Basic 2010 (10.0). In Chapter 23, you'll learn about the details of the new features and improvements.

Let's begin this overview with a review of where it all began for Visual Basic.

# THE ROOTS OF VISUAL BASIC

Visual Basic today is an object-oriented programming (OOP) language that shifts toward being a multi-paradigm programming language. However, it started its life in the mid-1960s as a high-level language that allowed the masses to program computers.

The original BASIC (Dartmouth BASIC) was designed by John G. Kemeny and Thomas E. Kurtz to provide computer access to non-science students. The language got its name from the acronym for *Beginner's All-purpose Symbolic Instruction Code*. BASIC was a real breakthrough, because, at that time, nearly all use of computers required writing custom software, which was something only computer scientists and mathematicians tended to be able to do. In contrast to the user experience that required first writing a computer program and then compiling it (which was a laborious and tedious task at that time), BASIC was an interpreted language that could be used interactively. The first programs were very simple and could be used from the command line. For example, a user may have typed something such as the following:

```
PRINT 2 + 2
```

The interpreter immediately showed 4 on the console as the result of this simple calculation.

BASIC as a language gained a great popularity in the late 1970s and 1980s when its variants became widespread on microcomputers such as on Atari, Commodore, Tandy, Sinclair models, and on many others.

## Structured and Unstructured BASIC

The first versions of the BASIC language were unstructured. The order (control flow) of the instructions was determined by line numbers. The execution (interpreting the source code) started at the line with the smallest number. The language had a GOTO statement to change the control flow, a GOSUB statement to call subroutines, and a FOR statement to organize cycles. At that time, formal and actual parameters were unknown in the language. Subroutines took input parameters and passed back results through global variables.

Listing 21-1 shows a simple calculation written with unstructured BASIC.

**LISTING 21-1:** Square Numbers Calculation with Unstructured BASIC

```
10 INPUT "ENDING NUMBER"; E
20 FOR I=1 TO E
30 A=I
40 GOSUB 100
50 NEXT I
60 END
100 PRINT A;"*";A;" = ";A*A
110 RETURN
```

Both the input and output of the programs were generally the console of the personal or microcomputer on which the interpreter was run. Figure 21-1 shows how users could run the previous code snippet on a Commodore 64 computer.

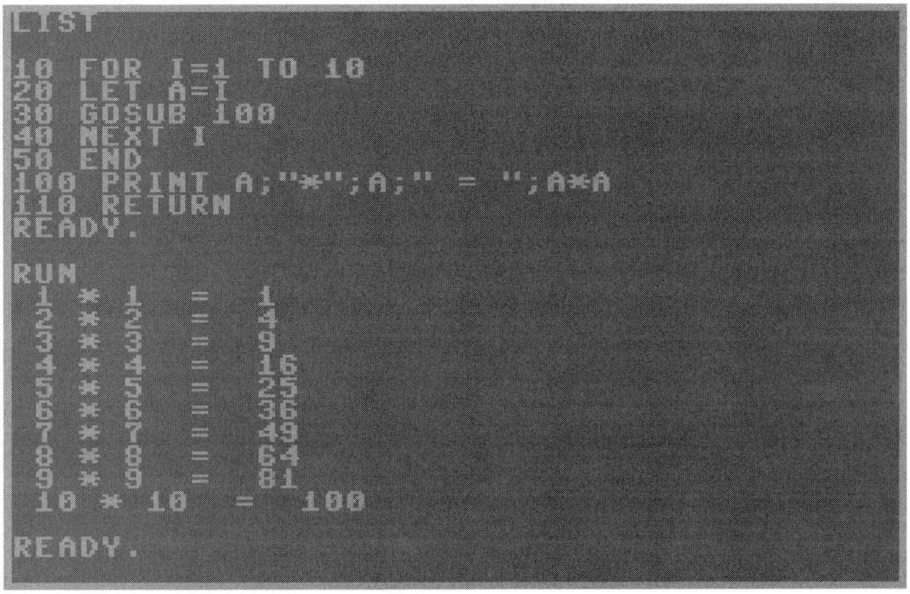

**FIGURE 21-1:** Simple BASIC program running on Commodore 64

Despite the fact that unstructured BASIC had poor features to define control flow, very complex applications (including business applications such as accounting, banking, simple CAD programs, technical computations, and many more) were programmed with it.

The second generation of BASIC variants (for example, GW-BASIC and its successor, QuickBASIC by Microsoft and PowerBASIC) introduced a number of features into the language, primarily related to structured and procedure-oriented programming.

> *The first version of QuickBASIC was released in 1985 for MS-DOS, and its last version was 4.5 released in 1988. There are many successors of the language (including its pure IDE), which are still in use. For example, QB64 released version 0.85 at the end of December 2009, and it even runs on Windows 7.*

These versions removed the need for line numbers (which were replaced by labels for GOTO) and added procedures to the language with formal parameters. Several new cycle types were already added, such as DO WHILE ... LOOP, DO ... UNTIL, and so on. Listing 21-2 shows how the calculation in Listing 21-1 could be transformed to the structured style defined by QuickBASIC.

**LISTING 21-2:** Square Numbers Calculation in QuickBASIC

```
CLS
INPUT "ENDING NUMBER: ", E
I = 0
DO WHILE I < E
  I = I + 1
  R = SQUARE(I)
  PRINT I; "*"; I; " = "; R
LOOP

FUNCTION SQUARE(I)
  SQUARE = I * I
END FUNCTION
```

# Moving to "Visual"

No doubt, BASIC implementations developed by Microsoft gave a solid ground for the company (think about the Commodore C64 Basic interpreter, GW-BASIC, and QuickBASIC for MS-DOS). The BASIC language was about console applications for a long time — reading input the user typed in, and writing output to the console. Early microcomputers extended the language with instructions for graphical applications. For example, C64 had Simon's BASIC. Sinclair ZX Spectrum had Sinclair BASIC that allowed developers to draw lines, circles, polygons, and other shapes utilizing the graphical capabilities of their host computers.

In the late 1980s and early 1990s, graphical user interfaces (GUIs) became very popular. That was the era when Microsoft's name had been tied with its Windows operating system, mainly because of the success of Windows 3.1.

For a long time, Windows application development was a privilege of C (and later C++) programmers. They had to carry out a lot of tasks for creating the simplest UI — such as defining and registering Windows classes, implementing the Windows message loop, dispatching Windows messages, painting the client in Windows, and so on. The smallest "Hello, World" program for Windows was about a hundred lines of code, where you could not meet any explicit statement to print out the "Hello, World" text. The UI missed the concept of controls — there were windows and child windows, all of them represented by window handles (HWNDs).

At that time, developers accepted this way of Windows software creation as a price for interacting with a GUI.

The first tool that dramatically changed Windows application development was Visual Basic 1.0, released in May 1991. Visual Basic introduced (or, perhaps, invented) such concepts as forms, controls, code-behind files — all of which are still in use in contemporary development tools. Instead of writing resource files and addressing UI elements through 16-bit constants, you could drag and drop predefined UI controls to your forms, and program their events. The hundred-line "Hello, World" program was so simple with Visual Basic:

```
Private Sub Form_Load()
    MsgBox("Hello, World!")
End Sub
```

Visual Basic 1.0 was released at the Comdex World Trade show in Atlanta, Georgia, and it immediately became a great success.

## Visual Basic in the 1990s

Visual Basic was not only a single language, but also a development environment. To understand how the language advanced, you must understand the technological trends and context that influenced the evolution of both the language and the development environment.

The great success of the concept Visual Basic represented gave a spin for the product, and Microsoft released five major versions up until 1998. The next version, Visual Basic 2.0, was released in November 1992. It did not add new concepts to the language, but its programming environment was much easier to use than its predecessors, and its speed was improved. While Visual Basic 1.0 used static forms, 2.0 allowed instantiating them.

In November 1992, after creating a tool allowing Windows development for the masses, Microsoft released Microsoft Access 1.0 as another visual tool — for database development — and in May 1993 Access 1.1 was released that included the Access Basic programming language.

Visual Basic 3.0 was a new version that shipped with two editions, Standard and Professional. The main theme of this version released in July 1993 was database programming with the Microsoft Jet Database Engine. The engine was the same as the one used in Access 1.1, and, because it was included in the installation kit, Visual Basic 3.0 could read and write Access databases.

When Windows 95 (the first 32-bit version of the Windows operating system) was launched in August 1995, the next Visual Basic, version 4.0 (which was released in the same month as Windows 95) was ready to create both 32-bit and 16-bit applications. Having a development tool with the capability to create 32-bit programs was an important factor to the success of Windows 95.

Unfortunately, Visual Basic 4.0 had several releases and introduced some compatibility issues. While the previous releases had used VBX controls, Visual Basic 4.0 later started using OLE controls (that is, filenames ending with an .ocx extension). This version also took a turn toward object-oriented principles — it allowed created non-GUI classes to implement Component Object Model (COM) interfaces, and encapsulate data and functionality. Although it was a different kind of object orientation than .NET offers today, admittedly, it was an important step.

Visual Basic 5.0 released in February 1997 and became an exclusive 32-bit version ready to convert 16-bit Visual Basic 4.0 programs to the new platform. While the previous versions compiled and executed an intermediate code (P-code), this version had the capability to compile native Windows executable code. This new compilation model helped significantly in the performance of calculation-intensive applications.

Another main theme for version 5.0 was *componentization*. Developers could create business components (middleware layer components) running in Microsoft Transaction Server (MTS, later renamed to COM+), and started moving toward three-tier distributed applications. This version also had a free Control Creation Edition to develop ActiveX controls (OLE controls were renamed to ActiveX controls).

The last version of Visual Basic for the Windows 32-bit platform was version 6.0 released in June 1998. The language and the development environment were equipped with features to create real distributed, multi-tier enterprise applications with database support, as well as the capability to create COM+ middleware components, thick-client, and web UI. Figure 21-2 shows the project types developers could use with Visual Basic 6.0 out-of-the-box.

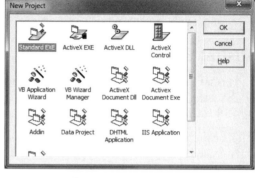

To emphasize this new position of Visual Basic, in addition to the Standard and Professional editions, 6.0 had an Enterprise edition — which was a sort of alternative for the Java language and platform born in 1995.

**FIGURE 21-2:** Project types in Visual Basic 6.0

Visual Basic 6.0 was long-lived product. Even today, there are business applications (with many COM+ components) developed with Visual Basic 6.0, which are still being used in production. Microsoft supported this application until March 2008, but the Enterprise edition still can be downloaded from MSDN.

## VISUAL BASIC IN THE .NET FRAMEWORK

After the release of Visual Basic 6.0, a long time passed before a new release of the language was announced. Meanwhile, Microsoft was working on its Common Object Run-time platform that was announced as the .NET Framework in July 2000 at Professional Developers Conference (PDC) held in Orlando, Florida. That PDC focused on the .NET Framework, and it spotlighted the new C# programming language. But it was clear that Visual Basic had a large camp of developers that Microsoft couldn't ignore.

When .NET Framework 1.0 was released as part of a pair with Visual Studio.NET in February 2002, the new Visual Basic 7.0 — called Visual Basic.NET — was born. This change for the programming language was at least as significant as the step from unstructured to structured BASIC in the mid-1980s.

### Design Goals and Debates

The most important goal of the Visual Basic language was to transform it to a real object-oriented (OO) language free from common programming flaws. While Microsoft communicated the pre-.NET versions as OO ones, only the encapsulation principle was fully implemented by Microsoft, while inheritance and polymorphism were very poor — object classes could implement COM interfaces.

The Common Type System (CTS) of the .NET Framework dictated the features language designers had to take into account. The real question was not which CTS features to implement, but rather which ones could be omitted from the language. In addition to this paradigm shift, another reasonable design goal was to change the language syntax and semantics with the best achievable level of backward compatibility.

The design resulted in a language that was not backward compatible with the previous versions. It contained significant breaking changes. While method bodies had the same structure and instructions (of course, a few new instructions were added, such as the ones supporting structured exception handling), other structures like namespaces and type nesting were totally unusual for Visual Basic developers.

Within a few months after the release, a rift developed within the developer community. Many developers said Visual Basic.NET was a new language, because the language had been decorated with unusual things that had been tuned for .NET. Companies with relatively small Visual Basic codebase were weighing whether to learn the new Visual Basic version, or to change to C#. Many of them decided to learn C#. Despite the debates surrounding Visual Basic.NET, the last eight years have seen Visual Basic become a modern multi-paradigm language successfully used by a large community for developing applications with the .NET Framework.

# Visual Basic .NET (7.0) and .NET 2003 (7.1)

Microsoft's opinion in the debate on whether or not Visual Basic .NET was a new language can be clearly seen from the continuous version number (7.0) it used. The next language release (7.1) that is often used as Visual Basic .NET 2003 (or simply Visual Basic 2003) did not change the language.

**FIGURE 21-3:** "Hello User" application UI

The new language became a bit more verbose than its pre-.NET versions. If you wanted to implement a simple "Hello User" application that displayed a user name typed in a `TextBox` (as shown if Figure 21-3), you had to use the following code with Visual Basic.NET (2003):

```
Public Class Form1
  Private Sub CommandBtn_Click(ByVal sender As System.Object,
      ByVal e As System.EventArgs) _
    Handles CommandBtn.Click
    WelcomeLabel.Text = "Welcome, " & NameBox.Text & "!"
  End Sub
End Class
```

With Visual Basic 6.0 you had a thinner surrounding for the statement setting the label text:

```
Private Sub CommandBtn_Click()
  WelcomeLabel.Caption = "Welcome, " & NameBox.Text & "!"
End Sub
```

If you compare the two code snippets, you can see a few things that characterize the .NET version:

➤    The .NET event mechanism is used, and it allows you to pass event arguments.

➤    Events and related response methods are no longer connected by names.

➤    Forms are explicit classes.

➤    The `Caption` property of a label was renamed to `Text` in .NET.

The list of differences in syntax and semantics (compatibility breaks) may underpin the opinions of those who feel that Visual Basic.NET is a new language. However, the style of the language — indentation (including the underscore as a line-continuation character) — is remarkably Visual Basic.

Microsoft and C# programmers often mention C# as the "native programming language for .NET." The bulk of the differences between C# and VB.NET from a technical perspective are syntactic sugar. Visual Basic has few features that cannot be found in C#:

➤   Visual Basic supports the IDE with the `WithEvents` construct so that a programmer may select an object from the Class Name drop-down list, and then select a method from the Declarations drop-down list to have the event method signature automatically inserted.

➤   C# introduced optional method parameters and named arguments only in C# 4.0 (released with Visual Studio 2010), while Visual Basic had it from the beginnings.

➤   The `With ... EndWith` construct allows marshaling an object for multiple actions using an unqualified dot reference.

➤   Inline date declarations can be used with the `#12/31/2009#` syntax.

➤   Interface member implementations can be mapped to any methods with matching signatures, and not just to methods having the same name as the interface member declaration.

## Type System

Visual Basic.NET has a unified type system that is the CTS in the .NET Framework. Each type has a root ancestor, namely `System.Object`. This type system separates data types into two categories:

➤   *Value types* — These are plain aggregations of data, and their instances do not have either referential identity or referential comparison semantics at all. Operations on value types are carried out with the actual data within the instances.

➤   *Reference types* — These have the notion of referential identity. Each instance of a reference type is inherently distinct from every other instance, even if the data within both instances is the same.

There are no standalone global variables or global functions in Visual Basic. All methods and data members must be declared within types or modules. The following "Hello, World" example mirrors this fact:

```
Module ExampleModule

  Sub Main()
    Console.WriteLine("Hello, World")
  End Sub

End Module
```

Visual Basic is *type safe*. The set of implicit conversions depends on the compilation environment and the `Option Strict` statement. If strict semantics are being used (`Option Strict On`), only widening conversions may occur implicitly. If permissive semantics are being used (`Option Strict Off`, which is the default), all widening and narrowing conversions may occur implicitly.

*Multiple inheritance* is not supported by the language. A class can have only one base class, but is allowed to implement any number of interfaces. This was a design decision to avoid complication, avoid dependency hell, and simplify architectural requirements throughout the CTS.

### Memory Management

The language has the `New` operator to allocate type instances from memory. However, it does not have any statement, function, or operator to explicitly free the allocated managed memory. Instead, it is automatically garbage-collected. *Garbage collection* addresses memory leaks by freeing the programmer of the responsibility for releasing memory that is no longer needed. It is a non-deterministic mechanism.

Visual Basic does not allow directly using *pointers*. However, reference types physically use pointers as their implementation, and you can use them only for referencing the objects behind them. No pointer arithmetic is available.

Visual Basic programs can still store and compare pointers through the `System.IntPtr` type (which provides interoperability between managed and unmanaged code), but objects and values behind `IntPtr` instances cannot be dereferenced.

## Visual Basic 2005 (8.0)

.NET 2.0 brought great changes into the CTS. The feature of *generic types* that really had been missing from the previous versions was added to the framework, and the Visual Basic language also implemented this feature. Most changes in Visual Basic 2005 were related to generic types.

However, in addition to generic types, there were several other great features added to the language in response to the community feedback and experiences, including the following:

➤ Partial types

➤ Nullable types

➤ Documentation comments

➤ Operator declarations

➤ New unsigned and signed integer types

➤ Using construct

Let's dive into some detail for these features.

### Generic Types

*Generic types* allow you to define type-safe data structures, without committing to actual data types. This results in higher-quality code, because you can reuse data processing algorithms without duplicating type-specific code.

There is a similar concept in C++, called *templates*, but while templates in C++ are supported by a compiler, .NET generic types are implemented at the Common Language Run-time (CLR) level. Although there are entire books dedicated to generics, this section provides a brief overview without deeper explanation.

The CLR before generics never offered a type-safe way to encapsulate common behavior into a type. For example, if you wanted to create a behavior describing how a queue works, and intended to use it with both `Integer` and your own `Transfer` type, you had to create a workaround. Either you implemented two separate types called `IntegerQueue` and `TransferQueue`, or created a single `Queue` type that accepted `System.Objects`. The first implementation has issues with code maintenance, while the second has issues with providing type safety and performance.

Generics in Visual Basic allow you to use *type parameters* with type and method definitions. These definitions are called *open type definitions*, as shown in the following example:

```
Public Class Queue(Of T)
    Public Sub Enqueue(ByVal item As T)
        ' ...
    End Sub

    Public Function Dequeue() As T
        ' ...
    End Function

    Public ReadOnly Property IsEmpty() As Boolean
        Get
            ' ...
        End Get
    End Property
End Class
```

In this sample definition, `T` is the type parameter. When it is time to use the definitions for concrete types, `T` is substituted with the type you intend to use, together with the behavior `Queue` offers:

```
Dim intQueue As Queue(Of Integer) = New Queue(Of Integer)
intQueue.Enqueue(42)
Dim transferQueue As Queue(Of Transfer) = New Queue(Of Transfer)
While Not transferQueue.IsEmpty
    Dim transfer = transferQueue.Dequeue()
    transfer.Process()
    ' ...
End While
```

The types where the type parameter is substituted with a concrete type are called *closed types*. You are not limited to using only one type parameter; you can use more. For example, the following declaration lets you define a node in a linked list, where `K` represents the type used as the key of the node, and `N` is the type representing the value of a node:

```
Public Class LinkedNode(Of K, N)
    ' ...
End Class
```

You can also add *type parameter constraints* to your types to restrict them to a subset of types. For example, when you allow only value types for being keys, and want to be sure that node elements can be compared, the previous type definition can be constrained like this:

```
Public Class LinkedNode(Of _
  K As Structure, _
  N As {IComparable(Of N), New})
  ' ...
End Class
```

There is a special type constraint called New that requires that the type be able to be used in New expressions. There are also two special type constraints that limit the kind of type that can be used to satisfy the constraint:

➤ Class constrains the type parameter to references types only.

➤ Structure constrains the type parameter to value types only, with the exception of nullable types.

You can use generic types as base types using either open or closed types, as shown in the following examples:

```
Public Class SortedNode(Of _
  K As Structure, _
  N As {IComparable(Of N), New})
  Inherits LinkedNode(Of K, N)
  ' ...
End Class

Public Class CodeNode(Of N As {IComparable(Of N), New})
  Inherits LinkedNode(Of Integer, N)
  ' ...
End Class

Public Class TransferNode
  Inherits LinkedNode(Of Integer, Transfer)
  ' ...
End Class
```

Not only types, but you can also use methods with generics, as shown here:

```
Public Class MyUtilities
  Public Sub WriteToDebug(Of T)(ByVal item As T)
    ' ...
  End Sub
  Public Sub Serialize(Of T As ISerializable)(ByVal item As T)
    ' ...
  End Sub
End Class
```

Even Shared, MustOverride and Overridable methods can leverage on generics, as shown here:

```
Public MustInherit Class BaseClass
  Public Shared Sub WriteToDebug(Of T)(ByVal item As T)
    ' ...
  End Sub
  Public MustOverride Sub AbstractMethod(Of T)(ByVal item As T)
```

```
     Public Overridable Sub SomeMethod(Of T)(ByVal item As T)
        ' ...
     End Sub
  End Class

  Public Class SubClass
     Inherits BaseClass

     Public Overrides Sub AbstractMethod(Of T)(ByVal item As T)
        ' ...
     End Sub
     Public Overrides Sub SomeMethod(Of T)(ByVal item As T)
        ' ...
     End Sub
  End Class
```

Operators and delegates are implemented as methods behind the scenes, and both of them support generics with all the power of generic methods. Here is a small example of defining and consuming generic delegates:

```
  Public Class UtilityClass(Of T)
     Public Delegate Sub GenericDelegate(ByVal arg As T)
     Public Sub SomeMethod(ByVal arg As T)
        ' ...
     End Sub
  End Class

  ' --- Use the delegate
  Dim obj As UtilityClass(Of Integer) = New UtilityClass(Of Integer)()
  Dim del As UtilityClass(Of Integer).GenericDelegate = _
     New UtilityClass(Of Integer).GenericDelegate(AddressOf obj.SomeMethod)
  del(3)
```

In .NET 2.0, reflection was extended to support generic type parameters. The type `System.Type` could now represent generic types with specific type arguments (closed types), or unspecified (open) types.

Also, many types in .NET 2.0 — especially collections — had been changed or added to support generics. For example, `Array` type now had about a dozen new generic methods, and there were many new generic collection classes to provide a new and performance-boosted experience related to the old .NET 1.1 collection types.

## Partial Types

The limitation that type definitions had to be entirely in only one physical file was a bottleneck in preceding Visual Basic versions, making the life of developers unnecessarily difficult. Large type definitions could not be split, and that was especially disadvantageous for those who used code generation intensively, because generated code could not be easily separated from user-defined code.

*Partial types* solve this issue. By using the `Partial` keyword, class, structure, and interface definitions can be split to spread in multiple files or multiple segments in the same file. This solves the problem of separation of user-defined and generated code. During compile time, the partitions of the type definition are merged, including attributes, base classes, interfaces, and access modifiers.

For example, you can split `SampleClass` into two parts, as shown in the following example:

```
' --- SampleClass1.cs
<Serializable()> _
Partial Public Class SampleClass
  Private _IsDisposed As Boolean
End Class

' --- SampleClass2.cs
Partial Class SampleClass
  Implements IEquatable(Of SampleClass)

  Public Function EqualsWithSample(ByVal other As SampleClass) As Boolean _
    Implements System.IEquatable(Of SampleClass).Equals
    ' ...
  End Function
End Class
```

The result of merging the partitions is a public class named `SampleClass` implementing the `System.IEquatable(Of SampleClass)` interface, and decorated with the `Serializable` attribute.

## Nullable Types

In CLR 1.0, one of the weaknesses of value types versus reference types was the lack of value type's "nullability." To eliminate this weakness, the CLR 2.0 designers added the concept of *nullable types* to the run-time. A new generic type, the `System.Nullable(Of T)` structure, was introduced, where `T` should be a value type.

The Visual Basic 2005 syntax allowed assigning `Nothing` to a `System.Nullable(Of T)` instance, and to compare an instance value with `Nothing`. The `HasValue` Boolean property tells if a nullable instance has a value, and, if it has, it can be obtained through the `Value` property.

Using these properties, you could define the `Nothing`-aware `Square` method, as shown in the following example:

```
Public Function Square(ByVal n As Nullable(Of Integer)) As Nullable(Of Integer)
  Return IIf(n.HasValue, n.Value * n.Value, Nothing)
End Function
```

The `Nullable(Of T)` also defines a `Narrowing` cast operator from `Nullable(Of T)` to `T`, and a `Widening` cast operator from `T` to `Nullable(Of T)`, so the following declarations are all correct when using `Option Strict On`:

```
Dim firstValue As Nullable(Of Integer) = 4
Dim secondValue As Nullable(Of Integer) = 5
Dim sumValue As Nullable(Of Integer) = firstValue + SecondValue
Dim squareValue As Integer = CType(Square(sumValue), Integer)
```

However, because the implicit conversion from `Nullable(Of T)` to `T` is not allowed, the last two of the following assignments will result in compilation errors with `Option Strict On`:

```
Dim firstValue As Nullable(Of Integer) = 4
Dim secondValue As Nullable(Of Integer) = 5
' --- Cannot convert Nullable(Of Integer) to Integer:
Dim myValue As Integer = secondValue
Dim sumValue As Integer = firstValue + SecondValue
```

## Documentation Comments

The C# language has been inspired by Javadoc and has its own XML-based documentation system since the first release of C# in 2002. Visual Basic 2005 introduced the similar concept with a slightly different syntax coming from the fact that C# and Visual Basic have separate tokens for comments.

Document comments in Visual Basic are special comments that begin with ''' (three single quotation marks). They must immediately precede the type or type member that they document. All adjacent document comments are appended together to produce a single document comment. Here is an example of documentation comments:

```
''' <summary>
''' This abstract class defines an attribute with a simple string value.
''' </summary>
''' <remarks>
''' The class is intended to derive new attributes having a simple string value.
''' Do not use this class to add other properties to the attribute!
''' </remarks>
Public MustInherit Class StringAttribute
  Inherits Attribute
  ''' <summary>
  ''' Creates a new instance of this attribute and sets its initial value.
  ''' </summary>
  ''' <param name="val">Initial attribute value.</param> */
  Protected Sub New(ByVal val As String)
    Value = val
  End Sub
  ' Other parts of the declaration omitted
End Class
```

During compilation, document comments are transformed into an XML file that can be utilized by tools to generate human-readable source code documentation. The documentation generator accepts and processes any tag that is valid according to the rules of XML. The Visual Basic language specification defines almost 20 tags that provide commonly used functionality in user documentation.

## Operator Declarations

*Operator declarations* are methods that define the meaning of an existing Visual Basic operator for the containing class. When the operator is applied to the class in an expression, the operator is compiled into a call to the operator method defined in the class. You can declare unary, binary and conversion operators. Defining an operator for a class is also known as *operator overloading*.

Operator declarations must always be Public and Shared, and the type of at least one of the operands (or the return value) must be the type that contains the operator. There is no function return variable defined for operators. Therefore, the Return statement must be used to return values from an operator body. Only the following unary and binary operators can be overloaded:

➤ Unary (+, unary -, logical Not, IsTrue, and IsFalse)

➤ Binary (+, -, *, /, Mod, and ^)

➤ Relational operators (=, <>, <, >, <=, and >=)

➤ Like, & (concatenation), logical And, Or, Xor

➤ <<, >>

Relational operators must be declared in pairs — = with <>, > with <, and >= with <=.

The following code extract demonstrates operator declarations:

```
Public Structure Vector2D
  Public X, Y As Double

  Public Sub New(ByVal xc As Double, ByVal yc As Double)
    X = xc
    Y = yc
  End Sub

  Public Shared Widening Operator CType(ByVal v2D As Vector2D) As Vector3D
    Dim v3D As Vector3D
    v3D.X = v2D.X
    v3D.Y = v2D.Y
    v3D.Z = 0
    Return v3D
  End Operator

  Public Shared Operator +(ByVal v1 As Vector2D, ByVal v2 As Vector2D) As Vector2D
    Dim result As Vector2D
    result.X = v1.X + v2.X
    result.Y = v1.Y + v2.Y
    Return result
  End Operator
  ' --- Other operators...
End Structure

Public Structure Vector3D
  Public X, Y, Z As Double

  ' --- Create omitted
  Public Shared Narrowing Operator CType(ByVal v3D As Vector3D) As Vector2D
    Dim v2D As Vector2D
    v2D.X = v3D.X
    v2D.Y = v3D.Y
    Return v2D
  End Operator
  ' --- Other operators...
End Structure
```

Vector2D defines a Widening conversion operator to Vector3D, while Vector3D has a Narrowing conversion operator to Vector2D. Widening operators can be used for implicit conversions, while Narrowing operators can be used only for explicit conversions (when Option Strict On is used).

Vector2D defines a binary + operator. The following statements compile and work successfully when using Option Strict On:

```
Dim vector1 As Vector2D = New Vector2D(1.0, 5.0)
Dim vector2 As Vector2D = New Vector2D(2.0, 4.0)
Dim result3D As Vector3D = vector1 + vector2
```

## New Unsigned and Signed Integer Types

However, although the CLR defines many unsigned integer types, Visual Basic 2002 and 2003 defined only Byte, Short, Integer, and Long as primitive (identified through keywords) types, and only Byte was unsigned.

Visual Basic 2005 extended the primitive types with the following new integer types:

➤ SByte (1-byte signed integer)

➤ UShort (2-byte unsigned integer)

➤ UInteger (4-byte unsigned integer)

➤ ULong (8-byte unsigned integer)

These types map to System.SByte, System.UInt16, System.UInt32, and System.UInt64, respectively.

## Using Construct

The CLR supports deterministic finalization with the dispose pattern (IDisposable behavior). C# leverages on this CLR feature with its using statement from C# 1.0, but the first versions of Visual Basic did not have this construct.

Visual Basic 2005 introduced the Using keyword to support the IDisposable pattern. Here is a short example:

```
Imports System.IO

Public Class UsingSample

  Public Sub LogEntry(ByVal entry As String)
    Using fs As FileStream = New FileStream("log.txt", FileMode.Append)
      Using log As StreamWriter = New StreamWriter(fs)
        log.WriteLine(entry)
      End Using
    End Using
  End Sub

End Class
```

The `Using` statement automates the process of acquiring a resource, executing a set of statements, and then disposing of the resource. For example, the inner `Using` statement is handled by the compiler as if you wrote this:

```
Dim log As StreamWriter = New StreamWriter(fs)
Try
  log.WriteLine(entry)
Finally
  If log IsNot Nothing Then
    log.Dispose()
  End If
End Try
```

The statement can take two forms. In one, the resource is a local variable declared as a part of the statement and treated as a regular local variable declaration statement. In the other, the resource is the result of an expression. A `Using` statement that has a local variable declaration statement may acquire multiple resources at a time, which is equivalent to nested `Using` statements. So, the previous nested `Using` statements could also be written as follows while preserving exactly the same semantics as the nested version:

```
Using fs As FileStream = New FileStream("log.txt", FileMode.Append), _
  log As StreamWriter = New StreamWriter(fs)
  log.WriteLine(entry)
End Using
```

## Visual Basic 2008 (9.0)

.NET 3.5 shipped with the new Language Integrated Query (LINQ) technology. Like C# 3.0, Visual Basic 2008 added several great features to the language to allow programmers to create data-processing operations where they express what they want to get, instead of expressing how they want to obtain the results.

The most exciting feature of this version was definitely the support of LINQ via the query expressions that became very popular because of their readability and expressiveness. To achieve that strength, the following other "syntax noise-reduction" features were put into the language, which have proven useful, even if you grab them out of the context of query expressions:

- ➤ Local variable type inference
- ➤ Extension methods
- ➤ Object-creation expressions
- ➤ Lambda expressions
- ➤ Query expressions
- ➤ Partial methods
- ➤ XML literal expressions
- ➤ Nullable value type modifier
- ➤ A true conditional operator

Let's take a look at these features in more detail.

## Local Variable Type Inference

There are a few points in the Visual Basic language where you could say the syntax is "noisy" — that is, developers must type many characters to express their intention. For example, when you want to declare a local variable for a dictionary and immediately initialize it, you do it with some code similar to the following:

```
Dim myCodeTable As Dictionary(Of Integer, String) =
    New Dictionary(Of Integer, String)
```

In this definition, writing the `Dictionary(Of Integer, String)` expression twice is what you could call *syntax noise*.

Visual Basic 2008 has a new option, `Infer`, that can be used to turn on or off the *local variable type inference* feature. Turning it on, you can reduce this noise, as shown here:

```
Option Infer On
'  ...
Dim myCodeTable = New Dictionary(Of Integer, String)
```

When you use `Option Infer On`, the compiler parses the expression to the right of the equal sign and infers its type. This will be used as the type of the variable.

The default value of `Infer` is `On`. If you turn off the type inference (with `Option Infer Off`), the previous declaration is still syntactically correct and the compiler will accept it. However, while, in the first case, the type of `myCodeTable` is `Dictionary(Of Integer, String)`, with `Option Infer Off`, it will be `System.Object`!

You can use this type of implicitly typed local variable declaration in `For`, `For Each`, and `Using` statements, as well.

## Extension Methods

Developers often write wrapper methods for objects that, in reality, could be the parts of the object itself. A good example is a method to check whether or not all characters in a string are in uppercase. This declaration can be put into a standard module, just like in the following code extract:

```
Module StringHelper

  Public Function IsAllUpper(ByVal s As String) As Boolean
    For Each c In s
      If Not Char.IsUpper(c) Then Return False
    Next
    Return True
  End Function

End Module
```

When using this helper class, you write code something like this:

```
Dim myString = "This is a String"
Dim isUpper = StringHelper.IsAllUpper(myString)
```

*Extension methods* provide a way to implement the same pattern and use it with a nicer (and more readable) syntax. Extension methods are methods with the `System.Runtime.CompilerServices.ExtensionAttribute` attribute applied to them. They can only be declared in standard modules, and must have at least one parameter, which specifies the type the method extends. The following slight change in the `IsAllUpper` method declaration makes it an extension method:

```
Imports System.Runtime.CompilerServices

Module StringHelper

  <Extension()> _
  Public Function IsAllUpper(ByVal s As String) As Boolean
    ' ...
  End Function

End Module
```

This extension method can be syntactically used as if it were the instance method of `String` — the type it extends:

```
Dim myString = "This is a String"
Dim isUpper = myString.IsAllUpper
```

## Object-Creation Expressions

Types within the .NET Framework rely heavily on the use of fields and properties. When instantiating and using new classes, it is very common to write code like this:

```
Public Class Customer
  Public ID As Integer
  Public Name As String
  Public IsKeyAccount As Boolean
End Class
' ...
Dim customer As Customer = New Customer
customer.ID = 112
customer.Name = "John Doe"
customer.IsKeyAccount = True
```

*Object-creation expressions* allow you to rewrite the preceding code with exactly the same semantics, but with a shorter and more expressive syntax:

```
Dim customer = New Customer With {.ID = 112, .Name = "John Doe", _
                                  .IsKeyAccount = True}
```

An object-creation expression can optionally specify a list of *member initializers* after the constructor arguments. These member initializers are prefixed with the keyword `With`, and the initializer list is interpreted as if it were in the context of a `With` statement.

One of the most convenient features of Visual Basic 2008 is the capability to create new types "on-the-fly" using *anonymous object-creation expressions*. An object-creation expression with member initializers can also omit the type name entirely. In that case, an anonymous type is constructed based on the types and names of the members initialized as a part of the expression. Consider the following example:

```
Module AnonymousType
  Sub Main()
    Dim order = New With {.ID = 101, .Date = #1/1/2010#, _
                          .ProductID = "Q3456", .Quantity = 123}
    Console.WriteLine("ProductID: {0}, Quantity: {1}", _
                      order.ProductID, order.Quantity)
  End Sub
End Module
```

Of course, there is no magic here. The compiler creates a real type behind the scenes, but does not expose its name to you. With `Option Infer On`, you can declare variables for the anonymous type instance without the need to name the type explicitly, as shown here:

```
Dim order2 = order ' --- declared above as anonymous type
order2.Date = #12/31/2009#
```

By default, the properties generated by the anonymous type are read-write. It is possible to mark an anonymous type property as read-only by using the `Key` modifier:

```
Dim order = New With { Key .ID = 101, .Date = #1/1/2010#, _
                       .ProductID = "Q3456", .Quantity = 123}
```

The `Key` modifier specifies that the field can be used to uniquely identify the value the anonymous type represents.

## Lambda Expressions

*Lambda expressions* provide a new and concise syntax to describe an anonymous function that can contain an expression, and can be used to create delegates. A lambda expression defines an anonymous method called a *lambda method*. Lambda methods make it easy to pass "in-line" methods to other methods that take delegate types.

In Visual Basic 2005, you should have used explicit delegates like this:

```
Module VB2005Module

  Delegate Function BinaryOperation(ByVal op1 As Double,
       ByVal op2 As Double) As Double

  Sub Main()
    Dim op1 As Double = 12.3
    Dim op2 As Double = 23.4
    Dim operation As BinaryOperation = AddressOf MyOperation
    Dim result As Double = operation(op1, op2)
  End Sub

  Function MyOperation(ByVal op1 As Double, ByVal op2 As Double) As Double
```

```
        Return (op1 + op2) / op2
    End Function

  End Module
```

Lambda expressions provide more concise syntax and type inference so that the operation delegate can even be described in a more straightforward way:

```
Sub Main()
   Dim op1 As Double = 12.3
   Dim op2 As Double = 23.4
   Dim operation As BinaryOperation = Function(x As Double, y As Double) (x + y) / y
   Dim result As Double = operation(op1, op2)
End Sub
```

A lambda expression begins with the keyword `Function` and a parameter list. Parameters in a lambda expression cannot be declared `Optional` or `ParamArray`, and cannot have attributes. Unlike regular methods, omitting a parameter type for a lambda method does not automatically infer `Object`. Instead, when a lambda method is reclassified, the omitted parameter types are inferred from the target type.

## Query Expressions

*Query expressions* provide the "language-integrated" experience of LINQ, because they provide syntax similar to SQL to describe a query. A query expression begins with a `From` or `Aggregate` operator and can end with any query operator. Other valid clauses for the middle of the expression include `From`, `Let`, `Where`, `Join`, `Distinct`, `Take`, `Take While`, `Skip`, `Skip While`, `Aggregate`, `Order By`, and `Group By` operators.

Let's take a look at an example:

```
        Dim fruits() As String = {"Apple", "Peach", "Orange", "Banana", "Lemon", _
                                  "Pear", "Grapefruit", "Watermelon", "Plum"}

        Dim filteredFruits = _
          From fruit In fruits _
          Where fruit.StartsWith("P") And fruit.Length < 20 _
          Order By fruit _
          Select fruit
```

The strength of this notation is that it describes the intention of what you would like to get as a result, instead of defining how you want to obtain it.

The Visual Basic compiler translates a query expression into method invocations. For example, the `Where` clause will translate into a call to a `Where` method, the `Order By` clause will translate into a call to an `OrderBy` method, and so on. These methods must be extension methods or instance methods on the type being queried. So, in the preceding example, the type representing `fruits` must have this characteristic. The method (not the compiler) will determine how to execute the query at run-time.

This kind of extensibility of query expressions makes LINQ a very powerful feature that enables the shift from an imperative data-processing model to the declarative one.

*Using LINQ and query expressions is definitely a topic out of the scope of this book. You can find many books treating LINQ in detail, such as Scott Klein's Professional LINQ (Indianapolis: Wiley, 2008). You can also examine the Visual Basic Language Specification for more information.*

*MSDN also supports you with Visual Basic LINQ samples at* http://msdn .microsoft.com/en-us/library/bb397978.aspx.

## Partial Methods

*Partial methods* live in partial types. A method is partial if it specifies a signature but not the body of the method. The body of the method can be supplied by another method declaration with the same name and signature, most likely in another partial declaration of the type.

This improves the performance because you are not loading/creating unwanted methods. Here is an example:

```
' --- Collection.vb: This is the class that would normally be autogenerated.
Partial Public Class CustomTypedCollection
    Partial Private Sub BeforeAddingElement(ByVal element As CustomElement)
    End Sub

    Public Sub AddElement(ByVal element As CustomElement)
      BeforeAddingElement(element)
    End Sub
End Class

' --- Customization.vb: This part is the one added by developers as customization
Partial Public Class CustomTypedCollection
    Private Sub BeforeAddingElement(ByVal element As CustomElement)
      Console.WriteLine("Element " & element.ToString() & " is being added.")
    End Sub
End Class
```

If the Customization.vb file did not contain an implementation part for the BeforeAddingElement partial method, no code would be compiled for this method call in Collection.vb.

Of course, partial methods have a few restrictions. For example, they must be Subs, and they are not allowed to have ByRef parameters, nor can they have access modifiers, and they cannot be Overridable.

## XML Literal Expressions

The simplicity with which it handles XML literal expressions is a unique feature for Visual Basic 2008 among the core .NET programming languages. An XML literal expression represents an XML 1.0 value, and can take the form of an XML document, an XML element, an XML processing instruction, an XML comment, or a CDATA section. There are so many things you can do with XML literals that this section is enough only to whet your appetite. Here is a short example:

```
Module XMLLiterals

  Dim Customer As XElement = _
    <Customer ID="112" Name="John Doe" IsKeyAccount="True"/>

  Dim name = "Jane Doe"
  Dim Customers As XDocument = _
    <?xml version="1.0"?>
    <Customers>
      <Customer ID="112" Name="John Doe" IsKeyAccount="True"/>
      <Customer ID="113" Name=<%= name %> IsKeyAccount="True"/>
      <Customer ID="114" Name="Alf Kiter" IsKeyAccount="False"/>
    </Customers>

End Module
```

The result of an XML literal expression is a value typed as one of the types from the `System.Xml.Linq` namespace. If the types in that namespace are not available, then an XML literal expression will cause a compile-time error.

In the previous sample, `Customer` defines an XML element, `Customers`, which is an XML document right from the XML literal expressions. You can see that `Customers` uses an embedded expression (name) to create the XML document with the `Name` attribute set to Jane Doe.

XML elements can contain XML namespace declarations, as defined by the XML namespaces 1.0 specification. You can also use the `Imports` section of the source file to define XML namespaces:

```
Imports <xmlns="http://myOrg.com">
Imports <xmlns:db="http://myOrg.com/myDb">

Module XMLNamespaces
  Dim Customers As XDocument = _
  <?xml version="1.0"?>
  <Customers>
    <Customer db:ID="112" Name="John Doe" IsKeyAccount="True"/>
    <Customer db:ID="113" Name="Jane Doe" IsKeyAccount="True"/>
    <Customer db:ID="114" Name="Alf Kiter" IsKeyAccount="False">
      <db:Order xmlns:db="http://myOrg.com/OrderDB">
        <db:ProductID>Q123</db:ProductID>
        <db:Amount>100</db:Amount>
      </db:Order>
    </Customer>
  </Customers>

End Module
```

The first Import statement sets the default XML namespace to `http://myOrg.com`, the second defines the `db` namespace prefix. In the `Customer` elements, the `db` prefix is used for the namespace defined in the second `Import` clause. However, the `Order` element overrides the `db` prefix for its local context to `http://myOrg.com/OrderDB`.

You can also use member access expressions to access elements and attributes in the hierarchy represented by an XML document or element. The following example shows how to access the hierarchy represented by `Customers` within the `XMLNamespaces` module:

```
Dim thirdCustomer As XElement = Customers...<Customers>(2)
Dim thirdCustomerName As String = thirdCustomer.@Name
Dim thirdCustomerID As Integer = thirdCustomer.@<db:ID>
Dim order As XElement = thirdCustomer.<db:Order>
```

The `...<descendants>` member access operator allows you to go down to the descendants' collection of the element from which it is applied. The `.<qualifiedname>` element access operator navigates down to a single element. The `.@name` and `.@<qualifiedname>` operators access element attributes.

*If you want more information about this great Visual Basic feature, navigate to* `http://msdn.microsoft.com/en-us/library/bb384808.aspx`.

## Nullable Value Type Modifier

.NET 2.0 introduced the `Nullable(Of T)` type to represent nullable value types. Because of `Nullable(Of T)` type is supported by the CLR, you can use it just like any other generic types:

```
Dim firstValue As Nullable(Of Integer) = 4
Dim secondValue As Nullable(Of Integer) = 5
Dim sumValue As Nullable(Of Integer) = firstValue + SecondValue
' ...
Public Function Square(ByVal n As Nullable(Of Integer)) As Nullable(Of Integer)
    Return Iif(n.HasValue, n.Value * n.Value, Nothing)
End Function
```

Visual Basic 2008 introduced the `?` modifier for value types. It can be added to a type name to represent the nullable version of that type. The previous code can be shorten with the `?` modifier:

```
Dim firstValue As Integer? = 4
Dim secondValue As Integer? = 5
Dim sumValue As Integer? = firstValue + secondValue
' ...
Public Function Square(ByVal n As Integer?) As Integer?
    Return Iif(n.HasValue, n.Value * n.Value, Nothing)
End Function
```

## A True Conditional Operator

The language has the `Iif` run-time function so that you can embed conditional evaluation into expressions. Because `Iif` is a function, the following expression will raise a `NullReferenceException` when `customer` is `Nothing`, because all the three expressions are evaluated and put to the evaluation stack before calling the `Iif` function.

```
Iif(customer Is Nothing, customer.Name, "<unknown>")
```

A conditional `If` expression tests an expression and returns a value. Unlike the `Iif` run-time function, however, a conditional expression only evaluates its operands if necessary. Using `If` in the code above instead `Iif` no exception occurs.

The operator has two forms:

➤   `If(CondExpr, Expr1, Expr2)` — Evaluates `CondExpr`, and, when it's true, evaluates `Expr1` as the operation result; otherwise evaluates `Expr2`.

➤   `If(Expr, NullExpr)` — Evaluated as if it were `If(Expr IsNot Nothing, Expr, NullExpr)`.

## SUMMARY

Currently an object-oriented language with functional programming features, Visual Basic began its life in the 1990s as a general-purpose, high-level language with very simple constructs. The ancestor of Visual Basic was BASIC developed by John G. Kemeny and Thomas E. Kurtz in 1964; today, you can still recognize the roots of that unstructured language.

At the end of the twentieth century, Visual Basic 6.0 became a very popular programming language with a large camp of developers using it. .NET turned Visual Basic into a real object-oriented language, and launched debates within the community as to whether it is still the same language or a new one.

Visual Basic evolved in parallel with the .NET Framework. New features and changes in the CLR and in the framework's class libraries inspired the language to embed new paradigms beside the object-oriented programming (OOP) principles.

In Chapter 22, you will learn the new features of Visual Basic 2010, including auto-implemented properties, multi-line lambda expressions, dynamic support, covariance, and contravariance.

# 22

# Visual Basic 10.0 Language Improvements

In Chapter 21, you learned that Visual Basic has a 19-year history under the Windows platform. During this long time, Visual Basic evolved from a general-purpose, high-level programming language to a multi-paradigm one. The first version of Visual Basic.NET turned the language into a real object-oriented one, and also launched debates within the community as to whether it is still the same Visual Basic or a new language.

Visual Basic 2005 added support for generic types, and got great performance-boosting features (such as partial types, operator declarations, Using statement, and nullable types). Visual Basic 2008 started embracing functional programming principles, such as LINQ and query expressions, and added XLM literal expressions to the language — which is unique among the core .NET languages.

The newest version, Visual Basic 2010, is about enhancing its functional features and providing seamless cooperation with dynamic programming languages. While a few years ago there were separate teams in Microsoft responsible for Visual Basic and C#, today the Managed Languages Team makes tremendous efforts toward the co-evolution of these two languages. Compare the new Visual Basic 2010 features with the new C# 4.0 improvements in Chapter 24 and you can see this co-evolution.

After reading this chapter, you will be familiar with the following improvements of the Visual Basic 2010 language:

➤ *Implicit line continuation* — You can get rid of the underscore character used at the end of a line when your statement goes on to the next consecutive line.

➤ *Auto-implemented properties* — You can quickly specify a property of a class without having to write code to Get and Set the property.

➤ *Collection initializers* — These provide a shortened syntax that enables you to create a collection and populate it with an initial set of values. Collection initializers are useful when you are creating a collection from a set of known values.

➤ *Multiline lambda expressions* — Lambda expressions now support subroutines and multiline functions.

➤ *Working with dynamic objects* — Visual Basic binds to objects from dynamic languages such as IronPython and IronRuby with the help of the Dynamic Language Run-time (DLR).

➤ *Variance* — .NET developers used to be constrained by the fact that an `IEnumerable(Of Object)` could not be substituted with an `IEnumerable(Of String)`. Now, this substitution can be done! Visual Basic embraces type-safe covariance and contravariance. The common Base Class Library types (primarily generic collection interfaces) also have been updated to support this behavior.

## NEW PRODUCTIVITY-IMPROVING SYNTAX

There are a few new features of the language that neither change how you program with Visual Basic nor provide you brand-new paradigms. However, they are still very useful, because they make your code shorter and more readable and altogether improve your productivity. This section provides an overview of them.

## Implicit Line Continuation

For a very long time, the underscore (_) line continuation character at the end of code lines was a hallmark of Visual Basic, and often referred to by C# programmers as an example why Visual Basic is a "noisy" language. Even in Visual Basic 2008, you had to use underscores, as shown here:

```
Dim fruits() As String = {"Apple", "Peach", "Orange", "Banana", "Lemon", _
                          "Pear", "Grapefruit", "Watermelon", "Plum"}

Dim filteredFruits = _
  From fruit In fruits _
  Where fruit.StartsWith("P") And fruit.Length < 20 _
  Order By fruit _
  Select fruit
```

The explicit line continuation has several issues:

➤ It is cumbersome to use it.

➤ The underscore does not give real value to developers. (Some would question whether it gives any value at all.) It is rather about helping the language parser find out which consecutive lines form a statement. It probably originates from the era when Basic programs were analyzed, tokenized, and compiled to P-code, line by line.

➤ As the language evolves and moves toward functional principles, there is a natural wish of developers to break statements into separate lines to improve readability. (Take a look at the earlier `filteredFruits` query expression.) Typing an extra underscore at the end of the lines goes against this wish.

After a long time, the Managed Language Team made a big leap. Visual Basic 2010 allows omitting the line-continuation character in most of the cases. For example, you can write the earlier code snippet like this:

```
Dim fruits() As String =
  {
    "Apple", "Peach", "Orange",
    "Banana", "Lemon", "Pear",
    "Grapefruit", "Watermelon", "Plum"
  }

Dim filteredFruits2 =
  From fruit In fruits
  Where fruit.StartsWith("P") And fruit.Length < 20
  Order By fruit
  Select fruit
```

Following is a list of the cases where you can continue a statement on the next consecutive line without using the underscore character:

➤  After a comma (,).

➤  After an open parenthesis (() or before a closing parenthesis ()).

➤  After an open curly brace ({) or before a closing curly brace (}).

➤  After an open embedded expression (<%=) or before the close of an embedded expression (%>) within an XML literal.

➤  After the concatenation operator (&).

➤  After assignment operators (=, &=, :=, +=, -=, *=, /=, \=, ^=, <<=, >>=).

➤  After the Is and IsNot operators.

➤  After a member qualifier character (.) and before the member name. However, you must include a line-continuation character (_) following a member qualifier character when you are using the With statement, or supplying values in the initialization list for a type.

➤  After an XML axis property qualifier (. or .@ or ...). However, you must include a line-continuation character (_) when you specify a member qualifier when you are using the With keyword.

➤  After a less-than sign (<) or before a greater-than sign (>) when you specify an attribute. Also, after a greater-than sign (>) when you specify an attribute. However, you must include a line-continuation character (_) when you specify assembly-level or module-level attributes.

➤  Before and after query operators. You cannot break a line between the keywords of query operators that are made up of multiple keywords (Order By, Group Join, Take While, and Skip While).

➤  After the In keyword in a For Each statement.

➤  After the From keyword in a collection initializer. (You'll learn about these later in this chapter.)

*This list of options to leave the underscore means that you can actually omit underscores from every location where it seems natural. If you would like to see samples and more details about statements and line continuation, navigate to* `http://msdn.microsoft.com/en-us/library/865x40k4(VS.100).aspx.`

Getting rid of the mandatory line continuation means that now you can break and indent your Visual Basic code easier than ever before.

## Auto-Implemented Properties

C# 3.0 introduced *automatic properties* in 2008. As a sign of co-evolution, Visual Basic 2010 also implements this feature — even better then C# did! *Auto-implemented properties* (the name is intentionally different from the C# terminology) enable you to quickly specify a property of a class without having to write code to Get and Set the property. When you write code for an auto-implemented property, the Visual Basic compiler automatically creates a private field to store the property variable, in addition to creating the associated Get and Set procedures.

The following code snippet shows an example defining several auto-implemented properties:

```
Public Class Order
  Public Property ID As Integer
  Public Property CustomerName As String = "Unknown"
  Public Property OrderDate As Date = DateTime.Now.Date
  Public Property Items As New List(Of OrderItem)
End Class

Public Class OrderItem
  ' ...
End Class
```

With auto-implemented properties, a property (including a default value) can be declared in a single line. Type inference also works, so if you provide a default value, the compiler infers the property type (assuming Option Infer On is used). Should you turn off type inference, properties with default values will have type of System.Object.

The Order class defines four properties, the last three with default values. While CustomerName and OrderDate explicitly define their types, the type of Items is inferred from the default value.

An auto-implemented property is equivalent to a property for which the property value is stored in a private field. When you declare an auto-implemented property, Visual Basic automatically creates a hidden private backing field to contain the property value. The backing field name is the auto-implemented property name preceded by an underscore (_). For example, the compiler generates the following code for the Items property:

```
Private _Items As List(Of OrderItem)
Public Property Items As List(Of OrderItem)
```

```
      Get
        Return _Items
      End Get
      Set(ByVal AutoPropertyValue As List(Of OrderItem))
        _Items = AutoPropertyValue
      End Set
   End Property
```

The backing field access modifiers are set by the compiler. The backing field is always `Private`, even when the property itself has a different access level (such as `Public` or `Protected`). When the property is `Shared`, the backing field is also `Shared`. No attributes specified for the property apply to the backing field.

If you add a member to your class that is also named the same as any of your properties having a preceding underscore, you produce a naming conflict, and Visual Basic reports a compiler error.

The backing field can be accessed from code within the class, just as if you declared it, so you can add the following declaration to the `Order` class:

```
   Public Overrides Function ToString() As String
      Return String.Format("ID={0}, Customer={1}, Date={2}, #of Items={3}",
                           _ID, _CustomerName, _OrderDate, _Items.Count)
   End Function
```

 *Despite the fact you can access the backing field from code, it is not a good practice to do so. Use direct backing field access only when it is really necessary — generally because of performance considerations.*

Although you access the backing field from the code, it does not show in an IntelliSense word-completion list. The backing field can also be accessed and from debugging tools such as the Watch window.

The compiler also takes care of setting the initial values of the properties in constructors. When creating the constructor, the code for property initialization precedes your custom constructor body. The compiler also takes care of that if you initialize one of the auto-implemented properties. It does not set the default value for it.

Let's assume you have the following two constructors in the `Order` class:

```
   Public Class Order
      Public Sub New()
      End Sub

      Public Sub New(ByVal initialID As Integer)
         ID = initialID
      End Sub
      ' --- Other members omitted
   End Class
```

The compiler will generate the following code:

```
Public Sub New()
  Me.CustomerName = "Unknown"
  Me.OrderDate = DateTime.Now.Date
  Dim temp_var As New List(Of OrderItem)
  Me.Items = temp_var
End Sub

Public Sub New(ByVal initialID As Integer)
  Me.CustomerName = "Unknown"
  Me.OrderDate = DateTime.Now.Date
  Dim temp_var As New List(Of OrderItem)
  Me.Items = temp_var
  Me.ID = initialID
End Sub
```

Following are a few restrictions concerning defining default values for auto-implemented properties:

➤ You cannot initialize an auto-implemented property that is a member of an `Interface` or one that is marked `MustOverride`.

➤ When you declare an auto-implemented property as a member of a `Structure`, you can only initialize the auto-implemented property if it is marked as `Shared`.

➤ When you declare an auto-implemented property as an array, you cannot specify explicit array bounds. However, you can supply a value by using an array initializer, and the array bounds are inferred from this initializer.

You cannot use auto-implemented properties in every case. Following are the cases when you must use the standard property definition syntax:

➤ You want the `Get` and `Set` procedures to have different accessibilities.

➤ You need `ReadOnly` or `WriteOnly` or parameterized properties.

➤ You want to add code for the `Get` or `Set` procedures.

➤ You need to extend the backing field with attributes or comments.

## Collection Initializers

Visual Basic provides you with a simple syntax to set up the initial values of arrays:

```
Dim PrimesUnder50() As Integer = {2, 3, 5, 7, 11, 13, 17, 19, 23,
    29, 31, 37, 41, 43, 47}
Dim SeaCreatures() As String = {"Stingray", "Potato cod", "Surgeon fish", _
  "Anemone fish", "Grey shark", "Stonefish"}
```

However, if `PrimesUnder50` and `SeaCreatures` were not arrays, but collections (for example, lists), with Visual Basic 2008, you must initialize them with longer procedural code:

```
Dim PrimesUnder50 As New List(Of Integer)
PrimesUnder50.Add(2)
PrimesUnder50.Add(3)
```

```
PrimesUnder50.Add(5)
'...
PrimesUnder50.Add(43)
PrimesUnder50.Add(47)
'  ...
Dim SeaCreatures As New List(Of String)
SeaCreatures.Add("Stingray")
SeaCreatures.Add("Potato cod")
'  ...
SeaCreatures.Add("Grey shark")
SeaCreatures.Add("Stonefish")
```

In 2008, C# 3.0 introduced a new syntax for collection initializers. Visual Basic 2010 took over the same semantics with a syntax tailored to the Basic language.

A collection initializer starts with the From keyword and consists of a list of comma-separated values that are enclosed in braces ({}). PrimesUnder50 and SeaCreatures can be initialized in Visual Basic 2010, as the following code extract shows:

```
Dim PrimesUnder50 As New List(Of Integer) From
    {2, 3, 5, 7, 11, 13, 17, 19, 23, 29, 31, 37, 41, 43, 47}
Dim SeaCreatures As New List(Of String) From
    {"Stingray", "Potato cod", "Surgeon fish",
     "Anemone fish", "Grey shark", "Stonefish"}
```

Behind the scenes, the Visual Basic compiler uses the same approach as you would use it with the List(Of T).Add method, but it makes for a safer approach, as the following example shows:

```
' --- Compiler generated code for initializing SeaCreatures:
Dim Temp_var As New List(Of String)
Temp_var.Add("Stingray")
Temp_var.Add("Potato cod")
Temp_var.Add("Surgeon fish")
Temp_var.Add("Anemone fish")
Temp_var.Add("Grey shark")
Temp_var.Add("Stonefish")
SeaCreatures = Temp_var
```

The collection is initialized in a temporary list (Temp_var), and the collection is set to this temporary list only after all elements have been successfully added to the collection. This approach is used to keep the initialization operation atomic. If any exception happened during the call of any Add method, SeaCreatures would not become partially initialized. At the end, it fully initializes or stays uninitialized.

You can initialize Dictionary(Of K, V) collections with a similar syntax as well:

```
Dim PrimesUnder10 As New Dictionary(Of Integer, String) From
  {
    {2, "Two"},
    {3, "Three"},
    {5, "Five"},
    {7, "Seven"}
  }
```

The mechanism behind is defined so that you can apply it for any valid collection type (classes implementing ICollection or ICollection(Of T)). The type that intends to use the collection initializer syntax must also expose an Add method that meets the following criteria:

➤ The Add method must be available from the scope in which the collection initializer is being called. If you are using the collection initializer in a scenario where non-public methods of the collection can be accessed, the Add method does not have to be Public.

➤ The Add method must be an instance member or Shared member of the collection class, or an extension method.

➤ An Add method must exist so that it can be matched, based on overload resolution rules, to the types that are supplied in the collection initializer.

Let's have a look at several simple examples to help understand these criteria. Assume that you have a Customer class defined like this:

```
Public Class Customer
    Public Property ID As Integer
    Public Property Name As String
End Class
```

You can create a CustomerCollection class by inheriting from List(Of Customer):

```
Public Class CustomerCollection
    Inherits List(Of Customer)
End Class
```

Because CustomerCollection is a collection type, you can use the collection initializer pattern to set up its initial value:

```
Dim Customers As New CustomerCollection From
    {
        New Customer With {.ID = 112, .Name = "John Doe"},
        New Customer With {.ID = 113, .Name = "Jane Doe"}
    }
```

This seems a bit noisy, and, in addition to the initial field values, you must type many other characters. Adding a constructor to the Customer class helps to reduce this noise a bit:

```
Public Class Customer
    Public Property ID As Integer
    Public Property Name As String

    Public Sub New(ByVal id As Integer, ByVal name As String)
        Me.ID = id
        Me.Name = name
    End Sub
End Class
' ...
```

```
Dim Customers As New CustomerCollection From
{
  New Customer(112, "John Doe"),
  New Customer(113, "Jane Doe")
}
```

To achieve the simplicity and clearness as with the `PrimesUnder10` dictionary in the previous code sample, you must append a new `Add` method to `CustomerCollection` with the signature accepting customer `ID` and `Name`. The compiler recognizes this `Add` method and can use it to initialize your collection:

```
Public Class CustomerCollection
  Inherits List(Of Customer)

  Public Overloads Sub Add(ByVal id As Integer, ByVal name As String)
    MyBase.Add(New Customer(id, name))
  End Sub
End Class
' ...
Dim Customers As New CustomerCollection From
  {
    {112, "John Doe"},
    {113, "Jane Doe"}
  }
```

There are situations when you cannot define an `Add` method within the collection class — for example, in a third-party assembly. In this case, extension methods are there to help you. When you define `Customers` as `List(Of Customer)`, you can still create an extension method to use the shorter collection initializer syntax:

```
Imports System.Runtime.CompilerServices

Module CustomerExtensions

  <Extension()>
  Public Sub Add(ByVal collection As ICollection(Of Customer),
                 ByVal id As Integer, ByVal name As String)
    collection.Add(New Customer(id, name))
  End Sub

End Module
' ...
Dim Customers As New List(Of Customer) From
  {
    {112, "John Doe"},
    {113, "Jane Doe"}
  }
```

Collection initializers can be nested. Listing 22-1 shows an example where `OrderCollection` is a nested collection in `Customer`.

**LISTING 22-1:** Class Definitions to Use in Nested Collection Initializers

```vb
Public Class Customer
  Public Property ID As Integer
  Public Property Name As String
  Public Property Orders As OrderCollection

  Public Sub New(ByVal id As Integer, ByVal name As String,
              ByVal orders As OrderCollection)
    Me.ID = id
    Me.Name = name
    Me.Orders = orders
  End Sub
End Class

Public Class CustomerCollection
  Inherits List(Of Customer)

  Public Overloads Sub Add(ByVal id As Integer, ByVal name As String,
                      ByVal orders As OrderCollection)
    MyBase.Add(New Customer(id, name, orders))
  End Sub
End Class

Public Class Order
  Public Property CustomerID As Integer
  Public Property OrderDate As Date

  Public Sub New(ByVal cid As Integer, ByVal odate As Date)
    CustomerID = cid
    OrderDate = odate
  End Sub
End Class

Public Class OrderCollection
  Inherits List(Of Order)

  Public Overloads Sub Add(ByVal cid As Integer, ByVal odate As Date)
    MyBase.Add(New Order(cid, odate))
  End Sub
End Class
```

With these classes, you can use the following initialization:

```vb
Dim Customers As New CustomerCollection From
  {
    {112, "John Doe", New OrderCollection From
      {
        {112, #12/1/2009#},
        {112, #12/2/2009#}
      }
    },
```

```
    {113, "Jane Doe", New OrderCollection From
      {
        {113, #12/20/2009#},
        {113, #12/22/2009#},
        {113, #12/23/2009#}
      }
    }
  }
```

As a special form of collection initializers, Visual Basic 2010 allows you to use *array literals* that provide a compact syntax for declaring an array whose type is inferred by the compiler. So, you do not have to declare an array as follows:

```
Dim PrimesUnder50() As Integer = {2, 3, 5, 7, 11, 13, 17, 19, 23,
        29, 31, 37, 41, 4
    Dim SeaCreatures() As String = {"Stingray", "Potato cod", "Surgeon fish", _
  "Anemone fish", "Grey shark", "Stonefish"}
```

Instead, you can write it without the explicit type declarations:

```
Dim PrimesUnder50 = {2, 3, 5, 7, 11, 13, 17, 19, 23, 29, 31, 37, 41, 43, 47}
Dim SeaCreatures = {"Stingray", "Potato cod", "Surgeon fish",
  "Anemone fish", "Grey shark", "Stonefish"}
```

The compiler infers the type of the enumerated values, and sets the variable in the `Dim` declaration to the appropriate array type. For example, `PrimesUnder50` will be an array of integers, and `SeaCreatures` an array of strings. You can use this construct to initialize multidimensional arrays like this one:

```
Dim threeTimesThree =
  {
    {1, 2, 3},
    {4, 5, 6},
    {7, 8, 9}
  }
```

The compiler also infers the number of dimensions and bounds for the multidimensional arrays, and also checks for the consistent use of boundaries. For example, when the listed values show inconsistencies, an error is raised:

```
Dim threeTimesMany =
  {
    {1, 2, 3},
    {4, 5, 6, 10},
    {7, 8, 9}
  }
```

According to the `{1, 2, 3}` initializer list, the compiler infers the second array dimension's upper bound to 3, but the next line shows this value to be 4, so you'll be given an error message.

## Multiline Lambda Expressions

Lambda expressions introduced in Visual Basic 2008 represent a function without a name that calculates and returns a single value. Lambda expressions can be used wherever a delegate type is valid. They provide a simple and concise syntax to eliminate the need for defining separate functions to be passed as delegates.

For example, without lambda expressions, you could write similar code in Visual Basic 2005:

```
Module VB2005Module

  Delegate Function BinaryOperation(ByVal op1 As Double, _
    ByVal op2 As Double) As Double

  Sub Main()
    Dim op1 As Double = 12.3
    Dim op2 As Double = 23.4
    Dim operation As BinaryOperation = AddressOf MyOperation
    Dim result As Double = operation(op1, op2)
  End Sub

  Function MyOperation(ByVal op1 As Double, ByVal op2 As Double) As Double
    Return (op1 + op2) / op2
  End Function

End Module
```

With Visual Basic 2008 lambda expressions, it gets shorter:

```
Module VB2008Module

  Delegate Function BinaryOperation(ByVal op1 As Double, _
    ByVal op2 As Double) As Double

  Sub Main()
    Dim op1 As Double = 12.3
    Dim op2 As Double = 23.4
    Dim operation As BinaryOperation = _
      Function(x As Double, y As Double) (x + y) / y
    Dim result As Double = operation(op1, op2)
  End Sub

End Module
```

While Visual Basic 2008 lambda expression implementation is great, it has two significant constraints:

➤ Only single-line functions can be used to define the return value of the lambda expressions.

➤ Only `Function` definitions are allowed; subroutines cannot be used.

Visual Basic 2010 removed these restrictions, so you can define lambda expressions as in the following sample:

```
Dim LinearValue1 = Function(a, x, b) a * x + b
Dim LinearValue2 = Function(a, x, b)
                       Dim y = a * x + b
                       Return y
                   End Function
Dim EnglishWelcome = Sub(name)
                        Console.WriteLine("Hello, {0}!", name)
                     End Sub
Dim HungarianWelcome = Sub(name)
                          Console.WriteLine("Isten hozott, {0}!", name)
                       End Sub
```

LinearValue1 and LinearValue2 delegates define the same lambda expression, but LinearValue2 uses a multiline function (which was not available in preceding Visual Basic versions). As you can see, now you can create lambda expressions for delegates invoking subroutines, as EnglishWelcome and HungarianWelcome show you.

These improvements in lambda expressions are very useful. The .NET Framework heavily uses the Action(Of T), Action(Of T1, T2), Action(Of T1, T2, T3), and so on, types as well as the Func(Of T, TResult), Func(Of T1, T2, TResult), and so on. They have an important role in query expressions, and in the Task Parallel Library. Now, thanks to the new lambda expressions, you can use them to make your Visual Basic code more concise than ever before.

Listing 22-2 shows you the source code of a simple Visual Basic console application that searches for a specific byte in a large byte array — using a parallel algorithm.

**LISTING 22-2:** Searching in a Large Byte Array

```
Imports System.Threading.Tasks

Module ParallelSearch

  Sub Main()
    Const ByteSeries = 100000
    Const BlobSize = 100
    Const ToSearch As Byte = 123

    Dim DumpInfo(ByteSeries)() As Byte

    Parallel.For(0, ByteSeries,
            Sub(index)
                Dim blob(BlobSize) As Byte
                Dim rnd = New Random(CType(DateTime.Now.Ticks, Integer))
                rnd.NextBytes(blob)
                DumpInfo(index) = blob
            End Sub)
```

*continues*

**LISTING 22-2** *(continued)*

```
Parallel.For(0, ByteSeries,
              Sub(index, state)
                If state.ShouldExitCurrentIteration Then Return
                Console.WriteLine("Search in blob #{0}", index)
                For Each b As Byte In DumpInfo(index)
                  If b = ToSearch Then
                    Console.WriteLine("Halt request in #{0}", index)
                    state.Stop()
                    Exit For
                  End If
                Next
              End Sub)

  End Sub

End Module
```

Without diving too deep into the code (you can find more details in Chapter 10), here is a brief explanation of this code.

The `Parallel.For` method executes the iteration bodies concurrently. The first and second argument define the range of indexes for the iterations. The third argument is a delegate for the iteration bodies. They are the concurrent versions of the sequential `For` cycles, where the method body uses a delegate passed in the third argument:

```
For index = 0 To ByteSeries - 1
  ' --- Here comes the iteration body
Next
```

The first `Parallel.For` call uses a delegate where the iteration index is passed. The second `Parallel.For` invokes a delegate where the iteration index and a variable representing the loop's state is passed.

Without the multiline lambda expressions, you had to move the iteration bodies out of the `Parallel.For` calls into separate methods. That would blow the readability of the code.

 *There are many subtle features of lambda expressions that are out of the scope of this book. You can read more about them at MSDN (*http://msdn.microsoft*.com/en-us/library/bb531253(VS.100).aspx).*

## WORKING WITH DYNAMIC OBJECTS

.NET developers are familiar with the fact that types and operations are strictly checked during the compilation process. The compiler generates Microsoft Intermediate Language (MSIL) code that explicitly carries out those operations by invoking methods. This behavior of the compiler is called *early binding*.

Early binding has the following characteristics:

➤ Early-bound objects (objects that have been assigned their values with early binding) allow the compiler to make important optimizations that yield more efficient applications.

➤ Early-bound objects are significantly faster than late-bound objects and make your code easier to read and maintain by stating exactly what kind of objects are being used.

➤ Early binding enables useful features such as automatic code completion and Dynamic Help because the Visual Studio integrated development environment (IDE) can determine exactly what type of object you are working with as you edit the code.

➤ Early binding reduces the number and severity of run-time errors because it allows the compiler to report errors when a program is compiled.

There is another galaxy in the universe of programming languages: *dynamic languages*. The compiler makes only a few checks over types and their operations. The majority of them are postponed to the execution of the corresponding operation at run-time.

In addition to the dynamic languages, there are *script languages* and *object models* (for example, COM objects over the Microsoft Office functionality, the DTE object model in Visual Studio, the HTML DOM in Internet Explorer, and so on) that also check operations at run-time.

In this complex world, these tools and languages should interoperate so that they can provide boosted developer performance. Scripting tools and languages such as JScript, PowerShell, and many others, as well as dynamic languages such as Python or Ruby, are very popular today.

Visual Basic was always very strong in interoperating with COM object models, because of the late binding mechanism provided by the compiler and the Visual Basic run-time. In Visual Basic 2010, this mechanism has been enhanced, so developers can bind to objects from dynamic languages such as IronPython and IronRuby much easier than ever before.

 *For a long time, C# could not compete with the interoperability features of Visual Basic, because the C# compiler did not know late binding. C# 4.0 improved C# by introducing a new variable type called* dynamic *to enable late binding. Chapter 24 describes how this works in C#.*

## Late Binding in Visual Basic 2010

Visual Basic implemented the mechanism of late binding a long time ago. When you compile your program with `Option Strict Off`, and you assign an object to a variable declared to by type of `Object`, the compiler generates code that postpones the assignment and other operations with that object until run-time. Listing 22-3 shows a simple console application utilizing this feature.

**LISTING 22-3:** Module1.vb: Console Application Demonstrating Late Binding

```vb
Option Strict Off
Module Module1

    Sub Main()
        Dim xlApp As Object
        Dim xlBook As Object
        Dim xlSheet As Object
        xlApp = CreateObject("Excel.Application")
        xlBook = xlApp.Workbooks.Add
        xlSheet = xlBook.Worksheets(1)
        xlSheet.Activate()
        xlSheet.Cells(1, 1) = "I"
        xlSheet.Cells(1, 2) = "I*I"
        For i = 1 To 10
            xlSheet.Cells(i + 1, 1) = i
            xlSheet.Cells(i + 1, 2) = i * i
        Next
        xlSheet.Application.Visible = True
    End Sub

End Module
```

*Code file [Module1.vb] available for download at Wrox.com*

This application creates an Excel worksheet with a small table and displays it using Microsoft Excel automation objects.

The `xlApp`, `xlBook` and `xlSheet` variables are declared as type of `Object`. At build time, the compiler does not know what kind of concrete objects they will represent at run-time. For example, it does not know how exactly to execute the following assignment:

```vb
xlBook = xlApp.Workbooks.Add
```

This is because it does not know how to access the `Workbooks` operation of `xlApp` and the `Add` operation resulted from the `xlApp.Workbooks` operation. The compiler does not even know which kind of operations (method invocation or property access) they are.

The compiler emits code that uses the types within the `Microsoft.VisualBasic.CompilerServices` namespace heavily to resolve and execute those operations at run-time. When you run the application, the following actions are carried out:

**1.** The run-time recognizes that `xlApp` is an Excel automation object (COM object)

**2.** It asks `xlApp` to execute the `WorkBooks` operation and retrieve its result.

**3.** When the `WorkBooks` object is returned, the run-time asks this object to execute its `Add` operation.

**4.** When `Add` is executed, its result is stored in `xlBook`.

The same mechanism is carried out when the run-time executes operations on xlSheet.

Visual Basic 2010 improves this mechanism by integrating the late binding with the Dynamic Language Run-time (DLR). If a late-bound call is made to an object that implements the IDynamicMetaObjectProvider interface of the System.Dynamic namespace, Visual Basic binds to the dynamic object by using that interface. If a late-bound call is made to an object that does not implement the IDynamicMetaObjectProvider interface, or if the call to the IDynamicMetaObjectProvider interface fails, Visual Basic binds to the object by using the late-binding capabilities of the Visual Basic run-time — just as it did before DLR integration.

From a Visual Basic syntax point of view, the DLR integration is transparent. You cannot see any difference if you work with a late-bound COM object or with a dynamic object (an object implementing IDynamicMetaObjectProvider). What you can observe is that now Visual Basic can bind to objects from dynamic languages such as IronPython and IronRuby. The world within which you can interoperate from Visual Basic is definitely larger than it was before.

---

**THE DYNAMIC LANGUAGE RUN-TIME**

An important component in the underlying implementation of dynamic lookup is the *Dynamic Language Run-time* (DLR), which is a part of .NET Framework 4.0. DLR is a run-time environment that adds a set of services for dynamic languages to the Common Language Run-time (CLR), and makes it easier to develop dynamic languages to run on the .NET Framework, as well as to add dynamic features to statically typed languages. DLR is built on the top of CLR, and uses *run-time binders* to access the physical object model addressed by dynamic expressions.

Chapter 10 provides more details about DLR.

---

## Accessing an IronPython Library

To learn how easy it is to use an IronPython library because of the DLR integration in Visual Basic, let's create a small console application that invokes an IronPython function to solve a quadratic equation. The function in IronPython will be so simple that you'll be able to understand it without any Python background.

To use IronPython, you must download and install the run-time from the Downloads tab of the IronPython project's home page on CodePlex at http://ironpython.codeplex.com.

Create a new Visual Basic console application project and name it IronPythonRunner. Double-click on My Project under the project node in Solution Explorer to display the project properties, and go to the References tab to add the IronPython reference assemblies. Click Add to display the Add References dialog. Use the Browse tab of the dialog to navigate to the IronPython run-time's installation folder, and add the selected assemblies shown in Figure 22-1 to the project.

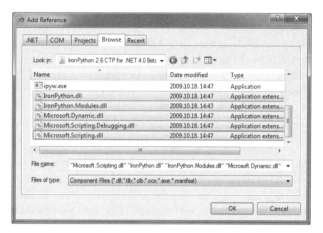

**FIGURE 22-1:** IronPython run-time assemblies

 *You will find this folder directly under your operating system's* Program Files *folder (on 64-bit systems, under the* Program Files (x86) *folder) in a folder with the* IronPython *prefix. As of this writing, a separate IronPython release was used especially created for Visual Studio 2010 Beta 2. Check the IronPython home page for the most current version.*

Add a new text file item and name it Quadratic.py, where .py is the standard extension for IronPython program files. This file should be in the same folder where the console application is started from. Set the Build Action property of Quadratic.py to Content, and the Copy to Output Directory property to Copy Always.

Listing 22-4 shows the content you should copy into the Quadratic.py file.

**LISTING 22-4: Quadratic.py**

```
import math

def SolveQuadratic(A, B, C):
  determ = B*B - 4*A*C
  solution1 = 0.0
  solution2 = 0.0
  hasSolution = determ >= 0.0
  if hasSolution:
    solution1 = (-B + math.sqrt(determ))/ (2*A)
    solution2 = (-B - math.sqrt(determ))/ (2*A)
  return hasSolution, solution1, solution2
```

*Code file [Quadratic.py] available for download at Wrox.com*

This small Python code snippet solves the quadratic equation defined in the form of $Ax^2 + Bx + c = 0$ and retrieves the results in a tuple of a Boolean (is there a solution, anyway?), and in two numbers (the two possible solutions).

Copy the code in Listing 22-5 into the `Module1.vb` file to invoke the Python code snippet.

**LISTING 22-5:** Module1.vb File of IronPythonRunner

```vb
Option Strict Off

Imports IronPython.Hosting

Module Module1

  Sub Main()
    Dim ipy As Object = Python.CreateRuntime()
    Dim calculator As Object = ipy.UseFile("Quadratic.py")
    SolveQuadratic(calculator, 1.0, 2.0, 3.0)
    SolveQuadratic(calculator, 2.0, 15.0, 6.0)
  End Sub

  Sub SolveQuadratic(ByVal calculator As Object,
                     ByVal A As Double,
                     ByVal B As Double,
                     ByVal C As Double)
    Dim result As Object = calculator.SolveQuadratic(A, B, C)
    Console.WriteLine("The quadratic equation {0}*x2 + {1}*x + {2} = 0",
                      A, B, C)
    If result(0) Then
      Console.WriteLine("  has the following solutions:")
      Console.WriteLine("    #1: {0}", result(1))
      Console.WriteLine("    #2: {0}", result(2))
    Else
      Console.WriteLine("  has no solution.")
    End If
    Console.WriteLine()
  End Sub

End Module
```

*Code file [Module1.vb] available for download at Wrox.com*

The code is really simple. The `Python` object located in the `IronPython.Hosting` namespace is responsible for managing the run-time environment. You can obtain a reference for an object (named `calculator` in this context) to access the operations defined by the `Quadratic.py` mini-program:

```vb
Dim ipy As Object = Python.CreateRuntime()
Dim calculator As Object = ipy.UseFile("Quadratic.py")
```

You can invoke the `SolveQuadratic` operation defined in the Python code snippet through the `calculator` object:

```
Dim result As Object = calculator.SolveQuadratic(A, B, C)
```

The result will be a tuple of three values that you can index from 0 to 2. Figure 22-2 shows the output of the console application.

```
C:\Windows\system32\cmd.exe
The quadratic equation 1*x2 + 2*x + 3 = 0
  has no solution.

The quadratic equation 2*x2 + 15*x + 6 = 0
  has the following solutions:
    #1: -0.423966326087482
    #2: -7.07603367391252

Press any key to continue . . . _
```

**FIGURE 22-2:** Output of the application

> *The IronPython run-time comes with a brief language tutorial. Open the* `Tutorial\Tutorial.htm` *file under the installation folder, and play with the language modifying the* `Quadratic.py` *and* `Module1.vb` *files. You can find a general (and more detailed) tutorial about the Python programming language at* `http://docs.python.org/tutorial/`.

## VARIANCE

Inheritance is a great object-oriented principle that is always directly or indirectly used when you create .NET applications or components. Visual Basic missed object-oriented programming (OOP) for a long time, but the first Visual Basic.NET version (2002) enabled the language to fully implement these principles. .NET Framework 2.0 and Visual Basic 2005 brought generic types into the picture, and boosted developer performance, as well as code reusability. However, generic types may sometimes surprise you because certain things are illegal, even if you thought they were allowed.

## Type Substitution

If you see the following Visual Basic console application, you would say, it's okay, and it runs:

```
Module Module1

  Public strings As IList(Of String) = New List(Of String)
  Public objects As IList(Of Object) = strings

  Sub Main()
    strings.Add("Hello")
```

```
        strings.Add("World")

        For Each item In objects
          Console.WriteLine(item)
        Next
    End Sub

  End Module
```

When you build it, the compiler does not show up any warning or error. However, when you set `Option Strict On`, the compiler gives an error message for the `objects` declaration telling you that there is no implicit conversion from an `IList(Of String)` to an `IList(Of Object)`.

The main reason is that the following kinds or relationships between types are often confused:

➤ *Inheritance* — A type descends from another type.

➤ *Realization* — A type implements an interface.

➤ *Generic parameter substitution* — A generic type's type parameters are substituted with concrete (closed) types.

Although `List(Of String)` realizes `IList(Of String)` (that is, a closed form of `IList(Of T)`) just as `List(Of Object)` realizes `IList(Of Object)` (that is, a closed form of `IList(Of T)`), it does not mean that `IList(Of String)` is assignable to an `IList(Of Object)`. Figure 22-3 shows a relationship diagram to help explain why this is so.

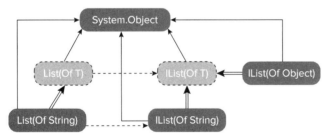

**FIGURE 22-3:** List(Of T) relationship diagram

The solid lines represent inheritance, dashed lines mark realization, and double lines stand for parameter substitution. It is obvious from the figure that the most common ancestor of these types is `System.Object`. While traversing through inheritance and realization in *linear inheritance* (like son, father, and grandfather in a family), parameter substitution means *collateral relation* (such as a second cousin in a family).

`IList(Of String)` and `IList(Of Object)` are in collateral relation. Often, at first sight, developers assume this is linear inheritance just because they share the same generic type as a kind of ancestor. So, there is a false expectation that `IList(Of String)` is assignable with a variable of `IList(Of Object)`.

It is not just an unnecessarily strict check of the compiler. The discussed assignment can even lead to hurting type safety. Look at the following code:

```
Module Module1

    Public strings As IList(Of String) = New List(Of String) From
      {"Zero", "One", "Two", "Three", "Four"}
    Public objects As IList(Of Object) = strings

    Sub Main()
      objects(3) = 3
      Dim three As String = strings(3)
    End Sub

End Module
```

If the `objects` = `strings` assignment were allowed, in the `objects(3)` = 3 assignment, an `Integer` was about to be inserted into a list of `Strings` and subsequently extracted as a `String`. This would be a type-safety violation, so that is why the assignment is invalid, resulting in compilation error.

Note that the whole situation is about how you can substitute instances of types with instances of other types. It is natural for OOP developers to think that substitutions are allowed by linear inheritance, but there are also other cases where theoretically collateral (and other types of) substitutions can be done.

The following code mirrors such a situation:

```
    Public strings As IList(Of String) = New List(Of String)
    Public objects As IEnumerable(Of Object) = strings
```

Note that `IEnumerable(Of T)` has a single method with the signature of the following:

```
    GetEnumerator() As IEnumerator(Of T)
```

Thus, there is no way you can make such an assignment as this in the previous code, so you have no opportunity to put the wrong type of things into `strings` through `objects`, because `objects` doesn't have any method that takes an element in:

```
    objects(3) = 3
```

So, here the assignment that hypothetically could work without issues:

```
    Public objects As IEnumerable(Of Object) = strings
```

If you can enumerate through instances of `System.Object` and use the elements in the enumeration for some operations over `System.Object`, those operations should work, even if you enumerate through instances of `System.String`. Why? Because `System.String` is assignable to a `System.Object`, so you can pass a `System.String` parameter to an operation (method) expecting `System.Object`.

The surprising fact is that this code compiles and works in Visual Basic 2010 with `Option Strict On`, although it does not compile with Visual Basic 2008.

This kind of substitution is called *covariance*. In programming languages, covariance provides the capability to use a more derived type than that originally specified. There is a pair of covariance, *contravariance*, that provides the capability to use a less derived type.

> *Understanding the basics of variance will help you in becoming a more productive developer. Read the "Bird's-Eye View of Variance" section in Chapter 24 to learn more about the concepts behind variance.*

## Variance in Visual Basic 2010

Right now, C# implements only a subset of behavior that theoretically could be achieved by covariance and contravariance. However, the result the CLR designers achieved with this new version are significant and really practical. Both Visual Basic 2010 and C# 4.0 have all features to utilize variance in CLR. The current Visual Basic 2010 variance implementation can be characterized with the following points:

➤ For non-generic types, nothing has been changed from the previous version of Visual Basic by means of variance.

➤ The way of providing variance for generic types is marking type parameters of a generic type as *variant*. Because of a restriction in the CLR, variant type parameters can be declared only on generic interface and delegate types.

➤ Variance only applies when there is a reference conversion between type arguments. For example, variance applies for `IEnumerable(Of String)` and `IEnumerable(Of Object)` because there is a reference conversion between `String` and `Object`. However, the conversion from `Integer` to `Object` is a boxing conversion, and so variance does not apply for `IEnumerable(Of Integer)` and `IEnumerable(Of Object)`.

➤ Variance is not automatic. The compiler will not infer whether a type parameter is covariant or contravariant. Developers must explicitly declare their intentions.

> *When `Option Strict Off` is used, Visual Basic allows any implicit conversion and does not raise any compilation error. When you intentionally use variance, it is highly recommended that you use `Option Strict On` to observe type cast and conversion issues during compile time.*

## Covariance

Following is an example of *covariance*:

```
Public strings As IList(Of String) = New List(Of String)
Public objects As IEnumerable(Of Object) = strings
```

Although this does not compile with Visual Studio 2008 when Option Strict is turned on, it works in Visual Basic 2010. The compiler accepts it, and generates proper code for executing the previous declarations. The key for this behavior is that IEnumerable(Of T) and IEnumerator(Of T) interfaces are declared with a variant type parameter T:

```
Public Interface IEnumerable(Of Out T)
  Inherits IEnumerable

  Function GetEnumerator() As IEnumerator
End Interface

Public Interface IEnumerator(Of Out T)
    Inherits IDisposable, IEnumerator
    ReadOnly Property Current As T
End Interface
```

The only change in the syntax of interface definitions — related to the previous language versions — is the Out modifier in the previous declarations. The Out modifier signifies that the T can only occur in an output position in the interface — otherwise, the compiler will raise an error. This restriction provides (of course, it can be proven) that the interface becomes covariant *in T*, which means that an IEnumerable(Of X) is considered an IEnumerable(Of Y) if X has a reference conversion to Y.

Because of this definition, a sequence of strings can substitute a sequence of objects, and the previous code works. This covariant behavior is very useful in correlation with LINQ query expressions.

To experiment with this, create a console application and name it CovarianceSample. Add a new code file named Pet.vb to the project and paste the code in Listing 22-6 into this new file.

**LISTING 22-6: Pet.vb**

```
Public MustInherit Class Pet
    Public Property NickName As String
    Public Property Age As Integer

    Public Shared Function ShackUpWith( _
      ByVal atHome As IEnumerable(Of Pet), _
      ByVal newComers As IEnumerable(Of Pet)) As IEnumerable(Of Pet)

      Return atHome.Union(newComers)
    End Function

End Class
```

```
Public NotInheritable Class Dog
  Inherits Pet
End Class

Public NotInheritable Class Macaw
  Inherits Pet
End Class
```

*Code file [Pet.vb] available for download at Wrox.com*

Here, you have abstract `Pets` with two concrete manifestations, `Dog` and `Macaw`. These types are intended to be used in a pet shop application, and so `Pet` has an operation named `ShackUpWith` accepting two sequences of pets and returns their union.

Modify the `Module1.vb` file of the application as shown in Listing 22-7.

**LISTING 22-7: Module1.vb of CovarianceSample**

```
Option Strict On
Module Module1

  Sub Main()
    Dim Dogs As New List(Of Dog) From
      {
        New Dog With {.NickName = "Spike", .Age = 3},
        New Dog With {.NickName = "Murray", .Age = 12},
        New Dog With {.NickName = "Peach", .Age = 2}
      }

    Dim Macaws As New List(Of Macaw) From
      {
        New Macaw With {.NickName = "Georgey", .Age = 32},
        New Macaw With {.NickName = "Bella", .Age = 4},
        New Macaw With {.NickName = "Grey", .Age = 11}
      }

    Dim Youngsters =
      From pet In pet.ShackUpWith(Dogs, Macaws)
      Where pet.Age < 5
      Select pet

    For Each pet In Youngsters
      Console.WriteLine(pet.NickName)
    Next
  End Sub

End Module
```

*Code file [Module1.vb] available for download at Wrox.com*

The `ShackUpWith` method used in the query expression expects `IEnumerable(Of Pet)` arguments. But in the previous code, `IEnumerable(Of Dog)` and `IEnumerable(Of Macaw)` instances are passed.

However, because `IEnumerable(Of T)` is covariant in `T`, the compiler accepts it. With Visual Basic 2008 — assuming that you would transform it in this source to the old syntax — this code would not compile with `Option Strict On`! In order to make it work with Visual Basic 2008, you must use a workaround. One possible solution is to cast `Dogs` and `Macaws` to `IEnumerable(Of Pet)`:

```
Dim DogsAsPets As IEnumerable(Of Pet) = Dogs.Cast(Of Pet)()
Dim MacawsAsPets As IEnumerable(Of Pet) = Macaws.Cast(Of Pet)()

Dim Youngsters =
  From pet In pet.ShackUpWith(DogsAsPets, MacawsAsPets)
  Where pet.Age < 5
  Select pet
```

It is much simpler with Visual Basic 2010, isn't it?

## Contravariance

*Contravariance* also works with generic interfaces and delegates in Visual Basic 2010. Create a console application and name it `ContravarianceSample`. Add the `Animal.vb` file to the project with the code in Listing 22-8.

**LISTING 22-8: Animals.vb**

```
Public MustInherit Class Animal
   Implements IComparable(Of Animal)

   Public Property Name As String

   Public Function CompareTo(ByVal other As Animal) As Integer _
     Implements IComparable(Of Animal).CompareTo
     Return Name.CompareTo(other.Name)
   End Function
End Class

Public Class Elephant
  Inherits Animal

  Public Shared Function CompareWithOther(
    ByVal first As IComparable(Of Elephant),
    ByVal other As Elephant) As Integer
    Return first.CompareTo(other)
  End Function
End Class
```

*Code file [Animals.vb] available for download at Wrox.com*

Modify the `Module1.vb` file as shown in Listing 22-9.

**LISTING 22-9:** Module1.vb of ContravarianceSample

```
Module Module1

    Sub Main()
      Dim Jack As New Elephant With {.Name = "Jack"}
      Dim Jane As New Elephant With {.Name = "Jane"}
      Dim compare = Elephant.CompareWithOther(Jane, Jack)
      Console.WriteLine("Jack compared to Jane: {0}", compare)
    End Sub

End Module
```

*Code file [Module1.vb] available for download at Wrox.com*

Although the `CompareWithOther` method in `Elephant` takes an `IComparable(Of Elephant)` instance as its first parameter, it still works in Visual Basic 2010 with an `Elephant` instance, despite the fact that `Elephant` does not implement `IComparable(Of Elephant)`. `Elephant` indirectly (through `Animal`) implements `IComparable(Of Animal)` that can substitute `IComparable (Of Elephant)`. This is because of the definition of `IComparable(Of T)`:

```
Public Interface IComparable(Of In T)
    Function CompareTo(ByVal other As T) As Integer
End Interface
```

The type parameter `T` here uses the `In` variant modifier, restricting `T` to occur only in input positions, and, just as in case of the `Out` modifier, the compiler will check the appropriate usage of `T`. This restriction provides (and, of course, it also can be proven) that the interface becomes *contravariant in T*, which means that an `IComparable(Of X)` is considered an `IComparable(Of Y)` if `X` has a reference conversion to `Y`.

In the example, `Elephant` has a reference conversion to `Animal`, and so `IComparable(Of Elephant)` can be substituted by `IComparable(Of Animal)`.

# A Few More Points on Variance

There are a few important things about the Visual Basic 2010 implementation of variance you should be aware of. These can help you understand the opportunities and limitations you have with this language version.

## Variance with Multiple Type Parameters

At first sight, many developers may think that to be covariant or contravariant is a property of a generic type. This is not true! Variance is a property of type parameters in generic types. When you have a generic type — let's say `MyType(Of T)` — you cannot say "`MyType` is invariant, covariant, or contravariant." What you can say is "`MyType` is invariant, covariant, or contravariant *in T*."

This means you can have generic types that have both covariant and contravariant type parameters. Before you think this is theoretical and might not have practical reason, consider the fact that there are generic types frequently used with such a behavior.

The Func(Of T, TResult) family of generic delegates is defined like this:

```
Public Delegate Function Func(Of In T, Out TResult)
    (ByVal arg As T) As TResult
Public Delegate Function Func(Of In T1, In T2, OutTResult)
    (ByVal arg1 As T1, ByVal arg2 As T2) As TResult
```

You can see that they have both kinds of type parameters. With a simple console application, it is pretty easy to show the power of the generic Func delegate.

Create a console application and name it FuncExample. Add a new Pet.vb file to the project with the code in Listing 22-10.

**LISTING 22-10: Pet.vb in FuncExample**

```
Public MustInherit Class Pet
   Public Property NickName As String
   Public Property Age As Integer
End Class

Public NotInheritable Class Dog
   Inherits Pet
End Class

Public NotInheritable Class Macaw
   Inherits Pet
End Class

Public NotInheritable Class Eagle
   Inherits Pet
End Class
```

*Code file [Pet.vb] available for download at Wrox.com*

You are going to use the Func(Of In T, Out TResult) delegate to define transformations among pets. Listing 22-11 shows the Module1.vb file implementing this functionality.

**LISTING 22-11: Module1.vb in FuncExample**

```
Option Infer On
Option Strict On

Module Module1

  Dim Dogs As New List(Of Dog) From
```

```
    {
      New Dog With {.NickName = "Spike", .Age = 3},
      New Dog With {.NickName = "Murray", .Age = 12},
      New Dog With {.NickName = "Peach", .Age = 2}
    }

  Dim Macaws As New List(Of Macaw) From
    {
      New Macaw With {.NickName = "Georgey", .Age = 32},
      New Macaw With {.NickName = "Bella", .Age = 4},
      New Macaw With {.NickName = "Grey", .Age = 11}
    }

  Sub Main()
    Dim macawsToDogs = TransformMacawTo(Macaws, AddressOf TransformToDog)
    Dim macawsToEagles = TransformMacawTo(Macaws, AddressOf TransformToEagle)
    Dim dogsToEagles = TransformDogTo(Dogs, AddressOf TransformToEagle)
  End Sub

  Private Function TransformMacawTo(
    ByVal pets As IEnumerable(Of Macaw),
    ByVal transformation As Func(Of Macaw, Pet)) As IEnumerable(Of Pet)

    Dim result As New List(Of Pet)
    For Each pet In pets
      result.Add(transformation(pet))
    Next
    Return result
  End Function

  Private Function TransformDogTo(
    ByVal pets As IEnumerable(Of Dog),
    ByVal transformation As Func(Of Dog, Pet)) As IEnumerable(Of Pet)

    Dim result As New List(Of Pet)
    For Each pet In pets
      result.Add(transformation(pet))
    Next
    Return result
  End Function

  Private Function TransformToDog(ByVal macaw As Macaw) As Dog
    Return New Dog With {.NickName = macaw.NickName, .Age = macaw.Age}
  End Function

  Private Function TransformToEagle(ByVal pet As Pet) As Eagle
    Return New Eagle With {.NickName = pet.NickName, .Age = pet.Age}
  End Function

End Module
```

*Code file [Module1.vb] available for download at Wrox.com*

In the `TransformMacawTo` function, the `Func(Of Macaw, Pet)` delegate is used, while in the `TransformDogTo` function, a `Func(Of Dog, Pet)` argument, is passed.

Two functions, `TransformToDog` and `TransfromToEagle`, are responsible for performing the "magical change" of pets. The following lines of codes utilize variance:

```
Dim macawsToDogs = TransformMacawTo(Macaws, AddressOf TransformToDog)
Dim macawsToEagles = TransformMacawTo(Macaws, AddressOf TransformToEagle)
Dim dogsToEagles = TransformDogTo(Dogs, AddressOf TransformToEagle)
```

In the first two `TransformMacawTo` calls, the `Func(Of Macaw, Pet)` arguments are substituted with `Func(Of Macaw, Dog)` and `Func(Of Pet, Eagle)`, respectively. In the invocation of `TransformDogTo`, a `Func(Of Pet, Eagle)` is used instead of the `Func(Of Dog, Pet)`. It is entirely valid, strongly typed, and no type conversion magic is done behind the scenes!

Why can, for example, `Func(Of Dog, Pet)` be substituted with `Func(Of Pet, Eagle)`? The fact that `Func(Of Dog, Pet)` is covariant in `Pet` means that you can return a `Pet` derived type, namely `Eagle`, because an `Eagle` is a `Pet`. The same thinking says that `Func(Of Dog, Pet)` is contravariant in `Dog`, and so any operation with `Pet` also will work on `Dog`, because `Dog` is derived from `Pet`. Therefore, `Func(Of Pet, Eagle)` is a good substitution for `Func(Dog, Pet)`.

## Variance with User Types

Obviously, you are not constrained to using only the existing generic types with variant type parameters. You can create your own generic interfaces and delegates. You can use the `In` modifier for signifying a contravariant, and the `Out` modifier for a covariant type parameter. Without a modifier, the type parameter remains invariant.

For example, consider the following declarations:

```
Public Interface IMyOperations(Of In T, U, V)
    '...
End Interface
Public Delegate Function MyDelegate(Of In T, U, Out X)
    (ByVal tPar As T, ByVal uPar As U) As X
```

Here, `X` is covariant, `T` is contravariant, and `U` and `V` are invariant type parameters.

The compiler checks to ensure that you keep within the rules for variant type parameters. For example, in the following interface definitions, all method declarations are invalid because one or more contravariant type parameters are in output positions:

```
Public Interface IMyOperations(Of In T, In U, V)
    Function OutputUnsafeOp1() As T
    Function OutputUnsafeOp2() As U()
    Function OutputUnsafeOp3() As List(Of T)
    Function OutputUnsafeOp4() As Func(Of V, U)
    Sub OutputUnsafeOp5(ByRef tpar As T)
    Sub OutputUnsafeOp6(ByRef par As Func(Of V, U))
End Interface
```

Similarly, in the following interface definition, all operations are invalid because covariant type parameters are in input positions:

```
Public Interface IMyOperations(Of Out T, U)
  Sub InputUnsafeOp1(ByVal tPar As T)
  Function InputUnsafeOp2(ByVal tPar() As T) As U
  Function InputUnsafeOp3(ByRef tPar As T) As Func(Of U, T)
End Interface
```

The Visual Basic 2010 language specification calls these invalid type parameters *output-unsafe* and *input-unsafe* types, and precisely defines the context they are unsafe within. With the introduction of variant type parameters, the type inference algorithm used by the compiler also has been modified.

## Variance and Reflection

The .NET Framework's reflection model can be used to obtain information about the variance of a type parameter. In Listing 22-12, you have a simple console application's `Module1.vb` file demonstrating the reflection model used to query variance information.

Available for download on Wrox.com

**LISTING 22-12: Module1.vb to Query Reflection About Variance**

```
Imports System.Reflection

Module Module1

  Sub Main()
    Dim Asm = GetType(IEnumerable()).Assembly
    Dim GenericTypes =
      From type In Asm.GetTypes()
      Where type.IsGenericTypeDefinition And type.IsPublic
      Select type
    For Each type In GenericTypes
      Console.WriteLine("{0}: ", type.Name)
      For Each typeParam In type.GetGenericArguments()
        Dim variance = typeParam.GenericParameterAttributes And
          GenericParameterAttributes.VarianceMask
        If (variance And GenericParameterAttributes.Covariant) <> 0 Then
          Console.WriteLine("  {0}: covariant", typeParam.Name)
        ElseIf (variance And GenericParameterAttributes.Contravariant) <> 0 Then
          Console.WriteLine("  {0}: contravariant", typeParam.Name)
        Else
          Console.WriteLine("  {0}: invariant", typeParam.Name)
        End If
      Next
    Next
  End Sub

End Module
```

*Code file [Module1.vb] available for download at Wrox.com*

This code iterates through all generic types in the `System` assembly and writes out their type parameter information. The nested `For Each` cycle goes through the type parameters, and uses the `GenericParameterAttributes` property of `System.Type` to obtain information about variance. This property's value is a `GenericParameterAttributes` enumeration instance with flags. The `VarianceMask` value of the enumeration can be used to separate the flags describing variance from the ones describing type parameter constraints. `Covariant` and `Contravariant` flags define the parameter behavior. If neither of them is set, the type parameter is invariant.

## SUMMARY

The Visual Basic language has received several great syntax improvements that neither change how you program with Visual Basic, nor provide you brand-new paradigms. However, they are still very useful, because they make your code shorter and more readable, altogether improving your productivity.

In Visual Basic 2010, you can omit the line continuation underscore from almost all places. Auto-implemented properties, collection initializers, and array literals allow you to type fewer characters to express the same thing as in the preceding version of the language.

Visual Basic 2010 allows using multiline lambda expressions, and now you can turn not only functions, but also subroutines, into lambdas. With this improvement, lambda expressions in Visual Basic become as powerful as the C# implementation.

Visual Basic has a great compiler feature, late binding, which allows the Visual Basic run-time to resolve and execute operations dynamically at run-time. This feature provides a significant simplification of consuming COM object models. Visual Basic 2010 improves this mechanism by integrating the late binding with the Dynamic Language Run-time (DLR). If a late-bound call is made to an object that is a dynamic object (implements the `IDynamicMetaObjectProvider` interface), Visual Basic binds to the dynamic object by using that interface.

Visual Basic 2010 introduces new forms of variance. With type parameters of generic interfaces and delegates signified as covariant or contravariant, from now on, the programming language has a much more flexible type substitution model than ever before.

In Chapter 23, you will learn about the history of C# — the other significant .NET programming language, often said to be "the native programming language of .NET."

# PART V
# C#

▶ **CHAPTER 23:** History of C#

▶ **CHAPTER 24:** C# 4.0 Language Improvements

# 23

# History of C#

Over the course of the past decade or so, the C# language (and, of course, the .NET Framework) has evolved to become a determining part of modern software development. From its first release in the beginning of 2002, the C# language has gone through an amazing progression, and attracted millions of developers into the .NET camp. As of today, C# is in its fourth version.

This chapter provides a brief overview of the history of the C# language. The discussions in this chapter do not teach you the language, which is definitely not in the scope of this book. Rather, the discussions in this chapter assume that you have already used the language. If you are a Visual Basic developer, this chapter also helps you to stay in context.

This chapter addresses the following topics:

> ➤ A brief history of the C# language

> ➤ The main characteristic of C# (as it was established in C# 1.0)

> ➤ A brief overview of features in C# 2.0 and C# 3.0

After having so many Visual Studio and .NET Framework releases in the past, it is now safe to say that every major Visual Studio release hosts a new version of the C# language. The same holds true for Visual Studio 2010, which introduces C# 4.0. In Chapter 25, you'll learn about the details of the new features found in C# 4.0.

## THE EVOLUTION OF C#

Today, C# is a multi-paradigm programming language. However, it started out as a general-purpose, object-oriented language.

The development team of the C# language was led by Anders Hejlsberg, who joined Microsoft in 1996 (and who is still the leader of the development team) after being exceptionally successful with Turbo Pascal and Delphi at Borland. At that time, Microsoft had already worked on something that later became the Common Language Run-time (CLR). Hejlsberg's team also put a lot of energy into getting rid of the common flaws found in major programming languages. Recognizing those flaws helped considerably in establishing the CLR, and also drove the development of the C# programming language.

Today, the name C# (pronounced as "C sharp") is used without any questions about what "#" really means in the name, because today's developers are used to languages ending with "sharp" (for example, J# or F#). The name of the programming language was inspired from the musical notation where a "sharp" indicates that the note should be made a half step higher in pitch. This kind of inspiration is not unique — just think of the C++ programming language, where "++" implies "something more than C". The "#" in the name simply means "++" in two rows — in other words, "(C++)++", suggesting to some that C# is superior to C++.

## Design Goals

The developers of C# got a lot of inspiration from C++ and Java in regard to both popular language features and flaws. The original design goal was to create a simple and modern general-purpose programming language that leveraged the object-oriented paradigms. The designers also wanted to create a language that was a first-class citizen in developing software components suitable for deployment in distributed environments. Less obvious was the fact that the team aimed C# to be suitable for writing applications for both hosted and embedded systems, independently of whether a large and sophisticated operating system was used or a very small one with dedicated functions.

Learning from the common flaws of major programming languages, the team focused on creating a language that provided support for software engineering principles such as strong types, array bounds checking, detection of attempts to use uninitialized variables, and automatic garbage collection.

## Short History

The history and evolution of C# cannot be uncoupled from the .NET Framework. Their origins have the same root, and their co-evolution is still inspired by the same forces moving the technology toward future trends.

The predecessor of the .NET Framework was called *Common Object Run-time* (COR). Traces of it can still be found, for example, in the name of the Microsoft Common Object Run-time Library (mscorlib.dll). At that time, the class library of COR was written in a managed code compiler called *Simple Managed C*. The team formed by Anders Hejlsberg started to develop the new language, and it wore the name *Cool*, which stood for "C-like Object Oriented Language." This name was so overloaded that Microsoft did not keep it because of trademark reasons, and renamed it to C#. By the time .NET was announced at PDC 2000, the class libraries were ported to C#.

According to the design goals, Microsoft decided to start the submission of the C# language specification as well as the Common Language Infrastructure (CLI) specification to the European Computer Manufacturers Association (ECMA). This submission was also co-sponsored by Hewlett-Packard and Intel Corporation. About 16 months later, the process resulted in the

ECMA-334 standard (December 2001). Microsoft also started the standardization at International Organization for Standardization (ISO), with C# becoming an ISO standard in 2003 with the moniker ISO/IEC 23270:2003.

In January 2002, the big leap reached the developer community. Visual Studio .NET (also known as VS 2002) was released with C# 1.0 (and Visual Basic .NET). The C# 1.0 compiler was the part of the .NET SDK, and Visual Studio included "only" the developer's workbench for the language. Although the .NET framework had been fixed and polished in 2003 and also a new Visual Studio version (VS 2003) had been released in April 2003, the C# language it used was the C# 1.0 specification.

The next roaring success of the language was C# 2.0 with its most appreciated feature: *generics*. In later interviews, Hejlsberg said the team had this feature on its list from the beginning, but there had simply not been enough time to implement it in .NET 1.0 or 1.1.

The implementation of generics was very important from the C# language point of view. It was not only a feature that enabled better code reusability, but also an important part in the move toward the functional programming paradigm. This new language version was released with Visual Studio 2005 in October 2005.

The related ECMA and ISO standards were also updated according to the new C# 2.0 features.

Released with Visual Studio 2008, C# 3.0 made another huge leap with the introduction of *Language Integrated Query* (*LINQ*) and *query expressions*. LINQ itself is a .NET Framework component that adds native data querying capabilities to .NET languages. Query expressions represent a new form of data query syntax that resembles the SQL language. With LINQ involved in C#, the language took a new programming paradigm shift from the imperative approach to the direction of declarative and functional programming. Parallel with the query expressions, the language included small (but significant) "syntactic sugar" features primarily intended to make the bed for LINQ, but these features individually were also very useful.

Microsoft has not submitted C# 3.0 for standardization. The most current versions of the standards for the C# programming language are ISO/IEC 23270:2006 and ECMA-334 4th edition.

The newest version of the language is version 4.0, released with Visual Studio 2010. The step from C# 3.0 to 4.0 signals that it really has become a multi-paradigm programming language. This new version introduces such new features as support for dynamic types, which introduces a great way to interoperate with dynamic languages. C# now has named and optional parameters that, among other things, allow using COM object hierarchies from C# with the same ease as in Visual Basic and scripts.

What will be in C# 5.0? Right now, there is no official information from Microsoft about what the language team is working on. But, because a new Visual Studio release is scheduled for every two years, you can be sure that the team is definitely working on new and exciting features to be encapsulated into C#.

## Implementations

Because the C# language is standardized, Microsoft Visual C# is not the only implementation, although it is the most used. There are other implementations that generally integrate the C#

language compiler, together with the CLI, which is also standardized. Following is a brief list of well-known C# and CLI implementations:

➤ *Mono project* — This is considered by some to be the best non-Microsoft implementation of an Open Source C# compiler, as well as a complete implementation of the CLI with the required framework libraries as they appear in the ECMA specification. Mono was led by Ximian for a long time; as of this writing, it is now led by Novell.

➤ *DotGNU* — A part of the GNU Project by Free Software Foundation, this also provides an Open Source C# compiler and CLI with framework libraries as required by the ECMA specification. However, this implementation is not yet complete.

➤ *Shared Source Common Language Infrastructure* — This Microsoft project is licensed for education and research only (formerly known as *Rotor*). This is a shared source implementation of a C# compiler and a subset of required framework libraries, according to the ECMA CLI specification.

## C# 1.0

This section provides a brief overview features included with this version of the programming language. Rather than teaching you C#, this discussion assumes that you have experience with this language — or at least with any other .NET language.

From its first version, C# has been the programming language that most directly reflects the underlying CLI by design, and this trait has not changed over time. Most of the intrinsic types in C# correspond to value types implemented by the CLI framework.

## Type System

C# has a unified type system that is the Common Type System in the .NET Framework. Each type has a root ancestor, namely System.Object. This type system separates data types into two categories:

➤ *Value types* — These are plain aggregations of data, and their instances do not have either referential identity or referential comparison semantics at all. Operations on value types are carried out with the actual data within the instances.

➤ *Reference types* — These have the notion of referential identity. Each instance of a reference type is inherently distinct from every other instance, even if the data within both instances is the same.

Both type categories can be extended by user-defined types. The value behind a value type instance can be converted into a value of a corresponding reference type by the *boxing operation* that is implicit in the C# language. The previously boxed value of a reference type can be converted into an instance of a value type with the unboxing operation. However, this requires an explicit type cast. The type system allows full type reflection and discovery.

There are no global variables or global functions in C#. All methods and data members must be declared within types. The following "Hello, World" example mirrors this fact:

```
using System;

class ExampleClass
{
  static void Main()
  {
      Console.WriteLine("Hello, world!");
  }
}
```

C# is *type safe*. It puts more emphasis on type safety than C++. The only implicit conversions by default are those that are considered safe (such as widening of integers). This is enforced by the C# compiler and even at run-time. C# has an intrinsic type for Booleans (the System.Boolean type), and there are no implicit conversions between Booleans and integers, or between enumeration members and integers (except for literal 0). Any user-defined conversion must be marked as explicit or implicit.

*Multiple inheritance* is not supported by the language. A class can have only one base class but is allowed to implement any number of interfaces. This was a design decision by the language's lead architect to avoid complication, avoid dependency hell, and simplify architectural requirements throughout the CLI.

## Memory Management

The C# language has the new operator to allocate type instances from the memory. However, it does not have any statement, function, or operator to explicitly free the allocated managed memory. Instead, it is automatically garbage-collected. *Garbage collection* addresses memory leaks by freeing the programmer of responsibility for releasing memory that is no longer needed. It is a non-deterministic mechanism.

The CLR supports deterministic finalization with the dispose pattern (IDisposable behavior). C# leverages on this CLR feature with its using statement, as shown here:

```
public class UsingExample
{
  public static void Main()
  {
    using(FileStream fs = new FileStream("log.txt"))
      using(StreamWriter log = new StreamWriter(fs))
      {
        log.WriteLine("This is a log entry.");
      }
  }
}
```

C# does not allow directly using *pointers*. However, reference types physically use pointers as their implementation, and you can use them only for referencing the objects behind them. No pointer arithmetic is available.

In C#, memory address pointers can only be used within blocks specifically marked as unsafe, and programs with unsafe code need appropriate permissions to run. Most object access is done through safe object references, which always either point to a "live" object or have the well-defined `null` value. It is impossible to obtain a reference to a random block of memory.

An unsafe pointer can point to an instance of a value type, array, string, or a block of memory allocated on a stack. Code that is not marked as unsafe can still store and manipulate pointers through the `System.IntPtr` type (which provides interoperability between managed and unmanaged code), but it cannot dereference them.

## Syntactic Sugar

The design team added some "syntactic sugar" to the language right at the beginning in C# 1.0 (and they kept adding this sugar from version by version).

*Enumeration members* in C# have their own scope, and can be used only by specifying the scope name. For example, consider the following enumeration type members:

```
enum MyPrimeNumbers
{
  Three = 3,
  Five = 5,
  Seven = 7
}
```

These can be used only when specifying `MyPrimeNumbers` as their scope:

```
MyPrimeNumbers pickFirst = MyPrimeNumbers.Three;
MyPrimeNumbers pickThird = MyPrimeNumbers.Seven;
```

C# includes concept of *properties,* which are members with *accessors* (getter and setter methods) that syntactically behave like fields. This concept was not new with the development of C#; it existed before in Delphi and Visual Basic 6. However, C# binds the accessors to the scope of a property declaration, as shown in the following example:

```
class MyClass
{
  private int _CountOfMembers;

  public int CountOfMembers
  {
    get { return _CountOfMembers; }
    set { _CountOfMembers = value; }
  }
}
```

The C# language has been inspired by Javadoc and has its own XML-based documentation system. Comments intended to be the part of the documentation use special comment tokens — `///` for "rest-of-the-line" comments, and `/**` and `*/` token pairs for multi-line comments. The ECMA C# standard provides a non-normative annex for defining the XML markups of documentation comments. This annex also treats comment processing rules, and their transformation to a plain

XML document in order to create the appropriate mappings between CLI elements (types, members, and so on) and related comments.

The following example illustrates how XML comments are used:

```
/// <summary>
/// This abstract class defines an attribute with a simple string value.
/// </summary>
/// <remarks>
/// The class is intended to derive new attributes having a simple string value.
/// Do not use this class to add other properties to the attribute!
/// </remarks>
public abstract class StringAttribute : Attribute
{
  /** <summary>
      Creates a new instance of this attribute and sets its initial value.
      </summary>
      <param name="value">Initial attribute value.</param> */
  protected StringAttribute(string value)
  {
    Value = value;
  }
  // ...
}
```

# C# 1.1

You can find many web pages and blog entries mentioning or picturing C# 1.1 as an individual release of the language. Well, there was a .NET Framework 1.1 release that came together with Visual Studio 2003. Of course, this version contained a new C# compiler, but it was still about implementing the C# 1.0 language.

Whenever C# 1.1 is mentioned, it probably means that the related examples are intended to be used together with Visual Studio 2003 and/or .NET Framework 1.1.

C# 1.1 never existed as a separate version of the programming language.

# C# 2.0

When C# 1.0 was designed, only a few dozen people had been involved in the process, and the specification mirrors mainly their programming experience. After the release of C# 1.0, the number of direct language influencers went to a few hundred, with tens of thousands indirectly having feedback on the strength and weaknesses of C#.

.NET 2.0 brought great changes into the Common Type System. The feature of *generic types* that really had been missing from the previous versions was added to the framework, and the C# language also implemented this feature. This change was so significant that the first word used to characterize C# 2.0 is almost always "generics."

However, in addition to generic types, there were several other great features added to the language in response to the community feedback and experiences that made C# 2.0 a very mature programming language, including the following:

➤ Partial types

➤ Static classes

➤ Iterators

➤ Anonymous methods

➤ Delegate inference

➤ Delegate covariance and contravariance

➤ Nullable types

➤ Property accessors

➤ Null-coalesce operators

➤ Namespace aliases

Let's dive into some details of these features.

## Generic Types

Generic types allow you to define type-safe data structures, without committing to actual data types. This results in higher-quality code, because you can reuse data processing algorithms without duplicating type-specific code.

There is a similar concept in C++, called "templates," but while templates in C++ are supported by a compiler, .NET generic types are implemented at the CLR level. Although there are entire books dedicated to generics, this section provides a brief overview without deeper explanations.

The C# world before generics never offered a type-safe way to encapsulate common behavior into a type. For example, if you wanted to create a behavior describing how a queue works and intended to use it with both `int` and your own `Order` type, you had to create a workaround. Either you implemented two separate types called `IntQueue` and `OrderQueue` or created a single `Queue` type that accepted `System.Objects`. The first implementation has issues with code maintenance, while the second has issues with providing type safety and performance.

C# generics allow you to use *type parameters* with type and method definitions. These definitions are called *open type definitions*, as shown in the following example:

```
public class Queue<T>
{
  public Enqueue(T item) { ... }
  public T Dequeue() { ... }
  public bool IsEmpty { get { ... } }
}
```

In this sample definition, T is the type parameter. When it is time to use the definitions for concrete types, T is substituted with the type you intend to use, together with the behavior Queue offers:

```
Queue<int> intQueue = new Queue<int>;
intQueue.Enqueue(42);
Queue<Order> orderQueue = new Queue<Order>
// ...
while (!orderQueue.IsEmpty)
{
  Order order = orderQueue.Dequeue();
  // ...
}
```

The types where the type parameter is substituted with a concrete type are called *closed types*. You are not limited to use only one type parameter; you can use more. For example, the following declaration lets you define a node in a linked list, where K represents the type used as the key of the node, and N is the type representing the value of a node:

```
public class LinkedNode<K, N> { ... }
```

You can also add type parameter constraints to your types to restrict them to a subset of types. For example, when you allow only value types for being keys, and want to be sure that node elements can be compared, the previous type definition can be constrained like this:

```
public class LinkedNode<K, N>
  where K: struct
  where N: IComparable
{ ... }
```

You can use generic types as base types using either open or closed types, as shown in the following examples:

```
public class SortedNode<K, N>: LinkedNode<K, N>
  where K: struct
  where N: IComparable
{ ... }

public class CodeNode<N>: LinkedNode<int, N>
  where N: IComparable
{ ... }

public class OrderNode: LinkedNode<int, Order> { ... }
```

Not only types, but you can also use methods with generics, as shown here:

```
public class MyUtilities
{
  public void WriteToDebug<T>(T item) { ... }
  public void Serialize<T>(T item)
    where T: ISerializable
  { ... }
}
```

Even static and virtual methods can leverage on generics, as shown here:

```
public class BaseClass
{
  public static void WriteToDebug<T>(T item) { ... }
  public virtual void SomeMethod<T>(T t) { ... }
}

public class SubClass: BaseClass
{
  public override void SomeMethod<T>(T t) { ... }
}
```

Operators and delegates are implemented as methods behind the scenes, and both of them support generics with all the power of generic methods. Here is a small example of defining and consuming generic delegates:

```
public class MyClass<T>
{
    public delegate void GenericDelegate(T t);
    public void SomeMethod(T t) { ... }
}

// --- Use the delegate
MyClass<int> obj = new MyClass<int>();
MyClass<int>.GenericDelegate del;

del = new MyClass<int>.GenericDelegate(obj.SomeMethod);
del(3);
```

In .NET 2.0, reflection is extended to support generic type parameters. The type `System.Type` can now represent generic types with specific type arguments (closed types), or unspecified (open) types.

Also, many types in .NET 2.0 — especially collections — had been changed or added to support generics. For example, `Array` type has now about a dozen new generic methods, and there are many new generic collection classes to provide a new and performance-boosted experience related to the old .NET 1.1 collection types.

## Partial Types

The limitation that type definitions had to be entirely in only one physical file was a bottleneck in C# 1.0, making the life of developers unnecessarily difficult. Large type definitions could not be split, and that was especially disadvantageous for those who used code generation intensively, because generated code could not be easily separated from user-defined code.

*Partial types* solve this issue. By using the `partial` keyword, class, structure, and interface definitions can be split to spread out in multiple files. This solves the problem of separation of user-defined and generated code. During compile time the partitions of the type definition are merged, including attributes, base classes and interfaces, and access modifiers.

For example, you can split MyClass into two parts, as shown in the following example:

```
// --- MyClass1.cs
[Serializable]
public partial class MyClass
{
  private bool _IsDisposed;
}

// --- MyClass2.cs
partial class MyClass : IDisposable
{
  public bool IsDisposed
  {
    get { return _IsDisposed; }
  }
  public void Dispose()
  {
    // --- Implement the logic here
    _IsDisposed = true;
  }
}
```

The result of merging the partitions is a public class named MyClass implementing the IDisposable interface and decorated with the Serializable attribute.

## Static Classes

*Static classes* are classes that cannot be instantiated, so you cannot use the new keyword to create a variable of the class type. Before C# 2.0, you could use only the singleton pattern to have types with exactly one instance.

By definition, static classes can contain only static members and no instance members, so they do not have instance constructors. The only base type allowed for static classes is Sytem.Object, and the class is sealed.

The MyMath class is an example of a simple static class, as shown here:

```
public static class MyMath
{
  private static double _LastResult;

  static MyMath() { _LastResult = 0.0; }
  public static double Add(double a, double b) {return _LastResult = a + b; }
  public static double Subtract(double a, double b) { return _LastResult = a - b; }
  public static double LastResult
  {
    get { return _LastResult; }
  }
}
```

You can use the class members directly by naming the class as you would for any ordinary static members, just like in the following code snippet:

```
double x = 2.0;
double y = 3.0;
doube result = MyMath.Add(x, y);
Console.WriteLine(MyMath.LastResult);
```

## Iterators

C# was designed with the capability to iterate over data structures implementing a GetEnumerator method that retrieves an instance with the IEnumerator behavior. The IEnumerable interface defines this behavior. However, implementing a data structure passing back an IEnumerator instance is laborious. You must implement IEnumerator's Current, MoveNext, and Reset methods.

C# 2.0 introduced the yield construct that is based on the proven theory that iterators can be implemented as deterministic state machines. You simply describe the iterator as a method using the yield return and yield break statements, as the following code snippet illustrates:

```
public IEnumerable<int> FibonacciUpToMillion()
{
  int fib0 = 0;
  int fib1 = 1;
  while(true)
  {
    int fibNext = fib0 + fib1;
    fib0 = fib1;
    fib1 = fibNext;
    if (fibNext > 1000000) yield break;
    yield return fibNext;
  }
}
```

This method creates numbers of the Fibonacchi-sequence, unless the subsequent number exceeds the value of 1 million. The yield return statement passes back the next item in the sequence, and the yield break statement stops the iteration. You can simply use the sequence just as any other data collection, as shown here:

```
foreach (int number in FibonacciUpToMillion())
{
  Console.WriteLine(number);
}
```

## Anonymous Methods

C# delegates provide operators and methods for adding and removing target methods, and are used extensively throughout the .NET Framework for events, callbacks, asynchronous calls, and multithreading. However, you are sometimes forced to create a class or a method just for the sake of using a delegate. The capability to create *anonymous methods* was a new feature in C# 2.0 that enabled you to define an anonymous (that is, nameless) method called by a delegate.

For example, the following is a conventional DoTheWork method definition and delegate invocation:

```
class MyClass
{
  delegate void MyDelegate();
  public void InvokeMethod()
  {
    MyDelegate del = new MyDelegate(DoTheWork);
    del();
  }
  void DoTheWork()
  {
    MessageBox.Show("Hello");
  }
}
```

You can define and implement this with an anonymous method, as the following snippet illustrates:

```
class MyClass
{
  delegate void MyDelegate();
  public void InvokeMethod()
  {
    MyDelegate del = delegate();
                     {
                        MessageBox.Show("Hello");
                     };
    del();
  }
}
```

## Delegate Inference

The C# 2.0 compiler featured *delegate inference*, which enables you to make a direct assignment of a method name to a delegate variable, without wrapping it first with a delegate object. You could write the following code:

```
public void InvokeMethod()
{
  MyDelegate del = new MyDelegate(DoTheWork);
  del();
}
void DoTheWork() { ... }
```

With delegate inference, the declaration of the del variable becomes as simple as the following:

```
MyDelegate del = DoTheWork;
```

## Delegate Covariance and Contravariance

C# 2.0 introduced *covariance* and *contravariance* to provide a degree of flexibility when matching method signatures with delegate types.

Covariance permits a method to have a more derived return type than what is defined in the delegate. The following example demonstrates covariance:

```
class Vertebrata { }
class Birds : Vertebrata { }
delegate Vertebrata Handler();

class Program
{
  Vertebrata FirstHandler() { return new Vertebrata(); }
  Birds SecondHandler() { return new Birds(); }

  static void Main()
  {
    Handler handler1 = FirstHandler;
    // --- Covariance allows this:
    Handler handler2 = SecondHandler;
  }
}
```

The data type returned by `SecondHandler` is of type `Birds`, which derives from the `Vertebrata` type defined in the delegate.

Contravariance permits a method with parameter types that are less derived than in the delegate type. With contravariance, you can now use one event handler in places where, previously, you would have had to use separate handlers. The following code snippet illustrates how it works:

```
public partial class Form1 : Form
{
  public Form1()
  {
    InitializeComponent();
    this.MouseDown += InputEvent;
    this.MouseUp += InputEvent;
    this.KeyDown += InputEvent;
    this.KeyUp += InputEvent;
  }

  private void InputEvent(object sender, EventArgs e)
  {
    Debug.WriteLine("Input event occured at {0}", DateTime.Now);
  }
}
```

The `InputEvent` handler accepts an `EventArgs` input parameter and uses it with the `MouseUp` and `MouseDown` events that send a `MouseEventArgs` type as a parameter, and also with the `KeyDown` and `KeyUp` events that send a `KeyEventArgs` parameter.

## Nullable Types

In C# 1.0, one of the weaknesses of value types versus reference types was the lack of value type's "nullability." To eliminate this weakness, the C# 2.0 designers added the concept of *nullable types* to the language.

This feature also required a change in the CLR. A new generic type, the System.Nullable<T> structure, was introduced, where T should be a value type.

The C# 2.0 syntax allows assigning null to a System.Nullable<T> instance, and to compare an instance value with null. You can also use shortcut syntax in form of T? instead of writing out Nullable<T>. The HasValue Boolean property tells if a nullable instance has a value, and, if it has, it can be obtained through the Value property.

Using these properties, you can define the null-aware Square method, as shown in the following example:

```
public int? Square(int? n)
{
  return n.HasValue
    ? n.Value * n.Value
    : null;
}
```

The Nullable<T> also defines an explicit cast operator from T? to T, and an implicit cast operator from T to T?, so the following declarations are all correct:

```
int? firstValue = 4;
int? secondValue = 5;
int? sumValue = firstValue + secondValue;
int squareValue = (int)sumValue;
```

However, because the implicit conversion from T? to T is not allowed, some of the following assignments will result in compilation errors:

```
int? firstValue = 4;
int? secondValue = 5;
int myValue = secondValue; // --- Cannot convert int? to int
int sumValue = firstValue + secondValue; // --- Cannot convert int? to int
```

## Property Accessors

Although a property's access modifier applies to both the get and set accessors, you can add a separate modifier to one of them. This modifier can narrow the accessibility scope of the corresponding accessor, but never widen it.

For example, the following declaration allows reading the MyValue property for everyone, but only derived classes can change it:

```
public int MyValue
{
  get { return _MyValue; }
  protected set { _MyValue = value; }
}
```

## Null-Coalesce Operator

A minor (but nice) feature of C# 2.0 was the *null-coalesce operator* that helps in the substitution of the `null` value with appropriate replacement. You no longer had to write something like the following:

```
string name = nameSpecified == null ? "Type a name" : nameSpecified;
```

Instead, you can use the `??` null-coalesce operator as a shortcut for that expression, as shown here:

```
string name = nameSpecified ?? "Type a name";
```

## Namespace Aliases

C# 2.0 introduced the *namespace alias* qualifier (`::`) that provides more control over accessing namespace members. The `global ::` alias allows access to the root namespace that may be hidden by an entity in your code.

This operator can help you a lot in name and type resolution when you have exactly the same full names for different types in separate assemblies. Let's assume that you have two assemblies from two vendors where a nice label control is named as `Controls.NiceLabel` in both assemblies. The namespace alias qualifier helps to resolve this situation. You can use separate aliases for the assemblies, as shown here:

```
extern alias AcmeGadgets; // --- Alias for the assembly made by AcmeGadgets
extern alias SuperControls; // --- Alias for the assembly provided by SuperControls
```

When it is time to resolve the controls, you can use the namespace qualifier, as shown here:

```
AcmeGadgets::Controls.NiceLabel
SuperControls::Controls.NiceLabel
```

## C# 3.0

C# 3.0 probably added the most exciting features to the language. This version added a functional approach to the language in order to allow programmers create data-processing operations where they express what they want to get, instead of expressing how they want to obtain the results.

The pivotal feature of this version is definitely the support of LINQ via the query expressions that became very popular because of their readability and expressiveness. To achieve that strength, the following other "syntax noise-reduction" features were put into the language, which have proven useful even if you grab them out of the context of query expressions:

- ➤ Local variable type inference
- ➤ Extension methods
- ➤ Anonymous types

- ➤ Lambda expressions
- ➤ Query expressions
- ➤ Expression trees
- ➤ Automatic properties
- ➤ Object initializers
- ➤ Collection initializers
- ➤ Partial methods

Let's take a look at some the details of these features.

## Local Variable Type Inference

There are a few points in the C# language where you could say the syntax is "noisy" — developers have to type many characters to express their intention. For example, when you want to declare a local variable for a dictionary and immediately initialize it, you do it with some code similar to the following:

```
Dictionary<int, string> myCodeTable = new Dictionary<int, string>();
```

In this definition, writing the `Dictionary<int, string>` expression twice is what you could call *syntax noise*.

The *local variable type inference* feature introduces the `var` context-sensitive keyword that reduces this noise, as shown here:

```
var myCodeTable = new Dictionary<int, string>();
```

The `var` keyword can be used only for local variable declarations where the variable has an initialize expression. It is used as an "abbreviation," and the compiler will generate exactly the same code as if you explicitly declared the `myCodeTable` variable as `Dictionary<int, string>`. When you declare a local variable with `var`, you actually tell the compiler, "Please parse the expression to the right of the equal sign and infer its type. I want my local variable declared with the type you've inferred."

You can use this type of implicitly typed local variable declaration in `for`, `foreach`, and `using` statements, as well

## Extension Methods

Developers often write wrapper methods for objects that, in reality, could be the parts of the object itself. A good example is a method to check whether or not all characters in a string are in uppercase. This declaration can be put into a static helper class, just like in the following code extract:

```
public static class StringHelper
{
  public static bool IsAllUpper(string s) { ... }
}
```

When using this helper class, you write code something like this:

```
string myString = ...;
bool isUpper = StringHelper.IsAllUpper(myString);
```

*Extension methods* provide a way to implement the same pattern and use it with a nicer, and more readable, syntax. An extension method is a static method in a static class that accepts its first parameter (and maybe the only one) on its parameter list, signing it with the `this` keyword, just like in the following example:

```
public static class StringHelper
{
  public static bool IsAllUpper(this string s) { ... }
}
```

The type accepted in the first parameter is the type this method virtually extends. This "extension" means that this static method can be syntactically used as if it were the instance method of the type it extends:

```
string myString = ...;
bool isUpper = myString.IsAllUpper();
```

In order for the compiler to recognize extension methods, you must import the namespaces containing the extender class.

## Anonymous Types

One of the most convenient features of C# 3.0 is the capability to create new types "on-the-fly" using *anonymous types*. These are essentially compiler-generated types that you don't explicitly declare with a separate type declaration. Instead, you define the type inline as part of the code where you need to use the new type.

The syntax to declare an anonymous type looks something like this:

```
var customer = new
{
  ID = 112,
  Name = "John Doe",
  IsKeyAccount = true
};
```

Of course, there is no magic here. The compiler creates a real type behind the scenes, but does not expose its name to you. Because of the local variable type inference, you can declare variables for the anonymous type instance without the need to name the type explicitly, as shown here:

```
var myCustomer = customer;
customer.IsKeyAccount = false;
```

Anonymous types have a signature composed from the names and types of properties they have. When you declare several anonymous types having the same signature, they will share a common type declaration, because the compiler recognizes this scenario and creates optimized code.

# Lambda Expressions

*Lambda expressions* provide a new and concise syntax to describe an anonymous function that can contain expressions and statements, and can be used to create delegates or expression tree types. Lambda expressions use the lambda operator =>, which is read as "goes to." The left side of the lambda operator specifies the input parameters (if any), and the right side holds the expression or statement block. The lambda expression x => x * x is read "x goes to x times x."

With C# 2.0, you could create anonymous methods to avoid the need for a separate method declaration. In C# 1.0, you should have used explicit delegates like this:

```
class Program
{
  delegate double BinaryOperation(double op1, double op2);

  static void Main(string[] args)
  {
    double op1 = 12.3;
    double op2 = 23.4;
    BinaryOperation operation = MyOperation;
    double result = operation(op1, op2);
  }

  static double MyOperation(double op1, double op2)
  {
    return (op1 + op2) / op2;
  }
}
```

With C# 2.0 anonymous methods, this gets easier because there is no need for writing the MyOperation method explicitly:

```
static void Main(string[] args)
{
  double op1 = 12.3;
  double op2 = 23.4;
  BinaryOperation operation = delegate(double x, double y) { return (x + y) / y; };
  double result = operation(op1, op2);
}
```

Lambda expressions provide more concise syntax and type inference so that the operation delegate can even be described in a more straightforward way:

```
static void Main(string[] args)
{
  double op1 = 12.3;
  double op2 = 23.4;
  BinaryOperation operation = (x, y) => (x + y) / y;
  double result = operation(op1, op2);
}
```

Lambda expressions can contain statements as well and can refer to outer variables, just like in the following example:

```
double op1 = 12.3;
double op2 = 23.4;
double factor = 45.6;
BinaryOperation operation = (x, y) =>
                             {
                                Console.WriteLine(factor);
                                return factor * (x + y) / y;
                             };
double result = operation(op1, op2);
```

## Query Expressions

*Query expressions* provide the "language-integrated" experience of LINQ, because they provide syntax similar to SQL to describe a query. A query expression begins with a `from` clause and ends with a `select` or `group` clause. Other valid clauses for the middle of the expression include `from`, `let`, `where`, `join`, and `orderby`.

Let's take a look at an example:

```
string[] fruits = { "Apple", "Peach", "Orange", "Banana", "Lemon", "Pear",
                    "Grapefruit", "Watermelon", "Plum" };

var filteredFruits =
    from fruit in fruits
    where fruit.StartsWith("P") && fruit.Length < 20
    orderby fruit
    select fruit;
```

The strength of this notation is that it describes the intention of what you would like to get as a result, instead of defining how you want to obtain that.

The C# compiler translates a query expression into method invocations. For example, the `where` clause will translate into a call to a `Where` method, the `orderby` clause will translate into a call to an `OrderBy` method, and so on. These methods must be extension methods or instance methods on the type being queried. So, in the preceding example, the type representing `fruits` must have this characteristic. The method (not the compiler) will determine how to execute the query at run-time. The compiler would transform the previous query expression into the following:

```
var filteredFruits =
   fruits.Where(f => f.StartsWith("P") && f.Length < 20)
         .OrderBy(f => f)
         .Select(f => f);
```

The lambda expressions in this query are simple, like `f => f` in the arguments of `OrderBy` and `Select` methods.

Behind the scenes, the C# compiler is performing a translation of the query expression and looking for matching methods to invoke. This means that the compiler will use the `IEnumerable<T>` or `IQueryable<T>` extension methods, when available. When importing the `System.Linq` namespace with a `using` clause, the compiler would find appropriate extension methods for `Select` and `OrderBy`. You could also leave out the `System.Linq` namespace and write your own extension methods to replace the standard LINQ implementations completely.

This kind of extensibility of query expressions makes LINQ a very powerful feature that enables the shift from an imperative data-processing model to the declarative one.

## Expression Trees

LINQ expressions can run against objects sitting in the memory, as well as against external objects (for example, entities represented by a SQL Server database). Consider the following simple LINQ query:

```
var q = from o in orders, c in customers
        where o.ShipCity == "London" && (o.CustomerID == c.CustomerID)
        select new { o.OrderDate, c.CompanyName, c.ContactTitle, c.ContactName };
```

When the `customers` collection in this query represents a simple memory object, the query runs again this object. However, when `customers` collection represents a LINQ provider (that is, it implements the `IQueryable<T>`, where `T` is the type of the data in `customers`), something very different happens.

Instead of compiling instructions in the sample query to execute, the compiler creates code to prepare an *expression tree* representing the query. The code that is compiled is passing this expression tree to the LINQ provider implemented by the `customers` object (through the `IQueryable<T>` interface). The provider can analyze this expression tree, and execute the query accordingly.

For example, if `customers` represents a `Table<Customer>` object that implements the `IQueriable<Customer>` interface, the related LINQ provider creates a SQL query string and runs it on the appropriate SQL Server database. For the preceding query, the SQL query string generated by the provider looks something like this:

```
exec sp_executesql N'SELECT [t1].[CompanyName], [t1].[ContactName],
[t1].[ContactTitle], [t0].[OrderDate]
FROM [Orders] AS [t0], [Customers] AS [t1]
WHERE ([t0].[ShipCity] = @p0) AND ([t0].[CustomerID] = [t1].[CustomerID])',
N'@p0 nvarchar(6)', @p0 = N'London'
```

By using the `Expression<T>` class, you can direct the compiler to create an expression tree from a lambda expression. Consider the following example:

```
Expression<Func<int,int>> expression = x => x + 12;
```

The `expression` variable is a tree that can be manipulated, or, after the manipulation, it can be compiled and evaluated:

```
var value = expression.Compile().Invoke(42);
```

This discussion does not dive any deeper into this topic because several books dealing with LINQ explain it in more depth.

## Automatic Properties

*Automatic properties* are shortcuts to define properties that use simple backing fields with the trivial get and set accessors. For example, the following backing field and property declaration can be changed to automatic properties:

```
// --- Backing field
private string _Name;

// --- Property using the backing field
public string Name
{
  get { return _Name; }
  set { _Name = value; }
}
```

With automatic properties, that same snippet can be written much more briefly as follows:

```
public string Name { get; set; }
```

You must provide both the get and set accessors in the definition. If you want to narrow the scope (for example, if you intend to declare a read-only property), then you must use access modifiers. For example, the following property declaration allows read-only access from external entities:

```
public string Name { get; private set; }
```

Behind the scenes, automatic properties use backing fields, but per the C# language specification, these cannot be accessed from the code directly.

## Object Initializers

Types within the .NET Framework rely heavily on the use of properties. When instantiating and using new classes, it is very common to write code like this:

```
public class Customer
{
  int ID { get; set; }
  string Name { get; set; }
  bool IsKeyAccount { get; set; }
}
// ...
Customer customer = new Customer();
customer.ID = 112;
customer.Name = "John Doe";
customer.IsKeyAccount = true;
```

*Object initializers* allow you to rewrite the preceding code with exactly the same semantics but with a shorter and more expressive syntax:

```
customer = new Customer { ID=112, Name="John Doe", IsKeyAccount=true };
```

## Collection Intializers

Similar to object initialization, it is very common to set up collections like this:

```
List<Customer> custList = new List<Customer>();
custList.Add(new Customer { ID=112, Name="John Doe", IsKeyAccount=true });
custList.Add(new Customer { ID=113, Name="Jane Doe", IsKeyAccount=true });
custList.Add(new Customer { ID=114, Name="G.I Joe", IsKeyAccount=false });
```

*Collection initializers* allow you to reduce the related syntax noise, as shown here:

```
var custList = new List<Customer>
{
  new Customer { ID=112, Name="John Doe", IsKeyAccount=true },
  new Customer { ID=113, Name="Jane Doe", IsKeyAccount=true },
  new Customer { ID=114, Name="G.I Joe", IsKeyAccount=false }
};
```

Under the hood, the compiler generates initialization code in a similar way as is used with the Add methods to append the elements to the collection.

## Partial Methods

C# 2.0 introduced partial classes to help resolve code-generation issues stemming from the fact that C# types should have been entirely in the same source file before.

*Partial methods* live in partial types, and have two parts: a declaration and an implementation. These are generally in separate partitions — and so in separate files. If the compiler finds only the declaration part, but no implementation, no method call code will be generated for the partial method.

This improves the performance because you are not loading/creating unwanted methods. Here is an example:

```
// --- Collection.cs: This is the class that would normally be autogenerated.
public partial class CustomTypedCollection
{
  partial void BeforeAddingElement(CustomElement element);

  public void AddElement(CustomElement element)
  {
    BeforeAddingElement();
  }
}

// --- Customization.cs: This part is the one added by developers as customization
public partial class CustomTypedCollection
{
  partial void BeforeAddingElement(CustomElement element)
  {
    Console.WriteLine("Element " + element + " is being added.");
  }
}
```

The partial method cannot be seen from outside:

```
class Program
{
  static void Main(string[] args)
  {
    CustomTypedCollection c = new CustomTypedCollection();
    c.AddElement(new CustomElement());
  }
}
```

If the `Customization.cs` file did not contain an implementation part for the `BeforeAddingElement` partial method, no code would be compiled for this method call in `Collection.cs`.

Of course, partial methods have a few restrictions. For example, they must return `void`, and are not allowed to have `out` or `ref` parameters, nor can they have access modifiers, and they cannot be `virtual`.

## SUMMARY

Currently a multi-paradigm programming language, C# began life with version 1.0 in 2002 as a general-purpose, object-oriented language. The development team of the C# language was led by Anders Hejlsberg. The language name was inspired from the musical notation where a sharp indicates that the note should be made a half step higher in pitch.

The language evolved in parallel with the .NET Framework as the "native" programming language of the framework's class libraries. New features and changes in the CLR and in the framework's class libraries inspired the language that turned into a real multi-paradigm language supporting not only the original object-oriented programming (OOP) principles, but also declarative, functional, and (with C# 4.0) the dynamic paradigm.

Chapter 24 will familiarize you with the new improvements to the C# language, such as dynamic lookup, named and optional parameters, the new COM-specific features, and variance.

# 24

# C# 4.0 Language Improvements

In Chapter 23, you learned about how C# evolved from a general-purpose, object-oriented programming (OOP) language to a multi-paradigm language. After its first release in 2002 (C# 1.0), the language matured amazingly. Version 2.0 added support for generic types and got great performance-boosting features such as iterators with the `yield`-construct, delegate inference, covariance and contravariance, and nullable types.

C# 3.0 gained a huge spin with the introduction of query expressions that allowed encapsulating LINQ technology into the language. This feature enabled the shift from the imperative data-processing model to the declarative one. In addition, many other "syntax noise-reduction" features were put into C# 3.0 to achieve the intended declarative strength.

The major theme for C# 4.0 is dynamic programming. Increasingly, objects are "dynamic" in the sense that their structure and behavior is not captured by a static type or, at least, not one that the compiler knows about when compiling your program. While C# remains a statically typed language, the Managed Languages Team targeted vastly improved interaction with the following:

➤ Objects from other programming languages, such as Python or Ruby

➤ Component Object Model (COM) objects accessed through the `IDispatch` interface

➤ Objects with dynamically changing structure, such the ones in HTML Document Object Model (DOM)

➤ Ordinary .NET types accessed through reflection

After reading this chapter, you will be familiar with the following improvements introduced with C# version 4.0:

➤ *Dynamic lookup* — You can write method, operator, and indexer calls; property and field accesses; and object invocations that bypass the C# compile-time static type checking. Instead, these invocations will get resolved at run-time with the help of Dynamic Language Run-time (DLR).

➤ *Named and optional parameters* — Parameters in C# can be specified as optional, and, in member invocations, optional arguments can be omitted. Furthermore, any argument can be passed by parameter name.

➤ *COM-specific interoperability features* — The language designers added a number of small features that, combined with the strength of dynamic lookup, further improved the programmer's interoperability experience.

➤ *Variance* — .NET developers used to be constrained by the fact that an `IEnumerable<object>` could not be substituted with an `IEnumerable<object>`. Now, this substitution can be done! C# embraces type-safe covariance and contravariance. The common Base Class Library types (primarily generic collection interfaces) also have been updated to support this behavior.

Before diving into the details of these topics, let's take a look at a short example demonstrating issues that were not previously addressed properly in C#, but have been adequately handled in version 4.0.

## PAINS WITH INTEROPERABILITY

Before Visual Studio 2010 and .NET 4, using COM object hierarchies in C# were much more cumbersome than in Visual Basic or in macros. To demonstrate those annoying details that prevented C# from being coequal with Visual Basic in the COM interoperability field, let's build a simple application using Microsoft Excel and Word. The application displays the top ten processes by means of memory usage, creates an Excel chart, and inserts it into a Word document.

In this example, you will create two versions of this application. First, you'll use the programming style you would use with Visual Studio 2008 and C# 3.0, and then you will create it again with C# 4.0 syntax. Comparing the source code between the two, you'll be able to see the marvelous improvements C# 4.0 offers. You do not have to install Visual Studio 2008 on your machine, because you can produce both applications with Visual Studio 2010.

## Creating the PainWithOffice Application

Start Visual Studio 2010, create a new Console Application project, and name it `PainWithOffice`. Be sure that the target framework is .NET Framework 4, as shown in Figure 24-1; otherwise, the application will not run properly.

**FIGURE 24-1:** Create the PainWithOffice project for .NET Framework 4

Add the following two assembly references to the project with the Add Reference dialog:

➤ Microsoft.Office.Interop.Excel

➤ Microsoft.Office.Interop.Word

Change the content of Program.cs file, as shown in Listing 24-1.

**LISTING 24-1: Program.cs**

```
using System;
using System.Linq;
using System.Diagnostics;
using Excel = Microsoft.Office.Interop.Excel;
using Word = Microsoft.Office.Interop.Word;

namespace PainWithOffice
{
  class Program
  {
    static void Main(string[] args)
    {
      var excel = new Excel.Application();
      excel.Visible = true;
      excel.Workbooks.Add(Type.Missing);
      ((Excel.Range)excel.Cells[1, 1]).Value2 = "Process Name";
```

*continues*

**LISTING 24-1** *(continued)*

```csharp
    ((Excel.Range)excel.Cells[1, 2]).Value2 = "Memory Usage";

    var processes = Process.GetProcesses()
        .OrderByDescending(p => p.WorkingSet64)
        .Take(10);
    int i = 2;
    foreach (var p in processes)
    {
      ((Excel.Range)excel.Cells[i, 1]).Value2 = p.ProcessName;
      ((Excel.Range)excel.Cells[i, 2]).Value2 = p.WorkingSet64;
      i++;
    }

    Excel.Range range = (Excel.Range)excel.Cells[1, 1];
    Excel.Chart chart = (Excel.Chart)excel.ActiveWorkbook.Charts.Add(
        Type.Missing,        // --- Before
        excel.ActiveSheet,   // --- After
        Type.Missing,        // --- Count
        Type.Missing);       // --- Type
    chart.ChartWizard(
      range.CurrentRegion,   // --- Source
      Type.Missing,          // --- Gallery
      Type.Missing,          // --- Format
      Type.Missing,          // --- PlotBy
      Type.Missing,          // --- CategoryLabels
      Type.Missing,          // --- SeriesLabels
      Type.Missing,          // --- HasLegend
      "Memory Usage in " + Environment.MachineName,
      // --- Title
      Type.Missing,          // --- CategoryTitle
      Type.Missing,          // --- ValueTitle
      Type.Missing);         // --- ObjectTitle
    chart.ChartType = Excel.XlChartType.xl3DColumn;
    chart.CopyPicture(Excel.XlPictureAppearance.xlScreen,
        Excel.XlCopyPictureFormat.xlBitmap,
        Excel.XlPictureAppearance.xlScreen);

    var word = new Word.Application();
    word.Visible = true;
    object template = Type.Missing;
    object newTemplate = Type.Missing;
    object docType = Type.Missing;
    object visible = Type.Missing;
    word.Documents.Add(
      ref template,
      ref newTemplate,
      ref docType,
      ref visible);
    word.Selection.Paste();
    }
  }
}
```

This program is really simple, even if it takes about 70 lines. The `Main` method creates an Excel sheet and sets up a two-column table with process name and memory usage. With the LINQ query on `Process.GetProcesses`, it obtains the top ten processes by means of memory consumption. The method puts the process information into the Excel table, then creates a nice three-dimensional column chart with the `Charts.Add` method, and copies it to the clipboard. Finally, the code creates a new Word document and pastes the chart into the document body.

At this point, you are ready to build and run this application by pressing Ctrl+F5. You will see Excel and Word flickering for a few seconds, and then Word shows you the result that resembles the chart in Figure 24-2.

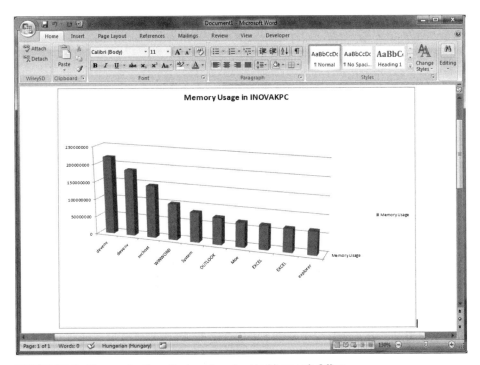

**FIGURE 24-2:** The application displays the chart in Microsoft Office

## Frustrating Issues

Although the previous code above seems simple and brief compared to the value it provides, it is full of syntax noise. If you happened to create the application in Visual Basic, it would be shorter and free from this noise.

The first and most eye-catching thing is that the code heavily uses the `Type.Missing` instances. Those are there as placeholders for optional parameters of COM methods. In this short code, you can count 17 occurrences of them, meaning 204 unnecessary characters altogether. The invocation of `ChartWizard` method contains 11 parameters, where only 2 of them use non-default values. Here you must pass nine `Type.Missing` instances to make your code compile.

Another annoying code snippet is where you set the values of Excel cells, as shown here:

```
((Excel.Range)excel.Cells[i, 1]).Value2 = p.ProcessName;
((Excel.Range)excel.Cells[i, 2]).Value2 = p.WorkingSet64;
```

Should this simple operation be so "noisy"? First, you must convert the object behind the cells to an `Excel.Range` instance, and then set its value through the `Value2` property. If you have never used Excel from C# before, it may take a little time before you get acquainted with this style. It can be called anything but "intuitive."

Have a look at the code where the `Document.Add` method is called. The four parameters it accepts must be passed to as `ref`.

```
object template = Type.Missing;
object newTemplate = Type.Missing;
object docType = Type.Missing;
object visible = Type.Missing;
word.Documents.Add(
  ref template,
  ref newTemplate,
  ref docType,
  ref visible);
```

This is not because the invoked method is about to modify them. (`Type.Missing` is immutable.) The `Add` method was implemented in this way, and your only choice is to use it as is. In order to call this method, you must create four temporary variables of type `System.Object` and assign `Type.Missing` to them. The whole effort is about being able to pass parameters by reference.

## Remove the Pain

The Managed Language Team has found the remedy for these frustrating issues. The solution is now part of the C# 4.0 language specification and is composed from several features that will be explained in detail later in this chapter.

Create a new console application and name it `PaneWithOfficeRemoved`. Change the `Program.cs` file in the project to the one shown in Listing 24-2. Build and run the project.

**LISTING 24-2:** Syntax noise removed from Program.cs

```
using System;
using System.Linq;
using System.Diagnostics;
using Excel = Microsoft.Office.Interop.Excel;
using Word = Microsoft.Office.Interop.Word;

namespace PainWithOfficeRemoved
```

```
{
  class Program
  {
    static void Main(string[] args)
    {
      var excel = new Excel.Application();
      excel.Visible = true;
      excel.Workbooks.Add();
      excel.Cells[1, 1].Value = "Process Name";
      excel.Cells[1, 2].Value = "Memory Usage";

      var processes = Process.GetProcesses()
          .OrderByDescending(p => p.WorkingSet64)
          .Take(10);
      int i = 2;
      foreach (var p in processes)
      {
        excel.Cells[i, 1].Value = p.ProcessName;
        excel.Cells[i, 2].Value = p.WorkingSet64;
        i++;
      }

      var range = excel.Cells[1, 1];
      var chart = excel.ActiveWorkbook.Charts.Add(After: excel.ActiveSheet);
      chart.ChartWizard(
        Source: range.CurrentRegion,
        Title: "Memory Usage in " + Environment.MachineName);
      chart.ChartType = Excel.XlChartType.xl3DColumn;
      chart.CopyPicture(Excel.XlPictureAppearance.xlScreen,
          Excel.XlCopyPictureFormat.xlBitmap,
          Excel.XlPictureAppearance.xlScreen);

      var word = new Word.Application();
      word.Visible = true;
      word.Documents.Add();
      word.Selection.Paste();
    }
  }
}
```

*Code file [Program.cs] available for download at Wrox.com*

As you can see, it works exactly like the one in Listing 24-1. However, this one is free from the annoying syntax noise.

From Listing 24-2 you can immediately recognize that there are no `Type.Missing` instances at all! Writing values to the Excel cells works as you expect. Look at the `Charts.Add` and `ChartWizard` methods. You can see that arguments are passed with parameter names. In Listing 24-2, no explicitly typed variable declarations are used.

Now, let's look behind the scenes, and examine the improvements that make this simplification possible.

# DYNAMIC LOOKUP

C# developers are familiar with the fact that types and operations are strictly checked during the compilation process. The compiler generates Microsoft Intermediate Language (MSIL) code that explicitly carries out those operations by invoking methods. The good side of this approach is the thorough checks that increase operation safety; the bad side is its rigidity.

There is another galaxy in the universe of programming languages: *dynamic languages*. The compiler makes only a few checks over types and their operations; the majority of them are postponed to the execution of the corresponding operation at run-time.

In addition to the dynamic languages, there are *script languages* and *object models* (for example, COM objects over the Microsoft Office functionality, the DTE object model in Visual Studio, the HTML DOM in Internet Explorer, and so on) that also check operations at run-time.

In this complex world, these tools and languages should interoperate so that they could provide boosted developer performance. Scripting tools and languages such as JScript, PowerShell, and many others, as well as dynamic languages such as Python or Ruby, are very popular today. They provide a unified approach to objects, and they operate independently of where they are coming from, and how they are working behind the scenes. These tools focus on the most important thing: providing the simplest and most intuitive way to use the object's exploited functionality.

For a long time, C# could not compete with the flexibility of these languages and tools. But that is no longer the case.

## Dynamic Binding

The new version of C# provides *dynamic binding* as a unified approach to selecting and carrying out operations dynamically. Operations can be uniformly applied on various objects independently of whether a specific object comes from COM (through interoperability), IronRuby, IronPython, the HTML DOM, or from any other dynamic context. The run-time takes this responsibility away from developers, and it will determine what a given operation means for a particular object.

This approach can greatly simplify your code (just compare the `Main` methods in Listing 24-1 and Listing 24-2), and affords you huge flexibility. However, the compiler assumes these dynamic objects support any operation, and this behavior has two drawbacks:

> ➤ It will turn out only at run-time if a specific object does not support a certain operation, and you will get an error. Contrast this to static typing, where the compiler gives an error message.

> ➤ Run-time checks incur a kind of performance penalty.

In many cases, these drawbacks do not come with any loss, because the objects providing the operations would not have a static type anyway. Of course, there are cases where a tradeoff should be made between safety and brevity. If brevity is important, safety can be strengthened by appropriate software development procedures (such as unit testing and code review).

Dynamic binding is implemented in C# 4.0 as an explicit mechanism where you can opt in or opt out whether you want to utilize this behavior. When you port your known and running C# 3.0 code to C# 4.0, it will not change its behavior implicitly. The compiler will make the same strong type and operation checks as before.

## The dynamic Type

The key to dynamic binding is a new static type introduced in C# 4.0 called `dynamic`. (That sounds funny — a static type that is dynamic — doesn't it?) When you have an object of type `dynamic`, you can ask it to do many things. The compiler will only check a few things by means of syntax and basic semantics, and let the run-time resolve operations. Here is a two-line sample:

```
dynamic dyn = GetDynamicObject(...);
dyn.DoSomething("C# 4.0 Rocks!", 42);
```

Assume the `GetDynamicObject` method retrieves an object of type `dynamic`. It is stored in `dyn`. The compiler analyzes the second line during compilation and creates code that can be described like this:

"Ask the run-time to call an operation named `DoSomething` with a `string` as its first argument, and an `int` as its second one. When the run-time recognizes this operation, call it with 'C# 4.0 Rocks!' and 42 as the actual parameters of the `DoSomething`."

At run-time, the actual object that `dyn` refers to will be examined to determine what it means to "call `DoSomething` with a `string` and an `int`," and if the `dyn` object knows how to handle the call, it executes it with the actual parameters passed to it.

The `dynamic` type can be thought of as a special version of the `System.Object` type, which signals that the object can be used dynamically.

It is easy to opt in or out of dynamic behavior — any object can be implicitly converted to `dynamic`, "suspending belief" until run-time. Listing 24-3 illustrates this with the dynamic form of "Hello, world."

**LISTING 24-3:** Program.cs file of HelloWorldDynamic

```csharp
using System;

namespace HelloWorldDynamic
{
  class Program
  {
    static void Main(string[] args)
    {
      dynamic dyn = Console.Out;
      dyn.WriteLine("Hello, {0} from dynamic console", "world");
    }
  }
}
```

*Code file [Program.cs] available for download at Wrox.com*

The run-time recognizes that `dyn` is an instance of `TextWriter` (this is the type of `Console.Out`) and tries to call the `WriteLine` method (utilizing .NET reflection) with the specified set of parameters. You can build and run this simple program, and it will work. Now, let's say that you change the `WriteLine` call to this:

```
dyn.WLine("Hello, {0} from dynamic console", "world");
```

The code still compiles, but raises a `RuntimeBinderException`, indicating a `TextWriter` instance does not support `WLine` operation.

Just as any object can be converted to `dynamic`, the compiler allows implicit conversion of dynamic expressions to any type:

```
dynamic dyn = 34 * 23 * 12;
int value = dyn;
Console.WriteLine(value);
```

While there is an implicit conversion from the type behind `dyn` to `int` (in this case, there is), the conversion will succeed at run-time. Otherwise (for example, try to use `string` instead of `int`), you get a `RuntimeBinderException` with a message describing what the issue was.

## Dynamic Operations

You can use the instances of `dynamic` type with a number of operations. Assuming that the variable `dyn` has a type of `dynamic`, you can execute all the operations summarized in Table 24-1.

**TABLE 24-1:** Operations with a `dynamic` instance

| OPERATION | SAMPLE |
| --- | --- |
| Method call | `dyn.SayHello("to have a good buy");` |
| Method call with passing arguments by name | `dyn.RunQuery(table: "customer",`<br>`filter: "City=='London'");` |
| Getting field, property, and indexer values | `int size = dyn.Count;`<br>`string value = dyn.Cells[1, 1];` |
| Setting field, property, and indexer values | `dyn.QuerySource = "customer";`<br>`dyn.Filters[0] = "City=='London'";` |
| Calling operators | `int increasedSize = dyn + 1024;` |
| Invoking as a delegate | `var opResult = dyn("GetPage", 10);` |
| Selecting constructors | `new MyType myType = new MyType(dyn);` |

The C# compiler checks the syntax and decides what kind of operation is to be carried out with `dyn`. According to the type of the operation, it packages the necessary information so that the run-time can pick it up and determine what the exact meaning of it is, given an actual object referenced by `dyn`. The result of most dynamic operations is itself of type `dynamic`; the exceptions are implicit or explicit conversion, and constructor call. These operations have a natural static type.

## Dynamic Dispatch

At run-time, a dynamic operation is dispatched to the target object `dyn` with the following steps:

**1.** If `dyn` is a COM object, the operation is dispatched dynamically through COM `IDispatch` interface. This allows calling to COM types that don't have a Primary Interoperability Assembly (PIA), and relying on COM features that don't have a counterpart in C # (such as indexed properties and default properties).

**2.** If `dyn` implements the interface of the `System.Dynamic` namespace, `dyn` itself is asked to perform the operation. (Of course, the run-time uses `IDynamicMetaObjectProvider` to do that.)

**3.** Otherwise, `dyn` is a standard .NET object, and the operation will be dispatched using reflection on its type, and a C# "run-time binder" that implements C#'s lookup and overload resolution semantics at run-time. (Run-time binders are explored in more detail later in this chapter in the section, "Dynamic Language Run-time.")

The `IDynamicMetaObjectProvider` type is a great way to completely redefine the meaning of dynamic operations, and so is an extensibility point to define a custom run-time binder to resolve any kind of dynamic type operations.

This is used intensively by dynamic languages such as IronPython and IronRuby to implement their own dynamic object models. It is also used by APIs (such as the HTML DOM) to allow direct access to the object's properties using C# property syntax.

## Compile Time Semantics

It seems the compiler has an easy job to make a decision on which operations to compile with static binding and which ones with dynamic binding. For example, you may think what the compiler does with the following code snippet is trivial:

```
dynamic someValue = DateTime.Now;
Console.WriteLine(someValue.Ticks);
```

You probably think the compiler works like this:

**1.** `DateTime.Now` is put into a dynamic object.

**2.** The property or field `Ticks` is resolved with dynamic binding.

**3.** `Console.WriteLine` is invoked with static (compile-time) binding.

Yes, it was easy. But, it would be a wrong solution if it worked this way! Why? Look at the following method call where `str` is a `string` and `dyn` is a dynamic variable:

```
Console.WriteLine(str, dyn);
```

The `Console.WriteLine` method has the following overloads that accept `string` as their first argument:

```
public void WriteLine(string);
public void WriteLine(string, object);
public void WriteLine(string, object, object);
public void WriteLine(string, object, object, object);
public void WriteLine(string, object, object, object, object);
public void WriteLine(string, object[]);
```

If you assume the second version is used by the compiler making a static binding, you think "statically." Look at the following two code snippets and you understand why this idea is wrong:

```
// --- Snippet #1
string str = "Value is {0}";
dynamic dyn = 1234.5;
Console.WriteLine(str, dyn);

// --- Snippet #2
string str = "{0} > {1}";
dynamic dyn = new object[] { 123, 12 };
Console.WriteLine(str, dyn);
```

It cannot be decided at compile time which `Console.WriteLine` method to call. In the case of `Snippet #1`, `WriteLine(string, object)` is the appropriate one; for `Snippet #2`, only `WriteLine(string, object[])` works. Generally, `dyn` gets its value during run-time, so the only thing the compiler can do is invoke `Console.WriteLine` with dynamic binding!

So, the compiler uses dynamic binding for the following operations if any of the constituent expressions is a dynamic expression:

➤ Member and element access

➤ Method, delegate, or constructor invocation

➤ Using overloaded operators (both unary and binary)

➤ Using compound assignment operators (such as +=, -=, and so on)

➤ Implicit and explicit conversions

Looking back at Table 24-1, you can see that the last row mentions "selecting constructors." This term comes from the fact that, for a constructor call with a dynamic parameter, the run-time selects which constructor to call according to the type of the dynamic expression.

## System.Object and dynamic

C# 4.0 defines `dynamic` as a new type, just like object, string, decimal, and so on. It means that where a type name is expected by the C# language grammar, `dynamic` can be used. For example, you can create methods using dynamic arguments and return a value, as shown here:

```
public dynamic MyOperation(int a, dynamic arg)
{
  return a + arg;
}
```

You can use them in types as members and also as constructor arguments, as shown here:

```
class MyClass
{
  dynamic _Arg;

  public MyClass(dynamic arg)
  {
    _Arg = arg;
  }
}
```

Compared to C# 4.0, the .NET Framework's Common Language Runtime (CLR) does not have a separate intrinsic type for dynamic. Instead, the compiler uses System.Object everywhere, and internally flags the variables as dynamic to use this information during compilation. This implementation has a few consequences:

➤ As with System.Object, there is an implicit conversion from every type (other than pointer types) to dynamic, and an explicit conversion from dynamic to every such type.

➤ If method signatures differ only by dynamic versus System.Object, they are considered to be the same.

➤ The typeof(dynamic) == typeof(System.Object) expression is true.

Although System.Object and dynamic are considered the same, the type inference algorithm prefers dynamic over System.Object if both are candidates for a certain expression.

## The Dynamic Language Run-time

An important component in the underlying implementation of dynamic lookup is the *Dynamic Language Runtime (DLR)*, which is a part of .NET Framework 4.0. DLR is a run-time environment that adds a set of services for dynamic languages to the Common Language Run-time (CLR), and makes it easier to develop dynamic languages to run on the .NET Framework, as well as to add dynamic features to statically typed languages. DLR is built on the top of CLR, and uses *run-time binders* to access the physical object model addressed by dynamic expressions.

The DLR provides most of the infrastructure behind not only C# dynamic lookup, but also the implementation of several dynamic programming languages on .NET (such as IronPython and IronRuby). DLR provides an excellent caching mechanism (named *Call Site Caching*) that greatly enhances the efficiency of run-time dispatch. To the user of dynamic lookup in C#, the DLR is invisible.

Although C# is said to be the .NET programming language that is closest to the CLR, there are some limitations when using dynamics:

➤ The DLR allows objects to be created from objects that represent classes. However, the current implementation of C# doesn't have syntax to support this.

➤ Lambda expressions are type-inferred by their nature, so the compiler uses the context of them to infer what they mean. If lambdas appeared as arguments to a dynamic method call, the compiler cannot decide what type the lambda expression is to be converted to. So, lambdas are not allowed to appear as dynamic method call arguments.

➤ Dynamic lookup will not be able to find extension methods. The dynamic lookup happens at run-time, while extension methods are compile-time artifacts. Whether extension methods apply or not (and which extension method, if there is more than one) depends on the static context of the call (that is, which `using` clauses occur in the source file). This context information is not kept in the compiled binaries, and so extension methods will not be found by the DLR.

## NAMED AND OPTIONAL PARAMETERS

Earlier, Listing 24-1 displayed some "code horror" in terms of using noisy and hard-to-read method invocations, like this one:

```
chart.ChartWizard(
    range.CurrentRegion, // --- Source
    Type.Missing,        // --- Gallery
    Type.Missing,        // --- Format
    Type.Missing,        // --- PlotBy
    Type.Missing,        // --- CategoryLabels
    Type.Missing,        // --- SeriesLabels
    Type.Missing,        // --- HasLegend
    "Memory Usage in " + Environment.MachineName, // --- Title
    Type.Missing,        // --- CategoryTitle
    Type.Missing,        // --- ValueTitle
    Type.Missing);       // --- ObjectTitle
```

End-of-line comments help you in guessing the role of arguments passed to the `ChartWizard` call, but without them, you could hardly decrypt what the `Type.Missing` arguments stand for.

Some APIs (most notably COM interfaces such as the Microsoft Office and Visual Studio automation APIs) are written specifically with *named* and *optional parameters* in mind. Up until now, it has been very painful to call into these APIs from C#, with sometimes as many as 30 arguments having to be explicitly passed, most of which have reasonable default values and could be omitted. With named and optional parameters introduced in C# 4.0, the preceding code looks exactly as it should look from the beginning:

```
chart.ChartWizard(
    Source: range.CurrentRegion,
    Title: "Memory Usage in " + Environment.MachineName);
```

Named and optional parameters are really two distinct features, but are often useful together. Optional parameters allow you to omit arguments to member invocations, while named arguments provide a way to utilize the name of the corresponding parameter, instead of relying on its position in the parameter list.

When you compare the two code snippets in Listing 24-1 and Listing 24-2 that invoke the `ChartWizard` method, you can see how powerful the combination of these new features is. Not only does the code become noiseless, but also the intention of the developer is obvious from the method invocation.

## Using Optional Parameters

Do not think that COM automation object models are the only candidates for these two language features! Even in APIs for .NET, you sometimes find yourself compelled to write many overloads of a method with different combinations of parameters in order to provide maximum usability to the callers. Optional parameters are a useful alternative for these situations.

Here is a sample to help you understand why:

```
public class MyClass
{
  public void DoTheWork(int taskID, string taskType, int timeOut,
    bool useMultipleCores)
  {
    // ...
  }

  public void DoTheWork(int taskID, string taskType, int timeOut)
  {
    DoTheWork(taskID, taskType, timeOut, false);
  }

  public void DoTheWork(int taskID, string taskType)
  {
    DoTheWork(taskID, taskType, 10000);
  }

  public void DoTheWork(int taskID)
  {
    DoThcWork(taskID, "Cleanup");
  }
}
```

Instead of writing four overloads for `DoTheWork`, you can create one method with optional parameters. A method parameter is declared optional simply by providing a default value for it:

```
public void DoTheWork(int taskID,
  string taskType = "Cleanup",
  int timeOut = 10000,
  bool useMultipleCores = false)
{
  // ...
}
```

Here, the `taskType`, `timeOut`, and `useMultipleCores` parameters are all optional ones and can be omitted in method invocations:

```
DoTheWork(123, "Processing", 4000, true);
DoTheWork(124, "Removing files", 6000);
DoTheWork(125, "Adding ID");
DoTheWork(126);
```

## Rules for Using Optional Parameters

C# 4.0 does not allow you to omit arguments between commas, so you cannot write something like this:

```
DoTheWork(123, , , true);
```

The designers of the language thought this could lead to highly unreadable comma-counting code — and they are right. Instead of writing commas, use named arguments.

There are a few rules for using required and optional parameters:

➤ Parameters with the `ref` or `out` modifiers cannot have default values.

➤ A required parameter (one without a default value expression) cannot appear after an optional parameter in the formal parameter list.

➤ The default values of optional parameters must be either constant expressions, or one of the new or the `default` operators with a value type. These can be resolved during compile time, while other expressions cannot.

## Optional Parameters and Indexers

*Accessors* of indexers are actually methods, so you can use optional parameters in getter and setter methods of indexers. For example, you can define a class implementing a sparse matrix as follows:

```
public class SparseMatrix<T>
{
  public struct SparseIndex
  {
    public int Row;
    public int Column;
  }

  Dictionary<SparseIndex, T> _Storage = new Dictionary<SparseIndex,T>();

  public T this[int row = 0, int column = 0]
  {
    get
    {
      T result;
      return _Storage.TryGetValue(
        new SparseIndex { Row = row, Column = column },
```

```
            out result) ? result : default(T);
        }
        set { _Storage[new SparseIndex { Row = row, Column = column }] = value; }
    }
}
```

This matrix allows you to omit the column value from the indexer. For example, you could write the following:

```
var matrix = new SparseMatrix();
// --- Initialize the matrix
Console.WriteLine(matrix[123]);
```

Although you can even omit the row information, you cannot omit all the indexes altogether. The following code would raise a syntax error:

```
Console.WriteLine(matrix[]); // --- This is not allowed
```

If your index has only one parameter and you declare it as an optional one, the compiler will display a warning. For example, you can have a SparseVector class similar to SparseArray with the following indexer:

```
public T this[int row = 0]
{
    get
    {
        T result;
        return _Storage.TryGetValue(row, out result)
            ? result : default(T);
    }
    set { _Storage[row] = value; }
}
```

Here row cannot be used as an optional parameter, because indexers cannot be used with zero parameters; they must have at least one. The warning lets you revise your intention.

## Using Named Parameters

In previous versions of C#, method, constructor, and indexer arguments could be passed only by their position. C# 4.0 now allows passing arguments by names. The method invocation may contain argument names that match with the name of the parameter in the method declaration. Use the name of the parameter, followed by a colon, to signal that you want to pass those by names, and not by position.

For example, you can call the DoTheWork method declared with the following signature:

```
public void DoTheWork(int taskID,
    string taskType = "Cleanup",
    int timeOut = 10000,
    bool useMultipleCores = false);
```

You use these invocations to set only the `taskID` and `useMultipleCores` parameters:

```
DoTheWork(123, useMultipleCores: true);
DoTheWork(taskID: 123, useMultipleCores: true);
```

As you can see, positional and named arguments can be mixed in the same call. However, no positional arguments are allowed to be used after named arguments. In the following code snippet, the second call will raise a compile time error:

```
DoTheWork(123, useMultipleCores: true);
DoTheWork(useMultipleCores: true, 123);
```

The reason behind this requirement is obvious. The named parameter explicitly signals the caller's intention to diverge from the original sequential positions. Could you tell the number of the position for `123` in the second method call?

## Overload Resolution

The introduction of named and optional parameters changed the way of resolving overloaded method invocations. Let's take a deeper look at these changes.

### Abstract and Virtual Members

C# allows using parameter names in overrides that are different than in the abstract or virtual definitions. For example, in the following sample, `MyMethod` has different parameter names in the base and the derived class:

```
public class BaseClass
{
  public virtual void MyMethod(int firstPar, string secondPar)
  {
  }
}

public class ChildClass : BaseClass
{
  public override void MyMethod(int firstArg, string secondArg)
  {
  }
}
```

How should `MyMethod` be called with named parameters? How should parameter names in `BaseClass` or in `ChildClass` be passed? Can any of them be used? The language specification says, "the parameter names that apply are the ones that appear in the most specific override of the function member with respect to the static type of the target of the member access."

To understand this rule, here is a short example showing how to use these names:

```
// --- Most specific context: BaseClass
var myClass = new BaseClass();
myClass.MyMethod(firstPar: 1, secondPar: "Hello");
myClass = new ChildClass();
```

```
myClass.MyMethod(firstPar: 1, secondPar: "Hello");

// --- Most specific context: ChildClass
var childClass = new ChildClass();
childClass.MyMethod(firstArg: 1, secondArg: "Hello");
```

When the `myClass` variable is initialized, the compiler infers its type as `BaseClass`. So, both `MyMethod` calls use the parameter names in the most specific override that can be found in `BaseClass`. The `childClass` variable is a type of `ChildClass`, so when calling `MyMethod` through `childClass`, the context for parameter name resolution is `ChildClass`.

## Resolving Applicable Signatures

When you have the same method with more than one overload, the compiler must resolve it during the build process. The compiler first filters the overloads to see which are applicable to the method call context. If there are more candidates, the compiler uses "betterness" rules to select the best one.

With named and optional arguments, this process changed a bit from C# 3.0 to C# 4.0.

➤   A signature is applicable if all its parameters are either optional, or have exactly one corresponding argument (by name or position) in the call that is convertible to the parameter type.

➤   "Betterness" rules on conversions are only applied for arguments that are explicitly given — omitted optional arguments are ignored for betterness purposes.

➤   If two signatures are equally good (by terms of "betterness"), one that does not omit optional parameters is preferred.

Here is a short sample to demonstrate the resolution steps. `MyClass` here defines four overloads for `MyMethod`:

```
public class MyClass
{
  MyMethod(string s, int i = 1) { ... }
  MyMethod(object o) { ... }
  MyMethod(int i, string s = "C#") { ... }
  MyMethod(int i) { ... }
}
```

The question is which method should be called in the following code snippet?

```
var myClass = new MyClass();
myClass.MyMethod(2010);
```

Now, you can see how the rules work. `MyMethod(string,int)` is not applicable, because `2010` doesn't convert to string. `MyMethod(int,string)` is applicable because its second parameter is optional, and `2010` matches with its first argument. Obviously, `MyMethod(object)` and `MyMethod(int)` are also applicable.

Because there are three candidates, the "betterness" rules are applied. `MyMethod(int,string)` and `MyMethod(int)` are both better than `MyMethod(object)` because the conversion from `2010` to `int` is better than the conversion from `2010` to `object`.

So, only two candidates remain. Finally `MyMethod(int)` is better than `MyMethod(int,string)` because no optional arguments are omitted, and, therefore, `MyMethod(int)` is called.

## COM-SPECIFIC INTEROPERABILITY FEATURES

The dynamic lookup in C# 4.0 solves a lot of issues related to interoperability with other object models, and this is especially true for COM objects such as the Office Automation API or the Visual Studio Extensibility object model (DTE). Optional and named parameters also add great value to reduce the syntax noise of using COM API from C# code.

The C# language design team felt that they should polish up the COM interoperability story in version 4.0, and they added a few missing pieces of the puzzle to complete the picture. In this section, you can get a closer look at these seemingly small, but really powerful, features.

### Dynamic Import

A majority of COM methods accept and return variant types. The Primary Interoperability Assemblies (PIAs) represent arguments and return values of the `System.Object` type. In a majority of cases, you already know the static type of a returned object from the call context, but explicitly have to perform a cast on the returned value. For example, when you access cells in Excel, you write the following:

```
var excel = new Excel.Application();
Excel.Range topLeftCell = (Excel.Range)excel.Cells[1,1];
```

Even if you know `Cells[,]` returns an instance of `Excel.Range`, you must explicitly cast it to the expected type.

To get rid of this syntax noise, you can now choose to import these COM APIs in such a way that variants are represented using the type `dynamic`. Many PIAs shipped with Visual Studio are created with `dynamic` — including Microsoft Office PIAs.

This means that you can easily access members of a returned object, or you can assign it to a strongly typed local variable, without having to cast. Instead of casting an Excel `Cells[,]` value to the type `Excel.Range`, you can now say the following:

```
var excel = new Excel.Application();
var oldValue = excel.Cells[1,1];
excel.Cells[1,1].Value = "Set To New Value";
```

Earlier in this chapter, in Listing 24-2, you could see this new C# feature in action.

### Omitting ref from Parameters

In C# (and in other .NET languages like Visual Basic or F#), you pass reference parameters in order for the called member to mutate it for the subsequent benefit of the caller. Because of a different programming model, many COM APIs utilize reference parameters. Contrary to references in C#, these are typically not meant to change a passed-in argument, but are simply another way of passing value parameters.

In Listing 24-1, a new Word document was created with the following code snippet:

```
var word = new Word.Application();
word.Visible = true;
object template = Type.Missing;
object newTemplate = Type.Missing;
object docType = Type.Missing;
object visible = Type.Missing;
word.Documents.Add(
  ref template,
  ref newTemplate,
  ref docType,
  ref visible);
```

This demonstrates very well that a C# programmer should have to create temporary variables for all such `ref` parameters and pass these by reference. `Type.Missing` is immutable, so passing a reference to it is not a real benefit for the called method.

Instead, specifically for COM methods, the C# 4.0 compiler will allow you to pass arguments by value to such a method, and will automatically generate temporary variables to hold the passed-in values. The compiler subsequently discards them when the call returns. Listing 24-2 carries out the same task more intuitively:

```
var word = new Word.Application();
word.Visible = true;
word.Documents.Add();
```

In this way, the caller sees value semantics and will not experience any side effects, but the called method still gets a reference.

## Indexed Properties

COM has a concept called *parameterized properties* that does not exist in C#. Until now, you had to use `get_X()` and `set_X()` methods to access the values of an indexed property `X`. For example, you could set the top-left cell's value of an Excel sheet as follows:

```
var excel = new Excel.Application();
excel.get_Range("A1").set_Value(Type.Missing, "Name");
```

Earlier, without indexed properties support, you had to use the ugly `Value2` property, because you otherwise had to call `get_Value()` or `set_Value()`:

```
var excel = new Excel.Application();
excel.get_Range("A1").Value2 = "Name";
```

Now, in C# 4.0, you can call parameterized properties declared in COM using the indexer syntax. For example, instead of `get_X()`, you can now write `X[]`. With this syntax, you can now set the cell value in the most intuitive way, just as scripts and dynamic languages already do:

```
var excel = new Excel.Application();
excel.Range["A1"].Value = "Name";
```

This is just syntactic sugar. The compiler still emits calls to the `get_` and `set_` accessors at the end of the day. This syntax does not mean that you can now create indexed properties in C#, because this feature still does not exist in the language. The language designers encourage you to use indexers and do not plan to introduce indexed properties.

## Compiling Without PIAs

To interoperate with a certain COM interface, you must use a .NET type wrapping the functionality of that COM interface. Building these wrapper types manually is very laborious, especially when you have hundreds of COM interfaces — for example, in the case of using the Microsoft Office automation model.

PIAs are .NET assemblies generated from COM interfaces to facilitate strongly typed interoperability. For large object models, the related PIAs are large as well. At run-time, these large assemblies can easily bloat your program. They can also cause versioning issues when they are distributed independently of your application.

For example, the Word 2007 interoperability assembly has a size about 800 KB, while the Excel 2007 PIA has about 1.2 MB. Contrast this to the `PainWithOffice` binary (the small application you saw earlier in this chapter), which takes only 18 KB. Is it normal to deploy about 2 MB of overhead (PIAs) for an application with a size of 18 KB?

The no-PIA feature allows you to continue to use PIAs at design time without having them around at run-time. Instead, the C# compiler will append the small part of the PIA that a program actually uses directly to its assembly. At run-time, the PIA does not have to be loaded.

You can turn on or off this feature for each interoperability assembly. Select the assembly in Solution Explorer and set the Embed Interop Types property to True (to turn on) or False (to turn off) no-PIA. Figure 24-3 shows the property window with no-PIA turned on for the Excel interoperability assembly.

**FIGURE 24-3:** Embed Interop Types property

When you use this option, the compiler checks for the interoperability types your code references, and, behind the scenes, puts the appropriate type definitions into your assembly. In Figure 24-4 you can see the referenced Excel interoperability types (and the ones those depended on) added to the `PainWithOfficeRemoved` assembly.

The no-PIA feature is not just a "compiler trick." There are a few new things in the .NET Framework 4.0 CLR that supports this behavior. You can read about them in Chapter 10, which discusses the enhancements to the .NET Framework's core.

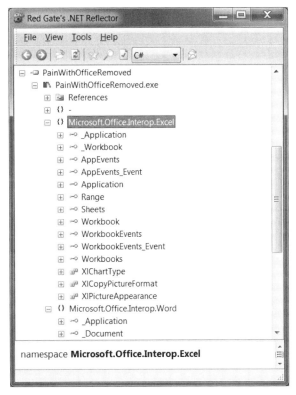

**FIGURE 24-4:** Embedded interoperability types in Reflector

## VARIANCE

Inheritance is a great object-oriented principle that is always directly or indirectly used when you create .NET applications or components. C# 2.0 brought generic types into the picture, and boosted developer performance, as well as code reusability. However, generic types may sometimes surprise you because certain things are illegal, even if you thought they were allowed.

### Type Substitution

Without a check, you would say the following declarations are legal, although the second one is invalid:

```
IList<string> stringList = new List<string>();
IList<object> objectList = stringList; // --- No implicit cast!
```

The main reason is that the following kinds or relationships between types are often confused:

➤ *Inheritance* — A type descends from another type.

➤ *Realization* — A type implements an interface.

➤ *Generic parameter substitution* — A generic type's type parameters substitute with concrete (closed) types.

Although `List<string>` realizes `IList<string>` (that is, a closed form of `IList<T>`) just as `List<object>` realizes `IList<object>` (that is, a closed form of `IList<T>`), it does not mean that

`IList<string>` is assignable to an `IList<object>`. Figure 24-5 shows a relationship diagram to help explain why this is so.

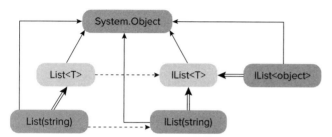

**FIGURE 24-5:** List<T> Relationship Diagram

The solid lines represent inheritance, dashed lines mark realization, and double lines stand for parameter substitution. It is obvious from the figure that the most common ancestor of these types is `System.Object`. While traversing through inheritance and realization in *linear inheritance* (like son, father, and grandfather in a family), parameter substitution means *collateral relation* (such as a second cousin in a family).

`IList<string>` and `IList<object>` are in collateral relation. Often, at first sight, developers take it into account as linear inheritance just because they share the same generic type as a kind of ancestor. So, there is a false expectation that `IList<string>` is assignable with a variable of `IList<object>`.

It is not just an unnecessarily strict check of the compiler; the discussed assignment can even lead to hurting type safety. Look at the following code:

```
IList<string> strings = new List<string> { "zero", "one", "two", "three", "four" };
IList<object> objects = strings;
objects[3] = 3;
string three = string[3];
```

If the `objects = strings` assignment were allowed, in the `objects[3] = 3` assignment, an `int` was about to be inserted into a list of `strings` and subsequently extracted as a `string`. This would be a type-safety violation, so that is why the assignment is invalid and results in compilation error.

Note that the whole situation is about how you can substitute instances of types with instances of other types. It is natural for OOP developers to think that substitutions are allowed by linear inheritance, but there are also other cases where theoretically collateral (and other types of) substitutions can be done.

The following code mirrors such a situation:

```
IList<string> strings = new List<string>();
IEnumerable<object> objects = strings;
```

Because `IEnumerable<T>` has a single method with the signature of

```
IEnumerator<T> GetEnumerator();
```

there is no way you can make such an assignment as

```
objects[3] = 3;
```

and so no opportunity to put the wrong type of thing into `strings` through `objects`, because `objects` doesn't have any method that takes an element in. So, here the assignment hypothetically could work without issues:

```
IEnumerable<object> objects = strings;
```

If you can enumerate through instances of `System.Object` and use the elements in the enumeration for some operations over `System.Object`, those operations should work even if you enumerate through instances of `System.String`. Why? Because `System.String` is assignable to a `System.Object`, so you can pass a `System.String` parameter to an operation (method) expecting `System.Object`.

The surprising fact is that this code works in C# 4.0, although it does not compile with C# 3.0.

## Bird's-Eye View of Variance

The concept of how types can be substituted with each other is called *variance*. Many forms of variance have been working in C# since the first language version. For example, method return values can be substituted with instances of derived types. Also, there are many forms that do not work.

Understanding the basics of variance will help you in becoming a more productive developer. This section provides a very brief overview about this topic from a higher (more theoretic) view without the intent of completeness.

Variance is an attribute of an operation related to a type in the type system of a programming language. The "operation" in this context can be a type conversion, some rule on the type, or any operation that carries out type transformations. In the type system, you can compare types X and Y, and the result of this comparison can be one and only one of the following:

➤ X and Y are equal.

➤ X is greater than Y.

➤ X is less than Y.

➤ X is not related to Y.

According to this comparison, you can define ordering (from the lowest to the highest) among the types, assuming they are related to each other. You say an operation over the types in the type system is one of the following:

➤ *Covariant* — This is if it preserves the ordering of types, or their unrelatedness;

➤ *Contravariant* — This is if it reverses the ordering of types, and keeps their equality and unrelatedness;

➤ *Invariant* — This is if neither of these apply.

One of the key factors that influences how the variance is interpreted for a concrete type system of a programming language is the type comparison operator between X and Y.

In the concrete example of the C# programming language, the type system is the .NET Framework's Common Type System (CTS). It's pretty easy to define that x and y are equal if and only if when `typeof(X).Equals(typeof(Y))`. It is also easy to imagine that x is greater than y if they are on the same inheritance chain, and x is closer to the root of the chain than y.

To define the complete ordering among the types of CTS, (including unrelatedness) is a complex task, — just think about generic types. The remaining discussions in this chapter focus on the practical side of variance, and its implementation in C# 4.0.

 *If you want to dive into this topic deeper and obtain more authentic information on variance, read Eric Lippert's blog, starting with this post:* `http://blogs .msdn.com/ericlippert/archive/2007/10/16/covariance-and-contra variance-in-c-part-one.aspx.`

## Variance in C# 4.0

Right now, C# implements only a subset of behavior that theoretically could be achieved by covariance and contravariance. However, the result the language designers achieved with this new version is significant and really practical. The current variance implementation can be characterized with the following points:

➤ For non-generic types, nothing has been changed from the previous version of C# by means of variance.

➤ The way of providing variance for generic types is by marking type parameters of a generic type as *variant*. Because a restriction in the CLR, variant type parameters can be declared only on generic interface and delegate types.

➤ Variance only applies when there is a reference conversion between type arguments. For example, variance applies for `IEnumerable<string>` and `IEnumerable<object>` because there is a reference conversion between `string` and `object`. However, the conversion from `int` to `object` is a boxing conversion, and so variance does not apply for `IEnumerable<int>` and `IEnumerable<object>`.

➤ Variance is not automatic. The compiler will not infer whether a type parameter is covariant or contravariant. Developers must explicitly declare their intention.

### Covariance

Following is an example of *covariance*:

```
IList<string> strings = new List<string>();
IEnumerable<object> objects = strings;
```

This works in C# 4.0. The compiler accepts it and generates proper code for executing the previous declarations. The key for this behavior is that `IEnumerable<T>` and `IEnumerator<T>` interfaces are declared with a variant type parameter `T`:

```
public interface IEnumerable<out T> : IEnumerable
{
  IEnumerator<T> GetEnumerator();
}

public interface IEnumerator<out T> : IEnumerator
{
  bool MoveNext();
  T Current { get; }
}
```

The only change in the syntax of interface definitions — related to the previous language versions — is the out modifier in the previous declarations. The out modifier signifies that the T can only occur in an output position in the interface — otherwise, the compiler will raise an error. This restriction provides (of course, it can be proven) that the interface becomes *covariant* in T, which means that an IEnumerable<X> is considered an IEnumerable<Y> if X has a reference conversion to Y.

Because of this definition, a sequence of strings can substitute a sequence of objects, and the previous code works. This covariant behavior is very useful in correlation with LINQ query expressions.

To experiment with this, create a console application and name it CovarianceSample. Add a new code file named Pet.cs to the project and paste the code in Listing 24-4 into this new file.

**LISTING 24-4: Pet.cs**

```
using System;
using System.Collections.Generic;
using System.Linq;

namespace CovarianceSample
{
  public abstract class Pet
  {
    public string NickName { get; set; }
    public int Age { get; set; }

    public static IEnumerable<Pet> ShackUpWith(
      IEnumerable<Pet> atHome,
      IEnumerable<Pet> newComers)
    {
      return atHome.Union(newComers);
    }
  }

  public sealed class Dog : Pet { }

  public sealed class Macaw : Pet { }
}
```

*Code file [Pet.cs] available for download at Wrox.com*

Here, you have abstract Pets with two concrete manifestations, Dog and Macaw. These types are intended to be used in a pet shop application, and so Pet has an operation named ShackUpWith accepting two sequences of pets and returns their union.

Modify the Program.cs file of the application as shown in Listing 24-5.

**LISTING 24-5: Program.cs**

```csharp
using System;
using System.Collections.Generic;
using System.Linq;

namespace CovarianceSample
{
  class Program
  {
    static void Main(string[] args)
    {
      var dogs = new List<Dog>
      {
        new Dog { NickName = "Spike",  Age = 3 },
        new Dog { NickName = "Murray", Age = 12 },
        new Dog { NickName = "Peach",  Age = 2 },
      };

      var macaws = new List<Macaw>
      {
        new Macaw { NickName = "Georgey" , Age = 32 },
        new Macaw { NickName = "Bella" , Age = 4 },
        new Macaw { NickName = "Grey" , Age = 11 },
      };

      var youngsters = from pet in Pet.ShackUpWith(dogs, macaws)
                       where pet.Age < 5
                       select pet;

      foreach (var pet in youngsters)
      {
        Console.WriteLine(pet.NickName);
      }
    }
  }
}
```

*Code file [Program.cs] available for download at Wrox.com*

The ShackUpWith method used in the query expression expects IEnumerable<Pet> arguments, but in the previous code, IEnumerable<Dog> and IEnumerable<Macaw> instances are passed. However, because IEnumerable<T> is covariant in T, the compiler accepts it. With C# 3.0 in Visual Studio 2008, this code would not compile! In order to make it work with C# 3.0, you must use a workaround. One possible solution is to cast dogs and macaws to IEnumerable<Pet>:

```
IEnumerable<Pet> dogsAsPets = dogs.Cast<Pet>();
IEnumerable<Pet> macawsAsPets = macaws.Cast<Pet>();
var youngsters = from pet in Pet.ShackUpWith(dogsAsPets, macawsAsPets)
                 where pet.Age < 5
                 select pet;
```

It is much simpler with C# 4.0, isn't it?

## Contravariance

*Contravariance* also works with generic interfaces and delegates in C# 4.0. Create a console application and name it `ContravarianceSample`. Add the `Animal.cs` file to the project with the code in Listing 24-6.

**LISTING 24-6: Animals.cs**

Available for download on Wrox.com

```
using System;

namespace ContravarianceSample
{
  public abstract class Animal : IComparable<Animal>
  {
    public string Name { get; set; }

    int IComparable<Animal>.CompareTo(Animal other)
    {
      return Name.CompareTo(other.Name);
    }
  }

  public class Elephant : Animal
  {
    public static int CompareWithOther(IComparable<Elephant> first, Elephant other)
    {
      return first.CompareTo(other);
    }
  }
}
```

*Code file [Animals.cs] available for download at Wrox.com*

Modify the `Program.cs` file, as shown in Listing 24-7.

**LISTING 24-7: Program.cs of ContravarianceSample**

Available for download on Wrox.com

```
namespace ContravarianceSample
{
  class Program
  {
    static void Main(string[] args)
```

*continues*

**LISTING 24-7** *(continued)*

```
    {
      var jack = new Elephant { Name = "Jack" };
      var jane = new Elephant { Name = "Jane" };

      var compare = Elephant.CompareWithOther(jane, jack);
    }
  }
}
```

*Code file [Program.cs] available for download at Wrox.com*

Although the CompareWithOther method in Elephant takes an IComparable<Elephant> instance as its first parameter, it still works in C# 4.0 with an Elephant instance, in spite of the fact that Elephant does not implement IComparable<Elephant>. Elephant indirectly (through Animal) implements IComparable<Animal> that can substitute IComparable<Elephant>. This is because the definition of IComparable<T>:

```
public interface IComparable<in T>
{
  int CompareTo(T other);
}
```

The type parameter T here uses the in variant modifier, restricting T to occur only in input positions, and, just as in case of the out modifier, the compiler will check the appropriate usage of T. This restriction provides (and, of course, it also can be proven) that the interface becomes *contravariant* in T, which means that an IComparable<X> is considered an IComparable<Y> if X has a reference conversion to Y.

In the example, Elephant has a reference conversion to Animal, and so IComparable<Elephant> can be substituted by IComparable<Animal>.

## A Few More Points on Variance

There are a few important things about the C# 4.0 implementation of variance you should be aware of. These can help you to understand the opportunities and limitations you have with this language version.

### Variance with Multiple Type Parameters

At first sight, many developers may think that to be covariant or contravariant is a property of a generic type. This is not true! Variance is property of type parameters in generic types. When you have a generic type, let's say MyType<T>, you cannot say "MyType is invariant, covariant or contravariant." What you can say is "MyType is invariant, covariant, or contravariant *in T*."

This means that you can actually have generic types that have both covariant and contravariant type parameters. Before you think this is theoretical and might not have practical reason, consider the fact that there are generic types frequently used with such a behavior.

The Func<> family of generic delegates is defined like this:

```
public delegate TResult Func<in T, out TResult>(T arg);
public delegate TResult Func<in T1, in T2, out TResult>(T1 arg1, T2 arg2);
```

You can see that they have both kinds of type parameters. With a simple console application, it is pretty easy to show the power of the generic Func delegate.

Create a console application and name it FuncExample. Add a new Pet.cs file to the project with the code in Listing 24-8.

**LISTING 24-8: Pet.cs in FuncExample**

```
namespace FuncExample
{
  public abstract class Pet
  {
    public string NickName { get; set; }
    public int Age { get; set; }
  }

  public sealed class Dog : Pet  { }

  public sealed class Macaw : Pet { }

  public sealed class Eagle : Pet { }
}
```

*Code file [Pet.cs] available for download at Wrox.com*

You are going to use the Func<> delegate to define transformations among pets. Listing 24-9 shows the Program.cs file implementing this functionality.

**LISTING 24-9: Program.cs in FuncExample**

```
using System;
using System.Collections.Generic;

namespace FuncExample
{
  class Program
  {
    static void Main(string[] args)
    {
      var dogs = new List<Dog>
      {
        new Dog { NickName = "Spike",  Age = 3 },
        new Dog { NickName = "Murray",  Age = 12 },
        new Dog { NickName = "Peach",  Age = 2 },
      };
```

*continues*

**LISTING 24-9** *(continued)*

```
    var macaws = new List<Macaw>
    {
      new Macaw { NickName = "Georgey" , Age = 32 },
      new Macaw { NickName = "Bella" , Age = 4 },
      new Macaw { NickName = "Grey" , Age = 11 },
    };

    var macawsToDogs = TransformMacawTo(macaws, TransformToDog);
    var macawsToEagles = TransformMacawTo(macaws, TransformToEagle);
    var dogsToEagles = TransformDogTo(dogs, TransformToEagle);
  }

  public static IEnumerable<Pet> TransformMacawTo(
    IEnumerable<Macaw> pets,
    Func<Macaw, Pet> tranformation)
  {
    foreach (var pet in pets)
      yield return tranformation(pet);
  }

  public static IEnumerable<Pet> TransformDogTo(
    IEnumerable<Dog> pets,
    Func<Dog, Pet> tranformation)
  {
    foreach (var pet in pets)
      yield return tranformation(pet);
  }

  static Dog TransformToDog(Macaw macaw)
  {
    return new Dog { NickName = macaw.NickName, Age = macaw.Age };
  }

  static Eagle TransformToEagle(Pet pet)
  {
    return new Eagle { NickName = pet.NickName, Age = pet.Age };
  }
 }
}
```

*Code file [Program.cs] available for download at Wrox.com*

In the `TransformMacawTo` function, the `Func<Macaw, Pet>` delegate is used, while in the `TransformDogTo` function, a `Func<Dog, Pet>` argument is passed.

Two functions, `TransformToDog` and `TransfromToEagle`, are responsible for performing the "magical change" of pets. The following lines of codes utilize variance:

```
    var macawsToDogs = TransformMacawTo(macaws, TransformToDog);
    var macawsToEagles = TransformMacawTo(macaws, TransformToEagle);
    var dogsToEagles = TransformDogTo(dogs, TransformToEagle);
```

In the first two `TransformMacawTo` calls, the `Func<Macaw, Pet>` arguments are substituted with `Func<Macaw, Dog>` and `Func<Pet, Eagle>`, respectively. In the invocation of `TransformDogTo`, a `Func<Pet, Eagle>` is used instead of the `Func<Dog, Pet>`. It is entirely valid, strongly typed, and no type conversion magic is done behind the scenes!

Why can, for example, `Func<Dog, Pet>` be substituted with `Func<Pet, Eagle>`? The fact that `Func<Dog, Pet>` is covariant in `Pet` means that you can return a `Pet` derived type, namely `Eagle`, because an `Eagle` is a `Pet`. The same thinking says that `Func<Dog, Pet>` is contravariant in `Dog`, and so any operation with `Pet` also will work on `Dog`, because `Dog` is derived from `Pet`. Therefore, `Func<Pet, Eagle>` is a good substitution for `Func<Dog, Pet>`.

## Variance with User Types

Obviously, you are not constrained to using only the existing generic types with variant type parameters. You can create your own generic interfaces and delegates. You can use the `in` modifier for signifying a contravariant, and the `out` modifier for a covariant type parameter. Without a modifier, the type parameter remains invariant.

For example, consider the following declarations:

```
public interface IMyOperations<in T, U, V> { ... }
public delegate X MyDelegate<in T, U, out X>(T t, U u);
```

Here, `X` is covariant, `T` is contravariant, and `U` and `V` are invariant type parameters.

The compiler checks to ensure that you keep within the rules for variant type parameters. For example, in the following interface definitions, all method declarations are invalid because one or more contravariant type parameters are in output positions:

```
public interface IMyOperations<in T, in U, V>
{
  T OutputUnsafeOp1();
  U[] OutputUnsafeOp2();
  List<T> OutputUnsafeOp3();
  Func<V, U> OutputUnsafeOp4();
  void OutputUnsafeOp5(out T t);
  void OutputUnsafeOp6(ref Func<V, U> t);
}
```

Similarly, in the following interface definition, all operations are invalid because covariant type parameters are in input positions:

```
public interface IMyOperations<out T, U>
{
  void InputUnsafeOp1(T t);
  U InputUnsafeOp2(T[] t);
  Func<U, T> InputUnsafeOp3(out T t);
  void InputUnsafeOp4(U u, ref T t);
}
```

The C# 4.0 language specification calls these invalid type parameters output-unsafe and input-unsafe types, and precisely defines the context they are unsafe within. With the introduction of variant type parameters, the type inference algorithm used by the compiler also has been modified.

## Variance and Reflection

The .NET Framework's reflection model can be used to obtain information about the variance of a type parameter. In Listing 24-10, you have a simple console application's `Program.cs` file demonstrating the reflection model used to query variance information.

**LISTING 24-10: Program.cs to query reflection about variance**

```csharp
using System;
using System.Reflection;
using System.Collections.Generic;
using System.Linq;

namespace VarianceAndReflection
{
  class Program
  {
    static void Main(string[] args)
    {
      var asm = typeof(IEnumerable<>).Assembly;

      var genericTypes = from type in asm.GetTypes()
                         where type.IsGenericTypeDefinition && type.IsPublic
                         select type;

      foreach (var type in genericTypes)
      {
        Console.WriteLine("{0}: ", type.Name);
        foreach (var typeParam in type.GetGenericArguments())
        {
          var variance = typeParam.GenericParameterAttributes &
            GenericParameterAttributes.VarianceMask;
          if ((variance & GenericParameterAttributes.Covariant) != 0)
            Console.WriteLine(" {0}: covariant", typeParam.Name);
          else if ((variance & GenericParameterAttributes.Contravariant) != 0)
            Console.WriteLine(" {0}: contravariant", typeParam.Name);
          else
            Console.WriteLine(" {0}: invariant", typeParam.Name);
        }
      }
    }
  }
}
```

*Code file [Program.cs] available for download at Wrox.com*

This code iterates through all generic types in the System assembly and writes out their type parameter information. The nested foreach cycle goes through the type parameters, and uses the GenericParameterAttributes property of System.Type to obtain information about variance. This property's value is a GenericParameterAttributes enumeration instance with flags. The VarianceMask value of the enumeration can be used to separate the flags describing variance from the ones describing type parameter constraints. Covariant and Contravariant flags define the parameter behavior. If neither is set, the type parameter is invariant.

## SUMMARY

The major theme for C# 4.0 is dynamic programming. You have a new feature called dynamic lookup to bypass the C# compile-time static type checking. Utilizing the new dynamic type operations on this type's instances will get resolved at run-time with the help of Dynamic Language Run-time (DLR).

Some APIs (most notably COM interfaces such as the Microsoft Office and Visual Studio automation APIs) are written specifically with named and optional parameters in mind. Up until now, it has been very painful to call into these APIs from C#. With named and optional parameters introduced in C# 4.0, this kind of discommodity has been finally removed from the language.

The C# design team felt that they should complete the COM interoperability picture in version 4.0, and they added great COM-specific features to the language, such as COM type import with the dynamic type, simplified syntax for indexed properties, automatic code generation for omitted ref parameters, and support for the no-PIA compilation.

C# 4.0 introduced new forms of variance. With type parameters of generic interfaces and delegates signified as covariant or contravariant, from now on, the programming language has a much more flexible type substitution model than ever before.

Chapter 25 provides an overview of other .NET languages, such as F#, IronPython, and IronRuby. You can learn the importance of functional programming through the great features of the F# language, and the chapter also will teach you to use F# with Visual Studio.

# PART VI
## F#

▶ **CHAPTER 25:** Visual F# and the Other .NET Languages

# 25

# Visual F# and the Other .NET Languages

One of the most exciting changes in Visual Studio 2010 is the inclusion of F# as a standard front end, bringing a true functional programming language into the .NET language ecosystem.

The importance of functional programming cannot be underestimated. Throughout this book, you have seen that many of the various enhancements to C# and Visual Basic (VB) are mostly about bringing functional programming concepts into those languages. This chapter will provide you with a basic understanding of functional programming, as well as an introduction to the F# language, a foundation that you can build on to better understand F# programs and write them yourself. By the end of this chapter, you will be familiar with the following:

➤ A brief history of the F# programming language.

➤ The core functional programming concepts from a pragmatic viewpoint — why they matter and how you can become a better programmer by using functional ideas.

➤ How you can get started with developing F# programs in Visual Studio, and try them interactively as you are developing them with F# Interactive.

➤ An overview of the F# language — basic syntax, major features (including pattern matching, active patterns, quotations, computation expressions (workflows), asynchronous computations, and units of measure), and how to use them to get the most out of the language.

➤ How you can develop a set of modules that you can use with F# Interactive to draw mathematical plots from your development session.

➤ A brief look at a couple of other .NET languages, IronRuby and IronPython.

# A BRIEF HISTORY OF F#

F# is a functional programming language that grew out of the work of Don Syme and his team at Microsoft Research (MSR) in Cambridge, United Kingdom. Syme and his team set out to implement a .NET front end for a functional programming language similar to OCaml. In fact, the initial goal of F# was to port OCaml to .NET, which, in turn, had identified many of the weaknesses of the early .NET 1.1 Common Type System (CTS).

One of the key features that differentiated OCaml and the standard .NET languages at the time was OCaml's more mature type system. In particular, the type system of .NET 1.1 languages was unable to express what is called *parametric polymorphism*, a key feature of many functional programming languages. This was eventually added to .NET 2.0 as Generics by, among others, Don Syme and Andrew Kennedy, making it possible to implement the first port of a functional programming language atop of .NET.

Although F# saw its beginnings somewhere around 2002, crowds didn't start building until around 2004–2005. These were silent but very productive years, and the occasional releases from Don Syme's MSR team (that included original team member James Margetson) delivered some impressive batches of new features every time, drawing more and more people's attention to F#. The community started to take shape, and many initiatives took off, including the HubFS (http://cs.hubfs.net), a community site that aims to be the primary place for F# enthusiasts — now numbering more than 16,000 members as of early January 2010.

The first books on F# appeared in 2007 — Robert Pickering's *Foundations of F#* (New York: Apress, 2007) and Don Syme's *Expert F#* (New York: Apress, 2007). These books helped to introduce F# to a multitude of developers, and the language gradually became well-known in professional .NET programming camps.

Undoubtedly, the growing interest in the functional paradigm, and the impressive coding experience that F# delivers, helped F# to make its way up to the strategic planners of Microsoft. Microsoft quickly realized the potential behind the language, and the project was promptly transferred from MSR Cambridge to Redmond, where it now resides with the other Visual Studio and programming languages teams.

This was followed by public announcements at the end of 2007 — the most notable one being that by Microsoft Developer Division Chief Soma Somasegar, who posted the news on his blog — emphasizing the company's strong commitment to "continue the flow of good ideas from functional programming world into mainstream development," and the importance of technology transfer from research to products to "productize" great research ideas.

As time has shown since 2007, F# is much more than a simple product glued together from a set of ideas from functional programming. It is a unique and amazingly effective combination of brevity and productivity, of imperative, object-oriented and mainly functional paradigms, and a mind-changer that offers a truly unrivaled developer experience.

A long time had to pass before F# reached its well-deserved membership in the Visual Studio standard languages, and this has made F# a robust and fully mature language that not only fills in where other .NET languages fall short, but also defines new approaches for many of the traditionally difficult problems developers face today — including the advent of multi-core programming, asynchronous and symbolic computations, and many others. It also reshaped what professional developers must know about problem solving, mutability, function-based abstractions, and, with its functional foundation, it prompts for exploring new ways to computing.

## F# AT FIRST GLANCE

F# is strongly typed functional programming language for .NET that also provides a unique and effective combination of object-oriented and imperative features — a sort of "best-of-breeds" language.

If you have a background in other .NET languages, the first question you may have when you first look at F# is about its support for object-oriented programming. While this chapter is primarily concerned with the basic functional aspects of F#, it is important to establish early in your language exploration that these functional core features sit on top of a small and well-defined object-oriented layer, inherent with the foundations of .NET.

One clear distinction you will observe in this chapter is the use of the word *object* versus *value*. While every object is a value, and ultimately every value is an object, you will see the word *object* refer to instances of class types only, and *value* for instances of any other F# type. As you will see shortly, there are a host of F#-specific types (such as records, tuples, lists, arrays, and others) that get special treatment in F# — although ultimately they all will be compiled to .NET classes to make interoperability with other languages possible.

There are several key characteristics of F# that stem from its functional origin. Understanding these will help you get up to speed with F# much quicker.

➤ *Immutability* — Once values are created and assigned to names (bindings), they do not change, or change only rarely via marked constructs (such as assigning to reference cells). Those data structures that break immutability are *mutable* or *imperative* data structures, as are most (if not all) of the data structures you have dealt with in your past C# or VB programming. With F#, you should think about your data structures mostly as *functional*, and avoid *mutation* wherever possible. You will see plenty of examples of defining and using functional data structures in this chapter.

➤ *Functions as first-class values* — The capability to pass functions or return them from other functions is the basic building block of functional, higher-level abstractions. You will learn about these abstractions in this chapter. You should think of higher-order functions and function values as a natural supplement to your coding that is now more readily available than ever before. In fact, as you will see shortly, these enable you to come up with better, more robust, and fundamentally simpler abstractions.

➤ *Algebraic data types* — These enable you to differentiate a group of "shapes" within a given type. For example, you may want to express that binary trees are either nodes (one shape) that carry some value, or trees (the other shape) that have two sub-trees and a value. This often distills into a more natural recursive definition of your data type. Also, by enumerating the cases or shapes that your values can take, you can effectively control and limit the complexity of your functions that deal with these values. You will see plenty of examples on how to use *discriminated unions*, an F# type used to define algebraic data types, and how to write functions that operate on these values via *pattern matching*.

➤ *Pattern matching* — You can use pattern matching to deconstruct complex values (algebraic data types, tuples, lists, and so on) into simpler ones in a type-safe and exhaustive way. You can apply pattern matching not only to discriminated unions and a few other collection types, but also to any value or object if you use *active patterns*, a unique F# feature that makes pattern matching extensible, and provides for complete encapsulation of data representations.

➤ *Type inference* — In F# code you will rarely see type annotations, simply because the compiler can infer types from their usage. This enables you to write less and accomplish more (for example, write better code that is more generic and reusable). For example, you can define functions without having to type their arguments, and you can just simply list the argument names instead. Then the compiler will try to find the most general signature for each argument, by solving various type constraints and "equations" that your code poses. You should always aim to write generic code, and eliminate any references, calls, and operators that are overly restrictive. This way, when the compiler infers the signature for your functions, they will be as general as possible, and you can make changes easily and apply them to as diverse data structures as possible.

➤ *Support for lazy evaluation* — You can delay the computation of certain values until these values are actually needed. This enables you to do/compute only as much as you really need to, and not more. F# offers various ways to enable lazy computations. Most notably, you will learn about *sequences* that can be enumerated on demand, via a lazy interface erected around most F# and .NET collections, Language Integrated Queries (LINQ), and computations that may yield a lot of data as results. You will also see how you can construct and evaluate lazy values directly through the .NET `Lazy` type and the F# helper module, and syntax sugar around it.

## Trying Things Out with F#

One of the fun sides of F# development is being able to quickly prototype things and try them out on-the-fly. In fact, this is also partially the reason for why developing with F# is a very satisfying and rewarding experience. A Visual Studio add-in called F# Interactive helps you to accomplish just that. You can also invoke F# Interactive as a command-line tool by locating `fsi.exe` from the F# distribution, and running it in a command window.

Working with the Visual Studio add-in for F# Interactive is the easiest way to get going. All you must do is to highlight some block of code and press Alt+Enter to send it to the interactive session. You can send any code you like; code will be interpreted just like if you typed it in directly into the F# Interactive window.

Your interactive session is alive from the time you start it until you decide to exit or restart it. Typically, you will want to have a session for the time you are developing a module or a piece of code that relates to a particular functionality in your application. As you add more code to the session, it is "remembered" — so you can refer to any function, type, or "variable" that you may have created and added earlier. You can also refer to the value of the last expression in the session as `it`.

Keep in mind, however, that redefining functions or types will not have any effect on what you have already entered unless you redefine the consuming functions also. In other words, anything you enter is parsed and interpreted using lexical scoping. You can think of redefinitions as creating a new definition with a new name that just happens to be the same as something that existed already, which now is unreachable.

If you want to restart your interactive session, type "`exit 1;;`".

# Understanding Syntax

Let's take a look at the syntax of F#. In this section, you will learn about a few characteristics, rules, and conventions for the language.

## First Taste

F# is a script-like language, with very light, concise, and almost math-like syntax. It lends itself to exploratory programming, and enables you to quickly prototype short (but powerful) functional programs that are also easy to maintain.

Listing 25-1 gives a taste of some of the functional core constructs of F#, including global and local nested functions, higher-order functions (HOFs), piping arguments, raising and catching exceptions, and pattern matching against values and types.

**LISTING 25-1:** A Simple F# Function with Various Language Constructs

```
/// Computes some number based on a list of integers.
/// Returns NaN and reports an error if any of the
/// numbers are prime or on division by zero.
let SillyComputation numbers =            // Global function
    let translate x =                     // Local, nested function
        let isEven n = n%2 = 0
        let isPrime n =
            if n > 1 then                 // If-then-else
                { 2 .. n/2 }              // Sequence
                |> Seq.exists (fun i -> n%i = 0)   // Piping into a HOF
                |> not
            else
                false
        if isPrime x then                 // If-then-elif-else
            failwith "Can't compute XYZ"  // Raising a failure
        elif isEven x then
            -1./float x
        else
            1./float x
    try                                   // try-with
        numbers
        |> List.map translate
        |> List.reduce (+)
        |> fun res -> -res                // Anonymous function
    with
    | Failure msg ->                      // Pattern matching
```

*continues*

**LISTING 25-1** *(continued)*

```
        printfn "Failure: %s" msg
        System.Double.NaN
    | :? System.DivideByZeroException ->          // Pattern matching over
                                                   // types
        printfn "Error: division by zero"
        System.Double.NaN

let _ =
    [ 1; 4; 6; 8; 12; 15 ]
    |> SillyComputation
    |> printfn "The result is=%f"
```

Several things should stand out if you are a C# or VB programmer (with many more standing out as you explore the content of this chapter):

➤ Indentation matters. The bodies of if-then-else blocks do not need to be enclosed in braces or between begin-end pairs. They are inferred using the indentation level.

➤ There are a series of let bindings that bind values to names, creating "variables" and "functions."

➤ The bindings you create do not change; there is no mutation. You can, of course, create bindings that can be updated, but those require extra notation and, thus, are easier to isolate.

➤ You can nest bindings, which creates nested local functions and bindings that are only visible in their own scope.

➤ Functions are called without parentheses, and these calls are often chained together with |>.

➤ There is no main function that triggers the execution. If you run the code in Listing 25-1 in F# Interactive, or if you compile it as a standalone program, it will print the result. The top-level binding that is discarded (via the underscore) causes the execution, and you may have multiple such blocks, even in multiple files.

➤ Thus, any value binding will trigger the evaluation of the value being bound, and all function bindings will postpone that evaluation until the function is called, as you would expect.

## Understanding Functions and Piping

Functional programming gets its name from one of its fundamental pillars: functions, the workhorses of F# development. In F#, functions can do the following:

➤ Appear anywhere other values can (they are *first-class values*)

➤ Be created on-the-fly (*anonymous functions*)

➤ Carry their *closures*

➤ Be passed to as arguments, or returned from other functions (*higher-order functions*)

As you will see in this chapter, functions are a powerful abstraction that can change the way you think about problems and their solutions.

In your C# or VB coding you were used to calling functions or methods supplying all of their arguments. For example, your call may have looked like this one:

```
MyFunction(1, "string value", 2)
```

In F#, this corresponds to calling `MyFunction` with a *single* tuple value that carries three values — the integer 1, the string `"string value"`, and the integer 2. You can phrase this in F# the same way, or slightly differently using *piping*:

```
(1, "string value", 3) |> MyFunction
```

Piping relies on the pipe (|>) operator, which is defined to take two arguments, and sends the first to the second. By flipping the order of the function and its argument, you gain two things. First, you get a more natural way of writing a function call. This becomes apparent when you have a chain of function calls that operate on a value:

```
GetAllCustomers()
|> FilterWomen
|> FilterThoseInCA
|> AllocateADiscount
```

Besides making nested function calls easier to read, piping also helps to drive type inference by propagating type information from left to right, from the arguments into the functions being called. In the previous example, the result type of `GetAllCustomers()` is known in advance, and is then propagated to the next call, and so on. This may not seem like a huge win in cases where the participating functions have specific type requirements, but it can be a lifesaver with generic ones, and will save you a few type annotations.

## Understanding Optional Parentheses Around Function Arguments

You may have noted in Listing 25-1 that in F#, parentheses around function arguments are optional, and you just saw that expressions such as (1, "string value", 2) are single tuple values. The following guidelines for writing function calls will help you write cleaner code:

➤ Use `f x` instead of `f(x)`. Function application binds stronger than most operators (unary negation being one notable exception), so you can safely write `1+f 2+3` instead of `1+f(2)+3`, saving a few keystrokes that can come in handy when prototyping code.

➤ Use `f (x, y)` or `f (x,y)` instead of `f(x, y)`. The extra space makes it clear that the function takes a tuple argument.

➤ Use `y |> f x` instead of `f x y`, if and when it makes sense (for example, if the result of `f` must undergo further transformations, or if it helps to drive type inference).

➤ Align your pipes on new lines. This makes code much easier to read and change.

F# encourages passing multiple values as multiple arguments, so they can be curried.

## Understanding Currying

*Currying* refers to functions taking arguments one by one, so they can be partially applied. This is in contract to passing all arguments at the same time as a single tuple value.

When the earlier `MyFunction` (assuming that it returns an integer) is defined in a curried form, it has the following type:

```
int -> string -> int -> int
```

This is opposed to its non-curried, tupled form:

```
(int * string * int) -> int
```

Curried functions offer a couple of advantages:

> ➤ They can be partially applied, yielding other, more specialized residual functions that take fewer arguments.

> ➤ They allow you to perform pre-computation on arguments that are known in advance.

To benefit the most from curried functions, you should order your arguments from the least varying, leaving the one that varies the most to the last. For example, the F# core library has a number of modules defined for operations on different data types (such as lists, arrays, sequences, sets, maps, and so on). A typical operation on these data types — say, mapping or transforming elements to yield another collection — is defined to take the collection after the transformation function itself. This is because you are more likely to apply the same transformation function to different collections, than vice versa.

Nonetheless, avoid exposing curried functions in .NET APIs that you will use from other .NET languages that don't have an implicit mechanism to call these without requiring you to supply each argument via an `Invoke` method call.

## Significant Whitespace, Indentation Matters

By default, the F# parser operates in what is called the "light" syntax, based on a simplified grammar where significant whitespace is used to eliminate the need for some keywords — providing for more concise code, and giving explicit recommendations on the coding style. The "full" F# language is slightly more verbose, and primarily it is rarely used, since the light syntax became the official standard.

 *Light syntax is often referred to as "#light" syntax. This is a parsing directive that you can use in your code to turn on (#light "on" or simply #light) or off (#light "off") the light mode.*

For example, the normal syntax mode for records requires that you use a semicolon to separate the fields, and places no restriction on how many you can fit on a single line. On the other hand, the light syntax requires no semicolon, but, to be able to disambiguate each field, it requires you to put each on a new line. You can see in Listing 26-1 that no `begin-end` or other organizational constructs were needed. The scopes of each identifier are clear by the indentation, and the code looks clean and concise.

As a general guideline, you should use the light syntax wherever possible, and only resort to normal syntax elements when absolutely necessary. The light syntax encourages a cleaner, shorter, and more robust coding style because of the added significant whitespace, so your code becomes easier to maintain.

## Naming Conventions

In addition to writing F# applications or F# libraries to be used from F# applications, you can use F# very effectively for writing libraries that you consume from other .NET languages. This is especially true in those domains where functional programming excels over other paradigms, including numerical and symbolic computing, data traversal and processing, parallel and asynchronous computations, and so on — which you then expose as a Windows Forms or web application with some C# or VB UI code.

Using F# for .NET components and libraries makes the naming conventions defined in the standard .NET Design Guidelines for libraries prevail, and, indeed, this is the recommended way to program, even in the small. F# itself has come a long way since its beginnings to wear off many of its early influences from OCaml, especially when it comes to naming conventions.

As a short summary, here are some naming and coding style recommendations that will help you to produce code that is easier to maintain and call from other .NET languages:

➤ Always use PascalCase for type names and type parameters (for example: `MyCustomerType<'T>`). Note that most of the standard F# type abbreviations (which you see all the time in F# code, such as `'T list`, `'T array`, `'T option`) are safe "exceptions" to this rule. As abbreviations, they will ultimately map to the underlying .NET type names that are PascalCase.

➤ Always use PascalCase for namespaces, modules, exceptions, class members (properties and methods), discriminated union cases, record labels, and, in general, everything that will be part of a public API.

➤ Always use camelCase for function and method parameters, and (internal) `let` values.

➤ Avoid using underscores in identifiers. There has been a strong movement motivated by standard .NET naming conventions to eliminate underscores from the F# core libraries, and, all in all, you should avoid using them as well.

## Using Comments

Comments in F# are the same as those in C#. Thus, you have the following:

➤ *Comments in between* (* *and* *) — These comments can be nested.

➤ *Single-line comments starting with* // — These comments apply from the comment opener to the end of the current line. Used for documenting inner code.

➤ *XDoc comments starting with* /// — Used to define comments for public APIs, such as member or type names, argument types, return types, member description, and so on.

# YOUR FIRST F# PROJECT

Now that you have seen some of F# and a bit of functional programming, it is time you created your first F# project. You can do this pretty much the same way you create any project, by going to File ➪ New in Visual Studio. Figure 25-1 shows a typical F# development environment with F# Interactive.

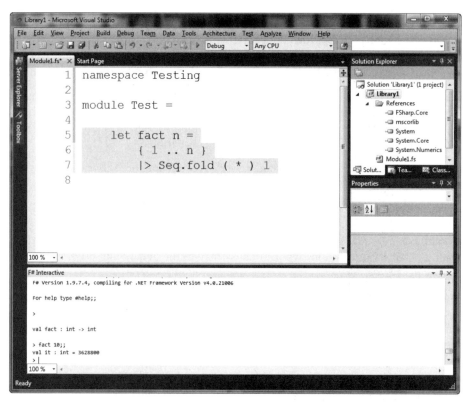

**FIGURE 25-1:** Developing F# projects

Once Visual Studio has created your project, note that a reference to `FSharp.Core.dll` has been added. For NET 4.0, this file resides under the following:

```
C:\Program Files\Reference Assemblies\Microsoft\F#\1.0\Runtime\v4.0\FSharp.Core.dll
```

`FSharp.Core.dll` contains all the core F# constructs, modules, types, and functions. Many of the miscellaneous functionality (including the primitives required to work with the F#-bundled lexer and parser generators) are placed in the F# PowerPack, which, as of this writing, is available as a separate download from MSDN Downloads and CodePlex.

There are certain types of F# files that you should become familiar with as you work with F# projects:

➤ *Source files* (*.fs) — These files contain F# code that will be compiled with your project. They are analogous to .cs or .vb files in other .NET languages.

➤ *Signature files* (*.fsi) — These files contain signatures and will be compiled with your project. You can use these signatures to give a public API to your corresponding source files, typically to restrict the visibility of certain members or types. In reality, because you can hide or expose members or functions within implementation modules using the appropriate access modifiers (such as private, public, or internal) signature files are of limited use, except when you want to hide the internals of certain types. Nonetheless, they are very effective in reiterating what the API should be.

➤ *Script files* (*.fsx) — These files can contain any code and will not be compiled with your project. You can use script files to experiment with certain parts of your code on-the-fly in F# Interactive, as you have already seen earlier in this chapter.

➤ *Lexer files* (*.fsl) — These files contain lexer definitions for your fslex-based lexers. fslex is a lexer generator for F#, similar to lex. To work with generated lexers, you must reference the F# PowerPack in your project.

➤ *Parser files* (*.fsy) — These files contain grammar definitions for your fsyacc-based parsers. fsyacc is a parser generator for F#, similar to yacc. To work with generated parsers (and lexers), you must reference the F# PowerPack in your project.

## PROGRAMMING WITH F#

You are now ready to take a deeper look at the F# language. In this section, you will learn about the fundamental concepts that underpin any F# programming.

## Namespaces and Modules

As with any .NET code, F# code is also organized into *namespaces*, which are logical containers of code and types. These namespaces may be provided via multiple physical libraries, and referencing a particular set of libraries will make the namespaces and the contents defined in them accessible.

For your F# projects, adding a project or library reference is all you need to access the namespaces therein. In F# Interactive, however, you must explicitly reference a particular library to work with it:

```
> #r "System.Xml.dll";;

--> Referenced 'C:\Windows\Microsoft.NET\Framework\v4.0.21006\System.Xml.dll'

> let xdoc = new System.Xml.XmlDocument();;

val xdoc : System.Xml.XmlDocument
```

F# also has another code organizational device: *modules*. Similar to namespaces, F# modules are also containers for functions and types, but they can also contain values/bindings, allowing you to group related functionality and their associated values into a single unit.

F# modules are translated to .NET classes, with the values exposed as static members and types as nested types. Modules can also contain sub-modules, which are simply translated to nested inner classes.

From those namespaces that are contained by the library references available to your project or your F# Interactive session, you can "open" any given namespace or module, making its contents available without having to qualify them with the parent namespace or module, by using the open keyword:

```
> open System.Xml;;
> let xdoc2 = new XmlDocument();;

val xdoc2 : XmlDocument
```

As shown in Table 25-1, there are a number of namespaces and modules opened by default in your F# projects.

**TABLE 25-1:** Namespaces and Modules Opened Implicitly

| NAMESPACE OR MODULE | TYPE | DESCRIPTION |
| --- | --- | --- |
| Microsoft.FSharp | Namespace | Parent namespace for all F#-related content. |
| Microsoft.FSharp.Core | Namespace | Contains the core F# constructs, including basic types such as tuples. |
| Microsoft.FSharp.Core.Operators | Module | Contains the core F# built-in operators and functions. |
| Microsoft.FSharp.Collections | Namespace | Contains the core F# collections, including support for sets, maps, lists, and arrays. |
| Microsoft.FSharp.Control | Namespace | Contains F# primitives for asynchronous and lazy programming. |
| Microsoft.FSharp.Core.ExtraTopLevelOperators | Module | Contains aliases for the top-level operators and functions, including pretty printing and common types. |

It is a good practice to always use a namespace declaration in the top of your source files, and nest modules underneath as you see fit:

```
namespace Your.Namespace

module FirstModule =

    open System.Xml
```

```
    let Foo () = new XmlDocument()
    ...

// Visible from outside as Your.Namespace.SecondModule
module SecondModule =

    let Bar () = FirstModule.Foo ()
    ...
```

In the absence of a top-level namespace declaration, the compiler will insist on a top-level module — and, in this case, all other modules will be implicitly nested underneath this module:

```
module FirstModule

open System.Xml

let Foo () = new XmlDocument()

// Visible from outside as FirstModule.SecondModule
module SecondModule =

    let Bar () = Foo ()
```

The only time you can get away with not giving a top-level namespace or module declaration (that is, simply giving a set of values, types, and/or functions) is when you have a single-file project. In that case, the compiler will generate a top-level module based on the filename, with a capital initial letter.

A useful module-level attribute is `RequireQualifiedAccess`. Adding this to a module requires that its contents are accessed via qualifying with the module name. For example, the `List` module in `Microsoft.FSharp.Collections` is marked with this attribute, and trying to open it will yield an error (or a warning in earlier versions of F#).

```
[<RequireQualifiedAccess>]
module YourModule =
    let Foo () = 1

module YourApplication =
    open YourModule            // Error

    let _ = Foo ()             // Error
    let _ = YourModule.Foo ()  // OK
```

## Attributes

As you just saw in the preceding example, you can add various attributes using the `[< ... >]` syntax. Attributes can apply to fields, members (properties, methods), types, modules, namespaces, as defined by their usage site. When adding an attribute whose name ends with `xxxAttribute`, you can simply use the name without that suffix.

## Literals and Bindings

In this section, you will learn more about simple values (ordinary and other literals, and syntax for various collections), bindings, and type signatures.

## Numbers, Booleans, and Unit

Having seen .NET code, you will not be surprised to find that most numeric literals are the same (or similar) as those you may have used in other .NET languages. Table 25-2 summarizes some of the basic numeric types and their associated literals. The list also includes the empty value (), which is the only value that inhabits the unit type, and it is roughly equivalent to the void type in C or C#.

**TABLE 25-2:** Some Basic Types and Literals

| F# TYPE | SAMPLE VALUES | .NET TYPE NAME |
|---------|---------------|----------------|
| bool | true, false | System.Boolean |
| byte | 16uy | System.Byte |
| sbyte | 16y | System.SByte |
| int16 | 16s | System.Int16 |
| uint16 | 16us | System.UInt16 |
| int, int32 | 16 | System.Int32 |
| uint32 | 16u | System.UInt32 |
| int64 | 16L | System.Int64 |
| uint64 | 16UL | System.UInt64 |
| single, float32 | 16.0f, 16.f | System.Single |
| float, double | 16.0, 16. | System.Double |
| decimal | 16M | System.Decimal |
| bigint | 16I | Math.BigInt |
| bignum | 16N | Math.BigNum |
| unit | () | Core.Unit |

In addition to the suffixes in Table 25-2, you can also specify binary, octal, and hexadecimal literals by prefixing them with 0b, 0O, 0x, respectively:

```
0b00010, 0O1234567, 0xFFFA00
```

## Strings

F# strings are immutable values, and they represent instances of the standard System.String type. Table 25-3 lists the most common string literals. The escape characters you can use are the same as in other .NET languages.

**TABLE 25-3:** String and Character Literals

| EXAMPLE | F# TYPE | DESCRIPTION |
| --- | --- | --- |
| `"Hello World!"` | `string` | Ordinary string |
| `"This is a line\nAnd another\n"` | `string` | String with escape characters |
| `@"c:\Program Files\"` | `string` | Verbatim string |
| `"This is a multi-line \ comment."` | `string` | Multi-line string |
| `"1234567890ABC"B` | `byte array` | Literal byte array |
| `'0'` | `char` | Character |
| `'\n'` | `char` | Escape character |

In addition to the static `System.String` members, the F# standard library provides the `Microsoft .FSharp.Core.String` module that contains a number of additional convenient operations on strings. These are summarized in Table 25-4.

**TABLE 25-4:** Static Members in the F# String Module

| MEMBER | TYPE | DESCRIPTION |
| --- | --- | --- |
| `collect` | `(char -> string) -> string -> string` | Maps each character of a string to build another by concatenating the resulting strings. |
| `concat` | `string -> seq<string> -> string` | Concatenates the given strings using the separator string in between elements. |
| `exists` | `(char -> bool) -> string -> bool` | Checks whether any character of the string satisfies the given predicate. |
| `forall` | `(char -> bool) -> string ->bool` | Tests whether all characters of the string satisfy the given predicate. |
| `init` | `int -> (int -> string) -> string` | Builds a new string by concatenating the results of the given function applied to values from 0 to the number given. |
| `iter` | `(char -> unit) -> string -> unit` | Applies the given function to each character of the string. |
| `iteri` | `(int -> char -> unit) -> string -> unit` | Applies the given function to each character and their position indexes in the string. |

*continues*

**TABLE 25-4** *(continued)*

| MEMBER | TYPE | DESCRIPTION |
|---|---|---|
| length | string -> int | Returns the length of the string. |
| map | (char -> char) -> string -> string | Builds a new string by applying the given function to each character in the string. |
| mapi | (int -> char -> char) -> string -> string | Builds a new string by applying the given function to each character and their position indexes in the string. |
| replicate | int -> string -> string | Builds a new string by appending the string by the specified number of times. |

## Syntax for Various Collections

F# provides special syntax for list and array values. These are summarized in Table 25-5. In addition, you can use range expressions (discussed later in this chapter) to generate sequences of numbers of various types.

**TABLE 25-5:** Common F# Collection Values

| F# TYPE | EXAMPLE | .NET TYPE NAME |
|---|---|---|
| list | [ ], [ 1 ], [ 1; 2 ] | Microsoft.FSharp.Collections.List |
| array | [\| \|], [\| 1 \|], [\| 1; 2 \|] | Microsoft.FSharp.Collections.Array |
| seq | { 1 .. 100 } | System.Collections.IEnumerable |

## Null Values

Generally, in pure F# programming, you will rarely (if ever) encounter null values. In other .NET languages, null is used as an indication that a particular value is not yet initialized or available, and some of the .NET APIs rely on passing and/or returning null values to indicate certain conditions. In F#, a common pattern for this is to return None option values. Option values, as you will see later in this chapter, are similar to Nullables, but they are truly generic and can be used with any type.

To accommodate .NET APIs returning or expecting nulls, F# also has a null value. When working with .NET APIs, you often need to check whether or not a result is null. You can do so by using pattern matching against the null pattern:

```
match SomeDotNetAPIFunction() with
| null ->
    ...
```

## Type Signatures

Before delving into the various forms of F# types and values, it is important to understand how the various types can be referred to, say, in another type definition or signature file.

F# type signatures (which cover the most common scenarios you will be seeing in this chapter) can contain the following:

- ➤ *Type names* — An example would be `System.Int32`. These type names can use the fully qualified type name, or the short type name if the containing namespace or module is opened.

- ➤ *Type variables* — An example would be `'T`. Here, `'T` stands for any type.

- ➤ *Type abbreviations* — Examples could be `int` or `float`. Table 25-2 shows many type abbreviations commonly used in F# code.

- ➤ *Tuples* — An example would be `T1*T2`. Here, the star (*) is used to "glue" values together into a tuple, an anonymous container of values of possibly different types.

- ➤ *Lists* — An example would be `'T list`. Lists are ubiquitous in functional programming, and you will see how to work with lists in the subsequent sections of this chapter.

- ➤ *Arrays* — An example would be `'T array` or `T[]`. Arrays are mutable collections (and, hence, fundamentally different from lists or tuples).

- ➤ *Function types* — Examples include `'T1->'T2->'T3`, or `('T1->'T2) ->'T3`. The arrow (->) type operator associates to the right, so `'T1->'T2->'T3` is the same type as `'T1->('T2->'T3)` — that is, a function that takes a value of type `'T1` and returns another function that takes a value of type `'T2` to produce a value of `'T3`. Essentially, both of these types describe a function that takes two arguments (of type `'T1` and `'T2`) in curried form to compute its result of `'T3`.

As this list shows, one way to write generic data types such as `List<'T>` is as `'T list`, and, indeed, this is the usual way you write the core F# container types such as lists and arrays. These two notations mean equivalent types.

## Bindings

Unlike in imperative languages, in F#, you rarely use "variables" (that is, memory locations that change their content). Instead, in most cases, when you assign a value to a "variable," it never changes. Functional programming encourages writing code that uses no mutation, and instead relies on applying *referentially transparent* functions (that is, functions that have no side effects, and consistently produce deterministic results).

You can bind a value to a name so that you can refer to it later by using a `let` binding, as you saw earlier in this chapter. You can bind any value, including functions. Occasionally, you may want to type annotate bindings, either to rule out ambiguities, or to assist the type inference algorithm. Here are a few cases that define how to do this:

- ➤ *Typing values* — You can type annotate a value simply by giving it a type and optionally wrapping it inside parentheses:

```
let amount: float = ...
```

➤ *Typing function arguments* — You can type annotate a parameter by wrapping it inside parentheses and giving it a type:

```
let WithdrawMoney customer (amount: float) = ...
```

➤ *Typing function return values* — You can simply give the function itself a return type (note the extra space for better readability):

```
let SomeFunction x y : float = ...
```

Bindings are visible in the scope they are defined in. So, your top-level bindings are visible everywhere beyond their definition, and your local bindings inside a function are only visible in that local scope. When you introduce a new binding, it is not yet available in the body of that binding, unless you make it so. You can introduce recursive bindings using the `rec` keyword:

```
let rec fact n = if n < 2 then 1 else n * fact (n-1)
```

Also, you may need to define mutually recursive bindings. For these you can combine `rec` and `and`:

```
let rec f x = if x > 0 then 1 + g x else 0
and g x = 1 + f (x-1)
```

The bindings you create are not mutable (that is, you can't update them once they are created, unless they point to mutable values). Mutable bindings can be created and later reassigned as follows:

```
let mutable counter = 0
//...
counter <- counter + 1
```

As you will see later in this chapter, you can also use mutable reference cells if you need mutable data.

## Access Control

You can control the visibility of your values, functions, types, members, and fields using the following access control specifiers:

➤ `public` — The entity is visible globally and can be referred to by all callers.

➤ `internal` — The entity is visible only inside the defining assembly.

➤ `private` — The entity is private to the enclosing type or module.

By default, in a module, all top-level `let` bindings and types are public. You will see type definitions later in this chapter. Members in a type are, by default, public also.

## Expressions

This section surveys some of the available F# operators and basic language constructs (conditionals and the imperative style looping). You should pay careful attention to the function operators, which you will see all the time in F# code.

## Operators

Tables 25-6, 25-7, and 25-8 summarize selected function, bitwise arithmetic, and logical operators.

**TABLE 25-6:** Function Operators

| OPERATOR | EXAMPLE | TYPE | DESCRIPTION |
|---|---|---|---|
| `|>` | `a |> f` | `'A -> ('A -> 'B) -> 'B` | Applies f to a. |
| `>>` | `(f >> g) a` | `('A -> 'B) -> ('B -> 'C) -> 'A -> 'C` | Applies f to a, then g to the result. Equivalent to g(f(a)). |
| `<<` | `(f << g) a` | `('A -> 'B) -> ('C -> 'A) -> 'C -> 'B` | Applies g to a, then f to the result. Equivalent to f(g(a)). |

**TABLE 25-7:** Bitwise Arithmetic Operators

| OPERATOR | EXAMPLE | RESULT | DESCRIPTION |
|---|---|---|---|
| `&&&` | `0b001 &&& 0b111` | `0b001` | Bitwise AND |
| `|||` | `0b001 ||| 0b111` | `0b111` | Bitwise OR |
| `^^^` | `0b001 ^^^ 0b111` | `0b110` | Bitwise EXCLUSIVE OR |
| `~~~` | `~~~0x100` | `0xFFFFFeff` | Bitwise negation |
| `<<<` | `0b001 <<< 2` | `0b100` | Left shift |
| `>>>` | `0b100 >>> 2` | `0b001` | Right shift |

Logical operators implement the usual shortcut logic, in `a&&b` and `a||b`, `b` is not evaluated if a is `false` and `true`, respectively.

**TABLE 25-8:** Boolean Operators

| OPERATOR | EXAMPLE | RESULT | DESCRIPTION |
|---|---|---|---|
| `&&` | `true && false` | `false` | Logical AND |
| `||` | `true || false` | `true` | Logical "OR" |
| `not` | `not true` | `false` | Logical negation |

Relational operators are standard, but do note the <> operator. Table 25-9 summarizes relational operators.

**TABLE 25-9:** Relational Operators

| OPERATOR | EXAMPLE | RESULT | DESCRIPTION |
|---|---|---|---|
| > | 1 > 0 | true | Greater than |
| >= | 1 >= 1 | true | Greater or equal |
| < | 2 < 1 | false | Less than |
| <= | 2 <= 0 | false | Less or equal |
| = | 2 = 2 | true | Equal |
| <> | 2 <> 2 | false | Not equal |

## Conditionals

*Conditionals* are expressions that are guarded by a Boolean condition, and, depending on this condition, evaluate one of their two branches. Unlike in C#, F# conditionals are not statements (that is, they do return values):

```
let a =
    if x>100 then
        2
    elif x>0 then
        1
    else
        0
```

As a consequence, all branches of a conditional must return a value of the same type. So, the following will yield a compile-time error:

```
let a =
    if x>100 then
        2
    elif x>0 then
        1
```

## Loops

F# provides various imperative looping constructs that will look familiar, although you rarely use them in functional code:

```
for i = 1 to 100 do
    printfn "%d" i

for (i, j) in [1,2; 2,3; 3,4; 4,5 ] do
    printfn "pair-%d-%d" i j

while someCondition do
    printfn "inside"
    ...
```

Here are these same code pieces using a more functional style:

```
{ 1 .. 100 }
|> Seq.iter (printfn "%d")

[1,2; 2,3; 3,4; 4,5 ]
|> List.iter (fun (i, j) ->
    printfn "pair-%d-%d" i j)

let rec loop () =
    if someCondition then
        printfn "inside"
        ...
        loop ()
```

The first two are a straightforward rewriting using pipelining and the higher-order functions for iteration. The third is an often-used technique to turn a block of code into a local recursive function, especially using an extra accumulator argument that collects a result through the iteration.

## Reference Cells

*Reference cells* are a type-safe way to maintain "links" to values. These links can later be updated to point to other values, effectively giving you a way to model imperative-style variables. You can create a new reference cell using the `ref` function as follows:

```
let counter = ref 0
```

This creates a reference cell, which is a core F# type called `ref`, and the `ref` function essentially translates any type `'T` to `'T ref`.

You can retrieve the value of a reference cell by invoking the `!` function on it, and you can update a reference cell via the `:=` operator:

```
counter := !counter + 1
```

Both reference cells and the mutable bindings you saw earlier can be passed to .NET functions that have *out parameters*, or expect referenced arguments.

## Core Functions — Formatted Printing

Opened by default, the `*.Core.ExtraTopLevelOperators` module contains a number of commonly used functions (such as `printf`, `printfn`, `sprintf`, and other formatted printing functions). In addition to the standard `String.Format` members, these are the most common ways to format objects. In particular, note the `%A` format specifier that you can use to print any value in a reasonably robust way.

The standard library is a collection of core functions that are part of every F# programmer's tool set, and this short chapter can't do justice to describing them in detail. Luckily, documentation is available at your fingertips in Visual Studio, where exploring the various namespaces is a breeze.

## Converting Literals and Values

You saw most of the numeric types and sample literals in Table 25-2. These types have a corresponding set of conversion functions defined in `Microsoft.FSharp.Core.Operators`, each having the same name as the type name, to convert between various numeric formats. This conversion may result in a loss of precision or overflow. Consider the case when there is no loss of precision — converting a 32-bit float value to a 64-bit one:

```
> System.Single.MaxValue;;
val it : float32 = 3.40282347e+38f
> float System.Single.MaxValue;;
val it : float = 3.402823466e+38
>
```

Underflowing is unchecked:

```
> sbyte -129;;
val it : sbyte = 127y
```

And so is overflowing:

```
> int16 System.Int32.MaxValue;;
val it : int16 = -1s
```

These conversion functions have alternatives in the `Microsoft.FSharp.Core.Operators.Checked` module that raise an exception if there is an over or underflow in the conversion:

```
> Microsoft.FSharp.Core.Operators.Checked.int16 System.Int32.MinValue;;
System.OverflowException: Arithmetic operation resulted in an overflow.
   at <StartupCode$FSI_0070>.$FSI_0070.main@()
Stopped due to error
```

Numeric literals can also be converted to other numeric types using the `System.Convert` class provided in the .NET framework. Note, however, that this conversion may fail in certain cases as documented for the various members of this class.

# Values and F# Types

Fundamentally, every value in your F# code will be compiled to .NET objects, making it easy to interoperate F# code with other .NET languages. However, the following are some of the multiple forms of types in the language that you should be aware of, and it is important to understand how these types will appear from a non-F# project:

➤ Tuples

➤ Discriminated unions (algebraic data types)

➤ Options

➤ Records

➤ Lists

➤ Arrays

## Class Types, Objects, and Object Expressions

You define class types by defining various *members* for them. Members can be *properties* or *methods*, similar to other .NET languages. Consider the following definition:

```
type Car(name: string, year: int) =
    member this.Name = name
    member this.Year = year
```

This defines a new class type called `Car` that has one constructor taking two arguments, and exposes those via two properties. Properties behave like method calls, except that they don't take arguments. This means that calling the same property multiple times will evaluate the body of the property every time. This is important to remember if you have state manipulation (for example, logging) in your property definitions. Also, note that all members are assumed to be public unless you otherwise specify by prefixing them with the appropriate access modifier.

```
member internal this.Year = year
```

### Inheritance

You can inherit from an existing type by adding the `inherit` clause. If you need to access the base instance, you can use the `base` keyword.

```
type BMW(model: string, year: int) =
    inherit Car("BMW", year)

    member this.Model = model
```

Inheritance is a less frequently used concept in F# programming. One of the many reasons is that inheritance is not a composable abstraction because it makes objects more complex and only conceivable up to a certain level, whereas functional programming aims to use simple (but powerful) composable building blocks such as higher-order functions.

### Interfaces

An alternative to implementation inheritance is using interfaces to define traits that can be supported without having to share a common object ancestry. Interfaces are abstract types, in the sense that they contain a "skeleton" or signature of a class type:

```
type ICar =
    abstract Name : string
    abstract Year : int
```

Note that interfaces can only describe instance member requirements, without having to name the instance itself in the signature. Also, they can't contain constructors or take arguments. Interfaces can also be inherited to create a *hierarchy of interface types*:

```
type ICarModel =
    inherit ICar

    abstract Model : string
```

## Object Expressions

You can instantiate interfaces using *object expressions*:

```
let audi2000 =
    { new ICar with
        member this.Name = "Audi"
        member this.Year = 2000 }
```

Object expressions are used for implementing interfaces on-the-fly. Any given object expression must give the implementation for all interface members:

```
let bmw525i2004 =
    { new ICarModel with
        member this.Name = "BMW"
        member this.Year = 2004
        member this.Model = "525i" }
```

You can also define new class types that implement interfaces, as many as you prefer:

```
type Citroen(model: string, year: int) =
    interface ICar with
        member this.Name = "Citroen"
        member this.Year = year
    member this.Model = model
```

## Objects

Ordinary class types can be instantiated using their constructors and the optional new keyword.

```
let audi2000 = Car("Audi", 2000)
let bmw525i2004 = new BMW("525i", 2004)
```

## Object State via let Bindings

Now that you have seen how to define class types and interfaces, how object expressions work, and you can instantiate both to create objects, there are a few additional details you should be aware of.

Foremost, you can add construction-time state to your objects using let bindings in the class definition:

```
type Rectangle(height, width) =
    let area = height*width
    let diagonal = Math.Sqrt(height**2.0 + width**2.0)

    member this.Area = area
    member this.Diagonal = diagonal
```

These let bindings, similar to the type/constructor arguments, are visible in the entire type definition, and they are computed only once as the object is being constructed. They need to be placed before the members; otherwise, you will get a compiler error.

## Object Initialization

You can also add initialization code to your classes using the `do` keyword. This code can be added before or after the `let` bindings. Usually, you can use initialization code to check various constraints that must hold for the object to be constructed. Here is an example for refusing to construct rectangles with negative dimensions:

```
type Rectangle2(height, width) =
    do if height < 0. || width < 0. then
        failwith "Can't construct rectangle with negative dimensions"

    let area = height*width
    let diagonal = Math.Sqrt(height**2.0 + width**2.0)

    member this.Area = area
    member this.Diagonal = diagonal
```

## Setters and Getters

In all previous class definition examples, the properties you defined were read-only. Another way to write these properties would be to specify the getter explicitly:

```
    ...
    member this.Area with get () = area
```

Because there is no setter defined by default, if you tried to set them, you would get an error:

```
let r2 = Rectangle2(100,100)
r2.Area <- 100                  // Error
```

Adding a setter is straightforward, and it usually comes defined together with the getter (unless you want only a setter):

```
type Rectangle2(height, width) =
    let mutable colorCode = 0
    ...
    member this.ColorCode
        with get () = colorCode
        and  set cc = colorCode <- cc
```

## Indexers

You can add further dot notation to your objects in the form of `object.[index]` and `object.[index] <- expr`. These *indexer* properties are special properties that take arguments, and can be defined with getters and setters as shown previously to a special property called `Item`.

For example, you may want to provide a mechanism to read the coordinates in a polygon via an index (starting at zero). You can implement this by creating a `Polygon` class with an indexer property:

```
type Polygon(coords: int list) =
    ...

    member self.Item
```

```
            with get idx =
                if Seq.length coords <= idx then
                    failwith "Index out of bound"
                else
                    Seq.nth idx coords
```

You can test the indexer property in F# Interactive:

```
> let p = new Polygon([1;2;3;4;5;6;7]);;

val p : Polygon

> p.[2] |> printfn "%d";;
3
val it : unit = ()
```

## Named and Optional Arguments to Constructors

You can make your code more readable by naming arguments and settable properties in your constructor calls. For example, you can construct a new rectangle this way:

```
let r2 = Rectangle2(height=100., width=100., ColorCode=5)
```

You can verify that this indeed initialized the object properly:

```
> r2.ColorCode;;
val it : int = 5
> r2.Area;;
val it : float = 10000.0
> r2.Diagonal;;
val it : float = 141.4213562
```

You can also add optional arguments to your constructors:

```
type Circle(radius, x, y, ?color: int) =
    let setColor =
        match color with
            | None ->
                128
            | Some c ->
                c
    member self.Everything = (radius, x, y, setColor)
```

Here, ?color defines an optional argument to the Circle class constructor. In F#, this is modeled as receiving an option value, which you check as part of the object initialization sequence, and assign the local setColor state variable accordingly (in this case, defaulting to 128 if no color code is given). You can test this in F# Interactive:

```
> let c1 = new Circle(radius=10, x=5, y=5);;
val c1 : Circle
> let c2 = new Circle(10, 5, 5, 100);;
```

```
    val c2 : Circle
  > c1.Everything;;
    val it : int * int * int * int = (10, 5, 5, 128)
  > c2.Everything;;
    val it : int * int * int * int = (10, 5, 5, 100)
```

## Anonymous Functions

You can create an anonymous function (a lambda expression in C# terminology) — that is, a new unnamed *function value* using the `fun` keyword, listing the formal parameters and the body of the function:

```
    fun x y -> System.Math.Sqrt(x**2. + y**2.)
```

You can name function values by binding them to a name:

```
    let diag = fun x y -> System.Math.Sqrt(x**2. + y**2.)
```

This, of course, is equivalent to the following:

```
    let diag x y = System.Math.Sqrt(x**2. + y**2.)
```

If you need a single argument function that pattern matches against its argument (you will learn about pattern matching later in this chapter), you can use the `function` keyword:

```
    let onlyOne = function | 1 -> 1 | _ -> 0
```

This defines a function that takes an integer and returns 1 if it was 1, and 0 otherwise. By convention, each pattern match case starts with a pipe character (|), including the first case.

The function values you create can be passed or returned from other functions. One particularly useful application of anonymous functions is writing *continuations*, also known as *continuation passing style* (CPS). You will see continuations later in this chapter in the discussion that deals with asynchronous programming, where an expression that is evaluated asynchronously takes place via registering a *callback function* (that is, a continuation that will receive the computed value and proceed with the rest of the computation).

For an example of explicit continuations, consider a CPS version of an evaluator (more of which you will be seeing later in this chapter in the discussion on discriminated unions):

```
    type Expr =
        | Number of float
        | Binop of (float -> float -> float) * Expr * Expr

        static member Add (e1, e2)  = Binop (( + ), e1, e2)
        static member Sub (e1, e2)  = Binop (( - ), e1, e2)
        static member Mul (e1, e2)  = Binop (( * ), e1, e2)
        static member Prod (e1, e2) = Binop (( / ), e1, e2)

    let rec Eval e cont =
        match e with
```

```
                | Number n ->
                    cont n
                | Binop (f, e1, e2) ->
                    Eval e1 (fun i1 ->
                        Eval e2 (fun i2 ->
                            f i1 i2 |> cont))
```

Here, the `Eval` function receives an expression and an explicit continuation that takes the result of the expression. When the expression is a number, you simply pass it to the continuation. If the expression is a binary operation, you evaluate the first operand with a continuation function that evaluates the second operand, which itself gets a continuation that takes both of the evaluated results, applies the binary operation on them, and passes the overall result to the original continuation.

CPS is a common functional pattern, often used for translating between different representations or traversing structured data types.

## Using Tuples

*Tuples* are a fundamental functional data structure, another workhorse of F# development. They are such a versatile data type that .NET 4.0 finally included them as a system type as `System.Tuple`, pioneered and inspired by F#.

Tuples are also referred to as *product types*, because they constitute the Cartesian product of their parts, and also because, in type theory, they are denoted by a star symbol (such as `T1*T2*T3`). As you saw earlier, in F# type signatures, tuples are marked with the star symbol (such as `T1*T2*T3`).

You can construct tuples by connecting values with a comma:

```
1, "my string", 3
```

Often, you must parenthesize to avoid precedence errors — for example, when you call a function that takes a tuple argument, as you saw in the beginning of this chapter:

```
(1, "my string", 3) |> MyFunction
```

Here, the function call (or the pipe operator) has higher precedence than a comma, and, without parentheses, it would only apply to the last value in the intended tuple.

Tuples are also called *n-tuples* for any n, where the tuple groups n separate values together. You can nest tuples in tuples, so the following are different values:

```
(1, "my string", 3)
(1, ("my string", 3))
((1, "my string"), 3)
```

You can use pattern matching to deconstruct tuples, as you will see later in this chapter. F# also provides some utility functions to work with pairs:

```
> fst (1, 2);;
val it : int = 1
> snd (1, 2);;
val it : int = 2
```

## Using Discriminated Unions

*Discriminated* (or *tagged*) *unions* are a form of algebraic data types that can take on a predefined set of shapes. One immediate advantage of using discriminated unions in your code is that the compiler can check that you handle all possible shapes where you operate on them, as you will see shortly in the discussion on pattern matching. However, fundamentally, an even more important advantage is that they provide type-safe access to the values they carry, as opposed to the C-style unions you may have encountered before. Discriminated unions are important data abstractions in functional programming because they partition a value space into a set of shapes, making it easier and conceptually cleaner to work on them.

Consider the following example:

```
type Expr =
    | Num of float
    | Var of string
    | UnOp of (float -> float) * Expr
    | BinOp of (float -> float -> float) * Expr * Expr

    static member Add (e1, e2) = BinOp (( + ), e1, e2)
    static member Sub (e1, e2) = BinOp (( - ), e1, e2)
    static member Mul (e1, e2) = BinOp (( * ), e1, e2)
    static member Div (e1, e2) = BinOp (( / ), e1, e2)
    static member Sin (e1)     = UnOp  (Math.Sin, e1)
    static member Cos (e1)     = UnOp  (Math.Cos, e1)
```

Here you created a discriminated union type to represent mathematical expressions with four basic shapes: numbers, variables, unary and binary operations. To make it easier to construct values (expressions) of this type, you have also added a few static members to represent the four basic arithmetic operations, and sine and cosine. You can also add any number of additional members the same way.

You can now construct mathematical expressions easily. Consider the following that represents $\cos(x+\pi)$:

```
let num = Expr.Cos (Expr.Add (Expr.Var "x", Expr.Num Math.PI))
```

Note that you have used the type name to qualify the occurrences of the basic four shapes (Var and Num) — this is not required as long as the type itself is in scope. However, because you may have union cases with the same name in different unions, it is good practice to qualify them with the appropriate type name.

You can examine union values (and others) using *pattern matching* — a machinery used to deconstruct and bind values via patterns. You will learn more about pattern matching later in this chapter, but as a preview, here is a function that evaluates expressions of your new type:

```
let rec Eval (env: Map<string, float>) = function
    | Num num ->
        num
    | Var v ->
        env.[v]
```

```
    | UnOp (op, e) ->
        op (Eval env e)
    | BinOp (op, e1, e2) ->
        op (Eval env e1) (Eval env e2)
```

You can play with the evaluator in F# Interactive a bit just to double-check that it works correctly:

```
> let env = ["x", 1.0] |> Map.ofList;;

val env : Map<string,float>

> Eval env num;;
val it : float = -0.5403023059
> Math.Cos (1. + Math.PI);;
val it : float = -0.5403023059
>
```

## Using Options

*Option values* are a generalization of the concept of "nullables" — that is, to represent that a value of some type T is given or not. One key difference from the `Nullable<'T>` .NET type is that F# options can be used with any arbitrary type, and not just value types. As you may expect, options can be implemented with discriminated unions. In fact, this is how it's done in the F# standard library:

```
type Option<'T> =
    | Some of 'T
    | None
```

You will also find a type alias (simply to define it as a lowercase type name) to this type in the standard library, and, in fact, this is the type you will be seeing in most F# code:

```
type 'T option = Option<'T>
```

Option values play an important role in making F# programming safe. One of the drawbacks of imperative languages is that they rely heavily on `null`s to represent that some computation can't proceed, or that the result is undefined. In fact, there are plenty of examples of standard .NET library functions returning `null`s in certain situations.

Consider the following F# function:

```
let FileExtension fname =
    if fname |> String.IsNullOrEmpty |> not then
        fname.LastIndexOf('.')
        |> function
            | n when n < 1 ->
                None
            | idx ->
                idx
                |> fname.Substring
                |> Some
    else
        None
```

This function returns the file extension from the filename parameter as an option. It will only succeed if the filename passed has a dot (.) in it, and then it will return the tail from that dot as a Some value. In every other case, it will return None. A bit of F# Interactive exploration helps to test these:

```
> FileExtension "data";;
val it : string option = None
> FileExtension "data.";;
val it : string option = Some "."
> FileExtension "data.dat";;
val it : string option = Some ".dat"
> FileExtension "";;
val it : string option = None
> FileExtension null;;
val it : string option = None
>
```

## Using Records

You can define a record type by listing its fields and their types inside braces:

```
type Person =
    { FirstName: string
      LastName: string
      Age: int
      Children: Person list
      mutable LastSeen: System.DateTime option }
```

You can just as easily create a new record value by giving the values of its fields inside braces:

```
let john =
    { FirstName = "John"
      LastName = "Smith"
      Age = 32
      Children = []
      LastSeen = None }
```

In both the definition and the value constructor, fields can be separated with semicolons — this comes in handy when you want to put multiple fields on the same line.

At times, you may need to copy records to create new ones, perhaps with certain fields changed:

```
let sally =
    { john with
        FirstName = "Sally"
        Age = 25 }
```

One important thing to remember is that records are not value types. Switching one of the fields to mutable will reveal this:

```
let shadowOfSally = sally
```

Now, in F# Interactive, you can experiment with what happens when you update `shadowOfSally`:

```
> shadowOfSally.LastSeen <- Some System.DateTime.Now;;
val it : unit = ()
> sally;;
val it : Person =
  {FirstName = "Sally";
   LastName = "Smith";
   Age = 25;
   Children = [];
   LastSeen = Some 12/16/2009 10:16:03 PM {Date = 12/16/2009 12:00:00 AM;
                                           Day = 16;
                                           DayOfWeek = Wednesday;
                                           DayOfYear = 350;
                                           Hour = 22;
                                           Kind = Local;
                                           Millisecond = 122;
                                           Minute = 16;
                                           Month = 12;
                                           Second = 3;
                                           Ticks = 633965985631224530L;
                                           TimeOfDay = 22:16:03.1224530;
                                           Year = 2009;};}
```

Type inference for records works by identifying field names and trying to match them to unique types. This can fail if you have multiple records types that overlap in their field names. In this case, you can prefix the field labels with the parent type to disambiguate — and even a single type annotation helps to fix the type error:

```
type PersonA = { FirstName: string; Age: int }
type PersonB = { FirstName: string; Age: int; Department: string }

let a = { PersonA.FirstName="Sally"; Age=32 }
let b = { FirstName="Peter"; Age=45; Department="Sales" }
```

## Using Lists

F# lists provide a hassle-free container for storing an ordered sequence of values of a given type, giving you fast access to the head and tail of the list. They are implemented as linked lists, so if you need random access to obtain the list elements, you should consider using sets or arrays instead.

Lists are at the core of functional programming, and, as such, they are your primary collection type as you work with F# code. They also receive extra attention in the language, which provides a clean syntax for constructing list values.

Table 25-10 shows the basic list-related language constructs.

**TABLE 25-10:** Language Constructs for Lists

| EXPRESSION | DESCRIPTION | EXAMPLES |
|---|---|---|
| [ ] | An empty list. | [ ] |
| expr :: expr | Adding an element to the head of the list ("consing"). | 1 :: [ 2; 3 ] |
| [ expr; ...; expr ] | A list with its elements. | [ 1; 2; 3 ] |
| [ expr .. expr ] | A range of numbers. | [ 1 .. 100 ], [ 1.0 .. 100.0] |
| [ expr .. expr .. expr ] | A range of numbers using a skip value. | [ 0 .. 2 .. 100 ] |
| expr @ epxr | Concatenation of two lists. | [ 1; 2 ] @ [ 3; 4 ] |
| [ for x in list -> expr ] | A list comprehension. | [ for x in 1 .. 100 -> x*x ] |

List values can be iterated, transformed, and aggregated using the static members available on the `List` module (defined as `Microsoft.FSharp.Collections.List`). Consider the following:

```
> let a = List.empty
  let b = []
  let c = 1 :: 2 :: 3 :: [ 4 ]
  let d = [ 1; 2; 3; 4 ];;

val a : 'a list
val b : 'a list
val c : int list = [1; 2; 3; 4]
val d : int list = [1; 2; 3; 4]
```

Here, both a and b contain the empty list, with a generic type because no list elements have been given. c and d are also equal, with 1, 2, 3, 4 as elements — and, thus, with the concrete type int list.

You can traverse (iterate) a list with `List.iter`, giving a "visitor" function that takes an element and returns nothing (so, a function value of type `'T -> unit`) and a list you want to traverse (of type `'T list`):

```
> List.iter (printfn "Printing a number: %d") c;;

Printing a number: 1
Printing a number: 2
Printing a number: 3
Printing a number: 4
val it : unit = ()
```

You can aggregate (fold) a list with `List.fold`, giving a function that takes an accumulator value and an element, and returns a new aggregate value (so, a function value of type `'T1->'T2->'T1`), an initial accumulator value (of type `'T1`), and a list (of type `'T2 list`):

```
> List.fold (+) 0 c
    |> printfn "The sum of all elements= %d";;

The sum of all elements= 10
val it : unit = ()
```

Here, both the accumulator and the list elements have the same type (`int`), so you can pass the ordinary addition operator (that has a relevant overload of type `int->int->int`) as the accumulator function.

You can also filter lists using `List.filter` and giving a predicate function. For example, you can define a Boolean function that checks whether its argument is a prime number:

```
> let IsPrime n =
      if n > 1 then
          { 2 .. n/2 }
          |> Seq.exists (fun i -> n%i = 0)
          |> not
      else
          false;;

val IsPrime : int -> bool
```

Armed with this function, you can then find all primes smaller than 100 as easily as the following:

```
> [ 1 .. 100 ] |> List.filter IsPrime;;

val it : int list =
  [2; 3; 5; 7; 11; 13; 17; 19; 23; 29; 31; 37; 41; 43; 47;
     53; 59; 61; 67; 71; 73; 79; 83; 89; 97]
```

Table 25-11 shows the most important list operations defined in the `List` module.

**TABLE 25-11:** Functions in the List Module

| FUNCTION | TYPE | DESCRIPTION |
|---|---|---|
| List.length | 'T list -> int | The length of the list. |
| List.head | 'T list -> 'T | The first element of the list (raises System. ArgumentException if the list is empty). |
| List.tail | 'T list -> 'T list | The tail (all but the first) elements of a list (raises System.ArgumentException if the list is empty). |
| List.init | int -> (int -> 'T) -> 'T list | Creates a new list of the specified size, and with elements generated by the function given in the second argument. |

| FUNCTION | TYPE | DESCRIPTION |
|---|---|---|
| `List.append` | `'T list -> 'T list -> 'T list` | Appends two lists that contain elements of the same type by copying the elements from the first list, followed by those in the second. |
| `List.filter` | `('T -> bool) -> 'T list -> 'T list` | Returns a new list containing the elements from the original list for which the given predicate function returns `true`. |
| `List.map` | `('T -> 'U) -> 'T list -> 'U list` | Maps a function to each element in a list, and returns the results in a new list. |
| `List.iter` | `('T -> unit) -> 'T list -> unit` | Iterates through the list by calling the given function on each element. |
| `List.unzip` | `('T * 'U) list -> 'T list * 'U list` | Takes a list of pairs and returns a pair of lists that each contain the elements from the original pairs. |
| `List.zip` | `'T list -> 'U list -> ('T * 'U) list` | Takes two lists, and returns a new list that contains the elements of the original two lists as pairs. Raises `System.ArgumentException` if the original lists are of different sizes. |
| `List.toArray` | `'T list -> 'T array` | Converts a list to an array. |
| `List.ofArray` | `'T array -> 'T list` | Converts an array to a list. |
| `List.toSeq` | `'T list -> 'T seq` | Converts a list to a sequence. |
| `List.ofSeq` | `'T seq -> 'T list` | Converts a sequence to a list. |

Finally, there are a few points to remember about lists:

➤ *Lists are immutable* — As you saw at the beginning of this chapter, immutability plays an important role in functional programming, and that is especially true for one of its fundamental data structures — lists. For example, when you cons (append to the front) a new element to a list, or concatenate two lists, you always get a new list value.

➤ *Lists are eager* — One way to ensure that a collection of values is fully computed is to convert it to a list. This is a typical pattern, and you will see it often when you work with lazy sequences (you will see what these are later in this chapter) and the kind of objects they wrap (for example, LINQ query results).

➤ *Lists are generic* — Because the standard .NET list collection type (of which the F# list type is a sub type) is generic, F# lists can store values of arbitrary types.

## Type Augmentations

Type augmentations make it possible to extend a type after it's been defined. The C# or VB extension methods you may have used fall under the very same umbrella, and, in fact, they can be modeled using F# type augmentations.

Here is an example of extending `System.Int32` with a new static member to check a number for primeness, reusing the `IsPrime` function you defined earlier:

```
type System.Int32 with
    static member IsPrime n = IsPrime n
```

You define type augmentations the same way you would add members to any of your types. The only difference is that the type being augmented is followed with the `with` keyword.

You should add type augmentations to a separate module that you can open whenever the augmentations are needed.

## Computation Expressions

*Computation expressions* (or F# *workflows*) are an important part of F# programming, and they underpin many useful formalisms such as sequence expressions, or asynchronous computations. Computation expressions are the F# way to express what's called *monads*, a term that originates from advanced mathematics, used for representing computations as a chain of operations. Monads are used extensively in various functional programming languages, most notably in Haskell.

The general syntax for computation expressions is strikingly simple:

```
builder { computation-expression }
```

Here, `builder` is any computation expression builder object, a special object that implements certain well-defined members that the various constructs in `computation-expression` are de-sugared into by the compiler. Table 25-12 summarizes the constructs, giving a subset of the F# language and some enhancements such as `let!` and `use!`, that you can use in computation expressions.

**TABLE 25-12:** Constructs in Computation Expressions

| CONSTRUCT | UNDERLYING REPRESENTATION |
|---|---|
| `()` | `b.Zero()` |
| `let pat = expr in cexpr` | `b.Let(expr, (fun pat -> [[cexpr]]))` |
| `let! pat = expr in cexpr` | `b.Bind(expr, (fun pat -> [[cexpr]]))` |
| `use pat = expr in cexpr` | `b.Using(expr, (fun pat -> [[cexpr]]))` |
| `use! pat = expr in cexpr` | `b.Bind(expr, (fun x -> b.Using(x, (fun pat -> [[cexpr]]))))` |
| `do expr in cexpr` | `b.Let(expr, (fun () -> [[cexpr]]))` |
| `do! expr in cexpr` | `b.Bind(expr, (fun () -> [[cexpr]]))` |
| `if expr then cexpr` | `if expr then [[cexpr]] else b.Zero()` |
| `if expr then cexpr1 else cexpr2` | `If expr then [[cexpr1]] else [[cexpr2]]` |

| CONSTRUCT | UNDERLYING REPRESENTATION |
|---|---|
| `cexpr1, cexpr2` | `b.Combine([[cexpr1]], b.Delay(fun () -> [[cexpr2]]))` |
| `while expr do cexpr` | `b.While((fun () -> expr), b.Delay((fun () -> [[cexpr]])))` |
| `for pat in expr do cexpr` | `b.For(expr, (fun pat -> [[cexpr]]))` |
| `return expr` | `b.Return(expr)` |
| `return! Expr` | `expr` |

Not all of the constructs in Table 25-12 are used in the various computation expressions available, and the designer of new *workflows* can decide what features to support by implementing the appropriate members, as listed in Table 25-13.

**TABLE 25-13:** Computation Expression API for Some Builder Type `M`

| MEMBER | DESCRIPTION |
|---|---|
| `Let : 'A * ('A -> M<'B>) -> M<'B>` | Used for `let` and `do`. |
| `Bind : M<'A> * ('A -> M<'B>) -> M<'B>` | Used for `let!` and `do!`. |
| `Delay : (unit -> M<'A>) ->M<'A>` | Used to execute an expression when expected. |
| `Using : 'A * ('A -> M<'A>) -> M<'A>, when 'A :> IDisposable` | Used for `use`. |
| `For : seq<'A> * ('A -> M<'B>) -> M<'B>` | Used for `for ... do ...` |
| `While : (unit -> bool) * M<'A> -> M<'A>` | Used for `while ... do ...` |
| `Combine : M<'A> * M<'A> -> M<'A>` | Used for sequencing. |
| `Zero : unit -> M<'A>` | Used for empty `else` branch. |
| `Return : 'A -> M<'A>` | Used for `return`. |

To implement a new computation builder, you must define a new type with some or all members from Table 25-13. As a short example, consider the following block of code:

```
let a = ComputeA ()
let b = ComputeB a
let c = ComputeC (a, b)
ComputeD c
```

Here, you would like to know how much time certain steps in the computation take, and log this timing information to the console (or a file, or the database, and so on).

You can start by defining a computation builder as follows:

```
type LoggerBuilder() =
    let mutable lastTime = None
    member self.Return e =
        lastTime <- None
        e
    member self.Bind (value, cont) =
        match lastTime with
        | None ->
            printfn "Time at let! = 0 sec"
        | Some (last: System.DateTime) ->
            let time = System.DateTime.Now - last
            time.TotalSeconds
            |> printfn "Time at let! = %f sec"
        lastTime <- Some System.DateTime.Now
        cont value

let logger = new LoggerBuilder()
```

Here, your new `logger` computation builder has special treatment for `let!` expressions. First, you keep a `lastTime` value in the builder that stores the timestamp of the latest invocation of a `let!` expression. Initially, this is not available, and you store that as a `None` option value. When a `let!` is encountered inside this builder, the `Bind` method will be invoked. Here, you first check if you have the last timestamp available, and report the elapsed time accordingly. As a last step, you update the `lastTime` counter, and invoke the continuation.

This will print the elapsed time since the last `let!` for each `let!`. One last tiny bit is resetting the timestamp when exiting from the `logger` block. This is useful if you are reusing the same logger builder instance across multiple sessions/blocks.

Now you can wrap your earlier code in a `logger` computation:

```
logger {
    let a = ComputeA ()
    let b = ComputeB a
    let c = ComputeC (a, b)
    let d = ComputeD c
    return d
}
```

This has no effect; everything executes like before. However, if you switch some of the instances of `let` to `let!`, you will see timing information:

```
Time at let! = 0 sec
Time at let! = 0.104006 sec
```

# Sequences

All F# collections, such as lists and arrays, implement the `System.Collections.IEnumerable<'T>` interface. In F# code, you most often see this interface type as `seq<'T>`, which is a type abbreviation for this interface type. As in other .NET code, sequences are lazy data structures. They are enumerated on demand, and sequence values are not computed until they are requested.

It is important to understand that, since sequences wrap collections, you can turn F# lists and arrays lazy by operating on them with the various `Seq.*` static members.

Table 25-14 shows the most important members, along with a brief description. As you will see, there is a lot of similarity between these and the aggregate operations defined in the `List` module in Table 25-11, and, indeed, this is true for all other F# collections as well. However, the `Seq` module also supports operations for calculating minimum, maximum, and average values, sort and average, and traverse in various ways to find or pick elements.

**TABLE 25-14:** Selected Aggregate Operators from the Seq Module

| FUNCTION | TYPE | DESCRIPTION |
| --- | --- | --- |
| Seq.append | seq<'T> -> seq<'T> -> seq<'T> | Appends two sequences, keeping the result lazy. |
| Seq.average | Seq<'T> -> 'T | Computes the average of the elements in the sequence. |
| Seq.cast | IEnumerable -> seq<'T> | Wraps an untyped collection to a typed sequence. |
| Seq.choose | ('T -> 'U option) -> seq<'T> -> seq<'U> | Returns a new sequence whose elements, when applied to the given predicate, return Some. |
| Seq.collect | ('T -> seq<'U>) -> seq<'T> -> seq<'U> | Applies the given function to each element, and returns a new sequence with the results concatenated. |
| Seq.concat | Seq<seq<'T>> -> seq<'T> | Concatenates the sequence of sequences into a single sequence. |
| Seq.distinct | Seq<'T> -> seq<'T> | Returns all distinct elements. |
| Seq.empty | Seq<'T> | Returns an empty sequence. |
| Seq.exists | ('T -> bool) -> seq<'T> -> bool | Tests if any element satisfies the given predicate. |
| Seq.filter | ('T -> bool) -> seq<'T> -> seq<'T> | Filters all elements that satisfy the given predicate. |
| Seq.find | ('T -> bool) -> seq<'T> -> 'T | Finds the first element that satisfies the given predicate. |

*continues*

**TABLE 25-14** *(continued)*

| FUNCTION | TYPE | DESCRIPTION |
|---|---|---|
| Seq.fold | ('State -> 'T -> 'State) -> 'State -> seq<'T> -> 'State | Applies the given function to each element in the sequence, threading a result throw each invocation. |
| Seq.forall | ('T -> bool) -> seq<'T> -> bool | Tests that the given predicate is satisfied by all elements in the sequence. |
| Seq.head | Seq<'T> -> 'T | Returns the head of the sequence. |
| Seq.isEmpty | Seq<'T> -> bool | Tests if the sequence is empty. |
| Seq.iter | ('T -> unit) -> seq<'T> -> unit | Applies the given function to every element of the sequence. |
| Seq.length | Seq<'T> -> int | Returns the length of the sequence. |
| Seq.map | ('T -> 'U) -> seq<'T> -> seq<'U> | Maps the given function to every element and returns a new sequence. |
| Seq.max | Seq<'T> -> 'T | Calculates the largest element in the sequence. |
| Seq.min | Seq<'T> -> 'T | Calculates the smallest element in the sequence. |
| Seq.nth | Int -> Seq<'T> -> 'T | Calculates the $n$th element in the sequence. |
| Seq.ofArray | 'T [] -> seq<'T> | Converts an array to a sequence. |
| Seq.ofList | 'T list -> seq<'T> | Converts a list to a sequence. |
| Seq.pick | ('T -> 'U option) -> seq<'T> -> U | Returns the first element for which the given function returns Some. |
| Seq.reduce | ('T -> 'T -> 'T) -> seq<'T> -> 'T | Applies the given function to the first two elements and threads the result with the others. |
| Seq.singleton | 'T -> seq<'T> | Builds a sequence with a single element. |
| Seq.skip | Int -> seq<'T> -> seq<'T> | Skips the specified number of elements and yields the rest of the sequence. |
| Seq.sort | Seq<'T> -> seq<'T> | Sorts the sequence (will enumerate all elements). |
| Seq.sum | Seq<'T> -> 'T | Returns the sum of the sequence. |
| Seq.take | Int -> seq<'T> -> seq<'T> | Returns the first $N$ elements. |
| Seq.toArray | Seq<'T> -> 'T[] | Converts the sequence to an array. |

| FUNCTION | TYPE | DESCRIPTION |
|---|---|---|
| Seq.toList | Seq<'T> -> 'T list | Converts the sequence to a list. |
| Seq.truncate | Int -> seq<'T> -> seq<'T> | Truncates a sequence to at most $N$ elements. |
| Seq.tryFind | ('T -> bool) -> seq<'T> -> 'T option | Same as Seq.find, but returns None if no element can be found that satisfies the given predicate. |
| Seq.tryPick | ('T -> 'U option) -> seq<'T> -> 'U option | Same as Seq.pick, but returns None if no element can be found that returns Some. |
| Seq.windowed | Int -> seq<'T> -> seq<'T []> | Returns a sequence of sliding windows, represented as fresh arrays, of the specified size. |
| Seq.zip | Seq<'T> -> seq<'U> -> seq<'T * 'U> | Combines two sequences (assuming equal length) to a sequence of pairs. |
| Seq.zip3 | Seq<'T> -> seq<'U> -> seq<'Z> -> seq<'T * 'U * 'Z> | Combines three sequences (assuming equal length) to a sequence of triplets drawn from each. |

## Range Expressions

In addition to using the various members in Table 25-14, sequences can be constructed in a variety of other ways. For example, numerical sequences can be constructed using *range expressions*, adding sugar to the more general sequence expressions you will see later in this chapter:

```
seq { 0 .. 100 }
```

This constructs a sequence of integers between 0 and 100, served on demand. If you need elements of another numerical type, you can add a type suffix to the initial and last element in the range expression, say, to yield a sequence of float32 values:

```
seq { 0.0f .. 100.0f }
```

You can also use a skip value to specify an increment. For example, the following will give you all even numbers between 0 and 100.

```
seq { 0 .. 2 .. 100 }
```

## Sequence Expressions

*Sequence expressions* are a form of computation expressions, built with the seq computation builder, that yield sequences. They are a versatile abstraction and receive special handling in terms of syntax from the compiler. You can use them for a host of different purposes — for example, to create a stream of computed elements, or serve large collections incrementally. Consider the following function, `AllFiles`, that returns all of the filenames in a given folder and all of its subfolders:

```
open System.IO

let rec AllFiles folder =
    seq { for file in Directory.GetFiles folder do
                yield file
            for subfolder in Directory.GetDirectories folder do
                yield! AllFiles subfolder }
```

This function has two parts. First it fetches all the files in the given folder using a single `System.IO` call, and serves their names one by one, on demand. Remember that sequences are lazy data structures, and their elements are only computed when they are requested.

Once all files in the specified folder have been served, the second part of the function fetches all the subfolders and calls itself for each recursively to enumerate the files within. Note the use of `yield!` to flatten the resulting sequence into the one that is being built.

In terms of the computation expression language that you can use inside a `seq` computation, the following constructs are not supported from the general computation expression capabilities:

➤   `let!`

➤   `use!`

➤   `return` (instead you must use `yield` to return a value from a sequence expression)

All others are available, and you can use them to build your sequence computations. Also, as you saw earlier, you can also use `yield!` to flatten a new sequence of values and return them as part of the original sequence you are building.

## Asynchronous Workflows

Asynchronous workflows enable you to write code whose execution is non-blocking. This is often highly desirable — for example, in situations where you need to keep a UI active while performing some intensive computation in the background. Here, your application must be designed not to be single-threaded to avoid the computation thread from becoming the bottleneck of your application.

An important characteristic of a computation is whether it is more CPU or more I/O bound — in other words, whether it spends most of its time calculating something spinning the CPU at 100 percent, or whether it simply waits for the inherently slower IO operations to complete.

Consider the following pseudo code, where `processUrl` involves both CPU and I/O bound activities. (For the purposes of this discussion, it downloads the content of a text file available via a URL and counts the number of words in it.) Let's assume that the two invocations of this function are independent.

```
let result1 = processUrl(...)
let result2 = processUrl(...)
...
```

As written, this code executing on a single thread will spend valuable time waiting for I/O operations to complete (for example, delays in addressing the server that contains the requested resources), whereas it could be instead working toward some CPU operations in the meantime. This may not seem like much. But if you have a multitude of similar calls, the overhead quickly adds up and the amount of "speed" you could gain by making your application more parallel can be very significant.

What you need is the capability to easily create threads, and, within a thread, designate the points of asynchronous execution that allow putting that thread to sleep until the asynchronous call returns, and letting another thread do something more useful in the meantime.

F# asynchronous workflows enable you to do just that. They use the workflow syntax you saw in the preceding sections to manipulate values of the `Microsoft.FSharp.Control.Async` class. This class provides the representation to model asynchronous computations, and contains various members for constructing and manipulating `Async` values by hand (in case you need finer control).

With the help of a couple `Async` members, you can easily rewrite the pseudo-code you saw earlier as follows.

First, create an `Async` value representing the computation to process a URL. Here you can see a quick-and-dirty implementation that yields a good enough approximation to counting the words in a text file accessed via a URL:

```
open Microsoft.FSharp.Control.WebExtensions

let processUrl url =
    async {
        let uri = new System.Uri(url)
        let client = new System.Net.WebClient()
        let! content = client.AsyncDownloadString uri
        let res =
            content.Split( [| '\n';'\r';'\t';'/';'\\';'=';'?';'-
                ';'*';'_';',';'.';';';' ' |])
            |> Seq.filter (fun s -> s <> "")
            |> Seq.distinct
            |> Seq.length
        return url, res
    }
```

The `Microsoft.FSharp.Control.WebExtensions` module that you opened before defining `processUrl` contains a couple of extension members (or, in F# terminology, *type augmentations*) that make it easier to create `Async` values from web-based activities. In particular, it defines `AsyncDownloadString`, which takes a `Uri` parameter and returns an asynchronous computation to download its content as a string.

Note that in the previous computation expression `AsyncDownloadString` is invoked using a `let!`. Indeed, in `async` computation expressions, a `let!` binding is implemented by calling the right-hand side asynchronously (thus, it must be an `Async` value), and putting the thread to sleep until that computation returns — in essence, giving you a nice syntax sugar to conveniently work with asynchronous computations.

To really benefit from making the `processUrl` asynchronous, you must fork off a few threads and let them compute in parallel. So, as a second step, you can take a few text file URLs, map them to `Async` values, run those in parallel, and collect their results in a single result by running the `Async` computation via `RunSynchronously`.

```
let pages =
    [ "http://www.google.com/robots.txt"
      "http://www.yahoo.com/robots.txt"
      "http://www.bing.com/robots.txt" ]
let res =
    pages
    |> List.map processUrl
    |> Async.Parallel
    |> Async.RunSynchronously
```

If you look carefully, this yields a list of (`string * int`) pairs, each representing the URL and the respective word count. And last, you can simply print these results on the screen:

```
res
|> Array.iter (fun (url, wcount) ->
    printf "The page at %s has approx. %d words)\n" url wcount)
```

This implementation performs far better as you scale up the number of URLs to be processed because of the relatively high latency in locating remote files via URLs. Instead of sequentially processing these URLs, this version is able to spread the work over several threads and minimize the idle time spent by keeping the CPU as busy as possible.

## Pattern Matching

Earlier in this chapter, you saw how you can use pattern matching to examine discriminated union values. But that's not all. You can use pattern matching to examine a whole host of different kinds of values. Take a look at Table 25-15.

**TABLE 25-15:** Basic Pattern Match Cases

| PATTERN CASE | EXAMPLE | DESCRIPTION |
| --- | --- | --- |
| null | null | Matches null |
| Lit | 12 | Matches the specified literal |
| Id | Str | Matches any value and binds it to id |
| _ | _ | Matches any value without binding it |
| id(patt,...) | Binop(f, op1, op2) | Matches a discriminated union case and its arguments |
| [] | [] | Matches an empty list |

| PATTERN CASE | EXAMPLE | DESCRIPTION |
|---|---|---|
| [ patt; ... ] | [ elem ] | Matches a list with its elements |
| id :: patt | hd :: tail | |
| hd1 :: hd2 :: [ last ] | Deconstructs a list into a head and a tail. | |
| [\| \|] | [\| \|] | Matches an empty array |
| [\| patt; ... \|] | [\| el1; _; el3 \|] | Matches an array with its elements |
| { id=patt; ... } | { FirstName=fn; LastName=ln } | Matches a record by matching against its fields |
| patt \| patt | [ ] \| [ elem ] | OR pattern |
| patt & patt | | AND pattern |

Pattern matching is a fundamental technique in functional programming and is absolutely ubiquitous in F# code. For example, all let bindings use pattern matching to bind the right-hand side of the binding to the left-hand side. Consider the following:

```
let (a, b, c) = 1, "my string", 2
let (x, y, _) = Compute3DCoordinates()
let (myList, Some x) = [1; 2], FindCustomerById 12
```

In addition to binding, pattern matching is also a control-flow device. The match ... with ... construct allows you to pattern match on an expression with various pattern cases, and return a value from the first pattern case that matches. The various cases are checked in the order of their definition, so the first you list in your match expression will be the first to be consulted.

```
let result =
    match myList with
    | [] ->
        printfn "empty"
        1
    | [ _ ] ->
        printfn "single element"
        1
    | _ :: [ _ ] ->
        printfn "two elements"
        2
    | _ ->
        printfn "more elements"
        3
```

A fundamental property of pattern matching is whether or not it is *exhaustive* — that is, whether it covers all possible cases or shapes of the value being matched. For example, a pattern match on a discriminated union value with three possible shapes must handle all three of those shapes to be exhaustive.

However, keep in mind that match cases can be arbitrarily complex, so deciding when you have an exhaustive set can be difficult in certain situations. Luckily, the F# compiler has a great deal of help to pinpoint pattern matches that are not exhaustive, and you will get a compiler warning in such cases:

```
> let result =
    match myList with
    | [] ->
        1
    | [ _ ] ->
        1
    | _ :: [ _ ] ->
        2;;

      match myList with
    ----------^^^^^^

C:\stdin(33,11): warning FS0025: Incomplete pattern matches on this expression.
    For example, the value '[_;_;_]' may indicate a case not covered
    by the pattern(s).

val result : int = 1
```

If you don't handle the missing cases, the compiler will insert an automatic "catch-all" case that simply does nothing but raise a `MatchFailure` exception. Therefore, it is imperative that you always have exhaustive pattern matches in production code (all code, really), because an unexpected run-time error can have disastrous consequences.

You may be tempted to use the wildcard pattern. However, you should take some extra precautions. Although using the wildcard pattern removes the compiler warning you just saw, it makes your code less extensible. Consider the following example where you have a discriminated union type representing how certain clients want to be contacted, and a function that determines whether a particular choice will cost anything. The original developer thought that only snail mail cost anything.

```
type ContactVia =
    | Email of string
    | Mail of string

let WillCost meth =
    match meth with
    | Mail _ ->
        true
    | _ ->
        false
```

However, in a subsequent iteration, another developer added a new contact method:

```
type ContactVia =
    | Email of string
    | Mail of string
    | Sms of string
```

At this point, the previous `WillCost` function compiled fine, and without knowing this code, this new developer would have never noticed that anything else needed to be addressed — which should raise some flags on its own right, of course. However, let's say that the original developer coded `WillCost` as follows:

```
let WillCost meth =
    match meth with
    | Mail _ ->
        true
    | Email ->
        false
```

It would have been immediately obvious that the additional contact method needs further code changes.

Functional programming encourages fast prototyping and incremental development, and you should learn to turn these to your (and your team's) advantage. As a case in point, try to avoid the wildcard pattern in match cases over most structured data, and spend the extra time to spell out all base cases/shapes.

And last, you can apply pattern matching not only to examine the shape of a particular value, but also of its type, as shown in Table 25-16. This comes in handy when you are dealing with catching exceptions. (You'll learn more about that later in this chapter.)

**TABLE 25-16:** Additional Pattern Match Constructs

| PATTERN CASE | EXAMPLE | DESCRIPTION |
| --- | --- | --- |
| patt when expr | lst when List.length lst > 0 | Conditional pattern |
| null | Null | Matches nulls |
| :? ty | :? System.Int32 | Checks whether the expression being matches has type ty. |

## Active Patterns

Ordinary pattern matching allows you to match on the structure of certain values such as lists, arrays, discriminated unions, tuples, or records. It does so by providing various pattern constructors for these shapes that, in turn, you can use to deconstruct structured values and bind their constituents, as you have seen in the previous section.

However, for other values such as objects, strings, or numbers, ordinary pattern matching is of little help. Consider matching on numbers, for example:

```
match i with
| i when i=0 ->
    0
| i when i<0 ->
```

```
      -1
| i when i>0 ->
      1
```

Although you can use *conditional pattern clauses* as shown in this example, and the F# compiler even warns you if not all possible values are matched. This forces you to have to remember what sets apart the different "types" of numbers with respect to a particular trait you are matching against. The same issue also holds for ordinary object values, which are "sealed" against ordinary pattern matching, and once again you must resort to various members that publish and use these to drive pattern matching.

What's needed is a mechanism to translate values of a given type to a set of "shapes" that you can then pattern match against. Luckily, F# provides this mechanism via its so-called *active patterns* feature. Active patterns (also called *active pattern recognizers*) allow you define for *any* value a set of named partitions called the *active pattern results* that you can pattern match against as if they were simply cases in a discriminated union.

Active pattern cases can carry values such as ordinary discriminated union constructors, allowing you to tag associated values of arbitrary complexity to each pattern result. Furthermore, your active pattern definitions can be *total* or *partial*.

There are three fundamental types of active patterns that you should be aware of, and each has its distinctive advantages and usage patterns. These are summarized in Table 25-17.

**TABLE 25-17:** Active Pattern Uses

| GOAL | TYPE | DESCRIPTION |
| --- | --- | --- |
| Conversion | Single-case, complete | Converts the given value to a new value. |
| Segmentation | Multi-case, complete | Groups all values of a given type into a set of shapes/groups. |
| Characterization | Single-case, partial | Provides a characteristic trait to *some* values in a given type. |

Active patterns have a distinct place in the language, and they are treated differently than ordinary pattern matches.

When you define active patterns, you must separate each pattern recognizer with a pipe (|) character, and also surround the entire set that belongs to a given active pattern by pipes.

Let's walk through the different active pattern families from Table 25-17.

Single-case complete active patterns behave much like a normal function that converts the value being matched to another value. This conversion is more convenient than a simple function, however, since it allows you to bind and extract the result in the same step. Consider the following example, where you get some input from your user and print it trimmed from leading and trailing white-space:

```
// Define a trimming function
let trim (s: string) = s.Trim()

// Read user input
let input = System.Console.ReadLine()

// Perform trimming
let trimmed = trim input

// Print the result
trimmed |> printf "Result=%s"
```

You can define an active pattern for the trimming "conversion":

```
// Define a conversion active pattern
let (|Trim|) (s: string) = s.Trim()

// Read user input and perform conversion
let (Trim trimmed) = System.Console.ReadLine()

// Print the result
trimmed |> printf "Result=%s"
```

Note how you can perform the trimming simply by pattern matching using the `Trim` active pattern case. You can also use active patterns like a function — in this case, you will need the pipes:

```
System.Console.ReadLine()
|> (|Trim|)
|> printf "Result=%s"
```

Multi-case *complete active patterns* can (in addition to these, you have just seen) be used to segment a given value space into multiple active pattern results. This is useful when you have a fixed set of "groups" that describe the values in a given type completely. A trivial example is splitting integers into even or odd numbers:

```
let (|Even|Odd|) (i: int) =
    if i%2 = 0 then
        Even
    else
        Odd
```

Another slightly more complex example is dividing string values into categories based on what they store. For example, the following active pattern splits strings into five different categories: nulls, empty (those strings that, when trimmed from white-space, yield an empty string), integers (those strings that store integer values), floats (those strings that store real numbers), and normal "strings" that don't fall into any of these categories.

First, both `System.Int32` and `System.Double` support a `TryParse` method that can be used to check whether a given string contains an integer or double, respectively. Instead of creating two nearly identical functions, you can create a generic one. This is parameterized over the type it can check. You can give it the "zero" value (or any value in that type for that matter) and the parse function that can take a string, and return whether it can be successfully converted to the given type and the converted value itself. Without having to worry about how `TryParse` is implemented (after some consideration, you would likely prefer a more consumable signature, such as mapping strings to `int` or `float` options), you have something like the following:

```
open System

let tryParseGeneric<'T> (zero: 'T) parse (s: string) =
    let i = ref zero
    if parse(s, i) then
        !i |> Some
    else
        None

let tryParseInt = tryParseGeneric<int> 0 Int32.TryParse
let tryParseFloat = tryParseGeneric<float> 0. Double.TryParse

let (|Empty|Null|Integer|Float|String|) (s: string) =
    if s = null then
        Null
    elif s.Trim() |> String.IsNullOrEmpty then
        Empty
    else
        match tryParseInt s with
        | Some i ->
            Integer i
        | None ->
            match tryParseFloat s with
            | Some f ->
                Float f
            | None ->
                String (s.Trim())
```

Basically, complete active patterns use some heuristics (most typically, a set of `if` statements or match cases) to figure out when to yield which active pattern result. Whenever a particular result is appropriate, you use it like you would any discriminated union case — that is, by giving its name and supplying any values you want to make available in the pattern match when that case is matched.

There is a subtle detail here that you should be aware of. The pattern cases you list in the definition of a complete active pattern will constitute the closed list of shapes that you can match against once the active pattern is applied to a value. So, even if you are not using a particular shape from those defined, you will still need to cover it in an actual match expression.

So, going back to the example, this implementation guarantees that a particular string value can only by matched by one of the active pattern cases, and it also guarantees that all strings fall into one of these pattern results. This is of great help, because the compiler can warn you of incomplete pattern matches. Simply try to remove any one of the match cases from the following function to see that in action:

```
let PrintString = function
    | Empty ->
        printfn "empty or whitespace"
    | Null ->
        printfn "null"
    | Integer i ->
        printfn "number:%d" i
    | Float f ->
        printfn "float:%f" f
    | String s ->
        printfn "other string:%s" s
```

Often, though, the difference between the various value "groups" is not so clear-cut, and you can either not characterize the entire value space at once (because you may not know about all the possible cases), or you don't care to.

Consider the following *partial active patterns*, reusing the functions you defined earlier:

```
let (|Integer|_|) = tryParseInt
let (|Float|_|)   = tryParseFloat
```

Here, the key difference from the previous complete active patterns is that there is only one case, with the "partial" nature being reflected in the "catch-all" wildcard case — and you will get a compiler error if you try to define a partial active pattern with more than one. This was a deliberate choice from the language designers, and you can think of partial active patterns as a means to define "traits" or "characterizations" that only apply to a particular set of values in the input type (and, for these, the partial active pattern recognizer returns a Some option value), leaving every other value "unmatched" (for those returning None).

In this example, tryParseInt and tryParseFloat have the following signature:

```
val tryParseInt : (string -> int option)
val tryParseFloat : (string -> float option)
```

Essentially, both take a string and return an option value of the appropriate type. Thus, you can use them as partial active patterns. Note how you can simply bind these functions to the partial active patterns without having to explicitly name the input parameter (the value to match against), making it obvious that these functions behave exactly like partial active patterns.

As you would expect, when matching with partial active patterns you always need a "catch-all" case:

```
match GetSomeNumber() with
| Integer i ->
    printfn "Is an integer=%d" i
| Float f ->
    printfn "Is a float=%f" f
| _ ->

    printfn "Unknown"
```

Finally, it is important to understand that you can apply both partial and complete active patterns in the same match expression, but the compiler will warn you if not all complete active pattern cases are covered. While normally an active pattern is executed only once for a given match expression, mixing different active patterns in the same match expression will cause the active patterns to execute, possibly more than once (depending on the order of the match cases and the value being matched).

## Exceptions

Exceptions are a way to signal an error to a calling site, breaking the normal flow of execution and exiting without a return value. .NET exceptions are relatively expensive to create, so you should not use exceptions as a control-flow device. Instead, you may try to return option values, and signal an error with a None value. However, there are situations where exceptions come handy, some even when they are inevitable.

F# provides a number of shorthand notations for dealing with exceptions. All F# exceptions are subtypes of the System.Exception class, the general .NET exception base class. Table 25-18 summarizes the primitives to raise and catch exceptions.

**TABLE 25-18:** Language Constructs for Exceptions

| CONSTRUCT | EXAMPLE | DESCRIPTION |
| --- | --- | --- |
| exception *id* of *ty* | exception CanNotCompute of string * int | Defines a new F# exception type. |
| raise | raise (new System.Argument Exception("message")) | Raises the given exception, either a type that inherits from System.Exception, or an F# exception. |
| | raise (MyException "message") | |
| try *expr* with *patt* -> *expr* | try | |
| | 1/num \|> Some | Evaluates an expression and catches any exceptions as specified. |
| | with | |
| | \| _ -> None | |
| try *expr* finally *expr* | | |
| failwith | failwith "Can't do it" | Raises a new instance of System.Exception with the given message. |
| failwithf | failwithf "Failed at number %d" i | Same as failwith, but allows to format the error message using a printf-style format string. |

F# exceptions can be defined using the `exception` keyword:

```
exception MyException of string * int
```

This defines a new exception type called `MyException`, a sub-type of `System.Exception`, that carries two values. It can be raised using the `raise` function defined in the `Core.Operators` module:

```
raise (MyException ("message", 1))
```

Since the return type of raising an exception is a generic type, it will unify with any type, so you can raise an exception anywhere where a value is expected, as indicated by the type of `raise`:

```
> raise;;
val it : (Exception -> 'a) = <fun:clo@11>
```

You can catch exceptions using a `try-catch` expression. If you want code that is executed regardless of whether any exception occurs you can wrap your `try-catch` expression in a `try-finally` expression:

```
try
    try
        MyException ("error", 0) |> raise
    with
        | MyException (msg, i) ->
            printfn "Caught - message=%s, value=%d" msg i
finally
    printfn "Done"
```

You can also use standard .NET exceptions. You simply define these as class types that inherit from `System.Exception`:

```
type MyDotNetException(msg: string, value: int) =
    inherit System.Exception()

    override self.Message = msg

    member self.Value = value
```

If you use .NET exceptions via class types, raising them requires you to instantiate them using the `new` keyword (although this is optional):

```
new MyDotNetException("error", 12) |> raise
```

Note that `MyException` (an F# exception) you defined earlier does not require instantiation — although underneath it is a .NET exception sub-type, it is not a class type directly. Instead, it receives special treatment from the F# compiler, and behaves like a function that takes the arguments of the exception and returns a new instance. Similarly, F# exceptions can be used in the `catch` cases to be matched against as if they were discriminated unions.

In contrast, `MyDotNetException` is not an F# exception, so you must catch it slightly differently by matching on its type:

```
try
    new MyDotNetException("error", 12) |> raise
with
    | :? MyDotNetException as exc ->
        printfn "Caught - message=%s, value=%d" exc.Message exc.Value
```

Now that you have seen how F# and .NET exceptions can be defined, raised, and caught, you can look at the rest of the exception primitives from Table 25-18.

You can signal a general failure using `failwith` or its format-enabled alternative, `failwithf`. This will raise an instance of `System.Exception`. Normally, you should use different exception subtypes to indicate different causes of failure so that the calling sites can recover appropriately, but when used in the small to yield a "general" failure these two functions are indispensable.

A companion to raising exceptions with `failwith`/`failwithf` is catching them via the `Failure` active pattern, defined in `Core.Operators`. This active pattern matches an exact instance (as opposed to a subtype instance) of `System.Exception` and binds the message it carries.

Consider implementing a special division function that reports the divisor of two integers, but with reporting division by zero and by a prime number. Reusing the `IsPrime` function you defined earlier in this chapter, you can implement this as follows.

```
let RequireNonPrime x =
    if IsPrime x then
        failwith "Prime"
    else
        x
let SpecialDiv x y =
    try
        x/RequireNonPrime y |> printfn "Result=%d"
    with
    | Failure msg ->
        printfn "Failure: %s" msg
    | :? System.DivideByZeroException ->
        printfn "Error: division by zero"
```

Experiment with this new function in F# Interactive, as shown here:

```
> SpecialDiv 1 0;;
Error: division by zero
val it : unit = ()
> SpecialDiv 1 17;;
Failure: Prime
val it : unit = ()
> SpecialDiv 10 4;;
Result=2
val it : unit = ()
```

# Units of Measure

One impressive feature of F# is its support for measures and their units. *Units of measure* enable you to associate various units with your numeric values and functions that operate on those values. The compiler will then verify that any operation that involves quantities with units produces the right unit of measure, saving precious time and preventing any programming mistakes. You will benefit most in your scientific coding by using units, but they can (and should) be used wherever you compute with various units to ensure that no bugs creep into your programming logic, and that you safely address unit conversions, and different systems of units.

You can define a unit of measure as a new type by adding the `Measure` annotation to it:

```
[<Measure>]
type g

[<Measure>]
type kg
```

This defines two units of measure, grams and kilograms. You can tag these units to a numerical quantity as follows:

```
let myWeight = 75<kg>
```

The unit and its quantity must follow each other without any white space for the compiler to correctly infer that this is a unit-tagged quantity. The type of this value will be derived as the type of the quantity (`int` in this example), enhanced with the specified unit, giving `int<kg>`.

Quantities with units participating in arithmetic expressions produce units that reflect the arithmetic operations performed. The unit language is quite expressive and follows the scientific conventions as closely as possible. In this unit language, you can use the following:

➤ *The literal* `1` — This represents a unitless quantity, and is equivalent to using a quantity without any units.

➤ *Units* — Examples would be `kg` or `m`. These must be measure-annotated types that are in scope.

➤ *Exponentiation* — Examples would be `kg^3` or `m^-3`. Powers must be integers, and can be negative to stand for reciprocal.

➤ *Division* — An example would be `m/s^2`. You can list other units separated by spaces following the division. They will all be assumed to be in the denominator.

➤ *Multiplication* — An example would be `kg * m`. You can omit the star and simply use spaces between the units that are to be multiplied, such as `kg m`. When you use the star together with division, the units following the star will be assumed to be in the numerator.

➤ *Parentheses* — An example would be `kg/(m/s)`.

The units you compose will be simplified and rearranged, eliminating negative powers, grouping units in the numerator and the denominator, and sorting them alphabetically.

When you write functions that require quantities with a certain unit, you must explicitly state that in its definition. For example, a typical conversion function looks like the following:

```
let GramsToKilos (x: int<g>) = x / 1000<g/kg>
```

Note how the division will cancel out the gram unit and yield kilograms. Explicitly stating the return type and its unit can also help to catch programming errors:

```
let BadGramsToKilos (x: int<g>) : int<kg> = x / 1000<g>
```

Here, the compiler will tell you that you are trying to return an integer value, whereas the function is defined to return int<kg>. By adding the right unit to the divisor, you can solve this problem.

Values carrying units are not compatible with the same values without units. This is the fundamental underpinning that ensures that the type system can assist you with finding programming errors in your unit-based computations. However, occasionally you may need to access the numerical value carried in a unit-enhanced value — for example, if you wanted to print someone's weight. In this case, you can either define a conversion with inverse units by multiplying your kilogram values with the constant 1<1/kg>, or you can simply throw away the unit annotation by applying the appropriate generic conversion function, int or float:

```
> let a = 1<kg>;;

val a : int<kg> = 1

> a*1<1/kg>;;
val it : int = 1
> float a;;
val it : float = 1.0
> int a;;
val it : int = 1
```

Units can also be treated in a generic way. For example, you may want to have an aggregate data type that has various parts sharing the same unit. You can define such types by utilizing the Measure annotation on the generic type variable:

```
type Expr<[<Measure>] 'U> =
    | Constant of int<'U>
    | Binop of (int<'U> -> int<'U> -> int<'U>) * Expr<'U> * Expr<'U>

    static member Sum  (e1, e2) = Binop (( + ), e1, e2)
    static member Diff (e1, e2) = Binop (( - ), e1, e2)
    static member Prod (e1, e2) = Binop (( * ), e1, e2)
    static member Div  (e1, e2) = Binop (( / ), e1, e2)
```

Here, you defined an expression type similar to the one you saw earlier in this chapter in the discussion on discriminated unions. But this new type is generalized over a particular unit of measure, 'U. Its two basic shapes carry this measure, so you either have an integer constant that has the required unit, or you have a binary operation that carries two operands that themselves have this unit.

The four static members on this type provide a convenient way to construct values of this type, but still adhering to the constraint that any expression must be quantified with the same unit. So, the following will not work:

```
let a = Expr<kg>.Sum(Constant 12<kg>, Constant 2<g>)
```

But once you bring the second constant to kilograms, you will be okay, and the compiler happily accepts your expression.

As this section has demonstrated, units of measure bring a tremendous value to your F# coding experience. Not only do they help produce code free of the typical and so-easy-to-make mistakes when it comes to computation with various measurements; they also make your programs easier to interpret, with the units guiding the reader.

You may wonder about the costs of using units for your computations. The good news is that there is no run-time cost associated. The unit information is only used during compilation to drive the compiler and pinpoint potential programming errors. Once your programs are compiled, this information is discarded, and your programs execute as if they were executing without using units of measure.

## Lazy Computations

As you saw earlier in this chapter, sequences provide one important way to express lazy computations as sequences of elements that are enumerated on demand, and indeed this is sufficient to model most scenarios with the need of lazy evaluation. The other most readily available way is to use Lazy values directly.

*Lazy computations* are effectively functions that need to be invoked to produce their result, as opposed to producing those results immediately. Consider the following:

```
let eagerResult = LongRunningComputation ()
let lazyResult = fun () -> LongRunningComputation ()
```

The difference between eagerResult and lazyResult is that the latter is wrapped in an anonymous function, and, thus, its value is a function that must be called first to return the result of LongRunningComputation.

This is essentially the idea behind explicit Lazy values. Lazy values are instances of the System.Lazy class, a standard .NET 4.0 class used to represent lazy values. This class is a bit of a pain to work with directly, so you will find the utility functions in the Microsoft.FSharp.Control.Lazy module, and the lazy keyword a joy to use. For example, you create a new lazy value as follows:

```
let a = lazy (LongRunningComputation ())
```

This is roughly equivalent to defining lazyResult as shown earlier, in the sense that it must be "pinged" to evaluate the lazy computation it carries. You can accomplish that by invoking the Value member:

```
a.Value
```

This will check that the lazy value a has been evaluated already, and, if not, it will evaluate it. Subsequent calls to the Value property will simply serve the value already calculated, so "caching" is automatically provided and this can be of great value. You can accomplish the same effect by calling Force().

## Quotations

Language Integrated Queries (LINQ) in C# and VB have received quite a bit of attention since their introduction and incorporation into those languages. The general idea of LINQ is to give you typed query access to various data sources using the same (language integrated) query language. Various SQL-like constructs were then added to C# and VB to utilize LINQ, including from, select, where, and so on.

Underneath the covers, when you use LINQ queries in C# or VB, the LINQ extensions to the compiler take care of translating those queries to *expression trees*, which are then evaluated at run-time and converted to various alternate representations and executed.

*Quotations* are the F# way of converting F# code into expression trees. These expression trees are different than those used by LINQ. They are defined in the Microsoft.FSharp.Quotations.Expr type. You will rarely use this type directly (if ever), but instead will create quotations using the convenient operators <@ ... @>:

```
> let q1 = <@ 1 @>;;

val q1 : Expr<int> = Value (1)

> let q2 = <@ 1+2 @>;;

val q2 : Expr<int> =
  Call (None, Int32 op_Addition[Int32,Int32,Int32](Int32, Int32),
      [Value (1), Value (2)])

> let q1 =
    <@ let add x y = x+y
       add 10 20 @>;;

val q1 : Expr<int> =
  Let (add,
     Lambda (x,
            Lambda (y,
                   Call (None,
                         Int32 op_Addition[Int32,Int32,Int32](Int32, Int32),
                         [x, y]))),
       Application (Application (add, Value (10)), Value (20)))
```

As these examples show, you can enclose any block of valid F# code inside quotations. They will be parsed and converted to quoted expressions. Furthermore, these quotations are typed, meaning that they preserve type information. If you need, there is also an untyped quotation expression representation. You can use <@@ ... @@> to wrap code and translate it to this untyped representation, or you can go directly from a typed quotation by invoking the Raw property on it.

Top-level bindings that aim to expose quoted expressions produce metadata for the quotations that will not be automatically compiled into the assembly. If you want to access your quotations from outside the assembly, you should add the `ReflectedDefinition` attribute to your binding.

Quoting F# code has a number of advantages, and it is the primary way to provide *alternate execution mechanisms* to F# code. As you will see in the next section, you can use quotations to author and effectively execute database queries. There are a number of Open Source and commercial projects that utilize F# quotations for other interesting applications. For example, one can translate F# quotations to code that can be executed on the GPU. Another, the `WebSharper` project, provides a framework to translate quotations to efficient JavaScript code to be executed in the browser, and it also manages many of the chores such as client-server communication and serialization, effectively freeing you from most of the painful details of web application development, and enabling you to write entire web applications with nothing but F# code.

## Working with Database Queries

As you saw in the previous section, quotations provide the mechanism to assign different execution strategies to F# code. The F# PowerPack includes a query builder that can construct SQL queries from quotations. Using this query builder, quoted LINQ-like queries that use sequence and other operations against relational data (for example, object-relational mappings generated by SqlMetal or another O/R tool) can be translated to SQL and executed against the database specified in the context handle of the generated mappings. The results are then fetched and served as prescribed in the queries, typically as sequences of objects that contain the extracted data fields.

Using higher-order functions to query, transform, or filter data is a fundamental functional abstraction, so, as you may expect, expressing such queries in native F# is straightforward. Consider the following code that computes the sorted list of CA customer last names for all orders that came in today:

```
// Get all orders
db.Orders
// Filter those that are from today
|> Seq.filter (fun o -> o.OrderDate = System.DateTime.Today)
// Filter those that are by CA customers
|> Seq.filter (fun o -> o.Customer.State = "CA")
// Map each order to the customer's last name
|> Seq.map (fun o -> o.Customer.LastName)
// Sort the results
|> Seq.sort
```

This code uses the `Seq` members you saw in Table 25-14 to filter, transform, and sort an initial sequence (all orders) you obtained from the database via SqlMetal-generated objects. You may also use other input collections to query in-memory collections or XML files.

Although queries using `Seq` members are highly expressive, they may not be the best or most efficient execution mechanism when used directly. In the previous example, for instance, each time you visit a new order, it must be brought in from the database (unless you have it "cached" in the database context you are using), and similarly for the associated customer records, an extra database read is necessary.

Instead, you can use the query builder `query` from `Microsoft.FSharp.Linq.Query`, found in the `Microsoft.FSharp.PowerPack.Linq.dll` assembly, and rephrase the previous query as follows:

```
query <@ seq { for o in db.Orders do
                  if o.OrderDate = System.DateTime.Today
                     && o.Customer.State = "CA" then
                       yield o }
           |> Seq.map (fun o -> o.Customer.LastName)
           |> Seq.sort @>
```

Here, you utilized a sequence expression to build a sequence of orders that came in today from customers in CA, then mapped and sorted this sequence using the standard `Seq` members. Above all, you wrapped this entire computation in a quotation and passed it to the `query` function.

The key part here is the use of the `query` function. This takes the quotation that describes what you want to do with the database — in this case, to query for some orders, filter those that are interesting, translate that entire quotation into .NET 4.0 expression trees, and pass it to the LINQ run-time for SQL generation and execution.

As with direct LINQ queries in C# or VB, there is a possibility that the run-time conversion from expression trees to SQL queries fails, most often because you are using primitives that are not supported inside database queries. Table 25-19 shows the various `Seq` and other members you can use inside quotations.

**TABLE 25-19:** Available Members in Database Queries

| MEMBER | MEMBER | MEMBER |
| --- | --- | --- |
| Query.contains | Seq.filter | Seq.toArray |
| Query.groupBy | Seq.find | Seq.toList |
| Query.groupJoin | Seq.forall | |
| Query.join | Seq.head | |
| Query.maxBy | Seq.length | |
| Query.minBy | Seq.map | |
| Seq.append | Seq.max | |
| Seq.average | Seq.min | |
| Seq.averageBy | Seq.sort | |
| Seq.collect | Seq.sortBy | |
| Seq.distinct | Seq.sum | |
| Seq.empty | Seq.sumBy | |
| Seq.exists | Seq.take | |

# A LARGER APPLICATION IN F#

Now that you have seen some of the core F# features, you can set out to develop a small application in F# that you might benefit from. Given that the F# Interactive is a great environment to test out your code incrementally, the idea of this section is to walk you through a series of module implementations that together allow you to use F# Interactive as a shell to explore plots of mathematical functions.

Figure 25-2 shows an example session.

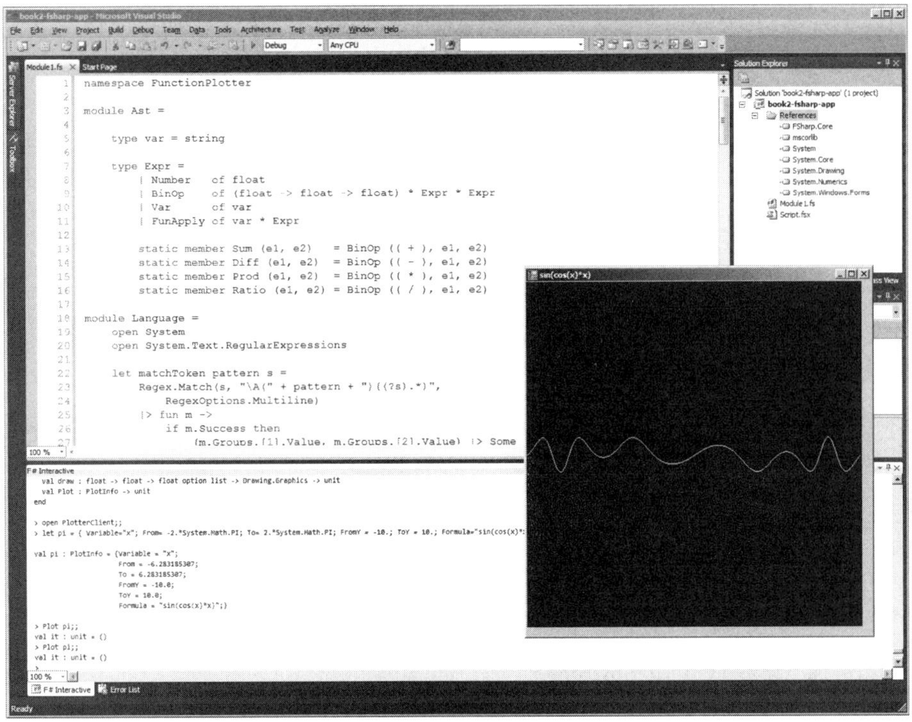

**FIGURE 25-2:** Using F# Interactive to plot functions

To build this code, you will need the following.

> Define your Abstract Syntax Tree (AST) representation for the mathematical expressions you want to plot. This will go into your `Ast` module.

> Implement a parser to parse formulas into this AST. This will go into your `Language` module.

> Implement a function that evaluates AST terms. This will go into your `Evaluator` module.

> Implement a function that creates a new window and plots your formulas in it. This will go into your `FunctionPlotter` module.

## The Ast Module

The Ast module defines the abstract syntax tree (AST) type for your arithmetic expressions. These consist of the following:

➤ Numbers, represented as floats

➤ Binary operations, such as addition or multiplication

➤ Variables, which will be the single variable used in the formulas you are going to be plotting

➤ Function calls, a couple of primitive ones of which you will support, such as sine and cosine

```
module Ast =

    type var = string

    type Expr =
        | Number   of float
        | BinOp    of (float -> float -> float) * Expr * Expr
        | Var      of var
        | FunApply of var * Expr

        static member Sum (e1, e2)   = BinOp (( + ), e1, e2)
        static member Diff (e1, e2)  = BinOp (( - ), e1, e2)
        static member Prod (e1, e2)  = BinOp (( * ), e1, e2)
        static member Ratio (e1, e2) = BinOp (( / ), e1, e2)
```

The static members you added to the type will make it easier later to create expressions that use the four basic arithmetic operators.

## The Language Module

The Language module contains functions to parse strings into the AST representation you defined earlier. The heart of the parser is matchToken, that takes a regex pattern and an input string and returns a Some value of a pair of strings (one for the matched, and one for the remaining string), or a None value (if the regex pattern can't be matched).

This function is then used to build various partial active patterns that can match different types of tokens (terminal symbols) and non-terminals. (These correspond to grammar productions that consist of various symbols that must be parsed before the production can "reduce.")

You build up expressions from sums that, in turn, can be products of terms that, in turn, can be various factors such as numbers, variables, or function calls.

```
module Language =
    open System
    open System.Text.RegularExpressions

    let matchToken pattern s =
        Regex.Match(s, "\A(" + pattern + ")((?s).*)",
            RegexOptions.Multiline)
        |> fun m ->
```

```
            if m.Success then
                (m.Groups.[1].Value, m.Groups.[2].Value) |> Some
            else
                None

let (|WHITESPACE|_|) = matchToken @"[ |\t|\n|\n\r]+"

let rec MatchTokenNoWS s pattern =
    match (|WHITESPACE|_|) s with
    | Some (_, rest) ->
        rest
        |> matchToken pattern
    | None ->
        s
        |> matchToken pattern

let MatchToken s f pattern =
    pattern
    |> MatchTokenNoWS s
    |> Option.bind f

let MatchSymbol s pattern =
    pattern
    |> MatchToken s (fun (_, rest) -> rest |> Some)

let rec (|Star|_|) f acc s =
    match f s with
    | Some (res, rest) ->
        (|Star|_|) f (res :: acc) rest
    | None ->
        (acc |> List.rev , s) |> Some

let (|NUMBER|_|) s =
    @"[0-9]+\.?[0-9]*"
    |> MatchToken s
        (fun (n, rest) -> (n |> Double.Parse, rest) |> Some)

let (|ID|_|) s =
    "[a-zA-Z]+"
    |> MatchToken s (fun res -> res |> Some)

let (|PLUS|_|)   s = @"\+" |> MatchSymbol s
let (|MINUS|_|)  s = @"\-" |> MatchSymbol s
let (|MUL|_|)    s = @"\*" |> MatchSymbol s
let (|DIV|_|)    s = "/"   |> MatchSymbol s
let (|LPAREN|_|) s = @"\(" |> MatchSymbol s
let (|RPAREN|_|) s = @"\)" |> MatchSymbol s

let rec (|Factor|_|) = function
    | NUMBER (n, rest) ->
        (Ast.Expr.Number n, rest) |> Some
    | ID (v, rest) ->
        match rest with
        | LPAREN (Expression (arg, RPAREN rest)) ->
```

```
                    (Ast.Expr.FunApply (v, arg), rest) |> Some
            | _ ->
                    (Ast.Expr.Var v, rest) |> Some
        | LPAREN (Expression (e, RPAREN rest)) ->
                    (e, rest) |> Some
        | _ ->
            None

    and (|Term|_|) = function
        | Factor (e1, rest) ->
            match rest with
            | MUL (Term (e2, rest)) ->
                    (Ast.Expr.Prod (e1, e2), rest) |> Some
            | DIV (Term (e2, rest)) ->
                    (Ast.Expr.Ratio (e1, e2), rest) |> Some
            | _ ->
                    (e1, rest) |> Some
        | _ ->
            None

    and (|Sum|_|) = function
        | Term (e1, rest) ->
            match rest with
            | PLUS (Sum (e2, rest)) ->
                    (Ast.Expr.Sum (e1, e2), rest) |> Some
            | MINUS (Sum (e2, rest)) ->
                    (Ast.Expr.Diff (e1, e2), rest) |> Some
            | _ ->
                    (e1, rest) |> Some
        | _ ->
            None

    and (|Expression|_|) = (|Sum|_|)

    let (|Eof|_|) s =
        if String.IsNullOrEmpty s then
            () |> Some
        else
            match s with
            | WHITESPACE (_, rest) when rest |> String.IsNullOrEmpty ->
                () |> Some
            | _ ->
                None
```

## The Evaluator Module

This module implements your evaluator — a function that takes AST terms and evaluates them with respect to an environment. You will model the environment as a list of string-float pairs that map a float value to a given variable.

The evaluator function works as follows:

➤ For numbers, it returns the number.

➤ For binary operations, it evaluates the two operands and calls the binary operation on them to calculate the result.

➤ For variables, it tries to locate the variable in the environment, and returns its bound value if successful. Otherwise, it raises an error message with the name of the variable that is not found.

➤ For function calls, it checks for the two built-in functions and calls them with the single argument evaluated.

➤ In every other case, it reports an error.

```
module Evaluator =
    open System
    open Ast

    let rec Eval (env: (string * float) list) e =
        match e with
        | Expr.Number num        -> num
        | Expr.BinOp (f, e1, e2) -> f (Eval env e1) (Eval env e2)
        | Expr.Var v             ->
            env
            |> List.tryFind (fun (_v, _) -> _v = v)
            |> function
                | None ->
                    "Unbound variable: " + v |> failwith
                | Some (_, value) ->
                    value
        | Expr.FunApply (f, e) when f.ToLower() = "sin" ->
            Eval env e |> sin
        | Expr.FunApply (f, e) when f.ToLower() = "cos" ->
            Eval env e |> cos
        | Expr.FunApply (f, _) ->
            "Unknown function: " + f |> failwith
```

# The FunctionPlotter Module

The FunctionPlotter module implements the plotting capabilities based on the modules you defined earlier. It defines a PlotInfo record type, which you will use to specify the information for the function plots — such as the formula itself, "sin(cos(x)*x)" or the formula variable, "x". This must match exactly the variable you use in your formulas. Also, only one variable is supported — the domain of this variable in which the plot will be made (between From and To) — and the range of the formula (between FromY and ToY), so you can "zoom" if you need to.

The entry point to this module is the Plot member that takes a PlotInfo value, creates a new window with a PictureBox, and plots the function given.

More refined implementations could do several optimizations, use better, more efficient drawing techniques, and implement further typical chores, such as calculating the optimal zooming to eliminate the need to specify range and domain limits, and so on. These are left to you for further exploration.

```
module PlotterClient =
    open System
    open System.Drawing
    open System.Windows.Forms
    open Microsoft.FSharp.Control

    let WIDTH = 500
    let HEIGHT = 500
    let POINTS = 500

    type PlotInfo =
        { Variable : string
          From : float
          To : float
          FromY : float
          ToY : float
          Formula : string }

    // A utility function to evaluate a formula with respect to the given
    // variable assigned with the given value.
    let EvalAt v formula x =
        Evaluator.Eval [v, x] formula

    // The function that plots a list of values with respect to a global
    // minimum and maximum.  It needs the graphics context of the canvas
    // to draw on.
    let draw min max values (ctx: Graphics) =
        let pen = new Pen(Color.White)
        // Increase range if min=max to 0..(max*2)
        let min = if min=max then 0. else min
        let max = if min=max then max*2. else max

        // Scale values into the box available (with height HEIGHT).
        let scaleY y = float32 HEIGHT - float32 HEIGHT / float32 ((max-min) /
            (y-min))

        // Break the computed values into segments (continuous lines)
        values
        |> List.fold (fun ((segments, current), x) y ->
            match y with
            | None ->
                (current :: segments, []), x+1
            | Some y ->
                y
                |> scaleY
                |> fun sy ->
                    if sy >= 0.f && sy <= float32 HEIGHT then
                        (segments,
                            PointF (float32 x * float32 WIDTH / float32 POINTS, sy)
                                :: current), x+1
                    else
```

```
                             (current :: segments, []), x+1) (([], []), 0)
         // Make sure that last segment is there
         |> fun ((segments, current), _) ->
             match current with
             | [] ->
                 segments
             | _ ->
                 current :: segments
         // Filter out "empty" and single segments
         |> List.filter (function | [] | [_] -> false | _ -> true)
         |> List.iter (fun segment ->
             // Draw each segment
             ctx.DrawCurve(pen, segment |> Array.ofList))

// Take a plot info object and draw it in a new window.
let Plot input =
    let form = new Form(Text=input.Formula)
    let bmp = new Bitmap(WIDTH, HEIGHT, Imaging.PixelFormat.Format16bppRgb555)
    let ctx = System.Drawing.Graphics.FromImage bmp
    let pbox = new PictureBox()
    pbox.Image <- bmp
    pbox.Width <- bmp.Width
    pbox.Height <- bmp.Height
    form.Width <- bmp.Width + 30
    form.Height <- bmp.Height + 50
    form.Controls.Add pbox
    form.Show()
    match input.Formula with
    | Language.Expression (formula, Language.Eof) ->
        try
            input.To - input.From
            |> fun range ->
                [ input.From .. (range / (float POINTS)) .. input.To ]
                // Calculate all Y's, returning None for undefined values.
                |> List.map (fun x ->
                    try
                        EvalAt input.Variable formula x
                        |> fun y ->
                            if y = infinity || y = -infinity then
                                None
                            else
                                Some y
                    with
                    | _ ->
                        None)
                |> fun values ->
                    draw input.FromY input.ToY values ctx
        with
        | e ->
            e.Message
            |> sprintf "Can not evaluate formula - %s"
            |> failwith
    | _ ->
        "Can not parse formula" |> failwith
```

## Running the Function Plotter

Although you could build an impressive UI around the function plotter functionality you built earlier, the easiest way to test it is via F# Interactive. You can highlight all the code and send it to a clean interactive session. At that point, you can start experimenting.

```
> open PlotterClient;;
> let pi = { Variable="x"; From= -2.*System.Math.PI;
      To= 2.*System.Math.PI; FromY = -10.; ToY = 10.;
      Formula="sin(cos(x)*x)" };;

val pi : PlotInfo = {Variable = "x";
                     From = -6.283185307;
                     To = 6.283185307;
                     FromY = -10.0;
                     ToY = 10.0;
                     Formula = "sin(cos(x)*x)";}

> Plot pi;;
val it : unit = ()
```

At this point, you should see a window pop up as shown in Figure 25-2.

## OTHER .NET LANGUAGES

Finally, to close this chapter, let's take a look at a few basic pointers concerning the Iron languages. These languages bring dynamic capabilities to the .NET language ecosystem, giving you another powerful toolset to combine with the functional paradigm you saw in this chapter.

### IronRuby

IronRuby is an implementation of the Ruby programming language for the .NET platform, spearheaded by John Lam, and running on the top of the Dynamic Language Runtime (DLR). The DLR is designed to enable language developers to create high-performance implementations of languages that rely on dynamic features, such as dynamic/duck typing and dynamic method dispatch.

Combined with the CLR and the DLR, Iron languages like IronRuby and IronPython offer developers a script-like syntax, and a dynamic run-time model that can be effectively used for quick exploration and problem-solving. They also enable developers to leverage the .NET libraries and its run-time support, and develop embedded languages, scripting capabilities, and other dynamic extensions.

You can find out more about IronRuby at the official site at `http://www.ironruby.net/`.

### IronPython

Another member of the Iron language, IronPython is a .NET implementation of Python, the popular general-purpose programming language, originally designed by Guido van Rossum in the early 1990s.

You can find out more about IronPython at `http://ironpython.net/`.

# SUMMARY

In this chapter you walked through the foundations and key features of Visual F#, a new functional, object-oriented programming language available in Visual Studio 2010. You learned about its origins and design motivations, and surveyed its core functional concepts, including immutability, functions as first-class values, algebraic data types, pattern matching, type inference, and lazy evaluation.

You saw how you can quickly get started with F#, how to create and run F# projects, and how to use the F# Interactive facility to quickly prototype F# programs and try them out on-the-fly as you develop your code.

You started your exploration of F# syntax with a short example that demonstrated defining and calling functions, binding values, currying and partial function application, and using piping to combine function calls to make them more readable. You then learned about using modules and namespaces to organize your code; ordinary, string, and other literals; the syntax for various collections; type signatures and annotations; and controlling access to parts of your code.

In a deeper look at the syntax of the language, you saw many of the available operators, conditionals, imperative features (such as loops and reference cells), and examples for converting between types. You worked with class types, objects, and object expressions, and surveyed the various object-oriented tools that enhance the dot-notation for values and objects.

You worked with anonymous functions, higher-order functions, and learned about continuations and CPS. You also saw many of the core functional data types (such as tuples, discriminated unions, option values, records, and lists).

In the second half of this chapter, you looked at some of the more advanced F# features, including computation expressions (also known as F# workflows), enumerable sequences, range and sequence expressions, asynchronous workflows, pattern matching, active patterns, exceptions, units of measure, lazy computations, and quotations. You saw how to work with database queries. As a more in-depth example, you developed a set of F# modules that you can use with F# Interactive to draw mathematical plots from your Visual Studio development session.

Finally, you took a tiny look at IronRuby and IronPython, and learned where you can obtain more information about these languages.

# INDEX

## Symbols

|> (pipe operator), F# syntax, 1109
=> (lambda operator), 1057

## A

About dialog box, VS Add-In Wizard, 232
About views, MVC, 770
abstract members, C# 4.0, 1082–1083
abstract syntax tree (AST), in F#, 1164
Access 1.1, release of, 985
access control, F#, 1120
accessors
    C# syntax, 1046
    indexers, 1080–1081
Accordion control
    AccordionSample.aspx, 924–925
    AccordionWithDataSample.aspx,
      926–927
    description of, 908
    overview of, 924
    properties, 928
action filtering, MVC, 821–822
ActionResult class, MVC, 822–824
actions
    designer-developer cooperation in Silverlight
      and WPF, 370
    in Macro Explorer, 216–217
actions, MVC controllers
    adding, 779
    child actions, 835
    Create view action, 786–787
    Delete view action, 787–789
    Details action, 779–782
    Edit view action, 782–785

active command scope, 156
active documents, components on Toolbox tabs,
    187–188
active patterns, F#
    complete, 1151–1152
    overview of, 1149–1151
    partial, 1152–1154
Active Server Pages. See ASP (Active Server
    Pages)
active solutions, Toolbox tabs, 187–188
active state, VisualStateGroup, 335
Active Template Library (ATL), for Visual Studio
    Gallery, 211
ActiveX controls, VB 5.0, 985
activities, WF 4.0. See also workflow activity
    library, WF 4.0
    adding flowchart to workflow, 500–504
    adding to workflow, 494
    assembling workflow, 490–491
    building in code-only workflows, 508
    extensions providing services to, 512–513
    workflow activity model changes, 513–517
    workflow architecture, 511–512
Activity class, WF 4.0, 511–512
<Activity> element, WF, 499
adaptive (smooth) streaming, Silverlight media,
    349–350
Add button, Code Snippets Manager, 52, 54
Add New Commands button, menus, 141–142
Add New Item dialog
    accessing online templates, 124
    adding item templates to project, 69–70
    customizing templates. See templates,
     customizing
    item template hierarchy, 84

Add New Menu button, 141
Add or Remove Buttons menu, 140, 144
Add Reference dialog, 19, 342
Add Tab command, Toolbox, 190
.AddIn file, 237–239
Add-In Manager, 231
Add-in Options page, Visual Studio Add-In
    Wizard, 231–232
add-ins
    architecture, 229–230
    creating with Connect class, 233–237
    creating with Visual Studio Add-In Wizard,
        230–233
    development of, 241–242
    managing and loading, 237–239
    overview of, 209–210
    using automation model, 239–241
AddNamedCommand2 method, implementing
    add-ins, 236
ad-hoc mode, WCF 4.0, 586
ADO.NET
    adding features to Visual Studio 2008 with,
        9–10
    creating Entity Data Model, 574
    Entity Framework. *See* Entity Framework
ADO.NET Data Services
    benefit of, 294
    Microsoft Ajax Library supporting, 879
    working with, 888–889
adornments, extensibility of new editor, 212
advanced data binding, Ajax, 872–875
AdvancedChartStateManagement.aspx page,
    serialization, 691–693
advertising, in SOA, 378
Aero glass, in Windows 7/WPF, 363
Ajax (Asynchronous JavaScript and XML)
    advanced data binding, 872–875
    ASP.NET and, 840–841
    client-side data binding with templates,
        859–860
    Content Delivery Network, 846–848
    Control Toolkit. *See* Ajax Control Toolkit
    custom converters in, 875–877
    DataView control, 860–863

DOM elements and, 852–855
interacting with events inside templates,
    867–871
jQuery leveraging Ajax infrastructure,
    976–977
live binding, 872–873
master-detail binding, 877–878
Microsoft Ajax Library, 666, 848–852
new in ASP.NET 3.5, 665–666
overview of, 665–666, 837–839
restoring framework libraries, 844–846
retrieving cross-domain data, 889–892
running code inside templates, 865–867
script loader, 855–859
server controls, 841–844
summary, 889–892
top-level binding, 874
two-way binding, 874–875
updating data on server, 883–888
using external templates, 871
using pseudo-columns in templates, 863–865
Visual Studio and, 841
WCF service enabled by, 392
working with ADO.NET data services,
    888–889
working with server-side data, 878–883
XMLHTTPRequest object, 839–840
Ajax chart interactivity
    handling click events, 698–701
    overview of, 697
    real time charts, 705–709
    triggering chart events, 701–705
Ajax Control Toolkit
    Accordion control, 924–928
    adding CascadingDropDown extenders to
        demo project, 901–902
    adding ExpertiseService class to demo
        project, 902–903
    adding ScriptManager to demo project, 901
    adding UpdatePanel to demo project,
        905–908
    animations, 956–962
    AsyncFileUpload control, 928–932
    button and checkbox extenders, 938–942

ComboBox control, 916–920

control extenders, 938

creating demo project, 896–900

discovering effect of CascadingDropDown extenders, 904–905

Editor control, 932–937

improving demo project, 900

installing, 894–895

list extenders, 947–949

list of controls in, 908–915

new server controls, 915–916

overview of, 841, 894

panel extenders, 949–952

popup extenders, 952–955

summary, 977

TabContainer control, 921–924

textbox extenders, 942–947

types of controls in, 895

upgrading to new version, 896

validator extenders, 955–956

Ajax Extensions. *See* also server controls, Ajax, 666, 841–842

Ajax Library, Microsoft

  client-side and, 666

  Core Services, 848–850

  cross-domain data requests supported, 889–892

  interoperability with web services, WCF services, and ADO.NET services, 879

  JavaScript library for use with Ajax, 837

  live binding, 872–873

  loading JavaScript files from Microsoft Ajax Library, 855–859

  Networking Layer, 850–852

  overview of, 841

  split script files in, 844–846

  top-level binding, 874

  two-way binding, 874–875

algebraic data types, in F#, 1105–1106, 1131

aliases, C# 2.0 namespace, 1056

AlignSeries method, DataManipulator, 644, 645

AllowRecomposition property, Import attribute, 481–482

Alt+F11, starting Macros IDE, 218

Alt+F7, changing active window, 159–160

AlwaysVisibleControlExtender control, 908

anchoring annotations, 636

Anders, Mark, 655–656

AnimationExtender

  Ajax Control Toolkit, 909

  XML animation declaration, 957–958, 962

animations

  defining with visual states, 334

  enhancing user experience with, 341

  jQuery library and, 975–976

  Silverlight, 341–345

  storyboards and, 342–344

  transformations, 344–345

animations, and Ajax Control Toolkit

  actions, 961–962

  events triggering, 959

  types of, 960

annotations

  anchoring, 636

  moving, 637–638

  overview of, 633

  properties of, 607–608

  types, 633–635

anonymous functions, F#, 1129–1130

anonymous methods, C# 2.0, 1052–1053

anonymous object-creation expressions, VB 9.0, 999–1000

anonymous types, C# 3.0, 1058

anti-aliasing, for text and graphics on charts, 622–623

application, MVC

  adding controller actions, 779

  adding pages to, 771

  Controller class, 769–770

  Create view action added, 786–787

  creating, 761–762

  creating controller for managing database items, 773–776

  creating database page for, 771–772

  creating model for, 772

  creating view for displaying items in database, 776–779

application, MVC (*continued*)
    Delete view action added, 787–789
    Details action added, 779–782
    Edit view action added, 782–785
    how it works, 764–766
    Index and About views, 770
    project structure, 763–764
    routing requests within, 766–768
application logic. *See* controllers, MVC
ApproveDomainNameRequest activity
    customizing tracking events, 549–550
    DomainNameWorkflowWithHost, 558–559
    resuming workflow instance, 543–544
ApprovementWorkflow activity, 557–560
architects, new tools for, 27–28
architecture
    add-in, 229–230
    DLR high-level, 405
    Entity Framework, 573–579
    extensibility of new editor, 212
    Model-View-Controller, 667–668
    .NET Framework, 289–290
    parallel programming, 420
    Visual Studio window, 128–131
    WCF building blocks, 378–381
    workflow. *See* workflow architecture
Architecture Explorer, 28
area charts, 612–613
areas, MVC 2 architecture, 668
areas, MVC architecture, 834
arguments, WF 4.0
    adding flowchart to workflow, 500
    adding input argument to workflow, 493
    adding output argument to workflow,
        495–496
    declaring in code-only workflows, 507–508
    explicit definition of, 511
    passing input argument to workflow,
        494–495
arithmetic expressions in F#, abstract syntax tree,
    1164
ArrangeOverride method, Silverlight layout, 317
array literals, as collection initializers, 1017
arrays, in F#, 1118, 1119

artifacts
    adding to VSIX project, 115–116
    building, 133
ASMX Web Services, 375–376
AsOrdered( ) method, and PLINQ behavior,
    427
ASP (Active Server Pages)
    ASP.NET improvements over, 657
    history of Microsoft web platforms and, 753
    as programming framework, 655
    in VS 97, 5
ASP+ platform, history of, 656
AsParallel( ) method, PLINQ, 425
<asp:Image> elements, 684–687
ASP.NET
    Ajax. *See* Ajax (Asynchronous JavaScript and
        XML)
    birth of, 5–6, 655–656
    chart controls. *See* chart controls, ASP.NET
    demo project. *See* FindAnExpertDemo,
        ASP.NET application
    Dynamic Data application. *See* Dynamic Data
        application, ASP.NET
    history of Microsoft's approach to web
        platform, 753–754
    improvements over ASP, 657
    Model View Controller. *See* MVC (Model
        View Controller)
    as .NET architecture service, 292
    overview of, 657–659
    release of, 655–657
    release of ASP, 654–655
    user experience in, 297
    version 1.0, 658, 659
    version 1.1, 658, 659
    version 2.0, 658, 659–664
    version 3.0, 658, 664–665
    version 3.5, 658, 665–666
    version 3.5 SPI, 659, 667
    version 4.0, 659, 667–668
    WCF RIA Services integration with, 354
    web development and, 653–654
AspNetCacheProfile attribute, HTTP caching
    in WCF 4.0, 589

assemblies
    interop (interoperability) assemblies, 211–212
    overview of, 463–464
    PIAs (Primary Interoperability Assemblies).
        *See* PIAs (Primary Interoperability
        Assemblies)
    referenced. *See* referenced assemblies
assembly catalog, programming with MEF, 468
<Assembly> element, for <References>
    element, 47
Assign button, keyboard shortcuts, 159
AST (abstract syntax tree), arithmetic expressions
    in F#, 1164
Ast module, F#, 1164
AsUnordered( ) method, PLINQ, 427
AsyncFileUpload control
    AsyncFileUpload.aspx.cs, 932
    AsyncFileUploadSample.aspx, 928–930
    description of, 909
    overview of, 928
    properties, 930–931
AsynchPostBackTrigger, chart events, 702–703
asynchronous communications, .NET vs.
    Silverlight, 352
asynchronous controllers, Model View Controller,
    835
Asynchronous Java Script and XML. *See* Ajax
    (Asynchronous JavaScript and XML)
asynchronous workflows, F#, 1144–1146
ATL (Active Template Library), for Visual Studio
    Gallery, 211
attached dependency properties, 318–319
AttachedToParent value, task control flow,
    444
attribute filters, jQuery, 968–969
Attributed Programming Model, MEF, 486
attributes
    customizing Dynamic Data validation,
        747–749
    MVC validation, 795–797
    programming in F#, 1115
    <Project> element for item templates, 94–95
    <Project> element for project templates,
        91–94
    <ProjectItem> element, 92–94

audio playback, Silverlight media, 345–347
authorization, in MVC, 819–821
AuthorizationAttribute, MVC, 819
AutoCompleteExtender, 909, 942
auto-encoding syntax, MVC, 771
Auto-Hide command, 136
auto-implemented properties, VB 10.0, 1007,
    1010–1012
automatic properties, C# 3.0, 1062
Automation API, 211–212
automation model
    functional parts of, 239–241
    programming macros using Visual Studio,
        208–209
Avalon, 301
axes, chart
    adding custom labels to, 629–630
    customizing appearance and behavior,
        623–627
    labels, 606–607
    titles, 606–607
AxisLabel property, customizing data point
    labels, 632

**B**

bandwidth
    in online video and movies, 349
    smooth streaming and, 349
bar charts
    candlestick charts as, 615
    defined, 610
    range, 614
Base Class Library
    development of, 7
    .NET Framework architecture, 290, 291
BASIC (Beginner's All-purpose Symbolic
    Instruction Code)
    moving to "visual," 984–985
    structured, 983–984
    unstructured, 982–983
Basic VSPackage Information page, 244–245
BasicChartStateManagement.aspx.cs,
    688–690, 691–693
BasicHttpBinding, Silverlight, 353

`BeforeOpeningFile` method, `iWizard`, 104, 106

behaviors

adding to workflow services, 560–561

customizing chart axis, 624–627

designer-developer cooperation in Silverlight/WPF, 370

enabling service discovery, 587

extension methods influencing PLINQ, 425–428

part creation, 482

Berners-Lee, Tim, and WWW, 653–654

`BetweenFilter` class, `DataManipulator` filtering, 643

binary operations

arithmetic expressions in F#, 1164

COM and reusability of, 281–282

overloading, 995–996

binary stream rendering, ASP.NET charts, 684–687

binding editor, WPF Designer property grid, 27

binding helpers, jQuery, 972–974

bindings, WCF

predefined, 379–380

specifying information, 387–388

Bing Maps, using Deep Zoom, 346–347

bitmap effects, Silverlight, 356

bitwise arithmetic operators, F#, 1121

BizTalk 2006, in .NET Framework 2.0, 286–287

Blend (Expression Blend)

creating complex animations, 342–344

editing Silverlight templates, 332

warning for conflicting visual state settings, 335–336

working with Silverlight and WPF, 313, 367–371

as WPF application, 302

blendability, 368–369

blocked components, and Toolbox, 191–192

`Blur` shader effect, Silverlight, 356

`Bmp` format, image files, 682

`body` delegate, `Parallel.For<TLocal>`, 436–437

`BookController` class, for MVC application, 773–776

bookmarks

resuming workflow instance with, 544

suspending workflow with, 539–540

Boolean operators, in F#, 1116, 1121

`BouncingCircle.xaml`, 342, 344–345

boxing operations, 1044

browser, running WPF application within, 359–361

Browser Compatibility Layer, ASP.NET Ajax, 841

`BrowserHttpStack`, Silverlight, 353

buffering, eliminating with stream smoothing, 349

Build ➪ Rebuild Solution function, VSPackage Wizard, 249

business processes

dynamic data and. *See* Dynamic Data application, ASP.NET

managing rules in MVC, 801–803

MVC controllers and. *See* controllers, MVC

.NET benefits, 294

`Buttons`

adding event handlers to Silverlight, 308–311

applying to templates, 337

`ControlTemplate`, 333

for data binding to list of objects, 326–328

for Silverlight layout containers, 316

`VisualStateGroups` for, 335

`ButtonTemplating.xaml`, `ControlTemplate`, 333–335

## C

C#

automatic properties, 1010

code snippet implementation in, 33–34, 40

design goals of, 1042

DLR high-level architecture diagram, 405

dynamic binding in, 185

evolution of, 1041–1042

history of, 1041

implementations of, 1043–1044

invoking code snippets, 35

.NET Framework and, 1042–1043

summary, 1064

user experience in VisualBasic.NET and, 297

variance in, 1029
VB.NET compared with, 988
C# 1.0
  memory management, 1045–1046
  overview of, 1044
  syntax, 1046–1047
  type system, 1044–1045
C# 1.1, 1047
C# 2.0
  anonymous methods, 1052–1053
  delegate covariance and contravariance,
    1053–1054
  delegate inference, 1053
  generic types, 1048–1050
  iterators, 1052
  namespace aliases, 1056
  nullable types, 1054–1055
  null-coalesce operator, 1056
  overview of, 1047–1048
  partial types, 1050–1051
  property accessors, 1055
  static classes, 1051–1052
C# 3.0, 1056–1064
  anonymous types, 1058
  automatic properties, 1062
  collection initializers, 1063
  expression trees, 1061
  extension methods, 1057–1058
  lambda expressions, 1059–1060
  local variable type inference, 1057
  object initializers, 1062
  overview of, 1056–1057
  partial methods, 1063–1064
  query expressions, 1060–1061
C# 4.0
  abstract and virtual members, 1082–1083
  addressing syntax noise, 1069–1071
  changes in CLR. *See* CLR (Common
    Language Run-time)
  COM-related interoperability issues,
    1084–1087
  contravariance, 1093–1094
  covariance, 1090–1093
  creating demo project, 1066–1069

dynamic binding, 1072–1073
Dynamic Language Run-time and, 1077–1078
dynamic lookup, 1072
dynamic operations, 1074–1077
dynamic type, 1073–1074
interoperability issues, 1066
issues before, 401
named parameters, 1081–1082
optional parameters, 1079–1081
overview of, 1065–1066
resolving applicable signatures, 1083–1084
resolving overloaded method invocations,
  1082
summary, 1099
type substitution and, 1087–1089
variance, 1089–1090
variance and reflection, 1098–1099
variance with multiple type parameters,
  1094–1097
variance with user types, 1097–1098
C+, roots of Visual Studio, 4
C++
  C# inspired by, 1042
  before .NET Framework, 280
  releasing Microsoft tools in, 4–5
  roots of Visual Studio, 4
  templates, 989, 1048
caching
  Call Site Caching in DLR, 1077–1078
  of command table in VS packages, 252
  WCF 4.0 support for HTTP, 589
CalendarExtender
  description of, 909
  textbox extenders, 942, 945
Call Hierarchy function, code navigation, 23
call site caching, in DLR
  DLR high-level architecture diagram, 405
  overview of, 403–404
  understanding, 1077–1078
cancellation, in compensating transaction model,
  528–530
cancellation primitives, 451, 455
CancellationToken property, Parallel class,
  430

candlestick charts, 615

Canvas, as layout container, 318–319

CascadingDropDown extenders
  adding to sample ASP.NET application, 901–902
  description of, 909
  discovering effect of, 904–905
  list extenders, 947

Case, types of animations, 960

catalogs, MEF, 475–476, 486

categories
  inserting, 35
  Options dialog, 146–147
  Visual Studio Gallery, 194–195

Ccheck.exe, 457, 462

Ccrefgen.exe, 457, 462

Ccrewrite.exe, 457, 462–463

CDN (Content Delivery Network), Ajax, 846–848

CERN (European Organization for Nuclear Research), 653

CF (Compact Framework), .NET, 289

chaining functions, jQuery, 970

ChangeRequestStatus method, resuming workflow, 544

character literals, in F#, 1117

Chart class, 607–608

chart components, .NET
  adding charts to WPF applications, 603–605
  adding data to chart programmatically, 598–603
  binding data to series, 638–641
  Chart class, 607–608
  chart coordinate system, 617–619
  chart data serialization, 648
  chart elements, 606–607
  chart elements, appearance of, 621–623
  chart elements, axes and related, 623–630
  chart interactivity, 649
  chart printing, 648
  creating simple chart, 594–598
  customizing chart drawing, 649
  data points, 630–633
  DataManipulator class. See DataManipulator class, Chart control

  overview of, 593
  three-dimensional charts, 619–621
  using annotations, 633–638

Chart control
  adding charts to WPF applications, 603–605
  adding data to chart programmatically, 598

chart controls, ASP.NET
  adding to page, 670–674
  binary stream rendering, 684–688
  binding data to chart, 676–678
  image URL rendering, 680–683
  overview of, 669–670
  rendering, 679–680
  setting up charts in event handler method, 674–676
  state management, 688–694
  user interactivity. See user interactivity, ASP. NET charts
  using charts with legacy web sites, 683–684

chart data serialization, 648

chart elements
  adding custom labels to axis, 629–630
  appearance of, 621–623
  axes, 623–627
  overview of, 606–607
  strip lines, 627–629

chart interactivity, 649

chart pictures, 606–607

chart printing, 648

chart state management, ASP.NET
  chart serialization basics, 690–691
  overview of, 688
  playing with serialization content, 693–694
  saving chart state, 688–690
  using serialization in state management, 691–693

chart types, .NET
  area charts, 612–613
  bar charts, 609–610
  candlestick charts, 615
  column charts, 609–610
  custom properties and, 616–617
  doughnut charts, 613–614
  line charts, 611

overview of, 609

pie charts, 613

point charts, 611–612

polar charts, 616

radar charts, 616

range charts, 614–615

step line charts, 615

stock charts, 615–616

ChartArea Collection Editor, 596, 598

ChartArea element, NET charts

adding new, 596

ASP.NET, 671–674

creating three-dimensional charts, 619–621

defined, 606–607

properties of, 607–608

ChartImages folder, ASP.NET charts, 680–681

/ChartImg.axd, rendering ASP.NET charts, 679–680

ChartSerializer, 691

CheckBox control, extenders, 938–942

child actions, MVC, 835

child tasks, 444–445

ChildActionOnlyAttribute, MVC authorization, 819

Choose a Collection of Settings to Import page, Import and Export Settings Wizard, 153

Choose Settings to Export page, Import and Export Settings Wizard, 152

Choose Template Type page, Export Template Wizard, 73

Choose Toolbox Items dialog, 190–191

class types, in F#, 1125

Class View, Architecture Explorer, 28

classes

C# 2.0 static, 1051–1052

macros using code in, 214

viewing in Macro Explorer, 215

Classic ASP. See ASP (Active Server Pages)

classification format, editor classifier, 262, 267–269

classification type, editor classifier, 262–263

classification type registry, 265

ClassificationChanged event, OrdinaryClassifier, 266–267

ClassificationFormat.cs file, 267–270

ClassificationRegistry field, classification type registry, 265

ClassificationType attribute, classification format, 268

ClassificationType.cs file

changing completely, 271–272

creating editor classifier, 262–263

modifying, 269–270

ClassificationTypeDefinition type, 263

classifier, creating simple

assigning to specified editor content, 212

classification format, 267–269

classification type, 262–263

classifier provider and classifier, 263–267

overview of, 260–262

playing with classification, 269–275

classifier provider, editor classifier, 263–267

Classifier.cs file, 263–267

ClassName() function, code snippets, 47, 49

CLI (Common Language Infrastructure)

history of C# and, 1042

implementations of, 1044

Click events

adding to Silverlight project, 310–311

ControlTemplate, 333

using Ajax for, 698–701

ClientHttpStack, Silverlight, 353–354

client-side

Ajax and jQuery as technologies on, 893

Ajax Library on, 666

data binding in Ajax on. See data binding, Ajax client-side

importance of user experience on, 297–299

validation in MVC on, 803–804

WCF on, 381

clock speed, computer CPU evolution and, 416–418

ClockSample.xaml, 323

ClockViewModel.cs, 323

closed types

in C#, 1049

in VB, 990

clouds, new in VS 2010, 12

CLR (Common Language Run-time)
    addressing flaws in major languages with, 1042
    birth of ASP.NET and, 656
    as bottom layer of .NET Framework, 290–291
    dispose pattern, 996–997
    DLR and, 402–411
    DLR integration, 1077–1078
    executing tasks in TPL, 448–449
    generic types implemented at CLR level, 989–990
    nullable types and, 1055
    overview of, 400
    in-process side-by-side execution and, 400–402
    support for LINQ, 564
    type equivalence, 411–415
    unsigned integers, 996
    user experience in VB.NET and, 297
    variance in, 1029
    Visual Studio 2005, 8
    VS 2008, 8–9
    in WCF, 379
code
    completion, 32
    inside templates, 865–867
    surround, with code snippets, 36
    XAML vs., 311–313
code contracts
    code contract library, 456–457
    declaring, 457–461
    defined, 400
    overview of, 455–456
    run-time behavior, 462–463
    system of, 456–457
    tools in Visual Studio for, 461–462
Code Definition window, code-navigation, 24
code editor
    Call Hierarchy function, 23
    Code Definition window, 24
    debugging, 24
    Navigate To dialog, 22
    new features in VS 2010, 12–13
    reference highlighting, 22
    UI enhancements, 20–22
    using code snippets with at least one, 34
code element, 43–44
code snippets
    adding and removing, 54
    adding text snippets to Toolbox, 192–193
    building online providers for, 59
    Code Snippets Manager, 52
    creating simple, 37–41
    editors, 59–60
    Export as Code Snippet, 60–61
    extending Visual Studio with, 205–207
    HTML, SQL, and JScript, 37
    importing, 54–55
    importing file with multiple, 56–57
    inserting, 34–36
    in other languages, 58
    overview of, 31–32
    Snippet Designer, 61–62
    Snippet Editor, 62–63
    specific Visual Basic features, 36–37
    storage, 53–54
    surrounding selected code with, 36
    types of, 33
    understanding, 32–33
    using, 34
code snippets, file structure
    functions, 47–51
    <Header>, 42–43
    language-dependent features, 46–47
    overview of, 41–42
    <Snippet>, 43–45
Code Snippets Manager
    adding and removing snippets, 54
    code snippet storage, 53–54
    importing code snippet, 39–41
    importing file with multiple snippets, 56–57
    importing snippets, 54–55
    overview of, 52
code-completion list, with snippets, 35
CodedHelloWorkflow, 505–509
code-navigation
    Call Hierarchy function, 23

Code Definition window, 24
    debugging, 24
    Navigate To dialog, 22
    reference highlighting, 22
code-only workflows, WF 4.0
    building activities, 508
    declaring variables, 508
    declaring workflow arguments, 507–508
    DomainNameWorkflow project, 533–534
    overview of, 505–507
    using expressions, 509
CodeOnly.xaml.cs, 311–313
CodePlex, downloading Ajax Control Toolkit
    from, 894
<CodeSnippet> element, 42
CollapsiblePanelExtender, 909, 949–951
collection initializers, in C# 3.0, 1063
collection initializers, in VB 10.0
    array literals, 1017
    examples of, 1013–1017
    how it works, 1012–1013
    new features in VB 10.0, 1007
collection-handling activities, in WF 4.0, 524–525
collections
    generics and, 1050
    programming in F#, 1118
Color, changing classification, 268–269
ColorAnimation, Silverlight, 343
ColorPickerExtender, 910, 942, 945
colors
    controlling chart appearance, 622–623
    customizing Text Content format, 274
    types of animations, 960
column charts, 609–610, 614
COM (Component Object Model)
    add-in components as, 229–230
    extensibility and, 211–212
    interoperability issues in C# 4.0, 1066,
        1084–1087
    issues before C# 4.0 with managed
        components, 401
    .NET 4 changes in CLR hosting, 401–402
    object-oriented programming and, 985

    programming before .NET Framework,
        281–282
    type equivalence and, 411–415
    VS 2010 and, 15
COM Components tab, Choose Toolbox Items
    dialog, 190
combined-page mode, Dynamic Data URL
    routing, 721–722, 729–730
ComboBox control
    AutoCompleteModeList, 919
    ComboBoxSample.aspx, 916–917
    ComboBoxSample.aspx.cs, 918–919
    description of, 910
    overview of, 916
    properties, 920
    SimpleComboBox_ItemInserting method,
        919–920
    using Dynamic Data web application for
        master-detail relationships, 729–730
ComImportAttribute attribute, equivalence in
    CLR, 415
command activation, package load mechanism for,
    204
command bar, workflow design surface, 491
command buttons, Start Page, 169–170
command groups, packages, 253
Command Options page, VSPackage Wizard,
    245–246
command table, package development, 252–254
command targets, command routing with, 156
CommandList_MouseDoubleClick, accessing VS
    object model, 184–185
CommandListStartPage, 184–185
CommandProcessor.cs file, simple item template,
    76–77
CommandProcessorItem.cs file, simple item
    template, 76–78
commands
    determining shortcut key assigned to, 158
    handling keyboard shortcuts, 155–157
    as menus and toolbars. See menus and
        toolbars, customizing
Commands tab, Customize dialog, 139–140

`CommentDescriptor.cs`, customizing templates, 104

comments
    F# syntax, 1111
    VB 7.0/7.1 documentation, 994

`CommentSelector.xaml`, 102–104

`CommentSelector.xaml.cs`, 103

`CommentWizard.cs`, iWizard, 106–107

Common Language Infrastructure (CLI)
    history of C# and, 1042
    implementations of, 1044

Common Language Run-time. *See* CLR (Common Language Run-time)

Common Language Specification, CLR, 290

Common Object Run-time (COR), 1042

Common Type System. *See* CTS (Common Type System)

`CommonStates`, `VisualStateGroup` for `Button`, 335–336

communication, between client and server, 297

community technology preview (CTP), of LINQ, 9

Compact Framework (CF), .NET, 289

`CompareMethod`, `DataManipulator` filtering, 643

compatibility, between versions of CLR, 400–401

compensating transaction model, WF 4.0
    `ConferenceWorkflow` example of, 527–528
    implementing cancellation, 528–529
    implementing compensation, 530–532
    implementing confirmation, 530
    transaction-handling activities implementing, 523–524

`CompilerGeneratedAttribute` attribute, equivalence in CLR, 415

compilers
    compile time semantics, 1075–1076
    compiling without PIAs, 1086–1087
    XAML, 308

complete active patterns, 1151–1152

Component Object Model. *See* COM (Component Object Model)

componentization, in VB 5.0, 985

components
    Model-View-ViewModel, 374

    pioneering role of COM, 281–282
    Visual Studio Gallery, 194–197

components, Toolbox
    adding, 190–191
    adding text snippets, 192–193
    blocked, 191–192
    overview of, 187–188

composition, MEF
    accessing metadata, 484–486
    defined, 471
    explicit and implicit, 478
    import notification, 480–481
    lazy instantiation, 480
    overview of, 477
    part instantiation, 478–480
    part lifetime, 482–484
    path instantiation, 478–479
    recomposition, 481–482

composition containers, MEF
    example of, 468
    overview of, 474–475
    part lifetime and, 482–484
    querying for parts, 486

computation expressions
    asynchronous workflows, 1144–1146
    F#, 1138–1140

Conceptual (C-Space layer), Entity Data Model, 574

Conceptual Schema Definition Language (CSDL), Entity Data Model, 574

Conceptual-Storage (C-S Mapping layer), Entity Data Model, 574

Concurrency Run-time, Parallel Computing Platform, 419

concurrent collection classes, 450–452

`Condition`, types of animations, 960

conditional operator, in VB 9.0, 1004–1005

conditional pattern clauses, 1150

conditionals, in F#, 1122

`ConferenceWorkflow`, 527–528

configuration, simplified in WCF 4.0, 583–585

`ConfigureWorkflow`, 548–549

confirmation, compensating transaction model, 528–532

ConfirmButtonExtender, 910

Connect class, creating add-ins, 233–237

constraints, type parameter, 990–991

Constructor Injection, MVC, 759

Consume First mode, IntelliSense, 21–22

containers, Silverlight layout
- Border, 317–318
- Canvas, 318–319
- concept of, 315–317
- Grid, 319–321
- StackPanel, 319
- Viewbox, 321–322

Content Delivery Network (CDN), Ajax, 846–848

Content Model View, XML Schema Designer, 27

Content property, Button, 308–309

ContentControl, as Silverlight container, 315–316

ContentPresenter control, ControlTemplate, 333

context
- changing using package load, 204
- sensitivity, 145
- Start Page accessing, 176–182
- in Visual Studio. See Visual Studio context

context menus
- adding menus and commands to, 143
- command handling for, 156
- initiating actions in Macro Explorer from, 216–217

ContextItem.cs file, 180

ContinueWith method, task control flow, 446

ContractException, 463

ContractFailed event, 463

ContractInvariant method, 458

contracts
- code. See code contracts
- name, 172
- programming with MEF, 471–472
- type, 472

CONTRACTS_FULL symbol, code contracts, 458

contravariance
- in C# 4.0, 1093–1094
- defined, 1029, 1089
- delegate covariance and contravariance in C# 2.0, 1053–1054

with multiple type parameters, 1033

in VB 10.0, 1032–1033

control extenders, Ajax Control Toolkit
- button and checkbox extenders, 938–942
- CascadingDropDown extenders, 901–902, 904–905
- list extenders, 947–949
- overview of, 895, 938
- panel extenders, 949–952
- popup extenders, 952–955
- textbox extenders, 942–947
- validator extenders, 955–956

control flow, and tasks, 444–446

control templates
- in Silverlight, 332–337
- in WPF, 365–366

Controller class, MVC, 769–770

Controller Factory, MVC routing details, 816–817

controllers, MVC
- architecture, 668
- asynchronous, 835
- authorization, 819–821
- child actions, 835
- Controller class, 769–770
- Controller Factory, 816–817
- Create view action added, 786–787
- creating for managing items in database, 773–776
- Delete view action added to MVC application, 787–789
- Details action added to MVC application, 779–782
- Edit view action added to MVC application, 782–785
- execution flow and, 817–818
- overview of, 752
- preparing for validation, 799–800
- testing, 824–826

controls
- adding own contributions to Visual Studio Gallery, 197
- displaying on Toolbox, 188
- Visual Studio Gallery, 194–195

controls, Ajax Control Toolkit
    `Accordion` control, 924–928
    `AsyncFileUpload` control, 928–932
    `ComboBox` control, 916–920
    `Editor` control, 932–937
    list of, 908–915
    new server controls, 915–916
    standard controls, 895
    `TabContainer` control, 921–924
    types of, 895
    `UpdatePanel` control, 905–908
`ControlStoryboardAction`, 342
contructs, in computation expressions, 1138–1139
converters, data binding and, 325, 875–877
coordinate system, charts, 617–619
coordination data structures
    cancellation primitives, 455
    concurrent collection classes, 451–452
    lazy initialization classes, 454
    overview of, 451
    synchronization primitives, 452–454
copying
    chart values in `DataManipulator`, 645
    files for exporting templates manually, 111
    project templates, 69
COR (Common Object Run-time), 1042
core functions, in F#, 1123
Core Services, Microsoft Ajax Library, 848–850
`CorrelationScope` activity,
    `DomainNameWorkflowWithHost`, 556
cost categories, Visual Studio Gallery, 195
covariance
    in C# 4.0, 1090–1093
    defined, 1029, 1089
    delegate covariance and contravariance in C#
        2.0, 1053–1054
    with multiple type parameters, 1033
    in VB 10.0, 1030–1032
Create New SQL Server Database, preparing
    workflow, 536
`Create` view action added, MVC controller
    actions, 786–787
`CreateBookmark` method, workflow, 540
`CreateDomainNameRequest` activity, workflow
    project, 536–537

cross-domain data, and Microsoft Ajax Library,
    889–892
`crossdomain.xml` file, Silverlight security, 352
CRUD (Create-Read-Update-Delete) operations
    creating Dynamic Data application for
        master-detail relationships, 726–730
    creating in Dynamic Data website, 712,
        718–724
    potential security risk of, 716
    using Entity Client for, 578
    WCF RIA Services addressing, 354
C-S (Conceptual-Storage) Mapping layer, Entity
    Data Model, 574
CSDL (Conceptual Schema Definition Language),
    Entity Data Model, 574
C-Space layer (Conceptual), Entity Data Model,
    574
`CssClass`, ASP.NET Dynamic Data websites
    customizing look and feel, 733
    working with field templates, 739–741
    working with page templates, 736–738
CTP (community technology preview), of LINQ, 9
Ctrl+Alt+X, 188–189
Ctrl+K, S, 34, 36
Ctrl+K, X, 34
Ctrl+K, Ctrl+B, 52
Ctrl+K, Ctrl+C, 155
Ctrl+Tab, 159–160
CTS (Common Type System)
    defined, 290
    in .NET Framework, 986
    ordering among types in, 1089
    VB 2005 (8.0) and, 989
    VB.NET (7.0/7.1) and, 988
    VS 2005 development, 7
current project scope, 156
currying, F# syntax, 1109–1110
custom converters, data binding, 875–877
custom error pages, in ASP.NET 2.0, 662–663
Custom Start Page Project Template
    accessing Visual Studio context, 178–182
    changing `StartPage.xaml` file, 173–176
    MyControl tab, 171–172
    Start Page, creating, 164

Start Page, more about, 186
Start Page solution structure, 165–167
customization
    ASP.NET Dynamic Data site page, 746–747
    ASP.NET Dynamic Data site validation,
        747–749
    chart axis labels, 629–630
    chart data points, 630–633
    chart drawing, 649
    extending Visual Studio with, 204–208
    features in MVC, 790
    Silverlight layout panels, 321–322
    templates. *See* templates, customizing
    templates in MVC, 811–814
    tracking workflow events, 549–550
customization, menus and toolbars
    adding menus and commands, 140–143
    context sensitivity, 145
    creating and rearranging toolbars, 144–145
    overview of, 138–140
Customize dialog
    adding menus and commands, 140–143
    creating and rearranging toolbars, 144–145
    overview of, 139–140
<CustomParameters> element, custom template
    parameters, 99–101

data. *See also* models, MVC
    adding to chart programmatically, 598–603
    manually adding to chart, 594–596
Data Annotation Attribute validation, MVC 2,
    668
data binding
    to charts in ASP.NET, 676–678
    dynamic binding in C# 4.0, 1072–1073
    early binding, 1020
    in F#, 1108, 1115, 1119–1120
    field templates rendering data, 738
    late binding in VB 10.0, 1021–1023
    to series in charts, 638–641
    to series in .NET charting components,
        638–641

several flavors of .NET, 639
data binding, Ajax client-side
    advanced, 872
    custom converters, 875–877
    DataView control, 860–863
    interacting with events inside templates,
        867–871
    live binding, 872–873
    master-detail, 877–878
    running code inside templates, 865–867
    with templates, 859–860
    two-way, 874–875
    using external templates, 871
    using pseudo-columns in templates, 863–865
data binding, Silverlight
    to list of objects, 326–328
    master-detail, 328–329
    overview of, 322
    simple, 322–325
    with templates, 337–341
    between two UI elements, 325
data binding, to data source in charts, 600–603
data context, adding data model to Dynamic Data
    website, 713–716
data contracts, WCF, 379, 386–387
data controls, ASP.NET, 660, 665
data labels, charts, 606–607
data models, Dynamic Data web applications
    creating for master-detail relationships,
        725–730
    creating using LINQ to SQL, 712–716
    mastering validations, 749
data points
    adding ASP.NET chart control to page with,
        671–672
    adding programmatically, 598–599
    adding tooltips to chart, 694–696
    anchoring annotations with, 636
    controlling color of, 622
    customizing, 630–633
    customizing for various chart types, 609
    filtering in DataManipulator, 642–643
    handling clicks on, 696–697
    in line charts, 611

data points (*continued*)
    overview of, 595
    properties of, 607–608
    in range charts, 614
    setting up in ASP.NET `Chart` control, 672
    sorting in `DataManipulator`, 644
data source
    binding chart to, 600–603
    binding to series, 638–641
    properties of, 608
Data Source Configuration Wizard, 601
data structures for coordination, parallel
    programming, 420
data types
    algebraic data types in F#, 1105–1106
    ASP.NET Dynamic Data field templates,
      738–741
databases
    creating Entity Data Model, 574–575
    creating pages in MVC, 771–772
    F# queries, 1161–1162
    preparing workflow, 536
    sending new request into, 536–537
`DataBindCrossTable.aspx` file, charts,
    676–678
`DatabindingList.cs`, 327–328
`DatabindingTemplates.xaml`, 337–341
`DataContext` property
    accessing Visual Studio context, 176–177,
      180–181
    `Grid_DataContextChanged`. *See* `Grid_`
      `DataContextChanged` method
    LINQ to SQL, 570–572
    master-detail data-binding, 329
    modifying for Start Pages, 186
    simple data-binding example, 324–325
`DataContract` attribute, WCF, 386–387
data-driven websites, with little or no coding. *See*
    Dynamic Data application, ASP.NET
`DataManipulator` class, `Chart` control
    applying financial formula to data, 647–648
    applying statistical formula to data, 646–647
    copying values, 645
    exporting data to `DataSet` object, 646
    filtering data, 642–643

overview of, 641–642
    sorting data, 644
`DataPager` data control, 665
DataPoint Collection Editor dialog, 595, 599
`DataPointCollection`, 640–641
datasets
    exporting chart data to, 646
    querying data with LINQ to DataSet,
      569–570
`DataView` control
    adding interaction events inside templates,
      867–871
    client-side data binding and, 860–863
    master-detail binding supported, 877–878
    using external templates, 871
`.dbmi` extension, Entity Data Model, 575
debugging
    add-ins, 237
    new in VS 2010, 12
    packages, 247, 254–255
    VS 2008, 11
    with WPF tree visualization, 27
Debugging category, Options dialog, 147
declarative data access, 660–661
declarative WCF services, 394–398
decomposition of tasks, into units, 440–441
`DecreaseTextEditorFontSize` macros,
    225–226
Deep Zoom, Silverlight, 347–348
default skins, 662
`Default.aspx` file
    adding ASP.NET chart control to page,
      670–674
    customizing ASP.NET Dynamic Data look
      and feel, 735
    setting up ASP.NET charts in event handler
      methods, 674–676
delegate covariance and contravariance, C# 2.0,
    1053–1054
delegate inference, C# 2.0, 1053
delegates, generics and, 1050
Delete button
    removing toolbar from list, 144
    removing Toolbox tab, 189

Delete view action added, MVC controller, 787–789

Delimiter attribute, code element, code snippets, 44

Delphi, programming in, 281

Dependency Injection (DI) design pattern for workflows, 512

Dependency Injection (DI), applying MVC to, 759–760

Dependency Object, actions and triggers, 370

dependency properties, animations working only with, 343

deployment
    macro project as smallest unit of, 215
    .NET Framework model for, 283

design patterns, in MVC, 752

design time sample data, in Blend, 369–370

designer-developer cooperation, in Silverlight and WPF, 367–371

designers
    skills of developers vs., 299–301
    WF 3.5 workflow design surface, 492
    WF 4.0 workflow design surface, 491
    WPF Designer, 26

designers, XML Schema Designer, 27

Details action, MVC controller, 779–782

DetailsView data control
    Dynamic Data website structure, 732
    new in ASP.NET 2.0, 660

developers, 299–301

Development Tools Extensibility (DTE), 239–241

devenv.exe, 229

DGQL (Directed Graph Query Language) file, Architecture Explorer, 28

DI (Dependency Injection), applying MVC to, 759–760

Directed Graph Query Language (DGQL) file, Architecture Explorer, 28

Directory column, Choose Toolbox Items dialog, 191

discovery
    in SOA, 378
    standard endpoints in 4.0, 586–588

discriminated (tagged) unions, in F#, 1106, 1131–1132

display area, Options dialog, 146

display templates, in MVC, 805–808

DisplayAttribute, in MVC, 810–811

DisplayColumnAttribute, in MVC, 808–809

DisplayFormatAttribute, in MVC, 809

DLINQ, 570–572

DLLs (dynamic link libraries)
    in C++, 280
    .NET Framework interoperability and, 283

DLR (Dynamic Language Run-time)
    accessing IronPython library from VB, 1023–1026
    C# 4.0 and, 1077–1078
    overview of, 1023

DLR (Dynamic Language Run-time), changes in CLR
    advantages of in .NET 4, 403–405
    dynamic object example, 409–411
    ExpandoObject example, 407–309
    expression trees in .NET 3.5 and, 402–403
    IronPython code example, 405–407
    overview of, 402

DNRequestTrackingBehavior, 560–561

DNRequestTrackingParticipant, 546–547, 548–549

docking windows
    document windows, 135–136
    tool windows, 131–132, 135
    using keyboard for, 160

DockPanel, WPF layout, 362

Document Object Model. See DOM (Document Object Model)

document outline window, VS 2010, 314

Document Outline window, WPF Designer, 26

document windows
    command handling for, 156
    defined, 16–17
    docking, 135–136
    floating, 134
    organizing into tab groups, 136
    overview of, 132–134
    setting position of new, 137–138
    splitting and duplicating, 136–137
    tabbed, 130

documentation comments, VB 2005 (8.0), 994

Documents tab, Options dialog, 137–138

DOM (Document Object Model)
 accessing elements via Microsoft Ajax
  Library, 851
 jQuery and, 964
 working with DOM elements in Ajax,
  852–855

domain logic. *See* controllers, MVC

domain model, in MVC, 826–827

`DomainNameWorkflow` project. *See* persistence
 and human interactions, WF 4.0

`DomainNameWorkflowTracking`. *See* workflow
 tracking, WF 4.0

`DomainNameWorkflowWithHost` project
 adding behaviors, 560–561
 approval workflow, 557–559
 changing main workflow, 554–556
 configuring `WorkflowServiceHost`,
  559–560
 overview of, 554
 running application, 561

DotGNU, implementation of C#, 1044

`DoubleAnimation`, Silverlight, 343

doughnut charts, 613–614

`DragPanelExtender`, 910, 949–950

`DrawChartButton_Click` handler, ASP.NET
 charts, 675–676

`DropDownExtender`, 910

`DropDownList` control, `CascadingDropDown`
 extenders, 902

`DropShadow` shader effect, Silverlight, 356

`DropShadowExtender`, 911, 949, 952

DTE (Development Tools Extensibility), 239–241

`DTE` property
 accessing Visual Studio context, 177
 accessing Visual Studio object model,
  182–185
 description of, 178
 macros accessing IDE options with, 226
 for MyControl tab in Start Page, 172

dynamic binding
 in C# 4.0, 1072–1073
 definition of, 185
 using C# 4.0, 400

dynamic composition, MEF, 464

Dynamic Data application, ASP.NET, 730–749
 customizing look and feel, 732–735
 customizing pages, 746–747
 customizing validations, 747–749
 displaying data from existing tables, 716–718
 with entity templates, 741–744
 with field templates, 738–741
 with filter templates, 744–746
 for master-detail relationships, 725–730
 overview of, 711
 with page templates, 735–738
 simple CRUD applications, 718–724
 summary review, 750
 understanding structure, 730–732
 working against data model, 711–716

dynamic data, MVC 2, 668

dynamic dispatch, in C# 4.0, 1075

dynamic HTML, evolution of, 653–654

dynamic import, COM-related interoperability
 issues, 1084

Dynamic Language Run-time. *See* DLR (Dynamic
 Language Run-time)

dynamic languages
 benefits of, 1072
 C# 4.0 as, 1065
 early vs. late binding and, 1021

dynamic link libraries (DLLs), 280, 283

dynamic lookup, 1065, 1072, 1078

dynamic object interoperability, of DLR
 example of, 409–411
 high-level architecture diagram of, 405
 overview of, 403–404

dynamic objects, in VB 10.0, 1008, 1020–1021

dynamic operations, in C# 4.0
 compile time semantics, 1075–1076
 dynamic dispatch, 1075
 overview of, 1074–1075
 `System.Object` and, 1076–1077

dynamic translation, in C++, 280

dynamic types, C# 4.0, 1073–1074

dynamically typed languages, using DLR,
 403–404

`DynamicPopulateExtender`, 911

## E

early binding, Microsoft Intermediate Language, 1020–1021

easings, applying to Silverlight animation, 343–344

EchoProcessor.cs file, 81

ECMA (European Computer Manufacturers Association), 1042–1043

Edit button, Dynamic Data website, 719

Edit view action added, in MVC, 782–785

editing
    basic template information, 121
    code snippet files, 59–62
    templates in MVC, 805–808

editions
    downloading correct versions of SDKs for, 114
    Visual Studio 2005, 8
    Visual Studio 2008, 11

Editor control
    CustomEditor.cs, 938
    description of, 911
    EditorSample.aspx, 933–934
    EditorSample.aspx.cs, 934–935
    overview of, 932–933
    properties, 935–936

editor extensibility
    with Managed Extensibility Framework, 256–258
    overview of, 255
    points, 258–260

editor extensibility, creating simple classifier
    classification format, 267–269
    classification type, 262–263
    classifier provider and classifier, 263–267
    overview of, 260–262
    playing with classification, 269–275

EDM (Entity Data Model), Entity Framework, 574–577

effects, jQuery visual, 975–976

80/20 rule, 418–420, 430

Ellipses, in Grid layout container
    ControlTemplate, 333, 336
    Silverlight layout, 320–321

EMF (Enhanced Metadata Format), image files, 682

EnableAction, animation, 961

encoding, in smooth streaming, 349–350

endpoints, WCF
    4.0 standard, 585–588
    Ajax-enabled, 393
    content of, 664
    creating, 382
    defined, 381

Enhanced Metadata Format (EMF), image files, 682

ENQUIRE software, 653

Enter a Name and Description page, Visual Studio Add-In Wizard, 231

Entity Client, Entity Framework, 578

Entity Data Model (EDM), Entity Framework, 574–577

Entity Data Model Wizard, 574–577

Entity Data Source control, 579

Entity Framework
    Dynamic Data web application requiring, 711
    Entity Client, 578
    Entity Data Model, 574–577
    Entity SQL, 578
    LINQ to Entities, 577
    as .NET architecture service, 293
    .NET benefit of, 294
    Object Services, 578–579
    overview of, 573

Entity SQL, Entity Framework, 578

entity templates, ASP.NET Dynamic Data site, 741–744

enumeration types, in C#, 1046

Environment category, Options dialog
    definition of, 146–147
    Extension Manager page, 148–149
    Keyboard page, 157–158
    Start Pages. See Start Page, customizing
    visual experience options, 148

equality comparisons, equivalence vs., 414

error-handling activities, WF 4.0, 522

Essential Windows Presentation Foundation (Anderson), 301

ETW (Event Tracking for Windows) events, 545–546

EtwTrackingParticipant, 545–546

European Computer Manufacturers Association (ECMA), 1042–1043

European Organization for Nuclear Research (CERN), 653

Evaluator module, in F#, 1166–1167

event handlers
    adding to Silverlight project using XAML, 308–311
    binding to list of objects, 327
    binding/unbinding, 974
    setting up ASP.NET charts, 674–676

Event Tracking for Windows (ETW) events, 545–546

event-driven recomposition, MEF, 481

eventing model, jQuery library, 971–975

events
    chart interactivity with Ajax. *See* Ajax chart interactivity
    customizing tracking, 549–550
    handling clicks on data points in charts, 696–697
    jQuery, 972–973
    package load mechanism, 204
    triggering animations, 959

exception handling
    in compensating transaction model, 529
    F#, 1154–1156
    in MVC routing details, 822
    WF 4.0, 522

Exec method, add-ins, 237

ExecuteCommand method, accessing VS object model, 185

execution
    flow in MVC, 817–818
    suspending workflow, 539–540

ExpandoObject example, DLR integration, 407–309

expansion snippets, 33–36

Experimental Hive
    creating editor classifier, 261
    debugging package, 247, 254–255

*Expert F#* (Syme), 1104

explicit composition, MEF, 478

explicit recomposition, MEF, 481

Export as Code Snippet, 60–61

Export attribute, MEF
    accessing metadata, 484–486
    attaching metadata to exports, 476–477
    in Attributed Programming Model, 486
    classification format, 267–268
    classification type, editor classifier, 263
    classifier provider, editor classifier, 265
    example of, 466
    part lifetime, 483
    parts and contracts using, 471–472
    using host services, 469–470
    working with, 472–474

Export Template Wizard dialog
    creating simple item template, 78–80
    creating simple project template, 72–74
    customizing project template, 75

Export Template Wizard, using
    Choose Template Type, 78, 112–113
    Select Item References, 79
    Select Item to Export, 79
    Select Template Options, 79

exporting
    chart data to DataSet object, 646
    IDE configuration, 153
    Import and Export Settings Wizard, 151–153
    keyboard mapping schemes, 161

exporting, in MEF
    attaching metadata, 476–477
    defined, 471
    overview of, 472–474
    path instantiation and, 478–480

exporting templates, 111–114

ExportMetadata attribute, MEF, 476–477, 484

ExportSeriesValues method, 646

Express Editions, Visual Studio 2005, 8

Expression Blend. *See* Blend (Expression Blend)

Expression Design, for Silverlight and WPF, 313–315

Expression Encoder 4, for live smooth streaming, 349–350

expression trees
    in C# 3.0, 1061
    in DLR, 402–405

expressions
    in code-only workflows using, 509
    in F#, 1120
    in WF 4.0 using VB syntax, 494
extended ORM. *See* Entity Framework
extensibility
    of add-ins. *See* add-ins
    customizing for, 204–208
    editor. *See* editor extensibility
    of MVC, 760–761
    overview of, 201–202
    of packages. *See* VSPackages (Visual Studio
        Packages)
    using macros for. *See* macros
    of Visual Studio SDK, 210–213
    of XAML, 308
extensibility points, editor, 258–260
Extensible Application Markup Language. *See*
    XAML (Extensible Application Markup
    Language)
Extension Manager
    browsing/installing online templates with,
        123–125
    Options page, 148–149
    removing Visual Studio Gallery components,
        196
    VS 2010 UI enhancements, 20, 110
extension methods
    in C# 3.0, 1057–1058
    influencing PLINQ behavior, 425–428
    in VB 9.0, 998–999
extensions
    adding tracking participant to workflow,
        545–546
    command handling for, 156
    Visual Studio Gallery and. *See* Visual Studio
        Gallery

**F**

F#
    access control, 1120
    active patterns, 1149–1154
    anonymous functions, 1129–1130

`Ast` module, 1164
asynchronous workflows, 1144–1146
attributes, 1115
bindings, 1119–1120
Booleans, 1116
building large applications in, 1163
characteristics of, 1105–1106
class types, objects, and object expressions,
    1125
comments, 1111
computation expressions, 1138–1140
conditionals, 1122
converting literals and values, 1124
core functions, 1123
currying, 1109–1110
database queries, 1161–1162
demo project, creating, 1112–1113
discriminated (tagged) unions, 1131–1132
`Evaluator` module, 1166–1167
exceptions, 1154–1156
expressions, 1120
function argument syntax, 1109
`FunctionPlotter` module, 1167–1170
functions, 1108–1109
history of, 1104–1105
indexers, 1127–1128
inheritance, 1125
interfaces, 1125
`Language` module, 1164–1166
lazy computations, 1159–1160
lists, 1134–1137
literals and bindings, 1115
loops, 1122–1123
modules, 1113–1115
named and optional arguments to
    constructors, 1128–1129
namespaces, 1113–1115
naming conventions, 1111
null values, 1118
numbers, 1116
object expressions, 1126
object initializers, 1127
object state via let bindings, 1126
objects, 1125, 1126

F# (*continued*)

    operators, 1121–1122

    option values, 1132–1133

    overview of, 1103

    pattern matching, 1146–1149

    piping, 1109

    prototyping and trying solutions on-the-fly, 1106–1107

    quotations, 1160–1161

    range expressions, 1143

    records, 1133–1134

    reference cells, 1123

    sequence expressions, 1143–1144

    sequences, 1141–1143

    setters and getters, 1127

    strings, 1116–1118

    summary, 1171

    syntax, 1107–1108

    Text Editor category options, 149

    tuples, 1130

    type augmentations, 1137–1138

    type signatures, 1119

    units, 1116

    units of measure, 1157–1159

    values and types, 1124

    whitespace and indentation, 1110–1111

F# Interactive, 1106, 1113

`Factory` property, `Task` class, 444

`FadeIn` animation, 960

`FadeOut` animation, 960

failure, cancellation vs., 529

Fibonaci sequence, with C# iterators, 1052

field templates, Dynamic Data websites, 738–741

fields, customizing Dynamic Data validation, 747–749

file associations, classification types and, 273

File System navigation, Architecture Explorer, 28

file templates, 70

files

    code snippet structure. *See* code snippets, file structure

    creating simple project template, 74

    custom parameters for naming, 100–101

    defining in project templates, 91–94

Dynamic Data website structure, 730–732

    VSIX project, 115–116

`Filter` method, `DataManipulator`, 643

filter templates, Dynamic Data websites, 744–746

Filter text box, Choose Toolbox Items dialog, 191

`FilterDataPoint` method, 643

`FilteredTextBoxExtender`, 911, 942, 944

filters

    `DataManipulator`, 642–643

    for master-detail relationships in Dynamic Data sites, 726–729

    MVC, 821–822

    Pascal IntelliSense lookup, 21

    Visual Studio Gallery, 195–196

    WCF 4.0 routing service, 589–591

filters, jQuery

    attribute filters, 968–969

    combining with selectors, 968

    form filters, 969–970

    list of, 966–967

financial formulas, for chart data, 647–648

Find and Replace window, 129

`FindAnExpertDemo`, ASP.NET application

    adding `CascadingDropDown` extenders to, 901–902

    adding `ExpertiseService` class to, 902–903

    adding `ScriptManager` to, 901

    adding `UpdatePanel` to demo project, 905–908

    Ajax Control Toolkit improving, 900

    creating, 896–897

    `DataAccess.cs`, 898–899

    `Default.aspx` for, 897–900

    discovering effect of `CascadingDropDown` extenders, 904–905

floating windows

    tool windows, 131–132

    using keyboard to dock, 160

    VS architecture, 130–131

    working with, 134–135

flow control activities, WF 4.0, 518–520

flow documents, WPF, 361–362

`Flowchart` activity, WF 4.0, 499

flowcharts, in WF 4.0

activities for creating, 521–522

adding `FlowDecision` activity, 500–502

adding `FlowSwitch` activity, 503–504

adding `ForEach<T>` activity, 502–503

adding to workflow, 500

overview of, 499–500

running workflow, 504–505

`FlowDecision` activity, flowchart workflow, 500–502

`FlowSwitch` activity, flowchart workflow, 503–504

`FocusedStates`, `ControlTemplate`, 335–336

folders

code snippet storage, 53–54

defining in project templates, 91–94

Dynamic Data website structure, 730–732

fonts

changing classification, 268–269

customizing Text Content format, 274

extensibility of new editor, 212

For method. *See* `Parallel.For`, Task Parallel Library

`For<TLocal>` method, `Parallel` class, 430, 436–438

`ForEach` method, `Parallel` class, 430, 439

`ForEach<T>` activity, flowchart workflow, 502–503

form filters, jQuery, 969–970

`Form_Init` method, chart state, 690

formats, changing image file, 682–683

`FormView` data control, 660

*Foundations of F#* (Pickering), 1104

framework libraries, restoring, 844–846

from clause, in query expressions, 1060

From property, Silverlight/WPF animations and, 343

from__ in ___, LINQ query structure, 566

full compatibility, 401

function arguments, in F#, 1109

function calls, in F#, 1164

function operators, in F#, 1121

functional programming languages. *See also* F#, 1103–1104

`FunctionPlotter` module, F#, 1167–1170

functions, code snippet, 47–51

functions, F#

anonymous, 1129–1130

capabilities of, 1108

currying and, 1109–1110

as first-class values, 1105

optional parentheses around function arguments, 1109

syntax, 1108–1109

type signature and, 1119

**G**

GAC (Global Assembly Cache), customizing templates, 101

garbage collection

in C#, 1045

memory management in VB.NET, 989

Garrett, Jesse James, 837

GDI+functions, drawing chart coordinates, 617

General page of Environment category, Options dialog, 146–148

Generate From Usage feature, 24–25

`GenerateSwitchCases(EnumLiteral)` function, code snippets, 47, 49

generic parameter substitution, type relationships, 1027, 1087

generic types

C# 2.0, 1048–1050

code reuse supported by, 1043

VB 2005 (8.0), 989–992

`GetChartDataConnection` method, 677

`GetClassificationSpans` method, editor classifier, 266, 273

`GetClassifier` method, editor classifier, 265–266

`GetData( )` method, WCF service interface, 384

`GetEmployeeList( )` method, WCF service interface, 384

`GetEnumerator` method, iteration, 1052

`GetOrCreateSingletonProperty` method, editor classifier, 266

`GetOutputWindowPane` method, output messages, 227

`GetService` method, package type definition, 250

getters
    C#, 1046
    F#, 1127
    property accessors, 1055

ghost frames, docking tool windows, 135

GhostDoc, 207–208

Global Assembly Cache (GAC), customizing templates, 101

Global scope
    command handling for, 156–157
    keys not assigned command in, 159
    overriding shortcut defined in, 158–159

global toolbars, creating and rearranging, 144

`Global.asax` file, 721

`GoToState` method, `ControlTemplate`, 334

GPU (graphics processing unit)
    acceleration in Silverlight, 357
    rendering in WPF, 301

Graph View, XML Schema Designer, 27

graphical user interfaces (GUIs), Windows OSs and, 984

`Grid` control
    "Hello World" application in WPF, 359
    as layout container, 319–321
    `StartPage.xaml`, 167–168

grid lines, chart, 606–607

`Grid_DataContextChanged` method
    accessing Visual Studio context, 179, 181–182
    accessing Visual Studio object model, 185

`GridView` data control
    Dynamic Data website structure, 732
    new in ASP.NET 2.0, 660
    working with page templates, 736–738

`group` clause, query expressions, 1060

`GuidAttribute` attribute, equivalence in CLR, 415

GUIs (graphical user interfaces), Windows OSs and, 984

Guthrie, Scott, 655–656

GW-BASIC, 983

**H**

H.264, Silverlight support for, 346

hardware graphics acceleration, 148

`HasMorePages` property, printing in Silverlight, 356

HD video, user playback problems in, 349

headers
    code snippets, 42–43
    customizing ASP.NET Dynamic Data look and feel, 734–736

Hejlsberg, Anders, 1041–1042

"Hello, World" application, Silverlight
    adding event handlers, 308–311
    creating new project, 304–311
    in Expression Blend, 314–315

"Hello, World" applications
    code-only workflows, 505–509
    in early Windows UI development, 4
    "Hello User" in VB.NET, 987
    jQuery, 963–964
    for workflow. See `HelloWorkflow` application
    in WPF, 359–361

`HelloWorkflow` application
    adding activities, 494
    adding input argument, 493
    adding output argument, 495
    adding variable, 496
    creating output value, 496
    extracting workflow output, 496–499
    overview of, 492–493
    passing input arguments to workflow, 494–495
    `SimpleHelloF35` workflow, 513–515
    `SimpleHelloF4` workflow, 515–517

`HiddenInputAttribute`, in MVC, 811

Hide Snippet Highlights, 37

`HideAction`, animation, 961

hierarchy
    code snippet folders, 54
    document windows, 133–134

item templates, 84

Macro Explorer, 215–216

project templates, 82–83

task control flow, 444–445

High level Shader Language (HSLS2.0), Silverlight bitmaps, 356

HKEY_CURRENT_USER hive, project template hierarchy, 82

horizontal tab groups, for document windows, 133, 136

host application

accessing extensions, 512–513

communicating with during workflow, 537–539

executing WorkflowApplication within, 510–511

hosting

with MEF, 469

.NET 4 changes in CLR and, 401–402

WCF 4.0 routing services, 590–591

WCF declarative services, 396

WCF services, 382–384, 388–389

HoverMenuExtender, 911

HSLS2.0 (High level Shader Language), Silverlight bitmaps, 356

HTML (Hypertext Markup Language)

ASP embedded in, 655

code snippets, 37

creating new Silverlight project, 308

as standard markup for web pages, 654

HtmlBrush class, available in OOB mode, 355

HtmlPageWithIFrame.html, charts with legacy web sites, 683–684

HTTP (HyperText Transfer Protocol)

network stacks for communication, 352–353

pipeline, and ASP.NET 3.5, 666

request flow in MVC, 768

WCF 4.0 support for caching, 589

human interactions, WF 4.0, 532

Hypertext Markup Language (HTML). See HTML (Hypertext Markup Language)

IBook interface, in MVC, 830–831

IClassifier interface, editor classifier, 266

IClassifierProvider type, 265

icons, exporting templates with, 111

IControllerFactory interface, 816

IDE configuration

for add-ins, 209

export and import options, 151–153

for macros, 225–226

option pages changes, 147–150

Options dialog, 145–147

using Macros IDE. See Macros IDE

Visual Studio settings, 150–151

.vssettings file, 154

IDE customization

keyboard shortcuts. See keyboard shortcuts

menus and toolbars. See menus and toolbars, customizing

overview of, 127–128

Start Page. See Start Page, customizing

Toolbox, 186

Visual Studio Gallery, 193–198

window management. See window management

identity metasystems, and CardSpace, 293

IDisposable pattern, in VB 8.0, 996–997

IDTCommandTarget interface, add-ins, 229, 235–237

IDTExtensibility2 interface, add-ins, 229, 235–236

IEnumerable interface, 1052

If operators, conditional expressions in VB 9.0, 1004–1005

<iframe> tags, charts with legacy web sites, 684

Iif function, conditional expressions in VB 9.0, 1004–1005

IIS (Internet Information Server), 7–8, 382

hosing WCF services, 382

VS 2005 changes in, 7–8

images, rendering ASP.NET charts, 679–683

immutability
  characteristics of F#, 1105
  of lists, 1137

implementations, of C#, 1043–1044

implicit composition, MEF, 478

implicit line continuation feature, in VB 10.0, 1007
  issues with explicit line continuation, 1008–1009
  new features in VB 10.0, 1007
  when you can use, 1009–1010

Import attribute, MEF
  accessing metadata, 485
  example of, 467–468
  import notification, 480–481
  lazy instantiation and, 480
  part lifetime, 483
  as part of Attributed Programming Model, 486
  parts and contracts using, 471–472
  recomposition, 481–482
  working with, 474

Import button, Code Snippets Manager, 54–55

import notification, MEF, 480–481

Imported FromTypeLibAttribute attribute, equivalence in CLR, 415

importing
  code snippets, 39–40, 54–55
  IDE configuration, 153
  with Import and Export Settings Wizard, 151–153
  keyboard mapping schemes, 161
  with MEF, 471–474, 478–480
  multiple snippets, 56–57
  templates, 111–114

ImportingConstructor attribute, MEF, 479–480

<Imports> element, code snippets, 46

IncreaseTextEditorFontSize macros, 225–226

indentation, in F#, 1108, 1110–1111

index files, of system folders, 54

Index view, 770, 776–779

indexed properties, in C# 4.0, 1085–1086

indexers, in F#, 1127–1128

Indigo. See WCF (Windows Communication Foundation)

inheritance
  as disadvantage of COM, 281
  F#, 1125
  multiple inheritance not supported by C#, 1045
  multiple inheritance not supported by VB, 989
  OOP and, 1026
  type relationships and, 1027, 1087

initialization, setting up Chart from code, 673–674

Initialize method, package type definition, 250

InitializeComponent method, event handler for Silverlight project, 310–311

initializers
  collection initializers in C#, 1063
  collection initializers in VB 10.0, 1012–1017
  object initializers in C#, 1062

InitServiceHost method, WorkflowServiceHost, 559–560

InitTrackingParticipant method, 548–549

inline styles, problems of, 330

INotifyCollectionChanged interface, 327

input, workflow services, 552–553

input arguments
  adding flowchart to workflow, 500
  adding to workflow, 493
  passing to workflow, 494–495

InputBox method, macros, 229

Insert button, Dynamic Data websites, 719

Insert Snippet function, expansion snippets, 34

inserting, code snippets, 34–36

installation kit, creating template
  creating VSIX installation kit, 114–119
  installing templates with Extension Manager, 123–125
  overview of, 114
  uploading to Visual Studio Gallery, 119–123

Installed Templates tab, New Project dialog, 164, 260–261

installing, Ajax Control Toolkit, 894–895

`InstanceStore` extension class, 512–513

integer types, unsigned and signed in VB 8.0, 996

Integrated Tools, Parallel Computing Platform, 419

IntelliSense

    changing presentation of, 212

    code editor window enhancements, 21–22

    creating code snippets, 38–40

    invoking code snippets from, 34–35

    Visual Basic code snippet features, 36–37

    writing LINQ queries in Silverlight using, 354

interactivity, chart, 648

interfaces

    applying MVC to development of, 756–757

    code contracts for, 458–459

    defining WCF services with, 384

    equivalence in CLR and, 415

    F#, 1125

`internal`, access control specifier, 1119

International Organization for Standardization (ISO), C# standard, 1043

Internet, development of, 653–654

Internet Information Server (IIS), 7–8, 382

interop (interoperability) assemblies, package development, 211–212

interoperability

    accessing Visual Studio context, 179

    advantages of DLR in .NET 4, 403

    C# and, 1066

    COM-related issues in C# 4.0, 1084–1087

    .NET Framework and, 283

`Interpolated` animation, 960

invariant, 1089

`Invoke` method

    `Parallel` class, 430–432

    passing input arguments to workflow, 494–495

`IPartImportsSatisfiedNotification` interface, 480–482

IronPython

    accessing library from VB 10.0, 1023–1026

    DLR high-level architecture diagram, 405

    DLR integration example, 405

    languages in .NET Framework, 1170

IronRuby, 405, 1167–1170

ISO (International Organization for Standardization), C# standard, 1043

isolated storage, Silverlight, 357–358

item templates

    `<TemplateContent>` elements, 91, 94–95

    `<TemplateData>` child elements, 88–89

    creating simple, 76–81

    hierarchical structure of, 84

    overview of, 69–70

    storage structure, 81–83

`ItemsPanelTemplate`, 338–339

iterators, C# 2.0, 1052

`IViewEngine`, 814–815

`IVsPackage` interface, 250

`IWizard` interface, 101–104

**J**

Java

    C# inspired by, 1042

    release of Visual J++1.0, 4

Java Virtual Machine (JVM), 4

Javadoc, C# and, 1046

JavaScript

    Ajax and jQuery built on, 893

    jQuery library, 962

    working with Ajax-enabled WCF service, 392–393

Jet Database engine, 985

JIT (Just In Time) compiler, VB.NET, 297

`join` clause, query expressions, 1060

`Jpeg` format, image files, 682

jQuery library

    Ajax features in, 976–977

    chaining and utility functions, 970–971

    eventing model, 971–975

    "Hello, World" example, 963–964

    `jQuery` object, 964–965

    overview of, 962

    publishing JavaScript file from Microsoft Ajax Library to, 846

    selectors and filters, 965–970

    summary, 977

    visual effects and animations, 975–976

jQuery object, 964–965
JScript, 37, 655
JSON, 666, 889–892
JSONP, 889–892
Just In Time (JIT) compiler, VB.NET, 297
JVM (Java Virtual Machine), 4

## K

Kennedy, Andrew, 1104
Kermeny, John G., 982
keyboard
    accessing Toolbox functions using, 188–189
    mapping schemes, 155, 160–162
Keyboard option page, 157–159
keyboard shortcuts
    command routing and command contexts,
        155–157
    creating new, 158–159
    determining key assigned to command,
        158–159
    Keyboard button in Customize dialog for, 140
    overview of, 155
    removing, 158
    using keyboard exclusively, 159–160
    using keyboard mapping schemes, 160–162
    working with, 157–158
keyframes, for Silverlight animations, 343
Kind attribute, code snippets, 44
Kurtz, Thomas E., 982

## L

labels, chart
    axis, 606–607, 629–630
    customizing data points, 632
lambda expressions
    C# 3.0, 1059–1060
    DLR and, 1078
    VB 10.0 multiline, 1007, 1018–1020
    VB 9.0, 1000–1001
lambda operator (=>), 1057
Language attribute, code snippets, 44
Language module, in F#, 1164–1166

language services, code snippets, 58
languages, in .NET Framework, 1170
languages, programming
    code snippets in other, 34
    DLR clients and, 405
    expression syntax and, 494
    history of Visual Studio, 4–5
    importing code snippets in other, 46–47,
        55, 58
    .NET as secure platform for multiple, 293
    .NET Framework, 1167–1170
    .NET full integration between, 283
    selecting for simple add-in, 231
    selecting in VSPackage Wizard, 244
    using Code Snippets Manager, 52
late binding, in VB 10.0, 1021–1023
"Latest News" tab, Start Pages, 186
layer diagram, as architectural tool, 28
layout. See also Silverlight layout
    customizing for table with entity templates,
        741–744
    WPF additional container and controls for,
        362–364
    WPF transformations, 345
LayoutRoot grid, Start Page
    accessing Visual Studio context, 182
    changing StartPage.xaml, 173
    properties of data context set for, 177–178
    structure of StartPage.xaml, 168
LayoutTransformer, Silverlight, 345
lazy computations, in F#, 1106, 1159–1160
lazy initialization classes, 451, 454
lazy instantiation, MEF, 480
left-brain thinking, developers vs. designers,
    299–300
legacy web sites, embedding charts into, 683–684,
    687
Legend Collection Editor, 597
legends
    adding, 597
    adding tooltips to chart, 694–696
    customizing items in, 709
    defined, 606–607
    handling clicks on, 697

pie charts and, 613
properties of, 608
Length animation, 960
let clause, in query expressions, 1060
lexer files (*.fsl), in F#, 1113
libraries
    jQuery. *See* jQuery library
    Microsoft Ajax Library, 848–852
    restoring framework, 844–846
"light" syntax, in F#, 1110–1111
line charts
    area charts based on, 612–613
    displaying range charts based on, 614
    overview of, 611
line continuation, VB 10.0 implicit, 1007–1010
line transformations, using new editor, 212
line-of-business (LOB) software, user experience
    and, 298
LINQ (Language Integrated Query)
    C#3.0 and, 1043
    expression trees, 1061
    LINQ to DataSet, 569–570
    LINQ to Entities, 577, 579
    LINQ to Objects, 567
    LINQ to XML, 568–569
    operators, 564–566
    overview of, 563–564
    PLINQ. *See* PLINQ (Parallel LINQ)
    query expressions in C# and, 1060
    query expressions in VB 9.0 and, 1001–1002
    released in VS 2008, 8–9
    supported in VB 9.0, 997
    WCF RIA Services and, 354
LINQ to SQL
    in Dynamic Data application. *See* Dynamic
        Data application, ASP.NET
    Dynamic Data for master-detail relationships,
        725–730
    LINQ to Entities vs., 579
    overview of, 570–572
List control, extenders for, 947–949
List module, F# functions, 1136–1137
List View option, Toolbox tabs, 189
ListBox, data binding with templates, 337–341

ListDatabinding.xaml, master-detail
    data-binding, 328–329
ListProj macro, 227–228
ListProjAux macro, 228
lists
    characteristics of, 1137
    data binding to object, 326–328
    F# type signature and, 1119
    programming in F#, 1118, 1134–1137
ListSearchExtender, 911, 947, 949
ListView data control
    new in ASP.NET 3.5, 665
    WPF layout, 362
literals
    converting in F#, 1124
    declaring in code snippets, 44–45
    programming in F#, 1115
    using code snippet functions, 49
live binding
    master-detail binding and, 877–878
    Microsoft Ajax Library supporting, 872–873
live encoding, smooth streaming and, 349–350
Live ID, Visual Studio Gallery, 119
LOB (line-of-business) software, user experience
    and, 298
local messaging, Silverlight, 356
local variable type inference
    in C# 3.0, 1057
    in VB 9.0, 998
localFinally delegate, Parallel.
    For<TLocal>, 436–437
localInit delegate, Parallel.For<TLocal>,
    436–437
localization, new in ASP.NET 2.0, 663
Location field, Code Snippets Manager, 52
Logical (Storage Layer or S-Space), Entity Data
    Model, 574
login controls, new in ASP.NET 2.0, 661
long-running transactions, 523
look and feel, customizing Dynamic Data,
    732–735
loops, in F#, 1122–1123
LoremIpsumQuery example, PLINQ, 421–425

**M**

machine templates, in item template hierarchy, 84

Macro Explorer, 215–218

macro system

    adding new macro project to, 217

    defined, 215

    viewing, 215–216

macros

    accessing IDE options, 225–226

    adding new module to macro project, 218

    automation model for, 208–209, 239–241

    creating, 213–218

    for dealing with user input, 229

    deploying, 224

    developing, 223–224

    Macro Explorer, 215–218

    Macros IDE, 218–221

    recording, 221–223

    responding to IDE events, 224–225

Macros IDE, 218–221

Main Menu bar, 141

`MainPage.xaml` file

    adding event handler to Silverlight project, 310–311

    with Hello World text block, 306–307

    in new Silverlight project, 306

Managed Code stack, Parallel Computing Platform, 419–420

Managed Extensibility Framework. *See* MEF (Managed Extensibility Framework)

managed mode, WCF 4.0, 586

Managed Package Framework (MPF), 212

manifest file

    advanced features, 95–98

    creating VSIX installation kit with, 116–117

    exporting templates by creating, 111

    general structure of, 85–86

    overview of, 84–85

    `<TemplateContent>` element, 91–95

    `<TemplateData>` element, 86–91

manipulation API, Windows 7/WPF, 363

many-core CPUs, 416–418

Mapping Specification Language (MSL), 574

Margetson, James, 1104

`MaskedEditExtender`, text boxes, 912, 942, 947

master pages, new in ASP.NET 2.0, 661

master-detail binding, 877–878

master-detail relationships

    creating Dynamic Data application for, 725–730

    data-binding and, 328–329

`MaxDegreeofParallelism` property, `Parallel` class, 430

MbUnit, unit testing with, 755

MDN (Microsoft Developer Network) library, 5

`MeasureOverride` method, Silverlight layout, 317

media, Silverlight

    audio and video playback, 345–347

    Deep Zoom, 347–348

    smooth streaming, 349–350

    webcam and microphone access, 350–352

`MediaElement` control, A/V playback with, 345–347

MEF (Managed Extensibility Framework)

    catalogs, 475–476

    challenge of, 463–465

    composition. *See* composition, MEF

    composition containers, 474–475

    defined, 15, 400

    exports and imports, 472–474

    extending editor with, 212, 256–258, 265

    more points about, 486

    overview of, 463

    parts and contracts, 471–472

    parts and metadata, 476–477

    simple example of, 465–471

memory

    managing in C# 1.0, 1045–1046

    managing in Visual Basic.NET (7.0/7.1), 988–989

    package integration and, 203–204

menu bar

    adding commands to, 141–143

    adding menus to, 141, 143

    removing menus and commands, 142–143

menus and toolbars, customizing

    adding commands, 141–143

    adding menus, 141, 143

context sensitivity and, 145
creating and rearranging toolbars, 144–145
Customize dialog, 138–140
overview of, 138–139
removing menus and commands, 142–143
messaging
Silverlight local, 356
SOA, 378
WCF service/client, 381
WF 4.0, 525–526
metadata
providers, 834
validation metadata, 798–799, 803–804
view interface, 485–486
metadata attributes, in MEF
accessing, 484–486
classification type, editor classifier, 263
classifier provider, editor classifier, 265
overview of, 258
programming with, 476–477
metadata attributes, in MVC
DisplayAttribute, 810–811
DisplayColumnAttribute, 808–809
DisplayFormatAttribute, 809
HiddenInputAttribute, 811
overview of, 808
ScaffoldColumnAttribute, 809
UIHintAttribute, 809–810
Method Call Injection, 759
MFC (Microsoft Foundation Classes), 4
Micro Framework, .NET, 289
microphone access, Silverlight media, 350–352
Microsoft
Ajax CDN, 846–848
Ajax Library. See Ajax Library, Microsoft
parallel computing approach ob, 418–420
Microsoft Developer Network Library, 5
Microsoft Foundation Classes (MFC), 4
Microsoft Intermediate Language. See MSIL
(Microsoft Intermediate Language)
Microsoft SQL Server 2005, 286–287
Microsoft.Expression.Interactions
assembly, in Blend SDK, 342–343
ModalPopupExtender

description of, 912
pop-up control extenders, 952, 954
Mode option, data binding, 325
model binders, MVC, 835
Model View Controller. See MVC (Model View
Controller)
Modeling project, as architectural tool, 27
models, MVC
architecture, 667–668
binding, 790–794, 835
creating, 772
domain model, 826–827
extending using validation metadata,
798–799
overview of, 752
models, MVVM, 372
Model-View-Presenter (MVP), 753
Model-View-ViewModel (MVVM)
design patterns in MVC, 753
overview of, 324, 372
ModifiedStartPage project, 173–176
Modify Selection button
changing name of custom toolbars, 145
creating and rearranging toolbars, 144
modules
adding to macro project, 218
creating demo project in F#, 1113–1115
organizing macros into, 213–214
viewing with Macro Explorer, 215
Mono project, 1044
Moore's law, 415–416
Move, types of animations, 960
Move Down
adding menus and commands, 142
creating and rearranging toolbars, 144
Toolbox tabs, 189
Move Up
adding menus and commands, 142
creating and rearranging toolbars, 144
Toolbox tabs, 189
MP3, Silverlight support for, 346
MPF (Managed Package Framework), 212
mscoree.dll file, CLR, 291
.msi file, deploying add-ins and, 209

MSIL (Microsoft Intermediate Language)
  creating expression trees in .NET 3.5, 402
  DLR integration in new CLR, 402
  early binding and, 1020
MSL (Mapping Specification Language), 574
msvbvm60.dll file, hiding Win32 API in Visual
  Basic, 280
MultiHandleSliderExtender
  description of, 912
  textbox extenders, 942, 946
multi-instanced windows
  document windows as, 132
  tool windows as, 131
multiline lambda expressions, in VB 10.0, 1008,
  1018–1020
multi-paradigm programming languages
  C# as, 1041
  VB as, 1007
multiple documents mode, Visual Studio 2008,
  130–131
multiple type parameters, variance in VB 10.0
  and, 1033–1036
multi-project templates
  composing, 67
  overview of, 95–98
MultiScaleImage (Deep Zoom) control,
  347–348
multi-targeting
  using Add Reference dialog, 19
  VS 2008, 8–9
multi-threading, 417–418
multitouch, Windows 7/WPF, 363
MutuallyExclusiveCheckBoxExtender, 912,
  938–942
MVC (Model View Controller)
  action and result filtering in, 821–822
  ActionResult class, 822–824
  adding controller actions, 779
  areas, 834
  asynchronous controllers in, 835
  attaching book item to IBook interface,
    830–831
  authorization in, 819–821
  auto-encoding syntax in, 771

business rule management, 801–803
child actions, 835
client-side validation, 803–804
Controller class, 769–770
Controller Factory, 816–817
Create view action, 786–787
creating controllers, 773–776
creating database pages, 771–772
creating models, 772
creating MVC applications, 761–762
creating views, 776–779
custom templates, 811–814
customization features, 790
Delete view action, 787–789
design patterns used by, 752
Details action, 779–782
DI (Dependency Injection), 759–760
display templates and edit templates in,
  805–808
DisplayAttribute, 810–811
DisplayColumnAttribute, 808–809
DisplayFormatAttribute, 809
displaying validation issues, 800–801
domain model for, 826–827
Edit view action, 782–785
exception filtering in, 822
execution flow in, 817–818
extending models using validation metadata,
  798–799
extensibility in, 760–761
features in ASP.NET 4.0, 667–668
HiddenInputAttribute, 811
how it works, 764–766
Index and About views, 770
interface-based development with, 756–757
metadata attributes in, 808
metadata providers, 834
Microsoft's approach to web platform and,
  753–754
model binding, 790–794, 835
MVVM pattern based on, 372
overview of, 751–752
preparing controller for validation, 799–800
project structure, 763–764, 826

repositories for projects, 827–830

Repository Design Pattern, 757–759

routing details, 816

routing requests within MVC applications, 766–768

ScaffoldColumnAttribute, 809

Service Locator Pattern, 760

summary, 835–836

TDD (test driven development) in, 755–756

templated helpers feature in, 804–805

testing controllers, 824–826

UI customization, 804

UIHintAttribute, 809–810

unit testing in, 831–833

validation attributes, 795–797

value providers, 834–835

view engines in, 814–816

what it is, 754–755

MVP (Model-View-Presenter), 753

MVVM (Model-View-ViewModel)

    design patterns in MVC, 753

    overview of, 324, 372

My Contributions link, Visual Studio Gallery, 197

My Documents virtual folder, code snippet storage, 53

MyControl tab, 171–172

MyControl.xaml file, Start Page, 172, 183–184

MyControl.xaml.cs file, Start Page, 130, 184–185

MyMacros, Macro Explorer, 215

MyTemplate.vstemplate file

    creating simple item template, 80

    creating simple project template, 74

    template storage structure, 81–82


**N**

named arguments for constructors, in F#, 1128–1129

named parameters

    abstract and virtual members and, 1082–1083

    in C# 4.0, 1066

    resolving applicable signatures, 1083–1084

    resolving overloaded method invocations, 1082

    using, 1081–1082

named skins, 662

namespaces

    aliases in C# 2.0, 1056

    in F#, 1113–1115

naming conventions

    F# syntax, 1111

    templates, 75

Navigate To dialog, code-navigation, 22

navigation

    displaying table data in Dynamic Data website, 718

    new in ASP.NET 2.0, 661

    Silverlight and, 358

navigation bar, workflow design surface, 491

navigation pane, Options dialog, 146

Nemerle programming language, 58

.NET Framework

    1.0, 5–6, 286

    1.1, 6, 286

    2.0, 286–287

    3.0, 8, 287, 375

    3.5, 8–10, 287–288, 301, 402–403

    4.0, 288–289

    architecture, 289–293

    before, 279–282

    C# history, 1042–1043

    chart types. See chart types, .NET

    Communications Framework enhancements. See WCF (Windows Communication Foundation) Framework 4.0 enhancements

    Compact Framework (CF), 289

    evolution of, 283–285

    history of Visual Basic and, 986

    languages in, 1170

    main benefits of, 293–294

    Micro Framework, 289

    origin and goals of, 282–283

    overview of, 279

    user experience and, 297

    and WCF, 379

    Workflow Framework enhancements. See WF (Workflow Foundation) 4.0

.NET Framework Components tab, Choose Toolbox Items dialog, 190

.NET Framework, Core Framework enhancements
  CLR. *See* CLR (Common Language
    Run-time)
  code contracts. *See* code contracts
  Managed Extensibility Framework. *See* MEF
    (Managed Extensibility Framework)
  overview of, 399–400
  parallel computing. *See* parallel computing
  shipping with new CLR, 400
  summary review, 487
.NET Framework, Data Framework enhancements
  choosing LINQ to Entities vs. LINQ to SQL,
    579
  Entity Data Source Control, 579
  Entity Framework, 573–579
  LINQ. *See* LINQ (Language Integrated
    Query)
  overview of, 563
  PLINQ, 572–573
networking, in Silverlight, 352–354
Networking Layer, Microsoft Ajax Library,
  850–852
New button, adding to toolbar, 144
New Project dialog
  accessing online templates, 124
  creating new Silverlight project, 304–305
  creating package with VSPackage Wizard,
    242–243
  creating Start Page with template, 164
  customizing templates. *See* templates,
    customizing
  project template hierarchy in, 82–84
  selecting installed project template, 67–69
  Visual Studio 2010 UI enhancements, 17–18
New Web Site dialog, 712
New Window command, 137
NeXT workstation, 653
NoBot control, 913
nodes, in project template hierarchy, 83–84
No-PIA example, of type equivalence, 412–414
*n-tuples*, F#, 1130. *See also* tuples
null values, in F#, 1118
nullable types
  C# 2.0, 1054–1055

Visual Basic 2005 (8.0), 993–994
nullable value type modifiers, in VB 9.0, 1004
null-coalesce operator, C# 2.0, 1056
<NumberOfParentCategoriesToRollUp>, in
  project template hierarchy, 84
numbers
  arithmetic expressions in F#, 1164
  programming in F# and, 1116
NumericUpDownExtender
  description of, 913
  textbox extenders, 942, 946
nUnit, unit testing with, 755

## O

object expressions, F#, 1125, 1126
object initializers
  C# 3.0, 1062
  F#, 1127
object invariants, code contracts, 457–458
object models
  accessing Visual Studio, 182–185
  early vs. late binding and, 1021
  LINQ integratation of queries into, 563
  macro programming using, 209
  .NET 4 changes in CLR, 402
object oriented programming. *See* OOP (object-
  oriented programming)
*Object Oriented Software Construction* (Meyer),
  464
Object Pascal, 281
Object Relational Designer (O/R Designer), 713,
  725–726
Object Services, Entity Framework, 578–579
<object> tag, HTML, 308
ObjectAnimation, Silverlight, 343
object-creation expressions, in VB 9.0, 999–1000
ObjectDataSource, new in ASP.NET 2.0, 661
objects
  data binding to list of, 326–328
  declaring in code snippets, 44–45
  dynamic, 1020–1021
  F#, 1125–1126
  LINQ to Objects, 567

.NET Framework, 283
package load mechanism for requesting, 204
selecting for EDM, 575
vs. values in F#, 1105
XAML describing hierarchy of UI, 308
Objects and Timeline panel, Blend, 315
OCaml, 1104
OldValue<T> method, 458
OLE controls, in VB 4.0, 985
OnClick, events triggering animations, 959
OnConnection method, 236
one-CLR-rules scenario, 401
100 percent stacked bar or column charts, 610
OnHoverOut, events triggering animations, 959
OnHoverOver, events triggering animations, 959
online code snippet providers, 59
online templates
browsing/installing, 124–125
creating project with, 68
OnLoad, events triggering animations, 959
OnMouseOut, events triggering animations, 959
OnMouseOver, events triggering animations, 959
OOB (out-of-browser) applications, Silverlight
settings, 355
OOP (object-oriented programming)
C# and, 1041
COM (Component Object Model), 985
F# support for, 1105
.NET Framework and, 282–283
variance and, 1087
Visual Basic and, 982, 986
OpacityAction, types of animation actions, 961
Open Packaging Convention, 114
open type definitions
in C#, 1048–1049
in VB, 990
Open/Closed Principle, MEF, 464–465
OperationContract attribute, in WCF, 379
operations, dynamic in C# 4.0, 1074–1077
operators
F#, 1121–1122
generics and, 1050
LINQ, 564–566
null-coalesce operator in C# 2.0, 1056

Visual Basic 2005 (8.0), 994–996
option values, F#, 1132–1133
optional arguments to constructors, F#,
1128–1129
optional parameters
in C# 4.0, 1066
indexes and, 1080–1081
overview of, 1078–1079
resolving applicable signatures, 1083–1084
resolving overloaded method invocations,
1082
using, 1079–1080
Options dialog
changing IDE configuration in, 150
customizing Start Page. See Start Page,
customizing
IDE configuration using, 145–147
new changes in pages of, 147–150
setting position of new document windows,
137–138
Visual Studio settings, 150–154
O/R Designer (Object Relational Designer), 713,
725–726
orderby clause, in query expressions, 1060
OrdinaryClassificationDefinition class,
263
OrdinaryClassificationType field, 263
OrdinaryClassifier class, editor classifier, 266
OrdinaryClassifierProvider, 265
Orientation attribute, StackPanel, 316–317
ORM (Object Relational Mapping)
benefits of LINQ for, 563–564
Entity Framework as extended. See Entity
Framework
out-of-browser (OOB) applications, Silverlight
settings, 355
output
adding arguments to workflow, 495
creating values in workflow, 496
extracting from workflow, 496–499
handling in workflow services, 552–553
running flowchart workflow, 504–505
writing messages with macros, 226–227

Output window
  defined, 130
  as docked tool window, 132
  writing output messages to, 226–227
`OutputItem` method, 228–229
`OutputString` method, 227
overloaded method invocations, resolving in C#
  4.0, 1082

## P

Package API
  managed code developers accessing, 211–212
  native code developers using, 211
`Package` class
  attributes decorating, 251–252
  overview of, 250–251
package load mechanism, 204
page templates, ASP.NET Dynamic Data
  creating custom, 746–748
  working with, 735–738
`Page_Init` method, ASP.NET Dynamic data,
  745–746
`Page_Load` method
  adding tooltips to chart, 695
  playing with serialization content, 693–694
  real time charts in Ajax, 706–708
  saving chart state, 688–690
  setting up `Chart` from code, 673–674
  triggering chart events with, 703
  using Ajax for click events, 701
  using serialization in state management, 692
pages, ASP.NET Dynamic Data website
  customizing, 746–747
  look and feel of, 734–736
`PagingBulletedListExtender`
  description of, 913
  list extenders, 947, 949
`Panel` control, extenders for, 949–952
`Parallel` class, Task Parallel Library
  overview of, 430
  `Parallel.For`, 432–436
  `Parallel.For<TLocal>`, 436–438
  `Parallel.ForEach`, 439
  `Parallel.Invoke`, 430–432

parallel computing
  challenge of many-core shift, 416–418
  Microsoft approach, 418–420
  overview of, 399–400, 415–416
  Parallel LINQ (PLINQ), 421–428
  Task Parallel Library. *See* TPL (Task Parallel
    Library)
Parallel Framework Extensions (PFX). *See* PLINQ
  (Parallel LINQ)
Parallel LINQ. *See* PLINQ (Parallel LINQ)
`Parallel.For`, Task Parallel Library, 429–430,
  432–436
`Parallel.For<SearchInfo>`, Task Parallel
  Library, 438
`Parallel.For<TLocal>`, Task Parallel Library,
  430, 436–438
`Parallel.ForEach`, Task Parallel Library, 430,
  439
`Parallel.Invoke`, Task Parallel Library,
  430–432
`ParallelLoopState` instances, 433–436
`ParallelOptions` instance, 430–433
parameters
  named. *See* named parameters
  optional. *See* optional parameters
  reference parameters, 1084–1085
  type parameters. *See* type parameters
parameters, template
  `$safeitemname$`, 77–78
  `$safeprojectname$`, 75
  customizing templates with, 98–101
parametric polymorphism, 1104
parent tasks, control flow, 444–445
parser files (*.`fsy`), in F#, 1113
part instantiation, MEF, 478–480
part lifetime, MEF, 482–484
`PartCreationPolicy` attribute, part lifetime,
  483
partial active patterns, 1152–1153
partial methods
  C# 3.0, 1063–1064
  in VB 9.0, 1002
partial types
  C# 2.0, 1050–1051
  partial methods and, 1002, 1063

Visual Basic 2005 (8.0), 992–993
parts, MEF
    composition containers and catalogs
      containing, 474–476
    matching with composition. *See* composition,
      MEF
    metadata and, 476–477
    multiple, 468–469
    overview of, 471–472
    querying composition container for, 486
Pascal IntelliSense lookup, 21
PasswordStrength
    description of, 913
    textbox extenders, 942, 944
path instantiation, MEF, 478–480
path of execution thinking, developers and, 440
Path option, data binding, 325
pattern matching, in F#
    active patterns, 1149–1154
    characteristics of F#, 1106
    examining union values with, 1131–1132
    overview of, 1146–1149
performance
    maximizing with PLINQ. *See* PLINQ
      (Parallel LINQ)
    situations when view state provides better,
      688
PerlScript, 655
persistence and human interactions, WF 4.0, 532
PersistenceParticipant extension class, 513
personalization services, new in ASP.NET 2.0,
    662–663
per-user extensions, 148
PetShopCharts sample, 670
PFX (Parallel Framework Extensions). *See* PLINQ
    (Parallel LINQ)
PIAs (Primary Interoperability Assemblies)
    compiling without, 1086–1087
    dynamic import and, 1084
    No-PIA example of type equivalence,
      412–414
    overview of, 411–412
pie charts, 613
pinning functionality, under Microsoft Windows
    7, 16

pipe operator (|>), F# syntax, 1109
placeholders
    inserting in code snippets, 35–36
    <Snippet> section, 43–44
    understanding code snippets, 32–33
    Visual Basic and, 36–37
PlaneProjection transform, 344
platform support, Visual Studio 2008, 11
PLINQ (Parallel LINQ)
    comparing LoremIpsumQuery
      implementations, 425
    extension methods influencing behavior of,
      425–428
    LoremIpsumQuery example, 421–425
    .NET Framework, Data Framework
      enhancements, 570–573
    overview of, 421
    as Parallel Computing Platform element, 419
    parallel programming architecture, 420
plot area, in charts, 606–607
Png format, image files, 682
point charts, 611–612
PointAnimation, Silverlight, 343
Pointer, Toolbox, 187
pointers
    not supported in C#, 1045
    not supported in VB, 989
points, editor extension, 258–260
polar charts, 616
PollingDuplexHttpBinding, Silverlight
    networking, 353
PopupControlExtender, 913, 952–955
Position property, Chart control, 617–619
postbacks, preserving chart state between,
    688 690
postconditions, code contracts, 457, 458
PowerBasic, 983
POX, ASP.NET 3.5 support for, 666
pre-compilation of full sites, new in ASP.NET 2.0,
    663
preconditions, code contracts, 457
Premium with MSDN edition, Microsoft Visual
    Studio 2010, 11
preview images, exporting templates by creating,
    111–113

Primary Interoperability Assemblies. *See* PIAs (Primary Interoperability Assemblies)

PrimaryInteropAssemblyAttribute attribute, 415

primitive activities, in WF 4.0, 518

primitive types, in VB 8.0, 996

printing
  charts, 648
  with Silverlight, 356

private, access control specifier, 1119

ProcessCommand method
  creating simple item template, 76–77, 81
  creating simple project template, 71–72

ProcessDomainNameRequest.cs class, 534–536, 554–556

product types, F#. *See also* tuples, 1130

Professional with MSDN edition, Microsoft Visual Studio 2010, 11

Program.cs file, 71–72

Programming Models, 419

Project Cool, 656

Project From Existing Code menu, options for creating new projects, 19

project structure, in MVC, 763–764, 826

project templates
  adding small customization to, 75
  creating, 71–75
  creating editor extensions with, 260–261
  hierarchical structure of, 82–84
  overview of, 67–69
  storage structure, 81–83
  <TemplateContent> elements, 91–94
  <TemplateData> elements, 89–90

project type root nodes, project template hierarchy, 83–84

<Project> element, 91–94

<ProjectCollection> element, 91, 95–97

ProjectFinishedGenerating method, 105–106

ProjectGroup type, 91, 95–97

<ProjectItem> element
  for item templates, 94–95
  for project templates, 91–93

ProjectItemFinishedGenerating method, 105–106

projects
  creating in new way, 19
  definition of, 133
  selecting in New Project dialog, 17–18
  <TemplateData> element and, 88

Projects and Solutions category, Options dialog, 147, 149

<ProjectTemplateLink>, 96–97

properties
  accessing Visual Studio context, 177–182
  accessors in C# 2.0, 1055
  anchoring annotations, 636
  animations changing, 343
  auto-implemented in VB 10.0, 1010–1012
  automatic in C#, 1062
  C# syntax, 1046
  Chart class, 607–608
  ClassificationFormatDefinition class, 268
  code contract tools, 461–462
  indexed properties in C# 4.0, 1085–1086
  macros accessing IDE options, 226
  moving annotations, 637–638
  tools for working with Silverlight and WPF, 314–315

properties, chart
  creating three-dimensional charts, 620
  customizing chart axes, 624–627
  determining appearance of chart elements, 621–623
  tailoring chart types with custom, 616–617

Properties grid, WPF Designer, 26–27

Properties window, as docked tool window, 132

Property (Setter) Injection, applying MVC to Dependency Injection, 759

Property Browser
  adding event handlers to Silverlight project, 310
  searching properties in, 314

PropertyChanged event, 324–325

prototyping, with F#, 1106–1107

provider class model, new in ASP.NET 2.0, 663–664

pseudo folder nodes, project template hierarchy, 83

pseudo-columns, using in templates, 863–865

public, access control specifier, 1119

Pulse, types of animations, 960

.py extension, IronPython, 405


## Q

query definition
  comparing implementations, 425
  implementing manually vs. using LINQ, 422
  implementing parallel query definition manually, 423–424
  implementing parallel query definition using PLINQ, 424–425

query expressions
  C# 3.0, 1043, 1060–1061
  VB 9.0, 1001–1002

QueryStatus method, 236

Quick Find button, 129

QuickBASIC, 983–984

quotations, F#, 1160–1161


## R

RAD (rapid application development)
  displaying UI in Visual Basic 6.0, 297
  Web Forms and, 755

radar charts, 616

range charts, 614–615

range expressions, F#, 1143

rapid application development (RAD)
  displaying UI in Visual Basic 6.0, 297
  Web Forms and, 755

Rating control, 914

RDBMS (relational database management system), 757

real time charts, Ajax displaying, 705–709

realization, type relationships and, 1027, 1087

Recent Projects
  definition on Start Page, 170–171
  pinning functionality of, 16

recomposition, MEF, 480–482

records, F#, 1133–1134

refactoring, using code snippets in C# for, 34

reference cells, F#, 1123

reference highlighting, code-navigation using, 22

reference parameters, 1084–1085

referenced assemblies
  creating simple item template, 79
  customizing templates with wizards, 101
  defining in item templates, 94–95
  Start Page, 166–167
  using item templates for, 70

references types
  in C#, 1044
  in VB.NET, 988

<References> element
  code snippets, 46–47
  item templates, 91, 94–95

referentially transparent functions, in F#, 1119

reflection
  C# type system and, 1044
  generic type parameters and, 1050
  variance in VB 10.0 and, 1037–1038

registering, data context with Dynamic Data website, 715–716

Regular mode, IntelliSense, 21–22

relational database management system (RDBMS), 757

relational operators
  F#, 1122
  VB 8.0, 995

Remove button, Code Snippets Manager, 52, 54

Remove button, removing shortcut key, 158

Remove Split command, document windows, 137

<RemoveShortcut> element, 162

rendering, ASP.NET charts
  binary stream, 684–687
  image URLs, 680–683
  overview of, 679–680

RenderType property, 680, 684–687

ReorderList control, 914

repository, implementing for book project in MVC, 827–830

Repository Design Pattern, 757–759

Representational Transfer State (REST), WCF and, 394, 588–589

RequestClient project files, DomainNameWorkflow project, 533–534

RequestClientProxy class, 538–539

RequiredCreationPolicy property, part lifetime, 483

RequireHttpsAttribute, 820

Requires<TException> method, 458

Reset Toolbox command, 190

ResizableControlExtender, 914

Resize, types of animations, 960

resolving applicable signatures, C# 4.0, 1083–1084

REST (Representational Transfer State), WCF and, 394, 588–589

result filtering, in MVC, 821–822

results, tasks with, 446–448

ResumeBookmark method, workflow, 544

reusability. See templates

RIA Services, WCF, 354

ribbons in Visual Studio, 139

rich client experience, 148

right-brain thinking, designers vs. developers, 299–300

RoundedCornersExtender, 914

round-trip, 838

routing algorithms, forwarding commands to command targets using, 156

routing details, in MVC
    action and result filtering in, 821–822
    ActionResult class, 822–824
    authorization, 819–821
    Controller Factory, 816–817
    exception filtering in, 822
    execution flow, 817–818
    overview of, 816

routing requests, within MVC applications, 766–768

routing service, in WCF 4.0, 589–591

RSS, ASP.NET 3.5 support for, 666

RunStarted method, 105–107

run-time
    behavior and code contracts, 462–463

binders in DLR, 1077

DomainNameWorkflowTracking, 550

IronPython, 407

Managed Extensibility Framework, 486

.NET Framework properties, 282

Parallel Computing Platform, 419

performing chart data-manipulation at. See DataManipulator class, Chart control

workflow activities in WF 4.0, 520–521

## S

$safeitemname$ template parameter, 77–78

$safeprojectname$ template parameter, 75

Samples, Macro Explorer, 215

Save Current Settings page, Import and Export Settings Wizard, 152

Saved DGQL Query mode, Architecture Explorer, 28

saving chart state, ASP.NET, 688–690

ScaffoldColumnAttribute, in MVC, 809

scaffolding mechanism, Dynamic Data, 711, 715–716

Scale animation, 960

schema, creating code snippets, 38

script files (*.fsx), in F#, 1113

script languages, .NET 4 changes in CLR, 402

Script Loader, 858–859

ScriptAction, animation, 961

ScriptManager
    adding to sample ASP.NET application, 901
    ASP.NET, 844–846
    ASP.NET Ajax server controls, 842–844
    using Ajax with, 698–699

scripts
    early vs. late binding in scripting languages, 1021
    loading JavaScript files from Microsoft Ajax Library, 855–859
    split script files in Microsoft Ajax Library, 844–846

SeaDragon, 347, 914

Search Engine Optimization. See SEO (Search Engine Optimization)

SearchInfo instance, Parallel class, 438
security
    Dynamic Data website risks, 716, 720
    .NET Framework, 283
    .NET multi-language platform and, 293–294
    .NET vs. Silverlight network access, 352
SecurityTokenException, 582
Select an Application Host page, Visual Studio
    Add-In Wizard, 231
select clause, query expressions, 1060
Select Programming Language page
    Visual Studio Add-In Wizard, 231
    VSPackage Wizard, 244
Select Template Options page, Export Template
    Wizard, 73
Select Test Project Options page, VSPackage
    Wizard, 246
selectors, jQuery, 965–968
Send activity, DomainNameWorkflowWithHost,
    556
SEO (Search Engine Optimization)
    creating pages in ASP.NET 4.0 for, 668
    Silverlight and, 308, 358
Seq Module, F#, 1141–1143
Sequence activity, WF, 499, 508
sequence expressions, F#, 1143–1144
sequences, F#, 1141–1143
sequential workflows, previous WF versions, 499
serialization, ASP.NET
    chart basics, 690–691
    playing with content, 693–694
    in state management, 691–693
serialization, of chart data in .NET, 648
SerializationContents enumeration
    chart serialization and, 690–691
    playing with serialization content, 693–694
    using serialization in state management, 692
Serializer property, Chart control, 691, 693
Series Collection Editor
    adding ASP.NET chart control to page,
        671–672
    adding data points to chart programmatically,
        599
    adding new chart area, 596

binding chart to data source, 601
    manually adding data to chart, 595
Series element, charts
    adding ASP.NET chart control to page,
        671–674
    adding to chart, 596
    binding data to, 638–641
    copying chart values in DataManipulator,
        645
    with custom properties that vary with chart
        types, 609
    defined, 606–607
    organizing chart data points into, 595
    pie charts and, 613
    properties of, 608, 622
    sorting data in DataManipulator, 644
server controls, Ajax, 837, 841–844
server-side
    ASP active scripting on, 654
    ASP.NET Ajax Extensions on, 666
    importance of user experience on, 297–299
server-side data, Ajax
    ADO.NET data services, 888–889
    Control Toolkit for, 894
    retrieving cross-domain data, 889–892
    updating data on server, 883–888
    working with, 878–883
Service Application template, WCF, 382–383
Service class, WCF, 382–386
service consumer(s)
    creating WCF service client, 391
    in SOA, 377
service contracts
    SOA, 377
    WCF, 379, 384, 395
service description, SOA, 378
service lease, SOA, 378
Service Locator Pattern, MVC, 760
service logic, declarative WCF services, 396–398
Service Oriented Architecture (SOA)
    quick look at, 376–378
    WCF based on. See WCF (Windows
        Communication Foundation)
service provider, SOA, 377

service proxy
    in SOA, 378
    WCF client, 389–391
service registry, SOA, 377
ServiceDiscovery behavior, 587
services
    accessing with Import attribute, MEF,
        257–258
    DLR, 404
    .NET architecture, 292–293
    SOA, 377
    WCF, creating, 382–384
    WCF, getting started with, 381
    WCF 4.0, simplified configuration, 583–585
    workflow. See workflow services
setters
    C#, 1046
    F#, 1127
    property accessors, 1055
SetValue method, 186
shader effects, Silverlight, 356
shadows, smoothing on charts, 623
Shared Source Common Language Infrastructure,
    C#, 1044
SharePoint, in VS 2010, 12
Shell, Visual Studio IDE, 203
<Shortcut> element, 162
shortcuts
    accessing expansion snippets with, 35–36
    invoking surrounding snippets with, 36
    keyboard. See keyboard shortcuts
<ShortcutsScheme> element, 162
ShouldAddProjectItem method, iWizard,
    105–107
Show All option, Toolbox controls, 188
Show Snippet Highlighting, 37
side-by-side execution, CLR, 401–402
signature files (*.fsi), F#, 1113
signed integers, VB 8.0, 996
Silverlight
    4.0, 302–304
    bitmap effects, 356
    choosing WPF vs., 366–367
    data binding. See data binding

designer-developer cooperation in, 300
emergence of, 9
GPU acceleration, 357
isolated storage, 357–358
local messaging, 356
MEF for, 486
MVVM pattern and, 372
navigation and SEO, 358
.NET using, 294
out-of-browser applications, 355
printing, 356
SDK for audio and video playback, 346
specifying version for new project, 18
Toolkit, 321–322
versions of, 302
WPF features not available in, 361–366
XAML, 304–311
XAML vs. code, 311–313
Silverlight, ten pillars of
    animations, 341–345
    data binding. See data binding
    layout. See Silverlight layout
    media. See media, Silverlight
    networking, 352–354
    overview of, 303
    styles, 330–332
    templates. See templates, Silverlight
    tools, 313–315
Silverlight Components tab, Toolbox, 190
Silverlight layout
    applying transformations, 345
    Border, 317–318
    Canvas, 318–319
    containers, 315–316
    custom layout panels, 321–322
    Grid, 319–321
    overview of, 315–317
    StackPanel, 319
    Viewbox, 321–322
Simple Comment wizard, 101–104
SimpleHelloF35 workflow, 513–517
SimpleHelloF35WF4 workflow, 515–517
SimplePackagePackage class, 248–249
SimplePackage.vsct file, 248, 252–254

`SimpleTypeName` function, code snippets, 47, 49

`Site.css` file, Dynamic Data
    customizing look and feel, 732–735
    working with field templates, 739–741
    working with page templates, 736–738

`Site.master` file, Dynamic Data, 734–735

64-bit architectures, ASP.NET 2.0 supporting, 659–660

SketchFlow, Blend, 370–371

skins, new in ASP.NET 2.0, 662

`SliderExtender`, 914, 943, 946

`SlideShowExtender`, 915

smooth (adaptive) streaming, Silverlight media, 349–350

Snippet Designer, 61–62

Snippet Editor, 62–63

`.snippet` files
    building online code snippet providers, 58
    creating snippets in XML, 38–41
    defined, 37
    editing, 59–62
    file structure. *See* code snippets, file structure
    importing, 54–55
    importing file with multiple snippets, 56–57
    Snippet Designer, 61–62
    storage, 53

`<Snippet>` section, `<CodeSnippet>`
    declaring literals and objects, 44–45
    defined, 42
    defining code, 43–44
    `<Imports>` and `<References>`, 46
    overview of, 43

`SnippetIndex.xml` file, Visual Basic, 54

`SnippetsIndex.xml` file, 54

SOA (Service Oriented Architecture)
    overview of, 376–378
    for WCF. *See* WCF (Windows Communication Foundation)

software
    challenges of many-core CPUs, 416–417
    development of web, 653
    using MEF for evolving, 463–464

Solution Explorer
    adding custom commands to context menu of, 143
    defined, 130
    as docked tool window, 132
    file structure of new Silverlight solution, 305

solution hierarchy, traversing with macros, 227–228

Solution View, Architecture Explorer, 28

`<SolutionFolder>`, multi-project templates, 96

`Sort` method, `DataManipulator`, 644

sorting data
    ordering of data points in ΔαταΜανιπυλατο, 644
    ordering of Toolbox tabs, 189

source code
    add-ins, 232
    in F#, 1113
    package type definition, 248–251
    VSPackage Wizard, 247–248

Source Control category, Options dialog, 147

`Source` option, data binding, 325

`source.extension.vsmanifest` file, 116–118, 130

Spec# project, 456

spline charts, 611–614

Split command, document windows, 137

split script files, 844–846, 855–856

splitter button, code editor window, 21

SQL
    code snippets, 37
    Entity SQL, Entity Framework, 578
    LINQ to SQL, 570–572
    using Entity SQL, 578

SQL Server database, preparing workflow, 536

`SqlDataSource`, new in ASP.NET 2.0, 660

`SqlWorkflowInstanceStore`, 536, 540–542

SSDL (Store Schema Definition Language), Entity Data Model, 574

stacked area charts, 613

stacked bar charts, 610

stacked column charts, 610

`StackedGroupName` property, stacked column charts, 610

`StackPanel`
data binding with templates, 339
overview of, 319
as Silverlight container, 316–317
standard endpoints, WCF 4.0, 585–587
standard query operators, LINQ, 564
star charts, 616
Start Page
choosing New Project dialog from, 17–18
enhanced features, 15–16
Start Page, customizing
accessing Visual Studio context, 176–182
accessing Visual Studio object model, 182–185
changing `StartPage.xaml` file, 173–176
command button definitions, 169–170
creating first, 163–165
definition of, 167–168
further tips about, 186
`MyControl` user control, 173–174
overview of, 16, 162–163
Recent Projects definition, 170–171
structure of, 165–167
Start View, XML Schema Designer, 27
`StartNew()` method, `Task` class, 444
`StartPage.xaml` file
accessing Visual Studio context, 178–179
changing, 173–176
command button definitions, 169–170
creating more tabs, 186
defined, 166
recent project list definitions, 170–171
structure of, 167–168
state management. *See* chart state management, ASP.NET
state-maching workflows, in WF versions, 499
static classes, C# 2.0, 1051–1052
static translation, in C++, 280
static types, 1073
statically-typed languages, using DLR, 403–404
statistical formulas, applying to chart data, 646–647
step line charts, 615
stock charts, 615–616
storage

code snippet, 53–54
template structure for, 81–82
Store Schema Definition Language (SSDL), Entity Data Model, 574
storyboards, 342–344
`Stretch` property, `Viewbox`, 321–322
String module, in F#, 1117–1118
strings, in F#, 1116–1118
`StyleAction`, animation, 961
styles, Dynamic Data
customizing look and feel with, 732–735
working with field templates, 739–741
working with page templates, 736–738
styles, Silverlight, 330–332
Surround With function, surrounding snippets, 34, 36
surrounding snippets, 33–34, 36
symbols, command table files for packages, 253–254
Syme, Don, 1104
synchronization primitives, 451–454
syntax
C# 1.0, 1046–1047
VB 10.0, 1008
syntax, F#
comments, 1111
currying, 1109–1110
function arguments, 1109
functions, 1108–1109
naming conventions, 1111
overview of, 1107–1108
piping, 1109
whitespace and indentation, 1110–1111
syntax noise
in C# applications, 1069–1070
local variable type inference and, 1057
removing from C# applications, 1070–1071
`Sys.get`, DOM elements in Ajax, 852–855
`Sys.require`, loading scripts, 855–856
system folders
code snippet storage, 53–54
taking care when removing, 54
as template storage structure, 82
`System.Object`, C# 4.0, 1076–1077

System.Threading.TaskScheduler class, 448–449

System.Threading.ThreadPool class, 448–449

System.Workflow Components, Choose Toolbox Items dialog, 190

## T

Tab Definition files, Start Page, 163

tab groups, for document windows, 133, 136

tabbed document windows, 130–131

TabContainer control
  description of, 914
  overview of, 921
  properties, 923
  TabContainerSample.asxp, 921–922
  TabContainerSample.asxp.cs, 922–923

TabControl, in Start Page, 171–172

tables, Dynamic Data
  customizing layout, 741–744
  displaying data, 716–718
  for master-detail relationships, 725–730

TabPanel control, properties, 923

tabs, Toolbox, 189–191

tagged (discriminated) unions, in F#, 1106, 1131–1132

tags, Visual Studio Gallery, 195

TargetControlID, Ajax control extenders, 938

Task class
  creating and starting tasks, 444
  defined, 450
  Task<TResult> derived from, 446–447

Task Parallel Library. See TPL (Task Parallel Library)

Task Scheduler, Parallel Computing Platform, 420

Task<TResult> class, 446–448, 450

taskbar integration, Windows 7/WPF, 364–365

TaskCancelledException class, 450

TaskCompletionSource<TResult> class, 450

TaskCreationOptions, task control flow, 444–445

TaskFactory, TaskFactory<TResult> class, 450

tasks, working with
  coordination data structures and, 450–455

creating and starting, 441–444

defining control flow, 444–446

executing, 448–449

overview of, 440–441

with results, 446–448

task-related types, 449–450

understanding, 428–430

TaskScheduler class, 450

TaskScheduler property, Parallel class, 430

TDD (test driven development)
  applying MVC to, 755–756
  Generate From Usage feature for, 27
  new in Visual Studio 2010, 12

Team Foundation Server, 11, 16

team settings file, Options dialog, 153

Team System Editions, Visual Studio 2005, 8

template folder nodes, project template hierarchy, 83–84

<TemplateContent> element
  custom templates, 99–101
  files and projects in project templates, 91–94
  files and referenced assemblies in item templates, 94–95
  multi-project templates, 96–97
  overview of, 91
  structure of manifest file, 85

templated helpers feature, in MVC, 804–805

Templated helpers, MVC 2, 668

<TemplateData> element
  display characteristics, 86–88
  general structure of manifest file, 85
  item template characteristics, 88–89
  meaning of, 90–91
  project and language characteristics, 88
  project template characteristics, 89–90

_TemplateIcon.ico file, 74, 80–81

templates
  C++, 989, 1048
  creating installation kit, 114–125
  creating simple item, 76–81
  creating simple project, 71–75
  creating Start Page, 164
  editor classifier, 260–262
  exporting and importing, 111–114

templates (*continued*)
   item, 69–70
   new in Visual Studio 2010, 12
   New Project dialog options, 18
   overview of, 65–66
   project, 67–69
   role of, 66–67
   storage structure. *See also* manifest file, 81–84
   summary review, 125
   using code snippets. *See* code snippets
   Visual Studio Gallery, 194–195, 197
   WCF Service, 382, 551
   Workflow Console Application, 492–493
templates, Ajax
   client-side data binding with, 859–860
   interacting with events inside, 867–871
   pseudo-columns in, 863–865
   running code inside, 865–867
templates, ASP.NET
   creating Dynamic Data site, 712–713
   Dynamic Data entity, 741–744
   Dynamic Data field, 738–741
   Dynamic Data filter, 744–746
   Dynamic Data page, 735
   overview of, 711–712
templates, customizing
   custom template parameters, 99–101
   overview of, 98
   template parameters, 98–99
   wizards, 101–110
templates, MVC
   custom templates, 811–814
   display and edit templates, 805–808
   templated helpers feature in, 804–805
templates, Silverlight, 332–341
   control, 332–337
   creating new project, 304–305
   for data binding, 337–341
   overview of, 332
   Silverlight Navigation Application, 358
test driven development. *See* TDD (test driven development)
Test Tools category, Options dialog, 147

testing
   add-ins, 238
   multi-threading issues in many-core CPUs, 417–418
   packages, 246
   webcam applications, 351
testing, with MVC
   attaching book to IBook, 830–831
   creating/running unit tests, 831–833
   domain model for, 826–827
   implementing repository for book project, 827–830
   overview of, 824
   project structure following refactoring, 826
   testing controller, 824–826
Text Editor category, Options dialog, 147, 149–150
text elements, properties controlling chart, 622
Text Model, editor, 212–213
Text properties, adding activities to workflow, 494
text snippets, adding to Toolbox, 192–193
Text View Model concept, editor, 212–213
TextBlock
   data binding with templates, 338–341
   "Hello World" application in WPF, 359
   master-detail data-binding, 329
   simple data binding example, 324–325
   using VideoBrush as foreground brush of, 346
TextBox control, extenders for, 942–947
TextBoxWatermarkExtender, 914, 943
themes and skins, new in ASP.NET 2.0, 661–662
third-party tools, with GhostDoc, 207–208
thread pool, executing tasks in TPL, 448–449
threads
   executing tasks in TPL, 448–449
   multi-threading issues in many-core CPUs, 417–418
3D, WPF, 366
three-dimensional charts
   adding effects to charts, 598
   creating doughnut charts as, 614
   overview of, 619–621

tick marks, chart, 606–607
time-based animations, Silverlight and WPF, 341
`Timer` control, real time charts in Ajax, 706–708
titles, chart, 596–597, 606–608
titles, customizing ASP.NET Dynamic Data look and feel, 734–736
Titles Collection Editor, 596–597, 601–602
`ToggleButtonExtender`, 914, 938–942
tokens, customizing data point labels, 632
tool windows
    auto-hiding, 136
    command handling for, 156
    defined, 16–17
    docking, 135
    document windows vs., 132
    floating, 134
    overview of, 131–132
    toolbars for, 144
    using keyboard exclusively in, 159–160
toolable, XAML as, 308
toolbars
    adding menu to Main Menu, 141
    adding menus and commands to, 143
    context sensitivity of predefined, 145
    creating and rearranging, 144–145
    customizing with Customize dialog, 138–140
    overview of, 138–139
    for window frames, 129
Toolbars tab, Customize dialog, 139–140, 144–145
Toolbox
    accessing functions using keyboard, 188–189
    adding items to, 190–193
    components in, 187–188
    customizing tabs, 189–190
    defined, 130
    further tips about, 193
    overview of, 186–187
    WF 4.0 workflow design surface, 492
    working with tabs, 189
    WPF Designer, 26
Toolkit. *See* Ajax Control Toolkit
`ToolkitScriptManager`, 901

tools
    adding own contributions to Visual Studio Gallery, 197
    code contract, 457, 461–462
    Visual Studio Gallery, 194–195
    VS 2008 diagnostic, 11
    for working with Silverlight and WPF, 313–315
Tools menu, 232
tooltips, adding to charts, 694–696, 709
top-level binding, Ajax Library supporting, 874
touch, Windows 7/WPF, 363
TPL (Task Parallel Library)
    coordination data structures and tasks, 450–455
    creating and starting tasks, 441–444
    defining control flow, 444–446
    executing tasks, 448–449
    overview of, 428–430
    as Parallel Computing Platform element, 419
    parallel programming architecture, 420
    PLINQ composed of, 573
    task-related types, 449–450
    tasks with results, 446–448
    working with tasks, overview, 440–441
TPL (Task Parallel Library), `Parallel` class
    overview of, 430
    `Parallel.For`, 432–436
    `Parallel.For<TLocal>`, 436–438
    `Parallel.ForEach`, 439
    `Parallel.Invoke`, 430–432
tracking participant
    adding to workflow instance, 545–546
    configuring, 548–549
    persisting tracking information with, 546–547
tracking profile, assigning to tracking participant, 545–546
tracking records, workflow, 544–545
`TrackingParticipant` extension class, 513
transaction-handling activities, WF 4.0, 523–524
Transact-SQL, Text Editor category for, 150
transformations, 344–345

transitions
    defining with visual states, 334
    enhancing user experience, 341
triggers
    for chart events with Ajax, 701–705
    jQuery, 972–973
    in Silverlight and WPF, 370
try-catch-finally exception handling, WF
    4.0, 522
tuples, F#, 1119, 1130
two-way binding, in Ajax Library, 874–875
type abbreviations, F# type signature, 1119
Type attribute, <VSTemplate>, 85, 91–95
type augmentations, in F#, 1137–1138
type equivalence
    in CLR, 415
    instead of equality, 414
    MSDN documentation vs., 415
    No-PIA example of, 412–414
    overview of, 411–412
type inference, in F#, 1106
type parameters
    in C#, 1048
    constraints on, 990–991
    variance with multiple type parameters in C#,
        1094–1097
    variance with multiple type parameters in VB
        10.0, 1033–1036
    in VB, 990
type safety
    in C#, 1045
    in VB.NET, 988
type signatures, in F#, 1119
type substitution
    in C# 4.0, 1087–1089
    in VB 10.0, 1026–1029
type system, C#
    1.0, 1044–1045
    dynamic type in 4.0, 1073–1074
    enumeration types, 1046
    generic types in 2.0, 1048–1050
    nullable types in 2.0, 1054–1055
    partial types in 2.0, 1050–1051
type system, F#

list of basic types, 1116
    type signatures, 1119
    values, 1124
type system, VB
    generic types in VB 8.0, 989–992
    local variable type inference in VB 9.0, 998
    nullable types in VB 8.0, 993–994
    nullable value type modifiers in VB 9.0, 1004
    overview of, 988–989
    partial types in VB 8.0, 992–993
    unsigned and signed integer types in VB 8.0,
        996
    variance with multiple type parameters in VB
        10.0, 1033–1036
    variance with user types, 1036–1037
TypeIdentifierAttribute attribute,
    equivalence in CLR, 415

U

udpDiscoveryEndpoint, service discovery in
    WCF 4.0, 587
UI (user interface)
    communicating with host application in
        workflow, 537–539
    customizing templates with wizards, 102–103
    data binding between two elements in, 325
    dynamic data using filter templates for,
        744–746
    in early Windows programming, 4
    popularity of Visual Basic because of
        complexity of, 280
    reasons to not ribbons in Visual Studio, 139
    synchronous vs. asynchronous, 838
    Visual Basic revolutionizing, 4
UI (user interface) enhancements, Visual Studio
    2010
    Add Reference dialog window, 19
    code editor window, 20–22
    code-navigation features, 22–24
    creating new projects in new way, 19
    Extension Manager, 20
    Generate From Usage feature, 24–25
    New Project dialog window, 17–18

new tools for architects, 27–28

overview, 15

Start Page, 15–16

understanding window management, 16–17

WPF Designer, 26–27

XML Schema Designer, 27

UI (user interface), in modern frameworks

developers vs. designers, 299–301

importance of user experience, 297–299

new generation of presentation frameworks, 301–303

Silverlight layout, 315–322

Silverlight tools, 313–315

ten pillars of Silverlight, 303–313

UI customization. *See* view, in MVC

UIElement

adding adornments to text in, 212

manipulation API for, 363

UIHintAttribute, in MVC, 809–810

Ultimate with MSDN edition, Microsoft Visual Studio 2010, 11

UML (unified modeling language), 27–28, 608

unary operators, overloading, 995

unboxing operations, 1044

underscore (_), line continuation character in VB, 1008

unified modeling language (UML), 27–28, 608

UniformGrid, WPF layout, 362–363

unit tests

creating/running in MVC, 831–833

Unit Testing Frameworks, 755

unit type, in F#, 1116

units

creating demo project in F#, 1116

decomposing tasks into, 440–441

of measure, in F#, 1157–1159

unsigned integers, in VB 8.0, 996

UpdatePanel control

ASP.NET Ajax server controls, 842–844

overview of, 905–908

triggering chart events with, 701–705

UpdatePanelAnimationExtender, 914, 957, 962

UpdateProgress control, Ajax, 705, 842–844

updates

checking for installed extension, 148

of data on server, 883–888

with host application in workflows, 537–539

upgrades, Ajax Control Toolkit, 896

uploading, template to Visual Studio Gallery, 119–123

<Url> element, 47

URLs

creating CRUD applications for Dynamic Data site, 719–721

customizing Dynamic Data's routing, 721–722

rendering ASP.NET chart images, 679–683

UseImageLocation property, rendering ASP.NET charts, 680

user experience (UX)

purchasing software based on, 297–299

in Silverlight and WPF, 367–371

user folders

importing snippets only to top-level, 55

removing snippets from, 54

storing code snippets in, 53–54

as template storage structure, 82

user input, collecting with macros, 229

user interactivity, ASP. NET charts

with Ajax, 697–709

handling clicks on data points, 696–697

more points about, 709

tooltips, 694–696

user interface. *See* UI (user interface)

user profiles, new in ASP.NET 2.0, 662

user templates, 84

user types

variance in C# 4.0 and, 1097–1098

variance in VB 10.0 and, 1036–1037

UserControl, adding styles to, 330–332

UserNamePasswordValidator class, in WCF with NET 3.5, 582

<UserShortcuts> element, 162

Using keyword, for IDisposable pattern in VB 8.0, 996–997

using statement, memory management in C#, 1045

utility functions, in jQuery, 970–971
UX (user experience)
    purchasing software based on, 297–299
    in Silverlight and WPF, 367–371

## V

`ValidateAntiForgeryTokenAttribute`, in MVC, 820
`ValidateInputAttribute`, in MVC, 820–821
validation
    binding between two UI elements and, 325
    Dynamic Data, 747–749
    in WCF 3.5, 582–583
validation, MVC
    attributes, 795–797
    client-side, 803–804
    displaying issues, 800–801
    extending model using metadata, 798–799
    managing business rules, 801–803
    overview of, 795
    preparing controller for, 799–800
validators, extenders for, 955–956
`VallidationCalloutExtender`, 914, 955–956
value providers, MVC, 834–835
value types
    in C#, 1044
    in VB.NET, 988
values
    converting, 1124
    copying in `DataManipulator`, 645
    F#, 1124
    vs. objects in F#, 1105
variables
    adding flowchart to workflow, 500
    adding workflow, 496
    assigning workflow without, 497
    declaring for incode-only workflows, 508
    F# arithmetic expressions and, 1164
    F# type signatures and, 1119
    WF 4.0 explicit definition of, 511
variance
    in C# 4.0, 1066, 1089–1090

delegate covariance and contravariance in
    C#2.0, 1053–1054
with multiple type parameters in C#,
    1094–1097
reflection and, 1098–1099
with user types in C#, 1097–1098
variance, in VB 10.0
    contravariance, 1032–1033
    covariance, 1030–1032
    with multiple type parameters, 1033–1036
    new features in VB 10.0, 1029
    overview of, 1029
    reflection and, 1037–1038
    type substitution and, 1026–1029
    with user types, 1036–1037
VBA (Visual Basic for Applications), macro
    development, 209
VB.NET, macro development, 209
VBScript, ASP pages using, 655
VCL (Visual Component Library), 281
vendors, Visual Studio Gallery, 195, 196
Version attribute, <VSTemplate>, 85
versions, Visual Studio Gallery, 195
vertical tab groups, for document windows, 136
video, Silverlight media, 309, 345–347
`VideoBrush`, 346–347, 355
view, in MVC
    custom templates, 811–814
    display templates and edit templates, 805–808
    `DisplayAttribute`, 810–811
    `DisplayColumnAttribute`, 808–809
    `DisplayFormatAttribute`, 809
    displaying items in database, 776–779
    displaying validation issues, 800–801
    `HiddenInputAttribute`, 811
    `Index` and `About` views, 770
    metadata attributes, 808
    overview of, 668, 752, 804
    `ScaffoldColumnAttribute`, 809
    templated helpers feature, 804–805
    `UIHintAttribute`, 809–810
    view engines in, 814–816
View, MVVM, 372

View Code command, VSIX installation kit, 117
view engines, MVC, 814–816
view state
  in ASP.NET Framework, 688
  using serialization in state management,
    692–693
Viewbox, as layout container, 321–322
ViewModel, MVVM, 372
__VIEWSTATE name, ASP.NET Framework, 688
ViewStateContent property, charts, 690–691
virtual members, C# 4.0, 1082–1083
VirtualizingStackPanel, data binding with
  templates, 338–339
Visual Basic
  1.0, 4
  2003, 987–989
  5.0, 5
  6.0, 297
  7.0/7.1 (VisualBasic.NET), 987–989
  9.0, 9
  code snippets in, 33–34, 36–37
  design goals and debates, 986–987
  DLR high-level architecture, 405
  history of, 981
  macros written in. See macros
  movement to "visual," 984–985
  .NET Framework and, 280–281, 986
  roots of, 982
  structured and unstructured BASIC and,
    982–984
  summary, 1005
  versions released in 1990s, 985–986
Visual Basic 10.0
  accessing IronPython library from, 1023–
    1026
  auto-implemented properties, 1010–1012
  collection initializers, 1012–1017
  contravariance in, 1032–1033
  covariance in, 1030–1032
  implicit line continuation feature, 1008–1010
  late binding in, 1021–1023
  multiline lambda expressions, 1018–1020
  new syntax in, 1008
  overview of, 1007

  summary, 1037–1038
  type substitution and, 1026–1029
  variance and reflection, 1037–1038
  variance in, 1029
  variance with multiple type parameters,
    1033–1036
  variance with user types, 1036–1037
  working with dynamic objects, 1020–1021
Visual Basic 8.0 (2005)
  documentation comments, 994
  generic types, 989–992
  nullable types, 993–994
  operator declarations, 994–996
  overview of, 989
  partial types, 992–993
  unsigned and signed integer types, 996
  Using keyword supporting IDisposable
    pattern, 996–997
Visual Basic 9.0 (2008)
  conditional operator, 1004–1005
  defined, 9
  extension methods, 998–999
  lambda expressions, 1000–1001
  local variable type inference, 998
  nullable value type modifiers, 1004
  object-creation expressions, 999–1000
  overview of, 997
  partial methods, 1002
  query expressions, 1001–1002
  XML literal expressions, 1002–1004
Visual Basic Editor, and code snippets, 36–37
Visual Basic for Applications (VBA), macro
  development, 209
Visual Basic.NET
  bundled into Visual Studio.NET, 6
  importance of user experience in, 297
  overview of, 987–989
Visual C#
  bundled into Visual Studio.NET, 6
  implementations of C#, 1043
  Microsoft release of, 5
Visual C++
  5.0, 5
  bundled into Visual Studio.NET, 7

Visual Component Library (VCL), 281
visual effects, jQuery library, 975–976
visual experience, Options dialog, 148
Visual F#. *See* F#
Visual FoxPro 3.0, 4–5
Visual InterDev, 5
Visual J#
    bundled into Visual Studio 97, 5
    bundled into Visual Studio.NET, 7
    released in 1995, 4
    retired in VS 2008, 9
Visual State Manager (VSM), WPF templates,
    365–366
visual states, in Silverlight, 333–336
Visual Studio 2002, 5–7
Visual Studio 2003, 7–8
Visual Studio 2005
    code snippets in, 37
    .NET Framework 2.0 for, 286–287
    overview of, 7–8
Visual Studio 2008, 8–10, 302
Visual Studio 2010, 10–13, 367–371
Visual Studio 6.0, 5
Visual Studio 97, 5
Visual Studio Add-in wizard, 210
Visual Studio Add-In Wizard, 230–231
Visual Studio Command Table (VSCT)
    expression, 252
Visual Studio contexts, 176–182, 204
Visual Studio Documentary, 3
Visual Studio Extensibility community, 198
Visual Studio Extension Installer, 117–118
Visual Studio Extensions category, 164
Visual Studio Gallery
    adding own contributions to, 197
    browsing, 194–196
    downloading and installing components, 196
    new in Visual Studio 2010, 12
    overview of, 193
    release of, 110
    uploading template installation kit to,
        119–123
    working with Visual Studio Extensibility
        community, 197

Visual Studio, history of, 3–13
    overview of, 3
    roots of, 3–5
    summary review, 13
    Visual Studio 2005, 7–8
    Visual Studio 2010, 10–13
    Visual Studio 97 and 6.0, 5
    Visual Studio .NET 2002 and 2003, 5–7
    VS 2008, 8–10
Visual Studio Integration Package Wizard.
    *See* VSPackage (Visual Studio Integration
    Package) Wizard
Visual Studio Library (VSL), and package
    development, 211
Visual Studio packages. *See* VSPackages (Visual
    Studio packages)
Visual Studio settings
    keyboard shortcuts in, 161–162
    managing with Import and Export Settings
        Wizard, 151–153
    overview of, 150–151
    .vssettings file, 154
Visual Studio Software Development Kit. *See* VS
    SDK (Visual Studio Software Development Kit)
VisualBrush, WPF, 366
visualizer, code editor window, 21
VisualStateGroups, 335–336
VisualStateManager, 334
VisualStudioIntegration folder, VS SDK
    directory, 210–211
VS SDK (Visual Studio Software Development Kit)
    creating editor extensions, 260–261
    creating packages with, 204
    downloading correct version of, 210
    extensibility, 210–213
    Start Page development with, 163–164
    for VSIX installation kit, 114
VsBrushes class, 168, 172
VSContextControl.xaml file, 179–180
VSContextControl.xaml.cs file, 180–182
VSCT (Visual Studio Command Table) expression,
    252
.vsct files, 253–254
.vsix file, 121, 123–125, 196

VSIX installation kit
  adding Visual Studio Gallery components, 196, 197
  creating for template, 123–125
  generating, 114
VSL (Visual Studio Library), and package development, 211
VSM (Visual State Manager), WPF templates, 365–366
.vsmacros extension, 215
VSPackage (Visual Studio Integration Package) Wizard
  creating package with, 243–247
  package type definition, 248–251
  source code structure, 247–248
VSPackage Options page, VSPackage Wizard, 245
VSPackages (Visual Studio packages)
  command table, 252–254
  creating Package API with VS SDK, 211
  creating package with VSPackage Wizard, 242–247
  debugging, 254–255
  implementing majority of IDE functions with, 203
  integrating, 203–204
  overview of, 204, 242
  package type definition, 248–251
  source code structure, 247–248
  Visual Studio Shell hosting, 203
.vssettings file
  automatic saving of settings in, 153
  IDE configuration, 154
  importing settings and, 152–153
  kinds of settings stored in, 154
  navigating to team settings file, 153
.vstdir file, project template hierarchy, 82, 84
.vstemplate file
  multi-project templates, 96–97
  project template hierarchy, 83
  as template manifest file. See manifest file
<VSTemplate> element
  in item templates, 94–95
  in project templates, 91–94
  structure of manifest file, 85

W

WaitForApproval method, workflows
  configuring, 540–542
  resuming, 543–544
  suspending and resuming, 539–540
WCF (Windows Communication Foundation)
  Ajax Library supporting, 879
  ASMX Web Services vs., 375–376
  ASP.NET 3.0 releasing, 287
  building blocks, 378–381
  creating service, 382–386
  creating service client (consumer), 391
  creating service proxy, 389–391
  creating workflow services. See workflow services
  defined, 375
  defining data contracts, 386–387
  hosting service, 388–389
  implementing declaratively, 394–398
  integration of messaging in workflows with, 525–526
  .NET 3.5 additions to, 581–583
  as .NET architecture service, 293
  overview of, 375
  released in .NET Framework 3.0, 664
  REST and, 394
  RIA Services, 354
  Service Library template, 382–383
  Service Workflow Application template, 551
  Silverlight networking and, 353–354
  SOA and, 376–378
  specifying binding information, 387–388
  working with Ajax-enabled, 392–393
WCF (Windows Communication Foundation)
  Framework 4.0 enhancements
  discovery, 586–588
  overview of, 583
  REST improvements, 588–589
  routing service, 589–591
  simplified configuration, 583–585
  standard endpoints, 585–586
WCS (Windows CardSpace), 293, 665
Web Browser tool window, 131–132

web charts, 616
web development, .NET benefits, 294
Web Forms
    ASP.NET 4.0, 667
    ASP.NET MVC compared with, 754–755
web parts, new in ASP.NET 2.0, 662
web platform, history of Microsoft's approach to, 753–754
web services
    Microsoft Ajax Library supporting, 879
    as .NET architecture service, 292
    .NET secure, 294
WebBrowser control, only in OOB mode, 355
webcam access, Silverlight media, 350–352
web.config file, Ajax-enabled WCF service, 392–393
WebFormViewEngine, 815
Welcome page, Import and Export Settings Wizard, 151–152
WF (Workflow Foundation)
    as .NET architecture service, 292
    released in .NET Framework 3.0, 287, 489
WF (Workflow Foundation) 4.0
    communicating with host application, 537–539
    compensating transaction model, 527–532
    configuring SqlWorkflowInstanceStore, 540–542
    creating code-only workflows, 505–509
    creating flowcharts, 500–505
    HelloWorkflow application, 492–499
    history of, 489
    main workflow, 534–536
    overview of, 490–491
    persistence and human interactions, 532
    persistence and human interactions in. See persistence and human interactions, WF 4.0
    preparing workflow database, 536
    project demonstrating, 533
    project structure, 533–534
    resuming workflow instance, 543–544
    storing new request into database, 536–537
    suspending workflow instance, 539–540
    workflow activity library. See workflow activity library

workflow architecture. See workflow architecture
workflow design surface, 491–492
workflow services. See workflow services
workflow tracking, 544–550
what you see is what you get (WYSIWYG), web development, 654
where clause, in query expressions, 1060
whitespace, F# syntax, 1110–1111
Win32 API, 279–281
window management
    architecture, 128–131
    arranging windows, 134–138
    document windows, 132–134
    overview of, 128
    tool windows, 131–132
Window root element, WPF, 359
Window_Loaded method
    SqlWorkflowInstanceStore, 541–542
    WorkflowServiceHost, 559–560
windows
    command handling for, 156
    enhanced features, 16–17
    frames, 129
    panes, 129
Windows 2000, 286
Windows 7, 363–365
Windows 95, 985
Windows 98, 286
Windows CardSpace (WCS), 293, 665
Windows Communication Foundation. See WCF (Windows Communication Foundation)
Windows Forms
    Chart control for. See chart components, .NET
    data binding in .NET 4, 639
    interoperability with WPF, 363
    as .NET architecture service, 292
    user experience in VB.NET and, 297
    using in Visual Studio 2008, 302
Windows Me, 286
Windows Media Audio (WMA) encoding format, in Silverlight, 346
Windows NT 4.0, 286
Windows Phone 7 (WP7) platform, 303

Windows Presentation Foundation. *See* WPF (Windows Presentation Foundation)
Windows Server 2003, 286, 287
Windows XP, 286, 287
`<WizardData>`, manifest file, 85
`<WizardExtension>`, manifest file, 85
wizards
    attaching to templates, 107–110
    customizing templates with, 101
    example of, 101–104
    implementing `iWizard`, 104–107
WMA (Windows Media Audio) encoding format, in Silverlight, 346
workflow activity library, WF 4.0
    collection-handling activities, 524–525
    error-handling activities, 522
    flow control activities, 518–520
    flow-chart specific activities, 521–522
    messaging activities, 525–526
    overview of, 517–518
    primitive activities, 518
    transaction-handling activities, 523–524
    workflow run-time activities, 520–521
workflow architecture, 509–510
    activities, 511–512
    activity model changes, 513–517
    extensions, 512–513
    `WorkflowApplication` and hosts, 510–511
workflow arguments, declaring in code-only workflows, 507–508
Workflow Console Application template, 492–493
Workflow Foundation. *See* WF (Workflow Foundation)
workflow run-time activities, in WF 4.0, 520–521
workflow services
    adding behaviors, 560–561
    approval workflow, 557–559
    changing main workflow, 554–556
    configuring `WorkflowServiceHost`, 559–560
    creating, 551–553
    running application, 561
    using `WorkflowServiceHost`, 553–554
workflow services, WF 4.0, 551–561
workflow tracking, WF 4.0, 544–550

configuring tracking participant, 548–549
custom events for, 549–550
overview of, 544
participating in tracking process, 545–546
persisting tracking information, 546–547
running `DomainNameWorkflowTracking`, 550
tracking records, 544–545
`WorkflowApplication` class, 510–513
`WorkflowInvoker` class, 494–495
workflows, in F#. *See* computation expressions
`WorkflowServiceHost`
    adding behaviors to, 560–561
    approval workflow, 557–559
    configuring, 559–560
    overview of, 510
    using, 553–554
`Workflow.xaml` file, adding flowchart to workflow, 500
workspace, Visual Studio 2010, 305
work-stealing, executing tasks in TPL, 449
World Wide Web (WWW), development of, 653–654
WP7 (Windows Phone 7) platform, 303
WPF (Windows Presentation Foundation)
    3D, 366
    4.0 features, 302
    adding charts to, 601–602
    animations, 342–345
    choosing between Silverlight and, 366–367
    code editor window enhancements, 20–21
    compared with Ajax Library, 875
    data-binding features, 862
    debugging using tree visualization, 27
    designer-developer cooperation in, 300, 367–371
    evolution of, 301–303?
    features not available in Silverlight, 361–366
    MVVM pattern, 372
    as .NET architecture service, 293
    .NET Framework 3.0 releasing, 287
    overview of, 359–361
    tools, 313–315
    VS 2010 based on, 12–13
    Windows Forms interoperability with, 363

WPF Components tab, Choose Toolbox Items
    dialog, 190
WPF Designer, 26–27
WPF/E (WPF Everywhere), 302
wrapped sets, jQuery, 964
WWW (World Wide Web) development, 653–654
WYSIWYG (what you see is what you get), web
    development, 654

# X

XAML (Extensible Application Markup
    Language)
    adding event handlers to Silverlight project,
        308–311
    code vs., 311–313
    creating new Silverlight project, 304–311
    defining declarative WCF services in,
        394–398
    defining Start Page, 163
    functionality of, 306
    goals and benefits of, 308
    as pillar of WPF, 301
    using Expression Blend with, 314–315
XBAP (WPF Browser) deployment, 359–361
XLINQ, 568–569
XML
    C# and, 1046–1047
    code snippets stored in, 53

creating simple code snippet, 38–41
Entity Data Model in, 576–577
LINQ to XML, 568–569
Schema Designer, 27
snippet editors, 58–59
VB 9.0 literal expressions, 1002–1004
VS 2008 literals, 9
XAML based on, 308
XmlDataSource, ASP.NET 2.0, 661
XMLHTTPRequest object, Ajax Extensions,
    839–842
XSP platform, history of, 656
xUnit, unit testing with, 755

# Z

Z coordinate, three-dimensional charts, 620
.zip archives
    creating multi-project templates, 96–97
    deploying template files, 113–114
    exporting templates manually, 111
    item template hierarchy, 84
    storing item templates, 80–82
    storing project templates as, 74
    template folders, 82–84
zoom, in code editor window, 21